REEF AND
SHORE FISHES
OF THE
SOUTH PACIFIC

Humphead Bannerfish, *Heniochus varius*

REEF AND SHORE FISHES OF THE SOUTH PACIFIC

New Caledonia to Tahiti and the Pitcairn Islands

John E. Randall

University of Hawai'i Press
HONOLULU

10 09 08 07 06 05   6 5 4 3 2 1

Library of Congress Cataloging-in-Publication Data

Randall, John E., 1924–
  Reef and shore fishes of the South Pacific : New Caledonia to Tahiti and
the Pitcairn Islands / John E. Randall
      p.cm.
  Includes bibliographic references (p.).
  ISBN 0–8248–2698–1 (cloth : alk. paper)
   1. Reef fishes—Oceania—Identification. 2. Marine
fishes—Oceania—Identification. I. Title.

QL636.5.O3R36 2003
597.177'89'0995—dc21
                                    2003051383

University of Hawai'i Press books are printed on acid-free paper
and meet the guidelines for permanence and durability of the
Council on Library Resources

Designed by Robert F. Myers
Printed by Everbest Printing Co., Ltd.

CONTENTS

Ribbon Moray, *Rhinomuraena quaesita*

ACKNOWLEDGMENTS

Support for fieldwork in the Pacific was provided by the National Geographic Society, National Science Foundation, Charles Engelhard Foundation, Bishop Museum, and the Hawai'i Institute of Marine Biology of the University of Hawai'i.

Donations for the publication of this volume were made by the Charles Engelhard Foundation, Foster Bam, Georgia Aquarium, Jefferson W. Asher, Jr., Mrs. Nadyne Taylor, and especially Roland S. Boreham, Jr. Without this support, the present volume with its many illustrations could not have been published.

The National Science Foundation, Charles Engelhard Foundation, Foster Bam, Roland S. Boreham, Jr., E. H. Chave, and the late William I. Follett have helped finance the publication of Indo-Pacific Fishes at the Bishop Museum, which has been fundamental to the author's systematic research.

I am most grateful to the following persons who have contributed a total of 55 fish photographs that were used in this book: Gerald R. Allen, Philippe Bacchet, James Collyer, John L. Earle, David W. Greenfield, Tomonori Hirata, John P. Hoover, Yves Magnier, Randall D. Mooi, Philip Munday, Robert F. Myers, Richard L. Pyle, Robert M. Pyle, Luiz A. Rocha, Barry C. Russell, Rodney Salm, Roger C. Steene, Hiroyuki Tanaka, Richard C. Wass, Jeffrey T. Williams, and Richard Winterbottom.

I also thank the following for assistance in the field, for help in South Pacific fish identification, or for providing loans of specimens: Gerald R. Allen, Kunio Amaoka, Willliam D. Anderson, Jr., Chuichi Araga, Nathan A. and Patricia Bartlett, Marie-Louise Bauchot, Lori J. Bell, David R. Bellwood, M. Boeseman, Charles J. Boyle, John C. Briggs, Bruce A. Carlson, Kent E. Carpenter, David H. Catania, J. Howard Choat, Eugenie Clark, Kendall D. Clements, Kathleen S. Cole, Patrick L. Colin, Bruce B. Collette, Leonard J. V. Compagno, Martine Desoutter, Terry J. Donaldson, John L. Earle, Alan R. Emery, William N. Eschmeyer, Jon D. Fong, Malcolm P. Francis, Thomas H. Fraser, Ronald Fricke, René Galzin, Anthony C. Gill, Martin F. Gomon, Ofer Gon, William A. Gosline, Brian Greene, David W. Greenfield, Antony S. Harold, Phillip C. Heemstra, Philip Helfrich, Dannie A. Hensley, J. Barry Hutchins, Hitoshi Ida, Walter Ivantsoff, Yukio Iwatsuki, Jeffrey W. Johnson, Richard H. Johnson, Scott Johnson, Leslie W. Knapp, Michel Kulbicki, Pierre Laboute, Ross Langston, Helen K. Larson, Peter R. Last, Yves Lefevre, Jeffrey M. Leis, Phillip S. Lobel, Kenneth R. Longenecker, Sara A. Lourie, Hajime Masuda, Keiichi Matsuura, Gerald McCormack, John E. McCosker, Mark A. McGrouther, Scott W. Michael, Mark Mohlmann, Randall D. Mooi, Sue M. Morrison, Hiroyuki Motomura, Bruce C. Mundy, Robert N. Myers, Anthony Nahacky, Tetsuji Nakabo, Joseph S. Nelson, Mike Neumann, James W. Orr, Brandon Paige, Paolo Parenti, Frank L. Pezold, Theodore W. Pietsch, Stuart G. Poss, Richard L. Pyle, Ernst S. Reese, Jacques Rivaton, D. Ross Robertson, Barry C. Russell, Johnson Seeto, Hiroshi Senou, Bernard Seret, Kwang-Tsao Shao, Larry Sharron, Jeffrey A. Siegel, David G. Smith, William F. Smith-Vaniz, Victor G. Springer, Wayne C. Starnes, Donald W. Strasburg, Randy Thaman, Kenneth A. Tighe, M. J. P. van Oijen, Robin S. Waples, Richard C. Wass, Alwynne C. Wheeler, Jeffrey T. Williams, Richard Winterbottom, David J. Woodland, Louise Wrobel, and Tetsuo Yoshino.

I am especially grateful for curatorial help at the Bishop Museum provided currently by Arnold Y. Suzumoto and Loreen R. O'Hara, and in the past by Gerald R. Allen, Marjorie Awai, Lori Buckley, Kent E. Carpenter, Jane B. Culp, David Erlenkotter, Ofer Gon, and A. Bradley Tarr. Malcolm P. Francis and David W. Greenfield carefully reviewed the manuscript and made corrections and valuable suggestions for improvement. Robert F. Myers, Patrice Marker, and Richard L. Pyle provided technical assistance with computer hardware and software.

And finally, with the most gratitude, I thank my wife Helen for her help in many ways, and in particular, her editorial skills.

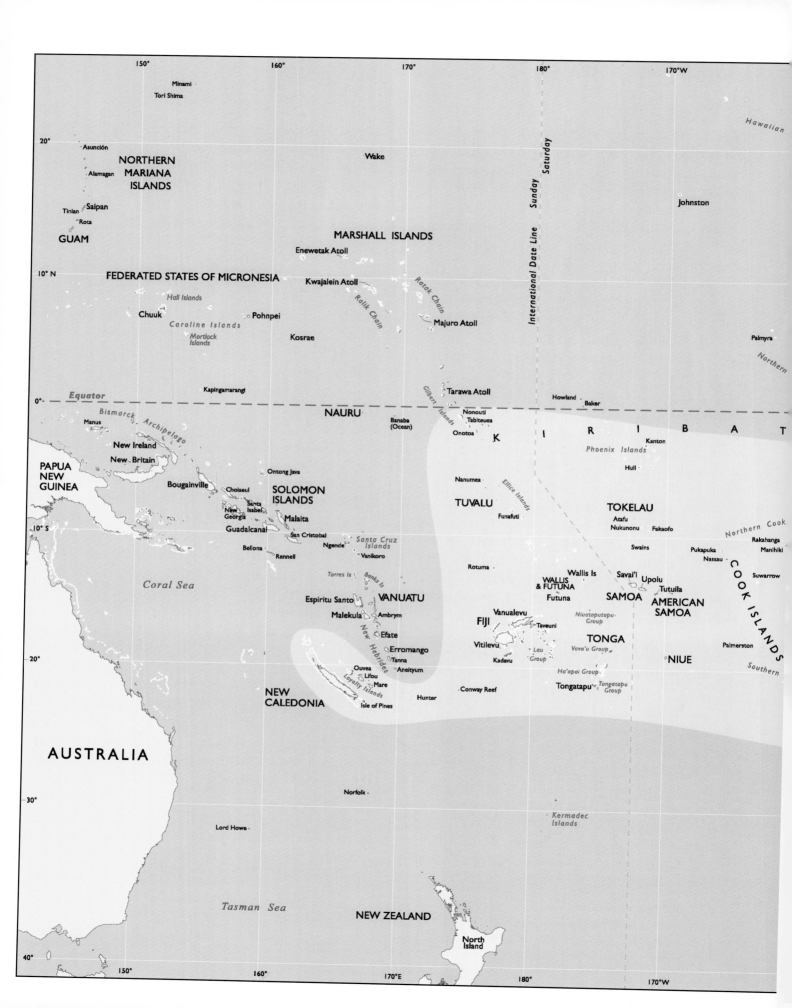

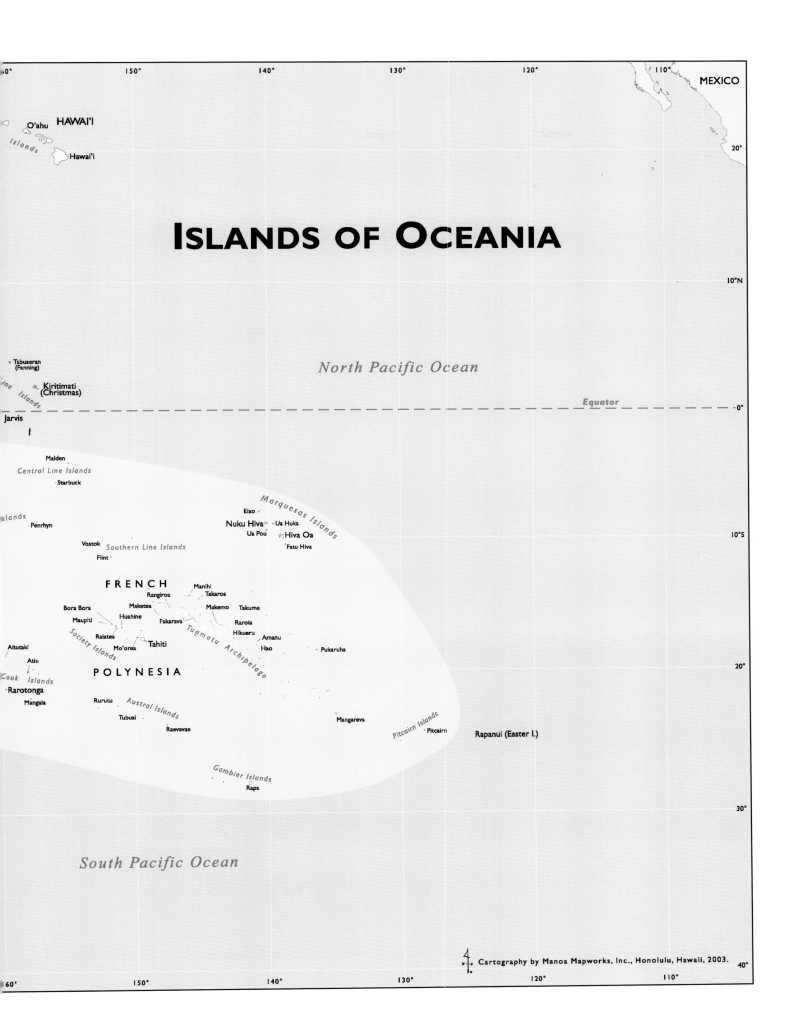

ISLANDS OF OCEANIA

MEXICO

150° 140° 130° 120° 110°

20°

O'ahu HAWAI'I

Islands

Hawai'i

10°N

North Pacific Ocean

Tabuaeran
(Fanning)

Kiritimati
(Christmas)

Line Islands

Jarvis

I

Equator 0°

Malden

Central Line Islands

·Starbuck

Marquesas Islands

Elao

Islands

Nuku Hiva · Ua Huka

·Penrhyn

Ua Pou   ·Hiva Oa

10°S

Vostok *Southern Line Islands*

·Fatu Hiva

Flint ·

FRENCH   Manihi

Rangiroa   ·Takaroa

Bora Bora   Makatea   Makemo   Takume

Maupiti   Huahine   Fakarava   Raroia

Raiatea   Tuamotu   Hikueru

Aitutaki   Mo'orea ·Tahiti   *Archipelago*   Amanu

Atiu   *Society Islands*   Hao

·Pukaruha

POLYNESIA

20°

Cook Islands

·Rarotonga

Mangaia   Rurutu   *Austral Islands*

Tubuai ·   Mangareva

Raevavae   *Pitcairn Islands*

·Pitcairn   Rapanui (Easter I.)

Gambier Islands

Rapa

30°

South Pacific Ocean

Cartography by Manoa Mapworks, Inc., Honolulu, Hawaii, 2003.   40°

160° 150° 140° 130° 120° 110°

Yellowstripe Goatfish, *Mulloidichthys flavolineatus*

INTRODUCTION

This book represents an eastward extension of *Fishes of the Great Barrier Reef and Coral Sea* (Randall et al., 1997a). The area covered lies between the equator and 27°S, beginning with New Caledonia and extending eastward to French Polynesia and the Pitcairn Islands. It includes the Loyalty Islands, Fiji, southern Gilbert Islands (Kiribati), Tuvalu, Wallis Islands, Tonga, Niue, Samoa Islands, Tokelau Islands, Phoenix Islands, Cook Islands, Austral Islands, Rapa, Society Islands, Tuamotu Archipelago, and the Marquesas Islands. It does not include the Solomon Islands and Vanuatu, which by virtue of their proximity to New Guinea and the other islands of the East Indies have a very rich fish fauna. Easter Island, the easternmost outpost of Polynesia, has also been omitted. This small isolated island has as high a percentage of endemic fishes as the Hawaiian Islands and is deserving of a separate study of its fish fauna. Nor does it include Lord Howe Island, Norfolk Island, or the Kermadec Islands, which lie south of 29°S and have a fish fauna dominated by subtropical species. A separate book of this series is planned for these islands by the author and Malcolm P. Francis.

The outer reef flat with surge channels, Onotoa Atoll, Kiribati.

The islands of the East Indies (Indonesia, New Guinea, and the Philippines) are estimated to have 2,600 species of shore fishes, defined as those occurring from the shore to a depth of 200 m (Randall, 1998a). This number drops from island group to island group eastward in the South Pacific. New Caledonia has 1,487 species of shore fishes; if one includes the Loyalty Islands and the Chesterfield Islands of the Coral Sea, the number is raised to 1,659 species (Kulbicki & Rivaton, 1997); Tonga has 1,163 species (Randall et al., 2004), the Samoa Islands have 915 species (Wass, 1984), the Society Islands 633 (Randall, 1985a), the Marquesas Islands 415 (Randall & Earle, 2000), the Pitcairn Islands 335 (Randall, 1999a), and Easter Island 126 (Randall, 1998a).

Shore of Opunohu Bay, Moorea, Society Islands.

The purpose of this book is to provide for the identification of the fishes that snorkelers or scuba divers may see on insular reefs or in adjacent habitats or that fishermen might catch while fishing inshore. It does not include offshore pelagic fishes, those that are found at depths greater than usually penetrated by divers, or fishes that occur only or primarily in fresh water. It also does not contain small species that live deep in the recesses of reefs by day and night, such as the small viviparous brotulas (Bythitidae) and the small false morays (Chlopsidae). Nor does it include the spaghetti eels (Moringuidae) and many of the snake eels and worm eels (Ophichthidae) that live in bottom sediment. These are species that have been discovered by ichthyologists mainly with the use of ichthyocides such as rotenone.

The order of presentation of fishes is phylogenetic, meaning treating first what we believe to be the most primitive groups. Sharks and rays are discussed family by family, followed by the bony fishes in their families. We are uncertain of the relationships of some of the families of fishes, so our concept of which family is more primitive than another may change.

Each species account begins with the English common name. Unfortunately, many of the fishes have more than one common name, even just in English. The common name used is usually the one that relates best to the scientific name when the latter was well chosen. The obvious

The author's ketch *Nani* at anchor in Opunohu Bay, Moorea, 1956.

1

The 30-m schooner *Westward* anchored at Mangareva, Tuamotu Archipelago.

Bounty Bay, Pitcairn, the only landing place, is dangerous when the surf is high.

A large tidepool during low tide at Down St. Paul, Pitcairn.

The spiny lobster *Panulirus pascuensis*, named for Easter Island, later found by the author at Rapa and Pitcairn.

advantage of the scientific name is its being universal, with only one valid name for each species. The first of the italicized two-part scientific name consists of the genus (which is capitalized). A genus is a group of related species; if a species has no close relatives, it may be in a genus by itself. The second part of the scientific name is the species name. Some species have been given more than one scientific name. The oldest name prevails, and the later names are referred to as synonyms. The species name is followed by the name of the author (or authors) who described it in the scientific literature and the date the name was published. Many fishes were described in the monumental 22-volume series *Histoire Naturelle des Poissons* by Georges Cuvier and Achille Valenciennes (1828–1849). To shorten species headings, these author names will be cited as Cuvier in C & V or Valenciennes in C & V. Some of the descriptions in Bloch & Schneider (1801) were prepared by Johann R. Forster. Rather than cite the authorship as Forster in Bloch and Schneider, only Forster's name is used. References are not included for the authors of species, except for a few recently described fishes. The older references may be found in Eschmeyer's three-volume *Catalog of Fishes* (1998).

An author's name in parentheses signifies that the specific name was initially published in another genus than that accepted today. For example, early naturalists describing new species of parrotfishes placed them in the genus *Scarus*. As more and more parrotfishes were given scientific names (there are now 85 in the world), it became apparent from major character differences that the genus *Scarus* needed to be divided into more genera. Today there are 10 genera in the parrotfish family Scaridae.

With so many islands covered by this volume, it would be impractical to list the native names of the fishes. The reader is therefore referred to the following publications for local names: southern Gilbert Islands (Kiribati) (Randall, 1955a); Tahiti (Randall, 1973); Rapa (Randall & Sinoto, 1978); Marquesas Islands (Lavondès & Randall, 1978); Samoa Islands (Wass, 1984); Tonga (Randall et al., 2004); islands of Polynesia (Rensch, 1999).

Genera of fishes are grouped into families, the scientific names of which end in "idae." Some families are divided into subfamilies, the scientific names of which end in "inae." An account is given for each family of fishes in larger type to present the principal characteristics and include remarks on the biology that may apply to all of the species of the family in general. Within a family or subfamily, the accounts of the fishes are presented alphabetically by genus and species. Separate systematic accounts are not given for subfamilies and genera. Diagnostic characters that are common to all species of a genus are presented in the first species account for the genus and are often followed by a parenthetical remark indicating that the character occurs in all species of the genus. The species accounts are written largely in telegraphic style, and numerals are used for numbers when designating counts.

Each species account includes a summary of the distribution of the fish, including the type locality—the location where the holotype (the principal specimen on which the original description was based) was collected. Only a few reef fishes, such as the Porcupinefish (*Diodon hystrix*), occur in all tropic seas, a distribution termed circumtropical. Many species are wide-ranging in the tropical Indian and Pacific Oceans from the east coast of Africa to the Hawaiian Islands and/or some islands of French Polynesia; such a wide distribution is referred to as Indo-Pacific. Some Indo-Pacific species have extended their range across the broad expanse of open ocean east of the islands of Oceania to the tropical coast of the Americas or offshore islands such as Clipperton and the Galápagos. The richest marine fish fauna in the world is found off the southeast coast of Asia, Philippines, Borneo, New Guinea, and the islands of Indonesia, collectively termed the Indo-Malayan region.

Fishes are divisible into five evolutionary lineages called classes that have been separated for many millions of years. These are the lampreys, the hagfishes, the cartilaginous fishes (sharks and rays), the lungfishes and coelacanths, and the ray-fin fishes. Only two of these are represented in shallow South Pacific seas, the Chondrichthyes (sharks and rays) and the Actinopterygii (largest class of the bony fishes).

It is necessary to use some scientific terminology when presenting the principal diagnostic characteristics of families and species of fishes. The major external features of fishes are shown in the illustrations on pages 4 and 5. A glossary of scientific terms is given at the back of the book before the references.

Most bony fishes have both spines and soft rays in their dorsal and anal fins. The soft rays are finely segmented, flexible, and usually branched. The spines are thicker, not branched, not segmented, and usually sharp-tipped. To differentiate the counts of spines and soft rays, roman numerals are used for the spines and arabic numbers for the soft rays. Thus a dorsal-ray count of X,12 means that a fish has a dorsal fin with 10 spines and 12 soft rays. If there are two separate dorsal fins, a plus sign (+) is used to indicate the separation. When the last dorsal and anal soft rays are divided to the base, they are still counted as if they are a single ray.

The majority of bony fishes have a longitudinal series of pores along the side of the body called the lateral line, one to a few pores in each scale, that lead to a sensory canal beneath the scales. It is this sensory system, along with pores on the head, that records low-frequency vibrations for the fish. It can detect, for example, the movements of prey, proximity of a near-by hard surface (from reflection of the fish's movements), or an onrushing predator. Counts of the lateral-line scales (or the scales in longitudinal series when the pores are difficult to detect or absent) are made from the upper end of the gill opening to the base of the caudal fin (the end of the vertebral column); sometimes pored scales continue onto the caudal fin, but either these are not counted or the caudal count is given separately.

Gill rakers are the slender bony projections on the anterior edge of each gill arch (opposite the red gill filaments). Fishes that feed on large prey have only a few small gill rakers (and rarely none), whereas those that feed on very small animals, such as zooplankton feeders, have numerous slender gill rakers. Gill-raker counts are often given in two numbers, the first for those above the angle of the gill arch and the second on the lower part (or lower limb). When there is a raker at the angle of the gill arch, it is included in the count of the lower part. Counts of gill rakers on small specimens generally require the use of a dissecting microscope.

Body proportions of fishes are often helpful in identification. For fishes with a normal caudal fin, these are often expressed in terms of the standard

The *Westward* at Îlots de Bass (Marotiri), 83 km southeast of Rapa.

Haurei Bay, Rapa, with village of Haurei and *Westward* at anchor.

Ua Pou, Marquesas Islands.

A cluster of Antenna Turkeyfish, *Pterois antennata,* and a cardinalfish, *Ostorhinchus relativus,* under a ledge, Nuku Hiva, Marquesas Islands.

3

External Features of Fishes

Cartilaginous Fishes (Sharks and Rays)

The two illustrations below and the four on the facing page are labelled to show the principal external parts of fishes.

Silvertip Shark
(*Carcharhinus albimarginatus*)

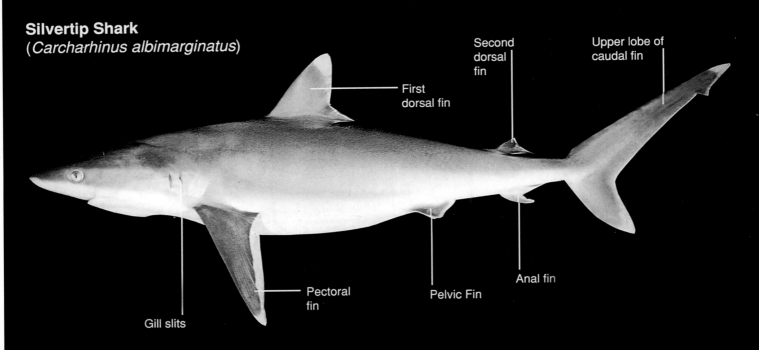

Second dorsal fin

Upper lobe of caudal fin

First dorsal fin

Pectoral fin

Pelvic Fin

Anal fin

Gill slits

Kuhl's Stingray
(*Dasyatis kuhlii*)

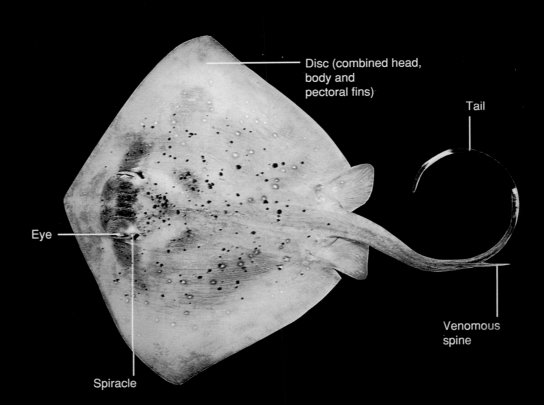

Disc (combined head, body and pectoral fins)

Tail

Eye

Spiracle

Venomous spine

awberry Rockcod
(ephalopholis spiloparaea)

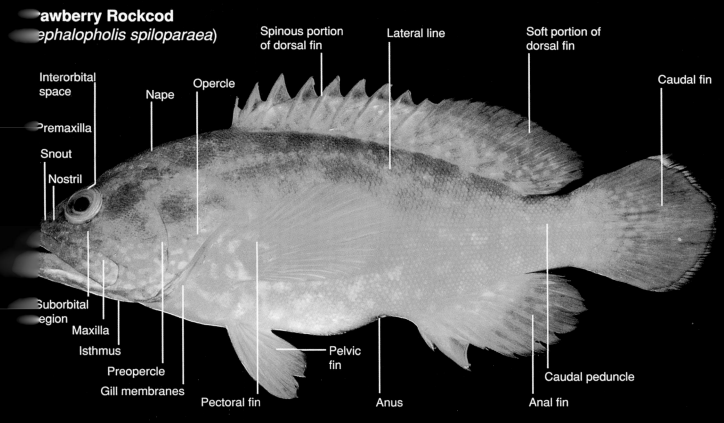

Interorbital space
Premaxilla
Snout
Nostril
Nape
Opercle
Spinous portion of dorsal fin
Lateral line
Soft portion of dorsal fin
Caudal fin
Suborbital region
Maxilla
Isthmus
Preopercle
Gill membranes
Pectoral fin
Pelvic fin
Anus
Anal fin
Caudal peduncle

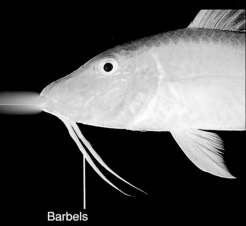

Barbels

The picture labelled **A** is the head of a goatfish (Mullidae) and shows the pair of barbels on the chin. These are moved over the bottom or thrust into the sediment during feeding to assist the fish in finding its food.

B shows the tail of a trevally (Carangidae) which has a falcate caudal fin; this shape is often found on fishes capable of swimming very rapidly. Because of the stress placed on the narrow caudal peduncle, fishes such as jacks and tunas usually reinforce it with scutes and/or keels.

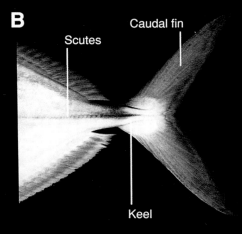

B
Scutes
Caudal fin
Keel

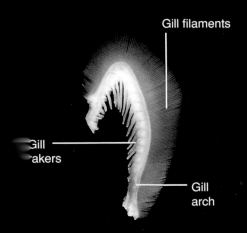

Gill filaments
Gill rakers
Gill arch

C depicts one of the gills (respiratory organs of fishes). The gill arch is the structural part. Gaseous exchange takes place in the gill filaments and the gill rakers keep food items from passing out of the gill opening along with expired water.

D is the roof of the mouth of a percomorph fish and shows the typical dentition of the premaxilla, vomer and palatine bones.

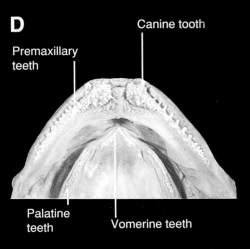

D
Premaxillary teeth
Canine tooth
Palatine teeth
Vomerine teeth

A Gilbertese fisherman with a sailfish caught while trolling from his sailing canoe. Onotoa Atoll, Kiribati.

The research vessel *Alis,* used for fieldwork on fishes in New Caledonia waters by the author and French colleagues (IRD, Nouméa).

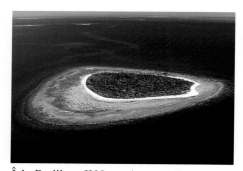

Île Redika off Nouméa, one of many dive localities around New Caledonia (IRD, Nouméa).

The 18-m ketch *Moku Makua Hine,* the base of ichthyological fieldwork in Fiji (K. R. Longenecker).

length, abbreviated SL, the length from the tip of the snout to the base of the caudal fin. For example, we might state that a fish is elongate, and to quantify it we might write that the body depth is 7 in the standard length, meaning that a measurement of the maximum depth of the body (not including the fins) is contained seven times in the length to the base of the caudal fin. For eels and sharks total length (TL) is used for such proportions; for jacks (with scutes to reinforce the narrow caudal peduncle, hence difficult to determine where the caudal fin begins), we use the fork length, abbreviated FL, the length from the tip of the snout to the end of the middle of the caudal fin.

The head of eels is measured from the front of the upper lip to the upper end of the gill opening, the trunk from the gill opening to the anus, and the tail from the anus to the tail tip.

The fieldwork in the South Pacific that is the basis for this volume began in the summer of 1951 when I was a member of a six-man expedition to Onotoa Atoll in the southern Gilbert Islands (now the major part of the nation Kiribati). Then a graduate student in zoology at the University of Hawai'i, I was to be the assistant of Dr. A. H. Banner. Because he was a marine invertebrate biologist, he asked me to collect the fishes. In 1955, after completing graduate school, I received a fellowship for one year from Yale University and the Bishop Museum in Honolulu to study the biology of fishes in the Society Islands under consideration for introduction to Hawaiian waters. I sailed to Tahiti with my family on our 11-m ketch *Nani;* most of the fieldwork was done in Moorea. This idyllic year was followed by academic positions in Florida, Virgin Islands, and Puerto Rico. In 1965 I returned to the Hawaiian Islands and resumed my study of Indo-Pacific fishes. In the last 35 years I have collected and photographed fishes at nearly all the island groups of the South Pacific. The most memorable fish expedition was one of seven months in 1970–1971 on the 30-m schooner *Westward,* with support of the National Geographic Society, to the Society Islands, Tuamotu Archipelago, Pitcairn Islands, Rapa, Austral Islands, Cook Islands, and the Marquesas Islands. Also productive were expeditions in New Caledonia waters from the 28-m R/V *Alis* with French colleagues, and recently to Fiji with David W. Greenfield and students from the 18-m ketch *Moku Makua Hine* with support of the National Science Foundation. The resulting Fiji fish collections have not been fully curated. They contain specimens that represent new records and new species that could not be added to this volume.

The majority of my fish collections from the Pacific and Indian Oceans have been deposited in the Bishop Museum in Honolulu during the period from 1966, when I joined the staff at a quarter-time position as the Curator of Fishes, to the present. In 1966 the fish collection consisted of 5,556 lots (a lot is a collection of one species at one time and place). There are now 39,291 lots of fishes, nearly all from the Indo-Pacific region.

The color photographs of fishes in this book are mine except for 55 from colleagues for which a credit line is given. Underwater photographs were taken with a Nikon F camera (manual F-stop selection and focusing) in an Ikelite housing with dual strobe lights. Photographs of fishes after removal from the sea were made by a method described by Randall (1961a). The locality of each photograph is given in small print beside the image.

SHARKS AND RAYS (CHONDRICHTHYES)

SHARKS

Only about 360 species of sharks are known in the world, compared with nearly 24,000 species of bony fishes. In spite of their low number of species, sharks play a major role in the seas of the world. Many are the top predators in the various food chains and serve to keep Nature in balance.

With the decline of so many major fisheries in the world, sharks are being exploited more as a source of food today. The demand for shark fins for use in the preparation of soup in Asia continues unabated. As a result, the populations of commercially important sharks are now seriously reduced. Because sharks have relatively few young, and most grow slowly, their populations can be quickly depleted by over-fishing.

Sharks differ in many ways from bony fishes. Their skeleton is cartilage, not bone. The jaws of sharks may seem as hard as bone, but it is only calcified cartilage. There are five to seven gill openings on each side of the head of sharks, compared with a single one for bony fishes. Most sharks have a spiracle, which is a rudimentary gill opening found behind or below the eye. In bottom-dwelling sharks and rays, it is functional as the incurrent opening for respiratory water. The skin of sharks is rough to the touch, due to the presence of numerous small dermal denticles that are close-set but not overlapping like the scales of most bony fishes. The mouth of most sharks is ventral on the head, thus the snout is overhanging. The teeth are modified, enlarged dermal denticles with a pulp cavity, dentine, and a thin layer of hard, enamel-like vitreodentine. They vary greatly in structure among the different species of sharks. Some teeth are sharp and blade-like, with or without serrations; others long and raptorial; and still others molariform for crushing mollusks and other hard-shelled invertebrates. When teeth are broken or worn, they are replaced from intact rows behind. The fossil record of sharks is based primarily on their teeth.

Sharks lack a swimbladder, the hydrostatic organ of bony fishes. To partially offset the greater density of their bodies than seawater, sharks have a very large liver containing much oil. Also they swim with pectoral fins outstretched and angled to give them lift.

All sharks have internal fertilization; the intromittent organ of the male is the pair of claspers, one developing along the medial edge of each pelvic fin (thus the sex of sharks is easily determined externally). Some sharks are oviparous; they lay eggs in leathery cases. Most sharks are ovoviviparous, meaning the eggs develop within the uterus. The requiem sharks (Carcharhinidae, except the Tiger Shark) and the hammerheads (Sphrynidae) are viviparous; the embryos are nourished by a placenta-like organ of the female. Most sharks have very few young, in some species only one or two (the Tiger Shark and the Blue Shark are exceptional in giving birth to as many as 80 and 135 pups, respectively, at one time). The intestine of sharks is very different from that of most bony fishes. It contains the spiral valve, much like an enclosed spiral staircase; indigestible items such as squid beaks cannot easily pass through the intestine; from time to time a shark may regurgitate such items from its stomach.

Sharks have exceptional sensory systems. Well known is their keen olfaction, which can detect attracting substances such as blood in minute quantities. Most sharks forage for food mainly at dusk or night (but may feed opportunistically during daylight hours); therefore their eyes are adapted to low levels of illumination. They have a tapetum lucidum behind the retina that reflects light (like a cat's eye at night); light

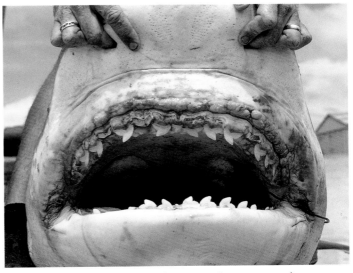

Jaws of the Tiger Shark showing strongly serrate teeth

passes through the light-receptor cells of the retina and is reflected back, thus doubling the stimulus. The highly developed lateralis system of sharks, a complex set of canals on the head and one along the side of the body with pores connecting to the surface, enables them to detect the sources of low-frequency vibrations at considerable distances. Thus they are aware of the movements of prey or predators that they may not see. Some pores on the head of sharks, concentrated on the snout, lead to dermal sensory organs called the ampullae of Lorenzini. These have been shown to act as electroreceptors. A shark is therefore able to detect the weak electromagnetic field around a sleeping fish at night.

Of greatest concern to all who venture into the sea is the threat of being bitten by a shark. However, as noted by many authors, shark attack as a cause of death in the world is negligible compared, for example, with automobile accidents. Even lightning causes more deaths than sharks.

The FAO volume on sharks of the world by Compagno (1984, partly revised in 2001) is the most useful reference for shark identification.

NURSE SHARKS (GINGLYMOSTOMATIDAE)

This family consists of three species, only one of which, the Tawny Nurse Shark (*Nebrius ferrugineus*), occurs in the South Pacific. They are characterized by small eyes, a barbel at each nostril, two close-set dorsal fins posteriorly on the body, and the caudal fin with a long upper lobe but very short lower lobe. Nurse sharks occur in shallow tropical and subtropical seas; they are ovoviviparous, bottom-dwelling, and nocturnal. Although contact with humans is usually without incident, there are records of divers being bitten following provocation, such as grabbing a nurse shark by the tail (Randall, 1961b).

Indonesia

Palau

TAWNY NURSE SHARK
Nebrius ferrugineus (Lesson, 1831)
First dorsal fin only slightly larger than second, its origin a little anterior to base of pelvic fins; caudal fin long, about 30% of total length; teeth small, in 3 or 4 functional rows, with a large central cusp and 4 to 6 small cusps on each side; spiracles very small. Grayish to yellowish brown, paler ventrally. Attains a length of at least 3.2 m. Indo-Pacific, including the Red Sea, but not Hawaiian Islands; described from specimens from New Ireland and Indonesia. Occurs at depths from 1 to at least 70 m. Feeds at night on a wide variety of prey, including reef fishes, spiny lobsters, crabs, and octopuses. Usually shelters in caves or beneath ledges by day; does well in captivity. *Nebrius concolor* Rüppell is a synonym.

8

ZEBRA SHARK FAMILY
(STEGOSTOMATIDAE)

This family consists of only a single species (see following account). There has been disagreement concerning the species name. Seba (1758: 105, pl. 34, fig. 1) illustrated the juvenile well and named it *Squalus varius*. Among the authors who have used Seba's name are Garman (1913), Klausewitz (1960), Dor (1984), and Randall (1995a). Others, most recently Compagno (2001), have used *Stegostoma fasciatum* (Hermann), which was based on Seba. Paolo Parenti (pers. comm.) provided a convincing explanation of why Seba's name for this shark should not be used. Many of Seba's names of fishes are polynomial, and the only binomial one that has been used is *Squalus varius*. His other identifiable fishes have been named by other authors, notably Cuvier in Cuvier et al. (1827).

South Africa

Juvenile, 58 cm, Bahrain

Egg case, Strait of Hormuz (R. Salm)

ZEBRA SHARK
Stegostoma fasciatum (Hermann, 1783)

Body with 5 prominent ridges on back, one of which is middorsal; snout short and broadly rounded; eyes small, the spiracles as large; nostrils with a short barbel; mouth small and nearly straight; teeth in several functional rows, each with a large central cusp and a short cusp to each side; dorsal fins on posterior half of body, the first about twice as large as second; caudal fin about as long as body with no lower lobe; grayish yellow with dark brown spots; juveniles whitish with black bars. Attains about 3 m. Red Sea and east coast of Africa to Samoa Islands, Marshall Islands, and Caroline Islands; southern Japan to Great Barrier Reef and New Caledonia; no type locality. Feeds at night, mainly on crustaceans and mollusks, occasionally on fishes. Oviparous, the egg cases 17 cm long (illustrated by Randall, 1995a). Young hatch at a length of 20–30 cm (van der Elst, 1981). Males mature at 147–183 cm, and females at 169–171 cm (Compagno, 1984).

REQUIEM SHARKS
(CARCHARHINIDAE)

The most important family of sharks from the standpoint of abundance, impact on marine communities, commercial value, and, for a few species such as the Tiger Shark and Bull Shark, as a threat to humans in the sea. The family consists of 12 genera and 49 species, most of which occur in coastal waters of tropic seas. All have five gill slits, no nasal barbels, a large mouth, the first dorsal fin near center of body, and a distinct pit at origin of upper lobe of caudal fin; most lack spiracles, and most have compressed serrate teeth in one functional row with a long, pointed cusp and no small basal cusps. These sharks feed mainly on bony fishes, but also on octopuses, squids, shrimps, and seabirds. The larger species prey, in addition, on smaller sharks, rays, sea turtles, and marine mammals. Except for the ovoviviparous Tiger Shark (*Galeocerdo cuvier*), the development is viviparous. Identification of the plain gray species of the genus *Carcharhinus* can be difficult. Garrick (1982) ably revised the genus, recognizing 25 species (though one, *C. wheeleri* Garrick, is now regarded as a synonym of *C. amblyrhynchos*).

New Britain

New Britain

SILVERTIP SHARK
Carcharhinus albimarginatus (Rüppell, 1837)
Snout moderately long, the preoral length 6.8–9.2% total length; ridge present between dorsal fins; origin of first dorsal fin over or slightly anterior to inner corner of pectoral fin; height of first dorsal fin 7.1–10.6% total length; first dorsal fin, lobes of caudal fin, and pectoral fins conspicuously tipped with white, the outer posterior margins of these and other fins narrowly white. Attains about 3 m. Indo-Pacific and the tropical eastern Pacific; type locality, Red Sea. Usually found on steep outer-reef slopes at depths greater than 30 m, but occasionally encountered in shallower water. Feeds on a wide variety of fishes (Fourmanoir, 1961), including other sharks (the author found a Gray Reef Shark in the stomach of one). Number of pups, 1–11 (usually 5 or 6); size at birth, about 65 cm. A dangerous species; a few attacks on divers have been reported.

GRAY REEF SHARK

Carcharhinus amblyrhynchos (Bleeker, 1856)

Snout moderately long, the preoral length 6.4–8.7% total length; interdorsal ridge absent; origin of first dorsal fin over or just anterior to inner corner of pectoral fin; height of first dorsal fin 8.3–11.9% total length; gray, shading to white ventrally; trailing edge of caudal fin black, very broad on lower lobe; second dorsal and anal fins black except basally. Attains about 1.8 m. Indo-Pacific; type locality, Java Sea; usually on coral reefs in clear water. Feeds mainly on reef fishes, occasionally on cephalopods and crustaceans (Randall, 1980a; Compagno, 1984). Number of pups, 1–6; size at birth, 45–60 cm. In spite of its small size, this shark can be dangerous, especially to spearfishers. Should not be approached if displaying threat behavior (exaggerated slow, sinuous swimming with pectoral fins lowered [see Johnson & Nelson, 1973]). Sometimes misidentified as *Carcharhinus menisorrah* (Valenciennes), a synonym of *C. falciformis* (Bibron).

GALAPAGOS SHARK

Carcharhinus galapagensis (Snodgrass & Heller, 1905)

Moderately slender for the genus; snout moderately long, the preoral length 6.0–8.2% total length; a low ridge on back between dorsal fins; first dorsal fin somewhat acute, its height 9.5–11.1% total length, the origin over about middle of inner margin of pectoral fin; gray to brownish gray, shading to whitish ventrally; no conspicuous markings on fins (fin tips, especially of pectorals, may be dusky). Reported to 3.7 m (Johnson, 1978). Circumglobal, mainly in subtropical seas (therefore expected only in the southern islands covered by this book); occurs especially in clear outer-reef areas. Feeds primarily on reef fishes, occasionally on flatfishes and other sedimentary bottom fishes and also on flyingfishes. Number of pups, 1–16 (in Hawaiian Islands); size at birth, 57–80 cm. Also reported to exhibit threat display like *Carcharhinus amblyrhynchos*. A dangerous shark; the author examined one 3 m long that killed a swimmer at St. Thomas, Virgin Islands (Randall, 1963a), the first published record for the Atlantic.

11

BULL SHARK

Carcharhinus leucas (Valenciennes in Müller & Henle 1839)
Heavy-bodied with a short, broadly rounded snout, the preoral length 4.6–6.7% total length; no interdorsal ridge; teeth nearly triangular (especially uppers) and strongly serrate; height of first dorsal fin 8.2–10.8% total length, its origin usually over posterior end of pectoral-fin base; gray, the young with tips and edges of fins black, these markings soon disappearing with growth. Largest recorded, 3.24 m. Circumtropical, mainly in continental waters or at large islands, hence New Caledonia, Fiji, and Samoa Islands, but a valid record from Rangiroa Atoll in the Tuamotus (Johnson, 1978); type locality, Antilles. Readily enters estuaries and rivers; some of its 10 synonyms were based on specimens from fresh water, such as *Carcharhinus zambezensis* (Peters) and *C. nicaraguensis* (Gill & Bransford). Feeds on a wide variety of fishes, including other sharks and rays, as well as invertebrates and offal. Number of pups, 1–13; size at birth, 56–81 cm. A very dangerous species; exceeded in attacks on humans only by the White Shark.

Fiji (R. L. Pyle)

Malaysia

70.9 cm, Bahrain

BLACKTIP SHARK

Carcharhinus limbatus (Valenciennes in Müller & Henle, 1839)
Snout pointed and moderately long, the preoral length 6.3–9.3% total length; no ridge between dorsal fins; upper teeth narrow-cusped for the genus; origin of first dorsal fin usually over axil of pectoral fins; height of first dorsal fin 8.2–13.8% total length; gray (may be bronze dorsally in life), with a pale band on side, white ventrally; second dorsal fin and lower lobe of caudal fin usually black-tipped (other fins may be black at tips, but the first dorsal often with only a black edge, and rarely entirely plain); Reaches 2.5 m. Fast-swimming and sometimes forms schools. Feeds mainly on small fishes, occasionally on cephalopods and crustaceans. Circumglobal in tropical to warm temperate seas; type locality, Martinique; may be found in turbid estuarine areas. Number of pups, 1–10; size at birth, 38–72 cm. Few attacks on humans have been attributed to this species, but spearfishermen have reason to fear it.

BLACKTIP REEF SHARK

Carcharhinus melanopterus (Quoy & Gaimard, 1824)

Snout short and rounded, the preoral length 5.6–6.3% total length; no interdorsal ridge; height of first dorsal fin 8.0–11.4% total length, its origin usually over inner corner of pectoral fin; second dorsal fin 3.4–5.0% total length; brownish gray to yellowish brown with conspicuous black tips on all fins. Largest, 1.8 m. Indo-Pacific; has penetrated the eastern Mediterranan Sea via the Suez Canal; type locality, Waigeo, Indonesia; generally found inshore, often in very shallow water. Number of pups, 2–5; size at birth, 33–52 cm. Ordinarily timid, but has bitten the feet or legs of persons wading on reef or sand flats (Randall & Helfman, 1973). One of the 3 most common inshore sharks of islands of Oceania (the others, *Carcharhinus amblyrhynchos* and *Triaenodon obesus*). Has been misidentified by some authors as *C. spallanzani* (Peron & Lesueur), now known to be a synonym of *C. sorrah* (Valenciennes).

SANDBAR SHARK

Carcharhinus plumbeus (Nardo, 1827)

Snout rounded, the preoral length 5.6–8.1% total length; a mid-dorsal ridge present between dorsal fins; first dorsal fin very large and erect, its height 13.6–16.5% total length, the fin origin over or a little anterior to pectoral-fin axil; grayish brown dorsally, shading to white below; no distinctive markings on fins (the tips and trailing edges may be dusky). Reaches 2.4 m. Cosmopolitan in tropical to warm temperate seas, especially continental shelf localities; reported from islands of Oceania only from New Caledonia and Hawaiian Islands; type locality, Adriatic Sea. Not yet positively implicated in attack on humans but potentially dangerous. Number of pups, 1–14; size at birth, 56–75 cm. Captive sharks in Hawai'i grew an average of 31 cm the first year, 21 cm the second, and 16 cm the third (Wass, 1973). *Carcharhinus milberti* (Valenciennes) is a synonym.

Hawaiian Islands

TIGER SHARK
Galeocerdo cuvier (Péron & Lesueur, 1822)
Stout-bodied anteriorly, but slender posteriorly, the narrow caudal peduncle reinforced by a low lateral keel; snout very short, the preoral length 3.7–4.8% total length, and only slightly rounded; spiracle a narrow slit behind eye about one-fourth eye diameter in length; teeth coarsely serrate, convex on the antero-medial edge and strongly notched on the posterolateral edge; narrow dark bars on side of body (may be faint on large adults); juveniles with more dark spots than bars, the markings darker. Fourmanoir (1961) reported a 7.4-m female, weighing 3,110 kg and bearing 75 embryos, from Vietnam. Circumglobal in tropi-cal to warm temperate seas; type locality, northwestern coast of Australia. Rarely seen inshore during the day. Tagging has

Embryo, 57.2 cm, Marshall Islands

shown a capability of long migrations, some over 1,000 nautical miles (1,853 km). Feeds on a great variety of marine animals, but also ingests garbage and refuse. Ovoviviparous; number of pups, 10–80; size at birth, 51–76 cm. Juveniles estimated to double their length the first year; maximum age estimated at 45–50 years. Randall (1992) reviewed the literature on the biology of this species. Well known as a very dangerous shark.

Indonesia

SICKLEFIN LEMON SHARK
Negaprion acutidens (Rüppell, 1837)
Snout short, the preoral length 4.6–6.4% total length, and broad-ly rounded; no interdorsal ridge; height of first dorsal fin 6.9–10.9% total length, its posterior edge deeply concave; second dorsal fin nearly as large as first; teeth usually smooth-edged (teeth of large adults may be finely serrate basally); yellowish gray to yellowish brown, the fins more yellowish than body.

Reported to 3.1 m. Indo-Pacific except Hawaiian Islands; type locality, Red Sea. The related *N. brevirostris* (Poey) occurs in the western Atlantic and eastern Pacific. An inshore species, the young often seen in very shallow water; may be found in estua-rine areas. Often seen at rest on the bottom. Feeds mainly on reef and shore fishes. Number of pups, 1–13; size at birth, 45–80 cm; growth slow, that of juveniles about 12 cm per year. Potentially dangerous.

14

Coral Sea

WHITETIP REEF SHARK
Triaenodon obesus (Rüppell, 1837)

A slender shark (hence the name *obesus* is not appropriate); head depressed, about twice as broad as deep; snout very short, the preoral length 3.1–4.5% total length, and broadly rounded; teeth in 2 or more functional rows in jaws, smooth-edged, with a large middle cusp and a small cusp (or 2 on posterior teeth) on each side; height of first dorsal fin 8.7–11.0% total length, its origin well behind inner corner of pectoral fin; second dorsal fin two-thirds to three-fourths size of first dorsal; brownish gray, shading to whitish or pale yellowish ventrally, usually with a few dark gray spots on body; conspicuous white tips on dorsal and caudal fins. To 1.75 m. Tropical and subtropical Indo-Pacific and eastern Pacific; type locality, Red Sea. Often seen at rest in caves or beneath ledges by day; feeds mainly on reef fishes at night; very adept at entering crevices and holes in reefs in quest of prey. Number of pups, 1–5; size at birth, 52–60 cm. Randall (1977) published on the biology. Sometimes classified in the families Hemigaleidae and Triakidae.

HAMMERHEAD SHARKS
(SPHYRNIDAE)

The sharks of this family are unmistakable with the blade-like lateral extensions of their head. This unusual head shape spreads the eyes and olfactory organs farther apart, thus improving binocular vision and providing better tracking of olfactory stimuli; it also serves as a forward rudder, making these sharks highly maneuverable. All are viviparous. Only a few attacks on humans are documented, but the responsible sharks were not identified to species. Gilbert (1967) revised the family and illustrated the dentition. Nine species of hammerheads are known, eight in the genus *Sphyrna* and one in *Eusphyra*. Two species of *Sphyrna* occur in the South Pacific.

Hawaiian Islands

Frontal view of the Scalloped Hammerhead, *Sphyrna lewini*

SCALLOPED HAMMERHEAD
Sphyrna lewini (Griffith & Smith, 1834)

Anterior margin of head broadly convex with a prominent median indentation and 2 lesser indentations on either side (thus giving the front of the head a scalloped appearance); preoral snout length 4.6–5.8% total length; height of first dorsal fin 11.9–14.5% total length; brownish gray, shading to white ventrally; tip of underside of pectoral fins dusky. Attains 4 m. Worldwide in tropical to warm temperate seas; type locality, southern Australia. Feeds mainly on fishes, including small sharks and stingrays, cephalopods, and crustaceans. Females tend to enter calm bays to have their pups; number of pups, 15–31; size at birth, 42–55 cm. Large semistationary schools are sometimes seen, the function of which is uncertain.

241.5 cm, Red Sea

GREAT HAMMERHEAD
Sphyrna mokarran (Rüppell, 1837)

Anterior margin of head nearly straight, with a median indentation and a second slight one to each side; first dorsal fin very high, erect, and pointed, its height 13.5–19.7% total length, the posterior margin strongly concave. The largest of the hammerheads; attains at least 6 m (with unconfirmed reports to 8 m). Circumglobal in tropical to warm temperate seas; type locality, Red Sea. Johnson (1978) reported the first record for French Polynesia. The author observed it at Rangiroa in the Tuamotu Archipelago. Some coastal populations are migratory, as indicated by movement to higher latitudes in warm months. Feeds on fishes, including stingrays, skates, guitarfishes, and other sharks; also squids and crabs. Number of pups, 13–42; size at birth, 50–70 cm.

RAYS (RAJIFORMES)

Rays are characterized by their flattened disc-like form. The enlarged laterally expanded pectoral fins are fused with the body to form the disc; the 5 (6 in one deep-sea family) pairs of gill openings are ventral on the disc. Respiratory water is taken into the spiracles (an opening behind each eye) and passed out the gill openings below. The mouth is ventral, the teeth generally flat and pavement-like. Rays share many of the general features listed earlier for sharks. Seven different families of rays are known to have a long, venomous spine or spines on their tail; the largest and best known are in the family Dasyatidae. Stingray spines have numerous small barbs on each side. The pain from wounds delivered by these spines is excruciating, and a few deaths have been reported. Immediate soaking of a wounded limb in water as hot as can be endured helps to alleviate the pain. Rays often bury in the sand with only their eyes and spiracles showing. They feed mainly on shellfish and worms and occasionally on small burrowing fishes that they excavate from the sediment. Reproduction is ovoviviparous; the nutrition for the developing eggs is initially from yolk, but later from albuminous fluid secreted from vascular filaments that line the uterine wall.

GUITARFISHES (RHINOBATIDAE)

The guitarfish family consists of 9 genera and about 52 species. The shape is variable, but most (such as those of the genera *Rhinobatos* and *Rhynchobatus*) are acutely wedge-shaped anteriorly, the body merging posteriorly and laterally with the pectoral fins; tail long, stout, and muscular with 2 well-developed dorsal fins; skin covered with close-set dermal denticles, often with a middorsal row of tubercles; spiracles large, directly behind eyes; teeth close-set, flat, and pavement-like. Most species occur on continental shelves or the insular shelves of large islands. Some species grow to a large size, but they are harmless to humans. Some authors classify the following species in the family Rhynchobatidae.

Great Barrier Reef

WHITESPOTTED GUITARFISH
Rhynchobatus djiddensis (Forsskål, 1775)
Snout long and pointed; pectoral fins merging with body, but juncture apparent; dorsal fins tall, narrow, and falcate, the first slightly posterior to origin of pelvic fins; caudal fin with a lower lobe; olivaceous to gray-brown with white spots along side of body. Reaches 3 m (one of 305 cm weighed 227 kg). Red Sea (type locality) to western Pacific, including New Caledonia. Variation of this ray over its range may result in it being divided into as many as 5 or 6 species. Reported to feed on crabs, cephalopods, and fishes. The individual in the photograph is being serviced by a pair of cleaner wrasses, *Labroides dimidiatus*.

STINGRAYS
(DASYATIDAE)

Stingrays have the head and body imperceptively fused with the broad pectoral fins to form a disc that varies from nearly circular to rhomboidal, often broader than long. The tail is slender, sometimes whip-like, without any fins (although folds of skin are present on the tail of some species); the venomous spine (sometimes two) is dorsally on the tail, nearer the base than the tip. More than 60 species of stingrays are known in the world; six are included here for the South Pacific region.

Solomon Islands

KUHL'S STINGRAY
Dasyatis kuhlii (Müller & Henle, 1841)
Disc rhomboidal, the anterior and lateral corners slightly rounded; eyes larger than spiracles; tail usually longer than disc, typically with 2 venomous spines; a middorsal row of tubercles on disc; yellowish to reddish brown with scattered dark-edged light blue spots of variable size; a short, transverse, dark brown band enclosing eyes and spiracles; end of tail with alternating bands of white and black, the tip usually white. Disc width to 38 cm; total length to 67 cm. East coast of Africa to Samoa Islands; described from specimens from India, New Guinea, and Vanikoro, Santa Cruz Islands; capable of burying itself completely in sand. Sometimes called the Bluespotted Stingray.

Marquesas Islands

PINK WHIPRAY
Himantura fai Jordan & Seale, 1906
Disc rhomboidal, the width about 1.2 times the length; tail (when intact) very long and slender, its length about twice disc width, and nearly cylindrical in cross-section; usually a single venomous spine about 2 spine lengths from base of tail; disc of adults with short, flat, well-spaced denticles, but no tubercles; color often given as grayish or brownish pink, but may be yellowish brown; edge of disc narrowly white. Disc width to at least 1.5 m; total length over 5 m. Palau, Guam, and Caroline Islands in the North Pacific; in the South Pacific from Queensland and New Caledonia to the Society Islands and Marquesas Islands; type locality, Western Samoa. Other than Western Australia, the distribution in the Indian Ocean is uncertain (Last & Stevens, 1994).

18

WHITETAIL WHIPRAY

Himantura granulata (Macleay, 1883)

Disc oval but nearly as wide as long; snout slightly pointed; tail 1.5–2 times disc width in juveniles, slightly longer than disc width in adults, tapering to a slender tip when intact; tail oval in cross-section, the depth at base of tail 1.3 in width; 1 or 2 venomous spines on tail about 2 spine lengths posterior to pelvic fins; disc dark gray to black dorsally with numerous very small white spots, white ventrally with black spots at edges; tail posterior to spines white. Reported to 97 cm disc width. Occurs from the Seychelles and Maldive Islands to Indonesia, Papua New Guinea (type locality), northern Australia and Queensland, Caroline Islands (Homma et al., 1991), Santa Cruz Islands, and New Caledonia (Laboute & Grandperrin, 2000). Known from the shallows to 85 m. Ishihara et al. (1993) redescribed the species and reported the following prey from 3 of 6 specimens containing food: fishes (*Siganus* sp., labrid, pomacentrid, several gobiids, including *Valenciennea* sp.), calappid crabs, octopus, and sipunculids. Last & Stevens (1994) stated that this stingray is called the Mangrove Whipray in Australia because it often occurs in mangrove habitats where it feeds mainly on crustaceans, especially crabs and shrimps. The individual photographed by the author was found at a depth of 2 meters in a narrow channel of a lagoon at North Malé Atoll in the Maldive Islands. The small black-striped blue fish on the disc of the ray is a cleaner wrasse, *Labroides dimidiatus*.

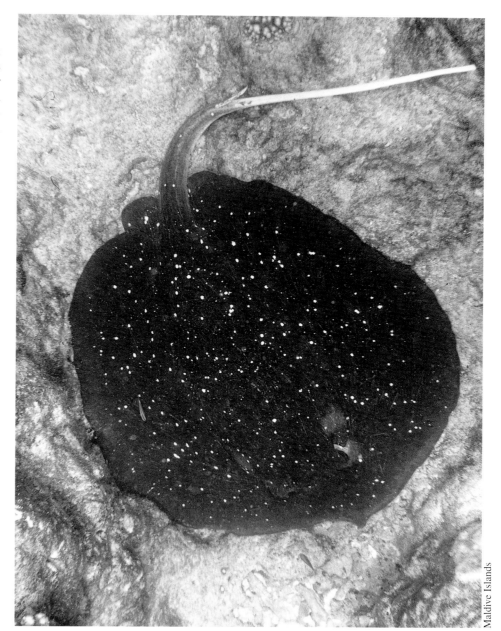

Maldive Islands

REEF STINGRAY

Taeniura lymma (Forsskål, 1775)

Disc ovate, a little longer than wide; tail nearly 1.5 times longer than disc; 1 or 2 venomous spines in about middle of tail; surface of disc usually smooth; yellowish brown with numerous round to oval, bright blue spots of variable size. Attains at least 70 cm total length. Red Sea (type locality), and east coast of Africa to western Pacific, from Philippines to Ningaloo Reef, Western Australia, Great Barrier Reef, Lord Howe Island, and New Caledonia. Nocturnal; reported to feed on mollusks, crustaceans, and polychaete worms. Hides on sand patches in caves or beneath ledges during the day. Also known as the Bluespotted Ribbontail Ray.

Papua New Guinea

Norfolk Island

BLACKBLOTCHED STINGRAY
Taeniura meyeni Müller & Henle, 1841
Disc nearly circular, slightly broader than long; tail about as long as disc, the venomous spine at about mid-length; a middorsal row of tubercles on disc, extending to spine; gray, densely blotched and mottled with black. Disc width to at least 1.8 m, and total length to 3.3 m. Red Sea and throughout the Indian Ocean to islands of Micronesia; in the western Pacific from southern Japan to Lord Howe Island, Norfolk Island, and New Caledonia; also reported from the Galápagos Islands (Grove & Lavenberg, 1997). Generally seen in shallow water, but 1 record from 435 m off Mozambique (Wallace, 1967); type locality, Mauritius. Two of 3 specimens with food in their stomachs contained only fishes (Randall, 1980a). Although not aggressive to humans, at least 2 persons have died from spine wounds (1 diver evidently thought the ray was a Manta and grabbed the front of the disc with his hands). *Taeniura melanospilos* (Bleeker) is a synonym.

Marshall Islands

PORCUPINE RAY
Urogymnus asperrimus (Bloch & Schneider, 1801)
Disc oval, a little longer than wide, and very thick centrally; tail about as long as disc and without a venomous spine; entire dorsal surface of disc and tail covered with large thorn-like tubercles; eyes of adults much smaller than spiracles; brownish gray, the tail blackish distally. Reported to reach a disc width of 1 m. Type locality, Bombay, India; occurs in the Indo-Pacific from east coast of Africa to the Marshall Islands and Fiji. Stomach contents of 5 specimens consisted of sipunculids, polychaetes, and crustaceans (Homma & Ishihara, 1994). *Urogymnus africanus* (Bloch & Schneider) from the Guinea coast of West Africa is considered a synonym (Last & Compagno in Carpenter & Niem, 1999a). Also known as the Thorny Ray.

EAGLERAYS
(MYLIOBATIDAE)

Eaglerays have the head distinct from the disc, with the eyes oriented more laterally than dorsally; the disc is at least 1.6 times broader than long, the outer corners acutely pointed; the tail is long and whip-like with a small dorsal fin near the base; one to several venomous spines are present on the basal part of the tail (except the species of *Aetomylaeus*). The teeth are flat and plate-like, either as single long transverse rows (as in *Aetobatis*) or with small hexagonal teeth at the end of the long middle plates (*Aetomylaeus* and *Myliobatis*); anterior nasal flaps long and fused medially to form a nasal curtain that overlaps mouth. A large elongate spiracle lies behind each eye, and five pairs of gill openings ventrally on anterior half of disc. Eaglerays feed mainly on hard-shelled mollusks and crustaceans. The mollusk shells are crushed in the powerful jaws, and the shell fragments ejected from the mouth. All are ovoviviparous. Compagno & Last in Carpenter & Niem (1999a) reviewed the family for the central and western Pacific; 10 species are known for the area, but only two extend their range to islands of Oceania.

Hawaiian Islands

SPOTTED EAGLERAY
Aetobatis narinari (Euphrasen, 1790)
Disc width 1.6–1.8 times longer than length, each side acutely pointed; anterior margin of disc nearly straight, the posterior a slight sinuous curve; head with a prominent rostral lobe (pointed in adults), nearly round in cross-section (flat dorsally); tail very long, as much as 3 times disc width, with 1 to 5 venomous spines near its base; nasal curtain deeply notched medially; dark gray to black dorsally with white spots or rings. Largest recorded, 2.3 m in width; weight to at least 200 kg. Cosmopolitan in all warm seas; type locality, St. Bartholomew, West Indies. Known from inshore, including estuarine habitats, to depths of 60 m. An active swimmer; sometimes leaps free of the surface. Reaches sexual maturity in 4–6 years; usual litter size, 4; size at birth, about 17 cm in disc width. Feeds primarily on a wide variety of gastropod and bivalve mollusks.

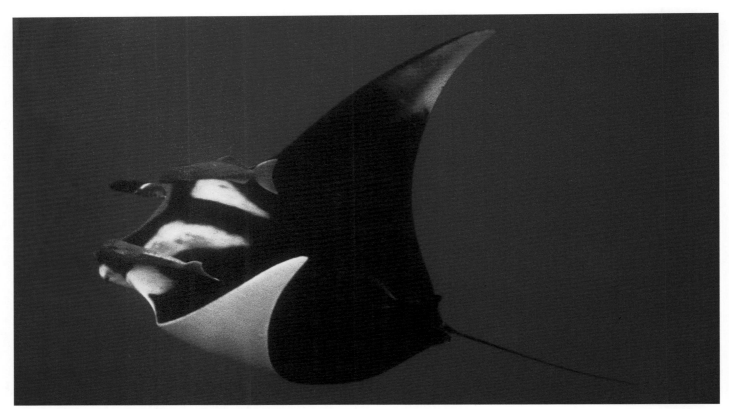

ORNATE EAGLERAY
Aetomylaeus vespertilio (Bleeker, 1852)
Disc width about twice disc length, each lateral tip acutely pointed; anterior margin of disc on each side slightly convex, the posterior concave; head with a prominent protruding rostral lobe, the snout duckbill-shaped; tail very long, nearly 3 times disc width when intact, without venomous spines; dorsal surface of disc gray with transverse wavy narrow dark bands on front half and a reticular pattern on posterior half. Reaches at least 16 cm in disc width and 38.5 cm in total length. Indo-Malayan region and northern Australia, north to Taiwan, east to New Caledonia (Laboute & Grandperrin, 2000), with Indian Ocean records of Maldive Islands and Mozambique; type locality, Java. Usually found inshore in turbid estuarine areas, but reported offshore to depths up to 110 m.

Manta, *Manta birostris,* Hawaiian Islands

MANTAS AND DEVILRAYS
(MOBULIDAE)

This family consists of two genera, *Mobula* (common name, devilrays) with nine species in the world (none recorded from the South Pacific) and *Manta* of which most authors recognize only one species. Mantas and devilrays feed on zooplankton, hence are usually actively moving in the sea. Like their eagleray relatives, they have a disc that is much wider than long, with pointed tips, a long whip-like tail, and a small dorsal fin on the base of the tail; one (rarely two) small barbed spines may be present near base of tail.

The head is broad, with a pair of unique cephalic flaps, one on each side of the mouth, that are used to direct food organisms into the mouth; the flaps are coiled into a spiral when not feeding; the anterior nasal flaps are joined to form a nasal curtain dorsally on mouth; the teeth are minute, in many rows. There are 5 pairs of internal gill slits in the pharyneal region with leaf-like appendages that act like sieves to capture the food organisms from the respiratory water that passes over the gills to exit through the 5 pairs of broad gill slits ventrally on the anterior part of the disc; there are no buccal papillae on the floor of the mouth; the spiracle is small and narrow. All are ovoviviparous, usually with a single embryo per female. Notarbartolo-di-Sciara (1987) revised the genus *Mobula*, and Compagno & Last in Carpenter & Niem (1999a) reviewed the family for the central and western Pacific.

Hawaiian Islands

MANTA
Manta birostris (Walbaum, 1792)

Disc about 2.2 times wider than long; head short and broad, the width just behind eyes less than 3 in distance from middle of front of snout to tip of pectoral fin; mouth terminal and broad, its width about 15 in disc width; cephalic flaps about half as broad at base as their length; teeth only in lower jaw and minute (may be concealed by skin), in about 18 rows centrally, narrowing to 12 to 14 rows at corners; tail slender, shorter than length of disc; no barbed spine on base of tail behind dorsal fin; skin with small, stellate dermal denticles; dark gray to black dorsally, sometimes with broad, oblique, whitish bands anteriorly, and white ventrally, often with irregular dark blotches. The largest of the rays; reported to a width of 7 m and a weight of 1,600 kg. Occurs in all tropical and subtropical seas; in the Pacific from Japan to New South Wales, east to the Hawaiian Islands and Tuamotu Archipelago. No type locality given. Usually seen at or near the surface. Feeds mainly on pelagic crustaceans and other small animals of the zooplankton, occasionally on small schooling fishes. The movements are probably related mainly to seeking areas where the plankton is dense. Often accompanied by the remora *Remorina albescens*. Young at birth, 122–127 cm in disc width. Capable of leaping free of the sea.

BONY FISHES

The bony fishes are distinguished from the sharks and rays by having a bony skeleton (though some primitive bony fishes such as sturgeons have a skeleton that is partly cartilage). Another obvious distinction is having a single gill opening on each side instead of the five to seven (mainly five) of sharks and rays (the chimaeras, a small, bizarre group of cartilaginous fishes, have one gill opening), and for nearly all, the spiracle is lacking. Except for some species, mainly those that rest on the bottom, bony fishes have a swimbladder (also called the gasbladder), which is a gas-filled sac just under the vertebral column that offsets the weight of the heavier tissues of the body. Most bony fishes have overlapping scales, at least on the body, and the scales for many extend variously onto the head and fins; the lateral line is usually present as a sensory canal beneath the scales connecting to the exterior via one or more pores through individual scales of the series.

The living bony fishes are divided into 2 classes One is the lobe-fin fishes (Sarcopterygii), which includes only the 3 lungfishes and 2 species of *Lati-meria*. The other is the ray-fin fishes (Actinopterygii). It is divided into 3 subclasses, the Chondrostei (sturgeons and their relatives), the Neopterygii (the bowfin and relatives), and the Teleostei, which includes nearly 24,000 species, hence about 96% of our living fishes. This very successful group has radiated into an incredible number of different forms and invaded nearly all aquatic habitats.

As mentioned in the Introduction, the order in which the fishes are presented is phylogenetically by family, beginning with families having characters considered to be primitive. Among these characters for the Actinopterygii are the low position of the pectoral fins on the side of the body, the origin of the pelvic fins in the posterior abdominal position, the lack of true spines in the fins, and the maxilla bearing teeth and forming a prominent part of the gape. The most primitive families considered here are those of tenpounders (*Elops*), tarpons (*Megalops*), bonefishes (*Albula*), and 3 families of eels. All have a ribbon-like transparent larval stage called the leptocephalus.

TENPOUNDERS
(ELOPIDAE)

The tenpounders, also called ladyfishes, are represented by a single genus, *Elops*, which is considered the most primitive of living bony fishes of the subclass Teleostei. It is characterized as follows: body elongate and moderately compressed; eyes large, covered anteriorly and posteriorly with transparent adipose tissue; mouth terminal or nearly so (upper jaw slightly anterior in young and lower jaw slightly projecting in adults); mouth large, the maxilla extending well beyond the eye; a broad, long, median bone called the gular plate between the mandibles; teeth very small, in bands in jaws, on bones of the palate, and on the tongue; branchiostegal rays numerous; a single dorsal fin near middle of body; anal fin entirely posterior to dorsal; neither fin with spines, the last rays short, and both fins folding into a scaly basal sheath; caudal fin deeply forked; pectoral fins very low on side of body; origin of pelvic fins below or slightly anterior to origin of dorsal fin; scales small and cycloid; lateral line commencing from upper end of gill opening, angling gradually downward to continue along middle of side of body, each scale with a single tubule. Whitehead (1962) revised the genus, recognizing six species in the world, only one of which, *E. hawaiensis* Regan, is found in the western and central Pacific.

HAWAIIAN TENPOUNDER
Elops hawaiensis Regan, 1909
Dorsal rays 23–27; anal rays 15–17; pectoral rays 16–17; pelvic rays 14–15; lateral-line scales 88–98; gill rakers long and slender, 7–8 + 12–15; branchiostegal rays 27–31; vertebrae 66–70; body depth 5.5–6.0 in standard length; head length 3.65–4.0 in standard length; upper jaw 5.9–6.7 in standard length; premaxillary teeth exposed when mouth closed; greenish gray dorsally,

Hawaiian Islands

silvery on sides and ventrally; fins gray, the edges of dorsal and caudal fins narrowly dark. Attains 105 cm; in spite of its common name, rarely reaches 10 lbs (5 kg). Eastern Indian Ocean from Andaman Sea to Western Australia; in the Pacific from southern Japan to New South Wales, east throughout most of Oceania to the Hawaiian Islands and Tuamotu Archipelago; euryhaline, occurring in the sea and in fresh water, but most often in brackish habitats. Prized as a gamefish, leaping when hooked, but not often eaten due to the numerous bones in the flesh. The similar *Elops machnata* (Forsskål) occurs in Indonesia and throughout the Indian Ocean, differing in having 63–64 vertebrae. Whitehead (1962) wrote that more of the premaxillary teeth of *machnata* are exposed when the mouth is closed than in *hawaiensis*, but he meant mandibular teeth.

TARPONS
(MEGALOPIDAE)

This family is sometimes combined with the Elopidae because of such shared characters as the presence of the gular plate in the lower jaw, numerous branchiostegal rays, dentition, adipose tissue over eye, position of the fins, and the leptocephalus larva. The tarpons are distinct in their projecting lower jaw with the mouth opening superior, deeper body, filamentous last dorsal ray, and differing meristic data. Two species are known in the family, the large Atlantic Tarpon, *Megalops atlanticus* Valenciennes, and the Indo-Pacific *M. cyprinoides* (Broussonet). Both are euryhaline.

INDO-PACIFIC TARPON
Megalops cyprinoides (Broussonet, 1782)
Dorsal rays 16–20; anal rays 23–31; pectoral rays 15–16; pelvic rays 10–11; lateral-line scales 36–40; gill rakers long and slender, 15–17 + 30–35; branchiostegal rays 23–27; vertebrae 67–68; villiform teeth in jaws, on vomer, palatines, pterygoids, and tongue; lateral line descending from upper end of gill opening to continue midlaterally on body; tubules on surface of scales of lateral line with many branches; body depth 3.5–4.0 in standard length; last ray of dorsal fin prolonged as a filament; anal fin entirely posterior to dorsal fin, its base 1.5 times longer than that of dorsal, the last ray longer than previous rays but not filamentous; caudal fin deeply forked; origin of pelvic fins anterior to origin of dorsal fin; silvery, the dorsal and caudal fins dark gray, the remaining fins whitish. Often reported to reach 1 m, but Weber & de Beaufort (1913) gave the maximum length as 55.5 cm, and van der Elst (1981) as 50 cm; the world angling record, from Queensland, is only 2.99 kg. Occurs throughout the Indo-

New Caledonia

Pacific region (except the Hawaiian Islands) where there is suitable estuarine habitat; able to live in fresh water. Preys mainly on small fishes and shrimps. The transparent ribbon-like leptocephalus larval stage recruits to fresh water, migrating up streams to ponds or lakes. When it transforms to the juvenile stage, it shrinks to half its length. Esteemed as a game fish, but not as food (the muscle tissue is very bony). Also widely known as the Oxeye or Oxeye Tarpon.

BONEFISHES
(ALBULIDAE)

The bonefish genus *Albula* was long believed to consist of two species, *A. nemoptera* (Fowler) from the western Atlantic and eastern Pacific, easily distinguished by its filamentous last dorsal and anal rays, and the circumglobal *A. vulpes* (Linnaeus), with a type locality of the Bahamas. Apart from *A. nemoptera*, Shaklee & Tamaru (1981) showed that there are two species in the western Atlantic and two different ones in the Indo-Pacific region, based mainly on specimens from the Hawaiian Islands. With the use of DNA, Colborn et al. (2001) identified eight populations of the genus in the world: three Indo-Pacific, two eastern Pacific, two western Atlantic, and one eastern Atlantic; four of these were designated only as *Albula* sp. A–D. Because so much of our information on bonefishes was thought to apply to a single species, *A. vulpes*, we are often unable to assign earlier data to the species level. The genus *Albula* is characterized by a long conical snout with a ventral mouth and broad patches of small molariform teeth on the roof and floor of the mouth; there is a single dorsal fin with no spines and 16–21 soft rays; the anal fin lies far behind the dorsal, with no spines and 7–9 soft rays; the caudal fin is deeply forked, the pectoral fins are low on body, and the pelvic fins lie behind the middle of the body; both fins have an axillary scale. The late postlarval stage is a leptocephalus. Bonefishes occur in all tropical and subtropical seas, generally in relatively shallow water on sand flats; they often penetrate brackish environments. Their food consists mainly of worms, small mollusks, and crustaceans that live on or beneath the surface of the bottom sediment, but small fishes have occasionally been found in stomachs. The species of *Albula* are not often eaten because of the numerous small bones in the muscle tissue (the probable basis for the common name). They are highly prized as game fishes. At the recommendation of the author, the International Game Fish Association changed its angling records for bonefish from *Albula vulpes* to *Albula* spp. The current all-tackle record for the genus is an 8.6-kg fish caught off KwaZulu, South Africa in 1962; before that, the world record was 8.2 kg from the Hawaiian Islands. The meristic data below for the two Hawaiian species of *Albula* were obtained from Shaklee & Tamaru (1981).

Hawaiian Islands

Sudan, Red Sea

LONGJAW BONEFISH
Albula forsteri Valenciennes in C & V, 1847
Dorsal rays 16–17; anal rays 7–8; pectoral rays 16–18; pelvic rays 9–11; lateral-line scales 62–72 (all pored scales counted); distance from front of snout to end of upper jaw 2.65–2.9 in head length; front of lower jaw somewhat pointed; silvery with a blackish mark at tip of snout. Maximum length about 70 cm. Occurs from Tahiti (type locality) and the Hawaiian Islands to the western Pacific. *Albula neoguinaica* Valenciennes is a synonym. First named *Esox argenteus* by Forster, but an invalid name because it was without a description. As a result of confusion in the subsequent use of the name *argenteus*, Valenciennes provided the new name *Albula forsteri* (clarification by Randall & Bauchot, 1999).

SHORTJAW BONEFISH
Albula glossodonta (Forsskål, 1775)
Dorsal rays 14–18; anal rays 7–9; pectoral rays 16–20; pelvic rays 9–11; lateral-line scales 69–78 (all pored scales counted); distance from front of snout to end of upper jaw 3.0–3.3 in head length; front of lower jaw rounded; silvery with a blackish mark at tip of snout. Maximum length about 70 cm. Type locality, Red Sea. Exact range uncertain, but probably occurs throughout most of the Indo-Pacific region. *Albula erythrocheilos* Valenciennes, described from Tonga, is a synonym. Vertebral count differences given by Shaklee & Tamaru (1981) to separate this and the preceding species are valid for Hawaiian specimens but not for the rest of the Pacific due to the presence of an apparent third species.

CONGER EELS AND GARDEN EELS
(CONGRIDAE)

The Congridae is one of 15 families of true eels of the order Anguilliformes. The species of this family have near-cylindrical bodies anteriorly, well-developed dorsal and anal fins, usually prominent pectoral fins, lips with a free margin on side of mouth, a complete lateral line, no scales, and a gill opening before or below the pectoral-fin base. Shallow-water species fall into 2 subfamilies, the Congrinae (conger eels) and Heterocongrinae (garden eels). Garden eels generally live in large colonies; each is in a separate burrow from which it rises to feed on zooplankton in the passing water mass, and into which it withdraws with the approach of danger. Epoxy casts of the burrows revealed that they are not straight but take the form of a series of sinusoidal waves (Tyler & Smith, 1992). The number of vertebrae (obtained from X-rays) is very important in the identification of congrids. The species treated here are those most apt to be seen in or near the reef environment. The genus *Conger* was revised by Kanazawa (1958), and the Indo-Pacific Heterocongrinae by Castle & Randall (1999). Clark (1980) and Clark et al. (1990) published on some aspects of the ecology and behavior of the garden eel *Gorgasia sillneri* Klausewitz of the Red Sea.

CONGER EELS (CONGRINAE)

BARRED CONGER
Ariosoma fasciatum (Günther, 1871)
Vertebrae 154–158; pectoral rays 13–14; lateral-line pores 145–149 (9–10 anterior to gill opening); body depth 14–21 in total length; origin of dorsal fin about one-half eye diameter before gill opening; whitish to pale yellowish, the adults with 12 double dark brown bars on body (solid bars and large spots on juveniles) and numerous dark brown spots on head, progressively larger posteriorly; dorsal fin with large, round, dark brown spots. Reaches about 60 cm. Reported from Sulawesi (type locality), Taiwan, Marshall Islands, Hawaiian Islands, Tahiti, and Madagascar; lives in a burrow in sand by day and forages at night; stiff caudal region an adaptation for rapid backward burrowing. *Ariosoma nancyae* Shen is a synonym. Originally described in the genus *Poeciloconger*; Shen (1998) referred this genus to the synonymy of *Ariosoma*.

Hawaiian Islands

MOUSTACHE CONGER
Conger cinereus Rüppell, 1830
Vertebrae 139–146; pectoral rays 15–19; lateral-line pores before anus 36–41; body depth 17–23 in total length; teeth at side of jaws compressed and close-set, forming a shearing edge; brownish gray with a blackish streak above and parallel to upper lip; median fins with a prominent black margin; pectoral fins often with a large blackish area; exhibits dark gray to black bars at night. Reaches 130 cm. Indo-Pacific (except the Hawaiian Islands where the very similar *Conger marginatus* Valenciennes occurs); type locality, Red Sea. A roving nocturnal predator of crustaceans and fishes. The author found an adult in the stomach of a Galapagos Shark at Rapa.

Hawaiian Islands (night)

GARDEN EELS (HETEROCONGRINAE)

GALZIN'S GARDEN EEL
Gorgasia galzini Castle & Randall, 1999
Vertebrae 178–188; pectoral fins small (12–16% head length), with 12–14 rays; lateral-line pores before anus 38–44; upper lip not continuous across front of snout; mouth only slightly oblique; body very elongate for the genus, the depth 60–74 in total length; dorsal fin origin over middle of pectoral fins; whitish, densely covered with minute dark spots; some white patches on postorbital head, especially just behind eye. Largest specimen, 44 cm. Society Islands, Marshall Islands (type locality, Enewetak Atoll), Samoa Islands, Coral Sea, and Guam; depth range 17–53 m, on sand.

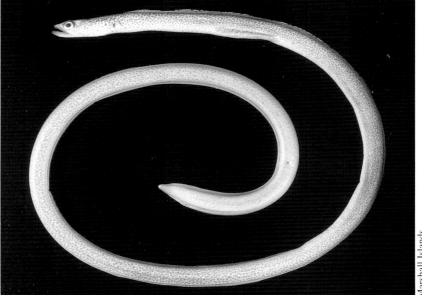
Marshall Islands

Maldive Islands

Cebu, Philippines

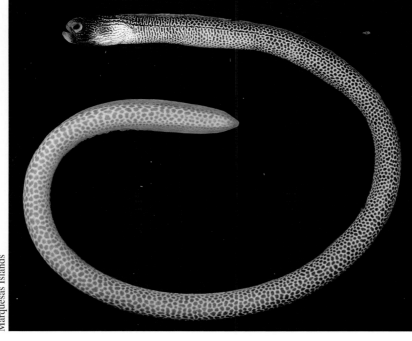

Marquesas Islands

SPLENDID GARDEN EEL

Gorgasia preclara Böhlke & Randall, 1981

Vertebrae 144–152; pectoral fins very small (8–11% head length), with 9–14 rays; lateral-line pores on body widely spaced, only 11–16 before anus; upper lip not continuous across front of snout; mouth only slightly oblique; body very elongate, the depth 42–52 in total length; dorsal-fin origin just posterior to pectoral fins; orange with white bars, those on head narrower and oblique, those on body progressively smaller posteriorly, ending as a series of small white spots. Attains 33 cm. Type locality, Cebu, Philippines; also known from Maldive Islands, Indonesia, Coral Sea, Guam, and Ryukyu Islands; depth range, 18–75 m; usually on sand-rubble substrata.

SPOTTED GARDEN EEL

Heteroconger hassi (Klausewitz & Eibl-Eibesfeldt, 1959)

Vertebrae 164–175; pectoral fins tiny (6–9% head length), with 11–12 rays; lateral-line pores before anus 59–64; upper lip continuous across front of snout; mouth strongly oblique; body very elongate, the depth 38–55 in total length; dorsal-fin origin slightly before gill opening; white with close-set small black spots and 3 large black spots, the first surrounding gill opening and pectoral fin, the second about halfway along trunk, and the third around anus; juveniles almost entirely black. Attains 40 cm. Natal and islands of the western Indian Ocean to Line Islands, Society Islands (Randall et al., 2002a), Tonga, Samoa Islands, and throughout Micronesia; Ryukyu Islands to Queensland and New Caledonia; type locality, Maldive Islands; occurs at depths of 7–45 m.

MASKED GARDEN EEL

Heteroconger lentiginosus Böhlke & Randall, 1981

Vertebrae 173–176; lateral-line pores before anus 63–64; upper lip continuous across front of snout; mouth strongly oblique; body moderately elongate, the depth 33–46 in total length; origin of dorsal fin far forward on head, above second lateral-line pore; pectoral fins very small, with 11–12 rays; yellowish white to white with numerous small olive to black spots; a broad blackish bar anteriorly on head, enclosing eye, followed by a large white area laterally and ventrally. Largest specimen, 37.6 cm. Collected to date only at the Marquesas Islands (type locality, Nuku Hiva), Society Islands, and Marshall Islands, from sand in 21–40 m, but it certainly can be expected in other areas of Oceania. The scientific name *lentiginosus* is from the latin meaning freckled, in reference to the numerous small dark spots. However, the more distinctive color marking is the broad blackish bar across the head enclosing the eye, hence the preferred common name Masked Garden Eel.

Headsaddle Snake Eel, *Ophichthus cephalozona*, in hole with cleaner shrimps, *Lysmata amboinensis*, Fiji

SNAKE EELS AND WORM EELS
(OPHICHTHIDAE)

The snake-eel family is the largest of the eel families, consisting of 59 genera and more than 260 species (McCosker, 1977a and subsequent papers), but they are not well known to divers because most of their time is spent buried in the sediment of the bottom or hidden deep in reef. Some species are nocturnal, and some are known to come to the surface at night, probably in association with spawning activity. Snake eels are very elongate, the body cylindrical or nearly so, and they have no scales. The anterior nostrils are usually tubular and project downward; the posterior nostrils open inside the mouth or through a valve in the upper lip. There are numerous branchiostegal rays that overlap ventrally. The eels of the largest subfamily (Ophichthinae) have a sharply pointed tail with no caudal fin; it is a burrowing organ that enables them to move easily tail-first in the sand or mud. Species of the other subfamily (Myrophinae) have the median fins continuous around the tip of the tail; they are small, less than 30 cm (systematic review by McCosker, 1970, 1977a). Snake eels are sometimes mistaken for sea snakes, but the latter may be readily distinguished by having scales, no fins (some snake eels are also finless), a highly compressed tail for swimming, and by their greater mobility (including trips to the surface for air). The species of snake eels that divers are most apt to encounter in the South Pacific area are treated here, but even these are rarely seen. Five species of worm eels of the genus *Muraenichthys* are listed by Wass (1984) from the Samoa Islands, all collected with ichthyocide; none observed alive by author. The worm eel *Scolecenchelys gymnota*, though ranging to the Society Islands, has not been seen by the author, but it was photographed in the open at night in Tahiti, so a species account of it is given here. *Glenoglossa wassi* McCosker, 1982, known from 2 specimens collected with rotenone from sand in 40 m in Tutuila, American Samoa, is unique in having a very elongate tongue that is modified into a lure.

Ambon, Indonesia

Tuamotu Archipelago

CROCODILE SNAKE EEL

Brachysomophis crocodilinus (Bennett, 1833)

Vertebrae 116–124; pores between gill opening and anus 50–52; head length 6.5–8 in total length; snout short, 13–19 in head length; eye far forward on head, over anterior third of gape; lower jaw of adults strongly projecting; side of jaws with a series of close-set cirri (some double, and some branched); 2 rows of teeth on upper jaw, those of inner row larger; a row of well-spaced canine teeth in lower jaw; largest canines in a row on intermaxilla and vomer; origin of dorsal fin over seventh or eighth lateral-line pore from gill opening; whitish, the upper two-thirds of body finely speckled with brown; lateral-line pores edged in brown. Largest specimen, 81.5 cm. Islands of western

Indian Ocean to Johnston Island and Society Islands; Ryukyu Islands to northern Great Barrier Reef. Buries in sand, usually with only part of the head visible. The type specimen from Mauritius is not extant; McCosker & Randall (2001) described a neotype. *Brachysomophis sauropsis* Schultz is a synonym.

Bali

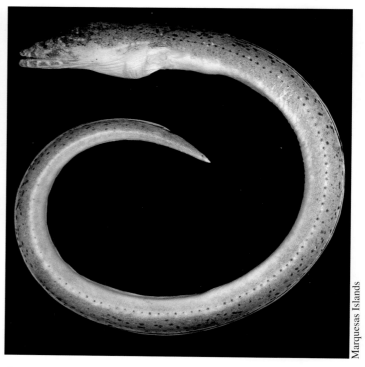

Marquesas Islands

REPTILIAN SNAKE EEL

Brachysomophis henshawi Jordan & Snyder, 1904

Vertebrae 128–134; pores between gill opening and anus about 53; body depth 19–32 in total length; head length 6.2–7.8 in total length; snout length 7.8–10.5 in head length; eye far forward on upper part of head, over anterior third of gape; mouth with lower jaw slightly projecting; a series of short cirri along side of jaws (larger on upper); dentition similar to that of *Brachysomophis crocodilinus*; whitish to light brown dorsally, with scattered small, dark brown spots above lateral line, the largest of about pupil size, shading to pale yellow or white ventrally; each lateral-line pore in a small, dark brown spot; head usually red anteriorly, often with white markings; dorsal fin black basally with a broad white margin. Attains about 100 cm. Known in the Indian

Ocean only from southern Oman, but ranges in the Pacific east to the Hawaiian Islands (type locality) and the Society Islands. Lives under the sand, generally near reefs, with just the upper part of the head barely visible; ambushes its prey of fishes and crustaceans that venture near. A diver's hand placed in front of the head of an adult of this eel might be savagely bitten.

BLACKSTRIPED SNAKE EEL
Callechelys catostoma (Forster, 1801)
Vertebrae 192–205; body very elongate, the depth 48–73 in
total length; tail short, 3.2–3.6 in total length; head length
18–20 in total length; eye centered over tip of lower jaw; a
median groove ventrally on snout extending to between anterior nostrils; intermaxilla with 2 to 4 retrorse canine teeth in
ventral groove on snout; remaining teeth in jaws and on
vomer small and uniserial; origin of dorsal fin above or
slightly behind corner of mouth; no pectoral fins; whitish to
cream with a broad black stripe on side from middle of head
nearly to tip of tail; edge of dorsal fin black. Largest specimen, 77 cm. Indo-Pacific; type locality, Tahiti; usually found
in shallow sandy areas, but the only specimen from Hawai'i
came from 32 m. *Callechelys melanotaenia* Bleeker and
C. striatus Smith are synonyms (Randall & Wheeler, 1991;
McCosker, 1998). The Greek *catostoma* means inferior mouth,
referring to the ventral position of the mouth (though true of
most snake eels).

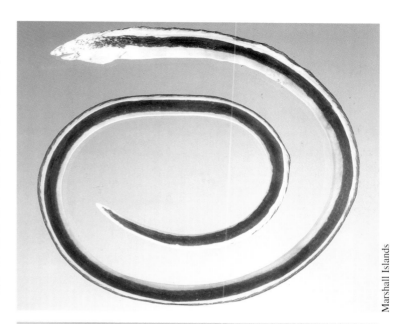

Marshall Islands

MARBLED SNAKE EEL
Callechelys marmorata (Bleeker, 1853)
Vertebrae 174–183; body very elongate, the depth 37–58 in
total length; tail short, 2.6–2.8 in total length; head length
14–16 in total length; median groove ventrally on snout containing 2–4 recumbent canine teeth; remaining teeth small,
slender, retrorse, uniserial in jaws and biserial on vomer; dorsal fin high, its origin slightly posterior to corner of mouth;
no pectoral fins; whitish to pale yellow with numerous
irregular, dark brown to black blotches, some interconnected,
those on head smaller (overall color may be more dark than
pale); dark spots present ventrally on body. Largest specimen,
the holotype, 86 cm, from Sumatra. Indo-Pacific; recently
found to coexist in the Hawaiian Islands with the endemic
Callechelys lutea Snyder; it is similar in morphology and
color but has 206–219 vertebrae and few or no spots ventrally on the body.

Bali

SADDLED SNAKE EEL
Leiuranus semicinctus (Lay & Bennett, 1839)
Vertebrae 162–171; body depth 35–60 in total length; snout
to anus 2.1–2.3 in total length; head length 12–15 in total
length; eye large, over middle of gape; snout moderately
pointed, its preoral length about equal to gape; a median
groove ventrally on snout containing about 5 nearly recumbent small canine teeth; remaining teeth in jaws small, in one
row, the uppers angling inward and posteriorly, the lowers
mainly at front of jaw; no teeth on vomer, or at most 1–3;
origin of dorsal fin above or a little posterior to gill opening;
white to pale yellowish with 22–30 broad, black, saddle-like
bars, only those on tail extending to ventral edge; saddles
varying from much broader than pale interspaces to nearly
equal in width; a black bar before and behind eye, the latter
continuing onto lower jaw. Largest specimen examined,
65.5 cm. Indo-Pacific; probable type locality, Hawaiian
Islands; a common shallow-water species of sand flats and
seagrass beds, but rarely seen in the open except when
attracted to night lights.

Balicasag Island, Philippines

31

Papua New Guinea

Maldive Islands (night)

Sulawesi (night)

RINGED SNAKE EEL
Myrichthys colubrinus (Boddaert, 1781)
Vertebrae 190–202; body very elongate, the depth 48–68 in total length; head length 17–20 in total length; teeth blunt, in 2 rows in jaws; anal fin ends on tail well before end of dorsal fin; white to pale yellowish with 25 to 32 black rings, most completely encircling head and body, the first enclosing eye; often with a round black spot (sometimes 2 or 3) in pale interspaces of adults. Reported to 97 cm. Indo-Pacific; type locality, Ambon, Indonesia. Occasionally seen by day moving slowly over open substrata as if foraging. Suggested as a mimic of the venomous banded sea snakes. *Myrichthys elaps* (Fowler) and *M. bleekeri* Gosline are among the 10 synonyms (McCosker & Rosenblatt, 1993).

SPOTTED SNAKE EEL
Myrichthys maculosus (Cuvier, 1816)
Vertebrae 185–189; body elongate, the depth 33–46 in total length, and compressed posteriorly; head 12.5–15 in total length; origin of dorsal fin in advance of gill opening; pectoral fins shorter than their base; white with large, well-separated, round black spots, more numerous in larger individuals (one row mid-dorsal on body, hence these spots semicircular when viewed from the side). Largest specimen, 99 cm. Indo-Pacific, but not Hawaiian Islands, where replaced by the similar *Myrichthys magnificus* (Abbott). Occurs in sandy areas from near shore to at least 30 m.

Sulawesi, with cleaning shrimp

HIGHFIN SNAKE EEL
Ophichthus altipennis (Kaup, 1856)
Vertebrae 177–179; body cylindrical, tapering to a hard finless point, its depth 25–40 in total length; preanal length 2.4–2.7 in total length; teeth conical, not enlarged, in one row in jaws; dorsal fin elevated, its origin above or slightly anterior to gill opening; pectoral fins 2.4–2.8 in head length; gray-brown to bronze, paler below, the head and lateral-line pores in small black spots, a white blotch on head before eye; sometimes a white blotch between pores on side of jaws; anterior part of dorsal fin and its margin black; pectoral fins black except occasional small individuals with clear fins. Reaches at least 103 cm. Known from Indonesia, Philippines, New Guinea, Queensland, Mariana Islands, Marshall Islands, and Society Islands; often seen with

anterior half of head exposed vertically from sand (note cleaning shrimp in figure); the author photographed one at night in Sulawesi swimming rapidly just off the bottom. Sometimes misspelled *altipinnis*; *Ophichthys melanochir* Bleeker and *Pisoodonophis zophistius* Jordan & Snyder are synonyms.

NAPOLEON SNAKE EEL

Ophichthus bonaparti (Kaup, 1856)

Vertebrae 156–164; body depth 28–38 in total length; snout to anus 1.7–1.8 in total length; head length 11–13 in total length; teeth in jaws and on vomer uniserial, sharply conical, and retrorse, origin of dorsal fin over tip of pectoral fins; pectoral fins small, about 7 in head length; pale yellow to cream with 14–23 broad dark brown to black saddles or bars; head with large, black-edged, orangish brown spots (bars may be nearly uniformly dark brown), progressively smaller anteriorly, some irregularly joined; a series of dark brown spots at edge of dorsal fin. Michael (1998) presented 3 illustrations to show variation in life color of the head. Attains 75 cm. Known from Natal, Mauritius, Maldive Islands, Indonesia (type locality, Ambon), southern Japan, Queensland, and Society Islands (the latter record as *Ophichthys garretti* Günther, a synonym). The specimen reported from the Hawaiian Islands by McCosker (2002) has been reidentifed as *Ophichthus fowleri* (Jordan & Evermann). Buries in sand by day (sometimes with just the front of the head showing) and may be seen in the open at night. The author removed a 65.8-cm one from the stomach of a 121.6-cm *Brachysomophis cirrocheilos* he speared in Ambon.

Papua New Guinea

HEADSADDLE SNAKE EEL

Ophichthus cephalozona Bleeker, 1864

Vertebrae 155–157 (2 counts); pectoral rays 13–15; body depth of adults 24–30 in total length; head length 9.5–11 in total length; slender, incurved conical teeth in a single row in jaws and on vomer; pectoral fins 3–4 in head length; origin of dorsal fin above end of pectorals; light brown, shading to white ventrally, with a large black saddle broadly edged in white on posterior part of head; each lateral-line pore in a small black spot; dorsal fin largely black; anal fin white with a broad black margin. Illustrated specimen from Fiji, 115 cm, the largest recorded. Described from specimens from Singapore and Ambon; also known from Queensland, Palau, Mariana Islands, Marshall Islands, and the Society Islands; reported as nocturnal.

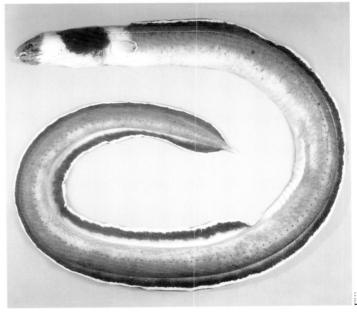

Fiji

WORM EELS (MYROPHINAE)

SLENDER WORM EEL

Scolecenchelys gymnota (Bleeker, 1857)

Vertebrae 126–136; body depth 32–44 in total length; head length 9–10 in total length; head and trunk 1.5 in length of tail; snout moderately pointed; eye 12–15 in head length; distance from tip of chin to font of snout about equal to eye diameter; anterior margin of eye closer to corner of mouth than tip of chin; dorsal fin low, its origin about half a head length posterior to anus; teeth conical, in 2 rows in upper jaw except posteriorly, and forming a median circle in 1 row anteriorly in jaw; side of lower jaw and vomer with 1 row of teeth, dividing to 2 anteriorly; translucent light gray-brown, with some blue iridescence, shading to nearly white on abdomen. Reaches at least 17 cm. Found throughout the Indo-Pacific region; type locality, Ambon, Molucca Islands. The author has collected specimens from tidepools in less than 0.2 m to caves in coral reefs in 17 m. Formerly classified in *Muraenichthys*.

Tahiti (P. Bacchet)

Barred Moray, *Echidna polyzona*, Sulawesi at night

MORAY EELS
(MURAENIDAE)

Like other eels, morays have a very elongate body, a small gill opening, and no pelvic fins. The caudal fin is joined with the dorsal and anal fins. Pectoral fins and scales are absent. Most species, such as those of the large genus *Gymnothorax,* have long fang-like teeth, some of which are inwardly depressible, but other species such as those of the genus *Echidna* have nodular to molariform teeth. Morays with long canines prey mainly on fishes, occasionally on crustaceans and octopuses, whereas the species that have blunt teeth feed primarily on crustaceans. Many morays remain hidden in the reef and are rarely seen. Some of the species exhibit great variation in color, not only with growth, but among individuals the same size. Depending on the species, morays may maintain separate sexes throughout life, change from female to male, change from male to female (*Rhinomuraena quaesita*), or be synchronously hermaphroditic (male and female at the same time) (Fishelson, 1992). Morays are rarely aggressive to humans, but divers are occasionally bitten; this happens most often from putting a hand into a hole or crevice in the reef and having a moray mistake it for a prey item such as an

octopus. The larval stage of morays is relatively large, in general, and the duration of life in the plankton is long. This has resulted in the broad distribution of many species within the vast Indo-Pacific region. As with snake eels, the number of vertebrae are often helpful in species identification. Böhlke (1982) has documented the vertebral counts of many of the type specimens of morays and other eels. Schultz in Schultz et al. (1953) reviewed the morays of the Marshall and Mariana Islands; of the 40 species he recognized, eight were described as new. Böhlke & Randall (1999) wrote a review of 40 species of morays from the Hawaiian Islands, and Böhlke & McCosker (2001) those of Australia and New Zealand. Still more systematic research is needed on Indo-Pacific morays, particularly the small cryptic species of the genus *Anarchias* (only 1 included here; 2 new species are known from the South Pacific). Also the generic classification of the Muraenidae may change. The morays are classified in 2 subfamilies, the Muraeninae and the Uropteryginae, the species of the latter have the median fins confined to the posterior end of the tail.

MORAYS (MURAENINAE)

WHITEFACE MORAY
Echidna leucotaenia Schultz, 1943
Vertebrae 121–130; body depth 13–19 in total length; anus a little anterior to middle of body; short conical teeth in one row at front of jaws; side of jaws with 1–2 irregular rows of small nodular to molariform teeth, increasing to 2 or 3 rows in lower jaw of larger individuals; vomer with 2 rows of small molariform teeth, increasing on large adults to an ovate patch with 5 or 6 teeth across widest point; dorsal-fin origin anterior to gill opening; brown, the snout paler than body (white in small individuals); corner of mouth dark brown, preceded by a large white spot; sensory pores of head and posterior nostril in a white spot; margin of fins white. Reported to 75 cm. Islands of Oceania (type locality, Phoenix Islands), including Johnston Island, but not the Hawaiian Islands; also reported from Aldabra and east coast of Africa; a shallow-water species of coral reefs and rubble bottoms.

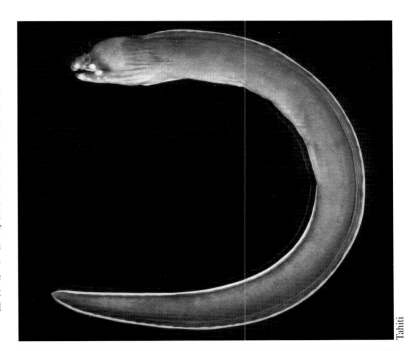
Tahiti

SNOWFLAKE MORAY
Echidna nebulosa (Ahl, 1789)
Vertebrae 119–126; body moderately elongate, the depth at gill opening 14–23 in total length; anus near midbody; no canine teeth; teeth in upper jaw in one row, those anteriorly stout and bluntly conical; 2 stout conical teeth in median row; lower jaw with an outer row of small nodular teeth and an inner row of 3–4 stout, bluntly conical treeth at the front; vomer with 2 rows of rounded molariform teeth that diverge anteriorly in large individuals; dorsal-fin origin over or slightly anterior to gill opening; white with about 3 longitudinal rows of dendritic black blotches containing one or more yellow spots; numerous small black spots among the black blotches. Reported to 75 cm. Indo-Pacific and tropical eastern Pacific; type locality, East Indies. More inclined than most morays to swim in the open. Feeds mainly on crabs. A popular aquarium fish, though not often available. *Echidna geographica* (Solander) is among the 8 synonyms.

Tonga

BARRED MORAY
Echidna polyzona (Richardson, 1845)
Vertebrae 119–126; body depth at gill opening 10–19 in total length; anus near midbody; no canine teeth; 5 irregular rows of short conical teeth across front of upper jaw (large males lose middle row); vomer a broad plate of molariform teeth (up to 7 rows and over 50 teeth in large individuals); lower jaw with 2 to 4 rows of teeth, the anterior teeth conical, the posterior ones molariform; origin of dorsal fin anterior to gill opening; juveniles pale brown with 25 dark brown bars broader than interspaces; bars become diffuse and the body strongly mottled with growth (bars evident only on tail of large individuals); corner of mouth dark. Largest specimen, 72.3 cm. Indo-Pacific; type locality not reported. Has been given 12 different scientific names, largely because of variation in color and dentition with growth.

Hawaiian Islands

35

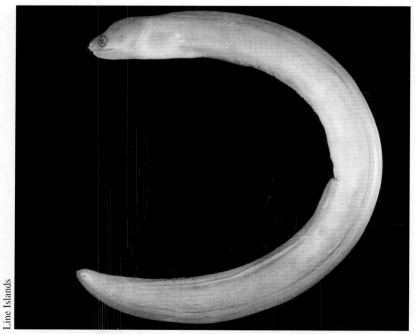

Line Islands

UNICOLOR MORAY

Echidna unicolor Schultz in Schultz et al., 1953
Vertebrae 122–131; body depth 18–25 in total length; anus before middle of body; stout conical teeth at front of upper jaw, the 2 largest in a median row; side of upper jaw with 2 rows of small teeth, the outer row nodular, the inner as slender conical teeth; lower jaw with 2 rows of nodular teeth, the largest in inner row at front of jaw; origin of dorsal fin about halfway between corner of mouth and gill opening; uniform tan to light brown with a narrow dark brown ring around eye. Largest specimen, 29 cm. The firrst record was a mis-identification of two Bishop Museum specimens as *Echidna amblyodon* (Bleeker) from the Marquesas islands by Seale (1906). First described from atolls in the Marshall Islands and subsequently reported from other islands of Micronesia, the Society Islands, Line Islands, and Johnston Island, but not the Hawaiian Islands; also reported from northwestern Australia, Maldive Islands, and Chagos Archipelago. Collected from shallow lagoon reefs to drop-offs in 25 m.

Maldive Islands

BAYER'S MORAY

Enchelycore bayeri (Schultz in Schultz et al., 1953)
Vertebrae 146–153; body depth 12–27 in total length; anus well before middle of body, the preanal length 2.4–2.55 in total length; jaws slender and hooked, with long canine teeth visible in gap between jaws when mouth closed (true of other species of *Enchelycore*); canines in jaws alternating with small sharp teeth, the upper jaw with an inner row of large canines; front of upper jaw with a median row of 3 very long canines; origin of dorsal fin over or slightly anterior to gill opening; brown with a yellowish green margin posteriorly on fins. Attains 70 cm. Known from the islands of Oceania except the Hawaiian Islands, Great Barrier Reef, Taiwan, Ryukyu Islands, Maldive Islands, and Chagos Archipelago; type locality, Rongelap Atoll, Marshall Islands; occurs on seaward reefs from surge channels to 38 m. Not seen by the author while diving, either by day or night.

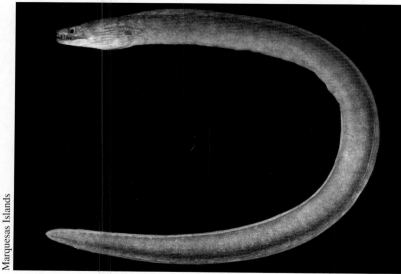

Marquesas Islands

BIKINI MORAY

Enchelycore bikiniensis (Schultz in Schultz et al., 1953)
Vertebrae 146–153; body depth 17–24 in total length; anus before middle of body; side of upper jaw with 3 rows of canines, the outer row at front of jaw alternating with small teeth; 3 very long canines in middle row at front of upper jaw; lower jaw with 2 rows of teeth, the inner row as canines; origin of dorsal fin over or slightly anterior to gill opening; posterior nostril oval, a little anterior to upper part of eye, with a slightly raised rim that becomes crenulate in adults; mottled light gray-brown. Reaches 60 cm. Reported from the Marshall, Mariana, Caroline, Samoa, and Marquesas Islands; inhabits seaward coral reefs exposed to wave action.

DRAGON MORAY

Enchelycore pardalis (Temminck & Schlegel, 1846)

Vertebrae 119–126; stout-bodied, the depth at gill opening 10–16 in total length; anus before midbody; teeth in jaws in 2 rows, those of outer row small but sharp and close to inner row of canines; 3 very long canines in a median row at front of upper jaw; tubular anterior nostril long; posterior nostril a very long tube above front of eye; adults brownish orange, becoming orange on head, with narrow, irregular, dark brown bars on body; head and body with numerous dark-edged white spots and some small black spots; many white spots on head vertically or obliquely elongate. Attains 92 cm. Wideranging from Zanzibar and Mauritius to the Hawaiian Islands and Marquesas Islands, but only from few localities, most of which are insular; type locality, Nagasaki, Japan. Often mistakenly placed in the genus *Muraena*.

Izu Islands, Japan

MOSAIC MORAY

Enchelycore ramosa (Griffin, 1926)

Vertebrae 145–151; depth of body 16.5–20 in total length; anus well before middle of body, the preanal length about 2.5 in total length; teeth in jaws in 2 rows, the inner row as slender canines, those anteriorly long; longest canines 3 in median row at front of upper jaw; aperture of posterior nostril of adults oval; origin of dorsal fin closer to gill opening than corner of mouth; whitish, often finely flecked with dark brown, overlaid by a striking anastomosing pattern of narrow dark brown bands. Attains about 100 cm. Southeast Australia, Lord Howe Island, Norfolk Island, northern New Zealand (type locality), Kermadec Islands, Rapa, and Easter Island. *Enchelycore mosaica* (Whitley) is a synonym.

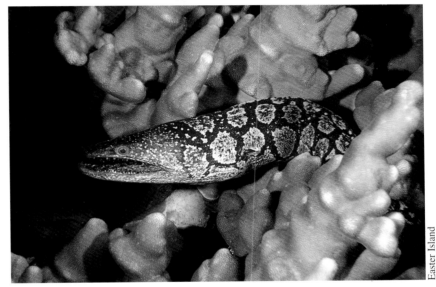

Easter Island

FUNNEL-NOSTRIL MORAY

Enchelycore schismatorhynchus (Bleeker, 1853)

Vertebrae 137–142; body depth 14–23 in total length; anus anterior to middle of body; front of upper jaw with a single row of large canines on each side, alternating with tiny teeth, and a median row of 3 very long canines; side of jaw with an inner row of lesser canines; front of lower jaw with an outer row of small teeth and an inner row of 3 canines on each side; tip of tubular anterior nostril expanded, funnel-like; dorsal fin high, its origin about halfway between corner of mouth and gill opening; light to medium brown, paler ventrally on head and trunk, the edge of fins white; distal end of anterior nostrils darker brown. Attains 120 cm. Reported from Chagos Archipelago, Indonesia (type locality, Sumatra), Ryukyu Islands, Palau, Mariana, Caroline, Samoa, Society, and Marquesas Islands; usually on seaward reefs; rarely encountered by divers.

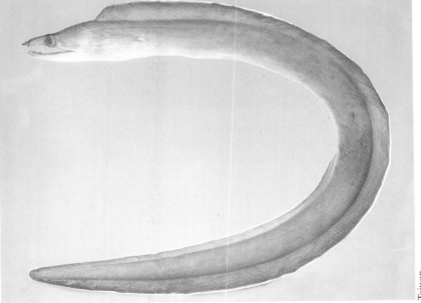

Taiwan

37

Hawaiian Islands

Hawaiian Islands

Waikīkī Aquarium

VIPER MORAY

Enchelynassa canina (Quoy & Gaimard, 1824)
Vertebrae 141–147; body depth at gill opening 11–20 in total length; anus near midbody; jaws concavely arched, only the tips meeting when mouth closed, exposing unusually large fangs; teeth in jaws in 2 rows, those of outer row small but sharp and close to inner row of canines; 3 very long canines in a median row at front of upper jaw; anterior nostril a short broad tube with a posterior bilobed flap; posterior nostril a very large oval opening with a short rim and a crenulate edge, about halfway between anterior nostril and eye; dorsal-fin origin between gill opening and corner of mouth; dark gray-brown, often with numerous vertical black lines. Reported to 152 cm (largest examined, 126 cm). Described from Rawak (Bismarck Archipelago) and Waigeo (Indonesia); most records from islands of Oceania, including the Hawaiian Islands and Pitcairn Islands; in the Indian Ocean from Cocos-Keeling Islands, Chagos Archipelago, and Mauritius; also known from the tropical eastern Pacific. Generally found inshore on reefs exposed to wave action, but rarely seen.

ZEBRA MORAY

Gymnomuraena zebra (Shaw in Shaw & Nodder, 1797)
Vertebrae 129–136; body depth at gill opening 15–21 in total length; anus far behind midbody, the tail about half length of pre-anal length; fins hidden in thick fleshy skin; teeth molariform, in 2 or 3 rows in jaws and 5 or 6 rows on palate (teeth more numerous with growth); orangish brown to dark brown with narrow white to pale yellow bars, varying from about 25 in small individuals to over 100 in large ones (some bars incomplete in adults); Reported to reach 150 cm, but such a length should be confirmed; certainly can attain 100 cm. Indo-Pacific and tropical eastern Pacific; type locality, Sumatra. Feeds principally on crabs, occasionally on mollusks and even sea urchins. Small ones of some value as an aquarium fish, but not in a tank with crustaceans.

Hawaiian Islands

WHITEMARGIN MORAY

Gymnothorax albimarginatus (Temminck & Schlegel, 1846)
Vertebrae 184–195; body depth at gill opening 11–25 in total length; tail slender and tapering; anus notably behind midbody, the preanal length 1.7–1.8 in total length; teeth in jaws in 1 row, long and well spaced; median row of 3 long fangs at front of upper jaw; large anterior teeth of adults serrate basally; dorsal fin high, its origin between corner of mouth and gill opening; light to medium brown, paler ventrally, the fins often darker and usually with a narrow white margin; pores on side of jaws in a white spot. Largest examined, 105 cm. Known from Japan (type locality), Taiwan, Indonesia, New Caledonia (*Gymnothorax* sp. 3 of

Laboute & Grandperrin, 2000), Hawaiian, Samoa, and Society Islands, generally in more than 30 m; largest specimen from a trap in 180 m. Often misidentified as *G. hepaticus*, a Red Sea–western Indian Ocean species. One colleague experienced more pain than expected from a bite to the wrist, the pain radiating to upper arm, thus indicating the probable presence of a venom.

SOUTH PACIFIC MORAY
Gymnothorax australicola Lavenberg, 1992

Vertebrae 138–148; body depth 16–23 in total length; anus well before midbody, the preanal length 2.2–2.4 in total length; front of upper jaw with a single row of canine teeth, followed by smaller, triangular compressed teeth and an inner row of longer, more slender teeth; 1 or 2 long canines in median row at front of upper jaw; teeth of lower jaw in 1 row; larger teeth in jaws serrate; origin of dorsal fin slightly anterior to gill opening; medium brown, the sensory pores on side of jaws in a white spot; a dark brown ring around eye, broader posteriorly; anal fin sometimes with a whitish margin. Reaches 40 cm. Known from Rapa, Pitcairn Islands, Easter Island (type locality), and San Felix Island, Chile; a common inshore species. Previously misidentified as *Gymnothorax panamensis* (Steindachner), which differs in having fewer vertebrae and 2 instead of a single branchial pore. Lavenberg's paratype of *australicola* from Lord Howe Island was reidentified as *G. atolli* (Pietschmann) by Böhlke & McCosker (2001).

Easter Island

BLACKCHEEK MORAY
Gymnothorax breedeni McCosker & Randall, 1977

Vertebrae 128–131; body robust, the depth about 14 in total length, the width about 1.7 in depth; anus before middle of body; short canine teeth in upper jaw in 1 row, the median row at front of upper jaw consisting of 2 long canines; 2 rows of teeth on each side at front of lower jaw, the inner row of 3 large canines; teeth in jaws finely serrate; dorsal-fin origin a little anterior to gill opening; finely mottled brown with an irregular oblique black band from eye to corner of mouth; gill opening edged in black. Attains 65 cm. Described from specimens from the Comoro Islands (type locality), Amirantes, Line Islands, and Marquesas Islands; also known from Natal, Maldive Islands, Indonesia, Palau, and the Caroline Islands. An aggressive species that is prone to bite; Allen & Steene (1979) referred to it as the "vicious moray" at Christmas Island, Indian Ocean, where both were bitten.

Marquesas Islands

LATTICETAIL MORAY
Gymnothorax buroensis (Bleeker, 1857)

Vertebrae 109–117; stout-bodied, the depth at gill opening 11–16 in total length; anus before midbody; canine teeth in 5 rows across front of upper jaw; teeth on side of upper jaw in 2 rows (3 rows in small individuals); teeth at front of lower jaw in 2 rows on each side, those of inner row larger; dorsal-fin origin anterior to gill opening; grayish brown, the body with about 5 longitudinal rows of small, dark brown blotches that tend to be aligned vertically, the blotches larger and more darkly pigmented posteriorly; head mottled grayish brown without distinct spots; tip of tail often yellow. Largest specimen, 38.7 cm; females may be fully mature as small as 18 cm. Indo-Pacific and tropical eastern Pacific; type locality, Buru, Molucca Islands. A shallow-water coral-reef species; common in tropical latitudes but rarely seen; only one specimen recorded for the Hawaiian Islands.

Bali

Sumatra

Bali

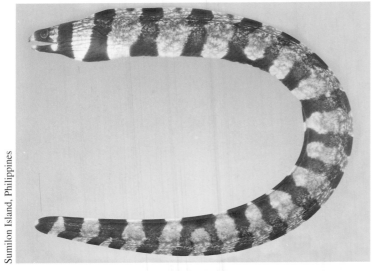

Sumilon Island, Philippines

Easter Island

LIPSPOT MORAY

Gymnothorax chilospilus Bleeker, 1865

Vertebrae 120–129; body depth at gill opening 14–22 in total length; anus before middle of body; teeth anteriorly in jaws in one row, the posterior canines usually alternating with 1 or 2 small teeth, 3 median canines at front of upper jaw the longest; side of jaw of females with 2 rows of teeth, the inner row of 1–3 long teeth (no inner teeth in males); teeth at front of lower jaw usually in 2 rows, those of inner row longest; origin of dorsal fin closer to gill opening than corner of mouth; light brown to whitish, finely mottled with darker brown, with 2 or more longitudinal rows of dendritic dark brown blotches (sometimes joined to form irregular bars); a dark brown spot at corner of mouth preceded by a larger white spot; each pore on side of jaws in a small white spot. A small species, the largest examined, 30 cm. Described from specimens from Sumatra and the Molucca Islands; also known from Mozambique (*Lycodontis perustus* Smith, a synonym), Seychelles, Chagos Archipelago, Ryukyu Islands, Philippines, Papua New Guinea, Great Barrier Reef, and Tahiti; generally found on shallow reefs.

ENIGMATIC MORAY

Gymnothorax enigmaticus McCosker & Randall, 1982

Vertebrae 126–134; body depth 15–23 in total length; anus before midbody; teeth in jaws in one row, the 3 anterior teeth on each side and 3 in a median row on upper jaw as canines; dorsal fin low, its origin just anterior to gill opening; whitish, becoming mottled dorsally, especially on larger individuals, with 17–21 black bars, narrower than pale interspaces, that completely encircle head and body. Reported to 58 cm. Natal, Maldive Islands, Chagos Archipelago, Indonesia, Philippines, Hong Kong, Okinawa, islands of Micronesia (type locality, Palau), Line Islands, and Samoa Islands; a shallow-water nocturnal species of coral reefs. Formerly misidentified as *Gymnothorax rueppellii*, a similar dark-barred species (see account for that species).

STOUT MORAY

Gymnothorax eurostus (Abbott, 1860)

Vertebrae 116–126; stout-bodied, the depth at gill opening 13–17 in total length; anus anterior to middle of body; canine teeth in 5 rows across front of upper jaw; teeth on side of upper jaw in 2 rows (3 rows in small individuals); teeth at front of lower jaw in 2 rows on each side, those of inner row larger; color highly variable, but usually brown, darker posteriorly, with numerous small, pale yellow to whitish spots; small black spots on about anterior half of body arranged in approximately vertical rows. Largest reported, 60 cm. Distribution antitropical: Japan, Taiwan, Minami-tori-shima (Marcus Island), Hawaiian Islands (type locality; the most common moray, but not often seen), Lord Howe Island, Norfolk Island, New Caledonia, Kermadec Islands, Austral Islands, Rapa, Marquesas Islands (low latitude, but sea cool), Pitcairn Islands, and Easter Island; in the Indian Ocean from southern Mozambique, Natal, and Mauritius; also known from the eastern Pacific. Randall (1985b) found food in 22 of 59 specimens examined: fishes in 8, the rest with crustaceans (mainly crabs). The name *eurostus* means stout in Greek, in reference to the robust body.

DARKSPOTTED MORAY
Gymnothorax fimbriatus (Bennett, 1832)
Vertebrae 128–142; body depth 14–18 in total length; anus a little anterior to middle of body; jaws narrow, the lower slightly curved; teeth at front of jaws in 1 row, the anterior canines of upper jaw alternating with small pointed teeth; side of upper jaw with a short inner row of canines; 2 pairs of long canines anteriorly in lower jaw; origin of dorsal fin a little anterior to gill opening; pale gray-brown, often with a greenish cast, with longitudinal rows of well-separated dark brown blotches; 2–3 oblique rows of dark spots behind eye; top of head dull greenish yellow; a large white spot at corner of mouth; edge of fins whitish. Reaches 80 cm. Mauritius (type locality) and Seychelles to islands of Micronesia, Society Islands, and Marquesas Islands; Ryukyu and Ogasawara Islands to Great Barrier Reef and New Caledonia; primarily nocturnal.

Papua New Guinea

YELLOWMARGIN MORAY
Gymnothorax flavimarginatus (Rüppell, 1830)
Vertebrae 132–140; body depth at gill opening 11–20 in total length (larger individuals heavier bodied); anus a short distance before midbody; no very long canine teeth in jaws, the largest in outer row at front of upper jaw with 2–4 small teeth flanking or in between; 1–3 canines in median row at front of upper jaw; side of upper jaw with a short inner row of 1–4 larger teeth; origin of dorsal fin anterior to gill opening; pale yellowish, densely and finely mottled with dark brown; snout and front of lower jaw purplish brown; gill opening in a prominent black spot; edge of fins green to yellow posteriorly. Reaches at least 120 cm. Indo-Pacific and tropical eastern Pacific; type locality, Red Sea. Generally seen in shallow depths, but known to 150 m. Only 7 of 24 with food in stomachs; 4 contained fishes, including *Mulloidichthys flavolineatus*, the rest crustacean remains (Randall, 1985b). Individuals have been tamed to leave the shelter of the reef and take food from the hand of divers.

Great Barrier Reef

BROWNSPOTTED MORAY
Gymnothorax fuscomaculatus (Schultz in Schultz et al., 1953)
Vertebrae 112–122; body depth at gill opening 4–20 in total length; anus before midbody; stout conical teeth at front of upper jaw in 1 row, none as canines, the median row with 2 teeth; side of upper jaw with 2 rows of teeth, those of inner row longer and more slender; stout conical teeth at front of lower jaw with an outer row of small rounded teeth; origin of dorsal fin far back, closer to anus than gill opening; usual color tan to light brown with small brown spots on body and fins (diffuse anteriorly on body, and few or none on head); head pores in prominent white spots. Reaches only 20 cm. Natal, Seychelles, Maldive Islands, and Chagos Archipelago to the islands of Micronesia (type locality, Rongerik Atoll, Marshall Islands), Hawaiian Islands, and Pitcairn Islands; a cryptic species known from the depth range of 1–22 m. Described in *Rabula*, an invalid genus.

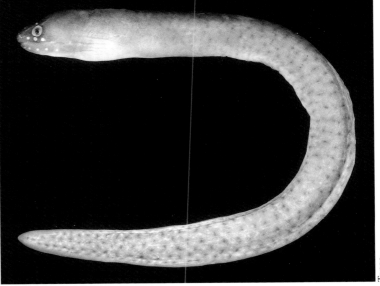
Tonga

41

Hawaiian Islands

SLENDERTAIL MORAY
Gymnothorax gracilicauda Jenkins, 1903
Vertebrae 127–135; body slender with tapering tail, the depth at gill opening 16–23 in total length; anus before midbody, the pre-anal length 2.2–2.3 in total length; usually 6 canines in outer row on each side at front of upper jaw, with a few very small lateral teeth between, the 3 longest teeth in middle row; side of upper jaw with a short inner row of lesser canines; front of lower jaw with an outer row of small teeth and an inner row of 3 or 4 canines on each side; origin of dorsal fin about halfway between corner of mouth and gill opening; mottled pale yellowish with about 40 narrow, dendritic, dark brown bars, many interconnected, those on head and trunk not extending ventrally; usually a median pale streak on snout; edge of median fins whitish. Largest specimen, 30.8 cm. Hawaiian Islands (type locality) and Pitcairn Islands to islands of Micronesia and the Great Barrier Reef; depth range, 1–20 m.

Tahiti, juvenile cleaner wrasse in gill opening

GIANT MORAY
Gymnothorax javanicus (Bleeker, 1859)
Vertebrae 137–143; body depth at gill opening 12–22 in total length, the large adults deep-bodied; tail strongly tapering; anus at or shortly anterior to middle of body; teeth large and stout, none extremely long; 5 or 6 teeth on each side at front of upper jaw, some with small teeth between; median row of teeth at front of upper jaw with 2 or 3 teeth; side of upper jaw with 2 or 3 inner teeth (lost in individuals over about 30 cm); lower jaw with a row of small sharp teeth and 3 or 4 inner canines anteriorly on each side; light to medium brown with large irregular dark brown

blotches (some may contain a pale spot or spots) and numerous small, irregular, dark brown spots; gill opening in a black spot. The largest of morays; attains at least 250 cm (the mud-dwelling *Strophidon sathete* is longer, but it is very slender). Indo-Pacific and Cocos Island, Costa Rica; type locality, Java. Fatalities have been reported from eating the flesh (from ciguatera fish poisoning). Brock (1972) opened the stomachs of 1,074 adult specimens from Johnston Island; only 158 contained food, 88.8% of which consisted of fishes from 17 families (the Scaridae predominating); a Whitetip Reef Shark was among the prey; also eaten were spiny lobsters and octopuses.

KIDAKO MORAY

Gymnothorax kidako (Temminck & Schlegel, 1846)
Vertebrae 136–149; body depth at gill opening 12–21 in total length; anus before middle of body, the preanal length 2.1–2.5 in total length; usually 6 canine teeth in 1 row on each side at front of upper jaw with a few very small teeth variously between, the 3 longest canines in middle row; side of upper jaw with an inner row of 1–3 lesser canines (in individuals smaller than 30 cm); front of lower jaw with 2–4 canines on each side, sometimes with a few small teeth forming a close-set outer row; origin of dorsal fin between corner of mouth and gill opening; white to yellowish brown with a complex dendritic reticular pattern of dark brown that tends to form bars posteriorly on body. Largest, 91.5 cm. Known from Japan (type locality), Taiwan, Hawaiian Islands (*Gymnothorax mucifer* Snyder is a synonym), Pitcairn Island, Society Islands, and Queensland south of 25°S, thus suggesting an antiequatorial distribution. Recorded from depths of 2–350 m (photograph taken in 49 m).

Ogasawara Islands

TRUNKSPOTTED MORAY

Gymnothorax margaritophorus Bleeker, 1865
Vertebrae 126–143; body depth 18–23 in total length; anus before middle of body, the preanal length 2.2–2.3 in total length; front of upper jaw with 3 rows of teeth, the outer row on each side with 3 or 4 canines and small teeth between, and the middle row of 2 large canines; side of upper jaw with an outer row of small teeth and an inner row of about 4 larger teeth; lower jaw with a single row of small teeth on each side and 2 pairs of canines at front of jaw; dorsal-fin origin on head a little closer to gill opening than corner of mouth; pale brown with a longitudinal series of 2–7 elongate dark brown blotches commencing dorsally on postorbital head and continuing as progressively less distinct round blotches posteriorly, disappearing before end of trunk; irregular dark bars developing faintly below round dark spots and becoming progressively more distinct posteriorly on tail; a median pale line dorsally on snout; 2 prominent dark brown spots sometimes present on head behind eye; corner of mouth and grooves on side of head behind mouth dark brown. Largest specimen, 38.7 cm. Mozambique and South Africa to Johnston Island, Line Islands, Society Islands, and throughout Micronesia; Ryukyu Islands to Great Barrier Reef; type locality, Ambon, Molucca Islands. A shallow-water coral-reef species rarely seen by divers.

Natal

DWARF MORAY

Gymnothorax melatremus Schultz in Schultz et al., 1953
Vertebrae 132–149; body depth at gill opening 13–20 in total length; anus before middle of body, the preanal length 2.2–2.4 in total length; teeth short and stout, none as canines, in one row at front of upper jaw, with 1 or 2 short stout median teeth; teeth in 2 rows on side of upper jaw, those of inner row longer and more slender; larger teeth at front of lower jaw often with an outer row of small teeth; origin of dorsal fin between corner of mouth and gill opening; color extremely variable, from bright yellow to brown, with or without small dark brown spots or a reticular pattern; gill opening in a dusky to blackish spot. Largest specimen examined, 29.9 cm. Indo-Pacific; type locality, Bikini Atoll, Marshall Islands; common in reefs to depths of at least 58 m, but not often seen by divers.

Hawaiian Islands

WHITEMOUTH MORAY

Gymnothorax meleagris (Shaw, 1795)

Vertebrae 127–132; stout-bodied, the depth at gill opening 11–18 in total length; tail not tapering much until posteriorly; anus before midbody, the preanal length 2.2–2.5 in total length; teeth in jaws mostly in 2 rows, those across front of upper jaw in 5 rows, the canines of middle rows longer than those of outer rows; side of upper jaw with an inner row of 7–12 lesser canines; origin of dorsal fin midway between corner of mouth and gill opening; color variable, but usually brown to orangish brown with numerous small, round, dark-edged white spots; tip of tail white; inside of mouth white; gill opening in a black blotch. Attains 100 cm. Coast of East Africa (but not the Red Sea) to Hawaiian Islands (where it is often seen by divers) and Pitcairn Islands; southern Japan to Great Barrier Reef, Lord Howe Island, and New Caledonia; also reported from the Galápagos Islands; type locality, "southern ocean"; known from depths of 1–30 m. Randall (1985b) opened the stomachs of 25 specimens; 7 contained fishes, one a portunid crab, and the rest were empty.

BROWN MORAY

Gymnothorax monochrous (Bleeker, 1856)

Vertebrae 134–145; body moderately elongate, the depth 19–22 in total length; anus before midbody, the preanal length about 2.1 in total length; head length 8–9 in total length, 2.7–2.9 in trunk length; a single row of compressed teeth in jaws, the upper with 2–4 canines interspersed anteriorly at side of upper jaw; a median row of long canines at front of upper jaw; dorsal fin moderately high, its origin halfway between corner of mouth and gill opening; brown without markings on body, darker dorsally than ventrally; fins colored like adjacent body; horizontal grooves on side of head behind eye darker brown. Reported to 56 cm. East coast of Africa to Indo-Malayan region (type locality, Ternate, Molucca Islands), east to New Caledonia; occurs in sheltered turbid waters, including mangrove habitats.

ONESPOT MORAY

Gymnothorax monostigma (Regan, 1909)

Vertebrae 129–133; body depth 16–20 in total length; anus anterior to middle of body; teeth in jaws in 1 row, conical anteriorly, slightly compressed on side of jaws, none as canines; 3 long teeth in a median row at front of jaw; 2 long teeth in an inner row on each side at front of lower jaw; teeth serrate along rear edge; origin of dorsal fin over or slightly anterior to gill opening; brown, the eye enclosed in a dark brown spot, most of which is posterior to eye; sensory pores on side of jaws and posterior nostril in a white spot; outer part of fins orange. Attains 65 cm. Maldive Islands, islands of Micronesia, Samoa Islands, Society Islands (type locality), Marquesas Islands, and Tuamotu Archipelago; no records from the East Indies, Australia, or Japan); found in surge channels of reefs exposed to wave action.

Hawaiian Islands

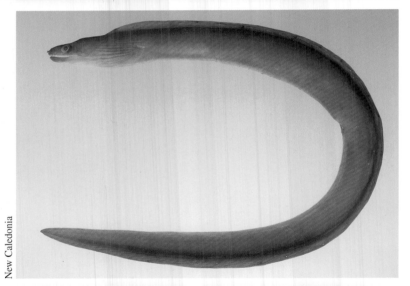

New Caledonia

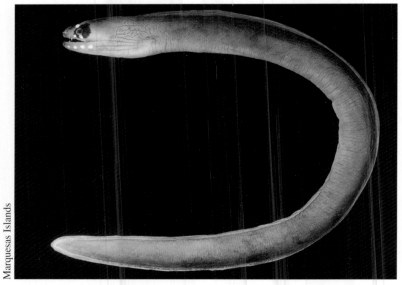

Marquesas Islands

EASTER ISLAND MORAY

Gymnothorax nasuta De Buen, 1961

Vertebrae 138 (1 count); body depth 14–17 in total length; anus well before midbody, the preanal length 2.3–2.45 in total length; teeth in jaws in one row, those anteriorly as canines, the longest a median row of 2 or 3 at front of upper jaw; tubular anterior nostril long, projecting well in front of snout; origin of dorsal fin between corner of mouth and gill opening; gray-brown, with discrete small white spots on head and anterior body; spots posteriorly grouping to form large dendritic blotches, leaving a narrow reticular pattern of gray-brown; dorsal fin with small white spots, the smallest a close-set series along margin of fin; anal fin with a prominent white margin and dark brown submarginal band; corner of mouth with a dark brown blotch containing a few small pale spots. Largest specimen, 71.2 cm. Known only from Easter Island (type locality), and 1 specimen from Pitcairn, but might be expected from the Austral Islands or Rapa; nocturnal.

Easter Island

YELLOWMOUTH MORAY

Gymnothorax nudivomer (Günther in Playfair & Günther, 1867)

Vertebrae 132–139; depth of body greatest at gill opening, 10–14 in total length, the trunk and tail strongly tapering; anus anterior to middle of body; teeth in jaws in 1 row, compressed and acutely triangular (none as canines); a single tooth or none in middle of front of upper jaw; largest teeth serrate; usually no teeth on vomer; origin of dorsal fin about halfway between corner of mouth and gill opening; light brown anteriorly with numerous very small, irregular, dark-edged white spots, becoming dark brown posteriorly with larger and more widely spaced white spots; gill opening in a large black blotch; inside of mouth bright yellow. Reaches at least 100 cm (a report of 180 cm should be confirmed). Red Sea, Oman, and east coast of Africa (type locality, Zanzibar) to Hawaiian Islands and Marquesas Islands; Ryukyu Islands to Great Barrier Reef and New Caledonia (but from few localities between); usually at depths greater than 30 m (one reported from 165 m), except the Red Sea where observed as shallow as 4 m. Often evokes a threat display by broadly opening its mouth. Secretes a skin toxin (Randall et al., 1981a).

Hawaiian Islands

PEPPERED MORAY

Gymnothorax pictus (Ahl, 1789)

Vertebrae 128–135; body depth at gill opening 15–22 in total length; anus in middle of body; teeth in jaws mostly in one row, short and conical anteriorly, compressed and triangular along side of jaws; 0–3 (usually 1) median teeth at front of upper jaw; vomerine teeth of large adults in 2 rows that diverge anteriorly; origin of dorsal fin over or slightly anterior to gill opening; whitish, finely specked with black, the dots sometimes grouped to form indistinct dark blotches. Reported to 120 cm (largest examined, 104 cm). Indo-Pacific and the tropical eastern Pacific; type locality, East Indies; a shallow-water species that may be exposed on reef flats when waves recede. Feeds mainly on crabs; has been observed to strike from the sea at grapsid crabs on rocks above the surface (Chave & H. A. Randall, 1971). Sometimes classified in the genus *Siderea*, now regarded as a synonym of *Gymnothorax*. *Gymnothorax hilonis* Jordan & Evermann is among the 13 synonyms.

Hawaiian Islands

45

Mauritius

Easter Island

New Caledonia

PINDA MORAY
Gymnothorax pindae Smith, 1962

Vertebrae 110–124; a stout species with tapering tail, the depth at gill opening 11–15 in total length; anus anterior to middle of body; teeth of adults in 1 row in jaws, compressed and triangular; usually 2 median teeth at front of upper jaw, the first short and conical, the second a slender canine; larger teeth anteriorly in jaws serrate; individuals less than about 17 cm with an inner row of teeth on side of upper jaw; origin of dorsal fin between corner of mouth and gill opening; uniform brown, becoming darker brown to almost black posteriorly on tail and fins; a diffuse dark brown ring around eye. Attains 33 cm. Indo-Pacific; type locality, Pinda, Mozambique; not uncommon but cryptic. Sometimes misidentified as *Gymnothorax moluccensis* (Bleeker).

LOWFIN MORAY
Gymnothorax porphyreus (Guichenot, 1848)

Vertebrae 137–142; body depth 14–19 in total length; anus located at or slightly anterior to middle of body; teeth in upper jaw in 2 rows, the outer row small, the inner row at front of jaw with 2 to 5 long canines, the middle row usually of 3 very long canines; teeth anteriorly in lower jaw in 2 rows, the inner row at front of jaw as canines; dorsal fin low, its origin anterior to gill opening; yellowish brown, densely mottled with dark brown spots averaging pupil in size. Largest examined, 81 cm. Peru, Chile, San Felix Island, Juan Fernandez Island (type locality), Easter Island, Rapa, Kermadec Islands, northern New Zealand, New Caledonia (*Gymnothorax* sp. 6 of Laboute & Grandperrin, 2000), Norfolk Island, and Lord Howe Island. Found at Easter Island from tidepools to 13 m; the most common moray seen while diving there; sometimes aggressive.

BARS 'N SPOTS MORAY
Gymnothorax punctatofasciatus Bleeker, 1863

Vertebrae 132–143; body depth 17–26 in total length; anus anterior to midbody, the preanal length 2.1–2.4 in total length; predorsal length 9.7–10.4 in total length; teeth along side of upper jaw in a single row (small individuals may have 1–3 inner maxillary teeth that are longer than the small lateral teeth and depressible); teeth finely serrate on about basal half (serrae may not be apparent on juveniles); light brown with numerous small dark brown spots and 25–35 irregular dark brown bars posterior to gill opening that are narrower than pale interspaces and sometimes branched dorsally. Largest specimen, 50.5 cm. Indonesia (type locality, Ambon), Sabah, Philippines, and New Caledonia (illustrated specimen, 20.2 cm, collected by M. Kulbicki and the author in a mangrove area, represents the first record from a Melanesian island; its vertebral count of 143 is higher than the count of 132–139 for remaining specimens, and the dark bars more irregular, but from other characters it appears to be this species [D. G. Smith, pers. comm.]. Smith & Böhlke (1997) reviewed the 7 Indo-Pacific species of the *Gymnothorax reticularis* complex, which includes *punctatofasciatus*, all with serrate teeth and strongly marked. One of this complex, *Gymnothorax chlamydatus*, bit the author on the hand; the pain was severe enough to suggest the presence of a venom.

REEVES' MORAY

Gymnothorax reevesii (Richardson, 1845)
Vertebrae 124–132; body depth 10–20 in total length (larger individuals deeper bodied); anus anterior to midbody, the preanal length 2.2–2.3 in total length; teeth in jaws in a single row (except juveniles may have an inner row of a few longer teeth on side of upper jaw), progressively longer anteriorly, but none of canine proportions except 3 teeth in median row at front of upper jaw; posterior nostril with a slight rim; origin of dorsal fin about equidistant from corner of mouth to gill opening; yellowish to orangish brown with numerous well-defined, dark brown spots on head, body, and fins, some round, some oval, but most with irregular margins; posterior nostril and sensory pores on side of head white. Reaches 70 cm. Southern Japan and Taiwan to the South China Sea; reported in the South Pacific from the Samoa Islands and Marquesas; type locality, China seas.

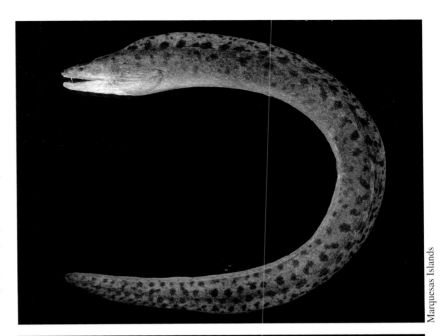

Marquesas Islands

RICHARDSON'S MORAY

Gymnothorax richardsonii (Bleeker, 1852)
Vertebrae 112–117; body depth 13–19 in total length; anus at or near middle of body, the preanal length 1.9–2.1 in total length; teeth triangular, compressed, and slanting posteriorly, none as canines; a median row of 1–3 teeth at front of upper jaw (sometimes none); a short inner row of teeth on side of upper jaw of juveniles and females; short conical teeth on vomer, in 2 rows in large adults; dorsal fin low, its origin over or slightly before gill opening; whitish to pale yellowish with a very fine dendritic reticular pattern of dark gray to dark brown; sensory pores on side of jaws in a white spot; tip of tail yellow. Reaches only 34 cm. Indo-Pacific (except Hawaiian Islands and Red Sea); described from Sumatra and the Molucca Islands; generally found on seaward reefs.

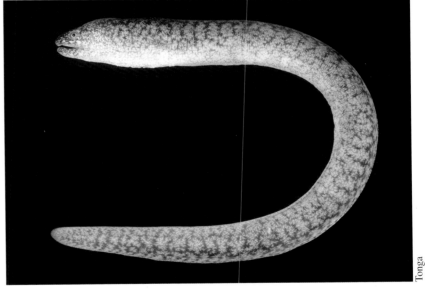

Tonga

BANDED MORAY

Gymnothorax rueppellii (McClelland, 1844)
Vertebrae 125–135; body depth at gill opening 13–25 in total length; anus before midbody, the preanal length 2.1–2.3 in total length; teeth anteriorly in jaws in 1 row, the long canines alternating with 2–3 small teeth; median row of 3 canines at front of upper jaw conspicuously long; side of upper jaw with an inner row of 1–3 slender canines; origin of dorsal fin closer to gill opening than corner of mouth; light grayish brown with 16–22 dark bars about as wide as pale interspaces on head, body, and fins, those on head and trunk not reaching ventral margin; a dark brown spot at corner of mouth; top of head yellowish; occasional large adults without dark bars. Attains 80 cm. Indo-Pacific; type locality, Red Sea; nocturnal and ill-tempered. Also known as the Yellowhead Moray. *Gymnothorax petelli* (Bleeker) is one of 8 synonyms.

Hawaiian Islands

Flores, Indonesia

Hawaiian Islands

Alor, Indonesia

WHITE-EYE MORAY

Gymnothorax thyrsoideus (Richardson, 1845)
Vertebrae 125–137; body depth 17–22 in total length; anus well before middle of body, the preanal length about 2.5 in total length; teeth conical, none as canines, in 2 rows on side of upper jaw and front of lower jaw; 2 conical teeth in median row at front of upper jaw; vomerine teeth in 2 rows that diverge anteriorly on large individuals; origin of dorsal fin about halfway between corner of mouth and gill opening; pale yellowish to whitish, densely mottled with dark gray or brown; front half of head uniform dark purplish gray; gill opening in a dusky blotch; iris white, the pupil small. Largest reported, 66 cm, but usually less than 40 cm. Ryukyu Islands to Great Barrier Reef, New South Wales, and New Caledonia, east to islands of Micronesia, Society Islands, and Tuamotu Archipelago; Christmas Island in the Indian Ocean; type locality, Guangzhou (Canton), China; inshore and not aggressive. *Gymnothorax prosopeion* (Bleeker) is a synonym.

UNDULATED MORAY

Gymnothorax undulatus (Lacepède, 1803)
Vertebrae 126–138; body depth at gill opening 12–21 in total length; anus at or slightly anterior to middle of body; long canine teeth anteriorly in jaws, some alternating with very small teeth; 3 very long fangs in median row at front of upper jaw; side of upper jaw with a few inner canines in small specimens; origin of dorsal fin anterior to gill opening; pale yellowish with large, irregular, dark brown blotches, the narrow pale interspaces with numerous irregular, small, dark brown spots; large spots joined posteriorly to form irregular bars that extend into fins; top of head often greenish yellow. Largest examined, 120 cm. Indo-Pacific and tropical eastern Pacific; type locality unknown. Primarily nocturnal; more prone to bite than most morays.

BARTAIL MORAY

Gymnothorax zonipectis Seale, 1906
Vertebrae 122–130; body depth 15–21 in total length; anus anterior to middle of body, the preanal length 2.2–2.3 in total length; a single row of canine teeth anteriorly in jaws, the upper jaw with 2 very long median canines; side of jaws with small sharp teeth, the upper often with an inner row of a few lesser canines; origin of dorsal fin closer to gill opening than corner of mouth; light brown with about 4 longitudinal rows of dendritic, dark brown blotches; head with irregular whitish and dark brown bands and spots; anal fin and posterior part of dorsal fin with oblique dark brown bars. Largest specimen, 47 cm. Indo-Pacific except the Hawaiian Islands and Red Sea; type locality, Tahiti. Has been observed to forage in the open at night.

REDFACE MORAY
Monopenchelys acuta (Parr, 1930)
Vertebrae 124–144; body slender, the depth at gill opening 19–38 in total length; anus anterior to middle of body, the pre-anal length 2.1–2.4 in total length; teeth in outer row in jaws small and slender, with an inner row of 3–5 canines at front of upper jaw and a median row of 3 longer canines; side of upper jaw with an inner row of 8–11 lesser canines; front of lower jaw with an inner row of 3 or 4 canines on each side; origin of dorsal fin about halfway between anus and tip of tail; reddish to orangish brown, the front of head orange-red; tip of tail yellowish. A small species, the largest specimen 20.9 cm. Tropical western Atlantic and Indo-Pacific, but only from scattered localities (in the Pacific only Hawaiian Islands and Fiji); type locality, West Caicos Island, Bahamas. Known from 13–45 m; specimens collected mainly with use of ichthyocide.

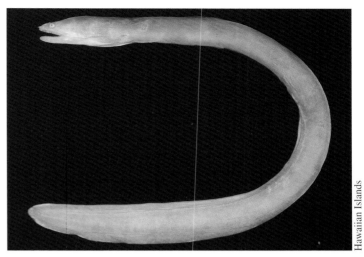
Hawaiian Islands

Bali

WHITE RIBBON MORAY
Pseudechidna brummeri (Bleeker, 1859)
Vertebrae 201–214; body very elongate, the depth 39–56 in total length; anus anterior to middle of body, the preanal length 2.1–2.3 in total length; teeth small, triangular, compressed, and backward-slanting, in 1 row in jaws of males; females with an inner row of teeth at side of upper jaw and front of lower jaw; dorsal fin as high as body depth, its origin between corner of mouth and gill opening; pale gray, shading to whitish ventrally; scattered small black spots on head; sensory pores of head

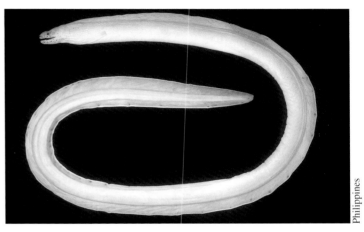
Philippines

rimmed in black; margin of dorsal fin white. Mozambique and Madagascar east to the Cook Islands; type locality, Timor. Reported to 103 cm. A shallow-water species of reef flats or seagrass beds; occasionally seen in the open. Böhlke (1997) redescribed the species.

Juvenile, Bali

RIBBON MORAY
Rhinomuraena quaesita Garman, 1888
Vertebrae 270–286; body extremely elongate, the depth 65–75 in total length, and very compressed; tail much longer than head and trunk, the preanal length 3.0–3.3 in total length; teeth in 1 row in jaws, small, slender, and slanted posteriorly; distal end of anterior nostril greatly expanded; a slender forward-projecting barbel at front of upper jaw and 3 on lower; juveniles and subadults black with a yellow dorsal fin and narrow white margin; males bright blue, the dorsal fin and anterior part of head yellow; females yellow except for black anal fin and white mar-

Male, Luzon

gin on fins. Attains at least 130 cm. Islands of the western Indian Ocean to Austral Islands and Tuamotu Archipelago; southern Japan to Great Barrier Reef and New Caledonia; type locality, Ebon, Marshall Islands. Females the result of sex change (Fishelson, 1990) and rarely seen. A valuable aquarium fish. *Rhinomuraena ambonensis* Barbour is a synonym based on the male phase.

Seaworld, Indonesia

Manila, Philippines

LONGTAIL MORAY
Strophidon sathete (Hamilton, 1822)
Vertebrae 183–196; body very elongate, the depth 38–47 in total length; head 10–14 in total length; tail about twice as long as head and trunk; teeth in jaws as moderate compressed canines in 2 rows at side of upper jaw and front of lower jaw; longest teeth a series of about 4 depressible canines medially on intermaxilla; grayish brown, paler ventrally, the fins darker. The longest of morays; reported to 375 cm. Red Sea and east coast of Africa

to western Pacific from the Ryukyu Islands to the Great Barrier Reef and New Caledonia; occurs on mud bottom in a burrow; believed to be nocturnal. Often identified as *Thyrsoidea macrura* (Bleeker); *Evenchelys* Jordan & Evermann and *Rhabdura* Ogilby are other generic synonyms (Böhlke, 1995).

SNAKEMORAYS (UROPTERYGINAE)

SEYCHELLES MORAY
Anarchias seychellensis Smith 1962
Vertebrae 121–132; body slender, the depth at gill opening 20–26 in total length; anus well before middle of body, the pre-anal length 2.2–2.5 in total length; teeth in jaws in 2 rows, the inner teeth long and slender; 3 median canines at front of upper jaw; anterior nostril in a short tube; posterior nostril above center of eye, with a low rim; a large sensory pore adjacent and posterior to posterior nostril; fins restricted to end of tail; origin of dorsal fin slightly anterior to origin of anal fin; color varying from nearly uniform brown, to mottled brown, to brown with 3 or 4 rows of stellate pale blotches; lower part of head whitish; head pores white; fins at tip of tail yellow. Reported to 29 cm. East coast of Africa to the Hawaiian Islands and Easter Island, mostly from insular localities; known from depths of less than 1 to 22 m; usually collected with ichthyocides.

Hawaiian Islands

Hawaiian Islands

SHORTTAIL SNAKEMORAY
Scuticaria okinawae (Jordan & Snyder, 1901)
Vertebrae 169–177; body elongate, the depth 24–32 in total length, and nearly cylindrical; anus far behind midbody, the pre-anal length about 1.5 in total length; long canines in 5 rows across front of upper jaw and 2 on side of jaw; teeth at front of lower jaw in 2 rows; dorsal and anal fins confined to posterior end of tail; uniform gray-brown. Largest specimen, 90.5 cm. Reported from Japan, Mauritius, Hawaiian Islands, and Tahiti. *Scuticaria unicolor* Seale and *S. sealei* (Whitley) are synonyms. Has been misidentified as *S. bennetti* (Günther), now known as a synonym of *Channomuraena vittata*. Böhlke & McCosker (1997) reviewed the genus *Scuticaria*.

TIGER SNAKEMORAY

Scuticaria tigrina (Lesson, 1828)

Vertebrae 166–174; body elongate, the depth 24–34 in total length, and nearly cylindrical; anus posterior, the tail less than one-third total length; jaws with an outer row of small sharp teeth; 5 rows of teeth across front of upper jaw, the 3 middle rows with 3 canines each; side of upper jaw with an inner row of 4–9 canines; front of lower jaw with an inner row of 3–8 canines on each side; fins rudimentary, evident only near tip of tail; pale yellowish to light brown with well-separated dark brown blotches of variable size. Attains about 120 cm. Indo-Pacific and tropical eastern Pacific; type locality, Bora Bora, Society Islands; nocturnal. Sometimes classified in the genus *Uropterygius*. *Uroptyerygius polyspilus* (Regan) is similar in color, with large and small dark spots, but its anus is near middle of body.

WHITESPECKLED SNAKEMORAY

Uropterygius alboguttatus Smith, 1962

Vertebrae 120–121; body elongate, the depth 25–30 in total length; anus before middle of body; head length about 7.5 in total length; teeth slender and sharp, in 2 rows in jaws, the inner row longer; gill opening on upper third of side; 2 lateral-line pores above and anterior to gill opening (other species of the genus except *U. xanthopterus* Bleeker with 1 pore); fins confined to tail tip; mottled brown with irregular pale blotches and scattered white dots, more numerous anteriorly; tip of tail and posterior margin of fins yellow. Attains 62 cm. Known from Mozambique, Seychelles (type locality, Assumption Island), Line Islands, Tuamotu Archipelago, Pitcairn Islands, and islands of Micronesia; occurs from shallow reefs to depths of 58 m. Smith (1962a) showed that specimens from the Marshall Islands identified by Schultz in Schultz et al. (1953) as *Uropterygius xanthopterus* Bleeker are *U. alboguttatus*.

BROWNSPOTTED SNAKEMORAY

Uropterygius fuscoguttatus Schultz in Schultz et al., 1953

Vertebrae 113–124; body depth 17–25 in total length; anus at or slightly anterior to middle of body; teeth in 3 rows in jaws, progressively longer inwardly; 2 or 3 canines in median row at front of upper jaw; gill opening well above midside; fins confined to tip of tail; marbled orangish brown with small dark brown spots posteriorly (spots only posteriorly on tail of small individuals; large adults with up to three-fourths of body spotted); dark spots on adults may form a reticular pattern posteriorly. Reaches 30 cm. Scattered insular localities from Maldive Islands and Chagos Archipelago to Hawaiian Islands and Pitcairn Islands; type locality, Bikini Atoll, Marshall Islands; coral reefs in 3–25 m. The species is larger in Hawai'i and Johnston Island than elsewhere in the Pacific, and with a higher number of vertebrae (120–124, compared with 113–120).

Hawaiian Islands

New Caledonia

Coral Sea

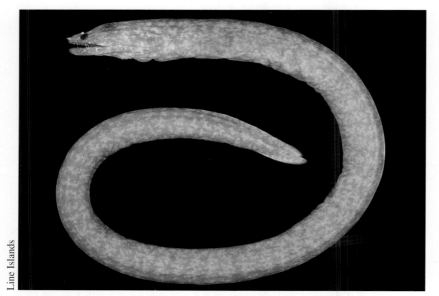

Line Islands

BARLIP SNAKEMORAY

Uropterygius kamar McCosker & Randall, 1977
Vertebrae 137–143; body slender, the depth of adults about 26 in total length; body width 1.4 in depth; anus well before middle of body, the preanal length 2.4–2.5 in total length; teeth in upper jaw in 3 rows, the outer row small and close-set, the inner rows as recurved canines; largest canines in middle of front of upper jaw; lower jaw with 3 rows of teeth anteriorly and 2 rows along side of jaw, the inner row as canines; median fins rudimentary at tip of tail; mottled reddish brown to dark brown with small white spots and short white bars on head; nostrils white. Attains 37 cm. Natal, Comoro Islands (type locality), and Chagos Archipelago to Pitcairn Islands; Palau and Marshall Islands in Micronesia; collected in the depth range of 3–55 m, often from coral rubble.

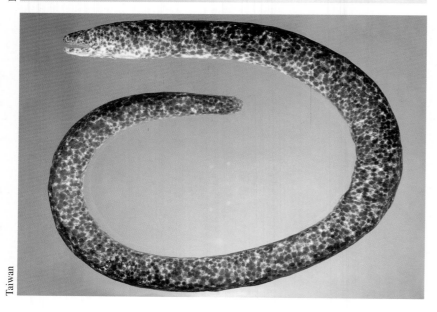

Marshall Islands

LARGEHEAD SNAKEMORAY

Uropterygius macrocephalus (Bleeker, 1865)
Vertebrae 102–119; body depth 13–21 in total length; anus before or behind midbody, the preanal length 1.9–2.3 in total length; head large, 6.4–8.0 in total length; gill opening low on side; posterior nostril above middle of eye, as a flared short tube in large adults; teeth numerous, in 2 rows in jaws, the inner row as slender canines; longest teeth medially at front of upper jaw; tail rounded, the fins confined to tail tip; dark gray-brown with 5 rows of large, complexly stellate, pale brown blotches (3 along side, 1 dorsal, and 1 ventral). Attains 45 cm. Seychelles (Randall & van Egmond, 1994) to the Hawaiian Islands and Society Islands; also known from the tropical and subtropical eastern Pacific; type locality, Ambon; occurs on reef flats, shallow reefs, rocky shores exposed to surf; greatest recorded depth, 14 m. *Uropterygius knighti* (Jordan & Starks), *U. necturus* (Jordan & Gilbert), and *U. reidi* (Schultz) are synonyms.

Taiwan

MARBLED SNAKEMORAY

Uropterygius marmoratus (Lacepède, 1803)
Vertebrae 131–139; body depth 22–30 in total length; anus well before middle of body, the preanal length 2.3–2.4 in total length; posterior nostril above eye, a broad short tube in large adults; teeth numerous slender and sharp, mostly in 3 rows in jaws, the inner rows progressively longer; gill opening at about midside; fins restricted to tip of tail; pale yellowish, densely spotted with dark brown, the spots of about eye diameter in average size (hence similar in color to *Gymnothorax flavimarginatus*). Largest examined, 62 cm. East coast of Africa to the Hawaiian Islands (where rare) and the Marquesas Islands; in the western Pacific from southern Japan to Queensland; type locality, New Britain. A shallow-water species, generally found in less than 2 m.

LARGESPOTTED SNAKEMORAY

Uropterygius polyspilus (Regan, 1909)
Vertebrae 130–136; body depth 20–25 in total length; anus at or slightly posterior to midbody, the preanal length 1.9–2.0 in total length; head short, 10–12 in total length; posterior nostril a broad tube, larger than anterior nostril in large adults; jaws short; teeth in jaws in 2 rows, the inner long and needle-like; 3 longest teeth in median row at front of upper jaw; gill opening slightly above midside; fins confined to tip of tail; pale brown with well-separated dark brown spots of variable size, the largest nearly half body depth; dark spots abruptly small and close-set on anterior third of head; nostrils white. Reaches 78 cm. Red Sea to the Hawaiian Islands and Society Islands (type locality, Tahiti); rare and known from few localities; only the Caroline Islands in Micronesia; a shallow-water species, usually found on reef flats.

TOOTHY SNAKEMORAY

Uropterygius supraforatus (Regan, 1909)
Vertebrae 117–136; body depth 16–19 in total length; anus at or before midbody, the preanal length 2.0–2.3 in total length; head short, 9–11 in total length; posterior nostril a short tube above middle of eye; sharp teeth in 5–7 rows in jaws, nearly filling mouth, progressively longer inwardly; gill opening about one-fourth body depth from upper edge of body; fins restricted to tip of tail; whitish to pale brown with numerous irregular, small, dark brown spots; nostrils white. Attains 40 cm. Maldive Islands, Chagos Archipelago, Taiwan (collected by author), islands of Micronesia, Samoa Islands (type locality, Savai'i), Hawaiian Islands, and Pitcairn Islands; usually from reefs in 1–15 m, but one depth record of 37 m. Also known from Clipperton Island off Mexico (Robertson et al., 2004). Vertebral counts in Hawai'i and Johnston Island 128–136, compared with 117–123 from other localities. *Uropterygius dentatus* Schultz from Johnston Island is regarded as a synonym.

WEDGETOOTH SNAKEMORAY

Uropterygius xenodontus McCosker & Smith, 1997
Vertebrae 154–157; body elongate, the depth 26–30 in total length; body width 1.6–1.7 in depth; anus at or slightly before midbody, the preanal length 2.0–2.1 in total length; posterior nostril in a very short tube over center of eye; teeth in jaws in 1 row and wedge-shaped, except for small canines on vomer and in middle of front part of upper jaw; gill opening at midside of body; fins restricted to tip of tail; brown with faint darker brown mottling. Largest specimen, 53 cm. Currently known only from Johnston Island, Samoa Islands, Marshall Islands, and the Chesterfield Islands, Coral Sea (type locality); specimens were collected from reefs in 6–9 m.

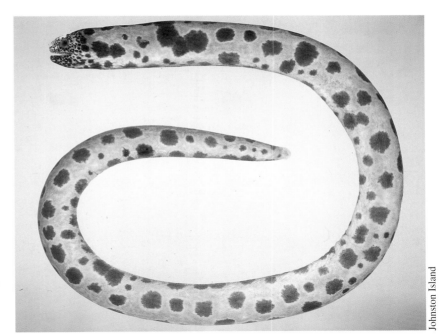

Johnston Island

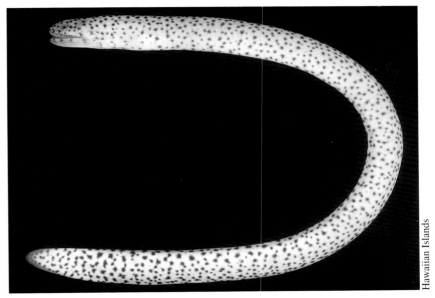

Hawaiian Islands

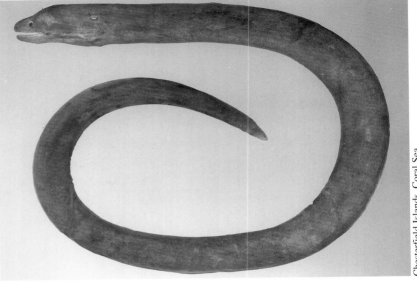

Chesterfield Islands, Coral Sea

Goldspot Herring, *Herklotsichthys quadrimaculatus,* Sudan, Red Sea

HERRINGS AND SARDINES
(CLUPEIDAE)

The species of this large family are small silvery fishes characterized by a single short dorsal fin near the middle of the body, no spines in fins, a forked caudal fin, pectoral fins low on body, pelvic fins in a posterior abdominal position, cycloid scales (usually easily lost), no lateral line, and gill rakers long and numerous. The mouth is terminal or with lower jaw projecting (except for the gizzard shads); and the teeth are usually small or minute (sometimes absent). Transparent adipose tissue usually present over eye except for a vertical slit over pupil (covers all of eye in *Etrumeus*). Most species have midventral scutes (modified scales with a median ridge ending in a sharp posterior point), and all have at least one pelvic scute. These fishes are nearly always found in schools above the bottom where most feed on the smaller animals of the zooplankton. Whitehead (1985) recognized 56 genera and 180 species in the family, but he estimated that there may eventually be about 60 genera and 200 species. Munroe, Wongratana & Nizinski in Carpenter & Niem (1999a) reviewed the species of the family for the central and western Pacific. The Clupeidae is divided into 5 subfamilies, of which 3 have representatives in the South Pacific, the herrings and sardines (Clupeinae), the roundherrings (Dussumieriinae), and the gizzard shads (Dorosomatinae). Clupeid and engraulid fishes in tropical or subtropical areas have been known to cause a severe toxemia when eaten. This has been called clupeoid poisoning (Melton et al., 1984). Although rare, it is often fatal.

HERRINGS AND SARDINES (CLUPEINAE)

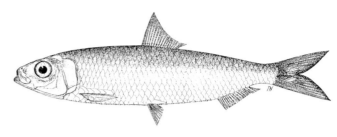

After Munroe et al. in
Carpenter & Niem 1999a

SMOOTHBELLY SARDINELLA
Amblygaster clupeoides Bleeker, 1849

Dorsal rays 18–19; anal rays 17–18, the posterior 2 rays enlarged; pectoral rays 16–17; pelvic rays 8; longitudinal scale series 40–43; median predorsal scales in a well-defined series (true of other *Amblygaster*); abdomen rounded, the ventral scutes not prominent (generic); prepelvic scutes 16–19, and postpelvic scutes 11–14; lower-limb gill rakers 26–31; body depth 3.7–4.2 in standard length; upper jaw without a median notch, the maxilla not reaching a vertical through anterior edge of eye; second supramaxilla symmetrical (generic); origin of pelvic fins below about seventh dorsal ray; anal fin very posterior (also generic); dark blue-green dorsally, silvery below; no series of dark spots along side of body. Maximum length, 21 cm. Reported from India, Indonesia (type locality, Sulawesi), and Fiji; a schooling coastal species; feeds on zooplankton, mainly copepods.

Ambon, Indonesia

SPOTTED SARDINELLA
Amblygaster sirm (Walbaum, 1792)

Dorsal rays 17–18; anal rays 15–19, the posterior 2 rays enlarged; pectoral rays 16–17; pelvic rays 8; longitudinal scale series 42–45; prepelvic scutes 16–18, and postpelvic scutes 13–15; lower-limb gill rakers 33–43; body depth 4.5–5.0 in standard length; upper jaw without a median notch, the maxilla not reaching a vertical through anterior edge of eye; origin of pelvic fins below about eighth dorsal ray; dark blue-green dorsally, silvery on side and ventrally, with a longitudinal series of 10–20 dark spots on upper side; dorsal and caudal fins dusky yellow. Reported to 27 cm. Red Sea (type locality) and east coast of Africa to southern Marshall Islands, Kiribati, Palau, Caroline Islands, and Fiji; Ryukyu Islands and Taiwan south to Western Australia, Queensland, and New Caledonia. Found mainly in lagoons and bays; schools located near the bottom during the day, dispersing into lesser depths at night to feed on zooplankton; life span 2–4 years.

FIJI SARDINELLA
Sardinella fijiense (Fowler & Bean, 1923)

Dorsal rays 17; anal rays 19; pectoral rays 15; pelvic rays 8; longitudinal scale series usually 39–40; median predorsal scales paired; abdomen strongly keeled, with a total of 29–30 ventral scutes; no perforations on posterior part of scales; lower-limb gill rakers 87–134 in fish 6–11 cm in standard length; body depth about 3.4 in standard length; maxilla reaching a vertical at front edge of eye; second supramaxilla paddle-shaped and symmetrical; origin of pelvic fins anterior to middle of dorsal fin; life color not known; a narrow faint dark line following middle of upper 3 longitudinal rows of scales on body; no dark spot at dorsal-fin origin; tip of dorsal fin black (possibly the caudal tips as well). Largest specimen, 14.5 cm. Currently known only from Fiji (type locality) and Papua New Guinea.

Sudan, Red Sea

GOLDSPOT HERRING
Herklotsichthys quadrimaculatus (Rüppell, 1837)

Dorsal rays 17–20; anal rays 17–19; pectoral rays 15–16; longitudinal scale series usually 38–40; median predorsal scales paired, with an elongate transverse scale beneath each pair; abdomen strongly keeled, the prepelvic scutes 16–19; postpelvic scutes 12–14; lower-limb gill rakers 30–37; body depth 3.3–5.0 in standard length; lower part of second supramaxilla larger than upper; origin of pelvic fins below middle of dorsal fin; silvery blue-green dorsally, grading to silvery on sides and ventrally, with a brassy spot behind upper end of gill opening, and another behind lower end. Reaches 14 cm. Red Sea (type locality) and east coast of Africa to Marshall, Caroline, and Samoa Islands; southern Japan to Queensland and New Caledonia; accidentally introduced into the Hawaiian Islands from the Marshall Islands; less apt to be found in brackish environments than most clupeids; forms dense schools during the day near shore or reefs and disperses at night for feeding on zooplankton; fast growing and short-lived (about 1 year). Of some value as a baitfish for tuna; 185 tons landed in Fiji in 1995.

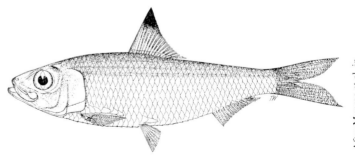

After Munroe et al. in
Carpenter & Niem 1999a

MARQUESAN SARDINELLA
Sardinella marquesensis Berry & Whitehead, 1968

Dorsal rays 16–17, the first 3 or 4 unbranched; anal rays 18–21, the first 2 or 3 unbranched; pectoral rays 13–15; pelvic rays 7–8 (usually 7); longitudinal scale series 35–42; median predorsal scales paired; abdomen strongly keeled, with 16–17 prepelvic scutes and 12–13 postpelvic scutes; no perforations on posterior part of scales; lower-limb gill rakers 25–84 (the number increasing with growth); body depth 3.5–4.35 in standard length; maxilla reaching posterior to a vertical at front edge of eye; origin of pelvic fins below about sixth dorsal ray; silvery with no dark markings. Attains 16 cm. Known naturally only from the Marquesas Islands where it occurs in protected bays; intentionally intro-

Marquesas Islands

duced as a baitfish to the Hawaiian Islands from 1955 to 1958; although the species established, it never became abundant. An opelu (*Decapterus*) fisherman on Kaua'i, Hawaiian Islands, died after eating 3 Marquesan sardines (Melton et al., 1984).

New Britain

BLACKTIP SARDINELLA
Sardinella melanura (Cuvier, 1829)

Dorsal rays 15–16; anal rays 18–19; pectoral rays 13–15; pelvic rays 8; longitudinal scale series 38–42; median predorsal scales paired; abdomen strongly keeled, with a total of 27–31 scutes; no perforations on posterior part of scales; lower-limb gill rakers 38–74; body depth 3.0–4.1 in standard length; maxilla nearly reaching a vertical at front edge of eye; origin of pelvic fins below about fifth dorsal ray; blue-green dorsally, silvery on side and ventrally; tips of caudal-fin lobes broadly black. Largest specimen, 15.2 cm. Gulf of Aden south to Mozambique and Madagascar, east to northwestern India; central Indonesia to New Guinea, northern tip of Queensland, Vanuatu, Fiji, American Samoa (Wass, 1984), and the Society Islands

Ambon, Indonesia

(Randall, 1985a); type locality, Vanikoro, Santa Cruz Islands. Mok in Shen (1993) recorded *Sardinella melanura* from Taiwan, but the illustration (showing a black spot at origin of dorsal fin) is *S. hualiensis* (Chu & Tsai). Motomura et al. (2001) recorded *S. melanura* from southern Japan.

ROUNDHERRINGS (DUSSUMIERIINAE)

There is a report of a slender undescribed species of *Dussumieria* from New Guinea, Caroline Islands, and Fiji (see Myers, 1999).

DELICATE ROUNDHERRING
Spratelloides delicatulus (Bennett, 1832)

Dorsal rays 11–13; anal rays 10–11 (usually 10); pectoral rays 11–13; pelvic rays 8; longitudinal scale series 35–41; abdomen rounded; no prepelvic or postpelvic scutes, but a W-shaped pelvic scute present (true of other *Spratelloides*); lower-limb gill rakers 26–32; body elongate and little compressed, the depth about 5–6 in standard length; second supramaxilla asymmetrical (lower half larger than upper) (also generic); origin of pelvic fins a little posterior to middle of dorsal fin; blue-green dorsally, grading to silvery on side and ventrally (no distinct silvery

Bahrain

stripe); 2 blackish streaks on base of caudal fin. Maximum length, 8.5 cm. Red Sea south to Natal, east to Tuamotu Archipelago and islands of Micronesia; southern Japan to Great Barrier Reef and Western Australia; type locality, Mauritius. Forms small schools inshore around reefs or in seagrass beds during the day. Spawning occurs at night, probably before midnight; reported to be capable of continuous spawning, but peak spawning believed to take place during full moon; sexually mature at about 2 months at 3.7 cm standard length in Kiribati; life span there 4–5 months.

Lord Howe Island

SLENDER ROUNDHERRING
Spratelloides gracilis (Temminck & Schlegel, 1846)
Dorsal rays 12–13; anal rays 11–14 (usually 12–13); pectoral rays 13–15; pelvic rays 8; longitudinal scale series 42–48; lower-limb gill rakers 27–37; body very slender and little compressed, the depth 5.8–7.6 in standard length; origin of pelvic fins a little posterior to middle of dorsal fin; bluish gray dorsally with a broad silvery stripe on side, sometimes with blue-green iridescence. Attains 10.5 cm. Red Sea south to Mozambique, east to Marshall Islands, Caroline Islands, Society Islands, and Tuamotu Archipelago; southern Japan (type locality, Nagasaki) to

Sulawesi

Queensland, Lord Howe Island, and New Caledonia. Also an inshore schooling species by day, generally in clear water; females mature at about 3.5–4.4 cm in fork length; limited data suggest peak spawning in October around full moon in Kiribati. *Spratelloides atrofasciatus* Schultz is a synonym.

GIZZARD SHADS (DOROSOMATINAE)

CHACUNDA GIZZARD SHAD
Anodontostoma chacunda (Hamilton, 1822)
Dorsal rays 17–19; anal rays 19–20; pectoral rays 15; longitudinal scale series 38–45; exposed edges of scales finely serrate; a straight series of median predorsal scales; ventral scutes about 28; lower-limb gill rakers 54–96; body depth increasing with age, 1.65–2.5 in standard length; snout rounded; mouth inferior; second supramaxilla slender; upper jaw with a median notch; body silvery, sometimes with golden reflections, with a large black spot behind upper end of gill opening; occiput golden; caudal fin often yellowish. Attains 22 cm. Persian Gulf along southern Asian shores to Indo-Malayan region, northern Australia, and New Caledonia; type locality, Ganges River estuary; ascends rivers to spawn; feeds on diatoms, radiolarians, mollusks, copepods, and other small crustaceans.

Cochin, India

ANCHOVIES
(ENGRAULIDAE)

Like the related herrings and sardines, the anchovies are classified in the order Clupeiformes, sharing such characters as a single short dorsal fin near middle of body (anterior in just the genus *Coilia*); no spines in fins, cycloid scales, a strongly forked caudal fin, pectoral fins low on side of body, and pelvic fins abdominal in position, those of Indo-Pacific genera with 7 rays (except *Coilia* with 8 or 9). The eyes are completely covered with transparent adipose tissue. All the Indo-Pacific anchovies except the species of the genus *Engraulis* have sharp midventral scutes. These fishes differ most clearly from the clupeids in the shape of the head; the snout is rounded and overhangs the long, slender lower jaw, which extends posterior to the eye (usually very posterior); the scales differ in having posterior striation, and are even more deciduous, in general, than those of the herrings and sardines. Anchovies are typically found as schools inshore in the quiet waters of bays and lagoons; many occur in brackish environments, and some are confined to fresh water. Whitehead et al. (1988) reviewed the family, recognizing 16 genera and 139 species in the world. Wongratana et al. in Carpenter & Niem (1999a) treated the species of the central and western Pacific, including a summary of available information on their biology and fisheries.

DE VIS' ANCHOVY
Encrasicholina devisi (Whitley, 1940)

Dorsal rays 15; anal rays 18–20 (initial 3 dorsal and anal rays unbranched, the first very small); pectoral rays 15; longitudinal scale series 39–42; needle-like prepelvic scutes 3–6 (usually 5); no postpelvic scutes and no predorsal scute (true of other species of *Encrasicholina*); lower-limb gill rakers 20–27; body elongate with slightly rounded abdomen; body width about half body depth; tip of maxilla pointed, reaching to subopercle; isthmus short, preceded by a small exposed bony portion of urohyal; origin of anal fin slightly posterior to rear base of dorsal fin; a broad bright silvery to brassy stripe on side of body bordered above by a blue line; dorsal part of body blue-gray. Maximum length, 9.5 cm. Gulf of

Madras, India

Aden along the Asian continent to the Indo-Malayan region and northern Australia (type locality, Gulf of Carpentaria); reported in Oceania from the Caroline Islands, Fiji, and Tonga; of value as a baitfish for tuna.

New Caledonia

Persian Gulf

SHORTHEAD ANCHOVY
Encrasicholina heteroloba (Rüppell, 1837)

Dorsal rays 14; anal rays 16–18 (first 2 dorsal and anal rays unbranched); pectoral rays 14; longitudinal scale series 39–43; needle-like prepelvic scutes 4–6 (usually 5); lower-limb gill rakers 22–30; body elongate, the depth about 5.5–6.0 in standard length, the abdomen rounded; body width about half body depth; posterior end of maxilla pointed, reaching to subopercle; origin of anal fin slightly posterior to rear base of dorsal fin; gray with a broad midlateral silvery stripe, the upper edge bordered with a blue line. A small species, probably not exceeding 9 cm. Red Sea (type locality) and continental Indian Ocean coasts to Indo-Malayan region and northern Australia, north to southern Japan, east to Caroline Islands and Samoa Islands. Spawns throughout the year around full moon at 2130 to 2300 hours; life span less than 1 year. Used as tuna baitfish, though less hardy than *E. devisi*. Marketed fresh or dried; also made into fish meal.

BUCCANEER ANCHOVY
Encrasicholina punctifer Fowler, 1938

Dorsal rays 14–15; anal rays 14–16 (first 2 dorsal and anal rays unbranched); pectoral rays 16–18; longitudinal scale series 39–43; needle-like prepelvic scutes 2–7 (usually 4 or 5); lower-limb gill rakers 23–26; body elongate, the depth about 6 in standard length; body width about half body depth; abdomen rounded; posterior end of maxilla blunt, not reaching anterior border of preopercle; isthmus short, preceded by a fleshy knob on urohyal; origin of anal fin clearly posterior to rear base of dorsal fin; pinkish gray with a broad midlateral silvery stripe, narrowly dark on upper edge. Maximum length 13 cm. Occurs throughout the tropical and subtropical Indo-Pacific from the Red Sea and east coast of Africa to the Society Islands (type locality, Huahine) and the Hawaiian Islands; occurs in schools inshore but also found hundreds of kilometers offshore. Highly regarded as a tuna baitfish. *Stolephorus buccaneeri* Strasburg is a synonym.

SAMOAN ANCHOVY
Stolephorus apiensis (Jordan & Seale, 1906)

Dorsal rays 14; anal rays 21–22 (first 2 or 3 dorsal and anal rays unbranched); pectoral rays 14–15; longitudinal scale series 34–42; needle-like prepelvic scutes 0–5 (usually 3); no predorsal scute; lower-limb gill rakers 27–31; body moderately elongate, the depth 5.0–5.6 in standard length; isthmus evenly tapering anteriorly; posterior border of preopercle rounded (not indented before posterior end of maxilla); tip of maxilla pointed, reaching to or beyond posterior margin of preopercle; origin of anal fin below middle of dorsal fin; pelvic fins reaching posterior to a vertical through dorsal-fin origin; gray with a midlateral silvery stripe on body that is narrow on its anterior fourth, then progressively broader posteriorly; silvery with blue-green iridescence over cheek and opercle; a nar-

Western Samoa (J. Collyer)

row black bar on side of occiput above level of eye; upper base of caudal fin with a blackish mark; lobes of caudal fin sometimes with a blackish area. Attains about 7 cm. Type specimens collected from the shore inside the reef at Apia, Western Samoa; also known from Fiji and Pohnpei (formerly Ponape).

Lombok, Indonesia

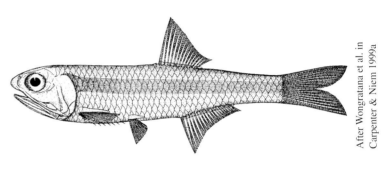

After Wongratana et al. in Carpenter & Niem 1999a

INDIAN ANCHOVY
Stolephorus indicus (van Hasselt, 1823)
Dorsal rays 15–17; anal rays 19–21; pectoral rays 15–17; longitudinal scale series 38–42; needle-like prepelvic scutes 2–6 (most often 4); no predorsal scute; lower-limb gill rakers 20–28; body depth 4.7–5.7 in standard length; isthmus evenly tapering anteriorly; posterior border of preopercle rounded (not indented before posterior end of maxilla); tip of maxilla pointed, reaching to or beyond posterior margin of preopercle; origin of anal fin below middle of dorsal fin; pelvic fins not reaching posterior to a vertical through dorsal-fin origin; translucent gray with a midlateral silvery stripe; head mainly silvery with patches of blackish pigment; base of dorsal and anal fins narrowly blackish; upper and lower edges of caudal fin broadly dusky to blackish. Largest species of the genus; reaches 18 cm. Red Sea and east coast of Africa to the Mariana, Caroline, and Society Islands; type locality, India. Does not form large schools, so not caught in large numbers; not hardy, hence unsuitable as a baitfish.

BAELAMA ANCHOVY
Thryssa baelama (Forsskål, 1775)
Dorsal rays 15–16; anal rays 29–32 (including initial 3 unbranched dorsal and anal rays, the first very small); pectoral rays 13–14; abdomen anterior to pelvic fins with 4–9 sharply pointed midventral scutes, none anterior to a vertical at base of pectoral fins; postpelvic scutes 12–18; lower-limb gill rakers 18–26; body depth about 4–5 in standard length; body width about 3 in body depth; tip of snout in front of center of eye; maxilla pointed and short, reaching slightly posterior to anterior border of preopercle; gray dorsally, silvery on side and ventrally; about 10 fine irregular orange lines extending posteriorly from upper part of gill opening; snout and interorbital translucent orangish. Reaches about 16 cm. Red Sea (type locality) south to Mozambique, Madagascar, and Mauri-

INSULAR ANCHOVY
Stolephorus insularis Hardenberg, 1933
Dorsal rays 15–16; anal rays 17–20; pectoral rays 15–17; longitudinal scale series 36–38; needle-like prepelvic scutes 4–8 (usually 6 or 7); a small predorsal spine on some specimens; lower-limb gill rakers 21–28; body depth about 4.7 in standard length; isthmus evenly tapering anteriorly; posterior border of preopercle slightly concave before rear end of maxilla; maxilla tapering and pointed, reaching to or beyond posterior margin of preopercle; origin of anal fin below middle of dorsal fin; pelvic fins just reaching a vertical at origin of dorsal fin; most characteristic marking a double dark-pigmented line dorsally behind dorsal fin; caudal fin deep yellow. Reaches 8 cm. Gulf of Aden and coast of Asia (not the Persian Gulf) to China and western Indonesia; reported in the Pacific from Caroline Islands and New Caledonia; described from Java and the Lingga Archipelago.

New Caledonia

tius, east through the Indo-Malayan region and northern half of Australia to New Caledonia, Fiji, Tonga, and the Mariana, Caroline, and Samoa Islands; typically found inshore in protected bays and lagoons, often in estuarine habitats. *Anchovia evermanni* Jordan & Seale is a synonym.

WOLF HERRINGS
(CHIROCENTRIDAE)

This family is grouped with the sardines and anchovies in the order Clupeiformes. It consists of a single genus and 2 species. They share the following characters with the clupeid fishes: elongate compressed body, no lateral line, 2 supramaxillae, very deciduous cycloid scales, transparent adipose tissue over eye, a single short dorsal fin; small pelvic fins with 7 rays, abdominal in position, and a deeply forked caudal fin. They differ in having very small scales, lacking scutes ventrally on the body, 8 branchiostegal rays (usually 6 or 7 in the Clupeidae), long canine teeth in the jaws, the posterior position of the dorsal fin, fewer gill rakers, and large size (over a meter). Fossil remains of the family from the Cretaceous. Unlike the clupeid fishes that feed on minute organisms of the plankton, the wolf herrings are voracious carnivores on small schooling fishes, squids, and shrimps. Dorsal and anal fin-ray counts here include the small initial unbranched rays.

Cochin, India

BLACKFIN WOLF HERRING
Chirocentrus dorab (Forsskål, 1775)

Dorsal rays 16–18; anal rays 29–36; pectoral rays 14–16; gill rakers 1–4 + 10–16; body depth about 7 in standard length; depth of head through center of eye 10.5–11.9 in standard length; pectoral fins relatively short, 7.7–9.1 in standard length (5.6–7.7 in the similar *C. nudus*); deep blue-green on back, silvery on side and ventrally; tip of dorsal fin blackish. Reported to 120 cm, but rarely exceeds 80 cm. Red Sea (type locality), Persian Gulf, tropical and subtropical continental shores of the Indian Ocean, and western Pacific from southern Japan to Solomon Islands and New Caledonia. Reported to occur from the surface to 120 m; a voracious feeder on small fishes (especially clupeids and engraulids), shrimps, and squids.

Sudan, Red Sea

MILKFISH FAMILY
(CHANIDAE)

This family consists of a single primitive teleost fish that is wide-ranging in the Indo-Pacific region (see following account).

Hawaiian Islands

MILKFISH
Chanos chanos (Forsskål, 1775)

Fins without spines; a short dorsal fin with 13–17 rays; anal rays 8–11; pectoral fins low on body, the rays 15–17; pelvic fins in about middle of body, with 10–12 rays; lateral-line scales 75–91; paired fins with an axillary scale; branchiostegal rays 4; more than 250 slender gill rakers; eye covered with adipose tissue; intermuscular bones numerous and long; caudal fin large and deeply forked; silvery blue-green on back, silvery on sides and ventrally. Maximum length reported as about 150 cm, but any over 120 cm would be exceptional. Indo-Pacific and tropical eastern Pacific; type locality, Red Sea. A valuable food fish, especially in Asia; the young are caught in fine-mesh nets and reared in coastal ponds; those in fresh water do not reach sexual maturity. Spawning takes place in the sea; duration of larval life 2–3 weeks. The young settle out inshore, including brackish environments. Juveniles feed mainly on diatoms, benthic cyano-bacteria (blue-green algae), and detritus, but also ingest filamentous green algae, small crustaceans, and nematodes (Hiatt, 1947). Adults are mainly herbivorous, but also feed on zooplankton, including larval fishes; the author has observed them swimming with mouth open at the surface, presumably for algal scums.

60

Lord Howe Island

EEL CATFISHES
(PLOTOSIDAE)

The eel catfishes are named for their elongate bodies and confluence of the caudal fin with the dorsal and anal fins. Other characteristics include the lack of scales, a complete lateral line extending nearly to caudal-fin base, no adipose fin (present in most other catfish families), and 4 pairs of barbels surrounding the mouth. The dorsal and pectoral fins have an initial venomous spine with a row of retrorse barbs on the edges; wounds from these spines are very painful. The author has been stung by the spines of 2 species and can attest to the virulence of the venom. There are 9 genera and about 40 species, more than half of which occur in fresh water in Australia and New Guinea.

STRIPED EEL CATFISH
Plotosus lineatus (Thunberg, 1787)

Dorsal rays I,4 + 69–115; anal rays 58–82; caudal rays 9–11; pectoral rays I,9–13; body depth 5.8–8.0 in standard length; 4 pairs of barbels on head, the nasal and maxillary pairs short; tubular anterior nostril dorsal to upper lip; gill membranes narrowly attached across isthmus; dorsal fins well-separated, the second originating posterior to a vertical through origin of pelvic fins; brown (the juveniles very dark brown) with 2 narrow white to pale yellow stripes; lower part of head and body white; edge of median fins black. Reaches 32 cm. Red Sea and east coast of Africa to Palau, Caroline Islands, and Samoa Islands; southern Korea and Japan to Western Australia, New South Wales, Lord Howe Island, and New Caledonia; type locality, Indian Ocean; occurs in a variety of habitats from coral reefs to estuaries. Forms dense aggregations for mutual protection from their venomous spines; adults disperse to forage at night. Feeds mainly on crustaceans, occasionally on mollusks and small fishes.

Juveniles, Ogasawara

Persian Gulf (night)

LIZARDFISHES
(SYNODONTIDAE)

Many common names of fishes are inappropriate, but the name is well chosen for the lizardfishes because of their reptilian head. They have a very large mouth, the nonprotractile upper jaw bordered by the premaxilla extending well posterior to the eye; there are numerous slender teeth in the jaws (none as canines), on the palatines, and on the tongue; the body is elongate and cylindrical; the eye is small to moderate in size with transparent adipose tissue on the anterior and posterior margins. The head and body have cycloid scales (except *Harpadon*, scaled only along lateral line); the gill rakers are rudimentary. There are no spines in the fins; the dorsal fin has 11–14 rays, followed by a very small adipose fin (no rays); the anal fin of 8–16 rays is set far back on body; the caudal fin of 19 principal rays is strongly forked; the pelvic fins are large with 8–9 rays. Lizardfishes are usually found on sand or mud bottoms into which they are able to quickly bury themselves; a few species occur in the coral-reef habitat and may be seen at rest on coral or rocky substrata. They are voracious ambush predators, mainly on fishes, occasionally on crustaceans and cephalopods. The species of the genus *Saurida* have numerous teeth on the side of the jaws that are visible when the mouth is closed; those of the large genus *Synodus* lack these small lateral teeth. Cressey (1981) revised the Indo-Pacific species of *Synodus*, Waples (1982) reviewed the Hawaiian species of *Saurida*, and Waples & Randall (1989) the Hawaiian species of *Synodus*. Russell in Carpenter & Niem (1999a) treated the central and western Pacific species of the family. The genera *Harpadon* (no representatives at islands of Oceania) and *Saurida* are classified in the subfamily Harpadoninae, the remaining 3 genera in the Synodontinae.

GRINNERS (HARPADONINAE)

REDMOUTH LIZARDFISH
Saurida flamma Waples, 1982
Dorsal rays 11 (rarely 12); anal rays 9–11; pectoral rays 13–15 (usually 14); pelvic rays 9 (true of other species of *Saurida*); branchiostegal rays 13 (also generic; 15–18 in *Synodus*); lateral-line scales 53–54 (usually 54); origin of dorsal fin at or anterior to midpoint between snout and adipose fin; a vertical from tip of pectoral fin passes through first to third predorsal scales; whitish, mottled with brown, with small blackish blotches, mainly in a row on lower side; a large blackish blotch in middle of body, another below adipose fin, and one at caudal-fin base; side of

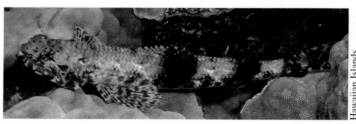

Hawaiian Islands

mouth red with narrow white bars. Reaches 33 cm. Currently known from the Hawaiian Islands (type locality, O'ahu), Johnston Island, Pitcairn Islands, Austral Islands, Rapa, and Niue, thus suggesting antitropical distribution; usually found in reef habitats; depth range 5–30 m.

SLENDER LIZARDFISH
Saurida gracilis (Quoy & Gaimard, 1824)
Dorsal rays 11–12 (rarely 12); anal rays 9–10; pectoral rays 12–14 (usually 13); lateral-line scales 49–52; origin of dorsal fin behind midpoint between snout and adipose fin; a vertical from tip of pectoral fin passes through second or third predorsal scales; whitish, mottled with brown dorsally, with 3 large blackish blotches, the first behind dorsal fin, the second below adipose fin, and the third at base of caudal fin; a row of blackish blotches on lower side. Attains 28 cm. Indo-Pacific; described from Mauritius and the Hawaiian Islands; a common shallow-water species usually seen at rest on sand or silty sand near protected reefs, but it may also occur on coral reefs.

Cebu, Philippines

NEBULOUS LIZARDFISH
Saurida nebulosa Valenciennes in C & V, 1850
Dorsal rays 10–11; anal rays 9–10; pectoral rays 11–13 (usually 12); lateral-line scales 50–52; origin of dorsal fin behind midpoint of distance between snout and adipose fin; a vertical from tip of pectoral fin passes through fourth to sixth predorsal scales; pectoral fins just reaching a vertical at origin of pelvic fins (pectorals extend beyond origin of pelvics in the other 2 species of

Tonga

Saurida); greenish gray, mottled with brown dorsally, with the same 3 blackish spots as the other *Saurida*, but generally smaller; a series of blackish blotches on lower side, with small blotches between except posteriorly. Largest specimen, 19 cm. Mauritius

BRUSHTOOTH LIZARDFISH
Saurida undosquamis (Richardson, 1848)
Dorsal rays 11–12 (usually 12); anal rays 10–11; pectoral rays 14–15; lateral-line scales 45–52; rows of scales above lateral line to base of dorsal fin 3.5–4.5; lateral series of palatine teeth in 2 rows; no teeth on vomer; first dorsal rays about 3 times longer than last ray; pectoral fins not extending beyond base of pelvic fins and not reaching origin of dorsal fin; brown dorsally, the scale edges darker, silvery white ventrally, with a series of about 9 elongate dark spots along lateral line; fins unmarked except for a series of small blackish spots along leading edge of dorsal fin and upper lobe of caudal fin. Reported to reach 50 cm. Red Sea

Persian Gulf

(and Mediterranean via the Suez Canal), Persian Gulf, and east coast of Africa, east to western Pacific from southern Japan to Australia; reported east to Fiji. Generally found on mud bottoms, but may be on sand; depth range 15 to at least 200 m.

(type locality) to Indonesia, Queensland, Tonga, Society Islands, Hawaiian Islands, and islands of Micronesia except the Marshall Islands; generally found in shallow water in muddy to silty sand habitats, including estuarine areas.

LIZARDFISHES (SYNODONTINAE)

Great Barrier Reef

TWOSPOT LIZARDFISH
Synodus binotatus Schultz in Schultz et al., 1953
Dorsal rays 12–13 (usually 13); anal rays 8–10; pectoral rays 11–12 (rarely 11); pelvic rays 8 (true of other species of *Synodus*); lateral-line scales 52–55; scale rows above lateral line 3.5; anterior palatine teeth longer than posterior teeth; flap on anterior nostril long and spatulate; pectoral fins long, reaching beyond a line connecting origins of dorsal and pelvic fins; whitish to light brown with 7 irregular dark red to dark brown bars on body, the first 2 indistinct, the third below front of dorsal fin, and the last at caudal-fin base; lower side of body with a series of large dark spots, each flanked by a smaller dark spot; a pair of small dark brown spots at tip of snout (the basis for the scientific name). Reaches 18 cm. East coast of Africa to the Hawaiian Islands and Tuamotu Archipelago; Ogasawara Islands and Taiwan to Great Barrier Reef; type locality, Kwajalein Atoll, Marshall Islands; usually found in less than 20 m, often in the coral-reef habitat on hard substratum.

Flores, Indonesia

Hawaiian Islands

CAPRICORN LIZARDFISH
Synodus capricornis Cressey & Randall, 1978
Dorsal rays 12–14; anal rays 8–10; pectoral rays 11–13; lateral-line scales 64–66; scale rows above lateral line 5.5; no scales on cheek behind mouth; anterior palatine teeth longer than posterior teeth; flap on anterior nostril short and triangular; pectoral fins short, not reaching a line between origins of dorsal and pelvic fins; whitish with a series of 8 large, dusky orange-red blotches along lateral line with a small spot between each pair extending as a streak onto ventral half of body; dorsal part of body mottled with dusky orange-red with a large, indistinct, irregular blotch extending dorsally from every other blotch of lateral line. Attains 21 cm. Described from Easter Island (type locality) and Pitcairn Island, hence the name *capricornis*, alluding to these southern localities. Waples & Randall (1989), however, recorded the species from the Hawaiian Islands, suggesting antitropical distribution; depth range 21–88 m.

CLEARFIN LIZARDFISH
Synodus dermatogenys Fowler, 1912
Dorsal rays 11–13 (rarely 13); anal rays 8–10; pectoral rays 11–13; lateral-line scales 59–62; scale rows above lateral line 5.5; eye small, the bony orbit diameter 3.4–5.3% standard length; anterior palatine teeth longer than posterior teeth; flap on anterior nostril slender; pectoral fins short, not reaching a line between origins of dorsal and pelvic fins; a series of 8 or 9 dark blotches, often with pale centers, along lateral line, the blotches narrower than pale interspaces and linked with a dark blotch

above; usually a narrow pale blue stripe on body behind upper end of gill opening; 6 small black spots on tip of snout. Attains 23 cm. Indo-Pacific; type locality, Hawaiian Islands. Generally found on sand or rubble near coral reefs from the shallows to at least 30 m. Misidentified by most recent authors as *S. variegatus*.

JAVELINFISH
Synodus jaculum Russell & Cressey, 1979
Dorsal rays 11–13; anal rays 8–10; pectoral rays 12–13; lateral-line scales 59–62; rows of scales above lateral line 5.5 (occasionally 6.5); no scales on cheek behind mouth; anterior palatine teeth longer than posterior teeth; nasal flap on anterior nostril very short; body with a complex pattern of irregular dark bars and longitudinal rows of dark spots, the most conspicuous markings a large dark blotch at base of caudal fin and a dendritic

Negros, Philippines

black spot dorsally on snout. Reaches about 20 cm. Gulf of Aden and east coast of Africa to the Line Islands, Marquesas Islands, and Society Islands; southern Japan to Great Barrier Reef (type locality, Lizard Island); reported from depths of 10–100 m. The most active of the lizardfishes, often rising well above the bottom to prey upon small fishes.

Hawaiian Islands

REDMARBLED LIZARDFISH
Synodus rubromarmoratus Russell & Cressey, 1979
Dorsal rays 10–12; anal rays 8–10; pectoral rays 11–12; lateral-line scales 54–55; rows of scales above lateral line 3.5; rows of scales on cheek 5; anterior palatine teeth not longer than posterior teeth; more than 30 teeth on free end of tongue; nasal flap on anterior nostril long and slender; anal-fin base shorter than dorsal-fin base; pectoral fins not reaching a line connecting origins of dorsal and pelvic fins; body with 5 dark bars of varying width, the upper half red with dark brown margin and the lower half dark brown; smaller and less distinct dark bars between each pair of principal bars, becoming darker ventrally; a small dark brown blotch between each pair of dark bars ventrally on body; a large red blotch on cheek and a smaller one on occiput. A small species, the largest specimen 8.4 cm. Great Barrier Reef (type locality, Lizard Island), Taiwan, Philippines, and Solomon Islands; Randall (1998b) extended the range to the Ogasawara Islands and Hawaiian Islands, Myers (1999) to Guam, and D. W. Greenfield recently collected the species in Fiji; occurs on coral reefs from the shallows to at least 15 m.

REEF LIZARDFISH
Synodus variegatus (Lacepède, 1803)
Dorsal rays 12–14; anal rays 8–10; pectoral rays 12–13; lateral-line scales 60–63; scale rows above lateral line 5.5; cheek fully scaled from behind mouth to edge of preopercle; anterior palatine teeth longer than posterior teeth; interorbital width broad, 3.9–4.7% standard length; anterior nostrils with a short triangular flap; pectoral fins not reaching a line connecting origins of dorsal and pelvic fins; whitish with a series of 5 irregular, hourglass-shaped, dark brown to reddish bars on upper half of body, the broad lower part on lateral line joined by a midlateral brown to red stripe; each dark bar with a narrow ventral exten-

Lord Howe Island

SOUTHERN LIZARDFISH
Synodus similis McCulloch, 1921
Dorsal rays 13–14 (usually 14); anal rays 9; pectoral rays 13; lateral-line scales 58–59; rows of scales above lateral line 3.5; rows of scales on cheek 4; anterior palatine teeth not longer than posterior teeth; fewer than 30 teeth on free end of tongue; nasal flap short and rounded; pectoral fins extending to a line from origin of pelvic fins to origin of dorsal fin; a series of squarish orangish red blotches along lateral line, each pair separated in their upper part by a smaller orangish red blotch; a row of dark reddish brown dots in upper part of each orangish red blotch; a faint narrow bluish stripe above orangish red blotches, and above this orangish red mottled with reddish brown dots; 2 or 3 oblique black spots dorsally on opercle; dorsal rays pale orange-red with well-spaced white spots; caudal fin with irregular white lines, the upper lobe tipped with white. Largest specimen the holotype, 18.5 cm, taken in 47–55 m off the Capricorn Group, Great Barrier Reef; also known from Lord Howe Island, Norfolk Island, New Zealand, New Caledonia, and Rapa; occurs on sand, generally near coral or rock; shallowest collection, 25 m.

Marshall Islands

sion, separating a series of rectangular white spots. Largest specimen, 28.3 cm. Indo-Pacific; type locality, Mauritius. Observed more often on coral reefs than any other lizardfish. *Synodus englemani* Schultz is a synonym.

SNAKEFISH
Trachinocephalus myops (Forster, 1801)
Dorsal rays 11–14; anal rays 13–18 (8–11 in other genera); pectoral rays 11–13; pelvic rays 8; branchiostegal rays 12; lateral-line scales 51–61; snout very short, equal to or shorter than eye diameter; interorbital space deeply concave; mouth strongly oblique; body with alternating stripes of pale blue and yellow, those on back edged in dark brown; an oblique black spot at upper end of gill opening. Tropical to warm temperate Indo-Pacific and Atlantic; type locality, St Helena. Reaches 32 cm. Reported from the shallows to 388 m. Occurs on sand or mud into which it can bury very rapidly, with only its eyes visible; rarely seen fully exposed.

Hawaiian Islands

BROTULAS AND CUSK EELS
(OPHIDIIDAE)

The fishes of this family, one of 5 of the large order Ophidiiformes, are moderately elongate with the caudal fin joined to the dorsal and anal fins; the pelvic fins are absent or reduced to 1 or 2 filamentous rays; some species have barbels around the mouth similar to those of catfishes. Scales are present. Most of the species occur in the deep sea; the few shallow-water species are cryptic, and the majority became known to ichthyologists only through the use of the ichthyocide rotenone. An example is the Slimy Cusk Eel (*Brosmophyciops pautzkei* Schultz), not described until 1960; it is often collected from coral reefs with rotenone. The author discovered by tasting the copious amount of mucus that a strong repelling substance is present. No research has been done on this proba-

Large-eye Brotula, *Brotula multibarbata,* Papua New Guinea (night)

ble skin toxin or whether it is also found in other species such as those of the genus *Dinematichthys.* The only species of the family apt to be seen by divers (and then only fleetingly at night) are discussed here.

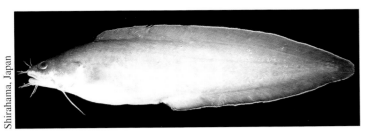

Shirahama, Japan

LARGE-EYE BROTULA
Brotula multibarbata Temminck & Schlegel, 1846
Dorsal rays 117–123; anal rays 88–100; pectoral rays 22–26; pelvic rays 2, the outer half of each free of membrane; longitudinal scale series 144–181; 3 pairs of barbels on snout and 3 pairs on chin; body depth 4.4–7.0 in standard length; eye large, equal to or larger than fleshy interorbital width; brown, shading to whitish on abdomen and ventrally on head; small juveniles translucent with dark gray spots. Attains 60 cm. Indo-Pacific; type locality, Nagasaki, Japan. Generally found in shallow reef areas, but 1 record from 650 m. Nocturnal; quickly retreating to shelter when illuminated. Hubbs (1944) revised the genus *Brotula,* but more taxonomic research is needed.

Johnston Island

SMALLEYE BROTULA
Brotula townsendi Fowler, 1900
Dorsal rays 97–105; anal rays 71–84; pectoral rays 24–26; branched caudal rays 9; pelvic rays 2, the outer half free of membrane; longitudinal scale series 124–133; 3 pairs of barbels on snout and 3 pairs on chin; body depth 4.2–5.0 in standard length; eye small, its diameter less than fleshy interorbial width; brown, the scales with narrow pale edges, shading to yellowish white ventrally; median fins darker brown posteriorly. Attains about 18 cm. Known from the Hawaiian Islands (type locality), Johnston Island, Marshall Islands, Tonga, Loyalty Islands, and Vanuatu.

PEARLFISHES
(CARAPIDAE)

This family of 7 genera and 31 species of small slender fishes is grouped with the brotulas and cusk eels in the order Ophidiiformes. These fishes are characterized by a very long tapering body without a caudal fin (the many-rayed dorsal and anal fins extend to the pointed tail tip); there are no spines in the fins; the pectoral fins are usually shorter than the head (fins lost in 3 species of *Encheliophis*); the pelvic fins are absent except in the 4 free-living deep-water species of the genus *Pyramodon*; there are no scales; the most unique feature is the anterior position of the anus (usually before the base of the pectoral fins). The body of many species is transparent, giving rise to one common name, glass eels; also known as fierasfers (from a generic name, now a synonym of *Carapus*). There are 2 different larval stages termed the vexiller and the tenuis. The vexiller has a very long predorsal filament, often ornamented such that it resembles a siphonophore. In view of the powerful stinging cells of siphonophores, mimicking them should enhance larval survival. Most carapids occur as commensals in sea cucumbers, cushion sea stars (*Culcita*), pearl oysters (*Pinctada*) and other large bivalve mollusks, and tunicates. A few of the genus *Encheliophis* (Jordan-

Fowler's Pearlfish, *Onuxodon fowleri*, Bali (night)

icus is a synonym, sometimes used as a subgenus) are parasitic, feeding on the respiratory tree and gonads of their host. The tenuis larval stage is the one that finds the echinoderm or molluskan host. The author has encountered these commensal species in the open only at night (and then rarely). One was observed in an aquarium to re-enter a sea cucumber by finding the cloacal opening with its snout, curving its long body in a U-shape, then quickly slipping in tail-first; pearlfishes are also known to enter sea cucumbers head first. The family was revised by Arnold (1956) and Markle & Olney (1990). Trott (1970) published a valuable paper on the biology of 8 species.

CUSHION STAR PEARLFISH
Carapus mourlani (Petit, 1934)
Pectoral rays 17–21; anal rays anterior to dorsal-fin origin 18–25; total vertebrae 102–114; precaudal vertebrae 15–17; body elongate, the depth 9.3–11.5 in total length, and compressed, the width about half the depth; anus anterior to pectoral-fin base; head length 6.5–7.1 in total length; maxilla extending well beyond posterior edge of eye; upper jaw with a pair of slender incurved canines at symphysis, followed by a band of very small teeth in 2–3 rows; lower jaw with a band of teeth, the outer row along side of jaw with about 7 enlarged teeth (progressively smaller posteriorly); protruding vomer with 2 or 3 large teeth; palatines with a band of short, stout, conical teeth; pectoral fins

PINHEAD PEARLFISH
Encheliophis boraborensis Kaup, 1856
Pectoral rays 15–21; anal rays anterior to dorsal-fin origin about 17; vertebrae 119–126; precaudal vertebrae 15–17; body elongate, the depth about 13 in total length, and compressed, the width nearly half the depth; head short, its length about 8–10 in total length; teeth in bands in jaws, those in lower jaw larger (none notably enlarged); protruding vomer studded with short conical teeth; palatines with a narrow band of stout conical teeth of variable size; pectoral fins about one-third head length; reddish brown, finely speckled with dark brown dots. Largest species

Marquesas Is.

2.1–3.0 in head length; translucent, silvery to coppery over cheek and abdomen, with numerous small dark brown spots. Attains 17 cm. Indo-Pacific; type locality, Mauritius. Usually commensal in sea stars, especially of the genus *Culcita*; other asteroid hosts: *Pentaceros hawaiiensis*, *Choriaster granulatus*, *Acanthaster planci*, and five species of holothurians (Markle & Olney, 1990); Randall et al. (1985b) reported two from *Stichopus* sp. taken in 103 and 116 m at Johnston Island.

Society Islands

of the genus; reaches 30 cm. Madagascar to Society Islands (type locality, Bora Bora); lives in sea cucumbers, often the large strongly papillate *Thelenota ananas*. Illustrated specimen from the holothurian *Bohadschia argus*. Feeds on shrimps and small fishes (Trott, 1970). *Encheliophis parvipinnis* (Kaup) is a synonym.

SLENDER PEARLFISH
Encheliophis gracilis (Bleeker, 1856)

Pectoral rays 17–19; dorsal and anal fins low; anal rays anterior to dorsal-fin origin 19–27; total vertebrae 136–140; precaudal vertebrae 26–32; body very slender, the depth about 20 in total length; head length 8.5–10.5 in total length; maxilla immobile, bound by skin to side of head; teeth in jaws in one row, well spaced, those of upper jaw hooked posteriorly; 2–4 large conical teeth on vomer; teeth in one row on palatines; pectoral fins 2.5–3.2 in head length; translucent, often heavily pigmented with small dark spots; posterior part of tail usually blackish. Largest specimen recorded, 27.5 cm; females generally larger

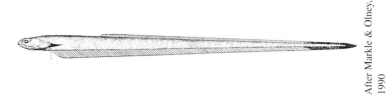

than males. Indo-Pacific; type locality, Banda, Indonesia. Parasitic in holothurians; feeds on the gonads and respiratory tree of the host. Trott (1970) found 44 in *Bohadschia argus*, all as male-female pairs.

SILVER PEARLFISH
Encheliophis homei (Richardson, 1846)

Pectoral rays 17–21; anal rays anterior to dorsal-fin origin 19–26; total vertebrae 116–128; precaudal vertebrae 16–19; head depth slightly greater than body depth, about 15 in total length; body width about half body depth; head length about 8 in total length; maxilla free from the cheek (maxilla attached to cheek in the Indo-Pacific *E. gracilis*, parasitic in sea cucumbers); jaws with 2 rows of incurved teeth, the inner row of upper jaw largest, the outer row of lower jaw largest (larger than upper teeth); 2 to 6 teeth in middle row of protruding vomer very large; palatine teeth in 2–3 rows, the inner largest; translucent, the vertebral column visible from being reddish with some dark pigment; cheek and abdomen silvery; side of jaws with some blackish pigment. Reaches 19 cm. Madagascar to Society Islands; Philippines to Queensland; type locality, Timor. Commensal in sea cucumbers; leaves its host at night to prey upon small fishes and shrimps.

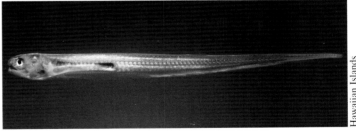

FOWLER'S PEARLFISH
Onuxodon fowleri (Smith, 1955)

Pectoral rays 13–17; anal rays anterior to dorsal-fin origin 2; total vertebrae about 90; precaudal vertebrae 19–22; body elongate, the depth 10–11.5 in total length, and compressed, the width about 2.5 in depth; head length 7.2–8.1 in total length; anus slightly posterior to base of pectoral fins (anterior on the other 2 species of the genus); a pair of prominent canine teeth at front of jaws, separated by a gap from narrow band of small teeth posteriorly; vomer and palatines with numerous small conical teeth; sensory papillae on head and anterior lateral line; pectoral fins 1.9–2.2 in head length; translucent, the vertebral column often darkly pigmented, especially posteriorly (sometimes entire posterior part of tail blackish). Attains 9 cm. East coast of Africa to the Hawaiian Islands and Pitcairn Islands; Philippines to New

South Wales and Kermadec Islands; type locality, Kiritimati (Christmas Island), Line Islands. Commensal in pearl oysters (*Pinctada*) and other large rock-dwelling bivalves (*Pteria, Avicula, Spondylus*); also reported from 2 holothurians (Markle & Olney, 1990). The related *Onuxodon margaritiferae* (Rendahl) is known only from the pearl oyster of Western Australia.

SHORTFIN PEARLFISH
Onuxodon parvibrachium (Fowler, 1927)

Pectoral rays 14–16; anal rays anterior to dorsal-fin origin 2; precaudal vertebrae 16–18; caudal vertebrae 48–65; body deep, the depth about 6–8 in total length, and strongly compressed; anus behind base of pectoral fins; head length about 6–8 in total length of adults; dentition as in *O. fowleri*; eye small, about 6–10 in head length; no sensory papillae on head or anterior lateral line; pectoral fins short, 3–6 in head length; translucent pink in life. Attains 10 cm. Known from Natal, Seychelles, Mal-

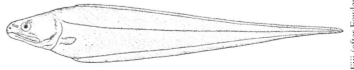

dive Islands, East Indies, eastern Australia, New Caledonia, Fiji, Hawaiian Islands, and Kiritimati (Christmas Island), Line Islands (type locality). Large oysters and "clams" (probably *Spondylus* spp.) reported as the hosts.

Giant Frogfish, *Antennarius commerson*, Papua New Guinea

FROGFISHES
(ANTENNARIIDAE)

Frogfishes are often called anglerfishes, but this is a general name best used for all 16 families of the order Lophiiformes, which are characterized by having the first dorsal spine modified into a lure consisting of the slender illicium, tipped with the esca (bait) that is used to attract prey near the mouth. Frogfishes have a laterally compressed body and a loose scaleless skin that may have spinules, wart-like protuberances, cirri, or slender branched tentacles. The mouth is very large and strongly oblique to vertical. There are 2 dorsal spines on the head behind the illicium; the third spine is usually curved and often broadly connected by membrane to the head; the prehensile pectoral fins have an "elbow" joint; the pelvic fins have a short slender spine and 5 soft rays. The gill opening is small, ventral on the base of the pectoral appendage (except for *Antennarius analis* and *A. duescus* in which it is distinctly posterior). The color of many species is extremely variable, often closely matching that of the surroundings; some of these fishes are capable of profound change in color within a few weeks. Frogfishes are able to swallow surprisingly large prey, even some fishes longer than themselves; they may also be cannibalistic. Except for the pelagic Sargassumfish (*Histrio histrio*), all are benthic, and most occur in shallow water. An account of the Sargassumfish is included here because it is sometimes found inshore as a result of drifting in with its associated floating algae. Because of the camouflage of frogfishes and their tendency to remain motionless, they are rarely seen. They are able to inflate their body by taking water into the stomach. Most species lay a mass of eggs that float like a raft on the surface; a few attach eggs to the male. An extensive review of the systematics and ecology of frogfishes was published by Pietsch & Grobecker (1987).

TAILJET FROGFISH

Antennarius analis (Schultz, 1957)

Dorsal rays I + I + I,12–13 (rarely 13); anal rays 6–7 (rarely 6); pectoral rays 9–10 (rarely 9); all pelvic rays unbranched; illicium about twice as long as second dorsal spine, 3.7–5.0 in standard length; esca a tuft of slender filaments from a fleshy base with up to 5 small dark spots on base; second dorsal spine straight and not broadly connected to head with a membrane; third dorsal spine straight to slightly curved, 3.9–5.25 in standard length; unique in the genus in having gill opening at base of anal fin; dorsal and anal fins ending at base of caudal fin (hence no caudal peduncle); usually no large dark spot at base of dorsal fin. Known from Japan (Kon & Yoshino, 1999), Hawaiian Islands (Waikīkī reef, type locality), Society Islands, Samoa Islands, Fiji, islands of Micronesia, and Christmas Island and Rowley Shoals in the eastern Indan Ocean; depth of capture 1.5–21 m. Kon & Yoshino (1999) corrected the authorship from Gosline to Schultz.

Palau (after Pietsch & Grobecker, 1987)

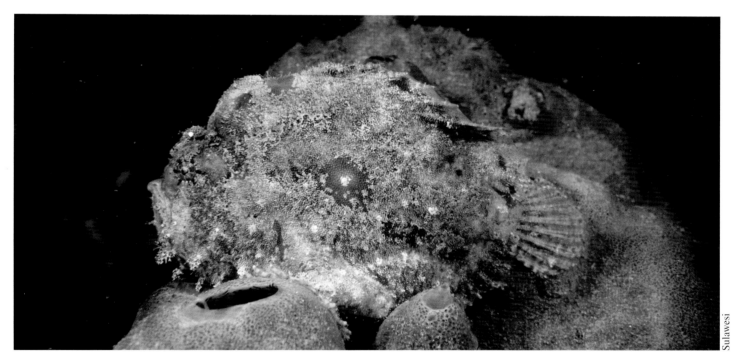

Sulawesi

WHITEBAIT FROGFISH

Antennarius coccineus (Cuvier in Lesson, 1831)

Dorsal rays I + I + I,12–13 (rarely 13); anal rays 7; pectoral rays 10–11 (rarely 9); last pelvic ray branched; illicium short, about as long as second dorsal spine; second dorsal spine curved and not connected to head with a membrane; a depressed naked area between second and third dorsal spines; dorsal and anal fins ending at base of caudal fin (hence no caudal peduncle); esca small, without long tentacles, and nearly always white; head and body usually mottled red or yellowish to reddish brown; a large dark spot rarely present at base of dorsal fin. Reaches 12 cm. Common and wide-ranging in the Indo-Pacific except the Hawaiian Islands where replaced by *Antennarius drombus* Jordan & Evermann (Williams, 1989); type locality, Mauritius; also known from the tropical eastern Pacific. Of specimens with data on depth of capture, 70% were taken in less than 10 m, but there is a record from 75 m.

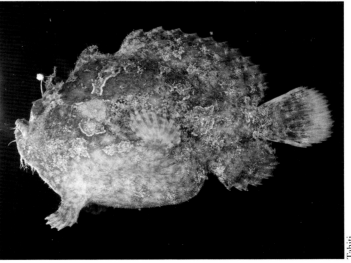

Tahiti

69

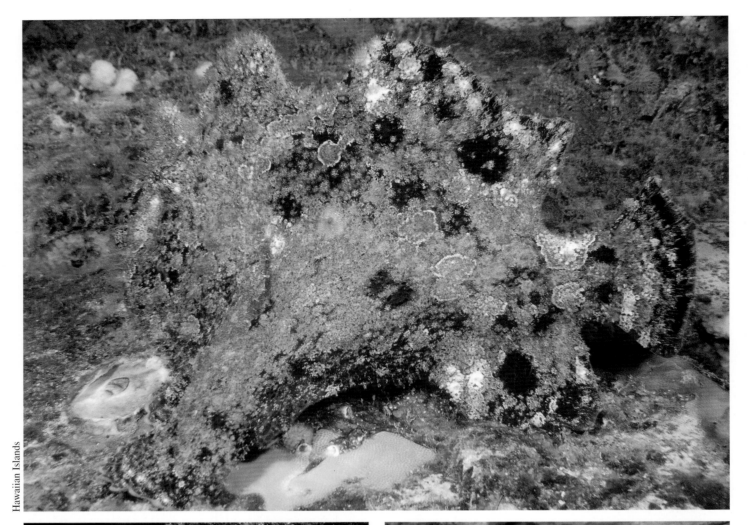

Hawaiian Islands

Hawaiian Islands

Komodo, Indonesia

GIANT FROGFISH

Antennarius commerson (Latreille, 1804)

Dorsal rays I + I + I,12–13 (rarely 12); anal rays 8; pectoral rays 11; illicium about twice as long as second spine; second dorsal spine joined to base of third dorsal spine by a thick membrane covered with small spinules; yellow, red, olive, brown, gray, black, or white, and variously mottled; often with 2 or more dark spots in caudal fin and one at base of dorsal and anal fins. Largest of Indo-Pacific frogfishes; reaches 38 cm. Red Sea and South Africa to Hawaiian Islands and Society Islands; southern Japan to New South Wales, Lord Howe Island, and New Caledonia (Laboute & Grandperrin, 2000); other Pacific localities include Guam, Palau, Fiji, and Samoa Islands; type locality, Mauritius; also occurs in the tropical eastern Pacific. Mostly found on reefs in less than 20 m, but ranges to at least 45 m. Often spelled *Antennarius commersonii,* but the original spelling is *commerson. Antennarius moluccensis* Bleeker is a synonym.

70

HISPID FROGFISH
Antennarius hispidus (Bloch & Schneider, 1801)

Dorsal rays I + I + I + 12 (rarely 11 or 13); anal rays 7; pectoral rays 10 (occasionally 7); last pelvic ray branched; illicium about as long as second dorsal spine, the esca a slender axial rod in line with illicium with many filaments radiating from it; second and third dorsal spines curved, the membrane of third spine not reaching base of dorsal fin; caudal peduncle about as long as length of second dorsal spine; yellow to light yellowish brown with elongate, narrow, dark spots or short bands on body angling downward and forward while those of cheek and opercle obliquely downward and backward; narrow dark bands radiating from eye; dark spots in fins, some on dorsal obliquely elongate. Attains about 19 cm. Reported from East Africa, India, East Indies, Vietnam, Taiwan, northern and eastern Australia, and Fiji. *Chironectes lophotes* Cuvier is a synonym.

After Bleeker, 1865

WARTY FROGFISH
Antennarius maculatus (Desjardins, 1840)

Dorsal rays I + I + I + 12 (rarely 11); anal rays 7 (rarely 6); pectoral rays 10 (rarely 11); illicium long, about twice as long as second dorsal spine, the esca with an eyespot resembling a small fish; second dorsal spine curved, with little membrane behind; third dorsal spine also curved, about one-fourth standard length, its membrane not joining dorsal fin; head, body, and fins with prominent wart-like protuberances; ground color varying from white or pale yellow to black, often with scattered ocellated dark spots (may be faint), typically with irregular bands of contrasting color radiating from eye; other irregular bands extending from front of soft dorsal fin and base of caudal fin. Largest specimen, 11 cm. Reported from Mauritius (type locality), Ryukyu Islands, Philippines, Singapore, Indonesia, New Guinea, New Britain, Solomon Islands, Guam, Tahiti (Randall et al., 2002a), and Hawai'i (Randall, forthcoming volume on reef and shore fishes of the Hawaiian Islands). Pietsch & Grobecker (1978) described the amazing resemblance of the esca of an individual of this species to a small fish. They filmed a luring sequence in which the esca was brought forward and vibrated, and another in which the esca was swept in arcs, allowing it to ripple like the undulations of a swimming fish.

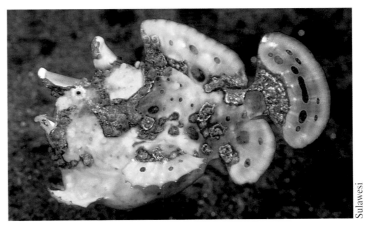

Sulawesi

Papua New Guinea

OPULENT FROGFISH
Antennarius nummifer (Cuvier, 1817)

Dorsal rays I + I + I,12–13 (rarely 13); anal rays 7; pectoral rays usually 10 or 11; illicium short, about as long as second dorsal spine; esca large, often filamentous; second dorsal spine nearly straight and not connected to head by membrane; a distinct caudal peduncle present; red, pink, orange, yellow, tan, or brown, usually with 1 to a few large round spots (the probable basis for the Latin scientific name meaning bearer of coins). Largest specimen, 12.5 cm. Indo-Pacific from the Red Sea to the Hawaiian Islands, and Marquesas Islands (one 14-mm specimen collected by author in Nuku Hiva), and islands of the eastern Atlantic. Generally found in shallow water, but known to a depth of 176 m. Fowler & Ball (1925) found a specimen 11.5 cm long on a beach at Laysan, Hawaiian Islands, that had eaten a *Myripristis* that they estimated was at least 12.5 cm long before being partially digested.

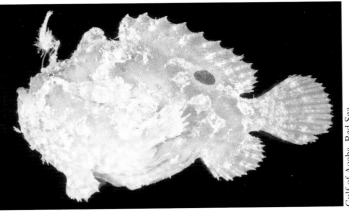

Gulf of Aqaba, Red Sea

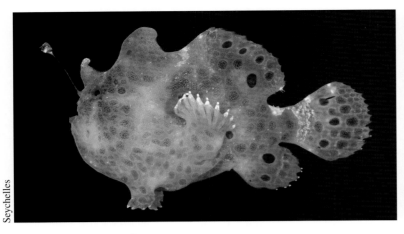

PAINTED FROGFISH

Antennarius pictus (Shaw in Shaw & Nodder, 1794)

Dorsal rays I + I + I,11–13 (usually 12); anal rays 6–7 (rarely 6); pectoral rays 10–11 (rarely 11); illicium about twice as long as second dorsal spine, the esca large and filamentous; second dorsal spine joined to head by membrane that is largely covered with spinules; a distinct caudal peduncle; white, red, yellow, gray, brown, or black, usually with many round spots or ocelli of various size, often with a triangle of 3 dark spots in caudal fin. Largest specimen, 21 cm. Indo-Pacific; type locality, Tahiti; depth range, shallows to 75 m. Similar to *Antennarius maculatus,* which differs notably in having large, wart-like protuberances on head, body, and fins (sometimes a few small ones in *pictus*). *Antennarius chironectes* Latreille is a synonym.

RANDALL'S FROGFISH

Antennarius randalli Allen, 1970

Dorsal rays I + I + I,12–13; anal rays 7; pectoral rays 9; all rays of paired fins unbranched; illicium distinctly shorter than second dorsal spine, the esca bilobed with numerous slender filaments; second dorsal spine curved, linked by a membrane to third dorsal spine; third dorsal spine also curved posteriorly, about 3 times longer than second, joined by membrane to dorsal fin, with only a slight indentation between; caudal peduncle present; red to mottled beige or brown to nearly black with a few scattered, round, white spots a little larger than pupil on dorsal half of body, dorsal fin, and 2 posteriorly in caudal fin, one at upper edge and the other at lower edge of fin. A small species, the largest 4.6 cm. Known from Japan (Senou & Kawamoto, 2002, with 10 color illustrations), Taiwan, Philippines, Molucca Islands, New Guinea (G. R. Allen, pers. comm.), Marshall Islands, Fiji, Hawaiian Islands, and Easter Island (type locality); depth range, 8–30.5 m. A relative of the diminutive *Antennarius pauciradiatus* Schultz of the Atlantic.

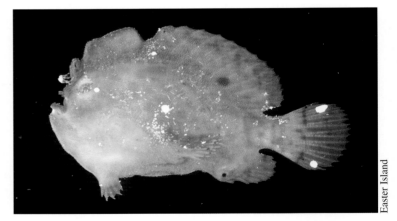

ROSY FROGFISH

Antennarius rosaceus Smith & Radcliffe in Radcliffe, 1912

Dorsal rays I + I + I,12 (rarely 11); anal rays 7 (rarely 6); pectoral rays 9 (rarely 8 or 10); illicium slender and long, 3.3–4.3 in standard length, nearly twice as long as second dorsal spine, the esca with a tuft of long filaments and about 5 dark spherical swellings at base; second dorsal spine nearly as long as third dorsal spine, narrow and tapering with 3 or more clusters of dermal spinules, and not connected by membrane to head; third anal spine curved at tip; a few slender flaps or tentacles may be present on head and body; ground color variable; a large ocellated black spot on back centered at base of eighth or ninth dorsal ray; small dark spots present or absent on abdomen; larger dark spots usually present on median fins. Largest specimen, 5.8 cm. Reported from the Red Sea, Indonesia, Philippines (type locality), Ryukyu Islands, Lord Howe Island, Marshall Islands, Gilbert Islands, and Samoa Islands from depths of about 1–130 m.

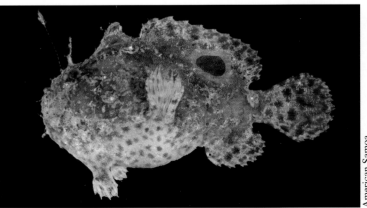

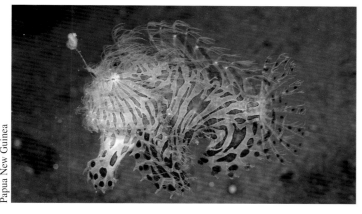
Papua New Guinea

Sulawesi

STRIATED FROGFISH

Antennarius striatus (Shaw in Shaw & Nodder, 1794)

Dorsal rays I + I + I,11–12 (rarely 11); anal rays 7; pectoral rays usually 10 or 11; illicium usually a little longer than second dorsal spine, the esca with 2 to 7 large worm-like projections, which may have a few filaments; numerous cirri or small, slender, branched tentacles often present on head, body, and fins; typically yellowish to orangish, but may be olivaceous, gray, black, or nearly white, usually with numerous oblique dark bands or elongate spots. Attains 22 cm. Tropical Atlantic and Indo-Pacific; type locality, Tahiti. Often on a bottom of algae, seagrass, or sponge. Occurs from the shallows to depths as great as 219 m; 86% of specimens with depth data were taken in 30 m or more. Less inclined to be hidden than other species. Has been given 25 different scientific names (Pietsch & Grobecker, 1987), but there is a possibility of more than one species now bearing the name *striatus* (Williams, 1989).

RETICULATED FROGFISH

Antennatus tuberosus (Cuvier, 1817)

Dorsal rays I + I + I,11–13 (rarely 11 or 13); anal rays 7–8 (rarely 8); pectoral rays 10–12 (usually 11, rarely 12); illicium long, 1.5–2 times longer than second dorsal spine, and without an esca; second dorsal spine cylindrical and not tapering; third dorsal spine only a rounded protuberance; usually pale yellow or gray with a dark brown or reddish brown reticular pattern and a dark bar across caudal fin; sometimes with large pink to whitish patches anteriorly. Reaches 9 cm. Indo-Pacific; type locality, Mauritius; often shelters in branching corals. Reported to a depth of 73 m, but 83% of captures from less than 20 m, and 66% from less than 8 m. *Antennatus reticulatus* (Eydoux & Souleyet) and *A. bigibbus* (Günther) are synonyms. Three other species in the genus: *A. strigatus* (Gill) from the eastern Pacific, *A. flagellatus* Ohnishi, Iwata & Hiramatsu from southern Japan, and *A. linearis* Randall & Holcom from the Hawaiian Islands, Aldabra, Mozambique, and Natal.

Hawaiian Islands

SARGASSUMFISH

Histrio histrio (Linnaeus, 1758)

Dorsal rays I + I + I + 11–13; anal rays 6–8; pectoral rays 10 (rarely 9 or 11); all pelvic rays unbranched; pelvic fins large, more than 25% standard length; median 7 caudal rays branched; skin smooth, usually without spinules (rarely with tiny unbranched spinules), densely covered with very small, low, round papillae; scattered cirri and slender cutaneous flaps usually present on head, body, fins, and dorsal spines; caudal peduncle distinct, about as long as second dorsal spine; illicium short, less than half length of second dorsal spine; pale yellow to orange with irregular black bands on head, body, and fins, those on body forming a broad reticulum; juveniles may be black. Reaches 19 cm. Pelagic in Atlantic and Indo-Pacific; probable type locality, China; 17 synonyms listed (Pietsch & Grobecker, 1987). Reports from the Galápagos Islands were considered false by Grove & Lavenberg (1997). Typically found in drifting masses of *Sargassum* but may occur in other floating plant material. Sometimes found inshore

Hawaiian Islands

when algae with which it is associated drifts in. A 2.5-cm juvenile from Taiwan with a bulging abdomen was opened and found to contain an alpheid shrimp with a body longer than the standard length of the fish.

73

Fringelip Mullet, *Crenimugil crenilabis*, Maldive Islands

MULLETS
(MUGILIDAE)

The mullets are typically found in brackish, mud-bottom, turbid habitats, but the 6 species treated here range into marine habitats and may be seen in the vicinity of coral reefs. Mugilid fishes are moderately elongate, only slightly compressed, with a small, terminal to slightly inferior mouth that is usually shaped like an inverted V when viewed from the front; the tip of the upper lip of most speces has a fleshy symphyseal knob; the preorbital is serrate; teeth are absent or minute, usually loosely attached on the lips; many species have adipose tissue covering the eye anteriorly and posteriorly; most have a gizzard-like stomach, and the intestine is very long; there are 2 widely spaced, short-based dorsal fins, the first of IV spines; the caudal fin varies from truncate to deeply emarginate or forked; the pelvic fins of I,5 rays lie well behind the pectorals; scales are cycloid or weakly ctenoid; there is no lateral line; instead most scales on the body have a longitudinal groove or a pit; vertebrae vary from 24 to 26. The color is silvery, sometimes with dark stripes. All mullets have a branchial filter-feeding mechanism involving their numerous slender gill rakers. They generally feed on the fine algal and detrital material from mud or sand substrata; after feeding on the bottom, they may be seen expelling sediment from their gill openings; some may ingest algal scums from the surface. Some mullets also feed opportunistically on zooplankton or small benthic crustaceans or worms. They often form schools, and they are prone to leap free of the surface, a habit that may enable them to escape a predator or an approaching seine. Many species are commercially important, and a few have been succssfully cultured. Opinions vary on where to place this family in relation to others, some favoring proximity to the atheriniform fishes (as here), and others within the perciforms. According to H. Senou (pers. comm.), 17 genera and 71 species are known in the family. The central and western Pacific species were treated by Harrison & Senou in Carpenter & Niem (1999b). According to H. Senou (pers. comm.), 17 genera and 71 species are known in the family. The generic classification follows Senou in Nakabo (2002).

LARGESCALE MULLET

Chelon macrolepis (Smith, 1846)

Dorsal rays IV + 8–9 (rarely 9); anal rays III,8–10 (usually 9); pectoral rays 15–18 (rarely 15 or 18, usually 16); longitudinal scale series 31–35 (usually 32–33); scales finely ctenoid; body depth 3.2–3.95 in standard length; head length 3.75–4.15 in standard length; head broad, the interorbital slightly convex; adipose tissue slight at rim of orbit or absent; a small slender part of maxilla exposed when mouth closed, between corner of mouth and serrate notched part of preorbital mouth, the posterior end nearly or just reaching a vertical at front edge of orbit; lower lip directed forward; upper lip with a row of very small, well-spaced, peg-like teeth; 1 or 2 irregular inner rows of small teeth well separated from outer row; origin of first dorsal fin closer to caudal-fin base than tip of snout; caudal fin forked; pectoral fins without an axillary scale, their tips not reaching below origin of first dorsal fin; gray to greenish gray dorsally, shading to silvery on sides and ventrally, with faint narrow gray stripes following scale centers on lower part of

New Caledonia

body; a narrow yellow bar often present at base of pectoral fins. Attains about 40 cm. Occurs throughout most of the Indo-Pacific region from the Red Sea and east coast of Africa (type locality, South Africa) to the Marquesas Islands and Tuamotu Archipelago; southern Japan to Great Barrier Reef and New Caledonia; usually seen in small schools, often in estuarine areas; known to penetrate fresh water.

OTOMENBORA MULLET

Chelon melinopterus (Valenciennes in C & V, 1836)

Dorsal rays IV + 9; anal rays III,8–10 (rarely 8 or 10); pectoral rays 15–17 (rarely 17); longitudinal scale series 26–31; scales finely ctenoid; body robust, the depth 3.0–3.6 in standard length; head broader than deep; snout shorter than eye; interorbital space slightly convex; adipose tissue narrow at edge of orbit; maxilla stocky, usually exposed posteroventral to closed mouth; lips thin, the lower lip directed forward; upper lip with an outer row of very small teeth, and less distinct tiny teeth in 1 or more inner rows; lower lip with few or no teeth; origin of first dorsal fin closer to caudal-fin base than front of snout; origin of second dorsal fin over or before middle of anal-fin base; both dorsal fins scaled except distally; caudal fin forked; axillary scale of pectoral fins rudimentary or absent; pectoral fins reaching to seventh or eighth scales in longitudinal series; olivaceous dorsally, sil-

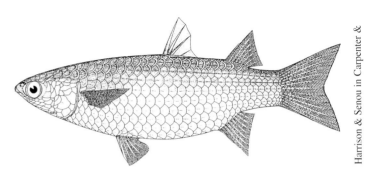

Harrison & Senou in Carpenter & Niem, 1999b

very white below; caudal fin dusky. Reported to reach 30 cm. East Africa to Marquesas Islands; South China Sea to northern Australia and Queensland; only Palau in Micronesia (Myers, 1999); apparently only Tonga and the Marquesas as records for the South Pacific.

GREENBACK MULLET

Chelon subviridis (Valenciennes in C & V, 1836)

Dorsal rays IV + 8–9 (rarely 9); anal rays III,8–10 (usually 9); pectoral rays 14–17; longitudinal scale series 27–33 (rarely 27 or 33); scales finely ctenoid; body depth 3.45–4.25 in standard length; head length 3.85–4.15 in standard length; snout short and blunt, usually shorter than orbit diameter; adipose tissue covering about half of iris in adults; a small oblique part of maxilla exposed posterior to corner of mouth when closed, the posterior end reaching or extending slightly beyond a vertical at front edge of orbit; lower lip directed forward; upper lip with an outer row of very small unicusp teeth; and 1 or 2 irregular inner rows of smaller teeth; origin of first dorsal fin midway between tip of snout and caudal-fin base or slightly closer to the latter; caudal fin emarginate; axillary scale of pectoral fins rudimentary or absent; pectoral fins not reaching to below origin of first dorsal fin; gray to greenish gray dorsally, silvery below, with faint narrow gray stripes following centers of scale rows; poste-

Lombok, Indonesia

rior margin of caudal fin blackish. Reported to 40 cm, but rarely exceeds 30 cm. Red Sea to Samoa Islands; Ryukyu Islands to Queensland and New Caledonia; type locality, Malabar, India. *Mugil dussumieri* Valenciennes and *M. javanicus* Bleeker are synonyms.

FRINGELIP MULLET

Crenimugil crenilabis (Forsskål, 1775)

Dorsal rays IV + 8–10 (usually 9); anal rays III,8–9 (rarely 8); pectoral rays 16–18; longitudinal scale series 36–41; scales cycloid, the edge membranous; no adipose tissue over eye; posterior end of maxilla not exposed when mouth closed, anterior to a vertical at front edge of eye; upper lip broad anteriorly, its lower part with a fringe of small papillae (absent in very small juveniles); lower lip finely folded with a forward-directed fringe of flattened papillae; no teeth on edge of lips; origin of first dorsal fin slightly closer to base of caudal fin than tip of snout; origin of second dorsal fin slightly posterior to origin of anal fin; caudal fin deeply emarginate; an elongate axillary scale above base of pectoral fins; pectoral-fin tips nearly or just reaching a vertical at origin of first dorsal fin; silvery olive-gray dorsally, silvery ventrally; caudal fin gray-blue with a blackish posterior border; pectoral fins yellowish with a prominent black spot at upper base. Largest specimen examined, 55 cm. Red Sea (type locality) and east coast of Africa to Line Islands and Tuamotu

Seychelles

Archipelago; southern Japan to New South Wales and Lord Howe Island; usually seen in small schools in shallow water and may occur in reef areas; juveniles have been found in tidepools. Spawning occurs in large aggregations near the surface at night (Helfrich & Allen, 1975).

SQUARETAIL MULLET

Ellochelon vaigiensis (Quoy & Gaimard, 1825)

Dorsal rays IV + 9; anal rays III,8–10 (rarely 8 or 10); pectoral rays 15–18 (rarely 15 or 18); longitudinal scale series 25–29; scales finely ctenoid, the sensory groove on each long; body depth 3.6–4.2 in standard length; head length 3.5–3.8 in standard length; head broad; a little of maxilla exposed when mouth closed, its posterior end reaching to below front edge of eye; edge of upper lip with a row of extremely small teeth; lower lip thin, the edge directed forward; origin of first dorsal fin slightly closer to base of caudal fin than tip of snout; origin of second dorsal fin over posterior one-third of anal-fin base; second dorsal fin higher than first dorsal; caudal fin slightly emarginate to truncate; no axillary scale above base of pectoral fins; pectoral-fin tips not reaching a vertical at origin of first dorsal fin; silvery gray dorsally, the edges of scales dark, shading to silvery below; narrow dark stripes on midside of body; median fins yellowish; pectoral fins largely black. Reported to reach 55 cm. Red Sea

Tuamotu Archipelago

and east coast of Africa to Tuamotu Archipelago; in the western Pacific from southern Japan to the Great Barrier Reef; type locality, Waigeo, Indonesia; occurs in small schools inshore in protected waters of lagoons or mangrove areas; tolerant of low salinity.

KANDA

Moolgarda engeli (Bleeker, 1859)

Dorsal rays IV + 9–10 (usually 9); anal rays III,8–9 (usually 9); pectoral rays 15–17; longitudinal scale series 31–35; scales cycloid with a crenulate membranous edge; body depth 3.6–3.9 in standard length; head length 3.6–4.0 in standard length; adipose tissue covering about half of iris; posterior end of maxilla not exposed when mouth closed, nearly or just reaching anterior edge of eye; lips thin, the lower directed forward; tiny teeth in a row on edge of lips (may be lost in large adults); origin of first dorsal fin closer to caudal-fin base than tip of snout; dorsal fins about equally high; origin of second dorsal fin in line with a vertical one-third along anal-fin base; caudal fin forked; pectoral fins nearly or just reaching a vertical at origin of first dorsal fin; axillary scale of pectoral fins about 40% length of fin; silvery, a little dusky dorsally; posterior edge of caudal fin narrowly blackish. A small species; attains about 20 cm. Western

American Samoa

Pacific from Ryukyu Islands to Indonesia, east to the islands of Micronesia and French Polynesia; type locality, Java; unintentionally introduced into the Hawaiian Islands. Forms small schools along sandy shores of lagoons or bays; also occurs in estuarine habitats.

Lombok, Indonesia

Hawaiian Islands

BLUESPOT MULLET

Moolgarda seheli (Forsskål, 1775)

Dorsal rays IV + 8–9 (rarely 8); anal rays III,8–9 (rarely 8); pectoral rays 17–19; longitudinal scale series 38–42; scales cycloid with a crenulate membranous edge; body depth 3.2–3.8 in standard length; head length 3.5–4.0 in standard length; adipose tissue covering posterior half of iris; maxilla concealed when mouth closed, its posterior end not or just reaching below front edge of eye; margin of lips thin with a series of tiny teeth; origin of first dorsal fin about equidistant to base of caudal fin and tip of snout; second dorsal fin slightly higher than first, its origin over or a little posterior to anal-fin origin; caudal fin forked; pectoral axillary scale long, about 38% fin length; pectoral-fin tips usually reaching a vertical at origin of first dorsal fin; silvery gray dorsally, silvery on side and ventrally, with narrow dark stripes, one for each scale row; median fins bluish gray; pectoral fins pale yellowish with a deep blue to black spot at upper base. Attains 50 cm. Red Sea (type locality) to South Africa, east to the Mariana Islands and Marquesas Islands; in the western Pacific from Japan to Norfolk Island; schools over sand flats of lagoons; also enters brackish and freshwater habitats.

STRIPED MULLET

Mugil cephalus Linnaeus, 1758

Dorsal rays IV + 8–9; anal rays III,8–9 (rarely 9); pectoral rays 16–19; longitudinal scale series 39–43; scales weakly ctenoid; body depth 3.8–4.5 in standard length; head length 3.45–3.7 in standard length; posterior end of maxilla not exposed when mouth closed, reaching to below front edge of eye; margin of lips thin with a series of tiny teeth; origin of first dorsal fin closer to tip of snout than base of caudal fin; second dorsal fin slightly higher than first dorsal, its origin on a vertical about one-fourth along anal-fin base; caudal fin forked; pectoral axillary scale long, about 35% fin length; pectoral fins short, not reaching a vertical at origin of first dorsal fin; olivaceous on back, silvery on sides with about 6 dark stripes along scale rows. Attains about 70 cm. Circumglobal in subtropical to warm temperate seas (type locality, Europe); in the South Pacific from Norfolk Island, New Caledonia, northern New Zealand (a commercial fishery), and Rapa; widely separated populations have been shown to be genetically distinct, and subspecies have been proposed; an important commercial species; occurs inshore in protected waters, including estuaries; young reported to enter fresh water. Migrates offshore to spawn.

SHARPNOSE MULLET

Neomyxus leuciscus (Günther, 1872)

Dorsal rays IV + 10; anal rays II,10–11; pectoral rays 15–16 (usually 16); longitudinal scale series 45–48; scales cycloid; body depth 4.0–4.5 in standard length; head length 3.6–4.0 in standard length; snout pointed, longer than eye; no adipose tissue; posterior end of maxilla not exposed when mouth closed, not reaching to below front edge of eye; upper lip thick and broad; lower lip thick, folded downward; lips with 2–3 rows of tiny trifid teeth on their edge; origin of first dorsal fin closer to base of caudal fin than tip of snout; second dorsal fin slightly higher than first, its origin on a vertical about one-fourth way along anal-fin base; caudal fin slightly forked; pectoral axillary scale not long, about 30% fin length; pectoral fins short, not approaching a vertical at origin of first dorsal fin; silvery greenish gray dorsally, silvery on sides and ventrally; a small yellow spot at upper base of pectoral fins. Reaches about 35 cm. Ogasawara Islands to Hawaiian Islands; Micronesia except Palau; Samoa Islands, Line Islands, French Polynesia, and Pitcairn Islands; type locality, Rarotonga. Occurs in small schools close to shore, over rocky bottom and sand. *Mugil chaptalii* Eydoux & Souleyet is a synonym.

Hawaiian Islands

SILVERSIDES
(ATHERINIDAE)

The silversides are small slender inshore fishes of tropical to temperate seas that usually form schools. They have 2 well-separated dorsal fins, the first of III to VIII flexible spines; the second dorsal and anal fins have an initial spine; the pectoral fins are high on the side of the body; the pelvic fins of I spine and 5 rays are distinctly posterior to the base of the pectorals; there is no lateral line; typically they have a lateral silver stripe on the body. These fishes feed on zooplankton, and they in turn are preyed upon by roving predaceous fishes such as jacks. They are attracted to a light at night. Many of the species occur in estuarine areas, and a few are confined to fresh water. The eggs are large and demersal with adhesive threads. Ivantsoff & Crowley in Carpenter & Niem (1999a) reviewed the family for the central and western Pacific.

Robust Silverside, *Atherinomorus lacunosus*, Red Sea

Ambon, Indonesia

Seychelles

LINED SILVERSIDE
Atherinomorus duodecimalis (Valenciennes in C & V, 1835)
Dorsal rays V-VI + 9–11; anal rays I,11–14; pectoral rays 14–17; longitudinal scale series 35–38; body depth 4.0–5.3 in standard length; eye large, 2.1–2.6 in head length; upper jaw not reaching a vertical at front edge of pupil; a tubercle at posterior end of lower jaw; teeth present on vomer, present or absent on palatines; caudal fin forked; gray to brown dorsally, silvery below, the 2 zones separated by a green line; 3 rows of scales on lower side with a blackish dash in center of each scale, hence forming longitudinal lines. Reaches 11 cm. Known from Sri Lanka (type locality), Ryukyu Islands, Philippines, Indonesia, New Guinea, Queensland, and New Caledonia. Found inshore from mangrove estuaries to open coast. Kimura et al. (2001a) distinguished this species from the similar *Atherinomorus endrachtensis* (Quoy & Gaimard), the latter redescribed and illustrated by Ivantsoff & Crowley (1991).

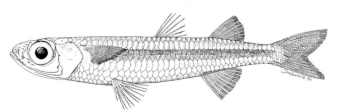

After Ivantsoff & Crowley in Carpenter & Niem (1999b)

ROBUST SILVERSIDE
Atherinomorus lacunosus (Forster, 1801)
Dorsal rays IV-VII + I,8–11; anal rays I,12–16; pectoral rays 15–19; longitudinal scale series 39–44; lower-limb gill rakers 18–25 (modally 22); body depth 4.1–5.6 in standard length; eye large, 2.4–3.1 in head length; upper jaw extending to or beyond front edge of pupil; teeth present on vomer and palatines; caudal fin forked; greenish gray with a broad silvery stripe on side of body (though less than full height of scales on side of body), its upper edge with an iridescent blue line. Reaches 13 cm. Red Sea to the Samoa Islands; probable type locality, New Caledonia; often seen in small schools in shallow water. Sometimes classified in *Pranesus*. *Atherinomorus pinguis* (Lacepède) and *A. forskalii* (Rüppell) are among the 8 synonyms listed by Whitehead & Ivantsoff (1983); however, one of them, *A. vaigiensis* (Quoy & Gaimard), was shown by Kimura et al. (2001b) to be a valid Australian endemic species.

FIJIAN SILVERSIDE
Hypoatherina ovalaua (Herre, 1935)
Dorsal rays IV-VII + I,8–10; anal rays I,9–12; pectoral rays 16–18; longitudinal scale series 38–42; predorsal scales 15–19; lower-limb gill rakers 22–25; mouth not large, the upper jaw just reaching to or slightly posterior to a vertical at front edge of eye; premaxilla with long ascending process (short in *Atherinomorus*) and 2 lateral

processes; small teeth present in jaws and on vomer; teeth on palatines larger; body depth 5.3–6.2 in standard length; eye large, 2.75–3.0 in head length; life color not recorded. Largest specimen, 7.8 cm. Reported from Fiji (type locality, Ovalau), Phoenix Islands, Marshall Islands, Mariana Islands, and New Britain.

Gulf of Aqaba, Red Sea

SAMOAN SILVERSIDE
Hypoatherina temminckii (Bleeker, 1853)
Dorsal rays V-VII + I,8–10; anal rays I,11–14; pectoral rays 14–18; longitudinal scale series 40–44; predorsal scales 16–18; lower-limb gill rakers 21–25; mouth small, the upper jaw just reaching to below front edge of eye; ascending process of premaxilla long, more than twice its width; lateral process of premaxilla short and wide; small teeth present in jaws and on vomer and palatines; body depth 5.6–6.9 in standard length; eye large,

about 3.0 in head length; translucent blue-green dorsally with a lateral silver stripe. Attains 12 cm. Red Sea and east coast of Africa to Samoa Islands; type locality, Java. *Atherina uisila* Jordan & Seale is a synonym.

PANATELA SILVERSIDE
Stenatherina panatela (Jordan & Richardson, 1908)
Dorsal rays V-VII + I,8–10; anal rays I,9–12; pectoral rays 17–19; longitudinal scale series 38–45; predorsal scales 17–20; lower-limb gill rakers 21–25; mouth small, the upper jaw just reaching to below front edge of eye; ascending process of premaxilla very long, extending into interorbital space, its lateral process long and sharp; villiform teeth in jaws and on vomer and palatines, those on vomer in a T-shape; body very slender, the depth about 6.8 in standard length; blue-green dorsally, silvery on side and ventrally, with a distinctive dark crescentic mark in front of eye, and a dark streak at base of caudal fin. Reported to 11 cm.

(Jordan & Richardson 1908)

Known from the East Indies (type locality, Calayan Island, Philippines), northern Australia, Solomon Islands, Vanuatu, Phoenix Islands, and Marshall Islands; preferred habitat, deep lagoons. Panatela is Spanish for a long slender cigar.

SURF FISHES
(ISONIDAE)

This small family, related to the Atherinidae, consists of 5 species of the genus *Iso*, all from the Indo-Pacific region. It is characterized by a very deep compressed body, with a fleshy keel ventrally, and a strongly tapering tail to a narrow caudal peduncle and forked caudal fin. There is a small first dorsal fin of III to VI spines, well-separated from the second dorsal of I,12–17 rays; the anal fin has I,20–28 rays; the pectoral fins of 11–14 rays are high on the body; the scales are cycloid, and there is no lateral line. These small silvery fishes are aptly named surf fishes because they live in the surf zone, often off rocky promontories. Some authors combine *Iso* with a species of *Notocheirus* from Chile in the family Notocheiridae. Saeed et al. (1993) is followed here in treating Isonidae as a family.

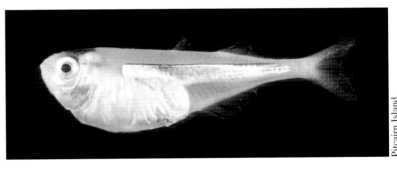

Pitcairn Island

INSULAR SURF FISH
Iso nesiotes Saeed, Ivantsoff & Crowley, 1993
Dorsal rays IV-VI + I,12–16; anal rays I,19–24; pectoral rays 11–13; longitudinal scale series 35–41; body deepest just before pelvic fins, the depth 2.4–3.7 in standard length, then strongly tapering; head length 4.1–5.0 in standard length; caudal peduncle slender, 12.5–16.2 in standard length; body translucent with a broad silvery stripe from beneath pectoral fin to midway along caudal peduncle; no oval silvery spot posteriorly on side of caudal peduncle. Largest specimen, 3.2 cm. Currently known only from Pitcairn Island and Tutuila, American Samoa (type locality). Two specimens from Rapa, 3.3–3.8 cm total length, identified as *Iso hawaiiensis* Gosline by Saeed et al. (1993) need to be reexamined; they lack the notch at the upper edge of the gill opening and the oval silvery spot posteriorly on the caudal peduncle; they are also larger than any specimens of *I. hawaiiensis*.

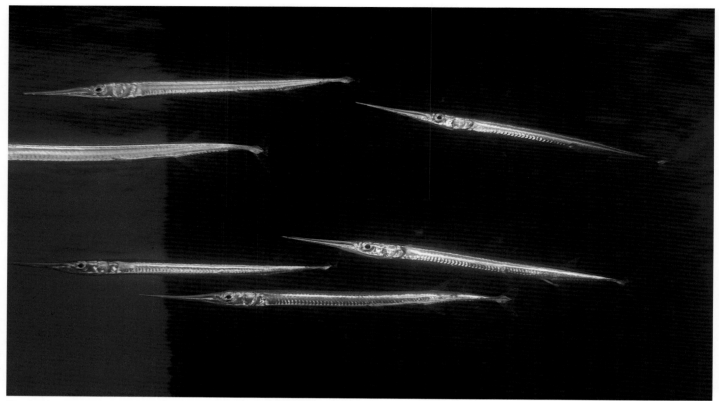

Keeltail Needlefish, *Platybelone argalus,* Hawaiian Islands

NEEDLEFISHES
(BELONIDAE)

Needlefishes are very elongate with long pointed jaws and numerous needle-like teeth; there are no spines in the fins; the dorsal and anal fins are posterior on the body; the pelvic fins of 6 rays are abdominal in position; the lateral line passes along the lower side; and the nasal organ is in a cavity in front of the eye. These fishes are surface-dwelling and protectively colored green or blue on the back and silvery below; some species have green bones. Needlefishes feed mainly on small fishes. When frightened, as by a predator, an approaching boat, or a light at night, they may skitter and leap at the surface at great speed. People in the path of these fishes have been struck by them and fatalities have resulted. The eggs of belonid fishes are large and are attached with adhesive filaments to floating objects. The following are the 4 most inshore species of needlefishes for the South Pacific area. A fifth needlefish, *Ablennes hians* (Valenciennes), is an offshore pelagic species. It is easily distinguished by its strongly compressed body, short dark bars on the side of the body, and 24–28 anal rays.

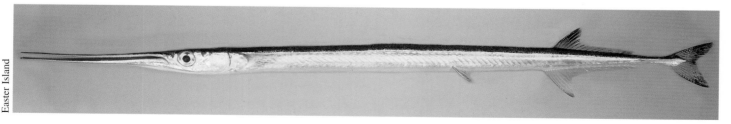

Easter Island

KEELTAIL NEEDLEFISH
Platybelone argalus (Lesueur, 1821)
Dorsal rays 12–15; anal rays 15–20; pectoral rays 10–12; body extremely elongate, the depth 20–25 in standard length, the width slightly greater than the depth; caudal peduncle about twice as wide as deep, with a scaly keel on side; caudal fin slightly emarginate, the lobes of about equal size; blue or blue-green dorsally, silvery on sides and ventrally. Attains 45 cm. Circumtropical; divisible into 5 subspecies (Parin, 1967), the one in the Indo-Pacific is *Platybelone argalus platyura* (Bennett) with a type locality of Mauritius; others are Arabian (Red Sea to Persian Gulf), eastern Pacific, North and South Atlantic. Occurs at the surface, mainly inshore, often in small aggregations; feeds on small fishes.

Marshall Islands

REEF NEEDLEFISH
Strongylura incisa (Valenciennes in C & V, 1846)
Dorsal rays 18–20; anal rays 21–23; pectoral rays 10–12; body depth of adults 13–15 in standard length (young much more slender); body compressed, the width about 1.4 in depth; no keel on side of caudal peduncle; caudal fin truncate in young, slightly emarginate in adults; origin of dorsal fin above second to sixth rays of anal fin; gray-green dorsally, silvery below. Attains at least 60 cm. Eastern Indian Ocean (type locality given as Indian Ocean), east to Samoa Islands and throughout Micronesia; Philippines and Hainan to Northern Territory of Australia and northern Queensland. Often found inshore in lagoons and over reef flats. May occur in small aggregations; feeds mainly on small fishes.

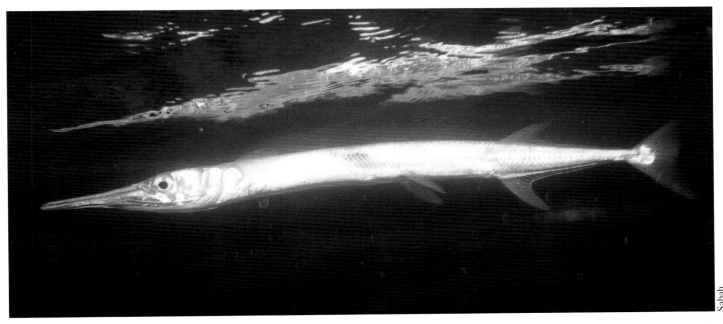

Sabah

AGUJON
Tylosurus acus (Lacepède, 1803)
Dorsal rays 24–27; anal rays 22–24; pectoral rays 13–14; no gill rakers; vertebrae 90–95; body elongate, the depth in adults 14.5–16 in standard length (in juveniles of 16.7–21 cm the depth is 23–24 in standard length); upper jaw curved, hence a gap present between jaws when mouth closed; teeth mainly perpendicular in jaws; a small black keel on side of caudal peduncle; caudal fin deeply emarginate, the lower lobe much longer than upper; origin of dorsal fin above origin of anal fin; blue on back, silvery on sides and ventrally; outer part of posterior half of dorsal fin blackish (juveniles with an elevated black posterior part of dorsal fin that is lost with growth; true of other species of the genus); margin of caudal fin blackish. Attains 100 cm. Divided into 4 subspecies, one in Indo-Pacific and eastern Pacific, *Tylosurus acus melanotus* (Bleeker) (type locality, Java), and 3 in Atlantic (Collette & Banford, 2001). Tends to occur more offshore than other species of the genus.

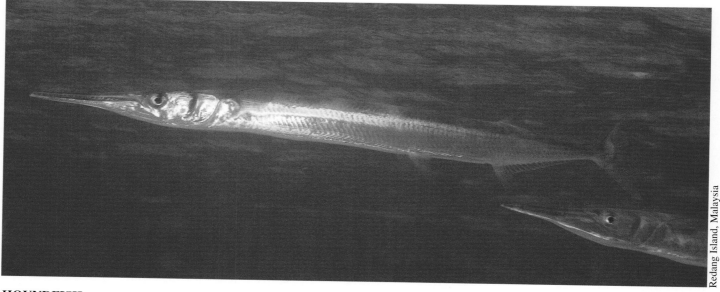

Redang Island, Malaysia

HOUNDFISH

Tylosurus crocodilus (Péron & Lesueur, 1821)
Dorsal rays 21–24; anal rays 19–22; pectoral rays 13–15; no gill rakers; vertebrae 75–80; body depth varying with growth, 19–23 in standard length in juveniles and 9–14 in large adults; jaws nearly straight, relatively shorter with growth; teeth usually inclined slightly forward; a black keel on side of caudal peduncle and base of caudal fin; caudal fin deeply emarginate, the lower lobe much longer than upper; green dorsally, grading to silvery below; bones green. Reaches at least 135 cm. The subspecies *Tylosurus crocodilus crocodilus* (type locality, Java) occurs in the tropical to warm temperate seas of the Atlantic and Indo-Pacific. The eastern Pacific subspecies is *T. c. fodiator.* Randall (1960b) documented injuries resulting from houndfish skipping at the surface and striking humans.

HALFBEAKS
(HEMIRAMPHIDAE)

The halfbeaks are related to the needlefishes and share many characters with them, such as elongate body, no spines in fins, abdominal pelvic fins with 6 rays, lateral line low on the body, and nasal organ in a cavity before the eye. They differ most obviously in having a short triangular upper jaw and a very prolonged lower jaw (lower jaw shortens on adults of species of 4 genera); tip of lower jaw red in some species. Halfbeaks live at or near the surface, and like the needlefishes they may leap and skip free of the surface (the ventral part of the body is nearly flat, thus facilitating their skipping). Two offshore species are able to glide in the air on outstretched pectoral fins like flyingfishes. Many halfbeaks feed on zooplankton and small fishes, whereas others ingest floating plant material such as pieces of seagrass. The family consists of 12 genera and about 85 species, 24 of which occur in fresh water. Most of the freshwater species are viviparous. The eggs of oviparous species have adhesive filaments and are usually attached to plants. Parin et al. (1980) reviewed the marine halfbeaks of the Indo-Pacific region, and Collette in Carpenter & Niem (1999b) the species of the central and western Pacific.

JUMPING HALFBEAK

Hemiramphus archipelagicus Collette & Parin, 1978
Dorsal rays 12–15; anal rays 10–13; pectoral rays 11–12; predorsal scales 32–37; gill rakers 25–32; body depth about 5.7 in standard length; upper jaw short and triangular (true of other halfbeaks); upper jaw without scales (generic); no preorbital ridge (bony ridge behind nasal pit); lower-jaw length beyond tip of upper jaw longer than head; anterior dorsal rays about twice as long as shortest ray; caudal fin forked, the lower lobe distinctly longer; pectoral fins short, not reaching nasal pit when extended forward; bluish gray dorsally, silvery white ventrally;

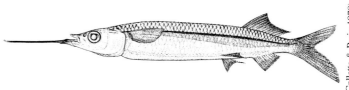

(Collette & Parin 1978)

tip of lower jaw bright red; upper lobe of caudal fin yellow. Reaches about 34 cm. West coast of India to Indo-Malayan region, east to Tonga and Samoa Islands; type locality, Gulf of Thailand; a coastal species, but young sometimes found offshore with drifting plants.

Hawaiian Islands

Philippines

POLYNESIAN HALFBEAK
Hemiramphus depauperatus Lay & Bennett, 1839

Dorsal rays 13–15; anal rays 12–13 (usually 13); pectoral rays 11; longitudinal scale series about 60; predorsal scales 37–44; body depth about 6.0–6.7 in standard length; body width 1.7–1.9 in body depth; head 4.0–4.4 in standard length; upper jaw naked; lower jaw 3.2–4.0 in standard length; origin of anal fin below fifth or sixth ray of dorsal fin; lower lobe of caudal fin much longer than upper; posterior tip of pelvic fins reaching to below origin of dorsal fin; greenish gray dorsally, silvery with blue-green iridescence on side and ventrally; tip of lower jaw orange-red. Largest specimen, 34.6 cm. Hawaiian Islands (type locality, Oʻahu), Line Islands, Marquesas Islands, and Society Islands. Parin et al. (1980) noted that there was no prolongation of the lower jaw in a 5-day larva that measured 8.4 mm in standard length, but by the fifteenth day, at a standard length of 15.8 mm, the long lower jaw is well-developed.

LUTKE'S HALFBEAK
Hemiramphus lutkei Valenciennes in C & V, 1847

Dorsal rays 12–15; anal rays 10–13 (usually 12); pectoral rays 10–12; predorsal scales 35–43 (usually 37–41); gill rakers 33–46 (usually 36–41); body depth about 6.7 in standard length; upper jaw scaleless; lower-jaw length beyond tip of upper jaw longer than head; anterior dorsal rays about 2.5 times longer than shortest ray; caudal fin forked, the lower lobe much longer than upper; pectoral fins long, reaching anterior to nasal pit when extended forward; dark bluish gray dorsally, silvery on side and ventrally; slender part of lower jaw nearly black with a red tip (but lower side may also be light red); caudal fin bluish, the upper and posterior margins blackish; a black spot at upper base of pectoral fins and a smaller one at base of pelvics. Reaches about 40 cm. East coast of Africa to Mariana, Caroline, and Samoa Islands, north to southern Japan; type locality, Buru, Indonesia; occurs more offshore than other species of the genus.

Papua New Guinea

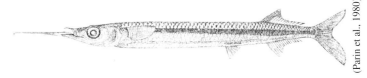

(Parin et al., 1980)

SPOTTED HALFBEAK
Hemiramphus far (Forsskål, 1775)

Dorsal rays 12–14; anal rays 10–12; pectoral rays 11–13; predorsal scales 32–39; gill rakers 25–36 (usually 29–33); body depth 5.7–7.3 in standard length; body width 1.3–1.8 in depth; upper jaw scaleless; lower-jaw length beyond tip of upper jaw longer than head; anterior dorsal rays about 3 times longer than shortest ray; caudal fin forked, the lower lobe distinctly longer; pectoral fins short, not reaching nasal pit when extended forward; green on back, grading to silvery on side, with a series of 3–9 black spots (often vertically elongate) on upper side. Attains about 45 cm. Red Sea (type locality) and east coast of Africa to Samoa Islands; southern Japan to tropical coasts of Australia and New Caledonia; only Palau in Micronesia. Feeds mainly on floating pieces of seagrass.

INSULAR HALFBEAK
Hyporhamphus affinis (Günther, 1866)

Dorsal rays 15–17; anal rays 15–18; pectoral rays 11–13; gill rakers 31–40; body depth 8.8–11.6 in standard length; body width 1.1–1.35 in depth; upper jaw scaled and pointed (viewed from above); preorbital bone (from front edge of eye to just behind corner of mouth) 1.35–1.65 in eye diameter; anal-fin origin below second or third dorsal ray; caudal fin forked, the lower lobe longer than upper; bluish gray dorsally, silvery below, with a blue line on body extending posteriorly from upper end of gill opening. Reaches 38 cm. Red Sea and Madagascar to the Tuamotu Archipelago; most localities insular (few records from the Indo-Malayan region); type locality, "South Sea," hence probably South Pacific. *Hyporhamphus australensis* (Seale) from Tubuai is a synonym.

ACUTE HALFBEAK
Hyporhamphus acutus (Günther, 1872)

Dorsal rays 13–15; anal rays 16–18; pectoral rays 10–11 (usually 11); body slender, the depth about 10–11 in standard length; body width 1.1–1.4 in depth; upper jaw scaled (generic); lower jaw very long, its length beyond upper jaw as much as 1.5 times head length; dorsal-fin origin over anal-fin origin; lower caudal lobe distinctly longer than upper; blue-green dorsally, grading

Easter Island

to silvery ventrally. Attains 30 cm. Islands of Oceania from Wake Island and Tonga to the east; type locality, Rarotonga, Cook Islands. Subspecifically different in the Hawaiian Islands (Collette, 1974).

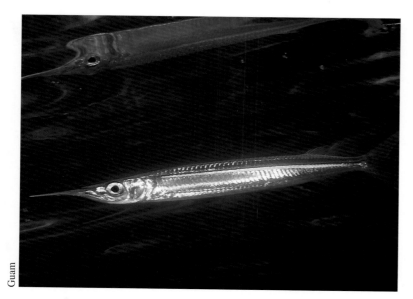

Guam

DUSSUMIER'S HALFBEAK

Hyporhamphus dussumieri (Valenciennes in C & V, 1847)
Dorsal rays 14–17; anal rays 14–17; pectoral rays 11–12; predorsal scales 37–44; gill rakers 33–47; body depth 8.1–10.6 in standard length; body width 1.1–1.3 in depth; upper jaw scaled, the tip (viewed from above) rounded; preorbital ridge (between eye and nasal pit) present; pre-orbital bone (from front edge of eye to just behind corner of mouth) 1.7–2.15 in eye diameter; anal-fin origin below second to fifth dorsal ray; caudal fin forked, the lower lobe slightly longer than upper; blue dorsally, shading to silvery on side and ventrally; tip of lower jaw red. Largest, 38 cm. Seychelles (type locality) to Austral Islands and Tuamotu Archipelago; Ryukyu Islands and Hong Kong to Western Australia, Queensland, and Great Barrier Reef. An inshore species often taken by seines. *Hyporhamphus laticeps* (Günther) from Fiji and *H. samoensis* Steindachner are synonyms.

Two-fin Flashlight Fish, *Anomalops katoptron*, Flores, Indonesia (night)

FLASHLIGHT FISHES
(ANOMALOPIDAE)

This small family of 6 genera and 7 species is classified in the order Beryciformes (comparative osteology studied by Zehren, 1979), along with the Holocentridae. The flashlight fishes are unique in possessing a large light organ under the eye that appears white by day but is luminescent at night. The light is produced by a symbiotic bacterium; the fish provides the medium for the bacterium to grow, and the bacterium produces the light as a by-product of metabolism. These fishes are able to turn their light on and off quickly either by rotating the organ inward, as in the species of *Anomalops*, or by covering it with an eyelid-like black curtain, as in the species of *Photoblepharon*. All in shallow water are nocturnal, hiding deep in the recesses of reefs by day and emerging at night to feed on zooplankton. The light enables the fishes to see the small animals of the zooplankton. It also may serve to confuse a predator by the fish rapidly changing direction after switching off the light, and to keep a school together as in *Anomalops katop-* *tron*; Howland et al. (1992) suggested communication in *Anomalops* by eye shine. The species of *Photo blepharon* are easily collected by divers by turning one's light off in a cave at night. After a few minutes of total darkness, the flashlightfish emerge from hiding and are readily seen by their bright light organ. An individual fish is then closely approached and the dive light turned on it. Usually the fish remains motionless and can be caught by hand. *Parmops coruscans* Rosenblatt & Johnson is known from one specimen taken from a grouper stomach in 350 m off Tahiti, and *Photoblepharon rosenblatti* Baldwin, Johnson & Paxton from one specimen from 274 m off Rarotonga.

TWO-FIN FLASHLIGHT FISH

Anomalops katoptron (Bleeker, 1856)

Dorsal rays IV or V + I,14,15; anal rays II,10–11; pectoral rays 18; lateral line nearly straight, the pored scales 57–60; midventral scutes well developed and continuous; light organ turned off by rotating inward; eye large, 2.5–2.7 in head length; posterior edge of orbit with a series of papillae; snout short and blunt, about half eye diameter; caudal fin deeply forked; dark purplish gray-brown; second dorsal and anal fins black with a pale blue margin and a whitish zone at base; caudal fin black with a blue margin. At depths of 1–30 m this species is small, at most 15 cm, but several specimens have been collected at 110–365 m that measure 29.5–34 cm in total length (McCosker & Rosenblatt, 1987). Known from southern Japan and Taiwan to the Great Barrier Reef, east to Guam and the Tuamotu Archipelago; type locality, Sulawesi. Swims in the open more than species of *Photoblepharon*; usually encountered at night in small aggregations as seen in the illustration for the family.

ONE-FIN FLASHLIGHT FISH

Photoblepharon palpebratus (Boddaert, 1781)

Dorsal rays II,18–19; anal rays II,13–15; pectoral rays 15; light organ turned off by elevating a black shutter from below; lateral line arched over pectoral fin, the pored scales about 35, much larger than remaining scales of body; midventral scutes reduced and discontinuous; eye large, about 2.3 in head; snout short and blunt, about half eye diameter; caudal fin deeply forked; dark purplish brown, the head nearly black; a white spot on lateral line scales, progressively smaller posteriorly; a bluish white area behind head and on pectoral-fin base; pectoral fins black; median fins dark brown with yellowish membranes and narrow pale blue margin. Attains about 10 cm. Known from Philippines, Indonesia (type locality, Ambon), Papua New Guinea, Great Barrier Reef, New Caledonia, islands of Micronesia, and Cook Islands; depth range 10 to at least 50 m. The closely related *P. steinitzi* occurs in the Red Sea and western Indian Ocean. The deepwater *P. rosenblatti* is easily distinguished by VI-I,14 dorsal rays, II,11 anal rays, and large size (229 mm SL).

Sabah (night)

Kakabia, Indonesia (night)

SQUIRRELFISHES AND SOLDIERFISHES (HOLOCENTRIDAE)

The fishes of this family are red or partly red with very large eyes, XI or XII (usually XI) dorsal spines, IV anal spines, and pelvic fins with I,7 rays; the caudal fin is forked with 17 branched rays; the scales are coarsely ctenoid (the edges with numerous sharp spinules); the lateral line is complete with 25–56 pored scales; the edges of the external bones are serrate or have small spines; the mouth is moderately large, terminal or with the lower jaw projecting; the upper jaw is protractile; two supramaxillae are present; the teeth are small, in villiform bands in the jaws, on the vomer and palatines (and for some on the ectopterygoids); the nasal organ is in a subtriangular cavity (called a fossa) in front of the eye. The family is divisible into 2 subfamilies, the Holocentrinae (squirrelfishes), with 3 genera and 32 species, characterized by a long sharp spine (which may be venomous) at the corner of the preopercle, a somewhat pointed snout, and 7–10 anal soft rays; and the Myripristinae (soldierfishes), with 5 genera and 36 species, that lack the preopercular spine or have only a short broad-based one (except the Atlantic *Corniger*), a blunt snout, and 10–16 anal soft rays. The holocentrid fishes are nocturnal; the soldierfishes feed mainly on the larger animals of the zooplankton, and the squirrelfishes mostly on benthic crustaceans. The genus *Myripristis* was revised by Randall & Greenfield (1996), and *Sargocentron* (*Adioryx* is a synonym) by Randall (1998c).

Epaulet Soldierfish, *Myripristis kuntee*, Hawaiian Islands

SOLDIERFISHES (MYRIPRISTINAE)

SHADOWFIN SOLDIERFISH
Myripristis adusta Bleeker, 1853

Dorsal rays X-I,14–16; anal rays IV,12–14; pectoral rays 15–17; lateral-line scales 27–29; scale rows above lateral line 2; 1 or 2 large scales in axil of pectoral fins (no small scales); gill rakers 35–40; silvery salmon pink, the scale edges dorsally on body deep blue to black; a black spot posteriorly on opercle; median fins with a broad black outer border (broadest on elevated anterior part of dorsal and anal fins). Largest of the soldierfishes; reaches 32 cm. East coast of Africa to the Line Islands and Tuamotu Archipelago; Ryukyu Islands to the Great Barrier Reef and New Caledonia; type locality, Ambon. Most common in protected waters of bays and lagoons; has been taken in as little as 2 m.

Palau

BRICK SOLDIERFISH
Myripristis amaena (Castelnau, 1873)

Dorsal rays X-I,13–16; anal rays IV,12–15; pectoral rays 15–16 (rarely 16); lateral-line scales 32–36; no scales in axil of pectoral fins; gill rakers 34–41; third and fourth anal spines about equal; light red, the scale edges dorsally on body dark red; outer part of spinous dorsal fin red; leading edges of median fins not white. Reaches 26.5 cm. Ryukyu Islands, Ogasawara Islands, islands of Micronesia, Society Islands, Tuamotu Archipelago, and Pitcairn Islands; no records from the Indo-Malayan region. Type locality reported as Knob Island, Torres Strait, a probable error (Randall & Greenfield, 1996). Generally found in less than 10 m. *Myripristis argyromus* Jordan & Evermann is a synonym.

Hawaiian Islands

BIGSCALE SOLDIERFISH
Myripristis berndti Jordan & Evermann, 1903

Dorsal rays X-I,13–15; anal rays IV,11–13; pectoral rays 14–16; lateral-line scales 28–31; small scales present on lower two-thirds of axil of pectoral fins; gill rakers 35–42; lower jaw of adults strongly projecting; interorbital space narrow, 4.5–5.2 in head length; silvery white to light red, the edges of scales red; opercular membrane black; outer part of spinous dorsal fin orange-yellow; leading edge of soft dorsal, anal, caudal, and pelvic fins white. Attains 30 cm. Occurs throughout the Indo-Pacific region except for Arabian waters, Bay of Bengal, and Easter Island; also known from islands of the tropical eastern Pacific. Type locality, Hawaiian Islands. Most specimens from depth range of 10–25 m, but reported from submarine observations to 159 m (Chave & Mundy, 1994).

Marshall Islands

Maldive Islands

Hawaiian Islands

Phoenix Islands (G. R. Allen)

BLACKTIP SOLDIERFISH
Myripristis botsche Cuvier, 1829

Dorsal rays X-I,13–15; anal rays IV,11–12 (usually 12); pectoral rays 14–16; lateral-line scales 27–29; no small scales in axil of pectoral fins; gill rakers 32–38; body moderately deep, the depth 2.1–2.45 in standard length; 2 pairs of tooth patches at front of lower jaw just outside gape; fourth anal spine usually slightly longer than third, 2.25–2.7 in head; scales of body white, the edges dusky red dorsally, red on side, and pale pink ventrally; front of head red; a dark red band from upper end of gill opening to axil of pectoral fin; opercular membrane black to or slightly below level of lower edge of eye; spinous dorsal fin whitish basally, broadly red distally; remaining median fins red with white leading edges, the elevated anterior part of soft dorsal and anal fins and caudal fin lobes tipped with black. Reaches 30 cm. South Africa and Seychelles to western Pacific from Ryukyu and Ogasawara Islands to New Caledonia; type locality, India. Usually found in protected waters at depths greater than 25 m. *Myripristis melanostictus* Bleeker is a synonym.

YELLOWFIN SOLDIERFISH
Myripristis chryseres Jordan & Evermann, 1903

Dorsal rays X-I,13–16 (modally 14); anal rays IV,11–13; pectoral rays 15–16 (rarely 16); lateral-line scales 32–38; no scales in axil of pectoral fins; gill rakers 33–39; front of lower jaw fitting into a distinct notch in upper jaw when mouth closed; third anal spine longer than fourth; red, the scale edges darker red; fins largely yellow. Reaches 25 cm. East coast of Africa to Hawaiian Islands and recently recorded from Society Islands and Tuamotu Archipelago (Randall et al., 2002a); type locality, Hilo, Hawaiʻi. Usually found at depths greater than 30 m; submarine observations in Hawaiian Islands to 230 m.

EARLE'S SOLDIERFISH
Myripristis earlei Randall, Allen & Robertson, 2003

Dorsal rays X-I,14–15 (usually 14); anal rays IV,12–13 (usually 12; pectoral rays 14–15 (usually 15); lateral-line scales 29–30 (usually 29); no scales present on lower two-thirds of axil of pectoral fins or only a few small scales ventrally; gill rakers 36–39; lower jaw of adults projecting; interorbital space narrow, 4.35–4.8 in head length; body pale red, the edges of the scales red; opercular membrane black to base of pectoral fin; fins red, the soft dorsal, anal, and caudal fins with no white leading edge; pelvic fins with a trace of white on lateral edge; iris red with a broad blackish bar extending dorsally and ventrally from pupil. Largest specimen 24 cm. Known only from the Marquesas Islands and Phoenix Islands. First identified as a color variant of *Myripristis berndti*.

DOUBLETOOTH SOLDIERFISH
Myripristis hexagona (Lacepède, 1802)
Dorsal rays X-I,13–15; anal rays IV,11–14; pectoral rays 14–16; lateral-line scales 25–29; lower two-thirds of axil of pectoral fins with small scales; gill rakers 36–50 (highest counts in Oceania, lowest in western Indian Ocean [Randall & Greenfield, 1996: table 7]); 2 pairs of tooth patches outside gape at front of lower jaw (other species of South Pacific region with 1 pair); scales silvery white, the edges dorsally on body reddish brown to dark red; a red band from upper end of gill opening to axil of pectoral fin; fins pale red, the outer part of spinous dorsal bright red. To 20 cm. East coast of Africa to Samoa Islands, Tonga, and Fiji; Philippines to Great Barrier Reef and New Caledonia; type locality unknown; usually found on protected reefs of bays and lagoons. *Myripristis macrolepis* Bleeker is a synonym.

Cebu, Philippines

EPAULET SOLDIERFISH
Myripristis kuntee Valenciennes in C & V, 1831
Dorsal rays X-I,15–17; anal rays IV,14–16; pectoral rays 15; lateral-line scales 37–44; no scales in axil of pectoral fins; gill rakers 33–41; third and fourth anal spines about equal; silvery orange-red, the scale edges darker; a broad reddish brown bar from upper end of gill opening to axil of pectoral fins; outer part of spinous dorsal fin yellow or orange-yellow; caudal fin and outer part of lobes of soft dorsal and anal fins bright red; leading edge of these and pelvic fins white. A small species, usually not exceeding 15 cm; largest 19 cm. Islands of the western Indian Ocean to the Hawaiian Islands, Society Islands, and Marquesas Islands; southern Japan to Great Barrier Reef and Lord Howe Island. *Myripristis multiradiatus* Günther is a synonym.

Hawaiian Islands

BLOTCHEYE SOLDIERFISH
Myripristis murdjan (Forsskål, 1775)
Dorsal rays X-I,13–15; anal rays IV,11–14; pectoral rays 14–16; lateral-line scales 27–32; small scales on lower part of axil of pectoral fins; gill rakers 36–44; interorbital space broad, 3.65–4.4 in head length; lower jaw slightly projecting when mouth closed; red to dusky red, shading to pinkish silvery below, the scale edges darker; black of opercular membrane not extending below level of lower edge of pupil; iris red with a large blackish blotch above pupil and a smaller one below; outer part of spinous dorsal red; leading edge of pelvic and remaining median fins white. Attains 27 cm. Red Sea (type locality) and east coast of Africa to Hawaiian Islands (recently found at Midway) and Samoa Islands; Ryukyu Islands to Great Barrier Reef and New Caledonia; reported from 1–50 m. *Myripristis parvidens* Cuvier and *M. axillaris* Valenciennes are synonyms.

Penyu Islands, Indonesia

SCARLET SOLDIERFISH

Myripristis pralinia Cuvier in C & V, 1829

Dorsal rays X-I,14–17 (modally 15); anal rays IV,13–15; pectoral rays 14–15 (rarely 14); lateral-line scales 34–40; no scales in axil of pectoral fins; gill rakers 35–42; interorbital space broad, 3.4–3.7 in head length; fourth anal spine longer than third; red dorsally, the scale edges darker red, shading to silvery ventrally, the scale edges light red; black of opercular membrane not extending below level of center of eye; median fins mainly red, the membranes at tip of anterior dorsal spines white; leading edges of soft dorsal, anal, caudal, and pelvic fins white. A small species, the largest examined, 20.3 cm. East coast of Africa to Society Islands and Tuamotu Archipelago; Ryukyu Islands to Great Barrier Reef and New Caledonia; type locality, New Ireland. Reported from depth range of 1 to 30 m. *Myripristis bleekeri* Günther and *M. sanguineus* Jordan & Seale are synonyms.

RANDALL'S SOLDIERFISH

Myripristis randalli Greenfield, 1974

Dorsal rays X-I,14–15 (usually 14); anal rays IV,12–13; pectoral rays 14–15; lateral-line scales 28–31; no scales in axil of pectoral fins; gill rakers 41–45; surface of bony shelf over eye irregularly striated and/or with tiny nodular projections; silvery pink dorsally with red-rimmed scales, shading to silvery below, the scales with pale red edges; black of opercular membrane extending slightly below level of center of eye; fins largely red, the spinous dorsal broadly white at base. Largest, 19.5 cm. Known at present only from the Pitcairn Islands, Austral Islands (Rurutu, type locality), American Samoa (Wass, 1984), and Tonga. Collected from the depth range of 15–53.5 m.

TIKI SOLDIERFISH

Myripristis tiki Greenfield, 1968

Dorsal rays X-I,14–16; anal rays IV,12–14 (rarely 12 or 14); pectoral rays 14–15 (usually 15); lateral-line scales 35–40; no scales in axil of pectoral fins; gill rakers 36–43; body elongate for the genus, the depth 2.5–2.95 in standard length; interorbital space broad, 3.8–4.2 in head length; lateral mucous channels dorsally on head very broad; third anal spine usually slightly longer than fourth, 2.05–2.45 in head length; light red dorsally, the scale edges red, silvery pink ventrally, with narrow red stripes between longitudinal scale rows, most evident on ventral half of body; opercular membrane red with dark pigment to level of lower edge of eye; fins largely red without white leading edges. Largest specimen, 26.5 cm. Known only from Easter Island (type locality), Pitcairn Islands, and Rapa; specimens collected from the depth range of 1.5–15 m.

LATTICE SOLDIERFISH
Myripristis violacea Bleeker, 1851
Dorsal rays X-I,13–16 (modally 15); anal rays
IV,12–14; pectoral rays 14–15; lateral-line scales
27–29; small scales on lower part of axil of pectoral fins; gill rakers 38–48; third and fourth anal
spines about equal, 2.2–2.5 in head length; silvery
to silvery pink (sometimes bluish silver dorsally),
the edges of scales dorsally on body dark brown to
nearly black (especially dark on nape); scales ventrally on body rimmed with red; median fins light
red, becoming red distally, usually with white
edges anteriorly on soft dorsal, anal, caudal, and
pelvic fins. Attains 22 cm. East coast of Africa to
the Line Islands, Marquesas Islands, and Tuamotu
Archipelago; Ryukyu Islands to Great Barrier Reef
and New Caledonia (Laboute & Grandperrin,
2000); type locality, Banda, Indonesia. Usually
seen on shallow protected reefs. *Myripristis
microphthalmus* Bleeker is a synonym.

Marshall Islands, with *Labroides pectoralis*

WHITETIP SOLDIERFISH
Myripristis vittata Valenciennes in C & V, 1831
Dorsal rays X-I,13–15; anal rays IV,11–12 (rarely
11); pectoral rays 14–16; lateral-line scales 35–40;
no small scales in axil of pectoral fins; gill rakers
33–38; interorbital space very broad, 3.1–3.4 in
head length; bony shelf over eye longitudinally
striated; third anal spine distinctly longer than
fourth; red to orange-red, the scale centers slightly
paler; opercular membrane dark red; fins red, the
membranes of dorsal spines tipped with white, the
leading edges of soft dorsal, anal, caudal, and
pelvic fins white. Attains 20 cm. Islands of western Indian Ocean (type locality, Mauritius) to
Hawaiian Islands and French Polynesia except
Rapa and the Austral Islands; southern Japan to
Great Barrier Reef and New Caledonia; usually
encountered in outer-reef areas at depths greater
than 15 m.

Penyu Islands, Indonesia

WHITESPOT SOLDIERFISH
Myripristis woodsi Greenfield, 1974
Dorsal rays X-I,13–15; anal rays IV,10–13 (usually 12); pectoral rays 14–16; lateral-line scales
30–34; no small scales in axil of pectoral fins;
third anal spine slightly longer than fourth; red
dorsally, shading to silvery white or pink ventrally,
the scale edges darker; opercular membrane red
with a variable amount of dark pigment to level of
lower edge of eye; axil of pectoral fins black, usually with a small white spot; a white streak on side
of lower jaw. Largest, 26.5 cm. Recorded from the
Marquesas Islands, Phoenix Islands, Line Islands,
Kiribati, Marshall Islands (type locality, Enewetak
Atoll), Minami-tori-shima (Marcus Island), Caroline Islands, and the Mariana Islands; a shallow-
water species of outer-reef areas exposed to wave
action.

Line Islands

91

Hawaiian Islands

Marshall Islands, with *Labroides bicolor*

Hawaiian Islands

SHY SOLDIERFISH

Plectrypops lima (Valenciennes in C & V, 1831)
Dorsal rays XII,14–16; anal rays IV,10–12; pectoral rays 16–17; lateral-line scales 39–42; scale rows above lateral line 4.5; gill rakers 7–8 + 14–15; scales coarsely ctenoid; no tooth patches outside gape at front of lower jaw; no large spine at corner of preopercle; dorsal spines short, the longest about 3 in head length; caudal-fin lobes broadly rounded; bright red with a light red square in each scale. Largest, 16 cm. East coast of Africa to the Hawaiian Islands and Easter Island; Japan to the Great Barrier Reef and Lord Howe Island; type locality, Mauritius; also reported from islands of the tropical eastern Pacific (Allen & Robertson, 1994). Hides in deepest recesses of coral reefs by day; rarely ventures out of caves at night. Only one other species in the genus, *P. retrospinis* (Guichenot), from the tropical western Atlantic.

SQUIRRELFISHES (HOLOCENTRINAE)

CLEARFIN SQUIRRELFISH

Neoniphon argenteus (Valenciennes in C & V, 1831)
Dorsal rays XI,11–13; anal rays IV,7–9; pectoral rays 12–14; lateral-line scales 38–43; scale rows above lateral line 2.5; gill rakers 5–7 + 9–12; lower jaw strongly projecting (true of other species of the genus); last dorsal spine close to first soft ray (also generic); silvery with blue and pink iridescence, each scale with a dark reddish brown spot; fins pale yellowish, the caudal with a broad red band in each lobe, the soft dorsal and anal with an anterior light red band. Indo-Pacific except Red Sea and Hawaiian Islands; type locality, New Guinea. Usually found on shallow protected reefs, often sheltering in branching corals by day. Distinguished from *N. opercularis* and *N. sammara* by lacking large black markings on dorsal fin. *Holocentrum laeve* Günther is a synonym. Individual in photo is being serviced by a Bicolor Cleaner Wrasse, *Labroides bicolor*.

GOLDLINED SQUIRRELFISH

Neoniphon aurolineatus (Liénard, 1839)
Dorsal rays XI,12–14; anal rays IV,8–9; pectoral rays 13–15; lateral-line scales 42–47; scale rows above lateral line 3.5; gill rakers 5–7 + 11–13; body depth 3.0–3.3 in standard length; last dorsal spine shortest (penultimate spine shortest on other species of *Neoniphon*); body silvery pink with narrow golden yellow stripes following scale rows; head with 2 silver streaks; fins largely red, the leading edge of anal and pelvic fins white. Reaches 22 cm. Islands of western Indian Ocean (Mauritius, type locality) to the Hawaiian Islands and Marquesas, but recorded from few localities (among them southern Japan, Ogasawara Islands, Indonesia, and Samoa Islands); generally found at depths greater than 40 m; submarine observations in the Hawaiian Islands to 188 m. As noted by Shimizu & Yamakawa (1979), this species resembles the West Indian *Neoniphon marianus*, which has significant meristic differences. *Flammeo scythrops* Jordan & Evermann is a synonym.

BLACKFIN SQUIRRELFISH
Neoniphon opercularis (Valenciennes in C & V, 1831)
Dorsal rays XI,12–14; anal rays IV,8–9; pectoral rays 13–15; lateral-line scales 36–41; scales above lateral line 2.5; gill rakers 5–8 + 11–13; silvery with yellow and green iridescence; a dusky purple to brownish spot on each scale; a wide red vertical zone basally on opercle broadly edged posteriorly with silvery white and pink posteriorly and anteriorly; spinous dorsal fin black, the triangular membrane tips white, with a large white spot at base of each membrane; caudal fin with yellow rays and a broad red band at edge of each lobe; soft portion of dorsal and anal fins with yellow rays and a red anterior band. Largest species of the genus; attains 35 cm. East coast of Africa to the Society Islands and Tuamotu Archipelago; Ryukyu Islands to New Caledonia and throughout Micronesia; type locality, New Ireland.

SPOTFIN SQUIRRELFISH
Neoniphon sammara (Forsskål, 1775)
Dorsal rays XI,11–13; anal rays IV,8; pectoral rays 13–15; lateral-line scales 38–43; scale rows above lateral line 2.5; gill rakers 6–8 + 10–13; silvery with blue-green iridescence; lateral line in a narrow pink stripe; a small dark reddish brown spot on each scale, most joining or nearly joining adjacent spots to form narrow dark stripes; spinous dorsal fin white with a very large round black spot on first 3 membranes, followed by a narrowing dark olive and red band; remaining fins as described for *N. opercularis*. Attains 30 cm. Widespread and common throughout the Indo-Pacific in shallow protected coral-reef areas; type locality, Red Sea. Not as secretive as other squirrelfishes. Thirty-three adults were collected by the author in early morning hours for food-habit study; about 70% of the diet consisted of crabs (xanthids, portunids, majids, and grapsids) and crab larvae, and about 15% small fishes (mostly postlarvae or transforming); other prey included shrimps and shrimp larvae, polychaete worms, hermit crabs and larvae, stomatopod larvae, and amphipods. Nine collected at 1300 hours had empty stomachs except one that contained a crab.

TAILSPOT SQUIRRELFISH
Sargocentron caudimaculatum (Rüppell, 1838)
Dorsal rays XI,13–15; anal rays IV,8–10; pectoral rays 13–15; lateral-line scales 38–43; scale rows above lateral line 2.5; oblique rows of scales on cheek 5; gill rakers 5–8 + 11–13; dorsal profile of head of adults nearly straight; premaxillary groove (middorsal on snout) not reaching or just reaching a vertical at front edge of eye; edge of nasal fossa (cavity in front of eye) with 1 or more spinules; red, the edges of scales narrowly silver; a prominent silvery white spot on caudal peduncle just behind rear base of dorsal fin; posterior one-third of body of some fish silvery white. Largest specimen, 25.3 cm. Red Sea (type locality) and east coast of Africa to the Line Islands and French Polynesia except Rapa and Australs; Ryukyu and Ogasawara Islands to Great Barrier Reef and New Caledonia; usually in 2–40 m, more often in outer-reef areas than in lagoons. *Holocentrum andamanense* Day is a synonym.

Penyu Islands, Indonesia

Coral Sea

Bali (night)

Ryukyu Islands

CROWN SQUIRRELFISH

Sargocentron diadema (Lacepède, 1802)

Dorsal rays XI,12–14; anal rays IV,8–10; pectoral rays 13–15; lateral-line scales 46–50; scale rows above lateral line 2.5; gill rakers 5–7 + 12–14; nasal fossa small, without spinules; preopercular spine short, 2–3 in eye diameter; body alternately striped with red and silvery white, the red 3 or more times broader than the white; spinous dorsal fin deep red with an anterior white band in low part of fin, and a posterior one in higher part of fin; membrane at tip of dorsal spines white. Largest examined, 17 cm, but rarely exceeds 13 cm. Occurs throughout the Indo-Pacific region; type locality unknown. Usually found in depths of 2–20 m. The most common species of the genus at most localities.

Pitcairn Islands

YELLOWSTRIPED SQUIRRELFISH

Sargocentron ensifer (Jordan & Evermann, 1903)

Dorsal rays XI,14; anal rays IV,9–11; pectoral rays 14–15 (rarely 14); lateral-line scales 42–47; scale rows above lateral line 3.5; gill rakers 6–8 + 13–14; first dorsal spine nearly as long as second; membranes of spinous dorsal fin not incised; body red with yellow stripes dorsally and narrow white stripes on side and ventrally; spinous dorsal fin yellow with a narrow red margin. Reaches 25 cm. Reported from the Hawaiian Islands (type locality), Japan, South China Sea, New Caledonia, Samoa Islands, and Pitcairn Island, mostly at depths greater than 20 m. Has been misidentified as *Sargocentron furcatum* (Günther), but this is a synonym of the Atlantic *Holocentrus adscensionis* (Osbeck) (Randall & Heemstra, 1985), the result of locality error.

Pitcairn Islands

BEADED SQUIRRELFISH

Sargocentron hormion Randall, 1998

Dorsal rays XI,13–14; anal rays IV,8–10; pectoral rays 14–15 (usually 15); lateral-line scales 51–56; scale rows above lateral line 2.5; gill rakers 5–7 + 13–15; body slender, the depth 2.8–3.1 in standard length; a small spine at edge of premaxillary groove; preopercular spine usually less than half eye diameter; nasal fossa of moderate size, without spinules; body striped with red and silvery white, the red about 3 times broader than the white; spinous portion of dorsal fin red except for white-tipped spines and a white spot near base of first 6 membranes. Largest specimen, 20 cm. Known only from Pitcairn Island (type locality), Rapa, and Rarotonga, Cook Islands, from depth range of 1–42 m.

DWARF SQUIRRELFISH
Sargocentron iota Randall, 1998

Dorsal rays XI + 12–14; anal rays IV,9; pectoral rays 14–15 (usually 15); lateral-line scales 43–47; scale rows above lateral line 3.5; gill rakers 5–7 + 10–13; body deep, the depth 2.3–2.5 in standard length; a small retrorse spine on nasal bone between nasal fossa and premaxillary groove, and another at edge of groove; spinous and soft portions of dorsal fin separate; caudal fin lobes broadly rounded; red with narrow darker red stripes on body. A small species, the largest specimen, 9.5 cm. Known to date from the Hawaiian Islands (type locality), Fiji, New Caledonia, Coral Sea, Palau, Papua New Guinea, Molucca Islands, and Christmas Island, Indian Ocean; never seen by day by the author; stays close to shelter of coral reef at night. Named for the smallest letter in the Greek alphabet in reference to the small size of the species.

Hawaiian Islands

SAMURAI SQUIRRELFISH
Sargocentron ittodai (Jordan & Fowler, 1902)

Dorsal rays XI,13–14 (rarely 14); anal rays IV,8–10; pectoral rays 14–16; lateral-line scales 43–49; scale rows above lateral line 2.5; gill rakers 5–7 + 12–14; snout length 3.65–4.15 in head length; nasal fossa small, without spinules; preopercular spine short, about one-third eye diameter; third anal spine long, 1.15–1.4 in head length; body with alternating stripes of red and silvery white; spinous dorsal fin dark red, with a row of white blotches, white-tipped spines, and a blackish blotch on each of first 2 membranes. Reaches 20 cm. Red Sea and east coast of Africa to Line Islands and Marquesas (but few localities from Oceania); common in Japan (type locality, Okinawa); depth range, 5–70 m.

Mauritius

YELLOWEYE SQUIRRELFISH
Sargocentron lepros (Allen & Cross, 1983)

Dorsal rays XI,12–14; anal rays IV,8–9 (rarely 8); pectoral rays 15; lateral-line scales 45–49; scale rows above lateral line 3.5; gill rakers 6–7 + 12–13; body depth 2.65–2.95 in standard length; a small retrorse spine on nasal bone between nasal fossa and premaxillary groove, but none at edge of groove; spinous and soft portions of dorsal fin separate; caudal fin lobes broadly rounded; red to orange-red with narrow darker red stripes on body; iris largely golden yellow. Reaches 10 cm. Recorded from Pitcairn Islands, Cook Islands, Samoa Islands, Rotuma, New Caledonia, and Cocos-Keeling Islands and Christmas Island (type locality) in the Indian Ocean.

American Samoa

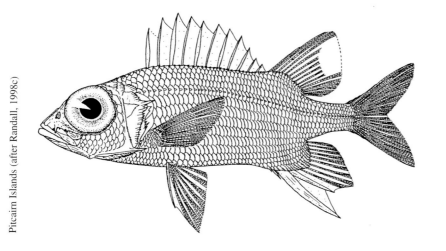

BIGEYE SQUIRRELFISH

Sargocentron megalops Randall, 1998

Dorsal rays XI,15; anal rays IV,10; pectoral rays 15; lateral-line scales 57–58; scale rows above lateral line 3.5; oblique rows of scales on cheek 5; gill rakers 6 + 13; no spinules in nasal fossa; body slender, the depth 3.1 in standard length; eye very large, 2.6 in head length; third anal spine 1.35 in head length; lobes of caudal fin pointed; life color unknown, but probably red; no dark markings in preservative. Known from only a single female specimen, 9.5 cm in total length, collected by the author at Henderson Island, Pitcairn Islands, in 49 m.

BLACKSPOT SQUIRRELFISH

*Sargocentron melanospilo*s (Bleeker, 1858)

Dorsal rays XI,12–14; anal rays IV,8–10; pectoral rays 14; lateral-line scales 33–36; scale rows above lateral line 2.5; oblique rows of scales on cheek 5; gill rakers 6–8 + 10–12; body depth 2.7–2.95 in standard length; upper jaw of adults projecting due to thickening of upper lip; nasal fossa with 1–4 spinules; third anal spine 1.5–1.75 in head length; body orange-red with narrow silvery stripes (brassy dorsally); a prominent black spot at base of soft dorsal, anal, and caudal fins; spinous dorsal fin red with a row of squarish white blotches and membrane at tip of spines white. Reaches 25 cm. East coast of Africa to Caroline Islands and Samoa Islands; Ryukyu Islands to Great Barrier Reef and New Caledonia; type locality, Ambon. Depth range, 5–90 m. Often misidentified as *Sargocentron cornutum*, a valid East Indian–Australian species.

SMALLMOUTH SQUIRRELFISH

Sargocentron microstoma (Günther, 1859)

Dorsal rays XI,12–14; anal rays IV,9–10 (rarely 10); pectoral rays 14–15 (usually 15); lateral-line scales 48–55; scale rows above lateral line 2.5; gill rakers 6–8 + 13–15; slender for the genus, the depth 2.9–3.5 in standard length; nasal fossa small, without spinules; preopercular spine short, its length one-fourth to one-third orbit diameter; third anal spine extremely long, 1.0–1.2 in head length; body with red and silvery white stripes, the white broader except narrow one following lateral line; spinous dorsal whitish with a submarginal red zone, usually with a large black spot on first 2 membranes. Largest specimen, 19.3 cm. Maldive Islands to the Line Islands, Tuamotu Archipelago, and Austral Islands; Ryukyu Islands and Ogasawara Islands to Great Barrier Reef and New Caledonia; type locality, Ambon. Usually in 1–35 m, but one photographed in 183 m from a submarine at Johnston Island (Randall et al., 1985b).

DARKSTRIPED SQUIRRELFISH
Sargocentron praslin (Lacepède, 1802)
Dorsal rays XI,12–13 (mainly 13); anal rays IV,8–9 (rarely 8); pectoral rays 13–15 (rarely 13); lateral-line scales 33–36; scale rows above lateral line 2.5; oblique rows of scales on cheek 4; gill rakers 6–8 + 10–12; snout short and blunt, 4.4–5.1 in head length; interorbital width 3.9–4.4 in head length; upper edge of first suborbital bone with a small lateral spine; body with dark reddish brown stripes alternating with silvery white stripes of about equal width; upper 2 dark stripes merging to form an elongate spot at base of soft dorsal fin; a dark spot below end of anal fin; dark pigment of pelvic fins mainly on first soft ray. Largest specimen, 21 cm. East coast of Africa to Caroline Islands and Society Islands; Ryukyu Islands to Great Barrier Reef; type locality, Solomon Islands. Usually in shallow, clear-water, seaward reef areas.

Penyu Islands, Indonesia

PEPPERED SQUIRRELFISH
Sargocentron punctatissimum (Cuvier in C & V, 1829)
Dorsal rays XI,12–14; anal rays IV,8–9 (rarely 8); pectoral rays 14–16; lateral-line scales 41–47; scale rows above lateral line 2.5; snout short, 4.0–4.65 in head length; interorbital width greater than snout length, 3.6–4.05 in head length; nasal fossa small, without spinules; second opercular spine nearly as long as first; silvery red, sometimes with blue-green iridescence dorsally, with an indistinct red-striped pattern; scales of head and body finely dotted with dark brown. Reaches 13 cm. Wide-ranging in Indo-Pacific from the Red Sea and South Africa to the Hawaiian Islands and Easter Island; type locality, Strong Island (= Kusiae), Caroline Islands. Common on reefs and rocky shores exposed to wave action; most specimens from less than 3 m, often taken in tidepools; stomach contents of 10 specimens consisted of crabs and crab larvae (mainly xanthids), shrimps and shrimp larvae; one had eaten a polychaete worm along with crustaceans.

Marshall Islands (night)

REDCOAT
Sargocentron rubrum (Forsskål, 1775)
Dorsal rays XI,12–14; anal rays IV,8–10 (rarely 10); pectoral rays 13–15; lateral-line scales 34–38; scale rows above lateral line 2.5; oblique rows of scales on cheek 5; gill rakers 6–8 + 9–12; snout short and blunt, 4.25–4.7 in head length; interorbital width narrow, 4.5–5.2 in head; upper edge of first suborbital bone with a small lateral spine; nasal fossa without spinules; body with alternating stripes of brownish red and silvery white, usually with an oblong dark brown spot at base of soft dorsal fin, and a lesser spot at base of anal and caudal fins; tips of pelvic rays 2–6 and adjacent membranes blackish red. Attains 27 cm. Red Sea (type locality) and east coast of Africa to Vanuatu, Lord Howe Island, and New Caledonia; Japan to New South Wales; known from 1–84 m, usually on silty reefs.

Bali

SABRE SQUIRRELFISH

Sargocentron spiniferum (Forsskål, 1775)

Dorsal rays XI,14–16 (usually 15); anal rays IV,9–10 (rarely 9); pectoral rays 14–16; lateral-line scales 41–46; scale rows above lateral line 3.5; gill rakers 6–8 + 12–14; body deep and compressed, the depth 2.4–2.6 in standard length; lower jaw strongly projecting; preopercular spine longer than eye diameter in adults; red, the scale edges silvery white; a vertically elongate crimson spot, partly bordered by silvery white, behind eye; spinous portion of dorsal fin solid red. Largest of the squirrelfishes; attains 45 cm. Occurs throughout the tropical Indo-Pacific region from the Red Sea (type locality) and South Africa to the Hawaiian Islands and Pitcairn Islands. Depth range, 1–122 m. Randall (1980a) summarized reports of food habits; most of the prey were crustaceans, largely crabs, but small fishes were also eaten. The author's wife was injured by the preopercular spine of this species; the pain was severe and long-lasting, indicative of the presence of a venom.

TAHITIAN SQUIRRELFISH

Sargocentron tiere (Cuvier in C & V, 1829)

Dorsal rays XI,13–15; anal rays IV,9–10 (rarely 10); pectoral rays 13–15; lateral-line scales 45–52; scale rows above lateral line 2.5; gill rakers 7–9 + 13–16; body depth 2.6–2.95 in standard length; preopercular spine of large adults may be slightly longer than eye diameter; the 2 opercular spines are nearly equal; dorsal spines short, the longest 2.6–3.5 in head length; nasal fossa large, without spinules; red with faint silvery red stripes, those ventrally often showing blue-violet iridescence; spinous dorsal fin red except for white-tipped spines and a row of white spots, one per membrane. Reaches 33 cm. Islands of western Indian Ocean to Hawaiian Islands and Pitcairn Islands; rare in Indo-Malayan region; type locality, Tahiti. Tiere is the Tahitian name for the species. Found more often on exposed than protected reefs; depth range 1–26 m. Six specimens were collected by the author for food-habit study; one had an empty stomach, the others all contained crabs (one of these had shrimp remains and another, 29.5 cm in standard length, had eaten *Sargocentron punctatissimum* 9.6 cm in standard length).

PINK SQUIRRELFISH

Sargocentron tiereoides (Bleeker, 1853)

Dorsal rays XI,12–14; anal rays IV,9–10 (usually 9); pectoral rays 13–15 (rarely 15); lateral-line scales 39–44; scale rows above lateral line 2.5; gill rakers 6–8 + 12–14; premaxillary groove extending distinctly posterior to a vertical at front edge of eye; nasal fossa moderately large, usually without spinules; red with silvery pink stripes a little narrower than red interspaces; spinous dorsal fin light red, the membrane at tips of spines white, with a deep red submarginal band. Largest specimen, 19.5 cm. East coast of Africa to Line Islands and French Polynesia except Rapa and the Marquesas Islands; Ryukyu Islands to Great Barrier Reef; type locality, Ambon. A coral-reef species known from the depth range of 6–45 m (mostly from more than 15 m).

Palau (night)

Fiji

VIOLET SQUIRRELFISH

Sargocentron violaceum (Bleeker, 1853)

Dorsal rays XI,12–15 (mainly 14); anal rays IV,9; pectoral rays 13–14 (rarely 13); lateral-line scales 33–37; scale rows above lateral line 2.5; gill rakers 6–8 + 12–13; body moderately deep, the depth 2.3–2.7 in standard length; nasal fossa with spinules; lower opercular spine nearly as long as upper; membranes of spinous dorsal fin very slightly incised; brownish to purplish red (more red at night), each scale of body with a vertical silvery white line; opercular membrane dark red and black; a triangular red spot above pectoral-fin base; spinous dorsal fin light purplish red with white-tipped spines and a submarginal bright red band. Largest specimen, 26 cm. East coast of Africa to the Line Islands and Samoa Islands; Ryukyu Islands to northern Great Barrier Reef; type locality, Ambon. A coral-reef species usually found in 1–15 m.

Penyu Islands, Indonesia (night)

Trumpetfish, *Aulostomus chinensis*, Tukangbesi Islands, Indonesia

TRUMPETFISHES
(AULOSTOMIDAE)

Trumpetfishes are very elongate, the body narrower than deep, with a very small oblique mouth at the end of a long tubular snout; the teeth are minute; scales are small and ctenoid, and there is a small barbel on the chin. The dorsal fin has slender isolated dorsal spines, followed posteriorly on the body by a soft-rayed fin; the caudal fin is rounded to rhomboid. These fishes usually swim slowly by undulating the soft dorsal and anal fins, but are capable of swift darting movements to capture fishes and shrimps; they suck in their prey by pipette-like action. They may align themselves vertically while hiding among plants or gorgonians and dart downward on their prey, or they may mingle with schools of plant-feeding fishes such as surgeonfishes to approach small fishes that are disrupted by the school. Also they sometimes hover over or beside larger fishes such as parrotfishes to get closer to prey. Fishes have been found in the stomachs that seem too large to have passed through the narrow snout, but the ventral part is membranous and elastic, expanding as needed for larger prey. There are 3 species of trumpetfishes in the world, all in the genus *Aulostomus*: one in the Indo-Pacific region, one in the western Atlantic, and one at islands of the eastern Atlantic (Wheeler, 1955; Bowen et al., 2001).

Hawaiian Islands

TRUMPETFISH
Aulostomus chinensis (Linnaeus, 1766)
Dorsal rays VIII-XII + 24–27; anal rays 26–29; pectoral rays 17; pelvic rays 6; caudal fin rounded to rhomboid; 2 color forms, yellow and the more common gray-brown or orangish brown, usually with faint whitish stripes, becoming blackish posteriorly with vertical rows of white spots; 2 black spots in caudal fin, 1 at base of each pelvic fin, and a black streak on upper jaw. Attains at least 76 cm. Indo-Pacific (though absent from the Red Sea to India) and tropical eastern Pacific; type locality, East Indies; a coral-reef fish reported from depths of 1–124 m. Of 18 specimens collected by the author with food in their stomachs, one had eaten a shrimp, the others fishes (pomacentrids, juvenile acanthurids, mullids, priacanthids, and apogonids). Prey fishes identified to species include *Mulloidichthys flavolineatus*, *Heteropriacanthus cruentatus*, *Pristiapogon kallopterus*, and *Stegastes nigricans*.

Smooth Cornetfish, *Fistularia commersonii*, Marshall Islands

CORNETFISHES
(FISTULARIIDAE)

Like the related trumpetfishes, the cornetfishes are very elongate with a long tubular snout, small mouth, very small teeth, and the dorsal and anal fins posterior in position. They differ notably in having a body that is broader than it is deep, no scales, no dorsal spines, and in having a forked caudal fin with 14 rays, the 2 middle rays prolonged to a long filament. Cornetfishes feed on small fishes and crustaceans in the same manner as trumpetfishes—by sucking in the prey like a giant pipette. The family consists of the single genus *Fistularia* and 4 species, 2 of which occur in the Indo-Pacific region, but only 1 is known from the South Pacific. The genus was reviewed by Fritzsche (1976).

SMOOTH CORNETFISH
Fistularia commersonii Rüppell, 1838
Dorsal rays 15–17; anal rays 14–16; pectoral rays 14–15 (usually 15); no row of slender embedded bony plates before dorsal fin; interorbital space with longitudinal ridges; dorsal and lateral ridges of snout of adults serrate; lateral line with ossifications, but without spines; green to olive dorsally, silvery white ventrally, with 1 or 2 pale blue stripes or rows of pale blue spots on back and dorsally on snout; tips of median fins pink. Reported to attain 150 cm in total length. Indo-Pacific and tropical eastern Pacific; type locality, Red Sea. Corsini et al. (2002) reported it from the Mediterranean Sea as a probable immigrant via the Suez Canal. An active fish generally seen over reefs, seagrass beds, or sand flats in the vicinity of reefs. At night or during the day when motionless on the bottom, it assumes a pattern of dark bars. Takeuchi et al. (2002) reported feeding on clupeid, carangid, labrid, mullid, scarid, chaetodontid, tripterygiid, gobiid, blennid, and bothid fishes, as well as mysids, euphausids, stomatopods, and decapod crustaceans. *Fistularia depressa* Günther is a synonym.

Bali

101

SEAMOTHS
(PEGASIDAE)

This bizarre family of 2 genera and 5 species is classified in the order Gasterosteiformes, along with the sticklebacks, pipefishes, and seahorses. The body of these small fishes is encased in bony plates formed from highly modified fused scales, those on the tail as rings, hence this part of the body is flexible; the carapace of the head and trunk is broader than high; there is a long rostrum from fused nasal bones extending well anterior to the small ventral mouth; the jaws are toothless; there are 2 lateral lines, one along the dorsolateral ridge and one along the ventrolateral ridge; the short dorsal and anal fins are on the second to fourth tail rings; the large pectoral fins are horizontally inserted and extend wing-like to each side; the pelvic fins of I spine and 2–3 soft rays are just behind the pectorals and serve for "walking" on the bottom; there is no swimbladder. The food is presumed to be very small invertebrates, primarily benthic crustaceans. The family was revised by Palsson & Pietsch (1989). Only 1 species ranges to the islands of the South Pacific.

Papua New Guinea

SHORT SEAMOTH
Eurypegasus draconis (Linnaeus, 1766)
Dorsal rays 5; anal rays 5; pectoral rays usually 10 or 11; tail rings usually 8, the last ring with a medial spine projecting posteriorly from the dorsal surface; dorsal surface of head with deep pits behind eyes; rostrum of variable length, 11–39% standard length; color variable, but often with a fine dark brown reticulum; membranes of pectoral fins hyaline with a broad white outer border, the rays with rows of small black spots. Attains 8 cm. The most wide-ranging species of the family, occurring from the Red Sea and east coast of Africa to French Polynesia; southern Japan south to New South Wales and Lord Howe Island; type locality unknown; replaced in the Hawaiian Islands by the similar *Eurypegasus papilio* (Gilbert). Generally seen on sand or sand-rubble bottoms, often with algal growth. Easily overlooked due to their camouflage and slow movement. The author has encountered them as male-female pairs. They are known from aquarium observations to periodically shed a complete outer body layer of mucus.

Ornate Ghost Pipefish, *Solenostomus paradoxus*, Alor, Indonesia

GHOST PIPEFISHES
(SOLENOSTOMIDAE)

This small family, allied to the pipefishes, consists of a single genus, *Solenostomus*. Like the pipefishes, these small fishes are encased externally in bony plates forming 27 to 35 complete or partial rings around the body; the snout is very long and narrow; there are 2 well-separated dorsal fins, the first long with V slender spines; both the second dorsal fin and the anal fin have 17–22 soft rays; the caudal fin is long. The pelvic fins of I spine and 6 soft rays are very large; they are modified by the female to form a brood pouch by being joined together ventrally and fused to the abdomen dorsally (unlike the pipefishes, the males of which brood the eggs). Ghost pipefishes are among the most perfectly camouflaged of all fishes. Those that shelter in gorgonians, black coral, or crinoids are colored like these sessile invertebrates and have numerous long cirri; others look like drifting pieces of algae or seagrass. They are often oriented with head downward, and they swim slowly. They feed on the small animals of the demersal zooplankton, especially crustaceans such as copepods and shrimp larvae. Three species were recognized in the revision by Orr & Fritzsche (1993), but a fourth was added by Orr et al. (2002).

Papua New Guinea

Alor, Indonesia

ROBUST GHOST PIPEFISH
Solenostomus cyanopterus Bleeker, 1854
Dorsal rays V + 17–22; anal rays 17–22; pectoral rays 24–28; body depth 4.0–6.7 in standard length; least snout depth 12–24 in standard length; caudal peduncle short, the average length 10 in standard length; membranes of caudal fin not or only slightly incised; cirri usually not present (when present small and mostly on snout); usually green to yellowish brown, but may be red or nearly black; often with scattered small whitish or pinkish blotches and/or small dark spots; an elongate dark spot often present on each of first 2 spinous dorsal membranes. Attains about 15 cm. Red Sea and east coast of Africa to Fiji; in the western Pacific from southern Japan to New South Wales and New Caledonia; type locality, Seram (Ceram), Indonesia. May occur on reefs, but more often found on algal flats or seagrass beds.

ORNATE GHOST PIPEFISH
Solenostomus paradoxus (Pallas, 1770)
Dorsal rays V + 17–21; anal rays 17–21; pectoral rays 25–28; body depth 4.3–7.6 in standard length; head, body, and fins usually with numerous slender cirri; snout slender, its least depth 18–36 in standard length; caudal peduncle slender and long, its average length 7.4 in standard length; caudal fin membranes deeply incised; color extremely variable, often translucent with small spots or short lines of white, black, red, orange, or yellow to match the pattern of the crinoids, gorgonians, soft coral, or black coral in which they usually hide. Reaches 11 cm. Red Sea and east coast of Africa to Fiji; in the western Pacific from southern Japan to New South Wales; type locality, Ambon, Molucca Islands.

Male-female pair of Gorgonian Pygmy Seahorse, *Hippocampus bargibanti*, Sulawesi

SEAHORSES AND PIPEFISHES
(SYNGNATHIDAE)

The pipefishes and seahorses are a large family of 52 genera and over 200 species of small fishes that occur mainly in shallow tropical to temperate seas; a few species live in fresh water. Syngnathids are characterized by an elongate body enclosed in a series of bony rings; it is generally quadrangular in cross-section, and there usually are distinct ridges dorsally and ventrally (termed superior and inferior) on both the trunk and the tail and a lateral ridge along the side. There is a single dorsal fin (absent in 3 genera), a small anal fin of 2–6 rays (rarely absent), small pectoral fins (absent in a few species), and no pelvic fins; a small caudal fin of 8–11 (usually 10) rays is present except in species with a prehensile tail such as the seahorses. The gill opening is very small. Many species have dermal flaps, tentacles, or cirri. The number of trunk rings (the first is the one bearing the base of the pectoral fins, and the last the one with the anus) and tail rings are important in the classification; also important is the configuration of the ridges on the body. The snout of these fishes is tubular, and the mouth very small; they feed mainly on very small crustaceans of the demersal plankton. Unique to the family is the parental care of the eggs and developing young by the male; the female attaches the eggs to the ventral surface of the male, often in a special pouch. Indo-Pacific pipefishes were well revised by Dawson (1985), and a guide to seahorses was published by Lourie et al. (1999).

Persian Gulf

Society Islands

SHORTBODIED PIPEFISH
Choeroichthys brachysoma (Bleeker, 1855)
Dorsal rays 18–26; pectoral rays 18–23; trunk rings 14–18; tail rings 17–20; superior trunk and tail ridges continuous; inferior trunk ridge ending on anal ring; lateral trunk ridge confluent with inferior tail ridge; head length 4.1–5.9 in standard length; snout length 1.8–2.4 in head length; least snout depth 3.8–5.8 in snout length; 2 rows of small dark spots usually present on side of trunk (upper row incomplete on males); a lateral stripe on side of snout passing through eye onto opercle. Reaches 6.5 cm. Indo-Pacific except Japan and the Hawaiian Islands; type locality, Batu Archipelago, Indonesia; occurs mainly on coral reefs or seagrass beds in about 5–25 m.

104

ZEBRA PIPEFISH

Choeroichthys cinctus Dawson, 1976

Dorsal rays 22–26; pectoral rays 20–23; trunk rings 15; tail rings 20–22; ridges on body as described for *C. brachysoma*; head length 3.4–3.9 in standard length; snout long and slender, 1.7–1.9 in head length; least snout depth 5.5–7.0 in snout length; white with narrow dark brown bars on body along margins of rings; small dark brown spots on operculum; a faint dark stripe on side of snout, darkest just before eye. A small species, the largest specimen 4.4 cm. Indonesia (type locality, Molucca Islands), northern Great Barrier Reef, Fiji, and Samoa Islands; coral reefs, mostly from the depth range of 9–38 m.

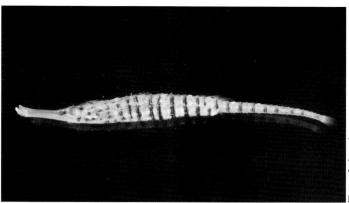

Flores, Indonesia

SCULPTURED PIPEFISH

Choeroichthys sculptus (Günther, 1870)

Dorsal rays 27–34; pectoral rays 18–23; trunk rings 18–21; tail rings 21–25; ridges on body as for the genus; head length 4.9–7.1 in standard length; snout length 2.0–2.5 in head length; least depth of snout 2.2–3.5 in its length; a horizontal ridge on scutella (small bony plates in 2 series on trunk and 1 series on tail); females with 3–4 longitudinal rows of small dark brown spots on trunk, continuing faintly in 1–2 rows on anterior part of tail; males with spots on trunk ocellated. Reaches 8.5 cm. East coast of Africa to Line Islands and Tuamotu Archipelago; type locality, Fiji; reefs and reef flats, generally in less than 3 m (illustrated specimen taken on a reef flat in 10 cm).

Line Islands

DARKBARRED PIPEFISH

Corythoichthys amplexus Dawson & Randall, 1975

Dorsal rays 23–30; pectoral rays 12–15 (modally 14); trunk rings 14–16; tail rings 35–39; superior trunk and rail ridges discontinuous; lateral trunk ridge straight, ending near anal ring; inferior trunk and tail ridges continuous (pattern of ridges generic); head length 8.4–12.0 in standard length; snout length 2.1–2.8 in head length; body with dark brown bars of 3–4 rings in width; no dark stripes on head behind eye. Attains 9 cm. Gulf of Oman and Seychelles to Samoa Islands; in the western Pacific from Ryukyu Islands to Great Barrier Reef; type locality, Fiji; depth range 0.2–30.5 m.

Flores, Indonesia

YELLOWBANDED PIPEFISH

Corythoichthys flavofasciatus (Rüppell, 1838)

Dorsal rays 26–36; pectoral rays 13–17; trunk rings 15–17; tail rings 32–39; ridges as described for *C. amplexus*; head length 6.8–10.9 in standard length; snout length 1.9–2.6 in head length; whitish with yellow stripes or rows of elongate spots and irregular dark reddish bars or reticulate spots; snout red and white; head with 2 dark stripes; a large bright blue spot (black in preservative) ventrally on anal ring of male. Attains about 11.5 cm. Red Sea (type locality) and Madagascar to the islands of Micronesia, Line Islands, and Tuamotu Archipelago (but remains unknown from Indonesia and the Philippines); generally found on coral reefs from the shallows to at least 25 m.

Society Islands

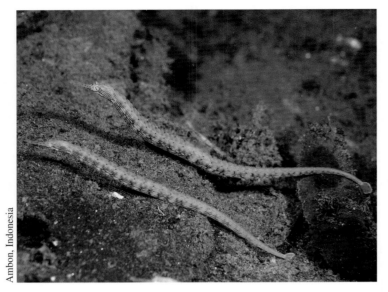

Ambon, Indonesia

SCRIBBLED PIPEFISH
Corythoichthys intestinalis (Ramsay, 1881)
Dorsal rays 26–32; pectoral rays 14–18; trunk rings 15–17 (modally 16); tail rings 31–37; ridges on body as in preceding species; head length 6.6–9.8 in standard length; snout length 1.8–2.4 in head length; color variable but usually whitish with longitudinal yellow lines and a series of 20 or more dark blotches composed of horizontal anastomosing black lines; head usually with prominent dark stripes (spots or a reticular pattern may be present on snout). Reaches 16 cm. Philippines, Indonesia, northwestern Australia and Great Barrier Reef east to islands of Micronesia, New Caledonia, Fiji, Tonga, Samoa Islands, and Rapa (Randall et al., 1990); type locality, Solomon Islands; most specimens from depth range of 0–3 m. *Corythoichthys haematopterus* (Bleeker) from east coast of Africa to Vanuatu is similar in color, differing in the absence of (or greatly reduced) dark markings on posterior one-third of tail, and in having modally 17 trunk rings.

BLACKCHEST PIPEFISH
Corythoichthys nigripectus Herald in Schultz et al., 1953
Dorsal rays 25–31; pectoral rays 13–17; trunk rings 16; tail rings 36–40; ridges on body as in others of the genus; head length 6.8–9.8 in standard length; snout length 1.9–2.3 in head length; whitish with a fine red reticular pattern dorsally on trunk and orange or yellow lines or rows of spots on lower side; tail with small red or orange spots (may be faint); ventral part of anterior trunk rings blackish; dorsal fin with 1–3 rows of orange to red

Marshall Islands

spots; caudal fin largely white. Reaches 11.5 cm. Distribution disjunct: northern Red Sea and islands of Micronesia (type locality, Bikini Atoll, Marshall Islands), New Caledonia, Fiji, and Society Islands; depth range 4.5–27.5 m.

SCHULTZ' PIPEFISH
Corythoichthys schultzi Herald in Schultz et al., 1953
Dorsal rays 25–31; pectoral rays 14–18; trunk rings 15–17; tail rings 32–39; ridges on body as in the genus; head length 6.0–8.1 in standard length; snout long and slender, its length 1.5–2.0 in head length; whitish with broken longitudinal dusky yellow to brown lines and rows of oval spots, the spots becoming red on tail. Attains 16 cm. Red Sea and islands of western Indian Ocean east to East Indies, Ryukyu Islands, Marshall Islands (type locality, Bikini Atoll), Fiji, and Tonga; in Australia from Rowley Shoals and Great Barrier Reef; occurs from shallow reefs to at least 30 m. The long-snouted *Corythoichthys ocellatus* Herald of the western Pacific is similar, differing in 22–25 dorsal rays, 29–32 tail rings, and a color pattern chiefly of rows of ocellated oval yellow spots.

Sulawesi

Southern Oman

BANNER'S PIPEFISH
Cosmocampus banneri (Herald & Randall, 1972)
Dorsal rays 16–20; pectoral rays 11–14; trunk rings 15; tail rings 27–30; superior trunk and tail ridges discontinuous; lateral trunk ridge straight, ending near anal ring; inferior trunk and tail ridges continuous; head length 7.1–8.3 in standard length; snout length 2.2–27 in head length; median ridge on snout with 2–4 dorsal projections; small dermal flaps on head, including eye; whitish to pale pink, often with 2 longitudinal rows of small dark spots on lower side of trunk. Maximum length about 6.5 cm. Red Sea, Natal, and islands of the western Indian Ocean to Marshall Islands and Fiji; Ryukyu Islands (type locality, Ishigaki) to New Caledonia; only Rowley Shoals and Christmas Island in eastern Indian Ocean; occurs on coral reefs to depths of 30 m.

MAX WEBER'S PIPEFISH
Cosmocampus maxweberi (Whitley, 1933)
Dorsal rays 23–27; pectoral rays 16–18 (usually 16); trunk rings 14–15 (usually 15); tail rings 29–32; ridges on body as for the genus, but not strongly developed; head length 5.3–6.8 in standard length; snout length 1.6–1.9 in head length; tan to light red, the ventral part of body usually with dark bars (1 per ring). Maximum length about 9 cm; males may be brooding as small as 6.2 cm. Recorded from the Red Sea, Indonesia (type locality, Sumbawa), Papua New Guinea, Great Barrier Reef, Marshall Islands, and Samoa Islands; illustrated specimen from 35 m.

BLUESTRIPE PIPEFISH
Doryrhamphus excisus Kaup, 1856
Dorsal rays 21–29; pectoral rays 19–23; trunk rings 17–19; tail rings 13–17; superior trunk and tail ridges discontinuous; lateral trunk ridge confluent with inferior tail ridge on second tail ring; principal ridges of trunk and tail with a spine on each ring; a blade-like ridge dorsally on snout with about 6 pointed projections; head length 3.9–4.9 in standard length; snout length 2.0–2.4 in head length; males usually with a fleshy flap on each ventrolateral ridge of snout; orange-yellow with a broad dark blue stripe on upper side continuing darker and narrower onto head to front of snout; caudal fin orange with large reddish brown blotches and white upper and lower margins. Largest, 7.5 cm. Indo-Pacific and tropical eastern Pacific; type locality, Massaua, Red Sea. Dawson (1981, 1985) regarded the eastern Pacific population as a subspecies, *Doryrhamphus excisus paulus* Fritzche, and the Red Sea population as *D. excisus abbreviatus* Dawson. Dawson (1985) noted that there is a clinal increase in the number of total rings and dorsal rays, with the highest values east of Fiji, adding that some specimens from southeastern Oceania (e.g., Austral Islands and Tuamotu Archipelago) may be largely brownish. More study of the latter population may result in its recognition as a subspecies or species. Cryptic; usually found in pairs; has been observed to clean other fishes (Randall & Helfman, 1972). *Doryrhamphus melanopleura* (Bleeker) is a synonym. Also known as the Fantail Pipefish.

RINGED PIPEFISH
Dunckerocampus dactyliophorus (Bleeker, 1853)
Dorsal rays 20–27; pectoral rays 18–22; trunk rings 15–17; tail rings 18–22; superior trunk and tail ridges discontinuous; inferior trunk ridge ending on anal ring; lateral trunk ridge continuous with inferior tail ridge; juveniles with 2 spines on ridges of body, reduced to 1 spine in adults, and this may be lost in large adults; head length 3.7–4.6 in standard length; snout long, 1.4–1.8 in head length; caudal fin moderately large; white to pale yellowish with 20–32 dark bars encircling head (including snout) and body; caudal fin red with a white margin and usually 1–3 white spots in middle. Reaches 18 cm. Ryukyu Islands to Great Barrier Reef, east to5 Marshall Islands and Society Islands; type locality, Java; occurs mainly on coral reefs at depths of 4 to 56 m. Classified in *Doryrhamphus* by some authors, such as Dawson (1985).

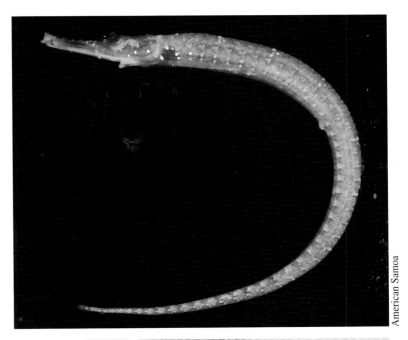

American Samoa

New Caledonia

Sulawesi

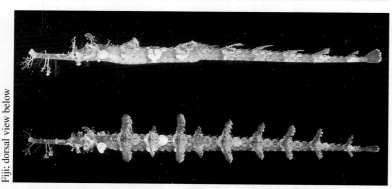

Norfolk Island

Fiji; dorsal view below

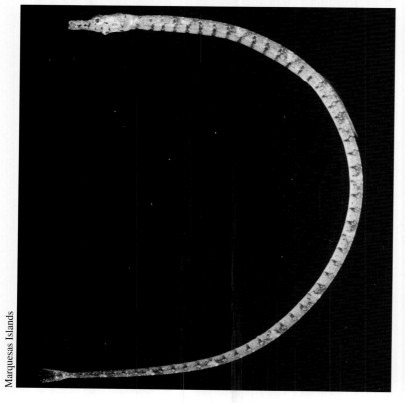

Marquesas Islands

BOOTH'S PIPEFISH

Halicampus boothae (Whitley, 1964)

Dorsal rays 18–24; pectoral rays 10–12; trunk rings 13–14 (usually 14); tail rings 37–52; superior trunk and tail ridges discontinuous; inferior trunk ridge ending at anal ring; lateral trunk ridge confluent with inferior tail ridge; median dorsal ridge on snout continuous; head length 12–17 in standard length; snout short, 3.0–3.8 in head length; caudal fin small; color variable, tan to dark brown, with series of well-separated white spots or short bars; tip of snout usually white. Attains 17 cm. Comoro Islands, Japan, Palau, Lord Howe Island (type locality), Norfolk Island, Chesterfield Islands (Coral Sea), and Fiji; specimens collected from depth range of 3–30 m. Very similar to *Halicampus dunckeri* (Chabanaud), a variable species from the Caroline Islands and Vanuatu to the western Indian Ocean and Red Sea. It differs from *H. boothae* chiefly in having 31–36 tail rings and smaller size (largest, 12.5 cm). Dawson (1985) noted that the Lord Howe Island population has a higher average number of dorsal rays and tail rings than elsewhere in its range.

LONGSNOUT PIPEFISH

Halicampus macrorhynchus Bamber, 1915

Dorsal rays 18–19; pectoral rays 16–19; trunk rings 14–15 (usually 14); tail rings 25–27; ridges on body as described for *H. boothae*; median ridge dorsally on snout low, consisting of a series of short projections; head length 4.7–5.1 in standard length; snout very long, 1.5–1.8 in head length; juveniles (7–10 cm) with 8–10 pairs of leaf-like fleshy flaps extending outward from superior ridge of body, and slender cirri, some with many branches, on head; color variable, but generally with alternating dark brown and whitish blotches. Reaches about 17 cm. Northern Red Sea (type locality), Papua New Guinea, Great Barrier Reef, Solomon Islands, and Fiji; usually found in diving depths on algal flats, seagrass beds, or coral rubble; one taken in a trawl from depths of 180–300 m.

MARQUESAN PIPEFISH

Halicampus marquesensis Dawson, 1984

Dorsal rays 21–22; pectoral rays 11–12; trunk rings 13–14 (usually 14); tail rings 39–40; ridges on body as in the genus; median dorsal ridge on snout continuous, finely denticulate posteriorly, with a parallel ridge to each side extending into interorbital; side of snout with a short low ridge; dorsal edge of orbit only slightly elevated; 2 lateral spines usually present on snout; head length 11.9–13.1 in standard length; snout length 2.4–2.7 in head length; light brown to olivaceous with 12 saddle-like whitish blotches dorsally on body and 14 narrow dark brown bars on ventral half of trunk; tail with irregular reddish brown bars containing pale blotches. Largest specimen, 7.2 cm. Positively known only from the Marquesas Islands (Tahuata, type locality); collected from 20–35 m on sand and rubble bottom; clumps of *Halimeda* present at type locality. One subadult from Fiji provisionally identified by Dawson (1985) as this species.

SAMOAN PIPEFISH

Halicampus mataafae (Jordan & Seale, 1906)

Dorsal rays 21–26; pectoral rays 12–14; trunk rings 15; tail rings 34–36; ridges on body as in the genus; median dorsal ridge on snout as 2 to 3 isolated spinous crests; 2 lateral spines usually present on snout; head length 10.2–13.0 in standard length; snout short, 2.5–4.0 in head length; caudal fin about as long as eye; mottled reddish to brown, often with 2 series of small pale spots on trunk and 1 on tail. Reaches about 13 cm. Red Sea to Natal, east to Marshall Islands and Samoa Islands (type locality); in the western Pacific from Ryukyu Islands to Great Barrier Reef; a shallow-water species; sometimes found in tidepools.

Southern Oman

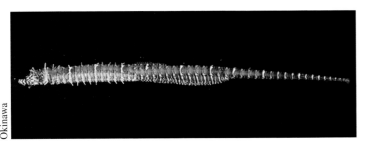

Okinawa

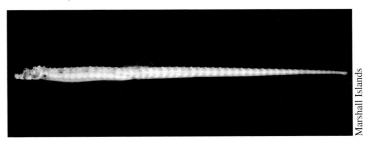

Marshall Islands

GLITTERING PIPEFISH

Halicampus nitidus (Günther, 1873)

Dorsal rays 18–22; pectoral rays 11–14; trunk rings 13–15 (usually 14); tail rings 30–32; ridges on body typical of the genus; margins of superior ridge serrate; median dorsal ridge on snout as 1–3 isolated spinous crests; usually 1 or 2 lateral spines on snout; small dermal flaps usually present on head and body; head length 8.2–10.7 in standard length; snout short, its length 2.9–3.7 in head length; gray-brown with irregular, narrow white bars corresponding to rings. Reaches 7.5 cm. Western Pacific from Ryukyu Islands to Great Barrier Reef, east to Fiji and west to Western Australia; type locality, Bowen, Queensland; known from coral reefs in about 1–20 m.

SPINYSNOUT PIPEFISH

Halicampus spinirostris (Dawson & Allen, 1981)

Dorsal rays 19–20; pectoral rays 13–14; trunk rings 14; tail rings 33–35; ridges on body as in the genus; median dorsal ridge on snout with 2–3 isolated spinous ridges; side of snout with 3 spines; head short, 10–11.3 in standard length; snout short, 3.1–3.8 in head length; whitish to light tan with a large dusky area on each ring above and below lateral ridge, thus giving a faint barred pattern; a large blackish blotch below eye, and smaller ones behind eye, on operculum, and pectoral-fin base. Largest specimen, 11.2 cm. Currently known only from Sri Lanka, Western Australia (type locality), Marshall Islands, and American Samoa.

PALEDOTTED PIPEFISH

Hippichthys cyanospilus (Bleeker, 1854)

Dorsal rays 20–28; pectoral rays 13–16 (usually 14–15); trunk rings 12–14; tail rings 32–35; superior trunk and tail ridges discontinuous; lateral trunk ridge deflected ventrally at posterior end; inferior trunk and tail ridges continuous; head length 7.5–9.8 in standard length; snout tapering, its length 1.3–2.6 in head length; light brown, densely dotted with whitish, with a pattern of orangish brown bars; dorsal fin whitish with small dark brown spots; some with a broad ventral red zone on trunk (perhaps only males). Reported to 16 cm. Northern Red Sea and

Lombok, Indonesia

Persian Gulf south to Natal, east to western Pacific from the Ryukyu Islands to Queensland; only Fiji and western Caroline Islands in Oceania; type locality, Banda Islands, Indonesia. Found in coastal and brackish habitats.

BARREDBELLY PIPEFISH

Hippichthys spicifer (Rüppell, 1838)

Dorsal rays 25–30; pectoral rays 15–18; trunk rings 14–16; tail rings 36–41; superior trunk and tail ridges discontinuous; lateral trunk ridge deflected ventrally to rear of last trunk ring; inferior trunk and tail ridges continuous; head length 6.9–10.3 in standard length; snout moderately long, 1.8–2.1 in head length; gray-brown, finely mottled with brown blotches and small pale spots, the abdomen with about 12 narrow dark bars, the tail with about 10 whitish bars; lower part of head usually with black dots.

New Caledonia

Reaches at least 17 cm. Red Sea (type locality) and east coast of Africa to Kiribati and Samoa Islands; in the western Pacific from southern Japan to the Great Barrier Reef and New Caledonia; occurs in shallow coastal waters, including estuarine habitats such as mangroves.

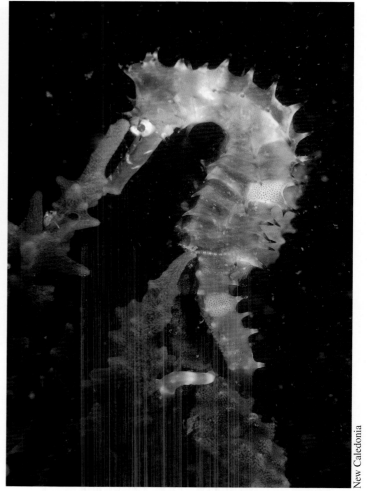

GORGONIAN PYGMY SEAHORSE
Hippocampus bargibanti Whitley, 1970

Dorsal rays 14; anal fin absent in adults; pectoral rays 10; head and body fleshy without recognizable bony segments; prominent bulbous tubercles of variable size on head and body; head length 5.1–5.9 in total length; snout very short, 2.95–4.1 in head length; no caudal fin (true of genus); color variable, to match the gorgonian on which it lives (generally seafans of the genus *Muricella*). Attains only about 3 cm. Known from New Caledonia (type locality), northern Great Barrier Reef, Papua New Guinea, and Indonesia.

THORNY SEAHORSE
Hippocampus histrix Kaup, 1856

Dorsal rays 17–19; anal rays 4; pectoral rays 17–18; trunk rings 11; tail rings 33–34; prominent sharp spines on ridges of rings of body, those on superior ridge longest; coronet (at top of head) with 5 short spines; a long median spine anterior to coronet and one equally long to either side, preceded by a smaller spine at posterior edge of eye; supraorbital spine long; snout longer than half length of head; color variable, the spines from dorsal part of head and body often black-tipped. Attains 15 cm. Indo-Pacific except the Red Sea and Gulf of Oman where replaced by *H. jayakari* Boulenger; type locality, Japan.

SMOOTH SEAHORSE
Hippocampus kuda Bleeker, 1852

Dorsal rays 15–18; anal rays 4; pectoral rays 15–17; trunk rings 11; tail rings 34–37; ridges not well-developed and tubercles short and blunt; coronet low, rounded, slanting posteriorly, with 5 short nodules; snout about equal to length of postorbital head; color usually yellow or yellowish (one common name, Yellow Seahorse), often with small dark spots; may also be black or brown, usually with scattered pale blotches. Reported to reach 30 cm. Indo-Pacific; type locality, Singapore; current research may result in the recognition of populations now identified as *H. kuda* as subspecies or different species (Lourie et al., 1999).

Sulawesi/female

THREE-SPOT SEAHORSE

Hippocampus trimaculatus Leach, 1814

Dorsal rays 18–22; pectoral rays usually 17 or 18; trunk rings 11; tail rings usually 40–41; coronet very low; spines small and low; a sharp hook-like spine on cheek and one above eye; snout long, 1.9–2.4 in head length; color variable from whitish to orange or black; some individuals zebra-striped; may have a large dark spot dorsally on side of body on first, fourth, and seventh trunk rings. India to western Pacific; Tahiti is the only locality recorded for Oceania; described from specimens from "Indian and Chinese seas."

ANDERSON'S PIPEFISH

Micrognathus andersonii (Bleeker, 1858)

Dorsal rays 17–24; pectoral rays 11–13; trunk rings 15–17; tail rings 27–32; superior trunk and tail ridges discontinuous; inferior trunk ridge ending on anal ring; lateral trunk ridge continuous with inferior tail ridge; ridges of posterior tail rings without backward-projecting spines; head length 8.1–10.4 in standard length; snout short, its length 2.7–3.4 in head length; color variable, often with 9–13 dusky-edged pale bars on body, sometimes with a few large blackish spots dorsally on trunk. Reaches about 8.5 cm. Red Sea and east coast of Africa to Tonga, Samoa Islands, and islands of Micronesia except the Marshall Islands; type locality, Cocos-Keeling Islands; a common shallow-water species often collected from tidepools.

Sulawesi/male

New Britain

(Dawson, 1985)

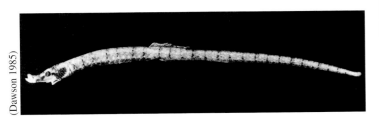

(Dawson 1985)

MYERS' PIPEFISH

Minyichthys myersi (Herald & Randall, 1972)

Dorsal rays 25–33; pectoral rays 12–13 (usually 13); trunk rings 17–19; tail rings 36–42; superior trunk and tail ridges discontinuous; inferior trunk ridge ending at anal ring; lateral trunk ridge confluent with inferior tail ridge; median ridge on snout with a distinctive small spike or elevated portion just before nostrils; head length 7.0–8.5 in standard length; snout length 2.3–3.2 in snout depth; snout depth 1.7–3.0 in snout length. Probably does not exceed 6.5 cm. Known to date only from the East Indies, St. Brandon's Shoals in the Indian Ocean, Guam (type locality), and the Society Islands from coral reefs or rubble substrata in the depth range of 6–35 m.

THORNTAIL PIPEFISH

Micrognathus brevirostris (Rüppell, 1838)

Dorsal rays 18–21; pectoral rays 10–13 (usually 11–12); trunk rings 15–16; tail rings 28–31; superior trunk and tail ridges discontinuous; inferior trunk ridge ending on anal ring; lateral trunk ridge continuous with inferior tail ridge; ridges of posterior tail rings flared laterally, with hook-like projections from posterior angles; head length 7.2–10.2 in standard length; snout length 2.6–3.3 in head length; color variable, often with about 10 irregular white bars across upper half of body, as in the figure of a female (after Dawson, 1985; his figure of the anterior part of a male lacks these bars, having instead many vertical rows of black spots). Attains about 6.5 cm. Fritzsche (1981) described *Micrognathus pygmaeus* from Tahiti; Dawson (1985) recognized this as a subspecies of *M. brevirostris* and gave the range as eastern Indonesia and northern Queensland to the Marshall Islands and Tahiti. *Micrognathus brevirostris brevirostris* is currently known only from the Red Sea (type locality) and Persian Gulf.

111

Fiji

ROCK PIPEFISH
Phoxocampus belcheri (Kaup, 1856)
Dorsal rays 20–24; anal rays 3–4; pectoral rays 11–13; trunk rings 16–17 (usually 16); tail rings 29–32; superior and inferior trunk and tail ridges continuous; lateral trunk ridge ending on first to fifth (usually third or fourth) tail ring; principal tail ridges ending posteriorly in a sharp point on each ring on at least posterior one-third of tail (true of other species of the genus); median ridge on snout low and nearly smooth; opercular ridge incomplete in adults; head length 7.1–9.4 in standard length; snout length 2.4–3.1 in head length; caudal fin small; pale gray to brown with 3 rows of dark spots along side of trunk, 1 on each ridge, the anterior ones sometimes partially joined to form bars; a dark bar across ventral surface of each trunk ring, progressively darker and more distinct anteriorly. Attains nearly 8 cm. Red Sea and east coast of Africa to Fiji; Japan to New Caledonia; not known from Australia or Micronesia; type locality, China; a shallow-water reef species.

Marshall Islands

TWOSPINE PIPEFISH
Phoxocampus diacanthus (Schultz, 1943)
Dorsal rays 20–24; anal rays 3–4; pectoral rays 13–15; trunk rings 15–16 (usually 16); tail rings 25–28; superior and inferior trunk and tail ridges continuous; lateral trunk ridge ending on last trunk ring or first tail ring; median ridge on snout low and finely serrate; a spiny projection on supraorbital ridge often present, and may bear a dermal flap; head length 6.4–7.9 in standard length; snout length 2.2–2.6 in head length; caudal fin small; pale to nearly black, variously blotched or barred. Attains nearly 9 cm. Sri Lanka and East Indies, Micronesia except the Caroline Islands, Fiji, and Samoa Islands (type locality, Tutuila); Hong Kong to Great Barrier Reef and New Caledonia; most specimens from coral reefs in 5–40 m.

Papua New Guinea

SEAGRASS PIPEFISH
Syngnathoides biaculeatus (Bloch, 1785)
Dorsal rays 38–48; pectoral rays 20–24; trunk rings 15–18; tail rings about 40–54; tail long, tapering, and prehensile, ending in a slender curled tip; no caudal fin; superior and inferior trunk ridges continuous with tail ridges; lateral trunk ridge deflected dorsally behind anal ring; head length 4.9–6.3 in total length; snout long, 1.7–1.8 in head length; green to greenish brown with variable white and dark markings. Largest specimen, 28.3 cm. Red Sea, east coast of Africa, Magadascar, India, Western Australia, East Indies (type locality), east to Samoa Islands and islands of Micronesia except the Marshall Islands; Japan to New South Wales; generally found in shallow lagoons or bays in seagrass beds or bottoms with heavy algal cover, the mottled green color matching that of the surrounding plants. Males as small as 18 cm may be brooding. Called the Alligator Pipefish in South Africa.

DOUBLE-ENDED PIPEFISH

Trachyrhamphus bicoarctatus (Bleeker, 1857)
Dorsal rays 24–32; pectoral rays 15–19; trunk rings 21–24; tail rings 55–63; superior trunk and tail ridges discontinuous, the superior tail ridge curving ventrally below dorsal fin; inferior trunk ridge ending at tail ring; lateral trunk ridge confluent with inferior tail ridge; body very slender, the depth at midtrunk 36–58 in total length; head length 9.9–13.0 in standard length; snout long, 1.5–2.0 in head length; caudal fin of adults often lacking or reduced in size; color variable, from nearly black to brown or whitish, with or without dark bars, and often with small pale and/or black spots. Attains about 40 cm. Red Sea, Persian Gulf, and east coast of Africa to Guam and New Caledonia;

Ambon, Indonesia

Japan to Western Australia and New South Wales; type locality, Ambon, Molucca Islands. Generally found on sand, rubble, or seagrass substrata; anchors in regions of current by putting tail tip in sand, the probable explanation for the reduction or loss of the caudal fin.

SHRIMPFISHES
(CENTRISCIDAE)

The shrimpfish family consists of 2 genera, each with 2 species. These bizarre fishes are encased in thin, transparent bony plates that are expansions of the vertebral column; the body is elongate and extremely compressed, the ventral edge sharp; the snout is long and tubular, the mouth small without teeth; there is no lateral line. The caudal fin and soft dorsal fin are displaced ventrally, and the spinous dorsal is in the usual position of the caudal fin; the long first dorsal spine is in alignment with the dorsal edge of the body. The first dorsal spine of *Aeoliscus* has a joint that allows the movement of the distal part; *Centriscus* lacks this joint. These fishes are usually encountered in aggregations just off the substratum, often swimming vertically with head down and all turning at the same time. They feed mainly on the small animals of the demer-

Coral Shrimpfishes, *Aeoliscus strigatus*, Sulawesi

sal zooplankton, especially crustaceans. Mohr (1937) revised the family; she treated *Aeoliscus* as a subgenus of *Centriscus*, but it is currently given generic rank.

CORAL SHRIMPFISH

Aeoliscus strigatus (Günther, 1861)
Dorsal rays III + 9–11; anal rays 10–12; caudal rays 9–10; pectoral rays 10–12; pelvic rays 3–5; first dorsal spine with a movable distal segment; body depth of adults 8.0–9.8 in total length (of juveniles about 6–7); head length 3.0–3.5 in total length; no median groove in interorbital space (present in *Centriscus*); snout long and slender in adults, 3.7–4.1 in total length (snout of juveniles much shorter, and the mouth upturned); whitish, becoming translucent ventrally, with a midlateral black stripe from front of snout through eye to base of soft dorsal fin; juveniles yellow to brown, the lateral black stripe confined to head; irregular rows of small dark brown spots anteriorly on side of body. Reaches 15 cm. Western Pacific from Japan to New South Wales, east to Pohnpei (Ponape), New Caledonia, and Fiji; in the Indian Ocean from the Seychelles (collected there by the author); type locality, Java. Occurs in sheltered waters of bays and lagoons, generally over coral reefs or in seagrass beds; usual depth range, 1 to 12 m; smaller individuals may take refuge among the long spines of sea urchins of the genus *Diadema*.

Palau

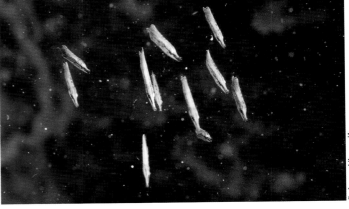

Sulawesi/juveniles

113

Bearded Ghoulfish, *Inimicus didactylus*, Papua New Guinea

SCORPIONFISHES
(SCORPAENIDAE)

The scorpionfish family, the largest of the order Scorpaeniformes, is named for the venomous spines possessed by many species. These fishes have a reinforcing bone called the suborbital stay from the second suborbital bone (usually referred to as the lacrimal) across the cheek to the preopercle. It is apparent externally as a horizontal ridge and usually has short posteriorly directed spines. Most species have numerous head spines, especially dorsally, including 3–5 on the edge of the preopercle, 2 on the opercle, and 2 or 3 on the lacrimal. Variation in the size and pattern of the spines is important in the classification of the species. There is a single dorsal fin with VIII to XVIII stout spines, notched between the spinous and soft portions; anal fin usually with III strong spines and 3–15 (frequently 5–6) soft rays. The pectoral fins are large, often with the upper rays branched and the lower rays unbranched and thickened; the pelvic fins have a single spine and 5 (occasionally 4) soft rays. The caudal fin is usually rounded, but may be truncate. The scales are small, ctenoid or cycloid, rarely entirely absent. Many species have dermal flaps, cirri, or small tentacles on the head and body, and some even have algae growing on the head. The mouth is moderately large, but the teeth in the jaws are small, conical, and in several rows. Most species are variably colored and generally match their immediate surroundings; therefore color is usually of little diagnostic value. However, the lionfishes and turkeyfishes of the subfamily Pteroinae generally have distinct color patterns. Scorpionfishes are benthic, or at least bottom-oriented. All are carnivorous, feeding mainly on small fishes and crustaceans (a few are known to feed on zooplankton). Many are ambush predators, relying on their superb camouflage to avoid detection by their potential prey (as well as the few predators that might prey upon them). Some of the scorpionfishes, in particular the lionfishes (*Dendrochirus* spp.) and turkeyfishes (*Pterois* spp.), may slowly stalk their prey. The venomous spines include those of the dorsal, anal, and pelvic fins. These spines are roughly T-shaped in cross-section; the glandular tissue producing the venom lies in the groove between the longitudinal ridges of the spine. The stonefishes are exceptional in having a large pyriform sac containing the venom that lies in the groove on each side of a spine but bulges laterally; the apical end of the sac narrows to a venom duct that passes to the spine tip. When the spine enters the flesh of the victim, any pressure on the sac forces the venom into the duct. Smith (1951) described the excruciating pain from a wound in the thumb by the Stonefish, *Synanceia verrucosa*, and Smith (1957a) documented fatalities from this species. An antivenin is available for stonefish stings (Halstead, 1970: 323). The wounds from lionfishes and turkeyfishes are also extremely painful (Ray & Coates, 1958; Steinitz, 1959). Unlike the stonefishes, the lionfishes and turkeyfishes are able to stab their spines into an intruder by quickly lowering their head and arching their back with the fully elevated dorsal spines pointing forward (Halstead, 1970: 287, fig. 1). The pain from scorpionfish stings can be greatly alleviated by placing the wounded member in water as hot as can be tolerated. The Scorpaenidae of the western and central Pacific was divided into 9 subfamilies by Poss in Carpenter & Niem (1999b), who is followed here for the 4 subfamilies that occur in shallow seas of the South Pacific area. Some authors, however, treat certain of the subfamilies as families. Eschmeyer & Rama Rao (1973) reviewed the subfamily Synanceinae.

LIONFISHES AND TURKEYFISHES (PTEROINAE)

Tahiti

Papua New Guinea

TWINSPOT LIONFISH
Dendrochirus biocellatus (Fowler, 1938)
Dorsal rays XIII,9; anal rays III,5; pectoral rays 20–21; longitudinal scale series 48–51; membranes of spinous portion of dorsal fin deeply incised, more so anteriorly; membranes of upper half of pectoral fin not incised, the rays of lower half unbranched, thicker, and free of membrane distally; a tentacle on lacrimal more than twice eye diameter in length; 2 large ocellated spots (sometimes a smaller third one) in outer part of soft portion of dorsal fin. Maximum length, 12 cm. East coast of Africa and Mauritius to the Line Islands and Tuamotu Archipelago; in the western Pacific from the Ryukyu Islands and Taiwan to New Caledonia; type locality, Jolo, Philippines; known from 1–40 m. Remains hidden in reefs during daylight hours.

SHORTFIN LIONFISH
Dendrochirus brachypterus (Cuvier in C & V, 1829)
Dorsal rays XIII,9–10; anal rays III,5; pectoral rays 17–18; longitudinal scale series 42–45; longest dorsal spine about 1.7 in body depth; membranes of spinous portion of dorsal fin deeply incised (nearly to base of fin between anterior spines); membranes of pectoral fins to fin margin except slightly incised between lower 7 unbranched rays; body with 5 or 6 broad dark brown bars, head with 5 irregular dark bars, and pectoral fins crossed by 8 to 10 narrow dark bars, the pale interspaces on body and fins varying from whitish to pale red or yellow. Attains 15 cm. Red Sea south to Durban, east to Tonga and Samoa Islands; in the western Pacific from the Philippines to the southern Great Barrier Reef, New South Wales, Lord Howe Island, and New Caledonia; type locality unknown; reported from depth range of 2–30 m. Inactive during the day, but forages for food, chiefly crustaceans, at night.

Ambon, Indonesia

ZEBRA LIONFISH

Dendrochirus zebra (Cuvier in C & V, 1829)

Dorsal rays XIII,10 (rarely 11); anal rays III,6; pectoral rays 17; longitudinal scale series 45–48; longest dorsal spines equal to or greater than body depth; anterior membranes of spinous portion of dorsal fin incised nearly to fin base; membranes of pectoral fins to fin margin except between lower 7–8 unbranched rays where incised from one-fourth to nearly one-half length of rays; a slender fimbriate tentacle above eye; body with 6 dark brown to dark red bars, each whitish interspace bisected by a narrow dark bar; last dark bar on caudal peduncle with a midlateral band extending to base of caudal fin; a dark brown bar through eye, and one across operculum; a large black spot on subopercle. Reaches 20 cm. East coast of Africa to Samoa Islands and islands of Micronesia except the Mariana Islands; southern Japan to Great Barrier Reef and New South Wales; reported from the shallows to 73 m. The author was stuck on the hand by a spine of a specimen in New Caledonia that had been on ice several hours. The severe pain was alleviated by immersion in hot water for 2.5 hours before it could be barely tolerated with the

Sulawesi

hand out of the hot water. Moyer & Zaiser (1981) studied the social organization and spawning in the Izu Islands. Females come to male rendezvous sites; spawning occurs after sunset at the peak of a short upward dash; females release 2 mucous sacks, each containing a few thousand eggs; well-known egg predators were repulsed by the mucus.

ANTENNA TURKEYFISH

Pterois antennata (Bloch, 1787)

Dorsal rays XIII,11–12; anal rays III,6; pectoral rays 16–17, all unbranched; scales largely ctenoid, those in longitudinal scale series 56–60; a long supraocular tentacle with black cross bands and small lateral flaps; longest dorsal spines clearly longer than body depth and free of membrane except basally; outer half to three-fourths of pectoral fins free of membrane, the long filamentous rays white to pale red, and the basal membranous part of fin with large black spots; body with numerous brown to brownish red bars of variable width, those on caudal peduncle narrow, irregular, and oblique; head with 3 dark brown bars, the anterior one through eye, the middle one leading to a large spot on subopercle; a small white spot often present above base of pectoral fin. Largest specimen examined, 19.5 cm, from the Austral Islands. Indo-Pacific except Red Sea, Persian Gulf, and Hawaiian Islands; type locality, Ambon, Indonesia. Found mainly on coral reefs, often in caves or upside down under ledges; reported to a depth of 76 m. Also known by the common names Spotfin Lionfish and Raggedfin Turkeyfish.

CLEARFIN TURKEYFISH

Pterois radiata Cuvier in C & V, 1829

Dorsal rays XII-XIII,11; anal rays III,5–6; pectoral rays 16, all unbranched, long and filamentous; scales mostly ctenoid, those in longitudinal series 49–56; dorsal spines longer than body depth, without membranes except basally; pectoral rays very long, the longest reaching well beyond base of caudal fin, and connected by membranes on only about basal one-third; pectoral rays red basally, soon becoming white; pectoral-fin membranes clear; body with dark reddish brown bars separated only by white lines that divide dorsally and ventrally to outline small reddish triangles; a slightly oblique white-edged reddish stripe on caudal peduncle; a white-edged dark bar through eye continuing narrowly onto long slender supraocular tentacle. Attains about 18 cm. Indo-Pacific except Hawaiian Islands; type locality, Tahiti.

Bali

Sulawesi

116

Sulawesi

TURKEYFISH

*Pterois volitan*s (Linnaeus, 1758)

Dorsal rays XIII,9–12 (usually 11); anal rays III,6–8 (usually 7); pectoral rays 14–16, all unbranched; scales cycloid and small, 90–105 in longitudinal series; supraocular tentacle of variable length, but usually long and slender, and rarely dark-banded; fimbriate flaps present on lacrimal and corner of preopercle; longest dorsal spines longer than body depth in adults; membranes of dorsal spines incised nearly to base of fin, with a broad membranous flap at spine tips; upper pectoral rays incised nearly to base, their lower edge with a broad plumose membrane (juveniles lack the expanded membranes at tips of dorsal spines and pectoral rays); lower pectoral rays incised about one-third distance to base; numerous dark brown to reddish brown bars of variable width on head and body, alternating with whitish lines. Reported to attain 38 cm. Western Australia and Cocos-Keeling Islands east to the islands of Oceania except the Hawaiian Islands; Japan and southern Korea to New South Wales and northern New Zealand (1 specimen); type locality, Ambon, Molucca Islands. Whitfield et al. (2002) reported the inadvertent introduction of this species to the western Atlantic where it now ranges from Florida to New York and Bermuda. Schultz (1986) sepa-

Papua New Guinea/juvenile

rated the Indian Ocean population west of the southwest coast of Sumatra as *Pterois mile*s (Bennett), primarily on the basis of modally 1 fewer dorsal and anal soft rays and shorter pectoral fins. Extremely venomous (see family introduction).

SCORPIONFISHES (SCORPAENINAE)

DECOY SCORPIONFISH

Iracundus signifer Jordan & Evermann, 1903

Dorsal rays XII,9–10 (rarely 10); anal rays III,5; pectoral rays 17–18 (usually 18); scales ctenoid, 65–75 in longitudinal series; palatine teeth absent; fourth dorsal spine notably elongate in adults; no spines on suborbital ridge except at posterior end; red, mottled with whitish, with a small black spot between second and third dor-

Hawaiian Islands

sal spines. Largest specimen, 13 cm. Scattered insular localities from the Hawaiian Islands (type locality, O'ahu) and Tuamotu Archipelago to Mauritius. Usually found on rubble substrata, often at the base of drop-offs. Shallenberger & Madden (1973) demonstrated that the front of the dorsal fin is used as a lure to resemble a small fish. The long fourth dorsal spine is the dorsal

fin of the lure, the black spot the eye, and the gap between the first and second dorsal spines is the mouth. The front of the dorsal fin is snapped back and forth, resulting in a sinuous wave passing posteriorly; the first and second dorsal spines are alternately closed together and separated, giving the effect of respiration. The resemblance to a small moving fish is remarkable.

Fiji

Taiwan

MCADAMS' SCORPIONFISH
Parascorpaena mcadamsi (Fowler, 1938)

Dorsal rays XII,8–9 (rarely 8); anal rays III,5; pectoral rays 15–16 (usually 16); longitudinal scale series 39–44; posterior lacrimal spine curved forward; no occipital pit; body depth 2.6–2.8 in standard length; supraocular tentacle often small or absent; reddish, mottled with whitish, usually without black blotches on body; males with a prominent black spot posteriorly near outer edge of spinous portion of dorsal fin; a small species, the largest examined, 7.7 cm, from Natal (usually less than 6 cm). East coast of Africa and Mauritius to Palau, Marshall Islands, islands of French Polynesia (except the Marquesas Islands) and the Pitcairn Islands; in the western Pacific from the Ryukyu Islands and Taiwan to the Great Barrier Reef; type locality, Jolo, Philippines; known from depths of 7–40 m.

MOZAMBIQUE SCORPIONFISH
Parascorpaena mossambica (Peters, 1855)

Dorsal rays XII,9; anal rays III,5; pectoral rays 15–16 (usually 16); longitudinal scale series 43–47; posterior lacrimal spine curved forward; a shallow to moderate occipital pit; body depth 2.45–2.6 in standard length; supraocular tentacle usually well developed (may be longer than eye diameter); color variable, orangish to reddish brown, mottled with white, with blackish blotches on head and body that persist in preservative. Largest specimen, 12 cm, from Mauritius. Wide-ranging in the Indo-Pacific from east coast of Africa to the islands of Micronesia, Society Islands, and Rapa; in the western Pacific from Miyake-jima, Japan, to New Caledonia. Typically a shallow-water species; the author collected it on the reef flat of Bali in less than 1 m.

Ambon, Indonesia

AMBON SCORPIONFISH
Pteroidichthys amboinensis Bleeker, 1856

Dorsal rays XI,11; anal rays II,6–7; pectoral rays 15; soft rays of median and pectoral fins unbranched; longitudinal scale series 39; no scales on head; body moderately elongate, the depth 3.0–3.5 in standard length, and strongly compressed; head, body, and fins with numerous branched cirri and tentacles, many branched or fringed; supraorbital tentacle generally longer than head and complexly fringed; dorsal fin deeply incised at end of spinous portion; caudal fin long, 2.5–3.0 in head length; mottled brown to reddish brown. Largest specimen, 8.2 cm. Reported from the Red Sea (Dor, 1984, after Frøiland), Indonesia (type locality, Ambon), Papua New Guinea (author's photo), Japan, here listed from Fiji from a specimen collected by D. W. Greenfield, and R. F. Myers (pers. comm.) has seen an underwater photograph from Saipan. Occurs in protected waters, generally on silty sand, often with plant debris; depth range about 10–30 m. Easily overlooked because of its superb camouflage.

Great Barrier Reef

LACY SCORPIONFISH

Rhinopias aphanes Eschmeyer, 1973

Dorsal rays XII,9; anal rays III,5; pectoral rays 16; scales small, cycloid, about 70 in longitudinal series; no scales on head; body deep, the depth about 2.2 in standard length, and compressed; mouth upturned and strongly oblique; numerous slender branched tentacles and cirri on head, body, and fins; a complex reticular pattern of black and yellowish green. Attains 24 cm.

LONG-RAYED SCORPIONFISH

Scorpaenodes albaiensis (Evermann & Seale, 1907)

Dorsal rays XIII,9; anal rays III,5; pectoral rays 16–17 (usually 16); longitudinal scale series 38–43; body slender, the depth 3.3–3.7 in standard length; spines on head low and retrorse; nasal spine absent; lower jaw strongly projecting; lower 6 or 7 (usually 7) pectoral rays unbranched, the upper 2 much longer than upper branched rays, 2.6–2.85 in standard length; dorsal fin deeply notched; supraocular tentacle present or absent; mottled red to reddish brown with a black spot larger than pupil on sub-opercle; a small black spot at rear base of anal fin; white cirri present on body. Reported to 8 cm. Described from the Philippines; also known from east coast of Africa, Seychelles, Maldive Islands, Chagos Archipelago, Great Barrier Reef, Papua New Guinea, Solomon Islands, New Caledonia, Tonga, and Fiji. Sometimes classified in the genus *Hypomacrus*, along with *Scorpaenodes minor*.

Described from New Caledonia; also known from Queensland, New Guinea, and Japan. Randall (2001a) extended the range to the southern end of the Great Barrier Reef. Poss in Carpenter & Niem (1999b) and a few authors have used the common name Weedy Scorpionfish for this species, but most apply this name to *Rhinopias frondosa* (and more aptly, in view of the scientific name). Several authors have noted the resemblance of this species to crinoids, in particular *Comantheria briareus*.

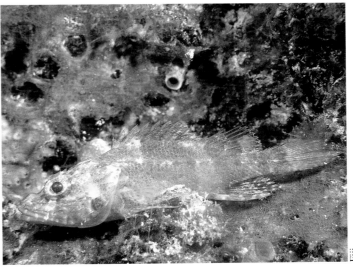

Fiji

119

Hawaiian Islands

CORAL SCORPIONFISH
Scorpaenodes corallinus Smith, 1957

Dorsal rays XIII,8; anal rays III,5; pectoral rays 17–18 (usually 17); longitudinal scale series 42–44; suborbital ridge with 3 spines; coronal spines present (between tympanic spines); lower jaw strongly projecting; dark brown to reddish brown with numerous small white flecks; a white bar across front of caudal peduncle, and an irregular pale band from above pectoral-fin base to middle of spinous portion of dorsal fin; a triangular dark brown band across base of pectoral fin. Largest specimen, 10.5 cm. Recorded from Mozambique (type locality) to Kenya, Seychelles, Mentawai Islands, Hawaiian Islands, and Society Islands. Smith (1957b) reported it as occurring only in coral; depth range, 1–18 m.

GUAM SCORPIONFISH
Scorpaenodes guamensis (Quoy & Gaimard, 1824)

Dorsal rays XIII,8; anal rays III,4–5 (usually 5); pectoral rays 18–19; longitudinal scale series 40–45; suborbital ridge with 3 spines; dorsal spines short, the longest 2.5–3.1 in head length; a pale-edged black spot nearly as large as eye on opercle at about level of eye; body irregularly blotched and spotted with dark brown or red, the blotches sometimes forming 3 irregular bars on body and 1 across base of caudal fin; 4 irregular bands radiating from eye, 2 of which extend ventrally from eye across cheek; Largest specimen examined, 12.5 cm, from Mauritius. Occurs from the Red Sea and east coast of Africa to the Society Islands and throughout Micronesia; in the western Pacific from southern Japan to Great Barrier Reef, Lord Howe Island, Norfolk Island, and New Caledonia. Primarily a shallow-water species, but reported to at least 30 m. Usually hides in reef or coarse rubble by day; feeds at night, mainly on benthic crustaceans. Some authors have considered *S. scaber* (Ramsay & Ogilby) from New South Wales as a synonym, but it is a

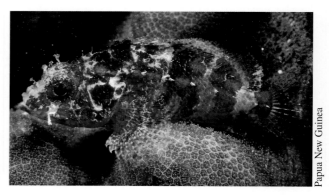

Papua New Guinea

valid species with coronal spines and sloping suborbital ridge with 4 spines. Terry J. Donaldson (pers. comm.) was spined on the finger by *S. guamensis* at Guam and experienced strong pain for 4 hours that radiated at intervals to his axilla.

HAIRY SCORPIONFISH
Scorpaenodes hirsutus (Smith, 1957)

Dorsal rays XIII,8–9 (usually 8); anal rays III,5; pectoral rays 17–18 (usually 17); longitudinal scale series about 30; suborbital ridge with 4 spines; a large oblique pore with a bony rim extending below first, second, and third and fourth suborbital spines; a small retrorse spine on each interorbital ridge; white cirri present or absent on head, body, and fins; unique color markings include 4 dark brown bands radiating from eye (none directly back from eye, 2 passing mainly ventrally), and a hemispherical red or dark brown area on about basal one-third of pectoral fin (sometimes red with a blackish blotch). Attains 5.5 cm. Occurs from east coast of Africa (type locality, Mozambique) and the Red Sea to the Hawaiian Islands and Cook Islands; in the western Pacific from southern Japan to the Great Barrier Reef. The author has collected specimens from the depth range of 8–54 m.

Cook Islands

DWARF SCORPIONFISH
Scorpaenodes kelloggi (Jenkins, 1903)

Dorsal rays XIII,8; anal rays III,5; pectoral rays 18–20 (usually 19, rarely 20); longitudinal scale series 30–33; suborbital ridge usually with 3 (occasionally 4) spines; a pair of small interorbital spines, one on each ridge; no coronal spines; body moderately elongate, the depth 3.0–3.4 in standard length; dorsal spines low, the longest 3.1–3.4 in head length; mottled dark brown, often with a pattern of 4 dark bars on body and 1 at base of caudal fin; dark bands radiating from eye. Largest specimen examined, 4.8 cm. East coast of

Seram, Indonesia

Africa to the Hawaiian Islands (type locality), Society Islands, and Marquesas Islands. Known from relatively few localities, probably because of its small size and cryptic habits. Occurs in coral reefs and coral rubble from less than 1 to at least 24 m.

CHEEKSPOT SCORPIONFISH

Scorpaenodes littoralis (Tanaka, 1917)

Dorsal rays XIII,9; anal rays III,5; pectoral rays 17–19 (usually 18, rarely 17); scales in longitudinal series 43–48; suborbital ridge with 3 spines; a pair of small interorbital spines usually present; small coronal spines sometimes present; a dark brown to dark reddish oval spot about as large as pupil on subopercle behind preopercular spines, usually pale-edged; short dark bands radiating from eye, the 2 behind eye darkest; small whitish spots along lateral line. Largest specimen examined, 10.5 cm, from Oman. Appears to be antitropical. Recorded in the western Indian Ocean from the northern Red Sea, southern Oman (cool from upwelling) and Natal. In the western Pacific from Japan (type locality, Misaki), Taiwan, southern Great Barrier Reef, southern New South Wales, and Lord Howe Island. In Oceania

Izu Islands, Japan

from the Hawaiian Islands, Rapa, and the Marquesas (sea cool in spite of low latitude); coral reefs or rocky bottom from depth range of 1–40 m. *Scorpaenodes englerti* Eschmeyer & Allen from Easter Island is closely related.

Austral Islands

MINOR SCORPIONFISH

Scorpaenodes minor (Smith, 1958)

Dorsal rays XIII,8–9 (rarely 9); anal rays III,5–6 (rarely 6); pectoral rays 14–16; longitudinal scale series 29–34; body slender, the depth 3.2–3.45 in standard length; spines on head low and retrorse; no nasal spine; lower jaw strongly projecting; lower 6 pectoral rays unbranched, the upper 2 much longer than upper branched rays, about 2.7 in standard length; dorsal fin deeply notched, the spines short; supraocular tentacle present or absent, if present slender; dark gray-brown with an irregular whitish bar across body below notch of dorsal fin; an oval black spot nearly as large as eye on subopercle, rimmed anteriorly with white. Largest specimen, 5.2 cm. Indo-Pacific but known from few localities; in the South Pacific from New Caledonia, Fiji, Tonga, Samoa Islands, and the Austral Islands (illustrated specimen from Rurutu, 52 m); type locality, Mozambique. *Hypomacrus brocki* Schultz, described from Indonesia and the Philippines, is a synonym.

FOURSPINE SCORPIONFISH

Scorpaenodes quadrispinosus Greenfield & Matsuura, 2002

Dorsal rays XIII,9–10 (usually 9); anal rays III,4–5 (usually 5); pectoral rays 17–18 (usually 17); 39–43 scales in longitudinal series; spines on head short and retrorse; interorbital and coronal spines present, but small; suborbital ridge with 4 spinous points, the second extending dorsally above ventral margin of orbit; body depth 2.85–3.05 in standard length; dorsal spines very short, less than eye diameter, 3.4–4.3 in head length; supraocular tentacle not evident, and skin flaps few; pale yellowish, mottled mainly dorsally with dark brown; 6 squarish blackish spots on back and extending into base of dorsal fin; short dark bands radiating from eye; outer half of caudal fin with numerous small dark spots. Largest specimen, 9.7 cm. Currently known only from Fiji (type locality) and the Marshall Islands; previously misidentified as *Scorpaenodes parvipinnis*, which it resembles,

Hawaiian Islands

LOWFIN SCORPIONFISH

Scorpaenodes parvipinnis (Garrett, 1864)

Dorsal rays XIII,9; anal rays III,5; pectoral rays 17–19 (usually 18); 47–51 scales in longitudinal series; suborbital ridge with 5–15 spinous points; spines on head short and retrorse; interorbital and coronal spines present; body depth 2.7–2.95 in standard length; dorsal spines very short, usually not longer than eye diameter, 3.4–4.3 in head length; supraocular tentacle not evident; numerous white cirri on head and body of some individuals; color variable but often with a large white area from behind eye to body below base of eighth dorsal spine; a white bar across most of caudal peduncle. Reported to 13 cm. Widespread from the Red Sea and east coast of Africa to the Hawaiian Islands (type locality) and islands of French Polynesia; Ryukyu Islands to the Great Barrier Reef; occurs on coral reefs from the shallows to at least 46 m.

Fiji (D. W. Greenfield)

particularly with respect to the short dorsal spines; *parvipinnis* differs in having 5 or more suborbital spines, no distinct squarish dark spots on back, and usually has numerous skin flaps. Occurs on outer-reef flat and surge channels of exposed reefs; has been collected at same station with *parvipinnis*.

Fiji

Mauritius

Sulawesi

BLOTCHFIN SCORPIONFISH
Scorpaenodes varipinnis Smith, 1957
Dorsal rays XIII,8; anal rays III,5; pectoral rays 17–19 (rarely 17); longitudinal scale series 37–40; suborbital ridge with 3 spines; no interorbital or coronal spines; body depth 2.6–2.95 in standard length; longest dorsal spine 2.9–3.15 in head length; body with large red to reddish brown blotches that may coalesce to form irregular bars, especially one between the soft dorsal and anal fins and extending into their base; caudal peduncle with a white bar followed by a narrow red bar that extends onto base of caudal fin; a large, pale-edged black spot on opercle behind eye; a black spot covering most of dorsal fin between spines VIII to XII (presumably just in males); a blackish arc at base of pectoral fins; pelvic fins blackish. Reported to 7.5 cm. Red Sea and east coast of Africa (type locality, Zanzibar) to the western Pacific where it ranges from Taiwan to the Great Barrier Reef; in Oceania only from New Caledonia and Guam.

DEVIL SCORPIONFISH
Scorpaenopsis diabolus (Cuvier in C & V, 1829)
Dorsal rays XII,9; anal rays III,5; pectoral rays 17–19 (usually 18); longitudinal scale series 43–45; back elevated below spinous portion of dorsal fin, giving a humpback appearance; mouth very strongly oblique, forming an angle of about 60–70°; no palatine teeth (true of all *Scorpaenopsis*); interorbital space broad, 3.9–4.55 in head length; very deep occipital and suborbital pits; upper opercular spine double; color highly variable; axil of pectoral fins black with white flecks inwardly, then red and yellow bands with a black spot in upper middle part of fin. Largest specimen, 23.4 cm, from Hawaiian Islands. Wide-ranging throughout the Indo-Pacific region on shallow reefs and rocky substrata; type locality, New Guinea. When disturbed, it moves its pectoral fins foward to reveal the bright colors of the inner surface, hence a warning to the intruder of its venomous spines.

FLASHER SCORPIONFISH
Scorpaenopsis macrochir Ogilby, 1910
Dorsal rays XII,9; anal rays III,5; pectoral rays 16–18 (usually 17); longitudinal scale series 42–45; also humpbacked like *Scorpaenopsis diabolus* and also with a broad interorbital space, deep occipital and suborbital pits, and double upper opercular spine; mouth forming an angle of about 40–50°; color variable; axil of pectoral fins with small black spots, the inner surface orange with a broad submarginal black band; a narrow, triangular black mark inside mouth at front of upper jaw. Largest specimen, the holotype, 13.6 cm. Known in the Indian Ocean only from Mauritius and Australia; in the Pacific from the Ryukyu Islands to southern Queensland (type locality, Bulwer Island, Brisbane), east to Guam, Caroline Islands, and the islands of French Polynesia. May be found in brackish habitats; occurs from tidepools to 80 m (from trawls).

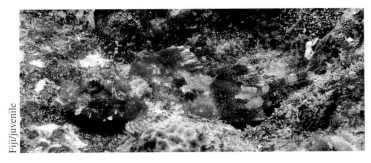

Fiji/juvenile

Fiji

PAPUAN SCORPIONFISH
Scorpaenopsis papuensis (Cuvier in C & V, 1829)
Dorsal rays XII,9; anal rays III,5; pectoral rays 18–20 (usually 19, rarely 20); longitudinal scale series 48–55; snout moderately long, 2.85–3.15 in head length; occipital pit shallow with a transverse ridge on its posterior edge in adults; longest dorsal spine 2.3–2.65 in head length; penultimate dorsal spine 1.9–2.2 in last spine; a long fimbriate supraocular tentacle often present; chin with prominent fringed flaps; nothing diagnostic in color pattern. Largest specimen, 19.5 cm, from Moorea. Western Pacific from the Ryukyu Islands to the southern Great Barrier Reef, east to Guam and the Society Islands; Western Australia and Mauritius the only Indian Ocean records; type locality, New Guinea. Found on coral reefs and rubble substrata; collected by the author from depths of 0.5–42 m. Sometimes misidentified as *Scorpaenopsis oxycephala*, which differs in having 59–67 scales in longitudinal series, no scales on the opercle between the opercular spines (present in *papuensis*), and usually 20 pectoral rays.

Papua New Guinea

POSS' SCORPIONFISH
Scorpaenopsis possi Randall & Eschmeyer, 2001
Dorsal rays XII,9; anal rays III,5; pectoral rays 17–18 (rarely 18); longitudinal scale series 43–50; body depth 2.6–3.05 in standard length; occipital pit present but not deep; an extra spine anterior to tympanic spine (absent in small juveniles); supraocular tentacle small to absent in adults; a fringe of small tentacles on chin and along lower jaw; mottled dark reddish to brownish gray. Largest specimen, 19.4 cm, from Rarotonga. Red Sea and east coast of Africa to Caroline Islands and Pitcairn Islands (type locality). Usually found on coral reefs or rocky bottom; depth range, 1–40 m. A southern form from Fiji to the southern Great Barrier Reef lacks the extra spine before each tympanic spine (Randall & Eschmeyer, 2001).

Marquesas Islands/subadult

123

Marquesas Islands

MARQUESAN SCORPIONFISH
Scorpaenopsis pusilla Randall & Eschmeyer, 2001
Dorsal rays XII,9; anal rays III,5; pectoral rays 17; longitudinal scale series 43; body depth 2.6–2.75 in standard length; snout short, its dorsal profile steep, 3.55–3.6 in head length; occipital pit moderately deep; coronal spines present or absent; upper opercular spine double; supraocular tentacle large; red with tips of spines of dorsal fin white. Known from only 2 specimens, 3.5–4 cm (the smallest a mature female) collected at Nuku Hiva, Marquesas Islands, in 17 m. Related to the small *Scorpaenopsis cotticeps,* which differs in having 33–37 scales and the interorbital ridges continuing to tip of tympanic spines.

Flores, Indonesia

RAMA RAO'S SCORPIONFISH
Scorpaenopsis ramaraoi Randall & Eschmeyer, 2001
Dorsal rays XII,9; anal rays III,5; pectoral rays 17–19; longitudinal scale series 45–49; snout not long, 3.2–3.45 in head length; suborbital ridge with 4 spines, the first on lacrimal short and more erect; ridge above this spine sharp and angling upward, with a pointed anterior tip; interorbital ridges prominent, ending on a short ridge at front of incurved margin of shallow occipital pit; no coronal spines and no extra spine anterior to each tympanic spine; fourth or fifth dorsal spines longest, 2.35–2.9 in head length; penultimate dorsal spine 1.4–1.8 in last spine; fimbriate supraocular tentacle varying from smaller than adjacent spine to as long as eye diameter; chin with prominent fringed flaps; color variable, often dark reddish to brownish gray, strongly mottled with dark brown. Largest specimen, 20.8 cm. Known from India and Sri Lanka (type locality) to the western Pacific; recently recorded from New Caledonia (Motomura, in press); collected by the author as shallow as 1 m, but taken by trawls as deep as 60 m.

BANDEDFIN SCORPIONFISH
Scorpaenopsis vittapinna Randall & Eschmeyer, 2001
Dorsal rays XII,9; anal rays III,5; pectoral rays 17–19 (usually 18, rarely 19); longitudinal scale series 40–44; body depth 2.75–3.2 in standard length; snout length 3.0–3.3 in head length; mouth slightly oblique; no median interorbital ridge; occipital pit shallow; upper opercular spine divided into 2 to 4 points; a broad black band across anal and pelvic fins. Reaches 8.5 cm. Known from the Red Sea, South Africa (type locality, Natal), Comoro Islands, Mauritius, Maldive Islands, East Indies, Caroline Islands, Coral Sea, Fiji, Samoa Islands, and Society Islands; occurs in coral reefs or on rubble bottom from depths of 7–28 m. Formerly identified as *Scorpaenopsis brevifrons,* a name now restricted to the related larger species of the Hawaiian Islands with a longer snout and modally 19 pectoral rays.

Fiji

YELLOWSPOTTED SCORPIONFISH

Sebastapistes cyanostigma (Bleeker, 1856)

Dorsal rays XII,9; anal rays III,5–6; pectoral rays 15–16 (rarely 15); scales ctenoid, 42–45 in longitudinal series; palatine teeth present; suborbital ridge double with a blunt spine at end; no coronal spines; 5 spines on lacrimal, 3 extending ventrally over upper lip; lower opercular spine not preceded by a ridge; gray to red with dense white dots and scattered large yellow to white spots on body. Reaches 7 cm. Red Sea and east coast of Africa to the Line Islands, Samoa Islands, and throughout Micronesia; in the western Pacific from the Ryukyu Islands to the Great Barrier Reef and New Caledonia; type locality, Buru, Molucca Islands, Indonesia; typically found among the branches of live coral (especially *Pocillopora*). *Sebastapistes albobrunnea* (Günther) and *S. kowiensis* (Smith) are synonyms.

Line Islands

FOWLER'S SCORPIONFISH

Sebastapistes fowleri (Pietschmann, 1934)

Dorsal rays XII,9; anal rays III,5; pectoral rays 16; scales ctenoid, 32–33 in longitudinal series; no palatine teeth (other *Sebastapistes* with palatine teeth); spines dorsally on head low; no occipital pit; no coronal, postorbital, or sphenotic spines; only a blunt spine at end of suborbital ridge, but an isolated spine below ridge; usually red to reddish orange, finely mottled with white, sometimes with blackish markings such as dark bands from eye. Attains only 4.7 cm; the smallest of the scorpionfishes; a mature female of only 2.4 cm total length. Islands of the western Indian Ocean to the Hawaiian Islands (type locality, O'ahu) and Pitcairn Islands; in the western Pacific from the Philippines to New Caledonia; collected from depths of 3–61 m; most specimens from more than 10 m in coral reefs or rubble bottoms. Formerly classified in *Scorpaenopsis* because of not having palatine teeth; reclassified in *Sebastapistes* by Randall & Poss (2002). *Sebastapistes badiorufus* Herre and *Sebastapistes klausewitz* are synonyms. Named for Henry W. Fowler, ichthyologist of the Academy of Natural Sciences of Philadelphia, whose many papers on fishes were published from 1899 to 1972.

Hawaiian Islands

Bali

MILKY SCORPIONFISH

Sebastapistes galactacma Jenkins, 1903

Dorsal rays XII,9; anal rays III,5; pectoral rays 15–16 (rarely 15); scales cycloid, 41–44 in longitudinal series; palatine teeth present; suborbital ridge with a spine at end and 1 just under ridge below eye; no occipital pit; no coronal spines; lower opercular spine preceded by a strong ridge; lacrimal with 2 spines that extend over upper lip; supraocular tentacle usually present, may be longer than eye; pink to red, finely dotted with white, usually with large indistinct white blotches on head and body. Largest, 10 cm, from Rapa (Randall et al., 1990). Known only from oceanic islands of the Pacific: Hawaiian Islands (type locality, O'ahu), Pitcairn Islands, French Polynesia, Caroline Islands, Mariana Islands, and Ogasawara Islands. Eschmeyer & Randall (1975) reported the habitat as coral and rubble areas, and the depth from near shore to 29 m. Sometimes found in branching coral.

Hawaiian Islands

Great Barrier Reef

Guam

Papua New Guinea

New Caledonia

MAURITIAN SCORPIONFISH
Sebastapistes mauritiana (Cuvier in C & V, 1829)
Dorsal rays XII,9; anal rays III,5; pectoral rays 15–16 (usually 16); scales ctenoid, 42–45 in longitudinal series; palatine teeth present; interorbital space only slightly depressed, the interorbital ridges nearly as high as supraocular ridges; occipital pit distinct; coronal spines present; suborbital ridge with a blunt spine at posterior end; lower opercular spine preceded by a ridge; lacrimal with 2 spines that extend over upper lip; brown to reddish brown, mottled with blackish and white. Largest specimen, 9.5 cm, from the Marquesas Islands. Occurs throughout most of the Indo-Pacific region; replaced in the Hawaiian Islands by the related *Sebastapistes ballieui* (Sauvage). Reported as having passed via the Suez Canal to the Mediterranean Sea. A shallow-water species, often found in tidepools. *Sebastapistes megastoma* (Sauvage) from Rarotonga is a synonym.

BARCHIN SCORPIONFISH
Sebastapistes strongia (Cuvier in C & V, 1829)
Dorsal rays XII,9; anal rays III,5; pectoral rays nearly always 15; scales ctenoid, 41–45 in longitudinal series; palatine teeth present; spines dorsally on head low; no occipital pit; no coronal spines; suborbital ridge with a spine at posterior end, sometimes one before it, and an isolated spine under eye below ridge; lower opercular spine preceded by a ridge; lacrimal with 2 spines that extend ventrally over upper lip; pores of cephalic lateralis system prominent (shared with *fowleri*); supraocular tentacle often present, and may be much longer than eye; brown to reddish brown, spotted and mottled with blackish and white; narrow dark bars along side of lower jaw; often a dark blotch below first 3 dorsal spines. Reported to 9.5 cm. Red Sea and east coast of Africa to the Caroline Islands (type locality, Strong Island = Kusiae) and Society Islands; in the western Pacific from the Ryukyu Islands to the Great Barrier Reef and New Caledonia. Known from tidepools to 37 m; most specimens from less than 3 m. *Scorpaena bynoensis* Richardson, *Scorpaena tristis* Klunzinger, *Scorpaena nuchalis* Günther, *Kantopus oglinus* Smith, and *Phenacoscorpius nebulosus* Smith are among the 13 synonyms.

DARKSPOTTED SCORPIONFISH
Sebastapistes tinkhami (Fowler, 1946)
Dorsal rays XII,9; anal rays III,5; pectoral rays 15–16 (rarely 15); scales ctenoid, 50–54 in longitudinal series; palatine teeth present; no occipital pit; no coronal spines; double suborbital ridge to below posterior edge of eye, one continuing to preopercular margin; lacrimal with 5 spines, 2 or 3 of which extend over maxilla; no obvious supraocular tentacle; lower opercular spine preceded by a scaled area (no ridge); body and fins with numerous small dark brown to dark red spots; head with dark bands or large spots around eye. Largest specimen, 10 cm, from the Marquesas Islands. Distribution subtropical: Natal in the Indian Ocean, Ryukyu Islands (type locality), Taiwan, and Minami-tori-shima (Marcus Island) in the North Pacific; New Caledonia to the Pitcairn Islands in the South. Collections from depths of 1–30 m.

Sabah

Sulawesi

LEAF SCORPIONFISH
Taenianotus triacanthus Lacepède, 1802

Dorsal rays XII,10–11 (usually 10); anal rays III,5–6 (rarely 5); pectoral rays 14–15 (usually 14); scales modified to small sharp papillae; body very compressed, the width about 3 in the depth; dorsal fin very elevated, its origin above posterior edge of eye, linked by membrane to basal half of caudal fin; extremely variable in color: black, red, yellow, brown, or nearly white, and var-

iously blotched. Reaches 10 cm. Occurs from east coast of Africa to the Hawaiian Islands and French Polynesia; in the western Pacific from southern Japan to New South Wales; one record from the Galápagos Islands; type locality unknown. Reported from depths of less than 1 to 135 m. Often rocks to and fro to simulate a bit of flotsom such as a leaf being moved by surge. Periodically sheds the outer layer of its skin. There seem to be no reports of venomous spines for this species.

STONEFISHES (SYNANCEINAE)

DARUMA STINGER
Erosa erosa (Langsdorf in C & V, 1829)

Dorsal rays XIV,9; anal rays II,5–6 (usually 6); pectoral rays 14–16; pelvic rays I,4; head very large and not depressed, the eyes lateral; snout extremely short, its dorsal profile nearly vertical; mouth strongly oblique; a bony ridge connecting orbits, followed by a deep occipital pit; lacrimal with 2 broad spines over upper lip; suborbital ridge without distinct spines; color variable. Western Pacific from southern Japan (type locality, seas of Japan) to the southern Great Barrier Reef, New Caledonia, and Tonga; in Western Australia to 21°S. Often taken in trawls to depths as great as 90 m. Dangerously venomous. Also known as the Pacific Monkeyfish.

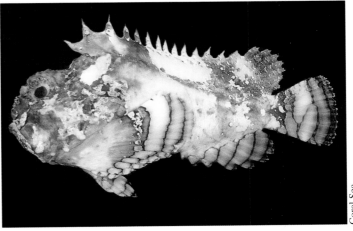

Coral Sea

CALEDONIAN STINGER
Inimicus caledonicus (Sauvage, 1878)

Dorsal rays XVII,8–9 (usually 8); anal rays II,11–12; pectoral rays 12, the lower 2 free from membrane (upper 2 filamentous only in juveniles); snout longer than postorbital length of head, the postorbital distance 1.2–1.4 in snout; first 3 dorsal spines broadly linked with membrane; remaining dorsal spines with membrane on only about basal one-fifth of spines; inside of pectoral fins most diagnostic, pale with a broad black band in outer middle part and a large black spot near base on upper one-third of fin (Eschmeyer et al., 1979: fig. 1 h). Largest reported, 22 cm. Known from New Caledonia (type locality), Queensland, Nicobar Islands, and Andaman Islands, in about 15–60 m.

Coral Sea

127

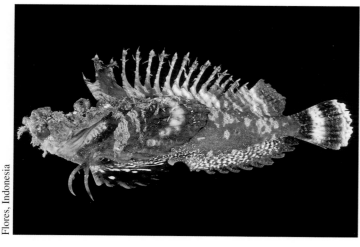

Flores, Indonesia

Sulawesi

BEARDED GHOULFISH

Inimicus didactylus (Pallas, 1769)

Dorsal rays XV-XVII (usually XVI),7–9; anal rays II,10–12; pectoral rays 12, the lower 2 free from membrane (upper 2 filamentous only in juveniles); snout longer than postorbital length of head, the postorbital distance 1.2–1.7 in snout; first 3 dorsal spines broadly linked with membrane; remaining dorsal spines with membrane on only about basal third of spines; inside of pectoral fins most diagnostic (see figure of 2 fish viewed from

Sulawesi

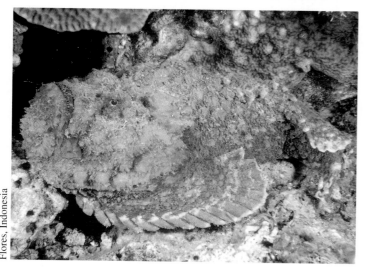

Flores, Indonesia

above flashing the warning coloration of the inside of their pectoral fins). Known from New Caledonia, Vanuatu, Solomon Islands, Papua New Guinea, Indonesia, Singapore, Thailand, Vietnam, and Philippines; type locality given as Indian Ocean (perhaps in error). Usually found on silty reefs and adjacent sand or mud-sand substrata in protected waters from near shore to about 80 m. Readily buries in sand. Wounds from the spines of this and other species of *Inimicus* are extremely painful.

ESTUARINE STONEFISH

Synanceia horrida (Linnaeus, 1766)

Dorsal rays XIII-XIV (usually XIII),6; anal rays III,5; pectoral rays 15–17 (usually 16); skin thick, with wart-like protuberances; head broad and depressed; eyes widely separated, directly mainly upward, strongly elevated with a pronounced bony ridge above posterior corner, joined by a continuous ridge between orbits; a deep pit behind and below each eye; mouth opening dorsal, the gape vertical, the lips with a fringe of cirri; dorsal spines nearly equal, the second to fourth largest, all with a venom gland in the lateral groove; pectoral fins large and fleshy; color variable. Attains at least 30 cm. Known from the Andaman Sea, Indo-Malayan region (type locality, East Indies), northern half of Australia, and New Caledonia. Occurs in protected waters of bays and lagoons, including estuarine areas; may be found in very shallow water of reef flats or seagrass beds. Wounds from the venomous spines can be lethal.

STONEFISH

Synanceia verrucosa Bloch & Schneider, 1801

Dorsal rays XII-XIV (usually XIII),5–7; anal rays III,5–6; pectoral rays 17–19 (usually 18); skin thick, with wart-like protuberances; head broad and dorsally flattened; eyes widely separated, directly mainly upward; a deep pit behind and a smaller one below each eye; mouth opening dorsal, the gape vertical; dorsal spines about equal in length; pectoral fins large and fleshy. Color variable, generally matching surroundings. Largest examined, 37.2 cm, from the northern Red Sea. Indo-Pacific except the Hawaiian Islands; type locality, Indian Ocean. Usually found on coral reefs, often in caves or under ledges, but may bury in sand with only the eyes and mouth barely visible. This and *Synanceia horrida* are the most feared venomous fishes in the sea (see family introduction).

WASPFISHES (TETRAROGINAE)

Sulawesi

Philippines

COCKATOO WASPFISH
Ablabys taenianotus (Cuvier, 1829)
Dorsal rays XVII-XVIII (usually XVII),6–7 (usually 7); anal rays III,4–5 (usually 5); pectoral rays 11–12; longitudinal scale series about 90; body strongly compressed; origin of dorsal fin above front edge of eye; anterior spinous portion of dorsal fin high and usually held fully erect; second dorsal spine longest, nearly as long as head length; color variable but usually brown or gray to brownish red, finely flecked with white; front of head sometimes abruptly white. Attains 12 cm. Andaman Islands and East Indies north to Taiwan and southern coast of China, south to coasts of Australia, and east to Lord Howe Island, Norfolk Island, New Caledonia, and Fiji; Poss in Carpenter & Niem (1999b) questioned the type locality of Mauritius. A shallow-water species that may be found among algal-covered rocks or on open silty sand bottom. It sways back and forth, thus emulating the effect of surge (even when there is no surge). Of some value in the aquarium trade.

WHITEBELLIED WASPFISH
Richardsonichthys leucogaster (Richardson, 1848)
Dorsal rays XIII,8; anal rays III,6; pectoral rays 15–16; skin scaleless; lacrimal with 2 spines that curve laterally and posteriorly, the posterior one nearly twice as long; upper preopercular spine more than half eye diameter in length; dorsal-fin origin over posterior one-third of eye, the first spine more than half length of second; membranes of spinous portion of dorsal fin deeply incised; color variable, but ventral half of body generally red (white in preservative); often a white patch over interorbital. Reaches 7 cm. Scattered localities from Zanzibar and Seychelles to New Caledonia; most records from Indonesia; type locality, Sea of China. Usually found in protected areas on silty sand in which it buries by day. Dangerously venomous.

LONGSPINE WASPFISH
Paracentropogon longispinis (Cuvier in C & V, 1829)
Dorsal rays XII-XV (usually XIII or XIV),7–8; anal rays II,5; pectoral rays II,10–11 (rarely 10); longitudinal scale series 65–75; body depth 2.7–2.9 in standard length; origin of dorsal fin above center of eye; membranes of spinous portion of dorsal fin deeply incised; grayish to reddish brown, finely dotted with white; front of head may be abuptly white; a small white spot often present above lateral line below base of tenth dorsal spine. Attains about 11 cm. Taiwan and southern China, south to northwestern Australia, west to India; 1 record from New Caledonia; type locality, Ambon, Molucca Islands. Inshore to 70 m, generally on coral reefs or rocky bottom; nocturnal. Poss in Carpenter & Niem (1999b) discussed regional variation, and Michael (1998) illustrated color variants. Highly venomous; Sadovy & Cornish (2000) noted that wounds inflicted by the spines have resulted in hospitalizations in Hong Kong.

Sulawesi

VELVETFISHES
(APLOACTINIDAE)

This small scorpaeniform family consists of about 17 genera and 37 species, most of which are restricted to Indo-Malayan and Australian seas. All are small, generally less than 7 cm. The body of the majority of species is covered with modified prickly scales, giving the skin a velvet-like texture; some have lost scales except for the lateral line, and the skin is smooth; most have a fleshy pad anteriorly on the isthmus. Instead of sharp head spines as found on scorpaenids, the head usually has knob-like protuberances, the most prominent on the lacrimal and edge of

129

preopercle. The origin of the dorsal fin is above or nearly above the eye, the spines (usually blunt) varying from IX to XIV, followed by 7–16 unbranched rays; the first 3–5 spines usually somewhat detached and often higher than the rest of fin (in 4 species forming a separate fin); anal fin with 0-V weak to blunt spines and 5–16 unbranched rays; pelvic fins with a strong spine and 1–3 rays; caudal fin rounded. Numerous small conical teeth present in jaws and usually on vomer, but none on palatines. Although believed to be related to the highly venomous subfamilies Synanceinae and Tetraroginae, there appear to be no reports of venomous aploactinids. Only 1 species is known from the South Pacific area covered by this book. Poss & Eschmeyer (1978) reviewed the genus *Paraploactis*, and Poss in Carpenter & Niem (1999b) listed the species of the western and central Pacific and provided a key.

INSULAR VELVETFISH
Paraploactis sp.

Dorsal rays VIII,11; anal rays II,8; pectoral rays 14; pelvic rays I,3; lateral-line tubes 11; skin with fleshy wart-like protuberances; lacrimal with 3 knob-like spines, and edge of preopercle with 5; suborbital ridge with a single blunt spine; a deep pit in interorbital bordered by a ridge to each side and one posteriorly; origin of dorsal fin over posterior half of eye; space between third and fourth dorsal spines much greater than that between other spines; third and fourth dorsal spines about twice as long as more posterior spines; reddish brown, finely mottled with darker spots and white flecks; a dark brown spot nearly as large as pupil at rear base of dorsal and anal fins. Known from a 5.3-cm specimen from Fiji, misidentified as *Aploactis milesii* Richardson by Seale (1935), and a 4.8-cm one from New

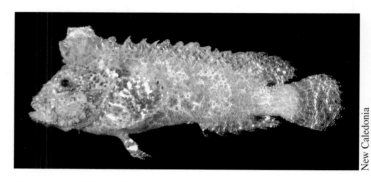

New Caledonia

Caledonia collected by the author outside the barrier reef in 3 m. Very similar to *Paraploactis obbesi* (Weber) from the Sulu Archipelago and *P. kagoshimensis* (Ishikawa) from Japan; specimens under study by Stuart G. Poss.

CORAL CROUCHERS
(CARACANTHIDAE)

Also known as orbicular velvetfishes, these small fishes are relatives of the scorpionfishes. The family consists of a single genus and 4 species, 2 wide-ranging in the Indo-Pacific region, 1 from the western Indian Ocean, and 1 endemic to the Hawaiian Islands. They are small (generally less than 5 cm), oval, compressed, and densely covered with fleshy tubercles that are larger and more firm anteriorly on the head and very small dorsally on the nape and below the dorsal fin. The lateral line is present as a series of tubed scales. The lacrimal (preorbital) bone beneath the front part of the eye has a large ventral spine that angles posteriorly, preceded by 1 or 2 small spines; the edge of preopercle with 5 well-spaced blunt spines; a continuous dorsal fin with VII or VIII spines and 11 or 12 soft rays; anal fin II,11–12; caudal fin rounded; pelvic fins small with I,2–3 rays. Found among the branches of coral of the genera *Pocillopora*, *Acropora*, and *Stylophora*, but easily overlooked. Not reported as venomous.

Line Islands

SPOTTED CORAL CROUCHER
Caracanthus maculatus (Gray, 1831)

Dorsal rays VII-VIII,12–13 (usually VIII,12); anal rays II,11–12; pectoral rays 13–14; body depth about 1.7 in standard length; lower anterior edge of lacrimal bone with a single small spine; dorsal fin deeply notched; gray with numerous small, irregular, dark red to dark brown spots on head, body, and basally on dorsal and caudal fins. Reaches 5 cm. Lives deep in the spaces among the branches of corals, particularly of the genus *Pocillopora*. Occurs throughout the tropical central and western Pacific except the Hawaiian Islands; type locality, Hao Atoll, Tuamotu Archipelago.

GRAY CORAL CROUCHER
Caracanthus unipinna (Gray, 1831)

Dorsal rays VII,12–13; anal rays II,11–13 (usually 12); pectoral rays 12–13 (usually 13); body depth about 1.8 in standard length; lower anterior edge of lacrimal bone with 2 small spines; dorsal fin moderately notched; uniform gray-brown in life. Reaches 5 cm. East coast of Africa to French Polynesia and throughout Micronesia; in the western Pacific from southern Japan to the Great Barrier Reef; type locality, Pacific Ocean. Lives among the branches of living coral.

Ogasawara Islands

Crocodile Fish, *Cymbacephalus beauforti*, Palau

FLATHEADS
(PLATYCEPHALIDAE)

The flathead family, one of the order Scorpaeniformes, consists of 19 genera and about 60 species, nearly all from the Indo-Pacific region. Most are found in coastal waters of continents or the large islands of the East Indies. They have a depressed body, and the head is even more flattened, with bony ridges usually bearing spines or serrations. The eyes are oriented more dorsally than laterally; the upper part of the iris has a lappet that extends over the upper part of the pupil; it varies from a simple lobe to a complexly branched structure. The mouth is large with the lower jaw projecting; villiform teeth are present in the jaws, on the vomer, and usually on the palatines (only a few species with canine teeth in the jaws). There are 2 dorsal fins, the first of VII to X (usually IX) spines, the first spine short and may be barely connected by membrane to the second spine or even separate; soft dorsal and anal fins with 10–15 rays; pelvic fins I,5, broadly separated, their bases distinctly posterior to those of the pectoral fins; the scales are small and ctenoid. The coloration is generally close to that of the surroundings. Most of the species occur on mud or sand bottoms, typically buried in the sediment, at least by day, except for their eyes and the slit of the mouth. Crustaceans and small fishes are the principal prey. Not known to be venomous. Only a few species range out to the islands of Oceania (none to the Hawaiian Islands). Those included here are ones that occur in the South Pacific area on coral reefs or adjacent sand areas. Knapp in Carpenter & Niem (1999b) reviewed the species of flatheads of the central and western Pacific.

131

Bali

CROCODILE FISH
Cymbacephalus beauforti (Knapp, 1973)
Dorsal rays IX-X + 11; anal rays 11; pectoral rays 19–21; lateral-line scales 50–55 (usually 52 or 53); vomerine teeth in 2 separate patches (true of other South Pacific species); a prominent pit behind eye; 10–12 dermal papillae on upper surface of eye; maxilla ending well before eye; usually 2 short, nearly equal, pre-opercular spines; suborbital ridge with only a few small spines posteriorly; numerous irregular gray-brown spots, the narrow space around them a pale reticulum; a series of broad black bars on body above anal fin, and a saddle-like black bar on caudal peduncle. Reported to 58 cm. Known from the Ryukyu Islands, Philippines, eastern Indonesia, New Guinea, Palau (type locality), Yap, and New Caledonia. A shallow-water species of coral reefs and sand-rubble areas. Easily overlooked in spite of its large size because of its camouflage; may be approached very closely.

BROADHEAD FLATHEAD
Eurycephalus arenicola (Schultz in Schultz et al., 1966)
Dorsal rays VIII-IX + 11–12 (usually 12); anal rays 11–13 (usually 12); pectoral rays 19–22; lateral-line scales 50–54; snout length 3.0–3.5 in head length; interorbital width broad, 1.0–2.0 in greatest eye diameter; maxilla just reaching or extending slightly posterior to a vertical through front edge of eye; no papillae on lips; suborbital ridge with 4 or 5 spines; preopercle with 2 or 3 spines at corner, the uppermost largest; tan, finely flecked with dark brown, shading to white ventrally; about 6 indistinct dark bars and scattered small pale blotches often present dorsally on body; fins without prominent black markings. Reported to 37 cm. East coast of Africa to the Mariana Islands, Marshall Islands (type locality, Rongelap Atoll), Caroline Islands, and Fiji; Ryukyu Islands and Taiwan to Great Barrier Reef. Found in sand in coral-reef areas from the shallows to at least 30 m. This species and *otaitensis* were reclassified from *Thysanophrys* to the new genus *Eurycephalus* by Imamura (1996).

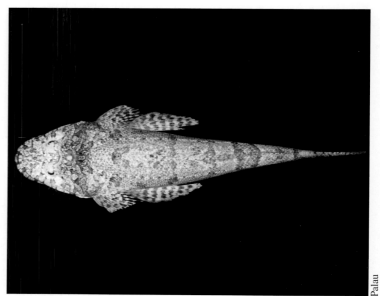
Palau

Ogasawara Islands

FRINGELIP FLATHEAD
Eurycephalus otaitensis (Cuvier in C & V, 1829)
Dorsal rays VIII-IX (usually IX) + 11–12 (usually 11); anal rays 11–12 (usually 12); lateral-line scales 50–54; snout 2.3–2.4 in head length; interorbital width 2.0–2.5 in eye diameter; maxilla extending posterior to a vertical at front edge of eye; lips with a row of fleshy papillae; suborbital ridge with about 5 stout spines; interopercular flap absent; preopercle with 2 or 3 spines at corner, the uppermost largest; whitish, finely and densely mottled with brown; scattered small white spots, particularly along lateral line; rays of fins with small black and white spots. Reaches about 25 cm. East coast of Africa to Society Islands and Tuamotu Archipelago; Ryukyu and Ogasawara Islands to Great Barrier Reef; type locality, Tahiti. Common in sand within and around coral reefs, but rarely seen. *Platycephalus malayanus* Bleeker and *Thysanophrys papillo-labium* Schultz are synonyms.

TWOSPOT FLATHEAD

Onigocia bimaculata Knapp, Imamura & Sakashita, 2000
Dorsal rays VIII-IX + 10–12; anal rays 10–12; pectoral rays
19–22; lateral-line scales 32–39, the anterior 2–4 with a spine;
scales on body ctenoid except some cycloid ventrally; gill rakers
6–9; head depressed; interorbital space narrow, 0.5–1.9% standard length; anterior edge of orbit usually with 3 spines; no postorbital spines; supraorbital ridge serrate; suborbital ridge serrate;
interopercular flap well developed; maxilla reaching to or a little
posterior to a vertical at front edge of eye; preopercle with 3
spines, the uppermost largest, with a supplemental spine at base;
no supraorbital flap or cirrus; iris lappet bilobed; light tan with 4
or 5 indistinct, brown, saddle-like bars dorsally on body; 2 small

Coral Sea

blackish spots anteriorly in first dorsal fin; pelvic fins with a
large black spot near base and 1 or 2 small black spots distally.
A small species, the largest of 67 specimens, 8.3 cm. Known
from Red Sea, Comoro Islands, Mauritius, Ryukyu Islands (type
locality), Philippines, Caroline Islands, Coral Sea, New
Caledonia, Tonga, American Samoa, and the Society Islands;
collections mainly from coral sand at depths of 3–30 m.

Flores, Indonesia (R. M. Pyle)

Seychelles

BROADBAND FLATHEAD

Onigocia pedimacula (Regan, 1908)
Dorsal rays IX + 11; anal rays 10–11 (usually 11); pectoral rays
19–23 (usually 21 or 22); lateral-line scales 29–33, the anterior
2–6 with a spine; gill rakers 4–5 (usually 4); head depressed and
broad; anterior edge of orbit with 3–5 spines, the posterior with
2 antrorse spines; supraorbital ridge serrate; a single finely serrate suborbital ridge; no interopercular flap; maxilla reaching to
or posterior to a vertical at front edge of eye; preopercle usually
with 3 spines, the uppermost largest and bearing a supplemental
spine at base; no supraorbital flap or cirrus; iris lappet with 2 to
several lobes; pale gray with dark bars, the broadest beneath first
dorsal fin, it and oblique bar below rear of second dorsal fin the
darkest; a narrow dark bar at base of caudal fin; pelvic fins with
a dark blotch in middle and a smaller one at base. Reaches 11 cm.
Reported from east coast of Africa, Pakistan, Maldive Islands
(type locality), Indonesia, Philippines, and northwestern Australia to Queensland, Solomon Islands, and Tonga; usually
caught in trawls; known from depths of 15–110 m.

SERRATED FLATHEAD

Rogadius serratus (Cuvier in C & V, 1829)
Dorsal rays IX + 11–12 (usually 11); anal rays 11; pectoral rays
20–23; lateral-line scales 50–54; scales above lateral line to base
of soft dorsal fin 8–10; maxilla reaching posterior to a vertical
through front edge of eye; iris lappet bilobed; usually 4 upper
preopercular spines, the dorsalmost longest and bearing a supplemental spine at base; lower edge of preopercle with a strong
antrorse spine; supraorbital and suborbital ridges finely serrate;
preocular spine with a supplemental spine; no interopercular
flap; 2 series of large dark brown blotches on upper half of body;
a dark brown bar under eye; dorsal and caudal fins with black
spots, those on caudal fin large. Reaches 24 cm. Western Indian
Ocean to East Indies and New Caledonia; type locality, Sri
Lanka. Recorded from 11 to 45 m; found on sand, generally near
coral reefs; buries by day, emerging at night.

THORNY FLATHEAD

Rogadius pristiger (Cuvier in C & V, 1829)
Dorsal rays IX + 10–12 (usually 11); anal rays 10–12 (usually
11); pectoral rays 20–24 (usually 22 or 23); lateral-line scales
49–55 (usually 52 or 53); scales above lateral line to base of soft
dorsal fin 5–7; maxilla reaching posterior to a vertical through
front edge of eye; iris lappet bilobed; usually 4 or 5 upper preopercular spines, the dorsalmost longest and bearing a supplemental spine at base; lower edge of preopercle with a strong
antrorse spine; supraorbital and suborbital ridges finely serrate;
no preorbital spine (instead a few small serrae); 1 preocular
spine; no interopercular flap; light brown dorsally, paler ventrally, with 4 or 5 dark bars; lower lip with 4–6 dark cross bands;
spinous dorsal fin with a black margin; dorsal soft rays with dark
spots; paired fins pale with many black spots, some nearly as
large as pupil; caudal fin with dark bars and a narrow white posterior margin. Reaches about 20 cm. Red Sea and Gulf of Oman
south to Mozambique and Madagasar, east to the Indo-Malayan
region, northern Australia, New Caledonia, and Tonga; described
from New Guinea and Sulawesi. Usually taken by trawls on sand
or mud bottoms; depth range, 15–95 m.

Sulawesi (night)

133

LONGSNOUT FLATHEAD
Thysanophrys chiltonae Schultz in Schultz et al., 1966

Dorsal rays IX + 11–13 (usually 12); anal rays 11; pectoral rays 19–22; lateral-line scales 50–55; snout long, 2.9–3.0 in head length; interorbital width narrow, 3.8–7.2 (usually 5–6) in greatest eye diameter; maxilla not reaching a vertical through front edge of eye; no papillae on lips; suborbital ridge with 4–7 spines; preopercle with 2 or 3 spines at corner, the uppermost largest; light gray-brown with 4 or 5 indistinct dark bars dorsally on body and scattered small dark brown blotches; usually a dark band across interorbital and extending as a bar below eye; dorsal and caudal fins with dark spots on rays, those on caudal larger and forming about 3 bars in fin; a blackish blotch in outer part of spinous dor-

Sulawesi

sal fin. Attains about 22 cm. Indo-Pacific except the Hawaiian Islands; type locality, Rongelap Atoll, Marshall Islands. Usually found in sand within or near coral reefs; collected by the author in 1–54 m.

HELMET GURNARDS
(DACTYLOPTERIDAE)

These distinctive fishes are usually called flying gurnards, but this is not an appropriate name because they do not "fly" like flyingfishes. They have very long pectoral fins that can be extended broadly to the side of the body; this is done when threatened and serves to make the fish seem much larger. The external bones of the head are united to form an armor, so helmet gurnards is a better common name for these fishes. This family has long been classified in the order Scorpaeniformes. Imamura (2000), however, related it instead to the Malacanthidae. This can be questioned, so the family remains here with the scorpaeniforms. The head has a very long spine at the corner of the preopercle, and the shoulder girdle extends shield-like posteriorly, ending in a sharp spine. The mouth is ventral and protractile, the teeth very small and nodular. The scales are scute-like, resulting in a longitudinal series of ridges on the body. The dorsal fin has I or II isolated spines, the first very long, just behind the head. The rest of the fin is divided into separate spinous and soft portions. The pectoral fins have 30 or more rays, including the anterior 5 that are separated from the rest of the fin and used for probing the substratum in search of food. The pelvic fins of I,4 rays are used for "walking" on the

Helmet Gurnard, *Dactyloptena orientalis*, Hawaiian Islands

bottom. These fishes live on sand, rubble, or mud bottoms where they feed mainly on benthic crustaceans and small mollusks. The late postlarval stage has a more massive helmet-like cover on the head and even larger preopercular and posttemporal (shoulder) spines; it is often caught after being attracted to a light at the surface at night. The family consists of 2 genera, the monotypic *Dactylopterus* of the Atlantic and the Indo-Pacific *Dactyloptena* with 6 species (Eschmeyer, 1997). Only one species, *D. orientalis*, ranges to the islands of Oceania.

134

HELMET GURNARD
Dactyloptena orientalis (Cuvier, 1829)

Dorsal rays I + I +V + 9; anal rays 6–7; pectoral rays 32–35; pelvic rays I,4–5; longitudinal scale series 45–47; body moderately elongate, the depth 5.1–6.6 in standard length; preopercular spine not extending posterior to posttemporal spine; interorbital space moderately concave, the least width 13–15% standard length; isolated first dorsal spine as long or longer than head (measured to end of preopercular spine); second isolated dorsal spine short, about half length of third spine; pectoral fins reaching to or beyond base of caudal fin, the distal end of the rays free of membrane; color variable, light yellowish brown to light greenish brown dorsally, usually with many round brown spots, shading to nearly white ventrally; pectoral fins of adults with prominent dark orangish to brown spots that may be more close-set basally in middle part of fin; pectoral fins of juveniles mostly black. Reported to reach 40 cm, but any over 30 cm would be unusually large. The only wide-ranging species of the genus, occurring from the Red Sea and east coast of Africa to the Hawaiian Islands and Tuamotu Archipelago; described from specimens from Mauritius and Waigeo, Indonesia.

Hawaiian Islands

GLASSFISHES
(AMBASSIDAE)

These fishes of this family, one of the many in the largest order, Perciformes, are often classified in the family Chandidae, but Ambassidae appears to have priority. The family consists of eight genera and 41 species, about 21 of which are confined to fresh water. The rest are brackish-water fishes, many of which can also be found in fresh water. Most species have a translucent body, hence the common name glassfishes or glass perchlets. They are small (most less than 10 cm total length) with moderately deep and strongly compressed bodies, and a somewhat pointed head with a highly oblique mouth and projecting lower jaw. There is a single dorsal fin with VII or VIII spines and 7–11 soft rays; anal fin with III spines and 7–11 rays; caudal fin forked with 15 branched rays. Glassfishes resemble the cardinal-fishes (Apogonidae) but differ in having a single (though deeply notched) dorsal fin, cycloid scales that extend onto the basal part of the dorsal fin, and III instead of II anal spines. Allen & Burgess (1990) reviewed the species of Australia and New Guinea.

New Caledonia

BURU GLASSFISH
Ambassis buruensis Bleeker, 1856

Dorsal rays VIII,9, deeply notched between spines VII and VIII; anal rays III,8–9 (usually 9); pectoral rays 15; lateral line interrupted, 8–13 + 11–14; horizontal rows of scales on cheek 2; predorsal scales 11–14; lower-limb gill rakers 23–26; a single retrorse supraorbital spine; nasal spine well developed; lower preopercular ridge with 7–11 spines; vertical edge of preopercle smooth, the lower edge with 17–24 serrae; body depth 2.55–3.0 in standard length; second dorsal spine longest, 3.05–3.6 in standard length; body translucent dorsally, the scale edges dotted with black, shading to silvery with iridescence ventrally; first 2 spines and membranes of dorsal fin blackish; caudal fin dusky yellow, the lobe tips blackish; preserved specimens with a thin, dark, midlateral line. Reaches 7.5 cm. Described from Buru in the Molucca Islands; also known from elsewhere in Indonesia, Philippines, Palau, Pohnpei, Guam, and here recorded from New Caledonia (specimen collected in a mangrove area near Bouraké in less than 1 m).

Waite's Splitfin, *Luzonichthys waitei*, Luzon

GROUPERS AND ALLIES
(SERRANIDAE)

The Serranidae, represented by nearly 500 species, is one of the largest of the order Perciformes. It has been variously subdivided at the subfamily and tribal level. To avoid designation of tribes, 5 subfamilies with species in the South Pacific are treated here: Anthiinae, Epinephelinae, Grammistinae, Pseudogramminae, and the Liopropominae. Such a large and diverse family is difficult to characterize, but these fishes share the following, in general: pelvic rays I,5 (soft rays reduced in a few species), the fins below or closely following the pectorals; caudal fin with 17 or fewer principal rays; mouth large, the maxilla not forming part of the gape, its posterior end fully exposed on the cheek; lower jaw usually projecting; jaws with bands of slender sharp teeth, the medial rows of which are depressible, usually a pair of stout canine teeth anteriorly in jaws; the preopercular margin is nearly always serrate; the opercle has 3 flat spines (rarely reduced to 2); scales are small and ctenoid (or secondarily cycloid). All of the serranid fishes are carnivorous, varying from the small species

of *Pseudanthias* that feed on zooplankton to the groupers that prey mainly on fishes and crustaceans, occasionally on cephalopods. Most of the serranids for which we know the reproductive strategy are protogynous hermaphrodites, meaning that they start their mature life as females and are able to change later to functional males. Males of species of *Pseudanthias* maintain a harem of females. Some groupers have been shown to form large aggregations year after year at the same spawning site. When fishermen discover these sites, they fish them heavily, resulting in a devastating decline of the populations. Grouper spawning sites should be set aside as preserves. Randall (1980b) reviewed the perchlets of the genus *Plectranthias*, subfamily Anthiinae, most of which occur below diving depths. The large anthiine genus *Pseudanthias* has not been revised; 57 valid species are currently known, but more await description. The species of 3 genera of soapfishes of the subfamily Grammistinae are unique in producing a strong bad-tasting skin toxin when threatened that provides protection from predation (Randall et al., 1971). Baldwin et al. (1991) illustrated the distinctive larvae of 3 species of soapfishes. The podges of the subfamily Pseudogramminae (revised by Randall & Baldwin, 1997) are small secretive reef fishes of the genera *Pseudogramma*, *Aporops*, and *Suttonia*; they are allied to the soapfishes but no skin toxin has been detected. Randall & Heemstra (1991) revised the Indo-Pacific groupers of the subfamily Epinephelinae, recognizing 110 species; Randall & Taylor (1988) monographed the 18 Indo-Pacific basslets of the genus *Liopropoma*; and Randall & McCosker (1992a) the 6 splitfins of the genus *Luzonichthys*. The species of *Plectranthias* and *Liopropoma* are cryptic and rarely seen by divers, whereas the species of *Pseudanthias* and *Luzonichthys* are conspicuous in zooplankton-feeding aggregations.

ANTHIASES, SPLITFINS, AND PERCHLETS (ANTHIINAE)

WAITE'S SPLITFIN

Luzonichthys waitei (Fowler, 1931)
Dorsal rays X + 15–17 (nearly always 16), the 2 fins entirely separate; anal rays III,7; pectoral rays 17–21 (modally 19 or 20); lateral-line scales 51–59; scales without enlarged cteni; gill rakers 7–10 + 19–20; body not very elongate for the genus, the depth 3.3–3.8 in standard length; caudal fin lunate, often with lobe tips as short filaments; paired fins relatively long, the pectorals 3.2–3.45 and the pelvics 3.7–4.7 in standard length; color in life variable, but usually dull yellow on upper third of head and body and lavender-pink below; a magenta band along upper and lower edges of caudal fin, the upper continuing forward onto dorsal part of caudal peduncle. Reaches at most 7 cm. Reported from the Seychelles, the islands of the East Indies (type locality, Luzon), southern Japan, and the Loyalty Islands. Known from the depth range of 1.5–50 m. Typically found in large aggregations feeding on zooplankton.

Widi Island, Indonesia

WHITLEY'S SPLITFIN

Luzonichthys whitleyi (Smith, 1955)
Dorsal rays X + 16; anal rays III,7; pectoral rays 19–22 (modally 21); lateral-line scales 65–74; scales without enlarged cteni; gill rakers 7–8 + 20–23; body moderately elongate, the depth 4.15–5.0 in standard length; caudal fin deeply forked without filamentous tips to lobes; pectoral fins 3.65–4.35 in standard length; pelvic fins 4.6–6.0 in standard length; body yellow or orange-yellow dorsally, abruptly lavender-pink below, shading to silvery lavender on abdomen and chest and to bluish silver on lower half of head. Attains about 6.5 cm. Currently known from the Line Islands, Phoenix Islands, Loyalty Islands, and Christmas Island in the eastern Indian Ocean; type locality, Nauru. This species forms feeding aggregations with *Pseudanthias dispar*, *P. bartlettorum*, *Lepidozygus tapeinosoma*,

Line Islands

and *Ecsenius midas* in the Line Islands and Phoenix Islands; all are similar in color, bright yellow above, abruptly bright pink below. Randall & McCosker (1993) cited this mixed school as an example of social mimicry. With the populations of 5 species forming the aggregations, the mutual benefit of schooling is enhanced.

WILLIAMS' SPLITFIN

Luzonichthys williamsi Randall & McCosker, 1992
Dorsal rays X + 16; anal rays III,7; pectoral rays 21–23 (modally 22); lateral-line scales 70–78; scales on body cycloid anteriorly and ctenoid posteriorly, many with enlarged flexible cteni, the central one often elongate; body elongate, the depth 5.2–5.4 in standard length; caudal fin forked, without filamentous tips to the lobes; pectoral fins 4.4–4.7 and the pelvics 4.8–5.8 in standard length; lavender-pink, darker dorsally, shading to silvery lavender on abdomen, chest, and lower head; a narrow orange stripe bordered by black-

(J. T. Williams)

ish along back; upper and lower edges of caudal fin with a broad deep pink band. Few specimens reported, the largest 5.8 cm. Known at the current time only from the Loyalty Islands from the depth range of 21.5–50 m.

RAPA PERCHLET

Plectranthias cirrhitoides Randall, 1980

Dorsal rays X,15; anal rays III,7; pectoral rays 13, none branched, the lower rays about twice as thick as upper; branched caudal rays 15; lateral line complete, the pored scales 29–30; top of head scaled almost to nostrils; 5 oblique rows of scales on cheek; no antrorse spines on lower margin of preopercle; body depth 3.15–3.35 in standard length; dorsal fin deeply notched between spinous and soft portions, the fourth spine longest; caudal fin rounded; body with 6 brown bars much wider than whitish interspaces; a large dark brown spot basally in anal fin and a smaller one at base of pectoral fin. Largest specimen, 7.2 cm. Known only from Rapa in southern French Polynesia from depths of 2.5–18 m.

BARRED PERCHLET

Plectranthias fourmanoiri Randall, 1980

Dorsal rays X,16–18 (usually 18); anal rays III,7; pectoral rays 12–13, none branched; branched caudal rays 12–14 (usually 13); lateral line complete, the pored scales 25; head scaled nearly to midinterorbital space; upper margin of preopercle of adults with 1–4 serrae, the lower margin usually with a single antrorse spine; body depth 2.65–3.0 in standard length; dorsal fin deeply notched between spinous and soft portions, the fourth spine longest; caudal fin rounded; white with scattered small yellow spots, the scales narrowly rimmed with light red; 4 dark bars on body and 5 prominent black spots (1 at origin of dorsal fin, 2 in dorsal fin, 1 at rear base of anal fin, and 1 midventral on abdo-

Rapa

Marshall Islands

men). Largest specimen, 4.7 cm. Reported from Christmas Island in the Indian Ocean, Mariana Islands, Marshall Islands (type locality, Enewetak Atoll), Samoa Islands, Cook Islands, Society Islands, Tuamotu Archipelago, and Pitcairn Islands from depth range of 5–44 m.

Fiji

Fiji

LONGFIN PERCHLET

Plectranthias longimanus (Weber, 1913)

Dorsal rays X,13–15 (rarely 15); anal rays III,6–7; pectoral rays 12–13 (usually 13), none branched and none thickened; lateral line incomplete, ending below soft portion of dorsal fin, the pored scales 12–15; head scaled anteriorly to midinterorbital space; upper margin of preopercle with 9–19 coarse serrae (the number increasing with growth), the lower margin with 2 antrorse spines; body depth 2.6–3.1 in standard length; dorsal fin deeply notched between spinous and soft portions, the fourth spine longest; caudal fin slightly rounded; large dark brown blotches forming 6 bars on body; a narrow, oblique, reddish brown streak across cheek; rear base of dorsal and anal fins and upper and lower base of caudal fin with a small dark brown to black spot, the 2 dorsal spots and the lower caudal-base spot with an adjacent white spot. Largest specimen, 3.6 cm. Known from east coast of Africa to Fiji and the Caroline Islands; southern Japan to Great Barrier Reef and New Caledonia; type locality, Paternoster Islands, Indonesia; more common on continental shores or those of large islands than off oceanic islands. Depth range, 6–73 m.

DWARF PERCHLET

Plectranthias nanus Randall, 1980

Dorsal rays X,13–15 (rarely 13); anal rays III,6–8 (usually 7); pectoral rays 14–16, none branched and none thickened; lateral line incomplete, ending below soft portion of dorsal fin, the pored scales 16–22; head scaled anteriorly to midinterorbital space; upper margin of preopercle with 4–17 coarse serrae (the number increasing with growth), the lower margin with 2 antrorse spines; body depth 2.9–3.6 in standard length; dorsal fin nearly separated into spinous and soft portions, the fourth spine longest; caudal fin rounded; color pattern almost identical to that of *Plectranthias longimanus*, but readily separated by having more pectoral rays and more lateral-line scales. Attains only 3.5 cm. Known from Christmas Island and Cocos-Keeling Islands in the Indian Ocean and the islands of Oceania, but not continental areas or large islands near continents such as those of the East Indies; type locality, Guam. Randall (1980b) noted that it was taken at the same locality as *P. longimanus* only at the Loyalty Islands and Ulithi Atoll in the Caroline Islands. Randall (1994) provisionally identified 2 specimens from the Red Sea as *P. nanus,* where *P. longimanus* remains unknown.

REDBLOTCH PERCHLET
Plectranthias winniensis (Tyler, 1966)

Dorsal rays X,16–17; anal rays III,7; pectoral rays 16–18, usually unbranched; branched caudal rays 13; lateral line incomplete, ending below soft portion of dorsal fin, the pored scales 14–20; head scaled anteriorly to midinterorbital space; upper margin of preopercle with 6–17 coarse serrae (the number increasing with growth), the lower margin with 2 antrorse spines; body depth 3.0–3.45 in standard length; dorsal fin deeply incised between spinous and soft portions, the fourth spine longest; caudal fin rounded; mottled orange, blotched with red posteriorly; a small white spot dorsally on caudal peduncle behind rear base of dorsal fin, and a large red spot anteriorly at base of dor-

Pitcairn Islands

sal fin. Largest specimen, 4.8 cm. Known from the northern Red Sea, Mauritius, Seychelles (type locality, St. Joseph Island, Amirantes), Vanuatu, New Caledonia, Austral Islands, Tuamotu Archipelago, Pitcairn Islands, and Hawaiian Islands. Specimens have been collected from depth range of 23–58 m.

BARTLETTS' ANTHIAS
Pseudanthias bartlettorum (Randall & Lubbock, 1981)

Dorsal rays X,17–18 (usually 17); anal rays III,7; pectoral rays 20–21 (usually 21); lateral-line scales 54–58; gill rakers 10–11 + 23–26; body depth 2.9–3.1 in standard length; no fleshy papillae on edge of orbit; rounded corner and upper edge of preopercle serrate, the lower edge smooth (true of other *Pseudanthias*); margin of subopercle and interopercle smooth; front of upper lip of males thickened and pointed; second dorsal spine of adults prolonged, especially that of males; caudal fin lunate with filamentous lobe tips; pelvic fins long, reaching origin of anal fin in females and beyond spinous portion of anal fin in males; females with upper one-third to half of head and body bright yellow, the lower part lavender-pink; dorsal fin yellow with a magenta margin that continues middorsally on nape; caudal fin with upper and lower margins magenta and a broad submarginal yellow band; males lavender-pink, the scale centers yellow, with a bright yellow band at base of dorsal fin that broadens posteriorly to entire base of caudal fin; a narrow yellow bar below eighth and ninth dorsal spines; dorsal fin violet anteriorly, shading to yellow posteriorly; caudal fin like that of female but upper and lower margins violet. Attains 6.2 cm. Known from the Line Islands, Phoenix Islands, Marshall Islands (type locality, Kwajalein Atoll), Caroline Islands, Nauru, and Palau, generally at depths of 10–15 m.

Line Islands

Marshall Islands/male

BICOLOR ANTHIAS
Pseudanthias bicolor (Randall, 1979)

Dorsal rays X,16–18; anal rays III,7–8 (rarely 8); pectoral rays 19–21 (usually 20, rarely 21); lateral-line scales 57–64; gill rakers 11–12 + 26–28; body depth 2.75–3.05 in standard length; no fleshy papillae on edge of orbit; rounded corner and upper edge of preopercle serrate, the lower edge smooth; margin of subopercle and interopercle smooth; front of upper lip of males thickened and somewhat pointed; third dorsal spine of adult females prolonged; second and third dorsal spines of males very elongate with a small membranous tip; caudal fin lunate with filamentous lobe tips; pelvic fins long, reaching to or beyond anus (beyond spinous portion of anal fin in males); upper half of body orange-yellow, the lower half lavender-pink; tip of second and third dorsal spines of adult males yellow. Reaches 13 cm. Mauritius and Maldive Islands to the Hawaiian Islands (type locality, O'ahu), Line Islands, and islands of Micronesia; in the western Pacific from the Ryukyu Islands to the Great Barrier Reef and New Caledonia. Reported from depths of 5–68 m.

Hawaiian Islands/juvenile

Hawaiian Islands/male

CARLSON'S ANTHIAS

Pseudanthias carlsoni Randall & Pyle, 2001

Dorsal rays X,16; anal rays III,7 (rarely 6); pectoral rays 14–16 (rarely 16); lateral-line scales 42–45; gill rakers 10–11 + 24–26; body moderately deep, the depth 2.7–3.1 in standard length; head length 3.05–3.2 in SL; no papillae on posterior edge of orbit; males without a fleshy protuberance at front of upper lip; third dorsal spine of males moderately elongate, 1.6–1.85 in head length; caudal fin deeply emarginate to lunate, the caudal concavity 1.5–2.15 in head. Females in life orange-pink with a vertically elongate dusky spot on each scale dorsally on body, the spots becoming yellow ventrally; a narrow, lavender-edged, yellow band from front of upper lip through lower edge of orbit to pectoral-fin base; males pink, shading to orange anteriorly and

pale lavender ventrally, with a red bar on side below eighth and ninth dorsal spines, the same yellow band on the head as females but brighter, and a conspicuous red spot in dorsal fin between sixth and seventh or eighth spines. Attains 10 cm. Known to date only from Fiji (type locality), Tonga (recently collected by Larry Sharron), Loyalty Islands, Solomon Islands, and Papua New Guinea from reefs in 37–46 m.

SILVERSTREAK ANTHIAS

Pseudanthias cooperi (Regan, 1902)

Dorsal rays X,15–17; anal rays III,7–8 (usually 7); pectoral rays 18–20; lateral-line scales 45–52; body depth 2.8–3.2 in standard length; no fleshy papillae on edge of orbit; margin of subopercle and interopercle serrate; last dorsal spine longest; caudal fin of adults lunate, the lobe tips of adult males prolonged as filaments; body ochre to dull orange-red, shading ventrally to whitish; head dull orange-red, abruptly white below a narrow oblique silvery white to lavender band from upper lip to pectoral-fin base; males with an indistinct orange band along back, red bar between lateral line and tip of pectoral fin, the dorsal fin orange-yellow with a lavender-blue margin, the first 4 membranes of dorsal fin deep red with a violet blotch at base of each; caudal-fin lobes of females tipped with orange-red; caudal fin of males red with narrow violet upper and lower margins. Reported to 14 cm. East

coast of Africa and Seychelles to Line Islands, Samoa Islands (*Anthias* sp. in Wass, 1984), and throughout Micronesia; in the western Pacific from southern Japan to New South Wales; occurs on reefs from 16 to at least 60 m. Sometimes misidentified as *Pseudanthias taeniatus (*Klunzinger), a Red Sea species, or as *P. kashiwae* (Tanaka), a synonym.

Bacan, Indonesia/females

Penyu Islands, Indonesia/male

REDFIN ANTHIAS

Pseudanthias dispar (Herre, 1955)

Dorsal rays X,16–18; anal rays III,7–8 (rarely 8); pectoral rays 18–20 (rarely 20); lateral-line scales 55–63; gill rakers 9–12 + 22–26; body depth 2.7–3.2 in standard length; no fleshy papillae on edge of orbit; 2 opercular spines; margin of subopercle and interopercle smooth; front of upper lip of males thickened and strongly pointed; first dorsal spine very short, the second prolonged; caudal fin deeply forked to lunate, the lobe tips often with a short filament; second pelvic soft ray slightly prolonged in females, very elongate in males; body light orange to orange-yellow, the head of males deeper orange to purplish to the violet-

edged bright orange band from front of snout to pectoral-fin base, white to pale yellowish below; dorsal fin of males bright red with a blue-violet margin; caudal lobes of females with orange-red tips; caudal fin of males orange, becoming yellow posteriorly, with violet upper and lower edges. Largest, 9.5 cm. Western Pacific east to Palau, Marshall Islands, Caroline Islands, Line Islands, Fiji, and Samoa Islands; also reported from Christmas Island in the eastern Indian Ocean; type locality, Solomon Islands. Replaced in the western Indian Ocean by *P. ignitus* (Randall & Lubbock). A shallow-water reef fish, the usual depth range 1–15 m. Suzuki (2001) studied the early development of this species and *Pseudanthias pascalus*.

Fiji/male

Fiji/female (above) and male

YELLOWTAIL ANTHIAS

Pseudanthias flavicauda Randall & Pyle, 2001

Dorsal rays X,16; anal rays III,7; pectoral rays 17 or 18; lateral-line scales 45–49; gill rakers 10–11 + 24–26; body depth 3.1–3.3 in standard length; no papillae on posterior edge of orbit; upper lip of males slightly fleshy and finely papillate anteriorly, but not developed to a protuberance; third dorsal spine of males moderately elongate, 1.5–1.95 in head length; caudal fin deeply emarginate to lunate. Females orange-pink, shading to pink ventrally, the scales dorsally on body with dusky yellow centers; head yellow dorsally; dorsal, anal, and paired fins mainly translucent pale yellow; caudal fin bright yellow. Body of males magenta with a large yellow area on back between base of fourth dorsal spine and

fourth or fifth dorsal soft rays; head pink, suffused with yellow dorsally, with a pink-edged yellow band from eye to pectoral-fin base; fins mainly yellow except anal, which is lavender with a yellow band. Reaches 9 cm. Currently known from the reefs of Fiji (type locality) at depths of 30–61 m, and Tonga (collected by Larry Sharron). Underwater photographs taken by Philippe Bacchet off the north coast of Tahiti at depths greater than 45 m were sent to the author; they appear to be this species.

MARQUESAN ANTHIAS

Pseudanthias hiva Randall & Pyle, 2001

Dorsal rays X,17 or 18 (usually 17); anal rays III,7; pectoral rays 19 to 21 (rarely 21); lateral-line scales 45–48; gill rakers 11–13 + 25–27; body depth 3.0–3.2 in standard length; no papillae on posterior edge of orbit; front of upper lip of males without a prominent fleshy protuberance; tenth dorsal spine longest, 2.05–2.3 in head length; caudal fin lunate. Females orange, shading to pink ventrally, the scales dorsally on body with dusky yellow centers, those ventrally with yellow; a narrow orange-red bar on body below eighth dorsal spine; a yellow-orange band, bordered below by violet, from lower part of eye to pectoral-fin base; dorsal fin orange with a violet margin; front half of anal fin magenta with a violet margin, the posterior half yellow; caudal fin orange, shading posteriorly to yellow, the lobe tips bright red; males lavender-red dorsally, shading to pale lavender ventrally, the scales below lateral line with yellow centers; head orange-red above a bluish white line from lower edge of orbit to lower base of pectoral fin, pale orange below; dorsal fin translucent orange-yellow with a lavender margin; anal fin translucent lavender with a row of small yellow spots on membranes; caudal fin red, the upper and lower edges and filaments pink; pelvic fins light red. Attains 14 cm. Known only from the Marquesas Islands (type locality, Hiva Oa); occurs on rocky substrata from 10 to at least 30 m.

STOCKY ANTHIAS

Pseudanthias hypselosoma Bleeker, 1878

Dorsal rays X,15–17 (usually 16, rarely 15); anal rays III,7; pectoral rays 18–20; lateral-line scales 44–48; gill rakers 11–13 + 26–29; body stocky, the depth 2.5–3.0 in standard length; no papillae on posterior edge of orbit; margin of subopercle and interopercle serrate; upper lip of males not developed to a protuberance; no dorsal spines prolonged, the fourth to tenth spines subequal; caudal fin of females emarginate, of males truncate to slightly rounded with prolonged tips at corners; tips of posterior rays of dorsal fin and anterior rays of anal fin protruding free of membrane; pelvic fins generally not reaching anal fin; scales of body with yellow centers, the edges pink to magenta in females and lavender in males; head and nape above a line from lower edge of eye to pectoral-fin base orange-red; caudal fin of females with a bright red posterior margin that broadens at lobe tips; fin of males red with a submarginal blue band at corners. Reported to 19 cm. Ranges from the Maldive Islands east to the Samoa Islands; in Micronesia only from Palau; in the western Pacific from the Ryukyu Islands to New South Wales; type locality, New Guinea. Usually found on well-protected reefs of lagoons or bays at depths of 6–50 m. *Pseudanthias truncatus* (Katayama & Masuda) is a synonym.

LORI'S ANTHIAS

Pseudanthias lori (Lubbock & Randall, 1976)

Dorsal rays X,16–17 (rarely 17); anal rays III,7–8 (rarely 8); pectoral rays 16–18 (rarely 16); lateral-line scales 49–52; gill rakers 8–9 + 21–24; body elongate, the depth 3.6–4.1 in standard length; fleshy papillae on posterior edge of orbit; margin of subopercle and interopercle smooth; front of upper lip of males a pointed protuberance; third dorsal spine of males prolonged; caudal fin lunate, the lobes of males more elongate; edges of longest pec-

toral rays finely serrate; pelvic fins of females reaching beyond anus, of males beyond origin of anal fin; pink, finely spotted with yellow, with a series of short red bars on back that are longer posteriorly (except the last, a spot at rear base of dorsal fin); a horizontal red band with whitish upper margin on caudal peduncle near dorsal edge; males may develop orange-yellow centers in bars and peduncular band. Attains 12 cm. Rowley Shoals and

Christmas Island in the eastern Indian Ocean to the Tuamotu Archipelago; only Palau in Micronesia; in the western Pacific from the Ryukyu Islands to the Great Barrier Reef and New Caledonia (type locality, Loyalty Islands). Usually seen in small aggregations on steep outer-reef slopes at depths of 18–70 m. Brief description by Lubbock & Randall in Fourmanoir & Laboute (1976); full description by Randall & Lubbock (1981).

MOOREA ANTHIAS
Pseudanthias mooreanus (Herre, 1935)
Dorsal rays X,16–17 (rarely 16); anal rays III,7; pectoral rays 18–21 (rarely 18 or 21); lateral-line scales 49–55; gill rakers 9–11 + 24–27; body depth 3.2–3.5 in standard length; no fleshy papillae on edge of orbit; margin of subopercle and interopercle finely serrate; no dorsal spines prolonged, the last 5 subequal; caudal fin lunate, the lobe tips prolonged as filaments; pelvic fins not reaching origin of anal fin; females greenish gray, the front of chin and snout red, continuing as band, edged in white below, to base of pectoral fins; a narrow red bar on side of body below lateral line, ending beneath outer part of pectoral fin; caudal fin

red in lobes, becoming yellow on membranes centroposteriorly, the upper and lower edges blue except red filamentous lobe tips; body of males pink anteriorly, developing longitudinal yellow lines along scale centers posteriorly, with the same narrow red bar on side of body. Attains 11 cm. Known only from the Society Islands (type locality, Moorea), Tuamotu Archipelago, and the Pitcairn Islands, usually on lagoon or bay reefs. Specimens collected by author in 6–46 m.

OLIVE ANTHIAS
Pseudanthias olivaceus (Randall & McCosker, 1981)
Dorsal rays X,17–18 (usually 17); anal rays III,7–8 (rarely 8); pectoral rays 17–20 (rarely 17 or 20, usually 18); lateral-line scales 44–49; gill rakers 8–11 + 24–28; body depth 2.9–3.2 in standard length; no fleshy papillae on edge of orbit; margin of subopercle with a few small serrae; margin of interopercle smooth; fourth or fifth dorsal spines longest, but remaining spines only slightly shorter; caudal fin lunate, the lobe tips filamentous; pelvic fins not reaching origin of anal fin; females olivaceous, the scales with yellow centers ventrally; an orange band

on snout continuing behind eye as a yellow band into base of pectoral fin; outer part of dorsal fin red; caudal fin bright yellow; males similar but with broad orange blotches anteriorly on side of body; band to pectoral fin and ventral scale centers orange; a dark reddish brown spot in outer upper part of pectoral fin; caudal fin yellow with a broad orange band in each lobe. Reaches 12 cm. Known only from the Society Islands, Tuamotu Archipelago, Austral Islands, Cook Islands (type locality, Rarotonga), Niue, Phoenix Islands, and Line Islands where most common. Collected from depth range of 1–33.5 m, mainly in outer-reef areas.

Fiji

Fiji/male

PURPLE QUEEN

Pseudanthias pascalus (Jordan & Tanaka, 1927)

Dorsal rays X,15–17; anal rays III,7–8 (rarely 8); pectoral rays 16–19 (modally 18); lateral-line scales 48–52; auxiliary scales present; gill rakers 9–11 + 23–27; body elongate, the depth 2.9–3.4 in standard length; fleshy papillae on posterior edge of orbit; 2 opercular spines; margin of subopercle and interopercle smooth; front of upper lip of males a pointed protuberance; fifth to tenth dorsal spines subequal, the fifth generally longest in small fish and the tenth in large adults; caudal fin deeply forked, the lobe tips of males prolonged; soft portion of dorsal fin of males elevated, often with some ray tips free of membrane; pelvic fins of males extending beyond origin of anal fin; purple to violet with a yellow spot on each scale; an orange band from snout to pectoral-fin base; males with a large orange-red area in outer part of soft portion of dorsal fin. Largest specimen, 17 cm. Western Pacific from the Ryukyu Islands (type locality, Okinawa) to the Great Barrier Reef and New Caledonia, east to islands of Micronesia, Fiji, Samoa Islands, Society Islands, and Tuamotu Archipelago; more common off oceanic islands than on continental reefs or large continental islands; occurs in aggregations on outer reef slopes from depths of 5–60 m. The male of the related *Pseudanthias tuka* (Herre & Montalban) is very similar, differing in being more yellow ventrally on the head and having a large deep red spot basally on the posterior part of the dorsal fin; the female of *tuka* is readily distinguished by a yellow band along the back and a yellow band in each caudal lobe; *tuka* does not range out into Oceania except to Palau.

Great Barrier Reef/female

Great Barrier Reef/male

PAINTED ANTHIAS

Pseudanthias pictilis (Randall & Allen, 1978)

Dorsal rays X,15–16 (rarely 15); anal rays III,7–8; pectoral rays 18–19; lateral-line scales 46–50; auxiliary scales on head and body; gill rakers 10–11 + 23–26; body notably deep for the genus, 2.4–2.7 in standard length; no papillae on posterior edge of orbit; margin of subopercle and interopercle smooth; no protuberance at front of upper lip of male; first and tenth dorsal spines longest; caudal fin emarginate; pelvic fins of males usually reaching anus, but not in females; females violet-pink ante-riorly, shading to yellow posteriorly; median fins yellow, the caudal with a narrow red posterior margin; males violet-pink to orange-red with an orange-edged violet to yellow bar below soft portion of dorsal fin; caudal fin deep orange with a broad yellow area near base and lavender lobe tips; dorsal fin mainly red with a narrow light blue margin. Attains 13.5 cm. Known from New Caledonia, Lord Howe Island (type locality), Norfolk Island, southern Great Barrier Reef, and New South Wales; adults occur in aggregations, generally at 20–40 m.

144

SQUARESPOT ANTHIAS

Pseudanthias pleurotaenia (Bleeker, 1857)

Dorsal rays X,16–18; anal rays III,7; pectoral rays 17–19; lateral-line scales 45–50; gill rakers 11–13 + 26–29; body deep for the genus, 2.4–2.7 in standard length; no papillae on posterior edge of orbit; margin of subopercle and interopercle weakly serrate; upper lip of males not developed to a protuberance; third dorsal spine prolonged; caudal fin lunate; pelvic fins reaching to or beyond origin of anal fin; females yellow, the scales edged in orange except ventrally, with a violet-edged yellow band from eye to pectoral-fin base, and 2 parallel violet lines passing from beneath pectoral fin to lower caudal peduncle; males orange and magenta with a very large, nearly square, violet to lavender spot anteriorly on side of body; dorsal fin yellow proximally, red distally, with a violet margin and spine tips, and a red spot or spots posteriorly in soft portion; anal fin lavender-blue with yellow streaks and red spots; caudal fin yellow with lavender-blue lobe tips. Reported to 20 cm. Western Pacific from the Ryukyu Islands to the Great Barrier Reef and New Caledonia, east to Samoa Islands and islands of Micronesia; type locality, Ambon, Molucca Islands. Occurs also at Rowley Shoals off northwestern Australia, but rare compared with the close relative there, *Pseudanthias sheni* Randall & Allen. Generally found on steep outer-reef slopes in 30 to 70 m, but has been observed in 10 m.

REGAL ANTHIAS

Pseudanthias regalis (Randall & Lubbock, 1981)

Dorsal rays X,17–18 (usually 17); anal rays III,7; pectoral rays 21–22 (usually 22); lateral-line scales 56–62; gill rakers 10–12 + 24–28; body depth 2.6–3.1 in standard length; no fleshy papillae on edge of orbit; margin of subopercle and interopercle smooth; front of upper lip of males thickened and pointed; second dorsal spine of adults prolonged, especially that of males; caudal fin lunate with filamentous lobe tips; pelvic fins long, reaching beyond anus in females and well beyond spinous portion of anal fin in males; females orange-yellow, shading to red posteriorly and to lavender ventrally, with a violet-edged orange band from snout to pectoral-fin base; males yellow dorsoanteriorly on body and on head above violet-edged yellow band; rest of body bright pink with a small yellow spot on each scale. Known only from the Marquesas Islands (type locality, Fatu Hiva), where it is found on rocky substrata from less than 10 to at least 30 m.

145

Rinca, Indonesia

Papua New Guinea/male

SCALEFIN ANTHIAS

Pseudanthias squamipinnis (Peters, 1855)

Dorsal rays X,16–18 (rarely 18); anal rays III,7; pectoral rays 16–18; lateral-line scales 37–43; auxiliary scales present; median fins heavily scaled; gill rakers 8–11 + 23–26; body depth 2.4–3.1 in standard length; no papillae on posterior edge of orbit; margin of subopercle and interopercle serrate; upper lip of males not developed to a protuberance; third dorsal spine prolonged in females, extremely elongate in males; caudal fin lunate, the lobes often greatly prolonged in males; pelvic fins of females not reaching origin of anal fin, but extending well beyond in males; females orange with a yellow spot on each scale; a violet-edged

orange band from lower part of eye to pectoral-fin base; males fuchsia with an orange spot on each scale; a large orange to magenta spot on outer upper part of pectoral fin. Attains 15 cm. Red Sea and east coast of Africa to Fiji and the Caroline Islands; in the western Pacific from southern Japan to New South Wales, Lord Howe Island, and Norfolk Island; type locality, Mozambique. Known from depths of 2–40 m, but usually less than 20 m. May occur in very large aggregations, then often the most common fish seen on shallow reefs. Shapiro (1981) documented the sex reversal and color change after removal of a male from its harem of females; the ranking female completed the change in sex and color pattern in 7–16 days.

Guam/female

Coral Sea/male

LONGFIN ANTHIAS

Pseudanthias ventralis (Randall, 1979)

Dorsal rays X,16–18; anal rays III,9; pectoral rays 15–16 (usually 15); lateral-line scales 39–45; gill rakers 7–9 + 21–25; body depth 2.85–3.15 in standard length; no papillae on posterior edge of orbit; margin of subopercle serrate, of interopercle smooth; upper lip of males not thickened to a protuberance; fifth dorsal spine usually longest, but not prolonged; caudal fin lunate; pelvic fins very long in adults of both sexes, reaching beyond spinous portion of anal fin; females pink to magenta, pale lavender to white ventrally with a broad yellow band dorsally on body, expanding to full depth of posterior caudal peduncle; an oblique

magenta band from eye to nape; median and pelvic fins yellow with a magenta margin; males deep pink to magenta, the yellow of head and dorsally on body with irregular bands and blotches of magenta; dorsal fin complexly colored with yellow, red, magenta, and blue; caudal fin yellow with a large blue-edged red spot posteriorly. Attains 7 cm. Ogasawara Islands to the Great Barrier Reef and New Caledonia, east to the islands of Oceania except Hawaiian Islands and Johnston Island (where replaced by the similar *Pseudanthias hawaiiensis*); type locality, Pitcairn Island. Common on deep-reef escarpments from 26 to 120 m, usually at depths greater than 40 m.

HAWK ANTHIAS
Serranocirrhitus latus Watanabe, 1949

Dorsal rays X,18–20; anal rays III,7; pectoral rays 13–14; lateral-line scales 33–38; body deep, the depth 1.9–2.2 in standard length; margin of subopercle and interopercle smooth; tenth dorsal spine longest, but eighth and ninth spines nearly as long; caudal fin lunate; pelvic fins reaching origin of anal fin; deep pink, each scale with a yellow spot, the spots progressively larger dorsally; yellow bands radiating from eye, and a yellow spot posteriorly on opercle. Attains 13 cm. Known from southern Japan (type locality, Okinawa) through Indonesia to northern Great Barrier Reef, east to Vanuatu, New Caledonia, and Fiji; only Palau in Micronesia; usually found in caves or beneath ledges on outer-reef drop-offs in the depth range of 15–70 m. *Dactylanthias mcmichaeli* Whitley is a synonym.

Palau

GROUPERS (EPINEPHELINAE)

Bali

REDMOUTH GROUPER
Aethaloperca rogaa (Forsskål, 1775)

Dorsal rays IX,16–18 (rarely 16); anal rays III,8–9 (rarely 8); pectoral rays 17–18 (usually 18); lateral-line scales 48–54; longitudinal scale series 94–104; scales ctenoid; gill rakers 8–11 + 15–17; palatine teeth present; body deep, the depth 2.1–2.4 in standard length; caudal fin truncate; fifth or sixth pectoral rays longest (middle rays longest in other South Pacific groupers); dark brown, sometimes with an orange cast; a whitish bar often centered on abdomen; outer part of spinous dorsal membranes deep orange to brownish red. Reported to 60 cm. Red Sea (type locality) and coast of Africa to Fiji; in the western Pacific from Japan to the Great Barrier Reef and New Caledonia. A clear-water, coral-reef species known from depths of 3 to at least 40 m; often found in the vicinity of caves. Juveniles mimic dark damselfishes, thereby getting closer to their prey (Snyder et al., 2001).

Bali/juvenile

Sulawesi/juvenile

Bali

SLENDER GROUPER

Anyperodon leucogrammicus (Valenciennes in C & V, 1828)

Dorsal rays XI,14–16; anal rays III,8–9 (usually 9); pectoral rays 15–17 (rarely 17); lateral-line scales 63–72; longitudinal scale series 110–125; scales ctenoid, becoming cycloid on chest and abdomen; gill rakers 7–9 + 14–17; no palatine teeth; body elongate, the depth 3.15–3.7 in standard length, and compressed, the width 2.3–2.8 in depth; lower jaw strongly projecting; caudal fin rounded; adults greenish to brownish gray with numerous orange-red spots; 4 white stripes often present on body (may be broken into series of dashes and may be lost in large adults); juveniles with stripes of orange-yellow and blue, a blue-edged black spot at base of caudal fin, and one in dorsal fin. Reaches about 60 cm. Red Sea and east coast of Africa to the Phoenix and Samoa Islands and the islands of Micronesia; in the western Pacific from the Ryukyu Islands to the Great Barrier Reef and New Caledonia; type locality, Seychelles. Reported from the shallows to depths of 80 m. Limited food-habit data indicate that it feeds mainly on small fishes. The juvenile stage is a mimic of wrasses of the genus *Halichoeres* (Russell et al., 1976; Randall & Kuiter, 1989). In the guise of a relatively harmless wrasse, it is presumed to be able to get closer to its prey.

PEACOCK HIND

Cephalopholis argus Bloch & Schneider, 1801

Dorsal rays IX,15–17 (rarely 15); anal rays III,9; pectoral rays 16–18 (rarely 18); lateral-line scales 46–51; longitudinal scale series 95–110; auxiliary scales present on body; scales ctenoid, becoming cycloid ventrally on abdomen; lower-limb gill rakers 17–19 (14–17 in other South Pacific *Cephalopholis*); body depth 2.7–3.2 in standard length; dark brown with numerous dark-edged blue spots on head, body, and fins, and a large pale area on chest; 5 or 6 broad pale bars often present on posterior half of body; triangular outer part of spinous dorsal membranes orange. Attains about 60 cm. Occurs throughout the Indo-Pacific except the Persian Gulf and Gulf of Oman; type locality, East Indies. Found more in outer-reef areas than in lagoons. Known from depths of 2–40 m. Introduced to the Hawaiian Islands in 1956 (Randall & Kanayama, 1972); because this species has caused ciguatera in Hawai'i, there is now little fishing effort for it. Randall & Brock (1960) examined 280 specimens for food-habit study; 77.5% of the prey were fishes, and the rest benthic crustaceans.

Maldive Islands

CHOCOLATE HIND
Cephalopholis boenak (Bloch, 1790)
Dorsal rays IX,15–17; anal rays III,8; pectoral rays
15–17; lateral-line scales 46–51; longitudinal scale
series 86–100; scales ctenoid on body, including
abdomen; body depth 2.6–3.05 in standard length;
brown with 7 or 8 dark brown bars in body, including 1 on nape; upper part of opercular membrane
nearly black; fins dark brown; posterior margin of
caudal fin white (often absent centrally); inside of
mouth partly orange. Largest specimen examined,
25.8 cm. East coast of Africa to the western Pacific
where it ranges from Japan (type locality) and
Shanghai to the southern Great Barrier Reef and
New Caledonia. Typical habitat, silty reefs of protected waters. Donaldson (1989a) documented the
pair spawning.

Great Barrier Reef

LEOPARD HIND
Cephalopholis leopardus (Lacepède, 1801)
Dorsal rays IX,13–15; anal rays III,9–10 (rarely 10);
pectoral rays 16–18; lateral-line scales 47–50; longitudinal scale series 79–88; scales on body ctenoid,
including abdomen; body depth 2.6–2.85 in standard length; light reddish brown, shading to whitish
ventrally, with numerous red-orange spots, most
evident ventrally; a black saddle-like spot dorsally
on caudal peduncle, with a small spot behind it; a
dark brown spot on upper part of opercular membrane. A small species, the largest 18.5 cm. East
coast of Africa to the Line Islands, Society Islands
and throughout Micronesia; in the western Pacific
from the Ryukyu Islands to the Great Barrier Reef;
type locality, Indian Ocean. A secretive coral-reef
species known from depths of 3–38 m.

Penyu Islands, Indonesia

FRECKLED HIND
Cephalopholis microprion (Bleeker, 1852)
Dorsal rays IX,15–16 (rarely 16); anal rays III,8;
pectoral rays 15–16 (usually 16); lateral-line scales
46–50; longitudinal scale series 84–98; scales on
body ctenoid, including abdomen; body depth
2.5–2.8 in standard length; dark brown with numerous very small, dark-edged blue spots on head and
anterior body; fins dark brown; caudal fin with a
gray-blue posterior margin except centrally; similar
margin on soft portion of anal fin; capable of displaying a pattern of 6 broad dark bars; another common color phase with a broad pale greenish yellow
area over most of body. Largest examined, 23 cm.
Western Pacific from the Ryukyu Islands to the
Great Barrier Reef, east to Vanuatu and New
Caledonia; type locality, Ambon, Molucca Islands.
Formerly recorded from the Andaman Sea, but this
population proved to be a related species,
Cephalopholis polyspila Randall & Satapoomin,
differing in have blue spots over all of body and fins
except the pelvics.

New Britain

149

Maldive Islands/juvenile

Maldive Islands

CORAL HIND
Cephalopholis miniata (Forsskål, 1775)
Dorsal rays IX,14–16; anal rays III,8–9 (rarely 8); pectoral rays 17–18 (usually 18); lateral-line scales 47–55; longitudinal scale series 94–114; scales on body ctenoid, becoming cycloid on abdomen; body depth 2.65–3.05 in standard length; orange-red to reddish brown with many bright blue spots (smaller than pupil and usually faintly dark-edged) on head, body, and median fins; outer edge of caudal fin and soft portion of dorsal and anal fins with a narrow blue margin and blackish submarginal line; capable of quickly assuming a disruptive pattern of irregular, oblique dark bars; juveniles may be yellow with scattered blue spots. Reported to 41 cm. Red Sea (type locality) and east coast of Africa to the Line, Phoenix, and Samoa Islands; Japan to Lord Howe Island in the western Pacific. Typically found on well-developed coral reefs in clear water, more often on exposed than protected reefs, usually in less than 40 m, but recorded to 90 m. Shpigel & Fishelson (1989) reported feeding mainly between 0700–0900 hours and 1400–1600 hours; 86% of the prey in the Red Sea consisted of small fishes (primarily *Pseudanthias squamipinnis*), and the rest crustaceans.

HARLEQUIN HIND
Cephalopholis polleni (Bleeker, 1868)
Dorsal rays IX,14–16; anal rays III,8–9 (rarely 8); pectoral rays 17–18; lateral-line scales 66–72; longitudinal scale series 112–135; scales on body ctenoid, including abdomen; snout before posterior nostrils scaleless; body depth 2.7–3.1 in standard length; head small, the length 2.65–3.05 in standard length; caudal fin truncate to slightly emarginate; greenish to yellowish brown on head and anterodorsally on body with a few blue stripes, shading to yellow on rest of body with 10–12 blue stripes about twice as broad as yellow interspaces, the upper stripes angling into basal soft portion of dorsal fin; caudal fin yellow with continuation of blue body stripes, some branching. Largest specimen, 32.2 cm. Islands of the western Indian Ocean (type locality, Réunion), Cocos-Keeling Islands, Indonesia, Philippines, Palau, Guam, Line Islands, and recently discovered by Yves Lefevre in Rangiroa, Tuamotu Archipelago; occurs on well-developed coral reefs, generally on steep outer-reef slopes, to depths of at least 70 m; rarely seen in less than 30 m, which may account for the paucity of records. The photograph of the pair from Kiritimati, Line Islands, was taken in 52 m.

Line Islands

Maldive Islands

SIXSPOT HIND
Cephalopholis sexmaculata (Rüppell, 1830)
Dorsal rays IX,14–16; anal rays III,9; pectoral rays 16–18; lateral-line scales 49–54; longitudinal scale series 95–108; scales on body ctenoid, including abdomen; body depth 2.65–3.05 in standard length; orange-red with small blue spots on head, body, and median fins; often with short blue lines on head; 6 quadrangular black blotches along back, the first 4 extending into dorsal fin. Largest specimen, 50 cm, from Natal. Red Sea (type locality) and east coast of Africa to the Line Islands, Marquesas Islands, Society Islands, and islands of Micronesia; southern Japan to the Great Barrier Reef and Lord Howe Island; few specimens in museum collections. A secretive coral-reef species often found in caves. A food-habit study revealed small fishes as the main item of diet, followed by crustaceans (Randall & Brock, 1960).

Bali/juvenile

Papua New Guinea

TOMATO HIND
Cephalopholis sonnerati (Valenciennes in C & V, 1828)
Dorsal rays IX,14–16; anal rays III,9; pectoral rays 18–20; lateral-line scales 66–80; longitudinal scale series 115–134; scales on body ctenoid except cycloid on abdomen; body moderately deep, the depth 2.3–2.75 in standard length; nape of adults prominently convex; opercular spines very flat; light reddish to yellowish brown with numerous very small, brownish red spots on head (where very close-set), body, and fins; a dark spot on upper part of opercular membrane; in the Indian Ocean orange-red to reddish brown, with close-set pale spots on head and often with scattered white blotches on body; juveniles dark reddish brown to nearly black with a bluish white marginal to submarginal band in caudal fin. Largest examined, 49 cm, from South Africa. Gulf of Aden and east coast of Africa to the Line Islands and Samoa Islands; in the western Pacific from southern Japan to the Great Barrier Reef and as juveniles to New South Wales; type locality, Pondicherry, India. Found on coral reefs and rocky substrata, usually at depths greater than 30 m; known to at least 100 m.

151

Marshall Islands

Line Islands

Wetar, Indonesia, with *Labroides pectoralis*

STRAWBERRY HIND

Cephalopholis spiloparaea (Valenciennes in C & V, 1828)

Dorsal rays IX,14–16; anal rays III,9–10 (rarely 10); pectoral rays 17–19; lateral-line scales 47–52; scales on body ctenoid except ventrally at front of abdomen; body depth 2.7–3.2 in standard length; light red, mottled and blotched with dark red or reddish brown; caudal fin with a bluish white posterior margin that becomes submarginal at corners. Largest specimen examined, 20.8 cm, from Rapa. East coast of Africa to the Pitcairn Islands, but unknown from the Red Sea to the Persian Gulf, India, and the Andaman Sea; in the western Pacific from southern Japan to the Great Barrier Reef and New Caledonia; type locality unknown but probably in Indian Ocean. Specimens have been collected from coral reefs in the depth range of 15–108 m, but usually not less than 30 m. The similar Golden Hind, *Cephalopholis aurantia* Valenciennes, is a deeper-water species (generally found in more than 100 m; 150–250 m in Tahiti). It differs in having a serrate subopercle and interopercle (smooth or with only a few serrae in *spiloparaea*) and pelvic fins that usually reach the anus (not to anus in *spiloparaea*).

DARKFIN HIND

Cephalopholis urodeta (Forster, 1801)

Dorsal rays IX,14–16 (rarely 14 or 16); anal rays III,8–9 (rarely 8); pectoral rays 17–19; lateral-line scales 54–68; scales on body ctenoid except ventrally on abdomen; body depth 2.75–3.1 in standard length; reddish brown to brownish red, darker posteriorly, with or without 6 broad irregular dark bars, the anterior 4 of which bifurcate ventrally; head and nape with numerous close-set orange-red spots, more evident ventrally; caudal fin with 2 oblique white bands that converge posteriorly; corners of fin above and below white bands red, the central part of fin dark reddish brown with small red spots; juveniles develop the white caudal bands at a length of about 5 cm; Indian Ocean fish lack the white bands in the caudal fin. Largest specimen, 26.5 cm, from the Marquesas Islands. East coast of Africa to the Line Islands, islands of French Polynesia (type locality, Marquesas Islands), and the Pitcairn Islands; southern Japan to Great Barrier Reef and New Caledonia. The Indian Ocean form was described as *Cephalopholis nigripinnis* by Valenciennes. When no morphological differences could be detected and specimens of intermediate color were found at Christmas Island in the eastern Indian Ocean, *nigripinnis* was placed in synonymy (Randall & Heemstra, 1991). Randall & Brock (1960) reported on the food habits of 25 of 71 specimens from the Society Islands with food in the stomachs. Small fishes represented 68% of the prey; the rest were crabs, shrimps, and mantis shrimps.

152

Great Barrier Reef

HUMPBACK GROUPER

Cromileptes altivelis (Valenciennes in C & V, 1828)
Dorsal rays X,17–19; anal rays III,9–10 (rarely 9); pectoral rays 17–18 (usually 18); lateral-line scales 54–62; longitudinal scale series 106–122; scales on body cycloid; body depth 2.5–3.0 in standard length, and compressed, the width 2.1–2.7 in depth; front of head containing eye small compared with greatly elevated postorbital head (hence dorsal profile of head very concave); greenish white to light greenish brown with scattered round black spots on head, body, and fins. Reported to 66 cm. Nicobar Islands and Indo-Malayan region (type locality, Java), north to southern Japan, and south to northwestern Australia and Great Barrier Reef; Palau, Guam, and New Caledonia the only records from Oceania. Several have been found in the Hawaiian Islands but were probable aquarium releases; the young enter the aquarium trade as Pantherfish. They tend to attract attention by exagerrated undulation of their fins. Adults are more secretive. Usually seen in silty reef areas but may occur off exposed shores. The author collected one from a tidepool off Broome, Western Australia. Highly esteemed as a food fish, especially in Australia where known as the Barramundi Cod.

Sulawesi/juvenile

153

Musandam, Oman/juvenile

Papua New Guinea

AREOLATE GROUPER

Epinephelus areolatus (Forsskål, 1775)

Dorsal rays XI,15–17; anal rays III,7–8 (rarely 7); pectoral rays 17–19 (rarely 19); lateral-line scales 49–53; longitudinal scale series 97–116; scales on body ctenoid, except chest and ventrally on abdomen; body moderately elongate, the depth 2.75–3.3 in standard length, and compressed; caudal fin slightly emarginate to truncate; whitish with numerous close-set, brown to yellowish brown spots on head, body, and fins; caudal fin with a white posterior border. Attains about 40 cm. Red Sea (type locality) and Persian Gulf to southern Mozambique, east to the western Pacific, where it ranges from southern Japan to New Caledonia, the only record for Oceania. Occurs in silty sand or seagrass habitats around small isolated patches of dead coral or sponge. One other species from the South Pacific area has an emarginate to truncate caudal fin and is densely spotted with dark brown, *Epinephelus chlorostigma* (Valenciennes). It differs in usually having 17 instead of 16 dorsal soft rays, and the edge of its anal fin is distinctly angular instead of rounded. It is known from 2 localities in Oceania, New Caledonia and American Samoa. Fourmanoir & Laboute (1976) reported the depth range in New Caledonia as 150–280 m.

New Britain

WHITESPOTTED GROUPER

Epinephelus coeruleopunctatus (Bloch, 1790)

Dorsal rays XI,15–17; anal rays III,8; pectoral rays 17–19 (rarely 19); lateral-line scales 51–61; longitudinal scale series 86–109; ctenoid scales on body of adults on a broad zone on side of body, cycloid elsewhere (ctenoid scale region larger in smaller fish); body moderately elongate, the depth 3.0–3.4 in standard length; head pointed, its dorsal profile nearly straight; posterior nostril of large adults enlarged and vertically elongate; upper edge of opercle straight to slightly convex; brownish gray with many small whitish spots and scattered, large, whitish blotches (nearly as large as eye) on postorbital head, body, and dorsal fin; a series of dark blotches along back; juveniles dark brown with scattered, round, white spots smaller than pupil. Reported to 76 cm. Persian Gulf and east coast of Africa to Fiji and the islands of Micronesia; in the western Pacific from Japan to New South Wales; type locality unknown. A shallow-water reef species that tends to be cryptic; the young have been found in tidepools.

ORANGESPOTTED GROUPER

Epinephelus coioides (Hamilton, 1822)

Dorsal rays XI,13–16 (rarely 13); anal rays III,8; pectoral rays 18–20 (rarely 18, usually 20); lateral-line scales 58–65; anterior lateral-line scales of adults with branched tubules; longitudinal scale series 100–118; ctenoid scales on body except for a zone along back; body elongate, the depth 2.9–3.7 in standard length; 2 rows of teeth on midside of lower jaw, increasing to 4–5 rows in large adults; light grayish brown, whitish below, with numerous brownish orange spots the size of pupil or smaller on head and body; 5 slightly oblique grayish brown bars on body that bifurcate ventrally, the first 4 extending into base of dorsal fin (bars may be broken on upper side); fins with small brownish orange to brown spots at least basally. Maximum length uncertain due to confusion with *Epinephelus lanceolatus* and *E. malabaricus*, but probably at least 100 cm. Red Sea, Persian Gulf, and east coast of Africa to western Pacific from Ryukyu Islands to New South Wales; east in Oceania only to Palau, Yap, New Caledonia, and Fiji; type locality, Ganges estuaries. This species and *E. malabaricus* are recorded from the Mediterranean Sea (via the Suez Canal). Often found in brackish areas, and will penetrate water of low salinity in rivers; recorded to depths of 100 m. Age, growth, and reproduction reported by Matthews et al. (1986) misidentified as *E. tauvina*. A valuable species for aquaculture; Doi et al. (1991) documented the successful artificial propagation and studied the development (as *E. suillus* Valenciennes, a junior synonym).

SPECKLED GROUPER

Epinephelus cyanopodus (Richardson, 1846)

Dorsal rays XI,15–17 (rarely 15); anal rays III,8; pectoral rays 18–20 (rarely 20); lateral-line scales 63–75; longitudinal scale series 128–147; scales ctenoid except anteriorly; body deep, the depth 2.4–2.7 in standard length; interorbital space distinctly convex; caudal fin truncate to slightly emarginate; light bluish gray with numerous very small black spots and scattered, irregular, larger black spots that are usually smaller than pupil; subadults lack the larger black spots and have a broad, black submarginal band in the caudal fin. Reported to 120 cm. Western Pacific from Japan to New South Wales, Lord Howe Island, and Norfolk Island, east to Fiji and the islands of Micronesia; type locality, Ghangzhou (Canton), China. Typical habitat, sand with isolated coral heads in lagoons and bays, but also occurs in deep outer-reef areas. *Epinephelus hoedtii* (Bleeker) and *E. kohleri* Schultz are synonyms.

Ryukyu Islands

BLACKTIP GROUPER
Epinephelus fasciatus (Forsskål, 1775)
Dorsal rays XI,15–17 (rarely 15); anal rays III,7–8 (rarely 7); pectoral rays 18–20 (rarely 20); lateral-line scales 49–75; longitudinal scale series 92–135; scales on body ctenoid except anteriorly; body depth 2.85–3.25 in standard length; interorbital space flat; caudal fin usually slightly to moderately rounded but some fish in Oceania with a nearly truncate fin; light greenish gray to pale yellowish red, the body with or without 5 orangish brown to dark red bars about equal to pale interspaces; rim of orbit narrowly black, circled by a blue line; outer triangular part of each spinous dorsal membrane black or deep red. Marquesan fish with scattered white spots. Reported to 38 cm. Occurs throughout the Indo-Pacific region except the Hawaiian Islands; type locality, Red Sea. There are at least 6 identifiable populations of this species, and 15 synonyms from *Epinephelus marginalis* (Bloch) to *E. emoryi* Schultz (Randall & Heemstra, 1991). One of the 2 most common species of Indo-Pacific *Epinephelus*.

Hong Kong

BROWNMARBLED GROUPER
Epinephelus fuscoguttatus (Forsskål, 1775)
Dorsal rays XI,13–15 (rarely 13); anal rays III,8; pectoral rays 18–20; lateral-line scales 52–58; longitudinal scale series 102–115; scales on body cycloid (ctenoid in juveniles); lower-limb gill rakers modally 18 (usually 16–17 in other *Epinephelus*); body moderately deep, the depth 2.6–2.9 in standard length; dorsal profile of head of adults indented in interorbital region, the nape distinctly convex; interorbital space flat to slightly convex; posterior nostril of adults subtriangular, as much as 4 times larger than anterior nostril; light yellowish brown, the head, body, and fins densely spotted with small dark brown spots; head and body with irregular dark brown blotches of variable size, the darkest dorsally on body; a black saddle-like spot on caudal peduncle. Largest examined, 95 cm. Red Sea (type locality) and east coast of Africa to Phoenix and Samoa Islands and islands of Micronesia; in the western Pacific from Ryukyu Islands to Great Barrier Reef and New Caledonia. A species of shallow coral reefs or rocky substrata; difficult to approach underwater. Limited data on food habits indicate feeding on fishes, crabs, and cephalopods (Harmelin-Vivien & Bouchon, 1976 and Randall, 1980a); has been implicated in ciguatera fish poisoning (Halstead, 1967; Randall, 1980a).

STARSPOTTED GROUPER

Epinephelus hexagonatus (Forster, 1801)

Dorsal rays XI,15–16 (rarely 16); anal rays III,8; pectoral rays 17–19 (rarely 17); lateral-line scales 61–70; longitudinal scale series 93–114; scales on body cycloid (ctenoid in juveniles); lower-limb gill rakers modally 18 (usually 16–17 in other *Epinephelus*); body depth 2.8–3.45 in standard length; interorbital space flat; second anal spine distinctly longer than third; midside of lower jaw with 3–5 rows of teeth; head and body with round to polygonal (mostly hexagonal) brown to reddish brown spots about size of pupil that partially merge on their sides, leaving only a triangular white dot at each angular corner (except ventrally where spots are separated); 5 groups of spots dorsally on body darker than others; a large yellow-brown spot behind eye and large elongate spot of the same color on opercle (the 2 spots sometimes joined). Largest examined, 25.4 cm. Kenya, Zanzibar, Comoro Islands, Mascarenes, Cocos-Keeling Islands, and Christmas Island in the Indian Ocean; Great Barrier Reef and islands of Oceania except Vanuatu, New Caledonia, and the Hawaiian Islands; few continental or large-island records (none from Indonesia or the Philippines); type locality, Tahiti. Usually found in shallow outer-reef areas exposed to surge.

Guam

BLACKSADDLE GROUPER

Epinephelus howlandi (Günther, 1873)

Dorsal rays XI,15–17; anal rays III,8; pectoral rays 17–19; lateral-line scales 49–52; longitudinal scale series 85–102; scales on body cycloid except beneath and just posterior to pectoral fins, where ctenoid; body depth 2.9–3.3 in standard length; interorbital space flat to slightly concave; midside of lower jaw with 2 rows of teeth (3–4 in large adults); pale gray, shading to white ventrally, with numerous well-separated, dark brown to black spots much smaller than pupil on head, body (except ventrally), and on fins (may be absent on pectorals); a blackish spot about as large as eye containing 4 to 8 black spots on back and basally in dorsal fin between spines IX and XI; a blackish spot containing 2 black spots dorsally on caudal peduncle; caudal fin with a white posterior margin and often a submarginal blackish zone. Largest examined, 44 cm.

Fiji

Known from Howland Island (type locality), Samoa Islands, Tonga, islands of Micronesia, Ogasawara Islands, Paracel Islands, Vanuatu, and Great Barrier Reef; depth range, 1–37 m. Often confused with *Epinephelus macrospilos* (see treatment of that species).

MARQUESAN GROUPER

Epinephelus irroratus (Forster, 1801)

Dorsal rays XI,16; anal rays III,8; pectoral rays 18–20 (rarely 18 or 20); lateral-line scales 70–75; longitudinal scale series 117–136; scales on body ctenoid except anteriorly; body depth 2.7–3.25 in standard length; interorbital space slightly convex; midside of lower jaw of adults with 3 rows of teeth; second dorsal spine prolonged, 1.85–2.4 in head; membranes of spinous portion of dorsal fin only slightly indented; caudal fin truncate to slightly rounded; reddish brown with a white dot on each scale; spinous portion of dorsal fin with a broad deep red border; median and pectoral fins with a narrow, white posterior margin. Largest specimen, 34 cm. Known only from the Marquesas Islands; a record from Minami-tori-shima (Marcus Island) was an error. *Epinephelus spiniger* (Günther) and *E. albopunctulatus* Boulenger are synonyms.

Marquesas Islands

157

Underwater World, Singapore

GIANT GROUPER
Epinephelus lanceolatus (Bloch, 1790)
Dorsal rays XI,14–16; anal rays III,8; pectoral rays 18–19 (usually 19); lateral-line scales 54–62; anterior lateral-line scales with branched tubules (except in small juveniles); longitudinal scale series 95–105; scales on body cycloid; body depth 2.35–3.4 in standard length; interorbital space flat to slightly convex; teeth on midside of lower jaw varying from 2 rows in juveniles to 15–16 rows in large adults; third to fifth dorsal spines longest in juveniles, last spine longest in adults; adults gray-brown with scattered, irregular, whitish blotches and numerous small black spots; juveniles yellow with irregular black bars. Reported to 270 cm. One of 250 cm from the Red Sea weighed about 300 kg. Occurs throughout the Indo-Pacific region from the Red Sea and east coast of Africa to the Hawaiian Islands, northern New Zealand, and Pitcairn Islands, though not recorded from many localities, and rare where known; type locality, East Indies. Reported as

Waikīkī Aquarium

deep as 100 m, but usually found in less than 30 m. Occurs in estuaries and harbors but also in clear water on coral reefs. The numbers of this huge fish have declined from angling and spearfishing. Spearing this species is banned in South Africa, and it should be elsewhere.

SNUBNOSE GROUPER
Epinephelus macrospilos (Bleeker, 1855)
Dorsal rays XI,15–17; anal rays III,8; pectoral rays 17–20 (usually 19); lateral-line scales 48–52; longitudinal scale series 86–103; scales on body cycloid except beneath pectoral fins, where ctenoid; body depth 2.95–3.6 in standard length; dorsal profile of head with an angularity over anterior interorbital space; snout short, 4.25–5.3 in head length; interorbital space flat to slightly concave; midside of lower jaw with 2–3 rows of teeth; pale gray-brown with well-spaced dark brown to orange-brown spots of unequal size (but not larger than pupil) on head, body, and fins except pectorals (though these fins may have a few spots basally); caudal fin with a yellow to white posterior margin; soft portions of dorsal and anal fins with a similar narrower margin; Indian Ocean fish with much larger spots, but otherwise not distinguished from the Pacific form. Largest reported, 51 cm. East coast of Africa to Fiji, Samoa Islands, Line Islands, Marquesas Islands, and islands of Micronesia except the Mariana Islands; Ryukyu Islands and Ogasawara Islands to the

Marshall Islands

Great Barrier Reef; type locality, Batjan, Molucca Islands. May be distinguished from *Epinephelus howlandi* by lacking the large blackish spot at rear of spinous portion of dorsal fin, having modally 19 instead of 18 pectoral rays, a more robust body (width 1.4–1.85 in depth, compared with 1.7–2.2 for *howlandi*), and a more strongly projecting lower jaw.

Papua New Guinea/juvenile

Great Barrier Reef

HIGHFIN GROUPER
Epinephelus maculatus (Bloch, 1790)

Dorsal rays XI,15–17; anal rays III,8–9 (rarely 9); pectoral rays 17–19 (nearly always 18); lateral-line scales 49–52; longitudinal scale series 102–120; scales on body ctenoid; body depth 2.75–3.1 in standard length; interorbital space slightly convex; midside of lower jaw with 2 rows of teeth; spinous portion of dorsal fin elevated, at least as high as soft portion, the third or fourth spines longest, 2.1–2.6 in head length; light brown to whitish with numerous close-set, round to hexagonal, dark brown spots on head, body, and fins, the spots on body about pupil size; 2 very large diffuse dusky areas on back that extend broadly into dorsal fin, where they are more heavily pigmented; dark areas on back separated by a pale (though still dark-spotted) area; juveniles yellowish brown to dark brown with large irregular white spots on head and body, the largest on back extending to margin of dorsal fin; larger juveniles with black spots developing within the darker areas of head, body, and fins. Attains about 62 cm. Western Pacific from Japan to Great Barrier Reef, Lord Howe Island, and as juveniles to New South Wales; east to Micronesia and the Samoa Islands; only Cocos-Keeling Islands in the Indian Ocean; type locality, East Indies. Generally found in protected waters such as isolated coral reefs in atoll lagoons; depth range, 2–100 m.

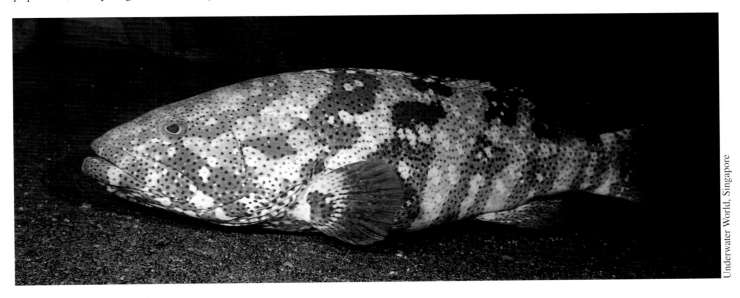
Underwater World, Singapore

MALABAR GROUPER
Epinephelus malabaricus (Bloch & Schneider, 1801)

Dorsal rays XI,14–16 (rarely 16); anal rays III,8; pectoral rays 18–20; lateral-line scales 54–64; anterior lateral-line scales of adults with branched tubules; longitudinal scale series 101–117; ctenoid scales on body except dorsoanteriorly and on chest and abdomen; body elongate, the depth 3.0–3.6 in standard length; width of body 1.4–1.9 in depth; 2 rows of teeth on midside of lower jaw, increasing to 4–5 rows in large adults; light grayish to yellowish brown with 5 slightly oblique, broad, dark brown bars on body that tend to bifurcate ventrally; head and body (and often fins) with small, well-separated, black spots; scattered pale spots and blotches on head and body (larger than black spots but smaller than eye). Reaches at least 115 cm. Red Sea, Gulf of Oman, and east coast of Africa to the western Pacific from Ryukyu Islands to New South Wales, east to Palau, western Caroline Islands, Fiji, and Tonga; type locality, Tranquebar, India. Differentiated from *Epinephelus coioides* by having black instead of orangish spots that are smaller, more widely spaced, and more sharply defined; also by the scattered whitish blotches; *coioides* has modally 20 pectoral rays compared with 19 for *malabaricus* and more rows of teeth on midside of lower jaw at a given size (maximum of 4–5 compared with 3). Occurs mainly on protected reefs and adjacent habitats; readily penetrates estuarine areas. Valuable in aquaculture.

159

BLACKSPOT GROUPER

Epinephelus melanostigma Schultz in Schultz et al., 1953
Dorsal rays XI,14–16; anal rays III,8–9; pectoral rays 17–19; lateral-line scales 56–68; longitudinal scale series 83–99; scales on body ctenoid in a broad zone on side, cycloid elsewhere; lower-limb gill rakers modally 18 (usually 16–17 in other *Epinephelus*); body depth 2.95–3.4 in standard length; caudal-peduncle depth 3.2–3.65 in head length; interorbital space flat to slightly concave; midside of lower jaw with 3–5 rows of teeth; second and third anal spines nearly equal; body and fins with numerous close-set, polygonal, dark orangish brown spots of approximate pupil size (the very narrow whitish space separating spots thus forming a fine reticulum); similar spots on head, progressively smaller anteriorly; a large black spot on back extending into dorsal fin between eighth spine and first soft ray. Largest specimen examined, 32.8 cm, from Taiwan. Wide-ranging from east coast of Africa to the Line Islands and northern Cook Islands, but not reported from many intervening localities; type locality, Swains Island, American Samoa. A shallow-water coral-

Line Islands

reef species; 17 juvenile to subadult specimens collected by the author on a Palmyra reef flat in less than 0.3 m. Long confused with other dark-spotted groupers, particularly *Epinephelus tauvina* and *E. spilotoceps*.

DWARF SPOTTED GROUPER

Epinephelus merra Bloch, 1793
Dorsal rays XI,15–17; anal rays III,8–9 (rarely 9); pectoral rays 16–18; lateral-line scales 48–53; longitudinal scale series 94–114; scales on body ctenoid except for a small anterodorsal area; body depth 2.85–3.3 in standard length; interorbital space flat to slightly convex; midside of lower jaw with 2 rows of teeth; whitish to light brown with numerous close-set (except ventrally), round to hexagonal, dark brown spots, a few of which may be joined to form short, dark, lengthwise bands; spots on head progressively smaller anteriorly; fins with dark brown spots that are progressively smaller distally except pectorals where nearly uniformly small and largely confined to rays. Largest specimen, 31 cm, from Tahiti. A shallow-water coral-reef species of calm areas such as lagoons and bays. Rivaled only by *Epinephelus fasciatus* as the most common and most widespread species of the genus; occurs throughout the Indo-Pacific region except seas of the Arabian Peninsula and the Hawaiian Islands; type locality, "Japanese Sea." An attempt in 1956 to introduce it to the Hawaiian Islands was not successful. Randall & Brock (1960) opened the stomachs of 481 adult specimens from the Society Islands of which 185 contained food (67.6% crustaceans, mainly

Ryukyu Islands

crabs; 28.7% fishes). Randall (1960a) reported ripe female fish in the Society Islands from January to April, with pair spawning occurring each month over a period of 3–4 days, with a peak at 2–3 days before full moon.

NETFIN GROUPER

Epinephelus miliaris (Valenciennes in C & V, 1830)
Dorsal rays XI,16–17; anal rays III,8; pectoral rays 17–18; lateral-line scales 48–52; longitudinal scale series 92–108; scales on body ctenoid except for a small anterodorsal area, on chest, and abdomen; body depth 2.85–3.2 in standard length; interorbital space slightly convex; midside of lower jaw with 2–4 rows of teeth; head and body whitish with numerous very small and very close-set, polygonal, brownish yellow to brown spots; 5 irregular dark bars on body (from spots being darker); broad outer soft portion of dorsal and anal fins, caudal fin, and paired fins with very close-set black spots, most of which are as large as or larger than pupil. Largest examined, 52.5 cm. East coast of Africa to Caroline Islands, Kiribati, Fiji, and Samoa Islands, but known from few localities; type locality, Vanikoro, Santa Cruz Islands.

Guadalcanal

Depth range, less than 1 to about 200 m; those from inshore areas mainly in protected waters of bays, lagoons, or mangrove channels. *Epinephelus gaimardi* (Valenciennes) and *E. diktiophorus* (Bleeker) are synonyms.

Negros, Philippines/juvenile

Bali

SPECKLEFIN GROUPER
Epinephelus ongus (Bloch, 1790)

Dorsal rays XI,14–16; anal rays III,8; pectoral rays 15–17; lateral-line scales 48–53; longitudinal scale series 95–109; scales on body ctenoid except anteriorly above lateral line, on chest, and abdomen; body depth 2.75–3.2 in standard length; interorbital space flat to slightly convex; midside of lower jaw with 2–4 rows of teeth; adults brown with numerous small white spots that tend to form irregular horizontal rows and may coalesce into narrow irregular stripes, especially posteriorly; whitish blotches as large as or larger than eye may be superimposed on the small-spot pattern; a prominent black streak on upper edge of maxillary groove; median fins grayish brown, finely spotted with white, the soft portion of dorsal and anal fins and posterior edge of caudal fin with a narrow white margin and black submarginal band; juveniles of about 70 mm dark brown with many discrete, small, round, white spots; with growth the spots tend to elongate horizontally. Largest examined, 30.5 cm. Reports of lengths to 70 cm may be the result of confusion with *Epinephelus coeruleopunctatus*. Kenya and Mozambique east to Marshall Islands and Caroline Islands and Fiji; in the western Pacific from Ryukyu and Ogasawara Islands to Great Barrier Reef and New Caledonia; type locality given as Japan. A shallow-water fish of coral reefs and rocky substrata, usually found in the vicinity of caves and ledges. Often misidentified as *E. summana* (Forsskål), a related species endemic to the Red Sea and Gulf of Aden (Randall & Ben-Tuvia, 1983).

Flores, Indonesia/juvenile

Marshall Islands

CAMOUFLAGE GROUPER
Epinephelus polyphekadion (Bleeker, 1849)

Dorsal rays XI,14–15 (more often 15); anal rays III,8; pectoral rays 16–18 (rarely 18); lateral-line scales 47–52; longitudinal scale series 95–113; scales ctenoid in a broad zone on side of body, cycloid elsewhere; body depth 2.7–3.1 in standard length; interorbital space usually flat; midside of lower jaw with 2–3 rows of teeth; posterior nostril of adults vertically ovate and larger than anterior nostril (may be twice as large); light brown with large, irregular, brown blotches on head and body; numerous small, close-set, dark brown spots superimposed on this pattern; small spots covering all of head, including lips and gill membranes; a prominent saddle-like black spot on caudal peduncle; all fins with numerous small, dark brown spots and scattered, larger white spots; juveniles with a pair of blackish spots dorsally on snout. Largest examined, 75 cm, from Rapa. Red Sea and east coast of Africa to the Line Islands and Tuamotu Archipelago; in the western Pacific from the Ryukyu Islands to the Great Barrier Reef and Lord Howe Island; type locality, Java. Most records from insular localities in clear water on coral reefs, both in lagoons and outer reef areas. Randall (1980a) reviewed the food-habit studies of Hiatt & Strasburg (1960), Randall & Brock (1960), and Helfrich et al. (1968). Crustaceans, especially crabs, comprised more than 60% of the diet, followed by fishes; a few had eaten cephalopods and gastropods. Often misidentified in older literature as *Epinephelus fuscoguttatus* (Forsskål) or *E. microdon* (Bleeker), the latter a synonym.

161

REDTIPPED GROUPER

Epinephelus retouti Beeker, 1868

Dorsal rays XI,16–17 (usually 16); anal rays III,8; pectoral rays 19–20 (rarely 20); lateral-line scales 64–76; longitudinal scale series 120–141; scales on body ctenoid except anteriorly; numerous auxiliary scales present on body; body depth 2.5–3.15 in standard length; interorbital space flat to slightly convex; maxilla not reaching a vertical at rear edge of orbit; nostrils nearly equal; caudal fin truncate to very slightly rounded; adults yellowish orange to brownish red, usually with 5 faint dark bars on body; orbit narrowly edged in deep red except anteriorly, with an adjacent outer blue line encircling eye; fins orangish except dorsal fin, which is gray-brown, the outer triangular part of each interspinous membrane deep red; upper one-fifth of caudal fin gray-brown. Juveniles with upper part of first 3 dark bars on body black, the second and third bars extending into dorsal fin; head above level of lower edge of eye black, the dorsal part with 4 irregular narrow whitish bars. Attains 47 cm. Known from

Taiwan

Mozambique Channel, Mauritius, and Chagos Archipelago to Line Islands, Society Islands, and Tuamotu Archipelago; in the western Pacific from Japan to New Caledonia; adults generally found in 70–220 m; juveniles may be seen at lesser depths. *Epinephelus truncatus* Katayama and *E. mauritianus* Baissac are synonyms.

HALFMOON GROUPER

Epinephelus rivulatus (Valenciennes in C & V, 1830)

Dorsal rays XI,16–18; anal rays III,8; pectoral rays 17–19 (rarely 19); lateral-line scales 48–53; longitudinal scale series 86–98; scales on body ctenoid except for chest, abdomen, and a zone of very small cycloid scales with numerous pores anterodorsally on body above lateral line and on nape; body depth 2.75–3.2 in standard length; interorbital space flat to slightly convex; midside of lower jaw with 2 close-set rows of teeth; reddish to greenish brown with a pale blue or white spot on each scale; 5 irregular, oblique, dark brown bars usually present on body; chest with 2 irregular, oblique, dark brown bands; head with broad, irregular, dark brown bands; base of pectoral fins with a large, dark red to reddish brown semicircular spot; fins without spots, the dorsal often with a black line along base. Largest examined, 39 cm, from New South Wales. Southern Arabian Peninsula and east coast of Africa to western Pacific from Japan to Western

Okinawa

Australia, New South Wales, and northern New Zealand; type locality, Réunion; localities from Oceania include Ogasawara Islands, Solomon Islands, New Caledonia, Norfolk Island, and Lord Howe Island. Known from depths of 1–150 m in a variety of habitats from coral reefs to seagrass and algal flats. *Epinephelus ryncholepis* (Bleeker) is one of 7 synonyms.

SURGE GROUPER

Epinephelus socialis (Günther, 1873)

Dorsal rays XI,14–16; anal rays III,8; pectoral rays 18–19 (usually 19); lateral-line scales 64–70; longitudinal scale series 97–111; scales usually ctenoid in a zone of variable size on side of body, cycloid elsewhere (1 large specimen with no ctenoid scales); body moderately elongate, the depth 2.95–3.4 in standard length; interorbital space flat to slightly convex; midside of lower jaw with 3–4 rows of teeth; whitish with numerous very small, close-set, dark brown to black spots on head and body except ventrally, those posteriorly on body often coalesced to form irregular longitudinal bands; 5 large blackish blotches usually present along back; median fins colored like body only basally, the caudal and soft portions of the dorsal and anal fins with small white spots; outer margin of these fins white, usually with a black submarginal band. Largest, 52 cm, from Pitcairn. Reported from the following islands of Oceania: Ogasawara,

Marshall Islands

Minami-tori-shima (Marcus), Mariana, Marshall, Phoenix, Samoa, Line, Society (type locality, Tahiti), Rapa, Tuamotu, and Pitcairn, mainly from atolls and low islands. A shallow-water species usually found in exposed outer-reef areas, often in tidepools.

FOURSADDLE GROUPER

Epinephelus spilotoceps Schultz in Schultz et al., 1953
Dorsal rays XI,14–16; anal rays III,8; pectoral rays
17–19 (usually 19); lateral-line scales 59–69; longitudinal scale series 86–100; lower-limb gill rakers
modally 18 (usually 16–17 in other *Epinephelus*);
scales on body ctenoid except anterodorsally, on
chest, and abdomen; body moderately elongate, the
depth 2.95–3.4 in standard length; caudal peduncle
slender, its depth 3.7–4.35 in head length; interorbital
space flat; second and third anal spines nearly equal;
midside of lower jaw with 3–4 rows of teeth; whitish
with many dark brown spots, those on body mostly
smaller than pupil, close-set except ventrally; dark
spots on head progressively shorter anteriorly, those
on snout black and size of nostrils, those on front of
upper lip in 3 or 4 irregular horizontal rows; a large
black spot on back and into base of last 4 dorsal
spines, 2 similar smaller spots below soft portion of dorsal fin,
and 1 dorsally on caudal peduncle; all fins with dark brown
spots. Largest examined, 31.2 cm. East coast of Africa and
islands of Indian Ocean to Marshall Islands (type locality, Bikini

Penyu Islands, Indonesia

Atoll), Caroline Islands, Line Islands, and Cook Islands; not
known from the Red Sea, shores of Asia, Australia, Philippines,
Taiwan, or Japan. A shallow-water coral-reef species found
mainly at oceanic islands.

Marshall Islands

GREASY GROUPER

Epinephelus tauvina (Forsskål, 1775)
Dorsal rays XI,13–16 (rarely 13); anal rays III,8; pectoral rays
18–19 (more often 19); lateral-line scales 63–74; longitudinal
scale series 95–112; scales on body ctenoid except anterodorsally, on chest, and abdomen; lower-limb gill rakers modally
18–19 (usually 16–17 in other *Epinephelus*); body elongate,
the depth 2.95–3.6 in standard length; interorbital space flat; second and third anal spines nearly equal; midside of lower jaw with
3–4 rows of teeth; posterior nostril of large adults (40 cm or
more) twice as large as anterior nostril; light greenish gray to
brown dorsally, whitish ventrally, with numerous roundish, well-
separated, reddish brown to dark brown spots on head, body, and
fins; 5 faint, dusky, oblique bars or series of large blotches often
present on body; a large blackish blotch or group of blackish
spots usually present at base of last 4 dorsal spines and extending into base of fin; 4 lesser groups of blackish spots often evident posteriorly along back; all fins dark-spotted, the spots on
pectorals small and faint or absent on outer fourth. Largest
examined, nearly 75 cm, from Wadge Bank, Sri Lanka.
Widespread from the Red Sea (type locality) and east coast of
Africa to the Line Islands and Pitcairn Islands; in the western
Pacific from Ryukyu Islands to New South Wales and Lord
Howe Island; no records from the Philippines or Indonesia; most
localities are insular clear-water areas with well-developed coral
reefs; depth range 0.3–52 m. Limited food-habit data indicate
feeding mainly on small reef fishes (Randall, 1980a). The
name *Epinephelus tauvina* has often been erroneously applied
to other large dark-spotted groupers. *Epinephelus elongatus*
Schultz is one of 5 synonyms.

New Britain

Kakabia, Indonesia/juvenile

Line Islands

SLENDERSPINE GROUPER

Gracila albomarginata (Fowler & Bean, 1930)

Dorsal rays IX,14–16; anal rays III,9–10 (usually 9); dorsal and anal spines slender; pectoral rays 18–19 (usually 19); lateral-line scales 66–76; longitudinal scale series 101–114; body depth 2.6–3.3 in standard length; head small, 2.9–3.2 in standard length; interorbital space slightly convex; side of lower jaw with 2 rows of teeth, the outer teeth fixed, the inner twice as long and depressible; caudal fin truncate to slightly emarginate; greenish to brownish gray or orangish brown, pale ventrally, with 16–20 narrow dark brown to orangish brown bars on side of body; 4 oblique blue lines (may be broken into dashes and spots) on head; a black spot about as large as eye posteriorly on side of

caudal peduncle; a transient color phase has a large white area in the middle of back flanked by 2 blackish areas of about the same size, and the caudal peduncle nearly white except for the black spot; juveniles strikingly colored purple to brown with a bright orange-red stripe in dorsal and anal fins and in each lobe of caudal fin extending onto upper and lower edges of caudal peduncle. Reaches nearly 40 cm. East coast of Africa to the Tuamotu Archipelago and Line Islands; in the western Pacific from the Ryukyu Islands to the Great Barrier Reef and New Caledonia; type locality, Danawan Island, Borneo. Occurs on coral reefs, generally at depths greater than 15 m to at least 100 m. More of a roving predator than most groupers.

164

Marshall Islands

Palau

BLACKSADDLE CORALGROUPER

Plectropomus laevis (Lacepède, 1801)

Dorsal rays VIII,11; anal rays III,8; pectoral rays 16–18; lateral-line scales 92–115; longitudinal scale series 123–153; no scales in interorbital space; 3 antrorse spines on lower margin of pre-opercle; a pair of stout canine teeth anteriorly in jaws and 1–4 on side of lower jaw (true of other species of *Plectropomus*); body elongate, the depth 2.95–3.65 in standard length; outer margin of anal fin straight; caudal fin slightly emarginate; 2 color phases, one white with 5 dark brown bars on head and body, scattered small dark-edged blue spots, and yellow fins; the other phase reddish brown with numerous small, dark-edged blue spots on head, body, and fins; dark bars as in first phase usually present but less conspicuous. Reaches about 125 cm. East coast of Africa to the Tuamotu Archipelago; in the western Pacific from the Ryukyu Islands to the Great Barrier Reef and New Caledonia; type locality, Indian Ocean; reported from 4 to at least 90 m. Preys mainly on reef fishes. One of the worst offenders in causing ciguatera fish poisoning when eaten. *Plectropomus melanoleucus* (Lacepède) is a synonym based on the first color phase. The young of this phase are remarkably similar to *Canthigaster valentini* and presumed to be a mimic of this small toxic puffer.

165

Coral Sea

LEOPARD CORALGROUPER

Plectropomus leopardus (Lacepède, 1802)

Dorsal rays VIII,11; anal rays III,8; pectoral rays 14–17 (modally 16); lateral-line scales 89–99; longitudinal scale series 112–127; no scales in interorbital space; 3 antrorse spines on lower margin of preopercle; body elongate, the depth 2.9–3.6 in standard length; outer margin of anal fin straight to slightly convex; caudal fin slightly emarginate; olivaceous to reddish brown with numerous dark-edged blue dots on head and body (except ventrally), and median fins; caudal fin with a narrow white posterior margin except near corners. Attains about 75 cm. Western Australia and western Pacific from southern Japan to the Great Barrier reef, east to Fiji and Caroline Islands; type locality not given. Reported from depths of 3–100 m. Goeden (1978) studied the biology; fish of 50 cm standard length were estimated to be 5 years old; spawning on the Great Barrier Reef occurs in late November and early December; 90% of the prey consisted of fishes.

Maldive Islands

ROVING CORALGROUPER

Plectropomus pessuliferus (Fowler, 1904)

Dorsal rays VIII,11; anal rays III,8; pectoral rays 15–16 (usually 16); lateral-line scales 85–104; longitudinal scale series 112–142; no embedded scales in interorbital space; 3 antrorse spines on lower margin of preopercle; posterior nostril of adults over 40 cm distinctly larger than anterior nostril; gill raker at angle of first gill arch shorter than gill filaments; outer margin of anal fin from fourth to eighth ray straight to slightly convex; caudal fin emarginate, the caudal concavity 4.2–6.2 in head length; pelvic fins 1.9–2.35 in head length; brown to orange-red with numerous small, dark-edged blue spots on head, body, and fins (only basally on pectorals); some spots on side of body vertically elongate. Largest specimen, 63 cm. Reported from Red Sea (where regarded as subspecifically different, *Plectropomus pessuliferus marisrubri* Randall & Hoese), Zanzibar, St. Brandon's Shoals, Maldive Islands, Sri Lanka, Sumatra (type locality), and Fiji; Red Sea subspecies may be seen in only a few meters, but depths recorded from elsewhere are 25–147 m.

Bali/juvenile

Papua New Guinea

LYRETAIL GROUPER

Variola albimarginata Baissac, 1952

Dorsal rays IX,14; anal rays III,8; pectoral rays 17–19; lateral-line scales 66–75; longitudinal scale series 109–127; a pair of large canine teeth anteriorly in jaws and 1 or 2 large curved canines on side of lower jaw; body elongate, the depth 2.85–3.5 in standard length; tenth and eleventh dorsal soft rays and fourth and fifth anal soft rays prolonged; caudal fin lunate; pelvic fins usually not reaching anus, 1.35–1.8 in head; body with red spots (sometimes with yellow centers), many coalesced to form irregular longitudinal bands separated by much narrower yellow bands; caudal fin with a narrow white posterior margin and dark submarginal band; juveniles brownish red with small blue spots. Attains 60 cm. East coast of Africa to western Pacific from Ryukyu Islands to southern Great Barrier Reef and New Caledonia, east to islands of Micronesia and the Samoa Islands; type locality, Mauritius. Occurs on coral reefs at depths of 15 to 90 m. Limited data indicate a piscivorous diet.

Papua New Guinea/subadult

Maldive Islands

CORONATION GROUPER

Variola louti (Forsskål, 1775)

Dorsal rays IX,13–14 (rarely 13); anal rays III,8; pectoral rays 16–19 (rarely 16 or 19); lateral-line scales 66–77; longitudinal scale series 113–135; a pair of large canine teeth anteriorly in jaws and 1 or 2 large curved canines on side of lower jaw; body elongate, the depth 2.8–3.2 in standard length; tenth and eleventh dorsal soft rays and fourth and fifth anal soft rays prolonged; caudal fin lunate; pelvic fins extending posterior to anus, 1.0–1.6 in head length; body yellowish brown (fish from deeper water orange-red), with many small spots and short dashes that may be blue, lavender, or pink; head with close-set, dark-edged, blue to lavender spots; fins with small blue to lavender spots, the posterior margin of median and pectoral fins broadly yellow; juveniles with very small pink to blue spots and a broad black stripe from eye to below rear of dorsal fin followed by a large black blotch dorsally at base of caudal fin; body above stripe orange, below white. Largest examined, 81 cm. Red Sea (type locality) and east coast of Africa to the Line Islands and Pitcairn Islands; in the western Pacific from southern Japan to New South Wales and Lord Howe Island. Reported from depths of 10–240 m; typically found on coral reefs in clear water, most often at oceanic islands. Randall (1980a) and Morgans (1982) have shown that the majority of the prey are fishes. Has been implicated in ciguatera fish poisoning.

Natal/juvenile

Maldive Islands

Cook Islands (R. L. Pyle)

Komodo, Indonesia

SOAPFISHES (GRAMMISTINAE)

ARROWHEAD SOAPFISH
Belonoperca chabanaudi Fowler & Bean, 1930
Dorsal rays VIII (rarely IX) + I,10; anal rays II,8; pectoral rays 13–15; lateral-line scales 69–76; scales ctenoid; body elongate, the depth 3.5–3.7 in standard length; head pointed; upper edge of opercle joined to body by membrane (true of other soapfishes); preopercle coarsely serrate; caudal fin truncate; basal half of inner pelvic ray joined by membrane to abdomen (also characteristic of soapfishes); olivaceous to brown, finely dotted with dark brown (as larger dark brown spots in juveniles); a bright yellow saddle-like spot on caudal peduncle; a large, blue-edged, black spot in spinous dorsal fin. Attains 15 cm. East coast of Africa to Tahiti (Randall et al., 2002a) and the islands of Micronesia; in the western Pacific from the Ryukyu Islands to the Great Barrier Reef and New Caledonia; type locality, Sulawesi. Occurs mainly on outer reef slopes from depths of 4–45 m; hidden in caves by day, becoming active at dusk (but still remains near cover). Reclassified as a soapfish after the discovery that it has a grammistin-like skin toxin (Randall et al., 1980).

ORANGESPOTTED SOAPFISH
Belonoperca pylei Baldwin & Smith, 1998
Dorsal rays IX,10, the fin moderately notched; anal rays III,7; pectoral rays 14; lateral-line scales 69–76; scales ctenoid; body very elongate, the depth 3.85–4.75 in standard length; head strongly pointed; preopercle serrate; caudal fin truncate; light yellow with a broad longitudinal band of close-set, irregular, pupil-size, orange spots on body; juveniles almost entirely yellow. Largest specimen, 8 cm. Described from 5 specimens taken in Rarotonga, Cook Islands, at depths of 68–122 m. Baldwin & Smith (1998) described the larva of a species of *Belonoperca* from the Philippines believed to be *pylei*, and a specimen was recently collected by Brian Greene at Kwajalein, Marshall Islands. Though slightly different in color, it is provisionally identified as *pylei*.

BARRED SOAPFISH
Diploprion bifasciatum Cuvier in C & V, 1828
Dorsal rays VIII,13–16, the fin deeply notched; anal rays II,12–13; pectoral rays 17–18; lateral-line scales 71–76; scales ctenoid; body deep, the depth 2.0–2.4 in standard length, and compressed, the width 3.3–4.0 in depth; preopercle coarsely serrate; caudal fin rounded; pelvic fins very long, reaching beyond spinous portion of anal fin; yellow with a black bar through eye and a broad one in middle of body continuing onto posterior two-thirds of spinous portion of dorsal fin; an occasional color form is black with caudal and soft portions of dorsal and anal fins yellow. Reported to 25 cm. India to the western Pacific from southern Japan to New South Wales, Lord Howe Island, and New Caledonia; type locality, Java. From coral reefs and adjacent habitats, generally in protected waters; reported from depths of 5–50 m. Secretes a skin toxin under stress from epidermal glandular cells; soapfishes of the genera *Grammistes*, *Pogonoperca*, and *Rypticus* produce more of the toxin in multicellular dermal glands.

SIXLINE SOAPFISH
Grammistes sexlineatus (Thunberg,1792)
Dorsal rays VII,13–14, the fin deeply notched; anal rays II,9; pectoral rays 16–18; lateral-line scales 60–72; scales cycloid; body depth 2.2–2.8 in standard length; posterior margin of preopercle with 2–4 short, broad-based spines; a small fleshy flap at tip of chin; caudal fin rounded; pelvic fins short; black with 6–8 yellow stripes and 1 mid-dorsal on head and nape; stripes of very large adults break into series of dashes; juveniles with fewer stripes; small juveniles with 2 longitudinal series of large pale yellow spots. Largest reported, 27 cm. Red Sea and east coast of Africa to islands of Micronesia and French Polynesia; in the western Pacific from Japan (probable type locality) to Lord Howe Island and the Kermadec Islands; a shallow-water species that usually hides in caves or beneath ledges during the day. The skin toxin is extremely bitter; the author once fed a live juvenile to a Turkeyfish (*Pterois volitans*) in an aquarium, which quickly released the soap-fish and then made 2 expelling movements of its mouth, suggesting a lingering bad taste.

Taiwan

Tahiti

OCELLATED SOAPFISH
Grammistops ocellatus Schultz in Schultz et al., 1953
Dorsal rays VII,12–13 (rarely 13), the fin deeply notched; anal rays II,8–9 (rarely 8); pectoral rays 14–15; lateral-line scales 58–67; scales cycloid; body elongate, the depth 3.1–3.7 in standard length; head pointed; posterior margin of preopercle smooth or with 1 or 2 short, broad-based spines; caudal fin rounded; pelvic fins short; gray-brown, the head yellowish brown with a large ocellated black spot on opercle (illustrated specimen unusual in the division of the opercular spot into 3 spots). Largest specimen, 13.2 cm. East coast of Africa to Tahiti, but otherwise reported only from the Ryukyu Islands and islands of Micronesia (type locality, Bikini Atoll). Never observed alive underwater by the author by day or night. Produces a skin toxin when threatened.

SPOTTED SOAPFISH
Pogonoperca punctata (Valenciennes in C & V, 1830)
Dorsal rays VIII,12–13, the fin nearly divided by a deep notch; anal rays II,8; pectoral rays 17–18; lateral-line scales 59–70; scales ctenoid; body depth 2.2–2.7 in standard length; posterior margin of preopercle with 3 to 5 short spines; a fleshy barbel about as large in area as eye oriented transversely at tip of chin; caudal fin rounded; pelvic fins short; head and body brown, densely covered with small white spots; a black bar through eye and 4 triangular black saddles on body, progressively smaller posteriorly; juveniles darker brown with larger white spots. Largest examined, 30 cm, from Okinawa. Andaman Sea to the Line Islands, Marquesas Islands, and Society Islands and throughout Micronesia; in the western Pacific from southern Japan to New Caledonia; type locality, Vanikoro Island, Santa Cruz Islands. Closely related to *Pogonoperca ocellata* Günther from the western Indian Ocean. Secretive and not common. Occurs mainly in outer-reef areas; reported from depths of 25–216 m.

Banda, Indonesia

169

Line Islands

Coral Sea

Fiji

PODGES (PSEUDOGRAMMINAE)

PORELESS PODGE
Aporops bilinearis Schultz, 1943
Dorsal rays VII,23–25; anal rays III,19–21; pectoral rays 15–17; 2 lateral lines, the first ending below soft portion of dorsal fin, the second midlateral on posterior part of body; longitudinal scale series 53–59; a prominent spine on preopercle (directed obliquely upward in this species, but obliquely downward on other podges); no large pores in interorbital space of adults; no canine teeth anteriorly in upper jaw; caudal fin small and rounded (true of other podges); light brown with scattered, vertically elongate, dark brown spots. Largest, 11.5 cm, from Taiwan. East coast of Africa to the Hawaiian Islands and Marquesas Islands, but no records from Southeast Asia, Philippines, or Indonesia; type locality, Hull Island, Phoenix Islands. A common shallow-water species, mainly from outer-reef areas exposed to surge; depth range from less than 1 to 15 m. Known only from collections made with ichthyocide; not seen alive by the author.

SPOTLESS PODGE
Pseudogramma astigmum Randall & Baldwin, 1997
Dorsal rays VII,21–23; anal rays III,17–18 (usually 18); pectoral rays 14–15 (usually 14); a single, incomplete lateral line; longitudinal scale series 50–51; no dermal flap or small tentacle above eye; a pair of large pores in interorbital space (true of other *Pseudogramma*); a small, stout canine tooth anteriorly on each side of upper jaw (also true of other *Pseudogramma*); longest pectoral ray reaching well posterior to a vertical at origin of soft portion of anal fin; light gray to yellowish or reddish brown with indistinct, interconnected, darker blotches of about eye size on body; a broad dark band extending posteriorly from eye, and a horizontal, broken, dark brown line across cheek; no black spot on opercle. Largest, 8.4 cm. Known to date only from Comoro Islands, Papua New Guinea, Coral Sea, Pohnpei, Marshall Islands (type locality, Enewetak Atoll), Vanuatu, and American Samoa from reefs at depths of 10–46 m.

PALE-SPOTTED PODGE
Pseudogramma polyacanthum (Bleeker, 1856)
Dorsal rays VII,19–22; anal rays III,16–18; pectoral rays 14–17; a single, incomplete lateral line (a few pored scales on caudal peduncle of a few specimens); longitudinal scale series 46–50; no dermal flap or short tentacle dorsally on eye; longest pectoral ray not reaching a vertical at origin of soft portion of anal fin; dark brown with 5 longitudinal rows of light brown to pale yellowish blotches about size of eye on body (pale spots much smaller and more sharply defined in juveniles); a large ocellated black spot on opercle. Largest specimen, 8.6 cm, from Hawaiian Islands. Known from east coast of Africa to the Hawaiian Islands and Pitcairn Islands; in the western Pacific from the Ryukyu Islands to the Great Barrier Reef, Lord Howe Island, and New Caledonia; not reported from the Red Sea to India; type locality, Ternate, Molucca Islands. One of the most common Indo-Pacific reef fishes; specimens have been collected with ichthyocide from depths of 1–64 m. The author has never observed it alive by day or night (photo is of rotenone specimen). Feeds primarily on small benthic crustaceans (Hiatt & Strasburg, 1960).

YELLOW PODGE
Pseudogramma xanthum Randall, Baldwin & Williams, 2002
Dorsal rays VII,19–21; anal rays III,16–18; pectoral rays 14–15; a single incomplete lateral line; longitudinal scale series 50–52; a broad-based dermal flap dorsally on eye; body yellow, shading to whitish on abdomen and chest, with indistinct white blotches and scattered dark red dots; head yellow dorsally with numerous dark red dots, white ventrally with fewer dark red dots, some forming lines; a blackish blotch on opercle containing dark red dots. Attains 5 cm. Known in the southern subtropical Pacific from Pitcairn Island, southern Tuamotu Archipelago (type locality, Temoe Atoll), Cook Islands, and Tonga. Collected with ichthy-

Tuamotu Archipelago

ocide from depths of 26–42 m and by dredging off Pitcairn to 100 m. First considered as a subspecies of *Pseudogramma australis* Randall & Baldwin from Easter Island, and was mistakenly named *P. a. australis*.

PALESTRIPE PODGE
Suttonia lineata Gosline, 1960
Dorsal rays VII,22–25; anal rays III,19–22; pectoral rays 15–17; a single lateral line ending beneath soft portion of dorsal fin; longitudinal scale series 52–56; scales ctenoid but cteni not projecting beyond membranous edge of scales (as in *Pseudogramma* and *Aporops*); no dermal flap dorsally on eye; a pair of large pores in interorbital space; a small canine tooth anteriorly on each side of upper jaw; body of adults dark red, mottled with dark brown, the median fins with less dark pigment; head dark red to reddish gray, the lower half generally abruptly paler; a dusky band sometimes present posterior to eye; a median pale pink stripe from tip of lower jaw to dorsal-fin origin; no distinct dark brown or black spot on opercle. Largest, 9.6 cm, from Hawaiian Islands (type locality, O'ahu). Also known from the Philippines, Indonesia, Great Barrier Reef, and islands of Oceania from Guam and New Caledonia to Palmyra and Tahiti; and Christmas Island and Cocos-Keeling Islands in the Indian Ocean.

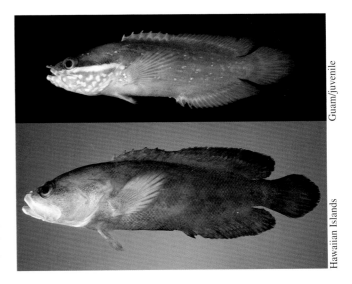

Guam/juvenile

Hawaiian Islands

BASSLETS (LIOPROPOMINAE)

YELLOW BASSLET
Liopropoma flavidum Randall & Taylor, 1988
Dorsal rays VI + I + I,12; anal rays III,8; pectoral rays 14; lateral-line scales 46; head nearly fully scaled; inner teeth at front of jaws and side of lower jaw about 5–6 times longer than outer teeth; lips smooth; posterior margin of preopercle with 8 poorly defined serrae; a pair of prominent pores anterior to posterior nostril, and another pair in anterior interorbital space; pelvic fins 1.75 in head length; bright yellow in life. Known from a single specimen collected by the author on a coral reef at Rurutu, Austral Islands, in 58 m.

Austral Islands

HEADBAND BASSLET
Liopropoma mitratum Lubbock & Randall, 1978
Dorsal rays VI + I (spine tip usually visible) + I,11–12 (rarely 11); anal rays III,8; pectoral rays 13–15 (usually 14); lateral-line scales 45–48; scales dorsally on snout reaching to or slightly anterior to posterior nostrils; lips finely papillate; posterior margin of preopercle with 19–30 serrae; an enlarged pore (sometimes bilobed or as a close-set pair) in front of each posterior nostril, but none in anterior interorbital space; pelvic fins 1.65–1.85 in head length; red to reddish brown, sometimes suffused with yellow posteriorly, with or without lengthwise dotted brown lines following scale rows on body; 1 to 3 dull yellow stripes on head extending posteriorly from eye. Largest specimen, 8.2 cm, from Tutuila. The most wide-ranging species of the

Luzon

genus, but not known from many localities; reported from the Red Sea (type locality), Christmas Island (Indian Ocean), Rowley Shoals (Western Australia), Seram (Indonesia), Papua New Guinea, Philippines, Palau, Caroline Islands, American Samoa, and Tuamotu Archipelago; specimens have been collected from depths of 3–46 m, most from more than 15 m.

Solomon Islands

Tahiti

LINED BASSLET

Liopropoma multilineatum Randall & Taylor, 1988

Dorsal rays VI + I + I,11–12 (rarely 11); anal rays III,8; pectoral rays 18–20 (modally 19); lateral-line scales 46–47; head nearly fully scaled; lips finely papillate; posterior margin of preopercle with 10–16 small serrae; a pair of pores anterior to posterior nostril and another pair in anterior interorbital space; pelvic fins 1.35–1.6 in head length; body yellow, becoming red posteriorly, with longitudinal red lines following scale rows; caudal peduncle with a narrow, mid-lateral white band; head light red; caudal fin with a broad red band in each lobe, continuous with red of caudal peduncle. Largest, 7.7 cm, from Fiji. Philippines to the Coral Sea, east to Fiji; also from Rowley Shoals off northwestern Australia; type locality, Florida Island, Solomon Islands; depth range, 25–46 m.

STRIPED BASSLET

Liopropoma susumi (Jordan & Seale, 1906)

Dorsal rays VI + I + I,11–12 (rarely 11); anal rays III,8; pectoral rays 15–16 (usually 15); lateral-line scales 44–47 (modally 46); scales dorsally on snout reaching only to posterior nostrils or slightly before; inner teeth at front of jaws and side of lower jaw 2–3 times longer than outer teeth; lips finely papillate; posterior margin of preopercle with 6–17 serrae; no enlarged pores anterior to posterior nostrils or in anterior interorbital space (instead groups of very small pores); pelvic fins short, 1.75–1.95 in head length; light gray, shading to red on caudal peduncle and fin, with 8 narrow, yellowish brown stripes on body, the middle 4 converging onto head to end at eye. Largest specimen, 9.1 cm, from Palmyra. Red Sea, coast of East Africa, and islands of the western Indian Ocean to Line Islands, Samoa Islands (type locality, Western Samoa), and islands of Micronesia except the Mari-

PALLID BASSLET

Liopropoma pallidum (Fowler, 1938)

Dorsal rays VI + I + I,12 (sixth spine may not be emergent); anal rays III,8; pectoral rays 15–16; lateral-line scales 46–47; scales dorsally on snout reaching only to posterior nostrils or slightly before; lips finely papillate; posterior margin of preopercle with 8–13 serrae; no enlarged pores anterior to posterior nostrils or in anterior interorbital space (instead groups of very small pores); pelvic fins short, 1.75–1.95 in head length; reddish gray to reddish brown anteriorly, shading posteriorly to orange-red or brownish red; faint brownish orange longitudinal lines following scale rows on body; iris yellow. Largest specimen, 7.8 cm, from Rurutu, Austral Islands. Otherwise known from the Pitcairn Islands, Society Islands, Ogasawara Islands, and the islands of Micronesia; type locality, Kiritimati (Christmas Island), Line Islands; depth of capture 15–40 m.

Fiji

ana Islands; in the western Pacific from the Ryukyu Islands to the southern Great Barrier Reef and New Caledonia. Judging from museum collections, the most common species of the genus. Known from depths of 2–34 m.

BARBERSHOP BASSLET

Liopropoma tonstrinum Randall & Taylor, 1988

Dorsal rays VI + I + I,12; anal rays III,8; pectoral rays 14; lateral-line scales 45–47; head nearly fully scaled; lips smooth; posterior margin of preopercle irregular, without obvious serrae; a pair of pores anterior to posterior nostril and another in anterior interorbital space; pelvic fins 1.4–1.7 in head length; head light red anteriorly, shading to yellow behind eye and onto nape and abdomen; body with 2 very broad red stripes continuing into caudal fin, separated by a narrow midlateral white band. Reaches 8 cm. Known from Christmas Island in the Indian Ocean, the islands of Micronesia (type locality, Palau), Fiji, Samoa Islands, and Tahiti (Randall et al., 2002a). Depth range, 11–50 m.

Palau

HAWKFISHES
(CIRRHITIDAE)

This family of 12 genera and 33 species is characterized by having X dorsal spines and 11–17 soft rays; anal fin with III spines and 5–7 (usually 6) soft rays; pectoral fins with 14 rays, of which the lower 5–7 are unbranched and thickened; pelvic fins with I spine and 5 soft rays; membrane at tip of each dorsal spine with a single cirrus (*Paracirrhites*) or a tuft of many cirri (other cirrhitid genera); 2 flat opercular spines; cycloid scales; and no swimbladder. All the species are benthic on coral reefs or rocky substrata, using their thickened lower pectoral rays to wedge themselves in place and to maintain position in areas of surge. All the species are carnivorous, darting out rapidly to prey on small fishes and crustaceans. *Cyprinocirrhites polyactis* frequently leaves the substratum to feed a meter or more above on zooplankton; *Oxycirrhites typus* makes quick forays into the water column for feeding from its usual perch on black corals or gorgonians. Protogynous hermaphroditism has been demonstrated for several cirrhitids (Sadovy & Donaldson, 1995), and most species are believed to be haremic. Randall (1963b) reviewed the family, and Randall (2001b) revised the generic classification. The South Pacific region is unusual in having 17 species of cirrhitid fishes, including 5 that are found only there.

TWINSPOT HAWKFISH
Amblycirrhitus bimacula (Jenkins, 1903)

Dorsal rays X,12; anal rays III,6; pectoral rays 14, the lower 5 unbranched; lateral-line scales 40–42; 3 rows of large scales above lateral line in middle of body; 4 or 5 rows of large scales on cheek; palatine teeth present; posterior margin of preopercle finely serrate (true of other *Amblycirrhitus*) body depth 2.8–3.0 in standard length; longest pectoral ray reaching a vertical at base of second anal spine; whitish with 10 dusky orange to dark reddish brown bars on body, some broken into elongate blotches, the sixth bifurcating dorsally to accommodate a large black spot below base of soft portion of dorsal fin; opercle with an ocellated black spot of nearly the same size. Largest examined, 8.5 cm. East coast of Africa and islands of western Indian Ocean to the Hawaiian Islands (type locality, Oʻahu) and Pitcairn Islands; in the western Pacific from Okinawa, Ogasawara Islands, and Taiwan to the Great Barrier Reef. A shallow-water species; the most cryptic of the hawkfishes; rarely seen in the open.

ONESPOT HAWKFISH
Amblycirrhitus unimacula (Kamohara, 1957)

Dorsal rays X,11; anal rays III,6; pectoral rays 14, the lower 5 unbranched; lateral-line scales 45–49; 4–5 oblique rows of large scales on cheek; a few small teeth anteriorly on palatines; body depth 2.8–3.2 in standard length; longest pectoral ray reaching at most slightly posterior to anus; whitish with 10 dark brown bars or as vertical rows of large dark brown blotches; an ocellated black spot larger than eye on back and extending partly into base of soft portion of dorsal fin; head with many irregular dark spots and short bands, but no large black spot on opercle; membrane behind tip of each dorsal spine black, the cirri pink. Largest specimen, 11 cm. Described from a single specimen from a tidepool in the Ryukyu Islands; specimens have been examined from Lanyu, Taiwan (Randall, 1963b); American Samoa (Wass, 1984); Îlots de Bass (Marotiri); Pitcairn Islands; Batanes Islands, northern Philippines; Eua, Tonga; and Erromango, Vanuatu (the last 3 localities provided by David G. Smith and Jeffrey T. Williams of the Smithsonian Institution). The known localities of this species suggest an antiequatorial distribution.

Hawaiian Islands

American Samoa (R. C. Wass)

DWARF HAWKFISH

Cirrhitichthys falco Randall, 1963

Dorsal rays X,12; anal rays III,6; pectoral rays 14, the lower 6 unbranched; lateral-line scales 40–47; palatine teeth present (true of other *Cirrhitichthys*); posterior margin of preopercle coarsely serrate (generic); body depth 2.9–3.4 in standard length; bony interorbital space narrow, about 2.2 in eye diameter; maxilla not reaching a vertical at front of eye; fourth dorsal spine longest, 1.7–2.1 in head length; a tuft of cirri near tip of each dorsal spine (also generic); caudal fin slightly emarginate; white with small red to dark brown spots grouped to form triangular bars on body that are broader anteriorly, the darkest centered below origin of dorsal fin (spots in this bar, and to a lesser extent the second bar, may be black); 2 narrow reddish bars extending ventrally from eye and a median dark reddish band dorsally on head; dorsal-spine cirri white, the membrane tips red. Reaches 7 cm. Western Pacific from southern Japan to Great Barrier Reef, New South Wales, and New Caledonia, east to the islands of Micronesia and

New Caledonia

Samoa Islands, and west to the Maldive Islands; type locality, Mindanao. Found mainly in outer-reef areas, often sheltering near live coral, from 4 to about 45 m. Donaldson (1986) described pair spawning after sunset in the Izu Islands, Japan. *Cirrhitichthys serratus* Randall is a synonym.

Bali

PIXIE HAWKFISH

Cirrhitichthys oxycephalus (Bleeker, 1855)

Dorsal rays X,12–13 (rarely 13); anal rays III,6; pectoral rays 14, the lower 6 unbranched; lateral-line scales 40–45; body depth 2.9–3.4 in standard length; bony interorbital space about 2.0 in eye diameter; maxilla reaching or extending posterior to a vertical at front of eye; fifth dorsal spine longest, 1.8–2.0 in head length; first dorsal soft ray of adults prolonged; whitish with 4 lengthwise series of large, close-set, red to dark brown spots and a fifth series of smaller blotches along lateral line; head, dorsal fin, and caudal fin densely spotted. Reaches 8.5 cm. Red Sea and east coast of Africa to the Marquesas Islands and islands of Micronesia; southern Japan to Great Barrier Reef and New South Wales; also in the eastern Pacific from the Gulf of California to Colombia and the Galápagos Islands; type locality, Ambon, Molucca Islands. A common coral-reef fish from the shallows to depths of at least 40 m.

Ogasawara Islands

WHITESPOTTED HAWKFISH

Cirrhitops hubbardi (Schultz, 1943)

Dorsal rays X,14; anal rays III,6; pectoral rays 14, the lower 6 unbranched; lateral-line scales 49–52; 4 rows of large scales above lateral line in middle of body; a few palatiane teeth anteriorly on palatines; upper three-fifths of preopercular margin finely serrate, the lower two-fifths smooth; body depth 2.6–3.0 in standard length; brown with 4 to 5 longitudinal rows of white spots on body and a row of smaller spots along base of dorsal fin; caudal peduncle and base of caudal fin orange with a very large black spot covering most of peduncle; head brown with numerous small, bluish white spots and lines, the lips crossed by lines. Attains about 7.5 cm. An unusual disjunct distribution: Pitcairn Islands (Randall, 1999a), Tuamotu Archipelago, Phoenix Islands (type locality, Enderbury Island), Line Islands, Tonga, Rarotonga, and Ogasawara Islands (Randall et al., 1997b). Reproductive behavior and early development studied by Tanaka & Ohyama (1991).

WHITEDOTTED HAWKFISH

Cirrhitus albopunctatus Schultz, 1950

Dorsal rays X,11–12; anal rays III,6; pectoral rays 14, the lower 7 unbranched; lateral-line scales 39–42; 4 rows of large scales above lateral line in middle of body; palatine teeth present; posterior preopercular margin finely serrate; suprascapular margin smooth (serrate on other species of *Cirrhitus*); body depth 3.1 in standard length; snout length 3.5 in head length (3.0–3.3 in other species of *Cirrhitus*); pectoral fins short, not reaching a vertical at tips of pelvic rays; color in alcohol brown with very small white spots on head, body, and fins, those on body one per scale, hence in about 13 longitudinal rows; 4 near-vertical rows of indistinct white blotches on body; a white spot nearly as large as eye at upper edge and another at lower edge of caudal-fin base; a small black spot at fin margin before and behind upper white spot. Largest specimen, the holotype, 12 cm. Known from just 2 specimens collected from the island of Niuafo'ou, Tonga, in 1930; no information on habitat or life color.

Tonga (after Randall, 1963b)

STOCKY HAWKFISH

Cirrhitus pinnulatus (Forster, 1801)

Dorsal rays X,11; anal rays III,6; pectoral rays 14, the lower 7 unbranched; lateral-line scales 39–42; 4 rows of large scales above lateral line in middle of body; palatine teeth present; posterior preopercular margin finely serrate; body robust, the depth 2.6–3.0 in standard length; snout short and blunt; pectoral fins short, not reaching a vertical at tips of pelvic rays; body brown to olivaceous, white ventrally, with scattered white blotches and many smaller dark red to dark brown spots. Attains 28 cm. East coast of Africa to the Hawaiian Islands and Pitcairn Islands; southern Japan to Great Barrier Reef, New Caledonia, and the Kermadec Islands; type locality, Tahiti. Lives in surge zone of exposed coral reefs or along rocky shores. Stomach contents of 12 specimens consisted of crabs (80%), shrimps and other crustaceans, fishes, sea urchins, and brittlestars (Randall, 1985b). Schultz (1950) treated the Red Sea form as a species, *Cirrhitus alternatus* Gill, and described the Hawaiian–Johnston Island form as *C. spilotoceps*, principally on the lack of dark brown spots on preserved specimens. The smaller spots on Hawaiian fish are mostly orange-red and do not persist in preservative. Although there is a difference in color, it is hardly enough to regard the Hawaiian form as a species.

Guam

SWALLOWTAIL HAWKFISH

Cyprinocirrhites polyactis (Bleeker, 1875)

Dorsal rays X,16–17 (usually 16); anal rays III,6–7 (usually 6); pectoral rays 14, the lower 6 unbranched; lateral-line scales 45–49; 3 rows of large scales above lateral line in middle of body; 4 rows of large scales on cheek, palatine teeth present; first dorsal soft ray elongate; caudal fin lunate (slightly emarginate to truncate in other cirrhitids); orange to brownish orange, mottled with orange-red to brown blotches; caudal fin mainly yellow. Reported to 14 cm. East coast of Africa to the western Pacific from southern Japan to Great Barrier Reef, New South Wales, New Caledonia, and northern New Zealand (1 specimen); only Palau in Micronesia; type locality, Ambon, Molucca Islands. Occurs in outer-reef areas at depths of 10–132 m, usually in more than 20 m; feeds well above the bottom on zooplankton.

Sulawesi

SIXBARRED HAWKFISH

Isocirrhitus sexfasciatus (Schultz in Schultz et al., 1960)

Dorsal rays X,11; anal rays III,6; pectoral rays 14, the lower 5 unbranched; lateral-line scales 44–45; interorbital scaled; 4 rows of large scales above lateral line in middle of body; 4 or 5 oblique rows of large scales on cheek; palatine teeth absent; upper third of posterior margin of preopercle finely serrate, the lower two-thirds smooth; light brown with 5 near-vertical dark brown bars slightly broader than pale interspaces and a narrow dark bar across caudal-fin base; a small dark spot dorsally on caudal peduncle behind dorsal fin. Largest 10.5 cm. Known from the atolls of Bikini (type locality) and Enewetak in the Marshall Islands, Raroia in the Tuamotu Archipelago (as *Paracirrhites cinctus* by Harry, 1953), and 3 specimens collected by the author at Makatea in the Tuamotu Archipelago; lives in surge channels on exposed seaward reefs.

REDRIMMED HAWKFISH

Itycirrhitus wilhelmi (Lavenberg & Yañez, 1972)

Dorsal rays X,12–14 (rarely 12 or 14); anal rays III,6; pectoral rays 14, the lower 6 unbranched; lateral-line scales 41–45; 4 rows of large scales above lateral line in middle of body; scales ventrally on chest one-half or more size of scales on side of body; a few small teeth anteriorly on palatines; first (most medial) branchiostegal ray nearly straight and not parallel to second ray; upper margin of preopercle coarsely serrate; body depth 2.6–3.05 in standard length; whitish with a short, vertical, dark brown bar below first 3 dorsal spines and 4 oblique dark brown bars on body, broader and darker dorsally, the upper half of fifth bar on caudal peduncle black; pale interspaces on body with brown streaks following oblique scale rows; scales on nape and body except chest and abdomen rimmed with bright red; an indistinct dark brown ocellus on opercle. Reaches 12 cm. Known only from Easter Island (type locality) and Pitcairn Island; occurs along rocky shores from less than 1 m to at least 55 m. Described in *Cirrhitus*; reclassified in the new monotypic genus *Itycirrhitus* (Randall, 2001b).

FLAME HAWKFISH

Neocirrhites armatus Castelnau, 1873

Dorsal rays X,13; anal rays III,6–7 (usually 7); pectoral rays 14, the lower 6 unbranched; lateral-line scales 42–45; interorbital without scales; 4 rows of large scales above lateral line in middle of body; small scales on cheek in more than 12 irregular rows; palatine teeth absent; posterior margin of preopercle coarsely serrate; body deep for a cirrhitid, the depth 2.0–2.4 in standard length, and compressed, the width 2.9–3.1 in depth; bright red with a broad black band on back and extending into base of dorsal fin; eye nearly rimmed by black, broadest posteriorly. Attains 9 cm. Most islands of Oceania from Pitcairn and Line Islands to the Ryukyu Islands and Great Barrier Reef; type locality, Nob Island, Queensland. An obligate coral-dwelling species usually associated with corals of the genus *Pocillopora*; takes refuge deep among the branches when threatened. Donaldson (1989b) has shown that it is normally monogamous. A popular aquarium fish.

176

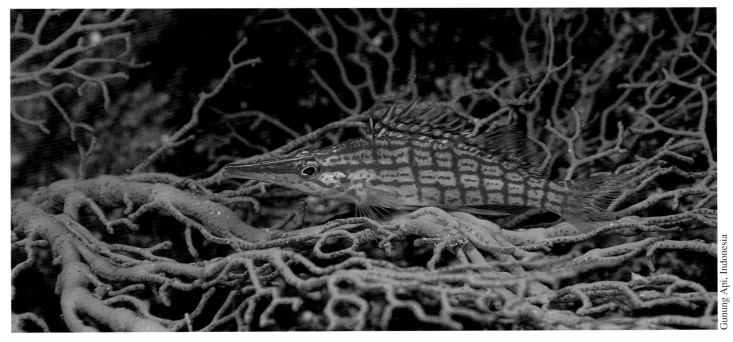

Gunung Api, Indonesia

LONGNOSE HAWKFISH
Oxycirrhites typus Bleeker, 1857
Dorsal rays X,13; anal rays III,7; pectoral rays 14, the lower 5 or 6 unbranched; lateral-line scales 51–53; 4 rows of large scales above lateral line in middle of body; 3–4 oblique rows of large scales on cheek; palatine teeth absent; posterior margin of preopercle coarsely serrate; body elongate, the depth 4.4–4.6 in standard length; snout very long and pointed, its length about 2.0 in head length; white with red to reddish brown stripes and bars forming a crosshatch pattern. Reaches 13 cm. Southern Japan to the Great Barrier Reef and New Caledonia, east to the Hawaiian Islands and Society Islands; in the Indian Ocean from the Chagos Archipelago, Maldive Islands, Seychelles, and Red Sea; occurs in the eastern Pacific from the Gulf of California to Colombia and the Galápagos Islands; type locality, Ambon, Molucca Islands. Reported from depths of 10 to 100 m, usually below 30 m; typically found on black coral or gorgonians; feeds mainly on small crustaceans, both benthic and pelagic. Reproductive behavior and early development documented by Tanaka & Ohyama (1991). A highly prized aquarium fish.

ARC-EYE HAWKFISH
Paracirrhites arcatus (Cuvier in C & V, 1829)
Dorsal rays X,11; anal rays III,6; pectoral rays 14, the upper 2 and lower 6 or 7 (usually 7) unbranched; lateral-line scales 45–50; 5 rows of large scales above lateral line in middle of body; 5 or 6 oblique rows of large scales on cheek with small basal scales (true of other *Paracirrhites*); no scales on snout anterior to nostrils; palatine teeth absent (also generic); posterior margin of preopercle smooth; body depth 2.4–2.6 in standard length; membranes of spinous portion of dorsal fin not incised, with a single cirrus from tip of each dorsal spine (generic); 2 color forms, one light grayish to orangish brown, the centers of scales paler, with a broad pale pink to white band along lateral line on posterior two-thirds of body; the other dark brown without the white band; both phases with an oblique U-shaped mark of orange, black, and blue behind eye and 3 orange bands on a light blue zone of interopercle. Attains 14 cm. Common and wide-ranging from east coast of Africa to the Hawaiian Islands and Pitcairn Islands; in the western Pacific from southern Japan to the Great Barrier Reef, Norfolk Island, and New Caledonia; described from specimens from Mauritius and Tahiti. Known from depths of 1–91 m (Chave & Mundy, 1994); usually seen at rest on live coral, particularly species of the genera *Pocillopora* and *Acropora*. Stomach contents of 15 specimens consisted of shrimps, small fishes, crabs, other crustaceans, and fish eggs (Randall, 1985b).

Marshall Islands

Marshall Islands

BICOLOR HAWKFISH
Paracirrhites bicolor Randall, 1963

Dorsal rays X,11; anal rays III,6; pectoral rays 14, the upper 2 and lower 7 unbranched; lateral-line scales 48–52; 5 rows of large scales above lateral line in middle of body; small scales dorsally on snout reaching anterior nostrils; upper two-fifths of preopercle finely serrate; body depth 2.5–2.65 in standard length; dark brown, abruptly bright orange on caudal peduncle and fin; lower brown part of body with lighter brown longitudinal bands; an oblique dark brown mark behind eye, edged in orange, black, and blue, this border continuing below and a little anterior to eye. Described from 2 specimens collected by the author at Caroline Atoll (10°S, 150°14′W), renamed Millennium Island; otherwise known only from the Tuamotu Archipelago; collections made in outer-reef areas in 5–14 m.

BLACKSIDE HAWKFISH
Paracirrhites forsteri (Bloch & Schneider, 1801)

Dorsal rays X,11; anal rays III,6; pectoral rays 14, the uppermost and lower 7 unbranched; lateral-line scales 45–49; 5 rows of large scales above lateral line in middle of body; 5 or 6 rows of large scales on cheek, often obscured by numerous small scales; snout almost entirely scaled; upper two-fifths of posterior margin of preopercle finely serrate; body depth 2.6–2.9 in standard length; ninth and tenth dorsal spines subequal; most common color phase gray-brown with a broad dark stripe, bordered by light yellow, on upper side of body that is brown anteriorly, soon becoming black, the black sometimes broken into large adjacent blotches; head and anterior body with many small red to dark reddish brown spots; a second color phase dark brown, shading to yellow or orange posteriorly; juveniles variably colored. Largest recorded, 22.5 cm. Red Sea and east coast of Africa to the Hawaiian Islands and Pitcairn Islands; in the western Pacific from southern Japan to northern New South Wales, Lord Howe Island, and Norfolk Island; type locality, Tahuata, Marquesas Islands. More common in outer-reef areas than on lagoon reefs; usually seen perched on live coral. Stomachs of 30 adult specimens were opened; 19 had eaten small fishes, 4 contained shrimps, and the rest were empty (Randall, 1985b). *Paracirrhites typee* Randall is a synonym.

HALFSPOTTED HAWKFISH

Paracirrhites hemistictus (Günther, 1874)

Dorsal rays X,11; anal rays III,6; pectoral rays 14, the uppermost and lower 7 unbranched; lateral-line scales 48–51; 5 rows of large scales above lateral line in middle of body; upper two-fifths of posterior margin of preopercle finely serrate; body elongate for the genus, depth 2.8–3.2 in standard length; tenth dorsal spine clearly longer than ninth; 2 color phases, one grayish to yellowish green, paler ventrally, densely spotted with black on about upper three-fourths of body (spots small anterodorsally) with a brilliant white stripe on lower side passing above upper edge of pectoral fin to front of snout (head may be suffused with pink, in which case stripe is pale pink); second phase reddish gray-brown on head, dark greenish gray on body, with the same black-spotted pattern (spots may be larger and more close-set), no white stripe, and a pure white spot about size of eye on lateral line below posterior dorsal spines. Reported to 29 cm. Great Barrier Reef and islands of Oceania except Hawaiian Islands, Easter Island, Rapa, Lord Howe Island, and Norfolk Island; also the Ogasawara Islands in Japan and Christmas Island and Cocos-Keeling Islands in the Indian Ocean; type locality, Raiatea, Society Islands. Not known from continental shores, the East Indies, or Taiwan. Occurs on exposed seaward reefs from the shallows to about 20 m, on rock or live coral. *Paracirrhites polystictus* (Günther) is a synonym based on the second color phase.

KING NISOS HAWKFISH

Paracirrhites nisus Randall, 1963

Dorsal rays X,11; anal rays III,6; pectoral rays 14, the upper 2 and lower 7 unbranched; lateral-line scales 48–49; 5 rows of large scales above lateral line in middle of body; 6 oblique rows of large scales on cheek; small scales middorsally on snout nearly reaching anterior nostrils; posterior margin of preopercle smooth or with only a few small serrae on upper part; body depth 2.6–2.7 in standard length; light brownish orange, with a white band, broadly bordered with black, along lateral line from below last dorsal spines into base of caudal fin; a narrow, oblique, dark gray band, bordered with yellow, black, and blue, extending upward from behind middle of eye, the tricolored border continuing above and below eye (may be broken to spots); a 25-mm juvenile was colored like the adult. Largest examined, 10 cm. Known from the Tuamotu Archipelago (type locality, Takapoto

Line Islands

Guam

Tuamotu Archipelago

Atoll), Oeno Atoll in the Pitcairn Islands, northern Cook Islands, and Phoenix Islands; a shallow-water species of exposed reefs; usually seen at rest on live coral. Named for a fabled Greek king said to have been changed into a hawk.

YELLOW HAWKFISH

Paracirrhites xanthus Randall, 1963

Dorsal rays X,11; anal rays III,6; pectoral rays 14, the upper 2 and lower 7 unbranched; lateral-line scales 49–52; 5 rows of large scales above lateral line in middle of body; 6 oblique rows of large scales on cheek; small scales middorsally on snout just reaching anterior nostrils; posterior margin of preopercle smooth or with only a few small serrae on upper middle part; body depth 2.5–2.65 in standard length; bright yellow overall, sometimes with a paler yellow streak posteriorly on lateral line; a narrow oblique dark gray band, bordered by lighter yellow, extending upward from behind middle of eye. Largest, 11.4 cm. Known from the Tuamotu Archipelago (type locality, Takapoto Atoll), Marquesas Islands, Society Islands (where rare), and Phoenix Islands. Found on shallow seaward reefs, generally on live coral.

Tuamotu Archipelago

MORWONGS AND TRUMPETERS (LATRIDAE)

Until the paper by Burridge & Smolenski (2004), the morwongs (formerly Cheilodactylidae) and the trumpeters (Latridae) were regarded as distinct families. These authors have joined them as a single family, now consisting of eight genera. The family Latridae is characterized by a long dorsal fin with XIV-XXIV spines and 19–40 soft rays; anal fin with III spines and 7–35 soft rays; a small mouth, the lips usually thickened in adults; teeth in jaws in villiform bands, none on vomer or palatines; caudal fin forked; pectoral fins of many species with the lower 4 to 7 rays usually thickened, elongate, and often partly detached from membrane. *Cheilodactylus* will be restricted to two South African species (C. P. Burridge, pers. comm.); therefore the subgenus *Goniistius* is the genus for the species in the review by Randall (1983a),

with the possible exception of the divergent *nigripes*, and with the addition of *G. francisi* (Burridge). *Goniistius* is represented by four species in Japan, China, Korea, and the Hawaiian Islands, and five in the South Pacific and Western Australia, hence antitropical in distribution. Although the species of *Goniistius* may prey directly on small invertebrates, they often feed by taking in mouthfuls of sand or by sucking in sediment and detritus from rocky surfaces; the fine inorganic matter is expelled from the gill opening, coarser sediment often from the mouth seconds later; and the tiny crustaceans, mollusks, and worms are retained. When not foraging, they may rest on the bottom, bracing themselves with pectoral fins as needed. Some species appear to be primarily nocturnal. The late postlarval stage of *Goniistius* (and at least some other latrids) is large, about 50–60 mm in total length, extremely compressed, with the ventral edge of the chest and abdomen a sharp-edged keel.

Lord Howe Island

Easter Island

MASKED MORWONG
Goniistius francisi (Burridge, 2004)
Dorsal rays XVI-XVII,31–34 (usually XVII,33); anal rays III,8; pectoral rays 13–14 (usually 14), the upper 2 and lower 6 unbranched; lateral-line scales 62–66; adults with a short bony knob above each posterior nostril, and a pair at front of snout; body depth 2.55–2.85 in standard length; first two dorsal spines very short, the third about twice length of second, and the fourth elongate, 0.85–1.6 in head length; pelvic fins reaching origin of anal fin; body white with two black bands, one from origin of dorsal fin curving broadly beneath pectoral fin and ending on abdomen, the second from posterior dorsal spines, along back at base of dorsal fin, across caudal peduncle, and ending at tip of lower caudal-fin lobe; three oblique black bands across head, pelvic fins and tip of upper caudal-fin lobe black. Attains about 40 cm. Known from Lord Howe Island (type locality), Middleton Reef, Norfolk Island, New Caledonia, and the Kermadec Islands. Very similar to *G. vittatus* (Garrett) from the Hawaiian Islands, differing slightly in color, in 5–6 upper-limb gill rakers (6–8, rarely 6, in *vittatus*), and species level in DNA.

PLESSIS' MORWONG
Goniistius plessisi (Randall, 1983)
Dorsal rays XVI-XVII,31–35; anal rays III,8–9 (rarely 8); pectoral rays 14, the upper 2 and lower 6 unbranched; lateral-line scales 65–71; adults with a short bony knob above each posterior nostril, and a pair at front of snout; body depth 2.35–2.75 in standard length; first 2 dorsal spines very short, the third about twice length of second, and the fourth elongate, 1.05–1.45 in head length; pelvic fins long, reaching origin of anal fin; light olivaceous with 4 oblique dark brown bands; a broad, near-vertical, dark brown bar from below middle of soft portion of dorsal fin to behind rear base of anal fin. Largest examined, 40 cm. Known only from Easter Island (type locality), Rapa, and nearby Marotiri (Îlots de Bass) from tidepools to 21.5 m. Gut contents of 4 adult specimens obtained in the morning consisted of shrimps (39%, mostly alpheids, the largest 17 mm), crabs (38%, the largest 8.5 cm), small gastropods, unidentified small crustaceans, bryozoans, ophiuroids, foraminifera, and algae and sand (4.5%). The alimentary tract of a fifth specimen taken at 1600 hours was completely empty.

CRESTED MORWONG
Goniistius vestitus (Castelnau, 1878)

Dorsal rays XVI-XVII,32–35; anal rays III,8–9 (usually 8); pectoral rays 14, the upper 2 and lower 6 unbranched; lateral-line scales 58–65; adults with a short bony knob above each posterior nostril, and a pair at front of snout; body depth 2.6–2.85 in standard length; first 3 dorsal spines very short, the fourth elongate, about equal to head length; whitish with 4 oblique dark brown bands: 2 on head that converge on pectoral-fin base, one from first 3 dorsal spines to below outer part of pectoral fin, and one from third to sixth dorsal spines across body to end at tip of lower lobe of caudal fin. Reaches at least 35 cm. Known from southern Queensland and the southern Great Barrier Reef to central New South Wales (type locality, Sydney), Lord Howe Island, Norfolk Island, and New Caledonia. Occurs on reefs to depths of at least 20 m, but also penetrates estuarine areas. Feeding appears to be nocturnal, because the alimentary tract is empty unless examined in early morning hours. Randall (1983a) examined the gut contents of 4 adults: crabs (25%, largest 7 mm), gastropods

Lord Howe Island

(13%, largest 7.5 mm), shrimps (12%), foraminifera, amphipods, polychaetes, chitons, bivalve mollusks, brittlestars, eggs, isopods, echinoids; sand, algae, and detritus comprised 28.7% by volume of the gut material. *Goniistius gibbosus* (Richardson) from Western Australia is a closely related species.

Fiveband Flagtail, *Kuhlia mugil*, Marshall Islands

FLAGTAILS
(KUHLIIDAE)

The fishes of this Indo-Pacific family are moderately deep-bodied and compressed, with 2 opercular spines, a deeply notched dorsal fin of X spines and 9–13 rays, and a scaly sheath at the base of the dorsal and anal fins. They have large eyes and are primarily nocturnal, at least as adults, feeding principally on planktonic crustaceans. They are usually silvery, often with dark markings on the caudal fin, the basis for the common name flagtails. The family consists of a single genus, *Kuhlia*, the species of which occur in tropical and subtropical waters of the Indo-Pacific region, with one ranging to the tropical eastern Pacific. Some species are found mainly in fresh water, whereas others are primarily marine. The latter tend to form schools by day and are typically found inshore; the young may be common in tidepools. At least some of the marine species are able to penetrate fresh water. Randall & Randall (2001) reviewed the 10 species that occur in central Pacific waters. Those that are mainly freshwater species include *Kuhlia malo* (Valenciennes) from the Society Islands; *K. salelea* Schultz from the Samoa Islands; *K. munda* (De Vis) from Fiji and New Caledonia to Queensland; *K. marginata* from the western Pacific east to Fiji; and *K. rupestris* (Lacepède) from East Africa to the Samoa Islands. Only the marine species are treated here.

Marshall Islands

Johnston Island

FIVEBAND FLAGTAIL
Kuhlia mugil (Forster, 1801)
Dorsal-fin rays X,10–11 (usually 10); anal-fin rays III,10–12 (usually 11); pectoral-fin rays 13–15; lateral-line scales 49–52 (usually 51); gill rakers 9–11 + 24–27; caudal fin deeply forked; silvery, the front of snout and chin blackish; caudal fin white with a median dark stripe and 2 broad, oblique, black bands across each lobe, the lobe tips white; a dusky band in outer part of soft portion of dorsal fin except for white tip of high anterior part. Small juveniles have median and outer black bands in caudal-fin lobes, but middle band is represented only by a black spot. Largest specimen examined, 24 cm, but recorded to 32 cm. Red Sea and east coast of Africa to islands of Oceania except Easter Island, Pitcairn Islands, Marquesas Islands, and Hawaiian Islands; in the western Pacific from southern Japan to New South Wales, Lord Howe Island, Norfolk Island, and the Kermadec Islands; in the eastern Pacific from Baja California to Colombia and all the offshore islands; type locality, Tahiti. Typically found along exposed rocky shores, the young often in tidepools; adults tend to occur in aggregations. *Kuhlia taeniura* (Cuvier) is a synonym.

RETICULATED FLAGTAIL
Kuhlia sandvicensis (Steindachner, 1876)
Dorsal-fin rays X,11–12 (rarely 12); anal-fin rays III,11–12 (rarely 12); pectoral-fin rays 13–15 (rarely 15); lateral-line scales 49–51 (usually 50, rarely 49); gill rakers 11–13 + 27–30; dorsal profile of head of adults straight; eye not very large, the orbit diameter 3.0–3.45 in head length; caudal fin strongly forked; silvery with a coarse silver and black reticulum dorsally on head in life; posterior edge of caudal fin blackish. Largest examined, 28 cm. Known from the Hawaiian Islands (type locality), Pitcairn Islands, Line Islands, Phoenix Islands, Marshall Islands, Kiribati, Wake Island, and Minami-tori-shima (Marcus Island); a common shallow-water species of coral reefs and rocky shores. Usually misidentified as *Kuhlia marginata* (Cuvier), a freshwater species of the western Pacific. Long overlooked in the Hawaiian Islands when it was believed that there was a single species of the genus there. The endemic Hawaiian species formerly identified as *sandvicensis* is now *K. xenura* (Jordan & Gilbert); San Salvador was given as the type locality of *xenura*, but this is an error (Randall & Randall, 2001).

PETIT'S FLAGTAIL
Kuhlia petiti Schultz, 1943
Dorsal-fin rays X,11–12 (usually 12); anal rays III,11–12 (usually 12); pectoral-fin rays 13–15 (rarely 13 or 15); lateral-line scales 51–53 (usually 51); gill rakers 9–11 + 24–27; caudal fin deeply forked; silvery, the front of the snout and chin a little blackish; caudal fin black with a large, C-shaped, white marking basally in each lobe, the lobe tips white; outer part of anterior half of soft portion of dorsal fin broadly blackish (nearly half of first few rays and adjacent membranes blackish). Largest specimen examined, 26 cm. Known only from the Phoenix Islands (type locality, Hull Island), Marquesas Islands, and Malden Island, Line Islands; occurs along rocky shores exposed to surge, often in aggregations.

Marquesas Islands

TERAPONS
(TERAPONIDAE)

The fishes of this Indo-Pacific perciform family are also called tigerperches, grunters, and trumpeters. The last two names allude to the sound produced by their unique swimbladders that are equipped with extrinsic muscles. Terapons have an oblong, moderately compressed body, small mouth with villiform teeth in jaws, and usually no teeth on vomer or palatines in adults; opercle with 2 spines, the lower notably larger; preopercular margin serrate; scales ctenoid and small; lateral line complete, extending onto caudal fin; dorsal fin with XI to XIV spines, the spinous portion folding into a basal scaly sheath; anal rays III,7–12. Most occur in fresh or brackish water, primarily in Australia. The family was revised by Vari (1978). Only 1 species ranges to the islands of Oceania.

Sabah

JARBUA
Terapon jarbua (Forsskål, 1775)

Dorsal rays XI-XII,9–11; anal rays III,7–10; pectoral rays 13–14; lateral-line scales 75–100; lower-limb gill rakers 13–16; exposed posterior end of posttemporal serrate; 2 opercular spines, the lower extending beyond opercular membrane; body depth 2.5–3.2 in standard length; dorsal fin deeply notched; caudal fin emarginate; silvery with 4 crescentic black bands on body (upper 2 may be broken into dashes), the third band continuing as a middle stripe to end of caudal fin; caudal fin with a black stripe above and below middle stripe, the lobes tipped with black; a large black area in outer part of dorsal fin between third and sixth spines; juveniles with dark spots arranged in horizontal and vertical rows; no large distal black spot on dorsal fin. Reported to 33 cm. Red Sea (type locality) and east coast of Africa to the Samoa Islands; only Palau in Micronesia; southern Japan to Lord Howe Island and New Caledonia in the western Pacific; often seen in very shallow water along sandy shores where their pattern of curved stripes serves as camouflage because of the ever-changing curved shadows on the sand from ripples at the surface; also occurs in brackish habitats. Feeds mainly on benthic invertebrates and small fishes. Not a good candidate for an aquarium because it is known to bite scales from other fishes.

BIGEYES
(PRIACANTHIDAE)

The fishes of this small circumtropical family of 4 genera and 18 species are distinctive in their extremely large eyes, relatively deep bodies, very rough scales, and usual red color. The scales are not ctenoid but modified cycloid scales with spinules. The eyes have a unique tapetum lucidum at the back that reflects the light, thus making vision more acute at low light levels. The opercle has 2 flat spines; the preopercle is serrate with a broad spine variously developed at the corner; the mouth is large, very oblique, with the lower jaw projecting; the teeth are in villiform bands in the jaws and on the vomer and palatines; dorsal fin continuous with X spines; anal fin with III spines; caudal fin with 16 principal rays; and pelvic fins I,5, the last ray broadly joined to abdomen by membrane. Although primarily red, some species can quickly alter their color to silver or to a barred or mottled red and silver pattern. Priacanthid fishes are recorded from depths of 2 to 400 m. They are primarily nocturnal and feed mainly on the larger animals of the zooplankton. Starnes (1988) revised the family.

Ogasawara Islands

GLASSEYE
Heteropriacanthus cruentatus (Lacepède, 1801)
Dorsal rays X,12–13 (usually 13); anal rays III,13–14 (usually 14); pectoral rays 17–19 (usually 18); lateral-line scales 63–81; gill rakers 21–25; flat spine at corner of preopercle nearly reaching edge of operculum; broad edge of preopercle (posterior to sensory canal) striated and without scales; body depth 2.3–2.7 in standard length; caudal fin truncate to slightly rounded or slightly double emarginate; pelvic fins not long, 1.5–1.7 in head length; solid red or silvery pink mottled with red; faint dark dots in median fins, especially the caudal. Largest recorded, 32 cm. Circumglobal in tropical and subtropical seas; type locality, Dominica, Lesser Antilles; more common in insular than continental waters. Inhabits shallow reefs, usually at depths less than 20 m; tends to hide in caves by day.

Bali

BLOCH'S BIGEYE
Priacanthus blochii Bleeker, 1853
Dorsal rays X,12–14; anal rays III,13–15; pectoral rays 17–19 (usually 17); lateral-line scales 69–77; gill rakers 17–22; preopercular spine of adults not reaching edge of operculum; body depth 2.6–2.9 in standard length; caudal fin rounded; pelvic fins equal to or slightly longer than head; pectoral fins small, 1.9–2.2 in head length; red or silvery blotched with red; about 14 small dark red spots along lateral line; a black spot at base of second and third pelvic rays. Largest measured, 30 cm. Southern Red

Luzon

Sea and south coast of Oman, Seychelles and western Pacific from the Philippines to the Great Barrier Reef; American Samoa is the only locality from Oceania (Wass, 1984); described from specimens from Java, Sumatra, and the Molucca Islands. Occurs on coral reefs from depths of 15–30 m.

Marshall Islands

GOGGLE-EYE
Priacanthus hamrur (Forsskål, 1775)

Dorsal rays X,13–15; anal rays III,13–16; pectoral rays 17–20 (usually 18 or 19); lateral-line scales 70–90; gill rakers 24–26; spine at corner of preopercle short in adults; body depth 2.5–2.9 in standard length; caudal fin emarginate (hence one common name, Crescent Bigeye); pectoral fins shorter than pelvic spine; pelvic fins long, reaching posterior to spinous portion of anal fin; usually deep red, but can alter to silvery pink with red bars; about 15 small dark red spots along lateral line; membranes of caudal and pelvic fins blackish distally. Reaches 40 cm. Red Sea (type locality) and east coast of Africa to Society Islands, Tuamotu Archipelago, and Marquesas Islands; in the western Pacific from southern Japan to New South Wales, Lord Howe Island, and New Caledonia; reported from depths of about 15 to 250 m; easily approached underwater; sometimes seen in small groups. Closely related to *Priacanthus meeki* Jenkins of the Hawaiian Islands and *P. arenatus* Cuvier of the Atlantic.

Luzon

DOTTYBACKS
(PSEUDOCHROMIDAE)

This Indo-Pacific family is divided into 4 subfamilies: the Anisochrominae (1 Indian Ocean genus of 3 species [Springer et al., 1977; Gill & Fricke, 2001]); the Pseudoplesiopinae (small fishes with I,3-I,4 pelvic rays, and 1 pored anterior lateral-line scale); the Congrogadinae (eel-like with loss of anal spines, and for many the loss of dorsal spines and pelvic fins as well (formerly regarded as a family but reclassified in the Pseudochromidae by Godkin & Winterbottom, 1985, and revised by Winterbottom, 1985a); and the speciose Pseudochrominae (revised by Gill, 2004), the only subfamily represented in the South Pacific area covered by this book. The fishes of this subfamily are moderately elongate with a long, continuous dorsal fin of I to III weak spines and 21–28 soft rays, anal fin with III spines and 11–21 soft rays, pelvic fins I,5, an interrupted lateral line, scaled head, and palatine teeth. Most species are small, many are very colorful, and some are sexually dichromatic. Dottybacks are well-known for being secretive; they rarely stray far from cover. The eggs are demersal and have filaments. The males of some species have been observed to guard a ball of eggs within a small shelter until hatching (Lubbock, 1975). The more colorful species enter the aquarium trade.

185

Solomon Islands/female

Solomon Islands/male

OBLIQUE-LINED DOTTYBACK

Cypho purpurascens (De Vis, 1884)

Dorsal rays III,22–24; anal rays III,13–15; pectoral rays 15–18; anterior lateral-line scales 23–32; posterior lateral-line scales 3–9; longitudinal scale series 30–37; scales on body ctenoid, becoming cycloid above lateral line anterior to base of about sixth dorsal soft ray; gill rakers 4–7 + 10–13; caudal fin slightly rounded; males red, females purplish gray anteriorly and pale orange-yellow posteriorly, both sexes with oblique dark purple

New Caledonia

Great Barrier Reef

lines following scale rows anteriorly on body, a blue margin on dorsal and anal fins, a blue line rimming eye ventrally and posteriorly, and blue dots on interorbital space and dorsally on snout; males may have an ocellated black spot in anterior one-third of dorsal fin. Reaches 7.5 cm. A shallow-water reef species known from Papua New Guinea, Great Barrier Reef, Solomon Islands, Vanuatu (type locality, Vila), Coral Sea, New Caledonia, and Tonga. *Pseudochromis mccullochi* Myers is a synonym.

FRECKLED DOTTYBACK

Ogilbyina salvati (Plessis & Fourmanoir, 1996)

Dorsal rays III,32–33; anal rays III,19–20; pectoral rays 17–18; pelvic rays I,5; anterior lateral-line scales 41–42; posterior lateral-line scales 4–12; longitudinal scale series 43–45; scales on body ctenoid, becoming cycloid above lateral line anterior to base of about sixth dorsal soft ray; gill rakers 4–5 + 9–11; body depth 2.85–3.3 in standard length; dusky red on back, shading to orange-red ventrally; bright blue spots on cheek and chest, and a blue ring nearly encircling eye, its inner edge dark brown posteriorly; caudal fin bright yellow; dorsal and anal fins red with irregular blue lines or series of dashes distally; pelvic fins whitish. Reaches about 8 cm. Known only from New Caledonia (type locality) and the Chesterfield Islands, Coral Sea. Illustrated specimen collected from an inshore reef in 1.5 m off Nouméa.

CORAL SEA DOTTYBACK

Pictichromis coralensis Gill, 2004

Dorsal rays III,21–22; anal rays III,11–12; pectoral rays 16–18; pelvic rays I,5; anterior lateral-line scales 21–28; posterior lateral-line scales 0–10; longitudinal scale series 36–43; scales on body ctenoid except above lateral line anterior to base of about fourth dorsal soft ray; gill rakers 5–7 + 14–16; caudal fin truncate to slightly rounded; anterior half bright purple, posterior half abruptly bright yellow; caudal fin solid yellow basally, clear on outer part, with yellow rays. Reaches 8.8 cm. Great Barrier Reef, western and southern Coral Sea, and New Caledonia; collected from depths of 6–40 m. Named *coralensis* for the type locality, Coral Sea. *Pictichromis paccagnellae* (Axelrod) from Indonesia to Vanuatu is colored the same but differs in having 13–15 anal soft rays and modally 17 instead of 18 pectoral rays.

186

MAGENTA DOTTYBACK
Pictichromis porphyreus (Lubbock & Goldman, 1974)

Dorsal rays III,21–22; anal rays III,11–13 (rarely 11); pectoral rays 16–18; pelvic rays I,5; anterior lateral-line scales 20–25; posterior lateral-line scales 3–8; longitudinal scale series 37–41; scales of head and anterior body cycloid, the remainder ctenoid; gill rakers 5–6 + 13–15; caudal fin truncate to slightly rounded; magenta, sometimes shading to purple on caudal peduncle and large semicircular basal area over most of caudal fin; outer part of caudal fin hyaline with yellow rays. Attains 6 cm. Reported from the Ryukyu Islands (type locality, Ishigaki), Taiwan, Philippines, Molucca Islands, Admiralty Islands, islands of Micronesia, and Samoa Islands; known from depths of 6–65 m.

Aquarium photo

Flores, Indonesia

Bali

BROWN DOTTYBACK
Pseudochromis fuscus Müller & Troschel, 1849

Dorsal rays III,25–28; anal rays III,13–15; pectoral rays 17–20; pelvic rays I,5; anterior lateral-line scales 23–36; posterior lateral-line scales 4–14; gill rakers 5–9 + 11–15; body deep for the genus, the depth 2.8–3.2 in standard length; color variable, dark brown, gray, or yellow with intermediate shades, all with a dark blue spot on each scale; caudal fin sometimes whitish; those with darker caudal fins may have a yellow streak dorsally and ventrally. Reaches 9 cm. Sri Lanka to Indo-Malayan region, north to Ogasawara Islands and Ryukyu Islands, south to Great Barrier Reef, east to New Caledonia, Palau, and the Caroline Islands (type locality, Sulawesi). Reported from depths of 1–30 m; occurs on coral reefs or adjacent rubble areas. *Pseudochromis aurea* Seale from the Philippines is a synonym.

SPOT-TAIL DOTTYBACK
Pseudochromis jamesi Schultz, 1943

Dorsal rays III,24–26; anal rays III,13–14; pectoral rays 18–20; pelvic rays I,5; anterior lateral-line scales 27–34; posterior lateral-line scales 4–12; longitudinal scale series 34–41; gill rakers 3–6 + 10–12; caudal fin rounded; males red, shading to orange on head, chest, and abdomen (or rarely orange dorsally, shading to yellow ventrally and to red posteriorly); females purplish gray, shading to white on lower part of head, on chest, and abdomen, both sexes usually with a black spot of pupil size or larger on upper base of caudal fin broadly edged with white dorsally. Reaches 5.5 cm. Southwestern Pacific from American Samoa (type locality, Rose Island), Fiji, and New Caledonia to the Great Barrier Reef.

New Caledonia

Fiji

187

Widi Island, Indonesia

ORANGESPOTTED DOTTYBACK

Pseudochromis marshallensis Schultz in Schultz et al., 1953
Dorsal rays III,21–23 (usually 25); anal rays III,11–14 (usually 12 or 13); pectoral rays 17–19; pelvic rays I,5; anterior lateral-line scales 23–32; posterior lateral-line scales 0–15; gill rakers 4–7 + 11–15; body depth 3.4–3.55 in standard length; body gray with an orange to orange-yellow spot on each scale; head dull orange, the scales edged in gray; lower edge of orbit narrowly rimmed in orange; dorsal fin sometimes with longitudinal red lines on basal half. Reaches about 6 cm. Indo-Malayan region north to Taiwan and Ogasawara Islands, south to Western Australia (Allen, 1985a), New Caledonia (Myers, 1999), and east to the Marshall Islands (type locality, Rongelap Atoll), and Caroline Islands. Collected from both lagoon and seaward reefs from less than 1 to 30 m. *Pseudochromis flavopunctatus* Gill & Randall from Indonesia is similar in color; it differs in having 16 anal soft rays and usually 26 dorsal soft rays.

BLUEBARRED DOTTYBACK

Pseudochromis tapeinosoma Bleeker, 1853
Dorsal rays III,22–23 (usually 22); anal rays III,12–13 (rarely 12); pectoral rays 16–20 (rarely 16 or 20); pelvic rays I,5; anterior lateral-line scales 24–31 (usually 25–29); posterior lateral-line scales 6–11; circumpeduncular scales 16; gill rakers 3–5 + 9–12; body depth 3.7–4.1 in standard length; lower lip not interrupted at symphysis or with a weak interruption; juveniles and females gray-brown, sometimes reddish on caudal peduncle; dorsal and anal fins gray basally, clear distally; caudal fin gray to orange-red basally, yellow to clear distally; males with lower part of head, chest, and anterior abdomen yellowish gray to yellow or orange; rest of head and body dark gray to black; anterior lateral line yellowish gray to yellow; a series of narrow bluish

Ambon, Indonesia

gray to blue bars posteriorly on body; median fins dark gray to black basally, light gray distally; paired fins yellow. Maximum length 6 cm. Ryukyu Islands and Hong Kong south to western and eastern Australia, east to New Caledonia, Vanuatu, and islands of Micronesia; tidepools to reefs at depths of 30 m.

Lord Howe Island

LORD HOWE DOTTYBACK

Pseudoplesiops howensis Allen, 1987
Dorsal rays I,23–24; anal rays I-II,14; pectoral rays 16–18; pelvic rays I,4; longitudinal scale series 30–35; a single tubed lateral-line scale; predorsal scales 6–9, posterior scales on body ctenoid to end of pectoral fins or a little before; gill rakers 2–4 + 8–14; vertebrae 11 + 18; body slender, the depth 3.5–4.4 in standard length; eyes large; pelvic fins nearly reaching anal fin origin; body and median fins brown to bright green; pelvic fins whitish to green. Largest specimen, 3.8 cm. Known from Great Barrier Reef, Lord Howe Island (type locality), and New Caledonia. Occurs on shallow lagoon reefs down to 30 m.

REVELLE'S DOTTYBACK

Pseudoplesiops revellei Schultz in Schultz et al., 1953
Dorsal rays I,27–28; anal rays I,17–18; pectoral rays 16–18; pelvic rays I,4; longitudinal scale series 34–38; predorsal scales 7–10; a single tubed lateral-line scale; scales ctenoid on about posterior half of body; gill rakers 2–3 + 9–10; body slender, the depth 3.9–4.1 in standard length; eye very large; a fleshy keel on underside of lower jaw; yellowish brown, shading to brownish yellow on chest and ventral half of head, with a pale-edged oblong black spot larger than pupil on upper base of opercle; inner rim of iris red; median fins yellowish brown, dorsal and anal fins with a bluish white submarginal line, the ray tips hyaline. Attains 4 cm. Known from the Mariana Islands, Marshall

Cook Islands

Islands (type locality, Bikini Atoll), Caroline Islands, Cook Islands, Society Islands, and Pitcairn Islands. Collected by the author from a lagoon reef at Oeno Atoll, Pitcairn Islands, in less than 2 m, and outside the barrier reef of Tahiti in 30.5 m.

LARGE-SCALED DOTTYBACK
Pseudoplesiops rosae Schultz, 1943
Dorsal rays I,22–23; anal rays I,13–14; pectoral rays 16–18; pelvic rays I,4; longitudinal scale series 26–29; a single tubed lateral-line scale; predorsal scales 7–10, extending forward nearly to above middle of eyes; posterior scales on body ctenoid; gill rakers 2–4 + 7–9; body slender, the depth 3.5–3.9 in standard length; eye very large, iris mainly red; olive to brown, red, or yellow; orbit rimmed posteriorly with black. Attains 3 cm. Andaman Sea; Ryukyu Islands to northwestern Australia and Great Barrier Reef, east to Samoa Islands (type locality, Rose Island), and throughout Micronesia; found on seaward reefs exposed to wave action to about 10 m.

Vanuatu (J. T. Williams)

WASS' DOTTYBACK
Pseudoplesiops wassi Gill & Edwards, 2003
Dorsal rays I,27–29; anal rays I-II,16–18; pectoral rays 16–18; pelvic rays I,3; longitudinal scale series 32–39; predorsal scales 6–9; a single tubed lateral-line scale; scales ctenoid anteriorly to end of pectoral fins or a little before; gill rakers about 2–4 + 9–13; body slender, the depth 3.5–4.7 in standard length; eyes large; pelvic fins long, reaching nearly to or slightly beyond origin of anal fin; head orange to yellow, the body dark brown, sometimes pink ventrally on chest and head; iris red; median fins orangish brown to yellow, the dorsal with a narrow blue margin; a bluish gray spot often present at base of every other ray of dorsal and anal fins; paired fins clear with orange rays. Largest specimen, 3.5 cm. First reported, as *Pseudoplesiops* sp., from American Samoa by Wass (1984); now known also from Caroline Islands (Pohnpei), Tonga, Fiji, Rotuma, Vanuatu, northern Great Barrier Reef, and Hermit Islands; collected from depths of 27–46 m.

Fiji

LONGFINS
(PLESIOPIDAE)

This Indo-Pacific family of small cryptic fishes receives its common name from the long pelvic fins. Prettyfins is another common family name, in reference to the colorful pattern of the dorsal and anal fins of many species. There are seven genera in the family, of which only two are represented by species at islands of the South Pacific; most species are found in Australian

Bluegill Longfin, *Plesiops corallicola*, Guam (R. F. Myers)

seas. The family is characterized by having the third branchiostegal ray projecting farther posteriorly than adjacent rays; no spines on opercle; edge of preopercle smooth; small canine teeth in bands in jaws and on vomer and palatines; lateral line incomplete or disjunct; most scales on body finely ctenoid; a continuous dorsal fin with XI-XV spines and 6–21 soft rays; anal fin with III spines and 7–23 soft rays; pelvic fins I,4, the fins long in most species; soft portions of dorsal and anal fins often prolonged posteriorly. The eggs of *Plesiops* are oblong with chorionic filaments clus-

tered about the micropyle (Mooi, 1990); the filaments are believed to attach the eggs to the substratum. The eggs of *P. coeruleolineatus* are deposited under a rock and guarded by the male parent (Mito, 1955). The eggs of *Assessor macneilli* are incubated in the mouth of the male (Allen & Kuiter, 1976). The larval stages of *Plesiops* were described by Leis & Carson-Ewart (2000). Allen & Kuiter (1976) revised the 3 species of the genus *Assessor*, and Mooi (1995) the 17 species of *Plesiops*. The species of the latter genus are rarely seen by divers; they are reported as nocturnal.

Great Barrier Reef

BLUE LONGFIN

Assessor macneilli Whitley, 1935

Dorsal rays XI,8–9; anal rays III,9; pectoral rays 15; lateral line scales 16–21 + 1–7; body depth 3.0–3.3 in standard length; scales cycloid; membranes of spinous portion of dorsal fin not incised; caudal fin forked; pelvic fins about equal to head length; dark blue with a narrow blue margin on dorsal, anal, and pelvic fins; pectoral fins translucent. Attains 6 cm. Great Barrier Reef and New Caledonia; also reported from the Chesterfield Islands, Coral Sea (Kulbicki et al., 1994); type locality, Hayman Island, Queensland. Found on coral reefs at depths of 2 to at least 15 m, often in aggregations, and always in caves or beneath ledges. Often swims upside down, especially when near the roof of a cave. Gut contents of 8 specimens consisted of copepods, ostracods, and amphipods (Allen & Kuiter, 1976).

COMET

Calloplesiops altivelis (Steindachner, 1903)

Dorsal rays XI,8–10 (rarely 10); anal rays III,9; pectoral rays 17–20; lateral-line scales 19–20 + 9–10; body depth 2.5–2.7 in standard length; head length 2.8–3.0 in standard length; dorsal and anal fins elevated posteriorly, the spinous membranes not incised; caudal fin longer than head, broad and somewhat pointed; pelvic fins very long, extending well beyond spinous portion of anal fin; dark brown with a small white spot on each scale; all fins except pectorals with small blue spots; a large, blue-edged, black spot at rear base of dorsal fin; pectoral fins clear with yellow rays. Reaches 16 cm. Red Sea and east coast of Africa to the Line

Red Sea

Islands and Tuamoto Archipelago; in the western Pacific from southern Japan to the Great Barrier Reef; type locality, Nias Island (off Sumatra); occurs from shallow reefs to 45 m. Hides in reef by day, emerging at dusk. When threatened, it moves headfirst into a hole but leaves the posterior part of its body

exposed. McCosker (1977b) suggested that it is mimicking the head of the Whitemouth Moray, *Gymnothorax meleagris*, the ocellated spot posteriorly on the dorsal fin appearing as the moray's eye. McCosker (1978) listed the 4 synonyms and provided localities.

REDTIPPED LONGFIN

Plesiops coeruleolineatus Rüppell, 1835

Dorsal rays X-XII (nearly always XI),6–8; anal rays III,8; pectoral rays 19–24; lateral-line scales 18–21 + 7–14; predorsal scales 5–8; gill rakers 3–6 + 6–11; total gill rakers modally 11–12; membranes of spinous portion of dorsal fin very deeply incised (true of other *Plesiops*); caudal fin rounded (also generic); pelvic fins long, reaching beyond origin of anal fin, the first soft ray branched and thickened (also generic); dark brown to nearly black, with no pale spots on body scales; head sometimes with a wash of yellow; no black opercular spot; dorsal spines broadly tipped with orange or red, bordered below by a blue line, then a black band bordered below by a blue line; anal fin with a pale margin and an inner blue line; caudal fin dark brown, with or without a pale yellowish submarginal band. Largest recorded, 8.5 cm; smallest gravid female, 3.4 cm. Red Sea (type locality) and east coast of Africa to the islands of Micronesia and Samoa Islands; in the western Pacific from southern Japan to the Great Barrier Reef and New Caledonia. Most collections from exposed outer-reef areas such as reef flats or tidepools, but has been taken

Marshall Islands

as deep as 15 m. *Plesiops melas* Bleeker is a synonym. *Plesiops polydactylus* Mooi (1995) was described from 9 specimens from Naviti Island, Fiji, with no information on life color. It differs from *coeruleolineatus* in having slightly higher gill-raker counts and 26–28 pectoral rays; Mooi wrote that it may represent a meristically aberrant population of *coeruleolineatus*.

BLUEGILL LONGFIN
Plesiops corallicola Bleeker, 1853

Dorsal rays XII,7–8; anal rays III,8; pectoral rays 20–22; lateral-line scales 18–21 + 7–14; predorsal scales 5–8; gill rakers 3–7 + 6–12; total gill rakers modally 14–15; dark gray with a small blue or white spot on each scale (spots may be round or vertically elongate); an ocellated black spot (may have large blue center) nearly as large as eye on lower part of opercle; 3 short dark bars extending posteriorly from eye; median fins with a white margin and blue spots; gill membranes bright blue. Attains 18 cm. Andaman Islands, Cocos-Keeling Islands, and Christmas Island in the Indian Ocean to the islands of Micronesia, Tonga, and the Cook Islands; type locality, Sumatra. Not known from Australia or New Caledonia.

Guam (R. F. Myers)

CORAL SEA LONGFIN
Plesiops insularis Mooi & Randall, 1991

Dorsal rays XII,6–8; anal rays III,7–9; pectoral rays 21–24; lateral-line scales 19–21 + 11–17; predorsal scales 6–8; band of cheek scales broad, about three-fourths eye diameter in width; gill rakers 4–6 + 10–19; total gill rakers modally 17–18; brown with no white spots on body and no dark ocellus on cheek; head brown but post-orbital part often suffused with yellow; 2 short dark brown bands diverging from behind eye, and a dark brown line extending from lower eye to above maxilla; dorsal and anal fins may have blue and orange stripes. Largest, 12.5 cm. New Caledonia, Lord Howe Island (type locality), Norfolk Island, Chesterfield Islands, Elizabeth and Middleton Reefs, and New South Wales. Occurs from about 1 m in tidepools to 25 m, but most specimens from less than 4 m.

New Caledonia

OBSCURE LONGFIN
Plesiops verecundus Mooi, 1995

Dorsal rays XII,7; anal rays III,8; pectoral rays 19–24 (rarely 19 or 24); lateral-line scales 18–20 + 10–16; predorsal scales 6–8; gill rakers 3–6 + 7–14; total gill rakers modally 14–15; dark brown with a pale spot basally on each scale of body; except for the body coloration, it can be similar to *Plesiops coeruleolineatus*; the illustration shows an unusually colorful specimen. Largest recorded, 12 cm. Western Australia to southern Great Barrier Reef, Indo-Malayan region north to Ryukyu Islands, east to New Caledonia, Tonga, and Fiji (type locality). An inshore species of reefs exposed to wave action.

Fiji

STEENE'S LONGFIN
Steeneichthys plesiopsus Allen & Randall, 1985

Dorsal rays IX,8–9 (usually 9); anal rays III,7; pectoral rays 17–18; pelvic rays I,4; branched caudal rays 14–15; a single lateral-line scale with a sensory tubule; longitudinal scale series 22–24; scales on head and body ctenoid but deciduous; gill rakers 2–3 + 7–8; body depth 2.5–3.2 in standard length; membranes of spinous portion of dorsal fin deeply incised; caudal fin rounded, 3.35–3.6 in standard length; pelvic fins very long (when intact may be more than half standard length); head whitish with 3 yellowish brown bars, the first through eye; body with 6 faint dark bars and a few white dots dorsally; tips of dorsal spines white; caudal fin with alternating narrow pale and broad dark bars. Largest specimen, 3 cm. Known from Rowley Shoals, Western Australia (type locality), Fiji, Tonga, and American Samoa; collected with ichthyocide from caves and crevices in outer-reef slopes from the depth range of 2 to 35 m; not observed alive.

American Samoa

Ringtail Cardinalfish, *Ostorhinchus aureus*, Ambon, Indonesia

CARDINALFISHES
(APOGONIDAE)

This large family (estimated 250 species) of small fishes is distinct in having 2 separate dorsal fins, the first of VI to VIII spines (first and eighth spines may be very small and easily overlooked); second dorsal fin of II spines and 8 to 18 rays, pelvic rays I,5; branchiostegal rays 7; vertebrae generally 24; scales usually finely ctenoid, but cycloid in some species and absent in the genus *Gymnapogon*; lateral line complete to base of caudal fin (except in *Foa* and *Fowleria*), with 1-4 pored scales extending onto base of caudal fin (lateral-line scale counts in species accounts here recorded to base of caudal fin); gill-raker counts often important in distinguishing related species (the counts include rudiments); eyes large; mouth large and oblique, the dentition variable (some with canines, but most with teeth in villiform bands); a single flat opercular spine; a ridge on preopercle preceding the edge (margin of both varying from smooth to serrate). The common name cardinalfishes refers to the red color of some species (most species are not red). These fishes are nocturnal, though some feed opportunistically by day; most feed on zooplankton, often well above the substratum, but some concentrate their feeding on or near the bottom. The species of *Siphamia* are unique in having a ventral luminous organ; the genus is in need of revision. Many species of the family are known to incubate the eggs in the mouth, releasing them at hatching (except for the one species of *Pterapogon* that holds the developing larvae in its mouth to the juvenile stage). Although the male is believed to be the oral-brooding sex in the Apogonidae, there are reports that it is the female of some species that assumes this role. Some of the cardinalfishes have surprisingly large distributions for mouth brooders. The finding of a transformed individual of *Pristiapogon kallopterus* well offshore in the Hawaiian Islands suggests that some of these fishes are able to cross broad expanses of ocean by existing as juveniles in the open ocean (B. C. Mundy, pers. comm.). Most apogonid fishes are marine, but some, such as the species of *Glossamia*, are found in fresh water. Fraser (1972) recognized 3 subfamilies: Apogoninae, Pseudaminae, and Epigoninae, but the last mentioned is now given family status. Baldwin & Johnson (1999) confirmed the placement of *Gymnapogon* in the Pseudaminae and added a new genus, *Paxton*, to the subfamily. Randall et al. (1985) revised *Pseudamia*, Gon (1993) the genus *Cheilodipterus*, and Gon & Randall (2003) the genus *Archamia*. Bergman (2004) has shown that the subgenera of *Apogon* in Fraser (1972) are now genera (except that *Ostorhinchus* Lacepède replaces *Nectamia* Jordan).

CAUDALBAR CARDINALFISH
Apogon caudicinctus Randall & Smith, 1988

Dorsal rays VI + I,9; anal rays II,8; pectoral rays 12; lateral-line scales 25; predorsal scales 7–8; gill rakers 3–4 + 12–13; body 2.95–3.45 in standard length; caudal peduncle nearly twice as long as deep; dorsal profile of head nearly straight; preopercular edge serrate; transparent red, the scale edges blackish, with a broad blackish bar posteriorly on caudal peduncle and base of caudal fin. Described from specimens from the Pitcairn Islands, Rapa (type locality), Fiji, Réunion, and the Ryukyu Islands, and reported from the Marquesas Islands by Randall & Earle (2000); a shallow-water fish of seaward rocky shores; collected from depths of 0.3–12 m.

Rapa

RUBY CARDINALFISH
Apogon crassiceps Garman, 1903

Dorsal rays VI + I,9; anal rays II,8; pectoral rays 13 (rarely 12 or 14); lateral-line scales 24; predorsal scales 5–6 (usually 6); a single large scale between lateral line and third dorsal spine; gill rakers 3–4 + 12–14; body depth 2.7–3.0 in standard length; snout short and rounded; dorsal profile of head from eye to first dorsal fin straight; a free edge of skin extending from above upper lip nearly to anterior nostril; vertical preopercular margin weakly serrate, the ridge smooth; caudal fin forked with broadly rounded lobes; transparent red, the red mostly on head, edges of body, and narrowly on scale edges; some blackish pigment may be present on scale edges dorsally on body. Attains 5 cm. Ryukyu Islands south to the Great Barrier Reef, east to the Line Islands and Tuamotu Archipelago; type locality, Fiji. Occurs on shallow reefs. Related to *Apogon coccineus* Rüppell, which appears to be restricted to the Red Sea and western Indian Ocean.

Fiji

DEETSIE'S CARDINALFISH
Apogon deetsie Randall, 1998

Dorsal rays VI + I,9; anal rays II,8; pectoral rays 11–12 (usually 12); lateral-line scales 24; predorsal scales 6; gill rakers 3–4 + 12–13; body of adults 2.9–3.15 in standard length; dorsal profile of head straight; posterior preopercular edge serrate, the corner and ventral edge with a protruding membranous lobe; preopercular ridge smooth; caudal fin slightly forked with very broadly rounded lobes; pale translucent red, the scale edges red, with 2 faint dark bars posteriorly on body (scale edges still red within bars), the first below posterior half of second dorsal fin, and the second posteriorly on caudal peduncle and extending partly onto caudal-fin base; outer fourth of caudal lobes blackish; tips of second dorsal and anal fins often dusky. Largest specimen, 6.7 cm. Currently known only from the Hawaiian Islands (type locality, O'ahu) and Rangiroa Atoll, Tuamotu Archipelago, from depths of 25–160 m.

Hawaiian Islands

LONGSPINE CARDINALFISH
Apogon doryssa (Jordan & Seale, 1906)

Dorsal rays VI + I,9; anal rays II,8; pectoral rays 11–12; lateral-line scales 24; predorsal scales 5–6; gill rakers 4–5 + 12–14 (usually 4 + 13); body depth 2.9–3.25 in standard length; dorsal profile of head nearly straight; posterior preopercular margin serrate, the ridge smooth; second dorsal spine long, nearly reaching rear base of second dorsal fin when depressed; caudal fin forked with rounded lobes; transparent red, the red mainly on head, edges of body, scale edges, vertebral column, and fin spines and rays. Reaches 5 cm. Maldive Islands east to Marshall Islands, Rapa, and the Tuamotu Archipelago; in the western Pacific from southern Japan to the Great Barrier Reef and New Caledonia; type locality, Upolu, Western Samoa. Remains well hidden by day, and never far from shelter at night.

Balicasag Island, Philippines (night)

SURGE CARDINALFISH

Apogon indicus Greenfield, 2001

Dorsal rays VI + I,9; anal rays II,8; pectoral rays 13; lateral-line scales 23–24 (usually 24); predorsal scales 6; 2 large scales between lateral line and third dorsal spine; gill rakers 2–3 + 12–13; body depth 2.6–3.1 in standard length; dorsal profile of snout strongly convex, of rest of head nearly straight; no free edge of skin extending from above upper lip nearly to anterior nostril; vertical preopercular margin serrate, the ridge smooth; caudal fin forked with broadly rounded lobes; translucent to transparent red with scattered small dark markings dorsally and on cheek. Reaches 5 cm. Known from islands of the Indian Ocean (type locality, Mauritius), Vietnam, Philippines, Palau, Mariana Islands, New

Bacan, Indonesia (night)

Caledonia, Tonga, and American Samoa; occurs on exposed outer reefs in the surge zone. One of a group of 4 small, transparent, often partly red species of *Apogon* termed the *erythrinus* complex (Greenfield, 2001).

BROADSTRIPE CARDINALFISH

Apogon lativittatus Randall, 2001

Dorsal rays VI + I,9; anal rays II,8; pectoral rays 13; lateral-line scales 25; predorsal scales 8–9; gill rakers 4 + 12–13; body depth 2.6–3.0 in standard length; dorsal profile of head straight; preopercular margin finely serrate, the ridge smooth; caudal fin slightly forked with broadly rounded lobes; adults red, the edges of scales dorsally on body blackish; a very broad, midlateral, blackish stripe posteriorly on body extending to end of caudal fin; a large dusky blotch behind and adjacent to eye and another at pectoral-fin base; a semicircular blackish spot behind preopercular margin; fins translucent with light red rays; juveniles similar but translucent red with a distinct blackish band from eye to pectoral-fin base. Largest specimen, 73.5 cm. Known only from the Marquesas Islands (type locality, Fatu Hiva) and 1 spec-

Marquesas Islands

imen from Tabuaeran (Fanning Island), Line Islands. Never observed underwater until the use of ichthyocide; depth of capture, 6–36.5 m. Related to *A. semiornatus* Peters, not reported from the Marquesas Islands.

MARQUESAN CARDINALFISH

Apogon marquesensis Greenfield, 2001

Dorsal rays VI + I,9; anal rays II,8; pectoral rays 13–14 (rarely 13); lateral-line scales usually 24; predorsal scales 6–7 (usually 6); 2 large scales between lateral line and third dorsal spine; gill rakers 3 + 11–13; body depth 2.4–2.75 in standard length; dorsal profile of snout strongly convex, rest of profile nearly straight; no free edge of skin extending from above upper lip nearly to anterior nostril; vertical preopercular margin weakly serrate, the ridge smooth; caudal fin forked with broadly rounded lobes; transparent with red over much of head, on upper and lower edges of body, and narrowly on scale edges; abdominal cavity obscured by a large, blackish green, oval patch; a little blackish midlaterally on caudal peduncle. Attains 5.5 cm.

Marquesas Islands (night)

Known only from the Marquesas Islands; collected from rocky substrata along shores exposed to wave action and in bays in less than 12 m. Related to *Apogon erythrinus* Snyder of the Hawaiian Islands.

Fiji

DOUBLEBAR CARDINALFISH

Apogon posterofasciatus Allen & Randall, 2002

Dorsal rays VI + I,9; anal rays II,8; pectoral rays 13; lateral-line scales 24; predorsal scales 6; developed gill rakers 2 + 11 (usually with 3 rudiments at each end of gill arch); body of adults 2.6–2.7 in standard length; dorsal profile of head straight; snout short, 4.4–5.1 in head length; posterior preopercular edge serrate, the corner and ventral edge membranous; preopercular ridge smooth; caudal fin slightly forked with very broadly rounded

194

lobes; body orange-yellow, the scale centers dusky, shading to light red on abdomen and chest, with 2 broad dusky bars, one connecting about posterior half of second dorsal and anal fins, and the other on posterior half of caudal peduncle, with some pigment continuing onto caudal-fin base; head mainly translucent pale red; first dorsal fin with pink spines; second dorsal and caudal fin with orange-yellow rays and near-transparent membranes. Attains 6.5 cm. Described from specimens from Indonesia, Philippines, and Solomon Islands (type locality, Florida Island); recently collected in Fiji by David W. Greenfield. *Apogon deetsie* is similar, with the same 2 posterior dusky bars, but it is more red overall and has 11 or 12 pectoral rays. It was described from the Hawaiian Islands, but is also reported from the Tuamotu Archipelago.

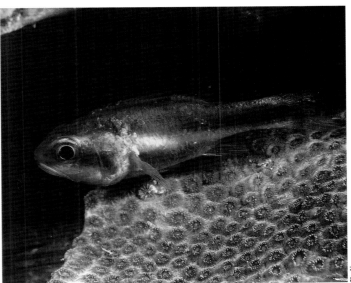

Bali

OBLIQUEBANDED CARDINALFISH
Apogon semiornatus Peters, 1876
Dorsal rays VI + I,9; anal rays II,8; pectoral rays 12; lateral-line scales 24–25; predorsal scales 6; gill rakers 4–5 + 12–13; body depth 2.7–3.0 in standard length; dorsal profile of head convex, especially snout; vertical margin of preopercular finely serrate, the ventral edge membranous and crenulate; preopercular ridge smooth; caudal fin forked with strongly rounded lobes; transparent light red with a broad dark brown band from eye to base of anal fin, and another following lateral line, broadening on caudal peduncle and base of caudal fin, then narrowing to end of fin. Reaches only 5 cm. Red Sea and Gulf of Oman south to Natal, east to western Pacific from southern Japan to the Great Barrier Reef and New Caledonia; no other localities reported from Oceania; type locality, Mauritius; a very secretive shallow-water species generally seen only at night (and then briefly, because it quickly seeks shelter when illuminated).

SUSAN'S CARDINALFISH
Apogon susanae Greenfield, 2001
Dorsal rays VI + I,9; anal rays II,8–9 (rarely 9); pectoral rays usually 14; lateral-line scales 23–25; predorsal scales 5–6; 2 large scales between lateral line and third dorsal spine; gill rakers 2–3 + 12–13; body depth 2.6–3.1 in standard length; dorsal profile of snout strongly convex, rest of head nearly straight; no free edge of skin extending from above upper lip nearly to anterior nostril; vertical preopercular margin serrate, the ridge smooth; caudal fin forked with broadly rounded lobes; life color unknown but probably transparent red like others of the *erythrinus* complex (revised by Greenfield, 2001). Attains 4.5 cm. Reported from Ogasawara Islands and New Caledonia, islands of Micronesia (type locality, Ifaluk Atoll, Caroline Islands), Line Islands, French Polynesia except the Marquesas Islands, and the Pitcairn Islands. Occurs inshore on seaward reefs exposed to wave action.

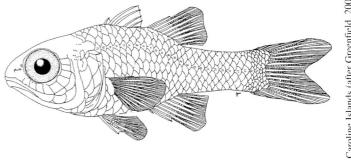

Caroline Islands (after Greenfield, 2001)

OCELLATED CARDINALFISH
Apogonichthys ocellatus (Weber, 1913)
Dorsal rays VIII (small eighth spine usually covered by skin) + I,9; anal rays II,8; pectoral rays 15; lateral-line scales 23; predorsal scales 4; gill rakers 14–15; no palatine teeth; ridge and edge of preopercle smooth; body depth 2.6–2.8 in standard length; anterior nostril with a long flap on hind edge; caudal fin broadly rounded; mottled dark brown with dark bands radiating from eye, the most prominent broad and oblique across cheek; a large, ocellated black spot posteriorly in first dorsal fin. Reaches 6 cm. East coast of Africa to the Marquesas Islands, but from scattered records between, including the Great Barrier Reef, Rapa, southern Japan, and islands of Micronesia; described from specimens from Sulu Archipelago, Sulawesi, and Molucca Islands. A cryptic species of calm shallow lagoons and bays.

Marquesas Islands

195

CAMOUFLAGE CARDINALFISH

Apogonichthys perdix Bleeker, 1854

Dorsal rays VIII (small eighth spine usually covered by skin) + I,9; anal rays II,8; pectoral rays 13–14; lateral-line scales 22–23; predorsal scales 5; gill rakers 1–2 + 11–12; no palatine teeth; ridge and edge of preopercle thin and crenulate; body depth 2.4–2.6 in standard length; caudal fin broadly rounded; reddish brown to olivaceous mottled with brown blotches and scattered white flecks; dark bands radiating from eye; posterior edge of caudal fin clear. Attains 6 cm. Red Sea south to Natal and east to the Hawaiian Islands and Rapa, but known from relatively few localities, among them southern Japan, Guam, and Flores (type locality); a very secretive species; never seen by day and rarely at

Hawaiian Islands

night; usually found in shallow protected waters of lagoons and bays, often on silty reefs with much algal growth or in seagrass beds. *Apogonichthys waikiki* Jordan & Evermann appears to be a synonym.

TWO-SPOT CARDINALFISH

Archamia biguttata Lachner, 1951

Dorsal rays VI + I,9; anal rays II,14–19 (usually 16–18); pectoral rays 13–15 (rarely 13 or 15); lateral-line scales 25; predorsal scales 5–6 (usually 6); gill rakers 5–7 + 15–18; body depth 2.3–2.85 in standard length; body width 2.3–2.7 in depth; preopercular margin nearly fully serrate; preopercular ridge angular and smooth except for a small flat spine at corner; caudal fin moderately forked; translucent gray with dusky orange lines on scale edges (vertical dorsally on body, curving forward as they pass ventrally); a broad, slightly oblique, blackish bar below eye; a large blackish spot above gill opening, often covering first lateral-line scale, sometimes extending diffusely on opercle to level of pectoral-fin base; a blackish spot present or absent at midbase of caudal fin; a narrow yellow stripe from front of snout to eye, sometimes edged in blue, the blue borders continuing as lines into eye. Largest examined, 9.8 cm.

Wetar, Indonesia

Ryukyu Islands to northern half of Australia, east to Guam and Western Samoa; type locality, Bacon Island, Luzon. Collected from depths of 0.1–33 m, but usually less than 15 m, on rocky or coral reefs, sometimes in association with branching corals.

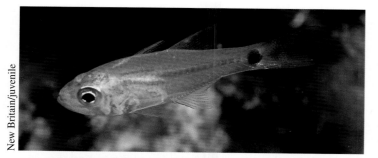

New Britain/juvenile

Sulawesi

ORANGELINED CARDINALFISH

Archamia fucata (Cantor, 1849)

Dorsal rays VI + I,9; anal rays II,15–18 (rarely 18); pectoral rays 13–15 (usually 14); lateral-line scales 24; predorsal scales 5–6; gill rakers 5–6 + 14–16; preopercular margin serrate only at corner and about posterior half of ventral margin; preopercular ridge angular, often with a small spine at corner; body deep, the depth 2.3–2.5 in standard length, and compressed, the width about 3.0 in depth; caudal fin slightly forked; translucent gray, sometimes with iridescence, with orange lines on scale edges (vertical dorsally on body, curving forward as they pass ventrally); a diffuse blackish spot larger than pupil (may be as large as eye) posteriorly on side of caudal peduncle; a blue-edged orange-yellow stripe on side of snout. Largest, 9.5 cm. Red Sea and east coast of Africa to Marshall Islands, Samoa Islands, and Tonga; in the western Pacific from southern Japan to the Great Barrier Reef and New Caledonia; type locality, Sea of Pinang. Generally found in aggregations on coral reefs, sometimes sheltering among branches of live coral in lagoons and bays, from depths of 0.5–35 m. Feeds at night as solitary individuals on the zooplankton well above the substratum. *Archamia dispilus* Lachner and *A. irida* Gon & Randall are synonyms, the latter described from subadults.

Norfolk Island

Norfolk Island (night)

LEA'S CARDINALFISH
Archamia leai Waite, 1916
Dorsal rays VII (the first spine very small) + I,9; anal rays II,12–14; pectoral rays 14–16 (rarely 16); lateral-line scales 25; predorsal scales 3–4 (rarely 3); gill rakers 5–7 + 16–19; preopercular margin serrate; body depth 2.5–2.8 in standard length; body width 2.05–2.8 in depth; caudal fin moderately forked; a dark brown bar on body linking front of second dorsal and anal fins, broader in middle, and 2 or 3 short bars on side of body above basal half of pectoral fin; body anterior to large bar mainly gray, posteriorly yellow; a blackish red stripe, edged in blue, from front of snout through eye, emerging behind eye without blue lines; fins mainly pink; gray with blue iridescence at night, the dark bars lost. Reaches 8.5 cm. Known only from the southern Great Barrier Reef, Coral Sea, Norfolk Island (type locality), and New Caledonia. Occurs in protected waters of bays and lagoons; known from depths of 0.5–15 m.

DUSKYTAIL CARDINALFISH
Archamia macroptera (Cuvier in C & V, 1828)
Dorsal rays VI + I,9–10 (rarely 10); anal rays II,13–15; pectoral rays 13–15 (rarely 13 or 15); lateral-line scales 25; predorsal scales 5–7; gill rakers 5–7 + 16–19; preopercular margin serrate; body depth 2.4–2.7 in standard length; caudal fin moderately forked; gray with dusky orange lines on body as described for *Archamia biguttata* but often obscure; body posterior to second dorsal and anal fins progressively more dusky; a black spot larger than pupil at midbase of caudal fin, its edges not distinct due to dusky surrounding area. Attains 9.5 cm. Sri Lanka and throughout the East Indies (type locality, Java), north to Ryukyu Islands, east from New Guinea to Vanuatu and Samoa Islands. A shallow-water species of lagoons and reefs of protected shores; usually seen in aggregations, sometimes with other species of the genus; may use branching coral for cover.

Bali

FRAIL CARDINALFISH
Cercamia cladara Randall & Smith, 1988
Dorsal rays VI + I,9; anal rays II,12–13; pectoral rays 10; scales deciduous (no counts made); gill rakers 3–4 + 14–16; vertebrae 9 + 15; preopercular margin and ridge smooth except for 2 small spines at corner of margin and 1 at angle of ridge; body very elongate, the depth 4.2–4.5 in standard length; caudal peduncle long and slender, its length 3.25–3.8 in standard length, its depth 3.35–4.05 in head length; caudal fin deeply forked; transparent with red dots; no obvious dark markings (at most a few melanophores behind eye of some specimens). Largest, 5.5 cm. Known from Pitcairn Islands, Society Islands, Rapa (type locality), Austral Islands, Cook Islands, Tonga, and Chesterfield Islands, Coral Sea, from depths of 10–52 m; has been observed in or near caves at night.

Tahiti

Papua New Guinea/subadult

New Britain

WOLF CARDINALFISH
Cheilodipterus artus Smith, 1961

Dorsal rays VI + I,9; anal rays II,8; pectoral rays 12–14 (usually 13); lateral-line scales 24–25; gill rakers 2–4 + 9–14; edge of preopercle smooth or with only a few minute serrae on vertical part; 3 pairs of canine teeth at front of upper jaw and about 6 on each side of lower jaw; body elongate, the depth 3.2–4.0 in standard length; caudal fin moderately forked; silvery gray with purple to green iridescence dorsally, silvery white ventrally, with 7 or 8 dusky yellow to yellowish brown stripes narrower than interspaces; young with a black spot at midbase of caudal fin within a yellow area; spot obscured by a blackish area over all of posterior caudal peduncle in adults. Attains 15 cm. East coast of Africa to the Marshall Islands and Tuamotu Archipelago; Ryukyu Islands to the Great Barrier Reef; type locality, Mahé, Seychelles. Usually found in lagoons or sheltered reef habitats between 3 and 10 m, sometimes retreating among branches of live coral.

Balicasag Island, Philippines (night)

TAILSPOT CARDINALFISH
Cheilodipterus isostigmus (Schultz, 1940)

Dorsal rays VI + I,9; anal rays II,8; pectoral rays 11–13 (usually 12); lateral-line scales 24; gill rakers 1–2 + 7–12; small canine teeth at front of lower jaw; edge of preopercle finely serrate except about anterior half of ventral part; body elongate, the depth 3.2–3.7 in standard length; caudal fin moderately forked; silvery gray, shading to silvery white ventrally, with 5 very narrow black stripes on body, the third passing from front of snout through eye to end at a large yellow area centered on base of caudal fin and containing a small black spot; with blue-green iridescence at night. Largest specimen, 10.5 cm. Known to date from the South China Sea, Philippines, Malaysia, New Guinea (type locality), New Britain, Solomon Islands, Vanuatu, Marshall Islands, and Tonga (from 1 specimen collected by the author in 15 m at Vava'u). Essentially the same in color as *Cheilodipterus quinquelineatus*. Lachner in Schultz et al. (1953) stated that *quinquelineatus* usually has more dark pigment on the upper and lower rays of the caudal fin, and Myers (1999) wrote that *isostigmus* has the peduncular spot in line with the midlateral stripe (whereas it is displaced slightly above in *quinquelineatus*). The only certain difference, however, is the presence of canine teeth at the front of the lower jaw of *isostigmus* and their absence in *quinquelineatus*. Schultz (1940) placed *isostigmus* in the new genus *Cheilodipterops*, later referred to synonymy. Gon (1993) noted that *isostigmus* is poorly represented in museum collections compared with the common *quinquelineatus*. The latter is most abundant on shallow patch reefs in lagoons, whereas most *isostigmus* have come from depths of 10 m or more in outer-reef areas, as well as deeper lagoon reefs.

198

Lombok, Indonesia

LARGE-TOOTHED CARDINALFISH
Cheilodipterus macrodon (Lacepède, 1802)
Dorsal rays VI + I,9; anal rays II,8; pectoral rays 12–14 (usually 13); lateral-line scales 24–25; gill rakers 1–2 + 6–9; canine teeth in jaws large; edge of preopercle serrate, but serrae relatively smaller with growth, and edge may be smooth in large adults; body elongate, the depth 3.1–3.8 in standard length; caudal fin moderately forked; adults silvery white to light brown with 8 to 10 dark brown stripes that are broader than pale interspaces; posterior caudal peduncle and base of caudal fin with a large black spot or a broad black ring; a whitish area separating black spot or ring from dark stripes; outer part of first dorsal fin blackish; upper and lower edges of caudal fin blackish. Reaches 25 cm. Red Sea and east coast of Africa to the islands of Micronesia,

Papua New Guinea/subadult

French Polynesia except the Marquesas Islands, and the Pitcairn Islands; in the western Pacific from southern Japan to New South Wales and Lord Howe Island; type locality, Mascarene Islands. Usually solitary in clear outer-reef areas in caves or beneath ledges by day, generally at depths of 4–30 m.

Sulawesi

Okinawa (night)

FIVE-LINE CARDINALFISH
Cheilodipterus quinquelineatus Cuvier in C & V, 1828
Dorsal rays VI + I,9; anal rays II,8; pectoral rays 12–13 (usually 12); lateral-line scales 24; gill rakers 1–2 + 7–12; no canine teeth at front of lower jaw; edge of preopercle finely serrate except about anterior half of ventral part; body elongate, the depth 3.1–3.7 in standard length; caudal fin moderately forked; silvery gray, shading to silvery white ventrally, with 5 very narrow black stripes on body, the third passing from front of snout through eye to end at a large yellow area centered on base of caudal fin and containing a small black spot; exhibits blue-green iridescence at night. Reaches 12.5 cm. Occurs throughout the Indo-Pacific region except the Persian Gulf and Hawaiian Islands; type locality, Bora Bora, Society Islands. Typically found on coral reefs in protected waters of bays or lagoons in 1–10 m, often hiding among the branches of coral or the spines of species of the sea urchin genus *Diadema*.

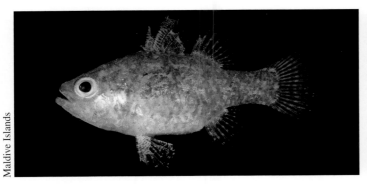

Maldive Islands

Marshall Islands

BIGHEAD CARDINALFISH
Foa fo Jordan & Seale, 1905

Dorsal rays VII + I,9; anal rays II,8; pectoral rays 12–13; lateral-line ending beneath end of first dorsal fin, the pored scales 9–11; scales in longitudinal series 22; gill rakers 3 + 9–11; ridge and edge of preopercle smooth; teeth present on palatines; body very deep, the depth 2.0–2.3 in standard length; head large, 2.15–2.35 in standard length; caudal fin broadly rounded; mottled brown, sometimes with narrow, irregular, dark bars on body, the first on nape, the second and third each below a dorsal fin, the fourth on caudal peduncle, and the fifth at base of caudal fin; tips of membranes of first dorsal fin black. Largest specimen, 6.8 cm. Scattered records from the Red Sea and east coast of Africa to Rapa and the Society Islands; type locality, Negros, Philippines. A shallow-water species from protected reefs, seagrass beds, or algal flats. Very similar to *Foa brachygramma* (Jenkins) from the Hawaiian Islands, which differs in having modally 15 total gill rakers (13–14 in *Foa fo*) and larger size (to 8.2 cm).

DOTTED CARDINALFISH
Fowleria isostigma (Jordan & Seale, 1906)

Dorsal rays VII + I,9; anal rays II,8; pectoral rays 13–14 (usually 14); tubed lateral-line scales 9–14; longitudinal scale series 23; median predorsal scales 6; gill rakers 3–4 + 13–14; posterior edge of preopercle smooth, the ventral edge membranous and crenulate; villiform teeth present in jaws and on vomer but not on palatines (true of other *Fowleria*); body depth 2.65–3.1 in standard length; caudal fin rounded; brown to yellowish brown with a very small round black spot basally on most scales of body (few or none above lateral line in some specimens), thus forming longitudinal rows of the scale pattern; an ocellated round black spot larger than pupil on opercle, with a dark brown line above; a dark-edged pale band from lower part of eye to upper corner of preopercle; fins dusky. Largest specimen, 9.2 cm, from Rapa. Southern Japan to Great Barrier Reef and New Caledonia, east to Mangareva and the islands of Micronesia; type locality, Upolu, Western Samoa. Collected from protected reefs in 1–15 m.

Line Islands

Solomon Islands

Bali (night: R. F. Myers)

CROSSEYED CARDINALFISH
Fowleria marmorata (Alleyne & Macleay, 1877)

Dorsal rays VII + I,9; anal rays II,8; pectoral rays 14–15 (usually 15); tubed lateral-line scales 10–13; longitudinal scale series 23; median predorsal scales 6; gill rakers 2–3 + 11–14; posterior edge of preopercle smooth, the ventral edge membranous and crenulate; body depth 2.7–3.1 in standard length; caudal fin rounded; reddish brown, usually with 10–12 dark brown bars on middle three-fourths of side of body; a white-edged round black spot larger than pupil on opercle with a horizontal black line above; a dark brown line from lower edge of eye to corner of preopercle; fins red. Reaches 9 cm. Red Sea south to Natal and east to the Line Islands, Society Islands, and Marquesas Islands; Ryukyu Islands to the Great Barrier Reef and New Caledonia; type locality, Cape Grenville, Queensland. Secretive and rarely seen; specimens collected from lagoon and seaward reefs in 7–30 m.

MOTTLED CARDINALFISH
Fowleria vaiulae (Jordan & Seale, 1906)

Dorsal rays VII + I,9; anal rays II,8; pectoral rays 13–14 (usually 14); tubed lateral-line scales 9–11; longitudinal scale series 22–23; predorsal scales 6; gill rakers 3 + 12–13; posterior edge and ridge of preopercle smooth; body depth 2.7–2.9 in standard length; caudal fin rounded; mottled brown or reddish brown and white, often with 6 to 8 narrow whitish bars on side of body; indistinct dark bands radiating from posterior half of eye; no ocellated dark spot on opercle. Attains 5 cm. Red Sea, Persian

Gulf, and Mauritius to Marshall Islands, Line Islands, and Society Islands; in the western Pacific from the Ryukyu Islands south to the Great Barrier Reef and New Caledonia; type locality, Upolu, Western Samoa. Occurs in a variety of habitats from reefs to seagrass and algal substrata; recorded from depths of 5–52 m. *Fowleria abocellata* Goren & Karplus is a synonym. The suggestion of Goren & Karplus (1983) that *abocellata* is a mimic of a scorpionfish has not been accepted.

Papau New Guinea

Palau

SPOT-TAIL CARDINALFISH

Gymnapogon urospilotus Lachner in Schultz et al., 1953
Dorsal rays VI + I,9; anal rays II,9–10 (usually 9); pectoral rays 13–14 (usually 13); head and body scaleless; small papillae on head, especially dorsally and on lower jaw; vertical rows of small papillae on body; gill rakers 2 + 10; a large spine at middle of preoperclular margin with a broad membraneous flap below, extending to margin of operculum; body elongate, the depth 3.55–4.5 in standard length; mouth large, the maxilla extending to below rear edge of eye; caudal fin forked with strongly rounded lobes; transparent, the individual dark vertebrae easily visible; a large double black spot (described as B-shaped) at base of caudal fin; a black spot on side of snout and one on lower jaw present or absent. Largest, 3.6 cm. Reported from Micronesia, Ryukyu Islands, Taiwan, Papua New Guinea, Great Barrier Reef, American Samoa, Tonga, and Society Islands; type locality, Kwajalein Atoll, Marshall Islands. Collected from tidepools to coral reefs at depths to at least 18 m; not observed in life (photographed specimen collected with ichthyocide; transparency already diminished).

EIGHTSPINE CARDINALFISH

Neamia octospina Smith & Radcliffe in Radcliffe, 1912
Dorsal rays VIII + I,9; anal rays II,8; pectoral rays 18; lateral-line scales 23; median predorsal scales 3–4; gill rakers 2 + 10–12; body depth 2.4–2.9 in standard length; preopercular ridge and edge smooth; mouth large, the maxilla reaching well posterior to eye; villiform teeth in jaws and on vomer, but none on palatines; caudal fin rounded; translucent whitish to yellowish with 3 narrow brown bands extending from posterior edge of eye. Reaches 5 cm. Red Sea and Mozambique to Pohnpei and Fiji; Ryukyu Islands to Great Barrier Reef and New Caledonia; type locality, Palawan. Fraser & Allen (2001) updated the distribution and described a second species of the genus, *Neamia notula*, from Mauritius. *Neamia octospina* is the only species of the Apogonidae with VIII distinct dorsal spines (in *N. notula* and the species of *Apogonichthys*, the eighth dorsal spine is hidden by skin). Gon (1987) discovered that *Apogon sphenurus* Klunzinger is a senior synonym but successfully petitioned the International Commission on Zoological Nomenclature to suppress *sphenurus* to conserve the well-known *octospina*.

VARIEGATED CARDINALFISH

Fowleria variegata (Valenciennes, 1832)
Dorsal rays VII + I,9; anal rays II,8; pectoral rays 12–14 (usually 13); tubed lateral-line scales 10–13; longitudinal scale series 22–23; predorsal scales 4; gill rakers 3–4 + 10–13; upper edge of preopercle smooth, the lower edge crenulate; preopercular ridge smooth; body depth 2.5–2.85 in standard length; caudal fin rounded; brown, densely spotted with dark brown; body before caudal peduncle sometimes with longitudinal rows of whitish dashes and small spots following scale rows; indistinct dark bars often present on body; a black spot larger than pupil on opercle, narrowly rimmed with yellow and nearly encircled with narrow dark brown segments, the one above spot straight; a dark-edged whitish band curving downward from lower posterior corner of eye; fins except pectorals with numerous small, dark brown spots tending to form irregular rows. Attains 7 cm. Red Sea and Persian Gulf south on east coast of Africa, east to Mariana Islands and Samoa Islands; in the western Pacific from the Ryukyu Islands to Great Barrier Reef and New Caledonia; type locality, Mauritius. A cryptic species of silty reefs, mangroves, and seagrass and algal flats from 0.3 to at least 27 m. Faded specimens have been misidentified as *Fowleria aurita* (Valenciennes), a species apparently not known from islands of Oceania. *Apogon punctulatus* Rüppell and *Apogonichthys polystigma* Bleeker are synonyms.

Fiji

Sangihe Islands, Indonesia

STRIPED CARDINALFISH

Ostorhinchus angustatus (Smith & Radcliffe, 1911)
Dorsal rays VII + I,9; anal rays III,8; pectoral rays usually 14; lateral-line scales 25; predorsal scales 3–4; gill rakers 5 + 14; body depth 2.75–3.15 in standard length; interorbital width 5.0–5.95 in head length; last anal ray longer than preceding ray, the outer border of anal fin distinctly concave; whitish with 5 dark stripes (varying from dark brown to yellowish brown) that are narrower than whitish interspaces; middle stripe ending in a nearly round black spot at base of caudal fin, its diameter a little larger than stripe width; fin rays light red, the membranes transparent. Reaches 9 cm. Wide-ranging in the Indo-Pacific from the Red Sea and east coast of Africa to the Line Islands and Pitcairn Islands; in the western Pacific from Taiwan to the Great Barrier Reef and New Caledonia; type locality, Malanipa Island, Philippines. Occurs mainly in clear outer-reef areas; reported from reef flats to 65 m.

Society Islands

GOLDBELLY CARDINALFISH

Ostorhinchus apogonides (Bleeker, 1856)
Dorsal rays VII + I,9; anal rays II,8; pectoral rays 14; lateral-line scales 26; predorsal scales 4–5; gill rakers usually 5–6 + 15–18; preopercular edge serrate, the ridge smooth; reddish gray dorsally, shading to brassy yellow ventrally on head and abdomen, and to red on rest of body; dark-edged blue spots in 2 to 3 rows midlaterally on body, narrowing to 1 row on caudal peduncle; a blackish stripe edged in bright blue from front of snout to eye, the blue borders continuing as lines through eye and across operculum; fins with pink rays and yellowish membranes, the first dorsal tipped with blackish. Reported to 10 cm. Red Sea and east coast of Africa to the Society Islands; in the western Pacific from Japan to New South Wales; type locality, Sulawesi; generally found in more than 30 m, but may occur in less than 2 m in calm waters of bays or lagoons.

RINGTAIL CARDINALFISH

Ostorhinchus aureus (Lacepède, 1802)
Dorsal rays VII + I,9; anal rays II,8; pectoral rays 13–15 (usually 14); lateral-line scales 24; predorsal scales 4–5; gill rakers 6–8 + 16–20; body moderately deep, the depth 2.25–2.85 in standard length (deeper with growth); preopercular margin serrate, the ridge smooth; caudal fin slightly forked; bronze to coppery dorsally, shading to golden yellow on sides and ventrally, paler posteriorly to a broad black ring around base of caudal fin (ring broader dorsally and ventrally in adults); a blackish stripe edged in bright blue from front of snout to eye, the blue borders continuing as lines through eye, breaking to dashes and spots across operculum; a blue line on upper lip continuing across maxilla; a small dark spot on each lateral-line scale except posteriorly. Largest specimen, 14.5 cm. Gulf of Oman to Natal, east to Tonga; not known from Micronesia; in the western Pacific from Japan to New South

Papua New Guinea

Wales; type locality, Mascarene Islands. Seems to be absent from atolls or low islands; occurs on coral reefs or rocky substrata from depths of 1 (where sea is calm) to at least 40 m. Often seen in aggregations. Also known as the Golden Cardinalfish.

BANDA CARDINALFISH

Ostorhinchus bandanensis (Bleeker, 1854)

Dorsal rays VII + I,9; anal rays II,8; pectoral rays usually 13; lateral-line scales 24; median predorsal scales 2; gill rakers 6–8 + 18–22 (usually 7–8 + 19–21); body depth 2.15–2.35 in standard length; snout very short and rounded; preopercular edge serrate, the ridge smooth; caudal fin very slightly emarginate, the lobes slightly rounded; light gray with pale blue-green iridescence (more at night) and 3 broad, dark gray bars, 1 under each dorsal fin and 1 posteriorly on caudal peduncle (complete across peduncle in juveniles, nearly so in adults); an oblique, wedge-shaped, dark band from eye, narrowing to a line to corner of preopercle; front of dorsal fins and upper and lower edges of caudal fin dark gray-brown. Largest specimen, 10.1 cm. Known to date from Banda (Indonesia), Tioman Island (Malaysia), Okinawa, Papua New Guinea, Guam, Marshall Islands, Rotuma, Fiji, and American Samoa.

Ogasawara Islands (night)

SHORTSPINE CARDINALFISH

Ostorhinchus brevispinis (Fraser & Randall, 2003)

Dorsal rays VII + I,9; anal rays II,8; pectoral rays 14; lateral-line scales 24; median predorsal scales 5; circumpeduncular scales 14; gill rakers 6 + 17; body depth 2.6–2.7 in standard length; preopercular edge serrate, the ridge smooth; first dorsal spine minute; last dorsal soft ray equal in length to preceding ray; last anal soft ray longer than preceding ray; caudal fin forked with rounded lobes; head and body with 5 golden brown stripes, the first middorsal and narrow, the next 3 very broad, becoming blackish as they end on base of caudal fin; fifth stripe from chin to base of anal fin; pale space between stripes as a white line; fins translucent pale yellow, the rays with pink edges; first 3 dorsal spines largely white; a white line at base of last 3 rays of second dorsal and anal fins, extending out to tip of last ray. Attains at least 8.5 cm. Described from 2 specimens collected by the author on a coral reef in 46–58 m at Rurutu, Austral Islands. A third specimen from 55 m off Rangiroa Atoll, Tuamotu Archipelago (illustrated here), was lost.

Tuamotu Archipelago

CAPRICORN CARDINALFISH

Ostorhinchus capricornis (Allen & Randall, 1993)

Dorsal rays VII + I,8–9 (rarely 8); anal rays II,9; pectoral rays 14; lateral-line scales 24; predorsal scales 4; gill rakers 5–7 + 17–18; body depth 2.9–3.3 in standard length; preopercular edge serrate, the ridge weakly crenate or with tiny serrae around angle; caudal fin slightly forked; yellowish brown dorsally, brassy yellow below, with narrow gray-brown bars following scale rows in middle of body; a black spot nearly as large as pupil at midbase of caudal fin; a blue-edged dark brown stripe from front of snout and tip of lower jaw to eye, the blue borders continuing through eye, the lower one to end of opercle. Reaches 8 cm. Described from specimens from the Capricorn Group of the Great Barrier Reef, Sydney Harbor, and the Chesterfield Bank, Coral Sea, from depths of 3–15 m; recorded from New Caledonia by Laboute & Grandperrin (2000). Aggregations are common during the day on the southern Great Barrier Reef, sheltering among branches of coral.

Great Barrier Reef (B. C. Russell)

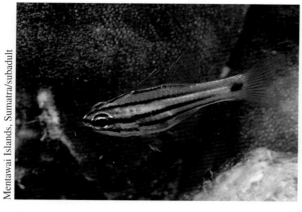
Mentawai Islands, Sumatra/subadult

New Britain

SPLIT-STRIPE CARDINALFISH

Ostorhinchus compressus (Smith & Radcliffe in Radcliffe, 1911)
Dorsal rays VI + I,9; anal rays II,9; pectoral rays 13 or 14; lateral-line scales 24; predorsal scales 7–8; gill rakers 7–8 + 20–22; body of adults about 2.7 in standard length; preopercular edge serrate, the ridge smooth; body silvery white with 7 maroon stripes, the second to fourth along middle of body much broader than white interspaces and breaking into spots at base of caudal fin; uppermost of the 3 principal stripes dividing in middle of body and continuing as 2 stripes to dorsal edge of eye; narrow dorsalmost stripe breaking into a series of spots along base of dorsal fins; fins with pink-edged rays; iris iridescent blue; juveniles colored much like *Cheilodipterus quinquelineatus*. Attains about 10 cm. Ryukyu Islands south to the Great Barrier Reef and New Caledonia; type locality, Bisucay Island, Cuyo Islands, Philippines. A shallow-water species of calm seas; usually seen by day oriented head-first into branching corals; while foraging at night, the white stripes are iridescent blue.

COOK'S CARDINALFISH

Ostorhinchus cookii (Macleay, 1881)
Dorsal rays VII + I,9; anal rays II,8; pectoral rays 15; lateral-line scales 24; predorsal scales 3–4; gill rakers 4–5 + 12–15; body depth of adults 2.5–2.8 in standard length; interorbital width 4.15–5.1 in head length; lower two-thirds and corner of preopercular edge serrate, the ridge smooth; last dorsal and anal rays not longer than penultimate rays; whitish with 6 dark brown stripes much broader than pale interspaces, the first middorsal, the third narrow, extending from upper edge of eye to below second dorsal fin, the broad fourth from snout through eye to base of caudal fin, where it ends in an oblong spot nearly twice as high as posterior end of stripe. Reaches 10 cm. Red Sea and Gulf of Oman south to Natal and east to the western Pacific, where it ranges from Japan to the Great Barrier Reef and New Caledonia; described from material from the Endeavour River and Darnley Island, Queensland. An inshore species generally found at depths less than 2 m.

Kenya

YELLOWSTRIPED CARDINALFISH

Ostorhinchus cyanosoma (Bleeker, 1883)
Dorsal rays VII + I,9; anal rays II,8; pectoral rays 14; lateral-line scales 24; predorsal scales 3–4; gill rakers 6–8 + 15–17; body depth of adults 2.7–3.0 in standard length; preopercular edge nearly fully serrate, the ridge smooth; body bluish silver with 6 orange-yellow stripes, the third, fifth, and sixth extending a short distance onto base of caudal fin, the narrow fourth from upper edge of eye, ending below second dorsal fin. Attains about 8 cm. Red Sea and Persian Gulf south to Mozambique and east to the western Pacific, where it ranges from the Ryukyu Islands to the Great Barrier Reef and New Caledonia; type locality, Solor, Indonesia. Occurs in a variety of habitats from depths of 1–50 m, usually in small aggregations in caves or under ledges by day; sometimes shelters among the spines of sea urchins of the genus *Diadema*. Similar to *O. rubrimacula* (see that account).

Sulawesi

204

FOURSTRIPE CARDINALFISH
Ostorhinchus doederleini (Jordan & Snyder, 1901)
Dorsal rays VII + I,9; anal rays II,8–9; pectoral rays 14 or 15; lateral-line scales 28; predorsal scales 4; gill rakers 2–3 + 10–12; body of adults 2.55–2.9 in standard length; preopercular edge finely serrate, the ridge smooth; second dorsal fin slightly higher than first dorsal fin; caudal fin slightly forked with rounded lobes; pale pinkish gray with 4 black to brassy yellowish brown stripes much narrower than pale interspaces and still narrower posteriorly; a round black spot smaller than pupil at midbase of caudal fin; fin rays pink, the membranes transparent. One of the larger species of the genus; reaches 12 cm. No records from Indonesia or New Guinea; in the north from Chiba Prefecture, Japan (type locality, Nagasaki), to Taiwan, Hong Kong (Sadovy & Cornish, 2000), and the Philippines; in the south from Western Australia to the Abrolhos and on the east coast to Sydney; east to Lord Howe Island, Norfolk Island, New Caledonia, Chesterfield Islands in the Coral Sea, and the Kermadec Islands, mostly from outer-reef areas, usually in small aggregations.

New Caledonia

BRASSY CARDINALFISH
Ostorhinchus flavus (Allen & Randall, 1993)
Dorsal rays VII + I,9; anal rays II,8; pectoral rays 15; lateral-line scales 24; predorsal scales 4; gill rakers 6–7 + 19–20; body depth of adults 2.6–2.8 in standard length; preopercular edge and ridge serrate; caudal fin slightly forked; yellowish gray dorsally, brassy yellow ventrally with a black spot, one-half to two-thirds pupil size, partly edged in pale blue, at midbase of caudal fin; a reddish black to blackish stripe, edged in pale blue or silvery white, from front of snout and lower jaw to eye, the blue borders continuing as lines through eye. Juveniles with tip of first dorsal fin blackish. Reaches 11 cm. Known from the southern Great Barrier Reef, Lord Howe Island, Norfolk Island (type locality), Coral Sea, and New Caledonia. The type specimens were collected from reefs in 10–21 m. Most similar to *Ostorhinchus capricornis* (Allen & Randall) from Southeast Australia and Coral Sea; it has 9 anal rays, 14 pectoral rays, and 22–24 gill rakers.

Norfolk Island

YELLOW-EDGED CARDINALFISH
Ostorhinchus fuscus (Quoy & Gaimard, 1825)
Dorsal rays VII + I,9; anal rays II,8; pectoral rays usually 13; lateral-line scales 24; median predorsal scales 2; gill rakers 6–8 + 18–22; body depth 2.25–2.5 in standard length; snout very short and rounded; preopercular edge serrate, the ridge smooth; caudal fin very slightly emarginate, the lobes slightly rounded; body gray-brown dorsally, pale pinkish gray on sides with numerous narrow, double, gray-brown bars ending anteriorly on caudal peduncle; a dark brown to black saddle-like bar posteriorly on caudal peduncle, ending in adults at lateral line but continuing ventrally in juveniles; an oblique, wedge-shaped, dark brown band from below eye to corner of preopercle; leading edges of second dorsal and anal fins and upper and lower edges of caudal fin yellow (pink at night); front of first dorsal fin broadly dark brown. Largest, 11.2 cm. Maldive Islands, Andaman Sea, and Cocos-Keeling Islands in the Indian Ocean; in the western Pacific from the Philippines and South China Sea to the Great Barrier Reef and New Caledonia; east in Oceania to the Line Islands and Tuamotu Archipelago; type locality, Guam.

Sulawesi (night)

GUAM CARDINALFISH

Ostorhinchus guamensis (Valenciennes, 1832)

Dorsal rays VII + I,9; anal rays II,8; pectoral rays usually 13; lateral-line scales 24; predorsal scales 3–4; gill rakers 6–8 + 18–21 (usually 6–7 + 18–20); body depth 2.4–3.7 in standard length; preopercular edge serrate, the ridge smooth; caudal fin very slightly forked, the lobes rounded; gray-brown, shading to silvery gray on sides, with a broad, blackish, saddle-like bar posteriorly on caudal peduncle extending slightly below lateral line; an oblique dark brown line from lower edge of eye to upper part of corner of preopercle; first dorsal fin dark from first to fourth spines and upper half of membrane between fourth and fifth spines; may show broad dark bars at night as seen in *Ostorhinchus bandanensis*. Attains 10 cm. Red Sea and east coast of Africa (but not the Mascarene Islands) to the Marshall Islands, Tonga, Phoenix Islands, and Samoa Islands; in the western Pacific from the Ryukyu Islands to the Great Barrier Reef; a shallow-water species that is well-hidden in reefs by day but feeds well above the substratum at night. *Apogon nubilus* Garman from Fiji is a synonym.

RIFLE CARDINALFISH

Ostorhinchus kiensis (Jordan & Snyder, 1901)

Dorsal rays VI + I,9; anal rays II,8; pectoral rays 14; lateral-line scales 24; predorsal scales 4–5; gill rakers 5–7 + 16–18; body depth 3.1–3.4 in standard length; vertical margin of preopercle serrate, the ridge smooth; caudal fin slightly forked; silvery gray to pale tan with a dark brown stripe about as wide as pupil, edged above by a white line and below by a pale blue line, from front of snout through eye to end of middle of caudal fin; a narrower dark brown stripe from dorsally on snout above eye, following contour of back to upper caudal peduncle, this stripe bordered above by an irregular pale blue line; some white flecks along lateral line. Attains 8 cm. East coast of Africa to the western Pacific, where it ranges from Japan (type locality, Wakanoura) to New South Wales, east to New Caledonia. Generally found in calm lagoons or estuaries, often over open stretches of silty sand; recorded from depths of 6–50 m.

PINSTRIPE CARDINALFISH

Ostorhinchus lateralis (Valenciennes, 1832)

Dorsal rays VI + I,9; anal rays II,8; pectoral rays 14; lateral-line scales 24; predorsal scales 6–7; gill rakers 5–7 + 16–18; body depth of adults about 2.5–2.7 in standard length; vertical margin of preoperculum serrate, the ridge smooth; caudal fin slightly forked; translucent gray with iridescence, silvery over abdomen and operculum, with a black line (faint on some fish) from upper end of gill opening, curving down to middle of body and extending to posterior caudal peduncle but usually not reaching a tiny black spot at midbase of caudal fin; a faint blackish line on side of snout and posterior to eye; leading edge of first dorsal fin black, the tip of fin broadly black. Reported to 10 cm. East coast of Africa to Samoa Islands; in the western Pacific from Taiwan to New Caledonia (misidentified as *Apogon ceramensis* by Laboute & Grandperrin, 2000). Type locality, Vanikoro, Santa Cruz Islands. A shallow-water species of protected waters of bays or lagoons; often in brackish areas such as mangrove sloughs and river mouths.

Papua New Guinea

Papua New Guinea

Cebu, Philippines

BLACKSTRIPED CARDINALFISH
Ostorhinchus nigrofasciatus (Lachner, 1953)

Dorsal rays VII + I,9; anal rays II,8; pectoral rays 13–14 (rarely 13); lateral-line scales 24–25 (usually 25); predorsal scales 3; gill rakers 5–7 + 15–17; body depth 2.6–3.1 in standard length; interorbital width 5.25–6.0 in head length; preopercular ridge serrate; preopercular ridge smooth; caudal fin slightly forked with rounded lobes; white to pale yellow with 5 dark brown to black stripes, suffused with red, the 3 middle bars broader than pale interspaces, the middle bar usually ending in a slightly broader, round to oblong, black spot at midbase of caudal fin, the second and fourth stripes slightly enlarged posteriorly and may converge a little to middle spot; fins transparent with light red rays. Largest examined, 8.8 cm. Red Sea and Gulf of Aden to the Marshall Islands and Tuamotu Archipelago; in the western Pacific from Japan to New South Wales; type locality, Bikini Atoll, Marshall Islands. Mainly a coral-reef inhabitant; collections from depths of 1–45 m. Early authors identified this species as *Apogon aroubiensis* Hombron & Jacquinot, but Randall & Lachner (1986) concluded that *aroubiensis* is not identifiable from its description, and no type specimen is extant.

Bonerate, Indonesia

Norfolk Island

NORFOLK CARDINALFISH
Ostorhinchus norfolcensis (Ogilby, 1888)

Dorsal rays VII-I,10; anal rays II,9; pectoral rays 14–15; lateral-line scales 24; predorsal scales 3; gill rakers 5–7 + 16–18; preopercular edge serrate, the ridge smooth; body depth 2.4–2.7 in standard length; front of second dorsal fin strongly elevated, the first dorsal soft ray 1.1–1.2 in head length; caudal fin slightly forked; silvery gray, the scales above lateral line and on caudal peduncle with a large dark brown or reddish brown spot, and scales below lateral line with broad dark brown or reddish brown edges; a small dark brown spot at midbase of caudal fin; caudal peduncle and a bar from below interdorsal space paler than rest of body (both may be almost entirely silvery white); a bluish white line from front of upper lip through eye; juveniles lack the dark bars on the body but have the same head markings and basi-caudal spot. Largest examined, 14.5 cm. Known only from Norfolk Island, Lord Howe Island, and New Caledonia. Most specimens from less than 2 m in mangrove areas or reefs in protected waters. More inclined than most apogonids to venture from cover, and will feed opportunistically by day.

New Caledonia/juveniles

207

Guam

Nuku Hiva, Marquesas Islands

Komodo, Indonesia (night)

NINESTRIPE CARDINALFISH
Ostorhinchus novemfasciatus (Cuvier in C & V, 1828)
Dorsal rays VII + I,9; anal rays II,8; pectoral rays 14; lateral-line scales 24–25; predorsal scales 3; gill rakers 2–3 + 10–13; body depth 2.7–3.1 in standard length; interorbital width 5.3–6.0 in head length; preopercular ridge serrate, the ridge smooth; last dorsal and anal soft rays longer than penulimate rays; caudal fin slightly forked with rounded lobes; whitish with 5 dark brown to black stripes, the uppermost middorsal except where it divides around dorsal fins (hence 9 stripes, counting both sides), the 3 middle stripes extending into middle of caudal fin, the second and fourth stripes converging on the third, the third not ending in a spot; middle stripe uneven in width. Attains 8.5 cm. Cocos-Keeling Islands in the Indian Ocean; southern Japan to the Great Barrier Reef and Coral Sea in the western Pacific, east to Line Islands, Samoa Islands, and the islands of Micronesia; described from Timor and Guam; occurs in shallow water of reef flats and lagoon reefs.

KIN CARDINALFISH
Ostorhinchus relativus (Randall, 2001)
Dorsal rays VII + I,9; anal rays III,8; pectoral rays 14; lateral-line scales 25; predorsal scales 4; gill rakers 5–6 + 14–16; body depth 2.85–3.4 in standard length; interorbital width 4.05–4.8 in head length; last anal ray longer than preceding rays (last ray 1.6–1.9 in head length in adults), thus outer border of anal fin distinctly concave; whitish with 5 dark brown stripes that are notably narrower than whitish interspaces; middle stripe ending in a vertically oval black spot at base of caudal fin (round in juveniles); fin rays pink, the membranes transparent. Largest specimen, 9.1 cm. Known only from the Marquesas Islands, where it is the most common apogonid fish; specimens were collected from less than 1 to 12 m on rocky substrata of bays and exposed shores. Closely related to the allopatric *O. angustatus*; *relativus* differs in having narrower dark stripes, a vertically oval basicaudal spot (seen on some specimens of *angustatus* from the Line Islands only), and a broader interorbital space (4.05–4.8 in head length, compared with 5.0–5.95 for *angustatus*).

REDSPOT CARDINALFISH
Ostorhinchus rubrimacula (Randall & Kulbicki, 1998)
Dorsal rays VII + I,9; anal rays II,8; pectoral rays 14; lateral-line scales 24; predorsal scales 4; gill rakers 6–8 + 17–20; body of adults 2.85–3.05 in standard length; preopercular edge nearly fully serrate, the ridge smooth to slightly crenulate; body silvery blue-gray with 6 orange-yellow stripes, the third, fifth, and sixth extending a short distance onto base of caudal fin, the narrow fourth from upper edge of eye, ending below second dorsal fin; third stripe ending in a red spot at caudal-fin base. Largest specimen, 5.4 cm. Described from Ryukyu Islands, Taiwan, Philippines, Indonesia, Great Barrier Reef, Coral Sea, Solomon Islands (type locality, Guadalcanal), and New Caledonia; collections were made on coral reefs from depths of 0.5–33 m. Randall & Kulbicki (1998) differentiated this species from the closely related *O. cyanosoma* (Bleeker), wide-ranging in the Indo-Pacific; *O. luteus* (Randall & Kulbicki) from Micronesia; *O. properupta* (Whitley) from eastern Australia and the Coral Sea; and *O. wassinki* (Bleeker) from Indonesia.

SAMOAN CARDINALFISH
Ostorhinchus savayensis (Günther, 1872)

Dorsal rays VII + I,9; anal rays II,8; pectoral rays usually 13; lateral-line scales 24; median predorsal scales 2–3; gill rakers 6–9 + 18–22 (usually 7–8 + 19–21); body depth 2.4–2.8 in standard length; snout very short and rounded; preopercular edge serrate, the ridge smooth; caudal fin very slightly emarginate, the lobes slightly rounded; body gray-brown dorsally, silvery gray on sides, often with lavender or blue-green iridescence; a broad, dark brown to black, saddle-like bar posteriorly on caudal peduncle extending to lateral line in adults, all the way across peduncle in juveniles; a wedge-shaped blackish band from lower edge of eye to corner of preopercle; front of dorsal fins dark brown; upper and lower edges of caudal fin dusky pinkish, the adjacent 2 or 3 rays darker than remaining rays. Largest, 11.3 cm. East coast of Africa to the Line Islands and islands of French Polynesia except the Marquesas Islands; in the western Pacific from the Philippines to the Great Barrier Reef, New Caledonia, Tonga, and Samoa Islands (type locality, Savai'i). Occurs on reefs in lagoons and deeper outer-reef areas; collections by the author from depths of 2–22 m.

Sumilon Island, Philippines (night)

METEOR CARDINALFISH
Ostorhinchus selas (Randall & Hayashi, 1990)

Dorsal rays VII + I,9; anal rays II,8; pectoral rays 13; lateral-line scales 24–25 (rarely 25); predorsal scales 4; gill rakers 3–4 + 11–14; body depth 2.9–3.6 in standard length; vertical margin of preopercular serrate, the ridge smooth; caudal fin forked; translucent pinkish gray, with a round black spot as large as eye, faintly edged with blue-green or yellow, centered on caudal-fin base; a midlateral red stripe on head, edged in iridescent blue-green (upper edge yellow where passing through eye) and overlaid with black pigment; stripe continuing as dusky orange on body; a large blue-green and blackish spot on abdomen above anus, followed along ventral part of body by a red stripe. Attains 4.5 cm. Known from southern Ryukyu Islands, Indonesia, Papua New Guinea (type locality, off Nagada Harbor, Madang Province), Solomon Islands, and New Caledonia; all localities from calm lagoons or bays with low coral growth or rubble and sand; depth range, 4–42 m.

Banda, Indonesia

BAY CARDINALFISH
Ostorhinchus sinus (Randall, 2001)

Dorsal rays VII + I,9; anal rays II,8; pectoral rays 14; lateral-line scales 25; predorsal scales 4; gill rakers 4–5 + 12–15; body depth 2.6–2.9 in standard length; interorbital space broad, the width 4.2–4.5 in head length; preopercular edge serrate, the ridge smooth; last dorsal and anal rays not clearly longer than penultimate rays; caudal fin slightly forked with broadly rounded lobes; iridescent pink with 7 narrow, reddish brown stripes, the upper 5 extending foward onto dorsal half of head; a short submarginal black bar on operculum anterior to pectoral-fin base. Largest specimen, 10.5 cm. Known only from the Marquesas Islands, where it was found only in bays in very shallow water, often from large tidepools. The scientific name *sinus* is from the Latin for bay. *Ostorhinchus taeniophorus* (Regan), which ranges from the east coast of Africa to the islands of French Polynesia except the Marquesas Islands, is the probable sister species.

Marquesas Islands

209

Mauritius

REEF-FLAT CARDINALFISH
Ostorhinchus taeniophorus (Regan, 1908)

Dorsal rays VII + I,9; anal rays II,8; pectoral rays 14; lateral-line scales 24; predorsal scales 3–4; gill rakers 4–5 + 12–14; body depth 2.7–3.0 in standard length; interorbital width 4.15–5.35 in head length; preopercular edge serrate, the ridge smooth; last dorsal and anal rays not longer than penultimate rays; whitish with 6 dark brown stripes, the first middorsal, the narrow third extending from upper edge of eye at most to below second dorsal fin, the second, fourth, and fifth extending onto base of caudal fin, the middle fourth stripe not ending in a round black spot (may be expanded slightly to form an elliptical spot); a broad black band often present near base of second dorsal fin. Largest examined, 11.5 cm. East coast of Africa to the islands of Micronesia, Line Islands, French Polynesia except the Marquesas, and the Pitcairn Islands; in the western Pacific from southern Japan to New South Wales; type locality, Maldive Islands. A shallow-water species of variable habitat from surge channels of exposed reefs to rock and debris of mud bottoms in harbors or bays.

Cebu, Philippines (night)

NARROWSTRIPE CARDINALFISH
Pristiapogon exostigma (Jordan & Starks in Jordan & Seale, 1906)

Dorsal rays VII + I,9; anal rays II,8; pectoral rays 12–14 (usually 13); lateral-line scales 24; predorsal scales 5; gill rakers 3–5 + 13–15; body depth 2.85–3.6 in standard length; preopercular edge and ridge serrate; caudal fin forked with slightly rounded lobes; gray to tan dorsally, shading to pale gray ventrally with iridescence; a narrow, tapering, midlateral black stripe ending posteriorly on caudal peduncle; a black spot smaller than pupil at base of caudal fin, its lower edge on lateral line; leading edge of first dorsal fin blackish; upper and lower edges of caudal fin narrowly blackish. Largest specimen, 12 cm. Known in the Indian Ocean only from the Red Sea, Comoro Islands, Oman, and Cocos-Keeling Islands, but widespread in the western Pacific, ranging east to the Line Islands and Pitcairn Islands; type locality, Upolu, Western Samoa. Fraser & Lachner (1985) revised the subgenus *Pristiapogon* (now a genus), which includes this species, *P. fraenatus*, *P. kallopterus*, *P. taeniopterus*, and the Indian Ocean *P. abrogramma*.

Cebu, Philippines

SPURCHEEK CARDINALFISH
Pristiapogon fraenatus (Valenciennes, 1832)

Dorsal rays VII + I,9; anal rays II,8; pectoral rays 13–15 (usually 14); lateral-line scales 24; predorsal scales 5; gill rakers 4–5 + 12–14; body depth 2.4–3.1 in standard length; preopercular edge and ridge strongly serrate; caudal fin slightly forked; gray to tan dorsally, silvery white with iridescence on side and ventrally, with a narrow, midlateral, tapering black stripe ending in a black spot nearly size of pupil on lateral line at caudal-fin base; black stripe often bordered by pale iridescent blue-green; leading edge of dorsal fin blackish. Largest specimen, 10.5 cm. Red Sea and Gulf of Oman south to Natal, east to the Line Islands and Tuamotu Archipelago; in the western Pacific from southern Japan to New South Wales; type locality, New Guinea. A shallow-water species of coral reefs or rocky bottom, but reported to 30 m.

IRIDESCENT CARDINALFISH

Pristiapogon kallopterus (Bleeker, 1856)

Dorsal rays VII + I,9; anal rays II,8; pectoral rays 13–14 (rarely 14); lateral-line scales 24; predorsal scales 5; gill rakers 4–5 + 13–15; body depth 2.5–3.3 in standard length; preopercular edge and ridge strongly serrate; caudal fin slightly forked; light greenish brown dorsally, the scale edges darker, with a near-uniform, dark brown, mid-lateral stripe from snout through eye, disappearing on caudal peduncle (stripe may be obscure in large adults); a black spot nearly as large as pupil at caudal-fin base, its lower edge on lateral line; body with some iridescence during the day, but with much pale green iridescence at night. Largest of 4,000 specimens, 15.5 cm (Fraser & Lachner, 1985). Judging from museum collections, the most common and widespread apogonid fish of the Indo-Pacific region, ranging from the Red Sea and east coast of Africa to the Hawaiian Islands and Pitcairn Islands (Randall, 1999a); type locality, Sulawesi. Occurs in a variety of habitats; at night mainly over sand or rubble areas near reefs, oriented to the substratum. Known from the depth range of 1–158 m (Chave

Cebu, Philippines

& Mundy, 1994). Chave (1979) reported its food as crustaceans (74.9%), polychaetes (12.3%), fishes (6.0%), brittlestars (4.1%), and gastropods (2.7%). *Apogon snyderi* Jordan & Evermann is a synonym.

BANDFIN CARDINALFISH

Pristiapogon taeniopterus (Bennett, 1836)

Dorsal rays VII + I,9; anal rays II,8; pectoral rays 13–14 (rarely 14); lateral-line scales 24; predorsal scales 5–6 (usually 6); gill rakers 5–6 + 16–17; body depth 2.6–3.2 in standard length; preopercular edge and ridge strongly serrate; caudal fin forked, the lobes slightly rounded; brown dorsally, the scale edges dark brown, becoming iridescent pale green and pink in centers of scales on side, ventrally on body, and on lower head; membrane of leading edge of first dorsal fin black with a posterior pale blue to white border; a blackish band near base of second dorsal and anal fins, edged in pale blue or white on anal fin and with only the lower edge pale in second dorsal fin; upper and lower edges of caudal fin with a submarginal black band, sometimes linked or nearly linked by a bar across basal one-third of fin. Largest specimen, 19.6 cm. An insular species known from Mauritius (type locality), Christmas Island, and Cocos-Keeling Islands in the Indian Ocean, and most of the oceanic islands of Oceania, including those of Micronesia,

Line Islands

New Caledonia, French Polynesia, Pitcairn Islands, and the Hawaiian Islands [where it has been regarded as a different species, *Pristiapogon menesemus* (Jenkins); however, there are no meristic differences, and Pitcairn specimens have the same caudal coloration as the Hawaiian].

THREESPOT CARDINALFISH

Pristicon trimaculatus (Cuvier in C & V, 1828)

Dorsal rays VI + I,9; anal rays II,8; pectoral rays 13–15 (rarely 13 or 15); lateral-line scales 24; predorsal scales 4–5 (usually 6); gill rakers 5–6 + 14–17 (most often 5 + 16); body moderately deep, the depth 2.45–2.7 in standard length; preopercular edge finely serrate; preopercular ridge serrate at sizes larger than 60 mm SL; caudal fin forked with rounded lobes; light gray-brown to olivaceous, the centers of scales darker than edges, with a short dark brown bar below origin of second dorsal fin, a longer oblique band from rear base of second dorsal fin, and a dark brown spot on opercle; juveniles may have a small dark spot at midbase of caudal fin. Largest specimen, 19.4 cm. Ryukyu Islands south to the Great Barrier Reef and New Caledonia, east to the Marshall Islands, Samoa Islands, and Tonga; type locality, Buru, Molucca Islands. Collected from depths of 1–32 m. *Apogon koilomatodon* Bleeker is a synonym.

Flores, Indonesia (night)

211

Rapa

Marshall Islands (night)

GELATINOUS CARDINALFISH
Pseudamia gelatinosa Smith, 1955
Dorsal rays VI + I,8; anal rays II,8; pectoral rays 15–17 (usually 16); scales cycloid, thin, and easily lost (true for the genus); 2 inconspicuous lateral lines, only the first few scales with pores (generic); longitudinal scale series 39–43; gill rakers 2–4 + 11–14; margin of preopercle serrate on corner and lower edge, the ridge smooth; body elongate, the depth 4.05–4.7 in standard length; caudal fin rounded, 2.7–3.3 in standard length; translucent, the sides and ventral part of head and body with gold to silver iridescence; numerous small brown spots of variable size on head and body; a dark brown spot as large as eye present or absent on base of caudal fin; caudal fin dusky to blackish with a broad hyaline posterior border. Largest, 10.2 cm. Red Sea and east coast of Africa to the Line Islands, Society Islands, and Rapa; in the western Pacific from Japan to New South Wales; type locality, Aldabra, Seychelles. Occurs on coral reefs in calm areas of lagoons and bays from depths of 0.5–40 m; collected with ichthyocide in caves or beneath ledges; not observed in life.

LONGTAIL CARDINALFISH
Pseudamiops gracilicauda (Lachner, 1953)
Dorsal rays VI + I,8; anal rays II,8; pectoral rays 15–16; scales cycloid, thin, and easily lost; longitudinal scale series 23–24; predorsal scales 5–6; small papillae in a crosshatch pattern on head; gill rakers 3 + 8; preopercular margin smooth except for 2 small spines at corner; a V-shaped bony process projecting downward from rear edge of maxilla; mouth large, the maxilla extending posterior to a vertical at rear edge of eye; front of upper jaw with 1–3 pairs of slender canine teeth; longest teeth on lower jaw in inner row about halfway back in jaw; small palatine teeth in a single row; body elongate, the depth 4.1–5.55 in standard length; caudal peduncle long and slender; caudal fin long, broad, and rounded; body transparent, the light red vertebral column clearly visible, as are the bright red gill filaments; a cluster of small dark spots on head behind eye. Reported to 5 cm. Western Pacific from Ryukyu Islands and Taiwan to the Great Barrier Reef, east to Marshall Islands (type locality, Bikini Atoll), and Rapa; well hidden in reefs by day, rising above bottom to forage on zooplankton at night.

Palau (night)

FANTAIL CARDINALFISH
Pseudamia zonata Randall, Lachner & Fraser, 1985
Dorsal rays VI + I,9–10; anal rays II,9; pectoral rays 15–16; longitudinal scale series 23–25; gill rakers 8 + 16–19; rounded corner and ventral margin of preopercle with 4–9 serrae, the vertical margin with a few poorly defined serrae; body elongate, the depth 3.75–4.45 in standard length; interorbital space flat; caudal fin very large and rhomboid, 2.2–2.9 in standard length; gray with 2 broad dark brown bars on body and an elliptical dark bar at base of caudal fin; median and pelvic fins dark brown. Largest specimen 11.5 cm. Known from the Ryukyu Islands, Philippines (type locality, Mactan Island, Cebu), Papua New Guinea, Solomon Islands, Vanuatu, New Caledonia, Fiji, and Palau; collected from caves in 18.5–30.5 m.

PHANTOM CARDINALFISH
Pseudamiops phasma Randall, 2001
Dorsal rays VI + I,8; anal rays II,8; pectoral rays 19; scales cycloid, thin, and vey easily lost; longitudinal scale series about 25; lateral line not detected; small papillae in a crosshatch pattern on head; gill rakers 4 + 12–13; lower two-thirds of preopercular margin finely serrate; a V–shaped bony process projecting downward from rear edge of maxilla; mouth large, the maxilla extending posterior to a vertical at rear edge of eye; front of upper jaw with 3 pairs of slender canine teeth; longest teeth on lower jaw in inner row about halfway back in jaw; small teeth in an irregular row on palatines; body

Marquesas Islands

elongate, the depth 4.3–4.5 in standard length; caudal fin rhomboid, 3.0 in standard length; largely transparent in life. Known from only 2 specimens from bays in the Marquesas Islands, the largest 4.7 cm.

Banda Islands, Indonesia

SWALLOWTAIL CARDINALFISH

Rhabdamia cypselura Weber, 1909

Dorsal rays VI + I,9; anal rays II,9; pectoral rays 14–16; scales cycloid, thin, and deciduous; lateral-line scales 25; predorsal scales 4; gill rakers 4–5 + 12–14; preopercular margin and ridge smooth; villiform teeth in jaws; palatine teeth present or absent; body elongate, the depth 3.8–4.3 in standard length; a pair of luminous organs under operculum; fin spines slender, caudal fin strongly forked; transparent with orange dots, becoming silvery to golden over abdomen and operculum; a narrow black stripe on side of snout, continuing faintly behind eye onto opercle; a submarginal blackish band in each lobe of caudal fin. Attains 6 cm. Red Sea, Persian Gulf, and east coast of Africa to islands of Micronesia;

Papua New Guinea

in the western Pacific from the Ryukyu Islands to the Great Barrier Reef, Loyalty Islands (Kulbicki & Williams, 1997), and Chesterfield Islands, Coral Sea (Kulbicki et al., 1994); type locality, Seram, Molucca Islands. Typically seen in dense aggregations in caves in lagoon reefs.

SLENDER CARDINALFISH

Rhabdamia gracilis (Bleeker, 1856)

Dorsal rays VI + I,9; anal rays II,12–13; pectoral rays 13; scales cycloid, thin, and deciduous; lateral-line scales 24; predorsal scales 4; gill rakers 6–7 + 21–22; preopercular margin and ridge smooth; teeth in jaws villiform; few or no teeth on palatines; body moderately elongate, the depth 3.3–3.6 in standard length, and compressed; fin spines slender; caudal fin strongly forked; transparent, the vertebral column showing clearly; an iridescent pale blue-green line from gill opening at level of eye to a small black spot (when present) at lower base of caudal fin; a dusky line along base of anal fin continuing ventrally on caudal peduncle; a blackish line dorsally on front of snout to above gill opening; often a small black

Great Barrier Reef

spot at tip of upper caudal lobe. Attains 6 cm. East coast of Africa to Marshall Islands, Caroline Islands, and Fiji; southern Japan to the Great Barrier Reef and New Caledonia; type locality, Ternate, Molucca Islands; forms dense schools in lagoon reefs, especially in caves.

213

Papua New Guinea

Palau

Tonga

SEA-URCHIN CARDINALFISH

Siphamia versicolor (Smith & Radcliffe in Radcliffe, 1911)

Dorsal rays VII + I,9; anal rays II,8; pectoral rays 14–16 (rarely 14); scales cycloid and deciduous; lateral-line scales 23–24; predorsal scales 4; developed gill rakers (higher than their base) 1 + 7–8; margin of preopercle serrate; a subcutaneous luminous organ, unique to the genus, ventrally on body from anteriorly in gill chamber to ventral caudal peduncle; body depth 2.4–2.6 in standard length; caudal fin forked with rounded lobes; black to silvery, or silvery with 3 broad black stripes (individuals can quickly change from one color pattern to another); fins translucent with orange-red rays; first dorsal fin with scattered black dots; surface of tongue with a large blackish patch on each side. Attains 4 cm. Gulf of Oman and Maldive Islands to western Pacific; Ryukyu Islands and Ogasawara Islands to the Great Barrier Reef and New Caledonia, east to Mariana Islands and Caroline Islands; type locality, Masbate, Philippines. Often found sheltering among long-spined sea urchins, especially species of the genus *Diadema*.

PAJAMA CARDINALFISH

Sphaeramia nematoptera (Bleeker, 1856)

Dorsal rays VI + I,9–10; anal rays II,9–10; pectoral rays usually 12; scales finely ctenoid; lateral-line scales 24; predorsal scales 8; total gill rakers 32–37; margin of preopercle serrate, the ridge smooth; body deep, the depth 1.8–2.0 in standard length; dorsal, anal, and pelvic fins long; first dorsal soft ray prolonged as a filament; caudal fin forked with strongly rounded lobes; whitish, shading to yellow on head, with a broad black bar anteriorly on body, continuing into anterior three-fourths of first dorsal fin and posterior three-fourths of pelvic fins; body posterior to black bar with about 30 round brown spots. Attains 9 cm. Ryukyu Islands to Great Barrier Reef and New Caledonia, east to Fiji and the Caroline Islands; type locality, Sulawesi. Usually seen in small aggregations on shallow protected reefs hovering just above branching coral.

ORBICULAR CARDINALFISH

Sphaeramia orbicularis (Cuvier in C & V, 1828)

Dorsal rays VI + I,9–10; anal rays II,8–9; pectoral rays 12–13 (usually 12); scales finely ctenoid; lateral-line scales 24; predorsal scales 6–7; total gill rakers 24–27; margin of preopercle serrate, the ridge smooth; body deep, the depth 1.8–2.0 in standard length; dorsal, anal, and pelvic fins long, the 2 dorsals equally long; caudal fin slightly forked with strongly rounded lobes; silvery to yellowish or greenish gray with iridescence; a narrow blackish bar from below origin of first dorsal fin to abdomen; small dark spots on head and body anterior to blackish bar, and larger ones posterior to bar; outer part of each pelvic-fin membrane with a large black area. Attains 12 cm. Southern Red Sea and east coast of Africa to Tonga and islands of Micronesia except Marshall Islands; type locality, Java. A shallow-water species of mangroves or protected rocky shores, usually seen in small aggregations. Allen (1975a) determined from a study in Palau that the food consisted of crabs (28.8%), insects (22.9%), copepods (12.9%), and the rest mainly polychaetes, ostracods, and other crustaceans. Mature males were found as small as 6.9 cm standard length, and mature females as small as 6 cm. Males incubate the eggs, which hatch at a length of 3.3 mm total length in about 8 days; developmental stages were illustrated. The young after settlement average about 10 mm total length; growth of juveniles ranged from 3.3 to 6.4 mm per month.

214

ODDSCALE CARDINALFISH
Zapogon evermanni (Jordan & Snyder, 1904)
Dorsal rays VI + I,9; anal rays II,8; pectoral rays 12; lateral-line scales 24; longitudinal scale series 45–48; predorsal scales 10–12; gill rakers 4–6 + 15–17; body depth 2.7–3.7 in standard length; dorsal profile of head straight; preopercular edge finely serrate, the ridge smooth; caudal fin forked, the lobes rounded; red with a dark brown streak from front of snout through eye and across operculum; a black spot at rear base of second dorsal fin, followed by a small white spot. Largest specimen, 12.2 cm. Unique among apogonids in the small size of the body scales compared with the lateral-line scales. Tropical western Atlantic and scattered localities from east coast of Africa to the Hawaiian Islands (type locality, O'ahu) and Marquesas Islands; occurs on seaward reef slopes, generally in deep caves; known from depths of 8 to 120 m, generally more than 20 m. *Apogon anisolepis* Randall & Böhlke from the West Indies is a synonym.

Kakabia, Indonesia

FRAGILE CARDINALFISH
Zoramia fragilis (Smith, 1961)
Dorsal rays VI + I,9; anal rays II,8; pectoral rays 14; lateral-line scales 24; predorsal scales 6; gill rakers 5–7 + 19–22; body depth 2.3–3.3 in standard length; lower preopercular edge serrate, the ridge smooth; caudal fin slightly forked; translucent gray, often with a few small blue spots on post-orbital head and anterior body and a wash of iridescent blue-green over posterior abdomen; a black spot about half diameter of pupil at caudal-fin base; a faint dusky stripe on side of snout; tips of caudal lobes often blackish. Largest specimen, 5.7 cm. Mozambique (type locality, Pinda), Madagascar, and Seychelles to the East Indies and Great Barrier Reef, east to Marshall Islands and Samoa Islands; forms aggregations by day, often near branching coral in calm bays and lagoons. This and the following species were formerly classified in the genus *Apogon*. Bergman (2004) has elevated the subgenus *Zoramia* Jordan to a genus.

Papua New Guinea

THREADFIN CARDINALFISH
Zoramia leptacantha (Bleeker, 1856)
Dorsal rays VI + I,9; anal rays II,9; pectoral rays 13–14; lateral-line scales 24; predorsal scales 6; gill rakers 6–9 + 21–24; body deep, the depth 2.1–2.6 in standard length; preopercular margin and ridge irregular but not serrate; first dorsal fin very high, the second spine filamentous, and third spine also long; caudal fin slightly forked, the lobes a little rounded; translucent gray with yellow-edged blue streaks on head and anterior body, those on cheek oblique, the others vertical; a greenish white line along back from origin of first dorsal fin to upper base of caudal fin; eye iridescent blue. Reaches 5.5 cm. Red Sea and east coast of Africa to the Marshall Islands and Samoa Islands; in the western Pacific from the Ryukyu Islands to the Great Barrier Reef and New Caledonia; type locality, Ternate, Molucca Islands. Typically found in aggregations in calm shallow water by day, sheltering as needed among the branches of coral. Strasburg (1966) reported huge aggregations associated with *Montipora gaimardi* in the lagoon at Majuro Atoll, Marshall Islands.

Palau

SILLAGOS
(SILLAGINIDAE)

Also known as whitings in Australia, these fishes are found only in shallow marine waters of the tropical western Pacific and Indian Oceans on open sand or mud bottoms. They may occur in estuaries or off sandy beaches. They are characterized by an elongate body; opercle with a single sharp spine; long pointed snout; small terminal mouth with villiform teeth in bands in jaws; small teeth anteriorly on vomer but none on palatines; maxilla slipping under preorbital when mouth closed; small ctenoid scales; complete lateral line; 2 dorsal fins with little or no space between, the first of IX to XI slender spines, the second of I spine and 16–26 rays; anal fin with II spines and 14–26 rays; pelvic fins I,5, inserted beneath the pectorals; caudal fin emarginate to truncate. The family was revised by McKay (1985, 1992). Burchmore et al. (1988) reported on the biology of 4 species of *Sillago* from New South Wales; the fishes fed principally on polychaete worms, crustaceans (amphipods, copepods, various shrimps including *Callianassa*), and small bivalve mollusks; when feeding on fossorial prey, they thrust their conical snout into the sediment. When threatened, they can dive into the sand or mud. The family consists of 3 genera and 39 species, 29 of which are classified in *Sillago*. Only 2 species are known from the South Pacific area, both at New Caledonia.

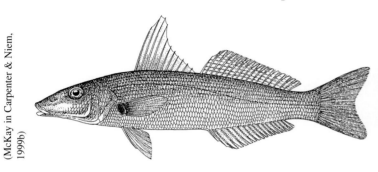

(McKay in Carpenter & Niem, 1999b)

SAND SILLAGO
Sillago ciliata Cuvier in C & V, 1829
Dorsal rays I,16–18; anal rays II,15–17; lateral-line scales 60–69; cheek scales in 4–5 rows, cycloid and ctenoid (but more cycloid); vertebrae 32–34; body depth 4.35–4.75 in standard length; second dorsal spine longest, about 1.5 in head length; caudal fin slightly forked; swimbladder with short lateral outpocketings anteriorly, not bifurcating posteriorly; color uniform silvery without dark markings except a large dark spot at base of pectoral fins. Reported to 51 cm. Type locality given by Cuvier as southern seas; known from east coast of Australia, mainly to the south, Lord Howe Island, and New Caledonia. Juveniles are usually found in small groups on sand flats or off beaches; adults tend to congregate off mouths of estuaries down to 5 m, but have been taken as deep as 40 m in the southern winter; feeds mainly on polychaete worms (61%) and crustaceans.

Lombok, Indonesia

SILVER SILLAGO
Sillago sihama (Forsskål, 1775)
Dorsal rays I,20–23; anal rays II,21–23; lateral-line scales 66–72; scales on cheek cycloid, in 4–5 (usually 5) rows; vertebrae 34; body depth 5.0–6.25 in standard length; second dorsal spine longest, about 1.8 in head length; caudal fin slightly emarginate to truncate; swimbladder without lateral extensions, bifurcate posteriorly, the 2 tapering parts extending into caudal region; silvery, sometimes with a lavender sheen. Reaches about 35 cm. The most wide-ranging species of the family, occurring along all continental shores from South Africa to the Red Sea, east throughout the East Indies to Korea; Western Australia to Queensland, east to Solomon Islands and New Caledonia; an inshore species of sandy beaches and sand flats; may occur in estuaries, even to fresh water; known to escape beach seines by diving into sand, but fishermen feel for the fish with their feet and dig them by hand. McKay (1992) summarized what is known of the biology.

TILEFISHES
(MALACANTHIDAE)

The tilefishes are characterized by an elongate body, opercle with a single spine; mouth terminal or slightly inferior; jaws with small canine teeth and a band of villiform teeth; no teeth on palate, but pharyngeal teeth well-developed; 6 branchiostegal rays; scales ctenoid on most of body, cycloid on head; dorsal and anal fins long, without a notch, the dorsal with I-X spines, and the anal with I or II spines; pelvic fins I,5. The family is small, with 5 genera and 39 species; it is divided into 2 subfamilies, the Latilinae (formerly Branchiosteginae) and the Malacanthinae (sandtilefishes) (Nelson, 1994; Eschmeyer, 1998). Dooley in Carpenter & Niem (1999b) preferred to treat these two subfamilies as families. Only one species of the Latininae occurs in the South Pacific, *Branchiostegus wardi* Whitley, with a single record from 250 m off New Caledonia (Dooley, 1978). Four species of the Malacanthinae are found in the South Pacific area. The species of this subfamily lack a predorsal ridge on the nape, are less blunt-headed, have a more elongate body, and some have a large spine at the corner of the preopercle. The genus *Malacanthus* has 3 species (one of which occurs in the Atlantic), and

Hoplolatilus contains 12 (Randall, 1981a; Clark et al., 1998). Three of the heavier-bodied species of *Hoplolatilus* construct large mounds of rubble in which they take shelter; the other species use burrows; all are able to live over barren sand or rubble-sand areas away from reefs. The species of *Hoplolatilus* feed on zooplankton, hence are generally found in areas of current.

GRAY SANDTILEFISH

Hoplolatilus cuniculus Randall & Dooley, 1974
Dorsal rays III-V,29–34; anal rays I,19–20; pectoral rays 16–18 (usually 17); lateral-line scales 116–140; gill rakers 21–24; no spine at corner of preopercle, but 1–2 serrae slightly enlarged; body depth 5.1–6.3 in standard length; penultimate dorsal and anal rays not prolonged; caudal fin forked; gray-brown on back, shading on lower half of body to pale gray or white; a blue area on dorsal and postorbital part of head; posterior caudal peduncle and caudal fin deep yellow except for narrow upper and lower edges and centoposterior area, which are white. Reaches 16 cm. East coast of Africa and Mauritius to Society Islands; Ryukyu Islands to Great Barrier Reef and New Caledonia; type locality, Tahiti. Reported from depths of 2–115 m, usually in more than 30 m; shelters in a burrow in sand, muddy sand, or sand and rubble bottom; 2 fish may share the same burrow.

Sumilon Island, Philippines

Molucca Islands, Indonesia/subadult

Palau

BLUEHEAD SANDTILEFISH

Hoplolatilus starcki Randall & Dooley, 1974
Dorsal rays VIII,21–23; anal rays II,15–16; pectoral rays 18–19; lateral-line scales 100–118; gill rakers 22–27; no spine at corner of preopercle, the margin with 30–57 serrae; body depth 3.7–4.6 in standard length; penultimate dorsal and anal rays not prolonged; caudal fin deeply forked, the lobe tips somewhat rounded; tan, shading to white ventrally, with a broad area of blue to purple over side and lower part of head and body below basal half of pectoral fin; caudal fin yellow except for upper and lower

margins and a distal area in middle of fin; young entirely blue. Reaches 15.5 cm. Philippines to the Great Barrier Reef and New Caledonia, east to the islands of Micronesia and the Tuamotu Archipelago; in the Indian Ocean from Rowley Shoals off Western Australia; type locality, Guam. Reported from depths of 21–105 m. Young *Hoplolatilus starcki* may school with *Pseudanthias tuka* or *P. pascalus,* which they resemble in color, hence examples of social mimicry (Randall & McCosker, 1993; Myers, 1999). The Queensland record is based on a single specimen from Yonge Reef, now in the Australian Museum.

217

Hawaiian Islands

FLAGTAIL SANDTILEFISH
Malacanthus brevirostris Guichenot, 1848
Dorsal rays I-IV,52–60; anal rays I,46–55; pectoral rays 15–17 (nearly always 16); lateral-line scales 146–189; gill rakers 9–20; margin of preopercle smooth; opercular spine large; body very elongate, the depth 6.3–8.3 in standard length; snout not pointed, about 3.0 in head length; caudal fin truncate; gray on about dorsal half of body, white below, the lower part of gray zone broken into about 20 short dark bars; 2 broad black stripes in caudal fin; iris blue and white; an arc of yellow just above eye. Reaches 30 cm. Red Sea and east coast of Africa to the Hawaiian Islands and French Polynesia; southern Japan to New South Wales, Lord Howe Island, and northern New Zealand; type locality, Madagascar. Also recorded from the tropical eastern Pacific. Typically found in pairs over sand-rubble areas, often near reefs; live in a burrow of their own construction, generally under a rock; small piles of rubble often indicate the site of the burrow; reported from depths of 14–61 m (Chave & Mundy, 1994). *Malacanthus hoedtii* Bleeker is a synonym.

Papua New Guinea

BLUE SANDTILEFISH
Malacanthus latovittatus (Lacepède, 1801)
Dorsal rays III-IV,43–47; anal rays I,37–40; pectoral rays 16–17 (usually 17); lateral-line scales 116–132; gill rakers 6–14; margin of preopercle smooth; opercular spine large; body elongate, the depth 5.0–6.7 in standard length; snout long and pointed, 2.1–2.7 in head length; caudal fin truncate with upper rays slightly prolonged; head and anterior body blue, shading to bluish white posteriorly, with fine black lines and spots in a linear pattern on back; a broad midlateral black stripe on body, continuing irregularly into caudal fin; juveniles white with a broader black stripe that extends through lower part of eye to front of head. Largest specimen, 44 cm. Red Sea and east coast of Africa to the Line Islands and Samoa Islands; southern Japan to New South Wales, type locality, "Great Equatorial Ocean." Usually seen in 6–15 m. Occurs in monogamous pairs that build a burrow. Difficult to approach underwater; retreats from an

Sulawesi/subadult

intruder rather than seeking shelter in the burrow. Clark & Pohle (1992) studied the reproduction and plotted the large foraging areas; feeding in the sand was often preceded by ejecting water to reveal buried prey such as worms and even small fishes.

218

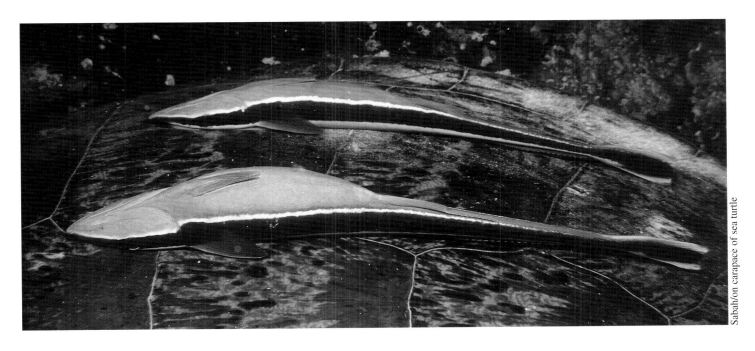

Sabah/on carapace of sea turtle

REMORAS
(ECHENEIDAE)

These fishes are unique in possessing an oval sucking disc dorsally on the head with which they attach to other fishes, cetaceans, or sea turtles. Other common names are shark suckers and discfishes. The disc consists of a series of transverse laminae, the number of which is useful in classification. From a study of development it was determined that the disc is derived from the spinous dorsal fin. Other characteristics of the family include no spines on opercle; small cycloid scales (may be embedded); no swim-bladder; 8–11 branchiostegal rays; villiform teeth in jaws; dorsal and anal fins with numerous rays, no spines, and elevated anteriorly; pelvic fins I,5. Some species are host specific or nearly so. *Remorina albescens* is commensal primarily with Manta rays. *Remora osteochir* (Cuvier) and *R. brachyptera* (Lowe) usually attach to billfishes, and *R. remora* to sharks. When small, echeneids often enter the mouth or gill chamber of their hosts, and some are known to feed on the host's ectoparasites (Cressey & Lachner, 1970). The 2 species of *Echeneis* attach to a wide variety of hosts and are free-living part of the time.

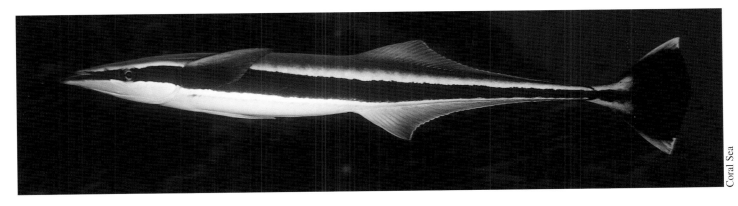

Coral Sea

SHARKSUCKER
Echeneis naucrates Linnaeus, 1758

Dorsal rays 34–42; anal rays 31–41; pectoral rays 21–24; lower-limb gill rakers 11–16 (not including rudiments); disc laminae 21–28; disc extending posteriorly to above middle of pectoral fins; body elongate, the depth 8–14 in standard length; caudal fin lanceolate in young, emarginate in adults; gray with a lateral, white-edged, black stripe from tip of lower jaw to base of caudal fin. Attains 90 cm. Circumglobal in tropical to warm temperate seas; type locality, Indian Ocean. Found on a wide variety of hosts, but most often on sharks; frequently observed free-living. One left a sea turtle and attached to the author's chest when he was snorkeling. John (1950) studied the early development.

Grand Bahama Island

Lord Howe Island

REMORA
Remora remora (Linnaeus, 1758)

Dorsal rays 21–27; anal rays 20–24; pectoral rays 25–32; lower-limb gill rakers 26–28 (including 1 or 2 rudiments); disc laminae 16–20; vertebrae 27; disc extending nearly to above end of pectoral fins, its length 2.4–2.95 in standard length; body depth about 6–8 in standard length; caudal fin emarginate; uniform tan to dark brown. Reaches 62 cm. Occurs in all tropical and subtropical seas; type locality, Indian Ocean. Found more on sharks than other hosts (reported from 12 different species of sharks of 8 different genera). Strasburg (1959) examined the stomach contents of seven specimens; he found hyperiid amphipods, decapod crustacean larvae, euphausids, mysids, copepods, and larval and juvenile fishes, but no parasitic copepods. Cressey & Lachner (1970) found parasitic copepods in 70% of the 147 stomachs containing food that they examined. Young remoras are more active in feeding on the host's parasites.

WHITE REMORA
Remorina albescens (Temminck & Schlegel, 1850)

Dorsal rays 15–22; anal rays 20–26; pectoral rays 18–21; lower-limb gill rakers about 10 (including rudiments); disc laminae 12–13; vertebrae 27; posterior end of disc nearly or just reaching a vertical at tip of pectoral fins; body depth 5.0–7.5 in standard length; caudal fin truncate to slightly rounded; pelvic fins narrowly attached to abdomen (broadly attached in species of *Remora*); pale gray to nearly white. Reported to 30 cm. Worldwide in tropical and subtropical seas; type locality, Nagasaki, Japan. *Manta birostris* and species of *Mobula* are the usual hosts, but *R. albescens* has been found on sharks; the illustrated specimen was taken from a Black Marlin (*Makaira indica*). This species enters the mouth and gill chamber of its host more than any other echeneid. The stomach contents of 17 specimens were examined for parasitic copepods by Cressey & Lachner (1970), but none was found.

JACKS
(CARANGIDAE)

This large family (about 32 genera and 140 species) consists of strong-swimming, open-water carnivorous fishes that are usually silvery, often with iridescence. They are highly variable in shape, from slender species such as scads of the genus *Decapterus* to deep-bodied ones like the threadfin jacks of the genus *Alectis*. They have a strongly forked or lunate caudal fin and a slender caudal peduncle, reinforced in most species by a series of overlapping bony plates called scutes (from modified scales). The eye is usually protected and streamlined by the transparent adipose tissue often referred to as the adipose eyelid. There is no spine on the opercle, and the edge of the preopercle is smooth. The mouth is usually large and slightly to strongly oblique. Most species have only bands of very small teeth in the jaws; those of the genera *Gnathanodon* and *Selaroides* lack teeth in the upper jaw. Some of the species of the genus *Caranx* have stout canines. Scales are small and cycloid, and they may be embedded. The lateral line is usually arched over the pectoral fins, becoming midlateral posteriorly and extending onto the caudal fin. There are 2 dorsal fins, the first of IV to VIII spines, the second of a single spine and numerous soft rays. The anal fin has II anterior spines (except *Elagatis* and *Seriolina* with I) that are detached from the rest of the fin of a single spine and numerous soft rays. The separate initial anal spines may be covered by skin in large individuals. A few species have finlets following the dorsal and anal fins. Pectoral fins vary from short to long and falcate. Pelvic fins I,5 (rudimentary in some species and lost in one). Because scutes mask the end of the vertebral column, fork length (from tip of snout to end of middle caudal-fin rays) is used for proportional measurements. Many species are valuable as food and game fishes. Most form schools or small aggregations. Those with numerous gill rakers, such as the species of the genus *Decapterus*, feed on zooplankton. Most of the larger jacks, such as the species of *Caranx* and *Seriola*, feed mainly on fishes. Some of them may also cause ciguatera poisoning when eaten. Smith-Vaniz in Carpenter & Niem (1999b) reviewed the Carangidae of the central and western Pacific.

Thicklipped Jack, *Pseudocaranx dentex*, Ogasawara Islands

Hawaiian Islands

Hawaiian Islands/juvenile

THREADFIN JACK
Alectis ciliaris (Bloch, 1787)
Dorsal rays VII + I,18–20 (spines of first dorsal fin embedded at a fork length greater than about 17 cm); anal rays II + I,15–17 (first 2 anal spines also embedded with growth); anterior 4 or 5 dorsal and anal soft rays of juveniles extremely long and filamentous (suggesting that juveniles may be mimicking venomous jellyfishes such as the virulent cubomedusae with long thread-like tentacles); scutes 12–30; scales minute and embedded; gill rakers 4–6 + 12–17 (excluding rudiments); villiform teeth in jaws, disappearing with age; body very deep in young, the depth about 1.5 in fork length, becoming less deep with growth; dorsal profile of head very steep; suborbital depth 1.7–3.0 in upper-jaw length (0.8–1.3 in *A. indicus*, a species of the Indian Ocean and western Pacific); silvery blue dorsally, silvery on sides and ventrally; juveniles with 5 dark bars that are slightly chevron-shaped. Reaches at least 130 cm; world angling record, 22.9 kg. Circumtropical; type locality, India. Reported to feed mainly on crustaceans, occasionally on small fishes.

HERRING SCAD
Alepes vari (Cuvier in C & V, 1833)
Dorsal rays VIII + I,24–27; anal rays III + I,20–23; curved portion of lateral line with 42–50 scales, of which 0–2 are small scutes; straight portion of lateral line with 0–7 scales and 48–69 scutes; total lateral-line scales and scutes 86–119; juncture of curved and straight portions of lateral line below first 3 soft rays of dorsal fin; transparent adipose tissue well developed only on posterior half of eye; supramaxilla

New Caledonia

relatively large with an anterior spine-like projection; silvery with a dusky spot posteriorly on opercle; caudal fin dusky. Largest reported, 56 cm. Red Sea and Persian Gulf to western Pacific from Taiwan to Queensland and New Caledonia; type locality, Pondicherry, India; occurs in shallow coastal waters; illustrated specimen collected from a mangrove area in New Caledonia in less than 1 m depth. Feeds mainly on crustaceans and small fishes.

YELLOWTAIL SCAD
Atule mate (Cuvier in C & V, 1833)

Dorsal rays VIII + I,22–25; anal rays II + I,18–21; curved part of lateral line with 39–57 pored scales; straight part of lateral line with 0–10 scales and 36–49 scutes; total scales and scutes in lateral line 92–103; juncture of curved and straight parts of lateral line below sixth to eighth dorsal soft rays; gill rakers 10–13 + 26–31; transparent adipose tissue covering eye except for a vertical slit in center; body moderately elongate, the depth of adults about 3.6–3.8 in fork length; front of upper jaw with 2 to 3 rows of small canines; rest of jaw and all of lower jaw with a single row of small teeth; last ray of dorsal and anal fins about twice as long as preceding ray and more separated than previous rays, joined only near base by membrane; silvery blue-green dorsally, silvery on side and below, often displaying about 10 dark bars on side of body; a prominent black spot posteriorly on opercle at level of upper part of eye; dorsal and pectoral fins translucent yellowish;

Hawaiian Islands

caudal fin yellow. Reaches 30 cm. Western Indian Ocean (including Red Sea and Persian Gulf) to the Hawaiian Islands and Society Islands; southern Japan to the Great Barrier Reef and New Caledonia; described from specimens from India, Seychelles, and New Guinea. Often seen in small schools; occurs to depths of at least 50 m; feeds on zooplankton and small fishes.

COASTAL TREVALLY
Carangoides coeruleopinnatus (Rüppell, 1830)

Dorsal rays VII + I,20–23 (usually 22 or 23); anal rays II + I,16–20; curved portion of lateral line slightly longer than straight; curved part with 77–97 scales, and straight part with 16–20 small scutes; juncture of curved and straight portions of lateral line below dorsal soft rays 12 and 14; chest scaleless ventrally to behind origin of pelvic fins and laterally to pectoral-fin base; gill rakers 5–8 + 15–19 (including rudiments); body moderately deep, the depth about 2.3–2.5 in fork length; anterior lobe of second dorsal fin filamentous in young, shorter with growth, shorter than head in adults larger than 25 cm fork length; pectoral fins long and falcate, reaching juncture of straight and curved parts of lateral line; silvery blue-green dorsally, silvery on side and ventrally; numerous small yellow spots usually present on body; a small black spot on operculum at level of upper part of eye. Attains 40 cm. Reported from the Sechelles, Maldive Islands, and coastal continental waters of the Indian Ocean to the western Pacific from Japan to Queensland, east in Oceania to Guam, Fiji, and Samoa Islands; type locality, Red Sea. Usually caught on deep coastal reefs; rarely taken inshore.

Seychelles

SHADOW JACK
Carangoides dinema Bleeker, 1851

Dorsal rays VIII + I,17–19; anal rays II + I,15–17; curved portion of lateral line slightly longer than straight, the latter with 0–6 scales and 23–30 small scutes; juncture of curved and straight portions of lateral line below dorsal soft rays 10–12; naked area of chest usually separated from naked base of pectoral fins by a band of scales; gill rakers 7–9 + 16–19; a band of small teeth in jaws, broader anteriorly, the outer row larger in upper jaw (and outer row may be larger in lower jaw as well in large individuals); body depth about 2.6–2.7 in fork length; anterior lobe of dorsal fin elongate, longer than head length and may be longer than base of second dorsal in large adults; pectoral fins long and falcate, reaching to or beyond juncture of straight and curved parts of lateral line; silvery with blue-green and pink iridescence; a diffuse, vertically elongate blotch posteriorly on opercle; a black spot in scaled basal part of each of last 10 rays of second dorsal fin, the spots larger posteriorly. Largest specimen 58.5 cm, 2.6 kg. In the Indian Ocean from Tanzania to South Africa; in the western Pacific from southern Japan to Indonesia, east to New Caledonia, Tonga, and the Samoa Islands; type locality, Borneo.

Lombok, Indonesia

BARRED JACK

Carangoides ferdau (Forsskål, 1775)

Dorsal rays VIII + I,26–34; anal rays II + I,21–26; curved portion of lateral line much longer than straight, the latter with 10–30 scales and 21–37 small scutes; juncture of curved and straight portions of lateral line below dorsal soft rays 15–20; chest scaled except for a broad, midventral, naked zone, narrowing to origin of pelvic fins; gill rakers 7–10 + 17–20; a narrow band of villiform teeth in jaws, disappearing with age; body depth 2.25–2.75 in fork length; anterior part of second dorsal and anal fins strongly elevated, the longest dorsal ray 2.75–4.0 in fork length; pectoral fins long and falcate, reaching juncture of curved and straight portions of lateral line; silvery blue to blue-green dorsally, silvery with iridescence below, with 8–10 gray bars a little narrower than silvery interspaces (bars in life vary from faint to strongly marked); numerous small yellow spots present or absent (when present, mostly on upper half of body). Reaches about 55 cm; world angling record, 2.26 kg, from Midway, Hawaiian Islands. Wide-ranging throughout the Indo-Pacific; type locality, Red Sea. Usually seen over sand near reefs, sometimes in small groups; occurs from inshore to depths of at least 60 m. Reported to feed mainly on benthic crustaceans, occasionally on small fishes.

YELLOWSPOTTED JACK

Carangoides fulvoguttatus (Forsskål, 1775)

Dorsal rays VIII + I,25–30; anal rays II + I,21–26; straight part of lateral line with 18–27 scales, followed by 15–21 small scutes; curved portion of lateral line longer than straight; juncture of curved and straight portions of lateral line below dorsal soft rays 13–16; chest nearly scaleless or with a scaled zone between naked prepectoral area and broad naked ventral zone; gill rakers 6–8 + 17–21; a band of villiform teeth in jaws and in an ovate patch on vomer; body moderately elongate, the depth 3.35–3.9 in fork length; dorsal profile of head to above posterior edge of eye nearly straight; first dorsal fin about half as high as anterior second dorsal; pectoral fins long and falcate, nearly or just reaching juncture of straight and curved portions of lateral line; silvery blue-green with iridescence, with 6–7 broad gray bars (can be turned on or off), usually with small yellow to blackish spots on dorsal half of body within gray bars; large adults often with 3 midlateral blackish blotches. Largest reported, 103 cm. Red Sea (type locality) and east coast of Africa to western Pacific from Ryukyu Islands and Ogasawara Islands to Great Barrier Reef and New Caledonia, east to Palau and Caroline Islands; often seen in small schools.

Bahrain

BLUDGER

Carangoides gymnostethus (Cuvier in C & V, 1833)
Dorsal rays VIII + I,28–32; anal rays II + I,24–26; straight part of lateral line with 14–25 scales, followed by 20–31 small scutes; curved portion of lateral line longer than straight; juncture of the two below dorsal soft rays 16–20; chest scaleless to base of pelvic fins; gill rakers 6–8 + 17–21; a band of villiform teeth in jaws and in an ovate patch on vomer; body moderately elongate, the depth 3.0–3.7 in fork length; dorsal profile of head smoothly convex; anterior second dorsal and anal fins not very high, the longest dorsal ray less than half head length; pectoral fins long and falcate, nearly or just reaching juncture of straight and curved portions of lateral line; silvery blue-green dorsally, shading to silvery ventrally with iridescence, sometimes with a few scattered, dark brown to yellow spots on side; a small dusky opercular spot. Reported to 90 cm. Indian Ocean to western Pacific from Ryukyu Islands to Great Barrier Reef and New Caledonia, east to Kapingamarangi Atoll, Caroline Islands; type locality, Seychelles. Reported to depths of 100 m; often seen in small schools.

Lombok, Indonesia/subadult

Lombok, Indonesia/male

BUMPNOSE TREVALLY

Carangoides hedlandensis (Whitley, 1934)
Dorsal rays VIII + I,20–22; anal rays II + I,24–26; straight part of lateral line with 29–41 scales and weak scutes, the last 17–28 as scutes; curved portion of lateral line longer than straight, the juncture of the two below dorsal soft rays 10 to 12; chest scaleless posterior to base of pelvic fins and laterally to pectoral-fin base; gill rakers 6–11 + 14–17 (including rudiments); a band of villiform teeth in jaws and in a wedge-shaped patch on vomer; body moderately deep, the depth 2.2–2.4 in fork length; dorsal profile of snout steep; a slight protuberance before upper part of eye; anterior lobe of second dorsal and anal fins filamentous; 3 to 8 of central rays of these fins produced as filaments in mature males; pectoral fins long and falcate, reaching juncture of straight and curved portions of lateral line; silvery with iridescence; a small blackish blotch posteriorly on opercle at level of eye; pelvic fins black in juveniles less than 10 cm fork length. Reaches 32 cm. Reported from South Africa, Seychelles, southern India, and Sri Lanka in Indian Ocean; western Pacific from Ryukyu Islands and Taiwan to east and west coasts of Australia; only Samoa Islands in Oceania (Wass, 1984).

225

Papua New Guinea

COACHWHIP TREVALLY

Carangoides oblongus (Cuvier in C & V, 1833)

Dorsal rays VIII + I,20–22; anal rays II + I,18–19; curved portion of lateral line slightly shorter than straight, the latter with 0–2 scales and 37–45 scutes; juncture of curved and straight portions of lateral line below dorsal soft rays 8–9; naked area of chest separated from naked base of pectoral fins by a band of scales; gill rakers 7–9 + 17–21; a band of small teeth in jaws, broader anteriorly, the outer row larger in upper jaw (and outer row may be larger in lower jaw as well in large individuals); body depth about 2.6–2.8 in fork length; filament of anterior lobe of dorsal fin elongate, longer than head length and may reach well beyond base of caudal fin in large adults; pectoral fins long and falcate, reaching beyond juncture of straight and curved parts of lateral line; silvery bluish gray, sometimes with scattered faint blackish flecks dorsally, silvery below; dorsal and caudal fins yellowish gray, the dorsal filament pale gray; anal fin more yellowish with a white outer margin; paired fins yellowish, the pelvics with a white lateral edge. Largest specimen, 46 cm. Occurs from the east coast of Africa to the western Pacific, where it ranges from southern Japan to the Great Barrier Reef and east to Fiji (type locality, Vanikoro, Santa Cruz Islands).

ISLAND JACK

Carangoides orthogrammus (Jordan & Gilbert, 1882)

Dorsal rays VIII + I,28–31; anal rays II + I,24–26; curved part of lateral line with 21–34 scales, followed by 19–31 small scutes in straight part; curved portion of lateral line longer than straight; juncture of the two below dorsal soft rays 15–19; chest scaleless ventrally to base of pelvic fins (occasionally a small patch of prepelvic scales), separated by a scaled zone from naked prepectoral area; gill rakers 8–10 + 20–23; a band of villiform teeth in jaws, obsolescent with age; body depth of adults 2.6–2.8 in fork length; dorsal profile of head nearly straight to above eye; lips of adults fleshy; anterior part of second dorsal and anal fins very high, the longest dorsal ray from three-fourths to longer than head length; pectoral fins long and falcate, usually reaching juncture of straight and curved portions of lateral line; silvery blue to blue-green dorsally, silvery with iridescence ventrally, typically with several elliptical bright yellow spots (sometimes with dusky centers) on side of body; gray bars sometimes faintly visible on body. World angling record, 79 cm, 8.3 kg, from Lāna‘i, Hawaiian Islands. East coast of Africa to the islands of Oceania; in the eastern Pacific from the

Palau

Revillagigedo Islands (type locality) and coast of Mexico to the Galápagos Islands; in the western Pacific from southern Japan to New South Wales and Lord Howe Island; submarine observations to 168 m (Chave & Mundy, 1994); may occur as solitary individuals or in small schools; reported to feed primarily on sand-dwelling crustaceans.

BARCHEEK JACK

Carangoides plagiotaenia Bleeker, 1857

Dorsal rays VIII + I,22–24; anal rays II + I,18–20; straight part of lateral line with 20–26 scales, followed by 11–18 small scutes; curved portion of lateral line longer than straight; juncture of the two below dorsal soft rays 13–15; chest fully scaled; gill rakers 8–14 + 19–27; lower jaw large and projecting; a band of villiform teeth in jaws, narrowing to an irregular row posteriorly on lower jaw; vomerine teeth in a triangular patch; body depth 2.8–3.3 in fork length; anterior part of second dorsal and anal fins low, the longest dorsal ray at most half head length; pectoral fins long and falcate, but not reaching juncture of straight and curved portions of lateral line; silvery blue-green with iridescence; adults with a prominent black margin on posterior edge of preopercle. Largest specimen reported, 41.5 cm.

Rowley Shoals, Western Australia

Red Sea and east coast of Africa to western Pacific from the Ryukyu Islands to the Great Barrier Reef and New Caledonia, east to Marshall Islands and Samoa Islands; type locality, Ambon, Molucca Islands. Usually found off seaward reefs as solitary individuals.

Hawaiian Islands

GIANT TREVALLY

Caranx ignobilis (Forsskål, 1775)

Dorsal rays VIII + I,18–21; anal rays II + I,15–17; straight part of lateral line longer than curved portion, with 0–4 scales, followed by 26–38 scutes; chest scaled to median ventral area, which is naked, except for occasional presence of a small patch of prepelvic scales; gill rakers 5–7 + 15–17; transparent adipose tissue short anteriorly, to center of eye posteriorly; upper jaw extending to below posterior edge of eye or a little beyond; jaws with an outer row of well-spaced strong canine teeth; body depth of adults 3.0–3.5 in fork length; dorsal profile of snout steep and nearly straight, the rest of profile smoothly curved with no angularity; anterior part of second dorsal and anal fins moderately high, the longest dorsal ray up to two-thirds head length; pectoral fins long and falcate, reaching beyond juncture of straight and curved portions of lateral line; silvery gray dorsally, shading to silvery white ventrally, with numerous scattered, very small black spots; centers of scutes blackish; no black spot on opercle; large males may be nearly completely blackish. Reaches at least 165 cm; world angling record, 66 kg, from Maui, Hawaiian Islands. Found throughout the tropical Indo-Pacific; type locality, Red Sea. May occur in small schools where population not reduced by fishing. Reported from depths of 1–188 m (Chave & Mundy, 1994); ranges into surprisingly shallow water for so large a fish. Feeds primarily on fishes; has been implicated in ciguatera poisoning (Randall, 1980a).

BLACK TREVALLY

Caranx lugubris Poey, 1860

Dorsal rays VIII + I,20–22; anal rays II + I,16–19; straight portion of lateral line longer than curved part, with 26–33 scutes; chest scaled; gill rakers 6–8 + 17–22; transparent adipose tissue narrow anteriorly, to center of eye posteriorly; upper jaw nearly or just reaching a vertical through center of eye; jaws with an outer row of well-spaced strong canine teeth; body deep, the depth of adults 2.4–2.8 in fork length; dorsal profile of head steep and slightly concave to above eye, where it is angular before curving onto nape; anterior part of second dorsal and anal fins very high, the longest dorsal ray of adults usually as long as or longer than head length; pectoral fins long and falcate, reaching well beyond juncture of straight and curved portions of lateral line; dark olive gray to nearly black dorsally, shading to silvery gray ventrally; scutes black; a small blackish spot at upper end of gill opening; fins dark gray, the anal with a narrow white margin. Reaches at least 80 cm; world angling record, 12.9 kg, from the Revillagigedo Islands, Mexico. Circumtropical; type locality, Cuba. Usually seen on outer-reef slopes in more than 30 m; submarine observations to 354 m (Chave & Mundy,

1994). Randall (1980a; 1995a) reported that fishes dominate its prey. Smith-Vaniz & Randall (1994) successfully petitioned the International Commission on Zoological Nomenclature to suppress the older but little-used name *C. ascensionis* Cuvier in favor of *C. lugubris*.

BLUEFIN TREVALLY

Caranx melampygus Cuvier in C & V, 1833

Dorsal rays VIII + I,21–24; anal rays II + I,17–20; straight portion of lateral line longer than curved part, with 0–10 scales and 27–32 scutes; chest scaled; gill rakers 5–9 + 17–21; transparent adipose tissue narrow anteriorly, to edge of pupil posteriorly; upper jaw not reaching a vertical through center of eye; jaws with an outer row of well-spaced strong canine teeth; body depth of adults 2.85–3.2 in fork length; dorsal profile of head to above eye nearly straight and forming an angle of about 45°; anterior part of second dorsal and anal fins moderately high, the longest dorsal ray of adults from one-half to three-fourths head length; pectoral fins long and falcate, reaching well beyond juncture of straight and curved portions of lateral line; brassy to silvery dorsally, finely blotched with blue, shading to silvery with iridescence ventrally; postorbital head and upper two-thirds of body with scattered, very small, black spots; scutes a little blackish; median fins bright blue. Reported to 100 cm; world angling record, 12 kg, from Clipperton Island off Mexico. Occurs throughout the tropical Indo-Pacific and eastern Pacific; described from specimens from Santa Cruz Islands, East Indies, and Mauritius. The most common trevally in Oceania; submarine observations to 188 m. Large individuals may be poisonous to eat in areas where ciguatera is prevalent. Randall (1980a) summarized our knowledge of food habits (almost entirely reef fishes).

BRASSY TREVALLY

Caranx papuensis Alleyne & Macleay, 1877

Dorsal rays VIII + I,21–23; anal rays II + I,16–19; straight portion of lateral line longer than curved part, with 0–3 scales and 31–39 scutes; ventral part of chest naked, usually with a small patch of scales before pelvic fins; gill rakers 7–9 + 18–21; adipose eyelid narrow anteriorly and posteriorly; upper jaw reaching a vertical through center of eye; jaws with an outer row of well-spaced, strong, canine teeth; body depth of adults 3.0–3.6 in fork length (depth decreasing with growth); dorsal profile of head to above eye nearly straight and forming an angle of about 50°; anterior part of second dorsal and anal fins moderately high, the longest dorsal ray of adults about three-fourths head length; pectoral fins long

and falcate, reaching well beyond juncture of straight and curved portions of lateral line; brassy to silvery blue-green dorsally, silvery with iridescence ventrally; large adults with very small black spots on upper half of body; a small dusky spot at upper end of gill opening, followed by a silvery white spot nearly as large as pupil; fins yellowish gray, the anal and lower lobe of caudal with an outer white border. Largest reported, 68 cm; world angling record, 4.4 kg, from the Ryukyu Islands. East coast of Africa to the Marquesas Islands and islands of Micronesia except the Marshall Islands; southern Japan to the Great Barrier Reef and New Caledonia; type locality, Papua New Guinea.

BIGEYE TREVALLY

Caranx sexfasciatus Quoy & Gaimard, 1825

Dorsal rays VIII + I,19–22; anal rays II + I,14–17; straight portion of lateral line longer than curved part, with 0–3 scales and 27–36 scutes; chest fully scaled; gill rakers 6–8 + 15–19; transparent adipose tissue over eye moderate anteriorly, to pupil posteriorly; upper jaw nearly or just reaching a vertical through rear edge of eye; jaws with an outer row of well-spaced canine teeth; body depth varying from 2.5 in fork length of juveniles to 3.8 in large adults; dorsal profile of head smoothly convex; longest dorsal ray of adults one-half to two-thirds head length; pectoral fins long and falcate, reaching beyond juncture of straight and curved portions of lateral line; silvery gray to greenish gray dorsally, silvery ventrally, with a distinct, small black spot at upper end of gill opening; scutes blackish; a white spot at tip of lobes of dorsal and anal fins; caudal fin with a black posterior margin; juveniles brassy yellow with 5 or 6 dark bars. Attains 85 cm; world angling record, 14.3 kg, from Seychelles. Occurs throughout the tropical Indo-Pacific and eastern Pacific; type locality, Waigeo, Indonesia. Forms large semistationary schools by day, feeds individually at night, mainly on fishes, sometimes on squids. Courtship observed at dusk with pairs swimming together, the male assuming black color. Juveniles commonly found in brackish environments, even penetrating fresh water.

Sri Lanka

TILLE TREVALLY
Caranx tille Cuvier in C & V, 1833
Dorsal rays VIII + I,20–22; anal rays II + I,16–18; straight portion of lateral line longer than curved part, with 0–2 scales and 33–42 scutes; chest completely scaled; gill rakers 6–8 + 15–17; transparent adipose tissue over eye moderate anteriorly, to pupil posteriorly; upper jaw extending beyond a vertical through rear edge of eye; jaws with an outer row of well-spaced, strong, canine teeth; body elongate for the genus, the depth varying from 3.0 in fork length of a 14-cm juvenile to 3.9 in large adults; dorsal profile of snout steep and straight to slightly concave, becom-

ing strongly convex on nape; longest dorsal ray about half head length; pectoral fins long and falcate, reaching beyond juncture of straight and curved portions of lateral line; silvery gray with iridescence; a black spot half pupil size or larger at upper end of gill opening, followed by a smaller white spot; scutes blackish posteriorly; no white spot at tip of second dorsal and anal fins. Largest recorded, 69 cm. East coast of Africa to Guam and Fiji; type locality, Pondicherry, India. Most common in coastal areas of continents and large islands; few records from oceanic islands.

MACKEREL SCAD
Decapterus macarellus (Cuvier in C & V, 1833)
Dorsal rays VIII + I,30–36 + 1; anal rays II + I,26–30 + 1; curved part of lateral line with 58–75 scales; straight part of lateral line with 18–38 scales and 25–39 scutes; scales on top of head extending forward to above anterior margin of pupil; gill rakers 10–13 + 34–41; transparent adipose tissue covering eye except for a narrow gap over center of pupil (true of other *Decapterus*); body elongate and little compressed, the depth about 5.0–5.65 in fork length; posterior end of maxilla straight, slanting anteroventrally; upper jaw without teeth; edge of shoulder girdle under operculum with an upper small and lower large papilla (also generic); pectoral fins short, 1.4–1.7 in head length; silvery blue-green dorsally, silvery white ventrally; a small black spot on edge of opercle at level of eye; caudal fin yellowish. Reaches 32 cm. Circumtropical; type locality, Martinique, Lesser Antilles. A

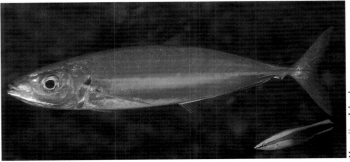

Hawaiian Islands

schooling species known from near the surface to 200 m (Chave & Mundy, 1994); like others of the genus, feeds on zooplankton. Clarke & Privitera (1995) determined that maturity is reached at a length of about 28 cm, and spawning in Hawai'i takes place, probably during the day, from April through August.

SHORTFIN SCAD
Decapterus macrosoma Bleeker, 1851
Dorsal rays VIII + I,32–38 + 1; anal rays II + I,26–30 + 1; curved part of lateral line with 58–72 scales; straight part of lateral line with 14–29 scales and 24–40 scutes; scales on top of head not extending forward of a vertical at anterior margin of pupil; gill rakers 10–12 + 34–38; body very slender and little compressed, the depth 5.5–6.5 in fork length; upper part of posterior end of maxilla straight to slightly concave, the lower part strongly rounded and protruding ventrally; upper jaw without teeth, the lower jaw with a single row of minute teeth; pectoral fins short, 1.35–1.65 in head length; metallic blue dorsally, silvery below, the indented upper part of opercular membrane blackish; caudal fin pale to slightly dusky; remaining fins pale, or anterior lobe of

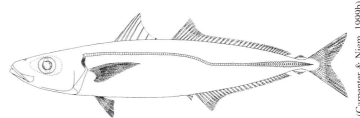

(Carpenter & Niem, 1999b)

dorsal fin a little dusky. Smallest species of Indo-Pacific *Decapterus*; maximum length 32 cm, but usually less than 25 cm. Occurs throughout the Indo-Pacific region except the Persian Gulf; also in the eastern Pacific from the Gulf of California to Peru; type locality, Java. Known from depths of 30 to at least 170 m.

AMBERSTRIPE SCAD

Decapterus muroadsi (Temminck & Schlegel, 1844)

Dorsal rays VIII + I,29–33 + 1; anal rays II + I,24–28 + 1; curved part of lateral line with 54–76 scales; straight part of lateral line with 5–15 scales and 32–42 scutes; scales on top of head extending forward to above anterior margin of pupil; gill rakers 13–15 + 36–42; body elongate and little compressed, the depth about 4.9–5.7 in fork length; posterior end of maxilla straight, only slightly slanting anteroventrally; upper jaw with a narrow band of minute teeth anteriorly, disappearing with age; lower jaw with a single row of minute teeth; pectoral fins short, 1.1–1.4 in head length; silvery blue-green dorsally, silvery below, often with a yellow stripe on side of body; a black spot posteriorly on opercle near upper end of gill opening; outer elevated anterior part of second dorsal fin dusky. Attains at least 45 cm. In the Indo-Pacific: Japan and Northwestern Hawaiian Islands, east and west

Easter Island

coasts of Australia, Rapa, and Easter Island; in the eastern Pacific from Gulf of California to Peru; also reported from St. Helena in the Atlantic; type locality, Nagasaki, Japan. A coastal pelagic schooling species; feeds on zooplankton. Should not be confused with the similar-named Japanese species *D. maruadsi* Temminck & Schlegel. *Decapterus scombrinus (*Valenciennes) from the Galápagos is a synonym.

New Britain

RAINBOW RUNNER

Elagatis bipinnulata (Quoy & Gaimard, 1825)

Dorsal rays VI + I,23–28 + 2; anal rays I + I,18–22 + 2; lateral-line scales about 100, none as scutes; anterior half of lateral line slightly arched; gill rakers 9–10 + 25–28; body elongate, the depth about 4.0–4.8 in fork length; head pointed; mouth small, the upper jaw not reaching a vertical at anterior edge of eye in adults (just reaching edge in juveniles); teeth in villiform bands in jaws; first dorsal fin low, about one-third height of anterior part of second dorsal; the single detached spine of anal fin scaled over in large adults; last 2 rays of dorsal and anal fins as a sep-

arate finlet; a notch posteriorly in caudal peduncle at base of upper and lower lobes of caudal fin; pectoral fins short, about half head length; pelvic fins about equal to pectorals; olive green dorsally, shading to greenish white ventrally, with 2 well-separated, bright blue stripes on side of body, extending forward onto head. Recorded to 107 cm; world angling record, 17.05 kg, from Revillagigedo Islands off Mexico. Circumtropical; type locality, New Guinea. Coastal pelagic, often in small schools. Feeds mainly on small fishes and the larger crustaceans of the zooplankton. Highly esteemed as a food fish and highly prized as a game fish.

232

Red Sea

GOLDEN TREVALLY
Gnathanodon speciosus (Forsskål, 1775)

Dorsal rays VII + I,18–20; anal rays II + I,15–17; straight part of lateral line with 17–24 scales and 17–26 scutes; juncture of curved and straight parts of lateral line below dorsal soft rays 9–14; chest completely scaled; gill rakers 7–9 + 19–22; adipose tissue weakly developed; upper jaw of adults not reaching a vertical at front edge of eye (just reaching in juveniles); mouth strongly protractile; lips thick and papillose; upper jaw without teeth; lower jaw with a few small teeth in young, disappearing with growth; body depth varying from 2.5 in fork length in young to 3.5 in large adults; first dorsal fin low, about two-thirds height of elevated anterior part of second dorsal fin; pectoral fins long and falcate, reaching juncture of straight and curved portions of lateral line; juveniles yellow with a dark bar through eye and 5 black bars on body with a narrow black bar in each yellow interspace; adults silvery gray with iridescence, the bars faint to absent, and a few scattered black blotches on body. Reaches about 120 cm; world angling record, 14.15 kg, from Port Hedland, Australia. Indo-Pacific and tropical eastern Pacific; type locality, Red Sea. Usually seen over open sand substrata; feeds by rooting in the sand for fossorial invertebrates, and occasionally eats small fishes.

Great Barrier Reef/subadults

Waikīkī Aquarium/juvenile

233

TORPEDO SCAD

Megalaspis cordyla (Linnaeus, 1758)

Dorsal rays VIII + I,18–20, the last 7 to 9 as separate finlets; anal rays II + I,16–17, the last 8 to 10 as separate finlets; curved part of lateral line short, with 21–28 scales, the straight with 51–59 huge scutes; caudal peduncle very slender, the scutes forming a lateral keel; ventral part of chest scaleless; gill rakers 8–11 + 18–22; transparent adipose tissue covering eye except for a narrow slit over pupil; body depth 3.6–4.3 in fork length; first dorsal fin three-fourths or more height of elevated anterior part of second dorsal fin; pectoral fins long and falcate, extending well posterior to origin of anal fin; silvery bluish gray dorsally, shading to silvery ventrally; a large black spot at edge of operculum at level of eye. Reported to 80 cm. Indian Ocean to western Pacific from southern Japan to New South Wales, east to New Caledonia and Fiji; only Palau in Micronesia; type locality, "America," hence in error. A pelagic schooling species that ranges into inshore waters; feeds mainly on fishes and squids.

THICKLIPPED JACK

Pseudocaranx dentex (Bloch & Schneider, 1801)

Dorsal rays VIII + I,24–28; anal rays II + I,20–24; curved portion of lateral line with 57–78 scales, straight portion with 2–27 scales and 16–30 scutes; juncture of curved and straight parts of lateral line below dorsal soft rays 12–14; chest fully scaled; gill rakers 9–11 + 20–24; transparent adipose tissue over eye rudimentary; head pointed; dorsal profile of snout forming an angle of about 35°; lips thick and papillose; both jaws with a row of blunt conical teeth, the upper sometimes with an inner row anteriorly; body depth of adults 2.8–3.1 in fork length; first dorsal fin slightly higher than second; last dorsal and anal rays longer than preceding rays and more widely separated; silvery blue-green dorsally, shading to silvery with iridescence below, with a midlateral yellow stripe (better developed in young); a prominent black spot on opercle at level of upper edge of eye; median fins yellowish. Reported to 82 cm. Circumglobal and antitropical; in the North Pacific from Japan and Northwestern Hawaiian Islands; in the south, Australia, New Zealand, Lord Howe Island,

Lombok, Indonesia

New Caledonia

Norfolk Island, Kermadec Islands, New Caledonia, Rapa, Pitcairn Islands, and Easter Island; type locality, Brazil. Found from near shore to depths of 200 m; often caught in trawls. Sazima (1998) reported on food habits (benthic crustaceans, small fishes, squids) and documented feeding on zooplankton by swimming with mouths open and opercles flared. Also known by the common names White Trevally and Silver Trevally.

DOUBLESPOTTED QUEENFISH

Scomberoides lysan (Forsskål, 1775)

Dorsal rays VI-VII + I,19–21; anal rays II + I,17–19; scales small, strongly pointed, and partially embedded; no scutes; gill rakers 3–8 + 15–20 (rudiments not counted); head small, the dorsal profile slightly concave; mouth large, the upper jaw extending to or slightly beyond a vertical at rear edge of eye; body elongate, the depth 3.7–4.8 in fork length, and strongly compressed; spines in first dorsal fin very short, flattened anteriorly-posteriorly, folding into a groove, and joined only basally by membrane in groove; posterior dorsal and anal soft rays joined only basally by membrane to preceding rays; anterior part of second dorsal and anal fins elevated, the dorsal lobe 7.05–11.0 in fork length; pelvic fins joined by membrane to abdomen; silvery greenish gray dorsally, silvery below, with a double series of 6–8 dark gray spots on side (spots may also appear silvery, depending on angle of light); outer half or more of lobe of second dorsal fin black. Largest reported, 67 cm. Distributed throughout the Indo-

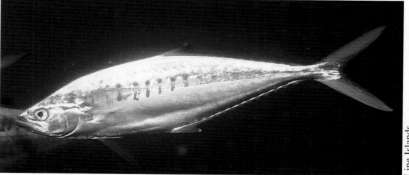

Line Islands

Pacific region; type locality, Red Sea. Occurs from the surface to 100 m, but usually seen in shallow water; juveniles also inshore, sometimes in brackish habitats. Adults feed mostly on small schooling fishes; juveniles known to bite scales and epidermal tissue from other fishes (Major, 1973). Spines of first dorsal and anal fins venomous (wounds painful, though not as serious as those from most scorpionfishes). *Chorinemus sanctipetri* Cuvier is a synonym.

NEEDLESCALE QUEENFISH
Scomberoides tol (Cuvier in C & V, 1832)

Dorsal rays VI-VII + I,19–21; anal rays II + I,18–20; scales small, strongly pointed, and partially embedded; no scutes; gill rakers 4–7 + 17–20 (rudiments not counted); head small, the dorsal profile slightly concave; upper jaw extending to below rear edge of pupil; body elongate, the depth 4.05–5.0 in fork length, and strongly compressed; spines in first dorsal fin very short, flattened anteriorly-posteriorly, folding into a groove, and joined only basally by membrane in the groove; posterior dorsal and anal soft rays joined only basally by membrane; anterior part of second dorsal and anal fins not very high, the dorsal lobe 8.9–13.0 in fork length; pelvic fins joined by membrane to abdomen; bluish silver dorsally, silvery on side and ventrally, with 5 to 8 vertically oblong dark gray spots (silvery depending on light angle), the first 4 or 5 on lateral line; outer three-fifths of lobe of second dorsal fin black. Largest specimen, 51 cm. Red Sea and Indian Ocean to western Pacific from Japan to southern Queensland, east to Fiji; type locality, Malabar, India. Often seen in small schools. Juveniles rasp tissue from other fishes. Spines of first dorsal and anal fins venomous.

OXEYE SCAD
Selar boops (Cuvier in C & V, 1833)

Dorsal rays VIII + I,23–25; anal rays II + I,19–21; no finlets; curved part of lateral line short with 21–24 scales and 0–4 scutes; straight part with 37–46 large scutes; scutes large, their height 1.3–1.6 in eye diameter; gill rakers 8–12 + 25–29; eye very large, slightly longer than snout length; transparent adipose tissue covering eye except for a narrow gap over center of pupil; upper jaw extending to below middle of eye; body depth about 3.4 in fork length; teeth in jaws small, mostly in 1 row; a deep furrow at lower edge of shoulder girdle under operculum, with a large papilla above it and a small one near upper end; first dorsal fin slightly higher than second; pectoral fins shorter than head length; silvery blue-green dorsally, silvery below, with a yellow stripe from upper end of gill opening to upper part of caudal peduncle; a black spot at edge of opercle in line with middle of eye. Attains 26 cm. East Indies and northern Australia, west to the Andaman Sea and east to Caroline Islands and New Caledonia; type locality, Ambon, Molucca Islands. Occurs in schools by day and disperses to feed at night. The photograph of a school shown above was taken at Bali in 2 m; the school was in the same place 1 year later.

235

Hawaiian Islands

BIGEYE SCAD
Selar crumenophthalmus (Bloch, 1793)
Dorsal rays VIII + I,24–27; anal rays II + I,21–23; pectoral rays 21; no finlets; curved part of lateral line short with 48–56 scales and 0–4 scutes; straight part with 0–11 scales and 29–42 scutes; scutes not large, their height 2.1–2.9 in eye diameter; gill rakers 9–12 + 27–31; eye large, but slightly shorter than snout length; transparent adipose tissue covering eye except for a narrow gap over center of pupil; upper jaw extending to below middle of eye; body depth 3.4–4.1 in fork length; teeth in jaws small, mostly in 1 row; a deep furrow at lower edge of shoulder girdle under operculum, with a large papilla above it and a small one near upper end; first dorsal fin and anterior lobe of second dorsal fin about equal in height; pectoral fins nearly as long as head; silvery blue-green, shading to silvery with iridescence below; a yellow stripe present or absent from upper end of gill opening to dorsal part of caudal peduncle; a blackish spot at edge of opercle at level of eye. Reaches 30 cm. Worldwide in tropical and subtropical seas; type locality, Acara, Guinea, West Africa. Occurs from near shore to depths as great as 170 m; nocturnal; feeds on zooplankton; forms semistationary schools by day. Maturity is reached at a total length of about 23 cm, and spawning takes place, probably during the day, in Hawai'i from April through September or October (Clarke & Privitera, 1995).

Hawaiian Islands

GREATER AMBERJACK
Seriola dumerili (Risso, 1810)
Dorsal rays VIII + I,29–35 (first spine usually embedded in large adults); anal rays II + I,18–22; no finlets; lateral-line scales 141–163; no scutes; gill rakers in juveniles less than 7 cm fork length 5–6 + 20–24, decreasing with growth to a total count of 11–19 in adults (excluding rudiments); vertebrae 10 + 14; upper jaw reaching to below pupil, the posterior edge very broad (supramaxilla large, its posterior corner well rounded); villiform teeth in bands in jaws; body depth 3.1–4.1 in fork length; a notch posteriorly on caudal peduncle before each lobe of caudal fin; anterior part of second dorsal fin more than twice height of first dorsal, its length 5.6–7.7 in fork length; pelvic fins longer than pectorals; silvery bluish gray to silvery olive gray dorsally, shading to silvery ventrally; an oblique, dark yellowish brown band from nape through eye to edge of upper lip; a lateral yellowish stripe sometimes present; tip of pelvic fins and anal-fin lobe often white; juveniles brassy with many irregular bars. Reported to 188 cm and 80.6 kg; world angling record, 70.6 kg, from Bermuda. Indo-Pacific and Atlantic; type locality, Nice, France. Ranges from near shore to depths as great as 385 m. Humphreys (1980) determined that adults in the Hawaiian Islands feed mainly on fishes, particularly the genus *Decapterus*, but also on cephalopods and shrimps. One of the worst offenders for causing ciguatera fish poisoning. Juveniles often associated with drifting algae or debris.

236

Lord Howe Island

YELLOWTAIL AMBERJACK
Seriola lalandi Valenciennes in C & V, 1833

Dorsal rays VIII + I,30–35 (first spine usually embedded in large adults); anal rays II + I,19–22 (rarely 19); no finlets; lateral-line scales about 160; no scutes; gill rakers 7–10 + 15–20 (excluding rudiments); vertebrae 11 + 14; surpaneural bones 3; posterior edge of upper jaw not very broad, the upper corner well rounded; villiform teeth in bands in jaws; body depth of adults 4.2–5.1 in fork length; a notch posteriorly on caudal peduncle before each lobe of caudal fin; side of caudal peduncle with a slight, lateral, fleshy keel; anterior part of second dorsal fin more than twice height of first dorsal, its length 7.5–9.1 in fork length; pelvic fins longer than pectorals; a broad, yellow to dark brown stripe from front of snout through eye to base of caudal fin; body above stripe usually silvery blue-green, below silvery; fins yellow to yellowish brown; young with 10–12 dark bars on body. Attains at least 150 cm; world angling record, 52 kg, from New Zealand. Circumglobal in subtropical to warm temperate seas; in the South Pacific from Australia (southern Queensland to Tasmania), Lord Howe Island, Norfolk Island, New Caledonia, New Zealand, Kermadec Islands, Rapa, Pitcairn Islands, and Easter Island; type locality, Brazil. A highly prized game fish. Some of the disjunct populations had different scientific names (*S. dorsalis* in the eastern Pacific, *S. grandis* in Australia, *S. aureovittata* in Japan, and *S. pappei* from South Africa). Feeds mainly on small fishes and squids.

Ogasawara Islands

ALMACO JACK
Seriola rivoliana Valenciennes in C & V, 1833

Dorsal rays VIII + I,27–33 (first spine usually embedded in large adults); anal rays II + I,18–22; no finlets; lateral-line scales 122–143; no scutes; gill rakers of juveniles 6–9 + 18–20, decreasing with growth to a total count of 22–26 (excluding rudiments) in adults; posterior edge of upper jaw very broad; villiform teeth in bands in jaws; body depth of adults 2.9–3.8 in fork length; a notch posteriorly on caudal peduncle before each lobe of caudal fin; anterior part of second dorsal fin about 4 times height of first dorsal, its length 4.5–5.55 in fork length; pelvic fins longer than pectorals; silvery blue-green to silvery olive dorsally, shading to silvery ventrally; a midlateral yellowish stripe usually present on body; an oblique, dark yellowish brown band from nape through eye to edge of upper lip; fins yellowish gray, the leading edge of pelvics and margin of anal fin white. Attains about 120 cm; world angling record, 59.87 kg, from La Paz, Baja California. Circumglobal in tropical to warm temperate seas; type locality, Greek Archipelago. Known from depths of 1–245 m; tends to range into deeper water (generally 30–160 m or more) in tropical areas.

Coral Sea

SMALLSPOTTED POMPANO
Trachinotus baillonii (Lacepède, 1801)
Dorsal rays VI + I,20–24; anal rays II + I,20–24; longitudinal scale series 89–97; gill rakers 7–13 + 15–19; villiform teeth in bands in jaws, in a chevron-shaped patch on vomer, and in a long band on palatines; body strongly compressed and moderately deep, the depth 2.4–2.9 in fork length; dorsal and ventral profiles of head about equally convex; anterior lobes of second dorsal and anal fins very long, slender, and posteriorly curved, the anal lobe of adults longer than the dorsal; longest dorsal soft ray 2.5–4.2 in fork length; caudal fin very large and deeply forked; pectoral fins about 1.4 in head length; pelvic fins about half length of pectorals; bluish silver dorsally, shading to silvery below, with 1 to 5 black spots smaller than pupil along lateral line (number of spots increasing, in general, with growth; spots absent in fish less than about 10–13 cm fork length); leading edges of second dorsal, anal, and caudal fin black. Largest reported, 53.5 cm. Red Sea and east coast of Africa to Line Islands, Society Islands, and Rapa; in the western Pacific from southern Japan to Lord Howe Island and Norfolk Island; type locality, Madagascar. Usually found in shallow water, often along sandy shores or near the surface, generally in small schools.

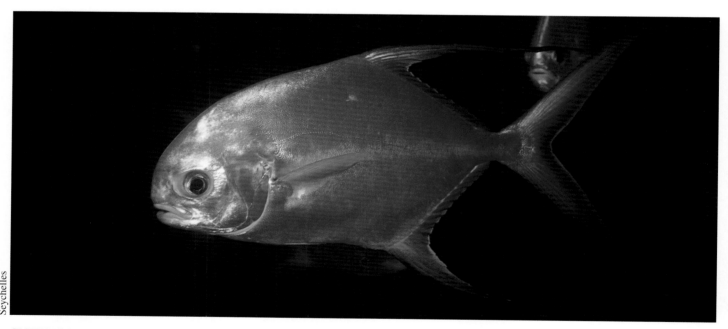

Seychelles

SNUBNOSE POMPANO
Trachinotus blochii (Lacepède, 1801)
Dorsal rays VI + I,18–20; anal rays II + I,16–18; anterior dorsal spines and first 2 anal spines often embedded in large adults; gill rakers 5–8 + 8–10; villiform teeth in bands in jaws; body compressed and moderately deep, the depth decreasing, in general, with growth, 1.8 in fork length of a 20-cm fish and 2.5 in fork length of a 69-cm specimen; dorsal profile of head very steep and strongly convex; snout short and bluntly rounded; anterior lobes of second dorsal fin longer than the anal, the longest dorsal soft ray 2.75–3.55 in fork length (relatively shorter with growth); caudal fin large and deeply forked; pectoral fins about 1.2 in head length; pelvic fins small, 1.7–2.0 in pectorals; bluish silver dorsally, shading to silvery or golden ventrally; front of snout and lips golden; fins yellow to yellowish gray, the leading edges and tips of second dorsal, anal, and caudal fins blackish. Attains at least 70 cm. Red Sea and east coast of Africa to the Marshall Islands and Samoa Islands; in the western Pacific from southern Japan to Norfolk Island and New South Wales; type locality, Madagascar. Reported to feed mainly on benthic mollusks; one of 64.5 cm collected by the author in the Solomon Islands had eaten gastropods (mainly *Strombus*, but some *Conus*) and hermit crabs.

PONYFISHES
(LEIOGNATHIDAE)

The ponyfishes are also called slipmouths (for their protrusible mouths) and soapies (for their excessive mucus). They are known only from the Indo-Pacific region except for one Red Sea species that has immigrated via the Suez Canal to the Mediterranean Sea. They are characterized by a compressed body of variable depth; two bony ridges dorsally on the head that converge on the nape; a median bony ridge anterior to the dorsal-fin origin; two short spines behind each nostril (may be little more than bumps on some species); ventral edge of the preopercle serrate; a small, highly protractile mouth that forms a tube when protruded; very small conical teeth in jaws, usually in a villiform band, but in a single row in a few species, except for the two species of *Gazza*, which have a single row of sharp teeth that become canines anteriorly; no teeth on vomer or palatines; gill membranes attached to isthmus; branchiostegal rays 5 or 6; small cycloid scales that are easily shed; dorsal rays VII-IX (usually VIII),14–17; anal rays III,13–15; second dorsal and anal spines longest; slender caudal peduncle; and forked caudal fin. The family consists of 3 genera and about 24 species. These fishes are bottom-dwelling on mud or sand substrata, mainly in shallow coastal waters, often in estuaries. Most feed on small invertebrates from the bottom, but the 2 species of *Gazza* prey in part on small fishes. The anterior dorsal and anal spines can be locked in an erect position (Seigel, 1982). Ponyfishes are also unique in possessing a light organ that encircles the posterior part of the esophagus (Haneda & Tsuji, 1976). The light is produced continuously by luminous bacteria but is not usually visible due to an opaque membrane covering the organ except for two window-like areas; a layer of guanine crystals serves to reflect the light through the two windows. The light from the ventral window shines through the translucent muscles of the isthmus and chest, and that from the dorsal window enters the anteroventral end of the swimbladder, which reflects it into the translucent abdominal muscles. The Leiognathidae of the central and western Pacific was reviewed by Woodland et al. in Carpenter & Niem (2001a).

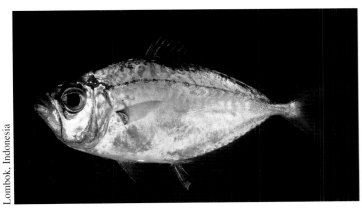

Lombok, Indonesia

Lombok, Indonesia

TOOTHPONY
Gazza minuta (Bloch, 1795)
Dorsal rays VII-VIII,15–17; anal rays III,13–14; pectoral rays 16–17; lateral-line scales 58–60; no scales on head, chest, or abdomen; gill rakers 4–6 + 16–17; body depth 2.2–2.5 in standard length; lower jaw slightly projecting when mouth closed; mouth moves slightly downward when protruded; upper jaw with a single pair of long canines at symphysis followed by a row of small sharp teeth; teeth of side of lower jaw progressively larger anteriorly, becoming canines at front; silvery, the upper one-third of body with irregular, dark gray to dark orange-yellow bars; caudal fin yellowish. Reported to 20 cm. Occurs throughout the tropical and subtropical Indian Ocean; in the western Pacific from the Ryukyu Islands to Queensland, east to the Samoa Islands; type locality, Malabar, India. Reported to depths of 75 m. Feeds on small fishes, shrimps and other crustaceans, and polychaete worms.

COMMON PONYFISH
Leiognathus equulus (Forsskål, 1775)
Dorsal rays VIII,15–16; anal rays III,14–15; pectoral rays 18–20; lateral-line scales 55–64; no scales on head or chest; gill rakers short, 5–6 + 15–17; body depth 1.7–2.1 in standard length; head length 2.9–3.3 in standard length; second dorsal spine 3.85–4.85 in standard length; silvery gray dorsally, silvery below, with narrow, slightly irregular, dark gray bars that extend to or slightly below lateral line; dorsal edge of caudal peduncle dark brown; caudal fin with a broad, dusky to blackish, posterior margin; anal and pelvic fins often pale yellowish. Largest of the leiognathids; reaches 24 cm. Red Sea (type locality), Persian Gulf, and east coast of Africa to Mariana Islands, Caroline Islands, and Samoa Islands; Ryukyu Islands to Queensland and New Caledonia; shallow coastal waters, including estuaries, to depths of 40 m. Young feed on zooplankton, larger fish on benthic crabs, shimps, and marine worms (van der Elst, 1981).

239

STRIPED PONYFISH

Leiognathus fasciatus (Lacepède, 1803)

Dorsal rays VII-VIII,16; anal rays III,14; pectoral rays usually 19; lateral-line scales 58–64; no scales on head or chest; gill rakers short, 4–6 + 14–16; body depth 1.6–2.05 in standard length; head length about 3.0 in standard length; dorsal profile of head nearly vertical to about level of center of eye, then slightly concave to above posterior edge of eye, and convex to origin of dorsal fin; second dorsal spine very long and filamentous, varying from 70% of body depth to greater than body depth; second anal spine 28–50% body depth; caudal fin deeply forked; color note made by the author of a 22-cm specimen from Tongatapu: silvery with bluish iridescence; 2 horizontally elongate brassy spots on side of body, with a row of smaller spots between these and lateral line; back above lateral line with narrow dusky yellowish bars, most broken into spots ventrally. This appears to be the largest specimen recorded. Red Sea and Gulf of Oman south to Madagascar and Mauritius (type locality), east to Fiji (after Jordan & Dickerson, 1908), and Samoa Islands; Ryukyu Islands to Queensland. Opinions differ whether *Leiognathus smithhursti* (Ramsay & Ogilby) is a syn-

Lombok, Indonesia

onym or a valid species; the only difference appears to be the second anal spine, which can be as long as the second dorsal spine. Fowler (1959) placed it in the synonymy of *fasciatus*; James (1975) regarded it as valid; Jones (1985) listed it for Australia but added that further study is needed to be certain of its validity.

SPLENDID PONYFISH

Leiognathus splendens (Cuvier, 1829)

Dorsal rays VIII,16; anal rays III,14; pectoral rays usually 17; lateral-line scales 49–56; no scales on head, but chest fully scaled; gill rakers 3–4 + 22–23; body depth 1.8–2.1 in standard length; head length 2.95–3.35 in standard length; mouth when closed in alignment with lower edge of eye; second dorsal spine 1.3–1.5 in head length; second anal spine 1.5–1.8 in head length; caudal fin deeply forked; bluish silver dorsally with very irregular, narrow, dark gray bars, shading to silvery ventrally; side of snout below nostrils dark brown; outer half or more of second to sixth membranes of dorsal fin black. Attains 14 cm. James (1975) gave the localities as Red Sea, Madagascar, Mauritius, India (type locality, Vishakhapatnam), Sri Lanka, Andaman Islands, Thailand, China, Taiwan, Philippines, Indonesia, Queensland, and Fiji.

Lombok, Indonesia

SPATTERED PONYFISH

Leiognathus stercorarius Evermann & Seale, 1907

Dorsal rays VIII,17; anal rays III,14; pectoral rays usually 17; lateral-line scales 55–57; small scales present on cheek and chest; gill rakers short, 6 + 14; 2 widely separated broad and low supraorbital spines; adipose tissue anteriorly and posteriorly at upper edge of orbit; body slender, the depth 3.0–3.2 in standard length; head length about 3.7 in standard length; dorsal profile of head nearly vertical to about level of center of eye, then nearly straight to origin of dorsal fin; second dorsal spine 1.4–1.75 in head; caudal fin deeply forked; silvery, the upper half of body with very irregular, narrow, dark markings that are short and mainly vertically oriented; front of snout with a dark brown band that continues above upper lip to corner of mouth; males with a broad blackish streak extending posteriorly on side of body from beneath pectoral fin. Attains 13 cm. Indo-Malayan region (type local-

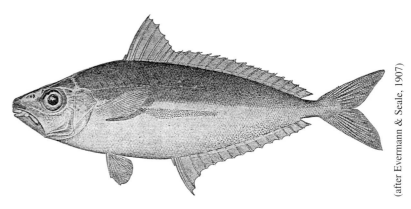

(after Evermann & Seale, 1907)

ity, Sorsogon, Philippines) east to Guam, Tonga, and Samoa Islands. This species was regarded as a synonym of the similar *L. elongatus* until Dunlap & McFall-Ngai (1984) differentiated the two.

PUGNOSE PONYFISH
Secutor insidiator (Bloch, 1787)

Dorsal rays VIII,16–17; anal rays III,14; pectoral rays 17–18; lateral-line scales about 80, ending below penultimate ray of dorsal fin; no scales on cheek; gill rakers 5–7 + 17–19; body moderately deep and compressed, the depth 1.7–2.5 in standard length, increasing with age; head length about 3.5 in standard length; dorsal profile of head deeply indented above front of eye; ventral profile of chin forming an angle of about 80°; mouth angling upward when protruded; maxilla ending well below level of lower edge of eye; silvery, the back greenish to bluish silver with dark gray spots or short bars in vertical series; a black line from eye to lower end of chin; a black spot distally on each of second to fifth membranes of spinous portion of dorsal fin; a broad dusky bar narrowing as it passes below basal part of pectoral fin. Attains 8 cm. East coast

Cochin, India

of Africa to Indo-Malayan region north to Taiwan, south to northern Australia and New Caledonia; type locality, Surat, India. Occurs in coastal waters, including estuaries; reported to 150 m; feeds on zooplankton (van der Elst, 1981).

DEEP PUGNOSE PONYFISH
Secutor ruconius (Hamilton, 1822)

Dorsal rays VIII,16; anal rays III,14; pectoral rays 17–18; lateral-line scales 40, ending below middle of soft portion of dorsal fin or a little beyond; small scales present on cheek (easily lost); gill rakers 5–6 + 16–17; body deep and compressed, the depth 1.5–1.75 in standard length, increasing with age; head length 3.5–3.7 in standard length; dorsal profile of head deeply indented above front of eye; ventral profile of chin forming an angle of about 80°; mouth angling upward when protruded; silvery, the back greenish to bluish silver with dark bluish gray bars or spots forming vertical series; a black line from eye to lower end of chin; tip of dorsal fin black, often bordered below by yellow; a broad, narrowing dusky bar often present below basal part of pectoral fin. Attains 8 cm. East coast of Africa, Madagascar, Mascarenes, and Seychelles to Indo-Malayan region and northern Australia, north to Taiwan, south to New Caledonia (M. Kulbicki, pers. comm.); type locality, Ganges estuary.

(after Woodland et al. in Carpenter & Niem, 2001a)

SNAPPERS
(LUTJANIDAE)

The Lutjanidae is a large family of 17 genera and 103 species (Allen, 1985b). Many of the snappers are commercially important, particularly those of the genus *Lutjanus* and the deeper-water species of the genera *Etelis* and *Pristipomoides*. The family is characterized by having a moderately large mouth with terminal jaws or the lower jaw projecting; teeth vary from small and conical to large and caniniform (none incisiform or truly molariform); vomer and palatines usually with small teeth; upper edge of maxilla slipping under the preorbital when mouth closed; no spines on the opercle; ctenoid scales on body; a single continuous or notched dorsal fin with X–XII,9–17 rays; anal rays III,7–11; caudal fin emarginate, forked, or lunate; pelvic rays I,5, their base slightly posterior to base of the pectoral fins. All snappers are carnivorous; most feed heavily on crustaceans, but a few prey mainly on fishes. Those that are piscivorous generally have large canine teeth, and some of the larger shallow-water species have caused ciguatera fish poisoning. Many of the snappers are nocturnal, and some of these form semistationary aggregations during the day. The 2 species of *Macolor* feed on zooplankton (genus revised by Kishimoto et al., 1987). The largest genus is *Lutjanus*, with 39 species in the Indo-Pacific alone (Allen & Talbot, 1985); 4 of these from the East Indies are known only from fresh and brackish-water habitats.

Yellowbanded Snappers, *Lutjanus adetii*, Great Barrier Reef

SMALLTOOTH JOBFISH

Aphareus furca (Lacepède, 1801)

Dorsal rays X,10–11 (rarely 10); anal rays III,8; pectoral rays 15–16; lateral-line scales 68–75; no scales on dorsal or anal fins; gill rakers 6–12 + 16–18; body depth 3.0–3.5 in standard length; lower jaw projecting; teeth in jaws small, disappearing with age; no teeth on palate; dorsal fin without a notch, the third spine longest; last dorsal and anal rays greatly prolonged; caudal fin forked; pectoral fins long, reaching to above anus; silvery purplish brown dorsally, light silvery bluish gray ventrally; lower jaw silvery; vertical edge of opercle and preopercle blackish; median fins yellow to yellowish brown; one rare color form bright yellow on top of head. Largest examined, 55 cm; 1.46 kg (caught trolling). Indo-Pacific except western and northern Australia, Persian Gulf, and Gulf of Oman; type locality, Mauritius; also reported from the eastern Pacific (Robertson et al., 2004). An open-water, usually solitary, roving carnivore of coral reefs; depth range, 1–122 m (Chave & Mundy, 1994). The author collected 17 adult specimens for food-habit study; 7 had empty stomachs; one had eaten six 5-mm crab megalops, and the rest contained fish remains (including *Chromis* sp. and *Pseudanthias evansi*) except one that had also eaten crab megalops and larvae of spiny lobster.

RUSTY JOBFISH

Aphareus rutilans Cuvier in C & V, 1830

Dorsal rays X,10–11 (rarely 10); anal rays III,8; pectoral rays 15–16; lateral-line scales 69–75; no scales on dorsal or anal fins; gill rakers 16–19 + 30–34; body depth 3.0–3.3 in standard length; lower jaw projecting; teeth in jaws small, none on palate; dorsal fin without a notch, the fourth to sixth spines longest; last dorsal and anal rays greatly prolonged; caudal fin lunate; pectoral fins long, reaching to above anus; silvery lavender-brown to silvery red, shading to silvery ventrally; edge of maxilla and lower jaw black; vertical edge of preopercle narrowly black; fins reddish. Reported to 110 cm. Red Sea (type locality) and east coast of Africa to the Hawaiian Islands and Samoa Islands (1 probable sight record off Tahiti); usually found in 100–250 m, but the author has observed the species as shallow as 10–15 m off South Africa and Western Australia; difficult to approach underwater. Judging from the numerous gill rakers, probably feeds mainly on the macroplankton.

Lombok, Indonesia

GREEN JOBFISH

Aprion virescens Valenciennes in C & V, 1830

Dorsal rays X,11 (rarely 10); anal rays III,8; pectoral rays 16–18; lateral-line scales 48–50; no scales on dorsal or anal fins; gill rakers 7–8 + 14–16; body depth 3.7–4.2 in standard length; snout as long as postorbital head; lower jaw projecting; villiform teeth in jaws with a pair of canines at front; teeth on vomer in a crescent-shaped patch; dorsal fin without a notch, the fifth spine longest; last dorsal and anal rays only slightly longer than penultimate rays; caudal fin lunate; pectoral fins shorter than pelvics, less than half head length; greenish gray dorsally, shading to white below; a black area often present at base of last 5 interspinous membranes of dorsal fin. Reaches 110 cm; world angling record, 14.5 kg, from the Ryukyu Islands. Occurs throughout the Indo-Pacific region; type locality, Seychelles; found from near shore to at least 100 m. A roving, coastal, open-water predator that is difficult to approach. Ommanney in Wheeler & Ommanney (1953), Talbot (1960), Randall (1980a), and van der Elst (1981) reported feeding mainly on fishes, but also on macroplankton, swimming crabs, and occasionally on benthic invertebrates such as octopus, calappid crabs, and stomatopods. Has caused ciguatera (the author suffered a light case from eating one in Mauritius).

Maldive Islands

YELLOWBANDED SNAPPER

Lutjanus adetii (Castelnau, 1873)

Dorsal rays X,14; anal rays III,8; pectoral rays 17; lateral-line scales 48–51; scale rows on back oblique; soft portion of dorsal and anal fins scaly (true of other *Lutjanus*); gill rakers 7–9 + 19–20; teeth on vomer in a triangular patch; tongue with a patch of granular teeth; lower edge of vertical margin of preopercle with a moderate notch, and interopercular knob moderately large; body depth 2.5–2.8 in standard length; caudal fin emarginate; reddish dorsally with a white spot on each scale, thus forming oblique rows, shading to white ventrally, with a narrow, yellow to greenish stripe from behind opercle at level of upper part of eye to caudal peduncle; caudal fin light red with a dark red posterior border; edges of soft portion of dorsal and anal fins broadly white; eye rimmed by greenish yellow; iris largely golden yellow. Reported to 50 cm. Known from northern Queensland to New South Wales, Lord Howe Island, and New Caledonia (type locality); forms near-stationary aggregations around coral heads or rocky outcrops during the day, mainly in protected waters. *Lutjanus amabilis* (De Vis) is a synonym.

New Caledonia

243

Great Barrier Reef

RIVER SNAPPER
Lutjanus argentimaculatus (Forsskål, 1775)
Dorsal rays X,13–14; anal rays III,8; pectoral rays 16–17; lateral-line scales 44–48; scale rows on back parallel lateral-line anteriorly, becoming oblique posteriorly; gill rakers 6–8 + 9–12; anterior canine teeth in jaws very large; teeth on vomer in a crescentic patch; tongue with a patch of granular teeth; lower edge of preopercle with a poorly developed notch; interopercular knob indistinct or absent; body depth 2.5–3.1 in standard length (depth decreasing with growth); caudal fin truncate; each scale of body with a vertically elongate, diamond-shaped, brown spot, the edges of scales light greenish gray dorsally and silvery to silvery pink ventrally; fins reddish brown, the caudal with a narrow, blackish posterior margin; juveniles with broad dark bars on body. Attains at least 100 cm. Red Sea (type locality), eastern Mediterranean (via the Suez Canal) to South Africa, east to the Line Islands and Samoa Islands; in the western Pacific from

Lombok, Indonesia/juvenile

Ryukyu Islands to New South Wales. Juveniles and subadults generally found in mangrove areas and even the lower reaches of rivers and streams; adults in silty protected reef areas from inshore to depths of 100 m; not observed on exposed outer reefs. Reported to feed mainly on fishes and crustaceans. Also called the Mangrove Snapper.

TWOSPOT BANDED SNAPPER
Lutjanus biguttatus (Valenciennes in C & V, 1830)
Dorsal rays XI,10–12; anal rays III,8; pectoral rays 15–16; lateral-line scales 47–50; scale rows on back oblique; gill rakers 7–8 + 16–19; teeth in jaws in a villiform band with a pair of moderate canines at front of upper jaw (one on each side) and 3 lesser canines along side of lower jaw; teeth on vomer in a diamond-shaped patch, or triangular with a median posterior extension; preopercular notch and knob poorly developed; body slender for the genus, the depth 3.5–3.8 in standard length; preorbital depth narrow, less than half eye diameter, 9.2–16.3 in head length; caudal fin truncate; top of head and back greenish gray, red below, with a broad, silvery white stripe from tip of chin across lower side of body to base of caudal fin; 2 bright white spots about half pupil size on back, one below seventh dorsal spine and the other below middle of soft portion of dorsal fin; median fins yellow; paired fins whitish, the pectorals with a small black spot at upper base. Attains

Sumilon Island, Philippines

20 cm. Maldive Islands to the Indo-Malayan region, east to Fiji, Palau, and Kapingamarangi in the Caroline Islands; described from Sri Lanka and Ambon, Molucca Islands. Usually found in aggregations on outer-reef slopes; recorded from depths of 2–36 m.

TWINSPOT SNAPPER
Lutjanus bohar (Forsskål, 1775)

Dorsal rays X,13–14; anal rays III,8; pectoral rays 16–17; lateral-line scales 48–51; scale rows on back oblique; gill rakers 6–7 + 16; anterior canine teeth in jaws very large; teeth on vomer in a crescentic patch; tongue with a patch of granular teeth; lower edge of preopercle with a moderately developed notch and interopercular knob; nostrils of adults in an oblique groove anterior to eye; body depth 2.4–2.9 in standard length; caudal fin emarginate; gray to reddish brown dorsally, paler below, with a whitish spot on each scale forming oblique lines above lateral line and horizontal lines below; juveniles and small adults with 2 silvery white spots on back, one below middle of dorsal fin and one below last dorsal rays (anterior spot sometimes wanting); fins dark reddish gray; juveniles with a black submarginal band in soft portions of dorsal and anal fins and each lobe of caudal fin. Small juvenile illustrated here was sheltering in a crinoid. Attains 80 cm; world angling record, 12.5 kg, from the Ogasawara Islands. Indo-Pacific except the Persian Gulf, Gulf of Oman, and Hawaiian Islands; type locality, Red Sea. Especially common on seaward reefs of atolls and low islands; generally found at depths of 10–70 m. Food habits extensively studied by Talbot (1960), Helfrich et al. (1968), and Randall (1980a). Fishes, expecially reef species, are the principal prey (about 70% by volume); also important, crustaceans and cephalopods. Juveniles mimic damselfishes of the genus *Chromis*; when mimicking *C. iomelas*, the posterior half of the body and caudal fin are entirely white (Russell et al., 1976). One of the worst offending species causing ciguatera poisoning (Helfrich et al., 1968; Randall, 1980a); banned from sale at some localities in Oceania.

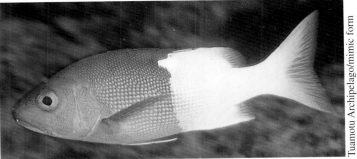

245

Sudan, Red Sea

BLACKSPOT SNAPPER

Lutjanus ehrenbergii (Peters, 1869)

Dorsal rays X,13–14; anal rays III,8–9; pectoral rays 15–16; lateral-line scales 48–51; scale rows on back parallel to lateral line; gill rakers 6–7 + 10–14; body depth 2.5–3.0 in standard length; preopercular notch indistinct; interopercular knob small or absent; vomerine teeth of adults in a triangular patch with a median posterior extension (patch crescentic in juveniles); tongue of adults with a patch of granular teeth; caudal fin truncate to slightly emarginate; body gray-brown dorsally, shading to silvery gray on sides and ventrally, with 4 or 5 narrow yellow stripes below lateral line and a large black spot on lateral line below juncture of spinous and soft portions of dorsal fin; fins yellow. Attains about 35 cm. Red Sea (type locality) and Persian Gulf south to Natal and east to Caroline Islands, and Fiji (recently collected by D. W. Greenfield and the author); an inshore species of coral reefs and rocky substrata; young sometimes found in estuaries; adults often encountered in aggregations.

DORY SNAPPER

Lutjanus fulviflamma (Forsskål, 1775)

Dorsal rays X,12–14; anal rays III,8; pectoral rays 15–17; lateral-line scales 42–47; scale rows on back oblique; gill rakers 6–7 + 9–12; anterior canine teeth in jaws moderately large; teeth on vomer in a triangular or diamond-shaped patch with a median posterior extension (except juveniles); tongue of adults with a patch of granular teeth; lower edge of preopercle with a shallow notch and indistinct interopercular knob; body depth 2.6–2.9 in standard length; caudal fin slightly emarginate; greenish to gray dorsally, silvery white below, with 5 or 6 orange-yellow stripes on body below lateral line, and a black spot (usually oblong) on lateral line beneath anterior soft portion of dorsal fin (most of spot below lateral line); fins yellow; juveniles and subadults usually with a dark brown streak from side of snout through eye to end of opercle. Attains

Great Barrier Reef

about 35 cm. Red Sea (type locality) and Persian Gulf to South Africa, east to Samoa Islands; only Palau in Micronesia; in western Pacific from Ryukyu Islands to New South Wales and Lord Howe Island; occurs on coral reefs and rocky substrata by day, from inshore to about 35 m, often in small aggregations; young enter brackish habitats.

BLACKTAIL SNAPPER

Lutjanus fulvus (Forster, 1801)

Dorsal rays X,13–14; anal rays III,8; pectoral rays 16; lateral-line scales 47–50; scale rows on back oblique; gill rakers 6–7 + 10–13; teeth on vomer in a V-shaped patch; no teeth on tongue; lower vertical edge of preopercle with a deep notch, and interopercular knob well developed; body depth 2.3–2.8 in standard length; caudal fin slightly emarginate; brownish to yellowish gray dorsally, pale yellowish ventrally; caudal fin reddish black with a narrow white posterior margin; dorsal fin reddish with a narrow white margin and broad blackish submarginal band; remaining fins yellow. Indonesian and Indian Ocean fish with narrow yellow stripes following every other scale row and continuing onto head. Reported to 40 cm. Southern Oman to South Africa, east to the islands of French Polynesia; in the western Pacific from southern Japan to the Great Barrier Reef, Norfolk Island, and New Caledonia; type locality, Tahiti. Introduced to the Hawaiian Islands; occurs on coral reefs from the shallows to at least 40 m; young often found in brackish habitats. Randall & Brock (1960) reported

Marshall Islands

in detail on the food habits in the Society Islands (where it is the most common snapper): crustaceans (mainly crabs) 54.3%, and fishes 42.4%. *Lutjanus vaigiensis* (Quoy & Gaimard) and *L. marginatus* (Cuvier) are synonyms.

HUMPBACK SNAPPER
Lutjanus gibbus (Forsskål, 1775)

Dorsal rays X,13–14; anal rays III,8; pectoral rays 16–17; lateral-line scales 47–51; scale rows on body except caudal peduncle oblique; gill rakers 9–10 + 15–20; teeth on vomer in a V-shaped patch; no teeth on tongue; lower vertical edge of preopercle with a deep notch, and interopercular knob well developed; body moderately deep, the depth 2.2–2.5 in standard length; dorsal profile of head a sinuous curve; caudal fin forked, the lobes broadly rounded in adults (the basis for one common name, Paddletail Snapper); reddish gray to red (those in deeper water more red); lower part of opercle and axil of pectoral fins yellow; median fins dark reddish with a narrow white margin; paired fins red; juveniles reddish gray with a pale blue spot on each scale, thus forming oblique lines on body; a very large black spot on base of caudal fin and posteriorly on caudal peduncle, continuing as a band dorsally on peduncle and into base of soft portion of dorsal fin. Reaches about 50 cm. Red Sea (type locality) and east coast of Africa to the Line Islands, French Polynesia, and all of Micronesia; southern Japan to the Great Barrier Reef and New Caledonia. When abundant, forms large, nearly stationary schools by day; disperses to feed individually at night. Randall (1980a) summarized his and previous food-habit data: crabs the dominant prey, followed by shrimps, fishes, mollusks (cephalopods, prosobranchs, opisthobranchs, and amphineurans), and echinoids.

Java/juvenile

Cochin, India

JOHN'S SNAPPER

Lutjanus johnii (Bloch, 1792)

Dorsal rays X,13–14; anal rays III,8; pectoral rays 16; lateral-line scales 46–49; scale rows on back parallel to lateral line; gill rakers 6–7 + 11; teeth on vomer in a crescent-shaped patch without a median posterior extension; tongue with a patch of fine granular teeth (may be absent on young); preopercular notch and knob poorly developed; body depth 2.4–2.9 in standard length; caudal fin truncate to slightly emarginate; gray dorsally, silvery to light bronze on side and ventrally, with a crescentic blackish spot or vertical streak on each scale, those dorsally on body joined by a longitudinal blackish line in middle of each scale row; a large black spot (the crescentic streaks darker within) on lateral line below anterior half of soft portion of dorsal fin (spot three-fourths above lateral line); fins reddish to yellowish brown; blackish spot on juveniles more distinct and may be pale-edged. Reaches about 70 cm. Djibouti south to Natal and Madagascar; Persian Gulf and India (type locality, Suratta) to Indo-Malayan region and northern Australia, north to Taiwan, east to Fiji; a continental and large-island species; juveniles in estuaries and mangrove habitats; adults in deeper water, to at least 80 m; often taken by trawls.

Ogasawara Islands

BLUESTRIPED SNAPPER

Lutjanus kasmira (Forsskål, 1775)

Dorsal rays XI,14–15; anal rays III,7–8; pectoral rays 16–17; lateral-line scales 46–49; scale rows on back oblique; gill rakers 7–8 + 13–14; vomerine teeth in a crescent-shaped patch; no teeth on tongue; lower edge of preopercle with a moderately deep notch, and interopercular knob well developed; body depth 2.4–2.8 in standard length; caudal fin slightly forked; yellow, becoming reddish gray on snout, with 4 dark-edged blue stripes on upper three-fifths of body, the first, second, and fourth stripes continuing onto head; a narrow blue stripe across lower part of head to corner of mouth (lacking on the very similar *Lutjanus bengalensis*, not known from the South Pacific); lower part of body white with rows of pale yellow spots, 1 per scale; fins yellow. Largest specimen, 32 cm. Occurs throughout most of the Indo-Pacific region; apparently not present from Oman to the Bay of Bengal; ranges in the western Pacific from southern Japan to New South Wales, Lord Howe Island, Norfolk Island, and the Kermadec Islands, and east in Oceania to the Pitcairn Islands; type locality, Red Sea. Introduced to the Hawaiian Islands, where it has undergone a population explosion that is believed to be at the expense of some species of greater commercial value; a common coral-reef species at most localities where it occurs, forming nearly stationary schools by day and feeding individually at night. Known from depths of 2–265 m (the latter depth from a fish caught by the author by hook and line in the Red Sea); generally found in more than 15 m. Feeds mainly on crustaceans (Randall & Brock, 1960; Talbot, 1960).

248

Redang, Malaysia

YELLOWLINED SNAPPER

Lutjanus lutjanus Bloch, 1790

Dorsal rays X-XII,12; anal rays III,8; pectoral rays 16–17; lateral-line scales 48–50; scale rows on back oblique; gill rakers 6–8 + 17–19; teeth on vomer in a triangular patch with a median posterior extension; a patch of small granular teeth on tongue; lower vertical edge of preopercle with a slight notch; interopercular knob not apparent; body slender, the depth 2.9–3.3 in standard length; suborbital depth 7.5–10 in head length; eye large, 2.9–3.7 in head length; caudal fin slightly forked; silvery gray on back with oblique brownish yellow lines following scale rows, silvery on sides and ventrally, with a yellow stripe from behind eye to upper base of caudal fin and longitudinal yellow lines following scale rows on lower half of body; median fins yellow. Reported to 33 cm. Red Sea and Persian Gulf to southern Mozambique, east to the western Pacific from Japan (type locality) to the Great Barrier Reef and New Caledonia; usually seen in aggregations on reefs; has been taken by trawls as deep as 90 m. *Lutjanus lineolatus* (Rüppell) is a synonym.

ONESPOT SNAPPER

Lutjanus monostigma (Cuvier in C & V, 1828)

Dorsal rays X,12–14 (rarely 14); anal rays III,8; pectoral rays 15–17; lateral-line scales 47–50; scale rows on back oblique; gill rakers 6–7 + 11–12; canine teeth at front of jaws very large; teeth on vomer in a crescentic patch without a median posterior extension; no teeth on tongue; lower vertical edge of preopercle with a slight notch; interopercular knob not well developed; body depth 2.6–3.0 in standard length; caudal fin slightly forked; silvery gray dorsally, the scale edges above lateral line gray-brown, pinkish to yellowish silver ventrally, with an oval blackish spot smaller than eye on lateral line below anterior soft portion of dorsal fin (spot may be faint or absent in large adults); fins yellow. Largest examined, 54.5 cm. Red Sea to Mozambique, east to French Polynesia and the Pitcairn Islands; in the western Pacific from the Ryukyu Islands to the Great Barrier Reef and New Caledonia; not known from the Persian Gulf or the Hawaiian Islands; type locality, Seychelles. Nocturnal, sheltering in reefs by day, often in the vicinity of caves; solitary or in small groups. Food-habit stud-

Bali

ies by Randall & Brock (1960), Talbot (1960), and Randall (1980a) indicate heavy feeding on fishes (about 90% of the diet), the rest mainly on crabs. Like *Lutjanus bohar*, large adults often reported to cause ciguatera. Banned from sale in Tahiti, where it is called Taivaiva.

FIVESTRIPE SNAPPER
Lutjanus quinquelineatus (Bloch, 1790)
Dorsal rays X,13–15; anal rays III,8; pectoral rays 16–17; lateral-line scales 47–50; scale rows on back oblique; gill rakers 7–8 + 13–15; teeth on vomer in a crescentic patch; no teeth on tongue; lower vertical edge of preopercle with a moderately deep notch; interopercular knob well developed; body depth 2.3–2.8 in standard length; caudal fin slightly forked; yellow, becoming reddish gray on snout, with 5 narrow, dark-edged blue stripes on body and 6 on head; a blackish spot, varying from smaller to slightly larger than eye, between second and third blue stripes below front of soft portion of dorsal fin, its lower edge on lateral line; all fins yellow. Largest examined, 25 cm. Persian Gulf and India to New Caledonia and Fiji; not reported from Micronesia; in the western Pacific from southern Japan to New South Wales and Lord Howe Island; in Western Australia south to Shark Bay; type locality, Java. Typically found in small

Great Barrier Reef

schools by day on coral reefs or rocky substrata from 2 to at least 40 m. The very similar *L. notatus* (Cuvier) ranges from Mauritius to South Africa. *Lutjanus spilurus* (Bennett) is a synonym.

Bali

SPECKLED SNAPPER
Lutjanus rivulatus (Cuvier in C & V, 1828)
Dorsal rays X,15–16; anal rays III,8; pectoral rays 17; lateral-line scales 47–49; scale rows on back oblique; gill rakers 6 + 11–13; teeth on vomer in a crescentic patch; no teeth on tongue; lips in adults thick (hence another common name, Blubberlip Snapper); preopercular notch and interopercular knob moderately developed; body deep, the depth 2.1–2.4 in standard length; suborbital deep, 3.1–4.5 in head length; soft portion of anal fin pointed; caudal fin slightly emarginate; yellowish gray, each scale of body of adults with 1 to 3 very small blue spots; head with longitudinal undulating lines of blue and dusky yellow; fins varying from yellow to blackish; caudal fin often blackish with a broad, yellow posterior border; juveniles with dark bars on body, the largest and darkest from origin of dorsal fin to base of pectoral fin; a prominent black spot and adjacent white spot on lateral line below anterior soft portion of dorsal fin (sometimes a second black spot following the white). Reaches about 80 cm. Red Sea to South Africa, east to Society Islands; in the western Pacific from southern Japan to Great Barrier Reef and New

Sulawesi/juvenile

Caledonia; reported only from Palau and the Mariana Islands in Micronesia; described from specimens from India and Java. The most wary species of the genus in spite of its large size. Usually solitary on coral reefs; reported to 100 m. Talbot (1960) wrote, "predominately a fish predator, also taking crabs, polychaetes, squid, octopus, echinoids, ascidians and polyzoa."

MOLUCCAN SNAPPER

Lutjanus rufolineatus (Valenciennes in C & V, 1830)

Dorsal rays X-XI,13–14; anal rays III,8; pectoral rays 16–17; lateral-line scales 45–48; scale rows on back oblique; gill rakers 6–7 + 13–15; teeth on vomer in a crescentic patch; no teeth on tongue; preopercular notch and interopercular knob well developed; body depth 2.4–2.6 in standard length; suborbital depth 5.3–6.6 in head length; eye large, 3.4–4.2 in head length; caudal fin slightly forked; silvery pink, becoming deep pink on snout, with 10–11 yellow stripes of variable width on body, those between lateral line and base of pectoral fins extending forward onto postorbital head; lower lip and ventral part of head white; fins yellow. Maximum length about 30 cm (largest examined, 25 cm). Indo-Malayan region north to southern Japan and east to Tonga and Samoa Islands; not known from Australia or the islands of Micronesia; type locality, New Guinea. Generally found in semistationary schools during the day on reefs from depths of 15–50 m; has been caught as deep as 160 m. Misidentified as *Lutjanus boutton* (Lacepède) by Allen & Talbot (1985) and Allen (1985b); corrected to *rufolineatus* by Allen (1995).

RUSSELL'S SNAPPER

Lutjanus russellii (Bleeker, 1849)

Dorsal rays X,14; anal rays III,8; pectoral rays 16–17; lateral-line scales 47–50; scale rows on back oblique; gill rakers 5–7 + 11–13; teeth on vomer in a triangular to diamond-shaped patch with a median posterior extension; tongue with a patch of small granular teeth; preopercular notch shallow; interopercular knob slightly developed; body depth 2.6–2.8 in standard length; caudal fin truncate to slightly forked; gray dorsally, silvery gray on sides and ventrally (scale edges narrowly pale), with a large, oblong, black spot on lateral line below anterior soft portion of dorsal fin (most of spot above lateral line); dorsal and caudal fins gray, remaining fins yellow, the pectorals with a small black spot at upper base; juveniles with 5 dark brown stripes, the 3 above lateral line oblique and curving onto head, the fourth extending posteriorly from eye and containing a large oblong black spot on lateral line; Indian Ocean adults with 6–8 very narrow, yellow to yellowish brown stripes that are horizontal on lower side but progressively more oblique dorsally. Attains 45 cm. Red Sea and Persian Gulf to South Africa, east to New Caledonia and Fiji; in the western Pacific from southern Japan to New South Wales; no records for Micronesia; type locality, Malay-Moluccan Archipelago. Found on coral reefs inshore but also taken in trawls to depths of 80 m; juveniles may occur in mangrove estuaries or the lower reaches of streams.

Bali

Ambon, Indonesia/juvenile

Great Barrier Reef

251

EMPEROR SNAPPER

Lutjanus sebae (Cuvier, 1816)

Dorsal rays XI,15–16 (rarely 15); anal rays III,10; pectoral rays 17; lateral-line scales 46–50; scale rows on back oblique; gill rakers 6–7 + 10–12; lips of adults thick; teeth on vomer in a triangular to V-shaped patch without a median posterior extension; no teeth on tongue; preopercular notch moderately deep; interopercular knob small; body deep, the depth 2.1–2.4 in standard length; dorsal profile of head to above eye steep and straight to slightly concave; soft portions of dorsal and anal fins pointed; caudal fin slightly forked; juveniles white with a broad black bar across anterior body continuing into dorsal and pelvic fins, a broad, oblique black band on head enclosing eye, and broad, oblique black band from below middle of dorsal fin to lower edge of caudal fin; upper edge of caudal fin broadly black except tip; margins of soft portions of dorsal and anal fins broadly black; dark bands less strongly pigmented with growth (and may be red instead of blackish); pattern still evident to a length of about 40 cm; large adults entirely pink to red on head and body, the scale centers pale. Reaches about 80 cm; world angling record, 17.9 kg, from Ogasawara Islands. Red Sea and east coast of Africa to western Pacific from southern Japan to New South Wales, east to New Caledonia; type locality, Pondicherry, India. Known from a few to at least 100 m; occurs on coral reefs but also ranges over open bottom; juveniles may be found in estuaries and sometimes take refuge among the long spines of venomous sea urchins such as *Astropyga radiata* in the photograph.

HALFBARRED SNAPPER

Lutjanus semicinctus Quoy & Gaimard, 1824

Dorsal rays X,13; anal rays III,8; pectoral rays 16; lateral-line scales 47–49; scale rows on back oblique; gill rakers 6–7 + 8–12; canine teeth at front of jaw enlarged; teeth on vomer in a crescentic patch without a median posterior extension; a patch of small granular teeth on tongue; preopercular notch slight; interopercular knob absent; body depth 2.6–3.1 in standard length; caudal fin truncate to slightly emarginate; pale yellowish to reddish gray dorsally, shading to silvery white or pink ventrally, with 6 or 7 slender black bars that narrow as they pass ventrally, ending in adults about halfway down side; a black band from upper lip to eye; caudal fin yellow to light red with a huge black spot on base of fin and extending broadly onto caudal peduncle. Attains about 35 cm. Philippines, eastern Indonesia and northern Great Barrier Reef to New Caledonia, Fiji, and islands of Micronesia; described from specimens from Waigeo, Indonesia, and Rewak, Bismarck Archipelago. A coral-reef species usually seen as solitary individuals in 10–30 m.

Solomon Islands

Rinca, Indonesia

BROWNSTRIPE SNAPPER

Lutjanus vitta (Quoy & Gaimard, 1824)

Dorsal rays X,12–13; anal rays III,8–9; pectoral rays 15–16; lateral-line scales 49–51; scale rows on back oblique; gill rakers 6–7 + 9–12; teeth on vomer in a triangular to diamond-shaped patch with a median posterior extension; a patch of small granular teeth on tongue; preopercular notch and interopercular knob indistinct; body depth 2.6–2.9 in standard length; suborbital depth 4.2–7.0 in head length; caudal fin slightly emarginate; pinkish to yellowish gray dorsally, shading to silvery white ventrally with a very narrow dark yellowish brown stripe from eye to caudal peduncle, where it broadens to a yellow area dorsally on peduncle; body above lateral line with oblique, yellowish brown lines following scale rows; body below with horizontal, yellowish brown lines; fins yellow; juveniles with a broader and darker stripe on side of body that continues through eye to front of snout. Reported to a maximum length of about 40 cm. Seychelles and India to western Pacific from southern Japan to Great Barrier Reef, east to New Caledonia, Kapingamarangi Atoll in the Caroline Islands, and the Marshall Islands; type locality, Waigeo, Indonesia. Usually seen on reefs in small aggregations; known from depths of 10–72 m.

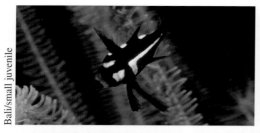
Bali/small juvenile

Banda Islands, Indonesia/subadult

New Britain

MIDNIGHT SNAPPER

Macolor macularis Fowler, 1931

Dorsal rays X,13–14 (usually 13); anal rays III,10; pectoral rays 17; lateral-line scales 50–55; scale rows on back parallel to lateral line; gill rakers 37–42 + 71–81; small conical teeth in jaws, larger anteriorly; teeth on vomer in a broad V-shaped patch; a deep notch in lower part of preopercle; body deep, the depth 2.2–2.4 in standard length; dorsal profile of head of juveniles nearly straight, of adults strongly convex; margins of soft portions of dorsal and anal fins smooth; dorsal fin of juveniles strongly elevated anteriorly and posteriorly, hence deeply notched in middle spinous portion; pelvic fins of juveniles extremely long (much longer than head); caudal fin slightly forked (rounded in small juveniles); body of adults dark gray-brown dorsally, shading to yellow on head and ventrally, with a vertical blue line on each scale except ventrally, where lines shorten to spots; iris yellow; juveniles complexly colored in black and white, changing with growth. Largest specimen, 60 cm. Maldive Islands to western Pacific from Ryukyu Islands to the Great Barrier Reef and New Caledonia, east to Fiji; only Palau and Mariana Islands in Micronesia; type locality, Luzon. Adults usually seen as individuals or in small aggregations off seaward reef escarpments from about 5 to 50 m.

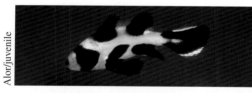
Alor/juvenile

Coral Sea/subadult

Banda Islands, Indonesia

BLACK-AND-WHITE SNAPPER

Macolor niger (Forsskål, 1775)

Dorsal rays X,13–15 (usually 14); anal rays III,10–11 (usually 11); pectoral rays 16–18; lateral-line scales 49–58; scale rows on back parallel to lateral line; gill rakers 26–38 + 60–71; small conical teeth in jaws, larger anteriorly; teeth on vomer in a broad V-shaped patch; a deep notch in lower part of preopercle; body deep, the depth 2.2–2.4 in standard length; dorsal profile of head of juveniles nearly straight, of adults strongly convex; margin of soft portions of dorsal and anal fins of adults ragged; dorsal fin of juveniles slightly elevated anteriorly and posteriorly, hence not deeply notched in middle spinous portion; pelvic fins of juveniles not longer than head; caudal fin slightly forked (rounded in small juveniles); body silvery gray, strongly blotched with blackish; snout and dorsal part of head with a fine dark gray and pale reticular pattern; juveniles complexly colored in black and white, the pattern changing with growth. Attains 60 cm. Red Sea (type locality) and east coast of Africa to the western Pacific from southern Japan to the Great Barrier Reef and New Caledonia, east to Samoa Islands and throughout Micronesia; usually observed in small aggregations on outer-reef drop-offs.

SMALLSCALE SNAPPER
Paracaesio sordida Abe & Shinohara, 1962

Dorsal rays X,9–10; anal rays III,8; pectoral rays 16–17; lateral-line scales 68–73; scale rows on back parallel to lateral line; no scales on dorsal or anal fins; gill rakers 5–11 + 19–22; mouth small and strongly oblique, the maxilla reaching slightly posterior to anterior edge of eye; jaws with an outer row of conical teeth and an inner band of villiform teeth; villiform teeth on vomer and palatines; body depth 2.5–2.7 in standard length; head small, 3.85–4.1 in standard length; dorsal profile of head strongly convex; snout very short, its length equal to or shorter than eye diameter; dorsal fin without a notch; caudal fin lunate; pectoral fins reaching to or beyond a vertical at origin of anal fin; centers of scales blue, the edges brown, particularly the upper and lower edges, thus imparting a fine blue and brown linear pattern to body; dorsal and caudal fins reddish brown, remaining fins gray. Reaches 35 cm. Known from the Red Sea to the Marquesas Islands and Pitcairn Islands, with scattered localities between: Oman, Maldive Islands, Sabah, southern Japan (type locality, Okinawa), New Caledonia, and American Samoa. Semipelagic, solitary or in small schools, from about 20 to 200 m.

Sabah

BLUE-AND-YELLOW SNAPPER
Paracaesio xanthura (Bleeker, 1869)

Dorsal rays X,10–11 (rarely 11); anal rays III,8–9 (rarely 9); pectoral rays 16; lateral-line scales 70–72; scale rows on back parallel to lateral line; no scales on dorsal or anal fins; gill rakers 9 + 18–20; mouth small and strongly oblique, the maxilla nearly or just reaching to below center of eye; jaws with an outer row of conical teeth and an inner band of villiform teeth; villiform teeth on vomer and palatines; body depth 2.5–2.9 in standard length; head small, 3.8–4.0 in standard length; dorsal profile of head strongly convex; eye large, about 3.5 in head length; snout very short, its length equal to or shorter than eye diameter; dorsal fin without a notch; caudal fin lunate; pectoral fins reaching a vertical at origin of anal fin; blue, shading to silvery ventrally on head and chest, with a very broad, bright yellow zone on posterior three-fourths of back, enclosing lateral line and continuing onto all of caudal fin; dorsal fin yellow; remaining fins translucent whitish. Attains 40 cm. Red Sea and east coast of Africa to Samoa

Ogasawara Islands

Islands; in the western Pacific from southern Japan to New South Wales, Lord Howe Island, Norfolk Island, and the Kermadec Islands; not reported from Micronesia; type locality, Madagascar. Known from depths of 20–200 m; feeds on zooplankton. *Paracaesio pedleyi* McCulloch & Waite is a synonym.

LEWIS' PINJALO
Pinjalo lewisi Randall, Allen & Anderson, 1987

Dorsal rays XII,13; anal rays III,8–9; pectoral rays 17–18; lateral-line scales 48–50; scale rows on back oblique, becoming horizontal on caudal peduncle; gill rakers 7–8 + 16–17; body depth 2.1–2.75 in standard length; second and third anal spines subequal, 2.7–3.2 in head length; caudal fin slightly emarginate, the caudal concavity 3.55–5.45 in head length; pectoral fins long, 2.5–3.05 in head length; pelvic fins short, 1.65–1.8 in head length; brownish red dorsally, shading to silvery pink ventrally; a large pale pink spot dorsally on caudal peduncle flanked by blotches of darker ground color; dorsal and caudal fins dark brownish red, the margins blackish. Largest specimen, 41 cm; probably attains about 50 cm. Oman and Persian Gulf to Indo-Malayan region, north to southern Japan and east to Fiji; type locality, Negros, Philippines. Usual depth range 40 to about 150 m, but the author observed a small aggregation in 30 m at Padang

Negros, Philippines

Bai, Bali. One other species in the genus, *Pinjalo pinjalo* (Bleeker). It is similar in color, but has oblique dark lines on about the dorsal half of the body from a spot on each scale, and 14 or 15 instead of 13 dorsal soft rays.

255

Kajoe Pangang, Indonesia/subadult

Papua New Guinea

Great Barrier Reef

SAILFIN SNAPPER
Symphorichthys spilurus (Günther, 1874)
Dorsal rays X,14–18; anal rays III,8–11; pectoral rays 16; lateral-line scales 53–59; gill rakers 4–6 + 14–15; front of jaws with small stout canines; side of jaws with nodular teeth; palate toothless, but pharyngeal dentition well developed; body deep, the depth 2.2–2.5 in standard length; dorsal profile of snout very steep and slightly concave, curving sharply on forehead to the slightly convex nape; dorsal profile of head of juveniles strongly sloping and straight; spines of dorsal and anal fins very low, the soft portions strongly elevated and pointed, the dorsal with one to several long filaments in juveniles and small adults; caudal fin slightly forked; yellow with numerous blue stripes (increasing in number with age) on head and body; a large ocellated black spot on dorsal half of caudal peduncle; a broad orange band across interorbital, and a narrower one from nape to posterior end of opercle; fins yellow; juveniles light yellowish gray with a broad midlateral white-edged black stripe. Reaches 60 cm. Western Pacific from the Ryukyu Islands to the Great Barrier Reef, Papua New Guinea, Vanuatu, and New Caledonia; only Palau (type locality) in Micronesia; usually seen over sand bottoms in the vicinity of reefs from 5 to 60 m, but not common at any locality. Feeds mainly on sand-dwelling mollusks and crustaceans. Generally solitary. Caught mainly with handlines or by trawling.

CHINAMANFISH
Symphorus nematophorus (Bleeker, 1860)
Dorsal rays X,15–16; anal rays III,9; pectoral rays 16–17; lateral-line scales 50–55; gill rakers 5 + 13; mouth large, the maxilla extending to below middle of eye; teeth in bands in jaws, the outer row enlarged; 4 strong canines at front of upper jaw; small teeth present on vomer and palatines; body depth 2.6–2.8 in standard length; suborbital depth great, about 2.6–2.7 in head length; soft portions of dorsal and anal fins elevated and pointed, the fourth to seventh or eighth rays produced as filaments in juveniles and subadults; caudal fin emarginate; brownish yellow to red with narrow blue stripes on body extending forward onto upper half of head; irregular, dark brown bars on body, some double or branching, and scattered small black spots, especially on head; fins mainly yellowish brown. Reported to 80 cm. Western Pacific to northern half of Australia, east to Vanuatu and New Caledonia; type locality, Sulawesi; a solitary species found on coral reefs from the shallows to at least 50 m; feeds mainly on fishes. Has caused ciguatera poisoning.

Scissortail Fusiliers, *Caesio caerulaurea*, Marshall Islands

FUSILIERS
(CAESIONIDAE)

Some authors, such as Nelson (1994), have classified the fusiliers as a subfamily of the Lutjanidae, but Carpenter (1987, 1988) revised the group and is followed here in giving it family status. These fishes have a continuous dorsal fin without a notch, with X-XV slender spines, the third or fourth longest, and 8–22 soft rays; anal fin III,9–13; pelvic fins I,5, their origin distinctly posterior to base of pectorals; caudal fin deeply forked; body fusiform; caudal peduncle slender; head small; snout short, its length equal to or less than orbit diameter; mouth small, terminal, oblique, and highly protrusible, the long median ascending process of the premaxilla a separate ossification; one or two slender bony processes present on side of premaxilla that slide medially to the maxilla;

teeth in jaws small to minute (absent in *Dipterygonotus*); teeth on vomer and palatines present or absent; opercle with a single flat spine; scales weakly ctenoid, 45–88 in lateral line; a supratemporal band of scales separated by a narrow naked zone from scales of rest of nape (this scale band not distinct in *Dipterygonotus*). Carpenter did not find the number of gill rakers of diagnostic value. Caesionids are diurnal, midwater, zooplankton-feeding fishes that are usually encountered in aggregations, generally over or in the vicinity of coral reefs. They do not take refuge in reefs by day, but depend on their swift swimming and elusive movements to escape predators. They come to cleaning stations on reefs and retire to the shelter of reefs at night, at which time their coloration changes, often with red predominating. The family is represented by four genera and 20 species, all in the Indo-Pacific region.

Bali, with *Labroides dimidiatus*

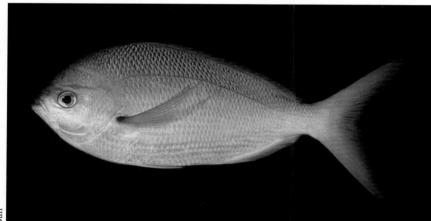

Bali

Great Barrier Reef (night)

SCISSORTAIL FUSILIER
Caesio caerulaurea Lacepède, 1801

Dorsal rays X,14–16; anal rays III,12–13; pectoral rays 19–22 (modally 21); lateral-line scales 57–65; supratemporal band of scales often interrupted middorsally; median fins scaled (true of other *Caesio*); a single lateral premaxillary process (also generic); body depth 3.0–4.2 in standard length; head length 2.8–3.6 in standard length; snout length 3.7–5.1 in head length; eye diameter 3.3–5.1 in head length; blue-green, shading to bluish white ventrally, with a yellow stripe nearly as broad as pupil and broadly bordered above and below by blue, its lower edge resting on lateral line for most of its length; lateral line narrowly blackish; caudal fin whitish with a broad black band in each lobe; base of pectoral fins white with a black triangular spot on upper half; axil of pectoral fins black. Largest examined, 29 cm; reported to 35 cm. Red Sea to South Africa and Madagascar, east to Samoa Islands and islands of Micronesia; in the western Pacific from the Ryukyu Islands and Ogasawara Islands to New South Wales and New Caledonia; type locality, Molucca Islands.

REDBELLY FUSILIER
Caesio cuning (Bloch, 1791)

Dorsal rays X,14–16; anal rays III,10–12; pectoral rays 17–20 (usually 18–19); lateral-line scales 45–50 (modally 49); predorsal scales usually 21–25; supratemporal band of scales confluent middorsally; spinous portion of dorsal fin with about its basal one-half covered by scales; body deep for the genus, the depth 2.2–3.1 in standard length; head length 2.7–3.4 in standard length; snout length 3.8–4.9 in head length; eye diameter 3.5–4.8 in head length; blue to bluegreen, yellow posteriorly to an oblique demarcation from beneath spinous portion of dorsal fin to lower base of caudal fin (yellow restricted to caudal peduncle and fin in some individuals); ventral part of head and body pinkish silver (tending to become red after death); a purplish blue streak over eye; caudal fin yellow; dorsal fin bluish anteriorly, yellow posteriorly; anal and paired fins white to pink. The largest of the fusiliers, reported to 50 cm. Ranges from Sri Lanka and Western Australia to the western Pacific from the Ryukyu Islands to New South Wales, east to Vanuatu and New Caledonia; type locality, East Indies. The most tolerant of murky water of all the caesionids, hence the one most often found in water of low visibility. One of the most important commercial species of the family. Because it often occurs over soft bottom, it is caught in trawls as well as drive-in nets, traps, and gill nets. Often misidentified as *Caesio erythrogaster* Cuvier, a synonym.

American Samoa

BLUE-AND-YELLOW FUSILIER
Caesio teres Seale, 1906
Dorsal rays X,14–16; anal rays III,12–13; pectoral rays 18–23 (modally 21); lateral-line scales 51–61 (modally 55); supratemporal band of scales interrupted middorsally by a narrow scaleless zone; body depth 2.7–4.2 in standard length; head length 2.6–3.6 in standard length; snout length 3.1–5.1 in head length; eye diameter 3.1–5.7 in head length; bright yellow on caudal fin, caudal peduncle, and body above an oblique demarcation from dorsal fin origin to ventral origin of peduncle; head and remainder of body bright blue, shading ventrally to silvery white; dorsal fin bluish proximally and yellow distally; remaining fins white, the axil and upper base of pectoral fins black. Attains at least 30 cm. East coast of Africa to Samoa Islands, Line Islands, and throughout Micronesia; in the western Pacific from the Ogasawara Islands to the Great Barrier Reef and New Caledonia; type locality, Solomon Islands. Bell & Colin (1985) observed mass spawning of this species in the Marshall Islands at or near full moon. *Caesio pulcherrimus* Smith & Smith is a synonym.

Marshall Islands (night)

MOTTLED FUSILIER
Dipterygonotus balteatus (Valenciennes in C & V, 1830)
Dorsal rays XII-XV,8–11; anal rays III,9–11; pectoral rays 16–19 (modally 18); lateral-line scales 68–80; median fins without scales; 2 lateral premaxillary processes; premaxilla without teeth; posterior end of maxilla tapered; body slender, the depth 4.4–5.7 in standard length; head length 3.3–4.0 in standard length; snout length 3.5–4.4 in head length; eye diameter 3.5–4.9 in head length; spines posterior to ninth short and connected only basally within groove on back; last dorsal spine less than half length of first dorsal soft ray; a narrow tan stripe from above eye to upper base of caudal fin; body dorsal of stripe dark gray-brown with 2 very irregular, longitudinal tan lines; body below stripe silvery; caudal fin unmarked; almost entirely reddish at night. Attains 12.5 cm. Indo-Malayan region west to Sri Lanka, Seychelles, and Gulf of Aden; south to Western Australia and Queensland, east to Solomon Islands and New Caledonia; type locality, Sri Lanka. An inshore pelagic species; often schools with clupeid fishes; rarely seen in clear coral-reef areas.

Sulawesi

259

SLENDER FUSILIER
Gymnocaesio gymnoptera (Bleeker, 1856)

Dorsal rays X-XI (rarely XI),14–16; anal rays III,11–13; pectoral rays 20–22; lateral-line scales 64–74 (modally 70); median fins without scales; 2 lateral premaxillary processes; no teeth on premaxilla or palatines; posterior end of maxilla tapered; body slender, the depth 3.3–6.0 (mean 5.1) in standard length; head length 3.0–4.3 in standard length; snout length 3.3–5.2 in head length; eye diameter 3.5–5.1 in head length; upper half of body light blue-green, the scale edges dark brown, lower half silvery to silvery pink; a narrow brownish yellow stripe following lateral line for about three-fifths its length, then continuing straight to base of caudal fin; a zigzag blackish line a scale row above and parallel to lateral line; caudal lobes broadly tipped with black. Maximum length about 18 cm. Known from Red Sea, Zanzibar, Seychelles, Maldive Islands, Sri Lanka, Indo-Malayan region (type locality, Ternate, Molucca Islands), and east through Solomon Islands and Vanuatu to Fiji. Forms schools in midwater, generally in the vicinity of coral reefs, sometimes with other caesionids.

TWO-STRIPE FUSILIER
Pterocaesio digramma (Bleeker, 1865)

Dorsal rays X,14–16; anal rays III,11–12; pectoral rays 20–23 (modally 21); lateral-line scales 66–76 (modally 72); median fins scaled (true of other *Pterocaesio*); 2 lateral premaxillary processes (also generic); body depth 3.5–4.1 in standard length; head length 2.9–3.7 in standard length; snout length 3.7–4.9 in head length; eye diameter 3.4–4.8 in head length; upper half of body bluish to greenish gray, the scale edges dark brown, the lower half silvery white to silvery pink; 2 very narrow yellow stripes, the first curving along back from top of head to dorsal edge of caudal peduncle, the second straight from upper edge of eye, passing under lateral line for three-fourths length of body, then crossing above lateral line to end at upper base of caudal fin; lateral line visible as a narrow dark line; caudal fin pale pink with a black spot at tip of each lobe sometimes edged anteriorly in deep pink; pectoral axil black. Attains 15 cm. Taiwan and Ogasawara Islands to Great Barrier Reef, Norfolk Island, and New Caledonia; also recorded from Western Australia; type locality, Ambon, Molucca Islands.

WIDEBAND FUSILIER
Pterocaesio lativittata Carpenter, 1987

Dorsal rays X,14–16; anal rays III,12–13 (rarely 13); pectoral rays 21–23; lateral-line scales 74–88; body elongate, the depth 4.1–5.3 in standard length; head length 3.1–3.7 in standard length; snout length 3.4–4.8 in head length; eye diameter 3.5–4.6 in head length; blue-green, the scales dorsally on body dark-edged, dull pink ventrally, with a yellow stripe that is broad anteriorly (including 2 scale rows above lateral line and 5 below), narrowing to 2 scale rows posteriorly on base of caudal fin above lateral line; tips of caudal lobes with a large black spot edged in red and preceded by a faint pale band; a large black spot in axil of pectoral fin but no black pigment on outer base of fin. Attains about 18 cm. Known to date only from the Chagos Archipelago, Maldive Islands, Cocos-Keeling Islands (type locality), Hermit Islands (Papua New Guinea), Palau, Line Islands (author's photograph at Kiritimati where observed in small aggregations), and Phoenix Islands (G. R. Allen, pers. comm.). Myers (1999) reported it in large schools in 28–40 m at Palau. *Pterocaesio chrysozona* (Cuvier) from the western Pacific to coast of East Africa and the Red Sea is similar; its yellow stripe is narrower, the upper edge along the anterior lateral line; it differs also in having 17–20 pectoral rays and 64–69 lateral-line scales.

MARR'S FUSILIER

Pterocaesio marri Schultz in Schultz et al., 1953

Dorsal rays X-XI,14–16; anal rays III,11–13; pectoral rays 22–24 (modally 23); lateral-line scales 68–76 (modally 73); body depth 3.4–4.6 in standard length; head length 3.0–3.7 in standard length; snout length 3.6–4.6 in head length; eye diameter 3.1–5.5 in head length; blue-green dorsally, the scale edges darker than centers, white ventrally (light red at night), with 2 narrow orange-yellow stripes, the uppermost from dorsally on nape, curving along back to end at rear base of dorsal fin; second stripe from upper end of gill opening, following lateral line to below rear part of dorsal fin, then crossing above and ending at upper base of caudal fin; both stripes progressively broader posteriorly; caudal fin white to light red, the lobe tips black; axil of pectoral fins black. Largest specimen, 31.5 cm. Known from east coast of Africa to the Marquesas Islands, Samoa Islands, and islands of Micronesia (type locality, Bikini Atoll). Carpenter (1987) showed that *Pterocaesio kohleri* Schultz is a synonym of *P. marri*.

BANANA FUSILIER

Pterocaesio pisang (Bleeker, 1853)

Dorsal rays X-XI,14–16; anal rays III,11–13; pectoral rays 18–20 (modally 19); lateral-line scales 63–71 (modally 66); body depth 3.6–4.8 in standard length; head length 3.0–3.5 in standard length; snout length 3.9–4.8 in head length; eye diameter 3.3–4.3 in head length; color variable, but usually grayish blue, the edges of scales dark brown, shading to light red ventrally, but may be almost entirely red; lateral line a conspicuous brown line; fins light red, the caudal-lobe tips with a deep red spot or a black spot edged in red; axil of pectoral fins black. Reported to 21 cm (largest examined, 17 cm). East coast of Africa to the Indo-Malayan region east to Pohnpei in the Caroline Islands, Kiribati (Gilbert Islands), and Fiji; in the western Pacific from the Ryukyu Islands south to New Caledonia; type locality, Ambon, Molucca Islands. An important food fish in the Philippines; caught mostly by drive-in nets, gill nets, and traps. Cabanban (1984) reported this species spawning year-around in the Philippines; its growth is rapid compared with that of other lutjanoid fishes. The species name *pisang* is taken from an Indonesian word for banana.

Pterocaesio marri, Marshall Islands (night)

Ogasawara Islands

Cebu, Philippines

Cebu, Philippines (night)

Marshall Islands

Cebu, Philippines

Flores, Indonesia (night)

NEON FUSILIER

Pterocaesio tile (Cuvier in C & V, 1830)

Dorsal rays XI-XII,19–22; anal rays III,13; pectoral rays 22–24 (modally 23); lateral-line scales 69–74 (modally 71); body depth 3.3–5.4 in standard length; head length 3.4–3.9 in standard length; snout length 3.7–4.4 in head length; eye diameter 2.9–4.9 in head length; a broad bright blue midlateral zone on body, narrowing as it passes to front of head, and narrowing posteriorly to end in midbase of caudal fin; a narrow black stripe at upper edge of blue zone following lateral line until posteriorly where the pored scales curve down to straight midlateral portion on caudal

Nil Desperandum Reef, Indonesia

peduncle; back above stripe dull green with black edges on scales; head and body below blue zone silvery pink to red; caudal fin whitish to pink with a black band in middle of each lobe, the upper band joining black stripe on body; a triangular black spot at upper base of pectoral fin, the axil black. Reaches 30 cm. Madagascar and Seychelles to the Line Islands and Pitcairn Islands; in the western Pacific from the Ryukyu Islands and Ogasawara Islands to the Great Barrier Reef and New Caledonia; type locality, Caroline Islands. Often the most common fusilier where it occurs.

THREELINE FUSILIER

Pterocaesio trilineata Carpenter, 1987

Dorsal rays X-XI (rarely XI),14–16; anal rays III,13; pectoral rays 19–21 (modally 20); lateral-line scales 62–75 (modally 66); body depth 4.0–4.9 in standard length; head length 3.1–3.5 in standard length; snout length 3.9–5.1 in head length; eye diameter 3.3–4.3 in head length; upper half of body light blue-green with 3 dark brown to yellow stripes, the upper stripe middorsal and narrow, the lower 2 broader than interspaces; lower stripe from upper edge of eye, following lateral line for most of its length, ending dorsally on caudal-fin base; lower half of body white to pink; caudal fin whitish, the lobes black-tipped; pectoral axil black. Largest specimen, 16 cm. Philippines south to Great Barrier Reef, New Caledonia, and Norfolk Island, east to Kiribati and Fiji (type locality). One Indian Ocean record from the Maldive Islands (Anderson et al., 1998).

Java

TRIPLETAIL FAMILY
(LOBOTIDAE)

The genus *Datnioides* has been included in the Lobot-idae, but Johnson in Moser et al. (1984) excluded it. The remaining single species of the family, *Lobotes surinamensis*, is discussed in the following account. Although resembling a serranid, it has sev-eral characters that distinguish it from that family: 2 weak opercular spines (nearly always 3 in serranids), 12 + 12 vertebrae (typically 10 + 14 in serranids), 6 instead of the usual 7 branchiostegal rays, and no supramaxilla.

TRIPLETAIL
Lobotes surinamensis (Bloch, 1790)
Dorsal rays XI-XII,15–16; anal rays III,11–12; pectoral rays 17; lateral-line scales 43–45; gill rakers 6–7 + 13–15; body depth 2.0–2.5 in standard length; head small; snout short; dorsal pro-file of head steep, slightly concave above eye; eye small; preo-percle serrate; no canine teeth, and no teeth on palate; rounded posterior lobes of dorsal and anal fins extending well beyond base of caudal fin (gives the impression, with the rounded cau-dal fin, of a 3-lobed tail); usually mottled silvery gray. Reports of lengths to 1 m seem exaggerated; world angling record, 19.2 kg, from South Africa. Circumglobal in tropical to warm tem-perate seas, but relatively few specimens known; Schmid & Randall (1997) summarized the distribution in a note reporting the first record for the Red Sea. Generally found in shallow brackish habitats, but may occur far offshore with drifting algae or flotsam; juveniles and subadults may lie on their side and match the color of material with which they are drifting from

Taiwan/juvenile

near black to yellow. The author would not have noticed a dark one in a marina in the Miami River in South Florida drifting on its side among blackened leaves had it not moved differently from the leaves.

Obliquebanded Thicklip, *Plectorhinchus lineatus*, Sipadan Island, Malaysia

GRUNTS
(HAEMULIDAE)

The grunts get their common name from the sounds they produce by grinding their pharyneal teeth together, the swimbladder acting as a resonating chamber. The family was long known as the Pomadasydae in the Indo-Pacific region and as the Haemulidae in the eastern Pacific and Atlantic; Haemulidae is the older name. In his review of western Indian Ocean species, Smith (1962b) used the invalid family name Gaterinidae. These fishes resemble snappers in general form and some characters such as the maxilla slipping under the edge of the preorbital when mouth is closed, no supramaxilla, no obvious spines on opercle, branchiostegal rays 7; ctenoid scales, and similar spine and soft-ray counts. They differ in having a small mouth that is often slightly inferior, small conical teeth in bands in jaws (teeth in outer row usually enlarged, but none approaching canine proportions); no teeth on vomer or palatines, but pharyngeal teeth well developed; preopercle serrate (serrae may be lost in large individuals); second anal spine longest and often much stronger than first and third spines; and enlarged pores on chin. Most grunts are nocturnal; they feed chiefly on benthic invertebrates, especially crustaceans. The family consists of 17 genera and about 150 species; it is divisible into three subfamilies; only the Haemulinae and Plectorhinchinae are represented at islands of the South Pacific. In Australia the fishes of the latter subfamily are called sweetlips; in South Africa rubberlips; the name used here is thicklips. Many undergo remarkable changes in color pattern with growth.

GRUNTS (HAEMULINAE)

SILVER GRUNT
Pomadasys argenteus (Forsskål, 1775)
Dorsal rays XII,14; anal rays III,7; pectoral rays 15–17; lateral-line scales 47–50; gill rakers 5–6 + 11–13; body depth 2.7–2.9 in standard length; head length 2.75–2.9 in standard length; dorsal profile of head intially straight, curving slightly on nape; tip of chin with a pair of sensory pores, followed by a large median pore; posterior margin and rounded corner of preopercle serrate; snout length 2.8–3.0 in head length; fourth dorsal spine usually longest, 1.7–1.8 in head length; penultimate dorsal spine about three-fourths length of last spine; caudal fin slightly emarginate; silvery with small dark brown spots on nape, upper three-fifths of body, and dorsal fin; juveniles with a large dark spot on opercle and blackish stripes that break into spots with

New Caledonia

growth. Reported to 52 cm. Red Sea (type locality) and Persian Gulf to the western Pacific from southern Japan and Taiwan to New Caledonia; illustrated specimen taken with gill net in mangrove area in less than 1 m.

THICKLIPS (PLECTORHINCHINAE)

Flores, Indonesia/small juvenile

Negros, Philippines/large juvenile

PAINTED THICKLIP
Diagramma pictum (Thunberg, 1792)
Dorsal rays IX-X (usually X),21–25; anal rays III,7; pectoral rays 16–18 (usually 17); lateral-line scales 57–74; gill rakers 5–9 + 13–17 (modally 6–7 + 14); body depth of adults 2.7–3.0 in standard length; head length of adults 3.2–3.6 in standard length; caudal peduncle slender and long, its length nearly as great as head length; chin with 6 pores and no median pit; outer row of teeth in jaws not enlarged; second dorsal spine longest, the first about one-third its length; outer margin of dorsal fin straight; caudal fin of juveniles slightly rounded, becoming truncate with age; small juveniles with 2 broad black stripes and black elevated anterior part of dorsal fin; more stripes added on body with growth; with further growth, stripes break into many spots that may be orange-yellow to brown; dorsal and caudal fins also with numerous brown spots; large adults may be entirely silvery gray, with or without large dark gray blotches of variable size. Reported to 90 cm (Smith, 1962b). Johnson et al. (2001) have divided this species into 5 subspecies; data here are for the subspecies *Diagramma pictum pictum*, which ranges from southern Japan (type locality) to the islands of the East Indies, southeast to the Solomon Islands, Vanuatu, and New Caledonia. *Diagramma pictum labiosum* occurs in Australia and southern Papua New Guinea.

New Caledonia

Great Barrier Reef

GIANT THICKLIP

Plectorhinchus albovittatus (Rüppell, 1838)

Dorsal rays XII-XIII (rarely XII),18–19 (usually 18); anal rays III,7–8; pectoral rays 17–18 (usually 17); lateral-line scales 55–60; gill rakers 8–9 + 19–21; body depth of adults 2.5–3.2 in standard length (depth decreasing with growth); chin with 6 pores and no median pit (true of other *Plectorhinchus*); lips greatly thickened, especially in adults; outer row of teeth in jaws slightly enlarged (also generic); third to fifth dorsal spines longest; dorsal fin notched between spinous and soft portions; caudal fin rounded in young, slightly emarginate in adults; small juveniles yellow to white with 2 broad black stripes on about upper two-thirds of body; stripes increasing to 4 with growth, disappearing with further growth; large adults gray with small pale spots and short irregular lines; a broad, diffuse, pale gray bar usually present from below spinous portion of dorsal fin to midabdomen; caudal fin with upper corner and lower margin broadly black; nearly anterior half of soft portion of dorsal fin black; remaining fins black. Largest species of the family, reaching at least 100 cm. Red Sea (type locality) and Madagascar to Fiji and the islands of Micronesia; Ryukyu Islands to the Great Barrier Reef and New Caledonia. Juveniles generally found in brackish habitats; adults occur on reefs and adjacent sand from depths of about 2 to 50 m. *Diagramma obscurum* (Günther) from Fiji, *D. giganteum* Günther from Pohnpei, and *Gaterin harrawayi* Smith from Mozambique are synonyms.

Sabah

HARLEQUIN THICKLIP

Plectorhinchus chaetodonoides Lacepède, 1801
Dorsal rays XI-XII (usually XII),18–20; anal
rays III,7–9; pectoral rays 17; lateral-line scales
58–62; gill rakers 10–11 + 26–28; body deep, the
depth 2.5–2.4 in standard length; third or fourth
dorsal spines longest; dorsal fin deeply notched
between spinous and soft portions; caudal fin of
juveniles deeply forked with broadly rounded
lobes, of adults slightly forked; juveniles brown
with 7 very large, dark-edged white spots or bars
on head and body; outer part of caudal fin white
with a large brown spot in each lobe; with growth
this pattern is obliterated by the formation of
small black spots on head, body, and fins; adults
pale green dorsally with numerous close-set black
spots on head, body, and median fins, abruptly
uniform light gray ventral to level of pectoral fins.
Attains about 50 cm. Mauritius and the Maldive
Islands to the western Caroline Islands and Tonga;
in the western Pacific from the Ryukyu Islands
to the Great Barrier Reef and New Caledonia;
no type locality given. Solitary on coral reefs.
Juveniles swim by rapid exaggerated undulating
movements, with the head usually oriented downward, but with little progression, suggesting that
they may be mimicking a toxic nudibranch or flat-
worm (Randall & Emery, 1971).

Palau/juvenile

Ambon, Indonesia/large juvenile

267

Kenya/subadult

Great Barrier Reef

YELLOWSPOTTED THICKLIP

Plectorhinchus flavomaculatus (Cuvier in C & V, 1830)

Dorsal rays XII-XIII (usually XIII),19–22; anal rays III,7; pectoral rays 17; lateral-line scales 56–59; gill rakers 11–14 + 17–20; body depth of adults 2.5–2.8 in standard length; fourth or fifth dorsal spines longest, about 2.6 in head length; margin of dorsal fin slightly concave; caudal fin of juveniles slightly rounded, of adults slightly emarginate; small juveniles with 8 orange-yellow stripes alternating with slightly narrower blue stripes on head and body, the yellow stripes on body breaking into spots with growth; dorsal and caudal fins with orange-yellow spots; lower edge of caudal fin broadly dusky; yellow spots relatively smaller and more numerous with further growth; yellow stripes on head only partially broken into spots; spots on body of big adults largely lost. Reaches 60 cm. Red Sea (type locality) and east coast of Africa to western Pacific from southern Japan to New South Wales and New Caledonia. Adults generally on protected reefs, juveniles in seagrass beds or algal flats. Also called the Lemon Thicklip.

Guam/juvenile

Ambon, Indonesia/subadult

Great Barrier Reef

GIBBOUS THICKLIP

Plectorhinchus gibbosus (Lacepède, 1802)

Dorsal rays XIV,15–16; anal rays III,7; pectoral rays 17; lateral-line scales 50–55; gill rakers 8–10 + 18–20; body depth of adults 2.1–2.7 in standard length (more elongate with growth); lips extremely thick in adults; fourth or fifth dorsal spines longest, 1.7–2.0 in head length (relatively longer in juveniles); a deep notch in dorsal fin between spinous and soft portions; spinous portion of dorsal fin of juveniles nearly twice as high as soft portion, about equal in height in large adults; caudal fin rounded in juveniles, slightly rounded to truncate in adults; dark gray, the centers of scales paler than edges; opercular membrane and a narrow zone adjacent to posterior edge of preopercle black; juveniles brown; unscaled part of caudal fin transparent; base of caudal fin and outer part of dorsal, anal, and pelvic fins broadly black. Reaches 70 cm. Red Sea to South Africa, east to Mariana, Caroline, and Samoa Islands; in the western Pacific from the Ryukyu Islands to New South Wales, Norfolk Island, and New Caledonia; no type locality given. Generally found in silty reef areas, the young penetrating estuarine habitats; small juveniles reported to float on their side at the surface, where they resemble drifting leaves. *Plectorhinchus nigrus* (Cuvier) is a synonym.

Taiwan/juvenile

Alor, Indonesia/subadult

Great Barrier Reef

LESSON'S THICKLIP
Plectorhinchus lessonii (Cuvier in C & V, 1830)
Dorsal rays XII-XIII (usually XII),18–21 (modally 20); anal rays III,7–8; pectoral rays 16–18 (usually 17); lateral-line scales 53–56; gill rakers 5–7 + 14–17; body depth 2.5–2.8 in standard length; dorsal profile of snout steep, forming an angle of about 60°, and nearly straight to above eye; profile of rest of head strongly convex; third to fifth dorsal spines longest; outer margin of dorsal fin slightly concave; caudal fin rounded in juveniles, slightly rounded to truncate in adults; juveniles with 3 very broad, dark brown stripes, often with red edges, separated by narrow, pale yellow stripes; first dark stripe extending into soft portion of

dorsal fin, the second into middle of caudal fin, and the third into anal fin; with growth, an additional dark stripe added dorsally and one ventrally; adults pale gray with 5 black stripes on body, the lowermost above base of pectoral fin; median fins yellow with black spots. Reaches 40 cm. Western Pacific from Ryukyu Islands and Ogasawara Islands to Great Barrier Reef and New Caledonia; type locality, Waigeo, Indonesia. A solitary coral-reef species. Some authors have used the name *Plectorhinchus diagramma* (Linnaeus) for this species; however, the fin-ray counts of D XI,15 and P 13 given by Linnaeus do not fit any species of *Plectorhinchus*, and no type specimen is extant.

Palau/subadult

Great Barrier Reef

OBLIQUEBANDED THICKLIP
Plectorhinchus lineatus (Linnaeus, 1758)
Dorsal rays XIII (rarely XII),18–20 (modally 19); anal rays III,7; pectoral rays 16–18 (usually 17); lateral-line scales 53–58; gill rakers 7–9 + 18–21; body depth 2.6–2.9 in standard length; third to fifth dorsal spines longest; outer margin of dorsal fin slightly concave; caudal fin rounded in juveniles, truncate in adults; very small juveniles with 2 black stripes, the number of stripes increasing with growth to as many as 10; at all these stages 1 stripe passes to middle of eye; those stripes continuing onto snout angle downward, thus forming a V if meeting stripe of

other side; median fins yellow, the black stripes breaking into spots with growth; with further growth, stripes disappear from about lower half of body; in final stage, black stripes more numerous on back and strongly oblique; a large red spot at upper base of pectoral fins. Reported to 60 cm (largest collected by the author, 49.5 cm, 1.64 kg). Western Pacific from Ryukyu Islands and Ogasawara Islands to the Great Barrier Reef and New Caledonia; no type locality. A coral-reef species, often seen in small groups in the shelter of reef by day; the same fish can be seen in the same small area months later. *Plectorhinchus goldmanni* (Bleeker) is a synonym.

Coral Sea

Sulawesi/small juvenile

Sumilon Island, Philippines/juvenile

Banda Islands, Indonesia/subadult

SPOTTED THICKLIP

Plectorhinchus picus (Cuvier in C & V, 1830)

Dorsal rays XII-XIV,18–20; anal rays III,7–8; pectoral rays 17–18; lateral-line scales 70–75; gill rakers 8–10 + 23–25; body depth 2.7–3.1 in standard length; third or fourth dorsal spines longest; outer margin of dorsal fin moderately concave; caudal fin rounded in juveniles, slightly emarginate in adults; juveniles of about 10 cm black, abruptly white ventrally, with white snout, 2 large white areas dorsally, and white and black caudal peduncle; with growth, black spots gradually replace this pattern; large adults greenish white on about upper two-thirds of head and body with numerous small black spots, uniform gray on lower one-third; small black spots in median fins; paired fins dark gray. Reaches about 60 cm. Mauritius and Seychelles to Rapa, Society Islands (type locality, Tahiti), and throughout Micronesia; in the western Pacific from southern Japan to New South Wales, Lord Howe Island, and New Caledonia; occurs on coral reefs, where it tends to hide in caves or beneath ledges by day; juveniles constantly in motion with strongly sinuous swimming, but progressing little.

270

ORIENTAL THICKLIP

Plectorhinchus vittatus (Linnaeus, 1758)

Dorsal rays XII-XIII (usually XIII),17–19 (modally 18); anal rays III,7–8; pectoral rays 17–18 (usually 18); lateral-line scales 57–65; gill rakers 9–11 + 19–24; body depth 2.6–2.9 in standard length; third or fourth dorsal spines longest; outer margin of dorsal fin moderately concave; caudal fin rounded in juveniles, truncate in adults; color of juveniles of about 10 cm similar to that described for *P. picus*, but white areas edged in orange or yellow; with growth, white areas complexly invade black, eventually ending in adults with 7 to 11 black stripes, the upper and lower narrow; front of head yellow with stripes passing horizontally across; no stripes on head to or through middle of eye; fins yellow; median fins initially with black stripes, most of which break into spots with growth. Attains 60 cm. Mozambique and islands of western Indian Ocean to Samoa Islands and Micronesia except the Marshall Islands; in the western Pacific from the Ryukyu Islands to the Solomon Islands; no type locality. Shelters on coral reefs by day, the juveniles usually solitary, the adults occasionally in small groups. Often identified as *Plectorhinchus orientalis* (Bloch), but Randall & Johnson (2000) showed that *P. vittatus* is the valid earlier name for this species.

Diurnal aggregation of Goldlined Emperors, *Gnathodentex aureolineatus,* Coral Sea

EMPERORS
(LETHRINIDAE)

The fishes of this family are represented by 39 species in 6 genera (preliminary revision by Carpenter & Allen, 1989); all but one Atlantic species of *Lethrinus* occur in the Indo-Pacific region. The lethrinids share the following family characters: dorsal fin with X spines and 9 or 10 soft rays; anal fin III,8–10; pectoral rays 13–15; pelvic fins I,5, with an auxiliary scale, scales finely ctenoid; no scales on fins except base of caudal fin; opercle with a single flat spine; vertebrae 10 + 14; supraneural bones 3; branchiostegal rays 6; gill rakers knob-like and few in number; mouth terminal, small to moderate, and protrusible; maxilla slipping beneath suborbital when mouth closed; no supramaxilla; front of jaws with an outer row of small to moderate canine teeth, and an inner band of small villiform teeth that narrows as it passes posteriorly; outer row of teeth on side of jaws either continuing progressively smaller posteriorly or replaced by nodular to molariform teeth; no teeth on vomer or palatines. Emperors are bottom-feeding fishes usually associated with coral reefs, rocky substrata, or adjacent habitats. The young of several species are found in seagrass beds or algal flats, and a few species may be seen there as adults. Only one species, *Wattsia mossambica,* occurs at greater than usual scuba-diving depths. All lethrinids are carnivorous; their prey varies from hard-shelled invertebrates for those species with molariform teeth to fishes for those of the genus *Lethrinus* with strong canine teeth. The species of *Lethrinus* are known for their ability to instantly change to a disruptive color pattern of irregular dark bars and blotches (see figures for *L. obsoletus*). The larger species of *Lethrinus* that feed in part on fishes may cause ciguatera poisoning when eaten.

GOLDLINED EMPEROR
Gnathodentex aureolineatus (Lacepède, 1802)

Dorsal rays X,10; anal rays III,8–9 (usually 9); pectoral rays 15; lateral-line scales 68–77; 5 scale rows above lateral line to base of middle dorsal spines; no scales in axil of pectoral fins; maxilla with a longitudinal serrate ridge; an outer row of conical teeth in jaws, and an inner band of villiform teeth that narrows posteriorly; 2 pairs of conical teeth at front of upper jaw and 3 at front of lower jaw of canine proportions; body depth 2.5–2.8 in standard length; snout shorter than eye and pointed; caudal fin forked; body above lateral line dark brown with a pale green spot on each scale above lateral line, this pattern interrupted by a yellow spot nearly as large as eye below rear base of dorsal fin; body below lateral line silvery with a broad, brown-edged, yellow stripe from behind upper end of gill opening to yellow spot on back, and 4 narrower stripes below that vary from brown to yellow; margins of dorsal and anal fins red. Reaches 30 cm. East coast of Africa to Line Islands and Pitcairn Islands; southern Japan to New South Wales, Norfolk Island, and New Caledonia; no type locality given. Nocturnal; resides in reefs by day, often in compact aggregations; feeds mainly on small benthic invertebrates. Only one species in the genus.

Line Islands

Coral Sea

SPECKLED EMPEROR
Gymnocranius euanus (Günther, 1879)

Dorsal rays X,10; anal rays III,10; pectoral rays 14; lateral-line scales 48–49; 4.5 scale rows between lateral line and base of middle dorsal spines; no scales on inner base of pectoral fins; molariform teeth on side of jaws; body depth 2.4–2.5 in standard length; eye large but less than interorbital width; caudal fin forked, the posterior edge of each lobe rounded; light silvery gray with scattered small black spots (at most covering a single scale), mainly on anterior half of body; head uniform light purplish gray. Attains about 45 cm. Southern Japan to Great Barrier Reef, Lord Howe Island, Norfolk Island, and New Caledonia, east to Mariana Islands, Caroline Islands, and Tonga (type locality, Eua); usually seen over sand and rubble bottoms near coral reefs at depths of 15–50 m, but recorded to 100 m; reported to feed mainly on benthic mollusks. *Gymnocranius affinis* (Whitley) and *G. japonicus* Akazaki are synonyms. Also known as the Japanese Large-eye Bream.

Seychelles/subadult

Maldive Islands

BLUELINED EMPEROR

Gymnocranius grandoculis (Valenciennes in C & V, 1830)
Dorsal rays X,10; anal rays III,10; pectoral rays 14; lateral-line scales 48–49; 5.5 rows of scales between lateral line and base of middle dorsal spines; no scales in axil of pectoral fins; no molariform teeth on side of jaws; body depth 2.4–2.5 in standard length; caudal fin forked; light silver gray; scales below lateral line with a silvery spot in center, resulting in a faint linear pattern; cheek with undulating, often broken, blue lines; dark bar under eye faint or absent; anterior half of head may be brown; a narrow dark bar across base of pectoral fins; juveniles silvery with dark brown bars and oblique bands on body, some complete and some short; a dark brown bar through eye. Reaches about 60 cm (reports of 80 cm may be in error). Occurs throughout the Indo-Pacific region except the Persian Gulf, Gulf of Oman, and Hawaiian Islands; type locality, Seychelles. Known from 10 to 100 m; often taken in trawls. *Gymnocranius rivulatus* (Rüppell), *G. lethrinoides* (Bleeker), and *G. robinsoni* (Gilchrist & Thompson) are synonyms.

Great Barrier Reef

Great Barrier Reef

ATKINSON'S EMPEROR

Lethrinus atkinsoni Seale, 1910
Dorsal rays X,9; anal rays III,8; pectoral rays 13; lateral-line scales 46–47; 4.5 rows of scales between lateral line and base of middle dorsal spines; 4–8 scales in supratemporal patch; no scales on cheek (true of other *Lethrinus*); small scales present in axil of pectoral fins; nodular or molariform teeth on side of jaws; body depth 2.3–2.6 in standard length; snout length varying from about 2.3 in head length of juveniles to 1.9 in adults; snout profile nearly straight, forming an angle of about 50° to horizontal axis of body; caudal fin slightly forked; body silvery bluish gray to silvery yellowish gray, the scale edges dorsally on body dark gray to black; one color phase with a broad midlateral yellow stripe on body that may expand dorsally on posterior part of body; head gray to gray-brown; caudal fin yellowish to yellow. Attains about 45 cm. Ryukyu Islands south to Cocos-Keeling Islands, Western Australia, Queensland, and Lord Howe Island, east to New Caledonia, Rarotonga (M. P. Francis, pers. comm.), and Tuamotu Archipelago (Carpenter & Allen, 1989); only Palau and Mariana Islands in Micronesia; type locality, Balabac Island, Philippines. Found on coral reefs, sandy areas, and seagrass beds, generally in less than 30 m; reported to feed on crustaceans, mollusks, and fishes. Also known as the Pacific Yellowtail Emperor.

Maldive Islands

ORANGEFIN EMPEROR

Lethrinus erythracanthus Valenciennes in C & V, 1830

Dorsal rays X,9; anal rays III,8; pectoral rays 13; lateral-line scales 47–48; 4.5 rows of scales between lateral line and base of middle dorsal spines; 5–7 scales in supratemporal patch; small scales present in axil of pectoral fins; conical teeth on side of jaws; body depth 2.5–2.7 in standard length; snout length from 2.3 in head length of juveniles to 1.8 in adults, its profile forming an angle of about 45° to horizontal axis of body; caudal fin slightly forked; body of adults gray-brown with black edges on scales; a broad, indistinct, pale yellowish to whitish zone on side of body passing from below dorsal fin beneath pectoral fin to abdomen, the scale edges in this zone blackish; head gray; fins varying from yellow to orange or red; juveniles yellowish to bronze with a blue spot on each scale, the blue spots joined to form an irregular line on every other row of scales below lateral line; pelvic fins white; subadults with vertical rows of whitish blotches. Reaches 70 cm. East coast of Africa to the Tuamotu Archipelago and islands of Micronesia (type locality, Luganor = Lukanor, Caroline Islands); Ryukyu Islands to the northern Great

Papua New Guinea/subadult

Barrier Reef; a coral-reef species, especially of outer-reef areas; reported to depths of 120 m. Randall (1980a) collected 13 adults in the Marshall Islands for food-habit study; 8 had food in the alimentary tract consisting primarily of sea urchins (including *Echinometra*), followed by mollusks (only 2 species of *Cypraea* identified), crinoids, and starfish. *Lethrinus kallopterus* Bleeker is a synonym.

LONGSPINE EMPEROR

Lethrinus genivittatus Valenciennes in C & V, 1830

Dorsal rays X,9; anal rays III,8; pectoral rays 13; lateral-line scales 46–47; 4.5 rows of scales between lateral line and base of middle dorsal spines; 5–8 scales in supra-temporal patch; third pair of canine teeth at front of lower jaw flaring laterally; small scales usually present in axil of pectoral fins; conical teeth on side of jaws; body moderately slender, the depth 2.7–3.2 in standard length; snout short, 2.2–2.5 in head length; its profile forming an angle of about 40° to horizontal axis of body; second dorsal spine of adults distinctly longer than other spines, 1.3–1.8 in head length; caudal fin slightly forked; pale gray with a large blackish blotch, varying from roundish to nearly square, below fourth and fifth dorsal spines, its upper edge on lateral line; smaller indistinct blackish blotches on body in about 10 vertical rows; head light brown to tan. Maximum length about 25 cm. Southern Japan south to New South Wales and to Perth in Western Aus-

Negros, Philippines

tralia, east to New Caledonia and Caroline Islands; probable type locality, Indonesia. A shallow-water species of seagrass beds, sand flats, and mangrove swamps. *Lethrinus nematacanthus* Bleeker is a synonym.

Kenya/juvenile

Papua New Guinea

New Caledonia

BLACKSPOT EMPEROR
Lethrinus harak (Forsskål, 1775)
Dorsal rays X,9; anal rays III,8; pectoral rays 13; lateral-line scales 46–47; 4.5–5.5 (usually 5.5) rows of scales between lateral line and base of middle dorsal spines; 4–7 scales in supratemporal patch; small scales present in axil of pectoral fins; nodular or molariform teeth on side of jaws; body depth 2.6–2.9 in standard length; snout varying from 2.4 in head length of juveniles to 1.9 in adults, its profile forming an angle of about 45–50° to horizontal axis of body; caudal fin slightly forked; silvery greenish gray, the scale edges brown; scales below lateral line with a round silvery spot; a large horizontally elongate black spot, usually broadly edged with dull yellow, on side of body between tip of pectoral fin and lateral line; posterior margin of caudal fin red. Attains about 45 cm. Red Sea (type locality) and east coast of Africa to Samoa Islands and all of Micronesia; Ryukyu Islands to the Great Barrier Reef and New Caledonia; occurs mainly in shallow, protected habitats such as seagrass beds, mangrove sloughs, and sand flats; rarely found on well-developed coral reefs; usually solitary.

GRASS EMPEROR
Lethrinus laticaudus Alleyne & Macleay, 1877
Dorsal rays X,9; anal rays III,8; pectoral rays 13; lateral-line scales 46–48; 4.5 rows of scales between lateral line and base of middle dorsal spines; 5–9 scales in supratemporal patch; small scales present in axil of pectoral fins; teeth conical on side of jaws; body relatively deep, the depth 2.2–2.4 in standard length; snout length 1.8–2.1 in head length; its dorsal profile slightly concave and forming an angle of about 45° to horizontal axis of body; caudal fin slightly forked; silvery gray, the edges of the scales blackish, and base of many scales on body with a vertically elongate, dark gray to black spot; head gray, often with short blue lines extending anteriorly and posteriorly from eye, and some blue dots on cheek; median fins yellowish; basal one-third of upper margin of pectoral fin blue. Largest reported, 56 cm. Southern Indonesia and northern half of Australia east to the Solomon Islands and New Caledonia; type locality, Percy Island, Queensland. Juveniles inhabit seagrass beds; adults found mainly on coral reefs. *Lethrinus fletus* Whitley is a synonym.

REDSPOT EMPEROR
Lethrinus lentjan (Lacepède, 1802)
Dorsal rays X,9; anal rays III,8; pectoral rays 13; lateral-line scales 46–47; 5.5 rows of scales between lateral line and base of middle dorsal spines; 4–9 scales in supratemporal patch; small scales usually present in axil of pectoral fins; teeth on side of jaws nodular, molariform, or molariform with a small tubercle on top; body depth 2.6–3.0 in standard length; snout varying from about 2.3 in head length of juveniles to 1.8 in adults; dorsal profile of head to above eye straight, forming an angle of about 35–40° to horizontal axis of body; caudal fin slightly forked; silvery gray, the edges of scales dorsally on body dark gray; head gray; a vertically elongate red spot posteriorly on opercle; upper base of pectoral fin often with a red spot. Reported to 50 cm; none over 30 cm observed by the author. Red Sea and east coast of Africa to Tonga and the Caroline Islands; Ryukyu Islands to the Great Barrier Reef and New Caledonia;

Underwater World, Singapore

probable type locality, Java. Juveniles mainly in seagrass beds and mangrove areas, often in small aggregations; adults usually solitary in deeper water. Crustaceans and mollusks are the principal prey. Also known as the Pink-eared Emperor.

TRUMPET EMPEROR

Lethrinus miniatus (Forster, 1801)

Dorsal rays X,9; anal rays III,8; pectoral rays 13; lateral-line scales 47–48; 4.5 rows of scales between lateral line and base of middle dorsal spines; 4–6 scales in supratemporal patch; small scales usually present in axil of pectoral fins; teeth on side of jaws conical; body depth 2.4–2.8 in standard length; snout moderately long, 1.65–2.0 in head length; dorsal profile of snout slightly concave, forming an angle of about 35–40° to horizontal axis of body; caudal fin slightly forked, the lobe tips rounded; silvery blue-green, the basal half of scales black on about upper half of body; alternate color phase with 10 brown bars on body, mostly broader than pale interspaces; head gray, sometimes with red markings around eye and in corner of mouth; a bright red spot in axil and base of pectoral fins; membranes of median fins reddish, the spinous membranes of dorsal fin often mostly bright red. Reported to attain 90 cm. Western Australia to southern Great Barrier Reef, Lord Howe Island, Norfolk Island, Coral Sea, and New Caledonia (type locality); a second population in the Ryukyu Islands. Known from less than 10 to 250 m. Resides in coral reefs by day and forages over adjacent habitats at night; feeds mainly on crabs, sea urchins, mollusks, and fishes. Not marketed in some areas for fear of ciguatera. *Lethrinus chrysostomus* Richardson and *L. amamianus* Akazaki are synonyms.

Great Barrier Reef

Coral Sea

Bahrain/subadult

Lord Howe Island

SPANGLED EMPEROR

Lethrinus nebulosus (Forsskål, 1775)

Dorsal rays X,9; anal rays III,8; pectoral rays 13; lateral-line scales 46–48; 5.5 rows of scales between lateral line and base of middle dorsal spines; 5–9 scales in supratemporal patch; small scales present in axil of pectoral fins; teeth on side of jaws conical; body depth 2.5–2.8 in standard length; snout length from 2.3 in head length of juveniles to 1.7 in adults; dorsal profile of head of adults to above eye slightly concave, forming an angle of about 40° to horizontal axis of body; caudal fin slightly forked; body greenish gray dorsally, silvery gray below, each scale with both a black and a pale blue or white spot (less evident ventrally); snout metallic tan, often with faint blue markings; a silvery white to blue spot at origin of lateral line; basal two-fifths of upper edge of pectoral fin bright blue; fins yellowish; small white spots on scales of juveniles tend to form short horizontal rows. Reported to 80 cm, but rarely more than 50 cm. Red Sea (type locality) and east coast of Africa to Samoa Islands; southern Japan to New South Wales, and Lord Howe Island; the most important commercial shore fish in New Caledonia. Juveniles occur in schools in sheltered inshore areas such as seagrass beds. Adults are found in a variety of habitats, sometimes in small groups, to depths of at least 75 m. Feeds chiefly on echinoderms, mollusks, and crustaceans, occasionally on polychaete worms and fishes. Carpenter in Carpenter & Allen (1989) listed the 19 synonyms.

New Britain/adult at rest

New Britain/same fish a few seconds later

Maldive Islands/juvenile

ORANGESTRIPE EMPEROR

Lethrinus obsoletus (Forsskål, 1775)

Dorsal rays X,9; anal rays III,8; pectoral rays 13; lateral-line scales 45–48; 5.5 rows of scales between lateral line and base of middle dorsal spines; 5–7 scales in supratemporal patch; small scales present in axil of pectoral fins; outer surface of maxilla with a small but distinct knob; teeth on side of jaws conical or nodular; body depth 2.6–2.9 in standard length; snout length varying from about 2.3 in head length of juveniles to 1.7 in adults; dorsal profile of head of adults to above eye straight to slightly concave, forming an angle of about 45° to horizontal axis of body; caudal fin slightly forked medially, the posterior lobe margins rounded; light greenish gray to tan dorsally, the edges of scales dark brown, shading to nearly white ventrally; a broad orange-yellow stripe on lower side at level of pectoral-fin base, often with 2 less distinct orange-yellow stripes above and 1 below; juveniles with 4 narrow orange stripes on body below lateral line, with a series of whitish dashes between each pair of stripes, the pattern often overlaid with brown blotches, the largest between lateral line and basal one-third of pectoral fin. The first adult figure here shows a fish at rest near the bottom;

the second figure is the same fish seconds later as it moved off the bottom. Reported to 60 cm, but rarely more than 35 cm. Red Sea (type locality) and east coast of Africa to Tonga, Samoa Islands, and throughout Micronesia; in the western Pacific from southern Japan to the Great Barrier Reef and New Caledonia; occurs singly or in small groups on coral reefs and adjacent habitats by day. One from the Marshall Islands with food in the gut contained the remains of heart urchin, pelecypod, crab, shrimp, and gastropod. Often identified as *Lethrinus ramak* (Forsskål), but Smith (1959b) noted that Forsskål listed this as the Arabic name.

Maldive Islands

LONGFACE EMPEROR

Lethrinus olivaceus Valenciennes in C & V, 1830

Dorsal rays X,9; anal rays III,8; pectoral rays 13; lateral-line scales 45–48; 5.5 rows of scales between lateral line and base of middle dorsal spines; usually 7–9 scales in supratemporal patch; no small scales in axil of pectoral fins; teeth on side of jaws conical; body elongate, the depth 3.0–3.4 in standard length; snout long, its length in adults 1.5–1.8 in head length; dorsal profile of

snout of adults slightly concave, forming an angle of about 30° to horizontal axis of body; caudal fin slightly forked; color usually greenish gray, the edges of scales narrowly dark, paler ventrally; capable of quickly assuming a dark reticular pattern (as when coming to rest on the bottom). Reported to attain 100 cm. Red Sea and east coast of Africa to Pitcairn Islands and islands of Micronesia; Ryukyu Islands to the Great Barrier Reef and

New Caledonia; a large solitary species that forages widely over coral reefs and adjacent habitats; known from depths of less than 10 to 185 m; the food habits of 8 of 14 adult specimens from the Marshall Islands with food in their stomachs were reported by Randall (1980a) (as *Lethrinus miniatus*): 3 had eaten fishes, including *Lethrinus* sp., and the rest contained crustaceans (stomatopods, crabs, alpheid shrimps). Randall & Wheeler (1991) showed that the species that most recent authors had identified as *L. miniatus* is *L. olivaceus*. The true *miniatus* is the more colorful species from the Southwest Pacific described on p. 277.

New Caledonia

Redang, Malaysia

DRAB EMPEROR

Lethrinus ravus Carpenter & Randall, 2003

Dorsal rays X,9; anal rays III,8; pectoral rays 13; lateral-line scales 48–49; 4.5 rows of scales between lateral line and base of middle dorsal spines; 6–8 scales in supratemporal patch; no small scales in axil of pectoral fins; teeth on side of jaws conical; body depth 2.7–2.9 in standard length; snout length in adults about 1.9 in head length; dorsal profile of head smoothly convex without a bump before eye; profile of snout nearly straight, forming an angle of about 40° to horizontal axis of body; caudal fin emarginate; body and postorbital head light brown, shading to white ventrally, with scattered irregular dark brown blotches, those above lateral line tending to form narrow bars; occasional scales on upper half of body with a small black vertical mark, a few in humeral region largest; snout purplish gray; fins unmarked. Attains at least 32 cm. Currently known from the Ryukyu Islands, Philippines, northwestern and northeastern Australia, New Caledonia (type locality), and Loyalty Islands. The illustrated specimen was collected by the author at Kindka Reef on the northeast coast of New Caledonia in 35 m.

SPOTCHEEK EMPEROR

Lethrinus rubrioperculatus Sato, 1978

Dorsal rays X,9; anal rays III,8; pectoral rays 13; lateral-line scales 47–49; 4.5 rows of scales between lateral line and base of middle dorsal spines; usually 7–10 scales in supratemporal patch; a broad naked area posteriorly on opercle just below level of eye; no small scales in axil of pectoral fins; teeth on side of jaws conical; body elongate, the depth 3.0–3.4 in standard length; snout length of adults about 1.8–2.0 in head length; dorsal profile of snout of adults slightly concave, forming an angle of about 40° to horizontal axis of body; a slight convexity in profile before eye; caudal fin deeply emarginate; light gray to light greenish gray, the scale edges darker; head uniform gray; a light red spot posteriorly on opercle at front of above-mentioned naked area; edges of lips at corner of mouth light red; may show a reticular pattern of blackish blotches on body. Maximum length reported, 50 cm. East coast of Africa to Marquesas Islands and Micronesia except the Marshall Islands; southern Japan

SLENDER EMPEROR

Lethrinus variegatus Valenciennes in C & V, 1830

Dorsal rays X,9; anal rays III,8; pectoral rays 13; lateral-line scales 45–47; 4.5 rows of scales between lateral line and base of middle dorsal spines; usually 4–7 scales in supratemporal patch; no small scales in axil of pectoral fins; teeth on side of jaws conical; body very elongate, the depth 3.4–3.9 in standard length; snout short, the length in adults 2.4–2.8 in head length; eye very large, nearly equal to snout length; dorsal profile of head straight to very slightly convex to eye, then angling slightly and continuing nearly straight on nape; snout forming an angle of about 35° to horizontal axis of body; caudal fin forked; light greenish to yellowish brown dorsally, shading to near white ventrally; scales on ventral half of body with a light brown to gray spot, resulting in a linear pattern; upper half of body sometimes with 2 rows of indistinct dark blotches; a dark stripe sometimes present under lateral line. Maximum length about 20 cm. Red Sea (type locality) and east coast of Africa to western Pacific from Ryukyu Islands to the Great Barrier Reef and New Caledonia; only Palau in Micronesia; usually found in seagrass beds, generally in less than 20 m.

Mauritius

(type locality, Okinawa) to the Great Barrier Reef and New Caledonia; not known from many intermediate localities, probably because it was regarded as the large adult of *L. variegatus* (as explained by Carpenter in Carpenter & Allen, 1989).

YELLOWLIP EMPEROR

Lethrinus xanthochilus Klunzinger, 1870

Dorsal rays X,9; anal rays III,8; pectoral rays 13; lateral-line scales 45–47; 4.5 rows of scales between lateral line and base of middle dorsal spines; usually 4–7 scales in supratemporal patch; no small scales in axil of pectoral fins; teeth on side of jaws conical; body moderately elongate, the depth 3.1–3.5 in standard length; snout length in adults 1.65–2.0 in head length; dorsal profile of head slightly concave to a point of flexure before upper part of eye, then nearly straight to origin of dorsal fin; snout forming an angle of about 35° to horizontal axis of body; interorbital space slightly concave; caudal fin slightly forked, the posterior edge of each lobe a slight, sinuous curve; light

Sabah

brown to light gray dorsally, the edge of scales darker, with indistinct dark blotches dorsally on body, the darkest between lateral line and middle of pectoral fin, and scattered small black spots (smaller than scales), mostly below and just above lateral line; upper lip yellow to light red; a bright red or yellow spot at upper base of pectoral fins; edges of median fins and leading edge of pelvic fins tinged with red; pectoral rays light red. Reported to 60 cm. Red Sea (type locality) to Mozambique, east to Line Islands, Marquesas Islands, and Society Islands; in the western Pacific from the Ryukyu Islands to the Great Barrier Reef and New Caledonia; a solitary species of coral reefs and adjacent habitats; difficult to approach underwater; found more often in lagoons than in outer-reef areas, from the shallows to 150 m, usually in less than 20 m. Randall (1980a) reported on the gut contents of 5 specimens: fishes, crabs (including a calappid), and echinoids.

Fiji/juvenile

Marshall Islands (night)

BIGEYE EMPEROR

Monotaxis grandoculis (Forsskål, 1775)

Dorsal rays X,10; anal rays III,9; pectoral rays 13–14 (rarely 13); lateral-line scales 44–47; rows of scales between lateral line and base of middle dorsal spines 5; scale rows below lateral line to origin of anal fin 13.5; small scales in axil of pectoral fins; side of maxilla with a denticulated ridge; side of jaws with a row of 5–7 large molariform teeth; body depth varying from 3.2 in standard length in juveniles to 2.2 in adults; eye very large, 2.7 in head length of juveniles to 3.8 in adults; snout length varying from 3.1 in head length in juveniles to 2.7 in adults; dorsal profile of snout of juveniles slightly convex, forming an angle of about 35–40° to horizontal axis of body; snout profile straighter and progressively steeper with growth, to about 70° in large adults; dorsal profile of head angular before eye, and continuing slightly convex to origin of dorsal fin; caudal fin moderately forked, the posterior margin of lobes slightly rounded; greenish gray dorsally, the edges of scales dark brown, shading to silvery white ventrally; can quickly assume a pattern of 4 broad, blackish bars on body, the white interspaces covering 3–4 rows of scales; lips often yellowish; a large dark brown to black spot at base of 3 or 4 membranes of soft portion of dorsal and anal fins; juveniles with 4 permanent broad black bars, 2 of which extend into dorsal fin, a black bar through eye, and an orange band in each lobe of caudal fin. Reaches 60 cm; largest collected by author, 56 cm, 3.4 kg. Occurs throughout the Indo-Pacific region except the Persian Gulf to western India; type locality, Red Sea. Found on coral reefs or adjacent areas. Feeds mainly at night, principally on hard-shelled invertebrates; Randall (1980a) summarized what is known of the prey, in the order of importance: gastropods, crabs, bivalve mollusks, echinoids, hermit crabs, and brittlestars.

Satonda Island, Indonesia/juvenile

Marshall Islands

REDFIN EMPEROR

Monotaxis heterodon (Bleeker, 1854)

Dorsal rays X,10; anal rays III,9; pectoral rays 13–14 (rarely 13); lateral-line scales 44–47; 5 rows of scales between lateral line and base of middle dorsal spines; other morphological characters as in *Monotaxis grandoculis* except the count of scales below the lateral line to origin of anal fin, 12.5; color similar to that of *grandoculis*, differing in having narrower white bars on body (covering 1–2 scales in width) when black bars are apparent, usually having brown or reddish lips, lacking the black spots at the base of the dorsal and anal fins, and generally having more red on fins; juveniles lack the dark bar that passes through the eye and have the narrow white bars; juveniles less than 40 mm have 2 black stripes on body. Rarely exceeds 30 cm. Known to date from the Seychelles, Maldive Islands, Sri Lanka, Indonesia, Malaysia, New Guinea, Great Barrier Reef, Marshall Islands, and New Caledonia; type locality, Halmahera, Molucca Islands (Fujioka & Yoshino, unpublished manuscript).

Lined Bream, *Scolopsis lineatus*, Tukangbesi Islands, Indonesia

BREAMS
(NEMIPTERIDAE)

This Indo-Pacific family of 5 genera and about 65 species shares the following characters with the Lethrinidae: dorsal rays X,9; forked or emarginate caudal fin; pelvic rays I,5; 10 + 14 vertebrae; 6 branchiostegal rays; mouth terminal with maxilla slipping under the suborbital when closed; no supramaxilla; no teeth on vomer or palatines; gill rakers knob-like and few in number; opercle with a single spine; and scales finely ctenoid. They differ from lethrinids in having III,7 anal rays; 14–19 pectoral rays; 2 supra-neural bones (lethrinids have 3); free margin on suborbital bones (with spines in the species of *Scolopsis*, often called spinecheeks), and in dentition. Nemipterids have small conical teeth in the jaws, those of the genera *Nemipterus* and *Pentapodus* with canines anteriorly. Many of the species of *Nemipterus* are of commercial importance, caught by trawling and by handlines; most occur in deeper-than-diving depths. The family was reviewed by Russell (1990); a few species remain to be described.

Sulawesi (night)

FORKTAIL BREAM
Nemipterus furcosus (Valenciennes in C & V, 1830)
Dorsal rays X,9; anal rays III,7; pectoral rays 16–18; lateral-line scales 47–50; scale rows below lateral line horizontal; 3 oblique rows of scales on cheek (true of other *Nemipterus*); gill rakers 9–12 (usually 10 or 11); 2 or 3 pairs of small, recurved canine teeth anteriorly in upper jaw; body depth 3.0–3.9 in standard length; caudal fin deeply forked, the lobes of equal length; pectoral fins 0.8–1.1 in head length; silvery pink with 9 red bars dorsally on head and body; dorsal fin translucent red with iridescent blue rays and margin; caudal fin light red with iridescent blue lower edge. Largest specimen, 28.5 cm. Sri Lanka (type locality) to western Pacific from southern Japan to northern half of Australia and New Caledonia; reported from sand and mud bottoms in the depth range of 8–110 m. Feeds during the day, mainly on crustaceans and small fishes. Russell (1990) listed the 8 synonyms of this species.

Bahrain

Lombok, Indonesia

NOTCHFIN BREAM
Nemipterus peronii (Valenciennes in C & V, 1830)
Dorsal rays X,9; anal rays III,7; pectoral rays 16–18; lateral-line scales 46–51; scale rows below lateral line horizontal; gill rakers 9–12 (usually 10 or 11); 3 or 4 pairs of small, recurved canine teeth anteriorly in upper jaw; body depth 3.3–3.5 in standard length; membranes of spinous portion of dorsal fin distinctly incised, the indentation greater in larger individuals (only species of the genus with incised dorsal membranes); caudal fin deeply forked, the upper lobe longer and more pointed, but not filamentous; pectoral fins 1.1–1.7 in head length; silvery pink with 7 or 8 dark pink, saddle-like bars on body reaching to or below lateral line; a diffuse light red spot below anterior part of lateral line; tips of spinous membranes of dorsal fin yellow. Attains 28 cm. Red Sea, Persian Gulf, and Gulf of Bengal to western Pacific from southern Japan to Queensland and New Caledonia; no type locality. A benthic species found over sand or mud substrata from 17 to about 100 m. Feeds during the day on fishes, crustaceans, mollusks, and polychaete worms (Said et al., 1983). *Nemipterus tolu* (Valenciennes) is a synonym.

SLENDER BREAM
Nemipterus zysron (Bleeker, 1857)
Dorsal rays X,9; anal rays III,7; pectoral rays 16–18; lateral-line scales 45–47; scale rows below lateral line horizontal; gill rakers 10–15; 3 or 4 pairs of small recurved canine teeth anteriorly in upper jaw; body very slender for the genus, the depth 3.8–4.6 in standard length; eye large, its diameter 2.6–3.5 in head length; snout short, equal to or shorter than eye diameter; caudal fin deeply forked, the upper lobe with a short filamentous tip; pectoral fins 1.1–1.4 in head length; silvery pink with a yellowish spot on each scale on side of body, thus forming indistinct stripes; a broad yellow stripe from upper lip to below eye; dorsal fin translucent pale yellow with a narrow, bright yellow margin; anal fin translucent lavender with a row of yellow spots near base; caudal fin pink to pale yellowish. Reaches 25 cm. Red Sea (but not the Persian Gulf or Gulf of Oman), east coast of Africa, and India to the western Pacific from Japan to northwestern Australia; Fiji and New Caledonia the only records for islands of the Pacific east of Indonesia; type locality, Nias (off Sumatra). Occurs in small aggregations at depths of 10–125 m.

Coral Sea/juvenile

New Caledonia

GOLDSTRIPE BREAM

Pentapodus aureofasciatus Russell, 2001

Dorsal rays X,9; anal rays III,7; pectoral rays 15–17 (usually 16 or 17); lateral-line scales 42–48 (usually 46 or 47); scales dorsally on head nearly reaching posterior nostrils; suborbital naked or with a small patch of scales below eye; lower limb of preopercle with 2 or 3 rows of scales; 2 or 3 pairs of small, recurved canines anteriorly in upper jaw, and a pair of larger, recurved, laterally flaring canines on each side at front of lower jaw (true of other *Pentapodus*); body depth of adults 3.4–3.6 in standard length; snout shorter than eye; pelvic fins nearly or just reaching anus; usually bluish gray on back, bluish white ventrally, with a

yellow stripe from behind eye to base of caudal fin, where its lower edge rests on lateral line; lateral line dark brown except posteriorly; a second faint narrow yellowish stripe passing just above anterior part of lateral line to rear base of dorsal fin; a blue-edged yellow stripe from front of upper lip to lower part of eye; a narrow, pale blue stripe from behind pelvic fins to lower part of caudal peduncle; caudal fin often pink or red; dorsal fin translucent pink; juveniles deep purplish blue with 2 bright yellow stripes. Attains at least 20 cm. Western Pacific from the Ryukyu Islands and Taiwan to Queensland, east to Tonga and Samoa Islands (type locality, Tutuila); generally found over sand near coral reefs.

Lombok, Indonesia/juvenile

Flores, Indonesia

Komodo, Indonesia (night)

SMALLTOOTH BREAM

Pentapodus caninus (Cuvier in C & V, 1830)

Dorsal rays X,9; anal rays III,7; pectoral rays 15–17 (usually 16); lateral-line scales 43–47 (usually 45–47); scales dorsally on head to or slightly before anterior nostrils, with a medial, naked, wedge-shaped notch between nostrils; suborbital scaly posteriorly; lower limb of preopercle with 2 or 3 rows of scales; body depth varying from 4.0 in standard length in juveniles to 3.1 in adults; snout short, about equal to eye diameter; caudal fin lunate, the lobe tips slender but not filamentous, the upper usually a little longer than lower; pelvic fins nearly or just reaching anus; tan to brown dorsally, pale tan to bluish white ventrally, with a yellow stripe from eye to upper side of caudal peduncle; a faint narrower yellow stripe often curving upward from eye and passing above lateral line to rear base of dorsal fin; a yellow-edged blue line from upper lip to lower edge of eye; a broader

blue and yellow band from lower edge of eye across operculum; caudal fin usually pale pink with red lobe tips; dorsal fin translucent red with a red margin, especially on soft portion; juveniles blue with 2 brown-edged yellow stripes. Largest collected, 26 cm. Southern Japan to East Indies, southeast to Vanuatu and New Caledonia and east throughout Micronesia; type locality, Doreh, New Guinea. Occurs on coral reefs and adjacent areas; free-swimming and mobile; feeds on macroplankton, benthic invertebrates, and small fishes. *Pentapodus macrurus* (Bleeker) is a synonym.

BRIDLED BREAM

Scolopsis bilineatus (Bloch, 1793)

Dorsal rays X,9; anal rays III,7; pectoral rays 16–18 (usually 17); lateral-line scales 45–48 (rarely 48); scales dorsally on head extending before anterior nostrils; a small antrorse spine just under eye; suborbital naked with a large retrorse spine dorsally on posterior edge and 2 or more small spines below (true of other *Scolopsis*); lower limb of preopercle with scales; margin of pre-opercle serrate (also generic); small conical teeth in bands in jaws, with no canines (generic); body depth of adults 2.5–3.0 in standard length; snout shorter than eye; caudal fin forked; pelvic fins long, nearly reaching origin of anal fin; a curved, black-edged, white stripe from below eye to a black spot below soft portion of dorsal fin, followed by a larger white spot at base of remaining part of fin; head and body below stripe pale gray, above blackish with 3 pale greenish lines; spinous portion of dorsal fin yellow, soft portion with a long, triangular, black and red anterior zone; front of anal fin black; juveniles variable in color as mimics of venomous-fanged blennies of the genus

Meiacanthus (Allen et al., 1975; Russell et al., 1976), in Fiji the yellow *M. oualanensis* (Günther). Largest, 19.5 cm. Maldive Islands and Laccadive Islands to the western Pacific from the Ryukyu Islands to New South Wales, Lord Howe Island, and New Caledonia, east to Fiji and Pohnpei; type locality given as Japan. A common, shallow-water, coral-reef species generally found in less than 20 m.

SILVERLINE BREAM

Scolopsis ciliatus (Lacepède, 1802)

Dorsal rays X,9; anal rays III,7; pectoral rays 16–18 (usually 17); lateral-line scales 41–43 (usually 43); scales dorsally on head extending to or slightly before anterior nostrils; a small antrorse spine just under eye; lower limb of preopercle with scales; edge of maxilla serrate; body depth 3.0–3.4 in standard length; snout shorter than eye; caudal fin forked; pelvic fins reaching to or beyond anus; gray dorsally, pale gray below, with a dusky-edged, silvery white stripe on back below posterior

three-fourths of dorsal fin; scales on dorsal half of body (except anteriorly) with a yellow to black spot (black dorsally and mostly yellow below lateral line); largest yellow spots in a posterior midlateral row; fins translucent, the rays tinged with pink; juveniles with 2 black-edged, greenish white stripes on dorsal half of head and body. Largest, 16.5 cm. Andaman Islands and western Pacific from southern Japan to Indonesia and Papua New Guinea, southeast to Solomon Islands, Vanuatu, and New Caledonia; no type locality. Found around shallow protected reefs and adjacent sand and weedy areas of lagoons and bays.

Tioman Island, Malaysia/juveniles

Guam

LINED BREAM
Scolopsis lineatus Quoy & Gaimard, 1824
Dorsal rays X,9; anal rays III,7; pectoral rays 14–17 (usually 16); lateral-line scales 40–46 (usually 42 or 43); scales dorsally on head extending slightly anterior to a vertical at front edge of eye; no antrorse spine just under eye; lower limb of preopercle naked; edge of maxilla serrate; body depth 3.0–3.4 in standard length; snout shorter than eye; caudal fin forked; pelvic fins reaching beyond anus; head and body black above a demarcation from front of snout to upper one-fourth of caudal peduncle, with 3 or 4 greenish gray bars and 2 irregular greenish white stripes, one from interorbital to rear base of dorsal fin and the other from upper part of eye to middle of body; head and body below demarcation bluish to greenish white; juveniles with 3 black and 2 yellow stripes on upper two-fifths of head and body, the lower part white. Largest, 22 cm. Cocos-Keeling Islands and Indonesia, north to southern Japan, south to Queensland and New Caledonia; type locality, Waigeo, Indonesia. A shallow-water fish of clear coral-reef areas; often seen in small aggregations. *Scolopsis cancellatus* (Cuvier) is a synonym.

BALDSPOT BREAM
Scolopsis temporalis (Cuvier in C & V, 1830)
Dorsal rays X,9; anal rays III,7; pectoral rays 18–19 (usually 18); lateral-line scales 46–49; scales dorsally on head nearly or just reaching a vertical at front edge of eye; no antrorse spine just under eye; a small scaleless area in temporal region behind eye; lower limb of preopercle scaly; body depth 2.7–3.1 in standard length; snout longer than eye; caudal fin deeply forked with pointed lobes; pelvic fins reaching to or beyond anus; body white with a pale blue spot on each scale; 3 broad blackish bands curving from behind and above eye to end dorsally on body and caudal peduncle; a black spot broadly edged anteriorly in bright blue next to eye at base of middle stripe; 3 black-edged orange stripes connecting across snout and interorbital from eye to eye, the broad lower stripe blackish anteriorly; caudal fin yellow, the lower lobe bluish gray. Attains about 40 cm. Sulawesi across northern New Guinea to the Solomon Islands and Fiji; type locality, Java. Usually seen over sand in the vicinity of reefs from depths of less than 10 to 30 m. Sometimes confused with the similar *S. monogramma*, which has the temporal region fully scaled; it is not known east of New Guinea or Australia.

Fiji

285

Cebu, Philippines

Cebu, Philippines (night)

Scolopsis trilineatus Kner, 1868

Dorsal rays X,9; anal rays III,7; pectoral rays 15–16 (usually 16); lateral-line scales 41–44; scales dorsally on head reaching only to above middle of eyes; no antrorse spine just under eye; lower limb of preopercle scaly; body depth 3.0–3.6 in standard length; snout length about equal to eye diameter; caudal fin forked; pelvic fins reaching to or beyond anus; gray dorsally, silvery white ventrally, with 3 narrow pale stripes extending posteriorly from eye, the uppermost light blue, curving upward from eye and ending below middle of dorsal fin, the second white, following lateral line anteriorly then curving upward to end at rear base of dorsal fin, the third white, bordered in yellow, from lower edge of eye, angling slightly upward nearly to middle of body, then abruptly upward to end at lateral line; a dark brown stripe edged in pale blue from front of snout through eye, continuing less pigmented between lower 2 white stripes. Reaches 20 cm. Philippines, Scott Reef, eastern Indonesia, Papua New Guinea, northern Great Barrier Reef, southeast to New Caledonia and east to Samoa Islands (type locality, Savai'i); only Palau in Micronesia; a shallow-water species generally found over sand near coral reefs, sometimes in small aggregations.

PORGIES AND SEABREAMS
(SPARIDAE)

The fishes of this family share many characters with the Lethrinidae and Nemipteridae such as the maxilla not fully exposed on the cheek when the mouth is closed, no teeth on the palate, a single flat spine on the opercle, 10 + 14 vertebrae, 6 branchiostegal rays, dorsal fin continuous without a notch between the spinous and soft portions, and the pelvic fins I,5 in thoracic position with an axillary scale. They are very diverse in general form; though usually deep-bodied, some are moderately elongate; the dorsal profile of the head varies from very steep to sloping. The dentition is highly variable, reflecting the food habits; the teeth may be conical, caniniform, molariform, or incisiform, with or without crenulations. The mouth is small, the cleft horizontal to slightly oblique, usually not reaching posterior to a vertical through center of eye, and slightly protrusible; the posterior end of the premaxilla overlaps the maxilla; the margin of the preopercle is smooth or with a few fine serrae; the scales are finely ctenoid or secondarily cycloid; the dorsal spines vary from X to XIII; most species have a scaly sheath at the base of the dorsal and anal fins. Most are carnivorous; those with molariform teeth feed principally on mollusks and crustaceans, but some such as the species of the genus *Diplodus* are omnivorous, feeding in part on benthic plants. Typically hermaphroditic; some have both male and female gonads developing at the same time; others change sex from male to female (protandrous), and still others from female to male (protogynous). Sparid fishes are found in tropical to temperate seas along continental shores or around large islands such as those of the East Indies; many occur at moderate depths, and a few penetrate brackish environments. There are 29 genera and about 100 species in the family; only one ranges east to New Caledonia.

PICNIC SEABREAM
Acanthopagrus berda (Forsskål, 1775)

Dorsal rays XI-XII (rarely XII),10–13; anal rays III,8–9; pectoral rays 14–15; lateral-line scales 43–46; scales above lateral line to base of fourth dorsal spine 4; gill rakers 6–7 + 9–11; body depth 1.9–2.4 in standard length; dorsal profile of head nearly straight to above eye; snout somewhat pointed; suborbital depth 6.0–7.5 in head length; 2 to 3 pairs of large compressed conical teeth at front of jaws, followed by 3 to 4 rows of molariform teeth, those in outer row bluntly conical; fourth to sixth dorsal spines longest; second anal spine stout, laterally flattened, and longer than third spine; caudal fin moderately forked; juveniles and subadults silvery, the lateral line dark; outer part of median and pelvic fins blackish; with growth, progressively more black pigment on scales (fish in turbid waters may be nearly black); opercular membrane blackish; often a blackish blotch at upper end of gill opening. Maximum total length about 75 cm. Continental shelf of Indian Ocean, including the Red Sea (type locality) and Persian Gulf, to the western Pacific from southern Japan to New Caledonia; a shallow-water species; freely enters estuaries, even into fresh water; feeds mainly on echinoids (especially sand dollars), crustaceans, polychaete worms, and mollusks (primarily small bivalves).

New Caledonia/subadult

Qatar Aquarium

Blacktip Mojarra, *Gerres oyena*, Bali

MOJARRAS
(GERREIDAE)

This small family of 8 genera and about 50 species is characterized as follows: body compressed, the depth variable; ventral profile of head to below eye concave; mouth terminal, very protractile, and angling downward when protruded; teeth in jaws setiform (very small, close-set, and numerous); no teeth on vomer or palatines; maxilla broad posteriorly and exposed on the cheek (except *Pentaprion*); gill membranes free from isthmus; branchiostegal rays 6; vertebrae 24; a single dorsal fin, elevated anteriorly, with IX or X spines and 9–18 soft rays; anal fin II-VI,6–18; dorsal and anal fins fold into a scaly sheath at base; caudal fin deeply forked; pelvic rays I,5; origin of pelvic fins slightly posterior to base of pectoral fins; scales moderately large, thin, cycloid, and easily detached; head scaled; the color is predominately silvery. The mojarras, also known as silver biddies or pursemouths, are inshore fishes found on sand to mud substrata in all tropical and subtropical seas; many occur in brackish environments, and one Central American species is confined to fresh water. They feed by taking in mouthfuls of bottom sediment (like the individual illustrated on p. 289) for the small fossorial fauna and expelling the sediment from the gill openings. They may be encountered as solitary individuals or in small schools.

287

WHIPFIN MOJARRA

Gerres filamentosus Cuvier, 1829

Dorsal rays IX,10; anal rays III,7; pectoral rays 15–16 (usually 16); lateral-line scales 43–46; scales above lateral line to middle dorsal spines 4.5–5.5; gill rakers 4–6 + 8–9 (rarely 9); body depth of adults 2.0–2.5 in standard length (juveniles less deep, to 3.0 in standard length); snout shorter than eye diameter; maxilla reaching or extending slightly beyond a vertical at anterior edge of eye; second dorsal spine of adults laterally compressed and very long (when intact, 1.7–2.0 in standard length); caudal fin large and deeply forked; pectoral fins reaching to or beyond a vertical at origin of anal fin; silvery with 7–10 columns of ovoid blackish spots on about upper half of body (as dark bars in juveniles); tip of lower lobe of caudal fin, apex of anal fin, and tip of pelvic fins white; a row of small, triangular, blackish spots in dorsal fin, 1 per membrane, except first few membranes. Reaches about 30 cm. Red Sea, Persian Gulf and east coast of Africa to Indo-Malayan region and northern Australia, north to southern Japan, east to Santa Cruz Islands and New Caledonia. Cuvier named *Gerres filamentosus* in a footnote based on the illustration in Russell (1803) from the Coromandel coast of

Cochin, India

India; the type locality, however, is Vanikoro Island from the neotype designation by Iwatsuki et al. (1996). A coastal species found along sandy shores and in estuarine areas; may be seen in small aggregations.

LONGTAIL MOJARRA

Gerres longirostris (Lacepède, 1801)

Dorsal rays IX,10; anal rays III,7; pectoral rays 17–18; lateral-line scales 45–49; scales above lateral line to middle dorsal spines 5.5; lower flange of preopercle scaled; gill rakers 6–7 + 7–9; body depth 2.3–2.8 in standard length; maxilla reaching or extending slightly beyond a vertical at anterior edge of eye; second dorsal spine 4.0–5.9 in standard length; caudal fin large and deeply forked; pectoral fins reaching to or beyond a vertical at origin of anal fin; silvery with 6 to 9 vertical series of oblong dark spots (may appear pink or blue); no black on dorsal fin; caudal fin with a blackish posterior margin. Largest specimen, 44.5 cm. Red Sea and east coast of Africa to the islands of Micronesia; southern Japan to the Great Barrier Reef and New Caledonia; type locality, "Great Gulf of India." Occurs over sand substrata, generally near reefs, but will range into mangrove areas. Iwatsuki et al. (2001) redescribed this species and placed *Gerres acinaces* Bleeker in its synonymy. Their listing of the Marquesas Islands among the localities is an error (Y. Iwatsuki, pers. comm.).

Marshall Islands

OBLONG MOJARRA

Gerres oblongus Cuvier in C & V, 1830

Dorsal rays IX,10; anal rays III,7; pectoral rays 16–17 (modally 16); lateral-line scales 43–46; scales above lateral line to middle dorsal spines 5.5; no small scales on lower flange of preopercle; gill rakers 6–7 + 7–9; body depth 2.8–3.3 in standard length; maxilla nearly reaching a vertical at anterior edge of eye; second dorsal spine longest, 3.85–5.25 in standard length; caudal fin deeply forked; pectoral fins not reaching to above origin of anal fin; silvery; dusky bars absent or indistinct (may be present in juveniles, those posteriorly on body oblique); adults sometimes with vertical columns of ovoid dark spots; no black on dorsal fin; caudal fin dusky, rarely with a dark posterior margin. Largest specimen, 33.5 cm. Red Sea and east coast of Africa to Samoa Islands, Tonga, and islands of Micronesia except the Marshall

New Caledonia/subadult

Islands; in the western Pacific from Ryukyu Islands to New Caledonia; type locality, Sri Lanka. Redescribed by Iwatsuki et al. (2001); *Gerres macrosoma* Bleeker and *G. gigas* Günther are synonyms.

BLACKTIP MOJARRA
Gerres oyena (Forsskål, 1775)
Dorsal rays IX,10; anal rays III,7; pectoral rays 16–17; lateral-line scales 35–40 (modally 38); scales above lateral line to middle dorsal spines usually 5.5; gill rakers 4–6 + 8; body depth 2.5–3.1 in standard length; maxilla reaching slightly posterior to a vertical at anterior edge of eye; second dorsal spine longest, 3.9–6.2 in standard length; caudal fin deeply forked, with long lobes; pectoral fins usually just reaching or extending slightly beyond a vertical at anus; silvery, sometimes with 6–8 faint dusky bars on body (especially in juveniles); dorsal fin tip broadly tipped with dusky or black. Largest specimen, 24 cm. Red Sea (type locality) to South Africa, east to Marshall Islands and Samoa Islands; Ryukyu Islands to the Great Barrier Reef and New Caledonia; occurs over shallow sand flats of protected waters. *Gerres argyreus* (Forster) is a synonym.

Red Sea

THREADFINS
(POLYNEMIDAE)

The pectoral fins of this family are its most distinctive feature; they are low on the body and divisible into an upper part with the rays joined by membrane and a lower part of separate rays that can be extended forward to make contact with the substratum; the number of rays vary with species from 3 to 7, except for one with 14 or 15; the rays are much longer in juveniles than in adults. Other family characters include an overhanging, obtusely conical snout; a large, near-horizontal mouth, the maxilla extending well beyond the eye; teeth in villiform bands in jaws and on palatines (on vomer of some species); adipose "eyelid" (firm transparent gelatinous tissue) covering eye; 2 well-separated dorsal fins, the first with VI to VIII spines, the second with an initial spine and 11–15 soft rays; caudal fin deeply forked to lunate; pelvic fins I,5, their origin distinctly posterior to base of pectoral fins; scales weakly ctenoid; small scales covering most of second dorsal, anal, and caudal fins; lateral line complete, continuing onto caudal fin; gill opening wide, the gill membranes separate and not attached to isthmus; branchiostegal rays 7; vertebrae 24–25; external bones of head with a well-developed muciferous system similar to that of the Sciaenidae. Once thought to be allied with the Mugilidae, the Polynemidae is now believed to be a distant relative of the Sciaenidae. Threadfins are found on sand or mud substrata; their separate lower pectoral rays have sensory capability as they are flicked over the sediment. Limited data suggest that the food consists mainly of small benthic crustaceans, polychaete worms, and occasionally small fishes. At least some of the polynemids are protandrous, meaning they commence mature life as males and change sex later to female. The family consists of 8 genera and 38 species (H. Motomura, pers. comm.); it is represented by species in all warm seas. All but one of the Indo-Pacific species are closely tied to freshwater drainage. The exception is *Polydactylus sexfilis*, which is often found mainly along sandy shores; it ranges east in Oceania to the Hawaiian Islands and Tuamotu Archipelago. Only 2 other species are known for the South Pacific, *P. plebeius*, which occurs east to Tahiti, and *P. microstomus* (Bleeker) that ranges only to New Caledonia; the latter inhabits mangrove creeks and rivers at depths less than 2 m; it has 5 free pectoral rays and an oblong black spot anteriorly on the lateral line. It was illustrated from New Caledonia by Laboute & Grandperrin (2000) as *P. sexfilis*.

Cochin, India/juvenile

Lombok, Indonesia

STRIPED THREADFIN

Polydactylus plebeius (Broussonet, 1782)

Dorsal rays VIII + 12–13 (usually 13); anal rays III,11–12 (usually 11); pectoral rays 15–18 (rarely 15, modally 17), all rays unbranched, + 6 separate filamentous lower rays; lateral-line scales 60–68; gill rakers 9–14 + 13–18; body depth about 3.5 in standard length; upper jaw short, 6.25–7.7 in standard length; teeth present on vomer; second dorsal soft ray 3.6–5.3 in stan-dard length; caudal fin large and deeply forked; swimbladder well developed; silvery white with narrow gray stripes following scale rows; leading edge of dorsal and caudal fins dark; pectoral fins blackish except basally; filamentous pectoral rays white. Attains about 60 cm. East coast of Africa to Tahiti (type locality); Japan to New Caledonia; usually found in brackish habitats. Redescribed and a neotype designated by Motomura et al. (2001a). *Polynemus lineatus* Lacepède is one of 7 synonyms.

Hawaiian Islands

SIXFEELER THREADFIN

Polydactylus sexfilis (Valenciennes in C & V, 1831)

Dorsal rays VIII + I2–13 (usually 13); anal rays III,11–12 (usually 11); pectoral rays 14–17 (usually 16), plus 6 separate fila-mentous lower rays; lateral-line scales 58–70 (modally 63); lat-eral line not branched; gill rakers 11–14 + 15–18; teeth present on vomer; body depth 3.1–3.85 in standard length; third dorsal spine longest, 4.4–5.55 in standard length; second soft dorsal ray longest, 3.35–4.75 in standard length; caudal fin large and deeply forked; swimbladder well developed; silvery to brassy, with narrow blackish stripes following longitudinal scale rows on body; fins dusky, the pelvics and anal with a white margin. Largest specimen, 60 cm, from Izu Islands, Japan (Motomura & Senou, 2002). Occurs from the Seychelles, Mauritius (type locality), Laccadive Islands, and India to the Hawaiian Islands,

Hawaiian Islands/subadult

Marquesas Islands, and Tuamotu Archipelago; in the western Pacific from southern Japan to New Caledonia; typically found along sandy shores, hence may be caught in beach seines; recently proven of value for aquaculture in the Hawaiian Islands. The species was redescribed by Motomura (2001); he showed that *Polynemus kuru* Bleeker is a synonym.

Yellowstripe Goatfish, *Mulloidichthys flavolineatus*, Hawaiian Islands

GOATFISHES
(MULLIDAE)

Goatfishes are easily recognized by the long pair of barbels on the chin. Other family characters include a moderately elongate body with a long, somewhat pointed snout; a small, slightly ventral, protrusible mouth; maxilla partly hidden under preorbital when mouth closed; a single sharp spine on opercle; preopercle smooth; scales finely ctenoid and moderately large, 27–38 in lateral line; 2 widely spaced dorsal fins, the first with VI to VIII spines (first spine may be very small), the second with 8 or 9 soft rays; anal fin with I or II spines and 5–8 soft rays; pelvic fins I,5, below or slightly posterior to pectorals; caudal fin forked; branchiostegal rays 4; vertebrae 24. The genera are distinguished primarily on dentition. The species of *Mulloidichthys* and *Parupeneus* lack teeth on the roof of the mouth, whereas those of *Upeneus* have small teeth on the vomer and palatines. The species of *Mulloidichthys* and *Upeneus* have bands of villiform teeth in the jaws in contrast to those of *Parupeneus* with a single row of moderately large conical teeth. The species of *Upeneus* are usually found on silty sand or mud bottoms; those of *Mulloidichthys* and *Parupeneus* are usually seen in reefs or adjacent environments. Goatfishes are carnivorous, feeding mainly on benthic invertebrates, particularly worms and crustaceans, but also taking brittlestars, small heart urchins, and small mollusks, and a few species feed in part on small fishes, notably the large *P. cyclostomus*. Goatfishes use their barbels, which possess chemosensory organs, to flick over the surface of the sediment or probe into it in search of prey. Once food is found, they thrust their snouts into the sediment in an effort to catch the prey. When not in use, the barbels are held back between the lower parts of the operculum (except males in courtship, which rapidly wriggle the barbels). Some species are primarily nocturnal and tend to form semistationary schools by day, but most of the reef-oriented species are active diurnal feeders. At night the color of most species is dominated by large, irregular, red bars or blotches. The family is represented by six genera and about 60 species in tropical to warm temperate seas. The Mullidae of the central and western Pacific was reviewed by Randall in Carpenter & Niem (2001a). *Parupeneus* was revised by Randall (2004b).

Hawaiian Islands

YELLOWSTRIPE GOATFISH

Mulloidichthys flavolineatus (Lacepède, 1801)

Dorsal rays VIII + 9; anal rays I,7; pectoral rays 16–18; lateral-line scales 33–36 (usually 34–35); gill rakers 7–10 + 18–22; body very elongate, the depth 3.7–4.8 in standard length; head length 3.1–3.45 in standard length; snout length 1.9–2.2 (2.4 in young) in head length; barbel length 1.4–1.65 in head; silvery white with a yellow stripe on body at level of eye; often a blackish spot in yellow stripe below first dorsal fin; fins whitish, the caudal often yellowish. Reported to 40 cm; largest specimen examined, 36.5 cm. Occurs throughout the Indo-Pacific region; type locality unknown. Tends to form inactive aggregations by day, sometimes with many individuals at rest on the bottom. Feeding has been observed during the day, but most appears to be nocturnal or crepuscular. Ten were collected by the author for food-habit study; 4 had empty stomachs; the rest contained small crabs, shrimps, polychaete worms, small bivalve mollusks, hermit crabs, crab megalops, heart urchins, small gastropods, amphipods, foraminifera, and unidentified eggs. Myers (1999) reported males mature as small as 12.3 cm standard length and females as small as 11.2 cm in the Mariana Islands; spawning takes place from December to September with peaks in March and April; large schools of silvery postlarvae settle on reef flats in March to June at a standard length of 6–8 cm. Spawning in Palau takes place over sandy areas near reef's edge for several days following new moon (Johannes, 1981). *Mulloides samoensis* Günther is a synonym.

Hawaiian Islands

Marquesas, with *Lutjanus kasmira* (J. L. Earle)

Line Islands

MIMIC GOATFISH

Mulloidichthys mimicus Randall & Guézé, 1980

Dorsal rays VIII + 9; anal rays I,7; pectoral rays 16–17; lateral-line scales 38–30; gill rakers 7–8 + 21–23; body moderately elongate, the depth 3.1–3.5 in standard length; head length 3.2–3.4 in standard length; snout length 2.2–2.4 in head length; barbels reaching slightly posterior to vertical margin of preopercle, their length 1.35–1.45 in head length; yellow with 5 dark-edged narrow blue stripes, the upper 2 slightly oblique; first

stripe ending below origin of second dorsal fin, and the second slightly posterior to that fin; fins yellow. Largest specimen, 30.5 cm. Known only from the Marquesas Islands (type locality, Nuku Hiva) and the Line Islands. Randall & Guézé (1980) named this species for its duplication of the color pattern of *Lutjanus kasmira*. It is frequently seen schooling by day with the snapper. The mimicry is believed to result from a predator preference for the softer, less spiny goatfish to the firm, more spiny snapper, as well as the protection provided by schooling.

Hawaiian Islands

Hawaiian Islands, with *Coris gaimard*

PFLUEGER'S GOATFISH
Mulloidichthys pfluegeri (Steindachner, 1900)

Dorsal rays VIII + 9; anal rays I,7; pectoral rays 17–18; lateral-line scales usually 35–37; gill rakers 6–8 + 19–22; body elongate, the depth 3.5–4.25 in standard length; head length 3.2–3.6 in standard length; snout length 1.85–2.2 in head length; barbel length 1.45–1.6 in head length; body and nape grayish red dorsally, pinkish white ventrally, with an indistinct midlateral brown stripe mainly visible as 3 separate dashes; head lavender-gray; when feeding (as in figure with *Coris gaimard*), pale with 4 broad red bars on body, the last at base of caudal fin; most of head red. Largest, 50 cm. Usually found over sand near reefs, generally at depths greater than 23 m. Indo-Pacific, but with few localities, all of which are oceanic islands: Hawaiian Islands (type locality, Oʻahu), Marquesas Islands, Society Islands, Tonga, Marshall Islands, Mariana Islands, Ogasawara Islands, Ryukyu Islands, and Réunion.

Marshall Islands (night)

Great Barrier Reef

YELLOWFIN GOATFISH
Mulloidichthys vanicolensis (Valenciennes in C & V, 1831)

Dorsal rays VIII + 9; anal rays I,7–8; pectoral rays 16–17; lateral-line scales 35–37; gill rakers 8–10 + 22–26; body elongate, the depth 3.5–4.5 in standard length; head length 2.95–3.4 in standard length; snout length 2.2–2.6 in head length; barbel length 1.2–1.5 in head; pale yellowish to greenish dorsally, the scale edges darker than centers, shading to whitish or pink ventrally, with a yellow stripe edged in pale blue from eye to base of caudal fin; fins yellow; night color pale with irregular red bars and blotches. Largest specimen, 38 cm. Occurs throughout the Indo-Pacific region; type locality, Vanikoro, Santa Cruz Islands. Pacific populations with slightly longer barbels and pectoral fins and slightly higher gill-raker counts than Indian Ocean populations; an electrophoretic study failed to show species-level divergence (Stepien et al., 1994). Closely related to *M. dentatus* (Gill) from the eastern Pacific and *M. martinicus* (Cuvier) from the western Atlantic. Habits much like *M. flavolineatus* but usually found in deeper water (generally more than 15 m; reported to 113 m). *Mulloidichthys auriflamma* (Forsskål) is an earlier name, but this was invalidated by the International Commission on Zoological Nomenclature.

293

Cebu, Philippines/juveniles

Marshall Islands

BICOLOR GOATFISH

Parupeneus barberinoides (Bleeker, 1852)

Dorsal rays VIII + 9; anal rays I,7; pectoral rays 15–16 (usually 16); gill rakers 28–33; body moderately elongate, the depth 3.2–3.5 in standard length; snout length 1.8–2.0 in head length; barbel length 1.3–1.5 in head length; head and anterior half of body reddish black, posterior half white and yellow with a black spot nearly as large as eye on upper side below rear base of second dorsal fin, followed by small blue spots; a white band from front of snout passing above eye along dorsal part of body, and a second nearly parallel one from corner of mouth to above pectoral fin; caudal fin pale yellow with a broad, dusky lower margin, and often with a small red spot at midbase; barbels red. Largest examined, 25 cm. Western Pacific from the Ryukyu Islands to Great Barrier Reef, New South Wales, and New Caledonia, east to Tonga, Samoa Islands, and the islands of Micronesia; ranges south on the northwestern coast of Australia to Ningaloo Reef; type locality, Seram, Molucca Islands. Usually encountered in the vicinity of coral reefs in calm areas such as bays and lagoons or in deeper outer-reef areas to at least 40 m.

DOT-DASH GOATFISH

Parupeneus barberinus (Lacepède, 1801)

Pectoral rays 16–18; gill rakers 26–31; body moderately elongate, the depth 3.3–3.7 in SL; head length 2.6–3.0 in SL; snout length 1.45–2.1 in head length (snout relatively longer with growth); barbel length 1.4–1.6 in head length; longest dorsal spine 1.15–1.75 in head length (longer with growth); whitish with a dark brown to black stripe (red on fish in deeper water) from upper lip through eye to below posterior part of second dorsal fin or anteriorly on upper caudal peduncle; body above stripe yellow or yellowish gray; body below whitish, the scale edges narrowly gray to brownish red; a black or red spot larger than eye at midbase of caudal fin; some large adults with centers of scales below dark stripe pale blue, the edges yellow or with yellow spots, especially posteriorly; Largest specimen examined, 53 cm, from Tahiti. East coast of Africa to Line Islands, Marquesas Islands, Tuamotu Archipelago, and islands of Micronesia; southern Japan to the Great Barrier Reef, Lord Howe Island, and New Caledonia; type locality, Molucca Islands. Usually seen over sand or sand-rubble substrata near coral reefs. Feeding is diurnal; 19 adult specimens were collected by the author for food-habit study; the prey by order by volume in the stomachs: crabs (portunid, anomuran, xanthid, and raninid), worms (mainly polychaetes but also sipunculids and unidentified), small bivalve mollusks, brachiopods, shrimps, small gastropods, isopods, amphipods, foramanifera, and an unidentified eel.

Great Barrier Reef

Bali (night)

294

WHITELINED GOATFISH

Parupeneus ciliatus (Lacepède, 1802)

Dorsal rays VIII + 9; anal rays I,7 pectoral rays 14–15 (rarely 14); lateral-line scales 27–28; gill rakers 30–34; body depth 2.95–3.5 in standard length; snout length 1.85–2.1 in head length; barbel length 1.55–1.9 in head length; last dorsal ray only slightly longer than preceding ray; body pale greenish to reddish gray dorsally, shading to pale red on sides and ventrally, the scale edges dark orange-yellow; an elongate white spot on 3 or 4 scales dorsally on anterior part of caudal peduncle, sometimes followed by a dusky blotch; head red with 3 white stripes, the upper 2 passing through edges of eye and continuing progressively fainter onto anterior half of body; third stripe from end of maxilla to pectoral-fin base. Largest specimen examined, 38 cm. Zanzibar, Madagascar, Mascarene Islands, and Seychelles to Line Islands and Pitcairn Islands; in western Pacific from southern Japan to Great Barrier Reef, New South Wales, Lord Howe Island, Norfolk Island, and New Caledonia; no type locality. Occurs on coral reefs and adjacent habitats to at least 40 m, often in small aggregations. *P. fraterculus* (Valenciennes) and *P. pleurotaenia* (Playfair) are synonyms.

THICKLIPPED GOATFISH

Parupeneus crassilabris (Valenciennes in C & V, 1831)

Dorsal rays VIII + 9; anal rays I,7; pectoral rays 15–16 (usually 16); lateral-line scales 27–28; gill rakers 35–38; body depth 2.9–3.2 in standard length; dorsal profile of snout concave, its length 1.6–1.9 in head length; barbels relatively short, 1.6–1.9 in head length; last dorsal ray only slightly longer than preceding ray and shorter than first ray; caudal fin forked, the posterior margin of lobes convex; gray to bluish gray, sometimes red or reddish brown, paler ventrally, the scales yellow-edged or with a yellow spot; a large, oval black spot from beneath pectoral fin to below anterior part of first dorsal fin; a broad black bar under second dorsal fin, a large dark brown to black spot behind and below eye, enclosing most of eye and extending as a broad band ventroanteriorly. A courting male was pale blue dorsally on the head and between the 2 large dark spots on the body, reddish ventrally on the head and below dark spots on the body, the yellow spots prominent. Attains at least 25 cm. Western Pacific from Ryukyu Islands through the Philippines and eastern Indonesia to Western Australia and the Great Barrier Reef, east to Vanuatu, New Caledonia, Palau, Caroline Islands, Fiji, Tuvalu, and Tonga; type locality, New Guinea. One of a complex of 3 species, the others *Parupeneus trifasciatus* from the Indian Ocean (*bifasciatus* is a synonym) and *P. insularis* from more eastern islands of Oceania. Often seen at rest on coral-reef substrata.

Great Barrier Reef

Sarosa, Indonesia

Great Barrier Reef

295

GOLDSADDLE GOATFISH

Parupeneus cyclostomus (Lacepède, 1801)

Dorsal rays VIII + 9; anal rays I,7; pectoral rays 15–17 (usually 16); lateral-line scales 27–28; gill rakers 6–7 + 22–26 (total rakers 29–33); body moderately elongate, the depth 3.3–3.9 in standard length; snout length 1.6–1.9 in head length; barbels long, extending to or beyond posterior end of head; last dorsal ray only slightly longer than preceding ray; large adults (perhaps only male) yellowish gray, the edges of the scales bright blue except ventrally, the edges more broadly blue posteriorly; a large, hemispherical, saddle-like, yellow spot covering most of upper half of caudal peduncle; region around eye yellow with radiating short blue bands; caudal fin with longitudinal blue bands; second dorsal and anal fins with narrow oblique blue bands; a second color phase (perhaps only female) entirely yellow, the dorsal peduncular spot sometimes apparent by being brighter yellow than rest of body. Attains about 50 cm. Occurs throughout the Indo-Pacific region; type locality, Mauritius. Inhabits clearwater, coral-reef habitats from less than 5 to 125 m; unusual for a goatfish in its heavy feeding on fishes (about 70% of its diet); uses its long barbels to frighten small fishes from their holes in the reef; of 21 collected by author with food in their stomachs, 18 had eaten fishes, though 6 of these also contained invertebrates: crabs, octopuses, stomatopods, shrimps, and sipunculids. *Parupeneus chryserydros* (Lacepède) and *P. luteus* (Valenciennes) are synonyms. Also known as the Blue Goatfish.

CINNABAR GOATFISH
Parupeneus heptacanthus (Lacepède, 1802)
Dorsal rays VIII + 9; anal rays I,7; pectoral rays 15–17 (usually 16); lateral-line scales 27–28; gill rakers 26–30; body depth 3.15–3.4 in standard length; snout length 1.75–2.1 in head length; barbels 1.15–1.4 in head length; dorsal profile of head strongly and evenly convex; rear of maxilla symmetrically convex (other South Pacific species with a dorsoposterior lobe at rear end of maxilla); yellowish to pinkish gray dorsally, the scale edges yellowish brown, shading to pinkish or bluish white ventrally, each scale with a blue spot (easily seen only on scales in the 2 rows above lateral line); a small red to reddish brown spot no larger than pupil usually present on ninth lateral-line scale and the scale below it. Largest specimen examined, 36 cm. Red Sea and east coast of Africa to the Samoa Islands and islands of Micronesia; southern Japan to the Great Barrier Reef, Lord Howe Island, and New Caledonia; no type locality given. Rarely seen on coral reefs, usually found on silty sand or weedy substrata, generally in more than 15 m. Often caught by trawling. Reports of specimens fished from as deep as 350 m need confirmation. *Parupeneus cinnabarinus* (Cuvier), *P. pleurospilos* (Bleeker), *P. seychellensis* (Smith & Smith), and *P. xanthopurpureus* (Fourmanoir) are synonyms.

INDIAN GOATFISH
Parupeneus indicus (Shaw, 1803)
Dorsal rays VIII + 9; anal rays I,7; pectoral rays 15–17 (usually 16); lateral-line scales 27–28; gill rakers 24–27; body moderately elongate, the depth 3.3–3.75 in standard length; snout length 1.65–2.0 in head length; barbels 1.3–1.55 in head length; body yellowish gray dorsally, pale gray ventrally, the scale edges narrowly yellowish brown; a large, horizontally elongate, bright yellow spot, sometimes with a bluish white center, on upper side centered below interdorsal space, the lateral line passing through its lower part; a midlateral, round, black spot larger than eye posteriorly on caudal peduncle; head with irregular, dark-edged blue lines and a broad brown band, bordered below by a blue line, from upper lip to eye; caudal fin with longitudinal blue lines, and second dorsal and anal fins with oblique blue lines. Attains at least 35 cm. East coast of Africa to the Caroline Islands, Samoa Islands, and Tonga; in the western Pacific from Ogasawara Islands and Taiwan to the Great Barrier Reef and New Caledonia; type locality, Vishakhapatnam, India. Typically found in shallow, silty sand areas of lagoons and bays; often seen in aggregations. *Parupeneus russelli* (Cuvier), *P. waigiensis* (Cuvier), *P. malabaricus* (Cuvier) and *P. griseofrenatus* (Kner) are synonyms.

Gulf of Aqaba, Red Sea

Papua New Guinea (night)

Papua New Guinea

Flores, Indonesia (night)

297

shrimps, heart urchins, sipunculids, bivalve mollusks, forami-nifera, brittlestars, fishes, amphipods, stomatopods, gastropods, and small crustaceans.

TAILSPOT GOATFISH
Parupeneus spilurus (Bleeker, 1854)
Dorsal rays VIII + 9; anal rays I,7; pectoral rays 15–17 (usually 16); lateral-line scales 27–28; gill rakers 28–32; body depth 3.1–3.5 in standard length; snout length 1.85–2.25 in head length; barbels 1.35–1.65 in head length; last dorsal soft ray not distinctly longer than preceding ray; brownish red dorsally, red ventrally, with 2 oblique, dark brown stripes bordered broadly by white from front of snout to a large yellow spot anteriorly on upper half of caudal peduncle; uppermost stripe passing through eye, the lower across cheek to middle of body, both broadening and progressively less pigmented posteriorly; a large black spot on upper half of caudal peduncle following yellow spot. Reaches at least 32 cm. Western Pacific from Korea, southern Japan (type locality, Nagasaki), and Taiwan to New South Wales, Lord Howe Island, Norfolk Island, New Caledonia, Tonga, northern New Zealand, and the Kermadec Islands; Western Australia from Geographe Bay (33°37′S) northward (Allen & Swainston, 1988). More common in subtropical than in tropical latitudes. Specimens from the southern part of the range with modally one more upper and one more lower gill raker. *Parupeneus signatus* (Günther), described from New South Wales, is a probable synonym. Also known as the Blackspot Goatfish.

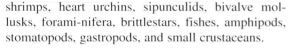

Bali (night)

Komodo, Indonesia

Komodo, Indonesia

299

INSULAR GOATFISH
Parupeneus insularis Randall & Myers, 2002

Dorsal rays VIII + 9; anal rays I,7; pectoral rays 15–17 (usually 16); lateral-line scales 27–28; gill rakers 8–10 + 29–32 (total rakers 37–41, modally 39); body depth 2.9–3.2 in standard length; dorsal profile of snout concave, its length 1.6–1.9 in head length; lips thick; barbels relatively short, 1.6–1.9 in head length; last dorsal ray only slightly longer than preceding ray and shorter than first ray; caudal fin forked, the posterior margin of lobes convex; gray to brown or red, the scale edges narrowly dark, with a dark brown bar on body below first dorsal fin and a broader one below second dorsal fin and extending onto adjacent caudal peduncle; most of peduncle and base of caudal fin often abruptly white; iris red. Largest specimen, 31.3 cm. Hawaiian Islands (type locality, Oʻahu) to Mariana Islands and Pitcairn Islands; French Polynesia to Phoenix and Samoa Islands. Occurs on or near coral reefs from depths of 1–80 m. The stomachs of 17 specimens were opened (5 empty), revealing feeding on crabs (44%), shrimps, octopuses, stomatopods, amphipods, other crustaceans, fishes, and polychaete worms. Stomachs are more apt to be full during early morning hours, suggesting that most feeding takes place at night or dawn. Differentiated from *Parupeneus crassilabris* of more western Pacific localities by color and a higher number of gill rakers (35–38 for *crassilabris*).

BANDTAIL GOATFISH
Upeneus arge Jordan & Evermann, 1903

Dorsal rays VIII + 9; anal rays I,7; pectoral rays 13–14; lateral-line scales 36–38; gill rakers 5–6 + 15–17 (total rakers 20–23); body very elongate, the depth 3.7–4.7 in standard length; snout length 2.2–2.4 in head length; barbels short, 1.3–1.6 in head length; greenish silver dorsally, the scales edged in bronze or with a bronze spot, silvery white on side and ventrally, with an orange stripe from eye to upper base of caudal fin and a narrower yellow stripe from corner of mouth to lower base of caudal fin; upper lobe of caudal fin of adults with 6 or 7 reddish black crossbands, and lower lobe with 4 or 5; dorsal fins with several oblique, dusky orange bands. Reaches 30 cm. The author has examined specimens only from the Hawaiian Islands (type locality, Oʻahu), Line Islands, Phoenix Islands, Society Islands, Tuamotu Archipelago, Macao, Maldive Islands, and Aldabra. Baissac (1976) included *Upeneus arge* in a checklist from Mauritius, and Yamakawa in Masuda et al. (1984) reported it from Ishigaki, Ryukyu Islands. Some authors have considered *Upeneus arge* to be a synonym of *U. taeniopterus* (Cuvier), type locality, Sri Lanka. Randall (after P. Guézé) in Carpenter & Niem (2001a) distinguished the two species.

SULPHUR GOATFISH
Upeneus sulphureus Cuvier in C & V, 1829

Dorsal rays VIII + 9; anal rays I,7–8; pectoral rays 14–17 (rarely 14 or 17); lateral-line scales 33–36 (rarely 33 or 36); gill rakers 8–9 + 19–21 (total rakers 26–30); body depth 3.25–3.85 in standard length; snout length 2.4–2.7 in head length; barbels short, 1.4–1.85 in head length (relatively longer in adults than in young); silvery greenish or pink dorsally, shading to silver on side and ventrally, with 2 narrow, brassy yellow stripes on side of body; first dorsal fin broadly tipped with black; caudal fin without dark crossbands; barbels white. Maximum total length about 20 cm. Southern Red Sea and coast of East Africa to Indo-Malayan region and northern Australia, north to Japan, east to Fiji; type locality, Anjer,

eastern Java; a species of continental shores and around large islands; generally found on mud substrata at depths of 20–60 m; often enters estuaries. Caught mainly by trawling, sometimes in large numbers.

FRECKLED GOATFISH
Upeneus tragula Richardson, 1846

Dorsal rays VIII + 9; anal rays I,7–8; pectoral rays 13–14 (usually 13); lateral-line scales 28–29; gill rakers 21–24; body very elongate, the depth 3.9–4.4 in standard length; snout length 2.25–2.65 in head length; barbels short, 1.45–1.85 in head length; greenish gray dorsally, densely flecked with red to reddish brown, white ventrally with numerous small red spots and a row of irregular red blotches on lower side; a red to brown stripe from front of upper lip through eye to midbase of caudal fin containing 6 sections that are more darkly pigmented; barbels yellow; lobes of caudal fin with transverse dark brown to black bands, increasing with growth to 5 in upper lobe and 6 in lower; upper part of first dorsal fin red to dark reddish brown with a few small yellow spots. Reaches 30 cm. East coast of Africa to western Pacific from southern Japan to the Great Barrier Reef and

New Caledonia; only Palau in Micronesia; type locality, Guangzhou (Canton), China. Occurs in calm waters of lagoons or bays on silty sand or mud bottom; also found in mangrove and seagrass habitats.

STRIPED GOATFISH
Upeneus vittatus (Forsskål, 1775)

Dorsal rays VIII + 9; anal rays I,7–8; pectoral rays 15–17 (usually 16); lateral-line scales 33–36; gill rakers 8–9 + 19–21 (total 27–30); body elongate, the depth 3.5–4.1 in standard length; snout length 2.5–2.8 in head length; barbels short, usually not reaching posterior margin of preopercle, their length 1.5–1.7 in head length; silvery green dorsally, silvery white on sides and ventrally, with 4 stripes, the upper 2 yellowish brown, the lower 2 orange-yellow; upper lobe of caudal fin of adults with 5 dark brown to black transverse bands, the lower lobe with 3, the outer band twice as broad and darker; dorsal fins with 3 horizontal, yellowish brown bands except band near tip of first dorsal, which is broad and black. Reported to 28 cm. Red Sea (type locality) and east coast of Africa to the Society Islands and Marquesas

Hawaiian Islands

Islands; southern Japan to Queensland and New Caledonia; unintentionally introduced to the Hawaiian Islands. Typically found in turbid, protected waters on silty sand to mud bottoms from a few to at least 100 m, often in small aggregations.

Parapriacanthus sp., Coral Sea

SWEEPERS
(PEMPHERIDAE)

This small family consists of only 2 genera, *Pempheris* with about 20 species, and *Parapriacanthus* with 10 small species, 2 of which from the South Pacific region are undescribed (the family is under study by R. D. Mooi). Sweepers, and especially those of the genus *Parapriacanthus*, may be difficult to identify from underwater photographs. All pempherid fishes are found in the Indo-Pacific region except for 2 in the western Atlantic. These fishes are distinctive in having a single short dorsal fin with IV-VII spines and 7–12 soft rays, and a long anal fin with III (rarely II) spines and 17–45 soft rays; the caudal fin is usually slightly forked with 15 branched rays; the pelvic fins have I,5 rays, their origin below the lower base of the pectorals. The body shape of *Pempheris* is

unusual in being very deep below the dorsal fin, then tapering strongly, especially on the ventral side, to the narrow caudal peduncle. The body of the species of *Parapriacanthus* is more slender and symmetrical. Other pempherid features include a very large eye, short snout, and strongly oblique mouth with projecting lower jaw; the maxilla is broad, exposed on the cheek, and reaching to below the pupil; teeth are small with incurved tips, in bands in jaws, on palatines, and in a V-shaped patch on vomer; the gill rakers are long. The scales vary from ctenoid and adherent to cycloid and deciduous. The species of *Parapriacanthus* and some of *Pempheris* have bioluminescent organs associated with the digestive tract (Haneda & Johnson, 1958, 1962). All the species are nocturnal. They are usually seen by day in aggregations in caves or beneath ledges, dispersing at night to feed individually on zooplankton.

DISPAR SWEEPER

Parapriacanthus dispar (Herre, 1935)

Dorsal rays VI,8–10 (rarely 8 or 10); anal rays III,21–25 (usually 22–24); pectoral rays 16–17, usually 16; lateral-line scales 54–64; gill rakers 5–7 + 16–19 (rarely 19); body depth 2.4–2.95 in standard length; head length 2.9–3.5 in standard length; eye about 2.2 in head length; anal-fin base 3.15–3.8 in standard length; caudal fin forked; dull pink dorsally, the scales rimmed with blackish, silvery on sides, densely spotted with dark-edged yellow dots; operculum silvery; head yellowish anteriorly, the front of snout and chin blackish; median fins with dusky pink rays and clear membranes; tip of caudal lobes blackish; a thin blackish line at base of caudal fin. Attains about 8 cm. Known

Sulawesi

from the Philippines, Indonesia, Solomon Islands (Ysabel Island, type locality), Great Barrier Reef, Chesterfield Islands, New Caledonia, and Loyalty Islands; illustrated specimen from a cave in 18 m.

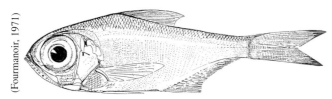

(Fourmanoir, 1971)

REDFIN SWEEPER

Parapriacanthus marei Fourmanoir, 1971

Dorsal rays VI,10–11; anal rays III,26–28; lateral-line scales 56–63; gill rakers 7–8 + 19–22; body depth 2.6–2.75 in standard length; head length 3.0–3.5 in standard length; eye large, about 2.0 in head length; anal-fin base 2.5–2.6 in standard length; caudal fin forked; pink, bluish on back, the scales dorsally and anteriorly edged in black, those posteriorly edged in brown; fins red, the caudal tips black (color note from Fourmanoir, 1971). Reaches about 10 cm. Described from a single specimen collected in 1.5 m at Maré, Loyalty Islands; also known from Vanuatu and Philippines (R. D. Mooi, pers. comm.).

COPPER SWEEPER

Pempheris oualensis Cuvier in Lesson, 1831

Dorsal rays VI,9–10 (usually 9); anal rays III,36–45; pectoral rays 16–18 (usually 17); lateral-line scales 54–79; scales above lateral line 5–7; small axillary scale at pelvic-fin angle; gill rakers 7–10 + 19–26; body depth 1.85–2.4 in standard length; prepelvic area narrow and keeled; caudal fin slightly forked; no light organs; bronze, the dorsal part of head and body with a dark greenish cast; base and axil of pectoral fins black; leading edge of dorsal fin broadly blackish to back; base of anal fin blackish; outer margin of anal and caudal fins often broadly dusky to blackish. Reaches 22 cm. Northwestern Australia, Cocos-Keeling Islands, and Christmas Island in Indian Ocean; in the Pacific from Philippines to Great Barrier Reef and New Caledonia, east to Line Islands and the islands of Micronesia (type locality, Oualan = Kusiae), and French Polynesia. *Pempheris otaitensis* Cuvier appears to be a synonym.

Line Islands

RAPA SWEEPER

Pempheris rapa Mooi, 1998

Dorsal rays VI,10–11; anal rays III,33–37; pectoral rays 16–17 (usually 16); lateral-line scales 72–84 (rarely fewer than 76); scales above lateral line 12–14; all scales ctenoid and adherent; no scales on throat; no pelvic axillary scale; gill rakers 11–13 + 26–29 (in specimens above 30 mm standard length); body depth 2.2–2.45 in standard length; prepelvic area broad, without a keel; caudal fin forked; no light organs; life color of adults not recorded but recalled as being bronze to coppery overall; a vertically elongate dark spot on opercle at level of eye of some specimens; leading edge and tip of dorsal fin blackish; tip of anterior rays of anal fin blackish; caudal fin pale. Largest specimen, 17.4 cm. Known only from the island of Rapa; all specimens were collected from caves in about 18 m.

Rapa (after Mooi, 1998)

SILVER SWEEPER
Pempheris schwenkii Bleeker, 1855

Dorsal rays VI-VII (rarely VII),8–9 (usually 9); anal rays III,34–43; pectoral rays 16–18 (usually 17); lateral-line scales 46–55; scales above lateral line 3–4; small axillary scale at pelvic-fin angle; gill rakers 6–9 +19–23; body depth 2.0–2.35 in standard length; prepelvic area narrow and keeled; caudal fin slightly forked; no light organs; deep purplish gray dorsally, silvery on sides and ventrally; tip and leading edge of dorsal fin dusky; scaled basal part of anal fin blackish; margin of caudal fin sometimes dusky; no black spot at base and axil of pectoral fins. Attains 15 cm. Red Sea and east coast of Africa to Vanuatu, Fiji, and Helen Reef in Micronesia; southern Japan to Great Barrier Reef. Western Australia south to Rottnest Island; type locality, Batu Island, Indonesia; reported from near shore to 40 m.

Seychelles

MONOS
(MONODACTYLIDAE)

The fishes of this small family of 2 genera, *Monodactylus* and the Australian *Schuettea*, are also called moonfishes. They are deep-bodied (some deeper than long) and compressed, with a very short snout and a very oblique mouth; the teeth in the jaws are small and brushlike, those on the vomer and palatines in villiform bands; there is a single dorsal fin of VII-VIII small spines and 26–36 soft rays, and an anal fin with III small spines and 27–37 soft rays; the anterior portion of dorsal and anal fins is strongly elevated; caudal fin slightly emarginate; scales small and weakly ctenoid; dorsal and anal fins nearly fully scaled; the color is predominantly silvery. Monos are usually encountered in schools; they are more apt to be found in estuarine or mangrove areas than in fully saline marine environments, but they can be seen at times over silty inshore reefs.

Silver Mono, *Monodactylus argenteus*, Papua New Guinea

SILVER MONO
Monodactylus argenteus (Linnaeus, 1758)

Dorsal rays VII-VIII,27–30; anal rays III,27–30; pectoral rays 16–18; pelvic fins I,2–3 (absent or vestigial in adults); lateral-line scales 52–58; gill rakers 8 + 18–22; upper jaw shorter than eye; teeth small, compressed, tricuspid (middle cusp longest) in bands in jaws; silvery, the juveniles with a dark bar through eye, and sometimes a second bar from nape through pectoral-fin base; median fins silvery proximally, yellowish distally, the leading edges of the dorsal and anal fins black (this edge much broader in anal fin). Reported to 25 cm, but rarely exceeds 20 cm. Red Sea and east coast of Africa to the Mariana, Caroline, and Samoa Islands; in the western Pacific from southern Japan to New South Wales and Norfolk Island; type locality, "Indiis." Typically found in active dense schools in brackish environments.

Aquarium photo

303

Blackfin Chub, *Kyphosus sydneyanus,* New Caledonia

SEA CHUBS
(KYPHOSIDAE)

Opinions vary on the limits of this family. Some authors include the Girellidae, Scorpididae, and Microcanthidae as subfamilies of the Kyphosidae; these are regarded here as families. The sea chubs, also called rudderfishes, consist of 4 genera: *Kyphosus* with about 10 species and the monotypic *Hermosilla, Neoscorpis,* and *Sectator.* These fishes are moderately deep-bodied and compressed with a small head, short snout, and a small terminal or slightly inferior mouth; the maxilla slips partially under the preorbital bone when the mouth is closed; the teeth are incisiform, in one row (in *Kyphosus*), or 2 rows, the inner row slender and incurved (in *Sectator*); the scales are small and ctenoid, those of *Kyphosus* and *Sectator* covering most of the head and fins; the dorsal fin is continuous, with XI (rarely X or XII) spines and 11–22 rays; the caudal fin is forked; the swimbladder is bifurcate posteriorly, extending into the tail. Sea chubs are omnivorous, but most feed mainly on benthic plants; the digestive tract is very long. They often occur in schools, a big advantage for those feeding on benthic algae because they are able to overwhelm the defenses of the territorial herbivores such as certain of the damselfishes and surgeonfishes. Juveniles of the species of *Kyphosus* and *Sectator* are often found well offshore with drifting algae and flotsam.

GRAY CHUB

Kyphosus bigibbus Lacepède, 1801

Dorsal rays XI,11–13 (rarely 11 or 13); anal rays III,10–12 (rarely 10 or 12); pectoral rays 18–20 (modally 19); lateral-line scales 51–55 (modally 53); gill rakers 21–24; body depth 2.15–2.5 in standard length; head length 3.2–3.9 in standard length; maxilla reaching to below anterior edge of eye when mouth fully closed; soft portion of dorsal fin not higher than spinous portion; base of spinous portion of dorsal fin longer than soft portion; longest anal soft ray (the second) 8.1–10.9 in standard length (in specimens over about 25 cm standard length); pelvic fins not approaching anus, 4.8–6.65 in standard length; caudal fin slightly forked; silvery gray, the edges of the scales brown, resulting in a longitudinal linear pattern on body; a broad silvery stripe from front of snout to below eye, bordered below by a gray streak extending posteriorly from end of maxilla; opercular membrane dark brown to black; fins dark gray. Reported to 75 cm. South African spearfishing record, 10 kg. Distribution appears antitropical in the Indian Ocean, northern Red Sea, South Africa, Madagascar (type locality), Mauritius, and Western Australia; in the Pacific, southern Japan, Queensland, New South Wales, Lord Howe Island, Norfolk Island, Kermadec Islands, New Zealand, and Rapa (Bishop Museum specimen).

PACIFIC CHUB

Kyphosus pacificus Sakai & Nakabo, 2004

Dorsal rays XI,11–13 (rarely 11 or 13); anal rays III,11; pectoral rays 18–20 (modally 19); lateral-line scales 52–56 (modally 53); gill rakers 26–29; body depth 1.95–2.55 in standard length; head length 3.4–4.3 in standard length (head decreasing in relative length with growth); maxilla reaching to below anterior edge of eye when mouth fully closed; soft portion of dorsal fin not as high as spinous; base of spinous portion of dorsal fin longer than soft portion; longest anal soft ray (the second) longer than longest dorsal spine, 6.7–8.0 in standard length (in specimens over 25 cm standard length); pelvic fins short, not approaching anus, 5.0–5.9 in standard length; caudal fin slightly forked; silvery gray, the edges of the scales brown, resulting in a longitudinal linear pattern on body; a broad silvery stripe from front of snout to below eye, bordered below by a gray streak extending posteriorly from end of maxilla; opercular membrane dark brown to black; fins dark gray; an occasional all-yellow color form may be seen, and rarely individuals that appear to be a cross of yellow and normal-colored fish; even more rare are albino individuals. Attains 65 cm. Except for the Marquesas Islands (where the sea is cool for that latitude), the distribution is antiequatorial: southern Queensland, Lord Howe Island, and Norfolk Island to French Polynesia, Pitcairn Islands, and Easter Island in the South Pacific, and southern Japan, Taiwan, Ogasawara Islands (type locality), Minami-tori-shima (Marcus Island), Mariana Islands, Wake Island, and the Hawaiian Islands in the North Pacific. *K. sandwicensis* (Sauvage) is an older name for *K. pacificus*, at least for the Hawaiian population. Occurs in schools on seaward reefs or rocky substrata. The stomach contents of 6 adults examined by the author consisted entirely of benthic algae of the genera *Sargassum, Ulva, Zonaria, Gelidium, Amansia, Polysiphonia, Herposiphonia, Gelidiella, Griffithsia, Hypnea,* and *Turbinaria* (the only fish known to eat such a tough alga, though others of the genus probably do as well).

Ogasawara Islands

The more common look-alike species in the Pacific, *K. pacificus* (see following account), was not distinguished from *bigibbus* until recently. The two are best separated by gill-raker counts (*pacificus* with 26–29). At standard lengths greater than about 25 cm, the length of the second anal ray provides separation, 6.7–8.0 in standard length for *pacificus*, compared with 8.1–10.9 for *bigibbus*. The two species occur together in the western Pacific, but currently only at Lord Howe Island and Rapa for islands of southern Oceania (Sakai & Nakabo, 2004).

Johnston Island

Ducie, Pitcairn Islands/yellow phase

305

Halmahera, Indonesia

Great Barrier Reef

Redang, Malaysia

HIGHFIN CHUB
Kyphosus cinerascens (Forsskål, 1775)
Dorsal rays XI,12; anal rays III,11–12 (usually 11); lateral-line scales 49–52; gill rakers 26–31; body depth 2.2–2.5 in standard length; head length 3.6–3.9 in standard length; dorsal profile of head with a protuberance anterior to upper part of eye; maxilla reaching slightly posterior to a vertical at front edge of eye; soft portion of dorsal fin much higher than longest dorsal spine, the longest dorsal spine contained 1.3–1.7 times in longest soft ray; base of spinous portion of dorsal fin slightly longer than base of soft portion; caudal fin slightly forked; silvery gray, the scale edges brown, especially the upper and lower edges, resulting in a pattern of longitudinal brown lines; opercular membrane dark brown. Reported to 50 cm. Occurs from the Red Sea (type locality) and east coast of Africa to the Hawaiian Islands, Line Islands, and Tuamotu Archipelago; in the western Pacific from Japan to New South Wales. Usually found in small aggregations over coral reefs or rocky substrata. The stomachs of 3 specimens were examined; all contained benthic algae.

BLACKFIN CHUB
Kyphosus sydneyanus (Günther, 1886)
Dorsal rays XI,12; anal rays III,10–11; lateral-line scales 55–59; body depth 2.2–2.4 in standard length; head length 3.6–3.9 in standard length; dorsal profile of head smoothly convex except for a slight protuberance anterior to upper part of eye; maxilla not reaching a vertical at anterior edge of eye; longest dorsal spine nearly twice as long as longest soft ray; spinous portion of dorsal fin nearly 1.5 times longer than soft portion; caudal fin slightly forked; silvery with a faint pattern of dark stripes following longitudinal rows of scales; silvery area of cheek bisected by an oblique dusky streak from corner of mouth; a distinct black spot just below axil of pectoral fin; fins dark gray to black except base of median fins. Attains 60 cm. Southern half of Australia on both coasts, east to Lord Howe Island, Norfolk Island, northern New Zealand, and New Caledonia. A coastal species usually found over rocky substrata; occurs from the shallows to about 30 m.

BRASSY CHUB
Kyphosus vaigiensis (Quoy & Gaimard, 1825)
Dorsal rays XI,14 (rarely 13 or 15); anal rays III,13 (rarely 12); lateral-line scales 51–55; gill rakers 8–10 + 20–24; body depth 2.3–2.5 in standard length; head length 3.4–3.65 in standard length; maxilla reaching to below anterior margin of eye when mouth fully closed; soft portion of dorsal fin not higher than spinous; base of spinous portion of dorsal fin shorter than soft portion; dorsal fin slightly forked; silvery gray with narrow brassy stripes along upper and lower edges of scales of body; 2 oblique brassy bands on snout and cheek, one from upper lip to upper corner of preopercle, the other from front of snout through lower part of eye; opercular membrane usually yellowish brown. Reported to reach 60 cm. Occurs from the Red Sea and east coast of Africa to the Hawaiian Islands and the islands of French Polynesia; type locality, Waigeo, Indonesia. *Kyphosus lembus* (Cuvier), *K. ternatensis* (Bleeker), *K. gibsoni* Ogilby, and *K. bleekeri* Fowler are synonyms (Sakai & Nakabo, 1995). Also known as the Lowfin Chub.

Hawaiian Islands

BLUESTRIPED CHUB

Sector ocyurus (Jordan & Gilbert, 1882)
Dorsal rays XI,15; anal rays III,13; pectoral rays 19–20; lateral-line scales 58–66; gill rakers 9 + 20–22; body depth 2.85–3.0 in standard length; head small, its length 3.7–4.0 in standard length; eye near middle of head; maxilla nearly reaching a vertical through front edge of eye; pointed incisiform teeth in a close-set row in jaws with a detached inner row of very slender, strongly incurved teeth; spinous portion of dorsal fin higher than soft; caudal fin deeply forked with slender lobes; brassy gray dorsally, bluish white ventrally, with 2 blue stripes on body, the uppermost along back beneath dorsal fin to upper base of caudal fin and the second midlateral with a broad, yellow ventral border; 2 blue streaks from snout, diverging as they cross head; fins yellow. Reaches about 38 cm (a report of 60 cm unconfirmed). An eastern Pacific species from southern California to Ecuador (type locality, Panama) that has turned up as apparent waifs in the Hawaiian Islands (where it was described as *S. azureus* by Jordan and Evermann, 1903), Society Islands (Randall, 1961c), Japan (Araga in Masuda et al., 1984), and Guam (Myers, 1999); in the Marquesas Islands, however, Randall & Earle (2000) observed aggregations of as many as 40 individuals in the water column off exposed promontories of Nuku Hiva and Eiao.

STRIPEYS
(MICROCANTHIDAE)

This small family consists of four genera, *Microcanthus*, *Atypichthys*, *Neatypus*, and *Tilodon*, and five species. These fishes have often been included as a subfamily of the Kyphosidae or the Scorpididae. Based on the lack of similarity of larval forms to the other families, Johnson in Moser et al. (1984) concluded that they warrant family rank, and he is followed here. With their ovate, deep, compressed bodies, small mouths, setiform (brushlike) teeth, small cycloid scales, scaled head, and striking color patterns, they resemble butterflyfishes, and they were once classified in the Chaetodontidae. They lack the tholichthys larval form typical of the latter family. They have a serrate preopercle; continuous unnotched dorsal fin with X-XI spines and 16–21 rays; anal fin with III spines and 14–18 soft rays; pelvic fins I,5, distinctly posterior to pectorals; and caudal fin varying from truncate to slightly emarginate or forked. The family is subtropical in Australia and New Zealand, and *Microcanthus* is antitropical in the western Pacific. The species are omnivorous.

STRIPEY

Microcanthus strigatus (Cuvier in C & V, 1831)
Dorsal rays XI,16–17; anal rays III,14–15 (rarely 15); pectoral rays 15–17; lateral-line scales 49–52; body deep, the depth 1.75–1.9 in standard length; head length 2.7–3.0 in standard length; eye large, its diameter greater than snout length; slender pointed teeth in many rows in jaws; caudal fin slightly emarginate; pale yellow with 6 oblique stripes on body that are narrower ventrally. Largest specimen examined, 19.5 cm. Antitropical; occurs in the north at the Hawaiian Islands, Japan (type locality), Taiwan, and China, and in the south in Western Australia, southern Queensland, Lord Howe Island, Norfolk Island, and New Caledonia. Typically found around rocky areas and coral reefs of sheltered waters of bays and harbors; also penetrates brackish habitats. The young in the Hawaiian Islands may be caught

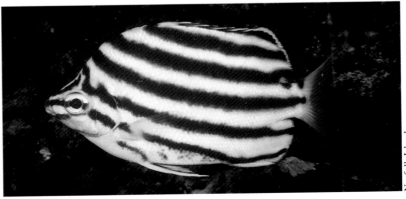

Norfolk Island

in tidepools from December to April. From a settlement size of about 1.2 cm, they grow to 4–5 cm in 4 months, and by the end of the year reach 7.5–10 cm. Feeds on small crustaceans and benthic algae.

Pennant Bannerfish, *Heniochus chrysostomus*, Marshall Islands

BUTTERFLYFISHES
(CHAETODONTIDAE)

The colorful fishes of this family are among the most popular with aquarists and fish watchers who snorkel and dive on coral reefs. They were included in the same family as the angelfishes until Burgess (1974) provided evidence that they should be given family status. The two families share such features as a deep, ovate, compressed body, a small mouth with small brush-like teeth (*Chaetodon* means bristle tooth), no teeth on the palate, ctenoid scales that extend onto head and well out on median fins, and a single unnotched dorsal fin. The butterflyfishes lack the spine at the corner of the preopercle that is always present in the angelfishes; they have a scaly axillary process at the base of the pelvic fins that angelfishes lack; and their scales are less strongly ctenoid. The larval stage, termed the tholichthys, is orbicular with large bony plates on the head and anterior body (the larval stage of angelfishes is very different). The dorsal fin of chaetodontids has VI-XVI strong spines (no

initial procumbent spine) and 15–30 soft rays; the anterior spinous membranes of the fin are deeply incised; anal fin with III-V (usually III) spines and 14–23 rays; caudal fin varying from slightly emarginate to slightly rounded; pelvic fins I,5, below or slightly posterior to the pectorals; a long, coiled intestine; and 24 vertebrae. Butterflyfishes are diurnal; at night they sleep in the cover of the reef, usually paler, but some species with significantly different night color pattern; a few of these are illustrated in the species accounts. Many of the chaetodontid fishes feed wholly or in large part on the polyps of corals or other coelenterates (Hiatt & Strasburg, 1960; Harmelin-Vivien, 1979; Sano, 1989). Those that are obligate coral-polyp feeders are obviously not good candidates for aquarium fishes. Other species feed on benthic algae or small benthic invertebrates such as worms and crustaceans. A few such as the species of *Hemitaurichthys* and *Heniochus diphreutes* are primarily zooplankton feeders. These are more inclined to form aggregations than other species. Most species are solitary or occur in monogamous pairs of long duration. Some species such as *Chaetodon trifascialis* have very small territories that they aggressively defend; others may cover rather large areas. Those that feed on coral take only one or a few bites of any one coral colony before moving on to another, and most feed only on the polyps, which the coral can regenerate. This is in sharp contrast to the coral-feeding Crown-of-Thorns Starfish (*Acanthaster planci*) that is able to kill entire coral colonies when it feeds. Most butterflyfishes are found on coral reefs or rocky sub-

strata in less than 30 m, but a few occur at depths of 200 m or more. The family consists of 123 species that are classified in 11 genera (Allen et al., 1998). Pyle & Randall (1994) provided references to 15 natural hybrids of chaetodontid fishes and noted that at least 12 others remain to be documented. Allen et al. (1988) published a well-illustrated guide to the butterflyfishes and angelfishes of the world; Pyle in Carpenter & Niem (2001a) reviewed the central and western Pacific species of these families.

Johnston Island

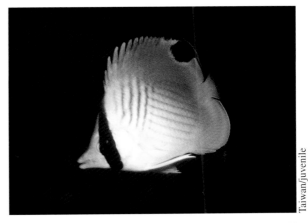

Taiwan/juvenile

Johnston Island (night)

THREADFIN BUTTERFLYFISH
Chaetodon auriga Forsskål, 1775
Dorsal rays XIII,22–25; anal rays III,19–22; pectoral rays 15–17; lateral line incomplete, ending below last rays of dorsal fin (true of other *Chaetodon*); longitudinal scale series 31–40; body depth 1.6–1.75 in standard length; snout moderately pointed, 2.2–2.8 in head length; fourth to sixth dorsal soft rays prolonged to a posterior filament that may extend well beyond caudal fin; caudal fin slightly rounded; white with 2 series of oblique blackish

lines set at right angles, shading posteriorly to orange-yellow; a black spot present in outer part of soft portion of dorsal fin (except the Red Sea population); a black bar through eye, very broad below eye. Reaches 20 cm. Occurs throughout the Indo-Pacific region, and a few have turned up as vagrants to the Galápagos Islands; type locality, Red Sea. A common species found in a variety of reef habitats from the shallows to at least 30 m; feeds mainly on coral polyps, anemones, small crustaceans, polychaete worms, eggs, and algae.

Palau

BARONESS BUTTERFLYFISH

Chaetodon baronessa Cuvier, 1829

Dorsal rays XI-XII,23–26; anal rays III,20–22; pectoral rays 15–17; longitudinal scale series 24–30; body very deep, the depth 1.2–1.4 in standard length; snout protuding, its length 2.6–3.0 in head length; dorsal and anal fins continuing to increase in height to about the sixth rays of these fins, giving the fish an approximate triangular shape; caudal fin slightly rounded; body with narrow, chevron-shaped, purplish gray bars alternating with yellow anteriorly, shading to dark purplish gray posteriorly with a narrow yellow slash across caudal peduncle into anal fin; head yellow with 2 curved, dark brown bars, one through eye; caudal fin gray with a transparent posterior margin and a yellow and black submarginal band. Attains about 12 cm. Cocos-Keeling Islands in the Indian Ocean and southern Japan south to the Great Barrier Reef and New Caledonia, east to Palau, Yap, and Fiji; no type locality. Occurs on coral reefs, especially where tabular *Acropora* is present; apparently feeds

Banda Islands, Indonesia/juvenile

only on coral polyps; occurs in pairs and is territorial. Also known as the Eastern Triangular Butterflyfish. Closely related to *Chaetodon triangulum* Cuvier of the Indian Ocean, which has a boomerang-shaped yellow mark in the basal part of the caudal fin in addition to the yellow streak across the caudal peduncle and into the anal fin.

BENNETT'S BUTTERFLYFISH

Chaetodon bennetti Cuvier in C & V, 1831

Dorsal rays XIII-XIV (rarely XIII),15–17 (rarely 15); anal rays III,20–22; pectoral rays 14–16; longitudinal scale series 36–40; body depth 1.4–1.7 in standard length; snout length about 3 in head length; caudal fin slightly rounded; yellow with a large, round, blue-edged black spot on upper side, a blue-edged, dark brown bar through eye, and 2 narrow curved blue bands, 1 above and 1 below pectoral fin. Attains about 17 cm. East coast of Africa to the islands of French Polynesia except the Marquesas Islands; in the western Pacific from southern Japan to the Great Barrier Reef and Lord Howe Island; type locality, Sumatra. Reported to feed mainly on coral polyps; sometimes seen in pairs. One of the more shy species of butterflyfishes.

Fiji

310

BURGESS' BUTTERFLYFISH

Chaetodon burgessi Allen & Starck, 1973

Dorsal rays XIII,18–19; anal rays III,15–16; pectoral rays 16; longitudinal scale series 35–37; body depth 1.6–1.7 in standard length; snout length 2.8–3.0 in head length; third or fourth dorsal spine longest, 1.1–1.3 in head length, the more posterior spines and rays progressively shorter, not extending posterior to base of caudal fin; caudal fin slightly rounded; white with a black band through eye, one from nape to below pectoral fin, and black on all the body and dorsal and anal fins posterior to an oblique line from the base of the fourth dorsal spine to the middle of the anal fin, except for white margin on these fins. Attains 14 cm. Known from the Philippines, Indonesia, Palau (type locality), Kiribati (reported to hybridize at Tarawa with *C. tinkeri* and *C. flavocoronatus*), Caroline Islands, and Tonga, generally at more than 40 m.

Palau

Sulawesi

Marshall Islands (night)

CITRON BUTTERFLYFISH

Chaetodon citrinellus Cuvier in C & V, 1831

Dorsal rays XIII-XIV (rarely XIII),20–22; anal rays III,20–22; pectoral rays 14–16; longitudinal scale series 36–42; body depth 1.6–1.9 in standard length; snout protuding, its length 2.7–3.0 in head length; caudal fin slightly rounded; body pale to bright yellow with a small round spot on each scale that is usually blue to violet but may be orange; head with a dark brown bar through eye; outer part of anal fin with a broad black margin and a pale yellow submarginal band. Reaches 13 cm. East coast of Africa to the Hawaiian Islands and French Polynesia; in the western Pacific from southern Japan to New South Wales, Lord Howe Island, and Norfolk Island; type locality, Guam. Often seen in pairs; feeds on coral polyps, polychaete worms, and benthic algae. Also known as the Speckled Butterflyfish.

Guam/juvenile

311

Line Islands/juvenile

Line Islands

MARQUESAN BUTTERFLYFISH

Chaetodon declivis Randall, 1975

Dorsal rays XIII,20; anal rays III,15–16; pectoral rays 15; longitudinal scale series 37–41; scales on side of body much larger than posterior scales; body depth 1.6–1.8 in standard length; snout length 2.9–3.5 in head length; third or fourth dorsal spines longest, the posterior spines and rays progressively shorter; dorsal fin not extending posterior to base of caudal fin; caudal fin slightly rounded; white, the scales of body with a blackish spot, to an oblique demarcation from base of fourth dorsal spine to rear part of anal fin, then orange-yellow with a variable amount of black; head with a broad yellow bar through eye. Attains about 12 cm. Known only from the Marquesas Islands (type locality, Fatu Hiva), the Line Islands, and observed in the Phoenix Islands (G. R. Allen, pers. comm.); occurs deeper than 20 m, and generally below 30 m. One of a complex of species that includes *C. tinkeri, C. mitratus, C. burgessi,* and *C. flavocoronatus.* The Line Islands population has more black in the orange-yellow posterior part of the body; it has been described as a subspecies, *Chaetodon declivis wilderi* (Pyle).

Palau/juvenile

Marshall Islands

SADDLED BUTTERFLYFISH

Chaetodon ephippium Cuvier in C & V, 1831

Dorsal rays XII-XIV (usually XIII),21–25; anal rays III,20–23; pectoral rays 15–17; longitudinal scale series 33–40; body depth 1.6–1.8 in standard length; snout protruding, its length 2.2–2.6 in head length; fourth dorsal ray (and adjacent rays) prolonged to a filament that may extend beyond caudal fin; caudal fin usually truncate; body yellowish gray with narrow purple stripes on ventral half, and a very large ovate black area on back, broadly bordered with white below, extending nearly to margin of dorsal fin; an arc of bright orange-red and yellow behind black area in dorsal fin; a large, irregular, orange-yellow zone ventrally on head and chest; an orange-red mark across posterior caudal peduncle. Reported to a maximum length of 23 cm. Southern India and Cocos-Keeling Islands to the Hawaiian Islands and French Polynesia (type locality, Society Islands); in the western Pacific from southern Japan to New South Wales. Its diet includes coral polyps, sponges, other benthic invertebrates, algae, and fish eggs. Reported to form hybrids with *Chaetodon auriga, C. semeion* (Randall et al., 1977), and *C. xanthocephalus.*

YELLOWSNOUT BUTTERFLYFISH
Chaetodon flavirostris Günther, 1874

Dorsal rays XII-XIII,24–27; anal rays III,20–21; pectoral rays 15–16; longitudinal scale series 40–46; body depth 1.4–1.6 in standard length; snout slightly protruding, its length 2.8–3.3 in head length; adults with a prominent protuberance anteriorly on nape; dorsal and anal fins low and rounded posteriorly; caudal fin slightly rounded; black, shading to gray dorsoanteriorly on body and posterior half of head, with a large, hemispherical, dusky yellow area on back; protuberance on nape black; snout orange-yellow except for white lips; a black bar below eye; caudal fin and soft portions of dorsal and anal fins with bands of yellow, orange-red, and black to gray. Reaches 20 cm. Southeastern Australia east in the South Pacific to the islands of southern French Polynesia and the Pitcairn Islands; type locality, Vava'u, Tonga. Occurs on reefs as solitary individuals, in pairs, and occasionally in aggregations. Reported to feed on coral polyps, algae, and small benthic invertebrates. Also called the Black Butterflyfish.

Great Barrier Reef

GÜNTHER'S BUTTERFLYFISH
Chaetodon guentheri Ahl, 1923

Dorsal rays XIII,20–23; anal rays III,18–20; pectoral rays 14; longitudinal scale series usually 39–40; body depth 1.5–1.7 in standard length; snout slightly protruding, its length 2.7–3.3 in head length; dorsal and anal fins low and rounded posteriorly; caudal fin truncate to slightly rounded; body white with a round, bluish gray to purple spot on each scale, shading to yellow dorsally and posteriorly and to orange on the soft portions of the dorsal and anal fins except for a white border and black submarginal line; head light gray with a broad, dark gray to black bar from top of nape to eye, continuing much narrower or only faintly below eye; caudal fin light yellow. Maximum length 14 cm. Western Pacific from southern Japan to New South Wales, Lord Howe Island, and New Caledonia; type locality, Sri Lanka. Reported from 5 to at least 50 m; usually found in deeper water in tropical localities except areas of upwelling such as Bali and Komodo.

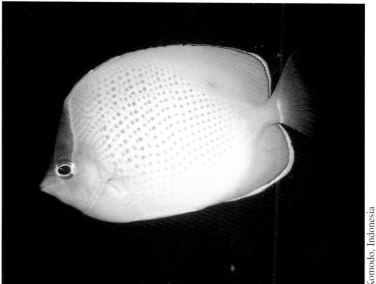

Komodo, Indonesia

BLACKLIP BUTTERFLYFISH
Chaetodon kleinii Bloch, 1790

Dorsal rays XIII-XIV (usually XIII),20–23; anal rays III,17–20; pectoral rays 13–16; longitudinal scale series 33–41; body depth 1.4–1.7 in standard length; snout length 2.5–3.2 in head length; caudal fin slightly rounded; posterior half of body orangish brown, anterior half and posterior head whitish, with a broad brown bar from below third to fifth dorsal spines to abdomen; each scale of body with a large pale bluish spot; head with a black bar from upper nape through eye to chest, the bar above eye blue in mature adults; snout bluish gray, the lips black; soft portions of dorsal and anal fins dusky orange-yellow with a white posterior margin and black submarginal line; caudal fin orange-yellow with a pale blue bar at base; pelvic fins black. Reaches 13 cm. East coast of Africa to the Hawaiian Islands, Line Islands, and Samoa Islands; southern Japan to New South Wales and Lord Howe Island; type locality, East Indies; one individual reported from the Galápagos Islands (Grove & Lavenberg,

Papua New Guinea

1997). Known from as little as 4 m to as much as 122 m (submarine observations by Chave & Mundy, 1994); feeds heavily on soft corals but also on zooplankton and benthic algae; may be seen singly or in pairs. *Chaetodon corallicola* Snyder is a synonym. Also called Klein's Butterflyfish.

LINED BUTTERFLYFISH

Chaetodon lineolatus Cuvier in C & V, 1831

Dorsal rays XII,24–27; anal rays III,20–22; pectoral rays 16–18; longitudinal scale series 26–33; body depth 1.5–1.8 in standard length; snout long and protruding, its length 2.0–2.7 in head length; caudal fin slightly rounded; pale gray to white, shading to yellow dorsally on posterior half of body, with a broad, oblique black zone on back below posterior half of dorsal fin, curving across caudal peduncle onto base of posterior part of anal fin; a very broad black bar across head from nape through eye; a small whitish spot anteriorly on nape within black bar; median fins yellow except for clear posterior margin of caudal. Largest species of the family; reaches 30 cm. Occurs throughout the Indo-Pacific region except the Arabian Sea to the Persian Gulf and the Gulf of Carpentaria to southern New Guinea; type locality, Mauritius. Reported from the depth range of 2–171 m; usually found in less than 30 m. Feeds mainly on coral polyps and sea anemones, also consumes other benthic invertebrates and algae. Closely related to *C. oxycephalus* Bleeker, which ranges from the Maldive Islands to the Solomon Islands; it differs in having the broad black bar through the eye broken in the middle of nape by an oblique white zone.

RACOON BUTTERFLYFISH

Chaetodon lunula (Lacepède, 1802)

Dorsal rays XI-XIII,22–25; anal rays III,17–19; pectoral rays 15–16; longitudinal scale series 35–44; body depth 1.4–1.7 in standard length; snout length 2.9–3.4 in head length; caudal fin slightly rounded; body orange-yellow with oblique reddish brown bands, overlaid dorsally with blackish pigment; a yellow-edged, curved black band centered at base of eighth dorsal spine and passing to upper half of gill opening; a broad black bar on head through eye, followed by an equally broad white bar; snout yellow; a yellow-edged black bar on caudal peduncle, continuing upward as an arc into base of dorsal fin. Attains 20 cm. Indo-Pacific except the Red Sea and Gulf of Aden where replaced by the similar *C. fasciatus*; also not known from the Persian Gulf and Arabian Sea except for southern Oman; type locality, Indian Ocean. Known in the eastern Pacific from single individuals at Cocos Island and the Galápagos Islands (Robertson et al., 2004). Common on shallow reefs but recorded to a depth of 158 m from submarine observation. Sometimes seen in small aggregations. Diet variable: opisthobranchs, nudibranchs, tube-worm tentacles, benthic algae, coral polyps, other benthic invertebrates, and zooplankton. Hobson (1974) reported this species as nocturnal, but the author has observed it only quiescent in its somber color pattern at night. Also has been observed feeding by day. Perhaps it is primarily a crepuscular feeder.

Line Islands

Line Islands

Hawaiian Islands (night)

Tuamotu Archipelago/juvenile

Marshall Islands

OVAL BUTTERFLYFISH
Chaetodon lunulatus Quoy & Gaimard, 1825
Dorsal rays XIII-XIV,20–22; anal rays III,18–21; pectoral rays 14–16; longitudinal scale series 30–39; body oval, the depth 1.5–1.8 in standard length; snout short, its length 3.0–3.8 in head length; caudal fin slightly rounded; orange-yellow with slightly oblique narrow purplish stripes on body; a yellow-edged black band across base of dorsal and anal fins, and one across middle of caudal fin; front of snout and forehead black; rest of head orange-yellow with a black bar through eye and a narrower one behind eye; a broad white bar at base of caudal fin. Attains about 15 cm. Western Australia and western Pacific from southern Japan to Great Barrier Reef, Lord Howe Island, Norfolk Island, and New Caledonia, east to the Hawaiian Islands (type locality) and the islands of French Polynesia except the Marquesas Islands; occurs on coral-rich reefs to depths of about 20 m; an obligate coral-polyp feeder that is nearly always seen in pairs.

Pair spawning occurs at dusk in Okinawa for a period of 5 days centered on full moon or new moon; pairs migrate 100–400 m from their feeding territories to the spawning site where the current is setting to the open sea (Yabuta, 1997). The very similar sister species in the Indian Ocean, *C. trifasciatus* Park, differs in having a broad orange bar at the base of the caudal fin; distributions of the 2 overlap in southeastern Indonesia; pairs consisting of one of each of the 2 species have been photographed in Bali.

Hong Kong/juvenile

Solomon Islands

BLACKBACK BUTTERFLYFISH
Chaetodon melannotus Bloch & Schneider, 1801
Dorsal rays XII-XIII,18–21; anal rays III,18–21; pectoral rays usually 14–15; longitudinal scale series 33–39; body depth 1.6–1.8 in standard length; snout slightly protruding, its length 2.6–3.3 in head length; caudal fin slightly rounded; body white with oblique black lines (dotted ventrally), ending in a broad black zone on back; a black bar through eye; head anterior to bar yellow, the posterior part white; a black saddle on caudal peduncle with a black spot on ventral edge; a black spot above anal spines; median and pelvic fins yellow. Reaches 15 cm. Red Sea and east coast of Africa to Samoa Islands; southern Japan to New South Wales, Lord Howe Island, and Norfolk Islands; not reported from the Persian Gulf to the Arabian Sea or northern or western Australia; type locality, Traquebar, India. Feeds mainly on coral polyps and soft corals. The similar *C. ocellicaudus* Cuvier of the Philippines, Indonesia, and northern Great Barrier Reef lacks the black area on the back and has an isolated black spot at the caudal-fin base.

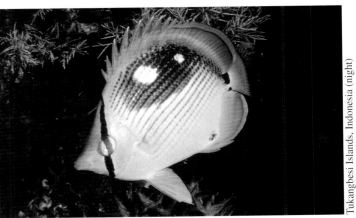

Tukangbesi Islands, Indonesia (night)

![Guam]

MERTENS' BUTTERFLYFISH
Chaetodon mertensii Cuvier in C & V, 1831
Dorsal rays XII-XIV,21–23; anal rays III,16–17 (usually 17); pectoral rays 14–16; longitudinal scale series 35–43; body depth 1.7–1.8 in standard length; snout slightly protruding, its length 2.3–3.0 in head length; caudal fin truncate to slightly rounded; anterior three-fourths of body white with 5–7 narrow, chevron-shaped black bars, the posterior one-fourth of body abruptly bright orange or yellow, this color continuing broadly onto soft portions of dorsal and anal fins; head gray dorsally, shading to white ventrally, with a white-edged black bar from nape to eye; a large blackish smudge dorsally at front of nape; basal half of caudal fin white, the outer part orange or yellow; median fins with a yellow posterior margin and black submarginal line. Reported to 12.5 cm. East coast of Africa to Rapa, Pitcairn Islands, Easter Island (DiSalvo et al., 1988), and throughout Micronesia; in the western Pacific from the Ryukyu Islands to New South Wales, Lord Howe Island, and Norfolk Island; type locality not given. Reported to feed on benthic invertebrates and algae. The Indian Ocean form has a shorter dark ocular bar, and the blackish smudge high at the front of the nape is replaced by a white-edged, black, U-shaped mark; some authors have called this a species, *C. madagaskariensis* Ahl; Allen et al. (1998) regarded it a color variety.

Palau

MEYER'S BUTTERFLYFISH
Chaetodon meyeri Bloch & Schneider, 1801
Dorsal rays XII-XIII (rarely XIII),23–25 (rarely 25); anal rays III,18–20; pectoral rays 16–17; longitudinal scale series 47–55; body depth 1.3–1.6 in standard length; snout slightly protruding, its length 2.6–3.2 in head length; caudal fin slightly rounded; body whitish to pale purplish gray, shading to pale yellow on nape, with 7 oblique, curving black bands, one of which arcs over operculum; head purplish gray with a yellow-edged black bar through eye, broader ventrally, and a yellow-edged black band around mouth; median fins yellow with black bands; paired fins yellow. Attains about 18 cm. East coast of Africa to Kiribati (Randall, 1955a), Line Islands, Phoenix Islands (Schultz, 1943), and Caroline Islands; in the western Pacific from the Ryukyu Islands to the Great Barrier Reef and Vanuatu; not reported from New Caledonia, Fiji, Tonga, and Samoa Islands; type locality, Molucca Islands. Two records from the eastern Pacific (Robertson et al., 2004). Occurs in clear-water, coral-rich areas; not common at any locality; may be seen as single individuals or in pairs; seems to feed almost exclusively on coral polyps.

Hawaiian Islands/juvenile

Marshall Islands

ORNATE BUTTERFLYFISH

Chaetodon ornatissimus Cuvier in C & V, 1831

Dorsal rays XII-XIII (rarely XIII),24–28; anal rays III,20–23; pectoral rays 15–17; longitudinal scale series 47–52; body depth 1.3–1.6 in standard length; snout slightly protruding, its length 2.6–3.2 in head length; caudal fin slightly rounded; bluish white with 6 oblique, bright orange bands; head yellow, the yellow continuing onto nape and below anteror part of dorsal fin, with black bars of varying width, one behind eye curving into dorsal fin as a narrow submarginal band, the margin yellow; anal fin colored like body basally, dusky orange distally, with a dark-edged, yellow submarginal band; caudal fin bluish white with 2 black bars. Reaches 18 cm. Occurs throughout the central and western Pacific; ranges into the Indian Ocean to the Maldive Islands; type locality, Tahiti. An obligate coral-polyp feeder that is usually seen in pairs.

Fiji/juvenile

Easter Island

DOT-DASH BUTTERFLYFISH

Chaetodon pelewensis Kner, 1868

Dorsal rays XIII,22–25; anal rays III,17–18; pectoral rays 14–15; longitudinal scale series 39–47; body depth 1.6–1.7 in standard length; snout slightly protruding, its length 2.4–3.1 in head length; caudal fin slightly rounded; yellowish gray anteriorly, shading to yellow posteriorly, with oblique rows of dark purplish brown spots, 6 of which become solid bands posteriorly; caudal peduncle and base of caudal fin abruptly bright orange; rest of fin yellow with a narrow, lens-shaped black bar and a clear outer zone; head purplish gray, shading to yellow on operculum, with a short, dark-edged orange bar through eye. Attains 12 cm. Papua New Guinea to New South Wales and Lord Howe Island, east to French Polynesia, Pitcairn Islands, and Easter Island; type locality given as Palau, but the species is not known from that archipelago. Usually observed in pairs. Overlaps with the closely related *C. punctatofasciatus* Cuvier on the Great Barrier Reef and Papua New Guinea; the two sometimes pair, and hybrids have been reported. Feeds mainly on coral polyps; also other benthic invertebrates and algae.

New Caledonia/juvenile

New Caledonia

BLUESTREAK BUTTERFLYFISH
Chaetodon plebeius Cuvier in C & V, 1831

Dorsal rays XIII-XIV,16–18; anal rays IV,14–16; pectoral rays 14–15; longitudinal scale series 36–41; body oval, the depth 1.6–1.8 in standard length; snout length 2.7–3.1 in head length; caudal fin slightly rounded; body yellow with narrow bluish to orangish gray stripes following scale rows, and a broad, bright blue streak on upper side; a blue-edged black bar through eye; a round, blue-edged black spot as large as or larger than eye on caudal peduncle; fins yellow except for clear outer zone of the caudal. Reported to 15 cm. Western Australia and southern Japan to New South Wales, Lord Howe Island, and Norfolk Island, east to New Caledonia and Fiji; only Palau (from one individual) in Micronesia; type locality, South Seas. Occurs singly or in pairs; feeds mainly on coral polyps.

Hawaiian Islands

FOURSPOT BUTTERFLYFISH
Chaetodon quadrimaculatus Gray, 1831

Dorsal rays XIII-XIV(rarely XIII),20–23; anal rays IV,16–18; pectoral rays 15–17; longitudinal scale series 38–45; body depth 1.4–1.7 in standard length; snout slightly protruding, the length 2.5–3.1 in head length; caudal fin slightly rounded; body orange-yellow, the back and base of dorsal fin dark brown, with 2 pure white spots just above lateral line; scales of orange-yellow lower part of body with a reddish to dark brown spot, the spots smaller ventrally; a dark brown bar covering most of caudal peduncle; head pale yellow with a blue-edged, dark brown bar to eye, changing to dark-edged orange below eye; fins yellow with a curved, dark-edged blue band in dorsal and anal fins. Reported to 16 cm. Ryukyu Islands and Taiwan to French Polynesia, Hawaiian Islands (type locality), and the Pitcairn Islands; only the Marshall Islands and Mariana Islands in Micronesia; no records for the East Indies or Australia east to Fiji; occurs on exposed seaward reefs, generally in 2–15 m; feeds principally on polyps of corals of the genus *Pocillopora*. Diurnal color pattern similar to the nocturnal color of several species.

Marshall Islands

LATTICED BUTTERFLYFISH
Chaetodon rafflesii Bennett, 1830

Dorsal rays XII-XIII (usually XIII),21–23; anal rays III,18–20; pectoral rays 15–16; longitudinal scale series 30–37; body depth 1.4–1.8 in standard length; snout slightly protruding, the length 2.1–2.6 in head length; caudal fin slightly rounded; yellow to orange-yellow, the scale edges reddish brown, resulting in a lattice effect; a black bar through eye, broader ventral to eye; forehead anterior to bar blue; a lens-shaped black bar in caudal fin; dorsal fin with a submarginal black band that broadens posteriorly; outer part of anal fin broadly orange with a narrow submarginal blue and black band. Attains 15 cm. Sri Lanka to the Tuamotu Archipelago; in the western Pacific from southern Japan to the northern Great Barrier Reef and New Caledonia; only Palau and the Caroline Islands in Micronesia; type locality, Sumatra. Most often on shallow sheltered reefs; feeds on sea anemones, coral polyps, polyps of octocorals, and polychaete worms.

RETICULATED BUTTERFLYFISH
Chaetodon reticulatus Cuvier in C & V, 1831
Dorsal rays XII-XIII (rarely XIII),26–29; anal rays III,20–22; pectoral rays 16–18; longitudinal scale series 45–48; body depth 1.35–1.6 in standard length; snout length 2.7–3.3 in head length; caudal fin rounded; body posterior to pectoral-fin base black with a round whitish spot on each scale; anterior body and posterior head white; a white- or yellow-edged black bar from high on nape through eye to chest; snout black except for white upper lip; an elliptical, white-edged blue band across interorbital; spinous portion of dorsal fin white, the soft portion gray with a white outer band; anal fin dark bluish gray, with a bright red edge posteriorly (red mark absent in juveniles), a black-edged, yellow submarginal band, and a white margin; a black bar across caudal peduncle and base of caudal fin; rest of fin white with a yellow-edged black bar near clear posterior margin. Reaches 16 cm. Islands of Oceania west to southern Japan, Philippines, Sulawesi, and north coast of New Guinea to the northern Great Barrier Reef; described from Tahiti and Ulea (= Woleai Atoll), Caroline Islands. Usually seen in pairs on coral reefs from a few to at least 30 m; feeds primarily on coral polyps and filamentous algae.

DOTTED BUTTERFLYFISH
Chaetodon semeion Bleeker, 1855
Dorsal rays XIII-XIV (rarely XIII),23–26; anal rays III,19–22; pectoral rays 14–15; longitudinal scale series 33–39; body depth 1.6–1.9 in standard length; snout length 2.4–2.9 in head length; dorsal fin with a posteriorly directed filament consisting of third soft ray and second and fourth rays at basal part; caudal fin slightly emarginate; orange-yellow to orange with a blackish dot on each scale; a very large blackish blotch sometimes present on back above pectoral fin; a very irregular black bar below eye, short and narrow above eye (relative size of black eye bar reduced with growth), continuing as a broad blue zone dorsally onto nape and anteriorly onto forehead; soft dorsal fin with a broad black middle band from posterior spinous portion to end of fin; anal fin with a similar black band but only on soft portion and narrowing anteriorly; caudal fin with orange rays, translucent membranes, and orange-yellow margin all around (narrow posteriorly); dorsal-fin filament orange-yellow; orange-yellow of head and body largely lost in night color pattern. Attains 24 cm. Sri Lanka, Andaman Sea, Cocos-Keeling Islands (type locality), and Christmas Island to the Line Islands, Tuamotu Archipelago, and throughout Miicronesia; in the western Pacific from the Ryukyu Islands to the northern Great Barrier Reef. Occurs on coral reefs in clear water from depths of 2–50 m, but usually in less than 20 m. Most often encountered in pairs. The most wary of the butterflyfishes.

Tuamotu Archipelago

Halmahera, Indonesia

Scott Reef, Western Australia (night)

Waikīkī Aquarium

BICOLORED BUTTERFLYFISH
Chaetodon smithi Randall, 1975

Dorsal rays XIII,23–24; anal rays III,19–20; pectoral rays 15–16; longitudinal scale series 37–46; body depth 1.7–1.9 in standard length; snout length 2.7–3.3 in head length; dorsal and anal fins broadly rounded posteriorly; caudal fin slightly emarginate; head, anterior half of body, and adjacent part of dorsal fin black, posterior half abruptly yellow; anal fin and yellow posterior part of dorsal fin with a pale blue margin and black submarginal line; pelvic fins black; outer one-fourth of caudal fin clear; juveniles similar in color to adults except the caudal fin mostly hyaline. Largest specimen, 16.4 cm. Known only from Rapa, Îlots de Bass (Marotiri), Pitcairn Islands (type locality, Pitcairn), and as a waif to Easter Island; specimens were collected from depths of 9–30 m. May occur in aggregations; limited observation indicated feeding on zooplankton and coral.

Hong Kong/juveniles

OVALSPOT BUTTERFLYFISH
Chaetodon speculum Cuvier in C & V, 1831

Dorsal rays XIV,17–18; anal rays III,15–16; pectoral rays 13–15; longitudinal scale series 37–42; body moderately deep, the depth 1.4–1.6 in standard length; snout short, its length 2.9–3.3 in head length; caudal fin slightly to moderately rounded; bright yellow with a huge, oval black spot in middle of upper side bisected by lateral line, its edges diffuse; a black bar from high on nape through eye to chest; outer one-third to one-fourth of caudal fin translucent. Reaches about 15 cm. Southern Japan to the Great

TINKER'S BUTTERFLYFISH
Chaetodon tinkeri Schultz, 1951

Dorsal rays XIII-XIV,18–22; anal rays III,16–17; pectoral rays 15–16; longitudinal scale series 36–40; body depth 1.5–1.7 in standard length; snout length 2.7–3.2 in head length; fourth dorsal spines longest, the more posterior spines and rays progressively shorter, not extending posterior to base of caudal fin; caudal fin slightly rounded; body white with a small blackish spot on each scale (spots large on the larger scales of midside of body) to a sharp demarcation from base of fourth dorsal spine to posterior part of anal fin, then black, the black extending into dorsal fin except for a white margin, submarginal black line, and orange band; head pale gray to whitish with an irregular black-edged orange-yellow bar through eye, and a yellow spot at front of snout; caudal fin yellow. Attains about 15 cm. Reported from the Hawaiian Islands (type locality, Oʻahu), Johnston Island, Marshall Islands, Cook Islands, and recently from an underwater photograph taken by Yves Lefevre in 70 m at Rangiroa Atoll,

Penyu Islands, Indonesia

Barrier Reef, Lord Howe Island, and New Caledonia, east to Fiji and Tonga; only Palau and Yap in Micronesia; Western Australia and Christmas Island in the eastern Indian Ocean; type locality, Java. Occurs in both lagoon and seaward reefs to depths of at least 30 m; not common; reported to feed on coral polyps and other benthic invertebrates.

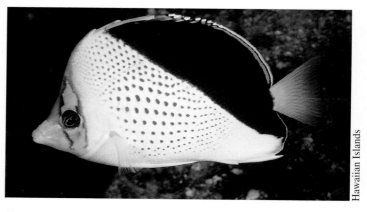

Hawaiian Islands

Tuamotu Archipelago. Known from depths of 40–183 m; feeds on a variety of benthic and planktonic invertebrates. A highly prized aquarium fish. One of a complex of deep-dwelling species that includes *C. burgessi*, *C. declivis*, *C. flavocoronatus*, and *C. mitratus*.

Society Islands

Marquesas Islands (night)

TAHITIAN BUTTERFLYFISH
Chaetodon trichrous Günther, 1874

Dorsal rays XIII,21–23; anal rays III,17–19; pectoral rays 14–15 (usually 15); longitudinal scale series 36–42; body depth 1.5–1.7 in standard length; snout short, its length 2.9–3.4 in head length; caudal fin slightly rounded; body posterior to rear base of pectoral fin dark brown, the centers of scales lighter brown; anterior body and head whitish with a black bar from high on nape through eye to front of chest; lips black; soft portion of dorsal and anal fins dark brown with a narrow, white posterior margin; caudal fin yellow with a narrow white bar at base and a broad translucent border. Reaches 12 cm. Known only from the Society Islands (type locality), Tuamotu Archipelago, and the Marquesas Islands; food habits not investigated but has been observed feeding on coral. Appears to be related to *C. kleinii*, a species not known from French Polynesia.

Chuuk/juvenile (R. F. Myers)

CHEVRON BUTTERFLYFISH
Chaetodon trifascialis Quoy & Gaimard, 1825

Dorsal rays XIII-XV,14–16; anal rays IV-V,13–15; pectoral rays 13–15; longitudinal scale series 22–29; the most elongate of the genus, the depth 1.7–2.2 in standard length; snout short, its length 2.8–3.3 in head length; spinous portion of dorsal fin low, the soft portion pointed and twice as high; caudal fin slightly rounded; white with numerous chevron-shaped, dark purple to black lines on body; head light gray with a yellow-edged black bar through eye; dorsal and anal fins orange-yellow with a narrow, pale blue margin and black submarginal line; caudal fin black with a yellow submarginal band, the upper and lower edges narrowly yellow. Attains 16.5 cm. Red Sea and east coast of Africa to Hawaiian Islands (very rare) and French Polynesia except the Marquesas Islands; southern Japan to the Great Barrier Reef, Lord Howe Island, Norfolk Island, and New Caledonia; type locality, Guam. Feeds primarily on the polyps of species of *Acropora*, occasionally on algae; has the smallest territory of the genus and is the most aggressive in its defense. Usually solitary; each male's territory typically includes 2–3 females. The spawning behavior was described by Yabuta & Kawashima (1997). Formerly classified in the genus *Megaprotodon*, now a subgenus. *Chaetodon strigangulus* Cuvier is a synonym.

Line Islands

Marshall Islands (night)

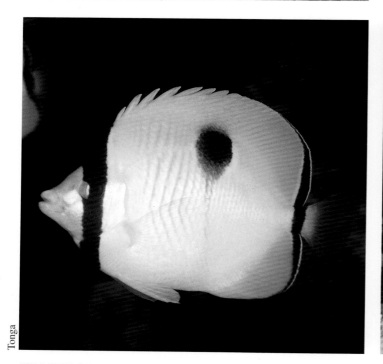

Tahiti

DOUBLEBARRED BUTTERFLYFISH
Chaetodon ulietensis Cuvier in C & V, 1831

Dorsal rays XII,23–24; anal rays III,19–21; pectoral rays 14–15; longitudinal scale series 32–37; body depth 1.5–1.8 in standard length; snout protruding, its length 2.1–2.5 in head length; caudal fin slightly rounded; head and anterior three-fourths of body white with vertical black lines following scale rows; 2 broad, blackish bars on body, one ending beneath pectoral fin, and the other on midside above middle of anal fin; posterior one-fourth of body and adjacent fins bright orange-yellow with a black spot about size of eye on side of caudal peduncle, its lower edge at ventral margin; a black bar through eye, broader below eye; caudal fin yellow with a clear posterior border and submarginal brown line. Reaches 15 cm. Southern Japan to New South Wales and Lord Howe Island, east to the Hawaiian Islands (as a waif) and the Pitcairn Islands (most common butterflyfish at Ducie Atoll); strays to Cocos-Keeling Islands in the Indian Ocean; type locality, Ulietea (= Raiatea), Society Islands. More common on protected reefs of lagoons and bays than on exposed reefs; may occur singly or in pairs; occasionally seen in small aggregations. Feeds on a wide variety of benthic invertebrates and algae. Overlaps in Sumatra with Indian Ocean relative, *Chaetodon falcula* Bloch.

Tuamotu Archipelago (right)

Tonga

TEARDROP BUTTERFLYFISH
Chaetodon unimaculatus Bloch, 1787

Dorsal rays XIII,21–23; anal rays III,18–20; pectoral rays 14–15; longitudinal scale series 38–47; body deep, the depth 1.4–1.6 in standard length; snout slightly protruding, its length 2.2–2.7 in head length; jaws strong; soft portions of dorsal and anal fins broadly rounded; caudal fin slightly rounded; white with faint, yellow, vertical lines following scale rows (slightly chevron-shaped anteriorly); a large round black spot on upper side in middle of body, its margin diffuse, usually with progressively narrower blackish streak extending ventrally; a broad black bar from upper nape through eye to chest; dorsal and anal fins yellow with a narrow white posterior margin and a broad black submarginal band that are in alignment with a black bar posteriorly on caudal peduncle; caudal fin white at base, soon becoming translucent; pelvic fins yellow. Attains 17 cm. Southern Japan to New South Wales, and Lord Howe Island east to the Hawaiian Islands, Pitcairn Islands, and Easter Island; western Australia, Christmas Island, and Cocos-Keeling Islands in the Indian Ocean; type locality, East Indies. Feeds on coral polyps (often getting some of the skeletal tissue as well), soft corals, polychaete worms, sponges, and algae. The similarly marked but all-yellow *Chaetodon interruptus* Ahl occurs in the Indian Ocean.

VAGABOND BUTTERFLYFISH
Chaetodon vagabundus Linnaeus, 1758

Dorsal rays XIII,23–25; anal rays III,19–22; pectoral rays 14–15; longitudinal scale series 34–40; body deep, the depth 1.5–1.7 in standard length; snout protruding, its length 2.6–3.1 in head length; caudal fin slightly rounded; body white with 2 sets of purplish to black lines set at right angles; head pale gray with a black bar from high on nape through eye, broader ventrally; orange lines across forehead; dorsal and anal fins yellow posteriorly, the dorsal with a narrow, black-edged blue margin; a broad black bar across caudal peduncle in line with a broad black band at base of dorsal fin that narrows and curves near edge of spinous portion of fin; peduncular bar also in line with a short narrower bar into base of anal fin; caudal fin yellow with a narrow black bar on outer half, a clear margin, and a thin, brown to black submarginal band; juveniles differ in having a black spot on outer anterior part of soft portion of dorsal fin and a translucent caudal fin except basally where orange-yellow. Attains about 20 cm. Ranges from the east coast of Africa and islands of the Indian Ocean to the Line Islands, Tuamotu Archipelago, and the islands of Micronesia; in the western Pacific from southern Japan to New South Wales; not known from the Red Sea, Gulf of Aden, Persian Gulf, Hawaiian Islands, Marquesas Islands, or the Pitcairn Islands; no type locality reported. Found in various coral-reef habitats, including turbid brackish areas. Feeds mainly on sea anemones, coral polyps, polychaete worms, and algae.

HIGHFIN CORALFISH
Coradion altivelis McCulloch, 1916

Dorsal rays VIII,30–33; anal rays III,19–22; pectoral rays 14–16; longitudinal scale series 49–54; body deep, the depth 1.4–1.5 in standard length; snout protruding, its length about 2.5 in head length; dorsal spines progressively longer, the first 3 soft rays even higher, the longest nearly as long as head length; caudal fin truncate to slightly rounded; head and body silvery white with a dark brown bar through eye and 2 on anterior half of body (sometimes containing small orange spots), darker ventrally, and joined there; a broad, dusky orange bar posteriorly on body, continuing into dorsal and anal fins, its middle part on body more brown than orange, its anterior edge on body blue; caudal peduncle with a white bar, followed by a black bar onto base of caudal fin; rest of fin translucent pale pink; second dorsal spine black; outer part of dorsal and anal fins yellow with a submarginal, dark-edged blue line; pelvic fins dark brown to black; juveniles with a large, ocellated black spot in soft portion of dorsal fin. Reaches 15 cm. Southern Japan to New South Wales, east to Vanuatu and New Caledonia, west to western Australia and eastern Andaman Sea; type locality, Queensland. Usually found on shallow protected reefs.

Palau

Bali (night)

New Caledonia

323

FORCEPSFISH

Forcipiger flavissimus Jordan & McGregor in Jordan & Evermann, 1898

Dorsal rays XI-XII (rarely XI),21–25; anal rays III,17–19; pectoral rays 15–17; lateral line complete, the pored scales 74–80; body depth 1.9–2.4 in standard length; snout extremely slender and very long, more than half length of head, and 3.6–4.5 in standard length; gape of mouth 1.3–3.4 in eye diameter; dorsal spines high, the membranes deeply incised; pelvic fins long with filamentous tips, reaching beyond origin of anal fin; caudal fin slightly emarginate to truncate; body and dorsal, anal, and pelvic fins yellow; nape and upper half of head black, chest and lower half of head white; a large black spot posteriorly in anal fin; caudal fin translucent. Largest specimen examined, 18.2 cm. Indo-Pacific (except Persian Gulf to Arabian Sea), including the Kermadec Islands and Easter Island; in the eastern Pacific from the Gulf of California to the Galápagos; type locality, Revillagigedo Islands. Randall (1985b) reported feeding on polychaetes and other worms (especially the tentacles of tube worms), pedicellariae and tube feet of sea urchins, mysid shrimps, amphipods and other small crustaceans, barnacle cirri, and fish eggs.

Palau

Hawaiian Islands

Hawaiian Islands

LONGNOSE BUTTERFLYFISH

Forcipiger longirostris (Broussonet, 1782)

Dorsal rays X-XI (rarely X),24–27; anal rays III,17–19; pectoral rays 15–17; lateral line complete, the pored scales 66–75; body depth 2.1–2.5 in standard length; snout extremely long and slender, much more than half length of head, and 2.6–3.0 in standard length; mouth with a very short gape, 4.3–6.0 in eye diameter; dorsal spines high, the membranes deeply incised; pelvic fins long and filamentous, reaching well beyond origin of anal fin; caudal fin emarginate, the upper lobe clearly longer than lower; 2 different color forms, the more common almost identical to *Forcipiger flavissimus*, differing in having a median black band

on top of snout and a small blackish spot on each scale of chest; other phase dark brown except for axil of pectoral fins, which is yellow; base of pectoral fins and caudal fin sometimes with a faint yellow bar. Largest specimen examined, 22 cm. East coast of Africa to Hawaiian Islands (type locality, Hawai'i), islands of French Polynesia except Rapa, and Pitcairn Islands; in the western Pacific from Ogasawara Islands to the Great Barrier Reef and New Caledonia; known from 5 to 60 m; generally found in deeper water than *F. flavissimus*. Feeds on small invertebrates, primarily crustaceans. *Forcipiger cyrano* Randall and *F. inornatus* Randall are synonyms, the latter based on the dark brown phase (once observed to change to yellow in an aquarium).

324

MULTISPINE BUTTERFLYFISH
Hemitaurichthys multispinosus Randall, 1975

Dorsal rays XV-XVI,18–20; anal rays V,15; pectoral rays 18–19; lateral line complete, the pored scales 80–91; body elongate for a chaetodontid, the depth 2.1–2.3 in standard length; snout somewhat protruding, its length 2.9–3.4 in head length; eye near center of head; dorsal and anal fins uniformly low; caudal fin emarginate; brown with a bluish cast; edges of median fins blackish. Largest specimen, 20.8 cm. Described from 12 specimens collected in 40–44 m on a coral reef at Pitcairn Island; photographed in 40 m at Rurutu, Austral Islands, by Yves Lefevre, who observed a group of 8 and found them difficult to approach.

Pitcairn Islands

PYRAMID BUTTERFLYFISH
Hemitaurichthys polylepis (Bleeker, 1857)

Dorsal rays XII,24–25; anal rays III,19–21; pectoral rays 18–19; lateral line complete, the pored scales 68–74; body depth 1.5–1.6 in standard length; snout slightly protruding, its length 2.7–3.2 in head length; dorsal and anal fins relatively low; caudal fin truncate; pelvic fins long and filamentous, reaching beyond origin of anal fin; head and body anterior to base of third dorsal spine brown, the rest of body yellow and white, the white in a broad, central, triangular zone, including caudal peduncle, caudal fin, and paired fins, with apex at base of eighth and ninth dorsal spines; dorsal and anal fins mainly yellow. Attains 16 cm. Southern Japan to Great Barrier Reef and New Caledonia, east to Hawaiian Islands, Austral Islands, and Pitcairn Islands; Christmas Island and Cocos-Keeling Islands in the eastern Indian Ocean; type locality, Ambon, Molucca Islands. Occurs on outer-reef slopes and drop-offs, particularly where currents are strong; feeds on zooplankton well above the substratum, sometimes in aggregations of several hundred individuals. Replaced by the brown and white *H. zoster* (Bennett) more to the west in the Indian Ocean.

Marshall Islands

THOMPSON'S BUTTERFLYFISH
Hemitaurichthys thompsoni Fowler, 1923

Dorsal rays XII,25–27; anal rays III,20–21; pectoral rays 18–19; lateral line complete, the pored scales 76–87; body depth 1.7–1.9 in standard length; snout protruding, its length 2.6–3.1 in head length; dorsal and anal fins relatively low; caudal fin slightly emarginate; pelvic fins reaching a little beyond origin of anal fin; gray-brown overall, sometimes paler on abdomen. Attains about 17 cm. Known only from Oceania: Hawaiian Islands (type locality, O'ahu) and Line Islands, Tuamotu Archipelago, Society Islands, Samoa Islands, Mariana Islands, and Ogasawara Islands (Senou et al., 1997); reported from the depth range of 10–114 m, generally in outer-reef areas; feeds on zooplankton, often in small aggregations.

Hawaiian Islands

Bali

LONGFIN BANNERFISH

Heniochus acuminatus (Linnaeus, 1758)

Dorsal rays XI-XII (rarely XII),22–27; anal rays III,15–18; pectoral rays 18–19; lateral line complete, the pored scales 47–54; body deep, the depth 1.25–1.45 in standard length; snout protruding, its length 2.7–3.3 in head length; fourth dorsal spine prolonged into a very long, tapering, white filament, often longer than standard length; caudal fin truncate to slightly rounded; pelvic fins broadly rounded and dark brown to black (true of other species of *Heniochus*); white with 2 broad black bands, the first from front of dorsal fin to abdomen, where it broadens posteriorly to anterior edge of anal fin, the second from middle of spinous portion of dorsal fin to posterior half of anal fin; a black band across interorbital space; top of snout blackish; caudal fin, pectoral fins, and soft portion of dorsal fin yellow; pelvic fins black. Reaches about 22 cm. East coast of Africa and Persian Gulf to French Polynesia (except Rapa and the Marquesas Islands), and throughout Micronesia; in the western Pacific from southern Japan to the Great Barrier Reef, Lord Howe Island, and New Caledonia; type locality, East Indies. Although known from as little as 2 m in calm areas, it usually occurs in more than 10 m and has been observed as deep as 75 m. Feeds both on zoo-

Marshall Islands/juvenile

plankton and benthic invertebrates; juveniles (and sometimes adults) have been observed cleaning other fishes; usually solitary or in pairs, but may occur in small groups. The identically colored *Heniochus diphreutes* Jordan differs in having XII (rarely XIII) dorsal spines; it forms large aggregations to feed on zooplankton, and is known from the Red Sea, Maldive Islands, New South Wales, Western Australia, southern Japan, and the Hawaiian Islands (Allen & Kuiter, 1978).

Tonga/juvenile

Marshall Islands

PENNANT BANNERFISH

Heniochus chrysostomus Cuvier in C & V, 1831
Dorsal rays XI-XII,21–22; anal rays III,17–18; pectoral rays 16–17; lateral line complete, the pored scales 56–61; body deep, the depth 1.4–1.6 in standard length; snout protruding but short, its length 3.1–3.8 in head length; a small bony protuberance on forehead in front of upper part of each eye of adults; fourth dorsal spine of juveniles prolonged into long, tapering filament that can be as long as standard length; filament much shorter and very broad in adults; caudal fin truncate to slightly rounded; white with 2 very broad, oblique, dark brown bands, one from nape and interorbital to abdomen, the other centered on fourth to fifth dorsal spines and passing into soft portion of anal fin; soft portion of dorsal fin and posterior spinous part yellowish brown; snout yellow with a blackish middorsal streak; caudal and pectoral fins with transparent membranes and yellowish rays; pelvic fins black; juveniles with a yellow-edged black spot in dark part of anal fin. Attains 16 cm. Southern Japan to New South Wales, east to Line Islands and Pitcairn Islands; in the Indian Ocean to western Australia and Cocos-Keeling Islands; type locality, Tahiti. Coral reefs to about 45 m, but usually in less than 15 m; reported to feed mainly on coral polyps; often seen in small aggregations.

MASKED BANNERFISH

Heniochus monoceros Cuvier in C & V, 1831
Dorsal rays XII,24–27; anal rays III,18–19; pectoral rays 16–17 (usually 17); lateral line complete, the pored scales 55–61; body deep, the depth 1.4–1.6 in standard length; snout protruding, its length 2.8–3.2 in head length; adults with a median protuberance on nape, and a short pointed bony protuberance in front of upper part of each eye; fourth dorsal spine prolonged into long, white, tapering filament; caudal fin truncate; silvery white with a black bar anteriorly on body, broadening as it passes ventrally to abdomen; a broad, oblique, blackish band from posterior spinous part of dorsal fin to posterior half of anal fin; body behind band yellow; black ocular bar commencing just behind corner of mouth, bifurcating a short distance above eye, the anterior part curving across interorbital, the posterior changing to brown but changing back to black on upper nape; front of knob on forehead black; caudal fin, posterior two-thirds of dorsal fin, and most of anal fin yellow; pelvic fins black. Reaches 25 cm. East coast of Africa to the Pitcairn Islands and throughout Micronesia; in the western Pacific from southern Japan to the Great Barrier Reef, New South Wales, Norfolk Island, and New Caledonia; type locality, Mauritius. Generally found on shallow coral reefs in lagoons and deeper seaward reefs; adults often seen in pairs.

Okinawa

327

HUMPHEAD BANNERFISH
Heniochus varius (Cuvier, 1829)

Dorsal rays XI,22–25; anal rays III,17–18; pectoral rays 15–16; lateral line complete, the pored scales 52–62; body very deep, the depth 1.3–1.5 in standard length; snout protruding, its length 2.6–3.1 in head length; adults with a large median protuberance on nape and a horn-like protuberance in front of upper part of each eye; profile of head between supraocular and nape protuberances strongly concave; fourth dorsal spine longest, the membrane broad but not prolonged to a filament in adults; caudal fin truncate; brown with a white bar from first 3 dorsal spines to chest, and an oblique white band from tip of fourth dorsal spine across dorsal fin and caudal peduncle to ventral base of caudal fin; head dark brown except ventrally; a pale bluish arc on side of snout; brown of pectoral region and below very dark; pelvic fins nearly black; anal fin dark brown with a narrow, pale blue posterior margin; caudal fin and outer soft portion of dorsal fin with yellowish rays and clear membranes. Reported to 19 cm. Southern Japan to Great Barrier Reef and New Caledonia, east to Society Islands and all of Micronesia; western Australia and Christmas Island in the Indian Ocean; type locality, Ambon, Molucca Islands. A clear-water, coral-reef species generally

Palau

found in less than 30 m; reported to feed on coral polyps and other reef invertebrates. Most similar to *H. pleurotaenia* Ahl from the Maldives to southern Indonesia (observed by the author at Komodo), hence overlapping with *varius* in southern Indonesia; it is easily distinguished by a white bar in middle of body.

Coral Sea

SINGULAR BANNERFISH
Heniochus singularus Smith & Radcliffe, 1911

Dorsal rays XI-XII,25–27; anal rays III,17–18; pectoral rays 17–18; lateral line complete, the pored scales 51–60; body deep, the depth 1.5–1.6 in standard length; snout protruding, its length 2.7–3.3 in head length; adults with a median protuberance on nape and a short, pointed, bony protuberance in front of upper part of each eye; fourth dorsal spine prolonged into long, white, tapering filament; caudal fin truncate; same basic color pattern on body as *H. monoceros*, but scales in the black bands with pale centers, and scales in broad middle white zone with a black dot or short dash; no yellow on anal fin; black ocular bar vertical and complete above eye (though short), separated by a narrow white bar from black of front of snout and lips. Attains 25 cm. Maldive Islands to Samoa Islands; in western Pacific from southern Japan to the Great Barrier Reef and New Caledonia; type locality, Ragay Gulf, Luzon. Often seen in pairs; difficult to approach underwater. Reported to feed on coral polyps, other benthic invertebrates, and algae.

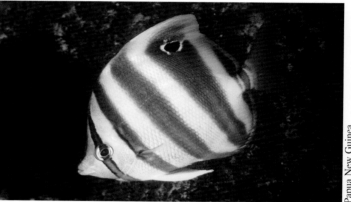

Papua New Guinea

OCELLATED CORALFISH
Parachaetodon ocellatus (Cuvier in C & V, 1831)

Dorsal rays VI-VII (rarely VII),28–30; anal rays III,18–20; pectoral rays 14–15; longitudinal scale series 39–46; body deep, the depth 1.3–1.4 in standard length; snout slightly protruding, its length 2.8–3.6 in head length; dorsal spines progressively longer, the first 2 soft rays even higher, the second about as long as head length; caudal fin truncate; silvery white with a median brown-edged band middorsally on snout, a brown-edged orange bar from top of head through eye to middle of chest, and 3 similar bars on body, broader posteriorly and with orange reduced; second and third bars of body extending into dorsal and anal fins, the third containing an ocellated black spot basally in dorsal fin; a brown-edged orange bar across caudal peduncle, preceded by a narrow white bar; posterior soft portions of dorsal and anal fins with an orangish brown band that parallels dark bars of body; caudal fin yellowish. Reaches 18 cm. Ogasawara Islands south through the East Indies to west coast of Australia and east coast to New South Wales, east through the Solomon Islands to Fiji; type locality not reported. Occurs in protected waters of bays and lagoons, including estuarine areas and seagrass beds; reported from depths of 2–60 m.

Flame Angelfish, *Centropyge loriculus*, Line Islands

ANGELFISHES
(POMACANTHIDAE)

As mentioned in the preceding family account, the angelfishes were once classified as a subfamily of the Chaetodontidae; they share such features as a deep compressed body, small mouth with brush-like teeth, ctenoid scales that extend onto head and well out on median fins, and a single unnotched dorsal fin. They differ in having a prominent spine at the corner of the preopercle, axillary scales as adults, the scales more strongly ctenoid, and no scaly axillary process at the base of the pelvic fins. The postlarvae lack the bony plates of the head and anterior body as seen on the tholichthys larval stage of butterflyfishes. Angelfishes are diurnal; the larger species feed mainly on sponges, supplemented by algae; those of *Centropyge* on algae and detritus; and those of *Genicanthus* primarily on zooplankton. The young of some of the species of *Pomacanthus* and *Holacanthus* have been observed cleaning other fishes. All the species of the family that have been studied are protogynous hermaphrodites, meaning they start life as females and change sex later to males. The first clue of such sex change was noted by Randall (1975) for the Red Sea *Genicanthus caudovittatus* when he observed the large, barred male spawning with a small female, noted that males are consistently larger than females, and later saw an individual of intermediate color pattern. Unlike other species of the family, those of *Genicanthus* are strongly sexually dichromatic. Males of many species of *Centropyge* can often be distinguished by the better-developed blue streaks posteriorly in the dorsal and anal fins. Angelfishes spawn in pairs, typically at dusk, following courtship with the male nuzzling the ventral body of the female (as shown in the author's photo of a pair of *Centropyge bispinosa*); spawning occurs at the apex of an upward rush. Males maintain a harem of two to several females. The species of *Pomacanthus* have juveniles that are very different in color from the adults. The species of *Centropyge* are often called pygmy angelfishes because of their small size; they never stray far from shelter. Several species are mimicked by juveniles of the surgeonfishes *Acanthurus pyroferus* and *A. tristis* (Randall & Randall, 1960; Randall, 2002a). Schneidewind (1999) published a well-illustrated guidebook to the pomacanthid fishes of the world, and Allen et al. (1998) one on both the pomacanthids and chaetodontids. The pomacanthids consist of 7 genera and 83 species (Pyle, 2003). Pyle's generic classification is the same as that of the 2 books except for placing *Paracentropyge* in the synonymy of *Centropyge*. Pyle & Randall (1994) reviewed 11 examples of naturally occurring hybrids of angelfishes. From a literature search to and including 1999, Schwartz (2001) listed 28 pomacanthid hybrids, more than any other marine family except the Pleuronectidae.

GRIFFIS' ANGELFISH
Apolemichthys griffisi (Carlson & Taylor, 1981)

Dorsal rays XIV,18; anal rays III,18; pectoral rays 17–18; lateral line usually discontinuous, the pored scales 38–47 + 4–6; preorbital bone finely serrate (true of other *Apolemichthys*); anterior end of interopercle serrate (also generic); body depth 1.65–1.8 in standard length; only the first 3 interspinous membranes of dorsal fin deeply incised (generic); caudal fin normally rounded (fish in illustration with abraded fin); body light brownish gray, each scale with a small white spot; an oblique black band commencing on back below fifth dorsal spine and broadening as it passes to rear base of anal fin and adjacent caudal peduncle; a pure white band above and adjacent to black band, extending into base of dorsal fin and base of caudal fin; a few small, dark brown spots anteriorly on upper part of body; head, chest, and abdomen bluish gray with a large black spot at front of nape well above eye, and a short, narrow, blackish bar through eye; opercular membrane orangish, becoming blackish on upper expanded part; dorsal fin black above white band. Largest specimen, 19.4 cm. First discovered in the Phoenix Islands (type locality, Kanton Island) in 1978; now known also from the Gilbert Islands

Aquarium photo

(Kiribati), Line Islands, Solomon Islands, Papua New Guinea, and northeastern Indonesia. Although observed in as little as 20 m, it is usually found at more than 40 m and has been video-taped at 110 m (R. L. Pyle, pers. comm.).

Seychelles

THREESPOT ANGELFISH
Apolemichthys trimaculatus (Lacepède in C & V, 1831)

Dorsal rays XIV,16–18; anal rays III,17–19; pectoral rays 17–18; lateral line discontinuous, the pored scales 38–47 + 4–6; body depth 1.6–1.8 in standard length; caudal fin rounded, usually with a short filament from upper corner; bright yellow, a dusky mark on each scale of body sometimes forming near-vertical lines; a black spot high on forehead, and an oval dusky spot behind upper end of gill opening; lips blue; preopercular spine pale blue; anal fin and adjacent body pale yellow to white, with a broad, outer black zone; small juveniles yellow with a narrow black bar through eye, irregular vertical dusky to orangish lines on body, and a black spot as large as or larger than eye on back, extending into base of soft portion of dorsal fin; larger juveniles lose the black ocular bar but gain the black spot on forehead. Reaches 25 cm. East coast of Africa to Samoa Islands; southern

Mauritius/juvenile

Japan to the Great Barrier Reef and New Caledonia; type locality, Molucca Islands. Usually seen on seaward reefs at depths of 15 to 60 m, either singly or in pairs. Feeds mainly on sponges and tunicates. Hioki & Suzuki (1995) studied the reproduction and early development.

Line Islands/juvenile

Line Islands

GOLDSPOTTED ANGELFISH

Apolemichthys xanthopunctatus Burgess, 1973

Dorsal rays XIV,17–18; anal rays III,17–19; pectoral rays 16; lateral-line scales 45–50; body depth 1.6–1.8 in standard length; caudal fin rounded; yellowish to greenish gray with a bright yellow spot on each scale of body except ventrally and on chest; a yellow-edged black spot on forehead and an oval, yellow-edged, dusky spot behind upper end of gill opening; lips bright blue; median fins black, except first 3 spines and base of spinous portion colored like body, with a narrow bright blue outer margin; juveniles yellow with irregular vertical gray lines on body, a large ocellated black spot on back, extending broadly into soft portion of dorsal fin; a narrow black bar through eye; outer part of anal fin and middle of caudal fin black. Attains about 25 cm. The author first collected this species at the type locality of Fanning Island (now Tabuaeran), Line Islands, in 1968 and later at Kiritimati (Christmas Island). Additional localities now include the Phoenix Islands, Gilbert Islands (Kiribati), and Kapingamarangi Atoll in the Caroline Islands; occurs in clear water on well-developed coral reefs, generally at depths greater than 10 m; deepest collection, 55 m. Usually found as solitary individuals. Highly prized as an aquarium fish.

GOLDEN ANGELFISH

Centropyge aurantia Randall & Wass, 1974

Dorsal rays XIV,16–17; anal rays III,17–18; pectoral rays 16–17; longitudinal scale series 42–46; preorbital strongly serrate to spiny (true of other *Centropyge*); anterior end of interopercle serrate (also generic); body depth 1.6–1.8 in standard length; first 8 membranes of dorsal fin incised more than one-fourth length of spines; cirrus at upper end of each interspinous membrane extending well above spine tip; posterior margin of dorsal and anal fins obtusely angular, the anal rays extending slightly posterior to midcaudal length; pelvic fins long, the filamentous tips reaching posterior to spinous portion of anal fin; caudal fin rounded; body orange with irregular, vertical yellow lines; head and chest orange with a reticular gray pattern; eye nearly rimmed with dark gray; median fins orange with longitudinal yellow bands basally, greenish gray distally, the fin margins clear (broad in caudal) with blackish rays and a black submarginal line; cirri at dorsal spine tips deep blue to black; a second color form (possibly related to occurrence in shallower water) with a gray-brown head and a gray body with vertical orange lines. Reaches 8 cm. Described from Tutuila, American Samoa; now known also from Pohnpei in the Caroline Islands, Palau, Solomon Islands, Papua New Guinea, northern Great Barrier Reef, and Sulawesi; reported from 3 to over 50 m. Divers seldom get more than a glimpse of this species, among the most wary of reef fishes, doubtless the reason for the few museum specimens. The species name *aurantia* is from New Latin for orange.

American Samoa

Aquarium photo (R. L. Pyle)

331

BICOLOR ANGELFISH

Centropyge bicolor (Bloch, 1787)

Dorsal rays XIV-XV,15–17; anal rays III,17–18; pectoral rays 16–17; longitudinal scale series 45–48; body depth 1.8–2.2 in standard length; only the first 3 spinous dorsal-fin membranes deeply incised; posterior margin of dorsal and anal fins strongly angular, usually reaching posterior to midcaudal length; caudal fin rounded; pelvic fins not reaching anal fin; body bright yellow anteriorly, abruptly deep blue posteriorly and on dorsal and anal fins; head bright yellow with a deep blue bar above eye, a diffuse dusky bar below, and an orange spot above gill opening; caudal and paired fins yellow. Reported to 15 cm. Southern Japan to New South Wales, east to Samoa Islands and islands of Micronesia; western Australia and Christmas Island (rare) in the Indian Ocean; type locality, East Indies. Found on coral reefs or rubble substrata, generally in 10–25 m.

TWO-SPINE ANGELFISH

Centropyge bispinosa (Günther, 1860)

Dorsal rays XIV,16–18; anal rays III,17–18; pectoral rays 15–17; longitudinal scale series 42–45; body depth 1.75–2.0 in standard length; only the first 3 interspinous membranes of dorsal fin deeply incised; posterior margin of dorsal and anal fins angular, usually reaching to midcaudal length; caudal fin rounded; pelvic fins nearly or just reaching anal fin; color variable, the body usually orange with irregular, often broken, deep blue to blackish, vertical lines; additional blue pigment often forming a narrow blue patch above pectoral fin; head and median fins deep blue, the fins with longitudinal broken dark bands, a thin black margin, and bright blue submarginal band; another color form almost entirely deep blue; a paler color variant from 30 m off Tahiti is illustrated. Largest reported, 11 cm. East coast of Africa to the Line Islands and Tuamotu Archipelago; in the western Pacific from the Ryukyu Islands to New South Wales, Lord Howe Island, and Norfolk Island; described from Vanuatu and Ambon, Indonesia. Forms hybrids with *Centropyge shepardi* Randall & Yasuda at Guam, Mariana Islands.

332

PEPPERMINT ANGELFISH
Centropyge boylei Pyle & Randall, 1992
Dorsal rays XIII,19–20; anal rays III,18–20; pectoral rays 15; longitudinal scale series 47–48; body depth 1.65–1.9 in standard length; spinous membranes of dorsal fin incised more than one-fourth length of spines for first 9 membranes; posterior margin of dorsal and anal fins rounded, the rays not extending posterior to base of caudal fin; caudal fin rounded; pelvic fins long, the 2 filaments of first soft ray reaching posterior to spinous portion of anal fin; white with 5 red bars on body, about twice as broad as white interspaces, extending into dorsal and anal fins; head with an orange bar from upper nape to eye, yellow below; caudal fin white; pelvic fins yellow and white. Maximum length, 7 cm. Known only from Rarotonga, Cook Islands, from the depth range of 56–120 m; the lack of other records is likely due to the deep habitat.

Cook Islands/inset: juvenile

COLIN'S ANGELFISH
Centropyge colini Smith-Vaniz & Randall, 1974
Dorsal rays XIV,16–17; anal rays III,17; pectoral rays 15–16; longitudinal scale series 47–48; body deep, the depth 1.7–1.8 in standard length; first 8 interspinous membranes of dorsal fin incised one-fourth or more length of spines; posterior margin of dorsal and anal fins broadly rounded, usually reaching to mid-caudal length; caudal fin rounded; pelvic fins extending beyond origin of anal fin; yellow, the spinous portion of dorsal fin and a broad adjacent zone of back anteriorly to nape abruptly deep purplish blue; a narrow blue ring around eye. Attains 8.5 cm. Reported from Cocos-Keeling Islands (type locality), Indonesia, Papua New Guinea, Palau, Guam, Marshall Islands, and Fiji; a secretive species usually found in caves and crevices on steep outer-reef drop-offs, generally at depths greater than 25 m; known to at least 75 m.

Palau/Aquarium photo

FISHER'S ANGELFISH
Centropyge fisheri (Snyder, 1904)
Dorsal rays XIV,15; anal rays III,17; pectoral rays 16; longitudinal scale series 40–45; body elongate for the genus, the depth 2.0–2.3 in standard length; only the first 3 or 4 interspinous membranes of dorsal fin incised one-fourth or more length of spines; posterior margin of dorsal and anal fins rounded, usually reaching slightly posterior to base of caudal fin; caudal fin truncate to slightly rounded; pelvic fins usually not reaching origin of anal fin; body deep blue or dark brown with a bluish cast, often with a large, deep blue area beneath and above pectoral fin; head dark brown to brownish orange, sometimes with a bluish cast; dorsal and anal fins colored like body, with a bright blue margin, the posterior edge with short blue streaks; caudal fin light yellow, the upper and lower edges often broadly brown one-half or more length of fin; pelvic fins with a broad, bright blue leading edge. Largest collected by author, 7.1 cm. East coast of Africa to the Hawaiian Islands (type locality), Marquesas Islands, and Tuamotu Archipelago; southern Japan to New South Wales. Generally found on rubble bottoms adjacent to coral reefs at depths of about 10–60 m. *Centropyge flavicauda* Fraser-Brunner, 1933, described from the Macclesfield Bank, South China Sea, is a synonym (Pyle, 2003).

Papua New Guinea

Tahiti/inset: juvenile, Marquesas Islands

LEMONPEEL ANGELFISH

Centropyge flavissima (Cuvier in C & V, 1831
Dorsal rays XIV,15–16; anal rays III,16; pectoral rays
16–17; longitudinal scale series 44–50; body depth
1.7–2.0 in standard length; first 8 interspinous membranes of dorsal fin incised one-fourth or more length
of spines; posterior margin of dorsal and anal fins
rounded to slightly angular, usually not reaching midcaudal length; caudal fin rounded; pelvic fins usually
reaching origin of anal fin; bright yellow; eye rimmed
with bright blue; opercular membrane orange (sometimes black or partially black), preceded by a narrow,
curving, bright blue band; preopercular spine blue;
posterior margin of median fins narrowly bright blue,
with a black submarginal line; juveniles with a large,
blue-edged black spot in middle of body. Attains
10.5 cm. Islands of Oceania except Hawaiian Islands,
Lord Howe Island, and Norfolk Island; in the western
Pacific from Ogasawara Islands to Great Barrier
Reef; Christmas Island and Cocos-Keeling Islands in
the Indian Ocean; type locality, Ulea (= Woleai),
Caroline Islands. Usually found in less than 25 m.
Common in French Polynesia and most of Micronesia, but rare at western Pacific localities. Hybridizes with *Centropyge vrolikii* and *C. eibli*. Mimicked
by juvenile *Acanthurus pyroferus*.

Marshall Islands

Fiji/color variant

HERALD'S ANGELFISH

Centropyge heraldi Woods & Schultz in Schultz et al., 1953
Dorsal rays XV,15; anal rays III,17; pectoral rays 16–17; longitudinal scale series 46–48; body depth 1.8–2.0 in standard
length; first 5 interspinous membranes of dorsal fin incised one-
fourth or more length of spines; posterior margin of dorsal and
anal fins angular, extending to or beyond midcaudal length; caudal fin rounded; pelvic fins usually reaching origin of anal fin;
bright yellow with a dusky olive patch containing yellow markings behind and adjacent to eye (sometimes covering most of
head); anal fin often with a faint orange band edged in greenish;

a color variant from South Pacific localities, common in the
Samoa Islands and Fiji, with a broad black outer zone in soft portion of dorsal fin beneath a pale blue margin. Largest specimen,
12 cm. Islands of Oceania except the Hawaiian Islands,
Marquesas Islands, Lord Howe Island, and Norfolk Island; in the
western Pacific from southern Japan, Taiwan, and the Great
Barrier Reef; type locality, Bikini Atoll, Marshall Islands.
Reported from depths of 8–40 m. Named for Earl S. Herald, former Superintendent of the Steinhart Aquarium in San Francisco.
Centropyge woodheadi Kuiter is a synonym based on the color
variety with the black band in the dorsal fin.

HOTUMATUA'S ANGELFISH

Centropyge hotumatua Randall & Caldwell, 1973

Dorsal rays XIV,17–18 (usually 17); anal rays III,18; pectoral rays 16–17 (usually 17); longitudinal scale series 43–46; body depth 1.8–1.9 in standard length; first 9 interspinous membranes of dorsal fin incised one-fourth or more length of spines; a black cirrus from membrane near tip of each dorsal spine; posterior margin of dorsal and anal fins rounded, extending beyond base of caudal fin but not reaching midcaudal length; caudal fin varying from slightly rounded to truncate with corners slightly prolonged; pelvic fins long, reaching well beyond origin of anal fin; broad middle zone of body and most of dorsal and anal fins dark brown, shading to bright orange-yellow on anterior body and head, and to orange-yellow posteriorly on caudal peduncle; an irregular blue arc around posterior half of eye; a black blotch posteriorly on opercle, with a few scattered blue markings; a large black area in outer posterior part of dorsal fin containing blue spots and dashes parallel with rays; anal fin with a bright blue margin and blue dashes at posterior edge; caudal fin orange-yellow basally and on lobes, transparent with brown rays on rest of fin. Largest specimen, 9 cm. Known only from Easter Island (type locality), Pitcairn Islands, Austral Islands, and Rapa; collected from depths of 15–45 m. Named for the legendary Polynesian chieftain who first colonized Easter Island.

FLAME ANGELFISH

Centropyge loriculus (Günther, 1874)

Dorsal rays XIV,16–18; anal rays III,17–18; pectoral rays 16–18 (rarely 18); longitudinal scale series 44–47; body depth 1.75–2.0 in standard length; first 5 interspinous membranes of dorsal fin incised one-fourth or more length of spines; posterior margin of dorsal and anal fins angular, approaching or just reaching midcaudal length; caudal fin rounded; double filament of first pelvic soft ray usually reaching anal fin; brilliant orange-red, shading to orange-yellow in middle of body, typically with a vertically elongate black spot beneath and above pectoral fin and 5 black bars on rest of body; small black spots often present on back or on basal part of dorsal fin; dorsal and anal fins bright orange-red, the posterior part broadly black with blue or purple streaks; caudal fin with light orange-yellow rays and transparent membranes; pelvic fins orange-red; pectorals with pale yellow rays and transparent membranes. Reaches 10 cm. Islands of Oceania, except Lord Howe Island and Norfolk Island, to Philippines, Indonesia, and northern Great Barrier Reef, but rare in East Indian localities; type locality, Society Islands. Known from depths of 4–60 m, but usually found below 20 m. Variably colored in the Marquesas Islands, many with only the single anterior black spot as in figure. A very popular aquarium fish. *Centropyge flammea* Woods & Schultz (type locality, Johnston Island) is a synonym. The Hawaiian population lacks blackish pigment on the opercular membrane and just above the pectoral-fin base. Both typical *loriculus* and the Hawaiian form occur at Johnston Island. A DNA study determined that these are not species.

Easter Island

Marshall Islands

Marquesas Islands

MULTICOLOR ANGELFISH

Centropyge multicolor Randall & Wass, 1974

Dorsal rays XIV,16–17 (usually 17); anal rays III,17; pectoral rays 16–17 (usually 17); longitudinal scale series 44–46; body depth 1.9–2.0 in standard length; first 5 interspinous membranes of dorsal fin incised one-fourth or more length of spines; posterior margin of dorsal and anal fins rounded, not reaching mid-caudal length; caudal fin rounded; pelvic fins reaching posterior to origin of anal fin; white dorsally, shading to yellow on caudal peduncle and fin, to dark brown ventrally, including anal fin, and to yellow on abdomen and chest; head yellow, the nape dark brown with irregular blue lines; dorsal fin white proximally, dark brown distally; outer part of dorsal and anal fins with a blue margin and black submarginal line. Reaches 8 cm. Recorded to date from Society Islands, Cook Islands, Samoa Islands, Kiribati, Caroline Islands, Marshall Islands (type locality, Enewetak Atoll), Fiji, Palau, Johnston Island, and Hawaiian Islands (1 specimen); depth range 20–90 m.

MULTIBAR ANGELFISH

Centropyge multifasciata (Smith & Radcliffe, 1911)

Dorsal rays XIII,17–19; anal rays III,17–18; pectoral rays 15–16; longitudinal scale series 45–47; body depth 1.55–1.7 in standard length; dorsal profile of head very steep; first 9 interspinous membranes of dorsal fin incised one-fourth or more length of spines, the membrane at tip of each spine with a white cirrus; posterior margin of dorsal and anal fins rounded, not reaching beyond base of caudal fin; caudal fin rounded; pelvic-fin tips extending posterior to spinous portion of anal fin; white with 7 or 8 dark brown bars on body that become yellow ventrally; bars extending into dorsal and anal fins; white interspaces sometimes with a faint, narrow yellow bar; a dark brown bar on head through eye, changing to yellow ventrally, and a narrow one middorsally on head; lips yellow and white; basal two-thirds of caudal fin with rows of brown spots that are progressively smaller posteriorly; pectoral fins translucent; pelvic fins yellow with a white lateral edge. Reported to 10 cm. Ryukyu Islands to northern Great Barrier Reef and New Caledonia, east to the Society Islands; type locality, Mindoro, Philippines. Usually found in caves in outer-reef drop-offs from depths of 15–70 m; a very shy species.

DEEPREEF ANGELFISH

Centropyge narcosis Pyle & Randall, 1992

Dorsal rays XIV,17–18; anal rays III,17–18; pectoral rays 16; longitudinal scale series 47–48; body deep, the depth 1.75–1.85 in standard length; first 7 interspinous membranes of dorsal fin incised one-fourth or more length of spines; posterior margin of dorsal and anal fins rounded, not reaching midcaudal length; caudal fin rounded; double filament of first pelvic soft ray reaching to base of third anal spine; yellow overall with a round black spot larger than eye on back below posterior spinous portion of dorsal fin, just under lateral line. Largest specimen, 7.2 cm. Known only from Rarotonga, Cook Islands, from depths of 100–112 m; occurs singly or in small groups. The species name alludes to the extreme nitrogen narcosis experienced by the collectors (Richard L. Pyle and Charles "Chip" Boyle) who caught the first specimens using conventional scuba gear.

Marshall Islands

Wakatobi Island, Indonesia

Cook Islands

OCELLATED ANGELFISH

Centropyge nigriocellus Woods & Schultz in Schultz et al., 1953
Dorsal rays XIII,15; anal rays III,15; pectoral rays 17; longitudinal scale series 44; body depth 1.9–2.0 in standard length; first 10 interspinous membranes of dorsal fin incised one-fourth or more length of spines; tip of each interspinous membrane of dorsal fin with a white cirrus; posterior margin of dorsal and anal fins rounded, not reaching midcaudal length; caudal fin rounded; double filament of first pelvic soft ray reaching posterior to spinous portion of anal fin; dorsal fin and dorsal part of body pale yellow, becoming white ventrally; head pale yellow, a little dusky above and anterior to eye; a large black spot covering all of pectoral-fin base; a second black spot as large or larger, narrowly rimmed in pale blue, at rear base of dorsal fin; caudal, anal, and pelvic fins white; pectoral fins transparent with dusky rays; juveniles with a large round black spot in middle of body and no spot in dorsal fin. Reaches about 6 cm. Known to date only from Johnston Island (type locality), Line Islands, Samoa Islands, Mariana Islands, and Admiralty Islands from depths of 4–15 m. Extremely secretive and rarely seen.

Line Islands/inset: juvenile, Tuamotu Archipelago

MIDNIGHT ANGELFISH

Centropyge nox (Bleeker, 1853)
Dorsal rays XIV-XV,16–17; anal rays III,16–17; pectoral rays 15; longitudinal scale series 42–48; body deep, the depth 1.7–1.8 in standard length; first 4 or 5 interspinous membranes of dorsal fin incised one-fourth or more length of spines; posterior margin of dorsal and anal fins angular, reaching beyond midcaudal length; caudal fin rounded; posterior ends of dorsal and anal fins aligned with contour of caudal fin to form a continuous curve; pelvic fins without a long filamentous first ray, not reaching origin of anal fin; uniform dark brown, appearing black underwater. Reaches 10 cm. Southern Japan to Great Barrier Reef, east to Palau, Caroline Islands, Vanuatu, New Caledonia, and Fiji; type locality, Ambon, Molucca Islands. Depth range 10–70 m. Very difficult to photograph underwater, due not only to its secretive nature but also to its dark coloration.

Papua New Guinea

KEYHOLE ANGELFISH

Centropyge tibicen (Cuvier in C & V, 1831)
Dorsal rays XIV,15–16; anal rays III,16–17; pectoral rays 15; longitudinal scale series 45–48; body depth 1.8–2.0 in standard length; first 4 interspinous membranes of dorsal fin incised one-fourth or more length of spines; posterior margin of dorsal and anal fins angular, sometimes reaching midcaudal length; caudal fin rounded; pelvic fins usually not reaching origin of anal fin; deep blue, the scale edges black, with a large, vertically elongate, pure white blotch on upper side off tip of pectoral fin; a deep purple, oval spot sometimes visible above pectoral fin; dorsal and caudal fins deep blue with a bright blue outer margin; anal fin deep blue to black with a very broad, yellow outer margin and blue submarginal line. Reported to 18.5 cm, largest for the genus (Araga in Masuda et al., 1984). Southern Japan to Great Barrier Reef, Lord Howe Island, Norfolk Island, and New Caledonia; east to Fiji and Caroline Islands; Christmas Island and northwestern Australia in the Indian Ocean; type locality not given. May be seen in various coral-reef habitats from depths of about 4–35 m.

Ambon, Indonesia

Lord Howe Island

CONSPICUOUS ANGELFISH

Chaetodontoplus conspicillatus (Waite, 1900)

Dorsal rays XIII,18; anal rays III,18; pectoral rays 15; scales very small, about 120 in longitudinal series; body depth about 2.0 in standard length; first 3 interspinous membranes of dorsal fin incised one-fourth or more length of spines; posterior margin of dorsal and anal fins rounded, not reaching beyond caudal-fin base; caudal fin rounded; pelvic fins without a filamentous first ray, not reaching origin of anal fin; body light grayish to yellowish brown dorsally, shading ventrally to dark brown, including chest; head orange except for bluish white lips, a zone of black around mouth, a broad dusky bar under eye, a blue ring with 2 anterior projections encircling eye; blue vertical margin of preopercle, and blue and black lines on edge of opercle; dorsal fin with a white margin and black submarginal band; anal fin dark brown with a pale blue margin; caudal fin yellow with a broad outer black zone and blue margin; pectoral fins dark brown and yellow; pelvics

Lord Howe Island, with *C. meredithi* (on left)

whitish. Maximum length about 30 cm. Queensland to New South Wales, Lord Howe Island (type locality), Norfolk Island, and New Caledonia; outer reefs, generally in 20–40 m. Reported to feed mainly on sponges.

Tahiti/female

Tahiti/male

ORNATE ANGELFISH
Genicanthus bellus Randall, 1975

Dorsal rays XV,15–16; anal rays III,16–17; pectoral rays 16–17; longitudinal scale series 46–48; lips not scaled; body depth 2.1–2.2 in standard length; only first 3 interspinous membranes of dorsal fin incised one-fourth or more length of spines (true of other *Genicanthus*); dorsal and anal fins strongly pointed posteriorly, the tenth soft ray longest in each fin; caudal fin lunate, the lobes of males greatly prolonged; females bluish white with a broad, curved, blue band from behind gill opening to above anal fin, a curved, dark brown band from base of pectoral fin upward across operculum to origin of dorsal fin, continuing along back below dorsal fin, and entering posterior soft portion of fin; an oblique dark brown band from curved band of upper part of head to lower part of caudal fin; a narrow brown band between oblique band and band on back; dorsal fin dark reddish brown with a bluish white margin; anal fin bluish gray with a blue margin and broad, submarginal orange band; caudal fin bluish gray with a white-edged brown band in each lobe; males with an orange stripe, bordered above by white from upper end of gill opening to midbase of caudal fin; head and body above stripe lavender-gray, below bluish white; an orangish brown band from snout before eye to origin of dorsal fin, continuing as an orange stripe along base of fin and breaking into short orange bands posteriorly in fin; an orange spot on lower base of pectoral fins; lobes of caudal fin lavender, the central part of fin with irregular orange bands. Reported to 18 cm. Known from Tahiti (type locality), Marshall Islands, Mariana Islands, Philippines, and Cocos-Keeling Islands; found off deep outer-reef escarpments from depths of about 25–100 m, but rare above 50 m.

BLACKSPOT ANGELFISH
Genicanthus melanospilos (Bleeker, 1857)

Dorsal rays XV,15–17; anal rays III,17–18 (rarely 17); pectoral rays 15–17; longitudinal scale series 46–48; lips naked or basal half or less of upper lip with small scales; body depth 1.9–2.15 in standard length; dorsal and anal fins strongly pointed posteriorly, the ninth soft ray longest in each fin; caudal fin lunate, the lobes greatly prolonged, especially in males; females lavender-gray on body below lateral line with a small yellow spot on each scale except ventrally; body above lateral line yellow, the scales edged in gray; head lavender-gray with a yellow band middorsally on nape; eye narrowly rimmed with light blue; dorsal fin gray with oblique yellow bands except posteriorly; anal fin lavender-gray with indistinct yellow lines in outer part; caudal fin white basally, shading to violet, with a broad black band in each lobe, the upper and lower edges narrowly violet; males pale blue dorsally, shading to bluish white ventrally, with about 12 narrow black bars across entire body, and 6 or 7 more dorsally on head; a midventral black spot as large as eye in front of pelvic fins; median fins bluish gray with numerous small yellow spots and blue margins. Reaches at least 25 cm (including caudal filaments). Ryukyu Islands to Great Barrier Reef, east to Mariana Islands, Palau, New Caledonia, and Fiji; type locality, Ambon, Molucca Islands. Occurs over coral reefs, generally at depths greater than 20 m.

Tonga/female

Great Barrier Reef/male

PITCAIRN ANGELFISH

Genicanthus spinus Randall, 1975

Dorsal rays XV,16–17; anal rays III,18–19; pectoral rays 16–17; longitudinal scale series 49–54; lips scaled; body depth 2.1–2.45 in standard length; anterior spine of preorbital enlarged, directed anteriorly before lips; dorsal and anal fins of females rounded posteriorly, angular in males; caudal fin lunate, the lobes greatly prolonged, especially in males; females light bluish gray overall (scales with bluish gray centers and white edges); caudal fin whitish with broad bluish gray margins, the entire fin finely dotted with brown; males lavender-gray, a little yellowish ventrally, with about 12 narrow, dark brown bars on body, those anteriorly reaching about halfway down body, the posterior 2 (on caudal peduncle and caudal-fin base) complete; head light bluish gray, the nape with irregular brown bars, the interorbital and forehead brown; rest of head and chest blotched with brown; fins light yellowish gray, the dorsal with a faint, orangish longitudinal band; caudal fin with an orange band in each lobe and a dark brown spot in center of fin. Largest specimen, 37.5 cm (including caudal filaments). First collected at Pitcairn Island (type locality), later from Austral Islands and Cook Islands; depth range 33.5–52 m.

WATANABE'S ANGELFISH

Genicanthus watanabei (Yasuda & Tominaga, 1970)

Dorsal rays XV-XVI (rarely XVI),15–16 (usually 16); anal rays III,17; pectoral rays 16; longitudinal scale series 45–48; lips not scaled; body depth 2.05–2.4 in standard length; dorsal and anal fins angular posteriorly; caudal fin lunate, the lobes greatly prolonged, especially in males; females pale lavender-gray; top of head bright blue with irregular black bands and spots; posterior edge of opercular membrane black; dorsal and anal fins pale blue-green with a narrow blue margin and black submarginal band; caudal fin pale blue green, the lobes black; axil of pectoral fins black; males lavender-blue on back, the scale edges narrowly dark, bluish white on side and ventrally with about 10 black stripes, ending with 2 on caudal peduncle; 3 or 4 of middle stripes changing to yellow posteriorly; head light gray, tinged with yellowish and lavender, sometimes with vestiges of black markings of female stage on nape; dorsal fin with a blue margin and broad, black submarginal band, edged below with blue; anal fin pale blue-green with a similar outer black band, the lower part with irregular extensions from 3 or 4 black stripes of body; caudal fin pale blue-green with broad purplish blue lobes. Largest examined, 27 cm, including caudal filaments. Records from Pitcairn Islands, Tuamotu Archipelago, Society Islands, Austral Islands, New Caledonia, Great Barrier Reef, Taiwan, Ryukyu Islands (type locality, Okinawa), Ogasawara Islands, Mariana Islands, and Marshall Islands; known from depths of 12–81 m, usually in more than 30 m. Hioki et al. (1995) studied the reproduction and early development of this species and *G. bellus* in an aquarium. Eggs measure 0.8 mm in diameter and hatch in about 17 hours.

EMPEROR ANGELFISH
Pomacanthus imperator (Bloch, 1787)

Dorsal rays XIII-XIV (usually XIV),19–21; anal rays III,19–21; pectoral rays 19–20 (usually 20); longitudinal scale series 77–99 (pored scales about 49); body depth 1.6–1.8 in standard length; middle rays of soft portion of dorsal fin of large adults prolonged into a retrorse filament; posterior soft portion of dorsal and anal fins rounded; caudal fin rounded; pelvic fins of adults not reaching anal fin; body and basal soft portion of dorsal and anal fins with alternating slightly oblique purple and yellow stripes; throat, chest, anterior abdomen, and a dorsal extension covering posterior head and anterior body deep purple, the part on head with a blue margin; a blue-edged, deep purple band across interorbital, enclosing eye, curving ventrally and narrowing to base of preopercular spine; head anterior to band pale lavender to bluish gray, posterior to band and on nape yellowish gray; juveniles deep blue to black with alternating narrow blue and wider white lines that are vertical anteriorly and progressively more curved posteriorly, 1 white line forming a complete circle anterior to caudal peduncle. Reaches about 40 cm. Occurs throughout the Indo-Pacific (only 1 natural record from Hawai'i); type locality, Japan. Recorded from depths of 6–60 m. The author examined the stomach and gut contents of 4 adult specimens; 95% of the food material of 3 of the specimens consisted of sponge, the rest algae (including *Halimeda*); the food of

the fourth fish was 65% sponge, 30% algae (mainly *Caulerpa urvilliana*), and 5% gorgonian. Adults are capable of producing a loud thumping sound when alarmed. Thresher (1982) reported in detail on the reproduction; males maintain a harem of 2 or more females; pair spawning occurs at dusk. He noted that the face of males anterior to the dark eye bar is deep blue, in contrast to the pale blue-gray of females, adding that this difference is more evident during courtship and spawning.

341

Halmahera, Indonesia

Bali/juvenile

SEMICIRCLE ANGELFISH
Pomacanthus semicirculatus (Cuvier in C & V, 1831)
Dorsal rays XIII,20–23; anal rays III,18–22; pectoral rays
19–21; longitudinal scale series 65–70; body depth 1.65–1.9 in
standard length; seventh soft ray of dorsal fin and sixth of anal
fin of adults prolonged into a retrorse filament that may extend
posterior to caudal fin (dorsal filament longest); caudal fin
rounded; pelvic fins reaching origin of anal fin; head, chest, and
nape of adults gray with bright blue edges on operculum and preopercle and its spine, shading on anterior half of body to yellow
with small black spots and larger elliptical spots, thence to black
on posterior half of body, including adjacent dorsal and anal fins
and caudal fin, with small, green or yellow spots and irregular
lines; median fins with a blue margin and black submarginal
band or line; juveniles deep blue with vertical blue lines on head
and anterior body, then alternating white and narrower blue lines
that are progressively more curved posteriorly (but never form a
complete circle); illustrated large juvenile just starting change to
adult coloration. Attains about 35 cm. East coast of Africa to
Palau and Fiji; southern Japan to New South Wales, Lord Howe
Island, and New Caledonia; described from specimens from
Indonesia and Bismarck Archipelago. Found on well-developed
coral reefs to depths of at least 40 m. Solitary, the juveniles
secretive and difficult to approach. Adults feed mainly on
sponges, tunicates, and algae.

342

SIX-BARRED ANGELFISH

Pomacanthus sexstriatus (Cuvier in C & V, 1831)

Dorsal rays XIV,18–20; anal rays III,18–19; pectoral rays 18–19; longitudinal scale series 47–50; body depth 1.7–1.9 in standard length; dorsal and anal spines and rays progressively longer to sixth or seventh soft rays, the longest about 3 in standard length, but not forming a filament; caudal fin rounded; pelvic fins long, reaching beyond origin of anal fin; body yellow with a grayish blue spot on each scale and 6 narrow slightly curved, blackish bars that are narrower dorsally and ventrally (scale patterns not obliterated by dark bars); head and chest black with an irregular white bar from nape, passing behind eye, and ending at base of preopercular spine; median fins yellow with blue margins, small blue spots, and short, irregular lines; paired fins black; juveniles deep blue with alternating white bars and vertical blue lines that are only slightly curved posteriorly (mainly basally into dorsal and anal fins). Reported to 46 cm. Ryukyu Islands to Western Australia and Queensland, east to Solomon Islands and New Caledonia; only Palau and Yap in Micronesia; type locality, Java. Found both in clear outer-reef areas and silty protected reefs from depths of 3–60 m. Difficult to approach underwater.

Great Barrier Reef

Society Islands/juvenile

Tahiti

REGAL ANGELFISH

Pygoplites diacanthus (Boddaert, 1772)

Dorsal rays XIV,17–19; anal rays III,17–19; pectoral rays 16–17; longitudinal scale series 48–50; preorbital finely serrate; no serrae on interopercle; body depth 1.75–2.0 in standard length; a narrow scaleless area at rim of eye posteriorly and ventrally (blue in life); dorsal and anal spines and rays progressively longer to eighth dorsal soft ray and ninth anal ray, the longest about 4 in standard length; posterior dorsal and anal fins not pointed but projecting posteriorly, reaching to about midcaudal-fin length; caudal fin rounded; pelvic fins nearly or just reaching origin of anal fin; body with slightly oblique dark blue to black-edged, pale blue bars alternating with orange; bars narrow and curve posteriorly into dorsal fin; head and chest yellowish gray with a dark bar above eye containing blue lines that rim front and rear of eye, a black-edged blue bar from nape to join blue opercular membrane; vertical edge of preopercle and its spine blue; lips yellow; soft portion of dorsal fin with a large, deep blue area containing blue dots; anal fin orange with curved blue bands paralleling outer margin; caudal and pelvic fins yellow; juveniles with a deep blue spot larger than eye in soft portion of dorsal fin, rimmed in pale blue and black. Attains about 25 cm. Red Sea and east coast of Africa to the Tuamotu Archipelago; in the western Pacific from the Ryukyu Islands to the Great Barrier Reef and New Caledonia; type locality, Ambon, Molucca Islands. Occurs from shallow protected reefs in bays and lagoons to outer-reef areas at depths of at least 50 m. Feeds mainly on sponges; juveniles cryptic, hiding in caves (often upside down on roof of caves). Indian Ocean population yellow on chest and with more yellow on the head, not yet given nomenclatural recognition.

343

ARMORHEADS
(PENTACEROTIDAE)

The fishes of this family (Histiopteridae is a synonym), called boarfishes in Australia, are easily distinguished by having the head encased in exposed striated bones; a small patch of embedded scales below the eye; snout profile concave; body moderately to very deep and compressed; the mouth is small with small teeth in bands in the jaws, sometimes on the vomer, but not on the palatines; a single dorsal fin with IV-XV strong spines and 8–29 soft rays; anal fin with II-VI strong spines and 6–17 soft rays; pelvic fins long with I spine and 5 soft rays; vertebrae 24–27. There are 8 genera and 12 species; 2 occur in the South Atlantic, the rest in the Indo-Pacific region, one of which ranges to the west coast of North America. The family was revised by Hardy (1983).

WHISKERED ARMORHEAD
Evistias acutirostris (Temminck & Schlegel, 1844)
Dorsal rays IV-V,26–28; anal rays III-IV,11–14; pectoral rays 16–18; scales small and ctenoid; vertebrae 27; body very deep, 1.3–1.8 in standard length (juveniles deeper bodied); head nearly covered with rugose bony plates; numerous small, whisker-like barbels on chin; dorsal profile of head a sinuous curve, the snout concave, and the forehead and nape convex; anterior soft portion of dorsal fin higher than spinous, the longest rays as long as or longer than head; caudal fin truncate; body white to pale yellow with 5 dark brown bars that are broader than pale interspaces except fifth at base of caudal fin; head dark brown except white bar from nape that crosses posterior part of operculum and the protruding snout, which is dark grayish blue; median and pelvic fins with yellow rays and clear or pale yellow membranes; pelvic fins dark brown. Attains 60 cm. Antitropical: Hawaiian Islands and Japan (type locality, Nagasaki) in the north, and New South Wales, Lord Howe Island, Norfolk Island, New Caledonia, New Zealand, and Kermadec Islands in the south; depth range in the Hawaiian Islands, 35–192 m; adults usually seen in pairs or small groups,

Hawaiian Islands

often resting in caves by day. One brought to Waikīkī Aquarium would not accept any food and wasted away; fecal pellets of a second fish revealed that it had eaten brittlestars. It was then successfully fed brittlestars and later adapted to other food.

JAWFISHES
(OPISTOGNATHIDAE)

The fishes of this family, well named for their very large mouths, are classified in three genera, *Opistognathus*, *Lonchopisthus*, and *Stalix*, and about 90 species (many still undescribed). They have moderately elongate, tapering bodies with a large head of steep profile, the eye far forward. The maxilla of the upper jaw extends well posterior to the eye; the teeth are conical, moderately large, and in several rows anteriorly in the jaws but narrowing to a single row posteriorly; there are no teeth on the palatines and few or none on the vomer. The scales are small and cycloid, often absent on the head. The lateral line is high on the body, ending below the soft portion of the dorsal fin. The dorsal fin is continuous, with X or XI spines that are usually flexible and 11–15 soft rays. The dorsal spines of the species of *Stalix* are unique in being distally forked. The anal fin has II or III slender spines and 10–16 soft rays. The caudal fin is rounded (lanceolate in *Lonchopisthus*, not from the Indo-Pacific). Pelvic fins anterior to the pectorals, the rays I,5, the first 2 soft rays thick and not branched. Most jawfishes occur on open bottoms, often sand and rubble near reefs, and generally in less than 30 m (though some have been taken at depths greater than 200 m). They live in vertical burrows of their own construction, typically lined with stones, coral fragments, or shell; an Atlantic species has been shown to have a chamber below the vertical shaft. These fishes usually have only the front of their head exposed above the burrow entrance. Depending on the species, they feed on zooplankton while hovering vertically above their burrow, or forage nearby for benthic invertebrates; usually they enter their burrow tail first. Their large mouths and powerful jaws serve them well to excavate and construct their burrow, but also, in the case of males, to incubate the eggs until hatching. The genus *Stalix* was revised by Smith-Vaniz (1989). His systematic research on the large genus *Opistognathus* is ongoing.

DWARF JAWFISH
Opistognathus sp. Smith-Vaniz (in prep.)

Papua New Guinea

Dorsal rays XI,11–13 (rarely 11 or 13); spines moderately stout and straight, some slightly curved distally but without flexible tips; anal rays II,11 or 12 (usually 12); pectoral rays 20 or 21; lateral line ending below verticals between first to third segmented dorsal rays; longitudinal scale series 40–45; body depth 5.1–5.6 in standard length; upper jaw extending about 0.5 to 0.7 eye diameters behind posterior margin of orbit. Adults with a partially ocellated black spot between third to sixth dorsal spines; body and fins dusky yellow; body and median fins of males blackish, in sharp contrast to pale yellowish head of large males. Attains 3.5 cm, with ripe females as small as 2.6 cm. Currently known from Indonesia (Komodo), Santa Cruz Islands, Fiji, and Samoa Islands; specimens collected from depths of 20–61 m.

Flores, Indonesia

CHINSTRAP JAWFISH
Opistognathus sp. Smith-Vaniz (in prep.)
Dorsal rays XI, 11; spines moderately stout, straight, and sharp-tipped; anal rays 10–11 (rarely 11); pectoral rays 19–22 (usually 20); lateral line ending below verticals between tenth spine and fourth segmented dorsal ray; longitudinal scale series 51–62; body depth 4.3–4.7 in standard length; upper jaw extending about 0.5 to 0.9 eye diameters behind posterior margin of orbit. Adults dusky yellow with a completely ocellated black spot between dorsal spines 3–4 and 6–7; dark chin bar, black blotch at posterodorsal corner of each eye, and 2 rows of roundish pale blotches on side extending to base of caudal fin. Attains 8 cm. Known from southern Japan, South China Sea, Philippines, Indonesia (Tidore and Flores), Great Barrier Reef, Papua New Guinea, Palau, Fiji, and Samoa Islands; depth range, 6–56 m.

Palau

HARLEQUIN JAWFISH
Stalix histrio Jordan & Snyder, 1902
Dorsal rays X-XI,11–12; first 7 or 8 dorsal spines bifurcate; anal rays II,10; pectoral rays 22–24; lateral line ending posterior to last dorsal spine; longitudinal scale series 47–50; body depth 5.1–5.4 in standard length; adults white with a broad, dusky to black stripe on upper side of body, and a vertically elongate black area posteriorly on opercle; top of head dusky with dark brown to black spots; median fins with black bands. Attains at least 7 cm. Known to date only from southern Japan (type locality, Nagasaki), northeastern Gulf of Carpentaria (from the stomach of a sea snake), northern Great Barrier Reef, Sulawesi, and New Caledonia.

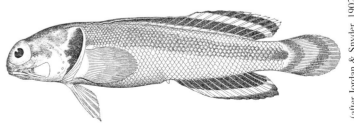

(after Jordan & Snyder, 1902)

Bluegreen Chromis, *Chromis viridis*, Tukangbesi Islands, Indonesia

DAMSELFISHES
(POMACENTRIDAE)

This family consists of 28 genera and 321 species (Allen, 1991); 30 new species have been described since Allen's review, nine from the South Pacific (Randall & McCosker, 1992b; Randall, 2001c, 2002b; Allen & Bailey, 2002). Most damselfishes are small, and many of them are colorful. The majority of the species are associated with shallow coral reefs or rocky substrata of tropic seas, but some are restricted to temperate waters. The family is characterized by a moderately deep and compressed body; a small mouth with conical or incisiform teeth; no teeth on the vomer or palatines; scales moderately large and ctenoid, extending onto head and basally on median fins; lateral line interrupted, the anterior end consisting of tubed scales, often followed by a few pored scales, the peduncular part only of pored scales (scale counts given for species are just the tubed scales of the anterior series); a single dorsal fin of VIII-XVII spines and 10–21 soft rays; anal fin with II spines and 10–16 soft rays; caudal fin varying from slightly emarginate to forked or lunate. Many of the damselfishes, such as those of the genera *Chromis*, *Dascyllus*, *Lepidozygus*, *Neopomacentrus*, *Pristotis*, and *Teixeirichthys*, swim well above the bottom to feed individually on the small animals of the plankton, returning to the reef for shelter and to sleep at night; these species are often seen in feeding aggregations. A few species such as *Cheiloprion labiatus* and *Plectroglyphidodon johnstonianus* feed primarily on coral polyps. Most of the other species are omnivorous, feeding on algae and a variety of small benthic invertebrates. Those that are primarily herbivorous are strongly territorial, and they may be very pugnacious, particularly the species of the genus *Stegastes*. In a sense, they farm their private pastures; they have been observed to nip off unwanted algae just as we pull weeds from a garden. Also aggressively territorial are the anemonefishes of the genera *Amphiprion* and *Premnas* that live symbiotically among the tentacles of sea anemones without being stung. They gain the protection provided by the anemones, and they in turn protect their host from being eaten by the few fishes that are able to prey upon anemones (notably certain butterflyfishes of the genus *Chaetodon*) (Fautin & Allen, 1992). Often only an adult monogamous pair of anemonefish share an anemone, sometimes with several juveniles. The species of *Amphiprion* are protandrous hermaphrodites, meaning that all begin mature life as males with the capability of changing sex to a female. If the female is removed, the male will change sex to female, and the dominant juvenile will mature into a male. The eggs of damselfishes are elliptical and demersal; the male parent guards the nest very vigorously until hatching. The anemone-fishes have the shortest larval life of the Pomacentri-dae (7–22 days), whereas the larvae of some species of *Chromis* have the longest sojourn in the pelagic realm for the family, up to 42 days (Thresher et al., 1989; Wellington & Victor, 1989).

Marquesas Islands

Marquesas Islands (night)

MARQUESAN SERGEANT

Abudefduf conformis Randall & Earle, 1999

Dorsal rays XIII,13–14 (usually 13); anal rays II,12–13 (usually 13); pectoral rays 19–20 (usually 19); tubed lateral-line scales 21–23; gill rakers 27–30; margin of preopercle and suborbital smooth (true of other *Abudefduf*); teeth incisiform and in 1 row (also generic); body deep, the depth 1.75–2.0 in standard length; caudal fin forked; body pale green, the scale edges blackish, with 5 blackish bars across body about half as wide as pale inter-spaces, extending into base of dorsal fin; head and chest green-ish gray; caudal fin gray without a black band in each lobe. Largest specimen, 17 cm. Known only from the Marquesas Islands; collected from depths of 0.5–12 m; juveniles and sub-adults from tidepools. One of a complex of 5 species of *Abudef-duf* worldwide: *A. saxatilis* of the Atlantic, *A. troscheli* of the eastern Pacific, *A. vaigiensis* of the Indo-Pacific, and *A. abdom-inalis* of the Hawaiian Islands.

SEVEN-BAR SERGEANT

Abudefduf septemfasciatus (Cuvier in C & V, 1830)

Dorsal rays XIII,12–14; anal rays II,11–13; pectoral rays 17–19; tubed lateral-line scales 20–22; gill rak-ers 20–26; body deep, the depth 1.7–1.9 in standard length; caudal fin forked with lobes rounded poste-riorly; body whitish with 6 blackish bars (scale cen-ters brown, the edges black), slightly broader than pale interspaces, and a seventh short one dorsally on head with small black spots below; a dark band across upper interorbital space; median fins gray, the base of caudal a little darker than rest of fin; a small black spot at upper base of pectoral fins. Reaches 20 cm. East coast of Africa to Line Islands and Tuamotu Archipelago; southern Japan to Great Barrier Reef and New Caledonia; type locality, Mauritius. Occurs along rocky shores in about 1–3 m, usually at localities exposed to moderate surge; juveniles may be found in tidepools. The author examined the stomach contents of 8 specimens from

Marshall Islands

the Marshall Islands and Society Islands; all had eaten algae (especially *Jania* and *Calothrix crustacea*), with animal mate-rial (including crustaceans and limpets) varying from 0 to 20% by volume.

Tahiti

Bali

Penyu Islands, Indonesia

SCISSORTAIL SERGEANT
Abudefduf sexfasciatus (Lacepède, 1801)
Dorsal rays XIII,12–14; anal rays II,11–13; pectoral rays 17–19; tubed lateral-line scales 18–22; gill rakers 23–30; body depth 1.6–2.0 in standard length; caudal fin forked; pale green, shading to white ventrally, the edges of scales dusky to blackish, with 5 black bars on body about equal in width to pale interspaces, 3 extending into base of dorsal fin and 1 into anal fin; caudal fin gray with a black band in each lobe, the upper band connecting dorsally with caudal-peduncle bar. Attains 19 cm. Red Sea to Mozambique, east to French Polynesia except the Marquesas Islands; southern Japan to New South Wales, Lord Howe Island, and Norfolk Island; type locality uncertain. Coral or rocky reefs, usually in 1–15 m; often seen in small aggregations. Feeding on zooplankton has been observed. Harmelin-Vivien (1979) analyzed the stomach contents of 40 specimens from Madagascar. The dominant food item was calanoid copepods, followed by small amounts of filamentous algae, shrimps, and larval polychaetes. *Abudefduf coelestinus* (Cuvier) is a synonym.

BLACKSPOT SERGEANT
Abudefduf sordidus (Forsskål, 1775)
Dorsal rays XIII,14–16; anal rays II,13–15; pectoral rays 18–20; tubed lateral-line scales 21–23; gill rakers 20–28; body depth 1.5–1.8 in standard length; caudal fin forked, the posterior margin of lobes slightly rounded; body with 6 brown bars alternating with 5 narrower white interspaces; a large black spot dorsally on peduncular bar; head brown with a white bar from nape to opercle, an oblique row of small black spots on nape, and scattered smaller black spots on head above eye; fins gray-brown. Largest specimen examined, 23.7 cm. Occurs throughout the Indo-Pacific region; an inshore species of rocky bottom, often where surge is strong; young common in tidepools. Randall (1985b) reported the diet as varied: some stomachs mainly with algae, others with crabs and other crustaceans (including barnacle appendages), sponges, and polychaete worms.

INDO-PACIFIC SERGEANT
Abudefduf vaigiensis (Quoy & Gaimard, 1825)
Dorsal rays XIII,12–14; anal rays II,11–13; pectoral rays 17–20; tubed lateral-line scales 21–23; gill rakers 19–23; body depth 1.5–1.8 in standard length; caudal fin forked, blue-green dorsally, the scales on body darker blue-green, shading to silvery white below, with 5 deep blue to black bars on body, the first ending at pectoral axil and base, the last on caudal peduncle; dorsal part of body between first and third stripes often yellow; fins without dark markings except ends of first to third black bars extending into base of dorsal fin and a vertically elongate blackish spot at rear base of dorsal fin. Reaches 18 cm. Wide-ranging in the Indo-Pacific, including 2 records from northern New Zealand; absent in the Pacific from the Marquesas Islands and Pitcairn Islands; only recently discovered as an apparent natural colonization of the Hawaiian Islands, where it coexists with the similar *A. abdominalis*. The introduction may have resulted from the proximity of adults on lost, algal-covered drift nets north of the Hawaiian Islands (Mundy, in press).

WHITLEY'S SERGEANT
Abudefduf whitleyi Allen & Robertson, 1974

Dorsal rays XIII,13; anal rays II,12–13; pectoral rays 19–20; tubed lateral-line scales 20–22; gill rakers 22–25; body depth 1.7–1.9 in standard length; caudal fin forked; light blue green, the scale edges dusky, with 5 indistinct narrow dark bars (from darker edges on the scales) on body, sometimes only the first 3 bars evident; opercular membrane blackish; a black spot at upper base and axil of pectoral fins; caudal fin black; dorsal and anal fins blackish, becoming black distally. Attains 19 cm. Great Barrier Reef (type locality, Pixie Reef) to New South Wales, Coral Sea, Lord Howe Island, Norfolk Island, and New Caledonia; shallow outer-reef areas to a maximum depth of 15 m. Feeds on zooplankton well above the bottom, usually in aggregations.

New Caledonia

GOLDEN DAMSELFISH
Amblyglyphidodon aureus (Cuvier in C & V, 1830)

Dorsal rays XIII,12–14; anal rays II,14–15; pectoral rays 16–18; tubed lateral-line scales 16–17; gill rakers 25–29; edge of pre-opercle and subopercle smooth (true of other *Amblyglyphidodon*); teeth in jaws in 1 row with flattened or notched tips (also generic); suborbital not scaled; body deep, the depth 1.5–1.7 in standard length; interspinous membranes of dorsal fin deeply incised (generic); soft portion of dorsal fin long and very pointed posteriorly; caudal fin forked; common color form bright yellow overall with small pale blue spots and short lines on head and chest; eye with a bright blue ring around iris and a blue rim at top of eye; second phase pale gray with faint broad bars on body, only the pelvic, anal, and caudal fins yellow. Attains about 12 cm. Andaman Sea, Christmas Island, and Rowley Shoals of northwestern Australia; in the eastern Ryukyu Islands to Great Barrier Reef and New Caledonia, east to Fiji and islands of Micronesia; type locality, Java. Occurs on well-developed lagoon or seaward coral reefs at depths of 2–45 m, often in the vicinity of gorgonians; observed to feed on zooplankton a short distance above the substratum.

Papua New Guinea

STAGHORN DAMSELFISH
Amblyglyphidodon curacao (Bloch, 1787)

Dorsal rays XIII,12–13; anal rays II,13–15; pectoral rays 17–18; tubed lateral-line scales 16–17; gill rakers 24–27; suborbital scaled; body deep, the depth 1.6–1.7 in standard length; soft portion of dorsal fin moderately long and pointed posteriorly; caudal fin forked; light blue-green dorsally, shading to white or yellowish white ventrally, with 5 blackish blue-green bars on body, the first indistinct from nape to axil of pectoral fins and merging with the same color dorsally on head and posteriorly on operculum, the fifth on caudal peduncle also indistinct; upper and lower edges of caudal fin and anterior edge of soft portion of dorsal fin blackish. Reaches 11 cm. Cocos-Keeling Islands and northwestern Australia; Ryukyu Islands, South China Sea, Gulf of Thailand, and East Indies to Great Barrier Reef and New Caledonia; east to Samoa Islands and islands of Micronesia; type locality of Curaçao an obvious error; most likely described from East Indian material. Typically found in lagoons and sheltered bays; often associated with staghorn coral (*Acopora*); depth range 1–40 m; feeding observed on both zooplankton and algae.

New Britain

349

Tonga

Tonga

BLACKFIN DAMSELFISH

Amblyglyphidodon melanopterus Allen & Randall, 2002
Dorsal rays XIII,11–13; anal rays II,11–13; pectoral rays 16–18; tubed lateral-line scales 15–17; gill rakers 31–32; suborbital scaled; body deep, the depth 1.6–1.7 in standard length; soft portion of dorsal fin long and pointed posteriorly; caudal fin forked; light grayish green dorsally, the scale edges dusky, shading on

Fiji

Coral Sea

sides and ventrally to yellowish white with a faint wash of pink; spinous portion of dorsal fin greenish gray; soft portions of dorsal and anal fins black except basal scaled part colored like body; caudal fin black; pectoral fins with transparent rays, dusky membranes, and a very small dusky spot at upper edge of base. Largest specimen, 14 cm. Known only from Tongatapu and Vava'u, Tonga; specimens collected from coral reefs in 1.5–15 m.

ORBICULAR DAMSELFISH

Amblyglyphidodon orbicularis (Hombron & Jacquinot, 1853)
Dorsal rays XIII,12–13; anal rays II,12–14; pectoral rays 17; tubed lateral-line scales 14–17 (modally 15); gill rakers 29–31; suborbital scaled; body deep, the depth 1.6–1.7 in standard length; soft portion of dorsal fin long and pointed posteriorly; caudal fin forked; head and nape gray, shading on body silvery white with a suffusion of yellow, becoming more yellow ventrally and posteriorly; dorsal fin gray with no black markings; anal and pelvic fins yellow to yellowish gray; caudal fin with whitish rays and transparent membranes, the upper and lower edges narrowly black to blackish; a very small black spot at upper edge of base. Reaches 13.5 cm. Currently known only from Samoa Islands, Fiji, and New Caledonia (*Amblyglyphidodon* sp. of Laboute & Grandperrin, 2000); no type locality given, but probably either Fiji or Samoa Islands. Collected from coral reefs at depths of 12–27 m. Previously identified as *Amblyglyphidodon leucogaster* (Bleeker), a valid species of Micronesia and the western Pacific.

GREAT BARRIER REEF ANEMONEFISH

Amphiprion akindynos Allen, 1972
Dorsal rays X-XI,14–17; anal rays II,13–14; pectoral rays 18–20; tubed lateral-line scales 31–40; gill rakers 19–22; opercle, subopercle, and interopercle strongly serrate (true of other *Amphiprion*); hind margin of preopercle finely serrate; teeth in jaws conical and in 1 row (also generic); body depth 1.8–2.0 in standard length; caudal fin emarginate; brownish orange to orangish brown with 2 dark-edged, pale blue to white bars, a narrow one in middle of body and a broad one from nape across operculum; snout pale orangish; caudal fin white. Reaches 12 cm. Great Barrier Reef (type locality, One Tree Island) to northern New South Wales, east to New Caledonia and the Loyalty Islands; symbiotic with the anemones *Heteractis aurora*, *H. crispa*, *H. magnifica*, *Stichodactyla haddoni*, *S. mertensii*, and *Entacmaea quadricolor*; lagoon and seaward reef slopes to about 30 m.

350

ORANGE-FIN ANEMONEFISH
Amphiprion chrysopterus Cuvier in C & V, 1830

Dorsal rays X-XI,15–18; anal rays II,11–13; pectoral rays 18–21; tubed lateral-line scales 35–42; gill rakers 18–21; hind margin of preopercle finely serrate; body depth 1.8–1.9 in standard length; caudal fin slightly emarginate; dark brown, becoming bright orange on lower abdomen, chest, and anterior head, with a bright blue bar in middle of body and a broader one from nape across operculum; caudal fin white; remaining fins orange except a color variant with dark brown anal and pelvic fins. Maximum length about 15 cm. Philippines, New Guinea, and northern Great Barrier Reef east to the Tuamotu Archipelago and throughout Micronesia; no type locality given. Symbiotic with the same anemones as *Amphiprion akindynos*; occurs mainly in outer-reef slopes from below the surge zone to about 30 m.

CLARK'S ANEMONEFISH
Amphiprion clarkii (Bennett, 1830)

Dorsal rays X-XI,14–17; anal rays II,12–15; pectoral rays 18–21; tubed lateral-line scales 34–45; gill rakers 18–20; hind margin of preopercle finely serrate; body depth 1.7–2.0 in standard length; caudal fin emarginate, the lobes sometimes rounded; black, usually with a variable amount of orange on abdomen, chest, and head; a white bar across middle of body, usually very broad, a second bar across posterior caudal peduncle and base of caudal fin, not well differentiated from the orange-yellow caudal fin, and a broad white bar from nape across operculum; snout pale orangish; dorsal and anal fins dark brown; pectoral fins yellow; pelvic and anal fins varying from orange to dark brown; juveniles from Vanuatu and New Caledonia are almost entirely orange with only the 2 anterior bars. Attains 14 cm. The most wide-ranging of anemonefishes: Persian Gulf and southern Oman to the Mariana Islands, Caroline Islands, and Fiji; in the western Pacific from the Great Barrier Reef to Chiba Prefecture,

Marshall Islands

Izu Islands, Japan

Japan, the most northern occurrence of an anemonefish; an adult at Miyake-jima was observed in the same anemone over a period of 13 years. Type locality, Sri Lanka. Known to associate with all 10 species of anemones that host anemonefishes (Fautin & Allen, 1992).

Great Barrier Reef

Fiji

DUSKY ANEMONEFISH
Amphiprion melanopus Bleeker, 1852

Dorsal rays IX-XI,15–18; anal rays II,13–15; pectoral rays 17–20; tubed lateral-line scales 32–42; gill rakers 16–20; hind margin of preopercle finely serrate; body depth 1.7–1.9 in standard length; caudal fin rounded to very slightly emarginate with rounded lobes; adults usually dark brown to black over most of body, becoming orange to orange-red anteriorly with only 1 blue bar of variable width (usually very broad) from high on nape across operculum; fins usually orange, but anal and pelvic fins may be dark brown or black; individuals from the Solomon Islands to New Caledonia have the dark brown area reduced to a small patch on side, and those from Fiji, Tonga, and Samoa Islands are entirely orange except for a bluish white bar on head. Reaches 12 cm. Indonesia from Bali through New Guinea to the northern Great Barrier Reef, east to Samoa Islands and all of Micronesia; type locality, Ambon, Molucca Islands. Usually symbiotic with the bubble anemone, *Entacmaea quadricolor*, a species that is often closely associated with coral. May be seen in shallow water of reef flats and lagoons but ranges to at least 20 m.

Palau

Marquesas Islands

Guam

PINK ANEMONEFISH

Amphiprion perideraion Bleeker, 1855

Dorsal rays IX-X,16–17; anal rays II,12–13; pectoral rays 16–18; tubed lateral-line scales 32–43; gill rakers 17–20; hind margin of preopercle finely serrate; body elongate for the genus, the depth 2.1–2.7 in standard length; caudal fin very slightly emarginate with rounded lobes; orange-pink with a narrow, median white band extending from midinterorbital space broadly along base of dorsal fin to top of caudal peduncle, and a narrow white bar from nape across opercle; rest of dorsal fin and caudal fin whitish to pale yellowish; remaining fins pale orange. Maximum length, 10 cm. Ryukyu Islands south through the East Indies to northwestern Australia and Queensland, east to Samoa Islands and all of Micronesia; type locality, Obi Island, Indonesia. Usually found in association with *Heteractis magnifica*, but also symbiotic with *H. crispa, Macrodactyla doreensis,* and *Stichodactyla gigantia*; occurs on lagoon reefs deeper than about 3 m and on exposed outer reefs generally in 10–30 m.

MARQUESAN WHITETAIL CHROMIS

Chromis abrupta Randall, 2001

Dorsal rays XII,11–13; anal rays II,11–12 (usually 12); upper and lower spiniform caudal rays 2; pectoral rays 16–18; tubed lateral-line scales 16–18 (rarely 16); gill rakers 25–29; hind margin of preopercle irregular but not serrate; free margin of suborbital nearly reaching a vertical at rear margin of pupil; outer row of conical teeth in jaws, larger anteriorly, with an inner band of much smaller teeth (true of other *Chromis*); body depth 1.95–2.1 in standard length; caudal fin deeply forked with second branched rays of upper and lower lobes prolonged as filaments; dark gray-brown (looks black underwater), the centers of scales darker than edges, with a pure white caudal fin; posterior part of dorsal and anal fins clear; 3 faint, longitudinal purplish lines and rows of small blotches ventrally on body, and irregular purplish markings on operculum. Largest specimen, 8 cm (including caudal filaments). Known only from the Marquesas Islands over rocky bottom from depths of 1–21.5 m.

MIDGET CHROMIS

Chromis acares Randall & Swerdloff, 1973

Dorsal rays XII (rarely XIII),11; anal rays II,10–11 (usually 11); upper and lower spiniform caudal rays 2; pectoral rays 16–18; tubed lateral-line scales 15–17; gill rakers 26–30; hind margin of preopercle slightly crenulate; margin of suborbital free only anteriorly; body elongate for the genus, the depth 2.4–2.6 in standard length; caudal fin lunate; bluish to purplish gray; ventral half of head and prepectoral area yellow, brightest on operculum; a small pale yellow spot at rear base of dorsal fin; lobes and base of caudal fin orange, the lobes shading to yellow distally; anterior half of anal fin black, bordered anteriorly by bright blue; an oblique black bar through pupil. Largest specimen, 5.5 cm. Ogasawara Islands and Mariana Islands to Hawaiian Islands (where rare); Solomon Islands and Vanuatu to Cook Islands (type locality, Rarotonga), Austral Islands, Tuamotu Archipelago, and Pitcairn Islands; depth range 2–37 m; feeds principally on zooplankton like others of the genus, but not far off the substratum; usually seen in small aggregations.

AGILE CHROMIS
Chromis agilis Smith, 1960

Dorsal rays XII,12–14; anal rays II,12–14; upper and lower spiniform caudal rays 2; pectoral rays 17–18 (usually 17); tubed lateral-line scales 15–17; gill rakers 27–30; hind margin of preopercle slightly crenulate; margin of suborbital free to a vertical at front edge of pupil; body depth 1.7–2.0 in standard length; caudal fin forked, the second branched rays of upper and lower lobes prolonged as filaments; orange-brown, suffused with lavender or pink over lower head and chest; caudal fin whitish; a large black spot at base and axil of pectoral fins. Reaches 11 cm. East Africa and Seychelles (type locality, Astove Island) to the Hawaiian Islands and Pitcairn Islands; in the western Pacific from Ogasawara Islands to the Great Barrier Reef and New Caledonia; more common at oceanic islands than off large islands or continents; reported from depths of 6–65 m.

Coral Sea

ALPHA CHROMIS
Chromis alpha Randall, 1988

Dorsal rays XII-XIII (rarely XII),12–13 (usually 12); anal rays II,11–13; upper and lower spiniform caudal rays 3; pectoral rays 16–18 (rarely 16); tubed lateral-line scales 14–16; gill rakers 27–31; margin of preopercle not serrate; margin of suborbital free to a vertical at front edge of pupil; body depth 1.8–2.0 in standard length; caudal fin forked; greenish to brown, the scales narrowly edged with dark brown, shading to blue ventrally, often with a yellow blotch on scales of head and dorsally on body; hind edge of preopercle blackish; rear edge of opercle and adjacent gill opening blackish; a black spot at upper base of pectoral fins; upper and lower edges of caudal fin broadly blackish; anal fin blue. Largest specimen examined, 12.4 cm. Papua New Guinea to the Great Barrier Reef and New Caledonia, east to islands of Micronesia and French Polynesia except the Marquesas Islands (type locality, Tetiaroa Atoll, Society Islands); also known in the eastern Indian Ocean from reefs off northwestern Australia and Cocos-Keeling Islands; replaced to the west by *Chromis nigroanalis* Randall. Occurs on steep outer-reef slopes; reported from depths of 18–95 m.

Tuamotu Archipelago

AMBON CHROMIS
Chromis amboinensis (Bleeker, 1873)

Dorsal rays XII,12–13; anal rays II,12–13; upper and lower spiniform caudal rays 2; pectoral rays 16–17; tubed lateral-line scales 13–14; gill rakers 26–29; margin of preopercle not serrate; margin of suborbital free to below middle of eye; body depth 1.6–1.8 in standard length; caudal fin deeply forked, the second upper and lower branched rays prolonged as double filaments; fifth dorsal and seventh anal soft rays also prolonged as filaments; gray to yellowish or orangish gray, the base and axil of pectoral fins bright yellow (yellow may be only on top of fin base); lobes of caudal fin dark brown; outer margin of anterior soft portion of dorsal and anal fins broadly blackish; iris blue with a black bar through pupil. Largest, 9.8 cm (including caudal filaments). Philippines and Indonesia to Great Barrier Reef and New Caledonia, east to Tonga, Samoa Islands, and all of Micronesia; Cocos-Keeling Islands in the eastern Indian Ocean; inhabits lagoon and outer coral-reef areas; recorded from depths of 5–65 m; stays near reef while feeding on zooplankton.

Cebu, Philippines

Bali/juvenile

Balicasag Island, Philippines

YELLOW CHROMIS
Chromis analis (Cuvier in C & V, 1830)

Dorsal rays XIII,11–13; anal rays II,11–12; upper and lower spiniform caudal rays 3; pectoral rays 18–20; tubed lateral-line scales 16–19; gill rakers 23–28; margin of preopercle not serrate; margin of suborbital free to below front edge of pupil; body depth 1.75–2.0 in standard length; caudal fin deeply forked, the lobe tips acute but not filamentous; yellowish brown, shading ventrally to yellow; fins yellow except scaly basal sheath of dorsal, colored like back; a small blackish spot at upper base of pec-toral fins; suborbital often bluish white; juveniles entirely bright yellow. Largest specimen examined, 20 cm. Southern Japan to Great Barrier Reef and New Caledonia, east to Fiji and the islands of Micronesia except the Marshall Islands; type locality, Ambon, Molucca Islands. Typically found on outer-reef slopes, most abundant on drop-offs; although known from as little as 10 m, not common in less than 30 m; maximum depth reported, 144 m, from off Guam (Myers, 1999). Related to *Chromis pembae* Smith of the western Indian Ocean, in spite of the obvious difference in color (dark brown with white caudal and pelvic fins).

BLACK-AXIL CHROMIS
Chromis atripectoralis Welander & Schultz, 1951

Dorsal rays XII,9–10 (rarely 9); anal rays II,9–10 (usually 10); upper and lower spiniform caudal rays 3; pectoral rays 18–20; tubed lateral-line scales 15–16; gill rakers 28–33; margin of preopercle smooth; suborbital covered with scales, without a free margin below eye; body depth 2.0–2.15 in standard length; interspinous membranes of dorsal fin not incised; caudal fin deeply forked, the lobe tips slightly filamentous; blue-green, shading to white ventrally; a wedge-shaped dusky bar on upper two-thirds of pectoral-fin base; axil of pectoral fin black; a bright blue line from tip of snout to eye; iris mainly bright blue. Attains 11 cm. Ryukyu Islands to Great Barrier Reef and Lord Howe Island, east to the islands of Oceania except the Hawaiian, Marquesas, and Pitcairn Islands; west in Indian Ocean to Maldive Islands and Seychelles; type locality, Bikini Atoll, Marshall Islands. Usual depth range, 2–15 m; closely associated with branching coral (especially species of *Acropora* and *Pocillopora*) for shelter and laying eggs on dead coral branches; typically seen in feeding aggregations above the corals; Hiatt & Strasburg (1960) noted the feeding on zooplankton, especially copepods, shrimp nauplii, and mysids.

Wetar, Indonesia

DARKFIN CHROMIS
Chromis atripes Fowler & Bean, 1928
Dorsal rays XII,12–13 (usually 12); anal rays II,12–13 (usually 12); upper and lower spiniform caudal rays 2; pectoral rays 15–17; tubed lateral-line scales 14–16 (rarely 16); gill rakers 24–29; margin of preopercle smooth; margin of suborbital free nearly to a vertical at rear edge of pupil; body depth 1.8–2.05 in standard length; caudal fin deeply forked, the second upper and lower branched rays prolonged as double filaments; orangish brown; upper half of caudal peduncle dusky, becoming black on upper edge; caudal fin yellow, shading outwardly to translucent, the upper and lower edges broadly blackish basally, progressively narrower posteriorly; a wedge-shaped black spot on upper half of pectoral-fin base, the rest of base orange-yellow; upper half of pectoral axil black; iris pale yellow with a black bar through pupil; dorsal and anal fins with a black outer margin. Reaches 8 cm, including caudal filaments. Western Pacific from southern Japan to Great Barrier Reef and New Caledonia east to Fiji, Caroline Islands, Kiribati, and Marshall Islands; in the Indian Ocean at reefs off northwestern Australia, Christmas Island, and Cocos-Keeling Islands; type locality, Mindoro, Philippines; replaced in the western Indian Ocean by *Chromis xutha* Randall. Occurs on coral reefs from depths of 2–40 m; usually solitary and stays close to shelter of the reef.

BAM'S CHROMIS
Chromis bami Randall & McCosker, 1992
Dorsal rays XII,13–14 (usually 13); anal rays II,12–14; upper and lower spiniform caudal rays 2; pectoral rays 16–18; tubed lateral-line scales 14–16; gill rakers 28–32; margin of preopercle smooth; free edge of suborbital reaching to a vertical at rear edge of pupil; body depth 2.05–2.2 in standard length; caudal fin deeply forked, the second upper and lower branched rays prolonged as filaments; dark brown, shading to brownish yellow on chest, abruptly white at anterior edge of caudal peduncle; a large black spot at base and axil of pectoral fins (axil yellow in an underwater photo of one from Vava'u, Tonga); posterior dorsal and anal rays transparent behind a vertical demarcation. Largest specimen, 8.5 cm. Known to date only from the Pitcairn Islands (type locality), Austral Islands, Rarotonga, Niue, and Tonga; coral reefs at depths of 12–44.5 m.

STOUT CHROMIS
Chromis chrysura (Bliss, 1883)
Dorsal rays XIII,14–15 (usually 14); anal rays II,11; upper and lower spiniform caudal rays 2; pectoral rays 18–19; tubed lateral-line scales 17–19; gill rakers 24–29; margin of preopercle smooth; free edge of suborbital short, ending below front edge of eye; body depth 1.65–1.8 in standard length; caudal fin forked, the tips pointed but not filamentous; body yellowish brown with a dark brown spot or dark edges on each scale; caudal peduncle white; caudal fin whitish to light gray, the upper and lower edges dark brown, the posterior margin dusky; dorsal and anal fins colored like body, abruptly white posteriorly. Largest specimen, 18.7 cm. Antitropical in 3 populations: Mauritius (type locality) and Réunion; southern Japan and Taiwan; and Great Barrier Reef to New South Wales, east to New Caledonia, Vanuatu, and Fiji; over coral reefs or rocky bottom in 5 to at least 30 m; ranges more widely in its feeding on zooplankton than most other species of *Chromis*.

Flores, Indonesia

Sulawesi

Marquesas Islands (L. Rocha)

DEEP-REEF CHROMIS
Chromis delta Randall, 1988
Dorsal rays XII,12–14 (rarely 12 or 14); anal rays II,12–14 (rarely 12 or 14); upper and lower spiniform caudal rays 2; pectoral rays 15–17 (usually 16); tubed lateral-line scales 12–14 (rarely 14); gill rakers 26–29; margin of preopercle irregular, but not serrate; free edge of suborbital reaching posterior to a vertical at rear edge of pupil; body depth 1.95–2.15 in standard length; caudal fin deeply forked, the second upper and lower branched rays with 2 filaments; dark brown to dark gray, the scale edges darker than centers, abruptly white on caudal peduncle and posterior part of dorsal and anal fins; sometimes with a black bar preceding peduncle; caudal fin transparent with dusky rays; a large black spot covering pectoral-fin base, the axil bright deep blue; suborbital suffused with pale blue or violet; iris blue, brightest at edge of pupil. Attains 7 cm, including caudal filaments. Taiwan to northern Great Barrier Reef, east to Palau and Fiji; only Christmas Island in the Indian Ocean; type locality, Guadalcanal, Solomon Islands. Known from steep outer reefs in 10–80 m; not common in less than 20 m; the most common pomacentrid of reefs in Palau from depths of 60–70 m (Allen, 1975b).

TWINSPOT CHROMIS
Chromis elerae Fowler & Bean, 1928
Dorsal rays XII,11–12; anal rays II,10–12; upper and lower spiniform caudal rays 2; pectoral rays 17–18; tubed lateral-line scales 15–17; gill rakers 29–31; margin of preopercle serrate; free edge of suborbital reaching to or posterior to a vertical at rear edge of pupil; body depth 2.0–2.2 in standard length; caudal fin forked, the second upper branched ray longest; grayish brown, the edges of scales a little darker than centers; posterior half of soft portion of dorsal and anal fins pale; a prominent white spot as large as or larger than pupil at rear base of dorsal and anal fins; pelvic and anal spines blue; a small black spot at upper base of pectoral fin. Reaches 6.5 cm. Taiwan and Philippines (type locality, Luzon) to Great Barrier Reef, west to Maldive Islands and east to Fiji and islands of Micronesia except the Marshall Islands; usually seen in caves or beneath ledges at depths of 12–70 m.

FATU HIVA CHROMIS
Chromis fatuhivae Randall, 2001
Dorsal rays XII,12–13 (usually 13); anal rays II,12–13; upper and lower spiniform caudal rays 2; pectoral rays 17; tubed lateral-line scales 15; gill rakers 29–31; margin of preopercle smooth to slightly irregular; free edge of suborbital reaching to a vertical at rear edge of pupil; body depth 1.9–2.0 in standard length; caudal fin deeply forked, the upper and lower second branched rays filamentous; dark bluish-gray, the body and fins posterior to a vertical just anterior to caudal peduncle abruptly white; a black spot at base of pectoral fins. Largest specimen, 8.8 cm. Known only from Fatu Hiva, the southernmost island of the Marquesas Islands. The type specimens were collected from above rocky bottom off a promontory in 18–21 m. First recognized as an undescribed species by Gerald R. Allen (1975b) in his book *Damselfishes of the South Seas*. He illustrated it from a photograph of a preserved specimen as *Chromis* sp. G.

Marquesas Islands/juvenile

Marquesas Islands

YELLOWTIPPED CHROMIS
Chromis flavapicis Randall, 2001
Dorsal rays XII,12–13 (rarely 13); anal rays II,11; upper and lower spiniform caudal rays 3; pectoral rays 18–20 (rarely 20); tubed lateral-line scales 16–18; gill rakers 27–32; margin of preopercle smooth; free edge of suborbital to below rear edge of pupil; body depth 1.9–2.25 in standard length; caudal fin forked, the lobe tips acute but not filamentous; gray-brown; interspinous membrane tips of dorsal fin bright yellow; a dark brown spot at base of pectoral fins; caudal fin dark brown, becoming translucent bluish white on outer one-fifth except dark brown lobe tips; young bright yellow with a small blackish spot at upper base of pectoral fins; caudal fin dusky with a broad yellow band in each lobe. Largest specimen, 13.5 cm. Known only from the Marquesas Islands (type locality, Fatu Hiva); collected from depths of 15–30.5 m on rocky bottom off exposed promontories; observed feeding on zooplankton, usually in small aggregations as high as 5 m above the substratum.

Ogasawara Islands

YELLOWSPOTTED CHROMIS
Chromis flavomaculata Kamohara, 1960
Dorsal rays XIII-XIV (rarely XIV),11–13; anal rays II,10–11 (usually 11); upper and lower spiniform caudal rays 2; pectoral rays 18–20; tubed lateral-line scales 17–19; gill rakers 29–34; margin of preopercle smooth; free edge of suborbital nearly or just reaching below front edge of pupil; body depth 2.0–2.35 in standard length; caudal fin forked, the lobe tips pointed but not filamentous; usually olivaceous to yellowish gray, the edges of the scales dusky to blackish, shading to yellowish on caudal peduncle; a large black spot over all of pectoral fin and axil; spinous portion of dorsal fin black except for basal scaled part colored like body and spine tips that are often pale blue; anal fin largely black with a blue leading edge; caudal fin yellow at base and broadly on lobes becoming nearly clear posteriorly except for blackish tips of lobes; some populations with a small yellowish spot at rear base of dorsal fin. Attains 17 cm. Antitropical: southern Japan (type locality, Susaki, Kochi Prefecture) to Taiwan in the north and southern Great Barrier Reef to New South Wales, Lord Howe Island, Norfolk Island, and New Caledonia in the south. The most common *Chromis* at many localities, forming large aggregations; depth range 6 to at least 40 m. Spawning in Miyake-jima, Izu Islands, takes place in spring and autumn when sea temperature reaches 21–23°C (Randall et al., 1981b). *Chromis kennensis* Whitley, described from Kenn Reef in the Coral Sea, is a synonym.

SMOKY CHROMIS
Chromis fumea (Tanaka, 1917)
Dorsal rays XIII-XIV (rarely XIV),10–12 (rarely 10); anal rays II,9–11 (rarely 11); upper and lower spiniform caudal rays 2; pectoral rays 18–20; tubed lateral-line scales 17–19; gill rakers 26–33; hind margin and corner of preopercle serrate; free edge of suborbital reaching to below front edge of pupil; body depth 2.05–2.45 in standard length; caudal fin forked, the lobe tips long and pointed in juveniles, often slightly rounded in adults; yellowish brown dorsally, shading on ventral half of body to whitish with blue-green iridescence; a small, bright white spot below and adjacent to rear base of dorsal fin, followed by a broad black band that continues as a submarginal band dorsally in caudal fin; lower lobe of caudal fin with a similar band; dorsal and anal fins with an outer blue margin, and upper and lower edges of caudal fin blue; axil of pectoral fins black, the pigment extending slightly above base of fin. Largest specimen, 12.7 cm. Distribution spotty: southern Japan (type locality, Nagasaki), Taiwan, New South Wales, Norfolk Island, northern New Zealand, New Caledonia (*Chromis* sp. of Fourmanoir and Laboute, 1976, and *C. nitida* of Laboute and Grandperrin, 2000); Allen &

Norfolk Island

Swainston (1988) reported it from Western Australia from Point Quobba north, and the author collected 4 specimens at Pulau Chebeh (2°56′N, 104°6′E), Malaysia, in 20–22 m; G. R. Allen (pers. comm.) observed it in South Komodo Island; occurs on rocky or coral-reef substrata from depths of 3–25 m.

HALF-AND-HALF CHROMIS
Chromis iomelas Jordan & Seale, 1906
Dorsal rays XII,13–14; anal rays II,12–14 (rarely 12); upper and lower spiniform caudal rays 2; pectoral rays 16–18; tubed lateral-line scales 15; gill rakers 26–29; margin of preopercle irregular, but not serrate; free edge of suborbital reaching below front edge of pupil; body depth 1.9–2.1 in standard length; caudal fin deeply forked, the second upper and lower branched rays prolonged as filaments; body dark brown to a vertical demarcation at origin of anal fin, then pure white; anal fin, posterior half of dorsal fin, and caudal fin white except transparent membranes posteriorly in fins; a large black spot at base and axil of pectoral fins. Attains 8.5 cm. New Guinea to the Great Barrier Reef and New Caledonia east to Tuamotu Archipelago; no records from Micronesia; type locality, Tutuila, American Samoa. Found on coral reefs at depths of 3–35 m. Nearly identical in color to *Chromis dimidiata* (Klunzinger) of the Indian Ocean and Red Sea; differs in lower fin-ray counts.

Tuamotu Archipelago

SCALY CHROMIS
Chromis lepidolepis Bleeker, 1877
Dorsal rays XII,11–13; anal rays II,11–12 (rarely 12); upper and lower spiniform caudal rays 2; pectoral rays 17–19; tubed lateral-line scales 15–18; auxiliary scales present on nape and back; gill rakers 27–32; hind margin and corner of preopercle serrate; free edge of suborbital extending to below rear edge of pupil; body depth 1.9–2.2 in standard length; caudal fin forked; greenish to yellowish gray; tips of dorsal spines white, the edge of each interspinous membrane black; a dark band usually present at upper and lower edges of caudal fin; tip of each caudal lobe black; iris white with a black bar through pupil. Attains 8 cm. Red Sea and east coast of Africa to islands of Micronesia, Fiji, and Line Islands; southern Japan to Great Barrier Reef; a coral-reef species generally found in less than 20 m; found in lagoons and outer-reef areas; stays close to shelter. *Lepidochromis brunneus* Smith is one of 3 junior synonyms.

Flores, Indonesia

WHITETAILED CHROMIS
Chromis leucura Gilbert, 1905

Dorsal rays XII,14; anal rays II,11–12 (rarely 11); upper and lower spiniform caudal rays 2; pectoral rays 16–17; tubed lateral-line scales 13–15; gill rakers 24–27; margin of preopercle smooth; free edge of suborbital reaching to below rear edge of pupil; body depth 1.9–2.0 in standard length; caudal fin forked, the second upper and lower branched rays prolonged as filaments; body dark brown to deep blue, the posterior half of caudal peduncle and base of caudal fin white; rest of fin translucent whitish tinged with pale pink or pale blue; dorsal and anal fins dark brown to a vertical black zone posteriorly in each fin ending in alignment with color demarcation on peduncle, the rest of fins translucent whitish; a large black spot at base and axil of pectoral fins, often followed by a yellow band; pelvic fins yellow with a brown leading edge. Reaches 8.5 cm, including caudal filaments. Known from scattered insular Indo-Pacific localities: Hawaiian Islands, Marquesas Islands, New Caledonia, Ryukyu Islands, Pulau Weh at northwestern end of Sumatra (G. R. Allen, pers. comm.), Mauritius, and Réunion; type locality, Timor. A deeper-water species; the known depth range, 29–118 m, doubtless the reason for the paucity of localities.

Hawaiian Islands

BICOLOR CHROMIS
Chromis margaritifer Fowler, 1946

Dorsal rays XII,12–13 (usually 12); anal rays II,11–12 (rarely 11); upper and lower spiniform caudal rays 2; pectoral rays 16–18; tubed lateral-line scales 16–18 (rarely 16); gill rakers 25–30; margin of preopercle smooth; free edge of suborbital reaching to below posterior edge of pupil; body depth 1.9–2.0 in standard length; caudal fin forked, the second upper and lower branched rays prolonged as filaments; body dark brown, the caudal peduncle abruptly white; caudal fin and posterior dorsal and anal fins white; a large black spot at base and axil of pectoral fins, often with a white edge posteriorly on spot at base of fin. Reaches 9 cm. Ryukyu Islands (type locality, Aguni Shima) to New South Wales and Lord Howe Island, east to Line Islands and Tuamotu Archipelago; northwestern Australia, Christmas Island, and Cocos-Keeling Islands in the Indian Ocean; a common shallow-water coral-reef fish in Oceania. *Chromis bicolor* (Macleay) is an earlier name, but invalid as a homonym.

Wetar, Indonesia

GREAT BARRIER REEF CHROMIS
Chromis nitida (Whitley, 1928)

Dorsal rays XIII,11–13; anal rays II,10–11; upper and lower spiniform caudal rays 2; pectoral rays 19; tubed lateral-line scales 17–18; gill rakers 28–31; margin of preopercle not serrate; free edge of suborbital scaled over; body depth 1.9–2.2 in standard length; snout very short and blunt; caudal fin forked, the lobe tips pointed but not filamentous; an oblique black band with jagged lower edge from front of snout through eye to margin of dorsal fin at juncture of spinous and soft portions and continuing on outer part of sort portion; head and body above band brownish yellow, below white with blue-green iridescence; lobes of caudal fin with a narrow, pale blue margin and broad, black submarginal band, the dorsal band continuing on upper edge of caudal peduncle to base of dorsal fin; axil and upper edge of pectoral-fin base black. Reaches 9 cm. Queensland (type locality, Hayman Island), central and southern Great Barrier Reef, Coral Sea, Lord Howe Island, and New Caledonia.

Great Barrier Reef

359

Pitcairn Islands

Flores, Indonesia

PAM'S CHROMIS
Chromis pamae Randall & McCosker, 1992

Dorsal rays XV,10–11; anal rays II,10–12; upper and lower spiniform caudal rays 2; pectoral rays 20–21; tubed lateral-line scales 18–21; gill rakers 33–37; margin of preopercle smooth to slightly irregular; free edge of suborbital scaled over; small fleshy papillae at posterior and ventral edge of orbit; body fusiform, elongate for the genus, the depth 2.7–3.1 in standard length; caudal fin deeply forked, the lobe tips pointed but not filamentous; metallic light blue-green, the edges of scales dorsally on body brown; median fins dark brown to black, becoming transparent posteriorly; a large black spot on base and axil of pectoral fins. Largest specimen, 13.7 cm. Known only from the Pitcairn Islands (type locality, Pitcairn, where common), Gambier Group of the Tuamotu Archipelago, Austral Islands, and Rapa; collected from depths of 4.5–44.5 m. Closely related to *Chromis randalli* Greenfield & Hensley from Easter Island.

BLACKBAR CHROMIS
Chromis retrofasciata Weber, 1913

Dorsal rays XII,12–13; anal rays II,12–13; upper and lower spiniform caudal rays 2; pectoral rays 15–16; tubed lateral-line scales 12; gill rakers 24–26; margin of preopercle smooth; free edge of suborbital reaching to below rear edge of pupil; body depth 1.8–2.0 in standard length; caudal fin forked, the second upper and lower branched rays prolonged as filaments; brownish yellow to yellow, the top of head and nape blackish, with a slightly oblique black bar from margin of posterior spinous portion of dorsal fin across caudal peduncle to margin in posterior half of anal fin; caudal fin and posterior part of dorsal and anal fins translucent; narrow row of scales rimming ventral and posterior edge of orbit pale blue. Largest specimen, 5.9 cm, including caudal filaments. Ryukyu Islands to Great Barrier Reef and New Caledonia, east to Fiji and Tonga; only Palau in Micronesia; type locality, Kur Island, Indonesia. Reported from depths of 5–65 m; stays close to the shelter of reefs.

TERNATE CHROMIS
Chromis ternatensis (Bleeker, 1856)

Dorsal rays XII-XIII (rarely XIII),10–12; anal rays II,11; upper and lower spiniform caudal rays 3; pectoral rays 17–19; tubed lateral-line scales 14–17; gill rakers 27–31; margin of preopercle smooth; free edge of suborbital ending below front edge of pupil; body depth 1.8–2.0 in standard length; interspinous membranes of dorsal fin not incised; caudal fin deeply forked, the lobe tips long and pointed but not as trailing filaments; olivaceous to yellowish gray dorsally, the scales edged with yellowish brown, shading to yellowish ventrally, the scale centers often iridescent pale blue; dorsal and anal fins colored like body with a very narrow blue margin; caudal fin with a broad black band in each lobe, the upper and lower margins narrowly blue. Reaches 10.5 cm. Red Sea and east coast of Africa to Samoa Islands and islands of Micronesia; Ryukyu Islands to Great Barrier Reef and New Caledonia; common on shallow, protected coral reefs of lagoons and bays, often using branching corals for shelter and their dead branches for nesting; feeds in aggregations, sometimes with *Chromis atripectoralis*. The author discovered that *C. caerulea* (Cuvier) is the earliest name for this species. Because *caerulea* was then incorrectly used for another common species of

Great Barrier Reef

Chromis that really is blue (or at least blue-green), the International Commission on Zoological Nomenclature was successfully petitioned (Randall et al., 1987) to suppress the name *caerulea* so that *ternatensis* could be maintained. The fish that was *Chromis caerulea* is now *C. viridis*.

VANDERBILT'S CHROMIS
Chromis vanderbilti (Fowler, 1941)

Dorsal rays XII,10–12; anal rays II,10–12; upper and lower spiniform caudal rays 2; pectoral rays 16–18; tubed lateral-line scales 16–18; gill rakers 23–28; margin of preopercle smooth; free margin of suborbital scaled over; body elongate for the genus, the depth 2.3–2.9 in standard length; caudal fin deeply forked, the lobes somewhat filamentous; dusky yellow dorsally, yellow on side, shading to bluish white ventrally; a narrow blue stripe following middle of scale rows below lateral line; operculum and cheek yellow with scattered blue spots; a small, bright yellow spot at rear base of dorsal fin; spinous portion of dorsal fin with a broad, bright yellow margin, the spine tips blue; anterior three-fourths of anal fin black with a blue margin, the posterior fourth translucent; upper lobe of caudal fin with a broad yellow band, the lower lobe with a broad black band. Largest

Marshall Islands

specimen, 7 cm. Southern Japan to New South Wales, east throughout all of Oceania except Easter Island; type locality, Oʻahu, Hawaiian Islands. Reported from depths of 2–20 m; feeds on zooplankton, primarily copepods.

BLUEGREEN CHROMIS
Chromis viridis (Cuvier in C & V, 1830)

Dorsal rays XII,9–10; anal rays II,10; upper and lower spiniform caudal rays 3; pectoral rays 17–18 (rarely 17); tubed lateral-line scales 15–16; gill rakers 28–33; margin of preopercle smooth; free edge of suborbital scaled over; body depth 2.05–2.2 in standard length; interspinous membranes of dorsal fin not incised; caudal fin deeply forked, the lobe tips long and pointed without trailing filaments; blue-green, shading to white ventrally; a faint dusky spot at upper base of pectoral fins; axil of pectoral fins pale; a blue line from front of snout to eye; a male in courtship color, with yellow and black largely replacing the blue-green, is illustrated here. Reaches 10 cm. Red Sea (type locality) and east coast of Africa to the Line Islands and Tuamotu Archipelago; Ryukyu Islands to the Great Barrier Reef and New Caledonia; typically found on shallow coral reefs in protected waters, retreating to spaces among branching corals for shelter, the young in more closely branched corals; feeds mainly on copepods and crustacean larvae of the zooplankton; Hiatt & Strasburg (1960) reported that 60% of 11 specimens from Arno Atoll, Marshall Islands, collected at the time of spawning, had eaten their own ova. Stays closer to the shelter of reefs than *Chromis atripectoralis*, which it resembles (*atripectoralis* differs in having the axil of the pectoral fins black). Swerdloff (1970) described the courtship and spawning.

Luzon

Luzon/male, breeding coloration

WEBER'S CHROMIS
Chromis weberi Fowler & Bean, 1928

Dorsal rays XIII,11; anal rays II,11; upper and lower spiniform caudal rays 3; pectoral rays 18–20; tubed lateral-line scales 17–19; gill rakers 27–31; margin of preopercle smooth or slightly irregular; free edge of suborbital nearly or just reaching below front edge of pupil; body depth 2.15–2.5 in standard length; caudal fin deeply forked, the lobes finely pointed, the upper longer than lower; olivaceous to bluish gray dorsally, the scale edges dark brown, shading to pale yellowish ventrally; a narrow blackish bar at hind edge of preopercle and on opercular membrane; a black spot at upper base of pectoral fins; upper and lower edges of caudal fin with a broad, dark brown band, the tip of lobes black. Attains 13.5 cm. Red Sea and East Africa to Fiji and Samoa

Great Barrier Reef

Islands; southern Japan to New South Wales and New Caledonia; only Palau in Micronesia; records from Line Islands and Pitcairn Islands in error; type locality, Java. Usual depth range 3–20 m; solitary or in small aggregations.

VARIABLE CHROMIS

Chromis xanthura (Bleeker, 1854)

Dorsal rays XIII,10–11 (rarely 10); anal rays II,10–11 (rarely 10); upper and lower spiniform caudal rays 3; pectoral rays 18–20; tubed lateral-line scales 16–19; gill rakers 26–30; margin of preopercle smooth; free edge of suborbital nearly or just reaching below front edge of pupil; body depth 2.15–2.5 in standard length; caudal fin deeply forked, the lobes finely pointed, the upper longer than lower; body of one color form varying from light blue-green with a large, diamond-shaped, black spot in each scale, the head with a broad blackish bar on hind margin of preopercle and another on upper edge of gill opening; caudal fin dark brown; a second color form black, the scale centers varying from pale blue-green to pale yellowish, the head gray with 2 narrow black bars; caudal peduncle and fin white; juveniles deep blue with the same 2 black bars on head, the median and pelvic fins largely bright yellow. Attains 17 cm. Southern Japan to Great Barrier Reef and New Caledonia, east to Line Islands and Pitcairn Islands; northwestern Australia, Christmas Island, and Cocos-Keeling Islands in the Indian Ocean; type locality, Banda Islands, Indonesia. Found on outer-reef slopes, usually from 10–40 m; often solitary. Feeds on zooplankton high above the bottom; difficult to approach because it tends to keep its distance rather than head for cover. The white-tailed form is most common, but the dark-tailed one occurs in the Society Islands, Line Islands, and Guam. The author observed a white-tailed adult fighting with a dark-tailed one in Kiritimati, Line Islands, and has seen both forms and intermediates in Taiwan.

WHITE DAMSELFISH

Chrysiptera albata Allen & Bailey, 2002

Dorsal rays XIV,12; anal rays II,13; pectoral rays 15–16; tubed lateral-line scales 15–16; gill rakers 19–20; margins of preopercle and suborbital smooth (true of other *Chrysiptera*); teeth in jaws slender and uniserial; body depth 2.5–2.7 in standard length; caudal fin slightly forked with broadly rounded lobes; bluish white overall, except a light bluish gray zone on forehead. Described from 3 specimens, the largest 3.6 cm (observed to about 4.5 cm); collected in 42–45 m on seaward slope of Nikumaroro Atoll, Phoenix Islands. Typically found in gullies of sand and rubble that dissect the reef slope, usually in small groups, and always close to the bottom, quickly taking cover in a hole or

under a stone when approached. Differs from other *Chrysiptera* except *caeruleolineata* in having XIV dorsal spines; *caeruleolineata* is easily differentiated by being yellow with a brilliant blue band along the back.

Marshall Islands/juvenile

Marshall Islands

TWOSPOT DAMSELFISH

Chrysiptera biocellata (Quoy & Gaimard, 1825)

Dorsal rays XIII,12–14; anal rays II,13–14; pectoral rays 17–19; tubed lateral-line scales 16–18; gill rakers 23–25; teeth in jaws slender, incurved, and biserial, those of inner row slightly smaller and fitting between teeth of outer row near tips (true of most species of the genus); body depth 2.2–2.5 in standard length; caudal fin forked with rounded lobes; adults dark gray-brown with a white bar from base of fifth and sixth dorsal spines to below pectoral fin (faint in large adults); a black spot at rear base of spinous portion of dorsal fin and a smaller one at rear base of soft portion, extending onto adjacent caudal peduncle and fol-lowed by a small blue spot; caudal fin light yellowish gray; a small black spot at upper base of pectoral fins; juveniles dark brown with 2–3 blue dots on each scale, shading to yellow on abdomen, chest, and lower part of head; a blue line from snout to large, blue-edged black spot in dorsal fin; dorsal fin brown, shading to yellow posteriorly, with blue spots and an outer blue line; remaining fins yellow. Largest specimen, 11 cm. East coast of Africa to Samoa Islands and islands of Micronesia (type local-ity, Guam); Ryukyu Islands to New Caledonia; protected reefs in less than 5 m; feeds mainly on algae, occasionally on crustaceans and polychaete worms (Hiatt & Strasburg, 1960).

Guam

Wakatobi Islands, Indonesia

SURGE DAMSELFISH

Chrysiptera brownriggii (Bennett, 1828)

Dorsal rays XIII,12–13; anal rays II,12–13; pectoral rays 18–19; tubed lateral-line scales 18–19; gill rakers 19–21; teeth biserial; body depth 2.2–2.5 in standard length; caudal fin slightly forked, the lobe tips rounded; 2 distinct color varieties not related to sex (occasional intermediates seen): one yellow with small blue spots and a bright blue band from top of snout through upper part of eye, across back, extending basally into soft portion of fin where it encloses a black spot, and ending narrowly on caudal peduncle; fins yellow, the dorsal with blue lines; the other dark gray-brown with a white bar from below sixth and seventh dor-sal spines to posterior abdomen and a second white bar across caudal peduncle; a yellow bar posteriorly on opercle, followed by a black spot. Reaches 8 cm. East coast of Africa to French Polynesia except Rapa; southern Japan to New South Wales; type locality, Sri Lanka. Occurs in areas of strong surge such as rubble bottoms of surge channels and seaward reef flats; feeds on algae and zooplankton near the substratum (Hiatt & Strasburg, 1960). Indian Ocean form of yellow phase with an elongate sec-ond black spot enclosed in blue stripe, and dark brown form with a blue-edged black spot at rear base of dorsal fin. *Chrysiptera leucopoma* (Cuvier) and *C. amabilis* (De Vis) are synonyms.

Papua New Guinea

BLUELINE DAMSELFISH
Chrysiptera caeruleolineata (Allen, 1973)
Dorsal rays XIV,11–13; anal rays II,13–14; pectoral rays 15–16; tubed lateral-line scales 12–15; gill rakers 20–23; teeth biserial; body depth 2.3–2.7 in standard length; caudal fin slightly forked, the lobes rounded; yellow with a broad black-edged bright blue band from front of snout through upper part of eye along back to end below middle of soft portion of dorsal fin; scales on yellow part of head and upper side of body below blue band with a vertical blue or violet spot; a small black spot at upper base of pectoral fin. Attains 5.2 cm. Ryukyu Islands to Coral Sea, east to Marshall Islands and Samoa Islands, west to Rowley Shoals and Scott Reef, Western Australia; type locality, Madang, New Guinea. Occurs on outer-reef slopes at depths of 24–64 m, usually in small groups; reported to feed primarily on copepods.

CANARY DAMSELFISH
Chrysiptera galba (Allen & Randall, 1974)
Dorsal rays XIII,13–15; anal rays II,14–16; pectoral rays 17–18; tubed lateral-line scales 17–18; gill rakers 21–23; teeth uniserial; body depth 2.4–3.0 in standard length; caudal fin lunate; bright yellow overall; 2 oblique blue lines through eye; dorsal and anal fins with narrow blue margins and faint submarginal blue lines; blue dots posteriorly in dorsal and anal fins and in central part of caudal fin. Largest specimen, 9.5 cm. Occurs in southeastern Oceania at the Pitcairn Islands, southern Tuamotu Archipelago, Austral Islands, Rapa (type locality), and Cook Islands; collected from depths of 1–21 m.

Rapa

Marshall Islands/juvenile

Tuamotu Archipelago

GRAY DAMSELFISH
Chrysiptera glauca (Cuvier in C & V, 1830
Dorsal rays XIII,12–13; anal rays II,12–13; pectoral rays 17–18; tubed lateral-line scales 17–19; gill rakers 21–24; teeth biserial; body depth 2.0–2.4 in standard length; caudal fin slightly forked with rounded lobes; adults gray with faint blue dots on scales, shading to white ventrally; often an oblique blue line dorsally on head and on side of snout; dorsal and anal fins with a blue margin; juveniles gray with bright blue vertical lines or rows of dots on scales; a blue line from front of snout through upper part of eye, continuing partially broken along base of dorsal fin; head and dorsal fin with numerous blue dots and short lines. Reaches 11.5 cm. East coast of Africa to Line Islands and Pitcairn Islands; southern Japan to Great Barrier Reef, Lord Howe Island, and Norfolk Island; type locality, Guam. A shallow-water species of rubble or rubble-sand areas of lagoons and outer-reef flats where not exposed to strong surge; feeds mainly on algae, occasionally on small crustaceans and polychaete worms (Hiatt & Strasburg, 1960).

KING DAMSELFISH

Chrysiptera rex (Snyder, 1909)

Dorsal rays XIII,13–14; anal rays II,13–14; pectoral rays 16–17; tubed lateral-line scales 16–17; gill rakers 17–19; teeth biserial; body depth 2.4–2.7 in standard length; caudal fin slightly forked with rounded lobes; head and sometimes chest gray to purplish gray with many very small, bluish to pinkish gray spots, this pattern continuing variably dorsoanteriorly on body, then shad-ing through orange and pale yellowish to white; a small black spot at upper end of gill opening; median fins pale yellow, the dorsal with longitudinal rows of pale blue dashes or small spots; juveniles with a U-shaped blue line dorsally on snout and interorbital space. Reaches 7.2 cm. Southern Japan (type local-ity, Okinawa) to Great Barrier Reef, New South Wales, and New Caledonia; only Palau in Micronesia; shallow coral reefs where not subjected to heavy surge.

ROLLAND'S DAMSELFISH

Chrysiptera rollandi (Whitley, 1961)

Dorsal rays XIII,10–11; anal rays II,12–13; pectoral rays 15; tubed lateral-line scales 14–16; gill rakers 21–22; teeth biserial; body depth 2.1–2.2 in standard length; caudal fin slightly forked with rounded lobes; head to an oblique demarcation from end of spinous portion of dorsal fin to chest dark brown (paler on chest), the rest of body and adjacent fins white; fish from New Caledonia and the Loyalty Islands with top of head and nape above a line from eye to base of fifth dorsal spine yellow. Attains 5.5 cm. Indo-Malayan region, including the Andaman Sea, to Great Barrier Reef, Vanuatu, and New Caledonia (type locality); only Palau in Micronesia; reported from depths of 2–35 m.

STARCK'S DAMSELFISH

Chrysiptera starcki (Allen, 1973)

Dorsal rays XIII,14–15; anal rays II,15–17; pec-toral rays 15–17; tubed lateral-line scales 15–17; gill rakers 21–22; teeth biserial; body depth 2.2–2.5 in standard length; caudal fin slightly forked, the lobe tips rounded; posterior head and body deep blue below a curved line from eye just above lateral line into basal half of soft portion of dorsal fin; head, body, and dorsal fin above this demarcation bright yellow; 2 oblique blue lines through eye, a short blue line on side of snout before eye, and one below eye; edge of dorsal fin blue; caudal fin yellow except for blue extending basally into lobes; anal and pelvic fins deep blue. Attains 9 cm. Known from southern Japan, Taiwan, Great Barrier Reef, New South Wales, Coral Sea (type locality, Osprey Reef), New Caledonia, and Fiji; reported from coral reefs in 25–52 m.

Great Barrier Reef

TALBOT'S DAMSELFISH
Chrysiptera talboti (Allen, 1975)
Dorsal rays XIII,11–12; anal rays II,11–13; pectoral rays 15–16; tubed lateral-line scales 14–16; gill rakers 18–20; teeth biserial; body depth 2.2–2.3 in standard length; caudal fin slightly forked, the lobes broadly rounded; body yellowish gray with a vertical blue to violet line on each scale, shading to bright yellow on nape and dorsally on head; 2 oblique blue lines through eye; an oval black spot about as large as eye at rear base of spinous portion of dorsal fin and extending onto adjacent back; median fins yellowish gray; pelvics bright yellow. Reaches 6 cm. Indo-Malayan region, including the Andaman Sea, to Great Barrier Reef (type locality, One Tree Island), east to Vanuatu and Fiji; only Palau in Micronesia; mainly on seaward reefs at depths of 6–35 m.

New Caledonia/male

Coral Sea/female

American Samoa

SOUTH SEAS DEVIL
Chrysiptera taupou (Jordan & Seale, 1906)
Dorsal rays XIII,11–12; anal rays II,11–13; pectoral rays 15–16; tubed lateral-line scales 14–16; gill rakers 18–20; teeth biserial; body depth 2.2–2.3 in standard length; caudal fin slightly forked, the lobes rounded; bright blue dorsally and on side with scattered pale green dots, bright yellow ventrally and on pelvics, anal, and most of caudal fin; dorsal fin mainly yellow in female, blue in males except posteriorly; a black streak from front of snout through eye, and a black spot posteriorly in dorsal fin and adjacent back. Attains 8 cm. Northern Great Barrier Reef and Coral Sea to Fiji, Tonga, Niue, and Samoa Islands (type locality, Upolu, Western Samoa). Occurs on coral reefs in lagoons and outer reefs free of heavy surge, generally in less than 5 m. Replaced in the Ryukyu Islands, Indo-Malayan region, and islands of Micronesia by *C. cyanea* (Quoy & Gaimard).

THREE-BAR DAMSELFISH
Chrysiptera tricincta (Allen & Randall, 1974)
Dorsal rays XIII,13–14; anal rays II,12; pectoral rays 18–19; tubed lateral-line scales 16–18; gill rakers 22–23; teeth biserial; body depth 2.1–2.4 in standard length; caudal fin slightly forked, the lobes rounded; white with 3 broad black bars, the first on head through eye, the second anteriorly on body, continuing into dorsal and pelvic fins, and the third posteriorly, extending into rear of dorsal and anal fins; caudal fin white basally, dusky orange to dusky yellow on outer half. Largest specimen, 9.5 cm. Antiequatorial; southern Japan including Ogasawara Islands in the north; Great Barrier Reef, Coral Sea, New South Wales, New Caledonia, Fiji, and Samoa Islands (type locality, Tutuila) in the south; typically found around isolated reefs or rocky outcrops in sandy areas of lagoons or bays at depths of 10–38 m.

Djibouti/juvenile

Maldive Islands

ONESPOT DAMSELFISH
Chrysiptera unimaculata (Cuvier in C & V, 1830)
Dorsal rays XIII,13–14 (rarely 14); anal rays II,12–14; pectoral rays 18–19 (usually 18); tubed lateral-line scales 16–18; gill rakers 22–24; teeth biserial; body depth 2.1–2.4 in standard length; caudal fin slightly forked, the lobes rounded; color variable, but adults usually with centers of scales pale greenish to bluish, the edges dark gray, an oval spot, generally edged in blue, at rear base of dorsal fin; a short yellow streak usually present posteri-orly at edge of opercle; pectoral fins yellow or yellowish; juve-niles yellow with a dark-edged, brilliant blue stripe from top of snout over eye to end at a large blue-edged black spot posteri-orly at base of spinous portion of dorsal fin; a small blue-edged black spot at rear base of dorsal fin, the blue continuing on top of caudal peduncle. Attains 8 cm. Red Sea and Oman to South Africa, east to Fiji; Ryukyu Islands and Taiwan to Great Barrier Reef; type locality, Timor. Inhabits shallow reefs where wave action is mild to moderate.

HUMBUG DASCYLLUS
Dascyllus aruanus (Linnaeus, 1758)
Dorsal rays XII,11–13; anal rays II,11–13; upper and lower spiniform caudal rays 2 (true of other *Dascyllus*); pectoral rays 17–19; tubed lateral-line scales 15–19; gill rakers 21–26; teeth in jaws conical, in 1 row except an inner band of villiform teeth at front of jaws (also generic); margin of preorbital, suborbital, and preopercle finely serrate (generic); body depth 1.5–1.7 in standard length; caudal fin forked with rounded lobes; white with a broad black band from nape through eye to chin, leaving only a median white patch before eye; an oblique band from dorsal fin from between ends of sixth to eighth spines enclosing pectoral-fin base and ending on abdomen and pelvic fins; a broad black bar posteriorly on body, continuing as a broad curving band to join top of first bar in dorsal fin, and extending broadly into posterior part of anal fin; caudal fin and posterior half of cau-dal peduncle white. Reaches 7.8 cm. Occurs through-out most of the Indo-Pacific from the Red Sea and east coast of Africa to the islands of French Polynesia, and Ryukyu Islands to New South Wales and Lord Howe Island; type locality Aru Islands, Indonesia. Typically found in colonies taking refuge in branch-ing coral in isolated reefs on sand bottom of lagoons or bays in less than 12 m. H. A. Randall & Allen (1977) summarized the knowledge of the biology.

Lord Howe Island

Line Islands

GOLDFIN DASCYLLUS
Dascyllus auripinnis Randall & Randall, 2001
Dorsal rays XII,14–15; anal rays II,14–15 (usually 14); pectoral rays 19–20 (usually 20); tubed lateral-line scales 18–19 (usually 19); gill rakers 24–27; body depth 1.5–1.65 in standard length; caudal fin slightly emarginate with rounded lobes; body bluish gray dorsally, the scale edges black, becoming bright orange-yellow ventrally; usually with a bilobed white spot just above eleventh and twelfth lateral-line scales; spinous portion of dorsal fin gray with a broad black border, the soft portion with white rays and transparent membranes; a black spot at upper base of pectoral fins; caudal, anal, and pelvic fins bright orange-yellow with a narrow black margin. Largest specimen, 14.5 cm. Known only from atolls in the Line Islands (type locality, Fanning Island = Tabuaeran), Phoenix Islands, and northern Cook Islands; collected from coral reefs, mainly in lagoons, from depths of 1.5–30 m; juveniles observed commensal with large anemones. In addition to color, differs from the closely related *Dascyllus trimaculatus* in modally 1 fewer gill rakers, shorter paired fins, and slightly larger maximum size.

Tuamotu Archipelago

Tuamotu Archipelago/subadult

YELLOWTAIL DASCYLLUS
Dascyllus flavicaudus Randall & Allen, 1977
Dorsal rays XII,15–16; anal rays II,13–14 (usually 14); pectoral rays 21–22; tubed lateral-line scales 17–19 (rarely 17); gill rakers 26–29; body depth 1.4–1.6 in standard length; caudal fin moderately forked; body light purplish gray, the scales with black edges; head and nape yellowish brown, and chest brownish orange, the scale edges narrowly black; spinous portion and basal soft portion of dorsal fin black, the outer part of soft portion translucent whitish; anal and pelvic fins largely black; caudal fin colored like body at base, then a broad zone of yellow, shading to translucent whitish distally; juveniles pale bluish gray with black edges on scales; a black bar anteriorly on body, continuous with a broad black border on spinous portion of dorsal fin and with black pelvic fins. Largest specimen, 11.5 cm. Pitcairn Islands, Society Islands, Tuamotu Archipelago, Rapa (type locality), and Rarotonga; depth range, 3–40 m.

BLACKTAIL DASCYLLUS
Dascyllus melanurus Bleeker, 1854

Dorsal rays XII,12–13 (usually 12); anal rays II,12–13 (usually 13); pectoral rays 18–19 (usually 19); tubed lateral-line scales 15–19; gill rakers 23–27; body depth 1.5–1.7 in standard length; caudal fin slightly forked with rounded lobes; white with a broad black band from nape through eye to chin, leaving only a median white patch before eye and on lips; a broad black bar from anterior part of dorsal fin to abdomen and pelvic fins; a broad black bar posteriorly on body extending into dorsal and anal fins; caudal fin white on basal half, black on posterior half except for a narrow, pale blue margin. Attains 8.5 cm. Ryukyu Islands to northern Great Barrier Reef and New Caledonia, east to Caroline Islands; type locality, Banda Islands, Indonesia; coral reefs from shallow lagoons to depths of 68 m; feeds on zooplankton, descending to the shelter of branching corals as needed.

Solomon Islands

Bali

RETICULATE DASCYLLUS
Dascyllus reticulatus (Richardson, 1846)

Dorsal rays XII,14–16; anal rays II,12–14; pectoral rays 19–21; tubed lateral-line scales 17–19 (rarely 19); gill rakers 24–29; body depth 1.4–1.6 in standard length; caudal fin moderately forked; pale bluish gray, the edges of the scales narrowly black, with a blackish bar anteriorly on body continuing as a broad outer border on spinous portion of dorsal fin; often a second indistinct dark bar posteriorly, aligned with black basal soft portion of dorsal and anal fins; lips blackish; caudal fin bluish gray, becoming translucent posteriorly; pelvic fins black; pectoral fins with gray rays, transparent membranes, and a small black spot at upper base. Attains 8.5 cm. Southern Japan to Great Barrier Reef, Lord Howe Island, and New Caledonia, east to Tuamotu Archipelago, Pitcairn Islands, and islands of Micronesia; Western Australia, Cocos-Keeling Islands, and Andaman Sea in the Indian Ocean; type locality, "China seas." Replaced in the rest of the tropical Indian Ocean by *Dascyllus carneus* Fischer. Occurs in colonies, closely associated with branching corals for shelter; feeds on zooplankton a short distance above the coral; reported from depths of 1–50 m.

Lord Howe Island

369

Marquesas Islands/juvenile

Marquesas Islands

STRASBURG'S DASCYLLUS
Dascyllus strasburgi Klausewitz, 1960

Dorsal rays XII,14–16; anal rays II,13–15; pectoral rays 19–21; tubed lateral-line scales 18–19; gill rakers 22–25; body depth 1.5–1.6 in standard length; caudal fin slightly emarginate with rounded lobes; pale gray, the scale edges dorsally on body, on head, and chest darker gray, the scales anteriorly on side of body with a vertically elongate dark gray spot; a black spot at upper base of pectoral fins; fins pale gray; juveniles darker gray with a very large white spot on lateral line in middle of body and a transverse white band across nape. Largest specimen, 10.5 cm. Known only from the Marquesas Islands (type locality, Nuku Hiva); collected from rocky areas at depths of 5–12 m. Differs from the closely related *Dascyllus trimaculatus* in its pale coloration, modally one more lateral-line scale, modally one fewer lower-limb gill rakers, and smaller maximum size.

Flores, Indonesia/juveniles in *Astropyga radiata*

Fiji

THREE-SPOT DASCYLLUS
Dascyllus trimaculatus (Rüppell, 1829)

Dorsal rays XII,14–16; anal rays II,14–15 (rarely 15); pectoral rays 19–21; tubed lateral-line scales 17–19; gill rakers 22–26; body depth 1.4–1.6 in standard length; caudal fin slightly emarginate with rounded lobes; body bluish gray, the scale edges dark brown to black; head with a white spot on eleventh and twelfth scales of lateral line and the scale above each; head and chest dark orangish brown, the lips blackish; median fins black except scaled basal parts colored like body; pectoral fins with transparent membranes, dark-edged rays, and a black spot at upper base; pelvic fins black; juveniles with a much larger white spot on lateral line and a transverse white band across nape; individuals from Fiji and Tonga with a variable amount of yellow in caudal, anal, and pelvic fins. Largest specimen, 13.8 cm. Red Sea (type locality) and east coast of Africa to Pitcairn Islands; southern Japan to New South Wales and Lord Howe Island; replaced in the Hawaiian Islands by *Dascyllus albisella* Gill and the Marquesas Islands by *Dascyllus strasburgi*. Coral reefs and rocky substrata from depths of 1–55 m; juveniles commensal with large sea anemones or venomous long-spined sea urchins of the genera *Diadema, Echinothrix,* or *Astropyga.*

FUSILIER DAMSELFISH
Lepidozygus tapeinosoma (Bleeker, 1856)

Dorsal rays XII,14–15; anal rays II,15–16; pectoral rays 21–22; tubed lateral-line scales 19–20; scales in longitudinal series 33–39; gill rakers 25–29; teeth uniserial; edge of suborbital scaled over; edge of preopercle finely serrate; posterior edge of orbit with a series of fleshy papillae; body very elongate, the depth 2.8–3.1 in standard length; caudal fin deeply forked, the lobe tips pointed; color variable, but often greenish to yellowish dorsally, the scale edges dark green to dark brown, dull pink ventrally, sometimes with a longitudinal zone of green on side at level of pectoral fin; last few rays and membranes of dorsal fin yellow (the most conspicuous color marking in life). Attains 10.5 cm. East coast of Africa to Line Islands, Marquesas Islands, and Tuamotu Archipelago; Ryukyu Islands to Great Barrier Reef and New Caledonia; type locality, Ternate, Molucca Islands; coral reefs, particularly on outer reef slopes in about 5–30 m; feeds on zooplankton in aggregations well above the bottom, but quickly retreats to the shelter of the reef as needed. One color phase, bright yellow dorsally and abruptly pink on side and ventrally, forms feeding aggregations with 3 species of anthiine fishes and the blenniid *Ecsenius midas* of the same color pattern in the Line Islands and Phoenix Islands, an example of social mimicry (Randall & McCosker, 1993).

CARLSON'S DAMSELFISH
Neoglyphidodon carlsoni (Allen, 1975)

Dorsal rays XIII,13–14; anal rays II,12–13; pectoral rays 18–19; tubed lateral-line scales 17–18; no notch between preorbital and suborbital (true of other *Neoglyphidodon*); margin of suborbital and preopercle smooth (also generic); suborbital scaled; teeth biserial anteriorly (generic); gill rakers 25–29; body depth 1.9–2.1 in standard length; caudal fin emarginate; adults dark orangish brown, the scale centers bluish or greenish gray; unscaled part of spinous portion of dorsal fin brownish orange; remaining median fins dark orangish brown; pelvic fins dark brown; pectorals with dark brown rays and transparent membranes; juveniles with a curving blue line on back between lateral line and base of dorsal fin. Reaches 11 cm. Currently known only from Fiji (type locality) and Tonga; usually found on shallow seaward reefs on the lee side of islands. This species was first collected in 1974 by Bruce A. Carlson while a member of the Peace Corps in Fiji (later he became director of the Waikīkī Aquarium). Gerald R. Allen (1975b) described the species in his book *Damselfishes of the South Seas*. He placed it in the genus *Paraglyphydodon,* but when he discovered that the type species of this genus is a species of *Chrysiptera*, he provided the new generic name *Neoglyphidodon*.

Line Islands

Line Islands/mimicry phase

Fiji/juvenile

Tonga

371

Great Barrier Reef/juvenile

Philippines

Norfolk Island

Norfolk Island

YELLOWFIN DAMSELFISH
Neoglyphidodon nigroris (Cuvier in C & V, 1830)

Dorsal rays XIII,13–14; anal rays II,13–15; pectoral rays 17–18 (usually 17); tubed lateral-line scales 15–17; gill rakers 22–26; body depth 1.7–2.0 in standard length; spinous portion of dorsal fin low; soft portion of dorsal and anal fins long and pointed, the longest dorsal ray 3 or more times longer than longest dorsal spine; caudal fin forked, the lobe tips pointed, sometimes with 1 or more short filaments; adults brown, shading to yellow posteriorly, including caudal fin and most of soft portions of dorsal and anal fins; a dark brown bar behind hind edge of preopercle; opercular membrane usually dark brown; unscaled spinous portion of dorsal fin yellow, becoming black distally, including cirrus at tip of each membrane; pectoral fins yellowish at base with a deep blue to black spot at upper edge followed by a small yellow spot; pelvic fins dark brown; juveniles (as small as 25 mm standard length) bright yellow with 2 black stripes, one midlateral, and one from front of snout along back following lateral line. Reaches 11.5 cm. Andaman Sea and northwestern Australia in the eastern Indian Ocean; Ryukyu Islands to the Great Barrier Reef, Vanuatu, and New Caledonia; only Palau in Micronesia; no type locality. Occurs on reefs in calm areas from depths of about 2–25 m; feeds on zooplankton and benthic algae. *Neoglyphidodon behnii* (Bleeker) is a synonym.

MULTISPINE DAMSELFISH
Neoglyphidodon polyacanthus (Ogilby, 1889)

Dorsal rays XIV,13–14; anal rays II,14; pectoral rays 18; tubed lateral-line scales 18–19; gill rakers 22–23; body depth 1.8–2.1 in standard length; soft portion of dorsal and anal fins pointed, the longest dorsal ray about twice as long as longest dorsal spine; caudal fin moderately forked, the lobe tips often with 1 or more short filaments; adults yellowish gray-brown, the scale edges dark gray; a small black spot at upper end of gill opening and one at upper edge of pectoral-fin base; a narrow blue margin on dorsal and anal fins; juveniles yellow with blue dots or a faint bluish bar on each scale; a black-edged blue line from front of snout through upper edge of eye to or nearly to a large blue-edged black spot posteriorly at base of spinous portion of dorsal fin and adjacent back; scattered small blue spots on head; a small black spot partly rimmed in blue at rear base of dorsal fin, the blue extending dorsally on caudal peduncle. Reaches 16 cm. Southern Great Barrier Reef to New South Wales, Lord Howe Island (type locality), Norfolk Island, and New Caledonia; occurs on rocky substrata or coral reefs from depths of 2–30 m.

Ambon, Indonesia

New Caledonia

FILAMENTOUS DAMSELFISH
Neopomacentrus filamentosus (Macleay, 1883)
Dorsal rays XIII,10–11; anal rays II,11–12; pectoral rays 16–17; tubed lateral-line scales 15–17; gill rakers 20–23; teeth biserial anteriorly, the outer row incisiform, the inner buttressing the outer (true of other *Neopomacentrus*); edge of preopercle crenulate; suborbital margin exposed; body depth 2.2–2.6 in standard length; soft portion of dorsal and anal fins long and pointed (when intact) extending to or beyond midlength of caudal fin; caudal fin deeply forked, the lobe tips long and pointed; posterior ends of median fins sometimes filamentous; greenish gray with an iridescent green blotch at upper end of gill opening; a black spot at upper base and upper axil of pectoral fins; a narrow blue margin on dorsal and anal fins, upper and lower edges of caudal fin, and lateral edge of pelvic fins; a black submarginal band in each lobe of caudal fin. Reaches 8 cm. Indo-Malayan region (type locality, New Guinea) and Western Australia east to New Caledonia; inshore silty reefs of lagoons, bays, and harbors; feeds primarily on zooplankton like others of the genus.

CORAL DAMSELFISH
Neopomacentrus nemurus (Bleeker, 1857)
Dorsal rays XIII,11–12; anal rays II,11–12; pectoral rays 16–17; tubed lateral-line scales 16–17; gill rakers 21–22; edge of preopercle crenulate; suborbital margin scaled over; body depth 2.4–2.5 in standard length; soft portion of dorsal and anal fins long and pointed, often ending in a filament; caudal fin lunate, the lobe tips usually filamentous; light greenish gray dorsally, with a broad, dark greenish gray edge on scales, shading to yellowish ventrally; small, bright blue spots on dorsal half of head, anterodorsally on body, and posterior body; a metallic green blotch at upper end of gill opening; a small black spot at upper base of pectoral fins; dorsal fin yellowish gray, shading to yellow on soft portion with small blue spots; anal fin mainly yellow with small blue spots; caudal fin yellow, brightest in lobes, with small blue spots; a narrow blue margin on dorsal and anal fins, upper and lower edges of caudal fin, and lateral edge of pelvic fins. Reaches 7.5 cm. Indo-Malayan region (type locality, Buru, Molucca Islands) east to Palau, Vanuatu, and New Caledonia; occurs on shallow coral reefs in areas protected from surge.

Fiji

Negros, Philippines

METALLIC DAMSELFISH
Neopomacentrus metallicus (Jordan & Seale, 1906)
Dorsal rays XIII,10–11; anal rays II,10–11; pectoral rays 18; tubed lateral-line scales 15–17; gill rakers 20–23; edge of preopercle not serrate; suborbital margin scaled over; body depth 2.4–2.6 in standard length; soft portion of dorsal and anal fins long and pointed, ending in a filament; caudal fin lunate, the lobe tips filamentous; body greenish gray with a vertically elongate dark gray spot on scales except ventrally where many scales have a small indistinct blue spot; postorbital head, chest, and lower abdomen yellowish gray; a blackish blotch over pectoral-fin base; a narrow blue margin on dorsal and anal fins, upper and lower edges of caudal fin, and lateral edge of pelvic fins; a dark gray submarginal band in each lobe of caudal fin. Attains 8 cm. Known only from Fiji and the Samoa Islands (type locality, Upolu); occurs on seaward reef slopes in 2–15 m.

HARBOR DAMSELFISH
Neopomacentrus violascens (Bleeker, 1848)
Dorsal rays XIII,11–12; anal rays II,10–11; pectoral rays 17–19; tubed lateral-line scales 15–17; gill rakers 19–21; hind edge of preopercle finely serrate; suborbital margin exposed; body depth 2.4–2.6 in standard length; soft portion of dorsal and anal fins long and pointed, often ending in a filament; caudal fin lunate, the lobe tips often filamentous; dark brown, the posterior caudal peduncle, caudal fin, and posterior dorsal fin bright yellow; a black blotch larger than pupil at upper end of gill opening; cheek, operculum, and chest with a few faint blue to violet spots; a narrow blue margin on dorsal and anal fins and lateral edge of pelvic fins. Reported to 9.2 cm. Indo-Malayan region (type locality, Sumbawa, Indonesia) east to Vanuatu and Fiji; occurs in sheltered waters of bays and harbors around isolated reefs or wreckage on silty sand or mud bottoms.

DICK'S DAMSELFISH

Plectroglyphidodon dickii (Liénard, 1839)
Dorsal rays XII,17–18; anal rays II,14–16; pectoral rays 18–19; tubed lateral-line scales 21–22; gill rakers 15–17; margin of suborbital and preopercle smooth (true of other *Plectroglyphidodon*); no notch between preorbital and suborbital (also generic); suborbital and top of head scaled to or beyond nostrils (generic); teeth in jaws uniserial, slender, incurved, and close-set (generic); body depth 1.8–1.9 in standard length; soft portion of dorsal and anal fins pointed posteriorly; caudal fin forked, the lobes rounded; a black bar across body from base of anterior soft portion of dorsal fin; head and body anterior to bar orangish brown, the scale edges blackish; body and fins posterior to bar white; pectoral fins yellow with transparent rays; pelvic fins brownish yellow. Attains 11.5 cm. East coast of Africa to the Line Islands, Marquesas Islands, and Tuamotu Archipelago; southern Japan to Great Barrier Reef, Lord Howe Island, Norfolk Island, and New Caledonia; lagoon and seaward coral reefs, often where there is surge; maintains a small territory in

Sangihe Islands, Indonesia

branching coral, especially *Pocillopora eydouxi*. In a study of the stomach contents of 40 specimens from Madagascar, Harmelin-Vivien (1979) found that filamentous algae, closely followed by coral polyps, were the dominant food items; calanoid copepods, other small crustaceans, and alcyonarian polyps were also eaten.

YELLOWBELLY DAMSELFISH

Plectroglyphidodon flaviventris Allen & Randall, 1974
Dorsal rays XII,18–19; anal rays II,15–16; pectoral rays 18–19; tubed lateral-line scales 21; gill rakers 12–13; body depth 1.7–1.8 in standard length; soft portion of dorsal and anal fins rounded posteriorly; caudal fin forked, the lobes rounded; body yellow, the outer edge of scales blackish except on chest and abdomen, becoming blackish posteriorly, the scales with purplish centers; snout and nape purplish gray; median fins dark gray except basal scaled part, colored like body; pectoral fins with a large bluish gray spot at base, the rays bright yellow, the membranes transparent; pelvic fins dull yellow. Reaches 8 cm. Known to date only from the atolls of Rangiroa (type locality) and Takaroa in the Tuamotu Archipelago on seaward reefs in 6–12 m; closely associated with the antler coral *Pocillopora eydouxi*.

Tuamotu Archipelago

BRIGHTEYE DAMSELFISH

Plectroglyphidodon imparipennis (Vaillant & Sauvage, 1875)
Dorsal rays XII,14–16; anal rays II,11–12; pectoral rays 19–21; tubed lateral-line scales 19; gill rakers 10–12; lips not thick and without ridges; body depth 2.1–2.3 in standard length; soft portion of dorsal and anal fins rounded posteriorly; caudal fin forked; pale gray, shading to white ventrally and yellow posteriorly (varying from pale to bright yellow); dorsal part of head, nape, and anterodorsal part of body sometimes abruptly darker gray; iris white with a black bar through pupil and extending slightly above edge of orbit. Rarely exceeds 6 cm. East coast of Africa to Hawaiian Islands (type locality, Oʻahu), French Polynesia except the Marquesas Islands, and the Pitcairn Islands; Ryukyu Islands to Great Barrier Reef and New Caledonia; seaward reefs exposed to wave action, usually in less than 4 m, but may occur to 15 m; stays close to shelter and difficult to photograph; stomach con-

Coral Sea

tents of 10 specimens contained mostly copepods and shrimp and crab larvae, but also polychaetes, one with a small, half-digested fish, and little algae. Replaced by *Plectroglyphidodon sagmarius* in the Marquesas Islands.

374

Tonga

Hawaiian Islands

BLUE-EYE DAMSELFISH

Plectroglyphidodon johnstonianus Fowler & Ball, 1924
Dorsal rays XII,18–19 (rarely 19); anal rays II,16–17; pectoral rays 19; tubed lateral-line scales 21–22; gill rakers 12–14; lips fleshy with vertical furrows; body depth 1.7–1.9 in standard length; soft portion of dorsal and anal fins rounded posteriorly; caudal fin slightly forked with rounded lobes; body pale yellowish gray with a very broad black bar posteriorly on body, its rounded ends extending into soft portions of dorsal and anal fins; head gray dorsally, shading to yellowish gray ventrally; a violet-blue line on side of snout; scales rimming posterior and ventral edges of eye lavender, and a row of scales posterior to mouth lavender; dorsal, anal, and pelvic fins yellowish gray, the dorsal with a blue margin; caudal fin grayish yellow; occasional individuals lack the broad black bar. East coast of Africa to the Hawaiian Islands, French Polynesia, and Pitcairn islands; Ryukyu Islands and Ogasawara Islands to Great Barrier Reef, Lord Howe Island, and Norfolk Island; type locality, Johnston Island. Occurs on exposed coral reefs, generally in 2–18 m; closely associated with corals of the genera *Acropora* and *Pocillopora*, especially *P. eydouxi;* its territory may be a single large head of this coral or adjacent heads; feeds mainly on coral polyps. *Plectroglyphidodon nitidus* Smith, described from Aldabra in the Seychelles, is a synonym.

Guam/juvenile

Fiji

JEWEL DAMSELFISH

Plectroglyphidodon lacrymatus (Quoy & Gaimard, 1825)
Dorsal rays XII,15–18; anal rays II,13–14; pectoral rays 18–20; tubed lateral-line scales 17–18; gill rakers 21–25; body depth 1.8–1.9 in standard length; soft portion of dorsal fin pointed posteriorly; caudal fin forked; dark brown with blackish edges on scales, shading to pale yellowish on caudal peduncle and fin; head, body, and dorsal fin with very small bright blue spots, those on body widely spaced and mainly on upper half; posterior part of dorsal and anal fins yellowish; a black spot at upper base of pectoral fins; juveniles with relatively larger blue spots, conspicuously black-edged, and a black spot posteriorly in spinous portion of dorsal fin well above base. Attains 11 cm. Red Sea and east coast of Africa to the Islands of Micronesia and French Polynesia except Rapa; in the western Pacific from the Ryukyu Islands to Great Barrier Reef, Lord Howe Island, and New Caledonia; type locality, Guam; occurs in clear-water lagoon and outer-reef areas from the depth range of 1–40 m; stomach contents of 88 specimens from Madagascar consisted mainly of benthic algae, but with substantial numbers of opisthobranchs and minor amounts of copepods, other small crustaceans, and ascidians (Harmelin-Vivien, 1979).

Coral Sea/juvenile

Guam

WHITEBAR DAMSELFISH
Plectroglyphidodon leucozonus (Bleeker, 1859)
Dorsal rays XII,15–16; anal rays II,12–13; pectoral rays 19–20; tubed lateral-line scales 19–20; gill rakers 15–23; body depth 1.8–1.9 in standard length; soft portion of dorsal and anal fins rounded posteriorly; caudal fin forked with rounded lobes; yellowish brown (centers of scales yellowish, the edges dark brown) with a white bar from below middle of spinous portion of dorsal fin to abdomen (bar broad in juveniles, may be faint or absent in large adults); fins dark brown, the pectorals with a black spot on upper half of base; juveniles with a large, yellow-edged, black

Guam

PACKSADDLE DAMSELFISH
Plectroglyphidodon sagmarius Randall & Earle, 1999
Dorsal rays XII,14–15 (usually 15); anal rays II,11–12 (rarely 12); pectoral rays 19–20 (usually 19); tubed lateral-line scales 19–21; gill rakers 10–13; body depth 2.1–2.35 in standard length; soft portion of dorsal and anal fins rounded posteriorly and short, not reaching beyond base of caudal fin; caudal fin forked with rounded lobes; body bluish white, the edges of scales dusky, with 3 broad, brownish yellow bars that merge above lateral line and narrow as they pass ventrally; a broad, saddle-like, black bar on caudal peduncle, becoming blackish below lateral line; spinous portion of dorsal fin dull orange-yellow with 2 rows of small gray-blue spots in outer part of fin; soft portion of dorsal, anal, caudal, and pelvic fins whitish; brownish yellow bars of juveniles not joined dorsally; a large, oblong, black spot basally in soft portion of dorsal fin extending onto back and continuous with a narrow black bar across caudal peduncle; a white spot dorsally on peduncle behind black bar. Largest specimen,

spot at posterior spinous part of dorsal fin, half in fin and half on back, and a small black spot dorsally on caudal peduncle at end of dorsal fin (reduced to a dark smudge in adults). Largest specimen examined, 11.5 cm. Red Sea (where named as a subspecies, *Plectroglyphidodon leucozonus cingulum*) and east coast of Africa to the Line Islands, Marquesas Islands, Tuamotu Archipelago, and Pitcairn Islands; southern Japan to Great Barrier Reef, New South Wales, and Lord Howe Island; type locality, Java. Usually found in surge zone along rocky shores or reef fronts; difficult to photograph in this habitat.

PINKBARRED DAMSELFISH
Plectroglyphidodon phoenixensis (Schultz, 1943)
Dorsal rays XII,16–17; anal rays II,13–14; pectoral rays 20–21; tubed lateral-line scales 21–22; gill rakers 14–16; body depth 1.9–2.1 in standard length; soft portion of dorsal and anal fins rounded posteriorly and short, not reaching beyond base of caudal fin; caudal fin forked; dark brown with 4 narrow pink bars, 1 from nape across operculum, 2 on body extending into dorsal fin, and 1 across front of caudal peduncle at edge of a black bar covering most of peduncle; caudal fin whitish. Attains 8.5 cm. East coast of Africa to Hawaiian Islands, Marquesas Islands, Tuamotu Archipelago, Phoenix Islands (type locality, Enderbury Island), and Pitcairn Islands; Ryukyu Islands to Great Barrier Reef. Lives in surge zone, generally in less than 2 m.

Marquesas Islands

6.4 cm. Known only from the Marquesas Islands (type locality, Fatu Hiva); occurs in surge zone along rocky shores; quickly seeks shelter when approached. Closely related to *Plectroglyphidodon imparipennis*, differing in color, deeper body, and modally 1 less pectoral ray.

OBSCURE DAMSELFISH
Pomacentrus adelus Allen, 1991

Dorsal rays XIII,14–15; anal rays II,14–15; pectoral rays 16–18; tubed lateral-line scales 17–18; gill rakers 22–24; margin of suborbital serrate; margin of preopercle serrate (true of other *Pomacentrus* herein); notch between preorbital and suborbital (generic); suborbital scaleless (applies to other species of the genus here except *philippinus*); body depth 1.8–2.0 in standard length; soft portion of dorsal and anal fins somewhat pointed posteriorly, not reaching beyond mid-length of caudal fin; caudal fin forked with rounded lobes; adults dark gray-brown overall with a small black spot at upper end of gill opening; juveniles with 2 blue lines dorsally on head and a blue-edged black spot in soft portion of dorsal fin that may persist in small adults; pupil narrowly rimmed in gold. Reaches 8 cm. Andaman Sea, Indo-Malayan region (type locality, Ashmore Reef, Timor Sea), northern Great Barrier Reef, Vanuatu, and New Caledonia; inshore coral reefs to depths of about 8 m.

Palau

AMBON DAMSELFISH
Pomacentrus amboinesis Bleeker, 1868

Dorsal rays XIII,14–16; anal rays II,14–16; pectoral rays 17; tubed lateral-line scales 16–17; gill rakers 22–24; margin of suborbital serrate; body depth 2.0–2.1 in standard length; soft portion of dorsal and anal fins pointed posteriorly, the dorsal reaching beyond midlength of caudal fin; caudal fin forked with rounded lobes; most common color form pale yellowish on body, the scales above lateral line edged in yellowish gray, below lateral line with vertical yellowish gray lines along scale edges; head yellowish brown with a small black spot at upper end of gill opening; fins pale yellow, the pectorals with a small black spot at upper base; juveniles yellow with a black spot edged in blue and black anteriorly in soft portion of dorsal fin and extending slightly into soft portion. Reaches 10.5 cm. Andaman Sea to Western Australia; Ryukyu Islands to Great Barrier Reef, New South Wales, New Caledonia, and throughout Micronesia; usually found on lagoon reefs in sandy areas.

Coral Sea/juvenile

Luzon

GOLDENBROW DAMSELFISH
Pomacentrus aurifrons Allen, 2004

Dorsal rays XIII,12; anal rays II,13; pectoral rays 16–17; tubed lateral-line scales 14–17; gill rakers 19–22; margin of suborbital serrate; margin of preopercle weakly serrate; body depth 1.9–2.1 in standard length; soft portion of dorsal and anal fins rounded posteriorly, just reaching base of caudal fin; caudal fin slightly forked with rounded lobes; head and nape above a demarcation from chin through eye to base of fourth dorsal spine yellow; rest of head and body pale blue-green with a narrow, dull pink bar on each scale; median fins with pale blue-green membranes and blue rays, the distal ends of spinous dorsal membranes bright orange-yellow. Reaches 7.5 cm. Papua New Guinea (type locality), southeast to New Caledonia. Usually found on reefs in protected waters from 2–15 m; appears to feed on zooplankton a short distance above the substratum; often shelters in branching coral. The closely related *Pomacentrus smithi* Fowler & Bean occurs in the Philippines and Indonesia.

New Britain

377

Cebu, Philippines/juvenile

New Britain

Balicasag, Philippines

Fiji

SPECKLED DAMSELFISH
Pomacentrus bankanensis Bleeker, 1853

Dorsal rays XIII,15–16; anal rays II,15–16; pectoral rays 18; tubed lateral-line scales 16–17; gill rakers 20–22; margin of suborbital serrate; body depth 2.0–2.1 in standard length; soft portion of dorsal and anal fins moderately pointed posteriorly, not reaching beyond midlength of caudal fin; caudal fin slightly forked with rounded lobes; orangish brown, the scale edges darker, with a blue dot on each scale; head and base of dorsal fin with small blue spots; a small blue and black spot at upper end of gill opening, and a small black spot at upper base of pectoral fin; a black spot posteriorly in soft portion of dorsal fin rimmed anteriorly in pale blue; caudal fin abruptly white; juveniles bright orange-red dorsally on head and spinous portion of dorsal fin with oblique bright blue lines edged in black, one of which is middorsal on head. Attains 8 cm. Christmas Island and reefs off northwestern Australia; Ryukyu Islands to Great Barrier Reef, New South Wales, and New Caledonia; east to Palau, Yap, and Fiji; type locality, Bangka Island, Indonesia; occurs on both lagoon and seaward reefs from depths of about 1–12 m.

CHARCOAL DAMSELFISH
Pomacentrus brachialis Cuvier in C & V, 1830

Dorsal rays XIII,13–15; anal rays II,14–15; pectoral rays 16–17; tubed lateral-line scales 16–17; gill rakers 19–21; margin of suborbital serrate; body depth 2.0–2.1 in standard length; soft portion of dorsal and anal fins slightly pointed posteriorly, reaching to or a little beyond base of caudal fin; caudal fin slightly forked, the lobes rounded; dark brown overall, the median fins darker than body, with a semicircular, jet black spot, rimmed posteriorly with light gray, covering all of base and axil of pectoral fin; pupil narrowly rimmed with gold. Reaches 10.5 cm. Ryukyu Islands to Great Barrier Reef and New Caledonia, east to Marshall Islands, Caroline Islands, Fiji, and Samoa Islands; type locality, Java. Occurs on coral reefs from depths of 6–40 m; reported to feed on algae and zooplankton. *Pomacentrus melanopterus* Bleeker is a synonym.

BLUE-GREEN DAMSELFISH
Pomacentrus callainus Randall, 2002

Dorsal rays XIII,14–15 (rarely 15); anal rays II,14–15 (rarely 15); pectoral rays 18–19 (rarely 19); tubed lateral-line scales 16–18; gill rakers 22–25; margin of suborbital smooth; vertical margin of preopercle serrate; suborbital scaled (naked in other *Pomacentrus* herein); body depth 2.0–2.3 in standard length; soft portion of dorsal and anal fins rounded to slightly angular posteriorly, reaching a little beyond base of caudal fin; caudal fin moderately forked with rounded lobes; dull blue-green overall, the scale edges dusky; a narrow, wedge-shaped, black spot on upper half of pectoral-fin base. Largest specimen, 9.5 cm. Fiji and Tonga (type locality, Tongatapu); shallow reefs; closely tied to coral for shelter. Similar to *Pomacentrus lepidogenys* Fowler & Bean of more western localities in the Pacific and eastern Indian Ocean; it is gray with yellow on the back posteriorly and adjacent dorsal fin, as well as caudal peduncle; also it has longer dorsal and anal spines.

YELLOWTAIL DAMSELFISH

Pomacentrus chrysurus Cuvier in C & V, 1830

Dorsal rays XIII,14–16; anal rays II,15–16; pectoral rays 18; tubed lateral-line scales 18–19; gill rakers 18–19; margin of suborbital serrate; body depth 1.9–2.2 in standard length; soft portion of dorsal and anal fins rounded to slightly angular posteriorly, reaching to or a little beyond base of caudal fin; caudal fin slightly to moderately forked, the lobes rounded; dark brown, the scale edges usually darker than centers; caudal fin abruptly yellow or white; small black spot at upper end of gill opening present or absent; a very small dark spot at upper base of pectoral fins; median and pelvic fins dark brown; pectoral fins with transparent membranes, the rays varying from yellow to brown; juveniles orange-yellow above a demarcation from chin through eye to end of spinous portion of dorsal fin, dark gray-brown below, with a large blue-edged black spot in soft portion of dorsal fin (may persist in adults to at least 7 cm). Reaches 9 cm. Maldive Islands to western Pacific from Ryukyu Islands to Great Barrier Reef, New South Wales, and New Caledonia; Palau in Micronesia; type locality, South Seas. A shallow-water species of coral reefs or rocky areas dominated by sand. *Pomacentrus rhodonotus* Bleeker and *P. flavicauda* Whitley are synonyms.

Redang, Malaysia

Sumatra

NEON DAMSELFISH

Pomacentrus coelestis Jordan & Starks, 1901

Dorsal rays XIII,13–15; anal rays II,14–15; pectoral rays 17–18; tubed lateral-line scales 17–18; gill rakers 20–22; margin of suborbital smooth; body elongate, the depth 2.5–2.6 in standard length; soft portion of dorsal and anal fins pointed posteriorly, reaching to or a little beyond base of caudal fin; caudal fin moderately forked; bright blue with a dark blue vertical line on each scale, abruptly yellow ventrally; a small dark blue spot at upper end of gill opening, and another at upper base of pectoral fin; caudal fin yellow, the caudal peduncle variably yellow; anal fin yellow with a blue margin, sometimes with a blue line and/or some blue dots; outer posterior soft portion of dorsal fin yellow. Attains 8 cm. Sri Lanka, Cocos-Keeling Islands, and Western Australia to Line Islands and French Polynesia except Rapa and the Austral Islands; Japan (type locality, Wakanura) to Great Barrier Reef, New South Wales, Lord Howe Island, and New Caledonia; usually found in rubble areas of coral reefs exposed to surge, generally in less than 12 m.

Fiji

IMITATOR DAMSELFISH

Pomacentrus imitator (Whitley, 1964)

Dorsal rays XIII-XIV (rarely XIV),13–14; anal rays II,13–14; pectoral rays 17–18; tubed lateral-line scales 15–18; a patch of scales on preorbital behind and below nostrils; gill rakers 22–24; margin of suborbital serrate; body depth 1.8–1.9 in standard length; soft portion of dorsal and anal fins pointed posteriorly, not reaching midlength of caudal fin; caudal fin forked with rounded lobes; gray-brown, the edges of scales narrowly black, usually shading to yellow on caudal peduncle and fin; a large black spot covering base and axil of pectoral fin; dorsal and anal fins yellowish gray with an outer blue margin. Attains 9.5 cm. Coral Sea (type locality, Lihou Reefs), New Caledonia, Tonga, Rotuma, and Fiji; outer-reef areas in about 2–15 m; generally above the substratum, where it seems to feed on zooplankton.

Fiji

Fiji

Tonga

New Caledonia/juvenile

Great Barrier Reef

Great Barrier Reef

LEMON DAMSELFISH

Pomacentrus moluccensis Bleeker, 1853

Dorsal rays XIII,14–15; anal rays II,14–15; pectoral rays 17; tubed lateral-line scales 17–18; gill rakers 23–24; margin of suborbital serrate; body depth 1.8–2.0 in standard length; soft portion of dorsal and anal fins moderately pointed posteriorly, usually not reaching midlength of caudal fin; caudal fin slightly forked with rounded lobes; yellow overall, the centers of scales a little dusky, with a very small black spot at upper end of gill opening and another at upper end of pectoral-fin base; a pale blue line on side of snout and other pale blue markings on head below eye; dorsal fin with a blue outer margin and a submarginal blue line; anal fin with a submarginal blue line, with or without a blue margin, and sometimes with a black margin; in Fiji and Tonga the broad middle zone of body overlaid with dusky, and most individuals in Tonga all dark brown except yellowish over ventral part of head and on chest and a bright yellow caudal fin; juveniles yellow. Attains 8 cm. Andaman Sea, Western Australia, and Ryukyu Islands to Great Barrier Reef, New South Wales, and Lord Howe Island, east to New Caledonia, Fiji, and Tonga; Palau and Yap in Micronesia; shallow reefs in clear water of lagoons or outer-reef areas free of heavy surge; usually near branching corals. *Pomacentrus popei* Evermann & Seale is a synonym.

NAGASAKI DAMSELFISH

Pomacentrus nagasakiensis Tanaka, 1917

Dorsal rays XIII,14–15; anal rays II,16–17; pectoral rays 17–18; tubed lateral-line scales 17–19; gill rakers 18–21; margin of suborbital serrate; body depth 1.9–2.2 in standard length; soft portion of dorsal and anal fins pointed posteriorly, usually not reaching midlength of caudal fin; caudal fin slightly forked with rounded lobes; dark gray-brown, the scale edges black; caudal fin whitish; a large black spot at pectoral-fin base; tips of interspinous membranes of dorsal fin black; juveniles with small blue spots and irregular blue lines on head, and a blue-edged black spot at rear base of dorsal fin. Reaches 11 cm. Maldive Islands and Sri Lanka to western Pacific from southern Japan to Great Barrier Reef, New South Wales, and New Caledonia; only Palau in Micronesia; reported from coral reefs at depths of 5–40 m. *Pomacentrus arenarius* Allen is a synonym.

BLACKMARGIN DAMSELFISH

Pomacentrus nigromarginatus Allen, 1973

Dorsal rays XIII,14–15; anal rays II,14–15; pectoral rays 16–17; tubed lateral-line scales 13–15; gill rakers 20–21; margin of suborbital serrate; body depth 1.9–2.2 in standard length; soft portion of dorsal and anal fins angular posteriorly, not reaching midlength of caudal fin; caudal fin very slightly forked with rounded lobes; gray, the scale edges darker gray, shading to yellow posteriorly, the scale edges grayish yellow; a large black spot covering base and axil of pectoral fins, the narrow area around spot a little paler; caudal fin yellow with a black posterior margin; dorsal and anal fins yellow to grayish yellow, the outer interspinous membranes of dorsal fin blackish, the terminal cirrus black. Reaches 9.5 cm. Ryukyu Islands to the northern Great Barrier Reef and Coral Sea, east to Fiji; type locality, Papua New Guinea; occurs on hard substratum of steep outer-reef slopes in 20–50 m.

PEACOCK DAMSELFISH

Pomacentrus pavo (Bloch, 1787)

Dorsal rays XIII,12–14; anal rays II,12–14; pectoral rays 17; tubed lateral-line scales 16–17; gill rakers 23–24; margin of suborbital serrate; body elongate, the depth 2.4–2.6 in standard length; soft portion of dorsal and anal fins pointed posteriorly, reaching to or beyond midlength of middle caudal rays; blue to blue-green with a vertical dark blue line and a vertical pale green line or row of pale green dots on each scale; head with many irregular blue to blue-green lines or dashes; an iridescent blue-green or black spot at upper end of gill opening; caudal fin pale yellow with light blue-green rays, the lobe margins narrowly blue. Attains 11 cm. East coast of Africa to the Society Islands and Tuamotu Archipelago; Taiwan to Great Barrier Reef, New South Wales, Lord Howe Island, and New Caledonia; type locality, East Indies. Typically found in lagoons or bays; occurs around isolated coral heads in about 1–15 m. Feeds mainly on small crustaceans, primarily from the plankton, occasionally on filamentous algae.

Marshall Islands

PHILIPPINE DAMSELFISH

Pomacentrus philippinus Evermann & Seale, 1907

Dorsal rays XIII,14–15 (usually 14); anal rays II,14–16; pectoral rays 18–19; tubed lateral-line scales 17–18; gill rakers 23–24; margin of suborbital serrate; suborbital scaled, at least posteriorly; a small patch of scales may be present on preorbital before lower half of eye; body depth 1.9–2.1 in standard length; soft portion of dorsal and anal fins usually pointed posteriorly but not extending much beyond base of caudal fin; caudal fin slightly to moderately forked, the lobes rounded to pointed; posterior ends of dorsal and anal fins and caudal lobes often with short exserted rays; centers of scales gray-brown, the edges broadly dark brown to black; head and chest dark brown; pectoral fins with a black spot covering base and axil; caudal fin and posterior part of dorsal and anal fins often yellow, sometimes with a black margin. Allen (1991) illustrated 3 extremes in color variation of this species; one with a dark caudal fin from the Great Barrier Reef also occurs from New Caledonia to the Samoa Islands (though without whitish scale centers). Largest specimen examined, 10.9 cm. Maldive Islands to Samoa Islands and Caroline Islands; Ryukyu Islands to Great Barrier Reef and New Caledonia; usually seen in small groups in outer reef areas, often near caves or under ledges; appears to feed mainly on zooplankton.

Bali/juvenile

Papua New Guinea

REID'S DAMSELFISH

Pomacentrus reidi Fowler & Bean, 1928

Dorsal rays XIV,13–15; anal rays II,15–16; pectoral rays 17–18; tubed lateral-line scales 16–17; gill rakers 19–21; margin of suborbital serrate; body depth 1.8–2.0 in standard length; soft portion of dorsal and anal fins rounded posteriorly, extending slightly beyond base of caudal fin; caudal fin slightly forked with rounded lobes; gray with vertical lavender lines on scales; head with numerous irregular violet spots; fins gray, the caudal yellowish posteriorly, the pectorals with a small black spot at upper base; iris blue with a narrow inner yellow ring. Attains 12 cm. Indo-Malayan region (type locality, Tawi Tawi Island, Philippines) to northern Great Barrier Reef and New Caledonia; only Palau in Micronesia; outer-reef slopes and deeper reefs of lagoons; reported from depths of 12–70 m.

Palau

Fiji/juvenile

Fiji

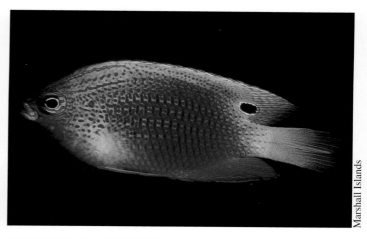

Marshall Islands

ORANGESPOTTED DAMSELFISH

Pomacentrus spilotoceps Randall, 2002

Dorsal rays XIII,14–15 (usually 15); anal rays II,15; pectoral rays 18; tubed lateral-line scales 17–18 (usually 18); total gill rakers 22–24; suborbital naked, the margin serrate; posterior edge of preorbital with a strong retrorse spine; body depth 1.95–2.1 in standard length; longest dorsal spine 1.55–1.65 in head length; second anal spine 1.4–1.5 in head length; yellowish brown, the scale edges blackish, with yellow to pale orange spots on opercle, pectoral-fin base, and a large triangular one above base; 2 blue lines on side of snout crossing upper lip; a small, vertically elongate, deep blue or black spot at upper end of gill opening, and a small black spot at upper pectoral-fin base; a blue-edged black spot posteriorly in lower half of dorsal fin present or absent in adults; caudal fin yellowish. Largest specimen, 7.8 cm. Currently known only from Tonga (type locality, Tongatapu) and Fiji. A shallow-water coral-reef species; not common.

TAHITIAN DAMSELFISH

Pomachromis fuscidorsalis Allen & Randall, 1974

Dorsal rays XIV,13; anal rays II,13; pectoral rays 19–20; tubed lateral-line scales 17–18; gill rakers 24–27; margin of suborbital and preopercle not serrate; teeth uniserial (irregularly biserial at front of jaws); body elongate, the depth 2.7–2.9 in standard length; spinous portion of dorsal fin not incised (generic); soft portion of dorsal and anal fins pointed posteriorly, the dorsal reaching at most slightly posterior to caudal-fin base; caudal fin forked, the lobe tips pointed; white with faint green edges on scales; a broad black band from eye along back above lateral line and continuing as a narrowing blue-edged band in upper lobe of caudal fin; lower lobe of caudal fin with a similar band; head and nape above black band pale yellowish; spinous portion of dorsal fin pale orange. Reaches 8.5 cm. Reported from the Society Islands

PRINCESS DAMSELFISH

Pomacentrus vaiuli Jordan & Seale, 1906

Dorsal rays XIII,15–16; anal rays II,15–16; pectoral rays 17–18; tubed lateral-line scales 17–18; gill rakers 20–21; margin of suborbital serrate; margin of preopercle weakly serrate; body depth 1.9–2.1 in standard length; soft portion of dorsal and anal fins pointed posteriorly, nearly reaching midlength of caudal fin; caudal fin slightly forked with rounded lobes; orange to orangish or yellowish brown with dark brown edges on scales and 2 to 3 bright blue spots on each scale in vertical series (only 1 on caudal peduncle); head with small blue spots and 1 or more oblique blue lines dorsally on head and nape; a small, dark green to black spot at upper end of gill opening; dorsal and caudal fin orange to brownish yellow with bluish rays, the dorsal with blue spots basally, blue margin, blue submarginal line, and a blue-edged black spot in soft portion; juveniles similar in color to the young of *Pomacentrus bankanensis*, with bright orange dorsally on head and nape containing bright blue lines and spots, but a median blue line on head is lacking. Attains 10 cm. Western Australia, where different in color (Allen, 1991) and western Pacific from southern Japan to Great Barrier Reef and New Caledonia, east to Samoa Islands (type locality, Tutuila), Rarotonga (M. P. Francis, pers. comm.), and throughout Micronesia; found on both lagoon and seaward reefs; reported from depths of 3–45 m; feeds mainly on algae, occasionally on small animals of the plankton, especially crustaceans.

Tahiti

(type locality, Tahiti), Tuamotu Archipelago, and Pitcairn Islands; observed at Rarotonga, Cook Islands, and Niue (M. P. Francis, pers. comm.); usually seen in small aggregations on exposed reef fronts or in surge channels at depths of 1–18 m; feeds on zooplankton.

382

RICHARDSON'S DAMSELFISH

Pomachromis richardsoni (Snyder, 1909)

Dorsal rays XIV,12–13; anal rays II,13; pectoral rays 18–19; tubed lateral-line scales 17; gill rakers 21; margin of suborbital and preopercle not serrate; teeth uniserial (irregularly biserial at front of jaws); body elongate, the depth 2.9–3.0 in standard length; soft portion of dorsal and anal fins pointed posteriorly, the dorsal reaching at most slightly posterior to caudal-fin base; caudal fin forked, the lobe tips pointed; body greenish gray dorsally, the scale edges black, shading to whitish ventrally; a small light green to white spot below rear base of dorsal fin; a broad black band below this spot continuing dorsally on caudal peduncle into upper lobe of caudal fin to lobe tip; a comparable black band in lower lobe of caudal fin but not extending onto peduncle; spinous portion of dorsal fin dull yellow with a blue margin and submarginal blue line, shading to black on anterior half of soft portion and to clear with dusky rays posteriorly. Largest specimen examined, 9.5 cm. Wide-ranging in the

Tonga

Indo-Pacific, but relatively few localities reported: Mauritius, Ryukyu Islands (type locality, Okinawa), Taiwan, Great Barrier Reef, Loyalty Islands, Fiji, Tonga, and Samoa Islands; habits similar to those of *Pomachromis fuscidorsalis*.

SHORTSNOUTED DAMSELFISH

Pristotis obtusirostris (Günther, 1862)

Dorsal rays XIII,12–13; anal rays II,12–14; pectoral rays 17–18; tubed lateral-line scales 19–20; predorsal scales to middle of interorbital space; gill rakers 26–28; margin of preopercle and subopercle serrate; no notch beween preorbital and suborbital; teeth uniserial; body depth 2.5–2.8 in standard length; membranes of spinous portion of dorsal fin not incised; caudal fin forked; pale blue to lavender-gray, the dorsal part of body often suffused with yellow; usually a blue spot on each scale; a small but prominent black spot at upper base of pectoral fin. Attains 13 cm. Persian Gulf and India to the western Pacific from Ryukyu Islands to Western Australia, Queensland, Great Barrier Reef, and New Caledonia; no type locality reported. Lives over silty sand substrata in protected waters of lagoons and bays, generally not near well-developed coral reefs; feeds on zooplankton. *Pristotis jerdoni* (Day) is a synonym.

New Caledonia/juvenile

Lombok, Indonesia

WHITEBAR GREGORY

Stegastes albifasciatus (Schlegel & Müller, 1839)

Dorsal rays XII,15–16 (usually 15); anal rays II,12–13 (usually 12); pectoral rays 18–20 (usually 20); tubed lateral-line scales 18–20; gill rakers 20–25; no notch between preorbital and suborbital (true of other *Stegastes*); margin of suborbital and preopercle serrate (also generic); suborbital scaled (generic); teeth slender, incisiform, and in 1 row (generic); inner base of pectoral fins scaly (naked on other species of the genus treated here); body depth 1.8–2.1 in standard length; anterior membranes of spinous portion of dorsal fin incised; dark gray, often with a vertically elongate blue spot on scales of body, and blue spots on cheek and opercle; a black spot on upper half of pectoral-fin base and in axil, and a vertically elongate black spot at rear base of dorsal fin extending slightly onto back, usually preceded by a white bar; males in breeding coloration with posterior half of body lighter gray and containing a broad white bar from middle of dorsal fin to anterior part of anal fin. Reaches 11 cm. Ryukyu Islands to Great Barrier Reef and New Caledonia, east to Line Islands, Tuamotu Archipelago, and throughout Micronesia; Indian Ocean

Tonga

localities include Aldabra, St. Brandon's Shoals, Chagos Archipelago, Cocos-Keeling Islands, and Christmas Island; type locality, Sulawesi. A shallow-water species usually found in areas of light surge, often on rubble or rubble-sand substrata; feeds almost entirely on algae, usually ingesting considerable sand; occasionally eats small crustaceans and fish eggs (Hiatt & Strasburg, 1960). *Stegastes eclipticus* Jordan & Seale is a synonym.

Rowley Shoals, Western Australia/subadult

Mauritius

DUSKY GREGORY
Stegastes nigricans (Lacepède, 1802)
Dorsal rays XII,15–17; anal rays II,12–14; pectoral rays 18–20; tubed lateral-line scales 17–19; scales above lateral line to base of middle dorsal spines 2.5; gill rakers 23–28; body depth 1.8–2.1 in standard length; anterior membranes of spinous portion of dorsal fin incised; caudal fin forked with broadly rounded lobes in adults; varies from light gray-brown to dark gray-brown, sometimes with a broad, vertical, paler zone in middle of body (which becomes intense white in male during courtship, with an added pale blue stripe from mouth across head); median and pelvic fins colored like body; a vertically elongate black spot at rear base of dorsal fin, extending onto adjacent back and caudal peduncle; pectoral fins with gray-brown rays, transparent membranes, and a black spot on about upper one-third of base; juveniles gray dorsally on head, nape, spinous portion of dorsal fin and back below, shading on sides and ventrally to pale yellowish; caudal fin, anal fin, and posterior soft portion of dorsal fin yellow. Attains 14 cm. Red Sea and east coast of Africa to islands of Micronesia, Line Islands, Marquesas Islands, and Tuamotu Archipelago; Ryukyu Islands and Ogasawara Islands to the Great Barrier Reef and New Caledonia; probable type locality, Mauritius; forms colonies in lagoons and bays at depths of 1–12 m, where often associated with staghorn coral (*Acropora*); maintains a territory in this habitat and very aggressively guards its private pasture of algae growing on dead parts of coral branches; not only drives away intruding herbivorous fishes but will at times nip divers that venture too near.

Palau/juvenile

Sulawesi

BLUNTSNOUT GREGORY
Stegastes punctatus (Quoy & Gaimard, 1825)
Dorsal rays XII,14–16; anal rays II,12–14; pectoral rays 18–19; tubed lateral-line scales 17–19; scales above lateral line to base of middle dorsal spines 1.5; gill rakers 23–29; depth of preorbital bone anteroventral to eye greater than eye diameter in specimens larger than 50 mm standard length (one-half to two-thirds eye diameter in other species of the genus); body depth 1.8–2.0 in standard length; anterior membranes of spinous portion of dorsal fin incised; caudal fin forked with very broadly rounded lobes in adults; adults dark gray-brown, the centers of scales paler, those ventrally and posteriorly often with a small pale spot; a very large, diffuse black spot basally on posterior part of dorsal fin and extending onto adjacent back; juveniles grayish yellow. Reaches 15 cm. Red Sea and east coast of Africa to the Line Islands, Tonga, and Society Islands (underwater photograph from Tahiti by P. Bachet); southern Japan to the Great Barrier Reef and New Caledonia; type locality given as Pacific Ocean. Occurs in shallow lagoons and protected outer-reef areas, generally in association with larger branching corals of the genus *Acropora*; maintains a territitory and feeds on the algae growing on dead basal parts of coral branches; very aggressive in the defense of its territory. Long misidentified as *S. lividus* (Forster), a species endemic to the Marquesas Islands.

386

Subadults of Feminine Wrasse, *Anampses femininus*, Easter Island

WRASSES
(LABRIDAE)

The Labridae is the second largest marine family of fishes (after the Gobiidae), with 68 genera and 453 species (Parenti & Randall, 2000). It is very diverse, with species ranging in adult size as small as 5 cm to the Giant Humphead Wrasse that has been recorded to 229 cm; they vary greatly in shape, from moderately deep-bodied to slender, from short-snouted to long, etc. The family can be defined collectively by the following characters: mouth usually terminal, protractile, and small to moderate in size, the maxilla not exposed on the cheek; lips often fleshy (hence the German common name Lippfische); teeth at front of jaws generally as well-developed canines that are often protruding; teeth absent from the palate (except for 1 or a few on vomer of some species of *Bodianus*); a canine tooth often present at the corner of the mouth; pharyngeal teeth well developed on paired upper pharyngeal bones and the single lower T- to Y-shaped pharyngeal plate, varying from stout and conical to molariform; head naked or with just the cheek and/or opercle scaled; lateral-line continuous or interrupted; a single dorsal fin of VIII-XXI spines, without a notch between spinous and soft portions (except in

the razorfish genus *Iniistius* with either a detached anterior part of fin of II spines or with a deeply incised membrane between the second and third spines) and 6–21 soft rays; anal spines usually III (a few species with II, and 2 European genera with IV-VI), and 7–18 soft rays; pelvic rays I,5, branchiostegal rays 5 or 6; vertebrae 23–42 (the high numbers in temperate species of the subfamily Labrinae). Most wrasses, and especially those of tropic seas, are very colorful. Juveniles may be very different in color from adults, and many species exhibit sexual dichromatism, maturing first as females and changing later to males (hence protogynous hermaphrodites). For some species, such as those of the genus *Thalassoma*, the first mature phase may be female or male, and spawning generally occurs in aggregations. This first phase, when either male or female, is termed the initial phase. The second color form, the terminal phase, is usually more colorful, and always male. These males usually have a harem of females within a territory that is strongly defended from other males. Males of the species of *Cirrhilabrus* and *Paracheilinus* display with vivid courtship colors, particularly of iridescent blue. Wrasses produce numerous tiny pelagic eggs (except for a few temperate species that build nests of seaweed and lay demersal eggs). All labrid fishes are carnivorous, but their food habits vary greatly. Most feed on invertebrates with hard parts such as crabs, hermit crabs, mollusks, sea urchins, and brittlestars that they crush with their pharyngeal teeth. Some of the smaller species, such as those of the genera *Cirrhilabrus*, *Paracheilinus*, *Pseudocoris*, and some species of *Thalassoma*, feed in aggregations on zooplankton. The scleral cornea of the eye of the fishes of the first two of these genera, and of *Pseudocheilinus* and *Pteragogus*, is divided into two adjacent circular parts; it has been speculated that the anterior part is used, bifocal fashion, to focus on small prey (Springer & Randall, 1974). Species of the genus *Labroides* and the young of some other genera, such as *Bodianus* and *Labropsis*, feed primarily on the ectoparasites and mucus of other fishes. Adults of *Labropsis*, *Labrichthys*, and *Diproctacanthus* feed mainly on coral polyps (for which their fleshy lips are believed to be a specialization). A few species, such as those of the genera *Hologymnosus* and *Oxycheilinus*, prey heavily on small fishes. The species of *Anampses* forcefully strike the substratum with the forward-projecting incisiform teeth in their jaws and at the same time apply suction to obtain tiny crustaceans, mollusks, worms, and foraminifera, along with sand and detritus. The species of *Stethojulis* have the same mode of feeding but tend to pick up more sand. Those of the genus *Hemigymnus* feed mainly by ingesting mouthfuls of sand, ejecting sand from the gill opening as they sort out the tiny animals within, and expelling the larger inorganic particles later from the mouth. Labrids are diurnal; most of the smaller species bury in sand at night; the larger ones sleep deep within the cover of the reef. Swmming is normally carried out with the pectoral fins; the caudal fin is brought into action only when speed is needed. Fifteen of the labrid genera have been revised for the Indo-Pacific region (see Parenti & Randall, 2000 for references). Current DNA studies (M. Westneat, pers. comm.) indicate that the largest genus, *Halichoeres*, may be divided into several genera.

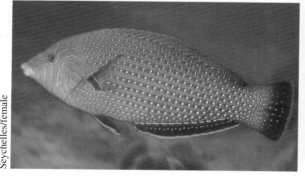

Rapa/juvenile

Seychelles/female

Andaman Sea/male

BLUESPOTTED WRASSE
Anampses caeruleopunctatus Rüppell, 1829

Dorsal rays IX,12; anal rays III,12; lateral-line scales 27 (not including 1 on caudal-fin base); head scaleless (true of other *Anampses*); gill rakers 18–21; body depth 2.3–3.0 in standard length; a single pair of forward-projecting teeth in jaws, the uppers somewhat flattened with pointed upcurved tips, the lowers nearly conical and curved downward; no remaining teeth or only a few small ones in jaws (also generic); caudal fin truncate to slightly rounded; pelvic fins short, 2.1–2.5 in head length; females olive to brown dorsally, shading to orangish ventrally, with small, dark-edged blue spots on body and fins, and dark-edged narrow blue bands on head, many radiating from eye; males olive with a dark-edged vertical blue line on each scale of side of body; head with narrow, dark-edged blue lines and a broad blue band across interorbital space; a broad, light green bar often present on body below sixth dorsal spine; small juveniles light olivaceous with a few scattered, small whitish spots. Largest examined, 42 cm. Occurs throughout the Indo-Pacific region from the Red Sea (type locality) to Easter Island except the Hawaiian Islands where replaced by *Anampses cuvier* Quoy & Gaimard. An inshore species, typically in areas exposed to surge, but may be seen as deep as 20 m. *Anampses diadematus* Rüppell is a synonym based on the male form.

FEMININE WRASSE

Anampses femininus Randall, 1972

Dorsal rays IX,12; anal rays III,12; lateral-line scales 26; gill rakers 15–17; body depth 3.0–3.4 in standard length; caudal fin rounded; pelvic fins short, 2.1–2.5 in head length; females bright orange with narrow, black-edged, blue stripes on head and body, shading to blue on caudal peduncle and caudal fin; males dusky yellow to blackish on body with a vertical blue line on each scale; head dusky orange, blue ventrally, with 4 diagonal blue bands, 2 of which extend onto chest; a small black spot posteriorly on opercle. Attains 24 cm. Reported in the South Pacific from Easter Island (type locality; first collected there by the author in 1969), Pitcairn Islands, Rapa, New Caledonia, Lord Howe Island, southern Great Barrier Reef, and New South Wales; adults are known from depths of 5–40 m; juveniles often seen in small aggregations, generally in shallower water than adults. Named *femininus* because the female is more beautiful than the male (unusual in the Animal Kingdom).

Easter Island/female

Easter Island/male

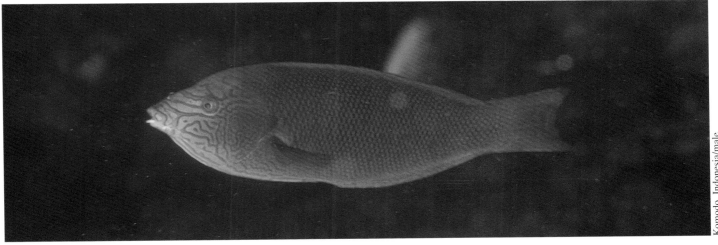

Komodo, Indonesia/male

GEOGRAPHIC WRASSE

Anampses geographicus Valenciennes in C & V, 1840

Dorsal rays IX,12; anal rays III,12; lateral-line scales 48–50; gill rakers 17–20; body depth 2.7–3.1 in standard length; caudal fin rounded in juveniles, becoming truncate to slightly emarginate in females and more emarginate in males; pelvic fins short, varying from 2.7 in head length in juveniles to 2.15 in males; females brown to reddish brown, sometimes shading to yellowish brown posteriorly; a large, yellow-edged black spot posteriorly in dorsal and anal fins; males reddish brown with a blue spot on each scale (vertically elongate in middle and anterior part of body); head and chest orange with a reticulum of bright blue; median fins orange, flecked with blue, with a submarginal blue line. Reaches 24 cm. Western Australia and western Pacific from the Ryukyu Islands to the Great Barrier Reef, east to Lord Howe Island, Fiji, and the Caroline Islands; type locality, Indian Ocean. Easily distinguished from other species of the genus by the high scale count. *Anampses pterophthalmus* Bleeker is a synonym based on the female form.

Coral Sea/subadult

Luzon/female

Bali/juvenile

Ogasawara Islands/female

Ogasawara Islands/male

BLACKTAIL WRASSE
Anampses melanurus Bleeker, 1857

Dorsal rays IX,12; anal rays III,12; lateral-line scales 26; gill rakers 14–17; body depth 1.95–2.5 in standard length; caudal fin rounded; pelvic fins 1.8–2.3 in head length; females dark brown with a white spot on each scale, the spots smaller posteriorly; head dark orangish brown with small white spots, many elongate or bilobed; a black spot posteriorly on opercle; lips gray and pink; caudal fin bright yellow basally, black distally with a pale bluish posterior margin that is broader at corners of fin; dorsal and anal fins dark brown with pale bluish margins and small white spots (only in a single basal row in anal fin); males with blue spots instead of white and a broad, yellow midlateral stripe on body; anal fin yellowish with blue stripes; juveniles dark brown with numerous small white spots, those on body and dorsal fin interspersed with larger irregular white spots; dorsal fin with a broad white border; anal fin with 3 rows of pale yellow spots; caudal fin colored like body basally, followed by a broad white bar, the outer three-fifths of fin transparent with pink rays. Reaches 14.5 cm. Ryukyu and Ogasawara Islands south to Indonesia and Scott Reef off northwestern Australia, east to Marshall Islands, Marquesas Islands, and Society Islands; type locality, Ambon, Molucca Islands. Usually seen in outer-reef areas from depths of 15–40 m. Replaced by *Anampses lineatus* Randall in the western Indian Ocean.

Philippines/female

Ogasawara Islands/male

SPOTTED WRASSE
Anampses meleagrides Valenciennes in C & V, 1840

Dorsal rays IX,12; anal rays III,12; lateral-line scales 26; gill rakers 18–20; body depth 3.1–3.4 in standard length; caudal fin truncate to emarginate; pelvic fins 1.5–2.0 in head length; females dark brown with a small, round white spot on each scale of body; head and dorsal and anal fins dark brown with small white spots; caudal fin bright yellow; males dark reddish brown

with a vertical blue line on each scale; head orangish brown with a blue reticulum; caudal fin orangish brown with small blue spots and a whitish crescent posteriorly edged in front with blue. Attains 21 cm. Red Sea and east coast of Africa to the Line Islands, Tuamotu Archipelago, Society Islands, and throughout Micronesia; southern Japan to Great Barrier Reef; type locality, Mauritius. Found on coral reefs and adjacent habitats. *Anampses amboinensis* Bleeker is a synonym based on the male phase.

NEW GUINEA WRASSE

Anampses neoguinaicus Bleeker, 1878

Dorsal rays IX,12; anal rays III,12; lateral-line scales 26; gill rakers 15–18; body depth 2.9–3.3 in standard length; caudal fin rounded; pelvic fins 1.5–2.5 in head length; females black dorsally, becoming yellowish white below a demarcation from front of snout to rear base of dorsal fin, with a small blue spot in each scale; a large, blue-edged black spot posteriorly on opercle; dorsal fin black with a row of blue spots at base and a blue-edged black spot posteriorly in fin; anal fin with a broad blue zone at base, black in outer part with a black spot edged partly in blue and partly in yellow posteriorly in fin; caudal fin mainly white; males similar with vertical blue lines replacing spots in white part of body; dark part of head with black-edged blue lines radiating from eye; ventral part of chest and abdomen salmon pink; an orange spot sometimes preceding black spot on opercle; no ocellus in dorsal and anal fins; outer part of anal and caudal fins salmon pink to orange with irregular blue lines, dots, and margins. Attains about 17 cm. Southern Japan to Great Barrier Reef, New South Wales, and Lord Howe Island; east to New Caledonia and Fiji; only Palau in Micronesia. *Anampses fidjensis* Sauvage is a synonym.

YELLOWBREASTED WRASSE

Anampses twistii Bleeker, 1856

Dorsal rays IX,12; anal rays III,12; lateral-line scales 26; gill rakers 16–19; body depth 3.0–3.3 in standard length; caudal fin rounded; pelvic fins 1.8–2.3 in head length; body and upper part of head dark brown, sometimes shading to dull salmon pink posteriorly, with a black-edged blue dot on each scale; abdomen, chest, and lower part of head yellow; a black and orange-red spot posteriorly on opercle; dorsal and anal fins dark orangish brown with dark-edged blue dots, a blue margin, a black submarginal line, and a large, blue-edged black spot posteriorly; caudal fin salmon pink to pale yellowish, usually with small, dark-edged, pale blue spots and a whitish posterior margin that is broadest at

Papua New Guinea/female

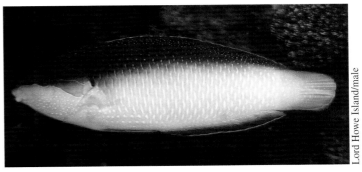

Lord Howe Island/male

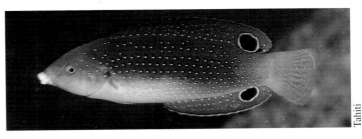

Tahiti

corners; males not very different in color from females. Largest reported, 18 cm. Red Sea and east coast of Africa to French Polynesia (except the Marquesas), Pitcairn Islands, and all of Micronesia; Ryukyu Islands and Ogasawara Islands to the Great Barrier Reef; type locality, Ambon, Molucca Islands.

Egypt, Red Sea/juvenile

Manuk, Indonesia

LYRETAIL HOGFISH

Bodianus anthioides (Bennett, 1832)

Dorsal rays XII,9–10 (usually 10); anal rays III,11–12 (usually 12); pectoral rays 15–17; lateral-line scales 29–30; a scaly sheath at base of dorsal and anal fins; gill rakers usually 16; 1 or more teeth present on vomer; posterior margin of preopercle serrate (true of most *Bodianus*); body depth 2.6–3.1 in standard length; snout short, 3.1–3.65 in head length, the dorsal profile of head steep and convex; caudal fin large and lunate; brownish orange to orange-red on head and about anterior one-third of body,

white posteriorly with scattered, irregular dark spots, the curved demarcation with a dark bar that continues into dorsal fin; lobes of caudal fin with a dark red to black band that continues onto caudal peduncle; lower part of head may be blackish; a large black spot anteriorly in dorsal fin. Reported to 21 cm. Red Sea and east coast of Africa to Line Islands, French Polynesia except the Marquesas Islands, and Pitcairn Islands; southern Japan to Great Barrier Reef and New Caledonia; type locality, Mauritius. Usually found at depths greater than 20 m.

AXILSPOT HOGFISH
Bodianus axillaris (Bennett, 1832)

Dorsal rays XII,9–10 (usually 10); anal rays III,11–12 (usually 12); pectoral rays 15–17; lateral-line scales 30–31; a scaly sheath at base of dorsal and anal fins; gill rakers 15–18; body depth 2.8–3.1 in standard length; snout short, 2.9–3.2 in head length; caudal fin rounded to slightly double emarginate; head and body of adults deep red to dark reddish brown anterior to a demarcation from chest to end of spinous portion of dorsal fin, white posteriorly; caudal fin, anal fin, and soft portion of dorsal fin with yellow rays and translucent membranes; a large black spot anteriorly in soft portion of dorsal and anal fins, and a black spot at front of dorsal fin; a large black spot at base and axil of pectoral fins; juveniles black with 2 rows of large white spots, one dorsal and one ventral. Reaches 20 cm. Red Sea and east coast of Africa to Line Islands, French Polynesia (except Rapa), and the Pitcairn Islands; southern Japan to Great Barrier Reef, New South Wales, Lord Howe Island, and New Caledonia; type locality, Mauritius. Juvenile color pattern in the western Indian Ocean retained in female stage. Juveniles usually found in caves where often seen cleaning other fishes; adults occasionally do the same.

SADDLEBACK HOGFISH
Bodianus bilunulatus (Lacepède, 1801)

Dorsal rays XII,9–10 (usually 10); anal rays III,12–13 (usually 12); pectoral rays 16–17 (usually 16); lateral-line scales 30–32; basal scaly sheath of dorsal and anal fins 2.5–3 scales in height; gill rakers 17–21; posterior margin of preopercle finely serrate in young, smooth in adults; body depth 2.6–3.0 in standard length; caudal fin truncate in young, emarginate to double emarginate in adults, with lobes moderately prolonged in large individuals; adult females light red dorsally, shading to white ventrally, sometimes to yellow posteriorly, with red longitudinal lines following scale rows on nape and body, the scales anteriorly on body with vertical red lines as well; a very large black spot beneath posterior part of dorsal fin and on adjacent peduncle, reaching to below lateral line; snout and dorsal part of head with dark red stripes; lower jaw and cheek white with a blackish streak extending posterior to mouth; a black spot on second dorsal membrane; males with pattern overlaid with dark purplish brown (illustration here of the male of the closely related Hawaiian endemic, *B. albotaeniatus*, which is essentially the same); juveniles with top of head and anterior body yellow and a very broad black bar across posterior part of body and dorsal and anal fins except for white posteriorly on caudal peduncle. Attains 55 cm. East Africa to the Hawaiian Islands (where subspecifically different), Marquesas Islands, and Pitcairn Islands, but distribution not continuous; southern Japan to Indonesia and New Caledonia; only Palau in Micronesia; type locality, Mauritius. Generally found at depths greater than 15 m.

Sermata Island, Indonesia/juvenile

Papua New Guinea

REDFIN HOGFISH

Bodianus sp. Gomon (in prep.)

Dorsal rays XII,9–10 (usually 10); anal rays III,10–12; pectoral rays 15–17; lateral-line scales 30–31; a broad sheath of scales basally on dorsal and anal fins; gill rakers 15–18; body depth 3.0–3.2 in standard length; snout pointed, 2.6–2.9 in head length; caudal fin slightly rounded in young, slightly emarginate to double emarginate in adults; head and dorsoanterior part of body reddish to purplish brown, shading to pale yellowish, the scales rimmed with reddish brown; scales dorsoposteriorly on body with a small black spot; a row of 4 or 5 small white spots widely spaced along back; fins largely red, the anal fin with 2 black spots, the caudal with one at midbase of fin, and the pelvics with a large black spot covering more than half the fins; juveniles dark red to reddish brown with numerous small white spots and 4 rows of larger elongate white spots, the same black spots on fins, plus 2 on dorsal fin. Reaches 25 cm. Southern Japan to Great Barrier Reef, New South Wales, New Caledonia, Tonga, and Phoenix Islands; Marshall Islands and Palau in Micronesia. Formerly identified as *Bodianus diana* (Lacepède), now regarded as a species restricted to the Indian Ocean; the latter differs in lacking the black spots on the anal and pelvic fins.

Papua New Guinea/juvenile

Great Barrier Reef

BLACKFIN HOGFISH

Bodianus loxozonus (Snyder, 1908)

Dorsal rays XII,9–11; anal rays III,11–12; pectoral rays 16–17; lateral-line scales 30–32; a broad scaly sheath at base of dorsal and anal fins; gill rakers 18–21; posterior margin of preopercle finely serrate; body depth 2.65–3.0 in standard length; caudal fin truncate with the corners slightly prolonged (upper longer than lower); pelvic fins of adults long, generally reaching to or beyond anus; head orange to yellow with narrow blue stripes; body orange to orange-red dorsally with dotted to dashed lines of pale blue or white, yellow and white striped ventrally; a very broad, oblique, black band from lower posterior part of dorsal fin, narrowing across body to posterior caudal peduncle and lower base of caudal fin; dorsal fin with a black spot anteriorly; anal fin with a broad black outer border; pelvic fins black; juveniles with a broad black bar posteriorly on body and base of caudal fin except for a white bar across peduncle. Reaches 40 cm. Ryukyu Islands (type locality, Okinawa) and Ogasawara Islands to the Great Barrier Reef and New Caledonia, east to islands of French Polynesia except the Marquesas Islands; Mariana Islands and Marshall Islands in Micronesia; known from depths of 3 to 50 m. Often misidentified as *Bodianus hirsutus* (Lacepède), a synonym of *B. macrourus* (Lacepède), the sister species from southwestern Indian Ocean.

SPLITLEVEL HOGFISH

Bodianus mesothorax (Bloch & Schneider, 1801)

Dorsal rays XII,9–11; anal rays III,11–12; pectoral rays 16; lateral-line scales 31–32; a broad scaly sheath at base of dorsal and anal fins; gill rakers usually 16; posterior margin of preopercle finely serrate; body depth 2.8–3.3 in standard length; snout pointed, 3.1–3.3 in head length; caudal fin truncate to slightly rounded; pelvic fins of adults long, generally reaching to or beyond anus; a broad, oblique, black band from spinous portion of dorsal fin to pectoral-fin axil; body anterior to band and head to a black streak across lower cheek dark purplish brown; body posterior to band whitish with narrow, orange-yellow stripes following scale rows; fins largely yellow except for black anterior part of dorsal fin and large black spot on pectoral-fin base; juveniles black with 2 series of bright yellow spots, one dorsal and one ventral. Attains 20 cm. Southern Japan to Great Barrier Reef (with juveniles south to Sydney), east to Fiji and Caroline Islands; Christmas Island in the Indian Ocean; type locality, East Indies. Reported from depths of 4–40 m.

FIVESTRIPE HOGFISH

Bodianus sp. Gomon (in prep.)

Dorsal rays XII,10; anal rays III,12; pectoral rays 16; lateral-line scales 30; predorsal scales about 18, reaching slightly anterior to a vertical through center of eye; a low scaly sheath at base of dorsal and anal fins; gill rakers 15–17; body depth about 2.8–3.2 in standard length; caudal fin slightly rounded to truncate; light red dorsally, paler ventrally, with 5 red to yellow stripes, the narrow first from interorbital to origin of dorsal fin, the middle 3 stripes commencing from eye, and the fifth stripe from corner of mouth along lower side; black dots within and between first 4 stripes for about half distance to caudal-fin base; a series of 3 or 4 small white spots below second red stripe on posterior half of body, the last dorsally on caudal peduncle; sometimes a few smaller white spots midlaterally on posterior third of body; a large black spot between first and fourth or fifth dorsal spines; pectoral-fin base and axil in a black spot; a 20-cm individual from Iejima Island,

Japan, was illustrated in color by Okamura & Amaoka (1997) as *Bodianus* sp.; it appears to be a terminal male, deeper-bodied with the black spot anteriorly on the dorsal fin largely replaced by red and yellow. To be described from 2 initial-phase specimens, 9.2–12.8 cm, the holotype from Rarotonga and the paratype from the D'Entrecasteaux Islands, Papua New Guinea; known also from photographs from Bali, Palau, and New Caledonia; depth range 50–115 m.

GOLDSPOT HOGFISH

Bodianus perditio (Quoy & Gaimard, 1834)

Dorsal rays XII,10; anal rays III,12; pectoral rays 17; lateral-line scales 30–31; a broad scaly sheath at base of dorsal and anal fins; body depth 2.7–2.9 in standard length; snout length 2.7–3.0 in head length; caudal fin round to truncate in young, truncate with prolonged lobes in adults; pelvic fins long, reaching beyond anus in adults; dull orange-pink, the head with small yellow spots, the scales of body edged in black except anteriorly; a large black to blackish area on back below posterior part of dorsal fin and extending basally into fin, preceded by a large, pale yellow spot or bar; anterior spinous portion of dorsal fin black above basal sheath; caudal fin colored like body on base, shading outwardly to yellow; small juveniles brownish red with a very large, elliptical black spot posteriorly in dorsal fin joined across body by a broad blackish bar to a similar spot in anal fin, the bar preceded by a white bar; an elliptical white spot on side of caudal peduncle; larger juveniles with the black area only above lateral line, the white bar reduced, and with small yellow spots on head and dorsoanteriorly on body. Reported to 80 cm. Antiequatorial

LONGNOSE HOGFISH
Bodianus prognathus Lobel, 1981

Dorsal rays XII,10; anal rays III,12; pectoral rays 16; lateral-line scales 30–31; small scales on cheek extending slightly anterior to front edge of orbit; a broad sheath of scales basally on dorsal and anal fins; gill rakers 16; posterior edge of preopercle smooth; body depth 3.2–4.0 in standard length; snout of adults and subadults extremely long and attenuate, 2.0–2.5 in head length; juveniles with shorter but still pointed snouts; caudal fin truncate; body of adults orange-red dorsally, shading ventrally to yellow or yellowish white, with a vertically elongate red spot on each scale below lateral line, the scales on upper half of body with a dark brown spot; a longitudinal row of 3 large white blotches on body above lateral line and often 1 on nape; head red, purplish over most of opercle and on side of lips; throat blue; iris bright red; median fins red except scaled basal part colored like body; juveniles dark reddish brown with white spots smaller than eye, many horizontally elongate, the larger ones on body mainly in 3 longitudinal rows; a large black spot at front of dorsal fin and another at front of soft portion of fin. Attains 22 cm. Known only from the Line Islands (type locality, Fanning Island

except for some caught trawling off northwestern Australia; Taiwan and southern Japan in the north; southern Tuamotu Archipelago and Rapa to New Caledonia, Norfolk Island, Lord Howe Island, and New South Wales in the south; also in southern Africa and the Mascarene Islands; type locality, Tongatapu. Occurs from 10 to at least 50 m.

Line Islands

= Tabuaeran) and the Phoenix Islands; remains close to the cover of coral reefs; adults have been collected in 10–15 m. Color pattern of adults and juveniles similar to that of *Bodianus diana* and *B. dictynna*. The 37-mm juvenile illustrated as this species by Lobel (1981) is a juvenile *B. axillaris*.

Fiji/juvenile

Tahiti/female

Tuamotu Archipelago/male

FLORAL WRASSE
Cheilinus chlorourus (Bloch, 1791)

Dorsal rays X,9 (rarely XI,8); anal rays III,8; pectoral rays 12; lateral line interrupted, the pored scales 14–16 + 7–9; a broad scaly sheath at base of dorsal and anal fins (true of other species of *Cheilinus*); gill rakers 11–14; body depth 2.4–2.8 in standard length; dorsal profile of head nearly straight, often with a slight concavity above eye; snout length 3.0–3.6 in head length; caudal fin rounded in females, the upper and lower rays prolonged in males; color variable but generally reddish brown to greenish gray, the head more green than body, with many small dots on head and body that may be white, pink, orange-red, or black; 2 or 3 oblique orange-red to black lines through lower part of eye and below eye; a series of white blotches along back extending into base of dorsal fin; pelvic, anal, caudal, and posterior dorsal fin with numerous white dots. Reaches 36 cm. East coast of Africa to islands of French Polynesia; in the western Pacific from the Ryukyu Islands to the Great Barrier Reef, New Caledonia, and throughout Micronesia; type locality, Japan, as restricted by Paepke (1999). Easily distinguished from other species of *Cheilinus* and those of the related genus *Oxycheilinus* by having X instead of IX dorsal spines.

Marshall Islands/juvenile

Papua New Guinea/female

Okinawa/male

REDBREASTED WRASSE

Cheilinus fasciatus (Bloch, 1791)

Dorsal rays IX,10; anal rays III,8; pectoral rays 12; lateral line interrupted, the pored scales 14–16 + 7–9; gill rakers 12–15; body depth 2.35–2.6 in standard length; dorsal profile of head convex, more so in large males; snout length 2.2–2.6 in head length; dorsal and anal fins angular posteriorly; caudal fin slightly rounded in juveniles, truncate with prolonged lobes in large males; pelvic fins short, not reaching anus; body and scaled basal part of dorsal and anal fins reddish brown to blackish with 6–7 narrow white bars, each scale with a vertical black streak; chest to posterior head orange; orange-red lines extending anteriorly and posteriorly to eye; caudal fin white with a broad black middle bar and black margin; red dots in soft portions of dorsal and anal fins; large males dark olive on head with a broad zone of bright orange-red from nape to chest and extending forward to eye, and red dots in white part of caudal fin. Reaches 36 cm. Red Sea and east coast of Africa to the Samoa Islands and islands of Micronesia; in the western Pacific from the Ryukyu Islands to the Great Barrier Reef, Lord Howe Island, and New Caledonia; type locality given as Japan (but it may have been one of the islands of the East Indies). More common on lagoon than seaward reefs. The least wary of the species of the genus. Donaldson (1995) described the spawning.

Coral Sea/juvenile

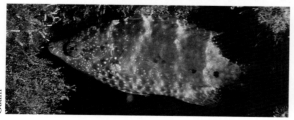

Guam

Marshall Islands

SNOOTY WRASSE

Cheilinus oxycephalus Bleeker, 1853

Dorsal rays IX,10; anal rays III,8; pectoral rays 12; lateral line interrupted, the pored scales 15–16 + 6–7; body depth 2.5–3.0 in standard length; dorsal profile of head from upper lip to above eye slightly concave, giving the snout an upturned appearance; snout short, the length 3.1–3.7 in head length; caudal fin rounded; pelvic fins usually reaching anus; mottled olivaceous brown to brownish red, often with a series of white blotches dorsally on body or narrow irregular white bars; head and anterior and ventral part of body with numerous white or pale orange-red dots; 3 or 4 blackish spots nearly as large as pupil in midlateral row on posterior half of body; a pair of black spots anteriorly on side of upper lip; lips may be crossed by white lines; a red and black spot anteriorly on dorsal fin. East coast of Africa to French Polynesia except Rapa; Taiwan and Ogasawara Islands to the Great Barrier Reef; type locality, Ambon, Molucca Islands. Attains 17 cm. Remains near shelter of coral reefs; among the most difficult fishes to approach while diving.

TRIPLETAIL WRASSE

Cheilinus trilobatus Lacepède, 1801

Dorsal rays IX,10; anal rays III,8; pectoral rays 12; lateral line interrupted, the pored scales 15–17 + 7–9; gill rakers 10–12; body moderately deep, the depth 2.3–2.6 in standard length; dorsal profile of head to above eye straight; snout length 2.7–3.2 in head length; caudal fin rounded, the upper and lower corners prolonged and middle part of fin protruding in large males; pelvic fins reaching anus except in small juveniles, extending well beyond in large adults; mottled olivaceous with red and green vertical lines across body, this pattern overlaid with indistinct, broad, blackish bars, one across posterior caudal peduncle preceded by a broad whitish bar, followed by a narrower whitish bar on caudal-fin base; head and chest olive-green with numerous small deep pink spots, the snout and suborbital region with a few irregular, deep pink lines; central part of caudal fin black, the posterior border greenish with red lines paralleling rays. Attains about 40 cm. East coast of Africa to the Society Islands, Tuamotu Archipelago, Austral Islands, and all of Micronesia; Ryukyu Islands and Ogasawara Islands to the Great Barrier Reef and New Caledonia; described from Madagascar, Réunion, and Mauritius. Feeds mainly on gastropods; also important: crabs, bivalve mollusks, and hermit crabs (food-habit study of 40 specimens from Madagascar by Harmelin-Vivien, 1979).

GIANT HUMPHEAD WRASSE
Cheilinus undulatus Rüppell, 1835

Dorsal rays IX,10; anal rays III,8; pectoral rays 12; lateral line interrupted, the pored scales 16 + 10; scaly sheath at base of dorsal and anal fins low; gill rakers 19–21; body depth varying from 2.2 in standard length in large adults to 2.7 in juveniles; dorsal profile of head straight to level of eye; adults developing a convexity on forehead that can protrude anterior to eye on large males; snout length 2.0–2.7 in head length; dorsal and anal fins of adults pointed posteriorly; caudal fin rounded; pelvic fins reaching anus in juveniles, extending beyond origin of anal fin in adults; olive green to blue-green with a narrow dark bar on each scale that breaks into irregular dark lines anteriorly on body with growth; head with a reticulum of dull pink and 2 slightly oblique black lines extending posteriorly from lower half of eye, often with 2 more from eye to rear part of upper lip; median fins crossed by numerous pale yellowish green lines; juveniles pale gray with a vertically elongate black spot on each scale, the body crossed by 4 narrow whitish bars; head with the same pair of parallel black lines before and after eye. A length of 229 cm and 190.5 kg (Marshall, 1964) needs verification. J. H. Choat (pers. comm.) noted that Marshall did not examine the fish. The largest Choat has observed is about 170 cm long. Widespread in the Indo-Pacific (only 2 records for the Hawaiian Islands); type locality, Red Sea. A study of food habits based on 72 specimens by Randall et al. (1978a) revealed feeding on gastropods, crabs and other crustaceans, sea urchins, bivalve mollusks, and fishes, with lesser amounts of brittlestars and sea stars. Also known as the Humphead Maori Wrasse; still another common name, Napoleonfish.

CIGAR WRASSE

Cheilio inermis (Forsskål, 1775)

Dorsal rays IX,12–13; anal rays III,11–12; pectoral rays 12–13; lateral line complete, the pored scales 45–47; head naked except for a few scales behind eye on preopercle and opercle; no scaly sheath at base of dorsal and anal fins; body very elongate, the depth 5.5–7.8 in standard length; snout long and pointed, 2.2–2.4 in head length; caudal fin rounded to slightly rhomboid; color variable: green, brown, orange-brown, or yellow, often with a narrow, midlateral, broken black stripe; large males without dark stripe, usually with a large pink to orange blotch or blotches behind pectoral fin, sometimes mixed with dark brown. Attains 50 cm. Occurs throughout the Indo-Pacific region from the Red Sea (type locality) to the Hawaiian Islands and Easter Island; may be seen on reefs, but more common on open substrata with seagrass or heavy growth of benthic algae. Harmelin-Vivien (1979) found gastropod mollusks to be the dominant food in Madagascar, with lesser feeding on crabs, other crustaceans, and small fishes; Randall (1985b) reported feeding on gastropods, bivalve mollusks, hermit crabs, crabs, sea urchins, and shrimps in the Hawaiian Islands.

Norfolk Island

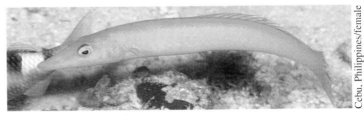

Cebu, Philippines/female

Bali/male

Luzon

ANCHOR TUSKFISH

Choerodon anchorago (Bloch, 1791)

Dorsal rays XIII,7; anal rays III,9; pectoral rays 15–16; lateral line a smooth continuous curve, with 27 pored scales to caudal-fin base (true of other *Choerodon*); scales on preopercle small, less than one-fourth size of those on body (also generic); 2 pairs of prominent curved canine teeth at front of each jaw (generic), the second pair in lower jaw larger than first and flaring laterally; body depth 2.4–2.7 in standard length; dorsal profile of snout steep and nearly straight; caudal fin truncate to slightly rounded; head and body olivaceus or gray-brown to an oblique white to pale yellow band passing upward from beneath pectoral fin, the head with orange dots; dorsal part of body posterior to pale band black to a large saddle-like white area under rear of dorsal fin and on anterior half of caudal peduncle; chin, lower part of head, and ventral part of body white to pale blue; some large individuals with a broad yellow zone midlaterally on body between the black and pale blue areas; pectoral-fin base dusky

Palau/juvenile

orange with 2 blue lines, the axil black; juveniles dark gray-brown with a crosshatch pattern of white stripes and bars. Ryukyu Islands to the Great Barrier Reef and New Caledonia; Palau and Yap in Micronesia; locality of lectotype given as Mediterranean (?) by Paepke (1999), an obvious error. A shallow-water species found in a variety of calm habitats, usually seagrass beds or rubble and sand with small patches of coral.

New Caledonia/juvenile

Great Barrier Reef

HARLEQUIN TUSKFISH

Choerodon fasciatus (Günther, 1867)

Dorsal rays XII,8; anal rays III,10; pectoral rays 14–15; small scales on cheek extending forward nearly to corner of mouth; predorsal scales reaching a vertical at rear edge of orbit; body deep, the depth 2.2–2.5 in standard length; caudal fin truncate to slightly emarginate; body light greenish gray anteriorly, soon shading to black posteriorly and to white ventrally, with a broad, blue-edged, orange-red bar from origin of dorsal fin to pelvic fins, followed by 3 narrower, blue-edged, orange-red bars; posterior one-third of body black except white rear part of caudal peduncle; head greenish gray to white with an orange-red bar across head through eye, 2 orange-red bands across front of head, and broad orange-red lips; teeth light blue; dorsal and anal fins orange-red with a narrow blue stripe and a black spot on first membrane of dorsal; caudal fin white, shading posteriorly to orange-red; juveniles white with red-edged brown bars, an ocellated black spot in soft portion of dorsal and anal fins, a black spot on pelvic fins, at front of dorsal fin, and a small black spot at upper and lower base of caudal fin. Attains 30 cm. Appears to be antiequatorial: southern Japan and Taiwan in the north, and southern Queensland, Lord Howe Island, and New Caledonia in the south; type locality given as Cape York, Queensland. Feeds on mollusks, crustaceans, worms, and echinoderms. Sometimes classified in the genus *Lienardella*, a synonym of *Choerodon*.

Great Barrier Reef/juvenile

New Caledonia

GRAPHIC TUSKFISH

Choerodon graphicus (De Vis, 1885)

Dorsal rays XII,7–8; anal rays III,10–11; pectoral rays 14–15; predorsal scales extending slightly anterior to a vertical at rear edge of preopercle; second pair of lower canine teeth much smaller than first and not flaring laterally; body depth 2.6–2.8 in standard length; caudal fin rounded; light yellowish with large, vertically elongate, dark brown bloches on body, some joining to form irregular bars; scales except anteriorly on body with a vertical pale blue line; head with dark brown bands radiating from eye; iris blue with an inner ring of yellow. Recorded to 46 m. Queensland (type locality, Cardwell) to New Caledonia. *Choerodon transversalis* Whitley is a synonym. Easily approached underwater.

400

Fiji/female

Fiji/male

JORDAN'S TUSKFISH
Choerodon jordani (Snyder, 1908)
Dorsal rays XIII,7; anal rays III,10; pectoral rays 15; predorsal scales just reaching a vertical at rear edge of preopercle; second pair of lower canine teeth largest in jaws, strongly curving outward and backward; body moderately elongate, the depth 2.8–3.6 in standard length; caudal fin truncate to slightly rounded; gray, shading to orange-yellow on snout and suborbital region, with a black stripe beginning posteriorly on opercle and above pectoral-fin base, broadening as it passes dorsoposteriorly on body, and ending below base of soft portion of dorsal fin where it encloses a large oval white spot. Reaches 17 cm. Known from southern Japan (type locality, Okinawa), Taiwan, Western Australia, Great Barrier Reef, Chesterfield Bank, New Caledonia, Tonga, and Fiji. Usually found over sand and rubble bottom or around small coral patches, generally at depths greater than 20 m. Tends to be wary of divers.

EXQUISITE WRASSE
Cirrhilabrus exquisitus Smith, 1957
Dorsal rays XI,9; anal rays III,9; pectoral rays 14–15 (rarely 14); lateral line interrupted, the pored scales 16–18 + 6–7; median predorsal scales 5; scale rows on cheek 2; gill rakers 19–21; posterior margin of preopercle serrate (true of other species of *Cirrhilabrus*); front of upper jaw with 3 pairs of forward-projecting canine teeth, larger laterally, the 2 lateral pairs outcurved (also generic); caudal fin rounded in juveniles and females, double emarginate in males; adult males olivaceous dorsally, shading to white, pale blue, or pink ventrally, with an oval black spot generally as large as or larger than eye posteriorly on caudal peduncle, its lower edge on lateral line; a blue line, sometimes broken, extending from below peduncular spot to beneath pectoral fin; an oblique blue line from corner of mouth above eye to nape and continuing along base of dorsal fin; another from behind eye, breaking up above pectoral fin, and a third from corner of mouth to upper edge of pectoral-fin base; base of pectoral fin with a blue-edged black bar, the margin of fin red; median fins with a variable amount of red (see 2 photos of males), the anal fin and posterior part of dorsal fin with a longitudinal row of black-edged blue spots; upper and lower edges of caudal fin with black-edged, pale blue spots; juveniles and small females red with an oval blue-edged black spot posteriorly on caudal peduncle, and a medial white spot at front of snout. Reaches 12 cm. The most widespread species of the genus: east coast of Africa (type locality, Pinda, Mozambique) to the Line Islands and Tuamotu Archipelago; Ryukyu Islands to the Great Barrier Reef, and the most inshore; usually found on exposed reefs from 2–10 m, but has been seen as deep as 32 m. The author speared one in the Line Islands that had male coloration but proved to be a female. Exhibits color variation over its broad range.

Tuamotu Archipelago

Tuamotu Archipelago/male

Palau/male

LABOUTE'S WRASSE

Cirrhilabrus laboutei Randall & Lubbock, 1982

Dorsal rays XI,9; anal rays III,8–9 (rarely 8); pectoral rays 15–16 (rarely 16); lateral line interrupted, the pored scales 16–18 + 5–7; median predorsal scales 5; scales on cheek mainly in a single row; gill rakers 17–21; first 2 anal spines of males prolonged; caudal fin rounded; pelvic fins short; adult females brownish yellow dorsally; a thin, white to pale pink line from front of snout above eye continuing along base of dorsal fin to end at upper base of caudal fin; a thin magenta stripe above and adjacent to white line from nape onward; a thin white line following upper part of lateral line; just below it a magenta stripe continuing forward to eye; a magenta band joining the first at upper end of gill opening passing down to below pectoral fin, then curving up to parallel first stripe and continuing to midbase of caudal fin, this stripe bordered below by yellow in its straight portion; broad anterior space between magenta stripes with a magenta streak; ventral part of head and body white to pale lavender; an oblique magenta band at pectoral-fin base and continuing below; males similar but magenta stripes deep purple,

New Caledonia/juvenile

New Caledonia

and the yellow borders more vivid; juveniles as illustrated. Reaches 12 cm. Known from Loyalty Islands, New Caledonia (type locality), reefs of the Coral Sea, and southern Great Barrier Reef; usually over rubble bottom near reefs; reported from depths of 8–55 m.

New Caledonia/female

Aquarium, male (H. Tanaka)

BLUELINED WRASSE

Cirrhilabrus lineatus Randall & Lubbock, 1982

Dorsal rays XI,9; anal rays III,9; pectoral rays 14–16; lateral line interrupted, the pored scales 15–17 + 4–6; median predorsal scales 5; scale rows on cheek 2; gill rakers 17–18; caudal fin rounded; pelvic fins of male reaching origin of anal fin; adult females lavender-pink, shading to pale yellow or white ventrally, with a blue stripe from eye along base of dorsal fin to

upper base of caudal fin; blue lines extending posteriorly from eye, breaking into dots and dashes as they pass posteriorly on body, 1 becoming a solid line midlaterally on caudal peduncle; median fins yellow with blue markings; males yellowish green with a blue stripe added ventrally on head and body. Reaches 12 cm. Known from Loyalty Islands, New Caledonia (type locality), reefs of Coral Sea, and southern Great Barrier Reef; collected from depths of 20–55 m.

Fiji/female (G. R. Allen)

Fiji/male (G. R. Allen)

MARJORIE'S WRASSE

Cirrhilabrus marjorie Allen, Randall & Carlson, 2003

Dorsal rays XI,9; anal rays III,9; pectoral rays 15; lateral-line scales 16 + 7; median predorsal scales 5; horizontal scale rows on cheek 2; gill rakers 18–19; caudal fin truncate to slightly emarginate in females, lunate in males; pelvic fins short in both sexes, 1.3–1.7 in head length, not approaching anal-fin origin; male with upper half of head and body bright red, the lower half whitish with 5 purplish gray stripes following scale rows; poste-

rior caudal peduncle and fin bright yellow; dorsal fin pale blue with a narrow blue margin and a broad black submarginal band; anal fin whitish with a narrow light blue margin; females pinkish red on about upper third of body, whitish ventrally, the scale edges pale red; an irregular round black spot larger than pupil posteriorly on upper part of caudal peduncle; dorsal and caudal fins pale translucent red, the dorsal with a pale blue margin. Attains about 8 cm. Currently known only from Fiji; occurs on rubble bottom in 20 to 50 m.

Great Barrier Reef/female

Tonga/male

Fiji/male, courtship

DOTTED WRASSE

Cirrhilabrus punctatus Randall & Kuiter, 1989

Dorsal rays XI,9; anal rays III,9; pectoral rays 15–16 (rarely 16); lateral line interrupted, the pored scales 16–18 + 6–9; median predorsal scales 5–7; scale rows on cheek 2; gill rakers 17–20; caudal fin rounded; pelvic fins of males very long, often half standard length; adult males with about upper three-fourths of body dark gray (sometimes reddish gray), finely flecked and dotted with blue; lower part of body white; an irregular blue line from corner of mouth below eye to end of opercle; head above blue line gray, head below and chest white; dorsal and anal fins with a broad basal black zone and an outer red zone, the two sometimes separated by a blue line; margin of median fins blue with black submarginal line; caudal fin gray with a curved blue line across middle of fin or with scattered, dark-edged blue dots; a broad black bar at base of pectoral fins; a New Caledonia male with a broad yellowish zone on back; females light red to light reddish brown dorsally with whitish to pale pink dots, white to pale pink ventrally; a deep blue spot at front of dorsal fin, black bar at base of pectoral fin, and a yellowish caudal fin; juveniles and subadult females with a small irregular black spot at upper base of caudal fin, black bar at pectoral-fin base, and a white spot dorsally on front of snout. Attains 13 cm. Papua New Guinea to Great Barrier Reef (type locality, One Tree Island, Capricorn Group), and New South Wales, east to Lord Howe Island, New Caledonia, Fiji, and Tonga; known from the depth range of 2 to 32 m. Courtship color of the male is shown in upper right figure, taken at Viti Levu, Fiji.

REDSTRIPE WRASSE

Cirrhilabrus roseafascia Randall & Lubbock, 1982

Dorsal rays XI,9; anal rays III,9; pectoral rays 15; lateral line interrupted, the pored scales 16–18 + 6–9; median predorsal scales 5; scale rows on cheek 2; gill rakers 17–20; caudal fin slightly rounded in juveniles, rhomboid in subadults, and lanceolate in adults, the fin of large males as much as 1.8 in standard length; pelvic fins small, 1.6–2.0 in head; juveniles dark red with 3 white lines on body, white spot on top of snout, and black spot on upper caudal peduncle; females light red with a red band from eye to upper side of body containing about 7 small white spots; a narrow red arc on upper cheek from corner of mouth to pectoral fin base; males orange-pink, the dorsal and anal fins yellow with magenta rays and a blue margin; pelvic fins with a large,

Fiji

deep purple spot posteriorly. Known from Samoa Islands, Fiji, New Caledonia (type locality), Palau, and the Philippines. Known from coral reefs at depths of 30–100 m; usually only juveniles seen in the lesser depths. Closely related to *Cirrhilabrus lanceolatus* Randall & Masuda from Japan.

Sulawesi/juvenile

Bali/female

Taiwan/male

REDMARGIN WRASSE

Cirrhilabrus rubrimarginatus Randall, 1992

Dorsal rays XI,9; anal rays III,9; pectoral rays 14–16; lateral line interrupted, the pored scales 16–18 + 6–9; median predorsal scales 5; scale rows on cheek 2; gill rakers 17–20; caudal fin rounded; pelvic fins of males very long, reaching well beyond origin of anal fin; females lavender-pink, the snout and dorsal part of head yellowish; irregular, broken yellow lines on head extending onto nape; dorsal and caudal fins with a broad, red outer zone and narrow blue margin, the dorsal with a submarginal blackish band anteriorly; males mixed light red and greenish dorsally with a broad, pale midlateral zone on body densely dotted with bright red; ventral part of head and body light blue-green, dotted with yellow; fins similar to those of female, but the black anteriorly in dorsal fin more extensive and outer red zones broader and brighter red with a blue margin and black submarginal line; juveniles pink, the top of the head bright yellow; a small, irregular black spot faintly edged in blue at upper base of caudal fin. Largest specimen, 15.2 cm. Ryukyu Islands (type locality, Okinawa), Taiwan, Philippines, and Indonesia, east to Palau, Vanuatu, Fiji, and Tonga; west to Cocos-Keeling Islands; collected from depths of 25–52 m on open sand or rubble bottoms near isolated small patch reefs of low profile.

Coral Sea/male

Tahiti/male

SCOTT'S WRASSE
Cirrhilabrus scottorum Randall & Pyle, 1989

Dorsal rays XI,9; anal rays III,9; pectoral rays 15–16 (usually 15); lateral line interrupted, the pored scales 15–18 + 5–8; median predorsal scales 5; scale rows on cheek 2; gill rakers 17–20; caudal fin rhomboid, large males with a filament from middle of posterior margin; pelvic fins short, not reaching origin of anal fin; adult males greenish dorsally with blackish dots on anterior upper half of body, white to pale orange or red ventrally; snout and chin yellowish; dorsal and anal fins usually red basally with a black outer zone that is finely dotted and flecked with blue, this zone progressively longer posteriorly, where it covers nearly full height of fins; unscaled part of caudal fin red; pectoral rays yellow, the base with a blackish bar; lateral edge of pelvic fins deep blue to black; females mainly red. Reaches 13 cm. Great Barrier Reef and reefs of Coral Sea to the Society Islands (type locality, Tahiti) and Pitcairn Islands; depth range, 3–40 m; more often seen in outer-reef areas than on lagoon reefs. Illustrations show color variation of males at east-west extremes of distribution in the Indo-Pacific region.

Ogasawara Islands/male

CLOWN CORIS
Coris aygula Lacepède, 1801

Dorsal rays IX,12–13 (rarely 13), the first 2 spines close together and prolonged in large adults; anal rays III,12; pectoral rays 14; lateral line continuous, deflected downward below posterior part of dorsal fin to straight peduncular portion (true of all *Coris*), the pored scales 59–67; gill rakers 18–21; a canine tooth (sometimes 2) at corner of mouth (absent in juveniles); body depth 2.6–3.4 in standard length (body deeper with growth); caudal fin rounded in juveniles, slightly rounded to truncate in adults with strongly exserted rays in large males; pelvic fins varying from about 1.8 in head length in juveniles to nearly head length in adults; females with a whitish bar below seventh and eighth dorsal spines; head and body before bar pale greenish with small black to dark red spots; body posterior to bar greenish with broad black edges on scales; large males dark green (often appearing black underwater), with a broad, pale green to blue-green bar below anterior soft portion of dorsal fin, often with a similar bar anterior to it; juveniles whitish with small black spots on head, anterior body, and dorsal fin; 2 large, semicircular, orange-red spots on back with a large ocellated black spot above each in dorsal fin. Largest specimen examined, 59.5 cm. Occurs throughout the Indo-Pacific

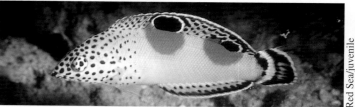

Red Sea/juvenile

Minami-tori-shima/female

region except the Persian Gulf, Gulf of Oman, and Hawaiian Islands; type locality, Mauritius. A major predator on shelled mollusks and crabs (Randall, 1999c). *Coris angulatus* Lacepède is among the 9 synonyms.

BATU CORIS
Coris batuensis (Bleeker, 1856)

Dorsal rays IX,11; anal rays III,11; pectoral rays 13–15; lateral-line scales 51–53; anterior lateral-line scales with 2 pores; gill rakers 16–21; anterior pair of canine teeth nearly twice as long as second pair of teeth; canine tooth present at corner of mouth; body depth 3.0–3.8 in standard length (body deeper with growth); first 2 dorsal spines not close together and not prolonged; caudal fin rounded; pelvic fins short, not reaching anus; females pale greenish gray, the scales ventrally on body with a small white spot, most evident on abdomen due to its being blackish; body with 6 indistinct dark bars narrower than pale interspaces, not extending more than halfway down body; short, narrow pale bars between dark bars, extending basally into dorsal fin; head with irregular pink bands and a small, dark blue-green spot behind eye; dorsal fin with a large ocellus in middle and a small one at front of fin; a dark bar at base of pectoral fins; males similar, but more green, the dark bars much broader and less distinct, the pale bars more distinct, and the blackish area over abdomen darker; juveniles have scattered, small orange spots, especially on head and abdomen, and a third ocellus posteriorly in dorsal fin. Largest specimen, 15.1 cm. Maldive Islands and Chagos Archipelago to Marshall Islands and Tonga; Ryukyu Islands to Great Barrier Reef, New South Wales, and New Caledonia; type locality, Batu Islands, Indonesia. Usually found on protected reefs, generally where there is more sand and rubble than coral; recorded from depths of 1–34 m. Formerly identified as *Coris variegata* (Rüppell), a closely related Red Sea endemic.

CENTRAL PACIFIC CORIS
Coris centralis Randall, 1999

Dorsal rays IX,12; anal rays III,12; pectoral rays 13; lateral-line scales 52–57, all with a single pore; gill rakers 17–20; anterior pair of canine teeth clearly longer than second pair; no canine tooth at corner of mouth; body elongate for the genus, the depth 4.0–4.7 in standard length; first 2 dorsal spines close together, those of males flexible and nearly twice length of third spine; caudal fin rounded; pelvic fins of males reaching anus; females with a narrow red stripe overlaid with dark brown, sometimes in a series of blotches, from front of snout through eye to base of caudal fin just above peduncular lateral line; a black spot in stripe on opercular membrane; body above stripe light brown, below white with a narrower yellow to orange stripe from upper end of pectoral-fin base to caudal fin just below lateral line; males with upper stripe breaking into blotches of deep pink and dark brown posteriorly, and a second series of pink or pink and brown blotches following lateral line and joining middle stripe on caudal peduncle; yellow lower stripe also replaced by spots that become pink posteriorly (and in larger males all pink and reduced in size); outer three-fourths of first 2 membranes of dorsal fin of males black (males elevate the front of the dorsal fin during courtship). Small for the genus; attains only about 10 cm. Known only from the Line Islands (type locality, Fanning Island = Tabuaeran) and the Phoenix Islands (G. R. Allen, pers. comm.); collected from depths of 4.5–46 m; usually found in lagoons in areas of sand and low-profile patch reefs.

Marshall Islands/juvenile

Sulawesi/female

Okinawa/male

Line Islands/female

Line Islands/male

PALEBARRED CORIS

Coris dorsomacula Fowler, 1908

Dorsal rays IX,12; anal rays III,12; pectoral rays 13; lateral-line scales 51–54, all with a single pore; gill rakers 17–19; a small canine tooth present at corner of mouth of males, none in juveniles or females; body slender, the depth 3.4–4.25 in standard length (body deeper with growth); space between first 2 dorsal spines about three-fourths space between second and third spines; first 2 dorsal-fin membranes slightly elevated by flexible extension of spines; caudal fin rounded; pelvic fins reaching to or beyond anus in adults (beyond third anal spine in large males); juveniles pale gray with a dark reddish stripe from front of snout through eye along upper side of body to caudal-fin base, interrupted by 7 pale bars; a black spot on opercle, edged posteriorly with yellow, and a small ocellus at rear base of dorsal fin; females similar, with the same pale bars, but light green with 2 pink stripes on lower half of body that break into blotches posteriorly, a black spot at upper base of pectoral fins, and a black spot on first 2 membranes of dorsal fin; males more variable in color but usually darker green with blackish bars, those in middle of body extending ventrally, where they may be deep blue; upper part of first 2 dorsal-fin membranes bright yellow; caudal fin green with 2 broad con-

Izu Islands, Japan/male

Sulawesi/female

Great Barrier Reef/juvenile

verging red bands. Reaches 19 cm. Southern Japan to eastern Australia (type locality, Victoria), east to Palau, New Caledonia, northern New Zealand, and Tonga; Cocos-Keeling Islands in eastern Indian Ocean; reported from depth range of 5–40 m.

Hawaiian Islands/juvenile

Hawaiian Islands/female

Hawaiian Islands/male

YELLOWTAIL CORIS

Coris gaimard (Quoy & Gaimard, 1824)

Dorsal rays IX,12; anal rays III,12; pectoral rays 13; lateral-line scales 68–77; median predorsal zone of adult males scaleless; gill rakers 16–19; anterior pair of canine teeth nearly twice as long as second pair of teeth; a small canine tooth present at corner of mouth of males; body depth 2.9–3.55 in standard length (body deeper with growth); space between first 2 dorsal spines about two-thirds space between second and third spines; dorsal spines of juveniles sharp-tipped, of adults flexible, the first 2 elongate (especially the first); caudal fin rounded; pelvic fins varying from 1.6 in head length of juveniles to 1.1 in males (in males reaching beyond spinous portion of anal fin); adult females orangish brown to dark greenish gray with many small, brilliant blue spots, progressively more numerous posteriorly; head orange with red-edged green bands; dorsal and anal fins orange with a blue margin and a narrow longitudinal blue band

in middle that breaks into spots posteriorly; unscaled part of caudal fin bright yellow; males similar but with a green or yellow bar on side of body above origin of anal fin, the blue spots on body much smaller and more posterior, and the outer part of the dorsal and anal fins dark brownish orange with irregular blue lines; juveniles completely different, bright orange or orange-red with 5 large, black-edged white spots dorsally on head and body. Largest examined, 31.4 cm. Western Australia, Cocos-Keeling Islands, and Christmas Island in eastern Indian Ocean; southern Japan to New South Wales and Lord Howe Island, east to Hawaiian Islands (type locality, Maui), and Tuamotu Archipelago; replaced by *Coris cuvieri* (Bennett) in the rest of Indian Ocean and by *C. marquesensis* in the Marquesas Islands. Data on food habits summarized by Randall (1999c); feeds chiefly on mollusks, brachyuran crabs, and hermit crabs; often observed turning over rocks to reveal hidden prey.

HEWETT'S CORIS

Coris hewetti Randall, 1999

Dorsal rays IX,12; anal rays III,12; pectoral rays 13; lateral-line scales 50–51 (usually 50); gill rakers 20–24; anterior pair of canine teeth nearly twice as long as second pair of teeth; canine tooth present at corner of mouth of males; body depth 3.55–4.15 in standard length; dorsal spines sharp-tipped only in juveniles and small females; dorsal spines and rays of adults progressively longer with growth, the ninth spine in small females 3.05 in head length, of large males 1.35; caudal fin rounded; pelvic fins at least to anus in mature females, reaching beyond spinous portion of anal fin in males; juveniles and small females whitish with a broad brown stripe from snout, through eye, and along upper side of body, containing a few small white spots, mostly in a line; a narrower dark stripe from nape along base of dorsal fin, also with a few white spots; larger females with blue and salmon pink bands on head; males green to olive green with a broad orange-red stripe on upper side containing 6 longitudinal rows of tiny blue or green spots or dashes; lower edge of stripe with about 17 narrow bars extending into ventral green part of body. Males in courtship flash the red areas to blue. Largest specimen, 16.7 cm. Known only from the Marquesas Islands (type locality, Nuku Hiva). Generally found on rubble or sand and rock bottoms; depth range, 1 to at least 40 m.

MARQUESAN CORIS

Coris marquesensis Randall, 1999

Dorsal rays IX,12; anal rays III,12; pectoral rays 13; lateral-line scales 72–76; gill rakers 16–18; anterior pair of canine teeth nearly twice as long as second pair of teeth; a small canine tooth present at corner of mouth of large female (no male specimens collected); body depth 3.2–3.85 in standard length; space between first 2 dorsal spines narrower than between second and third spines (latter gap broader with growth); dorsal spines of juveniles sharp-tipped, of adults flexible, the first 2 elongate, especially the first; caudal fin rounded; pelvic fins long, reaching to or beyond origin of anal fin in all but small juveniles; small females orange with 4 narrow blue stripes partly broken into series of spots; a large, blue-edged black spot at rear base of dorsal fin; larger females orangish brown on body with numerous very small blue spots, mostly not in rows; narrow pink to blue bands radiating from eye, oblique blue lines in dorsal and anal fins, and a yellow caudal fin; males wary, none photographed or collected; juveniles similar in color to *C. gaimard* juveniles but with narrower black margins on the white spots and a prominent black spot at rear base of dorsal fin. Largest collected, 31.8 cm, but much larger males were observed. Known only from the Marquesas Islands (type locality, Nuku Hiva) where it occurs from a few to at least 30 m.

Pitcairn Islands/subadult

Mangareva/female

Pitcairn Islands/male

RED-AND-GREEN CORIS
Coris roseoviridis Randall, 1999
Dorsal rays IX,11; anal rays III,11; pectoral rays 13–14 (rarely 14); lateral-line scales 51–52 (rarely 52); anterior lateral-line scales with 1 pore (except for occasional specimens over 150 mm standard length that have 2); gill rakers 15–18 (modally 17); a canine tooth at corner of mouth in specimens over about 90 mm standard length; body depth 3.5–4.5 in standard length; dorsal spines sharp-tipped; caudal fin rounded; pelvic fins not reaching origin of anal fin; small females with a red-edged orange stripe from front of snout through eye, along upper side to base of caudal fin; body above stripe pink, below white; a black spot

rimmed posteriorly in yellow on opercular flap; fins white; larger females with orange and green bands on head, a second orange stripe midlateral on body, breaking into vertically elongate spots posteriorly, and median fins green with orange markings; males more complexly colored green and rose red. Largest specimen, 24.2 cm. Known from the Pitcairn Islands, Mangareva, Austral Islands, Rapa (type locality), and Rarotonga; collections were made from tidepools to 58 m. One of a complex of 5 species, the others *venusta* from the Hawaiian Islands, *debueni* from Easter Island, *dorsomacula* from the western Pacific, and *caudimacula* from the Indian Ocean.

Marshall Islands/female

Bali/male

KNIFEFISH
Cymolutes praetextatus (Quoy & Gaimard, 1834)
Dorsal rays IX,12–13 (rarely 12), the first 2 spines flexible; anal rays II,12; branched caudal rays 10 (most wrasses with 11 or 12); pectoral rays 12; lateral line interrupted, the pored scales 50–60 + 15–21; head scaleless (true of the other 2 species of the genus); a pair of long slender canine teeth at front of jaws (also generic); body depth 4.1–4.6 in standard length; dorsal profile of head strongly convex (generic); caudal fin truncate to slightly rounded; females pale gray dorsally, white ventrally, with a faint, narrow, salmon pink stripe along back above lateral line and faint gray bars on posterior half of body; fish less than about 80 mm standard length with a small black spot at upper base of caudal fin; an oblique, white-edged black line on first membrane of dorsal fin; males with narrow upper stripe yellowish brown, a brown line above this, the bars posteriorly on body brownish yellow; a small, white-edged black spot on upper side below base of seventh dorsal spine; margin of dorsal and anal fins deep pink (broad on soft portion of dorsal), and upper and lower edges of caudal fin pink. Reported to 20 cm. East coast of Africa to Society Islands and Micronesia, but from few localities; known in the South Pacific from Phoenix Islands, Tonga, New Caledonia, Norfolk Island, and the Great Barrier Reef; type locality, Mauritius. Occurs in sparse seagrass beds and over open sand bottoms; dives into sand when threatened.

COLLARED KNIFEFISH
Cymolutes torquatus (Valenciennes in C & V, 1840)

Dorsal rays IX,12, the first 2 spines flexible; anal rays III,11–12 (rarely 11); pectoral rays 12; lateral line interrupted, the pored scales 56–69 + 16–22; body depth 4.2–4.5 in standard length; caudal fin slightly rounded; females light brown dorsally, shading to white ventrally, the posterior two-thirds of body with vertical brown lines, mostly joined dorsally by a narrow, dark brown stripe; a vertical dark brown streak posteriorly on opercle; dorsal fin with light red and green markings; body of males pale green, the lines posteriorly on body broader and orange; a narrow, oblique black streak with a pale center anteriorly on body from lateral line to below pectoral fin; head greenish dorsally, shading to yellowish, with an oblique blue line below eye and a blue-edged vertical orange streak posteriorly on opercle; dorsal fin red with a green reticulum; caudal fin with a broad, red posterior border. Reported to 20 cm. East coast of Africa to western Pacific from southern Japan to Great Barrier Reef, New South Wales, Lord Howe Island, and New Caledonia; occurs on sand flats and seagrass beds; quickly buries in sand with the approach of danger. Clark & Petzold (1998) studied the spawning behavior.

Negros, Philippines/female

Kenya/male

Marshall Is./juvenile

Fiji/female

Malaysia/yellow female

Palau/male

SLINGJAW WRASSE
Epibulus insidiator (Pallas, 1770)

Dorsal rays IX,10; anal rays III,8–9; pectoral rays 12; lateral line interrupted, the pored scales 14–15 + 8–9; gill rakers usually 5 + 12; body deep, the depth 2.0–2.3 in standard length; jaws extremely protractile; dorsal and anal fins of adults pointed posteriorly, especially in males, the anal sometimes reaching to or posterior to middle caudal rays; caudal fin slightly rounded in juveniles, emarginate to lunate in adults; females dark brown, light brown, or yellowish brown, usually with a vertical black mark on each scale, or entirely yellow; all phases with a narrow, pale blue edge on orbit and a black spot at front of dorsal fin; males with a pale gray head, a narrow black stripe from eye across operculum, a short black streak before eye, and another oblique one from lower edge of eye; nape and dorsoanterior body orange, shading posteriorly to a yellow bar that narrows as it passes behind pectoral fin; edges of scales green in lower part of orange and yellow areas; rest of body dark greenish gray with black edges on scales; juveniles dark brown with 4 narrow, black-edged white bars on body, a short one on chest, and 5 radiating from eye; 2 black spots in dorsal fin, and 1 on anal fin. Reaches 35 cm. Red Sea and east coast of Africa to the Hawaiian Islands (rare), Society Islands, and Tuamotu Archipelago; Ryukyu Islands to Great Barrier Reef and New Caledonia; type locality, Java. Found on coral reefs from depths of 2–40 m. Preys mainly on small fishes, shrimps, and crabs; feeding involves extremely rapid and long protrusion of the jaws (Westneat & Wainwright, 1989).

409

Wetar, Indonesia/juvenile

Penyu Islands, Indonesia/initial phase

New Britain/terminal-phase male

BIRD WRASSE

Gomphosus varius Lacepède, 1801

Dorsal rays VIII,13; anal rays III,11; pectoral rays 16; lateral-line scales 26–27; head naked except for a few small scales on upper part of operculum; snout of adults extremely long and slender, short in juveniles; preopercle with no free lower margin; body depth 3.5–4.0 in standard length; caudal fin slightly rounded in initial phase, truncate to emarginate in terminal males; head and anterior body of initial phase pale gray, shading to white ventrally and to black posteriorly, each scale in pale zone with a black spot, except on chest and anterior abdomen; scales in dark gray intermediate zone with black edges; a light red band from eye to front of snout; 2 rows of black spots extending posterior to eye (lower row of spots may be joined as a short stripe); caudal fin black with a broad translucent posterior border; body of terminal males dark green with a vertical deep pink line on each scale and a light yellowish green bar extending dorsally from beneath basal part of pectoral fin; head deep blue-green; caudal fin with a large blue-green crescent posteriorly; dorsal and anal fins blue-green; juveniles green with a very broad, black-edged, white stripe on lower side. Reported to 32 cm. Western Pacific from southern Japan to Great Barrier Reef, Lord Howe Island, Norfolk Island, and New Caledonia, east to Hawaiian Islands and Pitcairn Islands; Cocos-Keeling Islands and Christmas Island in the eastern Indian Ocean; type locality, Tahiti. Replaced by *Gomphosus caeruleus* Lacepède to the west. A very active coral-reef fish. The author examined the stomach contents of 4 adults and found small crustaceans (78% by volume, mainly crabs, shrimps, stomatopods, and hermit crabs), brittlestars (10%), small fishes (9.5%), and small mollusks. *Gomphosus tricolor* Quoy & Gaimard is a synonym based on the terminal male, and *Thalassoma stuckiae* Whitley a synonym based on the juvenile stage. Hybrids with 2 species of *Thalassoma* will be reported.

ARGUS WRASSE

Halichoeres argus (Bloch & Schneider, 1801)

Dorsal rays IX,11–12; anal rays III,11–12; pectoral rays 14; lateral line continuous, deflected sharply downward below rear of dorsal fin to straight peduncular part (true of other *Halichoeres*); lateral-line scales 27 (plus 1 on caudal-fin base); anterior lateral-line scales with 1 to 3 pores (usually 2); scales on chest much smaller than those on side of body (also generic); head scaleless; preopercle with about as much free margin ventrally as posteriorly (also generic); a single pair of canine teeth anteriorly in jaws; a canine tooth at corner of mouth, at least in adults (generic); females with 2 longitudinal rows of 6 or 7 large, dark gray blotches on body, one dorsal to lateral line and one along side; scales with a small green spot, forming longitudinal rows; 4 rows with a white dash replacing a green spot, separated from other white dashes by 2 or 3 green spots; males rose red with a black-edged green spot on each scale, each spot with a red center; rows of similar spots in dorsal and anal fins; head rose red with irregular green bands and large spots. Reported to 11 cm. Western Pacific from Taiwan to northern Australia, west in the Indian Ocean to Sri Lanka; known in the islands of Oceania to date only from Fiji. A shallow-water species, usually found in relatively protected waters. Randall (1981b) showed

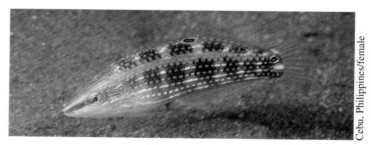

Cebu, Philippines/female

Cebu, Philippines/male

that *H. leparensis* Bleeker is the female form. De Beaufort (1940) suggested that *Halichoeres fijiensis* Herre is a hybrid of *argus* and *leparensis*, but Randall indicated that it is the intermediate form during sex reversal.

410

TWO-SPOTTED WRASSE
Halichoeres biocellatus Schultz, 1960

Dorsal rays IX,12; anal rays III,12; pectoral rays 13; lateral-line scales 27, the scales with a single pore; body depth 2.9–3.35 in standard length; caudal fin rounded; juveniles dark brownish red with narrow, white to pale green stripes, 2 large blue-edged black spots in dorsal fin (one at front and one at rear of soft portion of fin), and a small black spot at upper base of caudal fin; a small vertically elongate black spot usually present behind eye; females similar but lacking the black spot at caudal-fin base, the stripes now bright orange-red and green and breaking into rows of spots posteriorly; terminal males lose ocelli in dorsal fin, retain anterior stripes, now bright orange and green, the posterior half of body green, the scales with an orange spot at base. Attains 12 cm. Western Pacific from southern Japan to Great Barrier Reef and New South Wales, east to Samoa Islands and all of Micronesia (type locality, Bikini Atoll); coral reefs and adjacent sand and rubble; reported from depths of 7–40 m.

GOLDEN WRASSE
Halichoeres chrysus Randall, 1981

Dorsal rays IX,12; anal rays III,11–12 (rarely 11); pectoral rays 13–14 (rarely 14); lateral-line scales 27, the anterior scales with branched tubules (pores varying from 2 to 4, usually 2 or 3); head naked except for scales on nape; body moderately elongate, the depth 3.4–3.8 in standard length; caudal fin rounded; females bright yellow with a black spot behind eye, upper base of caudal fin, front of dorsal fin, and middle of dorsal fin (dorsal-fin spots often rimmed with light yellow or pale blue); males similar in color but with faint orange and greenish bands on head, chest, and median fins and loss of caudal and middle dorsal-fin spots; juveniles with a third black spot posteriorly in dorsal fin. Attains 12 cm. Southern Japan to Great Barrier Reef and New South Wales, east to New Caledonia, Caroline Islands, and Marshall Islands; type locality, Solomon Islands. Usual habitat, small iso-lated coral heads on sand or sand and rubble substrata; known from depths of 7–60 m, but rarely seen in less than 20 m. A popular aquarium fish. Closely related to *Halichoeres leucoxanthus* Randall & Smith of the Indian Ocean (the two overlap in western Indonesia).

Coral Sea/juvenile

Guam

Great Barrier Reef/female

Sangihe Islands/male

GOLDSTRIPE WRASSE
Halichoeres hartzfeldii (Bleeker, 1852)

Dorsal rays IX,11; anal rays III,11; pectoral rays 13; lateral-line scales 27; suborbital pores 8–11; head naked except for small scales on side of nape; body elongate, the depth 3.65–4.0 in standard length; caudal fin slightly rounded, becoming slightly double emarginate in large males; females pale green, shading to white ventrally, with a broad orange-yellow stripe from eye to base of caudal fin (where there may be a small black spot); a dull pink stripe from interorbital along back at base of dorsal fin; a small black spot at upper base of pectoral fin; males green dorsally, shading to light blue-green ventrally, with a salmon pink stripe beginning narrowly at upper end of gill opening, broadening along upper side of body to caudal-fin base, the edges of stripe wavy with a brighter pale blue-green margin; 3 black spots usually present posteriorly on upper edge of stripe; a short oblique dusky pink to blackish band on side of body from stripe to behind pectoral fin; head with irregular pink bands; usually a yellow spot above small black spot at upper pectoral-fin base. Attains 20 cm. Western Pacific to New South Wales, east to

Luzon/females

Bali/male

Samoa Islands and islands of Micronesia; type locality, Ambon, Molucca Islands. Occurs over open sand or rubble bottoms from depths of 10–85 m, often in small groups. Very closely related to *Halichoeres zeylonicus* of the Indian Ocean, and some may consider it a subspecies of *zeylonicus*.

Marshall Islands/juvenile

Marshall Islands/female

Line Islands/male

CHECKERBOARD WRASSE

Halichoeres hortulanus (Lacepède, 1801)

Dorsal rays IX,11; anal rays III,11; pectoral rays 14; lateral-line scales 26, the scales with 1 pore; suborbital pores varying from 12 in juveniles to 40 in adults; a patch of small scales dorsally on opercle and a near-vertical band of small scales in 2 or 3 rows just behind eye; 2 pairs of canine teeth anteriorly in upper jaw, the second pair strongly recurved; a single pair of canines at front of lower jaw; body depth 2.7–3.7 in standard length (relatively deeper with growth); caudal fin truncate to slightly rounded; females with longitudinal series of square, black-edged white spots following scale rows (or scales edged with black dots ventrally); a yellow spot on back at base of fourth and fifth dorsal spines and extending basally into fin; a similar but smaller spot in middle of base of soft portion of fin (lacking in Indian Ocean population); head yellowish green with irregular pink bands; caudal fin yellow; males with body green, each scale with a vertically elongate, purplish pink bar; caudal fin purple, shading at edges to red, with small, irregular green spots; juveniles white with a large, branching black bar in middle of body extending into dorsal fin, where it contains a yellow-edged black spot; a broad, mottled black bar across caudal peduncle; chest mainly black; a dusky orange streak across lower head, and a dark stripe on side of snout. Attains 27 cm. Red Sea and east coast of Africa to Line Islands, Society Islands, Tuamotu Archipelago, and Austral Islands; southern Japan to Great Barrier Reef, New South Wales, and New Caledonia; type locality, Mauritius. Coral reefs and adjacent sand and rubble, mainly in lagoons from 1 to at least 30 m. Feeds on small sand-dwelling gastropods, but also bivalve mollusks, crabs, hermit crabs, other crustaceans, polychaete worms, chitons, and foraminifera (author's data). *Halichoeres centiquadrus* was described by Lacepède in the same volume; Valenciennes (in C & V, 1839), as first revisor, selected *hortulanus* as the senior synonym.

WEEDY SURGE WRASSE

Halichoeres margaritaceus (Valenciennes in C & V, 1839)

Dorsal rays IX,11; anal rays III,11; pectoral rays usually 13; lateral-line scales 27, the anterior scales with 1–3 pores; head naked except for scales on side of nape; 2 pairs of canine teeth anteriorly in upper jaw, the second pair smaller and recurved; body depth 3.2–3.7 in standard length; caudal fin slightly rounded; females olivaceous on back, the scale edges often darker, whitish ventrally, with irregular blackish bars on upper half of body except posteriorly, and scattered, small white blotches; a broad, slightly oblique, bright pink bar posteriorly on abdomen, edged in white and often containing a vertical white line; a blue-edged yellow band from corner of mouth through eye; a black spot behind eye; a pink band on cheek paralleling band through eye; dorsal and anal fins with oblique dark red bands, the dorsal with a yellow-edged black spot in middle of fin and a small one on first membrane; body of males green, shading to yellow ventrally, the centers of some scales pink to purplish pink, forming a pattern of narrowing bars on body; head green with deep pink bands radiating from eye except ventrally; median fins green with irregular deep pink markings and an irregular black spot replacing ocellus of female. Reaches 12.5 cm. Western Pacific from southern Japan to Great Barrier Reef, New South Wales, Norfolk Island, New Caledonia, and the Kermadec

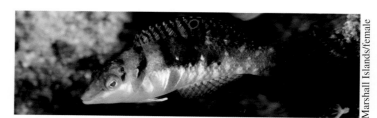

Marshall Islands/female

Ogasawara Islands/male

Islands, east to Line Islands, Society Islands, and Pitcairn Islands; Cocos-Keeling Islands in Indian Ocean; type locality, Vanikoro, Santa Cruz Islands. An inshore species of reef flats and rocky shores exposed to surge, often where algal growth is heavy. Kuiter & Randall (1981) distinguished this species from the very similar *H. nebulosus* (Valenciennes) and *H. miniatus* (Valenciennes), neither of which ranges to islands of Oceania.

Luzon/juvenile

Tonga/female

Marshall Islands/male

DUSKY WRASSE

Halichoeres marginatus Rüppell, 1835

Dorsal rays IX,13–14 (usually 13); anal rays III,12–13 (usually 12); pectoral rays 14–15 (usually 14); lateral-line scales 27–28, the anterior scales with 2–4 pores; head naked except for nape; teeth in jaws progressively longer anteriorly, the most anterior pair only slightly longer than the second; body depth 2.6–3.2 in standard length; caudal fin slightly rounded; females dark brown, usually with greenish lines following centers of scale rows that may be either darker or lighter than rest of scales; a large, deep blue ocellus in middle of dorsal fin and a small one at front of fin; caudal fin abruptly whitish (large females develop a blackish crescent posteriorly in fin); head of large males orangish with narrow, irregular, deep blue-green lines and a few spots, this pattern continuing as straighter dark

green lines anteriorly on body, soon changing to a pattern of a dark green spot edged with orange on each scale; often 3 rows of close-set red spots beneath pectoral fins; caudal fin with a bright green crescent at base, followed by a large orange crescent containing dark-edged blue-green spots, and an outer greenish yellow border; juveniles black with longitudinal yellow lines with periodic expansions to form spots, and the same 2 ocelli in dorsal fin as females. Reaches 17 cm. Red Sea (type locality) and east coast of Africa to the Hawaiian Islands (1 valid record), French Polynesia (except Rapa and the Marquesas Islands), Pitcairn Islands, and throughout Micronesia; southern Japan to Great Barrier Reef, and New South Wales; coral reefs from the shallows to about 30 m; feeds on a wide variety of benthic invertebrates, especially crustaceans, gastropods, and polychaete worms.

TAILSPOT WRASSE

Halichoeres melanurus (Bleeker, 1851)

Dorsal rays IX,12; anal rays III,12; pectoral rays 14; lateral-line scales 27, the anterior scales with 1–4 (usually 2) pores; head naked except for nape; a single pair of canine teeth anteriorly in jaws; body depth 3.1–3.6 in standard length; caudal fin rounded; females with alternating narrow orange-yellow and blue stripes; a blue-edged black spot about as large as pupil at upper base of caudal fin, a larger ocellus in middle of dorsal fin, and a small one at front of fin; body of males with green and orange stripes and 3 to 6 narrow green bars on upper side; head with orange and green bands; caudal fin blue to blue-green with 2 curved, orange-pink bands and a large vertically elongate black to blackish spot submarginally in middle of fin; base and axil of pectoral fins bright yellow with a small, triangular black spot at upper edge; a blackish blotch often present beneath pectoral fin. Largest specimen, 10.5 cm. Ryukyu Islands and Ogasawara Islands to Great Barrier Reef and New Caledonia, east to Tonga, Samoa Islands, and islands of Micronesia; type locality, Banda Islands, Indonesia. Collected from coral reefs from depths of 2–15 m. *Julis hoevenii* Bleeker is a synonym based on the female form.

Marshall Islands/female

Papua New Guinea/male

413

Ataoru, Indonesia/female

Cebu, Philippines/male

Hawaiian Islands/juvenile

Hawaiian Islands/female

Gunung Api, Indonesia/male

OCELLATED WRASSE
Halichoeres melasmapomus Randall, 1981

Dorsal rays IX,12; anal rays III,12; pectoral rays 13; lateral-line scales 27, the anterior scales with 2–7 pores (larger fish, in general, with more); suborbital pores 9–13; head naked except for nape; 2 pairs of canine teeth anteriorly in upper jaw, the second pair about two-thirds as long as first; body depth 2.95–3.3 in standard length; caudal fin rounded; body of adults light gray-brown, the scales with an indistinct orange-brown spot; head with a large black spot edged in blue and narrowly in black on opercle at level of eye, preceded by a small black spot rimmed in blue anteriorly and yellow posteriorly; a broad, bright green band from upper lip across head below eye, bordered above and below by a narrow, dark-edged orange stripe, the lower stripe bifurcating; females with 2 dark-edged blue lines before eye and 1 posteriorly from upper part of eye; snout and interorbital of males with irregular lines of dark green or blue and orange-red or orange-yellow; both sexes with a blue-edged black spot on upper basal part of caudal fin (may be lost in large males); females with 3 ocelli in dorsal fin, lost in the male. Largest specimen, 14 cm. Southern Japan to Great Barrier Reef; east to Line Islands, French Polynesia except Rapa, and the Pitcairn Islands (type locality); Christmas Island and Cocos-Keeling Islands in the Indian Ocean; reported from depths of 20–55 m, but rarely seen below 30 m. Kuiter & Tonozuka (2001) placed *Halichoeres melasmapomus* in the synonymy of *H. xanti* (Károli), type locality, Singapore. *Halichoeres xanti*, however, is a synonym of *H. bicolor* (Bloch & Schneider), one of the most common wrasses in Singapore's shallow waters.

ORNATE WRASSE
Halichoeres ornatissimus (Garrett, 1863)

Dorsal rays IX,12; anal rays III,12; pectoral rays 13; lateral-line scales 27, the anterior scales with 2–4 (usually 3) pores; suborbital pores 9–13; head naked except for nape; a single pair of canine teeth anteriorly in jaws; body depth 3.0–3.4 in standard length; caudal fin rounded; pelvic fins of large males nearly reaching origin of anal fin; pink to red, sometimes pale green ventrally, the body with a green spot on each scale (green spots absent ventrally on some individuals); head with lengthwise green bands, one from above eye often continuing onto anterior body replacing a row of spots; a small, vertically elongate spot, edged posteriorly in black, behind eye; juveniles with narrow, yellowish green and brownish orange stripes on head and body, a very large black spot with blue center and yellow edge in middle of dorsal fin, and a similar but smaller spot posteriorly in fin (which disappears at a length of about 85 mm). Attains 15 cm. Philippines and Indonesia to Great Barrier Reef and New Caledonia, east to the Hawaiian Islands (type locality, Hawai'i), Line Islands, and French Polynesia except the Austral Islands and Rapa; only Palau and the Mariana Islands in Micronesia; Cocos-Keeling Islands in the eastern Indian Ocean; replaced in Taiwan and southern Japan by *H. orientalis* Randall and in the western Indian Ocean by *H. cosmetus* Randall & Smith; mainly in outer-reef areas in sand and rubble bottoms from depths of 6–30 m. Shows a preference in its food habits for small benthic mollusks and crustaceans.

PALE WRASSE
Halichoeres pallidus Kuiter & Randall, 1995

Dorsal rays IX,12; anal rays III,12; pectoral rays 13; lateral-line scales 27, the anterior scales with 2–3 (usually 2) pores; gill rakers 15–16; suborbital pores about 12; head naked except for nape, the scales extending to above posterior edge of orbit; a single pair of canine teeth anteriorly in jaws; body depth 3.3–3.8 in standard length; caudal fin rounded; females pale pink, shading nearly to white ventrally, with 3 narrow red-edged pale blue stripes extending anteriorly and posteriorly from eye, the interspaces yellow; a large red spot on side of upper lip; dorsal fin with 3 blue-edged black spots, the one anteriorly in fin large; caudal fin pale yellow; males darker pink, the stripes on head green instead of pale blue; dorsal fin with only the large anterior black spot or with a vestige of the middle spot; caudal fin with 2 large semicircular green arcs; a narrow orange or yellow bar at base of pectoral fin. Attains 9 cm. Known from Indonesia (type locality, Gunung Api, Banda Sea), Palau, Kiritimati (Christmas

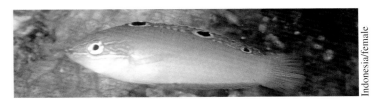

Indonesia/female

Indonesia/male

Island) in the Line Islands, and recently found in the Phoenix Islands by G. R. Allen; collected by the author from depths of 37–64 m. Closely related to *H. trispilus* Randall & Smith from the western Indian Ocean east to Java.

TWO-TONE WRASSE
Halichoeres prosopeion (Bleeker, 1853)

Dorsal rays IX,12; anal rays III,12; pectoral rays 13–14 (rarely 13); lateral-line scales 27, the anterior scales with 1–3 pores; head naked except for nape; 2 pairs of large canine teeth anteriorly in upper jaw, the second pair recurved; body depth 3.2–4.0 in standard length (body relatively deeper with growth); caudal fin of juveniles slightly rounded, of adults truncate; pelvic fins of adults usually extending beyond origin of anal fin; head and about anterior one-fourth of body purplish to bluish gray, shading gradually to pale gray posteriorly with vertical yellow lines on scales (as elongate spots ventrally and posteriorly); a small, vertically elongate, dark blue spot behind eye; dorsal fin light gray with a blue-edged black spot on second to fourth membranes, the membranes posterior to sixth spine with irregular yellow lines; caudal fin yellow with transparent membranes; base of pectoral fins pink with a narrow, deep blue, wedge-shaped mark; lateral edge of pelvic fins white; juveniles pale blue on snout, soon shading posteriorly to pale yellow, with 4 black stripes

Indonesia/juvenile

Palau

on head and body; a large black spot anteriorly on dorsal fin. Reaches 15 cm. Southern Japan to New South Wales (as juveniles), east to Samoa Islands; Palau in Micronesia; Scott Reef off northwestern Australia; type locality, Ambon, Molucca Islands. Lives on coral reefs from depths of about 5–40 m.

THREESPOT WRASSE
Halichoeres trimaculatus (Quoy & Gaimard, 1834)

Dorsal rays IX,11; anal rays III,11; pectoral rays 14–15 (usually 14); lateral-line scales 27, the anterior scales with 1 pore; a patch of small scales on upper part of opercle; 2 pairs of canine teeth anteriorly in upper jaw, the second pair about half as large and recurved; body depth 3.0–3.7 in standard length; caudal fin truncate to slightly rounded; females pale greenish gray with pale pink edges on scales and a large, irregular, pink to blackish spot on caudal peduncle above lateral line; upper half of head with oblique pink bands and a few spots; upper edge of pectoral-fin base with a small black spot; fins without markings; males more green, especially on head, with vertical pink lines on scales, becoming large, vertically elongate, pink spots anteriorly on body and postorbital head; dorsal and anal fins with pink lines; large males darker greenish gray dorsally on head and anteriorly on body, with fifth and sixth scales of lateral line and 1 or 2 scales below black and pale blue. Reported to 18 cm. Southern Japan to Great Barrier Reef, Lord Howe Island, Norfolk Island, and New Caledonia, east to Line Islands, French Polynesia except

Society Islands/female

Marshall Islands/male

Rapa, and the Pitcairn Islands; type locality, Vanikoro, Santa Cruz Islands. Typical habitat, sand or sand and rubble around small coral heads in shallow protected waters; may be found in less than 1 m, but reported to 18 m.

Penyu Islands, Indonesia/juvenile

Ogasawara Islands

BARRED THICKLIP WRASSE
Hemigymnus fasciatus (Bloch, 1792)

Dorsal rays IX,11; anal rays III,11; pectoral rays 14; lateral-line scales 27, a few rows of small scales on cheek; a pair of protruding canine teeth in jaws; a broad canine tooth at corner of mouth; lips very thick; gill opening restricted to side; body depth 2.3–2.6 in standard length; caudal fin slightly rounded to truncate; body of adults black with 4 slightly curved white bars across body and a short one on nape; head green with irregular, blue-edged pink bands, mainly around eye; lips yellowish; caudal fin greenish black, sometimes with a narrow white bar near base; juveniles dark brown, mottled with pale yellowish dorsally, with 5 narrow, pale yellow bars on body, the first from nape to chest, and 1 on caudal fin near base; narrow, pale yellowish bands radiating from eye, some branching. Reported to 80 cm; however, the author has observed none greater than 40 cm. Red Sea and east coast of Africa to the Line Islands, all of French Polynesia, and the Pitcairn Islands; Japan (type locality) to Great Barrier Reef, Lord Howe Island, and New Caledonia; found more on protected than exposed reefs; feeds mainly by extracting small animals from mouthfuls of sand; also preys on larger invertebrates such as mollusks and sea urchins. A reversal of the black and white bars of large adults occasionally observed with behavior suggesting a male in courtship.

Great Barrier Reef/juvenile

Papua New Guinea/female

Sabah/male

BLACKEYE THICKLIP WRASSE
Hemigymnus melapterus (Bloch, 1791)

Dorsal rays IX,11; anal rays III,11; pectoral rays 14; lateral-line scales 27, a few rows of small scales on cheek behind and below eye; lips extremely thick and fleshy; dentition, gill opening, and body shape as in *H. fasciatus*; caudal fin slightly rounded to truncate; head and chest of juveniles light gray; body with a white bar from front of dorsal fin to anterior half of abdomen; body behind bar dark gray to black with a pale gray or bluish spot on each scale; posterior caudal peduncle and fin bright yellow with a small black spot in middle; with growth, head above level of lower edge of eye and nape develop a reticulum of pink and green; with further growth, scales of black part of body reddish brown with green and black edges, the white bar pale pink with pale green edges, the reticulum of pink and green extending onto operculum and faintly onto cheek; a large area of darker green and pink, edged in blue, often present behind eye; caudal peduncle and fin dull yellow with blue lines on basal scales and blue lines paralleling rays. Reported to 90 cm, but any over 60 cm would be exceptional. Red Sea and east coast of Africa to Samoa Islands and islands of Micronesia; Ryukyu Islands and Ogasawara Islands to Great Barrier Reef, Lord Howe Island, and New Caledonia; type locality given as Japan. Food habits similar to those of *H. fasciatus*.

Red Sea/juvenile

Bali/female

Gulf of Aqaba, Red Sea/male

RINGWRASSE

Hologymnosus annulatus (Lacepède, 1801)

Dorsal rays IX,12, the spines thin and flexible; anal rays III,12; pectoral rays 13; lateral line continuous, deflected sharply downward posteriorly to straight peduncular part (true of other *Hologymnosus*); lateral-line scales 100–118, head scaleless; gill rakers 19–23; 2 pairs of canine teeth at front of jaws, but no canine at corner of mouth (also generic); body depth 3.3–5.1 in standard length (body depth increasing with growth); caudal fin slightly rounded in juveniles, emarginate in adults, the caudal concavity of large males about 5 in head length; pectoral fins of adults 1.65–1.9 in head length; initial phase brown to olive brown with 17–19 dark brown bars; a blue and black spot on opercular membrane; a black spot on side of lips, larger on lower; caudal fin with a large whitish crescent posteriorly; body

of terminal males green, sometimes shading to blue-green ventrally, with numerous purplish red bars, often with a pale yellowish bar on body above origin of anal fin; head light purplish with green to blue-green bands radiating from eye, one forward onto snout expanding broadly and branching; a broad, dull pink band in each lobe of caudal fin and a posterior green crescent; juveniles light yellow with a very broad, dark brown stripe on lower side of head and body, extending into caudal fin; a dark reddish to black line from top of snout along back above lateral line. Reaches 40 cm. Red Sea and east coast of Africa to the Marshall Islands, Line Islands, Society Islands, Pitcairn Islands, Austral Islands, and Rapa; southern Japan to the Great Barrier Reef; type locality, Mauritius. Not common; feeds mainly on fishes, occasionally on crustaceans. *Hologymnosus semidiscus* (Lacepède) is a synonym (Randall, 1982).

Philippines/juvenile

Okinawa/female

Okinawa/male

PASTEL RINGWRASSE

Hologymnosus doliatus (Lacepède, 1801)

Dorsal rays IX,12, the spines thin and flexible; anal rays III,12; pectoral rays 13; lateral-line scales 97–112, head scaleless; gill rakers 18–22; body depth 3.75–5.35 in standard length (depth increasing with growth); caudal fin slightly rounded in juveniles to double emarginate in large adults, the caudal concavity of large males about 11 in head length; pectoral fins of adults short, 1.9–2.1 in head length; initial phase pale bluish, greenish, or pinkish gray with 20–23 orange-brown bars on body; a black spot (may be edged in blue and yellow) on opercular flap; body of terminal males light blue-green, pinkish, or yellowish with

lavender-blue to purple bars, and often a pale yellowish bar in pectoral region bordered by purple bars; head pale green, yellow, or blue with pink bands; caudal fin green with a purplish red band in each lobe and elongate spots in central part; juveniles whitish with 3 narrow, orange-red stripes. Reported to 50 cm (largest examined, 38 cm). East coast of Africa to Line Islands and Samoa Islands; southern Japan to Great Barrier Reef, Lord Howe Island, and New Caledonia; type locality, Mauritius. Typically found in sand and rubble areas near reefs from the shallows to at least 30 m; juveniles often seen in small groups; reported to feed mainly on fishes and crustaceans, occasionally on brittlestars and polychaete worms.

SIDESPOT RINGWRASSE
Hologymnosus longipes (Günther, 1862)

Dorsal rays IX,12, the spines thin and flexible; anal rays III,12; pectoral rays 13; lateral-line scales 95–100, head scaleless; gill rakers 19–21; body depth 4.65–5.5 in standard length (depth increasing with growth); caudal fin slightly rounded to truncate, the corners a little prolonged; pectoral fins of adults short, 1.9–2.0 in head length; initial phase light greenish yellow to bluish gray with 2 series of vertically elongate orange spots on body that continue onto head as solid stripes; caudal fin orange to yellow; body of terminal male light greenish dorsally, white ventrally, with orange bars on side that become pale lavender-blue anteriorly on lower side; an oval black spot, rimmed in blue below and yellow above, on side of body dorsal to pectoral fin;

WHITEPATCH RAZORFISH
Iniistius aneitensis (Günther, 1862)

Dorsal rays IX,12; anal rays III,12; pectoral rays 12; lateral line interrupted, the pored scales 20–22 + 4–5; an oblique band of small scales from behind eye to below lower margin of eye; gill rakers 19–23; a pair of long, curved canine teeth anteriorly in jaws; body depth 2.4–3.1 in standard length (depth increasing with growth); origin of dorsal fin slightly anterior to a vertical at upper end of preopercular margin; first 2 dorsal spines flexible, the first not longer than longest dorsal ray; membrane between second and third dorsal spines incised more than half length of third spine; light gray with a black spot usually the size of eye or smaller on back below base of second to third dorsal soft rays; a very large, round, white to bluish white spot on upper abdomen centered below tip of pectoral fin, this spot usually preceded by a yellow to yellowish brown blotch; lesser blackish spots along back; juveniles may be entirely dark brown to black but usually pale with 2 dark bars on head and 3 on body. Reaches 22 cm. Zanzibar, Maldive Islands, and Chagos Archipelago in the western Indian Ocean to the Hawaiian Islands, Samoa Islands, and islands of Micronesia; Ryukyu Islands to Great Barrier Reef, Lord Howe Island, and New Caledonia; type locality, Aneiteum, Vanuatu. Lives on open, clean sand bottoms at depths of 6 to

MARQUESAN RAZORFISH
Iniistius auropunctatus Randall, Earle & Robertson, 2002

Dorsal rays IX,12; anal rays III,12; pectoral rays 12; lateral-line scales 19–21 + 5; gill rakers 18–20; body depth 2.75–3.2 in standard length; a broad band of small scales extending from below eye to slightly below corner of mouth; 2 or 3 scales dorsoanteriorly on opercle; first and second dorsal spines flexible, about twice length of third spine, slightly longer than longest dorsal soft ray, and not separated from remainder of fin; space between second and third dorsal spines about 1.5 times greater than space between third and fourth spines; membrane between second and third dorsal spines incised to about one-third length of third dorsal spine; a small black spot 1 scale row below eighth lateral-line scale (hence above tip of pectoral fin); both sexes with a row of orange dots along lateral line and scattered dots below; females with a large, roundish, pink patch dorsally on abdomen containing oblique orange lines on scale edges, ending dorsally in orange spots; males with black lines under edges of second to sixth lateral-line scales, sometimes extending to row above or below, and no pink patch on abdomen. Largest specimen, 15.5 cm. Cur-

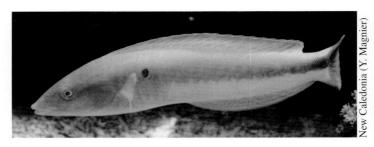

New Caledonia (Y. Magnier)

head green with pink bands radiating from eye; caudal fin blue with a large, whitish semicircular area posteriorly. Attains about 40 cm. New Caledonia, Loyalty Islands, Vanuatu (type locality, Aneiteum), and southern Great Barrier Reef; usually over sand or rubble near coral heads; depth range 5–30 m.

Papua New Guinea/juvenile

Papua New Guinea

91 m; like other razorfishes, dives into sand when threatened. Formerly classified in *Xyrichtys*, now retained for Atlantic and eastern Pacific razorfishes (except *Iniistius pavo,* which ranges to the eastern Pacific). *Xyrichtys niveilatus* Jordan & Evermann is a synonym.

Marquesas Is./female

Marquesas Is./male

rently known only from the island of Ua Pou in the Marquesas Islands; collected over sand in 15–17 m. Closely related to *Iniistius pentadactylus* (Linnaeus) from the Red Sea to the western Pacific, with only 2 records from islands of Oceania, Guam and Kiritimati (Christmas Island), Line Islands (Randall et al., 2002c). Photographs by J. P. Hoover.

BRONZESPOT RAZORFISH
Iniistius celebicus (Bleeker, 1856)

Ogasawara Islands/juvenile

Dorsal rays IX,12; anal rays III,12; pectoral rays 12; lateral-line scales about 20 + 6; gill rakers 18–22; body depth 2.3–2.9 in standard length; a single oblique row of small scales from below middle of eye to behind lower part of eye or a narrow triangular band of small scales that may extend nearly to level of corner of mouth; origin of dorsal fin slightly posterior to a vertical at posterior edge of eye; first 2 dorsal spines flexible, the first curved, neither longer than longest dorsal soft ray; membrane beween second and third dorsal spines incised more than three-fourths length of third dorsal spine; adults pale bluish gray, shading ventrally to white, with a large, vertically oval, dark yellowish brown to blackish red spot on side of body behind gill opening; a horizontally oval, yellowish brown spot midlaterally on caudal peduncle; juveniles with the same 2 spots, but the first nearly crossing body; also 2 brown bars on body that extend into soft portion of dorsal and anal fins, each bar in the dorsal with a large black spot. Largest specimen, 19.4 cm. Known from Indonesia, Philippines, Taiwan, Guam, Marshall Islands, Middleton Reef

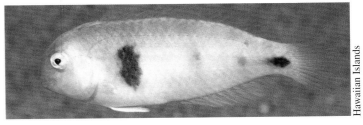

Hawaiian Islands

in the Coral Sea, Hawaiian Islands (Randall & Earle, 2002), American Samoa (Wass, 1984), and Rarotonga (M. P. Francis, pers. comm.); occurs on sand in about 8–20 m; more wary than other razorfishes.

Hawaiian Islands

PEACOCK RAZORFISH
Iniistius pavo (Valenciennes in C & V, 1840)

Negros, Philippines/juvenile

Dorsal rays II-VII,12; anal rays III,12; pectoral rays 12; lateral line interrupted, the pored scales 20–22 + 4–5; usually with 1–6 small scales (often embedded, sometimes absent) from behind lower part of eye to below posterior edge of eye; gill rakers 17–21; a pair of long, curved canine teeth anteriorly in jaws; body depth 2.3–3.3 in standard length; origin of dorsal fin over posterior half of eye; first 2 dorsal spines flexible (all flexible in adults), completely separated from third spine by a gap as great as 3 times space between other adjacent spines; first dorsal spine nearly twice as long as longest dorsal ray (may be 3 times longer in juveniles); adults light gray to brownish gray with 3 indistinct, broad, darker gray bars on body, and 1 across caudal-fin base; a black spot on eighth lateral-line scale and scale above; males with a dark-edged blue line on each scale of ventral half of body; juveniles with more distinct dark bars on body, 2 of which extend into dorsal fin, where they contain an ocellated black spot; other juveniles (and occasional adults) black except outer transparent part of caudal fin. Reaches 35 cm. Occurs throughout the Indo-Pacific region; also ranges to the tropical eastern Pacific; type locality, Mauritius. Collected from depths of 8–31 m, but observed to 100 m; lives over open stretches of sand, but usually not far from reefs. Juveniles hold the detached front part of dorsal fin forward over head and mimic drifting leaves. *Iniistius niger* (Steindachner) is among the 13 synonyms.

419

TUBELIP WRASSE
Labrichthys unilineatus (Guichenot, 1847)

Dorsal rays IX,11–12; anal rays III,10–11 (rarely 11); pectoral rays 14–15 (rarely 14); lateral line continuous, deflected downward below rear of dorsal fin, the pored scales 25–27; head fully scaled; lips thick and fleshy, forming a tube when mouth closed; front of upper jaw with 2 pairs of incurved canine teeth, a large canine tooth posteriorly, but no teeth between; lower jaw with a single pair of anterior canines, followed by 3–5 small teeth; body depth 2.6–3.2 in standard length; caudal fin strongly rounded; pelvic fins of males very long; females yellowish brown with blue longitudinal lines following scale centers; mouth yellow; males dark olive with blue longitudinal lines on body, a broad yellow bar in pectoral region (sometimes faint), and a blue reticulum on head; juveniles dark brown with 2 bluish white lines, one mid-lateral and one ventral; larger juveniles lose the lower line, and the lateral one becomes yellow. East coast of Africa to Samoa Islands and islands of Micronesia (type locality, Guam); southern Japan to Great Barrier Reef, Lord Howe Island, and New Caledonia; occurs in sheltered, coral-rich habitats; feeds on coral polyps. Largest examined, 17.5 cm. Only 1 species in genus; *Labrichthys cyanotaenia* Bleeker is a synonym.

BICOLOR CLEANER WRASSE
Labroides bicolor Fowler & Bean, 1928

Dorsal rays IX,11; anal rays III,10; pectoral rays 13; lateral line continuous, deflected downward below soft portion of dorsal fin, the pored scales 26; small scales on cheek, opercle, and nape; lips thick, the lower strongly bilobed; 1 pair of canine teeth anteriorly in jaws, a canine at corner of mouth, and several rows of small teeth on side of jaws; body depth 3.7–4.5 in standard length; caudal fin slightly rounded; females gray with a black lateral stripe anteriorly, pale yellowish posteriorly, with a semi-circular black band submarginally in caudal fin; males with head blue (younger males with black stripe still evident on head), middle of body black, posterior part yellow, and caudal fin green or blue with same submarginal black band; juveniles black with a narrow, brilliant yellow stripe on back; with growth, yellow stripe broadens and becomes white, the black reduced to middorsal and lateral stripes, the caudal fin pale yellowish (juvenile shown cleaning *Neoniphon sammara;* subadult shown with *Myripristis vittata;* see also figure of *Neoniphon argenteus* being cleaned by *L. bicolor* on p. 92). Reaches 14 cm. Indo-Pacific region except the Persian Gulf and Hawaiian Islands; type locality, Port Maricaban, Philippines. Feeds on ectoparasites and mucus of other fishes; moves more over the reef in search of host fishes than the following 3 species.

Moyo I., Indonesia/juvenile

Tuamotu Arch. color variant

Fiji/color variant

Great Barrier Reef, with *Plectropomus leopardus*

STRIPED CLEANER WRASSE

Labroides dimidiatus (Valenciennes in C & V, 1839)
Dorsal rays IX,11; anal rays III,10; pectoral rays 13; lateral-line scales 52–53; small scales on cheek, opercle, and nape; body depth 4.1–4.7 in standard length; caudal fin truncate to slightly rounded; adults with a black stripe from lips through eye, broadening as it passes posteriorly to end of caudal fin; head and anterior body above stripe light bluish gray, below white, becoming light blue posteriorly; some individuals in French Polynesia with a pale orange zone below and adjacent to black stripe anteriorly on body, and some in the Samoa Islands and Fiji with part of black stripe posteriorly on body replaced by yellow; juveniles black with a bright blue stripe dorsally on head to top of caudal fin. Attains 11.5 cm. Indo-Pacific except the Hawaiian Islands; in the western Pacific from Chiba Prefecture, Japan, to southern New South Wales, Lord Howe Island, and Norfolk Island; type locality, Gulf of Suez. Establishes "cleaning" stations on reefs to which fishes come to have crustacean ectoparasites removed; the mouth and gill chamber of larger fishes are often entered in quest of parasites. These include calagoid, lernaeid, and lichomolgid copepods, and larval gnathiid isopods (Randall, 1958); mucus is also ingested from the host fishes (for which the bilobed lower lip may serve as a scoop). Gorlick (1980) showed that considerable mucus is ingested by *Labroides phthirophagus* in Hawai'i, and it exhibits a preference for fishes such as labrids with much mucus. Kuwamura (1981, 1984) studied the reproduction and early life history of *L. dimidiatus* in Shirahama, Japan, where spawning was restricted to the warmer months of May to early September. Males pair spawn with 2–12 females within their home range. Maturity of females can be attained in 1 year. Sex change to males usually occurs shortly before age 3, but it can take place even in 1-year fish when no older or larger fish are in the vicinity.

BREASTSPOT CLEANER WRASSE

Labroides pectoralis Randall & Springer, 1975
Dorsal rays IX,10–12 (usually 11); anal rays III,9–10 (rarely 9); pectoral rays 13; lateral-line scales 26; cheek, opercle, and most of nape scaled; body depth 3.3–3.95 in standard length; caudal fin slightly rounded; adults with a black stripe from lips through eye, broadening greatly as it passes posteriorly to end of caudal fin; a median dorsal stripe from snout tip to dorsal fin; head and anterior body between black stripes yellow, shading posteriorly to orange; chest and anterior abdomen white, shading posteriorly to blue; a large black spot at lower edge of pectoral-fin base; lips orange-red and blackish; upper and lower edges of caudal fin lavender-pink to pale blue, the corners hyaline. Reaches 8 cm. Ogasawara Islands to Great Barrier Reef and New Caledonia, east to islands of Micronesia (type locality, Palau), west to Christmas Island, Cocos-Keeling Islands, and Rowley Shoals off northwestern Australia. Attains 8 cm. Habits as in *Labroides dimidiatus*. Senou & Ueda (2002) illustrated a hybrid of *Labroides bicolor* and *L. pectoralis* from Okinawa.

Papua New Guinea

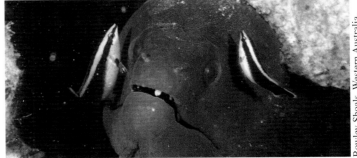

Rowley Shoals, Western Australia, with *Gymnothorax javanicus*

421

Line Islands

Line Islands

REDLIPPED CLEANER WRASSE
Labroides rubrolabiatus Randall, 1958

Dorsal rays IX,11; anal rays III,10; pectoral rays 13; lateral-line scales 26; cheek, opercle, and most of nape scaled; body depth 3.5–3.7 in standard length; caudal fin slightly rounded; adults with a black stripe from lips through eye onto anterior body, disappearing or reduced to dusky in middle of body, reappearing posteriorly and covering all of caudal fin except narrow upper and lower edges; a median black dorsal stripe from snout tip to dorsal fin; head and anterior body except for stripes whitish to greenish yellow; middle of body orange; abdomen pale blue, shading to pale yellow posteriorly; a blackish line from below corner of mouth to lower pectoral-fin base; edges of lips bright red; upper and lower edges of caudal fin pale lavender-blue; juveniles bright blue with a midlateral black stripe. Reaches 7.5 cm. Line Islands, islands of French Polynesia except Rapa (type locality, Moorea), Pitcairn Islands, Cook Islands, and Samoa Islands; habits like those of *Labroides dimidiatus*; often seen in pairs.

Tonga/juvenile

Great Barrier Reef/female

Great Barrier Reef/male

SOUTHERN TUBELIP WRASSE
Labropsis australis Randall, 1981

Dorsal rays IX,12; anal rays III,11; pectoral rays 13–15; lateral line continuous, deflected downward below rear of dorsal fin, the pored scales 35–40; head fully scaled; lips thick and fleshy, forming a tube when mouth closed; front of upper jaw with 2 pairs of recurved canine teeth, the second about half as large; a large canine tooth posteriorly, but no teeth between; lower jaw with a single pair of anterior canines, followed by 2–3 lesser canines; body depth 3.15–3.45 in standard length; caudal fin strongly rounded; pelvic fins not reaching anal fin; juveniles pale yellowish with 3 black stripes, the caudal fin black except for clear corners; females with a gray head and same 3 stripes as juveniles but less strongly pigmented, the body brown with a large, golden yellow spot on each scale; base of pectoral fin with a middle black spot merging above and below with an orange-red spot; adult males with a dark gray to black head, the dorsal profile with a protuberance before upper part of eye. Attains 10.5 cm. Solomon Islands, Great Barrier Reef (type locality, One Tree Island, Capricorn Group), and Lord Howe Island, east to New Caledonia, Fiji, and Samoa Islands. Adults feed on coral polyps; juveniles observed cleaning fishes.

Tahiti/female

Tahiti/male

POLYNESIAN TUBELIP
Labropsis polynesica Randall, 1981

Dorsal rays IX,11; anal rays III,10–11 (rarely 10); pectoral rays 13–14 (usually 14); lateral line continuous, deflected downward below rear of dorsal fin, the pored scales 43–47; head fully scaled; lips and dentition as in *Labropsis australis*; body depth 3.25–3.65 in standard length; caudal fin of females slightly rounded, of males emarginate, the caudal concavity of large males up to 1.9 in head length; pelvic fins short, 2.1–2.5 in head length; females dark brown with a small yellow spot on each scale (faint posteriorly) and 3 well-separated, narrow blue stripes from front of head to middle of body; lips white; yellow spots in males elongate to dashes to form nearly continuous lines on body; blue stripes absent; lips pale blue; a large yellow area on operculum. Largest specimen, 11.7 cm. Known from the Society Islands (type locality, Moorea), Tuamotu Archipelago, Austral Islands, and Cook Islands; seaward coral reefs; collections from depths of 15–38 m. Habits as in *L. australis*.

YELLOWBACK TUBELIP

Labropsis xanthonota Randall, 1981

Dorsal rays IX,11; anal rays III,10; pectoral rays 14–15 (rarely 15); lateral-line scales 46–49; postorbital head and posterior suborbital region scaled; lips and dentition as in *L. australis*; body depth 3.4–3.8 in standard length; caudal fin rounded in juveniles, less so in females, and emarginate in males; pelvic fins short, not reaching anus; juveniles bluish black with very narrow, pale blue to white stripes on head and body, becoming dotted posteriorly; dorsal fin largely pale yellow with a black anterior spot; females similar, but narrow stripes now as finely dotted, pale blue lines, the scales dorsally on body with a yellowish brown spot; head of males dark brown, shading to orange anteriorly, with a coarse reticulum of deep blue, and a broad bright yellow edge on opercle; body dark brown with a yellow dot on each scale, including base of median fins; outer part of caudal fin black with a V-shaped central posterior part of pale blue or white. Reaches 13 cm. East coast of Africa to Mariana Islands, Marshall Islands, and Samoa Islands (type locality, Tutuila); southern Japan to Great Barrier Reef and New Caledonia; reported from 7–55 m. Habits like those of *Labropsis australis*.

KUITER'S WRASSE

Macropharyngodon kuiteri Randall, 1978

Dorsal rays IX,12; anal rays III,12; pectoral rays 12; lateral line continuous, bent downward below rear of dorsal fin, the pored scales 27, the anterior scales with 1–3 (usually 2) pores; head naked except for scales on nape; teeth in jaws somewhat spatulate except for canine at corner of mouth; 2 pairs of enlarged teeth anteriorly in upper jaw, the second pair subtruncate and serving to buttress first pair; body moderately deep, the depth 2.3–2.5 in standard length; caudal peduncle short, its length 2.3–2.5 in its depth (1.4–1.9 for other species of the genus); dorsal spines progressively longer posteriorly; caudal fin rounded; juveniles and females orangish with a round, bluish white spot in center of each scale; a blue-edged black spot as large as eye on opercle; a small black spot behind upper part of eye; cheek and chest white with small orange spots; median fins orange to pale yellow with very small, dark-edged blue spots; males brownish orange anteriorly on body and above lateral line, with a pale blue spot on each scale; rest of body whitish with a vertically elongate, brownish orange spot on each scale; head light green with 5 or 6 orange bands radiating from eye except ventrally; 2 oblique, pale orange bands ventrally on head, and a large, irregular black spot posteriorly on opercle; median fins brownish orange, the dorsal with dull green spots at base and a blackish spot on each of first 2 membranes, the anal with 2 dull green stripes, and the caudal with dull green spots. Largest reported, 10 cm. Southern Great Barrier Reef to New South Wales (type locality, Seal Rocks), east to New Caledonia and Tonga; collected from depths of 5–55 m.

Ogasawara Islands/juvenile

Guam/female

Guam/male

BLACKSPOTTED WRASSE

Macropharyngodon meleagris (Valenciennes in C & V, 1839)
Dorsal rays IX,11; anal rays III,11; pectoral rays 13; lateral-line scales 27, the anterior scales with 2–4 pores; head naked except for scales on nape; 2 pairs of canine teeth anteriorly in upper jaw, the second pair recurved; body depth 2.55–3.05 in standard length; juveniles with middle dorsal spines notably shorter than second and last spines, the dorsal spines of adults nearly uniform in height; juveniles pale greenish with numerous small dusky orange blotches, many of which are interconnected, and a small ocellus posteriorly in dorsal and anal fins; larger juveniles with scattered, small, black and bluish white spots; adult females with a narrow orange band dorsally on head and body, the postorbital head and rest of body pale blue with large, irregular, interconnected black spots; irregular branching orange bands from ante-rior half of eye; base of dorsal and anal fins with a row of black spots, most connecting to irregular orange bands in outer part of fins; males dull orange-red with black-edged green spots on body and caudal fin, spots and short bands on head, and spots and a wavy stripe on dorsal and anal fins; a cluster of 3 black and yellow scales behind upper end of gill opening; a black spot on first 2 membranes of dorsal fin, edged above in yellow and red. Reaches 15 cm. Southern Japan to Great Barrier Reef, New South Wales, Lord Howe Island, and New Caledonia, east to Line Islands, French Polynesia except Rapa, and the Pitcairn Islands; type locality, Ulea, Caroline Islands. Typically found on shallow patch reefs of lagoons or bays or in adjacent sand and rubble areas. *Macropharyngodon pardalis* (Kner) is a synonym based on the female stage. Other synonyms are *M. nigromaculatus* (Günther) and *M. nigropunctatus* (Seale).

Negros, Philippines/juvenile

Cebu, Philippines/female

Palau/male

YELLOWDOTTED WRASSE

Macropharyngodon negrosensis Herre, 1932
Dorsal rays IX,11; anal rays III,11; pectoral rays 12; lateral-line scales 27, the anterior scales with 2–3 pores; head naked except for scales on nape; 2 pairs of canine teeth anteriorly in upper jaw, the second pair recurved; dorsal spines progressively longer posteriorly, body depth 2.65–2.95 in standard length; caudal fin truncate to slightly rounded; juveniles dark orangish brown dorsally, soon shading to black, with numerous pale yellow dots and small spots; dorsal fin dark orangish brown with pale yellow spots basally, shading to pale yellow distally; anal and pelvic fins black; caudal and pectoral fins clear with pink rays; females similar, with 4 mottled, pale yellow blotches along back at base, the dorsal fin pale yellow with oblique black lines; males black with pale blue-green edges on scales except for an interrupted narrow pale yellow zone along back; head with irregular, branching, pale yellow to green bands; caudal fin pale yellow with orange-red spots on rays, the upper and lower edges broadly blackish; pectoral fins with yellow rays, clear membranes, and a black bar at base. Attains 12 cm. Southern Japan to the Great Barrier Reef, and New South Wales, east to Marshall Islands and Samoa Islands; type locality, Negros, Philippines. Usually found on sand or rubble near coral reefs, generally deeper than 15 m. Also called the Black Wrasse, but this name should be restricted to the all-black *Halichoeres melas* Randall & Earle from Oman.

Batu Ata, Indonesia/juvenile

Hawaiian Islands

ROCKMOVER WRASSE

Novaculichthys taeniourus (Lacepède, 1801)

Dorsal rays IX,12; anal rays III,12; pectoral rays 13; lateral line interrupted, the pored scales 19–20 + 5–6; head naked except for 2 scales on upper part of opercle and a near-vertical row of small scales from below posterior edge of eye to behind middle of eye; a single straight pair of large canine teeth anteriorly in jaws; body depth 2.65–3.0 in standard length; body compressed, the width 2.4–3.0 in depth; first 2 dorsal spines flexible, greatly elongate in juveniles; caudal fin rounded; adults dark brown with a white spot or vertical white line on each scale; abdomen of some individuals red with white edges on scales; head light

gray, with or without narrow dark bands radiating from eye; an elongate black spot beneath basal part of pectoral fins; a small yellow spot often present at upper edge of pectoral-fin base; 2 black spots at front of dorsal fin; a broad whitish bar across base of caudal fin; juveniles brown, reddish, or greenish with dark bars and white spots; white and dark bands radiating from eye. Attains 30 cm. Occurs throughout the Indo-Pacific region except the Persian Gulf and ranges to the tropical eastern Pacific; type locality, Madagascar. Well known for its ability to overturn surprisingly large rocks to prey on invertebrates beneath, such as mollusks, crabs, and brittlestars; the young mimic drifting masses of algae.

SEAGRASS WRASSE

*Novaculoides macrolepidotus (*Bloch, 1791)

Dorsal rays IX,13; anal rays III,13; pectoral rays 12; lateral line interrupted, the pored scales 19–20 + 4–6; head naked except for 1–3 oblique rows of small scales from below to behind lower edge of eye; body depth 3.5–3.9 in standard length; dorsal profile of head forming an angle of about 45°; a pair of canine teeth anteriorly in each jaw, each curving strongly laterally; no canine at corner of mouth; longest dorsal soft ray nearly twice length of longest dorsal spine; pelvic fins of females not reaching anus; of males long and filamentous (may be longer than head); green to brownish yellow, females with an irregular, midlateral, dark brown stripe or row of spots, males with small dark spots only posteriorly; 2 curved dark brown bands from eye across upper part of operculum; a dark band or double line often presents from eye to front of snout; a black spot on

Cebu, Philippines

first membrane of dorsal fin; a large black spot usually present midventrally on chest; dorsal and anal fins with dull pink spots or bands. Attains about 16 cm. Red Sea and east coast of Africa to western Pacific; east to Mariana Islands, Palau, Lord Howe

Island, and Tonga. Lives in seagrass habitat or dense beds of algae where well camouflaged by its color. Formerly classified in the genus *Novaculichthys*, Randall & Earle (2004) placed it in the new genus *Novaculoides*.

LINED WRASSE

Oxycheilinus lineatus Randall, Westneat & Gomon, 2003

Dorsal rays IX,10; anal rays III,8; pectoral rays 13; lateral line interrupted, the pored scales to caudal-fin base 16 + 7; gill rakers 4 + 8; body moderately elongate, the depth about 3.4 in standard length; head length about 2.5 in standard length; snout long and pointed, about 2.5 in head; dorsal profile of snout nearly straight, of nape slightly convex; lower jaw slightly projecting; maxilla ending a half-eye diameter before anterior margin of orbit; caudal fin (of adult male) slightly rounded, the upper 3 principal rays slightly prolonged; pectoral fins short, about 3.2 in head length; body below lateral line with 12 narrow, slightly irregular, dark brown stripes separated by white lines; body above lateral line with similar but irregular bands; head with narrow, dark brown bands radiating from eye except anteriorly; snout bluish gray with brown dots; a blackish blotch on basal half

Cook Islands

of first membrane of dorsal fin. Total length of only specimen, 20 cm, from Rarotonga, Cook Islands, collected by Richard L. Pyle in 85 m. One was speared by the author in 76 m outside the reef from Papeete, Tahiti, but it escaped, as did another from 49 m off Henderson Island, Pitcairn Islands.

Coral Sea

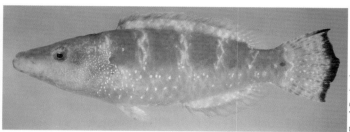

Coral Sea/male

BLACKMARGIN WRASSE

Oxycheilinus nigromarginatus Randall, Westneat, & Gomon, 2003

Dorsal rays IX,10; anal rays III,8; pectoral rays 13; lateral line interrupted, the pored scales to caudal-fin base 15 + 6; gill rakers 5–6 + 8–9; body moderately elongate, the depth 3.1–3.55 in standard length; head length 2.45–2.55 in standard length; snout long and pointed, 2.6–2.8 in head length; dorsal profile of snout straight or with a slight concavity of snout to above eye; lower jaw slightly projecting; maxilla reaching or nearly reaching a vertical at anterior margin of orbit; caudal fin of females slightly rounded, the upper 3 principal rays a little prolonged; fin of

males rhomboid with the upper 3 rays more strongly projecting; pectoral fins 2.6–2.95 in head; red in life on about upper half of body with 5 irregular pale bars from white edges on scales, pale red on lower half with 3 whitish stripes containing small white spots; white lines radiating from eye in females, pale orange in males; posterior edge of caudal fin broadly blackish to black. Known from New South Wales, Chesterfield Bank in Coral Sea (type locality), New Caledonia, and Tonga; collected from depths of 10–27 m in protected waters on a habitat of mixed sand and coral-reef patches.

RINGTAIL WRASSE

Oxycheilinus unifasciatus (Streets, 1877)

Dorsal rays IX,10; anal rays III,8; pectoral rays 12; lateral line interrupted, the pored scales 15–16 + 6–8; gill rakers 13–15; head pointed; dorsal profile of head straight to slightly convex; body depth 2.6–3.2 in standard length (larger fish deeper-bodied); caudal fin slightly rounded, the corners a little prolonged on large adults, resulting in a slight double-emarginate shape; color variable but usually greenish gray dorsally, shading to pale reddish, greenish, or whitish ventrally, with a deep pink to dark orangish brown vertical line on each scale except ventrally; head dull olive green with narrow, irregular, deep pink to reddish lines except for a broad band from eye to end of opercle bordered above and below by a dark reddish line, the lower ending at level of upper edge of pectoral-fin base; color within band often darker or paler than rest of head; deep pink reddish lines on cheek mostly oblique and parallel, but may be branching, joined, or broken into segments; a white bar across anterior caudal peduncle (may be faint); caudal fin usually greenish, sometimes with brown upper and lower edges; a dark spot basally on first 1 or 2 dorsal-fin membranes; juveniles with orangish brown spots

Tuamotu Archipelago/subadult

Guam/female

428

on scales instead of lines, a midlateral olive stripe, edged in reddish anteriorly, from front of snout to base of caudal fin, but broken on body by 4 irregular white bars (from white edges on scales); a yellow-edged, deep blue spot within stripe at base of caudal fin and another below fifth dorsal soft ray. Largest examined, 46 cm. Ryukyu Islands to Great Barrier Reef and New Caledonia, east to Hawaiian Islands and the islands of French Polynesia; type locality, Fanning Island (now Tabuaeran), Line Islands. Found on coral reefs from depths of 2–160 m. Capable of very rapid color change. Randall (1985a) examined the stomach contents of 33 adults in the Hawaiian Islands; 23 contained food items, 65% fish remains by volume; the remaining prey: crabs, brittlestars, heart urchins, and sea urchins. Has caused ciguatera fish poisoning. Often misidentified as *Cheilinus rhodochrous* Günther, a synonym of *Oxycheilinus orientalis* (Günther) (Randall & Khalaf, 2003).

Hawaiian Islands/male

REDTAIL FLASHERWRASSE
Paracheilinus rubricaudalis Randall & Allen, 2003
Dorsal rays IX,11; anal rays III,9; pectoral rays 14; lateral line interrupted, the pored scales 16 + 5; median predorsal scales 5; gill rakers 13–15; body depth 3.4–3.55 in SL; only the first dorsal soft ray of males prolonged as a filament; caudal fin slightly rounded; pelvic fins 1.75–2.0 in head length; males orange, shading to yellow ventrally, with 3 narrow pale blue stripes on side of body, the short middle one on anterior half of body and slightly oblique; three similar bands on postorbital head diverging from eye; a broad red outer zone in soft portion of dorsal fin; dorsal filament usually yellow (may be red); unscaled part of caudal fin mainly red; females smaller, more red overall, with the blue stripes barely visible. Described from two male specimens collected in 46 m in Fiji by Anthony Nahacky, the largest 6.6 cm. Also known from Vanuatu from photographs provided by Larry

Fiji/male

Sharron. Closely related to *P. mccoskeri* Randall & Harmelin-Vivien from the Indian Ocean with which it shares a single filamentous dorsal soft ray in the male. Differs from *mccoskeri* in having a more slender body, a red caudal fin, and the broad red zone in the soft portion of the dorsal fin.

CITRON WRASSE
Pseudocheilinus citrinus Randall, 1999
Dorsal rays IX,11; anal rays III,9; pectoral rays 14; lateral line interrupted, the pored scales 16–17 + 5–6; a series of elongate scales at base of dorsal and anal fins (true of other *Pseudocheilinus*); gill rakers 11–14; 3 pairs of canine teeth anteriorly in upper jaw, the third (most lateral) pair strongly curved and about twice as long as more medial teeth; body moderately elongate, the depth 3.4–3.65 in standard length; snout pointed (also generic), its length 2.5–2.85 in head length; first 2 dorsal spines with greatly prolonged filaments, the one from first spine varying from more than half length of spine to longer than spine; caudal fin rounded (generic); pelvic fins short, not reaching anus (generic); yellow to orange, often pale yellow to white ventrally on head and abdomen; a brownish orange stripe on side of snout; an oblique, pale lavender streak across cheek; fins pale whitish to yellowish, the dorsal and anal with an orange-red band at base.

Pitcairn Islands

Largest specimen, 8 cm. Known only from the Gambier Group of the Tuamotu Archipelago, Pitcairn Islands (type locality), Rapa, Austral Islands, and Cook Islands; collections from coral reefs at depths of 23–48 m.

429

Balicasag Island, Philippines

DISAPPEARING WRASSE

Pseudocheilinus evanidus Jordan & Evermann, 1903

Dorsal rays IX,11; anal rays III,9; pectoral rays 13–14 (rarely 13); lateral line interrupted, the pored scales 14–17 + 4–6; gill rakers 11–15; dentition as in *P. citrinus*; body depth 2.7–3.4 in standard length; snout length 2.65–2.95 in head length; first 2 filaments of dorsal fin not greatly prolonged; red to orange-red with about 25 fine, white, longitudinal lines on body; a pale blue to bluish white streak from corner of mouth nearly to upper corner of preopercle. Largest specimen examined, 9.1 cm. Red Sea and east coast of Africa to Hawaiian Islands (type locality, near Hilo, Hawaiʻi), Society Islands, and Tuamotu Archipelago; southern Japan to Great Barrier Reef and New Caledonia; collected from coral reefs from depths of 6–61 m. Stomach and gut contents of 9 specimens examined by the author; one contained fish, the rest crustaceans (none as crabs), except for 1 unidentified worm and a fragment of a brittlestar.

SIXSTRIPE WRASSE

Pseudocheilinus hexataenia (Bleeker, 1857)

Dorsal rays IX,11; anal rays III,9; pectoral rays 14–17 (modally 16); lateral line interrupted, the pored scales 16–19 + 4–8; gill rakers 12–18 (modally 15); 4 pairs of canine teeth anteriorly in jaws, the fourth pair curved and more than twice length of third pair; body depth 2.5–2.9 in standard length; snout length 2.8–3.5 in head length; upper two-thirds of body purple to purplish blue with 6 orange-yellow stripes, the upper 4 passing onto head; a blue-edged black spot of about pupil size posteriorly on upper part of caudal peduncle; cheek with numerous very small, yellow to orange spots; chin with a pair of small, bluish black spots; caudal fin green with a streak of yellow or orange on each membrane. Largest specimen examined, 7.5 cm. Red Sea and east coast of Africa to Johnston Island, Line Islands, and Tuamotu Archipelago; Ogasawara Islands to Great Barrier Reef, Lord Howe Island, and New Caledonia; type locality, Ambon, Molucca Islands. Judging from collections, the most common species of the genus, but this may be due to its occurrence in shallow water; known from less than 1 to 30 m, but rarely taken deeper than 20 m. Harmelin-Vivien (1979) reported on stomach contents of 31 specimens from Madagascar; she found mainly

Banda Islands, Indonesia

calanoid copepods, but also amphipods, gastropods, tanaids, shrimps, and polychaete worms; Hiatt & Strasburg (1960) found benthic crustaceans and foraminifera in 5 specimens from the Marshall Islands, and Sano et al. (1984) various demersal planktonic crustaceans and a few crustacean ectoparasites of fishes in 3 from Okinawa. Stays close to shelter, and difficult to approach.

MAGENTA WRASSE

Pseudocheilinus ocellatus Randall, 1999

Dorsal rays IX,11; anal rays III,9; pectoral rays 14–15 (usually 14); lateral line interrupted, the pored scales 16–17 + 4–7; gill rakers 11–14; dentition as in *P. citrinus*; body depth 3.05–3.5 in standard length; snout length 2.6–2.9 in head length; magenta with vertical white lines on body (may be faint); a black spot larger than pupil posteriorly on midside of caudal peduncle, narrowly rimmed in white and magenta and broadly in dull yellow; head anterior to vertical margin of preopercle yellow with narrow magenta and violet bands and a semicircular, bright red spot below and posterior to eye. Reaches 8 cm. Known to date from the following localities in Oceania: Ryukyu Islands, Ogasawara Islands, Palau, Caroline Islands, Marshall Islands (type locality, Majuro Atoll), Johnston Island, reefs in Coral Sea,

Marshall Islands

Vanuatu, Loyalty Islands, Fiji, Austral Islands, Society Islands, and Pitcairn Islands; all specimens and photographs from depths greater than 20 m, the deepest, 58 m; usually seen in caves or beneath ledges.

EIGHTSTRIPE WRASSE
Pseudocheilinus octotaenia Jenkins, 1901

Dorsal rays IX,11; anal rays III,9; pectoral rays 13–15 (strongly modal at 14); lateral line interrupted, the pored scales 16–18 + 5–7; gill rakers 12–17 (modally 15 and 16); dentition as in *P. citrinus*; body depth 2.9–3.5 in standard length; snout length 2.65–2.9 in head length; orange, pink, lavender, or light gray with about 8 narrow dark brown, red, dark pink, or violet stripes following middle of scale rows, the upper 3 or 4 stripes extending onto postorbital head; paler interspaces sometimes with a middle yellow stripe or series of dashes; numerous small yellow spots on opercle and cheek. Attains 11.5 cm. Islands of western Indian Ocean to Hawaiian Islands (type locality, Oʻahu), Line Islands, Marquesas Islands,

Line Islands

and Pitcairn Islands; Ryukyu Islands and Ogasawara Islands to New Caledonia; collections from depths of 6–41 m; feeds mainly on crustaceans, especially brachyuran crabs, occasionally on small gastropods, echinoids, and small fishes.

FOURSTRIPE WRASSE
Pseudocheilinus tetrataenia Schultz, 1960

Dorsal rays IX,11; anal rays III,9; pectoral rays 16–17 (rarely 17); lateral line interrupted, the pored scales 14–18 + 5–7; gill rakers 14–18 (modally 16); dentition as in *P. hexataenia*; body depth 2.8–3.3 in standard length; snout length 2.7–3.3 in head length; first 2 filaments of dorsal fin greatly prolonged, the first as much as twice spine length in males; orange to tan dorsally, usually green ventrally, with 4 black-edged blue lines, the upper 3 extending onto postorbital head; a pair of narrower blue lines from interorbital to origin of dorsal fin; a bright blue line from under eye to lower base of pectoral fin. Reaches 7 cm. Appears to be antiequatorial in the Pacific: Minami-tori-shima (Marcus Island), Mariana Islands, northern Marshall Islands (type locality, Bikini Atoll), Wake Island, and Hawaiian Islands in the north, and New Caledonia, Tonga, Samoa Islands, Cook Islands, Tuamotu Archipelago, Austral Islands, and Pitcairn Islands in

Hawaiian Islands

the south. Occurs primarily on exposed seaward reefs, often hiding under small heads of live coral, especially *Pocillopora meandrina*; extremely difficult to photograph underwater. The stomachs of 4 from Oʻahu contained mainly demersal plankton such as copepods, crab and shrimp larvae, and amphipods, but 1 had also eaten demersal fish eggs, and 1 a large alpheid shrimp (Randall, 1999b).

Gunung Api, Indonesia/female

Tuamotu Archipelago/male

ORANGEBARRED WRASSE
Pseudocoris aurantiofasciata Fourmanoir, 1971

Dorsal rays IX,12; anal rays III,12–13; pectoral rays 13–14 (usually 13); lateral line continuous, deflected downward below posterior part of dorsal fin, the pored scales 70–78; head scaleless; gill rakers 5–6 + 13–17; body depth 2.9–3.05 in standard length; snout short, 3.6–3.7 in head length; eye near center of head; a single pair of protruding canine teeth at front of jaws, the remaining teeth small with no canine at corner of mouth; first 2 dorsal spines close together, the first prolonged in large males, 1.65–1.9 in head length; caudal fin of females emarginate, of males lunate with long trailing filaments; females reddish to greenish gray, the snout and chin yellow; iris red; median fins

blue; a dark green bar at base of pectoral fins; males dark brown with narrow vertical orange and black bars on anterior half of body, sometimes with a pale yellowish one in middle of body. Reaches 30 cm, including caudal filaments. Described from Rangiroa Atoll, Tuamotu Archipelago; collected or photographed by the author in Takaroa and Tikahau in the Tuamotu Archipelago, Tetiaroa in the Society Islands, Rarotonga in the Cook Islands, Ani-jima in the Ogasawara Islands, and Gunung Api in the Banda Sea; only Palau in Micronesia; Cocos-Keeling Islands and Christmas Island in the eastern Indian Ocean; usually seen off escarpments of seaward reefs at depths greater than 30 m; feeds on zooplankon; stomach contents of 1 consisted mostly of copepods and appendicularian tunicates.

Papua New Guinea/subadult

Luzon/female

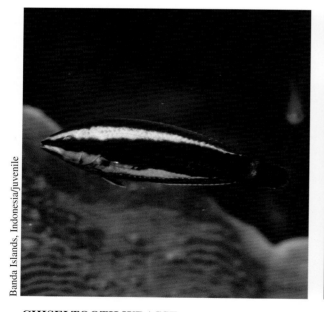

Okinawa/male

Banda Islands, Indonesia/juvenile

Bali

REDSPOT WRASSE

Pseudocoris yamashiroi (Schmidt, 1931)

Dorsal rays IX,12; anal rays III,12; pectoral rays 13; lateral line continuous, deflected downward below posterior part of dorsal fin, the pored scales 69–73; head scaleless; gill rakers 5–6 + 13–17; body depth 2.9–3.05 in standard length; snout short, 3.4–3.8 in head length; eye near center of head; dentition as in *P. aurantiofasciata*; first 2 dorsal spines close together, prolonged in large males; caudal fin of females slightly rounded to truncate, of males emarginate; body of females salmon pink, often with pale yellowish longitudinal lines, 2 of which continue more broadly and bluish white onto head, one above and one below eye; a large orange-red spot basally and in axil of pectoral fins; large females without pale lines on body but retaining the 2 on head; may be pale iridescent blue-green on abdomen and ventrally on head; upper two-thirds of body of males dark green, either with edges of scales black or with close-set vertical rows of small black spots joined to form lines, so dense on anterior one-fourth of body as to appear nearly black; lower one-third of body pale gray to white with small yellow spots above anal fin and on posterior abdomen; head dull green, the lower lip and throat blue; caudal fin black basally and on lobes, with a large, white crescentic area centroposteriorly. Attains 15 cm. Mauritius and the Maldive Islands to Samoa Islands and islands of Micronesia; southern Japan (type locality, Okinawa) to Great Barrier Reef, New South Wales, and Kermadec Islands; occurs in small aggregations, the females greatly outnumbering males; feeds on zooplankton.

CHISELTOOTH WRASSE

Pseudodax moluccanus (Valenciennes in C & V, 1840)

Dorsal rays IX,12; anal rays III,14; pectoral rays 15; lateral line continuous, without a sharp downward bend posteriorly, the pored scales 30–31; head scaled except for interorbital, snout, and chin; gill rakers 16–19; a pair of large spatulate incisiform teeth anteriorly in upper jaw, and 2 in lower, the second pair smaller; remaining teeth in jaws coalesced into a cutting ridge; pharyngeal dentition more like that of parrotfishes than of wrasses; body depth 2.6–3.3 in standard length; caudal fin rounded; adults gray with a reddish brown spot on each scale of body; a wash of orange-red on nape; upper lip yellow with a blue streak above that crosses lower cheek; teeth blue; caudal fin blackish with a narrow, blue posterior margin and a pale yellow bar at base; juveniles dark brown with 2 blue stripes on head and body, 1 dorsal and 1 ventral, narrower anteriorly and posteriorly. Reaches 25 cm. Red Sea and east coast of Africa to Society Islands, Marquesas Islands, and Tuamotu Archipelago; southern Japan to Great Barrier Reef and New Caledonia; juveniles have been observed cleaning other fishes.

TAHITIAN WRASSE
Pseudojuloides atavai Randall & Randall, 1981

Dorsal rays IX,11; anal rays III,12; pectoral rays 13; lateral line continuous, deflected sharply downward below posterior dorsal fin to straight peduncular portion, the pored scales 27; head scaleless; scales on chest and nape much smaller than those on body; gill rakers 16–18; a pair of canines anteriorly in jaws; side of jaws with chisel-like incisiform teeth; no canine at corner of mouth; body elongate, the depth 4.0–4.45 in standard length; caudal fin truncate to slightly rounded in females, slightly double emarginate in males, its length 1.3–1.5 in head length; females with a blue-green and black line from lower part of eye to upper base of caudal fin; head and body below line white, above orange to orange-red (may be blackish just above line); dorsal fin orange with a black spot on first 2.5 membranes; males with posterior two-thirds of body black, the centers of scales deep blue; anterior one-third light orange-red with a yellow spot on each scale; head orange-yellow with narrow violet-gray bands forming a reticulum; caudal fin black with a V-shaped orange area centroposteriorly; dorsal fin yellow with bluish black spot on each of first 3 membranes, and a narrow orange-red band at base; juveniles like females except head and body above blue line completely black. Reaches 14.5 cm. First discovered in Tahiti (*atavai* is Tahitian for pretty); collected later in the Tuamotu Archipelago, Pitcairn Islands, Rapa, and Austral Islands; M. P. Francis (pers. comm.) recently observed it at Niue. Known from depths of 12–30.5 m on seaward reefs. The author was surprised to photograph an initial phase underwater in Guam in 1986 (published by Myers, 1989); Senou et al. (1997) illustrated it from the Ogasawara Islands. However, photographs of a male of different color from *atavai* indicate that the Marianas-Ogasawara fish represents an undescribed species.

Society Islands/juvenile

Society Islands/female

Pitcairn Islands/male

Cebu, Philippines/female

Cebu, Philippines/male

SMALLTAIL WRASSE
Pseudojuloides cerasinus (Snyder, 1904)

Dorsal rays IX,11; anal rays III,12; pectoral rays 13; lateral line continuous, deflected sharply downward below posterior dorsal fin to straight peduncular portion, the pored scales 27; head scaleless; scales on chest and nape much smaller than those on body; gill rakers 15–19; dentition as in *P. atavai*; body elongate, the depth 3.8–4.44 in standard length; caudal fin truncate, slightly rounded, or slightly double emarginate, its length 1.55–1.9 in head length; females light red, shading to white or pale yellowish ventrally; snout often yellowish; males green dorsally, pale blue ventrally, with a yellow midlateral stripe on body broadly bordered by blue; head green with blue bands; caudal fin greenish yellow with a large, vertically elongate, blue-edged black spot posteriorly in fin. Largest specimen, 12 cm. East coast of Africa to the Hawaiian Islands (type locality, O'ahu), Line Islands, and Society Islands; southern Japan to Great Barrier Reef, New South Wales, Lord Howe Island, and New Caledonia; the report from Cocos Island, Costa Rica, by Allen & Robertson (1994) was considered a misidentification by Allen & Robertson (2002). Usually found on rubble bottom; recorded from depths of 2.5–61 m, but not often seen in less than 20 m.

433

Marquesas Islands/female

Marquesas Islands/male

FIERY WRASSE

Pseudojuloides pyrius Randall & Randall, 1981

Dorsal rays IX,11; anal rays III,12; pectoral rays 13; lateral line continuous, deflected sharply downward below posterior dorsal fin to straight peduncular portion, the pored scales 27; head scaleless; scales on chest and nape much smaller than those on body; gill rakers 14–17; dentition as in *P. atavai*; body elongate, the depth 4.15–4.7 in standard length; caudal fin truncate to slightly rounded, its length 1.55–1.6 in head length; females light red, faintly suffused with yellow, shading to white tinged

with pink on abdomen and chest; snout and upper lip yellow; dorsal and caudal fins pale yellow, the dorsal salmon pink basally; males with upper half of body bright yellow, the lower half abruptly red; head red except nape, which is yellow; dorsal and anal fins red with a whitish margin and black submaginal line, the dorsal with an anterior black spot; caudal fin red with a white crescentic area posteriorly. Largest collected, 8.5 cm. Known only from the Marquesas Islands; depth range 18.5–41 m; usually seen over open sand and rubble substrata.

TOROTAI WRASSE

Pseudolabrus torotai Russell & Randall, 1981

Dorsal rays IX,11; anal rays III,10; pectoral rays 12–13; lateral line continuous, bent downward below rear of dorsal fin to straight peduncular portion, the pored scales 25; head naked except for cheek and opercle; a low scaly sheath at base of dorsal and anal fins; gill rakers 20–22; a pair of large recurved canine teeth in upper jaw and 2 in lower, the second pair largest and recurved, side of jaws with 2 rows of conical teeth, the inner row smaller; a canine tooth at corner of mouth; body depth 2.9–3.0 in standard length; caudal fin truncate, the upper and lower corners slightly prolonged; pelvic fins short, not reaching anus; light red, shading to yellow ventrally on body, with 7 blackish bars, the first with small black spots, originating below first 2 dorsal spines, the last on base of caudal fin, the bars broader than pale interspaces dorsally, but equal or narrower ventrally; head above lower edge of eye with narrow, oblique

Rapa

blackish bands continuing as rows of spots on nape; dorsal fin red with blackish dots and a black spot anteriorly; anal and caudal fins light red, shading to yellow outwardly. Largest specimen, 19.2 cm. Known only from the island of Rapa (Torotai is the native name of the fish); collected from depths of 15–24 m. The more colorful *Pseudolabrus semifasciatus* (Rendahl) from Easter Island is a close relative.

CRYPTIC WRASSE

Pteragogus cryptus Randall, 1981

Dorsal rays X,9–10 (rarely 9); anal rays III,9; pectoral rays 12–13 (rarely 12); lateral line continuous, bent downward below fifth dorsal soft ray to straight peduncular portion, the pored scales 23–24 (rarely 23); head scaled except snout, interorbital, and chin; a row of elongate scales basally on dorsal and anal fins; scales on chest not much smaller than those on rest of body; gill rakers 12–17; vertical margin of preopercle with numerous sharp serrae; 2 pairs of canine teeth anteriorly in jaws, the anterior pair projecting, the second outcurved (strongly so in males); body depth 2.3–2.6 in standard length; membrane of first 4 dorsal spines prolonged as long filaments in males (filaments may be much longer than spines); caudal fin rounded; pelvic fins nearly or just reaching origin of anal fin; light red, the edges of scales variously white to pale pink, with a white streak from front of snout through dorsal part of eye to upper end of gill opening; an oblong, yellow-edged dark spot on opercle; anterior nostril in a small, dark brown spot; a small dark brown spot behind eye; a few small white spots along lateral line; scattered small dark brown spots present or absent on body (if present, some are on

Marshall Islands

lateral line); a small dark brown spot on first membrane of dorsal fin. Largest specimen, 9.5 cm. Red Sea (type locality), but no Indian Ocean records; western Pacific from Taiwan to Great Barrier Reef and New Caledonia, east to Samoa Islands and islands of Micronesia; very secretive, often hiding in soft coral or algae; known from depths of 4–67 m. Pacific population with modally 1 fewer gill rakers and smaller maximum size. Donaldson (1995) described the courtship and spawning.

434

COCKEREL WRASSE
Pteragogus enneacanthus (Bleeker, 1853)

Dorsal rays IX,11; anal rays III,9; pectoral rays 13; lateral-line scales 24; head scaled except snout, interorbital, and chin; a row of elongate scales basally on dorsal and anal fins; gill rakers 14–15 (3 counts); vertical margin of preopercle with numerous sharp serrae; dentition as in *P. cryptus*; body depth 2.3–2.5 in standard length; membranes of first 2 dorsal spines prolonged as filaments in males (filaments usually not as long as spines); caudal fin rounded; pelvic fins nearly or just reaching origin of anal fin; light red to brownish red, mottled with darker red, with longitudinal rows of interconnected whitish spots following centers of scales; an oblong dark green to black spot on opercle narrowly rimmed in orange and broadly in dark green; a few small, dark brown spots behind eye; small white and dark brown spots along lateral line; irregular, vertical, pale blue lines below eye and on operculum, forming a reticulum in large males. Reaches 15 cm. Taiwan to Great Barrier Reef and New South Wales, east to New Caledonia and Guam; type locality, Ambon, Molucca Islands. Like others of the genus, very cryptic, hiding among soft corals and algae. *Pteragogus amboinensis* (Bleeker) is a synonym based on the male color phase.

REDSHOULDER WRASSE
Stethojulis bandanensis (Bleeker, 1851)

Dorsal rays IX,11; anal rays III,11; pectoral rays 14–15 (rarely 15); lateral line continuous, deflected downward below soft portion of dorsal fin to straight peduncular portion, the pored scales 25; suborbital pores from behind center of eye to below front of orbit 9–13; head scaleless, no sheath of scales basally on dorsal and anal fins, and scales on chest not small (true of other *Stethojulis*); gill rakers 27–30 (modally 28); teeth incisiform, uniserial, and close-set (also generic); body depth 3.0–3.35 in standard length; caudal fin short and slightly rounded (generic); base of pectoral fins strongly oblique (generic); pelvic fins short (generic); initial phase greenish or grayish brown on dorsal half of head and body, finely dotted with pale blue-green to white; lower half of body whitish, the basal half of each scale blackish, with a broad reddish stripe superimposed on upper part of this zone; a semicircular, bright red spot above base of pectoral fin; 1–3 (usually 2) small blue-edged black spots midlaterally on posterior part of caudal peduncle; terminal male dark green to olive dorsally, light blue to light green ventrally, the 2 zones separated by a blue line; head with 4 black-edged blue lines, the uppermost continuing along base of dorsal fin, the second from behind eye to anterior body, the third from upper lip to below eye, dorsal to red spot above pectoral-fin base, and ending near middle of body, and the fourth across lower head. Largest specimen, 11.2 cm. Eastern Indian Ocean from Andaman Sea to southwestern Australia, including Christmas Island and Cocos-Keeling Islands; western and central Pacific except the Hawaiian Islands; also from islands of the tropical eastern Pacific. Feeds by quick bites of sand or algal-covered rock and extracting the tiny animals within, chiefly crustaceans, gastropods, polychaetes and other worms, and foraminifera. *Stethojulis linearis* Schultz is a synonym based on the terminal-male phase.

Taiwan/female

Taiwan/male

Papua New Guinea/juvenile

Marshall Islands/initial phase

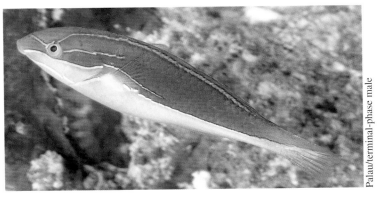

Palau/terminal-phase male

435

Marquesas Islands/initial phase

Marquesas Islands/terminal-phase male

Fiji/initial phase

MARQUESAN WRASSE
Stethojulis marquesensis Randall, 2000
Dorsal rays IX,11; anal rays III,11; pectoral rays 14–15 (rarely 15); lateral-line scales 25; gill rakers 26–28; suborbital pores from behind center of eye to below front of orbit 14–20; body depth 3.1–3.45 in standard length; upper half of head and body of initial phase brown, finely dotted with white, with an indistinct whitish line from snout, passing above eye, and ending below posterior part of dorsal fin; lower half of body whitish with a brown stripe across side at level of lower edge of pectoral fin, ending on ventral one-third of caudal-fin base; a pupil-size brown spot on upper base of caudal fin; terminal males with upper part of body dark olive-brown, shading to blackish brown posteriorly; ventral part of body bluish white; a blue band beneath basal part of pectoral fin, followed by a broad blackish band that curves downward onto abdomen; head dull yellowish green dorsally, light yellowish green ventrally, with a large, dark blue-green area over opercle and 2 blue lines, one from snout through upper part of eye across upper part of operculum, and the other from above corner of mouth to beneath eye. Largest specimen, 10.3 cm. Known only from the Marquesas Islands; occurs mainly in bays on mixed sand and rock substratum; specimens collected from less than 1 to 10.5 m.

Fiji/terminal-phase male

SOUTH PACIFIC WRASSE
Stethojulis notialis (Randall, 2000)
Dorsal rays IX,11; anal rays III,11; pectoral rays 13–14 (rarely 14); lateral-line scales 25; gill rakers 22–26; suborbital pores from behind center of eye to below front of orbit 6–8; body depth 3.6–3.9 in standard length; initial phase with a yellow stripe from front of snout, passing over eye and broadening as it continues along upper side of body to base of caudal fin; upper half of body below yellow stripe black with irregular, lengthwise, pale blue lines; lower half of body white with a small black spot on each scale and numerous gray flecks; terminal males green to blue-green along side of body shading to yellow dorsally and pale green ventrally, with a series of 4 or 5 short black bars in middle of body; a black spot at upper base and axil of pectoral fin with a yellow spot above; a small black spot on opercular flap; dark-edged blue lines as follows: first above eye along base of dorsal fin to upper part of caudal fin, second across front of interorbital space, passing through eye, across upper part of operculum, and

curving around to end behind a black spot on opercular flap; third from upper lip below eye to pectoral-fin base, continuing posteriorly to caudal-fin base (though often interrupted by a gap posterior to pectoral-fin base); a short blue line below pectoral-fin base. Largest specimen examined, 9.6 cm. Known to date from Fiji (type locality), New Caledonia, Norfolk Island, and Vanuatu (M. P. Francis, pers. comm.); occurs mainly on reef flats or around shallow patch reefs in sandy areas; all specimens from 0.5 to 5 m. Differs from the similar *Stethojulis interrupta* (Bleeker) in having a higher gill-raker count (20–24 in *interrupta*), in the yellow stripe of the initial phase, and in the black bars of the terminal male.

436

STRIPEBELLY WRASSE

Stethojulis strigiventer (Bennett, 1833)

Dorsal rays IX,11; anal rays III,11; pectoral rays 14–16 (rarely 14 or 16); lateral-line scales 25; gill rakers 24–30 (modally 26); suborbital pores from behind center of eye to below front of orbit 8–15; body depth 3.3–3.85 in standard length; initial phase greenish to brownish gray dorsally with faint, whitish, longitudinal lines, white ventrally with dark gray longitudinal lines; a small blue-edged dark spot at base of caudal fin above lateral line, and another at rear base of dorsal fin; terminal male greenish to yellowish brown dorsally, white ventrally, with dark-edged blue lines as follows: top of head along base of dorsal fin; snout through eye and upper end of gill opening to middle of caudal fin; upper lip to dorsal edge of pectoral-fin base; and edge of gill opening beneath lower pectoral-fin base to middle of body; region of overlap of the lower 2 blue lines at pectoral-fin base bright red; a small black spot at upper end of opercular flap; a small black spot at caudal-fin base. Attains 11 cm. East coast of Africa to the Society Islands, Tuamotu Archipelago, and Austral Islands; southern Japan to southwestern Australia, New South Wales, and New Caledonia; type locality, Mauritius. A shallow-water species that is found more often on sand substrata, seagrass beds, or algal flats than on coral reefs. Harmelin-Vivien (1979) collected 64 specimens for stomach-content analysis; she found small benthic copepods (primarily harpacticoids) as the principal prey; also of importance were foraminifera, ostracods, tanaids, and amphipods. *Stethojulis renardi* (Bleeker) is a synonym based on the terminal-male phase.

Guam/initial phase

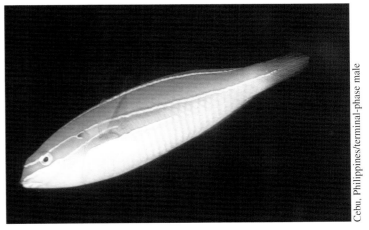

Cebu, Philippines/terminal-phase male

RAINBOW WRASSE

Suezichthys arquatus Russell, 1985

Dorsal rays IX,11; anal rays III,10; pectoral rays 13–14; lateral line continuous, deflected downward behind rear of dorsal fin, the pored scales 25–26; scales above lateral line 2.5; a low scaly sheath at base of dorsal and anal fins; gill rakers 18–20; body depth 3.3–3.85 in standard length; caudal fin of initial phase rounded, of terminal males rhomboid with the corners slightly protruding; initial phase yellowish brown dorsally with blue longitudinal lines, shading to pale yellow ventrally with rows of pale blue spots; a small black spot anteriorly and posteriorly in dorsal fin; 7 pale bars present or absent dorsally on body; terminal males olive with longitudinal blue lines dorsally, rows of blue spots on lower side, and a narrow white stripe on posterior half of body extending into middle of caudal fin; a male illustrated by Russell (1985) with median fins largely bright red. Largest specimen, 14.3 cm. Southern Queensland, New South Wales; northern New Zealand (type locality, Poor Knights Islands), Kermadec Islands, Lord Howe Island, Norfolk Island, and New Caledonia; also recorded from Japan from Izu Peninula, Honshu (Araga et al., 1988), to the Ogasawara Islands (Randall et al., 1997b). Of the name, Russell wrote, "This species is named arquatus from the Latin word for rainbow in reference to its beautiful, vivid, and many-hued coloration."

Lord Howe Island/initial phase

Lord Howe Island/terminal-phase male

DE VIS' WRASSE
Suezichthys devisi (Whitley, 1941)

Dorsal rays IX,11; anal rays III,10; pectoral rays 13–14; lateral line continuous, deflected downward behind rear of dorsal fin, the pored scales 25–26; scales above lateral line 1.5; no low scaly sheath at base of dorsal and anal fins; gill rakers 15–20; body slender, the depth 4.3–5.3 in standard length; caudal fin slightly rounded; initial phase pink dorsally, white ventrally, with an orange stripe, often dark-edged anteriorly and sometimes interrupted by pale bars, from eye along upper side, ending in a small black spot on caudal-fin base just above lateral line; a dark, iridescent blue spot in stripe above pectoral fin (lacking in small individuals); terminal male greenish yellow to orange-pink dorsally, yellowish white ventrally with an olive-green to blackish stripe on upper side extending into caudal fin, and the same dark blue spot within stripe as in initial phase; dorsal fin pink with 2 close-set, dusky blue stripes and a small black spot on first membrane; caudal fin with 2 orange-yellow bands that converge to form a V; axil of pectoral fin blackish, and upper edge of fin base with a small black spot. Reaches 16 cm. South-

New Caledonia/initial phase

ern Great Barrier Reef to New South Wales and New Caledonia; type locality, Frazer Island, Queensland. Usually found in sheltered waters of bays on sand near reefs. Formerly believed to be a synonym of *Stethojulis gracilis* (Steindachner & Döderlein) of Japan, Korea, and Taiwan, hence 1 antitropical species, but B. C. Russell (pers. comm.) now separates them (*gracilis* lacks the dark caudal spot).

Tuamotu Archipelago/initial phase

Papua New Guinea/initial phase

Taiwan/terminal-phase male

BLUNTHEADED WRASSE
Thalassoma amblycephalum (Bleeker, 1856)

Dorsal rays VIII,13; anal rays III,11; pectoral rays 15; lateral-line scales 26–27; head naked; scales of chest about half size of those on body (true of all *Thalassoma*); gill rakers 16–19; jaws with 1 pair of canine teeth anteriorly, followed by a row of progressively shorter conical teeth; no canine tooth at corner of mouth (dentition essentially the same for all *Thalassoma*); body slender, the depth 3.8–4.2 in standard length; caudal fin in initial phase truncate to slightly emarginate, becoming lunate in large males; initial phase with a broad blackish stripe from snout through eye to upper caudal-fin base; body above stripe greenish

to yellowish, below white; lobes of caudal fin with an orange band that is broader basally; terminal males reddish with vertical green lines on body; nape and body below first 4 or 5 dorsal spines yellow or yellow-green; head green with 2 golden lines; pectoral fins yellow with a large, elongate, black-edged blue spot on outer part. Attains 16 cm. East coast of Africa to Line Islands and French Polynesia except Rapa and Austral Islands; southern Japan to Great Barrier Reef, New South Wales, Lord Howe Island, Norfolk Island, northern New Zealand, and Kermadec Islands; type locality, Java. Occurs in aggregations over shallow reefs; feeds on zooplankton. Initial phase far more numerous than terminal males and often observed in group spawning.

438

Line Islands/initial phase

Bali/terminal-phase male

SIXBAR WRASSE
Thalassoma hardwicke (Bennett, 1830)
Dorsal rays VIII,13; anal rays III,11; pectoral rays 15–17; lateral-line scales 25; head naked except for a patch of 4–8 small scales dorsally on opercle; gill rakers 22–25; body depth 2.9–3.2 in standard length; caudal fin truncate in young, emarginate in adults; initial phase light green with 6 wedge-shaped, slightly diagonal, dark bars dorsally on body that are progressively shorter posteriorly; head light green with pink bands; terminal males green dorsally with scattered pink spots on scales, blue to blue-green ven-

HEISER'S WRASSE
Thalassoma heiseri Randall & Edwards, 1984
Dorsal rays VIII,13; anal rays III,11; pectoral rays 16; lateral-line scales 25; head naked except for a small patch of scales dorsally on opercle; gill rakers 21–27; body depth 3.45–4.05 in standard length; caudal fin varying from slightly rounded in juveniles to deeply emarginate in large males; initial phase orangish brown dorsally, abruptly white below, with a narrow green stripe from behind upper edge of eye along side of body just below lateral line to upper base of caudal fin, the stripe breaking into a series of vertically elongate spots over most of its length on body; an indistinct salmon pink stripe extending posteriorly from beneath lower part of pectoral fin; a pale blue-green band from upper lip across head to upper base of pectoral fin, and an angular blue-green band on opercle; dorsal fin with a black spot on first 2 membranes; a small bluish black spot at upper base of

MOON WRASSE
Thalassoma lunare (Linnaeus, 1758)
Dorsal rays VIII,13; anal rays III,11; pectoral rays 15; lateral-line scales 25; head naked except for a small patch of scales dorsally on opercle; gill rakers 18–20; body depth 3.1–3.7 in standard length; caudal fin varying from truncate in young to strongly lunate in large terminal males; initial phase green, shading to blue ventrally with vertical red lines on body; head green with rose-pink bands, those dorsally very irregular; caudal fin pinkish gray with an irregular black spot on midbase; a small black spot basally in middle of caudal fin; males entirely green on body, the red lines broken into segments, the head blue dorsally; rest of head about equally divided in green and lavender-pink bands; no black spot on dorsal fin or caudal-fin base, the caudal-fin lobes with a lavender-pink band edged in blue-green, the central posterior part of fin a large semicircular area of bright yellow; pectoral fins blue with a broad, deep pink band in upper part; males capable of quickly changing color to blue; juveniles similar to initial phase; may have 7 pale bars dorsally on body; caudal spot large and in a blue area, the dorsal spot rimmed in pale green. Maximum length, 25 cm. Red Sea

trally, with an irregular midlateral pink stripe posteriorly, the 6 bars solid black, extending into base of dorsal fin; 5 or 6 broad pink bands on head; 2 oblique, mixed black and dark reddish bands on nape; a black stripe in dorsal fin, and a black spot anteriorly in anal fin. Attains 18 cm. East coast of Africa to Line Islands and French Polynesia except Rapa and the Marquesas Islands; southern Japan to Great Barrier Reef, New South Wales, Lord Howe Island, Norfolk Island, and New Caledonia; type locality, Sri Lanka. An inshore reef species, ranging to about 15 m. *Thalassoma schwanefeldii* (Bleeker) is a synonym.

Pitcairn Islands/initial phase

pectoral fin with a blue band across rest of base, preceded by a pink band; only color note taken of an adult male: "reddish and bright blue-green; basal half of caudal fin white, the outer half black." Largest specimen, 13.7 cm. Known only from the Pitcairn Islands (type locality) and Temoe Atoll, Gambier Group, Tuamotu Archipelago; specimens were collected from seaward and lagoon reefs in 0.3–15 m.

Cebu, Philippines/terminal male

Papua New Guinea/juvenile

Line Islands/initial phase

and east coast of Africa to the Line Islands and Micronesia; southern Japan to Great Barrier Reef, New South Wales, Lord Howe Island, Norfolk Island, New Caledonia, Kermadec Islands, northern New Zealand, and Tonga; type locality, India. A very active and bold coral-reef fish (one bit the author's earlobe).

439

Mauritius/initial phase

Hawaiian Islands/terminal-phase male

CHRISTMAS WRASSE

Thalassoma trilobatum (Lacepède, 1801)

Dorsal rays VIII,13; anal rays III,11; pectoral rays 15–17 (usually 16); lateral-line scales 25; head naked except for a small patch of scales dorsally on opercle; gill rakers 17–24 (usually 21–23); body depth 2.75–3.6 in standard length; caudal fin of initial phase slightly rounded to truncate, of terminal males truncate to slightly double emarginate; initial phase colored almost the same as *Thalassoma purpureum*; the pink to maroon mark on side of snout in front of eye not a vertical line or Y but in a C shape; body of terminal males orange anteriorly, soon shading to red, with 2 longitudinal series of vertical green rectangles, every fourth pair of upper series joining as a single green bar across back; head orange to orangish brown; caudal fin yellowish green with blue upper and lower margins, the outer one-third of rays blue. Largest specimen, 30 cm. East coast of Africa to the Hawaiian Islands, islands of French Polynesia, and the Pitcairn Islands; Ryukyu Islands to Great Barrier Reef, New South Wales, Lord Howe Island, Norfolk Island, Kermadec Islands; type locality, Mauritius (Bauchot, 1963: 83). Also an inshore species; generally found on reefs and rocky shores exposed to wave action. Often identified as *T. fuscum* (Lacepède), but this name invalid as a homonym.

Cebu, Philippines

Maisel Islands, Indonesia

WHITEBANDED SHARPNOSE WRASSE

Wetmorella albofasciata Schultz & Marshall, 1954

Dorsal rays IX,10; anal rays III,8; pectoral rays 12; lateral line interrupted, the pored scales 13–15 + 5–7; head with large scales; preopercular margin scaled over; gill rakers 11–16; head pointed, the dorsal profile straight; body depth 2.8–3.3 in standard length; longest dorsal spine 1.9–2.25 in head length; third anal spine 2.0–2.3 in head; grayish to reddish brown with 3 white bars narrower than pupil on body and 3 radiating from eye; a large black spot on abdomen beween pelvic fins, and one on soft portion of dorsal, anal, and pelvic fins. Largest specimen, 5.5 cm. Tanzania to Hawaiian Islands and Society Islands, but not many records between: Micronesia, Samoa Islands, Fiji, Great Barrier Reef, Scott Reef, Agalega Islands, and Comoro Islands; type locality, Mabul Island, Philippines. Specimens collected from depths of 10–42 m, but most from more than 30 m; rarely seen underwater (only fleetingly in the deep recesses of caves).

SHARPNOSE WRASSE

Wetmorella nigropinnata (Seale, 1901)

Dorsal rays IX,10; anal rays III,8; pectoral rays 12; lateral line interrupted, the pored scales 13–15 + 5–7; head with large scales; preopercular margin scaled over; gill rakers 12–17; head pointed, the dorsal profile straight; body depth 2.55–3.15 in standard length; longest dorsal spine 1.7–2.05 in head length; third anal spine 1.7–2.1 in head; adults reddish brown with a dark-edged yellow bar on head behind and adjacent to eye and a second one at front of caudal peduncle; black spots on fins and ventrally on abdomen as in *W. albofasciata*; juveniles with 2 additional broad pale bars on body. Attains 8 cm. Red Sea to the islands of French Polynesia except Rapa and the Austral Islands, the Pitcairn Islands, and islands of Micronesia (type locality, Guam); Ryukyu Islands to Great Barrier Reef and New Caledonia; known from reefs at depths of 1–30 m; very secretive and rarely seen. *Wetmorella philippina* Fowler & Bean, *W. ocellata* Schultz & Marshall, and *W. triocellata* Schultz & Marshall are synonyms (Randall, 1983b).

REDBAND RAZORFISH

Xyrichtys halsteadi Randall & Lobel, 2003

Dorsal rays IX,12, the first 2 dorsal rays flexible and shorter than dorsal soft rays; anal rays III,12; pectoral rays 13; lateral line interrupted, the pored scales 20 + 5 (plus 2 pored scales on caudal-fin base); gill rakers 17–20; body depth 3.1–3.35 in standard length and very compressed; dorsal profile of head smoothly convex, forming an angle of about 45° to horizontal axis of body; anterior edge of head angular; juveniles and females whitish with a red band from above eye along back above lateral line; male purplish blue on head and along back, becoming pink posteriorly and ventrally; a prominent, pale-edged black spot on and below lateral line above pectoral fin. Largest male, 14 cm. Collected from the D'Entrecasteaux Islands, Papua New Guinea (type locality), Mariana Islands, and Wake Island at depths of 30–49 m; photographed underwater in Tahiti in 15 m. Typically found on sand or sand-rubble substrata into which it dives when approached.

Papua New Guinea/female

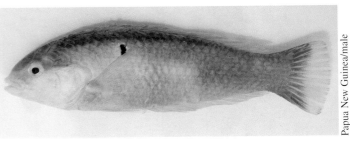

Papua New Guinea/male

Bumphead Parrotfish, *Bolbometopon muricatum*, Bali

PARROTFISHES
(SCARIDAE)

The parrotfishes are well named for their bright colors and the fusion of their teeth into beak-like plates. Ten genera and 90 species are currently recognized (Parenti & Randall, 2000), but a few species remain to be described. The family is clearly derived from the wrasses. In fact, some authors have preferred to clas-sify the parrotfishes as a subfamily of the Labridae. Bellwood (1994) is followed here in maintaining the group as a separate family, and his classification of the genera is accepted. Most authors have divided the parrotfishes into 2 subfamilies, the Sparisomatinae and the Scarinae; however, this division, according to Bellwood, does not seem justified. The fusion of the teeth into dental plates is the most unifying character of the family. Except for the genus *Calotomus*, these plates have a median suture, and there may be 1 to 3 sharp conical teeth on the side of the plates in adults. Also unique is the pharyngeal dentition in the throat; there are 2 interlocking upper pharyngeal bones with 1 to 3 longitudinal rows of molariform teeth that form a convex surface that bears against the molar-studded concave surface of the single lower pharyngeal bone. In addition to dentition, parrotfishes differ from wrasses in the loss of the supraneural (predorsal) bones, lack of a true stomach, very long intestine, and by being herbivorous. All species of the family have a continuous unnotched dorsal fin of IX,10 dorsal rays, and III,9 anal rays. The scales are large and cycloid; the lateral line is interrupted, the anterior series of pored scales 17–20, and the posterior midlateral series 5–7. The most useful meristic characters to identify species are the number of pectoral rays, which vary from 13–16, the number of median predorsal scales, varying from 2–7, the number of horizontal rows of scales on the cheek, and the number of scales within these rows, especially the lowermost. Unfortunately, closely related species may have no meristic differences, and other morphological characters may be lacking. The result is heavy reliance on coloration, in particular the life color. Faded museum specimens may prove impossible to identify. Parrotfishes are shallow-water fishes; most are closely associated with coral reefs. They feed mainly by scraping algae from rock or dead-coral surfaces. A few species are more often found in seagrass beds or algal flats. Bellwood & Choat (1990) identified 2 groups of parrotfishes based on jaw and tooth structure and their impact on the coral reef. The excavators include the monotypic genera *Bolbometopon* and *Cetoscarus* and the newly recognized genus *Chlorurus* (for *C. sordidus* and allies); with their more powerful jaws and stronger dental plates, these fishes remove part of the limestone or coral as they feed. The other group, called scrapers, ingests less inorganic matter with the surface algae. Some species feed in part on the algae growing on compact sand surfaces, taking in sand with the algal food. Some of the larger species feed in part on live coral and may leave a characteristic mark from the median suture of their dental plates. Parrotfishes are able to utilize the last stubble of algae on a reef that is no longer available to other grazing herbivores. The algae that is ingested with fragments of limestone and sand is triturated in the pharyngeal mill and hence made more digestible; the limestone fragments are ground into sand, and the sand into finer sand. Parrotfishes, therefore, are major producers of sand in coral-reef areas. Like the wrasses, juvenile parrotfishes are often very different in color from adults, and they may go through more than one color phase as juveniles (Bellwood & Choat, 1989). Also, like many of the wrasses, there are usually two strikingly different color phases as adults. The first mature phase, sometimes only female (monandric), but more often both male and female (diandric), is called the initial phase; it is generally drab, mainly brown or gray. Males in this phase are termed primary males. Females of most species in this phase are able to alter their sex to male and undergo a change in color to the terminal phase; primary males may also change to the terminal color form. Terminal males are more brightly—even gaudily—colored, the color usually dominated by green or blue-green. Initial-phase fish may be seen spawning in large aggregations that consist mainly of primary males. Terminal males tend to establish sexual territories, maintain a harem, and spawn individually with single females following a brief courtship display. In both pair spawning and group spawning, the eggs and sperm are released at the peak of a very rapid upward rush (Randall & Randall, 1963). Like the wrasses, normal swimming is achieved by the sculling of the pectoral fins, but when speed is needed, as during the spawning rush, to chase a rival male, or to escape a predator, the tail is brought into action. Scarid fishes sleep at night, usually well hidden in small caves or beneath ledges. Some species may have an accumulation of mucus around them at night referred to as the mucous cocoon; it is visible because of the particulate matter that adheres to it. The hypothesis that this might serve to deter nocturnal predators such as morays or repel ectoparasites has not been demonstrated.

A male Palenose Parrotfish, *Scarus psittacus*, asleep in its mucous cocoon.

Sabah (night)

Seribu Islands, Indonesia/juvenile

Sabah (night)

BUMPHEAD PARROTFISH
Bolbometopon muricatum (Valenciennes in C & V, 1840)
Pectoral rays usually 16; median predorsal scales 2–5 (usually 4); 3 rows of scales on cheek, the lower row with 1 or 2 scales; 1 row of scales on interopercle; dental plates largely exposed (only partly covered by lips), each of the fused teeth forming a small bump on plate surface; no conical teeth on side of plates; a prominent convexity on forehead of adults (evident on individuals as small as 25 cm); body deep, 2.05–2.5 in standard length (depth increasing with growth); caudal fin rounded, the lobes slightly prolonged in adults; adults dull green, the front of the head pale yellowish to pink; juveniles greenish to brown with 5 vertical rows of small whitish spots. Largest of the parrotfishes; attains 120 cm; one of 117 cm weighed 46 kg. Red Sea and east coast of Africa to the Line Islands and Samoa Islands; Ryukyu Islands to the Great Barrier Reef and New Caledonia; type locality, Java. Usually seen in small aggregations; difficult to approach underwater. Feeds on both benthic algae and live coral; one was observed by the author in the Line Islands to feed about half the time on coral.

445

Hawaiian Islands/initial phase

Hawaiian Islands/terminal-phase male

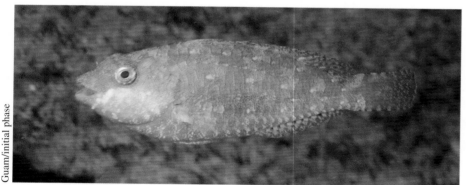

Guam/initial phase

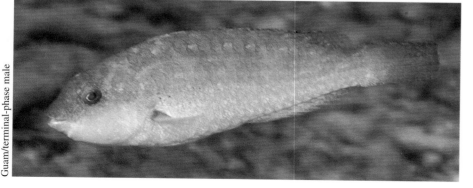

Guam/terminal-phase male

STAREYE PARROTFISH
Calotomus carolinus (Valenciennes in C & V, 1840)

Pectoral rays 13; median predorsal scales 3–4 (usually 4); a single row of 4 or 5 scales on cheek below eye; teeth not fully fused to form dental plates, the individual flattened teeth readily apparent on outer surface of jaws, imbricate, the tips of outer row forming a jagged cutting edge; lips nearly covering teeth; body depth 2.2–2.75 in standard length; caudal fin slightly rounded in juveniles, truncate in subadults and truncate with lobes prolonged in adults; initial phase mottled, dark orangish brown, shading ventrally to pale orangish; base of pectoral fins dark brown; posterior edge of caudal fin narrowly white; body of terminal males a mixture of brownish red and blue-green; head blue-green with orange-pink bands radiating from eye. Reported to 50 cm. East coast of Africa to the Hawaiian Islands, Pitcairn Islands, and throughout Micronesia (type locality, Caroline Islands); Ryukyu Islands and Ogasawara Islands to the Great Barrier Reef and New Caledonia; also known from the tropical eastern Pacific. Often misidentified as *Calotomus spinidens* (see next account). Bruce & Randall (1985) revised the genus *Calotomus*; they listed 8 synonyms, among them *Callyodon sandwicensis* Valenciennes and *C. brachysoma* Bleeker. Robertson et al. (1982) described the spawning at Aldabra Atoll.

RAGGEDTOOTH PARROTFISH
Calotomus spinidens (Quoy & Gaimard, 1824)

Pectoral rays 13; median predorsal scales 4; a single row of 4 or 5 scales on cheek below eye; dentition as in *C. carolinus*; lips nearly covering teeth; body slender, 2.7–3.1 in standard length; dorsal spines flexible; caudal fin rounded; initial phase mottled reddish to grayish brown, often with 3 longitudinal rows of whitish spots, and sometimes with faint broad stripes; upper and lower edges of caudal fin with small dusky spots; terminal males with faint orangish spots on body, and small orange spots and short lines on head; a blackish bar at pectoral-fin base, and a broad dark margin on anal fin. Largest reported, 19 cm. East coast of Africa to islands of Micronesia, Fiji, and Tonga; type locality, Waigeo, Indonesia. Lives in seagrass beds or on substrata with heavy algal growth; able to alter its color quickly to match its surroundings.

SPOTTED PARROTFISH

Cetoscarus ocellatus (Valenciennes in C & V, 1840)

Pectoral rays 14–15 (usually 14); median predorsal scales 5–7 (usually 6); 3 rows of scales on cheek, the lower row with 3–7 scales; outer surface of dental plates nodular (smooth on *Chlorurus*, *Hipposcarus*, and *Scarus*); no conical teeth on side of dental plates; lips largely covering dental plates; snout long, 1.8–2.2 in head length; caudal fin rounded in juveniles, emarginate in adults; head of initial phase purplish to reddish brown, finely spotted with black ventrally; body with a broad, pale yellowish zone dorsally, bluish gray below, the scales rimmed and spotted with black; median fins brownish red, the caudal with a whitish crescent posteriorly; terminal males green, the scales rimmed with pink, the head and anterior body with numerous small pink spots except below an orange line from corner of mouth to pectoral base and across upper abdomen, where solid green with a broad, pink, longitudinal ventral band; juveniles white with a broad, dark-edged orange bar covering head except snout and chin, a large, orange-rimmed black spot anteriorly in dorsal fin, and a broad, submarginal orange band in caudal fin. Attains about 80 cm. East coast of Africa to the Society Islands, Tuamotu Archipelago, and islands of Micronesia; type locality, Caroline Islands. Closely related to *Cetoscarus bicolor* (Rüppell) of the Red Sea (Randall & Choat, in prep.). The name *C. ocellatus* is based on the juvenile phase.

447

BLEEKER'S PARROTFISH

Chlorurus bleekeri (de Beaufort in Weber & de Beaufort, 1940)
Pectoral rays 15; median predorsal scales 4; 2 rows of scales on cheek; 1 or 2 conical teeth on side of upper dental plate; lips not covering dental plates; caudal fin truncate; initial phase dark brown with a narrow reddish bar on each scale (reduced to a spot on caudal peduncle), often with broad whitish to pale yellowish bars (pale bars can be quickly turned on or off); upper lip with a narrow orange margin and dull blue-green submarginal band; chin orange with 3 transverse, dull blue-green bands; dorsal edge of orbit blue; pectoral fins and unscaled part of caudal fin brownish red; terminal males green with a salmon pink bar on each scale; a large, white to pale yellow, quadrangular area bordered with green on cheek, linked anteriorly to 2 narrow blue-green bands on chin; juveniles dark gray-brown, shading to whitish posteriorly, often with 2 or 3 faint whitish stripes. Attains about 30 cm. Philippines to Great Barrier Reef, east to Fiji, Samoa Islands, and islands of Micronesia; type locality, Ternate, Molucca Islands. *Scarus cyanotaenia* Bleeker from Batavia (now Jakarta) is a probable synonym based on the initial phase.

448

Marshall Islands/male

REEFCREST PARROTFISH
Chlorurus frontalis (Valenciennes in C & V, 1840)
Pectoral rays 15; median predorsal scales 4; 2 rows of scales on cheek; adults with 2–4 conical teeth on side of upper dental plate; dental plates exposed, often with algae growing basally; dorsal profile of snout very steep; caudal fin of adults emarginate to lunate; unusual in not having 2 very different adult color patterns; green with a salmon pink bar on each scale; irregular salmon pink to lavender bands extending from eye except ven-

trally, a very broad one dorsally from eye and a broad oblique one onto snout; a similar broad band on chin. Reaches 50 cm. Ryukyu Islands to the Great Barrier Reef (where rare), east to islands of Micronesia, Line Islands, Tuamotu Archipelago, and Pitcairn Islands; type locality, Strong Island (= Kusiae), Caroline Islands. Appears to be absent from the islands of the East Indies; generally seen in small schools on reef flats. *Pseudoscarus jonesi* Streets, *Scarus lupus* Fowler, *Scarus brighami* Bryan & Herre, and *Callyodon latax* Jordan & Seale are synonyms.

Sulawesi/initial phase

Halmahera, Indonesia/terminal-phase male

REDTAIL PARROTFISH
Chlorurus japanensis (Bloch, 1789)
Pectoral rays 15; median predorsal scales 4; 2 rows of scales on cheek; no conical teeth on side of lower dental plate, 0–2 on upper plate of initial phase and usually 2 on terminal males; lips only slightly covering dental plates; front of head strongly rounded; caudal fin of initial phase slightly rounded to truncate, of terminal males slightly emarginate; initial phase dark brown, the caudal fin red with a narrow black margin; terminal male pale yellowish to pale greenish yellow with a pink bar on each scale, becoming blue-green on caudal peduncle, the pink bars

shortened to spots; a broad, oblique, dusky purplish zone overlying color pattern from nape and anterior body across pectoral region onto abdomen; top of head purplish gray; 3 blue-green bands extending posteriorly from eye and 2 anteriorly, the lower bifurcating, its upper branch continuing as a band across front of snout, the lower branch dividing again on chin. Reaches 30 cm. Ryukyu Islands to Great Barrier Reef (rare), east to Samoa Islands; only Palau in Micronesia; type locality given as Japan, but more likely Java. One of the most wary of the parrotfishes. *Callyodon pyrrhurus* Jordan & Seale and *C. abacurus* Jordan & Seale are synonyms.

Marshall Islands/juvenile

Marshall Islands

Marshall Islands/male (night)

STEEPHEAD PARROTFISH
Chlorurus microrhinos (Bleeker, 1854)

Pectoral rays 15–17 (usually 16); median predorsal scales 4; 3 rows of scales on cheek, the lower row with 1–8 (usually 5 or 6) scales; adults with 1 or 2 conical teeth on side of upper dental plate; dental plates broadly exposed, often with algae growing basally; dorsal profile of snout and forehead of adults very steep (the forehead may bulge anterior to mouth in large males); caudal fin of juveniles slightly rounded, of adults truncate with prolonged lobes; adults of both sexual phases green with a pink bar on each scale of body (lost in large males); a blue-green band on upper lip, and a broader one on chin joining posteriorly to an irregular band across cheek; head above this band purplish; dental plates blue-green; an occasional color morph red, shading to yellow ventrally, with yellow fins; juveniles dark brown with 3 narrow, pale yellowish stripes. Reaches 70 cm. Ryukyu Islands and Ogasawara Islands to the Great Barrier Reef, Lord Howe Island, and New Caledonia, east to the islands of Oceania except the Hawaiian Islands and Easter Island; type locality, Java. Often misidentified as *Chlorurus gibbus* (Rüppell), now restricted to the Red Sea. The similar *C. strongylocephalus* (Bleeker) occurs in the Indian Ocean east to western Indonesia.

450

Tonga/juvenile

Great Barrier Reef/initial

Hawaiian Islands/terminal-phase male

BULLETHEAD PARROTFISH
Chlorurus sordidus (Forsskål, 1775)

Pectoral rays 14–15 (rarely 14); median predorsal scales 4, progressively larger anteriorly; 2 rows of scales on cheek; no conical teeth on side of lower dental plates; large adults with 1–2 conical teeth on side of upper dental plate; lips covering less than half of dental plates; front of head strongly rounded, the dorsal and ventral profiles about equally convex; caudal fin of juveniles slightly rounded, of adults truncate (slightly emarginate in some large terminal males); initial phase dark reddish brown (often fading to light gray on anterior body and postorbital head), the ventral part of head and front of snout around mouth red; dental plates white; able to display 2 longitudinal series of small white spots on side of body; also evanescent, a broad whitish zone posteriorly with a large, round black spot on base of caudal fin; terminal males green with a pink bar on each scale except caudal peduncle, which is uniform light green; a broad zone of body often suffused with yellow; dental plates blue-green; edges of lips pink with a broad, submarginal green band; these join behind corner of mouth as a band that continues across head below eye; head above this band lavender to pale green with 2 green bands extending posteriorly from eye; juveniles dark brown with 4 narrow, whitish stripes on head and body. Attains 40 cm. Occurs throughout most of the Indo-Pacific region; type locality, Red Sea; the most common parrotfish of the genus at many localities. *Callyodon bipallidus* Smith is one of 16 synonyms (Parenti & Randall, 2000). Choat & Robertson in Reinboth (1975) found 11 primary males and 119 females of 130 initial-phase fish examined. Randall & Bruce (1983) reported pair spawning, and Yogo et al. (1980) both pair spawning and group spawning by initial-phase fish.

Guam/juvenile

Great Barrier Reef/initial

New Britain/terminal-phase male (night)

LONGNOSE PARROTFISH
Hipposcarus longiceps (Valenciennes in C & V, 1840)

Pectoral rays 15; median predorsal scales 4; cheek scales small, in a nearly isolated subtriangular patch; dental plates narrow, their height 1.5–2.0 in eye diameter and nearly covered by lips; terminal male with 1 or 2 conical teeth on side of upper dental plate; head pointed, the snout long, 1.8–2.2 in head length of adults; caudal fin rounded with slightly prolonged lobes in adults; initial phase pale yellowish gray to nearly white, the edges of scales darker gray; margin of dorsal and anal fins pale blue; caudal fin yellowish; terminal male pale blue-green, the edges of scales salmon pink; edge of upper lip narrowly bright salmon pink; dental plates white; dorsal and anal fins salmon pink with a blue streak on each membrane and a blue margin; juveniles light gray with a bright, orange-red, midlateral stripe ending in a black spot of about pupil size at base of caudal fin. Attains 50 cm. Ryukyu Islands to Great Barrier Reef and New Caledonia, east to the Line Islands, Society Islands, and Tuamotu Archipelago; Cocos-Keeling Islands and reefs off northwestern Australia in the Indian Ocean; type locality, Waigeo, Indonesia. An inshore species usually found in sand and rubble areas around shallow lagoon reefs, but may also occur over seaward reef flats; often seen in small aggregations. The related *Hipposcarus harid* (Forsskål) occurs in the western Indian Ocean and Red Sea.

451

Kenya/female

Easter Island/male

SEAGRASS PARROTFISH

Leptoscarus vaigiensis (Quoy & Gaimard, 1824)

Pectoral rays 13; median predorsal scales usually 4; a single row of scales on cheek below eye; oblique rows of teeth fused to form dental plates, the upper enclosed by lower when mouth closed; lips covering dental plates; body elongate for a scarid, the depth 2.9–3.8 in standard length; dorsal spines flexible, the interspinous membranes incised; caudal fin rounded; mottled olive to brown, shading to dull yellow or pale greenish ventrally; fins mottled yellowish; males with small blue spots on head, body, anal, and caudal fins, sometimes displaying a lateral whitish stripe on body. Reported to 35 cm. Wide-ranging from the Red Sea and East Africa to Easter Island, but known from scattered localities, most of which are subtropical; in the western Pacific from the Ryukyu Islands and Ogasawara Islands to New South Wales, Lord Howe Island, and New Zealand; in Western Australia south to Rottnest Island; type locality, Waigeo, Indonesia. Usually found in seagrass beds or substrata with heavy growth of algae, where it is well camouflaged. Also called the Slender Parrotfish and the Marbled Parrotfish.

Marshall Islands/terminal-phase male

Tonga/juvenile

MINIFIN PARROTFISH

Scarus altipinnis (Steindachner, 1879)

Pectoral rays 15; median predorsal scales 5–6; 3 rows of scales on cheek, the lower row with 1–3 scales; 1 or 2 conical teeth on side of upper dental plate; dental plates exposed, dark green in both color phases; spinous portion of dorsal fin distinctly higher than soft portion, the distal part of last spine and first soft rays extended as a short filament in adults; caudal fin rounded, the lobes prolonged in adults; initial phase reddish brown with 4 or 5 vertical series of small whitish spots on body; terminal male green, the scales narrowly edged with pink, those on anterior half of body densely spotted with pink; head lavender-gray with many small green spots and a few short green lines, shading to pale salmon pink ventrally; lips edged in bright salmon, the mouth surrounded by a broad, irregular, deep blue-green band that continues ventrally on head; juveniles dark gray with 4 vertical rows of white spots, whitish on caudal peduncle, and yellow on anterior head; dorsal, anal, and pelvic fins translucent with large black blotches. Attains about 50 cm. Great Barrier Reef and islands of Oceania except the Hawaiian Islands and Easter Island; type locality, southern Gilbert Islands (Kiribati). Usually found on seaward reefs, sometimes in large aggregations. *Scarus brevifilis* (Günther) is a synonym. Terminal males sometimes misidentified as *S. chlorodon* Jenyns, a synonym of *S. prasiognathos* Valenciennes of the western Pacific and Indian Ocean.

Marshall Islands/initial phase (night)

Great Barrier Reef/juvenile

Great Barrier Reef/initial

Fiji/terminal-phase male

Fiji/terminal-phase male

CHAMELEON PARROTFISH

Scarus chameleon Choat & Randall, 1986

Pectoral rays 14; median predorsal scales 4, preceded by a pair of medially overlapping scales; 3 rows of scales on cheek, the lower row with 1–3 scales; 1 or 2 conical teeth on side of dental plates of adults; lips covering about three-fourths of dental plates; caudal fin of initial phase varying from slightly rounded to slightly emarginate, of terminal males emarginate to lunate; initial phase usually gray, shading to white ventrally, each scale on about upper half of body with a yellow bar, the caudal peduncle gray with a yellow spot on each scale; caudal fin yellow; terminal male green, the scales either broadly edged in pink or vertically half pink and half green; a broad zone of salmon pink in pectoral region of body and extending posteriorly; body below pale green; dorsal half of head lavender with a green band extending anteriorly and posteriorly from lower part of eye, the anterior reaching edge of lips; a green band extending dorsally from eye, usually crossing interorbital space; a large, irregular green spot behind and above eye; caudal fin lavender with a D-shaped green marking posteriorly in fin and green spots on base; juveniles brownish gray, finely flecked with pink; whitish ventrally. Largest specimen, 31 cm. Ryukyu Islands to Great Barrier Reef, New South Wales, Lord Howe Island, and New Caledonia, east to Fiji; only Palau in Micronesia; Western Australia south to Abrolhos Islands; type locality, Sumilon Island, Cebu. Named for the ability of adults of both color phases to rapidly alter their basic color to different color patterns.

YELLOWBARRED PARROTFISH

Scarus dimidiatus Bleeker, 1859

Pectoral rays 14; median predorsal scales 5–6 (rarely 5); 3 rows of scales on cheek, the lower row with 1–4 scales; no conical teeth on side of dental plates; lips covering or nearly covering dental plates; caudal fin slightly rounded to truncate; body of initial phase light yellowish gray with 4 oblique yellow bars alternating with gray on about upper one-fourth of body, the bars less distinct posteriorly; head gray dorsally, pale yellowish below; median fins grayish yellow; pectoral fins with yellow rays; terminal males solid green on head above and posterior to eye, and on anterior body to below spinous portion of dorsal fin; rest of body green with lavender-pink edges or a bar on scales, shading to lavender on abdomen and chest; upper lip with a very broad blue-green border, the rest of snout lavender; chin very broadly blue-green, this color continuing dorsally and posteriorly as an irregular green band across head below eye; rest of cheek yellow, shading to lavender below; an irregular lavender stripe extending posteriorly from eye across operculum; unscaled part of caudal fin green; dental plates white; juveniles similar to initial phase. Reaches a maximum of about 30 cm. Ryukyu Islands south to Great Barrier Reef, east to Samoa Islands and islands of Micronesia except the Mariana Islands; type locality, Doreh, New Guinea. Usually found on shallow protected reefs of lagoons and bays; difficult to approach underwater.

Papua New Guinea/terminal-phase male

Papua New Guinea/initial, day

Papua New Guinea/initial, night

453

Flores, Indonesia/initial phase

Palau/terminal-phase male

FESTIVE PARROTFISH

Scarus festivus Valenciennes in C & V, 1840

Pectoral rays 13–14; median predorsal scales 4–5; 3 rows of scales on cheek, the lower row with 1–3 scales; dorsal profile of head of adults steep and often slightly concave to a distinct convexity dorsoanterior to eye (may be bulbous in large males); small adults with no conical teeth on side of dental plates; large males with 2–3 on upper plate and 1–2 on lower; lips covering half to two-thirds of upper dental plate and three-fourths or more of lower plate; caudal fin of adults emarginate to lunate; initial phase brown with an orange bar on each scale, abruptly white ventrally on head and body below level of pectoral-fin base; 2 indistinct green lines dorsally across interorbital space and 1 anterior to lower part of eye, continuing across dorsal part of upper lip; 2 transverse green bars on chin; caudal fin lavender-gray, with blue-green upper and lower edges, a bright green crescent in middle of fin, and a broad red posterior zone; terminal male green, the scales edged with pink or with a pink bar except on abdomen and chest; head lavender-gray, the 2 green bands across interorbital space distinct; a transverse orange band bordered in blue-green on upper lip, the borders joining and continuing as an irregular band to below eye; a short, transverse, blue-green band on front of snout and 2 on chin; caudal fin with a submarginal green crescent; very large males green, shading to purple ventrally, with vertical purple lines posteriorly on body. Attains about 45 cm. East coast of Africa to the Society Islands and islands of Micronesia; Ryukyu Islands and Ogasawara Islands south to Indonesia; no type locality given; not common at any locality. *Callyodon lunula* Snyder is a synonym.

Great Barrier Reef/initial phase

Great Barrier Reef/terminal-phase male

YELLOWFIN PARROTFISH

Scarus flavipectoralis Schultz, 1958

Pectoral rays 14; median predorsal scales 4, the second scale largest; 3 rows of scales on cheek, the lower row with 1–2 scales; terminal males with 1 or 2 conical teeth on side of lower dental plate and 1 on upper; lips nearly covering dental plates; caudal fin truncate in initial phase, emarginate in terminal male; initial phase yellowish gray, darker dorsally on head, with faint whitish stripes on abdomen; pectoral fins clear yellow, brighter yellow at base, with a small black spot at upper corner; terminal male with head and anterior body beneath and above pectoral fin lavender-gray with a green stripe from upper lip through lower part of eye and across operculum; body posterior to pectoral fins green with a lavender-pink bar on each scale except for a longitudinal mid-lateral zone of bright yellow posteriorly on body; lower lip edged in blue-green; an irregular, transverse green band farther back on chin; pectoral membranes clear, the rays yellow, the base with a dark green and lavender bar. Reaches 30 cm. Philippines (type locality, Papagas Bay, Luzon) to southern Great Barrier Reef and New Caledonia, east to the Marshall Islands and Caroline Islands; also known from Scott Reef off northwestern Australia. Occurs in sheltered waters, often into deeper water than most scarids.

WHITESPOT PARROTFISH
Scarus forsteni (Bleeker, 1861)
Pectoral rays 13–14 (rarely 13); median predorsal scales 6–7; 3 rows of scales on cheek, the lower row with 2–5 scales; large adults with 1 or 2 conical teeth posteriorly on side of upper dental plate; lips only partially covering dental plates; caudal fin of initial phase emarginate, of terminal male lunate; initial phase reddish brown to reddish gray dorsally, pale red or orange ventrally, with a broad, irregular, dark brown band from eye across operculum, broadening to a dark brown zone on side of body containing a large irregular area of dark iridescent blue and green in pectoral region, and usually a white or pink spot nearly as large as eye just off pectoral-fin tip; fins red; dental plates whitish; terminal males green, the scales with salmon pink edges or a bar of this color except solid pale green below a green line from pectoral-fin base along lower part of body, and dorsoanterior part of body, which is abruptly dark lavender-gray, continuing forward onto head above lower edge of eye; dental plates dark blue-green; upper lip edged in salmon pink with a broad, blue-green, submarginal band that continues across head below eye; lower lip broadly edged in blue-green; juveniles dark brownish red with 4 whitish stripes and vertical rows of whitish to pink spots. Largest specimen, 54.6 cm. Ryukyu Islands and Ogasawara Islands to Great Barrier Reef and New Caledonia, east to Rapa, Tuamotu Archipelago, Pitcairn Islands, and all of Micronesia; Rowley Shoals off Western Australia and Cocos-Keeling Islands in the eastern Indian Ocean; described from Sulawesi and the Molucca Islands. Usually encountered on seaward reefs. Sometimes misidentified as *Scarus lepidus* Jenyns and *S. tricolor* Bleeker. *Scarus lepidus* is a synonym of *globiceps*, and *tricolor* is a valid species (Choat & Randall, 1986).

BRIDLED PARROTFISH
Scarus frenatus Lacepède, 1802
Pectoral rays 14–15 (usually 14); median predorsal scales 6–7, preceded by a medial pair of small scales; 3 rows of scales on cheek, the lower row with 2–4 scales; adults with 0–2 conical teeth posteriorly on side of upper dental plate; lips nearly covering dental plates; caudal fin truncate in small adults, the lobes prolonged in large individuals; initial phase brownish yellow to reddish brown, usually paler on caudal peduncle, with 6 dark brown stripes on side of body following centers of scale rows; dental plates white; fins red; terminal male green, the scales of body anterior to caudal peduncle with vermiculations of orange or rose pink; head pink with green vermiculations, the upper lip pink with a middle green band that continues across head below eye and branches ventrally to green bands on lower lip and chin; caudal peduncle solid green, this color continuing onto caudal fin except for a large, pink, crescentic area with green markings; dental plates blue-green; small juveniles green with 4 whitish stripes and vertical rows of whitish spots; larger juveniles reddish brown, becoming white posteriorly. Largest specimen examined, 47 cm. Occurs throughout most of the Indo-Pacific region except for the Hawaiian Islands and Easter Island; type locality, Indo-Pacific region. Generally found on outer-reef areas exposed to wave action, sometimes in very shallow water. *Scarus sexvittatus* Rüppell, *Callyodon vermiculatus* Fowler & Bean, and *Scarus randalli* Schultz are synonyms.

Papua New Guinea/juvenile

Indonesia/subadult

Bali/initial phase

Palau/terminal-phase male

Tonga/juvenile

Great Barrier Reef/subadult

Marshall Islands/initial phase

Papua New Guinea/terminal-phase male

Marshall Islands/juvenile

Bali/initial phase

Bali/terminal-phase male

BLUEBARRED PARROTFISH

Scarus ghobban Forsskål, 1775

Pectoral rays 15–16 (rarely 16); median predorsal scales usually 6, preceded by a medial pair of small scales; 3 rows of scales on cheek, the lower row with 1–2 scales; large adults with 1–3 conical teeth posteriorly on side of upper dental plate; lips covering more than half of dental plates; posterior nostril oval and large; caudal fin slightly emarginate in small initial-phase fish to lunate in large terminal males; initial phase dull orange-yellow, whitish ventrally, the centers of scales blue or blue-green; 5 irregular blue or blue-green bars often present on body (from more intense blue or blue-green in scale centers within bars); fins orange-yellow, the dorsal and anal with blue margins, the upper and lower edges of caudal fin and upper edge of pectoral fins blue;

terminal males green dorsally, the scales rimmed with salmon pink, shading to pale green ventrally with a pale salmon pink bar on each scale; head green dorsally, shading to pale salmon on cheek and chin, with 2 transverse blue bands on chin and 3 narrow irregular green bands extending posteriorly from eye; juveniles yellowish with 1–3 irregular white blotches. Reaches 75 cm. The most wide-ranging of scarid fishes, from the Red Sea (type locality) and East Africa to the tropical eastern Pacific; islands of Oceania except the Hawaiian Islands and Easter Island; usually seen on shallow reefs and adjacent sandy areas of lagoons and bays; more inclined to penetrate silty environments than other parrotfishes. The name *S. ghobban* may be replaced in the Pacific by *S. pyrrostethus* Richardson (Choat & Randall, in prep.).

Line Islands/initial phase

Papua New Guinea/terminal-phase male

VIOLET-LINED PARROTFISH

Scarus globiceps Valenciennes in C & V, 1840

Pectoral rays 14; median predorsal scales 5–7 (rarely 7, usually 6), the third or fourth largest; usually a pair of small scales anterior to first median predorsal scale; 3 rows of scales on cheek, the lower row with 1–4 scales; initial phase with no conical teeth on side of dental plates; large terminal males with 1 or 2 conical teeth on side of upper and lower plates; lips nearly covering dental plates; terminal males with a slight convexity in dorsal profile of forehead; caudal fin of initial phase truncate, of terminal males emarginate; initial phase brownish gray with 3 longitudinal whitish lines on abdomen; fins reddish brown; terminal males green with salmon pink edges on scales except ventrally where the green forms stripes separated by pale violet to laven-

der bands, and anteriorly where the green breaks into numerous small green spots; head green with an oblique lavender-pink band passing through lower part of eye; snout mainly lavender-gray, becoming spotted with green in interorbital and nearly solid green on nape; head behind eye lavender-pink with small green spots and irregular lines; a small blackish spot at base of fourth dorsal spine. Largest specimen examined, 27 cm (Randall & Bruce, 1983). East coast of Africa to Line Islands, Society Islands (type locality, Tahiti), and Rapa; Ryukyu Islands and Ogasawara Islands to Great Barrier Reef, Lord Howe Island, and New Caledonia; a shallow-water coral-reef fish seen more in outer-reef areas than in protected waters; initial phase sometimes forms small aggregations. *Scarus lepidus* Jenyns from Tahiti and *Pseudoscarus spilonotus* Kner from Fiji are synonyms.

Marquesas Islands/initial phase

Marquesas Islands/terminal-phase male

MARQUESAN PARROTFISH

Scarus koputea Randall & Choat, 1980

Pectoral rays 15; median predorsal scales 6–7 (usually 6); 4 rows of scales on cheek, the lower row with 1–2 scales; adults with 1 or 2 conical teeth on side of upper dental plate; lips covering half or more of dental plates; caudal fin of juveniles slightly rounded, of initial phase truncate to slightly emarginate, of terminal males truncate with prolonged lobes; initial phase brownish red, becoming brownish yellow dorsally on body, the scales with dark brown to black edges and small dark brown to black spots, mostly in a vertical row; a large bluish white area on upper abdomen, the scales there with narrow dark brown edges and no dark spots; terminal males green, the scales rimmed with dark reddish brown anteriorly on body except dorsally where the edges are salmon pink; posterior part of body yellow, sometimes with a green spot on each scale; head pinkish gray with a broad pink band from upper lip to eye, bordered below and very broadly above by blue-green; caudal fin blue. Largest specimen, 37.4 cm. Known only from the Marquesas Islands, where common. Koputea is the native name for the initial phase.

New Caledonia/juvenile

Fiji/initial phase

Great Barrier Reef/terminal-phase male

HIGHFIN PARROTFISH

Scarus longipinnis Randall & Choat, 1980

Pectoral rays 14; median predorsal scales 3–4 (usually 4); 3 rows of scales on cheek, the lower row with 1–3 (usually 2) scales; body deeper than that of most *Scarus*, 2.55–2.8 in standard length; adults with 1 or 2 conical teeth on side of upper dental plate; large terminal males with 1 or 2 conical teeth on side of lower plate; lips covering all or nearly all of dental plates; dorsal fin elevated, the longest ray 1.7–2.1 in head length; caudal fin of initial phase slightly double emarginate, the lobes more prolonged in terminal males; initial phase light brownish orange, often with dark brown bars; 3 blue-green stripes ventrally on body; a green bar from in front of eye to chin, with a narrow branch onto upper lip, and continuing ventrally on head; a green band extending dorsally from eye, and another across cheek from lower edge of eye; a large black area in caudal fin, followed by a yellow bar nearly to margin; large terminal males purple with a green bar on each scale, shading to pale yellowish green anteriorly on body; head purple with the same green bands as in initial phase but broader, the cheek band with a narrow, deep purple band above; dorsal fin largely pale greenish yellow with a small black spot at base of first interspinous membrane; juveniles indistinctly striped with brownish gray and white, the caudal fin with a large black spot bordered posteriorly with yellow. Attains about 40 cm. Occurs mainly in the southern subtropical zone from the Pitcairn Islands (type locality), Rapa, Tonga, Lord Howe Island, and the Great Barrier Reef of Australia; may be seen in as little as 10 m in the southern Great Barrier Reef, but occurs deeper in northern sectors, generally more than 20 m; deepest record, 55 m.

Great Barrier Reef/juvenile

Great Barrier Reef/initial phase

Marshall Islands/terminal-phase male (night)

SWARTHY PARROTFISH

Scarus niger Forsskål, 1775

Pectoral rays 13–15 (usually 14); median predorsal scales 6–8 (usually 7), the fourth usually largest; 3 rows of scales on cheek, the lower row with 2–5 scales; initial phase usually without conical teeth on side of dental plates; terminal males usually with 2 on upper plate; dental plates largely covered by lips; caudal fin of small initial-phase fish slightly rounded; large adults with prolonged lobes; initial phase greenish gray, the scales narrowly rimmed with dark brown, those anteriorly on body with small dark brown spots; a small, black-edged, yellow-green spot at upper end of gill opening; head shading to orange anteriorly with a green band above upper lip, 1 on lower lip, and a third on chin continuing nearly to eye; body of terminal males green, the scales narrowly rimmed with dark reddish brown; head green with essentially the same green markings; pectoral fins magenta to red; juveniles dark brown with blue dots, shading to red on caudal peduncle and to white on caudal fin, with a large black spot basally at upper and lower edges of fin. Attains 35 cm. Red Sea (type locality) and East Africa to Society Islands and Tuamotu Archipelago; Ryukyu Islands and Ogasawara Islands to Great Barrier Reef, Lord Howe Island, and New Caledonia; in Western Australia south to Shark Bay. Males in courtship swim rapidly with the caudal fin angling upward and the posterior part of the anal fin downward.

Bali/initial phase

Bali/terminal-phase male

EGGHEAD PARROTFISH

Scarus oviceps Valenciennes in C & V, 1840

Pectoral rays 14–15 (rarely 15); median predorsal scales 6; 3 rows of scales on cheek, the lower row with 2–3 scales; no conical teeth on side of dental plates; lips covering dental plates; caudal fin of initial phase emarginate, of terminal males deeply emarginate; initial phase pale greenish to yellowish gray, the scales rimmed with dark gray; an oblique yellow bar on back at tip of pectoral fins separated by a dark gray bar from a yellowish blotch below soft portion of dorsal fin; body anterior to yellow bar and head above lower edge of eye dark gray, darkest adjacent to yellow bar and as a band anterior and posterior to eye; terminal males light blue-green, the scales rimmed with lavender-pink; head above lower edge of eye, and anterior body to a diagonal ending at base of eighth dorsal spine, dark purplish gray, becoming paler dorsally on head and nape; dental plates blue-green. Reaches about 30 cm. Ryukyu Islands and Ogasawara Islands to Great Barrier Reef and New Caledonia, east to Line Islands, Society Islands (type locality, Tahiti), and Tuamotu Archipelago; Cocos-Keeling Islands and Western Australia south to Shark Bay. Closely related to *S. scaber* Valenciennes of the western Indian Ocean.

PALENOSE PARROTFISH

Scarus psittacus Forsskål, 1775

Pectoral rays 13–15 (usually 14); median predorsal scales 4, the first largest in juveniles, the second in adults; 2 rows of scales on cheek; usually 1 conical tooth on side of upper dental plate of initial phase; usually 1 conical tooth on side of lower dental plate and 1 on upper plate of terminal males; lips largely covering dental plates; caudal fin of initial phase slightly emarginate, of large terminal males deeply emarginate; initial phase reddish brown to gray, the snout often paler than rest of head; a dark spot at base of first membrane of dorsal fin, and a small black and blue spot at upper base of pectoral fins; median fins colored like body; pelvic fins red; terminal male green posteriorly, the edges of scales pink, progressively more pink and less green on scales anteriorly; abdomen pink with longitudinal series of green spots following scale rows; head with a green band on edge of lips, joining at corner of mouth and continuing below eye; 2 additional green bands extending posterior to eye; snout to a vertical above posterior edge of eye dark purplish to lavender gray; dental plates white; some males with green of body partly or entirely replaced by yellow; juveniles colored much like initial phase. Rarely exceeds 30 cm. A common species found at nearly all Indo-Pacific localities; type locality, Red Sea. Initial phase often forms small feeding aggregations. *Scarus venosus* Valenciennes and *S. forsteri* Valenciennes are 2 of 18 synonyms.

Marshall Islands/juvenile

New Britain/initial phase

Tahiti/terminal-phase male

Great Barrier Reef/terminal-phase male

New Caledonia/initial phase

New Caledonia/terminal-phase male

SURF PARROTFISH

Scarus rivulatus Valenciennes in C & V, 1840

Pectoral rays 13–15 (nearly always 14); median predorsal scales 5–7 (usually 6), the third or fourth largest; a pair of small medial scales in front of most anterior predorsal scale; 3 rows of scales on cheek, with 2–4 scales in lower row; no conical teeth on side of dental plates of initial phase, usually 2 upper and 0–1 lower on terminal males; lips nearly covering dental plates; caudal fin of initial phase slightly rounded to truncate, of terminal males emarginate; initial phase gray to grayish brown with 3 whitish stripes on abdomen; terminal males green, the scales rimmed with lavender-pink anteriorly on body, with a lavender-pink bar on scales over most of middle of body, and scales half pink and half green posteriorly; postorbital head and interorbital space lavender-gray with scattered, small green spots and short lines; front of snout, suborbital region, and chin salmon pink with a reticulum of green; cheek salmon pink to yellow or orange. Largest examined, 40 cm. Ryukyu Islands to Great Barrier Reef, Lord Howe Island, Norfolk Island, and New Caledonia, east to Caroline Islands; Western Australia south to Ningaloo Reef; type locality, Java; often occurs in aggregations that may move onto reef flats at high tide for feeding. *Scarus fasciatus* Valenciennes is a synonym.

459

Bali/terminal-phase male

Maisel Islands, Indonesia/juvenile

Bali/initial phase

EMBER PARROTFISH

Scarus rubroviolaceus Bleeker, 1847

Pectoral rays 14–16 (usually 15); median predorsal scales 6; 3 rows of scales on cheek, with 1–3 (usually 2) scales in lower row; initial phase with 0–1 conical teeth on side of upper dental plate, terminal males with 1–3; lips covering half or more of dental plates; body moderately elongate, the depth 2.75–3.1 in standard length; dorsal profile of head very steep to level of eye, then curving sharply, the remaining contour to dorsal-fin origin nearly straight; caudal fin of initial phase slightly emarginate, of large terminal males lunate; initial phase reddish brown to gray, shading to light red ventrally, the scales of body with small black spots, irregular lines, and rimmed with black; fins red; dental plates white; terminal males green, the scale edges narrowly pink, with a wash of salmon pink or pale yellow over side of body, continuing anteriorly onto cheek; upper lip narrowly edged in salmon pink; lower lip edged in blue-green, separated by a salmon pink band from a blue-green band across chin, the lip and chin green bands joining at corner of mouth and extending to eye; dental plates blue-green; adults of both color phases able to darken the head and anterior body to pectoral-fin tips (brown on initial phase and purplish gray on the terminal males); juveniles white with 3 brown stripes partially broken by vertical rows of white blotches. Attains 70 cm. East coast of Africa to Hawaiian Islands, Line Islands, and French Polynesia except Rapa and Austral Islands; Ryukyu Islands and Ogasawara Islands to Great Barrier Reef, New South Wales, and New Caledonia; in Western Australia south to Point Quobba; type locality, Java; also known from the tropical eastern Pacific; usually found on seaward reefs or exposed rocky shores. *Scarus jordani* (Jenkins) and *Callyodon africanus* Smith are 2 of 9 synonyms. Also known as the Redlip Parrotfish.

New Caledonia/initial phase

Marshall Is./term. male (night)

New Caledonia/terminal-phase male

YELLOWBAR PARROTFISH

Scarus schlegeli (Bleeker, 1861)

Pectoral rays 13–15 (rarely 13, usually 14); median predorsal scales 4, the second scale largest; 2 rows of scales on cheek; no conical teeth on side of dental plates of initial phase, usually 1 upper and 2 lower on terminal males; lips nearly covering dental plates; caudal fin of initial phase slightly rounded to truncate, of terminal males slightly double emarginate; initial phase reddish brown to olivaceous with an orangish to reddish bar on each scale or the edges of the scales of this color; 5 curved whitish bars of 1–2 scales in width usually present on body; a small black spot at upper base of pectoral fins; snout and chin reddish with a dull blue band on upper lip and 2 on chin; terminal males with a short, bright yellow bar on back between last dorsal spine and second soft ray and continuing below as a green bar; body posterior to bar darker green, the scale edges pink or with a pink bar on each scale; body anterior to bar dark green dorsally or blue-green with pink-rimmed scales, abruptly purple to purplish red below; edge of upper lip blue-green, pink above, with a transverse dark green band at front of snout that continues to eye, dividing behind eye to 2 oblique green bands that join green zone of back. Largest specimen, 38 cm. Terminal males in the southern Great Barrier Reef have the yellow and green bar more anterior on body, and those from the Philippines and Ryukyu Islands may have a second narrower yellow and light green bar anterior to the principal one. Ranges south to Lord Howe Island and New Caledonia, east in Oceania to French Polynesia except the Marquesas Islands; in the Indian Ocean to Cocos-Keeling Islands and south on the Western Australian coast to the Abrolhos; type locality, Sulawesi. Occurs at a variety of coral-reef habitats; both adult phases make rapid changes in color pattern. Initial phase often misidentified as *Scarus venosus* Valenciennes, a synonym of *S. psittacus. Pseudoscarus pentazona* Bleeker and *Scarus cypho* Seale are synonyms.

Papua New Guinea/initial phase

Coral Sea/terminal-phase male

GREENCAP PARROTFISH

Scarus spinus (Kner, 1868)

Pectoral rays 13–14 (rarely 13); median predorsal scales 3–5 (usually 4, the anterior scale may be small and embedded); a small pair of medial scales anterior to first predorsal scale; 3 rows of scales on cheek, the lower row with 1–2 (usually 2) scales; initial phase generally with 1 conical tooth on side of lower dental plate, and terminal males with 1 or 2 on both plates; dental plates covered by lips; head bluntly rounded, especially in terminal males; caudal fin of initial phase slightly rounded to truncate, of terminal males moderately to deeply emarginate; initial phase dark brown, shading ventrally to reddish brown, often with 4 or 5 indistinct pale bars 1–2 scales in width on body (due to whitish centers of scales within bars); terminal males green, the scale edges lavender-pink; top of head and snout green to yellowish green, shading ventrally on chin to blue-green, where 2 salmon pink areas are enclosed; cheek and postorbital head broadly yellow. Largest specimen, 30 cm. Ryukyu Islands to Great Barrier Reef and New Caledonia, east to Fiji (type locality, Kandavu), the Samoa Islands, and Caroline Islands; Scott Reef off northwestern Australia. Often misidentified as *Scarus formosus* Valenciennes, a synonym of the Hawaiian *S. dubius* Bennett.

Line Islands/initial phase

Line Islands/terminal-phase male

TRICOLOR PARROTFISH
Scarus tricolor Bleeker, 1847

Pectoral rays 14–15; median predorsal scales 6–7; 3 rows of scales on cheek, the lower row with 2–6 (usually 3 or 4) scales; terminal males and occasional large initial-phase fish with 1 or 2 conical teeth posteriorly on side of upper dental plate; lips covering about half of dental plates; caudal fin of initial phase slightly to moderately emarginate, of terminal males lunate; body of initial phase with longitudinal zones of color from dark brown to brown on back through yellow, green, blue, and light red, the scales strongly rimmed with black; head and chest very dark brown except dorsally over eye, where gray; caudal and anal fins red; dental plates white to pale rose; body of terminal males green, the basal half of scales yellow to salmon pink except for a narrow green band along back and a series of green spots forming a stripe on lower side; chest and narrow ventral zone below stripe pale green; dental plates deep blue-green; upper lip salmon pink with a submarginal blue-green band that continues across head below eye; a pink band bordered by blue-green on chin; an oblique green band passing through upper part of eye. Attains at least 40 cm. East coast of Africa to Indonesia and Philippines, east to Line Islands and Samoa Islands; only Palau in Micronesia; type locality, Java. Occurs primarily on seaward reefs. *Scarus cyanognathus* Bleeker is a synonym based on the terminal-male phase.

Sulawesi/initial phase

Penyu Islands, Indonesia/terminal-phase male

RED PARROTFISH
Scarus xanthopleura Bleeker, 1853

Pectoral rays 14–15 (usually 15); median predorsal scales 6; 3 rows of scales on cheek, the lower row with 2–3 (usually 2) scales; initial phase with no conical teeth on side of dental plates; terminal males with 1 or 2 on side of upper plate; lips only partially covering dental plates; caudal fin of both phases lunate; initial phase reddish gray, the scale edges red, with alternating dark and pale bars, more evident posteriorly; head red, broadly suffused with brown over cheek; fins red; dental plates white to pale rose; terminal males blue-green, the edges of scales narrowly salmon pink; a very large, irregular blue patch ventrally on head; dental plates deep blue-green; an irregular blue-green band from corner of mouth to below eye; short blue-green lines extending anteriorly and posteriorly from eye, and a transverse blue-green line on snout. Largest specimen examined, 54 cm. Ryukyu Islands and Taiwan to Coral Sea, east to Marshall Islands and Tuvalu; type locality, Java. Not common. *Scarus atropectoralis* Schultz is a synonym based on the initial phase (Randall, 1997a). Masuda et al. (1975: 310, pl. 115 G) misidentified the initial phase as *Scarus caudofasciatus* (Günther), a valid western Indian Ocean species with similar color pattern.

462

SANDPERCHES
(PINGUIPEDIDAE)

These fishes are called grubfishes, weevers, or whitings in Australia and sandsmelts in South Africa; sandperches is gaining acceptance as the preferred common name in most of the English-speaking world. The scientific name for the family has also varied from Parapercidae to Mugiloididae, but is now Pinguipedidae (Rosa & Rosa, 1987). There are 4 genera; only the largest, *Parapercis*, occurs in the marine environment of the Indo-Pacific region. Sandperches have an elongate body that is nearly cylindrical anteriorly; the eyes are oriented as much dorsally as laterally; the mouth is moderately large, slightly oblique, and terminal or with the lower jaw slightly projecting; the maxilla is largely hidden beneath the preorbital when the mouth is closed; the jaws have stout incurved conical teeth in an outer row, the largest in lower jaw as 3 to 5 anterior pairs; an inner band of villiform teeth anteriorly in both jaws; teeth are present on the vomer and present or absent on the palatines; there is a single stout spine on opercle; the margin of the preopercle is smooth or finely and irregularly serrate; gill membranes are united, free from isthmus, with a fold across; branchiostegal rays 6. There is a long dorsal fin with IV-VII spines and 20–24 soft rays; anal fin with a slender spine and 14–22 rays; caudal fin with 15 principal rays, the posterior margin slightly rounded to deeply emarginate; pelvic fins I,5, inserted below or anterior to the pectorals; scales small, ctenoid on body, those on cheek cycloid or ctenoid; lateral line complete, with 38–89 scales. Several species of *Parapercis* have been shown to be protogynous hermaphrodites (Nakazono et al., 1985 for *P. snyderi*), meaning that they start mature life as females and change sex later to males (this may be expected for other species of the genus); usually there is some change in the color pattern with the sex change. The species of *Parapercis* are typically found on sand and rubble substrata near reefs, at rest on the bottom, propped on their pelvic fins. Most shallow-water species are easily approached underwater. Cantwell (1964) revised the genus, recognizing 27 species (not all valid, because some were males and females of the same species). With the recent descriptions of *Parapercis australis* and *P. lata*, the number of species is now 45.

SOUTHERN SHARPNOSE SANDPERCH
Parapercis australis Randall, 2003

Dorsal rays V,21; anal rays I,17; pectoral rays 14–16; lateral-line scales 48–59; about 5 predorsal scales; scales on cheek ctenoid; 10 canine teeth at front of lower jaw; palatine teeth present; a prominent sharp spine at upper edge of subopercle; body depth 4.4–4.55 in standard length; middle dorsal spine longest; membrane from last dorsal spine joined to base of first soft ray; whitish with a series of 10 quadrangular, dark brown blotches along back, progressively shorter posteriorly, each with a darker brown spot at upper corners that merge with small black spots at base of dorsal rays; first 5 blotches joined basally by a wavy, dark brown stripe; 10 dark brown bars on lower part of body, broadest in the middle, linked by 2 horizontal series of dark brown blotches; narrow upper end of each dark bar joining corresponding lower part of just-mentioned wavy stripe; a narrow dark brown bar below middle of eye; a large black spot basally on dorsal fin between spines II and V; caudal fin pale with numerous small black spots, a narrow white posterior margin, and black submarginal line. Attains about 12 cm. Great Barrier Reef (type locality, One Tree Island), Lord Howe Island, New Caledonia, Fiji, and Tonga; usually seen around shallow silty reefs or sparse seagrass. Differs from *Parapercis cylindrica* (Bloch) from Indonesia to the Ryukyu

Tonga

Islands by higher lateral-line scale counts (44–50 for *cylindrica*), more slender body, longer dorsal spines, and a longer caudal fin that is whitish instead of yellow. The New Caledonia–Fiji–Tonga population differs in having 52–59 lateral-line scales compared with 48–55 for the Great Barrier Reef population (Randall, 2003a).

Luzon/female

Luzon/male

LATTICED SANDPERCH

Parapercis clathrata Ogilby, 1911

Dorsal rays IV-V (rarely V), 20–21 (usually 21); anal rays I,17; pectoral rays usually 17; lateral-line scales 57–60; about 15 predorsal scales; scales on cheek cycloid; 6 canine teeth at front of lower jaw; no palatine teeth; a blunt spine at upper edge of subopercle; second and third dorsal spines longest; membrane from last dorsal spine linked to first soft ray nearly as high as spine; light brown to olivaceous dorsally with rows of small dark blotches, white below with a lower series of 9 or 10 vertically elongate brown or brown and red spots with black centers; an ocellated black spot above gill opening of males; caudal fin with a broad, yellow or white middle zone and scattered, small brown spots. Largest, 17.5 cm. Andaman Sea to Cocos-Keeling Islands, Christmas Island, and Western Australia south to Shark Bay; Ryukyu Islands to the Great Barrier Reef and New Caledonia, east to Samoa Islands, Phoenix Islands, and the islands of Micronesia; no type locality given; replacement name for the preoccupied *Percis tetracanthus* Lacepède. Known from depths of 4–50 m.

Great Barrier Reef/female

Fiji/male

SPECKLED SANDPERCH

Parapercis hexophtalma (Cuvier in C & V, 1829)

Dorsal rays V,21–22 (rarely 22); anal rays I,17–18 (rarely 18); pectoral rays 17–18; lateral-line scales 58–61; about 15 predorsal scales; scales on cheek cycloid; 8 canine teeth at front of lower jaw; palatine teeth absent; no prominent spine at upper edge of subopercle; fourth dorsal spine longest; membrane from last dorsal spine joined to first soft ray at level of spine tip; pale greenish dorsally with 2 irregular rows of short, brown to black markings; a midlateral series of 9 white rectangles narrowly separated by vertical greenish lines that continue ventrally, ending in a small black spot (thus dividing lower white part of body into 9 sections); each rectangle and section below with 1 or a pair of small black spots; head of females with scattered small black spots, of males with oblique black lines (yellow in large males); males with orange spots dorsally on head; both sexes with a very large, irregular black spot in middle of caudal fin. Reaches 23 cm. Red Sea (type locality) and east coast of Africa to Fiji; Ryukyu Islands to Great Barrier Reef, Lord Howe Island, and New Caledonia; Cocos-Keeling Islands in the eastern Indian Ocean; a shallow-water species of sand and rubble flats around coral reefs. Clark et al. (1991) determined that males maintain a harem of 2 or 3 females; they described the courtship and the pair spawning, which takes place from 22 minutes before to 15 minutes after sunset. *Parapercis polyophtalma* (Cuvier) is a synonym based on the female form.

Line Islands/female

Line Islands/male

Y-BARRED SANDPERCH

Parapercis lata Randall & McCosker, 2002

Dorsal rays V,21; anal rays I,17; pectoral rays 18–19 (usually 18); lateral-line scales 59–60; about 15 predorsal scales; scales on cheek very small, cycloid, and embedded; 6 canine teeth at front of lower jaw; no palatine teeth; anterior body wider than deep; no blunt spine at upper edge of subopercle; third and fourth dorsal spines longest, less than half length of longest soft ray; membrane from last dorsal spine linked to first soft ray at level of spine tip; a dark band across occiput, angling down over pectoral base and chest; 8 narrow black bars on body, the middle 6 expanded dorsally to Y-shape; black dots dorsally on head and anterodorsally on body, many more on males than on females; males with an oblique, dark-edged yellow band below eye. Largest specimen, 21.2 cm. Known only from the Line Islands (type locality, Tabuaeran, formerly Fanning Island) and Phoenix Islands from sand or rubble at depths of 5–55 m, in both lagoons and outer-reef areas.

Ogasawara Islands

SPOTTED SANDPERCH

Parapercis millepunctata (Günther, 1860)

Dorsal rays IV,20–21 (usually 21); anal rays I,17; pectoral rays usually 17; lateral-line scales 55–58; about 10 predorsal scales; scales on cheek cycloid; 6 canine teeth at front of lower jaw; no palatine teeth; a spine at upper edge of subopercle; membrane from last dorsal spine linked to first soft ray at level of spine tip; whitish to pale greenish dorsally, with a longitudinal series of brown blotches, white below with a complex pattern of 3 rows of brown to dark brown spots joined by narrow dark stripes, the lower row of spots largest, the ventral end of each spot progressively narrower; 2 large dark spots ventrally on cheek and 1 behind on opercle; small, dark brown spots dorsally on snout; caudal fin greenish with small dark spots, a rectangular white area posteriorly in middle of fin, usually preceded by a large black blotch. Largest examined, 18 cm. Maldive Islands to Pitcairn Islands; Ryukyu Islands and Ogasawara Islands to the Great Barrier Reef and New Caledonia; type locality, Sri Lanka. The most common species of the genus at many localities. *Parapercis cephalopunctata* (Seale) is a synonym.

Luzon

REDBARRED SANDPERCH

Parapercis multiplicata Randall, 1984

Dorsal rays V,21; anal rays I,16–17; pectoral rays 14–16; lateral-line scales 56–58; about 12 predorsal scales; scales on cheek cycloid; 8 canine teeth at front of lower jaw; no palatine teeth; upper edge of subopercle serrate, without a spine; third or fourth dorsal spine longest; membrane from last dorsal spine linked nearly to base of first soft ray; upper one-fourth of body pale greenish to pale red, with or without series of small black spots; lower three-fourths white with 8 narrow red bars, each with 2 small, deep red to black spots; 2 indistinct, irregular, narrow orange stripes on side of body; a red spot, with or without a black center, below pectoral-fin base; very small black to deep red spots dorsally on head; a large black spot on first 3 membranes of dorsal fin, and a row of red dots in soft dorsal and anal fins. Attains 12 cm. Known to date from Ryukyu Islands (type locality, Okinawa), Indonesia, New Caledonia, Western Australia, Coral Sea, Mariana Islands, and Pitcairn Islands; usually found on rubble substrata from depths of 4–30 m.

REDSPOTTED SANDPERCH
Parapercis schauinslandi (Steindachner, 1900)
Dorsal rays V,21; anal rays I,16–17; pectoral rays usually 16;
lateral-line scales 56–59; about 12 predorsal scales; scales on
cheek cycloid and embedded; 6 canine teeth at front of lower
jaw; no palatine teeth; upper edge of subopercle with 2–5 close-
set spines (may be fused), the uppermost largest; middle dorsal
spine longest; membrane from last dorsal spine linked nearly to
base of first soft ray; caudal fin emarginate to lunate; body varying from white to pale greenish or pale red, with a series of 8
semicircular to squarish, yellowish gray or pink bars on back,
each containing in its lower part a small dark red to black spot,
pair of spots, or a dash; side and lower part of body with a series
of 8 orange to red short bars or squarish blotches, each below a
pale interspace of back, the series sometimes linked with an
orange stripe; 2 red bars at base of pectoral fin; a narrow orange
or red band from front of upper lip to eye; red markings on cheek;

U-MARKED SANDPERCH
Parapercis snyderi Jordan & Starks, 1905
Dorsal rays V,21; anal rays I,16–18 (usually 17); pectoral rays
13–15 (usually 14, rarely 13); lateral-line scales 38–43; 4–5 predorsal scales; scales on cheek ctenoid; 8 canine teeth at front of
lower jaw; palatine teeth present; a spine at upper edge of subopercle; middle dorsal spine longest; membrane from last dorsal
spine joined to base of first soft ray; pale greenish to pale red
dorsally, white below, with a series of 5 U-shaped dark bars on
back (varying from black to faint gray depending on color of
substratum), or with 2 series of black or red dots along side, one
above and one below lateral line, that are darker where the dark
bars would be; a series of 9 narrow dark bars on lower half of
body crossed by a 2 rows of orange dots, the upper more evident
and sometimes blackish; first dorsal fin largely black in male;
rows of small orange spots in dorsal and caudal fins; anal fin
with a single row of orange spots or short lines at base; a small
dark red to black spot on penultimate membrane of anal fin.
Reaches 10.5 cm. Specimens have been examined from southern

Society Islands

2 red spots in vertical alignment on base of caudal fin; first dorsal fin black except for a broad red margin. Reaches 13 cm. East
coast of Africa to the Hawaiian Islands (type locality, O'ahu), and
Pitcairn Islands; southern Japan to Great Barrier Reef and New
Caledonia; occurs on rubble or rubble-sand substrata; reported
from depths of 15–170 m; rare in less than 20 m.

Taiwan

Japan, Taiwan, Hong Kong, Sulawesi, Sumatra, and New Caledonia; type locality, Korea. Nakazono et al. (1985) determined
the spawning season at Kyushu as May to October; males maintain a harem of 1 to 4 females in their territories of about 20
square meters; pair spawning was observed at dusk. Sex change
from female to male was demonstrated histologically. The illustration from the Great Barrier Reef in Randall et al. (1997a),
identified as *P. snyderi*, is the closely related *P. lineopunctata*
Randall, 2003, which differs in having 45–51 lateral-line scales
and some features of color.

New Caledonia/female

Lombok, Indonesia/male

WHITESTRIPE SANDPERCH
Parapercis xanthozona (Bleeker, 1849)
Dorsal rays V,21; anal rays I,17; pectoral rays usually 17; lateral-
line scales 56–60; about 15 predorsal scales; scales on cheek
cycloid and embedded; 6 canine teeth at front of lower jaw; no
palatine teeth; upper edge of subopercle with a few serrae but no
spine; middle dorsal spine longest; membrane from last dorsal
spine joined to first soft ray nearly at level of spine tip; a midlateral whitish stripe on body continuing to end of caudal fin
(pure white in fin); body above stripe pale greenish with a series
of small, paired, dark brown blotches along back at base of dor-

sal fin; a second series of larger squarish blotches in line with
the first, resting on lateral stripe, the scale edges dark brown,
forming little crosses within blotches; body below stripe pale
greenish with 9 narrow bars that vary from gray-brown to orange-
yellow; dorsal fin with 3 rows of small black spots; anal fin with
a single row of small black spots; caudal fin with scattered small
black spots, few in middle white stripe; males with curved,
oblique, black-edged white lines on cheek. Reaches 23 cm. East
Africa to Fiji; southern Japan to Great Barrier Reef and New
Caledonia; only Palau in Micronesia; type locality, Java. Usually
found in protected waters of bays and lagoons.

SANDDIVERS
(TRICHONOTIDAE)

This small Indo-Pacific family consists of a single genus, *Trichonotus*, and 10 species (including two probable undescribed species). The family was characterized by Nelson (1986), who provided osteological characters to distinguish it from the Creediidae. The most useful external characters are as follows: body very elongate; head pointed, the lower jaw strongly projecting; mouth large and only slightly oblique, the jaws, vomer, and palatines with small conical teeth; eyes oriented as much dorsally as laterally; eyes with a dorsal iris flap consisting of numerous strands extending downward; gill membranes separate and not joined to isthmus, the branchiostegal rays 7; dorsal fin very long with III-VI slender spines and 39–47 soft rays; anal fin I,34–42; branched caudal rays 11–13; pelvic rays I,5, the fins inserted slightly in advance of the pectorals; scales cycloid; lateral line complete, on midside of body, the pored scales 52–59, each with a posterior V-shaped notch. These fishes live in aggregations over sand. They feed on zooplankton a short distance above the bottom; when alarmed they dive into the sand, coming to rest with just the upper part of the head visible. If approached while in hiding, they dart out for about a half meter and dive again into the sand. Shimada & Yoshino (1984) stated that *Trichonotus elegans* appears to be a protogynous hermaphrodite. The author collected an intersex specimen of *T. halstead* in Indonesia (reported by Clark & Pohle, 1996). Males maintain a harem of females (for *T. elegans*, about 12 females in the harem of one male). Males are much larger than females, with longer fins, some with very prolonged and filamentous dorsal spines. In courtship and during aggression, the males fully elevate their dorsal fin and lower their anal and pelvic fins.

ELEGANT SANDDIVER
Trichonotus elegans Shimada & Yoshino, 1984
Dorsal rays III,43–45; anal rays I,39–42; pectoral rays 12–14; lateral-line scales 56–59; anterior half of body without scales except at base of dorsal and anal fins and along lateral line; head naked except for several scales on occiput; and a row of 3 or 4 behind and below eye; vertebrae 53–56; body depth 14–18 in standard length; dorsal spines of males greatly prolonged and filamentous; soft portion of dorsal fin of males about twice height of fin of females; caudal fin of females rounded, of males asymetrically lanceolate; whitish to brown, depending on whether living on white or dark sand, the females with 3 longitudinal dark lines or rows of dots on dorsal half of body and black anteriorly on dorsal fin; males with a row of dark-edged whitish blotches on upper side and a midlateral row of small, pale blue spots grouped to form dashes; a curved black band, partly edged in blue, from base of first 2 dorsal spines to upper end of gill opening; small, dark-edged blue spots on head; base of spinous

Ambon, Indonesia/female and male

portion of dorsal fin black, the filaments banded with white and brown; a row of small, dark-edged blue spots in dorsal fin, the ray tips white; caudal fin with small white spots. Attains 17 cm. Ryukyu Islands (type locality, Yaeyama Islands) to the Great Barrier Reef and New Caledonia, east to Fiji and the islands of Micronesia, from depths of 1–40 m; generally in aggregations.

SPOTTED SANDDIVER
Trichonotus setiger Bloch & Schneider, 1801
Dorsal rays V-VII,39–41; anal rays I,34–36; pectoral rays 12–15; lateral-line scales 52–55; body fully scaled; head naked except for 2 oblique rows of scales from corner of mouth to behind eye; vertebrae 49–51; body depth 12–14 in standard length; dorsal spines of males greatly prolonged and filamentous; soft portion of dorsal fin of males about twice height of fin of females; caudal fin of females rounded, of males rounded to rhomboid; whitish to brown with 9 dusky blotches on upper side and 6 longitudinal rows of dark-edged blue or yellow spots, 1 per scale; head with small, dark-edged blue to yellow spots, some of which may be obliquely elongate; side of lower jaw often dusky; dark-edged, pale blue spots basally in median fins; pelvic fins black-

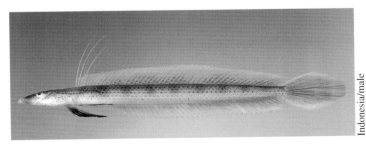

Indonesia/male

ish. Reaches 19 cm. India (type locality, eastern India) to Indo-Malayan region, north to Ryukyu Islands, south to Great Barrier Reef, and east to New Caledonia and Fiji. As noted by Randall & Tarr (1994), the records of *Trichonotus setiger* from the Persian Gulf are erroneous.

SANDBURROWERS
(CREEDIIDAE)

This Indo-Pacific family consists of seven genera and 16 species. Osteological and other characters were given by Nelson (1985), and a key to the species was provided by Nelson & Randall (1985). All of the species are very small, elongate, with the upper jaw projecting slightly anterior to the lower; lower jaw with a fringe of cirri and a dorsally projecting knob at the symphysis; eyes dorsolateral and protruding, the interorbital space very narrow; no iris flap dorsally on eyes; a continuous dorsal fin with 12–43 unbranched soft rays; pectoral rays 9–17; pelvic rays I,3–5 (fins absent in 1 species); lateral line abruptly or gradually descending from upper end of gill opening to lower base of caudal fin; some species largely scaleless (lateral-line scales always present). These tiny fishes are white or translucent, generally with dark markings to match the sand in which they live. They remain buried in the upper layers of sand, generally with only the top of the head or their eyes visible. They dart quickly upward and back down to the sand as they feed on individual animals of the demersal zooplankton. Most occur in shallow water, even in the sand of tidepools, but there are reports to depths of 150 m. Some species have been shown to be protandrous hermaphrodites (R. C. Langston, pers. comm.), meaning that they commence mature life as males and change sex later to females.

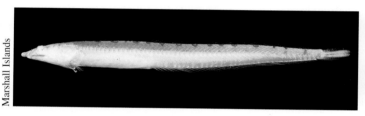

Marshall Islands

SADDLED SANDBURROWER
Chalixodytes chameleontoculis Smith, 1957
Dorsal rays 35–40; anal rays 36–40; pectoral rays 12–14; pelvic rays I,4; branched caudal rays 7 or 8; lateral-line scales 55–59; lateral-line scales rounded (not trilobed); median predorsal scales about 18; body scaleless except for lateral line, a row of scales along base of dorsal and anal fins, and a few scales posteriorly on body (however, the body of 1 of 3 specimens from Mangareva is fully scaled); body depth 11–15.5 in standard length; origin of dorsal fin over that of anal fin; translucent with about 16 brown saddle-like markings on back; eyes and sometimes tip of snout black. Reaches 4.6 cm. Known from the east coast of Africa, Seychelles (type locality), Chagos Archipelago (Winterbottom et al., 1989), Cocos-Keeling Islands, Christmas Island, and the following islands of the Pacific: Tuamotu Archipelago, Samoa Islands, Marshall Islands, and Mariana Islands; occurs in sand or fine gravel on shallow seaward reefs to a depth of about 10 m. *Chalixodytes tauensis* Schultz is a synonym (Rosa, 1993).

Hawaiian Islands

Pitcairn Islands

SOUTH PACIFIC SANDBURROWER
Crystallodytes enderburyensis Schultz, 1943
Dorsal rays 40–43; anal rays 38–41; pectoral rays 12–13; pelvic rays I,5; branched caudal rays 8; rays of other fins unbranched; lateral line descending gradually from upper end of gill opening to lower edge of caudal peduncle, the pored scales 57–60; lateral-line scales rounded; head and body naked except for scales of lateral line; body depth 9.3–12.5 in standard length; upper lip fleshy; no cirri on lips; origin of anal fin below fourth or fifth ray of dorsal fin; translucent whitish in life, some individuals with small dark saddles on back. Largest specimen, 7.4 cm. Schultz (1943) described *Crystallodytes cookei enderburyensis* as a new subspecies from the Phoenix Islands and Samoa Islands, differentiating it from the Hawaiian subspecies, *C. cookei cookei* Fowler, by higher meristic data. The differences in counts, however, seem specific in magnitude; the dorsal and anal rays for *cookei* 36–39, anal rays 35–37, pectoral rays 10–11, and the lateral-line scales 54–57. Also *cookei* is a smaller species, the largest specimen examined, 5.8 cm. Other localities for *enderburyensis* include the Society Islands and Pitcairn Islands; occurs in coarse sand or fine gravel in exposed tidepools and the spur and groove habitat to a maximum of about 15 m.

RADIANT SANDBURROWER
Limnichthys nitidus Smith, 1958
Dorsal rays 19–22; anal rays 23–26; pectoral rays 11–13; pelvic rays I,5; branched caudal rays 8; rays of other fins unbranched; lateral line descending gradually from upper end of gill opening to lower edge of caudal peduncle, the pored scales 36–42; lateral-line scales trilobed; body fully scaled; body depth 8.5–10 in standard length; lower lip with a series of cirri; origin of dorsal fin slightly posterior to origin of anal fin; whitish, typically with 11 narrow orange, brown, or gray bars on body that broaden and

join a midlateral stripe, the bars often broader and darker dorsally; irregular narrow dark bands radiating from eye. Probably does not exceed 3 cm. Reported from the Red Sea and east coast of Africa (type locality, Pinda, Mozambique) to the Hawaiian Islands and Pitcairn Islands. Found in coarse sand or fine gravel from depths of 4–20 m, generally in more protected waters than *Crystallodytes* spp., but never in calm bays. Schultz in Schultz et al. (1960) described *Limnichthys donaldsoni* from the Marshall Islands, with paratypes from the Hawaiian Islands, and the name has been used for specimens from the Samoa Islands, Pitcairn Islands, Ogasawara Islands, and Rowley Shoals off Western Australia. Rosa (1993) regarded *donaldsoni* as a subspecies of *nitidus*. Yoshino et al. (1999) placed *donaldsoni* in the synonymy of *nitidus*; they found Japanese specimens intermediate in meristic characters to *nitidus* and *donaldsoni* and concluded that the latter is only a geographical variant of *nitidus*.

SANDLANCES
(AMMODYTIDAE)

This small family of five genera and about 18 species is circumglobal in tropical to Arctic seas. These fishes are very elongate with a pointed head and strongly projecting lower jaw, a protractile premaxilla (except one genus), teeth present or absent; no spines in dorsal and anal fins, the dorsal very long with 36–69 rays; anal rays 14–36; caudal fin forked; pectoral rays 13–17; pelvic fins absent (except in *Embolichthys*); scales very small and cycloid or absent; lateral line high on body; no swimbladder; gill membranes separate, with 7 branchiostegal rays; vertebrae 52–78. As the common name suggests, they dive into sand when threatened. Typically they form schools and feed on zooplankton. An overview of the development and relationships of the family was provided by Stevens et al. in Moser et al. (1984). Only 1 species is known for the South Pacific area.

Pitcairn Island

PITCAIRN SANDLANCE
Ammodytoides leptus Collette & Randall, 2000
Dorsal rays 50–53; anal rays 24–25; pectoral rays 16–17; pelvic fins absent; lateral line incomplete, the pored scales 114–118 + 4–6; 10–12 rows of predorsal scales; head scaleless; fins scaleless except caudal; gill rakers 6–7 + 22–25; vertebrae 61–63; body elongate, the depth 10.5–11.5 in standard length; head pointed, the lower jaw projecting; dorsal and anal fins low; caudal fin forked; pelvic fins absent; grayish green dorsally, shading to silvery with iridescence on side and ventrally; fins clear except the caudal, which is yellowish. Largest specimen, 13.2 cm. Currently known only from Pitcairn Island, but should be expected from other subtropical islands of the South Pacific. Type specimens collected over sand from a depth of 10.5 m from a school of about 25 individuals; another school of about 100 fish seen in 30 m. Feeds well above the substratum on zooplankton; forms fast-swimming schools when threatened, diving into sand only as a last resort. One was found in the stomach of a jack (*Carangoides ferdau*).

STARGAZERS
(URANOSCOPIDAE)

The common name for this family is derived from the dorsal position of the eyes. The body is moderately elongate and tapering, naked or with small cycloid scales in oblique rows; the lateral line is high on the body. The head is large, flattened dorsally and ventrally, and partly covered with bony plates that may be granular or rugose; there is a stout cleithral spine at the upper end of the gill opening that is venomous in at least some species (deaths have been reported from stargazer wounds but not well documented). The cleft of the mouth is vertical or nearly so, and the lower jaw is strongly projecting; small teeth are present in the jaws and on the vomer and palatines; the lips are fringed with papillae; the gill opening is very broad, the gill membranes separate and free from the isthmus; branchiostegal rays 6. The spinous dorsal fin is small, generally with IV or V spines, but may be absent or may be joined to the soft dorsal fin; the anal fin is long, without spines; the pectoral fins are inserted on the lower half of the body; the pelvic fins, with I,5 rays, are close together in the throat region. Stargazers are rarely seen, because they are generally buried in sand or mud with only the eyes and fringed mouth barely exposed. Many have a slender fleshy lure developed from tissue of the oral valve inside at the front of the lower jaw that can be wriggled, worm-like, to attract their prey of small fishes. The family consists of 8 genera and about 50 species that inhabit tropical to warm temperate seas of the Indo-Pacific and Atlantic Oceans.

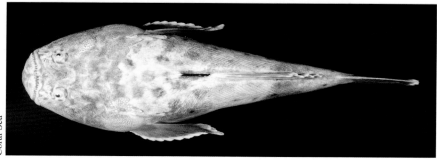

Coral Sea

Coral Sea

WHITEMARGIN STARGAZER
Uranoscopus sulphureus Valenciennes in C & V, 1832

Dorsal rays IV + 12–13, the spinous dorsal fin almost continuous with the soft; anal rays 13; pectoral rays 18–19; lower edge of preopercle with 5 small spines; fleshy edge of operculum lined with cirri; spinous dorsal fin low, less than half height of soft dorsal; third dorsal soft ray longest, about 2.5 times longer than first or last rays; caudal fin slightly rounded; grayish brown dorsally, with a faint, broad dark bar on upper half of head and 2 on body, white ventrally; a row of small, dark brown spots on upper side, and some brown blotches anterodorsally on body; spinous dorsal fin largely black; pelvic fins white; remaining fins with white outer margins. Attains about 35 cm. Reported from Tonga (type locality), Fiji, Samoa Islands, Indonesia, and the Red Sea. *Uranoscopus fuscomaculatus* Kner is a synonym.

TRIPLEFINS
(TRIPTERYGIIDAE)

The triplefins are small blennioid fishes (usually less than 6 cm long) of the order Perciformes that are found in tropical to temperate seas. The greatest number are in the Indo-Pacific region. Their most distinctive feature is having three separate dorsal fins, the first of III-X spines, the second of VII-XXVI spines, and the third with 7–17 soft rays; the anal fin has 0-II (rarely IV) spines and 14–31 soft rays; the caudal fin with 9–11 branched rays; the pelvic fins have a spine and 2–3 soft rays, the fins inserted distinctly anterior to the pectorals. The body is scaled, the scales usually ctenoid; there is either a single continuous lateral line that may end beneath the second dorsal fin or continue to the caudal peduncle, or a disjunct lateral line with an anterodorsal part of pored scales and a midlateral posterior part of notched scales. The jaws have bands of conical teeth that are broadest anteriorly, the largest teeth in the outer row at the front of the jaws. The gill membranes are broadly attached across the isthmus. Triplefins are usually found on coral reefs or rocky substrata. Most occur in shallow water, often on reef flats or in tidepools too shallow to be photographed underwater. Many of those occurring in diving depths are so cryptic that they are known only from collections with ichthyocide. Males usually have a different color pattern from females. Fricke (1994) recorded a total of 30 genera and "at

High-hat Triplefin, *Enneapterygius tutuilae*, Ternate, Indonesia

least 125 species" for the family. New Zealand has the most diverse triplefin fauna, with nine endemic genera and 23 endemic species. The tropical Indo-Pacific region has only six genera, but numerous species, of which 33 were recorded by Fricke (1997) for the South Pacific region covered by this book. Species accounts and illustrations are provided for 30 of these here; the reader is referred to Fricke (1997) for new species descriptions of *Enneapterygius fuscoventer*, *E. ornatus*, and *E. signicauda*. A revision of *Helcogramma* was published by Hansen (1986), of *Ceratobregma* by Holleman (1987), of *Norfolkia* by Holleman (1991), and of *Ucla* by Holleman (1993). Fricke's (1997) review of western and central Pacific species of the family was followed for the large genus *Enneapterygius*, but it is clear that much systematic research needs to be done on this genus. The number of sensory pores in the lower jaw of triplefins is of value in the classification of some species; the mandibular pore formulas given here consist of 3 numbers, the middle one is the number of pores at the front of the jaw (termed symphyseal), usually 1 or 2; the other 2 numbers represent the pores along each side of the jaw.

Tonga/female

HELEN'S TRIPLEFIN
Ceratobregma helenae Holleman, 1987
Dorsal rays III + XV-XVI + 9–10; anal rays I,19–21; pectoral rays 15–17; pelvic rays I,2; lateral line interrupted, 15–17 + 22–24; head naked; nape with small scales; pectoral-fin base naked, but abdomen scaled; lateral ethmoid bones expanded to form bony ridges in front of eyes, bearing spines in males; orbital tentacle lobate; mandibular pores 2 + 2 + 2; whitish with a coarse, yellowish brown reticulum on body; many scales rimmed in orange or yellow; a large orange-red area may be present on opercle. Reaches 3.5 cm. Described from Christmas Island, eastern Indian Ocean; otherwise known from the Pacific: Taiwan (Shen & Wu, 1994: fig. 3) to Great Barrier Reef, east to Fiji, Tonga, Caroline Islands, and American Samoa; reported from 4–37 m.

BLACKTHROAT TRIPLEFIN
Enneapterygius atrogulare (Günther, 1873)
Dorsal rays III + X-XIV + 8–11; anal rays I,16–20; pectoral rays 14–16; pelvic rays I,2 (true of other *Enneapterygius*); lateral line interrupted, 15–20 + 15–20; head, chest, and pectoral-fin base naked (also generic); palatine teeth present (generic); mandibular pores 4 + 2–3 + 4; orbital tentacle present; first dorsal fin higher in males, but shorter than second dorsal fin; whitish with 4 double, reddish brown bars on body and a dark blotch or narrow vertical bar on caudal peduncle; males blackish over head below eye, chest, and prepectoral area; first dorsal fin black, the second black with a white submarginal line, and the third black on basal two-thirds. Largest specimen, 5.3 cm. Described from Bowen, Queensland; ranges north to Cape York and south to New South Wales; otherwise known only from Herald Cays in the Coral Sea and Tonga; a shallow-water species. *Enneapterygius annulatus* (Ramsay & Ogilby) is a synonym.

Great Barrier Reef (R. C. Steene)

ELEGANT TRIPLEFIN
Enneapterygius elegans (Peters, 1876)
Dorsal rays III + X-XIV + 7–10; anal rays I,14–19; pectoral rays 15–16; lateral line interrupted, 15–20 + 14–21; mandibular pores 3–9 + 1 + 3–9; first dorsal fin about half as high as second; females greenish, the scales broadly marked with red; head whitish with orange-red markings, a broad, oblique blackish band on side of snout, and a large blackish blotch on opercle; pectoral-fin base with 2 dark red bars; males red, the lower three-fourths of head black, continuing to chest and pectoral-fin base, sometimes with a white spot below eye; both sexes with a few short, narrow white bars (from broad white edges on scales) and 2 black spots, one above the other (the lower may be small and indistinct), posteriorly on caudal peduncle, followed by a narrow, curved white bar bordered in red. Attains 3.5 cm. East coast of Africa to Taiwan, New Caledonia, Rotuma, Tonga, and American Samoa; no records from Indo-Malayan region except the Trobriand Islands; type locality, Mauritius. A species of shallow water, including tidepools.

Seychelles/male

Seychelles/female

471

YELLOWNAPE TRIPLEFIN

Enneapterygius flavoccipitis Shen & Wu, 1994

Dorsal rays III + XI-XII + 8–10; anal rays I,17–18; pectoral rays 14–17; lateral line interrupted, 15–17 + 17–22; ventral part of abdomen naked; mandibular pores 3 + 1 + 3; orbital tentacle slender; first dorsal fin short, about half height of second dorsal fin; females with 5 double dark bars on body, a black bar across caudal peduncle with 2 white spots, one above the other; anal with oblique dark streaks; body of males dark gray with a coarse blackish reticular pattern; dorsal part of head to below front of second dorsal fin bright yellow, this continuing as a bar to pec-

toral axil and fin; rest of head to base of pectoral fin black. Largest specimen, 3.2 cm. Taiwan (type locality), and Ryukyu Islands to Western Australia and Queensland, east to Vanuatu and New Caledonia; recorded from depths of 0.3–22 m.

HALFBLACK TRIPLEFIN

Enneapterygius hemimelas (Kner & Steindachner, 1867)

Dorsal rays III + XI-XIV + 6–10; anal rays I,15–20; pectoral rays 14–18; lateral line interrupted, 13–20 + 15–23; mandibular pores 3–4 + 1–2 + 3–4; supraorbital tentacle short; first dorsal fin slightly more than half height of second dorsal fin; females pale greenish, mottled with reddish brown and blotched with white; a dusky bar at base of dorsal fin, followed by a narrow white bar (may be broken midlaterally); males orange-red, finely mottled with blackish and white, abruptly black posterior to rear of second dorsal fin except for a whitish bar or pair of whitish spots below rear base of third dorsal fin; snout and lips red with a narrow black band from front of upper lip to eye; chest and rest of head below lower edge of eye black. Largest specimen, 4.8 cm. Ryukyu Islands to New South Wales, east to American Samoa (Tutuila, type locality); reported to 30 m, but most specimens from less than 5 m, and many from reef flats or tidepools.

PYGMY TRIPLEFIN

Enneapterygius nanus (Schultz in Schultz et al., 1960)

Dorsal rays III + XI-XIV + 7–11; anal rays I,16–20; pectoral rays 14–16; lateral line interrupted, 10–15 + 18–20; mandibular pores 3–4 + 2 + 3–4; supraorbital tentacle small; females translucent, finely dotted with black (most dense over opercle), the scale edges variously dark reddish brown; scattered small white spots, most numerous ventrally on head; males blackish on snout and head below a line from eye to lower edge of pectoral-fin base. Largest specimen, 2.8 cm. Andaman Sea and northwestern Australia; Taiwan to Coral Sea and New Caledonia, east to Mariana Islands, Marshall Islands (type locality), and Caroline Islands; reported to a depth of 20 m, but most specimens from shallow lagoon or ocean reefs, including tidepools.

BLACK TRIPLEFIN

Enneapterygius niger Fricke, 1994

Dorsal rays III + IX-XII + 7–10; anal rays I,16–20; pectoral rays 14–16; lateral line interrupted, 13–19 + 17–22; mandibular pores 4–6 + 1–2 + 4–6; supraorbital tentacle prominent; first dorsal fin nearly as high as second; females mottled reddish brown and white with 5 indistinct, double, dark brown bars on body; anal fin yellow; a white bar at base of caudal fin; New Caledonia male described (from author's slide, since lost) as dark brown, the sides with 2 rows of whitish spots; a narrow white bar below eye; caudal fin white; remaining fins blackish; Vanuatu males plain black, the caudal fin translucent; anal fin red in some specimens; a narrow white bar below eye in large specimens. Largest, 4.1 cm. Known only from New Caledonia (type locality), Vanuatu, Pohnpei (Ponape), and Taiwan; collected from tidepools to 15 m; most specimens from less than 3 m.

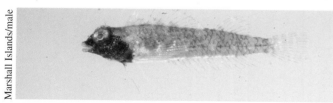

472

BLACKTAIL TRIPLEFIN

Enneapterygius nigricauda Fricke, 1997

Dorsal rays III + XI-XIV + 7–10; anal rays I,16–19; pectoral rays 15–17; lateral line interrupted, 15–20 + 15–20; mandibular pores 3–4 + 1 + 3–4; suprorbital tentacle short; first dorsal fin of female about half height of second dorsal, of males about three-fourths height; females translucent greenish gray with indistinct reddish blotches along back, a midlateral row of reddish blotches about size of pupil, a row of 3 quadrangular reddish blotches just above anal fin, and 1 in front of anal-fin origin; head with oblique orange-red bands; males bright red with darker red double bars; lower half of head blackish; basal two-thirds to three-fourths of caudal fin black, preceded by a vertical white line; pectoral and anal fins bright red. Reaches 3.5 cm. Ogasawara Islands, Taiwan, Philippines, and Vanuatu, east to islands of Micronesia, Line Islands, Society Islands, Samoa Islands, and Tonga (type locality); seaward and lagoon reefs, generally in less than 5 m.

Marshall Islands/female

Marshall Islands/male

New Caledonia

Marshall Islands

RETICULATE TRIPLEFIN

Enneapterygius paucifasciatus Fricke, 1994

Dorsal rays III + XIII + 8–9; anal rays I,20; pectoral rays 18–19; lateral line interrupted, 17–18 + 20–21; mandibular pores 5 + 2 + 5; supraorbital tentacle short; first dorsal fin three-fourths height of second dorsal fin; male paratype whitish, finely speckled with black dots (darkest over opercle), the body with a coarse reticular pattern of dark reddish brown; a broad, dark reddish brown bar at base of pectoral fin; first 2 dorsal fins and anal fin dusky with pale red rays; caudal fin transparent with a reddish white bar at base, the proximal half with reddish dots in vertical alignment. Largest specimen, 3.3 cm. Known from 4 specimens from coral reefs in 2–4 m off New Caledonia.

PYRAMID TRIPLEFIN

Enneapterygius pyramis Fricke, 1994

Dorsal rays III + XI-XVI + 7–11; anal rays I,16–20; pectoral rays 16–17; lateral line interrupted, 15–20 + 15–20; mandibular pores 3–5 + 0–2 + 3–5; supraorbital tentacle short and slender; first dorsal fin about three-fourths height of second dorsal fin; body of females white with black dots, most numerous on posterior half and on head, with 6 Y-shaped red bars on body; life color of male unknown but described from preserved specimens as having 5–6 large, triangular-shaped, dark brown spots on lower side of body (joined ventrally), numerous small dark brown spots on cheek, and a suborbital dark band. Largest specimen, 3.3 cm. Recorded from Great Barrier Reef, Vanuatu, Rotuma (type locality), Tonga, American Samoa, Society Islands, Tua-

MINUTE TRIPLEFIN

Enneapterygius philippinus (Peters, 1869)

Dorsal rays III + X-XIII + 7–10; anal rays I,14–17; pectoral rays 14–15; lateral line interrupted, 10–15 + 16–22; mandibular pores 2–3 + 1 + 2–3; supraorbital tentacle short and broad; translucent, finely dotted with black, with dark reddish edges on some scales forming blotches on body; a series of blackish spots along base of anal fin. Reaches 2.9 cm, but most specimens less than 2.5 cm. Islands of the western Indian Ocean to the islands of Micronesia and Samoa Islands; Ryukyu Islands to New Caledonia; type locality, Luzon; nearly all specimens collected from less than 2 m, many from high tidepools. *Enneapterygius minutus* (Günther) and *E. tusitalae* Jordan & Seale are among the 8 synonyms listed by Fricke (1997).

Pitcairn Islands/female

motu Archipelago, Pitcairn Islands, Pohnpei, and Guam; most specimens have been collected from depths greater than 5 m; the author's collections at Pitcairn varied from less than 1 m in a large tidepool to 30 m.

Rapa/female

Rapa/male

Marquesas Islands/female

RAPA TRIPLEFIN
Enneapterygius randalli Fricke, 1997

Dorsal rays III + XI-XIII + 8–10; anal rays I,15–17; pectoral rays 15–17; lateral line interrupted, 17–21 + 14–18; mandibular pores 4–5 + 1 + 4–5; supraorbital tentacle short; first dorsal fin about half height of second dorsal fin; females dark bluish gray on body with black double bars; a series of pink blotches along back (the pink on scale edges); abdomen, chest, cheek, and lips pale gray with black dots; top of head red; a broad, oblique black band from eye to mouth and chin; dorsal fins transparent with red rays; anal and caudal fins dusky, the caudal black at base; males black overall except for abdomen and a broad oblique band on cheek that are light gray with black dots; fins colored as in female, but with more black on caudal. Reaches 3.4 cm. Known only from Rapa and Îlots de Bass (Marotiri); collected from depths of 1–27 m.

SURF TRIPLEFIN
Enneapterygius rhothion Fricke, 1997

Dorsal rays III + XI-XIV + 7–10; anal rays I,17–21; pectoral rays 16–17; lateral line interrupted, 14–18 + 16–20; mandibular pores 4–5 + 2 + 4–5; supraorbital tentacle small; first dorsal fin about half height of second dorsal fin; females translucent pale gray to white with red or dark brown double bars on body; an oblique, red to dark brown band from upper lip to eye; a red or dark brown blotch on opercle and pectoral-fin base; median fins transparent with red rays; males red with faint, dark brown bars; chest and lower half of head dark gray with scattered black spots nearly as large as pupil. Largest specimen, 3.7 cm. Known only from New Caledonia (type locality), Loyalty Islands, and Vanu-

UMPIRE TRIPLEFIN
Enneapterygius rhabdotus Fricke, 1994

Dorsal rays III + XI-XV + 7–11; anal rays I,15–20; pectoral rays 15–17; lateral line interrupted, 15–20 + 15–20; mandibular pores 3–4 + 3–4 + 3–4; supraorbital tentacle long and slender; first dorsal fin one-half or less height of second dorsal fin; females mustard yellow with 3 broad, dark brown bars, edged in whitish, on body, the first with 2 bluish gray lines, the second and the very broad third divided by a bluish gray line; a broad black bar across base of caudal fin and adjacent peduncle; head pale gray with irregular, dark reddish brown lines; caudal fin with a broad, median blackish bar; males described as black on anterior three-fourths of body and fins; a broad, oblique black band across body linking posterior part of third dorsal fin and anal fin. Largest specimen, 3.2 cm. Reported from the Marquesas Islands (type locality), Society Islands, Tonga, Rotuma, Vanuatu, Solomon Islands, Palau, Papua New Guinea, Gulf of Thailand, Philippines, and Taiwan; collected from depths of 1–7.6 m.

New Caledonia/female

atu. Fricke named this species for its "favorite habitat on rocks in surge channels or around fringing reef exposed to the ocean surf." Most collections were made in less than 3 m, but 1 lot was taken in 15 m.

REDCAP TRIPLEFIN
Enneapterygius rufopileus (Waite, 1904)

Dorsal rays III + X-XIV + 8–12; anal rays I,16–21; pectoral rays 14–17; lateral line interrupted, 15–20 + 15–21; mandibular pores 4 + 1 + 4; supraorbital tentacle small; first dorsal fin of female about half height of second dorsal fin, of male about three-fourths height; both sexes translucent gray, the scale edges varying from pink to dark reddish brown, the pink-edged scales grouping to form blotches along back; a white bar at base of caudal fin; top of head red; rest of head of female brown with small white spots on cheek, the lower lip and posterior upper lip red; lower part of head of male black except for bright red lower lip to end of maxilla and red on upper part of opercle. Attains 4.5 cm. Known from Lord Howe Island (type locality), Elizabeth and Middleton Reefs, Norfolk Island, New Caledonia, Tonga, and Fiji; occurs from intertidal pools to 6 m. Waite

Lord Howe Island/male

Lord Howe Island/female

(1904) wrote with respect to the species at Lord Howe Island, "These little fishes swarmed in every rock-pool, and it was observed that the colouration is correlated to their surroundings. Examples taken in the coral rock are of reddish hue, those from sand bottoms yellow, while the specimens obtained in the dark volcanic troughs are the dark variety."

BLACK-AND-RED TRIPLEFIN
Enneapterygius similis Fricke, 1997
Dorsal rays III + XI-XV + 8–10; anal rays I,16–21; pectoral rays 16–17; lateral line interrupted, 14–19 + 14–21; mandibular pores 2–4 + 2 + 2–4; supraorbital tentacle small, lobate or branched; first dorsal fin about half height of second dorsal fin; females translucent gray, the edges of the scales faintly red; white flecks forming bars on dorsal half of body, each ending in a white spot on midlateral line; a broad, dark red band across interorbital; males red on anterior half of body, black on posterior half; third dorsal fin, posterior anal fin, and caudal fin black; forehead and snout black; cheek, chest, and pectoral-fin base pale greenish, densely dotted with black. Largest specimen, 3.9 cm. Philippines (type locality), Sabah, Indonesia, New Britain, Great Barrier Reef, New South Wales, Vanuatu, and New Caledonia. Collected from depths of 0–13 m in tidepools and on reef crests with some wave action and good algal growth. Named *E. similis* because of its similarity in color and habits to *E. hemimelas*.

WHITESPOTTED TRIPLEFIN
Enneapterygius triserialis Fricke, 1994
Dorsal rays III + XI-XIV+ 7–11; anal rays I,17–21; pectoral rays 15–18; lateral line interrupted, 14–20 + 14–21; mandibular pores 3–4 + 1 + 3–4; supraorbital tentacle small and slender; first spine of first dorsal fin of males higher than first spine of second dorsal fin; first dorsal fin of females slightly more than half height of second dorsal fin; body of females whitish, finely dotted with black, with a reticular pattern of red or brown, thus isolating the white into 2–3 longitudinal rows of blotches; color of males similar but darker overall. Attains 4.5 cm. Holmes Reefs in Coral Sea, New Caledonia (type locality), Loyalty Islands, Rotuma, Fiji, Tonga, Niue, American Samoa, Rapa, and Society Islands; collected from depths of 0.3–17 m.

HIGH-HAT TRIPLEFIN
Enneapterygius tutuilae Jordan & Seale, 1906
Dorsal rays III + XI-XIII + 7–10; anal rays I,15–20; pectoral rays 13–18; lateral line interrupted, 7–13 + 18–25; mandibular pores 2–4 + 2 + 2–4; supraorbital tentacle lobate; first dorsal fin high, the first spine higher than first and second spines of second dorsal fin, and may be higher than longest spine of second fin; apparently no sexual dichromatism (Fricke, 1997); color variable, but often translucent greenish with faint, irregular narrow bars from red to brown pigment on scale edges; an indistinct white bar often extending down from rear of second dorsal fin, and another from rear of third dorsal fin; usually a blackish blotch distally on third to fifth membrane of second dorsal fin that may continue as a curved dark band to base of ninth and tenth spines. Largest specimen, 2.8 cm. The most widespread and common species of the genus; Red Sea and Madagascar to Line Islands and Society Islands; Taiwan to reefs of Coral Sea and New Caledonia; known from tidepools to 55 m (collection at that depth by the author in the Gulf of Aqaba, Red Sea).

New Britain/female

Komodo, Indonesia/male

Loyalty Islands/female

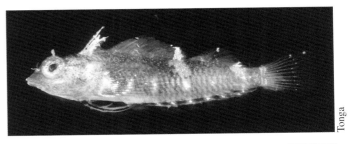

Tonga

Ogasawara Islands

(J. T. Williams)

(J. T. Williams)

WILLIAMS' TRIPLEFIN
Enneapterygius williamsi Fricke, 1997

Dorsal rays III + XI-XIV + 7–10; anal rays I,16–20; pectoral rays 17–18; lateral line interrupted, 14–20 + 15–21; mandibular pores 2–3 + 1–2 + 2–3; supraorbital tentacle minute; first dorsal fin of female about half height of second dorsal fin, of males about two-thirds height; males dark gray, mottled with light gray, with a narrow whitish bar below eye; large males with an oblique suborbital blue streak; fins translucent with gray spots and mottlings; females paler with 2 indistinct, dark double bars on anterior half of body that unite below lateral line. Largest specimen, 3.3 cm. New Caledonia, Loyalty Islands (type locality), Vanuatu, and Tonga; collections from depths 0.3–10 m, mostly from rocky shores exposed to surge.

HUDSON'S TRIPLEFIN
Helcogramma hudsoni (Jordan & Seale, 1906)

Dorsal rays III + XII-XIV + 9–11; anal rays I,17–20 (usually 19); pectoral rays 15–17; lateral line continuous, the pored scales 20–29; mandibular pores 4–5 + 3 + 4–5; supraorbital tentacle small; nasal tentacle simple or bilobed; first dorsal fin low; females whitish with 5 oblique, H-shaped maroon bars; male blackish on lower half of head, sometimes with a narrow white streak across cheek; anal fin of male dark. Largest specimen, 4.7 cm. American Samoa (type locality), Fiji, Rotuma, New Caledonia, and Vanuatu; collections from depths of 0–3 m. Hansen (1986) placed *Tripterygium gymnauchen* Weber and *Enneapterygius inclinatus* Fowler in the synonymy of *Helcogramma hudsoni*, but Fricke (1997) regarded these as valid species.

Guam/female

Marshall Islands/male

Palau/female

HOODED TRIPLEFIN
Helcogramma capidatum Rosenblatt in Schultz et al., 1960

Dorsal rays III + XIII-XV + 10–12; anal rays I,19–21 (rarely 19); pectoral rays 16; pelvic rays I,2 (true of other species of *Helcogramma*); lateral line continuous, the pored scales 20–27; no scales on head (also generic); mandibular pores 5–10 + 1 + 5–10; supraorbital tentacle absent; palatine teeth present (generic); upper jaw ending below posterior half of eye; females white with 7 narrow, double, red or reddish brown bars that extend about two-thirds of body depth; head with irregular, oblique, brownish red bands; dorsal fins without dark bands; males pale gray with the same 7 double bars, but most pairs meet below and extend farther ventrally; snout, lower three-fourths of head, and pectoral-fin base with numerous black dots (most dense on snout). Largest specimen, 4.1 cm. Caroline Islands (Kapingamarangi Atoll, type locality), Marshall Islands, Mariana Islands, southern Gilbert Islands (Kiribati) (color note by Randall, 1955a as *Helcogramma* sp.), Fiji, Tonga, Niue, and Sabah (the only record for Indo-Malayan region); known from depths of less than 1 to 30 m; most collections from depths greater than 3 m.

LITTLE HOODED TRIPLEFIN
Helcogramma chica Rosenblatt in Schultz et al., 1960

Dorsal rays III + XIII-XV + 9–12; anal rays I,18–20; pectoral rays 14–16; lateral line continuous, the pored scales 18–23; mandibular pores 3–4 + 1 + 3–4; supraorbital tentacle absent; upper jaw ending below anterior half of eye; females translucent gray, the vertebral column showing through as alternating broad bands of white and dark reddish brown along its upper edge; indistinct, narrow, Y-shaped, reddish brown bars on body, and a row of reddish brown spots along lower side; dorsal and caudal fins largely transparent; anal fin dusky; males blackish on lower half of head and pectoral-fin base. Attains 4 cm, but most specimens less than 3 cm. Phoenix Islands (Hull Island, type locality), Society Islands, Samoa Islands, Tonga, Rotuma, Vanuatu, Trobriand Islands, Marshall Islands, Mariana Islands, Ogasawara Islands, and Palau; in the Indian Ocean Christmas Island, Cocos-Keeling Islands, and Andaman Sea off Thailand; collected from 0.1–32 m, including tidepools. Hansen (1986) reported the stomach contents of several specimens as small crustaceans (about 50%) and the rest eggs (fish and others).

NEW CALEDONIA TRIPLEFIN
Helcogramma novaecaledoniae Fricke, 1994

Dorsal rays III + XIII-XV + 9–12 (modally 11); anal rays I,20–22 (counts by Fricke, but 18 on illustrated specimen); pectoral rays 15–17; lateral line continuous, the pored scales 34–38; mandibular pores 4–5 + 1 + 4–5; no supraorbital tentacle; jaws terminal, the upper reaching to or slightly beyond below middle of eye; first dorsal fin shorter than second in both sexes, lower in females; females whitish when fresh (probably partly translucent in life) with 6 oblique, H-shaped, dark reddish brown bars that are progressively darker posteriorly, the upper part of each mainly as dark flecks; head with small, dark reddish brown spots; first membrane of first dorsal fin pale, the rest of fin dark reddish brown; males reported by Fricke as more darkly pigmented. Largest specimen, 6.3 cm. Known only from New Caledonia and the Solomon Islands; collected from depths of 1.5–36 m. Identification by Fricke.

Solomon Islands

YELLOWSPOT TRIPLEFIN
Helcogramma sp. Williams & Holleman (in prep.)

Dorsal rays III + XII-XV + 10–12; anal rays I,20–21; pectoral rays 15–17; lateral line continuous, the pored scales 22–39; mandibular pores 3–5 + 1 + 3–5; supraorbital tentacle very short; jaws terminal, the upper reaching to below middle of eye; translucent greenish, the top of vertebral column showing as alternating white and dark red bands, the white longer; body with red to maroon double bars, faint to well marked, the anterior ones irregular and branching; a midlateral row of thin maroon dashes often present; a median maroon line on snout and a branching one from front of upper lip to eye; median fins of females largely transparent; first dorsal fin of male with a large black area containing a yellow spot on last membrane; second dorsal dusky except red blotches along base; third dorsal with oblique red bands, dusky at margin; caudal fin red; anal fin dusky. Attains 6.5 cm. Andaman Sea off Thailand and northwestern Australia; Ryukyu Islands to Great Barrier Reef and New Caledonia, east to Marshall Islands and American Samoa; collected from coral reefs in 1–21 m. Often misidentified as *Helcogramma ellioti* (Herre), a species from India and Sri Lanka.

Flores, Indonesia/female

New Caledonia/male

LINED TRIPLEFIN
Helcogramma striatum Hansen, 1986

Dorsal rays III + XI-XV (usually XIV) + 9–12 (usually 11); anal rays I,17–23 (usually 20–21); pectoral rays 15–17; lateral line continuous, the pored scales 14–20; mandibular pores 3 + 2 + 3; supraorbital tentacle absent; first dorsal fin less than half height of second dorsal fin; upper two-thirds of body red, lower one-third white, with 3 bluish to greenish white longitudinal lines, the lowermost at demarcation of red and white sectors; a midlateral series of 6–7 small whitish spots between lower 2 white lines; head with a greenish white line from corner of mouth to pectoral-fin base; snout and interorbital with greenish white spots; a middorsal greenish white line on nape. Attains 5 cm. Sri Lanka, Andaman Sea off Thailand, and northwestern Australia; Japan (type locality, Miyake-jima) to Great Barrier Reef, east to Gilbert Islands (Kiribati), Line Islands, and Fiji; coral reefs from depths of 1–30 m, often at rest on live coral. Usually the most common species of the genus in areas where it occurs, and the one most often observed and photographed by divers.

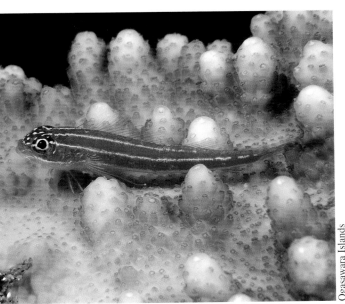
Ogasawara Islands

REDFIN TRIPLEFIN
Norfolkia brachylepis (Schultz, 1960)

Dorsal rays IV + XII-XV + 8–11; anal rays II,17–20; pectoral rays 15–16 (usually 16); pelvic rays I,2 (spine hidden; rays united only basally [true of other species of *Norfolkia*]); lateral line discontinuous, 14–19 + 16–24; scales ctenoid except cycloid on abdomen (also generic); scales on cheek, opercle, prepectoral region, and dorsal part of head to interorbital space; mandibular pores 4 + 1 + 4; no palatine teeth (generic); supraorbital tentacle a small flap; second dorsal fin usually slightly higher than first; whitish, the scale edges dusky yellow, with 6 irregular, slightly oblique brown bars on body; head mottled white and brown, with an oblique brown bar below eye bordered in white; second and third dorsal fins of male red, crossed by narrow whitish bands. Largest specimen, 7.3 cm. Red Sea and east coast of Africa to Mariana Islands, Marshall Islands (type locality, Bikini Atoll), and Fiji; Japan and Taiwan to New Caledonia, Great Barrier Reef, New South Wales, and south to Perth in Western Australia; coral reefs from depths of 1–25 m.

SCALYHEAD TRIPLEFIN
Norfolkia squamiceps (McCulloch & Waite, 1916)

Dorsal rays IV + XIV-XV (usually XV) + 10–11 (usually 11); anal rays II,20–21 (usually 21); pectoral rays 15–16 (usually 16); lateral line discontinuous, 21–24 + 14–19; scales on head to eye and over all of preopercle; mandibular pores 5–6 + 1 + 5–6; supraorbital tentacle small and palmate; body light gray or light brown with 2 longitudinal series of irregular brown blotches, the dorsal series larger (some upper blotches connected with lower); an oblique, dark brown bar bordered by white below eye; rest of head dark brown, shading to white ventrally; second and third dorsal fins of females with oblique dark bands, darker as they cross rays; caudal fin with irregular, vertical dark bars; males with dorsal and caudal fins yellow or orange. Largest specimen, 6.6 cm. Great Barrier Reef, Elizabeth and Middleton Reefs, Lord Howe Island (type locality), Norfolk Island, New Caledonia, and Loyalty Islands; rocky shores and reefs in 0.5–12 m, including tidepools. *Norfolkia lairdi* Fowler is a synonym.

THOMAS' TRIPLEFIN
Norfolkia thomasi Whitley, 1964

Dorsal rays IV + XIV-XV + 9–11 (usually XV + 10); anal rays II,20–22; pectoral rays 14–16 (usually 15); lateral line discontinuous, 12–15 + 24–27; scales on head to behind eye, but not on cheek; mandibular pores 3 + 2 + 3; supraorbital tentacle lobate; white, the scales rimmed with yellow or orange, with 6 irregular, oblique, dark brown bars that bifurcate ventrally; an irregular brown bar below eye bordered posteriorly by white; second and third dorsal fins of females with narrow oblique bands of red and white, these fins of males dull orange. Reaches 5 cm. Ryukyu Islands and Ogasawara Islands in the north; in the south, Great Barrier Reef (type locality), east to Vanuatu, New Caledonia, Fiji, Tonga, Samoa Islands, Rapa, Society Islands, Tuamotu Archipelago, and Pitcairn Islands; coral reefs in 1–20 m.

KULBICKI'S TRIPLEFIN
Springerichthys kulbickii (Fricke & Randall, 1994)

Dorsal rays III + XI-XV + 6–10; anal rays II,18–21; pectoral rays 16–18; pelvic rays I,2; lateral line discontinuous, 21–22 + 17–19; head and prepectoral area naked; snout very short, the dorsal profile steep; mandibular pores 3 + 2 + 3; supraorbital tentacle slender; first dorsal fin about one-third height of second dorsal fin; gray with 5 indistinct, broad, double brown bars on body; head and anterior body with irregular bright orange spots, the spots small on posterior half, many as orange posterior edges of scales; caudal fin black at base, gray centrally with a midlateral orange-red band, a narrow white margin, black submarginal line, and a broad arc of bright orange-red. Reaches 3.5 cm. Great Barrier Reef, Coral Sea, New Caledonia (type locality), Fiji, Tonga, and American Samoa; collected from depths of 3–15 m.

LONGJAW TRIPLEFIN
Ucla xenogrammus Holleman, 1993

Dorsal rays III + XII-XV + 11–14; anal rays II,18–22; pectoral rays 15; pelvic rays I,2, the spine short and hidden; lateral line continuous, with 3–13 pored scales, followed by 28–34 scales with a groove; mandibular pores 2–3 + 2 + 2–3; no supraorbital tentacle; body elongate, the depth 5.5–6.2 in standard length; head pointed, the snout long, 3.5–4.5 in head length, the lower jaw strongly projecting; mouth large, the maxilla extending to or slightly posterior to center of eye, the jaw length 2.0–2.4 in head length; both sexes translucent, the vertebral column sometimes apparent from alternating, long red and short white bands on its dorsal edge; maroon dots on body forming faint Y- or H-shaped bars, and a midlateral row of narrow dashes; a maroon line on snout bifurcating at nostrils; males green on head with faint dusky bands in second and third dorsal fins. Largest specimen, 5.7 cm. Andaman Sea off Thailand, Christmas Island, northwestern Australia, and St. Brandon's Shoals in the Indian Ocean; Ryukyu Islands to Great Barrier Reef (type locality, Lizard Island), and New Caledonia, east to Guam, Pohnpei, American Samoa, and Tonga; occurs on coral reefs in 2–41 m.

Papua New Guinea/female

Solomon Islands/male

Bluestriped Fangblenny, *Plagiotremus rhinorhynchos,* New Britain

BLENNIES
(BLENNIIDAE)

The Blenniidae is a large family of 53 genera and about 345 species of small, slender, agile fishes that lack scales; most are blunt-headed with the mouth low on the head and not protractile; the teeth in the jaws are numerous and slender, either fixed or movable. Teeth may be present on the vomer, but none on the palatines. The fangblennies (tribe Nemophini), also called sabertooth blennies, have a very large pair of incurved canine teeth in the lower jaw. Many blennies have cirri or small tentacles on the head, especially above the eye and on the anterior nostril, and some have a median fleshy crest on the head, often only in males. There is a single long dorsal fin with III-XVII flexible spines; all have II anal spines but one or both may be reduced in size or embedded in females; in males these spines may be capped by fleshy tissue believed to secrete an attracting substance at spawning time. The last soft ray of the dorsal and anal fins may be joined by membrane to the caudal peduncle or the base of the caudal fin. Pelvic fins anterior to pectorals, the rays I,2–4 (the spine small and embedded, hence easily overlooked). Many species, such as those of the genera *Alticus, Entomacrodus, Istiblennius,* and *Praealticus* live inshore on rocky substrata, sometimes in the surf-swept intertidal zone; they may be seen leaping from one pool to another (hence the common name rockskipper). Blennies generally take refuge in small holes in the reef, which they enter tail-first. The majority of tropical blennies are herbivorous. The Shortbodied Blenny (*Exallias brevis*) is unusual in feeding on coral polyps. The fangblennies of the genus *Plagiotremus* (*Runula* is a synonym) bite skin tissue and mucus from other fishes (but not with their large fangs, which are used for defense); they are sometimes called scale-eating blennies. The Cleaner Mimic (*Aspidontus taeniatus*), in its guise of a cleaner wrasse (*Labroides dimidiatus*), feeds in part by tearing pieces from the fins of other fishes. The 2 large

canines of the fangblennies of the genus *Meiacanthus* are venomous; these fishes are often seen swimming fearlessly a short distance above the bottom. Because they are avoided by predaceous fishes, some other small fishes, including blennies of the genera *Ecsenius, Plagiotremus,* and *Petroscirtes*, mimic them in color pattern and behavior (Losey, 1972; Springer & Smith-Vaniz, 1972; Russell et al., 1976; Smith-Vaniz, 1987). The blennies for which the reproductive habits are known lay demersal eggs that are guarded by the male parent. Springer (1993) characterized the Blenniidae in detail and compared it with other blennioid families. No subfamilies other than the Blenniinae are recognized; instead there are 5 tribes, of which 3 have representatives in the South Pacific: Salariini (Smith-Vaniz & Springer, 1971; Springer & Spreitzer, 1978; Bath, 2001), Omobranchini (Springer, 1972a; 1981), and Nemophini (Smith-Vaniz, 1976; 1987). Generic revisions have been published on *Entomacrodus* (Springer, 1967), *Stanulus* (Springer, 1968), *Omobranchus* (Springer & Gomon, 1975), *Ecsenius* (Springer, 1988), *Cirripectes* (Williams, 1988), *Praealticus* (Bath, 1992), and *Blenniella* and *Istiblennius* (Springer & Williams, 1994).

LEAPING ROCKSKIPPER
Alticus arnoldorum (Curtiss, 1938)

Dorsal rays XIV-XV,22–24; anal rays II,26–27; pectoral rays 15; pelvic rays I,4; caudal rays 13, unbranched; teeth in jaws very numerous and freely movable; margin of lips crenulate; no fleshy disc behind lower lip; supraorbital tentacle branched; no nuchal cirri; a well-developed fleshy occipital crest on male; body elongate, the depth at origin of anal fin about 7–8 in standard length; dorsal fin notched between spinous and soft portions, the last ray joined in part by membrane to caudal peduncle; last anal ray not linked by membrane to peduncle; caudal fin rounded; gray-brown, abruptly white on lower one-sixth of body, with narrow, dark-edged white bars,

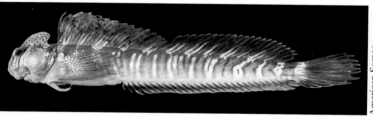

American Samoa

most as double bars; head, crest, and basal one-third of pectoral fin with dark brown dots. Largest specimen examined, 9 cm. Described from Tahiti; known also from Samoa Islands, Niue, Rotuma, and Guam; lives inshore on rocky substrata in the surge zone, more out of the sea than in, though wet with spray.

GARLANDED ROCKSKIPPER
Alticus sertatus (Garman, 1903)

Dorsal rays XIV-XV,22–24 (usually XV,23); anal rays II,27–28; pectoral rays 15; pelvic rays I,4; caudal rays 12, unbranched; 1 canine tooth on each side of lower jaw of males, lacking in females, small teeth in jaws very numerous, about 300 in upper jaw and 250 in lower, and freely movable; margin of lips crenulate; no fleshy disc behind lower lip; nasal cirrus unbranched; supraorbital cirrus branched; no nuchal cirri; fleshy occipital crest on males; body elongate, the depth at origin of anal fin about 7–8 in standard length; dorsal fin notched between spinous and soft portions, the last ray joined by membrane to caudal peduncle; last anal ray not bound to peduncle by membrane; male light lavender-gray, shading to white ventrally, with dark lines bordering narrow, irregular white

Tonga (Williams)

bars on side of body; orange-red margin along anterior half of spinous portion of dorsal fin; a row of saddle-like darker spots of about eye size along back extending onto base of dorsal fin; head with black dots and short lines; a curving black line behind eye; crest with numerous small black spots; a black submarginal band in anal fin and caudal fin except dorsally. Largest specimen, 8 cm. Known from the Solomon Islands to Tonga. Habitat as in *A. arnoldorum*.

MARQUESAN ROCKSKIPPER

Alticus simplicirrus Smith-Vaniz & Springer, 1971

Dorsal rays XIII,23–24; anal rays II,26; pectoral rays 15; pelvic rays I,3; caudal rays 13, unbranched; teeth in jaws very numerous, about 300 in upper jaw and 250 in lower, and freely movable; margin of lips crenulate; no fleshy disc behind lower lip; supraorbital cirrus short and unbranched; no nuchal cirri; fleshy occipital crest on males; body elongate, the depth at origin of anal fin about 7–8 in standard length; dorsal fin deeply notched between spinous and soft portions, the last ray joined by membrane to caudal peduncle; last anal ray not bound to peduncle by membrane; male gray-brown, shading to white ventrally, with vertical white lines or rows of white dashes that continue into dorsal fin parallel with spines and rays; a row of small, dark

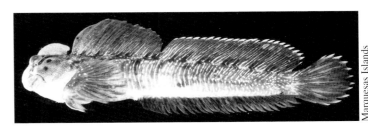

Marquesas Islands

brown spots along back extending into base of dorsal fin; head finely dotted with white, becoming white on branchiostegal membranes; a curving black line behind eye and 2 small black spots on cheek; tips of caudal and soft dorsal rays white. Largest specimen, 12 cm. Known only from the Marquesas Islands. Surge-zone habitat as in *A. arnoldorum*.

ELUSIVE ROCKSKIPPER

Alticus sp. Williams (in prep.)

Dorsal rays XIV,23–24; anal rays II,27–28; pelvic rays I,4; caudal rays 13, unbranched; teeth in jaws very numerous and freely movable; margin of lips crenulate; a well-developed occipital crest on male; body elongate, the depth at origin of anal fin about 7–8 in standard length; dorsal fin only slightly notched between spinous and soft portions, the last ray joined in part by membrane to caudal peduncle; last anal ray not linked by membrane to peduncle; caudal fin asymmetrically rounded; pale gray with vertical to oblique brownish red lines on body; an oblique, black-edged white band from occiput to upper lip, passing behind

Pitcairn Island/male

eye; outer half of anal fin black; lower and posterior margin of caudal fin broadly black; tips of dorsal soft rays and pectoral rays black. Largest specimen examined, 8 cm. Known from Pitcairn Island, Rapa, and Rarotonga. Surge-zone habitat as in other species of *Alticus*.

Pantar, Indonesia/female

LANCE BLENNY

Aspidontus dussumieri (Valenciennes in C & V, 1836)

Dorsal rays X-XII,28–34 (rarely 28); anal rays II,25–28; pectoral rays 13–15; pelvic rays I,3; segmented caudal rays 11; mouth slightly ventral; teeth in jaws small and slender except for a very large recurved canine (not venomous) on each side at front of lower jaw; origin of dorsal fin less than an eye diameter behind eye, the fin nearly uniform in height; caudal fin slightly rounded, becoming lanceolate in adults, the 2 middle rays occasionally filamentous in adults; light yellowish gray with a white-edged black stripe from front of snout to basal one-third of caudal fin, nearly uniform in width on body; dorsal fin yellowish with a broad black stripe; only the female with a black spot at front of fin (Smith-Vaniz, 1976). Reaches about 12 cm. Red Sea and east coast of Africa to Tuamotu Archipelago; southern Japan to southern New South Wales; type locality, Réunion. Stays closer to the reef than the following species, backing into an empty worm tube or other small hole when threatened.

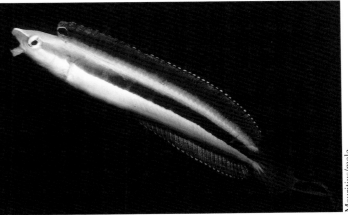

Mauritius/male

Mauritius

CLEANER MIMIC

Aspidontus taeniatus Quoy & Gaimard, 1834

Dorsal rays IX-XI,26–29; anal rays II,25–28; pectoral rays 13–15; pelvic rays I,3; segmented caudal rays 11; mouth ventral, the conical snout overhanging; teeth in jaws small and slender except for a very large recurved canine (not venomous) on each side at front of lower jaw; 4 small cirri in a transverse row on chin; body moderately elongate, the depth 5.0–6.5 in standard length; origin of dorsal fin less than an eye diameter behind eye, the fin nearly uniform in height (except in late postlarval stage, where the anterior part is elevated); color variable, depending on the local coloration of its model, the Striped Cleaner Wrasse, *Labroides dimidiatus*; hence it is often whitish or pale yellow anteriorly, soon shading to blue posteriorly, with a black lateral stripe from snout to end of caudal fin that is progressively wider posteriorly. A common color phase of *L. dimidiatus* in French Polynesia has a pale orange streak next to lower edge of the black stripe in middle of body; the blenny (or often a pair) lurking nearby has the same color. An occasional *L. dimidiatus* from Samoa and Fiji to the Coral Sea has the posterior one-third to half of the black stripe on the body nearly replaced by yellow, this color continuing anteriorly below the stripe; the blenny then has the same color pattern (see *L. dimidiatus* account). The blenny mimics the cleaner wrasse in the mode of swimming as well, thus gaining protection from predation and enabling it to closely approach unwary fishes from which it tries to bite pieces of skin tissue, especially from the fins (the fishes learn to discriminate the mimic from the model and avoid the former); it also feeds in part on demersal fish eggs and tentacles of polychaete tube worms. Attains 10.5 cm. The mimicry was first discovered in Moorea in 1956 (Randall & Randall, 1960). Ranges in the Indo-Pacific from the Red Sea to French Polynesia; type locality, New Guinea. Regarded as a different subspecies, *Aspidontus taeniatus tractus* Fowler, in the western part of its range. The unusually large late postlarval stage (to about 6 cm) was described as a new species, *A. filamentosus* (Valenciennes, 1836) and long regarded as valid; it was placed in synonymy by Smith-Vaniz & Randall (1973).

BROWN CORAL BLENNY

Atrosalarias fuscus (Rüppell, 1838)

Dorsal rays IX-XI (usually X),18–22; anal rays II,18–21; pectoral rays 15–18; pelvic rays I,2; segmented caudal rays 10–14 (usually 12 or 13); a short cirrus on nape and on hind edge of anterior nostril; a short tentacle above eye; body deep, the depth about 3 in standard length; dorsal and anal fins progressively longer posteriorly, the last ray of each attached by membrane to caudal peduncle; caudal fin rounded; adults uniformly dark brown (appear black underwater); juveniles bright yellow. Reaches 14.5 cm. Described from the Red Sea; ranges to the Society Islands; in the western Pacific from Ryukyu Islands to the Great Barrier Reef (where the caudal fin of adults is yellow); regarded as a different subspecies, *Atrosalarias fuscus holomelas* (Günther), in the Pacific and Western Australia. Lives on sheltered shallow reefs, often hiding among branches of live or dead coral; difficult to approach underwater.

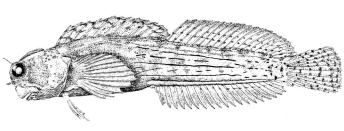

LINED-TAIL BLENNIELLA
Blenniella caudolineata (Günther, 1877)

Dorsal rays XII-XIV,19–22; anal rays II,20–23; pectoral rays 12–15 (usually 14); pelvic rays I,3; segmented caudal rays 13, the middle 9 branched (true of all *Blenniella*); no cirri on nape; supraorbital tentacle a simple filament; nasal cirrus small, simple or palmate; lateral line ending below sixth to tenth dorsal spines; mandibular pores 3–7 on each side; males with a low occipital crest; margin of lips smooth; a canine tooth posteriorly in lower jaw (also generic); females with 3 or 4 dark brown longitudinal lines on side of body behind pectoral fin, breaking into spots and dashes posteriorly; often with 1 or 2 additional longitudinal rows of dashes and small spots; dorsal and caudal fins with small, dark brown spots; males with up to 9 brown to olive bars on midside, some containing a pair of small, almond-shaped blue ocelli, one

above the other; numerous small pale spots ventrally, and traces of dark longitudinal lines in middle of body; caudal fin olive-brown with a few small pale spots in outer part and a broad pale pink distal margin. Largest male, 10 cm; largest female, 8.2 cm. Southern Japan to Molucca Islands and New Guinea, east to Mariana Islands, Howland Island, Tahiti (type locality), and Tuamotu Archipelago; often found in tidepools on exposed shores. Very close to *Blenniella cyanostigma* (Bleeker) from southwestern Indonesia, Andaman Sea, and east coast of Africa; *caudolineata* differs in having modally 1 fewer mandibular pores, slight modal difference in fin-rays counts, and females with 5 or 6 longitudinal dark lines on body; males of the two said to be indistinguishable (one of *cyanostigma* from Kenya illustrated here). *Salarias beani* Fowler from Vanuatu is a synonym.

REDSPOTTED BLENNIELLA
Blenniella chrysospilos (Bleeker, 1857)

Dorsal rays XII-XIV,18–22; anal rays II,20–23; pectoral rays 12–15 (usually 14); pelvic rays I,3; nape usually with a small cirrus on each side; supraorbital tentacle with 2–11 short branches at tip; nasal cirrus small and palmate; lateral line ending below ninth to twelfth dorsal spines; mandibular pores usually 6; males with a low occipital crest; margin of upper lip crenulate medially; a canine posteriorly on side of lower jaw of adults; females with 8 double, light red to dusky bars, partially interrupted by a pale stripe, many bars containing red to reddish brown dots in vertical series (also in some pale interspaces); head with red dots and an oblique red band behind eye; spinous dorsal with red or orange dots and dashes; pectoral fins with dark red dots; dorsal spines tipped with white and black; males bluish gray to brown with up to 9 dark brown to reddish blotches or short double bars along upper side (may be obscure on dark individuals), numerous small,

pale blue spots or dashes, mainly on lower half of body, and often a pupil-size black spot below anterior part of soft portion of dorsal fin; lower half of caudal fin blackish. Largest male, 13.5 cm; largest female, 11.5 cm. East coast of Africa to the Society Islands; Ryukyu Islands to the Great Barrier Reef and New Caledonia; type locality, Ambon. A shallow-water species of reef crests or fringing reefs exposed to surf. *Salarias coronatus* Günther is a synonym.

483

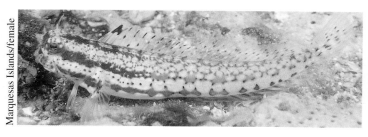

Marquesas Islands/female

Hawaiian Islands/male

Hawaiian Islands/male

BIGBROW BLENNIELLA
Blenniella gibbifrons (Quoy & Gaimard, 1824)

Dorsal rays XII-XIV,17–21; anal rays II,18–22; pectoral rays 13–14; pelvic rays I,3; cirrus on nape present or absent; supraorbital tentacle slender, rarely with 1 to a few small branches near tip; nasal cirrus small, usually with 4 or 5 short, slender branches; lateral line ending below eleventh to thirteenth dorsal spines; mandibular pores 5–7 on each side; no crest on head of either sex; margin of lips smooth; females with a fine reticular pattern of red to dark reddish brown that may consist partly of dots; side of body of both sexes with 2 longitudinal series of short double dark bars which may be linked by vertical lines or may be irregularly joined to form 2 stripes that continue onto head; head with red dots; dorsal fin of both sexes with small white and red spots (only white on some males), mainly on spines and rays, and 1 to a few black spots per membrane at front of fin; males with numerous small, elliptical, pale blue spots and short dashes on body and small blue spots on head. Largest male, 12.2 cm; largest female, 10.7 cm. Distribution disjunct east to west: east coast of Africa to Mauritius and Chagos Archipelago in the Indian Ocean, and islands of Micronesia (except Palau and Yap) to the Hawaiian Islands (type locality) and Pitcairn Islands on the Pacific Plate (apparently absent from the Samoa Islands); not present in the Indo-Malayan region north to the Ryukyu Islands; occurs on intertidal reef flats.

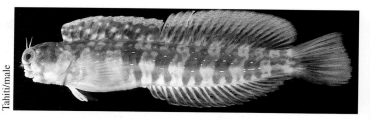

Tahiti/male

BULLETHEAD BLENNIELLA
Blenniella paula (Bryan & Herre, 1903)

Dorsal rays XII-XIV,18–22; anal rays II,19–23 (rarely 19 or 23); pectoral rays 13–15; pelvic rays I,3; cirrus on nape small; supraorbital tentacle slender, rarely with 1 to 4 small lateral branches; nasal cirrus short and palmate, rarely with more than 6 branches; lateral line ending below eighth to twelfth dorsal spines; mandibular pores 5–7 on each side; no crest on head of either sex, though occasional large males may have a thin ridge; males pale yellowish with 7 gray-brown bars on body that divide into 2 or more irregular short branches dorsally and bifurcate on lower one-fourth of body; 2 elongate, dark-edged, pale blue spots or dashes in each bar, one above the other, and sometimes scattered lesser blue spots on body; broad outer part of dorsal fin pale yellow with numerous small orange-red spots and dashes; life color of female not recorded, but probably similar to that of *Blenniella periophthalmus*, hence with numerous small orange-red or black dots superimposed on the barred pattern. In their revision of *Blenniella* and *Istiblennius*, Springer & Williams (1994) admitted to difficulty deciding whether to recognize *B. paula* as distinct from *B. periophthalmus*, the latter from the Indian Ocean and western Pacific from the Ryukyu Islands to Vanuatu, the former from the Coral Sea and islands of Oceania except the Hawaiian Islands; the type locality of *paula* is Minami-tori-shima (formerly Marcus Island). Reaches 16 cm.

Lord Howe Island

WHITEDOTTED BLENNY
Cirripectes alboapicalis (Ogilby, 1899)

Dorsal rays XII,15–17; anal rays II,16–18; pectoral rays usually 15 (true of other *Cirripectes*); pelvic rays I,4 (the spine and inner ray difficult to detect); segmented caudal rays 13, the middle 9 branched (also generic); lateral-line tubes 9–17, the last posterior to twelfth dorsal soft ray; small scale-like flaps over anterior part of lateral line (not present on other *Cirripectes* here); a transverse fringe of cirri on nape (also characteristic of the genus), with a median gap, the total nuchal cirri usually 32–39; edge of upper lip with 34–52 crenulae; middle of margin of lower lip crenulate; teeth in jaws movable and very numerous, and a canine tooth posteriorly on each side of lower jaw (generic); dorsal fin deeply incised above last spine; last dorsal ray joined by membrane to caudal peduncle; dark brown with white dots on head and at least anteriorly on body; a black spot on head behind eye. Largest specimen, 15.5 cm. A southern subtropical species ranging from Easter Island to Pitcairn Islands, Rapa, Tonga, Kermadec Islands, Norfolk Island, Lord Howe Island (type locality), and southern Great Barrier Reef. *Cirripectes patuki* De Buen from Easter Island is a synonym.

Fiji/female

Great Barrier Reef/male

Coral Sea/male

CHESTNUT BLENNY
Cirripectes castaneus (Valenciennes in C & V, 1836)
Dorsal rays XI-XIII,13–15 (nearly always XII,14); anal rays II,14–16; pelvic rays I,4; lateral-line tubes 1–13, the last below or posterior to sixth dorsal soft ray; cirri on nape divided into 4 groups, those on lower part of ventral group on a slightly expanded base; total nuchal cirri usually 32–40; upper lip with 29–50 crenulae; dorsal fin deeply incised above last spine; last dorsal ray joined by membrane to caudal-fin base; females dark brown to dark reddish brown with close-set light olive spots of pupil size or smaller (occasional females uniform dark brown); males dark brown, the head and body lighter brown, with slightly oblique, orange-red to reddish brown bars. Largest specimen, 11.5 cm. Red Sea and east coast of Africa to Caroline Islands, Fiji, and Tonga; southern Japan to southern Great Barrier Reef, New Caledonia, Norfolk Island, and the Kermadec Islands. Feeds on algae and detritus, like others of the genus. *Salarias sebae* Valenciennes is a synonym.

LADY MUSGRAVE BLENNY
Cirripectes chelomatus Williams & Maugé, 1984
Dorsal rays XII-XIII,14–16 (nearly always XII,15); anal rays II,15–17; pelvic rays I,4; lateral-line tubes 0–8, the last below space between last dorsal spine and tenth dorsal soft ray; cirri on nape divided into 4 groups, those on lower part of ventral group on a slightly expanded base; total nuchal cirri usually 27–32; upper lip with 29–43 crenulae; middle of lower lip smooth; dorsal fin with a very shallow notch above last spine; last dorsal ray joined by membrane to caudal-fin base; sexes similar in color, dark to medium brown with very small, bright red spots on head and body (absent on head and anterior body of illustrated male). Largest specimen, 12.3 cm. Described from Lady Musgrave Reef on the Great Barrier Reef; ranges north to eastern end of Papua New Guinea, south to Lord Howe Island, and east to Fiji and Tonga.

Tuamotu Archipelago

Marshall Islands/male

JENNINGS' BLENNY
Cirripectes jenningsi Schultz, 1943
Dorsal rays XII-XIII (rarely XIII),15–16 (rarely 16); anal rays II,15–17; pelvic rays I,4; anterior lateral-line tubes 2–11, the last posterior to fifteenth dorsal soft ray; cirri on nape not divided into groups, the total number usually 37–42; upper lip with 41–47 crenulae; middle of lower lip crenulate; dorsal fin with a very deep notch above last spine; last dorsal ray joined by membrane to caudal-fin base; no color photographs available; color note: head and anterior body rose red with scattered, small dark spots, rest of body purplish black to dark bluish with numerous small white spots. Largest specimen, 9.7 cm. Described from Swains Island in the Tokelau Islands; also known from the Gilbert Islands (Kiribati), Phoenix Islands, Line Islands, and Tuamotu Archipelago.

BROWNSPOTTED BLENNY
Cirripectes fuscoguttatus Strasburg & Schultz, 1953
Dorsal rays XII,13–15; anal rays II,14–16; pelvic rays I,4; anterior lateral-line tubes 0–3, the last posterior to thirteenth dorsal soft ray; cirri on nape generally divided into 4 groups, the 2 dorsal groups usually meet or overlap medially on nape, the lower group on an expanded flap; total nuchal cirri 47–66; upper lip with 40–55 crenulae; middle of lower lip smooth; dorsal fin with a very deep notch above last spine; last dorsal ray joined by membrane to caudal-fin base; yellowish on head and anterior body, shading to brown posteriorly, with numerous dark brown spots, those on head and anterior body more irregular, those posteriorly more close-set. Largest specimen, 13.3 cm. Taiwan and Philippines east to islands of Micronesia (Marshall Islands, type locality), Tonga, Phoenix Islands, Samoa Islands, Society Islands, and Tuamotu Archipelago.

Chagos/female (Winterbottom)

Chagos/male (Winterbottom)

BURNT BLENNY
Cirripectes perustus Smith, 1959

Dorsal rays XI-XII (rarely XI),14–15 (rarely 15); anal rays II,14–16; pelvic rays I,3; lateral-line tubes 0–3, the last below dorsal soft rays 5–11; cirri on nape divided into 3–4 groups (3 when the 2 dorsal groups fuse medially), the lower cirri of ventral group on a slightly expanded base; total number of nuchal cirri usually 34–42; upper lip crenulae 36–48; middle of lower lip smooth; dorsal fin not notched above last spine; last dorsal ray joined by membrane to caudal-fin base; females yellowish to grayish brown anteriorly, brown posteriorly, with brownish red spots; males light yellowish brown anteriorly, shading to brownish red posteriorly; spinous portion of dorsal fin yellow, the soft portion, anal, and caudal fins red and brown; upper part of pectoral fin yellow, lower part red. Largest specimen, 12.9 cm. First reported from the southern Gilbert Islands as *Cirripectes* sp. by Randall (1955a); named from Kenya in 1959; otherwise known from Madagascar, Seychelles, Chagos Archipelago, Nicobar Islands, Philippines, Taiwan, Papua New Guinea, Fiji, Palau, and Yap and Ifaluk in the Caroline Islands.

Great Barrier Reef/juvenile

Guam/female

BARRED BLENNY
Cirripectes polyzona (Bleeker, 1868)

Dorsal rays XI-XIII,13–15 (nearly always XII,14); anal rays II,14–16; pelvic rays I,4; lateral-line tubes 2–9, the last posterior to seventh dorsal soft ray; cirri on nape divided into 4 groups, the lower cirri of ventral group on a slightly expanded base; total number of nuchal cirri usually 37–41; upper lip with 32–45 crenulae; middle of lower lip smooth; dorsal fin deeply notched above last spine; last dorsal ray joined by membrane to caudal-fin base; adults gray, shading to brown posteriorly, with dark brown bars, the females with a dull red reticular pattern on head, the males with oblique red bars; juveniles gray with a broad, dark brown stripe on upper side, orange markings on head, a white bar below eye and a white spot in posterior interorbital. Small for the genus, the largest 8.5 cm. Gulf of Aden to South Africa, east to Johnston Island, Line Islands, and Samoa Islands; in the western Pacific from southern Japan through Indonesia (Ambon, type locality) to southern Great Barrier Reef. *Blennius canescens* Garman from Fiji is a synonym.

ZEBRA BLENNY
Cirripectes quagga (Fowler & Ball, 1924)

Dorsal rays XI-XIII,14–16 (nearly always XII,15); anal rays II,14–16; pelvic rays I,4; anterior lateral-line tubes 7–18, the last posterior to seventh dorsal soft ray; transverse row of nuchal cirri with a distinct gap medially on nape, the total number of cirri usually 26–32; upper lip with 32–46 crenulae; middle of lower lip smooth; dorsal fin deeply notched above last spine; last dorsal ray bound by membrane to caudal peduncle in adults; color highly variable, sometimes uniform brown, but often with 12–14 dark bars on body separated by narrow pale interspaces; or with vertical rows of white dots; a broad, bright red or yellow area posteriorly on body present or absent. Attains 9 cm. East coast of Africa to the Hawaiian Islands, French Polynesia, and Pitcairn Islands; Taiwan to the Great Barrier Reef; type locality, Wake Island. Although usually collected on coral reefs in less than 10 m, one lot was taken in the Marquesas Islands in 19 m. *Cirripectes lineopunctatus* Strasburg was described from the Hawaiian Islands mainly on its color pattern of vertical rows of white dots on the body, but Williams (1988) placed it in synonymy after finding this pattern at other localities.

Marshall Islands

Marquesas Islands

486

Coral Sea/female

Great Barrier Reef/male

RETICULATED BLENNY

Cirripectes stigmaticus Strasburg & Schultz, 1953

Dorsal rays XII,14–16; anal rays II,15–17; pelvic rays I,4; anterior lateral-line tubes 1–10, the last posterior to seventh dorsal soft ray; nuchal cirri in 4 groups, the lower cirri of ventral group on a slightly expanded base; total number of cirri usually 34–40; upper lip with 35–52 crenulae; middle of lower lip smooth; dorsal fin deeply notched above last spine; last dorsal ray joined by membrane to caudal-fin base; females usually olivaceous with a

reticular pattern of dull orange-red that tends to break into dark reddish spots posteriorly (or one could say orange-red with numerous olivaceous spots); males similar anteriorly but most of body dark brown with bright red spots and short irregular lines. Largest specimen, 12.1 cm. East coast of Africa to Marshall Islands (type locality), Caroline Islands, Tonga, and Samoa Islands; Indonesia to Great Barrier Reef and New Caledonia; common in surge channels in outer-reef areas, often on coral. *Cirripectes cruentus* Smith from Mozambique is a synonym.

Marshall Islands/female

Marquesas Islands/male

PACIFIC PLATE BLENNY

Cirripectes variolosus (Valenciennes in C & V, 1836)

Dorsal rays XI-XIII,13–15 (nearly always XII,14); anal rays II,14–16; pelvic rays I,4; anterior lateral-line tubes 1–11, the last posterior to seventh dorsal soft ray; nuchal cirri in 4 groups, the lower cirri of ventral group on a slightly expanded base; total number of cirri usually 34–40; upper lip with 37–51 crenulae; middle of lower lip smooth; dorsal fin deeply notched above last spine; last dorsal ray joined by membrane to caudal-fin base; both sexes gray to light brown or brownish red, the head with

small red spots and oblique bars; base of soft portion of dorsal fin often with oblique red streaks; head of a female from 30 m off Pitcairn Island was mostly bright red; some females with pupil-size dark brown spots posteriorly on body. Largest specimen, 11.2 cm. Occurs at islands of the Pacific Plate (sensu Springer, 1982), except the Hawaiian Islands (where the similar *Cirripectes vanderbilti* is found (both occur at Johnston Island); type locality, Guam. The species name is derived from the Latin *variola*, meaning smallpox (hence spotted).

FRINGEFACE BLENNY

Cirrisalarias bunares Springer, 1976

Dorsal rays X-XII (usually XI), 16–17; anal rays II,17–18 (rarely 17); pectoral rays 14; pelvic rays I,3; segmented caudal rays 13, none branched; lateral line short, consisting of 1–2 tubes; teeth in jaws relatively rigid, 23–28 in upper jaw and 22–26 in lower jaw; upper lip without a free dorsal margin medially; numerous large fleshy cirri on rims of anterior and posterior nostrils; supraorbital tentacle simple or palmate; no nuchal cirri; life color not known; pale in preservative, the males with a broad blackish zone across throat. Largest, 2.4 cm. Described from the Comoro Islands and Sri Lanka from specimens collected from surge chan-

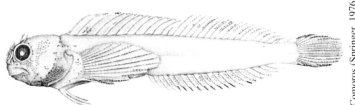
Comoros (Springer, 1976)

nels; reported from American Samoa (Wass, 1984); other previously unreported records from Christmas Island (Indian Ocean), Philippines, Solomon Islands, Tonga, and Fiji (V. G. Springer, pers. comm.).

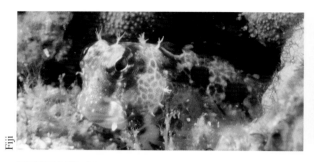

Fiji

New Britain

TRIPLESPOT BLENNY

Crossosalarias macrospilus Smith-Vaniz & Springer, 1971
Dorsal rays XII,16–18; anal rays II,18–20; segmented caudal rays 13, the median 9 branched; pectoral rays 15; pelvic rays I,3; numerous very small movable teeth in jaws, with a canine posteriorly on each side of lower jaw; a short barbel at corner of lower lip; gill opening ending at or slightly below level of lowermost pectoral ray; a palmate cirrus on each side of nape; a median fleshy flap at base and anterior to first dorsal spine; middle dorsal spines sometimes filamentous on large adults; dorsal fin deeply incised between spinous and soft portions; last anal

ray connected by membrane to base of caudal fin; whitish anteriorly, densely spotted with light brown, and light brown posteriorly densely spotted with pale greenish; a large, deep blue to black spot at base and median flap of first dorsal spine, and a similar pair on throat; an irregular dark brown blotch larger than eye at upper end of gill opening, followed by 2 or more lesser blotches on upper side of body. Largest specimen, 8.2 cm. Ryukyu Islands to Great Barrier Reef and New Caledonia, east to Fiji and Tonga; type locality, Bougainville. Occurs on coral reefs from less than 1 to 25 m (usually in less than 10 m). The only species of the genus.

BICOLOR BLENNY

Ecsenius bicolor (Day, 1888)
Dorsal rays XI-XII (usually XII),15–18 (rarely 15); anal rays II,17–21; pectoral rays 12–14; pelvic rays I,3, the third soft ray very small (true of all *Ecsenius*); segmented caudal rays (unbranched in all *Ecsenius*) 13–14 (usually 14), the third and eleventh very prolonged in large adults (presumed males); lateral line ending below tenth to thirteenth dorsal spines; usually a single canine tooth posteriorly on each side of lower jaw; a cirrus from both anterior and posterior rim of anterior nostril; no cirri on nape or above eye (also generic); edges of lips smooth (generic); dorsal fin incised between spinous and soft portions about half length of first soft ray; last anal ray bound by membrane to caudal peduncle (generic); 3 color phases: first uniform dark brown (head may be yellowish to reddish brown); second with head and anterior half of body dark bluish to purplish gray, the posterior half bright orange-yellow; and the third with a wide black stripe on upper side, broadly bordered by white below, ending in a yellow area posteriorly; all three with an oblique orange line behind eye. Reaches 11 cm (including caudal filaments). A common species ranging from Maldive Islands and

Guam

Indonesia

Guam

Sri Lanka to Marshall Islands and Samoa Islands; Taiwan south to the Great Barrier Reef; type locality, Burma; occurs on coral reefs at depths of 1–21 m. Suzuki et al. (2001) studied the reproductive behavior and early development.

FIJI BLENNY

Ecsenius fijiensis Springer, 1988
Dorsal rays XII,13–14 (usually 13); anal rays II,15–16; pectoral rays 13–14 (usually 13); segmented caudal rays 13; lateral line ending below tenth to twelfth dorsal spines; usually a single canine tooth posteriorly on each side of lower jaw; a cirrus present only on posterior rim of anterior nostril; dorsal fin deeply incised between spinous and soft portions; body whitish with 2 stripes that begin as red and change below soft portion of dorsal fin to series of vertically elongate black spots faintly connected with a narrow dusky stripe; upper stripe continuing on head to eye as a dark brown band edged in white or yellow. Attains 5 cm. Known only from Fiji; collected from coral reefs in 0.5–23 m, mostly from depths greater than 10 m. Springer (2002) described *Ecsenius niue* from the island nation of Niue, which lies east of

Fiji

Tonga. He differentiated it from *E. fijiensis* principally in having 2 vertical rows of 2 black spots on the caudal peduncle, whereas *fijiensis* has 1 vertical row of 2 black spots with a black streak extending posteriorly from each spot to the base of the caudal fin. Some, including the author, would be inclined to regard *niue* as a subspecies of *fijiensis*. A form similar to these two should be expected in Tonga.

FOURMANOIR'S BLENNY

Ecsenius fourmanoiri Springer, 1972
Dorsal rays XII,14–15 (usually 15); anal rays II,16–17 (usually 17); pectoral rays 12–13 (usually 13); segmented caudal rays 13; lateral line ending below tenth to twelfth dorsal spines; a single canine tooth posteriorly on each side of lower jaw; a cirrus present only on posterior rim of anterior nostril; dorsal fin deeply incised between spinous and soft portions; whitish with 3 black stripes on body, diffusely edged with orange, the middle one extending forward to eye; stripes posterior to anal fin joined by narrow, blackish orange bars that expand as they approach stripes, thus isolating a series of roundish whitish spots between stripes; anal fin with a broad black stripe. Reaches 6.2 cm. Described from New Caledonia; later collected from Fiji and Tonga. Named for the ichthyologist Pierre Fourmanoir.

New Caledonia

TWINSPOT BLENNY

Ecsenius isos McKinney & Springer, 1976
Dorsal rays XII,14–15 (usually 14); anal rays II,16–17 (usually 16); pectoral rays 13–14 (rarely 14); segmented caudal rays 13; lateral line ending below eighth to eleventh dorsal spines; a single canine tooth posteriorly on each side of lower jaw; a cirrus present only on posterior rim of anterior nostril; dorsal fin deeply incised between spinous and soft portions; 2 longitudinal rows of dusky red spots on side of body, becoming smaller and black posteriorly; head pale orange with a few small, dark brown spots, including a prominent pair on throat. Largest specimen, 4 cm. Described from Vanuatu; known otherwise only from New Caledonia.

New Caledonia

Bali

Papua New Guinea

MIDAS BLENNY

Ecsenius midas Starck, 1969
Dorsal rays XII,18–21 (usually 19 or 20); anal rays II,20–23 (rarely 20); pectoral rays 13–14 (rarely 14); segmented caudal rays usually 14; lateral line ending below seventh to ninth dorsal spines; usually a single canine tooth posteriorly on each side of lower jaw; a pair of anterior teeth at front of lower jaw about twice as large as adjacent slender teeth; total slender teeth in lower jaw 13–16 (more than 31 in other species of *Ecsenius*); a cirrus present only on posterior rim of anterior nostril; body very elongate, the depth about 5–6 in standard length; origin of dorsal fin over middle of head (more posterior on other *Ecsenius*); dorsal fin not incised; caudal fin deeply emarginate; color extremely variable; usually orange-yellow or dark slate blue, but always with a large black spot directly in front of anus. Largest species of the genus, reaches 13 cm, and the most wide-ranging: Red Sea (type locality) to the Marquesas Islands; occurs on coral reefs to at least 30 m. Orange-yellow phase observed to school with *Pseudanthias squamipinnis*, which it resembles in color. One color phase, bright yellow dorsally and abruptly pink on side and ventrally, forms feeding aggregations with 3 species of anthiine fishes and the damselfish *Lepidozygus tapeinosoma* of the same color pattern in the Line Islands and Phoenix Islands, an example of social mimicry (Randall & McCosker, 1993). Suzuki et al. (2001) studied the reproductive behavior and early development.

LEOPARD BLENNY

Ecsenius pardus Springer, 1988

Dorsal rays XII,13–15; anal rays II,16–17; pectoral rays 12–14; segmented caudal rays 13–14 (rarely 14); lateral line ending below tenth to twelfth dorsal spines; a single small canine tooth posteriorly on each side of lower jaw; a cirrus present only on posterior rim of anterior nostril; dorsal fin deeply incised between spinous and soft portions; reddish brown with a row of 5 ocellated black spots about as large as eye along upper side, a second row of 3 similar ocellated spots above anal fin, and a third row of smaller spots adjacent to dorsal fin; a black line extending from eye across head, bordered below by a white line to lower edge of middle of upper series of ocellated spots; a row

Fiji

of well-separated white spots or dashes before lower series of ocelli, ending in 2 white spots at pectoral-fin base; pectoral rays red. Largest specimen, 6.2 cm. Known only from Fiji; one of a group of 8 related allopatric species termed the *oculus* complex by Springer (1988), which could also be treated as subspecies.

PORTENOY'S BLENNY

Ecsenius portenoyi Springer, 1988

Dorsal rays XII,13–15 (usually 14); anal rays II,14–16 (usually 16); pectoral rays 12–13 (usually 13); segmented caudal rays 13; lateral line ending below tenth to twelfth dorsal spines; a single small canine tooth posteriorly on each side of lower jaw; a cirrus present only on posterior rim of anterior nostril; dorsal fin deeply incised between spinous and soft portions; brownish red with 3 longitudinal series of pale-edged black spots, the smallest adjacent to base of dorsal fin, merging posteriorly with spots of middle row; lower row of 4 or 5 spots above anal fin; a narrow white stripe from lower part of eye along body between 2 lower rows of spots, its upper edge blackish anteriorly. Largest specimen, 5.8 cm. Known only from American Samoa, Tonga, and Rotuma; also a member of the *oculus* complex, as is the following species.

American Samoa

TILED BLENNY

Ecsenius tessera Springer, 1988

Dorsal rays XII,14–15 (usually 14); anal rays II,16–17; pectoral rays 13; segmented caudal rays 13; lateral line ending below tenth to twelfth dorsal spines; a single small canine tooth posteriorly on each side of lower jaw; a cirrus present only on posterior rim of anterior nostril; dorsal fin deeply incised between spinous and soft portions; brown with 2 rows of black spots larger than eye on body posterior to pectoral fin, separated by a narrow, pale brown network; a row of semicircular black spots along base of dorsal fin to middle of soft portion; a black line from behind eye to above and behind a white spot above pectoral-fin base; dorsal spines and pectoral rays red; a broad red stripe

New Caledonia

on anal fin. Largest specimen, 5.9 cm, a male, as is normally true of blennies. Described from 3 specimens from New Caledonia (type locality) collected in 6–10 m outside the barrier reef, and 4 from Vanuatu.

BLACK BLENNY

Enchelyurus ater (Günther, 1877)

Dorsal rays VIII-X (rarely VIII or X),20–24 (modally 21); anal rays II,18–21 (modally 19); pectoral rays 14–16; pelvic rays I,2 (the spine hidden); segmented caudal rays 14 (unbranched); teeth incisiform, fewer than 50 in each jaw; a large canine on side of both upper and lower jaws; no cirri on head; dorsal fin without a notch; dorsal and anal fins fully confluent with caudal fin; dark brown to black, sometimes with a faint reticular or barred pattern; head with numerous small, irregular brown spots; paired fins yellow. Largest specimen 5.3 cm. Known from Lord Howe Island, New Caledonia, Fiji, Tonga, Samoa Islands, Society Islands (type locality, Tahiti), Rapa, and Tuamotu Archipelago; a cryptic coral-reef fish.

Coral Sea

KRAUSS' BLENNY
Enchelyurus kraussii (Klunzinger, 1871)

Dorsal rays VI-IX (modally VIII; VI only in Red Sea),21–24 (modally 22); anal rays II,18–20; pectoral rays 14–16; pelvic rays I,2 (the spine hidden); segmented caudal rays 14 (unbranched); teeth incisiform, fewer than 50 in each jaw; a large canine on side of both upper and lower jaws; no cirri on head; dorsal fin without a notch; dorsal and anal fins fully confluent with caudal fin; dark orangish brown, shading to dull brownish orange on head with a few black dots and short lines below and behind eye; outer part of dorsal fin broadly brownish orange except posteriorly, the outer half of first 2 membranes black. Largest specimen, 5.0 cm. Described from the Red Sea; recorded also from Comoros, Seychelles, Indo-Malayan region,

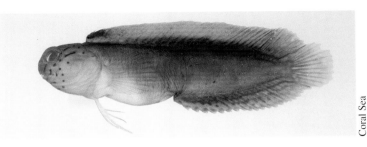

Coral Sea

Taiwan, Mariana Islands, Great Barrier Reef, Coral Sea, New Caledonia, and Tonga. Springer (1972a) noted that this species and *Enchelyurus ater* were not known then from the same locality, but the two coexist in New Caledonia (M. L. Kulbicki, pers. comm.) and the Chesterfield Bank, Coral Sea.

BARREDTAIL ROCKSKIPPER
Entomacrodus caudofasciatus (Regan, 1909)

Dorsal spines XIII,14–16; anal rays II,15–17; pectoral rays usually 14; pelvic rays I,4, the spine not visible externally (true of all *Entomacrodus*); segmented caudal rays normally 13, the middle 9 branched (also generic); lateral line ending in space below eighth dorsal spine and fifth soft ray; gill rakers 13–18; nape with 1 cirrus on each side; supraorbital tentacle with 1–8 branches (increasing in number with growth); cirri present posteriorly on anterior nostril (generic); margin of upper lip smooth medially, crenulate only on lateral one-third; over 100 freely movable slender teeth in each jaw (generic); dorsal fin deeply notched between spinous and soft portions (generic); last dorsal ray joined by membrane to caudal peduncle (generic); color highly variable with locality; most with a very dark humeral spot (below lateral line under third dorsal spine, but absent in French Polynesia and Cook Islands), followed by a series of 5 or 6 double, dark brown

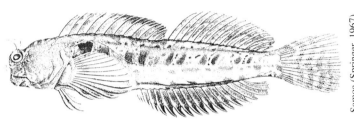

Samoa (Springer, 1967)

blotches along side of body; a dark spot usually not present behind eye; dark bars on upper lip present or absent. Largest specimen, 6.6 cm, from Tonga. Described from Christmas Island; otherwise known in the Indian Ocean only from Cocos-Keeling Islands and Andaman Islands; in the Pacific from Indo-Malayan region north to Taiwan and Japan, east to Marshall Islands, Tuamotu Archipelago, and Pitcairn Islands; also a record from the Kermadec Islands (Francis et al., 1987). *Salarias rarotongensis* Whitley is a synonym.

CORNELIA'S ROCKSKIPPER
Entomacrodus corneliae (Fowler, 1932)

Dorsal spines XIII,13–15 (rarely 13); anal rays II,16–17 (usually 16); pectoral rays usually 14; lateral line ending in space below second and fourth dorsal soft rays; gill rakers 16–17; nape with one cirrus on each side; supraorbital tentacle with 3–6 cirri; margin of upper lip smooth medially, crenulate only on lateral one-third; light gray-brown with 6 short double dark bars along side of body and numerous white spots and dashes, mostly in longitudinal rows; head pale brown with 2 oblique black lines behind eye and a brown band between, numerous dark brown dots dorsally, and dark brown lines ventrally. Attains at least 5 cm. Known only from the Marquesas

Marquesas Islands

Islands. Described from a specimen 17 mm in standard length in the late postlarval stage; linked to this species by Springer (1967), mainly by fin-ray counts. Very close to *E. sealei*, not known from the Marquesas but from islands to the south and west. *Entomacrodus corneliae* might best be treated as a subspecies of *E. sealei*.

SURF ROCKSKIPPER
Entomacrodus cymatobiotus Schultz & Chapman, 1960

Dorsal spines XIII,13–15; anal rays II,14–16; pectoral rays usually 14; lateral line ending in space below eleventh dorsal spine and sixth dorsal soft ray; gill rakers 10–16 (usually 12–14); nape with 1 cirrus on each side; supraorbital tentacle with 2–6

Marshall Islands

cirri; margin of upper lip completely crenulate; light brown with 6 short, double dark bars along side of body and longitudinal rows of white dashes; dorsal part of body finely dotted with dark brown; 2 parallel, oblique, dark orange lines behind eye. Largest

specimen, 5.7 cm. Described from the Marshall Islands; also known from Caroline Islands, Line Islands, Phoenix Islands, Tuamotu Archipelago, and Kermadec Islands; occurs on surf-swept seaward reefs.

Tonga

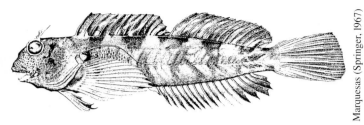

Marquesas (Springer, 1967)

WAVYLINE ROCKSKIPPER
Entomacrodus decussatus (Bleeker, 1858)
Dorsal spines XIII,16–18 (rarely 18, usually 17); anal rays II,16–19 (rarely 16, usually 18); pectoral rays usually 14; lateral line ending in space below eleventh dorsal spine and sixth dorsal soft ray; gill rakers 17–30 (increasing with growth); nape with 1 cirrus on each side (may have side branches in large individuals); supraorbital tentacle with many short cirri on each side; margin of upper lip of adults completely crenulate; body whitish with 6 short, double dark bars along side of body, overlaid by a pattern of wavy, longitudinal, dark gray lines; head with scattered small, dark brown spots; rays of dorsal fin with small white and black spots. Attains 19 cm. Western Australia and Indo-Malayan region (Indonesia the type locality) east to Mariana Islands, Tonga, and Samoa Islands.

RANDALL'S ROCKSKIPPER
Entomacrodus randalli Springer, 1967
Dorsal spines XIII,15–16 (usually 16); anal rays II,16–17 (usually 17); pectoral rays usually 14; lateral line ending in space below tenth and last dorsal soft rays; gill rakers 21–24; nape with 1 cirrus on each side; supraorbital tentacle with 4–8 cirri on medial edge; margin of upper lip completely crenulate; body with 5 irregular dark bars, the posterior 4 vaguely X-shaped; a dark spot at top of caudal peduncle and one directly below on ventral edge; anterior bar extending to a dark brown humeral spot below anterior part of lateral line; head with an irregular, oblique, dark brown line behind eye; suborbital region, snout, and upper lip with very small, close-set dark spots. Largest specimen, 10.9 cm. One of 3 species of the genus endemic to the Marquesas Islands.

Rapa

Marquesas Islands

Marquesas Islands

ZEBRALIP ROCKSKIPPER
Entomacrodus epalzeocheilos (Bleeker, 1859)
Dorsal spines XIII,14–16 (rarely 14); anal rays II,15–17 (rarely 15); pectoral rays usually 14; lateral line ending in space below second to eleventh dorsal soft rays; gill rakers 16–25 (usually more than 19 in specimens larger than 40 mm standard length); nape with 1–10 cirri on each side; supraorbital tentacle with 3–9 cirri on medial side; margin of upper lip of adults completely crenulate; whitish with numerous irregular gray-brown blotches on body and very small, gray to reddish brown spots dorsoanteriorly on body; head and pectoral-fin base with numerous very small orangish brown to brownish red spots; a large, vertically elongate, blackish spot behind eye; 3 oblique orange or red-edged gray bands across throat; upper lip with alternating narrow, vertical, white and orange-edged dark gray bands that extend a short distance onto snout. Largest specimen, 12.8 cm. Reported from Natal, Madagascar, Seychelles, Sri Lanka, Indonesia (type locality, Java), Ogasawara Islands, Mariana Islands, Norfolk Island, Kermadec Islands, Niuafo'ou, Tonga, Samoa Islands, Rapa, and Pitcairn Islands. Springer (1972b) wrote that it is "quite possible" that *Entomacrodus niuafoouensis* (Fowler) and *E. epalzeocheilos* are one species; *niuafoouensis* is here tentatively placed in synonymy.

BIGSPOT ROCKSKIPPER
Entomacrodus macrospilus Springer, 1967
Dorsal spines XIII,15–16 (usually 16); anal rays II,17–18 (usually 18); pectoral rays usually 14; lateral line ending in space below tenth and eleventh dorsal spines; gill rakers 13–14; nape without cirri; supraorbital tentacle without cirri; margin of upper lip completely crenulate; light brown with numerous small white spots and a lateral series of 7 dark reddish brown bars across body (bars double except first and last); a round black spot nearly as large as eye behind eye in males (irregular and dark brown in females); males may have a large yellow area over branchiostegal membranes. Largest specimen, 4.2 cm. Known only from the Marquesas Islands; specimens were collected along rocky shores exposed to strong surge, some as deep as 8 m.

ROFEN'S ROCKSKIPPER

Entomacrodus rofeni Springer, 1967

Dorsal spines XIII,16–17 (usually 16); anal rays II,17–18 (usually 18); pectoral rays usually 14; lateral line ending in space below tenth and eleventh dorsal spines; gill rakers 16–19; nape with 1 cirrus on each side; supraorbital tentacle with 5–8 cirri; margin of upper lip completely crenulate; white, finely flecked with small, dull orange blotches dorsally; a series of 7 faint gray blotches containing orangish and blackish dots along side of body; head with a fine reticular pattern of dull orange. Largest specimen, 6.7 cm. Described from Raroia Atoll in the Tuamotu Archipelago; collected by the author in 1971 in Rangiroa Atoll and Henderson and Ducie in the Pitcairn Islands along exposed rocky shores (Randall, 1999a).

SEALE'S ROCKSKIPPER

Entomacrodus sealei Bryan & Herre, 1903

Dorsal spines XIII,13–16 (rarely 13 or 16; usually 15); anal rays II,15–17; pectoral rays usually 14; lateral line ending in space below eleventh dorsal spine and fifth dorsal soft ray; gill rakers 15–21 (modally 17); nape with 1 cirrus on each side; supraorbital tentacle with 1–7 cirri (increasing with growth), all on medial side; margin of upper lip smooth in middle, and crenulate on lateral one1third; light brown, shading to pale gray ventrally with longitudinal rows of white dashes and 6 short, dark bars along side, the second to fourth as double bars; irregular branching dark orange lines on head, mainly vertical in orientation, and an oblique gray mark behind eye; an orange-edged bar before pectoral-fin base. Largest specimen, 7.8 cm. Described from

Minami-tori-shima (Marcus Island); also known from Mariana Islands, Marshall Islands, Caroline Islands, Malden Island, Tonga, Phoenix Islands, Samoa Islands, Tuamotu Archipelago, and the Pitcairn Islands.

BLACKSPOTTED ROCKSKIPPER

Entomacrodus striatus (Quoy & Gaimard in C & V, 1836)

Dorsal spines XIII,14–17 (rarely 14 or 17); anal rays II,15–18 (rarely 15 or 18; usually 17); pectoral rays usually 14; lateral line ending in space below eleventh dorsal spine and tenth dorsal soft ray; gill rakers 14–22 (usually 17 or 18); nape with 1 cirrus on each side (occasionally absent); supraorbital tentacle with 1–20 cirri (increasing in number with growth) on medial and usually lateral side as well; margin of upper lip usually completely crenulate; whitish with numerous small, irregular black spots, the darkest closely grouped to form a longitudinal series of 7 blotches, the first below anterior end of lateral line. Largest specimen, 11.8 cm. The most common and widespread species of the genus; found throughout the Indo-Pacific region except the seas around the Arabian Peninsula and the Hawaiian Islands; type locality, Mauritius. Occurs in the intertidal zone of both protected lagoons and wave-swept outer reefs. *Entomacrodus plurifilis* Schultz & Chapman is one of 5 synonyms.

REEFMARGIN ROCKSKIPPER

Entomacrodus thalassinus (Jordan & Seale, 1906)

Dorsal spines XIII,13–15; anal rays II,15–17; pectoral rays usually 14; lateral line ending in space below eighth to thirteenth dorsal spines; gill rakers 9–18 (usually 11 or 12); nape with 1 cirrus on each side (occasionally missing on 1 side and rarely on both); supraorbital tentacle with 1–8 cirri (increasing in number with growth); margin of upper lip smooth; body whitish with numerous small, dark brown to black dots and 7 faint, irregular dark bars on body, more heavily pigmented in middle portion, thus forming a longitudinal series of dark blotches; head, including lips, with numerous dark red dots and an oblique blackish line behind eye. Largest specimen, 6 cm. Springer (1967) described 2 subspecies, *Entomacrodus thalassinus longicirrus* from the Gulf of Thailand to Hong Kong, and *E. t. thalassinus* with a disjunct distribution, Seychelles and Maldive Islands (Randall & Anderson, 1993) in the Indian Ocean and southern Japan and Taiwan east to the Line Islands and Tuamotu Archipelago in the Pacific; type locality, Western Samoa.

Hawaiian Islands/female

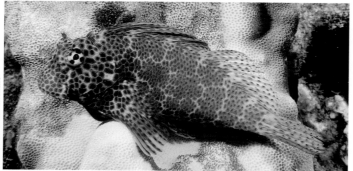

Hawaiian Islands/male

DELICATE BLENNY

Glyptoparus delicatulus Smith, 1959

Dorsal rays XII-XIII (usually XII),15–17; anal rays II,18–19; pectoral rays 13–14 (usually 14); pelvic rays I,3; segmented caudal rays 13; body elongate, the depth about 7 in standard length; teeth in jaws fairly rigid, 74–80 in upper jaw and 50–58 in lower; 2 or 3 canine teeth posteriorly on each side of lower jaw; occipital crest present; supraorbital cirrus minute or absent; a cirrus on anterior nostril and on each side of nape; dorsal fin deeply notched between spinous and soft portions; last dorsal and anal rays connected by membrane to caudal peduncle; caudal fin slightly rounded; pale gray with scattered, small white flecks and 4 rows of small black spots except those of 2 lower rows on anterior half of body as large as or larger than pupil; 2 oblique, dark gray bands behind eye; a dark gray or green transverse band on

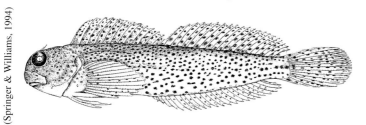

(Springer & Williams, 1994)

BEAUTIFUL ROCKSKIPPER

Istiblennius bellus (Günther, 1861)

Dorsal rays XII-XIV,20–22; anal rays II,20–23; pectoral rays 13–14 (usually 14); pelvic rays I,3; segmented caudal rays 13, the middle 9 branched (true of other *Istiblennius*); no cirri on nape; supraorbital cirrus usually a simple filament (occasionally with a small lateral branch); nasal cirri short; lateral line ending below fifth to tenth dorsal spines; mandibular pores 3–7 on each side; adult males with a blade-like occipital crest; margin of upper lip and middle of lower lip crenulate on most adults; no posterior canine teeth in lower jaw; dorsal fin notched between spinous and

SHORTBODIED BLENNY

Exallias brevis (Kner, 1868)

Dorsal spines XII,12–13 (usually 13); anal rays II,13–14 (usually 13); pectoral rays 15; pelvic rays I,4; segmented caudal rays 13, the middle 9 branched; lateral line ending in space below eighth to thirteenth dorsal spines; body deep, the depth at anal-fin origin 2.6–2.8 in standard length; teeth incisiform, very numerous, those in upper jaw movable, those in lower nearly fixed; no canine or vomerine teeth; lips crenulate; a transverse band of cirri on nape; supraorbital tentacle with many small branches; a pair of tiny barbels on each side of chin; dorsal fin deeply notched over last spine, the last ray connected by membrane to base of caudal fin; whitish with numerous, close-set, irregular spots, dark brown on female and bright red on male except head and abdomen. Largest specimen 14.5 cm. Occurs throughout the tropical Indo-Pacific; type locality given as China Seas. The only species of the genus. Feeds almost entirely on coral polyps; males prepare a nest by overgrazing a patch of live coral (often *Porites*) and may spawn with several females that come to the same nest site (Carlson, 1992). The eggs are bright yellow and not vigorously guarded by the male. Few fishes have been observed to feed on the eggs (though both females and males occasionally eat their own eggs), so it is believed that the eggs contain a repelling substance.

Flores/female (G. Allen)

chin and one on throat; a dark spot before pelvic-fin base; fins without dark markings. Attains 4.5 cm, but rarely exceeds 3.5 cm. Described from Kenya; also reported from Seychelles, Maldive Islands, Chagos Archipelago, Rowley Shoals, Ryukyu Islands, Great Barrier Reef, Tonga, Rotuma, Guam, Pohnpei, and Onotoa Atoll, Kiribati, the last as *Rhabdoblennius* sp. by Randall (1955a). The only species of the genus.

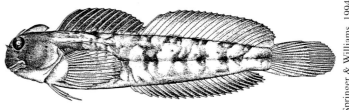

(Springer & Williams, 1994)

soft portions more than half length of first soft ray (true of all *Istiblennius*); last ray of dorsal fin joined by membrane to caudal peduncle or base of caudal fin (also generic); body of females with 7 or 8 irregular dark bars, this pattern overlaid with numerous small dark brown spots; small dark spots also present on head and fins; males with 7 or 8 irregular dark bars, the first 4 divided ventrally. Largest specimen. 16.5 cm. Distribution disjunct, Mariana Islands, Vanuatu, Tonga, Samoa Islands, and Marquesas Islands in the Pacific and east coast of Africa, Madagascar, Mauritius, Seychelles, and Christmas Island in the Indian Ocean. Type locality given as China seas, but probably in error.

DUSSUMIER'S ROCKSKIPPER
Istiblennius dussumieri (Valenciennes in C & V, 1836)
Dorsal rays XII-XIV,19–24; anal rays II,21–25; pectoral rays 13–15 (rarely 13); pelvic rays I,3; no cirri on nape; supraorbital tentacle variable, with up to 5 branches on each side; nasal cirri short, usually palmate; lateral line ending below fourth to tenth dorsal spines; mandibular pores 4–6 on each side; adult males with a blade-like occipital crest; edges of lips smooth; posterior canine tooth on each side of lower jaw present or absent; dusky gray with a series of 7 double, brownish orange bars on body, the bar of each pair posterior to pectoral fin divided ventrally (except posteriorly where the lower parts are separated as spots); females with scattered, small dark spots on body; males with outer part of median fins broadly dark; a black band on first 3 membranes of dorsal fin. Largest specimen, 12.9 cm. East coast of Africa,

Ambon, Indonesia/male

Arabian Sea, and India (type locality, Malabar) to Indo-Malayan region, north to Taiwan, south to Great Barrier Reef, and Norfolk Island, east to Palau, New Caledonia, and Fiji. The record from Lord Howe Island given by Springer & Williams (1994) is in error (specimen from Norfolk Island), but the species might be expected from Lord Howe Island (M. P. Francis, pers. comm.). *Salarias forsteri* Valenciennes is one of 12 synonyms.

Guam/male

RIPPLED ROCKSKIPPER
Istiblennius edentulus (Forster, 1801)
Dorsal rays XII-XIV,18–23; anal rays II,20–24; pectoral rays 13–14 (usually 14); pelvic rays I,3; a moderately long cirrus on each side of nape; supraorbital tentacle usually a long simple filament; nasal cirri usually 3; lateral line without vertical pairs of pores, ending below last dorsal spine and fifteenth soft ray; mandibular pores 5–6 on each side; adult males with a blade-like occipital crest; females sometimes with a low median ridge; edges of lips smooth; no posterior canine tooth on each side of lower jaw; pale greenish gray with dark gray double bars on body that extend basally into dorsal fin; irregular orangish lines in pale interspaces on posterior half of body; a pale-edged gray bar from eye across upper lip, and an oblique, pale-edged gray band behind

Okinawa/male

Okinawa/female

eye; females with orangish brown dots posteriorly on body and in dorsal and anal fins. Largest specimen, 17 cm, from Pitcairn Island. Occurs throughout the Indo-Pacific region except the Hawaiian Islands; type locality, Tahiti. Typically found along the edge of rocky shores where wave action is not severe. *Salarias quadricornis* Valenciennes, type locality Mauritius, is one of 17 synonyms.

LINED ROCKSKIPPER
Istiblennius lineatus (Valenciennes in C & V, 1836)
Dorsal rays XII-XIV,21–25; anal rays II,22–25; pectoral rays 13–15; pelvic rays I,3; no cirri on nape; supraorbital tentacle usually a triangular filament with short medial and lateral branches in adults; nasal cirri short and palmate; lateral line without vertical pairs of pores, ending below space between sixth dorsal spine and fifth soft ray; mandibular pores 3–7 on each side; adult males with a large, blade-like occipital crest; edge of upper lip crenulate, the lower lip smooth; posterior canine tooth present on each side of lower jaw; females pale yellowish with about 7 longitudinal, dark brown lines on body (may be irregular and broken), generally breaking into spots on caudal peduncle or a little before; dark vertical lines on head below and behind eye; soft portion of dorsal fin light gray with oblique dark gray lines; males with dark linear pattern subdued, more as pale lengthwise, often broken, lines; head crossed with vertical, irregular, orangish brown lines. Attains 14 cm. Laccadive Islands and Maldive Islands to the Tuamotu Archipelago and

Tahiti/male

Taiwan/female

Pitcairn Islands; southern Japan to Great Barrier Reef and New Caledonia; type locality, Java. The similar *Istiblennius steindachneri* (Pfeffer) occurs from east coast of Africa to Mauritius and the Seychelles, and *I. pox* Springer & Williams from the Red Sea to the Persian Gulf.

MEDUSA BLENNY

Medusablennius chani Springer, 1966

Dorsal rays XI-XII,17–18; anal rays II,19; pectoral rays 13; pelvic rays I,3; segmented caudal rays 13, none branched; lateral line as 1 or 2 short tubes above pectoral-fin base; teeth incisiform, 18–19 in upper jaw and 16–18 in lower; large complex cirri on nostrils, above eye, and in interorbital space; dorsal fin incised between spinous and soft portions about half length of first soft ray; color in preservative uniformly pale except a few black dots distally in spinous portion of dorsal fin. Largest specimen, 1.8 cm. Known from only 2 collections from surge channels in the seaward reef of Raroia Atoll, Tuamotu Archipelago.

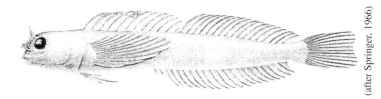

(after Springer, 1966)

YELLOWTAIL FANGBLENNY

Meiacanthus atrodorsalis (Günther, 1877)

Dorsal rays III-VI (rarely III or VI, usually IV),25–28; anal rays II,25–28 (usually 26 or 27); pectoral rays usually 14; pelvic rays I,3; segmented caudal rays usually 11 or 12, none branched; a short anterior lateral line; an enormous recurved canine tooth on each side of lower jaw, grooved and with a venom gland at base (true of other *Meiacanthus*); a pair of cirri on chin; swimbladder present (also generic); dorsal fin without a notch (generic); last dorsal and anal rays joined by membrane to caudal peduncle or base of caudal fin (true of all fangblennies); caudal fin lunate, the lobes prolonged in large adults of both sexes; Smith-Vaniz (1987) described 5 color morphs; the most common with head and anterior half of body gray-blue, shading to yellow posteriorly and on caudal fin; an oblique black band through eye; a black stripe in dorsal fin (absent in some populations); a black spot in lower part of axil of pectoral fin. Reaches 11 cm. Western

Coral Sea

Australia and western Pacific, east to islands of Micronesia and Samoa Islands (type locality); tends to be solitary. Mimicked by the blue-yellow phase of *Ecsenius bicolor* and *Plagiotremus laudandus*. Feeds on both benthic and planktonic animals, especially small crustaceans and worms.

BUNDOON FANGBLENNY

Meiacanthus bundoon Smith-Vaniz, 1976

Dorsal rays IV-V (usually V),26–27; anal rays II,16–17; pectoral rays 15–16; segmented caudal rays 11–13; caudal fin lunate, the lobes elongate in adults of both sexes; dark olive in life with a wedge-shaped, orange-yellow stripe on side of body; cheek and opercle green; base and lobes of caudal fin black, centroposterior part of fin transparent whitish with dusky rays. Largest specimen, 9.5 cm. Described from 5 specimens from Moala Island, Lau Group, Fiji; collected later at other localities in Fiji by Victor G. Springer and at Tongatapu by the author.

DOUBLEPORE FANGBLENNY

Meiacanthus ditrema Smith-Vaniz, 1976

Dorsal rays V-VI (rarely VI),22–25 (modally 24); anal rays II,15–18 (usually 16 or 17); pectoral rays usually 14; pelvic rays I,3; lateral line absent; mandibular pores 2 (3 in other *Meiacanthus*); supratemporal sensory canal ending in a pair of pores on top of head; caudal fin emarginate, the third and ninth segmented rays very prolonged in large males; pale bluish gray with a black stripe from above eye along back; 2 parallel black stripes on head, one on front of snout through eye and the other from mouth just below eye, joining as one broader stripe beneath pectoral fin and continuing along lower side to caudal fin. Largest, 6.7 cm, including caudal filaments. Western Australia and western Pacific east to Tonga and Samoa Islands; only Palau (type locality) in Micronesia; usually seen in small aggregations a short distance above the bottom.

Tonga

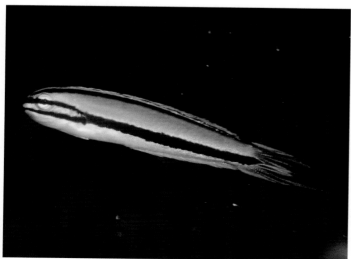

Indonesia

496

CANARY FANGBLENNY
Meiacanthus oualanensis (Günther, 1880)
Dorsal rays IV-V (rarely V),25–28 (usually 27); anal rays II,16–18; pectoral rays usually 14; pelvic rays I,3; segmented caudal rays 11–12 (usually 11); lateral line present; caudal fin lunate, the lobes prolonged in large adults of both sexes; bright yellow, a little greenish dorsally on head; a faint greenish stripe in dorsal fin; a dark spot in axil of pectoral fin; centroposterior part of caudal fin transparent with translucent dusky rays. Largest specimen, 10 cm. Known only from Fiji; named for the island of Ovalau, so the species name should have been *ovalauensis*. Mimicked by the yellow subspecies of *Plagiotremus laudandus*. Smith-Vaniz (1976) first treated this fish as a subspecies of *M. atrodorsalis*; Smith-Vaniz (1987) reclassified it as a species. *Petroscirtes auratus* Seale is a synonym.

TWILIGHT FANGBLENNY
Meiacanthus phaeus Smith-Vaniz, 1976
Dorsal rays IV,27; anal rays II,17; pectoral rays 16; segmented caudal rays 11; lateral line present; caudal fin lunate with prolonged lobes; bluish gray, shading nearly to white posteriorly on body and middle base of caudal fin; dorsal fin with a very narrow, pale bluish gray margin and broad, black submarginal band; anal fin black; lobes of caudal fin black, the membrane between transparent with pale bluish gray rays. Described from a single specimen from New Caledonia; the range extended west to the Chesterfield Bank, Coral Sea, by the photograph here.

SWALLOWTAIL FANGBLENNY
Meiacanthus procne Smith-Vaniz, 1976
Dorsal rays IV-V (rarely IV),25–26; anal rays II,15–16; pectoral rays 13–14 (rarely 13); pelvic rays I,3; segmented caudal rays 11–12 (usually 11); lateral line present; caudal fin lunate, the lobes prolonged in both sexes; upper half of body bluish black, the lower half abruptly bluish white with a few small black spots posteriorly; basal half of dorsal fin black with a pale blue stripe consisting of 1 spot per membrane broadly joined to the next; outer half of fin bluish gray with a narrow, pale blue margin and black submarginal line; lobes and base of caudal fin black, the upper and lower margins pale blue, the centroposterior part of fin transparent with dusky rays; no dark spot in axil of pectoral fins. Attains at least 7 cm. Known only from Vava'u, Tonga; 1 record from Tahiti is regarded as erroneous (Smith-Vaniz, 1987).

TONGA FANGBLENNY
Meiacanthus tongaensis Smith-Vaniz, 1987
Dorsal rays IV,27–28; anal rays II,17–18; pectoral rays usually 14; pelvic rays I,3; segmented caudal rays 11–12 (usually 11); lateral line present, ending below third to seventh dorsal soft rays; caudal fin lunate, the lobes prolonged in adults of both sexes; yellowish green on head and dorsally on body, shading to light yellow ventrally; dorsal and anal fins greenish yellow, the dorsal with a broad black stripe near base; base and lobes of caudal fin greenish yellow, the centroposterior part of fin transparent with pale greenish yellow rays. Reaches 10 cm. Known only from Tongatapu and Vava'u, Tonga; the holotype was collected by the author for Smith-Vaniz off the yellow jetty in Nukualofa in 1–2 m.

Komodo, Indonesia

Fiji

PYGMY BLENNY
Nannosalarias nativitatus (Regan, 1909)

Dorsal spines XII-XIII (rarely XIII),15–16; anal rays II,16–18; pectoral rays 14–15 (rarely 14); pelvic rays I,3; caudal fin with 13 segmented rays, the middle 9 branched; lateral line ending below seventh or eighth dorsal spine; gill rakers 12–14; margin of lips smooth; supraorbital tentacle slender and unbranched; nuchal and nasal cirri short; gray with numerous white dots, those ventrally mixed with irregular, vertical white lines; a mid-lateral series of short, deep red bars, most as double bars; double red spots along base of dorsal fin, 1 on each ray, and paired spots on back below; a broad, oblique, deep red band behind eye, its posterior edge dotted with white; a large black spot on each side of throat (sometimes merged as 1 spot). Largest specimen, 4.2 cm. Described from Christmas Island, Indian Ocean; also reported from Indonesia, Pratas Reef (South China Sea), Ryukyu Islands, Great Barrier Reef, Tonga, and Samoa Islands. The photograph was taken in a surgy area of Komodo in 1.5 m.

GERMAIN'S BLENNY
Omobranchus germaini (Sauvage, 1883)

Dorsal rays XII-XIV (usually XIII),18–23; anal rays II,21–26; pectoral rays usually 13; pelvic rays I,2; segmented caudal rays 13–14 (rarely 14), unbranched; lateral-line tubes 0–8 (rarely 0); interorbital pores 2–5 (usually 3); mandibular pores 3 on each side; gill opening extending ventrally from slightly above base of pectoral fin to opposite sixth pectoral ray (rarely below fourth ray); no crest on head; teeth incisiform, close-set, and rigid, 14–15 in upper jaw and 16–28 in lower; a large, recurved canine tooth posteriorly on each side of both jaws; no cirri on head (true of all *Omobranchus*); dorsal fin only slightly notched; last dorsal and anal rays bound by membrane to caudal peduncle (also generic); light brown with oblique blackish bands on side of body that pass downward and posteriorly on anterior half of body and downward and anteriorly on posterior half; 2 series of blackish spots or dashes dorsally on body, variously joined; a blackish spot behind eye; an oblique, pale-edged red spot posteriorly on opercle preceded by a curved blackish band; lower part of head with dark spots or oblique bands; an ocellated black spot present or absent near middle of soft portion of dorsal fin; females

MANGROVE BLENNY
Omobranchus obliquus (Garman, 1903)

Dorsal rays XI-XIII (usually XII),18–21 (rarely 21); anal rays II, 20–23; pectoral rays usually 13; pelvic rays I,2; segmented caudal rays 11–13 (rarely 11 or 13), unbranched; lateral-line tubes 0–6 (rarely 5 or 6); interorbital pores 1–4 (rarely 1); ventral end of gill opening extending to opposite pectoral rays 2–8; no crest on head; upper-jaw teeth 18–28; lower-jaw teeth 19–29; dorsal fin slightly notched; light brown with oblique blackish bands on side of body that pass downward and posteriorly on anterior half of body and downward and anteriorly on posterior half; white lines between blackish bands; 2 irregular series of black spots dorsally on body, the upper row as a spot at base of a dorsal spine or ray; a vertically elongate, pale-edged, dull red spot on opercle, flanked by black spots; a large, quadrangular blackish blotch behind eye; irregular black lines ventrally on head, continuing onto throat; a blackish spot (may be blue in middle) in dorsal fin centered on eleventh soft ray. Reaches 7 cm. Nicobar Islands, Indo-Malayan region, Palau, Yap, and Guam in Micronesia, Vanuatu, New Caledonia, Fiji (type locality), Tonga, and Samoa Islands; unintentionally introduced to the Hawaiian Islands. Inshore on rocky substrata in calm habitats, often mangrove areas. Springer & Gomon (1975) first treated this species as a subspecies of *Omobranchus rotundiceps* (Macleay).

New Caledonia/female

New Caledonia/male

less strongly pigmented than males. Largest specimen, 7.8 cm. Described from New Caledonia; also reported from Western Australia to Queensland, the Indo-Malayan region, and Taiwan. Stomach and gut contents of illustrated specimens consisted of algae and detritus.

New Caledonia/male (*above*) & female

Christmas Island (Allen)

OMOX BLENNY
Omox biporos Springer, 1972

Dorsal rays XII,15–17; anal rays II,17–19; pectoral rays 13; pelvic rays I,2; segmented caudal rays 13, unbranched; interorbital pores usually 4; lateral line absent; teeth in jaws incisiform, rigid, and close-set; a large curved canine posteriorly on side of both upper and lower jaws; no cirri and no crest on head; ventral end of gill opening extending to level of eighth to eleventh pectoral rays; dorsal fin slightly notched; males may have 2 prolonged caudal rays; brown with blackish bars or 2 rows of blackish spots of near-pupil size on body, one midlateral and the other at base of dorsal fin; head with large, close-set blackish blotches; white dashes may be present in narrow pale interspaces. Attains 6 cm. Described from specimens from the Gulf of Thailand (type locality), Papua New Guinea, and Palau; recorded here from New Caledonia.

HEPBURN'S BLENNY
Parenchelyurus hepburni (Snyder, 1908)

Dorsal rays XI-XIII,18–20; anal rays II,20–23; pectoral rays 13–14 (rarely 14); pelvic rays I,2; segmented caudal rays 13, unbranched; interorbital pores 3; mandibular pores on each side 2; lateral-line tubes 3–8; teeth in jaws incisiform, rigid, and close-set; a large curved canine posteriorly on side of both upper and lower jaws; no cirri and no crest on head; ventral end of gill opening extending to level of fifth pectoral ray; dorsal fin not notched; last dorsal and anal rays connected by membrane to caudal fin; dark brown to black, the male with small blue spots on body and median fins, those on body mainly in 2 or 3 longitudinal rows. Largest specimen, 4.2 cm. Western Pacific from Ryukyu Islands (type locality, Okinawa) to Great Barrier Reef, east to islands of Micronesia and Samoa Islands; also reported from Mauritius, Maldive Islands, and Chagos Archipelago; lives in intertidal zone beneath stones.

Lord Howe Island

Bahrain

WOLF FANGBLENNY
Petroscirtes lupus (De Vis, 1885)

Dorsal rays XI,19–20; anal rays II,18–20 (rarely 18); pectoral rays 13–14 (usually 14); pelvic rays I,3; segmented caudal rays 11, unbranched; teeth in jaws incisiform, rigid, close-set, increasing with age; a large, curved canine tooth posteriorly on side of lower jaw, and a lesser canine posteriorly on each side of upper jaw (dentition essentially the same in other *Petroscirtes*); lower end of gill opening above level of pectoral-fin base (also generic); a small unbranched cirrus on each side of chin; a small supraorbital cirrus and a small nuchal cirrus present or absent; body depth at anal-fin origin 4.5–7.0 in standard length; second dorsal spine of males prolonged; dorsal fin not notched; interradial membranes of caudal fin slightly incised, especially on males; ground color variable with habitat, gray, brown, or green, with 6 large, irregular dark blotches on upper side and numerous white dots and dashes and dark dots (the latter mainly ventral). Attains 13 cm. Queensland (type locality, Moreton Bay), New South Wales, Lord Howe Island, and New Caledonia; tends to hide in seagrasses, algae, or empty mollusk shells; often lays its eggs, guarded by the male, on the inner surface of a bivalve shell.

HIGHFIN FANGBLENNY
Petroscirtes mitratus Rüppell, 1830

Dorsal rays X-XI (rarely X),14–16; anal rays II,14–16; pectoral rays 14–15 (usually 14); pelvic rays I,3; segmented caudal rays 11, unbranched; snout short, its dorsal profile steep; a small flap on each side of chin; a slender flap on anterior rim of posterior nostril; supraorbital tentacle a slender flap, usually with short branches; a small cirrus usually present on each side of nape; body depth at anal-fin origin 4.65–6.75 in standard length; anterior part of dorsal fin (first 4 spines) elevated, higher in males than in females; caudal fin slightly rounded, the interradial membranes of rays incised; pelvic fins of males longer than those in females (may be one-third or more of standard length); whitish to pale brown or green, finely mottled and spotted with white and brown, with 6 large, irregular dark blotches on upper side, some containing a round white spot broadly edged in blackish; a longitudinal row of small orange or yellow spots often present on side of body. Largest specimen, 7.7 cm. Red Sea (type locality) and east coast of Africa to Marshall Islands, Samoa Islands, and Tonga; Ryukyu Islands to Great Barrier Reef and New Caledonia. A cryptic species. Judging from museum collections, the most common of the genus.

FLORAL FANGBLENNY
Petroscirtes xestus Jordan & Seale, 1906

Dorsal rays VIII-X (usually IX),27–30; anal rays II,22–24; pectoral rays usually 12; pelvic rays I,3; segmented caudal rays 11, unbranched; snout short, its dorsal profile steep; a small fringed flap on each side of chin; supraorbital tentacle small, varying from a filament to a short flap; a small cirrus on anterior rim of posterior nostril, and cirri elsewhere on head; body depth at origin of anal fin 5.25–6.6 in standard length; second dorsal spine ending in a short filament, longer in males; caudal fin slightly rounded, the second and tenth rays prolonged in males; pale gray or pale brown, finely spotted and dotted with white and brown; a narrow, dark brown stripe from eye to upper base of caudal fin, often faint or broken into a series of dark blotches; distal part of first dorsal spine black except for white tip; margin of dorsal fin, including filament, white; a row of small black spots in outer

Watabela Islands, Indonesia

part of fin, one near middle of fin larger and elongate. Reaches 7.5 cm. East coast of Africa to the islands of Micronesia, Line Islands, Samoa Islands (type locality), and Society Islands; few records for the western Pacific (Great Barrier Reef, Vanuatu, and Banda Sea); Smith-Vaniz (1987) added a record for Rowley Shoals, Western Australia. Usually found in flat sandy or weedy habitats; often uses empty mollusk shells for refuge.

BICOLOR FANGBLENNY
Plagiotremus laudandus (Whitley, 1961)

Dorsal rays X-XI (usually XI),14–16; anal rays II,14–16; pectoral rays usually 14; pelvic rays I,3; segmented caudal rays 11, no lateral line (true of other *Plagiotremus*); interorbital pores 2; body very elongate (also generic), the depth 6.5–8.5 in standard length; snout bluntly rounded, the mouth distinctly ventral; close-set incisiform teeth in jaws, increasing in number with age; a very large, recurved, nonvenomous canine tooth posteriorly on each side of lower jaw (dentition essentially the same in other species of the genus); origin of dorsal fin slightly posterior to eye and nearly uniform in height; last dorsal and anal rays connected by membrane to caudal peduncle (also generic); caudal fin lunate; pelvic fins small, shorter than eye diameter; grayish blue anteriorly, yellow posteriorly, with a black stripe in dorsal fin, hence remarkably similar to the color of *Meiacanthus atrodorsalis*, which it mimics (partially overcoming its more slender body by fully elevating its dorsal and anal fins). Reaches 7.5 cm. Western Australia and western Pacific, east to Micronesia and Samoa Islands; type locality, New Caledonia. Entirely yellow in Fiji, where it mimics the yellow *M. oualanensis*. Smith-Vaniz (1976) named the Fiji population *P. laudandus flavus*; in 1987 he extended the range of this subspecies to Tonga. By resembling the venomous-fanged but nonthreatening *M. atrodorsalis* and *M. oualanensis*, *P. laudandus*

American Samoa

Fiji

is believed to gain some protection from predation and get closer to its prey. Like others of the genus, it attacks fishes, usually much larger than itself, and removes mucus, skin tissue, and small scales.

BLUESTRIPED FANGBLENNY
Plagiotremus rhinorhynchos (Bleeker, 1852)

Dorsal rays X-XI (usually XI),31–37; anal rays II,29–33; pectoral rays usually 12; pelvic rays I,3; segmented caudal rays 11; interorbital pores 4; snout bluntly conical and strongly overhanging mouth; origin of dorsal fin slightly posterior to vertical margin of preopercle; caudal fin slightly emarginate; pelvic fins usually a little longer than eye diameter; ground color black, yellowish brown, or yellow, with 2 blue stripes; fins translucent yellow. Reported to 12 cm. Like others of the genus, attacks fishes to remove mucus and skin tissue. In its blue-striped black phase it mimics the cleaner wrasse *Labroides dimidiatus*. In its yellow phase with narrow blue stripes it mingles with the anthiine fish *Pseudanthias squami-*

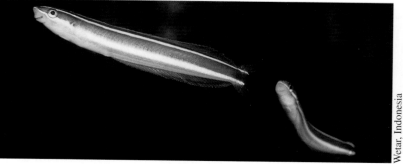

Wetar, Indonesia

pinnis. Occurs throughout the tropical Indo-Pacific region except the Hawaiian Islands, where replaced by the closely related *Plagiotremus ewaensis* (Brock). Type locality, Ceram (now Seram), Molucca Islands.

500

PIANO FANGBLENNY
Plagiotremus tapeinosoma (Bleeker, 1857)

Dorsal rays VII-IX (usually VIII),34–39; anal rays II,28–33; pectoral rays usually 12; pelvic rays I,3; segmented caudal rays 11; interorbital pores 2; snout bluntly conical and strongly overhanging mouth; origin of dorsal fin over or slightly posterior to vertical margin of preopercle; caudal fin slightly emarginate; pelvic fins distinctly longer than eye diameter, prolonged in males; a black stripe from front of snout through upper two-thirds of eye to caudal fin, consisting on body of contiguous, vertically elongate spots, reduced to half size posteriorly and replaced by yellow above; a white line above stripe, and a broad white stripe below; central part of head and body dull yellow; a narrow black stripe from dorsally on snout along back at base of dorsal fin; dorsal fin bluish basally with a broad, black outer stripe and narrow, bluish white margin. Attains 11 cm. Occurs throughout the tropical Indo-Pacific except the Hawaiian Islands, where replaced by *Plagiotremus goslinei* (Strasburg). Type locality, Ambon, Molucca Islands.

Norfolk Island

WHITEDOTTED ROCKSKIPPER
Praealticus bilineatus (Peters, 1868)

Dorsal rays XIII (the last spine very small),18–20; anal rays II,18–21; pectoral rays usually 15; pelvic rays I,3; segmented caudal rays usually 13–14, the middle 6–9 branched; lateral-line pores 5–10, without scalelike flaps; interorbital pores 3; upper lip without a free dorsal margin (true of other *Praealticus*); edges of lips smooth; teeth numerous, movable in jaws (also generic); a posterior canine present on each side of lower jaw but not in upper; supraorbital tentacle of adults pinnately branched (generic); no cirri on nape; a small cirrus, usually unbranched, on hind rim of anterior nostril (generic); occipital crest present, higher on male (generic); dorsal fin deeply notched between spinous and soft portions, the last ray connected by membrane to caudal peduncle (generic); dark gray-brown, the body with small white spots of variable size; head and fins except pelvic and caudal fins with white dots (dots on head and pectoral fins brown in preservative); an elongate dark spot on first membrane of dorsal fin (more evident in preservative). Reaches about 9 cm. Western Pacific from southern Japan to New Caledonia; type locality, Samar, Philippines; occurs on exposed rocky shores.

Okinawa

BLACKMARGIN ROCKSKIPPER
Praealticus caesius (Seale, 1906)

Dorsal rays XIII (last spine very small),17–20 (usually 19); anal rays II,19–22 (rarely 19 or 22); pectoral rays usually 15; segmented caudal rays 14 (middle 6–9 branched); pelvic rays I,3; lateral-line pores 5–9; edge of lips smooth; females whitish to light gray dorsally, white ventrally, with a series of 6 double black spots (anterior 2 pairs irregular, with a row of spots above) on upper side of body, and 1 spot on caudal peduncle, each connected by a gray bar to a lower series; a black line on back at base of spinous portion of dorsal fin, and 4 pairs of small black spots along base of soft portion; small bluish white spots on posterior half of body, mostly on upper half; narrow black bars ventrally on head angling onto throat; a white line at posterior edge of eye continuing below to upper lip; median fins with blackish margins; posterior part of crest with a narrow pink margin and a broad, submarginal black band; base of dorsal fin with alternating black and whitish blotches; a black spot at midbase of caudal fin; males similar but body darker; most bluish white spots on body elliptical; oblique black bands on throat less evident; oblique white lines in soft portion of dorsal fin. Largest specimen examined, 7.9 cm. Islands of South Pacific from Fiji to Tuamotu Archipelago, Rapa, and Pitcairn Islands; type locality, Tubuai, Austral Islands; illustrated specimens from a lot of 66 collected by the author from high tidepools on southwestern coast of Tongatapu.

Tonga/female

Tonga/male

CRINOID CLINGFISH

Discotrema crinophila Briggs, 1976

Dorsal rays 8–9; anal rays 7–8; pectoral rays 25–27; caudal rays 12–15; body slender, the depth 5.0–6.6 in standard length; head depressed; a single row of slender incisiform teeth with rounded tips in jaws; disc length 4.2–4.9 in standard length; anus much closer to origin of anal fin than to disc; usual color dark brown or dark red with 3 narrow. white or pale yellow stripes, one mid-dorsal and one on each side, all meeting at front of upper lip. Attains about 3 cm. Known from Fiji (type locality), Bismarck Archipelago, Ryukyu Islands (Masuda & Kobayashi, 1994), and New Caledonia (Laboute & Grandperrin, 2000); in addition, the author has collected it in Indonesia, Papua New Guinea, and the Philippines. Allen & Steene (1988) reported a similar and apparently undescribed species as *Discotrema echinocephala* (a misnomer for *D. crinophila*) from Christmas Island (Indian Ocean), Randall et al. (1997a) figured it as *Discotrema* sp. from the Great

Alor, Indonesia

Barrier Reef, and Laboute & Grandperrin (2000) as *D. crinophila* from New Caledonia. It lacks the middorsal stripe. Both species are usually commensal in crinoids, especially *Comanthus bennetti*.

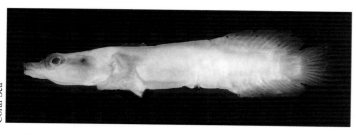

Coral Sea

BRIDLED CLINGFISH

Lepadichthys frenatus Waite, 1904

Dorsal rays 15–17; anal rays 12–15; pectoral rays 25–31; caudal rays 10–14; gill rakers on second gill arch slender and pointed, 12–14; body slender, the depth 6.2–7.3 in standard length; disc small, its length 4.9–5.8 in standard length; anus much closer to anal-fin origin than to rear edge of disc; upper end of gill opening at level of third to eighth pectoral rays; color variable: gray, pinkish gray, yellow, or whitish, usually with an indistinct dark stripe from front of snout through eye to edge of preopercle. Attains 6 cm. The known localities, Japan, Taiwan, southern Great Barrier Reef, Lord Howe Island (type locality), Norfolk Island, Vanuatu, New Caledonia, Fiji, and Pitcairn Islands, suggest an antiequatorial distribution; reported as usually found under the sea urchin *Diadema setosum*.

SMALLDISC CLINGFISH

Pherallodus indicus (Weber, 1913)

Dorsal rays 8–9; anal rays 5–7; pectoral rays 22–23; caudal rays 10–11; 6 short gill rakers on second gill arch; body slender, the depth 6.8–7.3 in standard length; head narrow but depressed; a single row of incisiform teeth in jaws, those at front pointed, those on side notched; disc small, its length 4.9–5.8 in standard length; anus much closer to anal-fin origin than to rear edge of disc; upper end of gill opening at level of ninth to tenth pectoral rays; purple to dark red with a network of white lines on dorsal half of head and body enclosing irregular spots of variable size. Reaches 3.5 cm. Described from the Sula Islands, Indonesia; also reported from Sumba, southern Japan, and Raroia Atoll in the Tuamotu Archipelago; in Japan it is usually commensal with the sea urchin *Stomopneustes variolaris*. The author collected specimens from Lord Howe Island and Henderson Island, Pit-

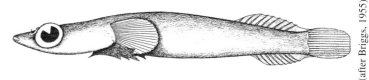

(after Briggs, 1955)

DWARF CLINGFISH

Lepadichthys minor Briggs, 1955

Dorsal rays 9–10; anal rays 8; pectoral rays 27–29; caudal rays 12; 5 blunt gill rakers on second gill arch; body slender, the depth about 6.4 in standard length; head depressed; eye large, about 3.4 in head length; disc small, its length 5.0–5.3 in standard length; anus about halfway between anal-fin origin and rear edge of disc; upper end of gill opening at level of twelfth to thirteenth pectoral rays; color note from original description: dark purple, whitish on abdomen and throat, with a number of white lines on head and body. Largest specimen, 2.5 cm. Described from Muaras Reef in the Sulawesi Sea; also known from the Molucca Islands, Mariana Islands, New Caledonia, and Samoa Islands; reported to occur in tidepools and reef flats on exposed shores; Bishop Museum has 1 specimen from Howland Island taken in 9 m.

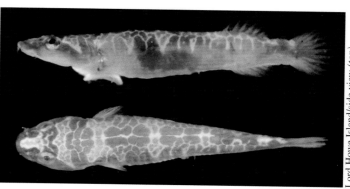

Lord Howe Island/side view (top)

cairn Islands; those from the latter locality were taken with the ichthyocide rotenone near the deep purple slate pencil urchin *Heterocentrotus trigonarius*; the fish were the same color and probably were commensal with the urchin.

DRAGONETS
(CALLIONYMIDAE)

The dragonets are small benthic fishes found in all tropical and subtropical seas, but mainly in the Indo-Pacific region. Their most unifying character is a strong spine at the corner of the preopercle that usually bears barb-like spinules; there is no spine on the opercle or subopercle; the body is elongate and moderately depressed; the head is broad and depressed, often almost triangular when viewed from above; the eyes can be elevated; there are no scales; the lateral line is continuous; the mouth is small with a very protrusible upper jaw; there are villiform teeth in the jaws, but none on vomer or palatines; the gill opening is reduced to a small opening on the upper posterior part of the head. There are two dorsal fins (except *Draculo*, which has only a soft dorsal), the first usually with IV flexible spines, and the second with 6–11 soft rays; anal fin without spines, the soft rays 4–10; the pelvic fins of I,5 rays are broadly separated, inserted before the pectorals, the fifth ray joined by membrane to the pectoral-fin base. Most species are found on sedimentary substrata, but a few occur in rocky or coral-reef habitats; they range in depth from the shallows to at least 400 m. Many of those that live on sand or mud are able to bury themselves quickly in the sediment. Dragonets feed mainly on small benthic invertebrates. Sexual dimorphism is usually evident, the males generally larger and often more colorful with a higher first dorsal fin and longer caudal fin. Pair spawning has been observed for several species; the eggs are pelagic. Fricke (1983) revised the Indo-Pacific species, recognizing nine genera and 126 species. Although followed here, his generic classification is not universally accepted. There are about 160 species worldwide. No account is provided here of *Synchiropus springeri* Fricke (1983: 673, fig. 208), known from 3 specimens, 10.6–18.4 mm standard length, collected in 20 m at Malolo Island, Fiji.

MANGROVE DRAGONET
Callionymus enneactis Bleeker, 1879

Dorsal rays IV + 7–8 (usually 8); anal rays I,7–8 (usually 8); pectoral rays 18–20; body depth 6.3–9.6 in standard length; head length 3.4–4.6 in standard length; preopercular spine 3.4–5.9 in head length, with 2 spinules on dorsomedial surface (not including upturned tip), and an antrorse spine at its base; first dorsal fin of male high, the first and third or fourth spines long and filamentous, the fin deeply incised; soft dorsal and anal rays unbranched except last ray in each fin; caudal fin 2.3–3.2 in standard length in male, 2.7–4.0 in female. Brown dorsally, mottled with white blotches, becoming white ventrally; fins mainly clear except for scattered, small dark spots, especially on caudal fin, and first dorsal fin of male with patches of yellowish brown and orange bands, edged in pale blue. Reaches 7.5 cm. Japan to Great Barrier Reef, east to New Caledonia, Palau, and Yap; type locality, Singapore; typically found in shallow mangrove areas.

FILAMENTOUS DRAGONET
Callionymus filamentosus Valenciennes in C & V, 1837

Dorsal rays IV + 9 (first spine detached in males); anal rays 9; pectoral rays 17–21; branched caudal rays 7, 1 branch of middle 2 rays extended posteriorly as a filament in male; body depth 7.4–10.8 in standard length; head depressed, its width about 4 in standard length; eye moderately large, 2.2–2.8 in head length; preopercular spine 0.8–1.1 in eye diameter, with 4–9 forward-curved spinules on dorsomedial edge and an antrorse spine anteriorly at its base; detached first dorsal spine of male 3.0–6.0 in standard length; first spine of female about 10–11 in standard length; first dorsal soft ray of male 4.7–5.4 in standard length, of female 5.9–6.5 in standard length; brown with numerous very small black spots and very small, dark edged, pale spots on postorbital head and body; pale-edged, oblique dark bands on cheek (more evident in male); fins except anal and lower half of caudal

Sulawesi (G. R. Allen)

Flores/female (*above*) and male

with small black spots; first dorsal fin of male posterior to third spine black with irregular pale lines (light blue in life); first dorsal fin of female with a large, irregular black spot posteriorly. Largest specimen, 16.5 cm. Red Sea (and the Mediterranean Sea via the Suez Canal) and east coast of Africa to the western Pacific from Taiwan to the Indo-Malayan region; a surprising record from the Society Islands by Randall et al. (2002a).

MARQUESAN DRAGONET

Callionymus marquesensis Fricke, 1989

Dorsal rays IV + 8; anal rays 7; pectoral rays 17–21; branched caudal rays 7; body elongate, the depth 6.9–10 in standard length, and depressed, the width 5.5–8.5 in standard length; eye moderately large, 2.1–2.6 in head length; preopercular spine 2.3–3.4 in head, with 4–7 (rarely 4) curved spinules on dorsomedial edge (not including upcurved tip), and an antrorse spine ventrally at base; first dorsal fin higher in the male, the first 2 spines higher than longest soft ray, 4.2–3.4 in standard length; first dorsal spine at most slightly longer than longest soft ray in female; caudal fin of male 1.5–1.9 in standard length, of females 3.25–3.5 in standard length; pale brown with a row of 5 round dusky spots with black centers along side of body above anal fin, dorsal part of body finely dotted with orangish brown, with a longitudinal row of small, faint white spots; ventral part of body with 2 rows of white dashes; black spots on middle caudal rays; head of

Marquesas Is./male (*above*) and female

males with bluish white spots and dashes, faint yellow spots, and yellow lower lip. Largest specimen, 5.5 cm. Known only from the Marquesas Islands; collected by the author and associates for Fricke's description from sand and rubble substrata in 21–33 m. First identified as *Callionymus simplicicornis*.

SIMPLE-SPINE DRAGONET

Callionymus simplicicornis Valenciennes in C & V, 1837

Dorsal rays IV + 8; anal rays 7; pectoral rays 16–18; branched caudal rays 7; body elongate and depressed, the depth 6.5–10.5 in standard length; eye diameter 2.1–3.1 in head length; preopercular spine 2.4–3.3 in head, with 5–13 (rarely fewer than 7) small serrae on dorsomedial edge; first dorsal fin of males about equal to height of second dorsal, the first spine 4.1–5.5 in standard length; first dorsal spine of females, 6.5–9.0 in standard length; caudal fin of male with middle and lower rays longer than upper, 1.7–3.0 in standard length; caudal fin of females rounded, 2.9–4.2 in standard length; light brown, finely flecked with white and dark brown dorsally, with 1 or 2 midlateral rows of small white spots or dashes and a row of large, round, dark gray blotches on lower side with a small spot between each pair;

Alor, Indonesia/male

lower half of caudal fin with dark spots; females with a large black spot in outer part of first dorsal fin; males with oblique blue dashes on head, chest, and first dorsal fin. Attains nearly 6 cm. Philippines and Indonesia east to Society Islands, Cook Islands, and islands of Micronesia; type locality, Guam; reported from the shallows to 40 m.

Seram, Indonesia/female

GORAM DRAGONET

Diplogrammus goramensis (Bleeker, 1858)

Dorsal rays IV + 8; anal rays 7; pectoral rays 17–20; branched caudal rays 7; body elongate and depressed, the depth 6.8–10.4 in standard length; a thin longitudinal fold of skin along lower side of body (true of all *Diplogrammus* and not found in *Callionymus*); operculum with a free flap of skin (also not on *Callionymus*); eye diameter 2.6–4.0 in head length; preopercular spine 2.1–2.6 in head, with tip upturned, 5–8 small spinules on dorsomedial edge, and a small antrorse spine on lower base; first dorsal spine of males prolonged as a filament, 2.4–4.1 in standard length; first dorsal spine of females not filamentous, 6.3–7.7 in standard length; caudal fin rounded, 3.5–3.7 in standard length; females light brown with large, irregular dusky blotches along back, small white spots and irregular white blotches, a midlateral row of dusky blotches, and the lower fold of skin with pairs of

Bali/female

Bali/male

white dashes alternating with a small blackish spot; males brown with dark brown spots and many very small blue spots on head, body, second dorsal, and caudal fins; anal fin dark brown to black except tips of rays with light blue dots and short lines. Attains 9 cm. Indo-Malayan region (type locality, Goram Archipelago), north to southern Japan (Masuda & Kobayashi, 1994), south to Great Barrier Reef and Norfolk Island, east to Society Islands (Randall et al., 2002a) and islands of Micronesia. *Callionymus cookii* Günther from Rarotonga and *Dermosteira dorotheae* Schultz from American Samoa are synonyms.

Fiji/female

Okinawa/male

MORRISON'S DRAGONET

Synchiropus morrisoni Schultz in Schultz et al., 1960

Dorsal rays IV + 8; anal rays 7; pectoral rays 18–23; branched caudal rays 7; body depth 4.4–6.5 in standard length; snout shorter than eye diameter, its profile steep (true of other *Synchiropus*); eye large, 1.8–2.6 in head length; preopercular spine short, 3.6–6.3 in head, with tip slightly upturned, only 2 curved spinules on dorsomedial edge, and no lower spine; first dorsal fin of males high, the spines nearly equal in length, 3.3–4.5 in standard length; first dorsal fin of females slightly lower than longest ray of second fin, the first spine 6.6–9.8 in standard length; caudal fin rounded, 2.9–3.4 in standard length; females light brown to red, densely spotted with dark brown and white spots of variable size, the most diagnostic as 2 longitudinal rows of white spots on lower side of body, those of upper row of about pupil size, those of lower row much smaller; males usually red with numerous white spots on body and usually a row of irregular dark blotches as large as eye; head below eye and membrane linking pelvic fin to pectoral-fin base with many bright blue dots; first dorsal fin yellow with curving, vertical, dark brown bands, narrowly edged in white and black; similar bands in second dorsal fin, but horizontal and edged in blue and black. Reaches 8 cm. Izu Islands (Japan), Great Barrier Reef, islands of Micronesia (type locality, Bikini Atoll), Fiji, Samoa Islands, and New Caledonia (*Synchiropus ocellatus* of Laboute & Grandperrin, 2000); occurs on coral reefs and adjacent rubble; reported at depths of 12–33 m. No records for the Indo-Malayan region.

Papua New Guinea/female

Marquesas Islands/male

OCELLATED DRAGONET

Synchiropus ocellatus (Pallas, 1770)

Dorsal rays IV + 8; anal rays 7; pectoral rays 18–23; branched caudal rays 7; body depth 4.4–5.6 in standard length; eye diameter 2.2–3.0 in head length; preopercular spine short, 4.1–7.2 in head, with tip upturned, only a single spinule on dorsomedial edge, and no lower spine; first dorsal fin of males high, the spines nearly equal in length (may have filamentous tips), 3.3–4.5 in standard length; first dorsal fin of females slightly lower than longest ray of second fin, the first spine 6.6–9.8 in standard length; caudal fin rounded, 3.0–3.7 in standard length; females white, finely flecked with red and brown, with 3 longitudinal rows of very irregular blotches, the uppermost brown and the lower 2 red; basal three-fourths of first dorsal fin black except first membrane; males with large blotches on body reddish brown, even more irregular, and variously interconnected; blue dots on head including eye; first dorsal fin yellowish to tan with irregular, dark brown bands narrowly edged with white and black and containing 2–4 black spots in outer part of fin; second dorsal fin with oblique, dark brown bands, narrowly edged in blue and black across each membrane, but not in alignment with bands of adjacent membranes; pelvic fins with blue dots and a blue line at base. Largest specimen, 8.9 cm. Southern Japan to Great Barrier Reef and New Caledonia (*Synchiropus* sp. of Laboute & Grandperrin, 2000), east to Marshall Islands, Caroline Islands, Marquesas Islands, and Pitcairn Islands; type locality, Ambon, Molucca Islands. Known from rocky substrata and coral reefs from large tidepools to at least 30 m (1 record from 73 m). *Callionymus microps* Günther from Tonga is one of 4 synonyms. Very closely related to *S. stellatus* Smith of the Indian Ocean; Fricke (1983) distinguished the two by color and a higher first dorsal fin of the male of *S. stellatus*.

MANDARINFISH

Synchiropus splendidus (Herre, 1927)

Dorsal rays IV + 8; anal rays 7; pectoral rays 28–35; branched caudal rays usually 8; body depth 3.4–4.2 in standard length; eye large, 1.9–2.7 in head length; preopercular spine 3.4–4.1 in head, with tip slightly upturned, 2–5 curved spinules on dorsomedial edge, and no lower spine; first dorsal fin low, the first spine of males filamentous, of variable length (maximum 1.9 in standard length); first dorsal fin of females shorter than second dorsal, the first spine 5.6–6.4 in standard length; caudal fin rounded, 2.7–3.2 in standard length; body, postorbital head, dorsal, anal, and pelvic fins orange with irregular, black-edged, green bands and spots; 4 blue lines across interorbital and front of snout; adults with a large black spot at corner of cheek containing short yellow lines and spots; outer edges of median and pelvic fins often bright blue; females with a large black spot in first dorsal fin. Reaches 7 cm. Ryukyu Islands to southern Great Barrier Reef, east to New Caledonia and Caroline Islands; also known from Rowley Shoals off northwestern Australia; type locality, Bungau, Philippines. Occurs in shallow protected reef or rocky areas; remains hidden in reef until dusk.

Palau

While the author was collecting gobies with icthyocide in Palau, a Mandarinfish headed slowly to the surface; it was seized but quickly expelled by 3 adult breams (*Pentapodus trivittatus*); this led to the discovery of a skin toxin in this species and also in *S. picturatus* (Peters) (Sadovy et al., in press). These 2 species are the most colorful of the dragonets; their brilliant color may serve as warning coloration. Both are popular aquarium fishes.

GOBIES
(GOBIIDAE)

The Gobiidae is the largest family of fishes in the marine environment, and many species also occur in fresh water. Larson in Carpenter & Niem (2001b) wrote that there are over 220 genera and more than 1,500 species in the family. Many more remain to be described. With so many species, it is difficult to find diagnostic characters that apply to all. One seems to be small size, because most gobies are less than 10 cm in length. *Trimmatom nanus* is the shortest fish in the world, with females maturing as little as 0.8 cm in standard length. However, some species have been reported as large as 50 cm. Most gobies are elongate, and the body of most is scaled, the scales either ctenoid or cycloid; usually the scales are relatively large posteriorly and progressively smaller anteriorly; there is no lateral line, but the head is usually well supplied with sensory pores or papillae, and some species have small barbels. The opercle is without a spine, and the edge of the preopercle is smooth except for a few species with one to a few short spines. The mouth is generally large and oblique, the teeth in the jaws conical, though sometimes enlarged as small canines; most species lack teeth on the vomer or palatines. There are 5 branchiostegal rays; the gill membranes are often broadly attached to the isthmus, thus restrict-

ing the gill opening to the side of the body. Nearly all gobies have 2 dorsal fins, the first usually with II-VIII flexible spines (frequently VI; exceptionally to XVII in mudskippers); second dorsal and anal fins usually with a weak initial spine and 6–15 soft rays; the caudal fin is variable in shape, but commonly rounded, the segmented rays usually 16–17; the pelvic fins are close together, typically with a short spine and 5 soft rays, often fully united to form a sucking disc; when united there may be an anterior transverse membrane called the frenum linking the spines. Gobies are carnivorous and bottom-dwelling; most rest directly on the substratum or live within burrows, but some hover a short distance above (these are more apt to have the pelvic fins separate). The division of the Gobiidae into subfamilies is not fully resolved, but there is one subfamily that is universally accepted, the Oxudercinae, popularly known as mudskippers (revised by Murdy, 1989); these unique fishes inhabit the mangrove habitat or mud flats and spend more time out of water than in it. Another well-established subfamily is the Sicydiinae, a freshwater group, but many have larvae that develop in the sea. The largest subfamily is the Gobiinae; all the species included below fall into this subfamily except 2 mudskippers of the genus *Periophthalmus*. Most gobiid fishes are found in shallow water, but some occur to depths greater than 200 m. They inhabit a variety of habitats from coral reef to

Taylor's Dwarfgoby, *Trimma taylori,* Tukangbesi Islands, Indonesia/aggregation

sand, mud, rubble, algal flats, or seagrass beds. Many live in close association with invertebrates, such as within sponges or on corals and gorgonians. The coral-dwelling gobies of the genus *Gobiodon* produce a strong skin toxin (see account of *G. axillaris*). Species of 13 genera, including *Amblyeleotris, Cryptocentrus, Ctenogobiops, Mahidolia,* and *Vanderhorstia,* are known to live symbiotically with snapping shrimps (Alpheidae) (Karplus, 1987). The shrimps (generally a pair) build and maintain a burrow in sand or mud, usually constructing an arch of coral, rock, or shell fragments at the entrance. The identifications of the shrimps were provided by Arthur Anker, who stresses that they are mostly tentative and based on color pattern. It is expected that many of these names will be shown to be represented by more than one species. The gobies use the burrow as a refuge; their mutualistic role is to serve as sentinels, drawing on their superior vision and lateralis sensory system. Nearly all gobies for which the reproductive habits are known lay demersal eggs that are guarded by the male par-

ent. Some gobies have been shown to be protogynous hermaphrodites—they begin mature life as females and change later to males (Robertson & Justines, 1982; Cole & Robertson, 1988; Cole & Shapiro, 1990). The following Indo-Pacific gobiid genera have been revised: *Bryaninops* (Larson, 1985); *Eviota* (Lachner & Karnella, 1980; Karnella & Lachner, 1981; Jewett & Lachner, 1983); *Exyrias* and *Macrodontogobius* (Murdy, 1985b); *Istigobius* (Murdy, 1985a); *Kelloggella* (Hoese, 1975); *Lubricogobius* (Randall & Senou, 2001); *Pleurosicya* (Larson, 1990); *Priolepis* (Winterbottom & Burridge, 1989, 1992, 1993a, 1993b); *Sueviota* (Winterbottom & Hoese, 1988); and *Valenciennea* (Hoese & Larson, 1994). Munday et al. (1999) has illustrated 16 species of *Gobiodon* from the Great Barrier Reef and Papua New Guinea in color, 4 of which appear to be undescribed. Randall (1995b) placed *Fusigobius* in the synonymy of *Coryphopterus,* and Randall (2001d) reviewed the Indo-Pacific species of the genus. New species of *Trimma* and *Trimmatom* are under study by Richard Winterbottom.

New Caledonia

Guadalcanal, Solomon Islands

PRETTYTAIL SHRIMPGOBY
Amblyeleotris bellicauda Randall, 2004

Dorsal rays VI + I,13; anal rays I,13; pectoral rays 19; longitudinal scale series 89; scales on body ctenoid posteriorly, becoming cycloid anterior to below fourth dorsal spine (scales ctenoid posteriorly on other *Amblyeleotris*); head naked (also generic); no predorsal or prepectoral scales; scales on side of nape extending forward only to above gill opening; villiform teeth in bands in jaws and continuing along side of upper jaw; a pair of well-spaced recurved canine teeth on each side at front of upper jaw, and three close-set canines nearly halfway back on side of lower jaw, followed by a single row of small teeth (dentition similar for other species of the genus); gill opening extending forward to below posterior margin of preopercle (gill opening also broad in other *Amblyeleotris*); body depth about 5.35 in standard length; caudal fin pointed, 2.9 in standard length; pelvic fins joined by membrane only basally; no pelvic frenum; fourth pelvic ray longest; fifth pelvic ray branched 3 times; white, densely marked with small blue spots, with 4 red bars on body, the first under first dorsal fin slightly oblique, the next 2 under second dorsal fin, broader ventrally, the last across caudal-fin base; a reddish brown bar from nape across opercle onto throat and branchiostegal membranes, with blue and yellow markings; caudal fin with a large elliptical dark red mark, partly edged in blue, the center of fin dusky orange. Known from one 6.7-cm specimen collected by author in 10 m outside barrier reef at New Caledonia.

Redang, Malaysia

TWINSPOT SHRIMPGOBY
Amblyeleotris biguttata Randall, 2004

Dorsal rays VI+I,13; anal rays I,13; pectoral rays 19; pelvic fins joined by membrane to tips of fifth rays; pelvic frenum present; fourth pelvic ray longest; fifth pelvic ray branching twice; longitudinal scale series 91–103; no median predorsal scales; scales on side of nape extending to above middle of opercle; gill opening reaching forward to a vertical about two-thirds orbit diameter behind eye; body depth 5.8–6.1 in SL; head length 3.6–3.8 in SL; caudal fin pointed and long, 2.2–2.6 in SL; pale brown dorsally, white ventrally, with three indistinct brown bars on body, and a slightly oblique brown bar from nape across opercle; pale interspaces with small brown blotches, faintly interconnected; a pair of prominent black spots on chin; dorsal fins yellowish gray, the first dorsal with small irregular dark-edged pale blue spots and orange-tipped spines, the second dorsal with a broad yellow border containing small dark-edged pale blue spots, the rays tipped with orange; caudal fin with a vertically elongate diffuse brown spot on base. Largest specimen, 10.4 cm. Described from four specimens from Guadalcanal, Solomon Islands, and New Caledonia that were collected from silty sand at depths of 11–50 m. The fish shared a burrow with an alpheid shrimp. Very similar to *Amblyeleotris masuii* Aonuma & Yoshino from Okinawa, which differs in its more slender body (depth given as 7.15–8.5 in SL), and in color, such as paler anal and caudal fins, and dark bars of body not extending into dorsal fins.

SLANTBAR SHRIMPGOBY
Amblyeleotris diagonalis Polunin & Lubbock, 1979

Dorsal rays VI + I,13; anal rays I,13; pectoral rays 19–20; longitudinal scale series 67–75; predorsal scales extending forward to above upper end of preopercular margin; pectoral-fin base scaled; body depth 5.2–6.7 in standard length; caudal fin longer than head, 2.8–3.6 in standard length; pelvic fins divided, joined by membrane only basally; white with 4 diagonal dusky orange to dark reddish brown bars on body, much narrower than pale interspaces; head with a comparable bar from nape across posterior part of operculum; an oblique dark brown line, bordered in yellow and blue, from occiput to corner of mouth (broken behind eye); a few small blackish spots dorsally in pale interspaces on body. Reaches about 9 cm. Red Sea, Persian Gulf, and east coast of Africa to western Pacific from Ryukyu Islands (Masuda & Kobayashi, 1994) to Great Barrier Reef (type locality, Lizard Island) and New Caledonia (Laboute & Grandperrin, 2000, as *Amblyeleotris* sp. 1). Known from depths of 6–30 m; lives symbiotically with snapping shrimps of the genus *Alpheus*.

512

ELLIPSE SHRIMPGOBY
Amblyeleotris ellipse Randall, 2004

Dorsal rays VI + I,13; anal rays I,13; pectoral rays 19–20 (usually 19); longitudinal scale series 80–89; no predorsal or prepectoral scales; scales on side of nape extending forward to above middle of opercle; body depth 4.6–5.35 in standard length; caudal fin rounded, 2.8–3.1 in standard length; pelvic fins joined by a short membrane at base, no frenum; fifth pelvic ray longest, branching once, but branches not separated; yellowish white with many small pale blue spots; 3 broad dusky red bars on body, a faint brown one posteriorly on caudal peduncle, merging with brownish red of caudal-fin base, and a narrower dark one from nape across opercle to throat; caudal fin with a large elliptical

American Samoa

blue-edged multicolor mark that extends to posterior margin, the center of fin white with gray streaks. Largest specimen, 7.3 cm. Currently known only from Tutuila, American Samoa; first collected by author in 1971 at Fagasa Bay in 23 m; a second collection by R. C. Wass and I. Swan from 32 m on Taema Bank.

BARRED SHRIMPGOBY
Amblyeleotris fasciata (Herre, 1953)

Dorsal rays VI + I,12; anal rays I,12; pectoral rays 18–20; longitudinal scale series 50–58; predorsal scales extending to above posterior margin of preopercle; body depth 4.5–5.2 in standard length; caudal fin rounded, only slightly longer than head; pelvic fins joined medially for nearly half length of fifth rays; whitish to pale yellow with 5 slightly oblique, dark reddish brown or red bars as broad as or broader than pale interspaces, the first behind eye diffuse and containing bright red and orange spots, the second from nape across opercle, also with red spots; red spots at corner of mouth; small pale blue spots on head, body, and often on fins except pectorals; small red to yellow spots on dorsal fins. Attains 8 cm. Red Sea to islands of Micronesia; in the western Pacific from the Ryukyu Islands to the Great Barrier Reef and New Caledonia. The most common shallow-water goby of the genus in the coral-reef environment at

Bali

many localities; occurs to depths of at least 30 m (dark bars on body may be entirely red in deeper water). Lives in association with snapping shrimps, most often *Alpheus ochrostriatus. Amblyeleotris wheeleri (*Polunin & Lubbock) is a synonym.

GIANT SHRIMPGOBY
Amblyeleotris fontanesii (Bleeker, 1852)

Dorsal rays VI + I,15; anal rays I,16–17; pectoral rays 20–21; longitudinal scale series about 110; predorsal scales extending to less than an orbit diameter from interorbital space; body depth 5.8–6.3 in standard length; outer margin of first dorsal fin rounded, its height a little greater than second dorsal fin; caudal fin somewhat pointed, longer than head; pelvic fins fully united, with a well-developed frenum; whitish with 4 dark brown bars nearly as broad as pale interspaces, the first from nape across posterior part of operculum, the second extending into middle of first dorsal fin; a large, vertically elongate, dark brown spot on base of caudal fin; pale interspaces on body often with 2 or 3 yellow lines (dusky yellow in juveniles, hence more visible); an oblique blue line under eye, and yellow dots on head, mostly on cheek. The largest of the shrimp gobies; reaches at least 20 cm. Indo-

Flores, Indonesia

Malayan region (type locality, Indonesia) to the Great Barrier Reef and New Caledonia; only Palau in Micronesia; occurs on mud bottoms; lives with the largest of the symbiotic snapping shrimps, *Alpheus fenneri.*

Marshall Islands

YELLOWSPOTTED SHRIMPGOBY

Amblyeleotris guttata (Fowler, 1938)

Dorsal rays VI + I,12; anal rays I,12; pectoral rays 19–20; longitudinal scale series 65–70; predorsal scales to above posterior margin of preopercle; body depth 4.5–5.2 in standard length; second to fourth (and sometimes the first) dorsal spines prolonged as short filaments, the third longest; pelvic fins connected by membrane at base of fifth soft rays; pale greenish gray with 4 faint blackish bars, the first across rear of head containing blue dots ventrally; numerous yellow spots of variable size on head, body, and dorsal fins, some on body larger than pupil, those in dorsal fins rimmed in blue; chest, most of pelvic fins, and ventral part of abdomen black, with a large triangular extension dorsally from abdomen to beneath pectoral fin; caudal fin with blue-edged orange spots; anal fin yellowish with 3 yellow spots along base, oblique blue lines, and a broad, middle blackish stripe. Attains 10 cm. Ryukyu Islands and Taiwan to southern Great Barrier Reef and New Caledonia, east to Samoa Islands and all of Micronesia; type locality, Marinduque Island, Philippines; lives mainly with *Alpheus ochrostriatus*.

KATHERINE'S SHRIMPGOBY

Amblyeleotris katherine Randall, 2004

Dorsal rays VI + I,12; anal rays I,12; pectoral rays 18–19 (usually 19); longitudinal scale series 67–73; predorsal scales extending forward to above upper end of preopercular margin; cycloid scales on pectoral-fin base and chest; body depth 4.6–5.35 in standard length; caudal fin rounded, 2.7–3.2 in standard length; pelvic fins joined by a very short membrane at base; no pelvic frenum; white, with many small bright yellow spots on head, body, and dorsal fins; 5 slightly oblique bright red bars narrower than eye diameter, the first from nape across operculum, and the last on caudal peduncle; a

Guam

small red spot above posterior end of maxilla; a blue-edged red arc in basal part of caudal fin. Largest specimen, 6 cm. Known from the Society Islands (type locality, Tetiaroa Atoll), Rarotonga, American Samoa, Niue (M. P. Francis, pers. comm.), Guam, and Enewetak, Marshall Islands; symbiotic with the shrimp *Alpheus ochrostriatus*; typically found on sand near lagoon patch reefs; collected from depths of 3–38 m. Formerly misidentified as *Amblyeleotris fasciata* (Herre).

MARQUESAN SHRIMPGOBY

Amblyeleotris marquesas Mohlmann & Randall, 2002

Dorsal rays VI + I,14; anal rays I,15; pectoral rays 18–19; longitudinal scale series 92–96; midline of nape, pectoral-fin base, and chest naked; scales on side of nape extending to above middle of operculum; body depth 6.6–7.7 in standard length; pelvic fins united only at basal 10% of fifth rays; no pelvic frenum; cau\dal fin pointed, longer than head, 3.1–4.1 in standard length; greenish white with a slightly oblique, brownish red bar from nape across operculum to throat and 3 brownish red bars on body, much wider than pale interspaces; bars broader in middle; each pale interspace with a narrow, irregular, brownish red bar; a broad, brownish red bar across caudal-fin base; top of head and front of snout purplish gray; some irregular orange markings on postorbital head. Attains about 8.5 cm. Known only from the Marquesas Islands; found at depths of 20–25 m living in association with the snapping shrimp *Alpheus randalli*.

Marquesas Islands

Great Barrier Reef

New Caledonia

OGASAWARA SHRIMPGOBY

Amblyeleotris ogasawarensis Yanagisawa, 1978

Dorsal rays VI + I,13–14; anal rays I,13–14; pectoral rays 18–20; longitudinal scale series 80–94; no predorsal or prepectoral scales; body depth 5.2–5.8 in standard length; caudal fin rounded to slightly pointed, longer than head; pelvic fins united to tips of fifth rays, without a frenum; whitish or pale yellow with 5 slightly oblique, dark reddish bars narrower than pale interspaces; first bar across nape and opercle containing a dark reddish spot smaller than pupil just above opercle; second bar ending dorsally in a semicircular dark reddish spot at midbase of first dorsal fin; a narrow dusky bar from eye to corner of mouth; each pale interspace of body bisected by a narrow, dusky reddish bar; scattered small, pale blue spots on head, and numerous pale blue spots in pale interspaces of body, most of which are at edges of both broad and narrow bars on body; a few small red spots on head, one beneath posterior end of maxilla; a dark reddish crescent in caudal fin. Attains about 11 cm. Described from the Ogasawara Islands (type locality) and Ryukyu Islands; collected by the author from the Capricorn Group and Lizard Island of the Great Barrier Reef, Negros in the Philippines, and photographed underwater at New Caledonia and the atoll of Kiritimati (formerly Christmas Island), Line Islands. Symbiotic with *Alpheus*.

BLOTCHY SHRIMPGOBY

Amblyeleotris periophthalma (Bleeker, 1853)

Dorsal rays VI + I,12; anal rays I,11–12 (usually 12); pectoral rays 18–19; longitudinal scale series about 80; no predorsal scales or only a few embedded scales just anterior to origin of first dorsal fin; body depth 4.6–6.4 in standard length; caudal fin longer than head, 2.8–3.4 in standard length; pelvic fins separate, joined only basally by membrane; pale greenish gray dorsally, soon shading to white below, with 4 gray bars on body overlaid with large, irregular, brownish orange blotches; pale interspaces with smaller, irregular dark blotches; a gray bar from nape across posterior operculum containing dark-edged orange-yellow spots; a less-distinct bar on occiput, also with orange-yellow spots; 2 red spots at corner of mouth. Attains 9 cm. Red Sea, Persian Gulf, Zanzibar, and Mauritius east to the Caroline Islands and Samoa Islands; Ryukyu Islands to the Great Barrier Reef and New Caledonia; type locality, Java. Shares a burrow most often with *Alpheus ochrostriatus*. *Cryptocentrops exilis* Smith and *Amblyeleotris maculata* Yanagisawa are synonyms.

NEW CALEDONIA SHRIMPGOBY

Amblyeleotris novaecaledoniae Goren, 1981

Dorsal rays VI + I,12–13 (usually 13); anal rays I,13; pectoral rays 18–20 (usually 19); longitudinal scale series 75–83; no predorsal scales; body depth about 5.4–6.1 in standard length; a membrane connecting tips of fifth rays of pelvic fins (when intact); no pelvic frenum; fourth pelvic ray slightly longer than fifth; fifth ray branched 3 times; caudal fin much longer than head, broadly rounded when spread, about 2.5 in standard length; whitish with 5 brownish red bars, narrower than pale interspaces, the first from nape across opercle, the last posteriorly on caudal peduncle; postorbital head and white interspaces of body with numerous small, pale blue spots that tend to form vertical rows; sometimes a faint narrow brownish red bar in middle of each pale interspace; a brownish red streak extending ventrally from eye to above posterior end of maxilla; median fins unmarked except caudal with a large, blue-edged orange crescent and 1 or 2 blue-edged orange spots ventrally; last three membranes of pelvic fins of preserved specimens with irregular narrow dark bands and spots. Reaches about 10 cm. Known to date only from New Caledonia; holotype collected by the author and L. A. Maugé in a muddy sand area of coral patches and seagrass at a depth of 3–5 m. Bishop Museum collections from 7–12 m. Like others of the genus, lives in association with snapping shrimps of the genus *Alpheus*.

Great Barrier Reef

515

RANDALL'S SHRIMPGOBY
Amblyeleotris randalli Hoese & Steene, 1978

Dorsal rays VI + I,12; anal rays I,12; pectoral rays 18–19; longitudinal scale series 54–63; midline of nape naked; small embedded cycloid scales on side of nape extending only to above upper end of gill opening; no scales on prepectoral area; body depth 4.9–5.7 in standard length; first dorsal fin broadly rounded and high, the second and third spines usually longer than head; caudal fin a little longer than head; pelvic fins linked by membrane to tips of inner rays; no pelvic frenum; pale gray, shading to white ventrally, with 5 narrow, slightly oblique orange bars, the first from nape across posterior operculum; a narrow orange band across interorbital and extending as a narrow bar below eye; first dorsal fin with a large, ocellated black spot at base. Reaches about 11 cm. Indo-Malayan region (type locality, Sumilon Island, Philippines) north to Ryukyu Islands, south to Great Barrier Reef, east to New Caledonia and Fiji. Usually found in the sand and rubble bottom of caves in reef drop-offs at depths of 20–48 m; the illustrated shrimp partner appears to be an undescribed species of *Alpheus* (A. Anker, pers. comm.).

REDMARGIN SHRIMPGOBY
Amblyeleotris rubrimarginata Mohlmann & Randall, 2002

Dorsal rays VI + I,13–14 (rarely 14); anal rays I,14–15 (rarely 15); pectoral rays 18–20; longitudinal scale series 77–94; midline of nape, chest, and pectoral-fin base naked; body depth 5.6–6.7 in standard length; third dorsal spine longest, 1.2–1.8 in head length; caudal fin pointed, longer than head, 2.3–3.2 in standard length; fifth rays of pelvic fins linked by membrane about 10% of their length; pelvic frenum present; whitish with 5 orange to orangish brown bars, distinctly narrower than pale interspaces, the first on nape passing down over operculum, and the fifth on caudal peduncle; dorsal part of pale interspaces with small brown spots and short irregular lines; a small black spot behind eye; an oblique blue and yellow line from below to nape, broken behind eye; caudal fin with an orangish brown arc or large spot; dorsal fins with yellow dots and small, pale blue dashes and dots, the margin red with a submarginal pale blue line. Attains about 11 cm. Philippines, Indonesia, Malaysia, Papua New Guinea, Great Barrier Reef (type locality, Lizard Island), and New Cale-

Sulawesi

Papua New Guinea

donia (*Amblyeleotris* sp. 9 of Laboute & Grandperrin, 2000); found on sand or silty sand near coral reefs or seagrass beds at depths of 3 to 26 m; shares a burrow with either of the snapping shrimps *Alpheus bellulus* or *A. ochrostriatus*; sometimes 2 fish occupy the same burrow.

STEINITZ' SHRIMPGOBY
Amblyeleotris steinitzi (Klausewitz, 1974)

Dorsal rays VI + I,12; anal rays I,12; pectoral rays 17; longitudinal scale series 72–78; head and median part of nape naked; scales on side of nape and those anteriorly on body to below base of third to fourth spines cycloid; scales on rest of body ctenoid; body depth 4.3–5.5 in standard length; first dorsal fin equal in height to second dorsal; caudal fin rounded, a little longer than head; head and body whitish with 5 slightly oblique, dark orangish to reddish brown bars narrower than pale interspaces, the first from nape to throat; a vertically elongate, dark orangish spot at caudal-fin base; pale interspaces with faint pale blue dots and yellow lines; dorsal fins with yellow dots. Attains about 8 cm. Red Sea (type locality) and Mauritius to islands of Micronesia and Samoa Islands; in the western Pacific from the Ryukyu Islands to Great Barrier Reef and New Caledonia; collected by author from depths of 2–43 m; symbiotic with 5 different alpheid shrimps, often *Alpheus djeddensis*.

Marshall Islands

THINBAR SHRIMPGOBY

Amblyeleotris stenotaeniata Randall, 2004

Dorsal rays VI + I,13; anal rays I,14; pectoral rays 19; longitudinal scale series 81; predorsal scales extending forward to within three-fourths orbit diameter behind eyes; small scales present on prepectoral area and chest; body depth about 5.5 in standard length; caudal fin pointed and long, 2.4 in standard length; pelvic fins joined at base by a very short membrane; fifth pelvic ray longest, branched once, the branches not separated; tan dorsally, white below; 5 oblique brown bars with a dark brownish red band in center of each, the first from nape onto opercle, and the last on caudal peduncle; a few small dark brown spots dorsally in pale interspaces; dorsal fins dusky yellow with small irregular dark-edged blue spots; a bright yellow spot rimmed below by a blue arc at margin of each membrane of second dorsal fin. Described from a single 9.5-cm specimen collected in Canala Bay on the northeast coast of New Caledonia in 11 m. Illustrated in Laboute & Grandperrin (2000) as *Amblyeleotris* sp. 4 by an underwater photograph taken in the New Caledonia lagoon; they gave the depth range as 10–20 m.

New Caledonia (T. Allen)

CROSSHATCH GOBY

Amblygobius decussatus (Bleeker, 1855)

Dorsal rays VI + I,14; anal rays I,14; pectoral rays 18–19; longitudinal scale series 55–60; predorsal scales 23–28; scales dorsally on opercle, none on cheek; scales on body ctenoid, those on nape, abdomen, and opercle cycloid; anterior half of upper limb of first gill arch with fleshy filaments, some more than half length of longest gill filaments (true of other *Amblygobius*); body depth 4.0–4.6 in standard length; first dorsal fin equal in height to second; caudal fin rounded, slightly longer than head; pelvic fins joined to form a disc; pelvic frenum present; light greenish gray dorsally, soon shading to white on side and ventrally, with 6 orange stripes, the uppermost broken into spots and short lines, the lowermost faint, the second and third extending onto head, where more distinct; second stripe through eye to front of snout, the third to corner of mouth; stripes on body crossed by 8 narrow orange bars; a pale-edged orange spot larger than pupil on caudal-fin base slightly above midlateral position. Reaches 8 cm. Western Australia, Cocos-Keeling Islands, and western Pacific from Ryukyu Islands to Great Barrier Reef, east to New Caledonia, Fiji, and islands of Micronesia; type locality, Manado, Sulawesi; occurs on silty sand substrata usually near

New Britain

protected reefs in depths of about 3–20 m; shelters in a vertical burrow. This and other species of the genus appear to feed by sifting small crustaceans, mollusks, worms, etc., from mouthfuls of sediment; perhaps the fleshy structure on the first gill arch aids in the filtering.

PAJAMA GOBY

Amblygobius nocturnus (Herre, 1945)

Dorsal rays VI + I,13–15; anal rays I,13–15; pectoral rays 19–20; longitudinal scale series 63–66; scales cycloid; no predorsal scales; scales on side of nape extending a short distance in front of gill opening; scales dorsally on opercle, none on cheek; body depth 4.7–6.4 in standard length; first dorsal fin about equal in height to second; caudal fin slightly pointed, equal to or a little shorter than head; pelvic fins joined to form a disc, with a weak frenum; pale greenish gray with an orange stripe bordered by black and pale blue from anterior nostril through eye and fading gradually to middle of body; a broad black band on upper lip, continuing as an orange band across lower part of head and then midlaterally as a faint stripe to end of caudal fin, where joined by pair of converging orange bands; a series of short dusky bars

New Caledonia

along back. Attains 7 cm. Red Sea and Persian Gulf to French Polynesia; Ryukyu Islands to Lord Howe Island; type locality, Busuanga, Philippines; occurs inshore in sheltered waters, generally seen hovering above a burrow in silty sand.

Marshall Islands

New Caledonia

SPHYNX GOBY
Amblygobius sphynx (Valenciennes in C & V, 1837)
Dorsal rays VI + I,13–15; anal rays I,14–15; pectoral rays 17–19; longitudinal scale series about 55; predorsal scales 20–22, reaching interorbital space; scales ctenoid, becoming cycloid on abdomen, chest, nape, and dorsally on opercle; body depth 3.5–4.2 in standard length; first dorsal fin equal to or slightly shorter than second; caudal fin rounded, equal to or a little longer than head; pelvic fins united to form a disc; pelvic frenum present; olivaceous with 4 broad dark bars with blue dots on body, the center of each with a narrow black bar; 4 or 5 small black spots along dorsal edge of body; a black spot nearly as large as pupil on base of caudal fin just above midlateral line; head below eye with narrow irregular orangish to olivaceous bars and blue flecks. Attains about 15 cm. East coast of Africa and Mauritius to western Pacific, where ranges from Ryukyu Islands to Great Barrier Reef, east to Palau and New Caledonia; type locality,

TWINSPOT GOBY
Asterropteryx bipunctata Allen & Munday, 1995
Dorsal rays VI + I,10; anal rays I,8–10; pectoral rays 17–18; longitudinal scale series 24; predorsal scales and scales on body ctenoid; scales on cheek, opercle, pectoral-fin base, and prepelvic area cycloid; 4–7 close-set spines on edge of preopercle just above corner; body depth 3.2–3.7 in standard length; fourth dorsal spine prolonged to a long filament in males (may be half standard length); caudal fin rounded, equal to or slightly longer than head length; pelvic fins joined by membrane nearly to end of innermost rays, with a weak frenum; pale gray with numerous orange-yellow spots on head, body, and dorsal and caudal fins; an ocellated black spot larger than pupil at midbase of caudal fin,

CALICO GOBY
Amblygobius phalaena (Valenciennes in C & V, 1837)
Dorsal rays VI + I,13–15; anal rays I,14; pectoral rays 18–20; longitudinal scale series 50–55; predorsal scales to interorbital space; scales ctenoid, becoming cycloid on abdomen, chest, nape, and dorsally on opercle; body depth 3.4–4.6 in standard length; third and fourth dorsal spines prolonged as short filaments (second and fifth may also have short free tips); caudal fin rounded, longer than head, 3.2–3.5 in standard length; pelvic fins united to form a disc; pelvic frenum present; 2 color phases, one nearly white, the other blackish, both with 5 black bars on body and dark stripes, one from snout to eye, dividing to 2 stripes behind eye, and one from corner of mouth across lower part of head (may be bordered with or replaced by rows of blue spots); 2 stripes continuing onto body as disjunct segments between bars; rows of orange to dark red or black spots dorsally on head and nape; a large black spot centered on fifth dorsal spine; a large dark spot near base of caudal fin on third to fifth branched rays. Attains 15 cm. Western Australia and Cocos-Keeling Islands to islands of Micronesia and French Polynesia; in western Pacific from Ryukyu Islands and Ogasawara Islands to Great Barrier Reef, Lord Howe Island, and New Caledonia; type locality, Vanikoro, Santa Cruz Islands. Typically found in lagoons or bays on sand or sparse seagrass; constructs a burrow by removing mouthfuls of sand; often seen in pairs. Closely related to *A. semicinctus* (Bennett) of the western Indian Ocean and *A. albimaculatus* (Rüppell) of the Red Sea.

Papua New Guinea

New Guinea; generally found in seagrass beds. Reported to depths as great as 20 m. Harmelin-Vivien (1979) analyzed the contents of the alimentary tracts of 22 specimens from Madagascar; she found mainly small crustaceans (primarily copepods and amphipods) and small gastropods (probably from sifting these organisms from mouthfuls of sand as has been observed for species of *Amblygobius*, in general).

Lombok, Indonesia

and a similar ocellus anteriorly at base of dorsal fin. Largest collected by the author, 4.2 cm. Known from Papua New Guinea (type locality, Madang), Indonesia, Sabah, Solomon Islands, and American Samoa (*Asterropteryx* sp. 7 of Wass, 1984); occurs on sand and rubble near reefs; collected from depths of 13–38 m.

CHEEKSPINE GOBY
Asterropteryx ensifera (Bleeker, 1874)

Dorsal rays VI + I,10; anal rays I,9; pectoral rays 17; longitudinal scale series 24; scales ctenoid; median predorsal scales 5, reaching into posterior interorbital space; cheek and opercle scaled; a single broad-based spine at corner of preopercle, its length about half to two-thirds pupil diameter; body depth 2.7–3.1 in standard length; third dorsal spine prolonged to a long filament in adults; caudal fin rounded, shorter than head length; pelvic fins completely separated, reaching to or beyond anus; light brown with a dusky stripe from eye along upper side of body, and short double bars extending upward from it to dorsal edge of body; dark-edged, pale blue spots in 5 longitudinal rows over full length of body, 1 spot per scale; another row from below first dorsal fin onto head, and a faint one on abdomen; sec-

Marshall Islands

ond dorsal and anal fin with rows of blue spots in lower part. Attains 4 cm. Ryukyu Islands to Great Barrier Reef, east to Marshall Islands and Society Islands; type locality, Buru, Molucca Islands; collected by the author from depths of 0.3–30 m from lagoon patch reefs, algal flats, and seagrass beds.

HALFSPOTTED GOBY
Asterropteryx semipunctata Rüppell, 1830

Dorsal rays VI + I,9–11; anal rays I,8–9 (usually 9); pectoral rays 16–18; longitudinal scale series 23–25; scales ctenoid; head scaled except for snout and interorbital space; gill opening ending below middle of opercle; 3–9 close-set spines on edge of preopercle just above corner; body depth 3.0–3.6 in standard length; third dorsal spine prolonged to a long filament in adults; caudal fin rounded or truncate with broadly rounded corners; pelvic fins separate, joined by membrane only at their extreme bases; color variable, dark to light gray with 3 longitudinal rows of large, dark brown blotches on body and numerous bright blue dots on head and body, mostly on ventral half. Attains 6.5 cm. Occurs throughout most of the tropical Indo-Pacific region; type locality, Red Sea; usually found in silty dead-reef areas at depths of 1–15 m; takes refuge in a burrow or hole in reef. Often classified in the earlier literature as a sleeper (Eleotridae) because of the divided pelvic fins (not a family character). Privitera (2001, 2002) studied the reproductive biology in the Hawaiian Islands. Spawning occurs at various times during the day, year-around, with a peak from May to July. Clutch size varied from 296 to 1,552 (mean 886), independent of length of the female. Eggs are ellipsoidal and varied from 067–0.84 mm in length, hence unusually small for a goby of this size. Eggs were laid beneath coral; egg tending was performed by the male, who periodically fanned them with the pectoral fins. Eggs hatched in laboratory

Palau

aquaria shortly after lights were turned off, 4–6 nights after being deposited in the nest. Newly hatched larvae had a mean notochord length of 1.88 mm. Minimum length at maturity, 17.5–19 mm, estimated at 4.5–5 months after hatching. Also known as the Bluespotted Goby, not a good name because the western Pacific *Asterropteryx striatus* Allen & Munday is more prominently blue-spotted.

SPINY GOBY
Asterropteryx spinosa (Goren, 1981)

Dorsal rays VI + I,9–10 (usually 10); anal rays I,9; pectoral rays 17–19; longitudinal scale series 24; predorsal scales 4–5, reaching to eyes; scales ctenoid on body, becoming cycloid anterior to paired fins; large scales on operculum; 3–7 spines on posterior edge of preopercle, the lowermost often largest; body depth 3.7–4.0 in standard length; fourth dorsal spine prolonged to a filament in adults; caudal fin rounded, a little longer than head; pelvic fins joined by membrane; no pelvic frenum; pale gray, the head, body, and dorsal and caudal fins densely covered with small, brownish orange spots of variable size; a narrow black bar extending ventrally from eye; a short, vertical black streak at midbase of caudal fin. Largest specimen, 4.3 cm. Known from New Caledonia (type locality), Micronesia except the Mariana Islands, Philippines, Ryukyu Islands, and Maldive Islands (Ran-

Palau

dall & Goren, 1993). Holotype collected by the author and L. A. Maugé in a muddy sand area with coral patches and seagrass in 3–5 m. Bishop Museum specimens have been collected from depths of 0.5–30 m.

WHITESPOTTED FRILLGOBY
Bathygobius coalitus (Bennett, 1832)

Dorsal rays VI + I,9; anal rays I,8; pectoral rays 18–20, the upper 4 or 5 branched to base, with membrane-free ends; longitudinal scale series 36–38; predorsal scales 15–20, reaching midway between posterior edge of preopercle and hind edge of eyes; operculum naked; scales on body ctenoid, becoming cycloid on abdomen, chest, and nape; no fleshy flap extending from edge of cheek into notch at posterior end of upper lip; a small posterior flap on anterior nostril; body depth 4.3–4.7 in standard length; head depressed, its width greater than its depth (true of other *Bathygobius*); caudal fin rounded, about equal to head length; pelvic disc pointed, nearly or just reaching anus; pelvic frenum present (generic), the free edge smoothly concave; brown, the scale edges darker, white on chest and lower abdomen, with a series of 7 or 8 dark blotches larger than pupil along side of body a little below midlateral line; numerous small white spots on head, body, and dorsal and anal fins; a narrow dusky stripe near base of first dorsal fin. Reported to 12 cm. East coast of Africa to the Hawaiian Islands and Marquesas Islands; Japan to Great Barrier Reef; type locality, Mauritius; typically found in the intertidal zone. *Bathygobius albopunctatus* (Valenciennes) and *B. padangensis* (Bleeker) appear to be synonyms.

COCOS FRILLGOBY
Bathygobius cocosensis (Bleeker, 1854)

Dorsal rays VI + I,9; anal rays I,8; pectoral rays 18–19, the upper 4 or 5 branched to base with membrane-free ends; longitudinal scale series 37–38; predorsal scales 10–12, nearly reaching to above posterior margin of preopercle; operculum naked; scales on body ctenoid, becoming cycloid on abdomen, chest, and nape; no fleshy flap extending from edge of cheek into notch at posterior end of upper lip; no posterior flap on anterior nostril; body depth about 5 in standard length; caudal fin rounded, about equal to head length; pelvic disc pointed, reaching anus; a well-developed frenum, the free edge smoothly concave; brown, most pigment on scale edges, becoming white on abdomen and ventrally on head; usually a series of large dark brown blotches along side a little below midlateral line; 5 irregular whitish blotches or narrow short bars often present dorsally on body; small white spots present or absent on body, cheek, and dorsal and caudal fins. Reported to 8 cm, but usually not exceeding 6 cm. Occurs throughout the tropical Indo-Pacific region; type locality, Cocos-Keeling Islands; typically found in tidepools or shallow reef flats.

CHEEKSCALED FRILLGOBY
Bathygobius cotticeps (Steindachner, 1879)

Dorsal rays VI + I,10; anal rays I,8; pectoral rays 23–24, the upper 5–7 partly free of membrane, the uppermost with 5–7 branches; longitudinal scale series 35–39; median predorsal scales 21–32, extending into interorbital space; scales present on cheek and opercle; scales on head and anterior body small and cycloid, becoming larger and ctenoid posteriorly; body depth 4.2–5.0 in standard length; head strongly depressed; anterior nostril with a slender flap on posterior edge; caudal fin rounded, shorter than head; pelvic disc round, not approaching anus; a fleshy pelvic frenum, the margin with a median convexity; brown, mottled with darker brown spots and small pale spots; a broad bar often present below each dorsal fin (obscure in large individuals); dark spots basally in dorsal and caudal fins tending to form bands; first dorsal fin may have a large black spot posteriorly near its base. Reaches 11 cm. Wide-ranging in the Indo-Pacific from East Africa to the Hawaiian Islands and Pitcairn Islands; Japan to the Great Barrier Reef; type locality, Society Islands; also an intertidal species.

ROUNDFIN FRILLGOBY
Bathygobius cyclopterus (Valenciennes in C & V, 1837)

Dorsal rays VI + I,9; anal rays I,8; pectoral rays 20–22, the upper 5 with free ends, and the sixth partly free; upper 4 rays with 3 branches, the fifth with 4; longitudinal scale series 37–38; predorsal scales 18–20, reaching or nearly reaching interorbital space; upper part of opercle with cycloid scales; scales on body ctenoid, becoming cycloid on abdomen, chest, pectoral-fin base, and nape; a fleshy double flap extending from edge of cheek into notch at posterior end of upper lip; a slender posterior flap on anterior nostril; body depth 4.3–5.5 in standard length; caudal fin rounded, about equal to head without snout; pelvic disc round, reaching about halfway to origin of anal fin, the margin of frenum with a slight convexity in the middle; color variable, with or without dark longitudinal lines following scale rows; outer part of dorsal and caudal fins often broadly yellow, the second dorsal and caudal fins with blackish margin; a blackish spot on last 2 membranes of first dorsal fin; small, dark reddish spots basally on second dorsal and caudal fins. Attains 7 cm. Red Sea and east coast of Africa to Samoa Islands; Japan to Indo-Malayan region; type locality, New Ireland. *Mapo crassiceps* Jordan & Seale is a synonym.

DUSKY FRILLGOBY
Bathygobius fuscus (Rüppell, 1830)

Dorsal rays VI + I,9; anal rays I,8; pectoral rays 17–19, the upper 3 partly free of membrane, the uppermost with 2–3 branches; longitudinal scale series 29–36; median predorsal scales 10–19, reaching from above middle of preopercle nearly to interorbital space; prepelvic area scaled; body depth 4.4–5.0 in standard length; first dorsal spine longest; caudal fin rounded, a little shorter than head length; pelvic disc with a well-developed frenum; posterior margin of frenum straight; pale yellowish brown with large, irregular, dark brown blotches on body and longitudinal rows of small, pale blue spots, one per scale; small

Tonga

blue spots in dorsal and caudal fins, the outer margin of first dorsal broadly yellow. Reaches 8 cm. Red Sea (type locality) and east coast of Africa to western Pacific from Japan and Korea to Great Barrier Reef, east to Samoa Islands and Micronesia.

LADD'S FRILLGOBY
Bathygobius laddi (Fowler, 1931)

Dorsal rays VI + I,9; anal rays I,8; pectoral rays 21–24, the upper 5 or 6 partly free of membrane; longitudinal scale series 28–32; median predorsal scales 9–13, not reaching above posterior margin of preopercle; no scales on cheek, opercle, pectoral-fin base, and prepelvic area; scales ctenoid on body a short distance anterior to first dorsal fin, cycloid before; body depth 4.65–5.85 in standard length; no flap on posterior edge of anterior nostril; caudal fin rounded, shorter than head; pelvic disc oblong, not reaching anus; scales of body with dark brown edges and pale centers; a faint pattern of dark bars sometimes evident; head mottled yellowish brown with dark spots or short bars below eye and on snout; a small dark spot behind eye; dorsal fins with oblique dark bands; caudal fin with dark spots forming irregular

Sri Lanka

bars; a black spot often present dorsally and ventrally on caudal-fin base. A small species; attains only about 5 cm. East Africa to Fiji (Viti Levu, type locality); Taiwan to Queensland and Western Australia; specimens collected by the author from tidepools, rocky shore, and mangrove and rock habitat in Sri Lanka, northern Taiwan, Dampier Archipelago (Western Australia), and Cooktown, Queensland.

Fiji

DIANNE'S GOBY
Bryaninops dianneae Larson, 1985

Dorsal rays VI + I,8; anal rays I,9; pectoral rays 15–16; branched caudal rays 11 (true of other *Bryaninops*); longitudinal scale series 50–54; no scales on head, nape, chest, and pectoral-fin base (also generic); scales ctenoid (generic); body slender, the depth at origin of anal fin about 8 in standard length; head width greater than head depth; snout longer than orbit diameter; gill opening reaching to just behind eye; a curved canine tooth at midside of lower jaw (true of other species of the genus here); pelvic disc reaching beyond anus, the frenum smooth, not curled under to form pockets; caudal fin truncate with rounded corners (generic); transparent, the vertebral column visible with a dark line on its upper edge; lower half of body finely dotted with black; a dusky orange stripe on side of snout; iris mainly yellow, dusky at outer edge, with an arc of red ventrally; a red line along base of dorsal fin; fins transparent except lower two-thirds of caudal light red. Largest specimen, 2.4 cm. Reported only from Fiji; found on green finger-like sponge of the genus *Haliclona* from depths of 6–15 m.

Sulawesi

LOKI'S GOBY
Bryaninops loki Larson, 1985

Dorsal rays VI + I,7–9 (usually 8); anal rays I,7–9; pectoral rays 13–17 (usually 14 or 15), the upper 3 or 4 and the lower 2 or 3 unbranched; longitudinal scale series 33–53 (mean, 47); body slender, the depth at origin of anal fin 5.6–9.5 in standard length; head width about equal to head depth; snout equal to or shorter than orbit diameter; gill opening reaching to below posterior edge of eye; pelvic disc short, round, and cup-like, not reaching anus; body transparent dorsally, a yellow line visible along top of vertebral column; ventral part of body with a series of large red blotches, joined ventrally, with 7 or 8 triangular extensions into upper part of body; a red stripe from upper lip to eye; iris red with an inner yellow ring; fins transparent with pale red rays. Largest specimen, 2.8 cm. Ryukyu Islands to Great Barrier Reef (type locality, Lizard Island) and Lord Howe Island, east to Fiji and Samoa Islands, west to Chagos Archipelago; photographed and collected by the author at Banda, Wetar, Sulawesi, and the Mentawai Islands in Indonesia, and Cebu in the Philippines; commensal on sea whips (*Junceella* sp. in illustration), sea fans, or black coral at depths of 6 to at least 45 m.

Sulawesi

Wetar, Indonesia

HOVERING GOBY

Bryaninops natans Larson, 1985

Dorsal rays IV-VIII (usually VI) + I,7–9 (usually 8); anal rays I,8–9 (usually 9); pectoral rays 14–17; body about half scaled, the longitudinal scale series 19–40 (mean, 31); body stout for the genus, the depth at origin of anal fin 4.4–6.2 in standard length; head width less than head depth; snout short, less than orbit diameter; gill opening reaching to or before a vertical at posterior edge of eye; pelvic disc a shallow cup, the spines with fleshy lobes; transparent, the vertebral column easily seen for its entire length; a large yellow area over abdomen; a broad orange-red band from pectoral-fin base to eye; a broad deep pink band across interorbital; iris bright red; edge of orbit partially black. Largest specimen, 2.4 cm. Known from Red Sea and Seychelles to the Cook Islands; Ryukyu Islands to Great Barrier Reef (type locality, Lizard Island). Generally seen in groups of 8–10, hovering 30–60 cm above coral thickets of the genus *Acropora* (Larson, 1985); rests on live coral.

Alor, Indonesia

WHIP GOBY

Bryaninops yongei (Davis & Cohen, 1969)

Dorsal rays VI + I,7–10 (usually 8 or 9); anal rays I,7–9; pectoral rays 13–17; body about half scaled, the longitudinal scale series 26–58 (mean, 40); body depth at origin of anal fin 5.4–8.1 in standard length; head width greater than head depth; snout slightly longer than orbit diameter; gill opening reaching ventrally to below pectoral-fin base; pelvic disc usually cup-like and short, not reaching anus, the spines with fleshy lobes; upper part of body transparent to translucent greenish, a pale yellow line visible along top of vertebral column; dorsal part of body crossed by 6 reddish bars; lower part of body dusky greenish or yellowish, sometimes red, with 2 narrow whitish bars on abdomen; a narrow red band from front of upper lip to eye; iris varying from orange-red to yellow. Largest specimen, 3.7 cm. Red Sea to the Hawaiian Islands, Marquesas Islands, Society Islands, and Rapa; Japan to Great Barrier Reef; type locality, Darvel Bay, Sabah. Lives on the antipatharian sea whip *Cirrhipathes anguina* at depths of 3 to at least 45 m, typically with 1 male and female pair per sea whip, sometimes with a few juveniles as well.

BLACKCORAL GOBY

Bryaninops tigris Larson, 1985

Dorsal rays VI + I,7–8 (usually 8); anal rays I,8–9; pectoral rays 12–14 (usually 13), the lower 3 or 4 rays unbranched and thickened; longitudinal scale series 32–59 (mean, 47), the scales usually reaching to above pectoral-fin base, occasionally a little anterior to it; midline of nape usually naked (rarely a few predorsal scales); abdomen naked midventrally, and usually the sides as well; body slender, the depth at origin of anal fin 6.9–8.6 in standard length; head width about equal to head depth; snout length about equal to orbit diameter; gill opening short, ending at lower edge of pectoral-fin base or slightly anterior; pelvic fins short and cup-like; side of body blackish to dusky red or orange; back transparent except for 6 or 7 narrow dusky orange or red bars that are continuous with color of side, and a series of small spots of the same color dorsally on body, one in each space between bars; a white line along top of vertebral column; a dusky orange or red stripe from front of snout through eye and across postorbital head; a prominent black blotch at base of caudal fin. Attains 3 cm. Known from the Chagos Archipelago, Gulf of Thailand, Solomon Islands, Great Barrier Reef (type locality, Lizard Island), Tahiti (Randall et al., 2002a), and the Hawaiian Islands; commensal on black coral (*Antipathes*); reported from depths of 15–53 m.

(Masuda et al., 1984)

TONGAREVA GOBY

Cabillus tongarevae (Fowler, 1927)

Dorsal rays VI-I,9; anal rays I,8; pectoral rays 18; branched caudal rays 13; longitudinal scale series 27; no median predorsal scales; no scales on prepectoral area, and none evident in prepelvic area; gill rakers very short, 1 + 4; body depth about 6 in standard length; head very depressed, the head depth about 1.3 in head width; gill opening restricted to base of pectoral fin; maxilla reaching slightly posterior to a vertical through center of eye; caudal fin somewhat pointed, shorter than head length; pelvic fins joined for at least basal fourth or fifth rays, the fin tips reaching origin of anal fin; no pelvic frenum; tips of pelvic rays branched and curved outward, thus providing a fringe effect to the lateral edge. Total length of holotype, 3.0 cm. Positively known only from the type locality, Tongareva (also known as Penrhyn Island) in the northern Cook Islands, Kanton Island in the Phoenix Islands (Schultz, 1943), and the Ryukyu Islands (Prince Akihito in Masuda et al., 1984). Winterbottom & Emery (1986) identified 39 specimens from the Chagos Archipelago as *Cabillus tongarevae*; they noted that Fowler's counts of 5 dorsal and anal soft rays (his illustration shows 7) are erroneous (the holotype in the Bishop Museum has 9 dorsal soft rays and 8 anal soft rays); Fowler gave 23 as the count of scales in longitudinal series, but the holotype has 27. The gill-raker count of Chagos specimens, 1 + 5–6 (mean, 5.9), is significantly different from 1 + 4 of the holotype of *tongarevae*. The photograph of the Ryukyu Islands specimen reproduced here agrees with Fowler's drawing, but is clearly different from Chagos specimens.

HASSELT'S GOBY
Callogobius hasseltii (Bleeker, 1851)

Dorsal rays VI + I,9–10; anal rays I,7–8; pectoral rays 16–18; longitudinal scale series 40–45; predorsal scales 20–22, just reaching interorbital space; a few embedded scales on opercle; scales ctenoid on about posterior half of body, cycloid anteriorly; short ridges of sensory papillae on head set at various angles (true of other species of the genus); body elongate, the length 5.4–6.0 in standard length; head width greater than head depth; second dorsal fin a little higher than first; caudal fin large and pointed, 2.4–3.0 in standard length; pectoral-fin tip reaching above origin of anal fin; pelvic fins united by membrane (when intact) to form a disc; pelvic frenum present; brown, usually with large, irregular, dark brown bars or blotches; an oval black spot larger than eye usually present at upper edge of caudal fin; 2 or 3 broad, oblique, dark brown bands in second dorsal fin. Attains

about 7.5 cm. Known from Japan to Philippines and Indonesia (type locality, Java), west to India, east to Fiji, Tonga, and islands of Micronesia except the Mariana Islands. A shallow-water species of bays and lagoons, including mangrove areas.

OSTRICH GOBY
Callogobius maculipinnis (Fowler, 1918)

Dorsal rays VI + I,9; anal rays I,7; pectoral rays 17–19; longitudinal scale series 22–25; predorsal scales 6–7; scales on body ctenoid, becoming cycloid on nape, pectoral-fin base, and chest; embedded cycloid scales on cheek and opercle; body depth about 4 in standard length; gill opening ending at lower edge of pectoral-fin base; first dorsal fin higher than second dorsal, the second spine prolonged as a short filament; caudal fin rounded, equal to or a little longer than head; pectoral-fin tip reaching above second or third anal soft ray; pelvic fins united to form a disc; pelvic frenum present; brown with numerous small, pale brown spots on body; papillae of fleshy ridges on head dark brown; first dorsal fin with wavy, oblique, brown bands much wider than pale interspaces; all fins except pelvics with very small white spots, most numerous on second dorsal and caudal fins. Reaches 9 cm. Known from Red Sea, east coast of Africa,

Seychelles, Philippines (type locality), Great Barrier Reef, Norfolk Island, New Caledonia, Fiji, Tonga, Samoa Islands, Palau, Guam, and Marshall Islands. *Drombus irrasus* Smith from Mahé, Seychelles, is a synonym.

TRIPLEBAND GOBY
Callogobius sclateri (Steindachner, 1879)

Dorsal rays VI + I,9; anal rays I,8; pectoral rays 16–17; longitudinal scale series 27–28; predorsal scales 11, increasing in size anteriorly, extending into interorbital space; scales on body ctenoid to base of sixth dorsal spine, cycloid anteriorly; cheek and operculum scaled; body depth 4.7–5.5 in standard length; head depressed; first dorsal fin about equal in height to second, without a filament; caudal fin rounded, equal to or a little shorter than head; pectoral-fin tip reaching above origin of anal fin; pelvic fins variously joined medially from base to two-thirds length of fifth rays; no pelvic frenum; pale brown to nearly white with 3 irregular dark bands, one from beneath pectoral fin into base of first dorsal fin, the second oblique from behind anal fin into second dorsal fin, and the third vertically across base of caudal fin. Attains 4.5 cm. The most common and widespread spe-

cies of the genus; Red Sea and east coast of Africa to the Society Islands (type locality) and Marquesas Islands; southern Japan to Great Barrier Reef; lagoon reef or rubble areas from depths of 1–35 m; very cryptic.

523

Komodo, Indonesia

Okinawa

TWOSPOT SANDGOBY

Coryphopterus duospilus (Hoese & Reader, 1985)

Dorsal rays VI + I,9; anal rays I,8; pectoral rays 18–20; longitudinal scale series 24–25; scales on body ctenoid, becoming cycloid anterior to paired fins; no scales on operculum; no median predorsal scales, but scales on side of nape to above posterior margin of preopercle; body depth 4.35–5.8 in standard length; interorbital space very narrow (true of other *Coryphopterus*); gill opening extending forward to or nearly to a vertical at posterior margin of preopercle; caudal fin rounded, slightly shorter than head length (also generic); pelvic fins united nearly to end of fifth rays, the frenum weak; translucent gray with scattered, brownish orange dots and small blotches and small white spots; a small blackish spot at midbase of caudal fin; 2 black spots in outer part of first dorsal fin, one on first membrane, often with a black line from it to base of third dorsal spine, and the other on fifth membrane. Largest specimen, 5.7 cm. East coast of Africa to the Hawaiian Islands and Marquesas Islands; Japan to Great Barrier Reef (type locality, Escape Reef); typically found on sand and rubble next to reefs, where it seeks shelter under coral or stones (also true of other species of *Coryphopterus*, in general); collections from depths of 1–46 m.

SHOULDERSPOT SANDGOBY

Coryphopterus humeralis Randall, 2001

Dorsal rays VI + I,9; anal rays I,8; pectoral rays 17–19; longitudinal scale series 25; scales ctenoid except nape, chest, and pectoral-fin base, where cycloid; no scales on operculum; no median predorsal scales, but scales on side of nape nearly to orbit; posterior nostril very close to orbit; gill opening to below anterior one-fourth of opercle; body depth 4.4–4.8 in standard length; snout short, 3.4–3.7 in head length; first dorsal fin not higher than second, the second and third spines longest; pelvic fins fully united by membrane (when intact); pelvic frenum present; translucent with numerous small, dusky orange-yellow spots on head and body (orangish brown on fish living on dark sand), those on head in oblique rows; a round black spot as large as or larger than pupil in humeral region above pectoral-fin base; a

SLENDER SANDGOBY

Coryphopterus gracilis Randall, 2001

Dorsal rays VI + I,9; anal rays I,8; pectoral rays 17–19; longitudinal scale series 25; scales on body ctenoid, becoming cycloid anterior to paired fins; no scales on operculum; no median predorsal scales, but scales on side of nape nearly to above posterior margin of preopercle; posterior nostril not close to orbit; gill opening extending forward to below middle of opercle; body slender, the depth 5.4–5.8 in standard length; snout length 3.0–3.4 in head length; first dorsal fin not higher than second, the second spine usually longest; pelvic fins fully united by membrane (when intact), without a frenum; translucent with numerous very small orange-yellow spots with blackish centers on head and body, those on head arranged in oblique rows; a black spot the size of pupil or smaller at midbase of caudal fin; a second smaller blackish spot above base of pectoral fin; dorsal and caudal fins with orange-yellow spots; a dusky orange line from upper part of first membrane of first dorsal fin to base of second spine. Largest specimen, 5.3 cm. Ryukyu Islands (type locality, Okinawa) to Great Barrier Reef and New Caledonia, east to Fiji; collections from depths of 6–18 m.

Bali

second black spot nearly as large at midbase of caudal fin. A small species, the largest examined, 4.4 cm. Red Sea to French Polynesia; Ryukyu Islands to Great Barrier Reef and New Caledonia; type locality, Maldive Islands. Collected from depths of 3–30 m.

INNERSPOTTED SANDGOBY

Coryphopterus inframaculatus Randall, 1994

Dorsal rays VI + I,9; anal rays I,7–8 (rarely 7); pectoral rays 17–20 (modally 19); longitudinal scale series 25–26; scales on body ctenoid; no scales on operculum; no median predorsal scales, but scales on side of nape nearly reaching orbit; posterior nostril very close to orbit; gill opening ending below posterior half of opercle; body depth 4.8–5.15 in standard length; snout length 3.15–3.45 in head length; first 2 dorsal spines prolonged to a filament, very long in males, up to 1.7 in standard length;

Sabah/female

524

pelvic fins fully united by membrane (when intact), with a frenum, reaching to or beyond anus; translucent with small dark-edged orange-yellow spots on head, body, and dorsal and caudal fins, the spots on head tending to align in oblique rows; an internal series of 5 large, horizontally elongate black spots, interspersed with white; a large, oval black spot at base of caudal fin; first interspinous membrane of dorsal fin blackish. Reaches 6 cm. Persian Gulf (type locality), Kenya, and Mauritius to western Pacific from the Philippines to southern Great Barrier Reef, east to Tonga; collected over sand or sand and rubble from depths of 1.5–15 m.

Great Barrier Reef/male

Sangiang, Indonesia

Flores, Indonesia

BLACKTIP SANDGOBY
Coryphopterus melacron Randall, 2001

Dorsal rays VI + I,10; anal rays I,9; pectoral rays 19–21; longitudinal scale series 27; head and most of nape naked; scales ctenoid except cycloid on chest, pectoral-fin base, and a few scales on side of nape; posterior nostril very close to orbit; gill opening to below posterior margin of preopercle; body depth 4.75–5.2 in standard length; snout length 3.2–3.4 in head length; first dorsal fin distinctly higher than second, the second and third spines longest, 3.25–3.45 in standard length; pelvic fins joined only basally by membrane, without a frenum; body translucent gray with small, greenish white spots and numerous small, yellowish brown or dusky orange-red spots, those ventrally on body forming longitudinal rows; outer part of first dorsal fin broadly dark brown to black. Attains 4.5 cm. Known from the Andaman Sea off Thailand, Ryukyu Islands, Philippines, Indonesia (type locality, Bali), Palau, Solomon Islands, and Fiji; collected from depths of 7–30.5 m.

NOVICE SANDGOBY
Coryphopterus neophytus (Günther, 1877)

Dorsal rays VI + I,9; anal rays I,8; pectoral rays 16–19 (rarely 16 or 19); longitudinal scale series 22–24; no median predorsal scales; only 5 or 6 scales on side of nape anterior to origin of dorsal fin; scales ctenoid, including those on nape, cycloid on chest and pectoral-fin base; an extra sensory pore over preopercle; gill opening extending forward nearly to a vertical at posterior margin of preopercle; body depth 4.0–4.6 in standard length; snout pointed, its length about equal to eye diameter; first dorsal fin about equal in height to second; pelvic fins fully joined; frenum well developed; translucent with an inner row of black dashes alternating with white; numerous small, dusky yellow spots externally; a black spot smaller than pupil at caudal-fin base; a short vertical black streak often present on lower midside of caudal peduncle; a U-shaped, dark brown mark dorsally on snout, and a

SIGNAL SANDGOBY
Coryphopterus signipinnis (Hoese & Obika, 1988)

Dorsal rays VI + I,9; anal rays I,8; pectoral rays 16–18 (rarely 16); longitudinal scale series 23–25; scales ctenoid except cycloid on chest, pectoral-fin base, and side of nape to above posterior margin of preopercle; gill opening slightly anterior to a vertical at posterior margin of preopercle; body depth 4.7–5.5 in standard length; snout length 3.0–3.4 in head length; first dorsal fin about equal in height to second dorsal fin; pelvic fins joined only basally by membrane, without a frenum; translucent gray with dark orange to dark brown dots; fins largely transparent except first dorsal, black at tip of first 2 membranes; below this a large, brownish orange blotch with white spots. Largest specimen, 6.3 cm. Ryukyu Islands to Great Barrier Reef (type locality, Lizard Island), east to Guam, Caroline Islands, Fiji, and Tonga; reported from depths of 5–25 m. Named for its habit of flicking its first dorsal fin up and down.

Great Barrier Reef

dark brown line on side of snout; a small black spot anteriorly in first dorsal fin, the outer margin white. Reaches 7 cm. Occurs throughout the Indo-Pacific region except the Hawaiian Islands; described from Pohnpei (Ponape), Upolu, Huahine, and Tahiti; collected from depths of 0.5–25 m.

Sulawesi

Maldive Islands/yellow phase

VARIABLE SHRIMPGOBY

Cryptocentrus fasciatus (Playfair in Playfair & Günther, 1867)
Dorsal rays VI + I,10; anal rays I,9; pectoral rays 17–18; longitudinal scale series 77–92; scales cycloid; small embedded scales on pectoral-fin base, prepelvic area, isthmus, and nape nearly to interorbital space; head naked except for a few scales dorsally on opercle; gill opening extending forward to below posterior one-third of preopercle; body depth 5.5–5.8 in standard length; dorsal profile of snout steep (true of other *Cryptocentrus*); first dorsal fin higher than second; caudal fin rounded, 3.2–3.8 in standard length; pelvic fins joined medially, nearly reaching anus; pelvic frenum present but thin; whitish to pale yellow with 5 dark brown bars broader than pale interspaces, the first on nape passing obliquely across most of opercle, the next 3 usually bifurcating dorsally; blue dots or dashes on head; another color phase dark brown, with or without blue dots; 6 whitish to pale yellow blotches dorsally on head and body; a third phase all dark brown; a fourth color phase yellow; all phases with lengthwise blue lines in anal fin. Reaches 9.5 cm. Red Sea, Oman, and Zanzibar (type locality) to Indonesia and Melanesia, including New Caledonia; lives symbiotically with snapping shrimps (most often *Alpheus bellulus*); known from the depth range of 6–20 m.

Tonga

Palau

SINGAPORE SHRIMPGOBY

Cryptocentrus leptocephalus Bleeker, 1876
Dorsal rays VI + I,10–11; anal rays I,10–11; pectoral rays 17–18; longitudinal scale series 77–92; head naked; scales cycloid, those anteriorly on body embedded; scales on side of nape extending forward nearly to above posterior margin of preopercle; gill opening nearly reaching to below posterior margin of preopercle; body depth 5.4–6.0 in standard length; head length 3.5–3.7 in standard length; first dorsal fin higher than second, the third and fourth spines longest (may be prolonged, making the fin pointed), varying from nearly as long as to longer than head; caudal fin rounded, much longer than head, about 2.6 in standard length; pelvic fins joined medially, usually reaching origin of anal fin; pelvic frenum well developed; body pale yellowish with 6 or 7 slightly oblique, brownish orange bars equal to or narrower than pale interspaces; small orange and blue spots, mostly on upper half of body; head with blue dots, larger pink to orange spots, and an oblique, broken, pink to orange line behind eye extending onto nape; first dorsal fin with many oblong orange to dark brown spots rimmed in blue. Reaches 10 cm. Indo-Malayan region east to Tonga; only Palau in Micronesia; type locality, Singapore; occurs in shallow, silty sand and rubble areas near protected reefs and in mangrove habitats; lives symbiotically with alpheid shrimps, including *Alpheus djeddensis*, *A. ochrostriatus*, and *A. rapax*. *Cryptocentrus geniornatus* Herre, *Smilogobius obliquus* Herre, and *S. singapurensis* Herre are regarded as synonyms.

526

SADDLED SHRIMPGOBY
Cryptocentrus leucostictus (Günther, 1872)
Dorsal rays VI + I,10–11; anal rays I,9–10; pectoral rays 16–17; longitudinal scale series about 90; head naked; scales cycloid, those anteriorly on body embedded; scales on side of nape extending forward nearly to above posterior margin of preopercle; gill opening nearly reaching a vertical at posterior margin of preopercle; body depth 5.2–6.6 in standard length; head length 3.9–4.2 in standard length; first dorsal fin lower than second, the fourth and fifth spines longest, about half head length; caudal fin rounded, longer than head, 3.0–3.4 in standard length; pelvic fins joined medially; pelvic frenum present, the fins short, 1.2–1.4 in head length; dark brown to black with whitish dots and small spots and 9 pale yellow to white blotches dorsally on head and body, the first on occiput, the last above base of caudal fin; front of head including chin white to pale yellow; upper and lower edge of pectoral-fin base white to pale yellow; rays of median

Papua New Guinea

fins banded with white and dark brown. Reaches 11 cm. Andaman Sea and Indo-Malayan region east to Palau, Tonga (type locality), and Samoa Islands; occurs on silty sand and rubble substrata from the shallows to at least 20 m; lives with alpheid shrimps, including *Alpheus rapax*.

Solomon Islands

TARGET SHRIMPGOBY
Cryptocentrus strigilliceps (Jordan & Seale, 1906)
Dorsal rays VI + I,9–10 (usually 10); anal rays I,9–10 (usually 9); pectoral rays 16–17; longitudinal scale series 54–61; scales ctenoid to below last dorsal spine, cycloid anteriorly; scales on side of nape extending to above posterior margin of preopercle; gill opening reaching to below posterior margin of preopercle; body depth 3.8–4.5 in standard length; head length 3.2–3.35 in standard length; first dorsal fin higher than second, the second and third spines long and filiform (can be longer than head length); caudal fin rounded, about as long as head; pelvic fins joined medially, the fins usually reaching anus; whitish with 3 broad brown bars dorsally on body, the first 2 soon dividing into 3 irregular branches, the third into 2; a lateral series of 4 large, roundish, dark brown spots within branches, the first beneath pectoral fin, about twice as large as others, and pale-rimmed; scattered small blue spots may be present on body; head with irregular, orangish brown spots and short bands, mostly in oblique rows. Reaches 6 cm. East coast of Africa to Marshall Islands and Samoa Islands (type locality, Upolu); Ryukyu Islands to Great Barrier Reef and New Caledonia; a shallow-water species of silty sand bottom; shares a burrow with *Alpheus djeddensis*, *A. rapacida*, or *A. ochrostriatus*. *Obtortiophagus koumansi* Whitley is a synonym. Very similar to *Cryptocentrus caeruleomaculatus* (Herre), which differs in having the first dorsal fin about equal in height to the second, the first dark spot on the side not much larger than the others, and oblique dark bands on the anal fin.

Flores, Indonesia

GOLDSTREAKED SHRIMPGOBY
Ctenogobiops aurocingulus (Herre, 1935)
Dorsal rays VI + I,11; anal rays I,11; pectoral rays 18–20; longitudinal scale series 48–56; no scales on head, chest, pectoral-fin base, or median zone of nape (true of other *Ctenogobiops*); scales cycloid anteriorly on body, ctenoid posterior to middle of first dorsal fin; gill opening reaching to or slightly beyond posterior margin of preopercle; body depth 4.7–5.5 in standard length; head length 3.1–3.45 in standard length; first dorsal spine longest, higher than second dorsal fin, about equal to head length; caudal fin longer than head length, the fifth and ninth branched rays slightly prolonged as filaments; pelvic fins joined medially to form a disc, and pelvic frenum present (generic), the fins nearly or just reaching origin of anal fin; pale greenish gray with 4 rows of dark brown spots on body, those of third row largest; short, vertical, dusky edged orange lines ventrally on body, sometimes associated with dark spots of lower row; oblique, dark-edged, orange and blue broken lines on cheek and operculum, 1 series beginning behind eye and curving upward onto nape; a white spot on pectoral fin, one at upper base of fin and one dorsoposteriorly on caudal peduncle; a black or black-edged orange arc at base of first dorsal fin; caudal fin with orange-red spots and streaks. Largest specimen, 8.8 cm. Ryukyu Islands to Great Barrier Reef and New Caledonia, east to Marshall Islands, Caroline Islands, and Samoa Islands; type locality, Ovalau, Fiji. The author was surprised to collect this species in Sri Lanka, otherwise unknown from the Indian Ocean. Occurs on sand-rubble bottoms from tidepools to at least 15 m; symbiotic with snapping shrimps of the genus *Alpheus*.

FIERCE SHRIMPGOBY

Ctenogobiops feroculus Lubbock & Polunin, 1977

Dorsal rays VI + I,11–12; anal rays I,11; pectoral rays 19–20; longitudinal scale series 54–57; scales ctenoid on body to below sixth dorsal spine (more anterior lower on body), cycloid anteriorly; gill opening extending forward to posterior margin of preopercle; body depth 4.7–5.5 in standard length; head length 3.1–3.45 in standard length; first dorsal spine longest, sometimes prolonged, 3.0–3.5 in standard length; caudal fin rounded, about equal to head length; pelvic fins nearly or just reaching anal-fin origin; whitish with 3 longitudinal rows of dark orangish brown spots, those of second row mostly as double spots and often forming a triangle with a spot of upper row; lower row of spots midlateral and consisting of 6 or 7 spots, the first 4 or 5 horizontally elongate; a dark blotch behind eye, and a more elongate one below on cheek, sometimes with blue and/or yellow line just below; often a short dark line behind corner of mouth; 2 dark

Marshall Islands

brown spots on opercle; a white spot, sometimes elongate or spindle-shaped, in lower one-third of pectoral fin near base; basal third of anal fin white, the outer two-thirds blackish; median part of pelvic disc blackish. Reaches 6.5 cm. Red Sea to islands of Micronesia and Society Islands; Ryukyu Islands to Great Barrier Reef and New Caledonia (type locality); occurs in protected areas of fine sand and rubble, generally in less than 4 m; sometimes seen in pairs; symbiotic with snapping shrimps, including *Alpheus djeddensis* and *A. rapax*.

Palau

GOLD-SPECKED SHRIMPGOBY

Ctenogobiops pomastictus Lubbock & Polunin, 1977

Dorsal rays VI + I,11–12 (usually 11); anal rays I,11; pectoral rays 18–20 (rarely 18); longitudinal scale series 50–55; no scales on head, chest, or nape except for a few oblique rows of small scales anterior to upper end of gill opening; scales cycloid anteriorly on body, ctenoid posterior to below middle of first dorsal fin; gill opening extending forward to a vertical at posterior edge of preopercle; body depth 4.5–5.0 in standard length; head length 3.1–3.4 in standard length; second dorsal spine longest (but third nearly as long), 3.3–5.1 in standard length; caudal fin rounded, about equal to head length; pelvic fins nearly or just reaching anal-fin origin; whitish to pale gray with 4 longitudinal rows of dark brown spots on body, those of third row largest and horizontally elongate, with a small brown spot between larger spots, the first 3 mainly yellow; second row of spots also with intermediate small spots, the anterior ones mainly yellow; anterior spots of lower row with yellow centers; spots of blue, brown, and yellow on cheek and operculum, the 2 most prominent behind eye and continuing as a broken line onto nape; upper half of iris with 3 black marks, the middle one semicircular; an oblique white spot, sometimes spindle-shaped, in lower one-third of pectoral fin near base. Attains 7 cm. Andaman Sea, Rowley Shoals off northwestern Australia; Ryukyu Islands to Great Barrier Reef (type locality, Lizard Island) and New Caledonia; occurs on silty sand and rubble near lagoon coral reefs, generally in less than 6 m; lives symbiotically with *Alpheus djeddensis*, *A. djiboutensis*, and *A. ochrostriatus*.

Papua New Guinea

TANGAROA SHRIMPGOBY

Ctenogobiops tangaroai Lubbock & Polunin, 1977

Dorsal rays VI + I,10–11 (usually 11); anal rays I,10–11 (usually 11); pectoral rays 18–20; longitudinal scale series 47–51; no scales on head, chest, or nape except for a few oblique rows of small scales anterior to upper end of gill opening; scales cycloid anteriorly on body, ctenoid posterior to below middle of first dorsal fin; gill opening extending forward to a vertical at posterior margin of eye; body depth 4.3–5.2 in standard length; head length 2.95–3.15 in standard length; first and second dorsal spines greatly prolonged, the second longer, generally more than half standard length; caudal fin rounded except middle 5 or 6 rays of equal length (so fin margin straight in central part), the fin length about equal to head length; pelvic fins reaching slightly posterior to anus; body translucent light gray with a midlateral row of 5 orange-yellow spots nearly as large as pupil; other smaller orange-yellow spots, white spots, and a scattering of pale blue dots on body; head with 2 oblique, dark-edged yellow lines behind eye, the upper continuing as a series of dashes to origin of first dorsal fin; small, dark-edged, orange-yellow spots on cheek and opercle, the darkest (may be black) behind corner of mouth; membrane between first and second dorsal spines blackish; a long, narrow white streak in lower one-third of pectoral fins (white spot in other species of the genus). Attains 6.5 cm. Ranges in the western Pacific from the Ryukyu Islands to Great Barrier Reef, east to Palau, Guam, Tonga, Fiji, and Samoa Islands; usually found in sand-rubble pockets on seaward reefs in from 4 to 40 m, generally in more than 15 m; symbiotic with the snapping shrimp *Alpheus ochrostriatus*. Named for the Polynesian god of the sea.

TONGA SHRIMPGOBY
Ctenogobiops tongaensis Randall, Shao & Chen, 2003
Dorsal rays VI + I,11; anal rays I,11; pectoral rays 18; longitudinal scale series 50–51; no scales on head, chest, or pectoral-fin base; nape without scales except for a few oblique rows of small scales anterior to upper end of gill opening; scales cycloid anteriorly on body, ctenoid dorsally on body posterior to fourth dorsal spine; gill opening extending forward to below about middle of preopercle; body depth 4.4–4.45 in standard length; head length 2.95–3.05 in standard length; second dorsal spine longest, greatly prolonged in male, 2.55 in standard length, and moderately long in female, 3.5 in standard length; caudal fin rounded, longer than head, 2.65–2.8 in standard length; pelvic fins reaching to base of second anal soft ray; pale gray, shading to whitish ventrally, with 4 longitudinal rows of round blackish spots, the largest in midlateral row; a row of 3 brown spots on cheek with

Tonga

a blue and yellow line below the first 2; a series of blue and yellow dashes forming an arc from behind eye to dorsal-fin origin; pectoral fin with a spindle-shaped white spot longer than pupil on lower third of fin near base. Known from 2 specimens, the largest 5.5 cm, collected in silty sand and rubble in 1 m in the inner harbor of Neiafu, Vava'u, Tonga. Observed to be symbiotic with an alpheid shrimp.

FLAME GOBY
Discordipinna griessingeri Hoese & Fourmanoir, 1978
Dorsal rays V + I,7–8 (rarely 7); anal rays I,8; pectoral rays 17–19; branched caudal rays 15–16; longitudinal scale series 22–25; scales ctenoid posteriorly, cycloid anteriorly; large cycloid scales on top of head; no scales on cheek or operculum; body depth 5.2–5.8 in standard length; head distinctly broader than deep; origin of first dorsal fin over upper end of gill opening, the fin widely separated from second dorsal; first 2 dorsal spines greatly prolonged, the second longest, about 1.5 in standard length; caudal fin somewhat pointed, 2.5–3.0 in standard length; pectoral fins large, about 2.3 in standard length, the rays with free tips; pelvic fins joined to form a disc, reaching to origin of anal fin; upper half of body white, the lower half red; head white with red-edged, dark brown spots; fins mainly red, the

Tahiti

second dorsal and upper half of caudal fin with 3 black spots. Largest specimen, 2.9 cm. Known from the Red Sea (type locality, Gulf of Aqaba), St. Brandon's Shoals, Cocos-Keeling Islands, Papua New Guinea, Great Barrier Reef, Fiji, Tonga, Tahiti, Tuamotu Archipelago, Marquesas Islands, and Hawaiian Islands; collected from depths of 2–37 m; cryptic, apparently in live coral; known only from collections with ichthyocide.

AFELEI'S PYGMYGOBY
Eviota afelei Jordan & Seale, 1906
Dorsal rays VI + I,8–9 (usually 9); anal rays I,8; pectoral rays 15–18, the eleventh to fifteenth almost always branched; longitudinal scale series 23–25; scales ctenoid, none on head, nape, or base of pectoral fins (true of all *Eviota*); no scales on chest; pelvic fins separated, only a thin membrane joining bases (also generic); fifth pelvic ray 10% length of fourth ray; fourth pelvic ray with 6–15 (average 11.5) branches; free tips of pelvic rays provide a lateral fringe to pelvic fins (generic); first 2 dorsal spines of male may be elongate; cephalic sensory pore system lacking the intertemporal pore (see Lachner & Karnella, 1980: fig. 4); body depth 4.3–4.8 in standard length; translucent greenish, usually with narrow, internal, orangish brown bars in body

Fiji

and a dark brownish orange line on edge of each scale; head pale gray with dark brown dots and vertically elongate orange spots (many bilobed). Largest specimen, 2.3 cm; smallest gravid female, 1.2 cm. Known from Ashmore Reef (Timor Sea), Ninigo Islands (Papua New Guinea), Great Barrier Reef, and islands of Oceania to the Tuamotu Archipelago (not the Hawaiian Islands); type locality, Tutuila, American Samoa.

WHITELINE PYGMYGOBY
Eviota albolineata Jewett & Lachner, 1983
Dorsal rays VI + I,8–9; anal rays I,8; pectoral rays 16–21, the fourth to eighteenth branched; longitudinal scale series 23–25; fifth pelvic ray 10–20% length of fourth ray; fourth pelvic ray with 6–12 branches; no elongation of spines of first dorsal fin observed; cephalic sensory pore system complete (see Lachner & Karnella, 1980: fig. 4); body translucent gray with scattered, small white flecks and short, vertical red streaks on scales; internally a line of long red and short white dashes above vertebral column (true of other *Eviota* when translucent and not obscured

Line Islands

by external markings); head with 2 broad red bands extending posteriorly from eye, separated by a white line reaching to upper pectoral-fin base; a white band on occiput with a median red dash anteriorly; a short white line from eye to upper lip; fins

529

STRIPED PYGMYGOBY
Eviota sebreei Jordan & Seale, 1906
Dorsal rays VI + I,8–10 (rarely 10); anal rays I,8–9 (rarely 9); pectoral rays 15–17 (rarely 15), none branched; longitudinal scale series 23–24 (usually 23); no scales on chest; fifth pelvic ray 50–80% length of fourth ray; fourth pelvic ray with 11 to 19 branches (mean, 14.3); second or third dorsal spines longest, not prolonged; pelvic fins usually extending to or beyond origin of anal fin; body slender, the depth 5.5–6.3 in standard length; cephalic sensory pore system lacking the paired supraotic pores (see Lachner & Karnella, 1980: fig. 4); a broad, internal, dark red to black stripe from occiput and behind eye extending narrowly along body to end in a white-edged black spot (usually larger than pupil); a series of white dashes along top of dark stripe, and a series of white spots along lower edge of stripe in abdomi-

Fiji

nal region; a dark red band from eye to tip of anterior nostril; reaches 3 cm. Red Sea and islands of western Indian Ocean to Samoa Islands (type locality, Upolu), Marshall Islands, and Caroline Islands; Ryukyu Islands to Great Barrier Reef and New Caledonia; known from depths of 1–33 m; a common species often seen in the open at rest on live coral.

EMERALD PYGMYGOBY
Eviota smaragdus Jordan & Seale, 1906
Dorsal rays VI + I,8–9 (usually 9); anal rays I,7–8 (rarely 7); pectoral rays 15–17, the second to seventeenth may be branched; longitudinal scale series 23–25; no scales on chest; fifth pelvic ray usually 20% length of fourth ray; fourth pelvic ray modally with 5 branches; first and second dorsal spines of males may be elongate and filamentous, the longest reaching to end of base of second dorsal fin when depressed; pelvic fins usually not reaching origin of anal fin and never beyond; cephalic sensory pore system complete; translucent green with a series of about 12 small orange-red spots along dorsal edge of body, a lateral series of 6 larger orange-red spots, and a ventral series of 7 reddish

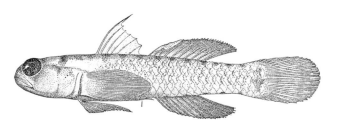

(Jordan & Seale, 1906)

brown spots; region over abdomen green with white blotches; a pair of blackish spots on occiput, 1 on each side, generally as large as pupil. Largest specimen, 2.4 cm; smallest gravid female, 1.35 cm. Known from the Ryukyu Islands, Guam, Vanuatu, Norfolk Island, Fiji, and Samoa Islands (type locality, Tutuila).

Ambon, Indonesia

SPECKLED PYGMYGOBY
Eviota sparsa Jewett & Lachner, 1983
Dorsal rays VI + I,8–10 (rarely 8 or 10); anal rays I,7–8 (rarely 7); pectoral rays 14–17 (rarely 14, modally 16); pectoral rays 8–17 may be branched, the twelfth to fifteenth usually branched; longitudinal scale series 23–25; chest scaleless; fifth pelvic ray 60–90% length of fourth ray; fourth pelvic ray with 2–8 branches; elongation of dorsal spines not common, but first 4 spines of male may be filamentous, the longest to middle of base of second dorsal fin; pelvic fins usually reaching origin of anal fin or beyond; cephalic sensory pore system lacking the intertemporal and preopercular pores (see Lachner & Karnella, 1980); translucent pale orange with dusky orange edges on scales; a double rectangular black spot, the pair separated by white, at side of occiput behind upper edge of eye; 6 internal dark spots ventrally on body from anal-fin origin to caudal-fin base; median fins dusky, the dorsal and caudal rays with small orange spots on rays, the anal with orange rays. Largest specimen, 2.9 cm (collected by the author in Vava'u, Tonga). Known from the Philippines, Indonesia, Palau, Great Barrier Reef, Tonga, and Samoa Islands (type locality, Tutuila).

Fiji

ZEBRA PYGMYGOBY
Eviota zebrina Lachner & Karnella, 1978
Dorsal rays VI + I,7–10 (rarely 7 or 10, usually 9); anal rays I,7–9 (rarely 9); pectoral rays 14–18 (usually 16 or 17), none branched; longitudinal scale series 21–24 (rarely 21 or 24); chest scaleless; fifth pelvic ray about one-tenth length of fourth ray; fourth pelvic ray with an average of 7.4 branches; first 4 dorsal spines of males may be filamentous, the longest may reach base of caudal fin; pelvic fins usually extending beyond origin of anal fin; cephalic sensory pore system lacking only the intertemporal pore; translucent whitish with narrow, internal blackish bars; a black spot posteriorly on midside of caudal peduncle with an adjacent black line at base of caudal fin; a series of about 14 small, dark reddish spots dorsally on body; a horseshoe-shaped black mark on snout; caudal fin with irregular, vertical blackish lines. Largest specimen, 2.4 cm; smallest gravid female, 1.4 cm. Red Sea, islands of Indian Ocean (type locality, Seychelles), Western Australia, Great Barrier Reef, and Fiji (first record for Oceania from collection of D. W. Greenfield and the author).

ZONED PYGMYGOBY

Eviota zonura Jordan & Seale, 1906

Dorsal rays VI + I,8–10 (rarely 8 or 10); anal rays I,7–8 (rarely 7); pectoral rays 15–17 (rarely 15), the eleventh to fifteenth usually branched; longitudinal scale series 23–24; chest scaleless; fifth pelvic ray absent or rudimentary; fourth pelvic ray with an average of 7.6 branches; first and second dorsal spines of males may be filamentous, the longest to base of fifth dorsal ray; pelvic fins nearly or just reaching origin of anal fin; cephalic sensory pore system lacking the intertemporal pore; translucent green with a series of 7 vertically elongate, dusky red blotches along upper side, the last overlying a vertically elongate, internal black spot posteriorly on caudal peduncle; a row of 8 similar dusky red blotches along lower side of body, the first 3 beneath pectoral fin; dusky orange spots and short bands on head; broad outer part of first dorsal fin blackish. Largest specimen, 2.6 cm; smallest gravid female, 1.4 cm. Reported from the Ogasawara Islands, Indonesia, Western Australia, islands of Micronesia, Fiji, and Samoa Islands (type locality, Tutuila).

Ataoru, Indonesia

BEAUTIFUL GOBY

Exyrias belissimus (Smith, 1959)

Dorsal rays VI + I,10; anal rays I,9; pectoral rays 17–19; longitudinal scale series 31–32; predorsal scales 10–12, extending to interorbital space; scales on cheek divided into 3 patches by 3 rows of papillae; scales of body ctenoid except cycloid on nape and isthmus; body depth 3.6–3.9 in standard length; head length 3.2–3.6 in standard length; mouth inferior; teeth conical, in 4–5 rows in each jaw, those of outer row largest; isthmus broad; tips of dorsal spines of adults free, the first 3 or 4 spines as long filaments in juveniles and subadults (Murdy, 1985b); caudal fin large and oblong, 2.0–2.7 in standard length; pelvic fins united to form a cup-like disc; body brown with small whitish and black spots, 1 per scale, in longitudinal rows; a few small blue dots above pectoral-fin base; head mottled brown with whitish and orange dots and an oblique double orange line from lower part of eye to upper lip; dorsal and anal fins with oblique, elliptical, brownish red spots on membranes; caudal fin gray with orange-red dots and small spots. Largest specimen, 16.5 cm. Type locality, Pinda,

Papua New Guinea

Mozambique; also in Indian Ocean from Seychelles and Chagos Archipelago; in the Pacific: Indo-Malayan region north to Ryukyu Islands, south to Great Barrier Reef and New Caledonia, east to Palau, Mariana Islands, Caroline Islands, Fiji, and Samoa Islands; usually found on silty sand bottoms in protected reef areas, taking refuge in reef when threatened; reported from depths of 1–20 m; feeds by taking mouthfuls of sand and filtering small organisms.

PUNTANG GOBY

Exyrias puntang (Bleeker, 1851)

Dorsal rays VI + I,10; anal rays I,9; pectoral rays 16–18; longitudinal scale series 30–33; predorsal scales 8–9; scales on cheek divided into 3 patches by 3 rows of papillae; scales of body ctenoid except cycloid on nape and isthmus; body depth 3.6–4.0 in standard length; head length about 3.5 in standard length; mouth inferior; teeth conical, in 4–5 rows in each jaw, those of outer row largest; isthmus broad; caudal fin rounded, 3.3–3.7 in standard length; pelvic fins united to form a cup-like disc. Orangish brown with longitudinal rows of small whitish and dark brown spots, 1 per scale, the most prominent as 3 pairs of double dark brown spots midlaterally on posterior one-third of body; a large, irregular, dark brown bar usually present below eye; median fins gray, the first dorsal with oblique, reddish black spots, the second dorsal with oblique, dark red spots, the anal

Ambon, Indonesia

with 4 longitudinal rows of oblique red dashes, the middle 2 most evident, and the caudal densely covered with small red spots. Attains 13 cm. Ryukyu Islands to Great Barrier Reef; east to Guam, Vanuatu, and New Caledonia, west to Andaman Islands and Sri Lanka; type locality, Java. Usually found on mud substrata in shallow turbid waters, including estuaries.

EYEBAR GOBY

Gnatholepis anjerensis (Bleeker, 1851)

Dorsal rays VI + I,11; anal rays I,11; pectoral rays 14–17 (modally 16); pelvic fins joined to form a disc, the frenum well developed (true of all species of *Gnatholepis*); longitudinal scale series usually 30; scales present on cheek and opercle; usually a few small scales on cheek anterior to black line below eye; scales medially on nape extending to interorbital space; lower lip with a ventral flap along side of lower jaw (generic); outer teeth at front of lower jaw enlarged as canines, the most lateral strongly recurved; body depth 3.9–4.6 in standard length; head compressed (generic); dorsal profile of snout very steep (generic); caudal fin rounded, usually slightly longer than head, 2.8–3.6 in standard length; whitish with numerous very small, dark brown spots on body, more numerous on dorsal half and few ventrally; a series of five irregular gray blotches on back, the small brown spots within blotches darker; a series of 5 blackish blotches on lower side, progressively smaller posteriorly; a blackish blotch containing a small yellow spot usually present above pectoral-fin base; a vertical black line ventral to eye, sometimes with dusky side branches; a black line dorsally on eye, centered over posterior half of pupil, not crossing interorbital space; black dots often present on median fins, except anal fin where few or absent. Largest specimen, 10.5 cm, but rarely exceeds 8 cm. Red Sea and East Africa to the Hawaiian Islands and islands of French

Society Islands

Polynesia; southern Japan to Great Barrier Reef and Lord Howe Island; the majority of specimens from less than 2 m, often from tidepools; deepest record, 46 m. Like others of the genus, lives on sand near reefs or rocky substrata in which it hides when threatened; also found in mangrove areas. Bleeker described this species from a drawing; he later made it the type species of his new genus *Gnatholepis*. In a preliminary review of the genus, Randall & Greenfield (2001) designated a neotype from Sulawesi to establish the name *anjerensis* that most authors have used for this species. *Gobius deltoides* Seale from Guam and *Gnatholepis knighti* Jordan & Evermann from Hawai'i are among the 5 synonyms.

SHOULDERSPOT GOBY

Gnatholepis cauerensis (Bleeker, 1853)

Dorsal rays VI + I,11; anal rays I,10–12; pectoral rays 16–19 (modally 17); longitudinal scale series usually 30; scales present on cheek and opercle; usually no scales on cheek anterior to black line below eye; scales medially on nape extending to interorbital space; outer teeth at front of lower jaw enlarged as canines, the most lateral strongly recurved; body depth 4.25–5.15 in standard length; head compressed, its length 3.2–3.55 in standard length; caudal fin rounded, usually slightly longer than head, 2.75–3.35 in standard length; color similar to that of *anjerensis*, having the same dark blotches on body, black vertical line through and below eye, and blackish shoulder spot with a small yellow spot; generally differs in having longitudinal dark lines following scale rows instead of numerous small dark brown spots; also the dark line dorsally on eye is more over the center of the pupil and usually extends across the interorbital space. Largest specimen, 5.3 cm, except for the Marquesas Islands, where the largest is 6.7 cm. Randall & Greenfield (2001) recognized 4 subspecies: *G. cauerensis cauerensis* from the Indian Ocean to the western Pacific from southern Japan to Great Bar-

New Caledonia

rier Reef (type locality, Sumatra) east to islands of Micronesia and Society Islands; *G. c. hawaiiensis* from the Hawaiian Islands; *G. c. australis* from the Austral Islands, Rapa, Pitcairn Islands, and Cook Islands; and *G. c. pasquensis* from Easter Island. The Marquesan population may also warrant subspecific recognition. *Gnatholepis cauerensis* tends to occur in deeper water than *anjerensis*; of 21 Bishop Museum lots with depth data, only 4 were from 2 m or less; 7 were from 30 m or more, and 3 from more than 45 m. *Gnatholepis scapulostigma* Herre is a synonym.

ROUNDHEAD CORALGOBY

Gobiodon axillaris De Vis, 1884

Dorsal rays VI + I, 9–10; anal rays I,8–9; pectoral rays 18–19 (usually 19); no scales (true of other *Gobiodon* except some with a few scales on caudal peduncle); body deep, the depth 2.3–2.5 in standard length, and strongly compressed; dorsal and ventral profiles of head strongly rounded; no median groove in isthmus; ventral edge of gill opening ending opposite last few pectoral rays (true of other *Gobiodon* herein); first dorsal fin distinctly lower than second, the second to fifth spines subequal; dorsal fins joined by membrane to about lower one-third of spine of

Great Barrier Reef (P. L. Munday)

536

second fin; caudal fin rounded, about equal to or a little shorter than head length; pelvic fins united to a small cup-like disc (also generic); brown to yellowish or greenish brown with 4 narrow red bars on side of head, the first through eye and the last through a black spot posteriorly on opercle at upper edge of gill opening; a dark red line at base of dorsal fins and often on base of anal fin. Attains about 4 cm. Western Australia, Great Barrier Reef, Vanu-atu (type locality, Banks Islands), and Fiji. Like others of the genus, commensal in corals of the genus *Acropora* (most often *A. nasuta* and *A. millepora* for this species). The species of *Gobiodon* produce a thick mucus with a stinging bitter taste. Hashimoto et al. (1974) showed that the mucus contains a skin toxin similar to grammistin, the crinotoxin of soapfishes. It probably serves to deter predators.

Red Sea

Palau

CITRON CORALGOBY
Gobiodon citrinus (Rüppell, 1838)
Dorsal rays VI + I,10–11 (usually 10); anal rays I,9; pectoral rays 18–19; body deep, the depth 2.3–2.7 in standard length, and slightly compressed, the width 1.9–2.2 in depth; no median groove in isthmus; first and second dorsal spines usually longest; dorsal fins barely linked ventrally by membrane; caudal fin rounded, slightly shorter than head; ground color variable,

brown to bright yellow; a small black spot at upper end of opercular flap; 2 blue lines extending ventrally from eye, another from nape across opercle, and a fourth from behind black spot across pectoral-fin base; a blue line at base of dorsal and anal fins. Largest specimen, 6.6 cm. Red Sea (type locality) and east coast of Africa to Marshall Islands and Samoa Islands, in the western Pacific from southern Japan to the Great Barrier Reef; found on branches of live coral of the genus *Acropora*.

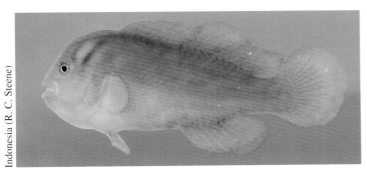

Indonesia (R. C. Steene)

Fiji

TOOTHY CORALGOBY
Gobiodon brochus Harold & Winterbottom, 1999
Dorsal rays VI + I,10–12; anal rays I,9–10; pectoral rays 18–20; a fleshy projection bearing small teeth medially at front of upper jaw (unique to this species); body deep, the depth about 2.5 in standard length, and strongly compressed; a median groove in isthmus, broadening posteriorly; dorsal spines progressively longer posteriorly; dorsal fins nearly fully joined by membrane; caudal fin rounded, slightly shorter than head; pelvic frenum present; usually dull green, shading to yellow on abdomen, chest, and lower part of head; an oblique pale zone on nape bordered by blackish bands less than orbit diameter in width. Largest specimen, 3.45 cm. Known from Fiji (type locality, Great Astrolabe Reef), Tonga, and the northern Great Barrier Reef; reported to inhabit the corals *Acropora loripes* and *A. elseyi*; commonly occurs in pairs. Previously identified as *Gobiodon micropus* Günther, a similar species that lacks the dentigerous pad at the front of the lower jaw.

ACTOR CORALGOBY
Gobiodon histrio (Valenciennes in C & V, 1837)
Dorsal rays VI + I,10; anal rays I,9; pectoral rays 19–21; body depth of adults 2.2–2.7 in standard length; eye relatively small; a median groove in isthmus that broadens posteriorly; membrane from tip of sixth dorsal spine joined to first spine of second dorsal fin about one-third distance from its base; caudal fin rounded and short, its length about 1.3 in head length; green with 4 red bars on side of head, the first passing through eye, the fourth enclosing a small black spot at upper end of opercular flap and continuing onto pectoral-fin base; body with several rows of red stripes, variously broken into series of spots. Attains about 3.5 cm. Red Sea to Samoa Islands; Ryukyu Islands to Great Barrier Reef. Valenciennes' description based on a drawing from Bantam, Indonesia, and a specimen from Tongatapu. *Gobiodon erythrospilus* Bleeker, a form lacking the small black opercular spot, is considered a synonym (Munday et al., 1999).

Palau

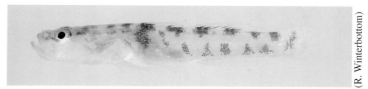

(R. Winterbottom)

OKINAWA CORALGOBY

Gobiodon okinawae Sawada, Arai & Abe, 1972

Dorsal rays VI + I,10–11; anal rays I,9–10; pectoral rays 16–17; body elongate for the genus, the depth 2.75–3.5 in standard length, and only slightly compressed; no median groove on isthmus; membrane from tip of sixth dorsal spine joined to spine of second dorsal fin about one-fourth to one-third distance from its base; caudal fin rounded, its length about 1.2 in head length; bright yellow overall. Reported to 3.8 cm, but usually less than 3 cm. Cocos-Keeling Islands and Rowley Shoals in Indian Ocean; southern Japan (type locality, Yaeyama Islands) to Great Barrier Reef; east to Marshall Islands, Palau, and New Caledonia. Like others of the genus, shelters in live coral of the genus *Acropora*; occurs in small groups in a coral colony.

SHORTBARBEL GOBY

Gobiopsis exigua Lachner & McKinney, 1979

Dorsal rays VI + I,10–11 (usually 10); anal rays I,10; pectoral rays 18–20; branched caudal rays 15–17; longitudinal scale series 30–37; predorsal scales 11–17, not reaching interorbital space; no scales on cheek or opercle; scales cycloid; 1 short pair of barbels on chin and 1 on snout; bands of sensory papillae on head prominent; body depth 5.5–6.8 in standard length; dorsal fins low, the first distinctly lower than second; caudal fin rounded, a little shorter than head; pelvic fins united nearly to tips of fifth rays, the fins not reaching anus; pelvic frenum present; pale with 3 narrow, dusky, transverse bands on postorbital head and nape, and 6 dusky saddles along back; 7 brown spots along lower side of body, the first under tip of pectoral fin, the last on base of caudal fin. Largest specimen, 5.3 cm. Known to date only from the Comoro Islands, Seychelles, Kiribati (type locality, Abaiang Atoll), Fiji, and Society Islands. Specimens collected by the author in Fiji were from rubble and coarse sand.

Sulawesi

Fiji

Negros, Philippines

FIVELINED CORALGOBY

Gobiodon quinquestrigatus (Valenciennes in C & V, 1837)

Dorsal rays VI + I,10–11; anal rays I,8–9; pectoral rays 19–20; body depth 2.6–2.9 in standard length; body slightly compressed; no median groove in isthmus; membrane from tip of sixth dorsal spine joined to spine of second dorsal fin one-fourth to one-third distance from its base; caudal fin rounded, its length about 1.3 in head length; head usually dark orange-red, shading anteriorly on body to dark reddish brown and posteriorly to black; fins black except dark orange-red base of pectoral fins; 5 vertical blue lines anteriorly, 2 through eye, 2 across operculum, and 1 across pectoral-fin base. Reaches 4.6 cm. Wakayama Prefecture, Japan, to Great Barrier Reef and New Caledonia, east to Society Islands; type locality, Tonga.

DECORATED GOBY

Istigobius decoratus (Herre, 1927)

Dorsal rays VI + I,10; anal rays I,9; pectoral rays 17–19; longitudinal scale series 28; scales on body ctenoid, becoming cycloid anterior to paired fins (true of all *Istigobius*); predorsal scales 8–10, reaching interorbital space; isthmus scaled to below posterior margin of preopercle; body depth 5.0–5.9 in standard length; head length 3.5–4.0 in standard length; front of snout obtuse and mouth slightly inferior (also generic); pelvic fins fully joined to form a disc, with a well-developed frenum (generic); caudal fin rounded, as long as or longer than head; upper two-thirds of body brown with a white spot in most scale centers (some spots may be yellow); a midlateral row of double, dark brown spots on body; 2 longitudinal rows of smaller dark spots dorsally on body; lower one-third of body white with a few dark spots on upper part; head with irregular brown or reddish lines; often a curved dark mark above corner of mouth; fins dark-spotted except pelvics; a black spot on first interspinous membrane. Reaches 12 cm. The most wide-ranging of the genus; Red Sea and east coast of Africa to islands of Micronesia and Samoa Islands; in the western Pacific from the Ryukyu Islands to Great Barrier Reef and Lord Howe Island; type locality, Leyte, Philippines. Typically found on sandy substrata near reefs in bays or lagoons. Kritzer (2002) estimated the maximum age from presumed daily increments of the sagittal otoliths as 266 days, suggesting at most an annual life cycle.

GOLDMANN'S GOBY
Istigobius goldmanni (Bleeker, 1852)

Dorsal rays VI + I,10–11 (rarely 11); anal rays I,9; pectoral rays 17–19; longitudinal scale series 30–32; no scales on opercle or cheek; predorsal scales 7–9, reaching interorbital space; prepelvic scales reaching to below middle of preopercle; body depth 4.9–5.6 in standard length; head length 3.4–4.1 in standard length; caudal fin rounded, about equal to head length; pectoral fins longest of genus, 3.2–3.85 in standard length; gray dorsally, white ventrally, with a midlateral row of 5 small, double black spots within a narrow white stripe of 1-scale thickness; a smaller single black spot in 3 interspaces; a second narrow white stripe above the midlateral one; back above with numerous small, irregular white spots and scattered small black spots; a blackish line across cheek from posterior upper lip; median fins faintly dark-spotted. Smallest species of the genus; largest specimen, 6.2 cm. Ryukyu Islands to northwestern Australia and southern Queensland, east to Palau and Fiji; type locality, Timor. Lives in protected sand or sand-rubble areas, generally in 1–7 m.

Great Barrier Reef

TRIANGLESPOT GOBY
Istigobius nigroocellatus (Günther, 1873)

Dorsal rays VI + I,10–11 (rarely 11); anal rays I,9–10 (rarely 10); pectoral rays 17–19; longitudinal scale series 30–32; no scales on opercle or cheek; predorsal scales 7–10, reaching interorbital space; body depth 4.8–5.75 in standard length; head length 3.55–4.45 in standard length; caudal fin rounded, slightly longer than head; color similar to that of *I. decoratus*, differing in a near-triangular blackish spot (3 black spots within) about as large as eye at midbase of caudal fin; midlateral double black spots often merged to a dash, and the median fins lightly spotted except for a prominent black spot between fifth and sixth dorsal spines. Also a small species; reaches 6.5 cm. Reported from the Ryukyu Islands, Philippines, Papua New Guinea, Western Australia to Queensland (type locality, Bowen), Solomon Islands, New Caledonia, and American Samoa. Generally found in shallow turbid areas.

Sulawesi

Great Barrier Reef

ORNATE GOBY
Istigobius ornatus (Rüppell, 1830)

Dorsal rays VI + I,10–11 (rarely 11); anal rays I,8–10; pectoral rays 17–20 (modally 19); longitudinal scale series 29–32; no scales on opercle or cheek; predorsal scales 9–12, reaching interorbital space; body depth 4.6–5.25 in standard length; head length 3.45–4.3 in standard length; no recurved canine tooth on side of lower jaw (present in other *Istigobius*); caudal fin rounded, slightly longer than head; upper 3 or 4 pectoral rays free of membrane; whitish to light gray-brown with numerous small, pale blue spots, 3 or 4 longitudinal rows of broken dark brown lines on back, a midlateral row of deep blue to black spots, many as double or triple spots, and a similar row on lower side; orange-

Fiji

red and pale blue spots and short lines on cheek and opercle; median and pelvic fins finely spotted. Reaches 10 cm. Red Sea (type locality) south to Mozambique, east to islands of Micronesia and Fiji; Ryukyu Islands and Ogasawara Islands to Great Barrier Reef and New Caledonia; generally found in silty inshore reefs and mangrove areas in less than 2 m.

ORANGESPOTTED GOBY
Istigobius rigilius (Herre, 1953)
Dorsal rays VI + I,10; anal rays I,9; branched caudal rays nearly always 13 (modally 13.05, compared with modal counts of 13.4–15.0 for other species of *Istigobius*); pectoral rays 16–19 (strongly modal 18); longitudinal scale series 29–32; no scales on opercle or cheek; predorsal scales 7–9, reaching interorbital space; body depth 4.75–6.1 in standard length; head length 3.4–4.1 in standard length; caudal fin rounded, distinctly longer than head, about 3.3 in standard length; pale gray with small white flecks, spots, and dashes on most of head and body in addition to larger white blotches ventrally on body; small orange spots in a comparable pattern to black of other species, the most prominent the midlateral row of double spots that may join to form dashes; ventral half of head, pelvic fins, and anal fin white; first dorsal fin whitish with oblique, oblong blackish spots; second dorsal fin with blackish spots forming 4–5 near-horizontal rows; caudal fin with brownish orange spots. Largest specimen, 9.5 cm. Ryukyu Islands to Great Barrier Reef, east to New Caledonia, Fiji, Tonga, Palau, Kiribati, and Marshall Islands (type locality, Enewetak Atoll); occurs in white sand and rubble areas in clear parts of lagoons and bays; recorded from depths of 1–30 m. *Bikinigobius welanderi* Herre from Bikini Atoll, Marshall Islands, is a synonym.

REDFIN SHOREGOBY
Kelloggella cardinalis Jordan & Seale, 1906
Dorsal rays VI + I,11–12 (usually 12); anal rays I,7–8 (usually 8); pectoral rays 13–15; pelvic rays I,5, united to form a disc (true of all species of *Kelloggella*); segmented caudal rays 15–16 (rarely 15); no scales and no head pores (also generic); teeth of jaws tricuspid, the outer row enlarged (generic); body depth about 6 in standard length; caudal fin rounded, about equal to head length; color of holotype given by Jordan & Seale: clear grass green, the median fins bright cherry red, the anal greenish in front; paired fins green; 2 larger specimens were greenish black, more greenish anteriorly; dorsal and anal fins bright orange, edged with black; paired fins bright golden green; caudal fin gray. Attains 3 cm. Recorded from the Ryukyu Islands, Philippines, Guam, Vanuatu, Tonga, and Samoa Islands (type locality, Tutuila); occurs in small high tidepools that are replenished only at high tide or when surf is strong. Larson (1983) provided notes on the biology: feeds on copepods, algae, ostracods, amphipods, mollusks, polychaetes, insect larvae, midges, and nematodes; has a broad tolerance to temperature and salinity.

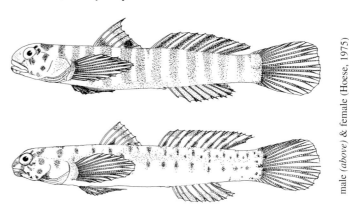

FIFTEEN-BAR SHOREGOBY
Kelloggella quindecimfasciata (Fowler, 1946)
Dorsal rays VI + I,9–11 (rarely 9 or 11); anal rays I,6–8 (rarely 6 or 8); pectoral rays 12–13 (usually 12); segmented caudal rays 15–16 (rarely 15); body depth about 6–7 in standard length; caudal fin rounded, shorter than head; body and dorsal part of head of males with 12 narrow dark bars, plus 3 more on cheek, a prominent black spot between fifth and sixth dorsal spines; female with 2 longitudinal rows of dark spots on upper half of body corresponding to bars of male; head with dark brown spots. Largest specimen, 2.6 cm. Reported from the Chagos Archipelago, Ryukyu Islands (type locality), Marshall Islands, and Cook Islands. *Kelloggella centralis* Hoese is a synonym (Yoshino in Masuda et al.,1984; Winterbottom & Emery, 1986)

MARQUESAN SHOREGOBY
Kelloggella tricuspidata (Herre, 1935)
Dorsal rays VI + I,12; anal rays I,7–9 (rarely 7 or 9); pectoral rays 13–15 (rarely 13); segmented caudal rays 15–16 (rarely 15); body depth about 6–7 in standard length; caudal fin rounded, about equal to head; pale gray with 8 narrow blackish bars that extend three-fourths distance down side of body except the first on nape that ends in axil of pectoral fin; head above level of mouth blackish with small, pale yellowish spots and irregular dashes; snout gray; dorsal fins with a broad, outer reddish margin. Attains 3 cm. Known only from tidepools in the Marquesas Islands. Named for the tricuspid teeth in the jaws.

RAINFORD'S GOBY
Koumansetta rainfordi Whitley, 1940

Dorsal rays VI + I,15–16; anal rays I,15–16; pectoral rays 16–18; longitudinal scale series 55–60; scales ctenoid posteriorly on body, becoming cycloid anterior to rear part of first dorsal fin; no scales on head or only 2 or 3 small cycloid scales dorsally on opercle; prepectoral and prepelvic areas with small scales; head pointed, the snout somewhat conical and overhanging mouth; mouth not large, the maxilla ending before a vertical at front edge of eye, the upper-jaw length 3.2–3.6 in head length; anterior half of upper limb of first gill arch fleshy but with only a few very short filaments (in contrast to species of *Amblygobius* with long filaments); body depth about 4.5 in standard length; first 2 dorsal spines elongate and may be filamentous in adults of both sexes; caudal fin rounded, usually slightly shorter than head length; pelvic fins united, but frenum absent; brown with 5 longitudinal, black-edged orange lines on head and body; a row of 5 small white spots dorsally on body; an ocellated black spot as large eye in middle of second dorsal fin, and a smaller oblong ocellus at upper base of caudal fin. Largest collected by author, 7.7 cm. Philippines to Great Barrier Reef (type locality, Whitsunday Islands, Queensland), and New Caledonia; occurs on well-developed but protected reefs from 2 to at least 30 m; typi-

Papua New Guinea

cally seen hovering above the substratum; aquarium fish collectors find it difficult to capture, because it usually darts to cover in the reef. This and *Seychellea hectori* Smith are usually classified in *Amblygobius* but are shifted here to *Koumansetta* Whitley. The species of *Amblygobius* have a larger mouth (maxilla extending posterior to front of eye), obtusely rounded snout, a pelvic frenum, and the longest dorsal spines not the first or the second; they are benthic and take refuge in burrows in sand.

WHITECAP SHRIMPGOBY
Lotilia graciliosa Klausewitz, 1960

Dorsal rays VI + I,9–10; anal rays I,9; pectoral rays 16; longitudinal scale series 44–50; scales on body ctenoid posteriorly, cycloid anteriorly; no scales on head, no predorsal scales; caudal fin rounded and large, clearly longer than head; pelvic fins joined; pelvic frenum present; black with a large white area dorsally on head and nape from upper lip through upper part of eye, including front of first dorsal fin; a large white spot basally at origin of second dorsal fin, and a saddle-like white spot posteriorly on caudal peduncle; a large black spot in first dorsal fin, usually narrowly rimmed in orange; caudal fin transparent; pectoral fins black at base, followed by a white zone, the broad outer part transparent with 2 rows of black spots. Reaches 4.5 cm. Red Sea (type locality) to Ryukyu Islands, south to Great Barrier Reef, east to Fiji, Phoenix Islands, and islands of Micronesia. Lives with the snapping shrimp *Alpheus rubromaculatus*, often larger than itself (this shrimp rarely seen with other gobies). Hovers above entrance to the burrow and stays over the shrimp when the latter moves away from the entrance; constantly moves its pectoral fins.

Tukangbesi Islands, Indonesia

FURTIVE GOBY
Lubricogobius ornatus Fourmanoir, 1966

Dorsal rays VI-I,8–10; anal rays I,7; pectoral rays 18–20; branched caudal rays 13–15; no scales; no sensory pores on head, but sensory papillae well developed; anterior nostrils present; body depth 2.95–3.85 in standard length; dorsal and ventral edges of caudal peduncle not keeled; caudal fin rounded, shorter than head; pelvic fins united to a disc; pelvic frenum present; orange-yellow with pale blue lines radiating from eye. Attains 4 cm. Known to date only from Ryukyu Islands, Vietnam (type locality), Arafura Sea and Timor Sea (Northern Territory of Australia), Dampier Archipelago (Western Australia), and New Caledonia; silty sand substrata; collections from depths of 17–79 m. Randall & Senou (2001) noted the possible presence of the

New Caledonia

Japanese species *L. exiguus* Tanaka in New Caledonia from a sighting in the Nouméa Aquarium; a specimen is needed for confirmation. *Lubricogobius exiguus* is yellow without blue lines on the head, modally 6 anal rays, modally 17 pectoral rays, and keeled upper and lower edges of the caudal peduncle.

LARGETOOTH GOBY

Macrodontogobius wilburi Herre, 1936

Dorsal rays VI + I,10; anal rays I,9; pectoral rays 15–17; segmented caudal rays 13–14; longitudinal scale series 27–31; scales ctenoid except cycloid before paired fins; cheek and operculum fully scaled; predorsal scales 7 or fewer, extending to interorbital space; mouth slightly inferior; a large recurved canine tooth on each side at front of lower jaw; gill opening extending slightly below pectoral-fin base; body depth 4.65–6.3 in standard length; caudal fin rounded, usually slightly longer than head, 3.9–5.0 in standard length; pelvic fins fully joined, extending past origin of anal fin; pelvic frenum well developed; whitish, densely spotted with brown, with double, darker brown spots in a midlateral row within a poorly defined, narrow white stripe, the first pair of spots beneath the pectoral fin and the last at caudal-fin base; an irregular dark brown to blackish blotch or bar under

Papua New Guinea

eye. Largest specimen, 6.7 cm. Seychelles and Maldive Islands to islands of Micronesia (except Mariana Islands), Line Islands, and Samoa Islands; Ryukyu Islands to Great Barrier Reef, Lord Howe Island, and New Caledonia; type locality, Palau. Typically found on sand and rubble areas near coral reefs in bays and lagoons from depths of 1–22 m.

FLAGFIN SHRIMPGOBY

Mahidolia mystacina (Valenciennes in C & V, 1837)

Dorsal rays VI + I,10; anal rays I,9; pectoral rays 15–17; longitudinal scale series 33–39; scales ctenoid to below middle of first dorsal fin, cycloid anteriorly; head and prepectoral area naked; predorsal scales about 8, extending to above middle of opercle; mouth very large, the maxilla extending well beyond eye, the upper-jaw length about 1.7 in head length; gill opening extending a little anterior to rear preopercular margin; body depth about 4.2 in standard length; first dorsal fin shorter than head in females, longer in males, the anterior spines longest; penultimate dorsal soft ray longest, longer than first dorsal spines in females; caudal fin rounded, shorter than head; pelvic fins fully joined; pelvic frenum present; body with 6 oblique dark bars; head, nape, and pectoral-fin base with small brownish orange spots; first dorsal fin with 3 dark-edged dusky pink crossbands, often with 1 or 2 iridescent, bright blue spots in outer posterior part; a yellow color phase sometimes seen. Reported to 8 cm. East coast of Africa to western Pacific from Japan to northern Australia and New Caledonia, east to islands of Micronesia; type locality, Java. Occurs in shallow silty sand or mud habitats, sometimes in estuaries. Lives with alpheid shrimps, including *Alpheus rapacida*; hovers above as the shrimp makes its forays away from the burrow.

Flores, Indonesia

SMOOTHCHEEK GOBY

Oplopomops atherinoides (Peters, 1855)

Dorsal rays VI + I,10; anal rays I,9–11; pectoral rays 17–18; longitudinal scale series 27–28; scales on body and nape ctenoid; head scaleless; prepectoral and prepelvic areas with cycloid scales; predorsal scales 8–10, reaching interorbital space; no spines on preopercular margin; body depth 5.5–6.1 in standard length; first spine of first dorsal fin and spine of second dorsal fin strong and sharp-tipped; second spine of first dorsal fin longest, may be filamentous; caudal fin slightly rounded, a little longer than head; pelvic fins united; pelvic frenum present; translucent gray with numerous small white spots and blotches, scattered small black spots dorsally on body, and a row of double blackish

Marshall Islands

spots along side below midlateral line; pale blue-green blotches ventrally on posterior half of body. Attains about 5 cm. East coast of Africa (type locality, Mozambique) to Marshall Islands and Phoenix Islands; occurs on sandy areas near protected reefs. *Oplopomus diacanthus* Schultz is a synonym (Smith, 1959a).

New Caledonia

Bali

TRIPLESPOT GOBY

Oplopomus caninoides (Bleeker, 1852)

Dorsal rays VI + I,10; anal rays I,10; pectoral rays 17–19; longitudinal scale series 28–29; scales on body and nape ctenoid; scales cycloid on prepectoral area, chest, cheek, and opercle; predorsal scales about 12, extending to interorbital space; 1 or 2 small spines on preopercular margin just above corner; gill opening reaching to below posterior margin of preopercle; body depth 4.2–4.7 in standard length; first spine in each dorsal fin strong and sharp-tipped; second to fourth dorsal spines subequal and longest, caudal fin rounded, a little shorter than head; pelvic fins united, with a well-developed frenum; whitish with a midlateral row of 5 black spots or merged double spots and numerous small spots, dark brown dorsally and brownish orange or yellow ventrally that tend to form longitudinal rows; a few short, oblique dark lines on snout and cheek; a vertical row of 3 prominent black spots near base of caudal fin, the middle one largest and in contact with last spot of midlateral series; dorsal fins with rows of black spots, 1 on sixth dorsal spine may be enlarged. Reported to 8.5 cm. Philippines, Indonesia (type locality, Ambon), and New Caledonia.

HORNED GOBY

Oxyurichthys cornutus McCulloch & Waite, 1918

Dorsal rays VI + I,12; anal rays I,13; pectoral rays 21; longitudinal scale series 61–80; scales on body ctenoid to below second dorsal fin, cycloid anteriorly; scales sometimes present on side of nape but not on chest, prepectoral region, cheek, or opercle; a slender tentacle on eye about three-fourths orbit diameter in length; a fleshy median ridge on nape; gill opening extending to beneath middle of opercle; a single row of slender conical teeth in upper jaw; body depth 4.3–5.9 in standard length; dorsal spines filamentous, the second longest, reaching to middle of base of second dorsal fin when depressed; caudal fin lanceolate, nearly twice length of head; pelvic fins united; pelvic frenum present; 5 roundish blotches along midside of body, the last at caudal-fin base smallest and often more triangular; 5 rectangular saddles dorsally on body, varying from diffuse to well defined; narrow dusky to brownish bars present across posterior half of

SPINECHEEK GOBY

Oplopomus oplopomus (Valenciennes in C & V, 1837)

Dorsal rays VI + I,10; anal rays I,10; pectoral rays 18–19; longitudinal scale series 29–30; scales on body ctenoid, cycloid on prepectoral area, chest, and abdomen; head naked; predorsal scales about 13, extending to above posterior margin of preopercle; 1–3 small spines on preopercular margin just above corner; gill opening extending forward to below posterior margin of preopercle; body depth 4.0–4.6 in standard length; first spine in each dorsal fin strong and sharp-tipped; fourth dorsal spine longest, prolonged in males (adjacent spines also long); caudal fin rounded, shorter than head; pelvic fins united; pelvic frenum well developed; light gray with small, pale blue-green and bright yellow spots on body, a midlateral row of dusky blotches, and a few small blackish spots, mainly dorsally; head with pale blue-green spots and short lines; outer half of fourth dorsal spine and adjacent membrane of male white; a black band centered on fifth and sixth spines, the one on sixth spine bordered in blue. Reaches 8 cm. Red Sea (type locality) and east coast of Africa to islands of Micronesia and Society Islands; Ryukyu Islands to Great Barrier Reef and New Caledonia; lives in silty sand areas of bays or lagoons at depths of a few to at least 50 m; shelters in a burrow, evidently not of its own making.

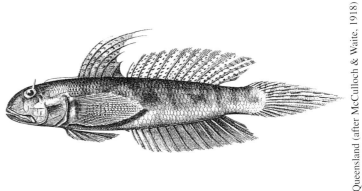

Queensland (after McCulloch & Waite, 1918)

body in some specimens. Reaches about 14 cm. Known from the Indo-Malayan region north to Japan, south to Australia (type locality, Cairns, Queensland), and east to Fiji and Samoa Islands; generally found in mangrove areas and tidal creeks.

Tahiti/female

Sulawesi

THREADFIN GOBY
Oxyurichthys notonema (Weber, 1909)
Dorsal rays VI + I,12; anal rays I,13; pectoral rays 20–23; longitudinal scale series 61–80; scales on body ctenoid to below second dorsal fin, cycloid anteriorly; scales sometimes present on side of nape but not on chest, prepectoral region, cheek, or opercle; no tentacle on eye; a fleshy median ridge on nape; gill opening extending to beneath middle of opercle; a single row of slender conical teeth in upper jaw; body depth 5.2–7.0 in standard length; first 4 dorsal spines (and to a lesser extent the fifth spine) long and filamentous in both sexes, the longest about 2.9 in standard length; caudal fin lanceolate, 2.3–2.7 in standard length; pelvic fins united; pelvic frenum present; pale bluish gray with 5 midlateral, round, brownish orange spots larger than eye, the first beneath pectoral fin and the last on caudal-fin base; irregular orange markings between spots; short blue lines or elongate spots set at various angles on head; an orange spot dorsally on eye; fleshy ridge on nape orange; dorsal fins orange with irregular blue lines. Attains 16 cm. Known from Mozambique, Indonesia (type locality, Sulawesi), Philippines, Japan, and Tahiti; occurs in silty sand or mud areas; shelters in a burrow.

Coral Sea

REDHEAD CORALGOBY
Paragobiodon echinocephalus (Rüppell, 1830)
Dorsal rays VI + I,9; anal rays I,9; pectoral rays 19–21; longitudinal scale series 23–25; scales ctenoid, except cycloid on abdomen; head and nape naked, with slender bristle-like papillae; gill opening ending ventrally at level of last pectoral ray; pelvic fins joined to form a cup-like disc, the pelvic frenum well developed (true of other *Paragobiodon*); body depth 3.0–3.2 in standard length, and body width about 1.7 in body depth (also generic); dorsal profile of head steep and strongly convex (generic); caudal fin rounded, shorter than head length; body and fins black or blackish orange; head orange, often with very small, pale blue spots. Attains 4 cm. Widely distributed in the Indo-Pacific region from the Red Sea (type locality) to the Marquesas Islands and Tuamotu Archipelago (but not the Hawaiian Islands); in the western Pacific from the Ryukyu Islands to the Great Barrier Reef and Lord Howe Island; lives mainly in corals of the genus *Stylophora*, especially *S. pistillata*.

FROGFACE GOBY
Oxyurichthys papuensis (Valenciennes in C & V, 1837)
Dorsal rays VI + I,12; anal rays I,13; pectoral rays 20–23; longitudinal scale series 75–80; scales on body ctenoid to below middle of first dorsal fin, cycloid anteriorly; scales present on side of nape to above posterior margin of preopercle and on chest, but not prepectoral region, cheek, or opercle; a short, red fleshy knob dorsally on eye; a fleshy median ridge on nape; gill opening nearly reaching a vertical at posterior margin of preopercle; upper jaw with a single row of slender conical teeth; upper part of eye elevated above dorsal profile; body depth 5.6–6.5 in standard length; caudal fin lanceolate, nearly twice length of head; pelvic fins united; frenum present; greenish gray, the scales edged in dark brown, with a midlateral row of 4 large brown blotches with lesser blotches between, all tending to expand dorsally and ventrally to form faint bars; a large black spot at caudal-fin base; a brown spot dorsally on pectoral-fin base with a narrow, curved orange bar extending below; dorsal fins crossed with irregular oblique orange lines. Reported to 17 cm. East coast of Africa to Indo-Malayan region, north to Ryukyu Islands and south to New Caledonia; type locality, New Guinea. Typically found in mud; takes refuge in a burrow, but is able to dive quickly into mud if threatened when away from its burrow.

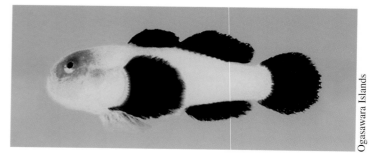
Ogasawara Islands

BLACKFIN CORALGOBY
Paragobiodon lacunicolus (Kendall & Goldsborough, 1911)
Dorsal rays VI + I,9; anal rays I,8; pectoral rays 21; longitudinal scale series 22–24; scales ctenoid, none on head, nape, prepectoral region, chest, and midventrally on abdomen; fleshy papillae on snout and cheek; ventral end of gill opening extending to level of first or second lower pectoral rays; caudal fin rounded and short, about three-fourths head length; body white to pale yellowish, shading to pale orange on head, the median and pectoral fins black, sometimes reddish at base. Attains 2.5 cm. East coast of Africa to Line Islands and Tuamotu Archipelago (Fakarava Atoll, type locality); Ryukyu Islands and Ogasawara Islands to New Caledonia and Lord Howe Island; reported to live in the coral *Pocillopora damicornis*.

Maldive Islands

Great Barrier Reef (R. C. Steene)

WARTHEAD CORALGOBY

Paragobiodon modestus (Regan, 1908)

Dorsal rays VI + I,8–9; anal rays I,9–10; pectoral rays 20–22; longitudinal scale series 22–24; scales ctenoid, none on head, nape, prepectoral region, chest, and midventrally on abdomen; numerous short bristle-like cirri on head and nape; ventral end of gill opening extending to level of third to seventh lower pectoral rays; caudal fin rounded, a little shorter than head length; head and nape dark brownish orange, grading to black anteriorly on body; median and pectoral fins black. Reaches 3.5 cm. East coast of Africa to the Marshall Islands and Society Islands (Randall et al., 2002a); Ryukyu Islands to Lord Howe Island; type locality, Chagos Archipelago. Lives among branches of corals of the genus *Seriatopora*.

YELLOWGREEN CORALGOBY

Paragobiodon xanthosomus (Bleeker, 1852)

Dorsal rays VI + I,8–9; anal rays I,8–9; pectoral rays 20–22; longitudinal scale series 22–24; scales ctenoid, none on head, nape, prepectoral region, chest, and midventrally on abdomen; numerous bristle-like cirri dorsally on head and nape and ventrally on head; ventral end of gill opening extending to level of lowest pectoral ray; dorsal fins joined by membrane at most to one-fourth length of spine of second dorsal fin; caudal fin rounded, a little shorter than head length; pale yellow to light green, with very small pale blue spots on head, sometimes extending anteriorly on body. Reported to 4 cm. East coast of Africa to the Marshall Islands and Samoa Islands; in the western Pacific from the Ryukyu Islands to Great Barrier Reef and Lord Howe Island; type locality, Seram, Molucca Islands; commensal in corals of the genus *Seriatopora*. The similar *P. echinocephalus* (Rüppell) seems to differ mainly in color; its distribution is uncertain. A revision of the genus *Paragobiodon* is needed.

Fiji

SILVERLINED MUDSKIPPER

Periophthalmus argentilineatus Valenciennes in C & V, 1837

Dorsal rays XI-XVI + I,9–12; anal rays I,8–11; pectoral rays 11–14; scales cycloid, 64–100 in longitudinal series; predorsal scales 22–37; eyes erectile; lower "eyelid" present; no canine teeth in upper jaw; a single row of teeth in lower jaw; body depth 5.8–7.8 in standard length; pelvic fins without a frenum; mottled brown, abruptly white ventrally, with short, white vertical lines and dots in lower brown part of body; lower half of operculum with scattered white dots; first dorsal fin red with a few dark-edged white dots basally, a broad submarginal black band with an adjacent red spot at outer edge on each membrane, and a translucent margin; second dorsal fin translucent with a broad red margin and a broad black submarginal band with a row of white dots between. Largest specimen, 11.6 cm. Red Sea and east coast of Africa to Samoa Islands and islands of Micronesia except the Marshall Islands; Ryukyu Islands to Queensland and Western Australia; described from Irian Jaya and the Molucca Islands. Amphibious in the mangrove and nipa palm habitats, more out of the water than in; caudal fin usually remaining in the sea except when flipping over mangrove roots and mud. Feeds mainly on small crustaceans, worms, and insects.

Djibouti

KALOLO MUDSKIPPER

Periophthalmus kalolo Lesson, 1831

Dorsal rays XI-XV + I,9–12; anal rays I,11–12; pectoral rays 12–14; scales cycloid, 66–86 in longitudinal series; predorsal scales 27–40; eyes erectile; lower "eyelid" present; no canine teeth in lower jaw; a single row of teeth in upper jaw; body depth 6.3–7.1 in standard length; pelvic fins with a frenum; light gray-brown, the scale edges dark brown, with scattered, small blackish flecks; cheek with dark-edged white spots; first dorsal fin reddish gray with white spots and a broad, white-edged black band at margin; second dorsal fin gray with white spots ventrally, a white-edged black band in outer middle part, and a broad red margin. Largest specimen, 17.5 cm. Gulf of Aden, Tanzania, and Madagascar to Samoa Islands and Pohnpei, Caroline Islands; sometimes coexisting with *Periophthalmus argentilineatus*, and with similar habits.

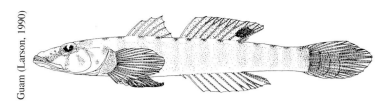

BILOBED GHOSTGOBY
Pleurosicya bilobata (Koumans, 1941)

Dorsal rays VI + I,7–8 (usually 8); anal rays I,7–9 (usually 8); pectoral rays 16–19 (rarely 19), the lower 3–7 unbranched; branched caudal rays 11 (true of other species of the genus here); longitudinal scale series 23–29; scales ctenoid, none on head, chest, or prepectoral area (true of other *Pleurosicya*); nape naked; body slender, the depth at anal-fin origin about 6.7 in standard length; tongue usually bilobed (basis of species name); dorsal fins low; pectoral fins short, reaching at most to below rear of first dorsal fin; pelvic fins united to a cup-like disc, with a forwardly folded pelvic frenum and fleshy lobes around the pelvic spines (also generic); translucent green to yellowish green with brown to yellowish brown bars on body and bands on head; males with a black spot posteriorly on second dorsal fin. Largest specimen, 2.75 cm. India (type locality) and St. Brandon's Shoals to western Pacific from Ryukyu Islands to New South Wales, east to New Caledonia, Palau, and Mariana Islands; generally found on seagrass. *Pleurosicya taisnei* Plessis & Fourmanoir from the Isle of Pines, New Caledonia, is a synonym; it was collected from the tunicate *Polycarpa aurata* in 30 m (Larson, 1990).

STAGHORN GHOSTGOBY
Pleurosicya fringilla Larson, 1990

Dorsal rays VI + I,7–9; anal rays I,7–9; pectoral rays 14–16 (rarely 14), the lower 4–6 unbranched; longitudinal scale series 23–31 (mean 27); head, nape, and area dorsally under first dorsal fin naked; body depth at anus 4.55–6.65 in standard length; head length about 2.3 in standard length; head width usually a little greater than head depth; tongue usually narrow and pointed; upper lip very large anteriorly; gill opening restricted to pectoral-fin base; body transparent; a brown stripe from eye to front of snout and another passing anteriorly from dorsal-fin origin; postorbital head orange-yellow, brown dorsally on opercle. Attains 2.2 cm. Natal and islands of western Indian Ocean to Tuamotu Archipelago; Ryukyu Islands to Great Barrier Reef; usually found on staghorn coral, especially *Acropora formosa* and *A. grandis*; clings to underside of the coral branches.

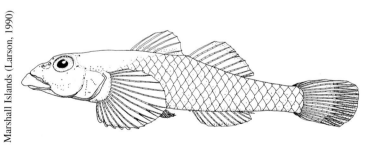

BLUE CORAL GHOSTGOBY
Pleurosicya coerulea Larson, 1990

Dorsal rays VI + I,7–9 (rarely 7 or 9); anal rays I,8–9 (rarely 9); pectoral rays 15–18 (rarely 15, modally 17), the lower 5–7 unbranched; longitudinal scale series 22–25 (modally 23); nape naked; body depth at anal-fin origin 3.9–6.9 in standard length; head broad; upper lip fleshy, overlapping mouth; gill opening restricted to pectoral-fin base; tongue round to pointed; translucent dull blue to blue-green with 2 reddish stripes on head and a dusky spot medially on nape. Largest specimen, 2.2 cm. Seychelles, Chagos Archipelago, and reefs off northwestern Australia to western Pacific from Ryukyu Islands to Great Barrier Reef and New Caledonia, east to Marshall Islands (type locality, Enewetak Atoll), Caroline Islands, and Gilbert Islands (Kiribati); commensal on blue coral (*Heliopora coerulea*).

MICHEL'S GHOSTGOBY
Pleurosicya micheli Fourmanoir, 1971

Dorsal rays VI + I,7–8 (usually 8); anal rays I,7–8 (usually 8); pectoral rays 16–19 (rarely 19), the lower 2–5 unbranched; longitudinal scale series 22–28 (modally 25); no median predorsal scales; side of nape scaled to above preopercle; body depth at anal-fin origin 5.0–7.1 in standard length; head width greater than head depth; gill opening broad, reaching at least to below posterior edge of eye; translucent with an internal red stripe that continues onto lower half of caudal fin (stripe may be blackish posteriorly); a pinkish white line on top of red stripe, broken into segments posteriorly. Attains 2.5 cm. Seychelles and Maldive Islands to Hawaiian Islands and Society Islands (Randall et al., 2002a); Ryukyu Islands and Taiwan to Great Barrier Reef and New Caledonia; type locality, Loyalty Islands; commensal on a variety of hard corals; seems to be the most common species of the genus, but this may be due to its being seen most often in the open at rest on corals; recorded from depths of 15–38 m.

Fiji

MOZAMBIQUE GHOSTGOBY
Pleurosicya mossambica Smith, 1959

Dorsal rays VI + I,7–8 (rarely 7); anal rays I,7–8 (rarely 7); pectoral rays 16–20 (rarely 16 or 20, modally 18), the lower 3–8 unbranched; longitudinal scale series 20–27 (modally 24); side of nape scaled to eyes; median predorsal scales 0–13; body depth at anal-fin origin 5.3–6.8 in standard length; head width usually greater than head depth; gill opening broad, reaching to below middle of eye; color variable, depending on the host species; usually with a broad dusky red stripe on lower side, continuing as blackish into lower half of caudal fin; some blackish pigment often at base of first dorsal fin. Reaches 2.5 cm. Red Sea, east coast of Africa, and Seychelles to Marshall Islands and Marquesas Islands; Kochi Prefecture to Great Barrier Reef, New South Wales, Lord Howe Island, and New Caledonia; commensal on a wide variety of benthic invertebrates, including sponges and soft corals; also lives on algae such as *Turbinaria* and *Dendrophyllia*; reported from depths of 2–28 m. *Pleurosicya sinaia* Goren from the Red Sea is a synonym.

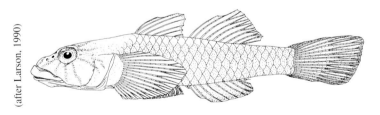

(after Larson, 1990)

SOFT CORAL GHOSTGOBY
Pleurosicya muscarum (Jordan & Seale, 1906)

Dorsal rays VI + I,7–8 (rarely 7); anal rays I,7–8 (rarely 7); pectoral rays 16–19 (rarely 16), the lower 1–7 unbranched; longitudinal scale series 21–25 (modally 23); nape naked; body depth at anal-fin origin 4.7–7.1 in standard length; head width greater than head depth; gill opening reaching at most to below posterior margin of preopercle; upper lip broad; tongue blunt to rounded; transparent bluish to greenish gray with red lines radiating from eye; snout sometimes yellow. Largest specimen, 2.6 cm. East Africa to Samoa Islands (type locality, Tutuila) and islands of Micronesia; Ryukyu Islands to Great Barrier Reef and Dampier Archipelago, Western Australia; commensal on a variety of alcyonarian soft corals; recorded from depths of 2–28 m. *Pleurosicyops timidus* Smith from Mozambique is a synonym.

Easter Island

LATTICED GOBY
Priolepis sp.

Dorsal rays VI + I,11–12 (usually 11); anal rays I,9; pectoral rays 19–20; longitudinal scale series 27–28; head naked; median predorsal scales 0–12; scales on body ctenoid, becoming cycloid on pectoral-fin base, midventrally on abdomen, and chest; body depth 4.4–5.2 in standard length; head length about 3.1 in standard length; gill opening reaching a little anterior to posterior margin of preopercle; caudal fin rounded, about equal to head length; pelvic fins united; no pelvic frenum; fifth pelvic ray branched, about nine-tenths length of fourth ray; pelvic fins usually reaching anus, sometimes to origin of anal fin; whitish, the scales strongly rimmed with dark orangish brown (thus the overall color is brown); head orangish brown, usually with 2 narrow, curved, brownish red bars extending ventrally from eye and 1 across operculum following margin of preopercle; dorsal and caudal fins with rows of dark orange-red spots. Largest specimen, 4.7 cm. Known only from Easter Island and Rapa; collected by the author in reefs from depths of 3–42 m; never seen in the open. As noted by Randall et al. (1990: 34, fig. 45), specimens of this new species of goby were sent to D. F. Hoese of the Australian Museum for the description.

female (R. Winterbottom)

MOURNFUL GOBY
Priolepis ailina Winterbottom & Burridge, 1993

Dorsal rays VI + I,9; anal rays I,8; pectoral rays 19; longitudinal scale series 23–24; scales on body ctenoid except midline of abdomen and dorsalmost row of scales on body, which are cycloid; head, nape, pectoral-fin base, and chest naked; body depth about 3.8 in standard length; head length about 3 in standard length; dorsal fins low, about equal in height; caudal fin rounded, shorter than head; pelvic fins united for about 50% fin length; no pelvic frenum; fifth pelvic ray branched, about half length of fourth ray; translucent yellow with faint dark bars on postorbital head and dorsally on body, the 2 most prominent on body below first dorsal fin; a black bar from below eye to corner of mouth, and a black spot behind and above eye; dorsal and caudal fins with small black spots. Largest specimen, 2.15 cm. Currently known only from Moorea, Society Islands; collections from 7 to about 20 m.

547

CONVICT GOBY

Priolepis cincta (Regan, 1908)

Dorsal rays VI + I,10–11 (rarely 10); anal rays I,8–9 (rarely 8); pectoral rays 17–19; longitudinal scale series 27–31; scales on body ctenoid except abdomen, prepectoral, and prepelvic areas, where cycloid; scales on nape extending to midinterorbital space; a patch of small scales, mostly cycloid, dorsally on opercle; no scales on cheek; body depth 3.8–4.6 in standard length; head length 2.95–3.3 in standard length; gill opening reaching to below posterior margin of preopercle; caudal fin rounded, shorter than head; pelvic fins united, not reaching anus; no pelvic frenum; body whitish with 7 dark-edged gray-brown bars, progressively narrower posteriorly (but always broader than whitish interspaces); bars continuing on nape and head, progressively narrower anteriorly, 4 crossing interorbital space, 2 extending below eye; dorsal and caudal fins with small orange or brown

Bali

spots on rays. Attains 5 cm. Red Sea, Persian Gulf, and east coast of Africa to islands of Micronesia, Fiji, and Tonga; Japan to Coral Sea; type locality, Chagos Archipelago. Very cryptic like others of the genus, and rarely seen by divers. *Priolepis naraharae* (Snyder) is a synonym.

CROSSROADS GOBY

Priolepis compita Winterbottom, 1985

Dorsal rays VI + I,8–9 (rarely 9); anal rays I,6–8; pectoral rays 17–19; longitudinal scale series 26; scales on body ctenoid, becoming cycloid anteriorly; no scales on head, nape, pectoral-fin base, or chest; body depth 3.5–4.2 in standard length; head length 2.85–3.0 in standard length; gill opening wide, reaching almost to below posterior edge of eye; caudal fin rounded, about equal to head length; pelvic fins united, usually reaching anal-fin origin; no pelvic frenum; body and fins translucent yellowish brown; black-edged white lines radiating from eye, 3 vertical lines on postorbital head and nape interconnecting at eye level,

Bali

and 3 anterodorsally on body. Attains 1.7 cm. Known from Natal, Chagos Archipelago (type locality), Indonesia, Great Barrier Reef, and Fiji. Gut contents included copepods, ostracods, and radiolarians (Winterbottom, 1985b).

EIGHTBAR GOBY

Priolepis fallacincta Winterbottom & Burridge, 1992

Dorsal rays VI + I,9–10 (rarely 10); anal rays I,8–9 (rarely 9); pectoral rays 17–19; longitudinal scale series 24–26; 13–15 ctenoid predorsal scales; scales on body ctenoid, cycloid on pectoral-fin base and chest, and mixed cycloid and ctenoid on opercle; no scales on cheek; no transverse anterior interorbital papillae; gill rakers 3–4 + 13–14; body depth about 4.5 in standard length; bony interorbital space half pupil diameter; gill opening reaching to below middle of preopercle; no elongate dorsal spines; caudal fin rounded; pelvic fins united; no pelvic frenum; body, including nape, with 8 brown bars, the scale centers pale, and 8 narrow light bars; head with dark brown and whitish bands radiating from

Negros (R. Winterbottom)

eye; no black spot in first dorsal fin. Largest specimen, 3.2 cm. Known from Taiwan, Philippines (type locality, Negros), Indonesia, Papua New Guinea, Great Barrier Reef, Solomon Islands, New Caledonia, and Fiji; coral reefs, 1–37 m.

BRICK GOBY

Priolepis inhaca (Smith, 1949)

Dorsal rays VI + I,9–10 (more often 10); anal rays I,8; pectoral rays 15–17; longitudinal scale series 26–28; predorsal scales of adults 12–17 (mean 15); scales on body ctenoid, becoming cycloid on pectoral-fin base, midventrally on abdomen, and chest; cycloid scales present on opercle of adults; posterior edge of tubular posterior nostril adherent to edge of orbit; body depth about 4 in standard length; head length about 3.4–3.7 in standard length; gill opening wide, reaching almost to below posterior edge of eye; caudal fin rounded, shorter than head; pelvic fins united; no pelvic frenum; color variable with habitat; generally light gray, the scale edges dark brown; 3 pale vertical lines on ventral half of head; fins often reddish, the rays of dorsal fins

Moorea (R. Winterbottom)

dotted with brown or orange; deeper-water individuals dominantly red. Attains 4 cm. East coast of Africa (type locality, Inhaca Island, Mozambique) to the Society Islands; Ryukyu Islands to Great Barrier Reef; only Guam and Gilbert Islands (Kiribati) in Micronesia; reported from depths of 12–26 m.

KAPPA GOBY
Priolepis kappa Winterbottom & Burridge, 1993
Dorsal rays VI + I,8–9 (rarely 8); anal rays I,7–8 (rarely 7); pectoral rays 18–19; longitudinal scale series 23–26; no scales on head or nape; scales on body ctenoid, except cycloid on abdomen; a few cycloid scales on prepectoral region in larger specimens; gill rakers 2–3 + 11–12; body depth about 4.7 in standard length; bony interorbital space half pupil diameter; gill opening reaching to below posterior end of preopercle; no elongate dorsal spines; caudal fin rounded; pelvic fins united; fifth pelvic ray subequal to fourth; no pelvic frenum; light yellowish brown, the scale edges dark brown; 6 narrow whitish bars on body; whitish lines radiating from eye, 1 on posterior edge of preopercle joining line on nape. A small species, the largest specimen 2.6 cm.

BLACKBARRED GOBY
Priolepis nocturna (Smith, 1957)
Dorsal rays VI + I,8–10; anal rays I,7–8; pectoral rays 20–21 (usually 20); longitudinal scale series 28; scales on body ctenoid to base of second dorsal spine, cycloid anteriorly, including pectoral-fin base, chest, and ventrally on abdomen; head and median part of nape naked; small embedded scales extending on side of nape to above middle of opercle; body deep for the genus, the depth 3.0–3.7 in standard length; head length about 3 in standard length; gill opening reaching to below posterior margin of preopercle; tips of spines of first dorsal fin free of membrane; caudal fin rounded, about equal to head length; pelvic fins united only basally, without a frenum, nearly reaching anus; white with 3 black bars on body, the first 2 as double bars, one below each dorsal fin and extending into fin as a large black spot; a black bar on nape across operculum; a black band across interorbital, and

PALEBARRED GOBY
Priolepis pallidicincta Winterbottom & Burridge, 1993
Dorsal rays VI + I,10–11 (rarely 11); anal rays I,8–9 (rarely 9); pectoral rays 18–20; longitudinal scale series 26–28; 13–14 ctenoid predorsal scales; scales on body ctenoid, cycloid on pectoral-fin base and chest; a maximum of 2 cycloid scales on opercle; no scales on cheek; gill rakers 3–4 + 12–13; body depth about 4.2 in standard length; bony interorbital space half pupil diameter; gill opening reaching to below posterior margin of preopercle; fourth and fifth dorsal spines longest, reaching to base of first dorsal soft ray when depressed; caudal fin rounded; pelvic fins united; no pelvic frenum; body in preservative with 6 double

HALFBARRED GOBY
Priolepis semidoliata (Valenciennes in C & V, 1837)
Dorsal rays VI + I,9, the rays unbranched; anal rays I,7; pectoral rays 16–18; longitudinal scale series 25–28 (modally 27); scales on body ctenoid, becoming cycloid anterior to middle of first dorsal fin; no scales on head, nape, or prepectoral area; scales present or absent on chest; body depth about 3.4–3.9 in standard length; head length 2.9–3.0 in standard length; gill opening reaching slightly anterior to a vertical at posterior margin of preopercle; caudal fin rounded, about equal to head length; pelvic fins united for at least half their length, without a frenum, reaching to or slightly beyond anus; translucent yellowish gray with narrow, dark-edged white bands radiating from pupil; one on nape bifurcating, with a branch crossing operculum and another

Bali

Reported from Comoro Islands (type locality, Anjouan), Indonesia, Papua New Guinea, Philippines, Taiwan, Wake Island, Great Barrier Reef, Fiji, and Rotuma; reef in 1–19 m. Named *kappa* for the Greek letter from the resemblance of the white lines on the postorbital head to K.

Marquesas Islands

2 narrow black bars extending ventrally from eye; a large black spot, rimmed posteriorly in white, in upper middle part of caudal fin. Attains 4.5 cm. Known only from the Seychelles (type locality, Aldabra), Maldive Islands, Indonesia, Philippines, Phoenix Islands, and Marquesas Islands. The western Indian Ocean form has a single dark bar below each dorsal fin and below the eye; the Pacific form may prove to be different enough to warrant description as a new species or subspecies.

(Winterbottom & Burridge)

brown bars, hence with about 12 narrow pale bars; no dark spots in fins. Attains 3.6 cm. Known from the Philippines, Indonesia, Papua New Guinea, Great Barrier Reef, Solomon Islands, Vanuatu, Kiribati, Caroline Islands, and Fiji (type locality, Great Astrolabe Reef); coral reefs in 1–56 m.

Saudi Arabia, Red Sea

across pectoral-fin base, and a variable number (0–9, often 3) anteriorly on body; median fins reddish; paired fins dusky yellow. Reaches 3 cm. Occurs throughout most of the Indo-Pacific region from the Red Sea to the Pitcairn Islands (but not the Hawaiian Islands); type locality, Vanikoro Island, Santa Cruz Islands; a common cryptic coral-reef species; the author has never seen one alive underwater.

Tahiti

(R. Winterbottom)

SCALEDCHEEK GOBY

Priolepis squamogena Winterbottom & Burridge, 1989

Dorsal rays VI + I,10–11 (rarely 10); anal rays I,9; pectoral rays 18–19 (usually 19); longitudinal scale series 29–30 (modally 30); scales on body ctenoid except prepectoral area and chest, where cycloid; 16–18 ctenoid predorsal scales on nape extending into middle interorbital space; ctenoid scales on dorsal one-third of opercle and posterodorsal quarter of cheek of adults; gill opening reaching to below posterior margin of preopercle; pelvic fins united, just reaching anus; no pelvic frenum; body proportions, meristic data, and color very similar to those of *P. cincta*. Largest specimen, 5.4 cm. Society Islands (type locality, Huahine), Tuamotu Archipelago, Marquesas Islands, Line Islands, and Howland Island; collections from tidepools to 52 m. Some might prefer to regard *P. squamogena* as a subspecies of *P. cincta*, differing chiefly in having scales on the cheek.

"THREE-EYED" GOBY

Priolepis triops Winterbottom & Burridge, 1993

Dorsal rays VI + I,11; anal rays I,9; pectoral rays 20–22; longitudinal scale series 25–28; predorsal scales of adults 9–15; scales on body ctenoid except pectoral-fin base, midventrally on abdomen, and chest, where cycloid; no scales on opercle or cheek; body depth about 4.3 in standard length; head length about 3.4 in standard length; gill opening reaching to below posterior margin of preopercle; caudal fin rounded, a little shorter than head length; pelvic fins united, reaching posterior to first anal soft ray; no pelvic frenum; pale gray, the scale edges a little darker than centers, with yellowish brown bars as follows: 3 narrow ones below eye, a short one on postorbital head, 1 on nape across operculum, and 7 on body (the last 2 on caudal peduncle faint); a dark stripe on upper and lower edges of caudal peduncle; opercle and abdomen suffused with red; a large black spot at front of first dorsal fin, broadly bordered by white posteriorly (the basis for the scientific name, meaning 3-eyed). Largest specimen, 2.6 cm. Known only from the Society Islands (type locality, Moorea) and Fiji; collections from depths of 12–24 m, mostly from rubble bottom.

Marquesas Islands

Marquesas Islands/juvenile

SENTINEL SHRIMPGOBY

Stonogobiops medon Hoese & Randall, 1982

Dorsal rays VI + I,12; anal rays I,11; pectoral rays 18; branched caudal rays 13–14; longitudinal scale series 100–115; no median predorsal scales; scales on body cycloid, extending forward to above posterior margin of preopercle, those on pectoral-fin base and chest small and embedded; head naked; no pores on head; body depth 5.05–5.75 in standard length; head length 3.3–3.5 in standard length; mouth large and oblique, the lower jaw projecting (true of other *Stonogobiops*); vomer with 2–4 large recurved teeth (also generic); gill opening reaching to below posterior edge of eye; first to third dorsal spines of adults greatly prolonged, the second 1.9–2.15 in standard length; caudal fin rounded, a little shorter than head length; pelvic fins united, not reaching anus in adults; pelvic frenum present; tan, the center of each scale pale; a broad, blue-edged dark brown band curving from nape onto upper preopercle; a blue-edged black streak above posterior half of upper lip; a dark spot in front of first dorsal spine, and 4 along base of dorsal fins; snout orange, the lips pale orange; juveniles white with 4 oblique black bands and yellow snout and chin (hence similar to *S. xanthorhinica*). Largest specimen, 6.7 cm. Known only from the Marquesas Islands; collections on flat or slightly sloping sand or sand-rubble substrata in 21.5–35 m; symbiotic with *Alpheus randalli*.

Kyushu (T. Hirata)

Flores, Indonesia

ORANGESTRIPED SHRIMPGOBY

Stonogobiops yasha Yoshino & Shimada, 2001

Dorsal rays VI + I,10–12; anal rays I,10–11; pectoral rays 16–17; branched caudal rays 14–15; longitudinal scale series 82–96; no median predorsal scales; scales cycloid, embedded anteriorly; head, pectoral-fin base, and chest naked; no pores on head except 2 median pores in interorbital; body depth 5.0–5.55 in standard length; head length 3.2–3.6 in standard length; gill opening reaching to below a point midway between posterior margin of preopercle and posterior edge of eye; first 2 dorsal spines greatly prolonged, the second longest, varying from 1.1 to greater than standard length; caudal fin rounded, usually shorter than head length; pelvic fins united, not reaching anus; pelvic frenum well developed; white with orange stripes on body and elongate orange spots on head and nape; filamentous part of first dorsal fin white; a large, triangular black spot in outer middle part of first dorsal fin. Largest specimen, 6.1 cm. Ryukyu Islands (type locality, Okinawa), Kashiwa-jima (Kochi Prefecture), Miyake-jima (Izu Islands), Bali, Palau, and New Caledonia; observed on outer-reef slopes in 15–40 m; usually seen in pairs; symbiotic with *Alpheus randalli* and *A. bellulus.* The long prevomerine teeth of this goby are the basis for the name *yasha,* a traditional female devil in Japan having a pair of long canine teeth in the upper jaw. First illustrated and briefly diagnosed in Masuda et al. (1984) as *Stonogobiops* sp.

REDSPOT PYGMYGOBY

Sueviota aprica Winterbottom & Hoese, 1988

Dorsal rays VI + I,10; anal rays I,8–9 (usually 9); pectoral rays 17–19, the first 11 or 12 unbranched, the next 4 or 5 branched; branched caudal rays 12; longitudinal scale series 26–27; scales cycloid, none on head, nape, pectoral-fin base, or chest; no preopercular pores; postocular pore present; no pelvic frenum; first and second dorsal spines of males elongate; body depth about 4.2 in standard length; caudal fin rounded, a little longer than head; 3 narrow, irregular, dark yellow or orange-red bars on postorbital head and a bright red spot as large as eye on side of occiput between second and third bars; 7 faint, dark yellow to

YELLOWNOSE SHRIMPGOBY

Stonogobiops xanthorhinica Hoese & Randall, 1982

Dorsal rays VI + I,11; anal rays I,10; pectoral rays 16–17 (usually 16); branched caudal rays 12–14 (rarely 12, usually 13); longitudinal scale series 75–92; usually no median predorsal scales; scales cycloid; pectoral-fin base and chest naked or with only a few scales; head naked; no pores on head; body depth 4.7–5.3 in standard length; head length 3.3–3.55 in standard length; gill opening reaching to below a point midway between posterior margin of preopercle and posterior edge of eye; first dorsal fin elevated only in male; caudal fin rounded, about equal to head length; pelvic fins united, sometimes reaching anus; pelvic frenum present; white with 4 strongly oblique, narrow black bands, the first from nape across operculum, the second curving into first dorsal fin to form a broad outer border, the third between second dorsal and anal fins, and the fourth posteriorly on caudal peduncle; front of head, including chin and most of eye, bright yellow. Largest specimen, 6.4 cm. Southern Japan to Great Barrier Reef, east to Palau and Fiji (Fiji record from an underwater photograph by Mike Neumann); type locality, Madang, Papua New Guinea. Occurs on sand or sand and rubble substrata; often a pair share the same burrow; the usual symbiotic shrimp is *Alpheus randalli*; collected from depths of 3–45 m.

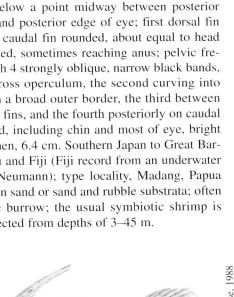

Winterbottom & Hoese, 1988

orange-brown bars dorsally on body; a midventral black spot on chin in line with anterior edge of eye. Largest specimen, 2.15 cm. Chagos Archpelago (type locality) and Fiji; collected from steep outer-reef slopes in 16–42 m.

LACHNER'S PYGMYGOBY

Sueviota lachneri Winterbottom & Hoese, 1988

Dorsal rays VI + I,8–9 (rarely 8); anal rays I,8; pectoral rays 16–18, 1–6 branched; branched caudal rays 12; longitudinal scale series 25–26 (rarely 25); ctenoid scales on body except near midline of abdomen, where cycloid; no scales on head, nape, pectoral-fin base, or chest; a postocular and 2 preopercular pores; no pelvic frenum; no elongate dorsal spines; body depth about 4.3 in standard length; caudal fin rounded, a little shorter than head; translucent pale yellowish gray, the scale edges rimmed in dusky orange; head with large, dusky orange spots; pectoral-fin base with 2 pupil-size spots; dorsal and caudal fins with dusky orange dots on rays. Largest specimen, 2.4 cm. Known from Chagos Archipelago (type locality, Salomon Atoll),

Ogasawara Islands

Maldive Islands, Ogasawara Islands, Philippines, Papua New Guinea, Great Barrier Reef, Osprey Reef (Coral Sea), and Fiji; collections from depths of 3–50 m. Gut contents included amphipods, isopods, and small gastropods, indicating probable benthic feeding (Winterbottom & Hoese, 1988).

RED DWARFGOBY

Trimma benjamini Winterbottom, 1996

Dorsal rays VI + I,10; anal rays I,9; pectoral rays 18–19, 7–11 branched; longitudinal scale series 23–25; no median predorsal scales, but scales on side of nape nearly to eye; head naked; scales ctenoid, becoming cycloid on pectoral-fin base, chest, and ventroanteriorly on abdomen; no pores on head (true of other *Trimma*); gill opening broad, reaching forward to below middle of eye (also generic); second dorsal spine usually elongate in both sexes; caudal fin slightly rounded; pelvic fins joined only basally by membrane; fifth pelvic rays branched, 60–75% length of fourth ray; no pelvic frenum; red overall; a pale blue to dusky white line nearly encircling eye, and 2 lines continuing ventrally from eye (lines persist as dusky in preservative); iris deep red with an inner rim of bright yellow; fins translucent pale red with light red rays. Attains 3 cm. Indo-Malayan region (type local-

Fiji

ity, Siquijor Island, Philippines), east to Marshall Islands, Palau, New Caledonia, Fiji, and Tonga; often found on reef drop-offs; collections from depths of 4–30 m; relatively easy to approach underwater.

GROOVED DWARFGOBY

Trimma caesiura Jordan & Seale, 1906

Dorsal rays VI + I,8; anal rays I,8; pectoral rays 17–18; longitudinal scale series 23–25; no median predorsal scales, but scales on side of nape nearly to eye; head naked; interorbital space a deep groove that bifurcates to Y-shape, 1 branch around each orbit; scales ctenoid, becoming cycloid on pectoral-fin base, chest, and ventroanteriorly on abdomen; second dorsal spine usually elongate in both sexes; caudal fin truncate; fifth pelvic rays branched, 60–75% length of fourth ray; no pelvic frenum; red dorsally, translucent gray ventrally, the scale edges dusky red; postorbital head and dorsoanterior part of body with a pale blue reticular pattern outlining red spots as large or larger than pupil; a series of 4 bluish white blotches on upper side of body

Palau

from below end of first dorsal fin to upper edge of caudal-fin base. Reported to 3.5 cm. Ryukyu Islands to New Caledonia, east to Samoa Islands (type locality, Upolu), and islands of Micronesia.

EMERY'S DWARFGOBY

Trimma emeryi Winterbottom, 1985

Dorsal rays VI + I,8; anal rays I,7–8 (usually 8); pectoral rays 16–18, none branched; longitudinal scale series 24–25; median predorsal scales 7–8; head naked; scales ctenoid, becoming cycloid on pectoral-fin base and chest; second dorsal spine longest but not elongate; caudal fin rounded; pelvic fins united about one-third length of fifth ray, which is branched and nearly as long as fourth ray, reaching to or a little beyond origin of anal fin; no pelvic frenum; translucent pale yellowish, the edges of scales orangish brown; head orangish, the iris mainly bright red.

Marshall Islands

Largest specimen, 2.4 cm. Known from Comoro Islands, Chagos Archipelago (type locality, Salomon Atoll), Maldive Islands, southern Ryukyu Islands, Guam, Marshall Islands, Pohnpei, and Tonga; depth range, 5–35 m.

LARGE-EYE DWARFGOBY
Trimma macrophthalma (Tomiyama, 1936)
Dorsal rays VI + I,9; anal rays I,8–9 (usually 9); pectoral rays 17–18 (usualy 18); longitudinal scale series 26–27; head and nape naked; scales on body ctenoid, becoming cycloid on pectoral-fin base, chest, and ventrally on abdomen; second dorsal spine longest and may be filamentous; caudal fin rounded; pelvic fins united about half fin length, reaching origin of anal fin; fifth pelvic ray branched, two-thirds length of fourth ray; no pelvic frenum; translucent red, the scale edges darker red, with orange-red spots on head and anterior body; 2 prominent deep red spots, one above the other, on base of pectoral fin; fins transparent with red rays. Attains 2.7 cm. East Africa to western Pacific from Japan (type locality) to Great Barrier Reef, east to Palau and Fiji. *Trimma flammea* (Smith) is regarded as a synonym (Winterbottom, 1984).

Solomon Islands

RED-EARTH DWARFGOBY
Trimma milta Winterbottom, 2002
Dorsal rays VI + I,9; anal rays I,8; pectoral rays 17–18 (usually 17); longitudinal scale series 22–24; median predorsal scales 6–8; scales on body ctenoid, becoming cycloid on pectoral-fin base, chest, nape, and ventrally on abdomen; 2 or 3 cycloid scales dorsally on opercle (may be absent in juveniles); first dorsal fin without elongate spines; caudal fin rounded; pelvic fins united by membrane on basal one-tenth of fifth ray; fifth pelvic ray unbranched, about half length of fourth ray; no pelvic frenum; translucent light orange-red, the scale edges dusky red, shading to orange-yellow ventrally on head and body; dorsal and anal fins with a red band at base and a yellow band above; cau-

Hawaiian Islands

dal fin yellow with broad pink upper and lower edges. Reaches 3 cm. Western Australia, East Indies north to Taiwan, south to Great Barrier Reef, and east to the Hawaiian Islands and Society Islands (type locality, Moorea); collected from depths of 9–26 m, usually off coral rock walls or in reef areas with sand and rubble.

OKINAWA DWARFGOBY
Trimma okinawae (Aoyagi, 1949)
Dorsal rays VI + I,9–10; anal rays I,8–9; pectoral rays 16–18; longitudinal scale series 26–27; no median predorsal scales, but scales on side of nape nearly to eye; head naked; interorbital space a narrow deep groove that bifurcates to Y-shape, 1 branch around posterior side of each orbit; scales ctenoid, becoming cycloid on pectoral-fin base, chest, and ventroanteriorly on abdomen; second dorsal spine usually elongate in both sexes; caudal fin rounded; pelvic fins joined by membrane only basally; fifth pelvic ray branched, about two-thirds length of fourth ray; no pelvic frenum; translucent with numerous close-set, yellow to orange-red spots on body, many vertically elongate; head with spots and bars of the same color; a row of yellow spots near base

Fiji

of first dorsal fin and 2 or more on second dorsal; a cluster of yellow spots in centrobasal part of caudal fin. Reaches 4.3 cm. Ryukyu Islands (type locality, Okinawa) and Ogasawara Islands to Great Barrier Reef, east to Samoa Islands and Palau.

STRIPEDHEAD DWARFGOBY
Trimma striata (Herre, 1945)
Dorsal rays VI + I,9; anal rays I,8; pectoral rays 16–17; longitudinal scale series 26–27; head and median predorsal region of nape naked; scales on side of nape extending forward nearly to eyes; scales ctenoid, becoming cycloid on pectoral-fin base, chest, and anteriorly on nape; second dorsal spine usually elongate and filamentous; caudal fin truncate; pelvic fins nearly fully united, reaching to or beyond origin of anal fin; a weak frenum present; fifth pelvic ray branched, about two-thirds length of fourth ray; translucent dusky gray, the scale edges narrowly dark; head with 6 narrow, bright red stripes that extend a short distance onto anterior body. Reported to 4 cm. Maldive Islands to Indo-Malayan

Palau

region, New Caledonia, and Palau; type locality, Busuanga Island, Philippines; usually seen at rest head-down on vertical surfaces of reefs near a hole or crevice for refuge. *Zonogobius capostriatus* Goren, named from New Caledonia, is a synonym.

Solomon Islands

Balicasag Island, Philippines

TAYLOR'S DWARFGOBY

Trimma taylori Lobel, 1979

Dorsal rays VI + I,10–11 (rarely 11); anal rays I,9–10 (rarely 9); pectoral rays 13–15; longitudinal scale series 23–24 (usually 24); predorsal scales 6–8; head naked; scales ctenoid, becoming cycloid on pectoral-fin base, chest, and ventrally on abdomen; second dorsal spine elongate and filamentous (sometimes the third as well); caudal fin truncate; pelvic fins united by membrane for about one-third length of fins, usually reaching to base of third anal soft ray; fifth pelvic ray branched, about four-fifths length of fourth ray; no pelvic frenum; translucent pale red (sometimes pale yellow) with small, faint yellow spots on body, operculum, and median fins. Reaches 2.5 cm. Red Sea (Winterbottom, 1995), Chagos Archipelago, and Maldive Islands to Hawaiian Islands (type locality, O'ahu), and Society Islands (Randall et al., 2002a); generally found in caves or under ledges, mostly in 20–50 m, often in small aggregations above the bottom. Gut contents consisted of copepods (Winterbottom, 1984).

BLUESTRIPE DWARFGOBY

Trimma tevegae Cohen & Davis, 1969

Dorsal rays VI + I,9; anal rays I,9; pectoral rays 13–14, all rays unbranched; longitudinal scale series 25–26; predorsal scales 12, extending into interorbital space; scales ctenoid, becoming cycloid on chest; opercle scaled; a few cycloid scales on cheek; interorbital space broad for genus; second dorsal spine elongate and filamentous; caudal fin truncate to slightly emarginate; pelvic fins united only at base by membrane; no pelvic frenum; brownish yellow with a blue line through eye at upper edge of pupil, continuing as a broad, pale blue stripe and ending in a large reddish black spot, rimmed posteriorly with red, covering basal one-third of caudal fin; outer part of caudal fin often with bright pink streaks; abdomen and ventral part of head white. Reaches 3.5 cm. Indo-Malayan region (type locality, New Britain), north to southern Japan, south to Great Barrier Reef, east to Tonga; usually seen in aggregations in small caves; depth range, 10–40 m; often oriented vertically with head up. *Trimma caudimaculata* Yoshino & Araga is a probable synonym (Winterbottom, 1984).

Hawaiian Islands

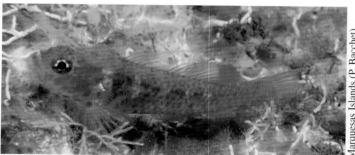

Marquesas Islands (P. Bacchet)

ONESCALE DWARFGOBY

Trimma unisquamis (Gosline, 1959)

Dorsal rays VI + I,7; anal rays I,7; pectoral rays 18; longitudinal scale series 25–26; top of head scaled forward to eyes; opercle nearly covered by 12 large scales; a single large embedded scale dorsally on cheek; pectoral-fin base and chest naked; scales ctenoid; first dorsal spine barely the longest, a little longer than longest dorsal soft ray; caudal fin truncate; pelvic fins united by membrane only basally, the fins reaching anus; pelvic frenum present; red, the scale edges blackish, with 4 narrow, pale bluish gray bars on body; a narrow red bar under eye and 1 from occiput down the posterior margin of preopercle; opercle blackish; a black bar basally on caudal fin; a broad black outer margin on dorsal fins, the margin only dusky to blackish on anal and caudal fins. Attains about 2.6 cm. Known from the Hawaiian Islands (type locality, O'ahu), Easter Island, Society Islands, Tonga, and Guam; depth range, 12–35 m.

MARQUESAN DWARFGOBY

Trimma woutsi Winterbottom, 2002

Dorsal rays VI + I,9–10 (usually 9); anal rays I,9; pectoral rays 17–19; longitudinal scale series 24–26; no predorsal scales; no scales on head, cheek, or opercle; pectoral base with small cycloid scales; chest and abdomen with cycloid scales; no deep postorbital groove; second dorsal spine elongate, reaching at least to base of second soft dorsal ray; no pelvic frenum; fourth pelvic ray reaching to base of anal spine; translucent orange with small orangish brown spots, the scale edges sometimes brown; alternating narrow white and broad dark internal blotches along vertebral column; an elongate white spot on upper edge of pectoral-fin base. Attains 3 cm. Known only from the Marquesas Islands (type locality, Hiva Oa); specimens collected about 5 to 30.5 m.

BLUE-BARRED DWARFGOBY
Trimmatom eviotops (Schultz, 1943)
Dorsal rays VI + I,9–10 (usually 9); anal rays I,8–9; pectoral rays 17–18, none branched; no scales on head or nape; first dorsal fin low, the first 4 spines about equal in length, about half head length; caudal fin rounded; pelvic fins with basal membrane rudimentary or absent, reaching to or a little beyond anus; no pelvic frenum; fifth pelvic ray rudimentary or absent; orange-red, shading to pink on abdomen and ventrally on head, with vertical, black-edged blue lines as follows: a short one below eye, 2 short ones on occiput, 1 on nape extending to and nearly enclosing pectoral fin base, 1 under first dorsal fin, 2 under second dorsal (the first at origin of fin), and a short horizontal line dorsally on caudal peduncle; a broad red stripe in middle of caudal fin.

PIXIE DWARFGOBY
Trimmatom nanus Winterbottom & Emery, 1981
Dorsal rays VI + I,8–9 (usually 9); anal rays I,7–9; pectoral rays 14–16, none branched; longitudinal scale series about 26 or 27; no scales on head or body; dorsal fins low, about equal in height, with no elongate spines; caudal fin rounded; pelvic fins with basal membrane vestigial or absent, the rays unbranched; no pelvic frenum; fifth pelvic ray absent or rudimentary, the fourth ray longest, reaching to base of fourth anal soft ray; translucent red. The shortest known vertebrate (Winterbottom & Emery,

ADORNED GOBY
Valenciennea decora Hoese & Larson, 1994
Dorsal rays VI + I,11; anal rays I,11; pectoral rays 21–23 (usually 21); longitudinal scale series 88–106; scales ctenoid on body except cycloid on abdomen (true of other *Valenciennea*); no scales on head or midline of nape (also generic); cycloid scales extending forward on side of nape to above rear edge of opercle; pectoral-fin base naked; prepelvic area of adults usually with a small patch of scales; dorsal fin rounded, no spines prolonged; caudal fin broadly rounded, a little shorter than head length, 3.0–4.0 in standard length; pelvic fins completely separate with no connecting membrane and no pelvic frenum (generic); pale gray, shading to white ventrally, with an orange stripe on lower side of body (faint on some individuals), connecting with 1–5 vertical orange bars (5 on Great Barrier Reef fish, 1 on Coral Sea and Fiji fish, and 4 in New Caledonia) that extend to dorsal edge of body; a broad, pale blue band, edged in dark blue, across head from above side of upper lip to upper part of opercle, and parallel rows of blue spots above; a black line along edge of upper lip;

Great Barrier Reef

Marshall Islands

Largest specimen, 1.9 cm. Known from the Society Islands, Tuamotu Archipelago, Samoa Islands (type locality, Rose Island), and islands of Micronesia. Specimens from the Chagos Archipelago and Great Barrier Reef provisionally identified as this species by Winterbottom (1984). Specimens similar in color to *eviotops* from Rapa and the Pitcairn Islands represent an undescribed species (R. Winterbottom, pers. comm.).

(R. Winterbottom)

1981), mature females as small as 0.8 cm standard length (1 cm total length). Chagos Archipelago (type locality, Salomon Atoll) to the Society Islands, with few records between; most specimens collected from seaward reef drop-offs in 20–30 m.

Coral Sea

a white-edged blackish band on outer part of first dorsal fin (only at tip of fin in an individual from Fiji). Largest specimen, 14.3 cm. Known from the Capricorn Group, southern Great Barrier Reef (type locality, One Tree Island), Osprey Reef in the Coral Sea, New Caledonia, Fiji, and Tonga; found on sand and rubble substrata of protected areas in 2–33 m.

TWOSTRIPE GOBY
Valenciennea helsdingenii (Bleeker, 1858)
Dorsal rays VI + I,11; anal rays I,11; pectoral rays 21–23; longitudinal scale series 127–146; cycloid scales extending forward on side of nape to above middle of operculum in adults; pectoral-fin base and prepelvic area of adults usually scaled; dorsal fin low and rounded, no spines prolonged; caudal fin truncate to slightly emarginate, the ray above and below the 3 central rays prolonged as a filament in adults; caudal-fin length 2.4–5.0 in standard length; gray, shading ventrally to white, with 2 narrow orange and black stripes, 1 passing through eye and 1 from upper lip, each ending in a caudal filament; a large, oval black spot rimmed above and below in white in outer posterior part of first

dorsal fin. Reported to attain 25 cm (Kuiter, 1993). Natal, Seychelles, and Maldive Islands to the Line Islands and Marquesas Islands; southern Japan to Great Barrier Reef, New South Wales, and New Caledonia; type locality, Goram Island, Indonesia. Like others of the genus, usually seen in pairs; lives in a burrow of its

own making; shell fragments and small pieces of coral rock often mark the entrance to the burrow. Depth range 1–40 m, but usually in more than 15 m; feeds by filtering small marine animals, such as copepods, ostracods, amphipods, various worms, and foraminifera, from mouthfuls of sand.

MUD-DWELLING GOBY

Valenciennea limicola Hoese & Larson, 1994

Dorsal rays VI + I,16–17; anal rays I,16–17; pectoral rays 20–21; longitudinal scale series 65–75; cycloid scales extending forward on side of nape to above middle of operculum; pectoral-fin base with a patch of scales in adults; prepelvic area scaled; dorsal fin low and rounded, no spines prolonged; caudal fin rhomboid, much longer than head, about 3 in standard length; greenish with a blue-green stripe bordered by orange on side of snout, continuing horizontally behind eye to caudal fin (faint on posterior half of body); dorsal fins with 2 pale orange stripes; roof and sides of mouth behind vomer black. Largest specimen, 8.2 cm. Known only from Suva Harbor, Fiji (type locality), New Caledonia, and the Gulf of Thailand (Hoese & Larson noted differences in the color of the specimen from Thailand). Specimens

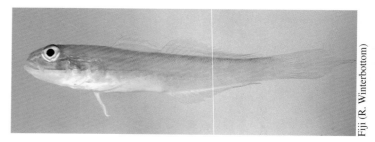
Fiji (R. Winterbottom)

were collected only from turbid areas of mud bottom (the name *limicola* means mud-dwelling), the holotype from 26 m. Hoese & Larson included an underwater photo identified as this species taken by the author at Banda, Indonesia; however, the color seems too different to be *limicola*, and the sea was clear with a bottom of sand and gravel.

LONGFIN GOBY

Valenciennea longipinnis (Lay & Bennett, 1839)

Dorsal rays VI + I,12–13 (rarely 13); anal rays I,11–13 (usually 12); pectoral rays 19–22 (rarely 19 or 22); longitudinal scale series 80–121; cycloid scales extending forward on side of nape to above middle of operculum; pectoral-fin base usually scaled in adults; prepelvic area partly or fully scaled in adults; first dorsal fin higher than second, the margin rounded with no prolonged spines; caudal fin rhomboid, much longer than head, about 2.7 in standard length; pale gray dorsally, shading to white on side and ventrally, with a midlateral series of 5 blue-edged, pink, urn-shaped spots, the center of the lower bulbous part of each with a reddish brown to black blotch; back with 3 longitudinal yellowish brown lines, the lowermost connecting the tops of urn-shaped spots; head with oblique pink lines and rows of blue spots; first dorsal fin with narrow, oblique, orangish brown bands; second dorsal with numerous dark-edged pale blue spots; caudal fin with 2 converging bands of orange spots.

Coral Sea

Attains 15 cm. Ryukyu Islands (type locality) to Western Australia and Great Barrier Reef, east to Palau, Yap, New Caledonia, Fiji, and Tonga; typically found in shallow water, generally less than 3 m, in sandy areas of lagoons and bays.

LADDER GOBY

Valenciennea parva Hoese & Larson, 1994

Dorsal rays VI + I,11–13 (rarely 11 or 13); anal rays I,11–13 (rarely 11 or 13); pectoral rays 18–20; longitudinal scale series 67–85; cycloid scales extending forward on side of nape slightly anterior to upper end of gill opening; pectoral-fin base naked; prepelvic area naked or partly scaled; margin of dorsal fin rounded, with no prolonged spines; caudal fin rounded and short, about equal to head length; greenish gray, the back sometimes mottled with brown, with 2 parallel, narrow orange stripes connected by narrow orange bars (hence ladder-shaped); an oblique, dark-edged, pale blue band from below eye to upper part of opercle; fins transparent with whitish rays, the caudal with continuations of the narrow orange body stripes. Smallest species of the genus, the largest 6.8 cm; females as small as 3.3 cm with developed ova. Seychelles and Maldive Islands to Marshall, Caroline, and

Great Barrier Reef

Samoa Islands; Ryukyu Islands to Great Barrier Reef (type locality, Lizard Island); occurs over clean sand in lagoons at depths of 1–15 m; may be seen in pairs or in small groups; when observed near its burrow, it often rocks back and forth.

MAIDEN GOBY
Valenciennea puellaris (Tomiyama, 1956)

Dorsal rays VI + I,11–13 (usually 12); anal rays I,11–13 (rarely 11, usually 12); pectoral rays 19–22 (rarely 19); longitudinal scale series 72–91; cycloid scales extending forward on side of nape to above middle of operculum; pectoral-fin base naked; prepelvic area partly to fully scaled; first dorsal fin pointed, the third spine longest, 4.6–6.4 in standard length; caudal fin rounded, 3.0–4.2 in standard length; pale gray, shading to white ventrally, with oblique orange-yellow bars or elongate spots on back, interspersed with small, faint, orange-yellow spots; an orange-yellow stripe, faintly edged in pale blue and usually containing more intense orange spots on side of body from beneath pectoral fin to lower base of caudal fin; head with round to oblong, dark-edged, pale blue spots. Reaches 14 cm. Red Sea and southern Oman to Madagascar and Mauritius, east to Caroline Islands, Samoa

Negros, Philippines

Islands, and Tonga; southern Japan (type locality, Kiragawa, Kochi Prefecture) to Great Barrier Reef and New Caledonia; usually found over moderately fine sand at depths of 10–30 m, but may occur in as little as 2 m in sheltered areas. Hoese & Larson (1994) documented the geographic color variation.

RANDALL'S GOBY
Valenciennea randalli Hoese & Larson, 1994

Dorsal rays VI + I,16–18; anal rays I,16–18; pectoral rays 19–21 (rarely 19); longitudinal scale series 76–81; cycloid scales extending forward on side of nape to above middle of opercle; pectoral-fin base and prepelvic area fully scaled in adults; first dorsal fin high and pointed, the third spine longest and prolonged in adults, 4.05–4.75 in standard length; caudal fin rhomboid, a little longer than head; light tan dorsally, shading to white ventrally, with a faint orange-yellow stripe, edged in bluish gray and broadly bordered above by white, from axil of pectoral fin to lower caudal-fin base; a pale green to yellow stripe bordered by bright blue-green, black, and orange from upper lip across head to end of opercle; a faint orange-red stripe basally in dorsal fins. Largest specimen, 10.8 cm. Indo-Malayan region north to Ryukyu Islands, south to Great Barrier Reef, New Caledonia, and Fiji; type locality, Guadalcanal, Solomon Islands. Lives over mud, silty sand, or fine sand; depth range, 8–21 m.

Fiji

SIXSPOT GOBY
Valenciennea sexguttata (Valenciennes in C & V, 1837)

Dorsal rays VI + I,11–13 (rarely 11 or 13); anal rays I,11–13 (rarely 11 or 13); pectoral rays 19–21; longitudinal scale series 71–99; small embedded cycloid scales extending forward on side of nape a short distance anterior to gill opening; pectoral-fin base naked to partly scaled; prepelvic area partly to fully scaled; first dorsal fin high and pointed, the third spine longest but not filamentous, 4.5–5.35 in standard length; caudal fin somewhat pointed, longer in males, 2.9–3.6 in standard length, in females 3.3–3.9; light gray, shading to white on side and ventrally, with a light red to pink stripe on lower side, sometimes with 4–7 pink to dusky bars extending upward from stripe, which may link with a faint pink stripe on upper side; 4–10 round to oval, iridescent, pale blue spots on cheek and opercle; a black spot at tip of membrane between third and fourth dorsal spines; anal fin with a blackish margin in adults. Reaches 14 cm. Red Sea and Persian Gulf south to Mozambique, east to Line Islands and Samoa Islands; Ryukyu Islands to Great Barrier Reef; type local-

Flores, Indonesia

ity, Sri Lanka; a shallow-water species of bays and lagoons, usually found over substrata of fine or silty sand, generally at depths of 1–10 m. Hoese & Larson (1994) discussed geographic variation. *Valenciennea violifera* Jordan & Seale is a synonym.

557

BLUESTREAK GOBY

Valenciennea strigata (Broussonet, 1782)
Dorsal rays VI + I,17–19; anal rays I,16–19 (usually 17); pectoral rays 20–23; longitudinal scale series 101–126; small embedded cycloid scales extending forward on side of nape to above or a little before middle of opercle; pectoral-fin base and prepelvic area fully scaled; second and third dorsal spines prolonged to filaments in individuals larger than about 4.5 cm; fourth spines filamentous to a lesser extent at a slightly larger size; caudal fin rounded, a little longer than head; gray to pale gray or white ventrally, with a narrow, bright blue stripe, narrowly edged in black and yellow from above corner of mouth across head to upper edge of opercle; curved blue lines ventrally on head; front of head yellowish in adults, bright yellow in subadults and juveniles; 2 faint pink stripes in caudal fin. Reaches 18 cm. East coast of Africa to the Line Islands, Society

WARD'S GOBY

Valenciennea wardii (Playfair in Playfair & Günther, 1867)
Dorsal rays VI + I,11–12 (rarely 11); anal rays I,11–12 (usually 12); pectoral rays 19–22 (usually 20 or 21); longitudinal scale series 70–88; small scales extending forward on side of nape a little anterior to gill opening; pectoral-fin base usually scaled, and prepelvic area fully scaled; margin of dorsal fin rhomboid, the third to fifth spines subequal, 4.5–5.85 in standard length; caudal fin rounded, equal to or a little shorter than head; white with 3 broad, orangish brown bars with blackish margins dorsally on body; a short, dusky to blackish bar dorsally in each pale interspace; head brownish gray with a narrow, oblique, black-edged blue band from behind corner of mouth to opercle; first dorsal with a large black ocellus posteriorly in outer part of fin; caudal fin with a black bar at base and a black spot dorsally and ventrally. Largest specimen, 12.3 cm. Known from

Papua New Guinea/subadult

New Britain

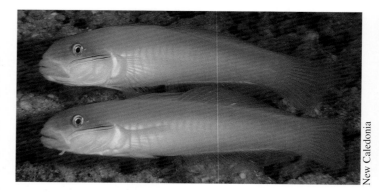

New Caledonia

Islands (type locality, Tahiti), and Tuamotu Archipelago; Ryukyu Islands to Great Barrier Reef, Lord Howe Island, and New South Wales; unlike others of the genus, occurs on seaward reefs, often in 1–6 m, though known to at least 24 m.

Gulf of Aqaba, Red Sea

Red Sea, Zanzibar (type locality), Maldive Islands, India, Thailand, Vietnam, Western Australia, China, southern Japan, Great Barrier Reef, and New Caledonia; most specimens taken by trawls.

AMBANORO SHRIMPGOBY

Vanderhorstia ambanoro (Fourmanoir, 1957)
Dorsal rays VI + I,13; anal rays I,13; pectoral rays 17–18; longitudinal scale series 73–85; scales cycloid; no scales on head or nape; body elongate, the depth 5.5–6.4 in standard length; first dorsal fin low and rounded, the fourth and fifth spines longest, about half head length; caudal fin with upper and lower margins converging posteriorly but ending in a near-truncate posterior margin, the fin about equal to head length or a little longer; pelvic fins united, the frenum well developed, not reaching anus; light gray-brown dorsally, shading to whitish ventrally, with a row of 5 or 6 dark brown to black spots of near-pupil size along upper side of body, often with lesser spots between; a second row of smaller spots above, and a third row along base of dorsal fins; several prominent black spots on occiput and behind eye; a reddish brown to black band bordered below and sometimes above by blue at margins of dorsal fins, and a similar oblique band in upper part of caudal fin. Largest specimen examined, 7.3 cm. Collected or photographed by the author in Red Sea, Kenya, Maldive Islands, Indonesia, Papua New Guinea, Solomon Islands, Palau, and Marshall Islands; type locality, Ambanoro Bay, Madagascar; known also from Caroline Islands, Mariana Islands, Samoa Islands, Tonga, and New Caledonia; occurs on silty sand in protected environments; shares a burrow with an alpheid shrimp; often seen hovering above the burrow entrance.

BLACKBLOTCHED SHRIMPGOBY
Vanderhorstia sp.

Dorsal rays VI-I,13–14 (usually 13); anal rays I,13; pectoral rays 18; longitudinal scale series 52–55; scales cycloid, none on head, nape, or pectoral-fin base; body elongate, the depth about 6 in standard length; third dorsal spine elongate and filamentous; caudal fin somewhat pointed, much longer than head; whitish with dark pigment on many scales, especially on upper half of body; 5 dark blotches in midlateral series on body, the first beneath pectoral fin, the last at caudal-fin base, the black pigment obscuring pale, blue-edged, orange double spots beneath; pale orange and blue spots between dark blotches more visible; head with oblique elongate spots or lines of blue and dusky yellow; base of dorsal fins with irregular, dusky yellow and black-edged, pale blue markings; anal fin blackish with a white band at base; caudal fin dusky yellow with a white-edged, dark red arc. Attains about

New Caledonia

7 cm. Distribution uncertain pending further study, but at least Great Barrier Reef to New Caledonia and Tonga; also appears to be the same in Palau and Guam (Myers, 1999: pl. 155 B); symbiotic with alpheid shrimps. Often misidentified as *V. ornatissima* Smith, which lacks the longiudinal row of 5 dark blotches and has a different pattern of blue-edged, pale orange spots (for color photos of *ornatissima*, see Allen & Steene, 1987: pl. 114, fig. 8; or Myers, 1999: pl. 155, fig. A).

SHADOW GOBY
Yongeichthys criniger (Valenciennes in C & V, 1837)

Dorsal rays VI + I,9; anal rays I,9; pectoral rays 17–19; longitudinal scale series 29–30; head naked; scales ctenoid except ventroanteriorly on abdomen, chest, pectoral-fin base, and lower side of nape, where small and cycloid; usually no median predorsal scales, but there may be 1 or 2 just before origin of first dorsal fin; gill opening not reaching a vertical at posterior margin of preopercle; a horizontal band of small sensory papillae across head from corner of mouth; body depth 3.2–3.4 in standard length; head length 3.2–3.4 in standard length; second dorsal spine elongate and filamentous, as is third spine and sometimes the fourth to a lesser extent; caudal fin rounded, a little shorter than head; pelvic fins united, the frenum well developed; light gray, densely blotched with dark brown, white ventrally; 3 large, dark brown blotches in a row along midside of body, the third at base of caudal fin; dorsal and caudal fins with brownish

Flores, Indonesia

orange spots on rays. Reported to 18 cm. Oman to Caroline Islands and Samoa Islands; Ryukyu Islands to Great Barrier Reef and New Caledonia; described from India and New Guinea. Lives on silty sand or mud bottom, including mangrove areas; takes refuge in a burrow. People have been poisoned in Japan and Taiwan from eating this goby (Noguchi et al., 1971). The toxin is strongest in the skin; Noguchi & Hashimoto (1973) demonstrated that it is tetrodotoxin.

SLEEPERS
(ELEOTRIDAE)

This family is closely allied to the Gobiidae, and several characters are shared, such as 2 separate dorsal fins and the absence of a lateral line. The principal basis for separating the families used to be the structure of the pelvic fins; if the pelvics of a fish were completely separate, it was classified as an eleotrid. We now know that many gobies have pelvic fins completely divided, some within genera containing species with the pelvics forming a typical disc. One consistent difference is the number of branchiostegal rays, 5 for Gobiidae and 6 for Eleotridae. Also the eleotrids never have a ventral mouth; usually the lower jaw is projecting. The great majority of species occur in freshwater or brackish habitats, though many have larval stages that develop in sea. Only 2 marine species are known for the South Pacific area.

female (R. Winterbottom)

TAILFACE SLEEPER
Calumia godeffroyi (Günther, 1877)

Dorsal rays VI + I,6–7; anal rays I,6–7; pectoral rays 16–17; pelvic rays I,5, the rays branched; longitudinal scale series 21–23; predorsal scales 7–9 (usually 7); cheek and opercle scaled, and an enlarged scale between eyes (generic); scales on body ctenoid, those on head cycloid; head broad and depressed; dorsal profile straight, the interorbital space slightly concave; no pores on head (generic); mouth short, the maxilla reaching to below anterior edge of orbit; tip of tongue pointed to slightly rounded; gill opening extending forward to below posterior margin of preopercle; dorsal and anal fins short-based but long (generic); third and fourth dorsal spines longest; caudal fin rounded, shorter than head; pale brown with 5 dark brown bars on body and a dark brown saddle on nape; median fins blackish, the caudal with 2 large black spots at base, one above the other. Attains 3.6 cm. East Africa to the Society Islands (type locality); also known from Great Barrier Reef, Papua New Guinea (collected by the author from a lagoon reef near Madang in 2 m), Mariana Islands, Pohnpei in the Caroline Islands, and Christmas Island in the Indian Ocean. *Calumia biocellata* Smith from Zanzibar is a synonym, as shown by Larson & Hoese (1980).

Fiji

WRIGGLERS
(XENISTHMIDAE)

The fishes of this small Indo-Pacific fish family have been classified previously in the Gobiidae, Eleotridae, and Microdesmidae. Springer (1983) regarded them as a subfamily within Gobiidae; however, Hoese in Moser et al. (1984) elevated the group to a family. These fishes differ from gobies in having a free ventral margin on the lower lip, 6 branchiostegal rays, the ascending process of the premaxilla absent or rudimentary, plus other osteological characters. They are elongate with a small depressed head and strongly oblique mouth. The dorsal and anal fins are relatively low, the first dorsal with VI spines (except the monotypic genus *Rotuma* with V, and the monotypic *Tyson* with none), and the second dorsal fin with a spine and 10–13 rays; the pelvic fins are separated. All wrigglers are small, none exceeding 4.5 cm; typically they live in sand patches adjacent to or within coral reefs. The family consists of five genera and about 20 species.

Marshall Islands

BIGMOUTH SLEEPER
Calumia profunda Larson & Hoese, 1980
Dorsal rays VI + I,6–7; anal rays I,7; pectoral rays 14–15; pelvic rays I,5, the rays unbranched; longitudinal scale series 24–25; predorsal scales 8; cheek and opercle scaled; scales on body ctenoid, those on head cycloid; lower-limb gill rakers 13–14; head broad and depressed; dorsal profile straight, the interorbital space slightly concave; mouth large, the maxilla reaching to below posterior half of pupil; tip of tongue bilobed; gill opening extending forward to below posterior half of pupil; second dorsal spine longest; pale gray, the scale edges dark, with 7 dark bars on body broader than pale interspaces (bars often with yellow vertical markings); dorsal and anal fins with a broad, submarginal, yellow or orange band; caudal fin variably brown and orange-yellow. Largest specimen, 2.2 cm. Described from the Solomon Islands (type locality) and Vanuatu; later collected by the author in Flores and Sulawesi, Indonesia. Named *profunda* from the type specimens being found in 38–55 m. Richard L. Pyle extended the depth range to 76 m from a collection made in Papua New Guinea; however, David W. Greenfield and the author recently obtained specimens from 18 m in Fiji.

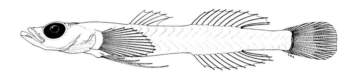

(after Springer, 1988)

LEWIS' WRIGGLER
Rotuma lewisi Springer, 1988
Dorsal rays V + I,9; anal rays I,9; pectoral rays 16, none branched; pelvic rays I,5, the spine and fifth soft ray vestigial; branched caudal rays 11; no scales on head or body; body slender, the depth about 7.5 in standard length; mouth oblique, the lower jaw strongly protruding; first dorsal fin low, the fourth and fifth spines longest, about 2.5 in head length; caudal fin rounded and short, about 1.4 in head length; no color markings evident in preservative; live color unknown. Described from 2 specimens from Rotuma (12°30′S, 177°E), the largest 2.3 cm; holotype collected from an isolated patch reef in 10.7 m.

BLACKSTRIPED WRIGGLER
Xenisthmus clarus (Jordan & Seale, 1906)
Dorsal rays V + I,12; anal rays I,11; pectoral rays 17; pelvic rays I,5; branched caudal rays 13; longitudinal scale series about 65; predorsal scales 19; no scales on head; body slender, the depth 5.5–6.5 in standard length; mouth oblique, the lower jaw strongly protruding; first dorsal fin about equal in height to second, the third and fourth spines longest, about 2.7 in head length; caudal fin rounded, nearly equal to head length; white with a brown stripe crossing lips, passing through eye and across head (where narrow and dark brown), becoming broad and diffuse across lower side of body to caudal fin; median fins translucent, the caudal with a median white stripe nearly reaching end of fin and 2 or more blackish blotches. Described from Tutuila, American Samoa; also known from the Marshall Islands (specimens from the outer reef flat of Enewetak Atoll), Ryukyu Islands, and northern Australia. Largest specimen, 3 cm.

BARRED WRIGGLER
Xenisthmus polyzonatus (Klunzinger, 1871)

Dorsal rays V + I,11; anal rays I,10; pectoral rays 15–17; pelvic rays I,5; branched caudal rays 13; longitudinal scale series about 60 (scales partially embedded and difficult to count); predorsal scales about 20, extending to above posterior margin of preopercle; cheek and opercle scaled; scales ctenoid posterior to pectoral fins; body slender, the depth 5.3–6.8 in standard length; mouth oblique, the lower jaw very strongly protruding; first dorsal fin lower than second, the fifth spine longest, about 2.7 in head length; caudal fin rounded, a little shorter than head length; body orange-red with 12 narrow, irregular, pale gray bars (sometimes dark-edged), shading to pale orange ventrally; a narrow red bar below eye; a black spot nearly as large as eye at midbase of cau-

Fiji

dal fin, rimmed in white or yellow, at least anteriorly; before that an arc of bright orange-red. Largest specimen examined, 3.1 cm. Reported from the Red Sea (type locality), Maldive Islands, Chagos Archipelago, Ryukyu Islands, and American Samoa; collections by the author include ones from Maldive Islands, Papua New Guinea, Chesterfield Bank (Coral Sea), Fiji, and Tonga, all from lagoon reefs in 9–24 m.

SAND DARTS
(KRAEMERIIDAE)

This is another small Indo-Pacific fish family with species that have been placed previously in other families, in this case the Gobiidae, Eleotridae, and the Trichonotidae. Gosline (1955) correctly classified the group in the suborder Gobioidei. Rofen (1958) gave it family status; in his review he recognized 2 genera and 7 species, 2 of which occur in the South Pacific. The record of *Kraemeria bryani* Schultz from the Society Islands in a checklist by Randall (1985a) may be in error, because no material of this species has been found in the Bishop Museum. These small fishes are elongate and scaleless; they have a strongly protruding lower jaw, the chin large and pointed; the eyes are small, oriented as much dorsally as laterally; there are 5 branchiostegal rays; the tongue is strongly bilobed; the dorsal fin is continuous, with IV-VI weak spines and 13–17 soft rays; the anal fin has a weak spine and 11–14 soft rays; the dorsal and anal soft rays are not branched; the pectoral fins are small, with 3–9 rays; principal caudal rays 11; pelvic fins I,5, the fins fully united only in the monotypic genus *Gobitrichinotus*. These fishes live in shallow sandy habitats. Like the sandburrowers, they hide in sand, usually with just the top of their head or eyes visible.

SAMOAN SAND DART
Kraemeria samoensis Steindachner, 1906

Dorsal rays VI,14, the spinous and soft portions broadly separated but fully linked by membrane; gap between fifth and sixth spines broader than that between previous spines; anal rays I,13; pectoral rays 7–9, usually all branched; pelvic fins separated to base, the rays branched; lower edge of gill cover with 10 cirri instead of a scalloped margin; body depth 8.5–10.2 in standard length; head length 3.9–4.3 in standard length; interorbital space very narrow, less than one-half orbit diameter; pale (probably transparent in life) with a scattering of melanophores dorsally on head; Marshall Islands specimens with a dark streak from lower edge of eye. Largest specimen, 3.1 cm. Reported from the east

(after Rofen, 1958)

coast of Africa, Chagos Archipelago, Marshall Islands, and the Samoa Islands (type locality). Smith (1959a) and Winterbottom & Emery (1986) collected their specimens from beach sand where freshwater streams entered the sea, the fish always facing upstream; Smith reported some as feeding on polychaete worms. He placed *Kraemeria nuda* (Regan) from the Seychelles in the synonymy of *K. samoensis*.

TONGAN SAND DART
Kraemeria tongaensis Rofen, 1958

Dorsal rays VI,14 (with a broad gap between the fifth and sixth spines); anal rays I,13; pectoral rays 8, the fourth to seventh branched; lower one-fifth of pelvic fins joined by membrane, all rays branched; edge of suborbital fold, lower edge of preopercle, and ventral edge of gill cover scalloped; body depth about 8 in standard length; head length about 4.0 in standard length; probably transparent in life; only dark pigment in preservative, a few small pigment spots in a diffuse streak in front of the eye. Described from a single 3-cm specimen from the shore of Namuka Island, Tonga; known otherwise only from Ishigaki, Ryukyu Islands (Hayashi in Masuda et al., 1984).

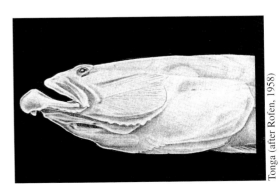

Tonga (after Rofen, 1958)

WORMFISHES
(MICRODESMIDAE)

Recent authors have included the dartfishes (*Ptereleotris* and allied genera) with the wormfishes in the Microdesmidae (Hoese in Moser et al., 1984); however, Thacker (2000) separated them as the family Ptereleotridae, and she is followed here. Externally there is some similarity in the 2 groups, but osteological characters such as the presence of a posterior pelvic process in the ptereleotrids and its absence in microdesmids, and 42–76 vertebrae for the Microdesmidae compared with 26 for the Ptereleotridae indicate separation at the family level. The wormfishes consist of 5 genera, of which only *Gunnellichthys* and *Paragunnellichthys* have species in the Indo-Pacific region. The microdesmids have extremely elongate and compressed bodies with small, embedded, often non-overlapping cycloid scales; the head is partially scaled; there is no lateral line; the gill opening is restricted to the side; the mouth is strongly oblique, the lower jaw heavy and protruding. There is a long, low, continuous dorsal fin with X-XXVIII flexible spines and 28–66 soft rays, and a long anal fin with no spine and 23–61 soft rays; the pelvic fins are small, with a spine and 2–4 rays, inserted beneath the pectoral fins. There are 15–17 principal caudal rays, the fin of some species joined to the dorsal and anal fins. Wormfishes are agile, eel-like, and secretive. They are closely associated with sand or mud bottoms, either burrowing or burrow-inhabiting in the sediment. None is known to reach 30 cm in length, and they seldom exceed 20 cm.

CURIOUS WORMFISH
Gunnellichthys curiosus Dawson, 1968

Dorsal rays XX-XXI,40–42; anal rays 38–40; pectoral rays 14–15; pelvic rays I,4; vertebrae 58; scales dorsally on head to nostrils; cheek and opercle scaled; body very elongate, the depth 10–13 in standard length, and compressed, the width about half the depth; lower jaw massive and strongly projecting (true of other species of genus); dorsal-fin low (also generic), the origin above anterior one-third of pectoral fin; caudal fin rounded; pelvic fins about 1.5 times longer than orbit diameter; light blue dorsally, white ventrally, with a dusky orange stripe from front of lower jaw through eye and across head, becoming bright orange on body, broadening posteriorly where it covers more than ventral half of body, and ending in a large, elliptical black spot on basal half of caudal fin; a small black spot within orange stripe posteriorly on opercle. Largest specimen, 11.5 cm. Described from a single specimen from Curieuse Island in the Seychelles

Flores, Indonesia

(so the scientific name is not based on the fish being curious); now known to be widely distributed in the Indo-Pacific to the Hawaiian Islands and Society Islands and southern Japan to the Great Barrier Reef and New Caledonia; occurs on seaward reefs from depths of 9–60 m, sometimes in pairs. Difficult to approach; either retreats or pops down a burrow (also true for other species). Reported to feed on both zooplankton and small benthic crustaceans.

ONESPOT WORMFISH
Gunnellichthys monostigma Smith, 1958

Dorsal rays XXI,36–40; anal rays 36–41; pectoral rays 14–15; pelvic rays I,4; vertebrae 58; no scales on head; body elongate, the depth 10–13 in standard length, and compressed; gill opening ending a short distance below pectoral-fin base; dorsal-fin origin a little anterior to upper end of gill opening; caudal fin slightly rounded to rhomboid; pelvic fins about twice orbit diameter in length; whitish with a yellow to orange lateral stripe variously develped (in white sand areas, the stripe is only faint on posterior half of body; in darker habitats, stripe is full length of head and body and continues to end of caudal fin); a prominent, elliptical black spot posteriorly on opercle; iridescent blue lines on head. Reaches 11 cm. Red Sea (Randall & Shen, 2001) and East Africa (type locality, Pinda, Mozambique) to Society Islands, Marquesas Islands, and islands of Micronesia; Ryukyu Islands to Great Barrier Reef and New Caledonia. Strasburg (1967) reported the species common in the lagoon of Enewetak Atoll in 2–6 m, where it hovers 20–30 cm above the sand; when approached, the fish dives into a burrow in the sand. He found

Papua New Guinea

them in colonies with their burrows about a meter apart. He placed 3 in an aquarium with 30 cm of sand in the bottom, expecting them to construct a burrow; but they did not. He then placed glass tubes in the sand, which they readily accepted as sanctuaries. Stomach contents of 10 specimens yielded amphipods, harpacticoid copepods, pelagic copepods, ostracods, shrimps, and crab fragments; Strasburg concluded that the species feeds on both pelagic and benthic crustaceans.

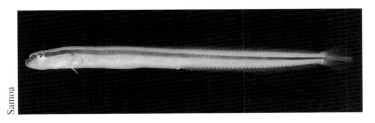

Samoa

BROWNSTRIPE WORMFISH
Gunnellichthys pleurotaenia Bleeker, 1858
Dorsal rays XX-XXI,38–41; anal rays 36–40; pectoral rays 12–13; pelvic rays I,4; vertebrae about 60 (Smith, 1958); head partly scaled; body very elongate, the depth 11.5–16 in standard length, and compressed; dorsal-fin origin slightly posterior to pectoral-fin base; caudal fin rounded; pelvic fins small, about 1.5 times longer than orbit diameter; whitish with a brown to dusky orange stripe, narrower than pupil diameter, from front of upper jaw through eye and across body, narrowing posteriorly to end at midbase of caudal fin; stripe continuous with a broader median orange stripe in caudal fin. Attains 9 cm. East coast of Africa to the Samoa Islands and islands of Micronesia; Ryukyu Islands to the Great Barrier Reef; type locality, Manado, Sulawesi. Swims by sinuous movement of the body (as is typical for the genus); found more often over sandy substrata with algae and seagrass than on reefs.

Papua New Guinea

YELLOWSTRIPED WORMFISH
Gunnellichthys viridescens Dawson, 1968
Dorsal rays XX-XXI,38–41; anal rays 36–40; pectoral rays 12–13; pelvic rays I,4; vertebrae 57–59; cheek and opercle scaled; body very elongate, the depth 12–16 in standard length, and compressed; dorsal-fin origin slightly posterior to pectoral-fin base; caudal fin rounded, its length 1.5 in head length; pelvic fins small, about equal in length to eye diameter; whitish to pale blue with a narrow, dark-edged yellow stripe from front of lower jaw, across snout, through eye, and continuing along side of body to end of caudal fin. Largest specimen, 7.2 cm. Known from the Persian Gulf, Seychelles (type locality), Maldive Islands, Great Barrier Reef, New Caledonia, and islands of Micronesia except the Marianas. Usually found over sand, algal flats, or seagrass beds from depths of about 5–50 m.

DARTFISHES
(PTERELEOTRIDAE)

As mentioned in the preceding family account, the dartfishes are now recognized as a family instead of a subfamily of the Microdesmidae (Thacker, 2000). These fishes are also elongate, though not to the degree of the more slender microdesmids, and they have a similar oblique mouth and projecting lower jaw, 5 branchiostegal rays, no lateral line, and small, embedded, often nonoverlapping, cycloid scales (except for 2 species with a few weakly ctenoid scales posteriorly). Noteworthy differences from the wormfishes include a naked head, a divided dorsal fin (except *Ptereleotris monoptera*), with IV-VI flexible spines and 9–39 soft rays; anal fin with a spine and 9–36 soft rays, and 26 vertebrae. The family includes 5 genera: *Ptereleotris, Nemateleotris, Parioglossus, Oxymetopon,* and *Ailiops*. The first 3 have species that occur in the South Pacific islands covered by this book. Dartfishes move higher in the water column than wormfishes, where they feed on zooplankton; they are difficult to approach underwater. The best photographic opportunity is when they are hovering above their burrow. One has to approach very gradually and make no sharp movement to get closer. Usually the fish dart head-first into the burrow with

Smallscale Dartfish, *Ptereleotris microlepis,* Guam

incredible rapidity before photographic range is attained. The burrow is not of their own making; it may be the burrow of a shrimpgoby where they are unwelcome guests. *Nemateleotris* was revised by Randall & Allen (1973), *Ptereleotris* by Randall & Hoese (1985), and *Parioglossus* by Rennis & Hoese (1985).

563

Halmahera, Indonesia

Marshall Islands

ELEGANT DARTFISH

Nemateleotris decora Randall & Allen, 1973

Dorsal rays VI + I,27–32; anal rays I,28–31; pectoral rays 20–21; pelvic rays I,5; longitudinal scale series about 135–160; body depth 4.8–5.7 in standard length; a low fleshy ridge on head (true of other species of *Nemateleotris*); elongate anterior part of first dorsal fin variable in length, 2.5–5.4 in standard length; caudal fin slightly emarginate with rounded lobes, 4.7–5.6 in standard length; body whitish anteriorly, gradually shading to deep purple posteriorly; head whitish except lips, snout, and a broad, median dorsal band that are violet; elevated anterior part of first dorsal fin orange-red, the leading edge magenta; median fins colored like body basally, then mainly orange-red with magenta bands and spots; caudal fin broadly purple medially, the lobes orange-red with purple streaks. Largest specimen, 8.3 cm. Red Sea (Randall & Shen, 2001) and islands of the western Indian Ocean to western Pacific from Ryukyu Islands to Great Barrier Reef, east to New Caledonia, Caroline Islands, and southern Marshall Islands; type locality, Palau. Generally found on seaward rubble slopes, often in pairs occupying the same hole for shelter; depth range, 27–67.5 m.

FIRE DARTFISH

Nemateleotris magnifica Fowler, 1938

Dorsal rays VI + I,28–32; anal rays I,27–30; pectoral rays 19–20; pelvic rays I,5; longitudinal scale series about 110–130; body depth 4.4–4.9 in standard length; anterior part of first dorsal fin extremely long and filamentous, 1.2–2.0 in standard length; caudal fin rounded, 3.5–4.2 in standard length; body whitish anteriorly, gradually shading to red in middle of body and to blackish red on caudal peduncle; head yellow anteriorly with a median violet and pale blue band from interorbital to origin of first dorsal fin; pale blue spots on cheek and opercle; first dorsal fin white with small, pale blue spots at base, the leading edge red and blue; caudal fin blackish red with 2 converging, narrow, dark olive bands. Reaches 8 cm. East Africa to the Hawaiian Islands (where rare) and Pitcairn Islands; Ryukyu Islands to New South Wales; type locality, Gulf of Tomini, Sulawesi. Reported from depths of 6–61 m, but not often seen deeper than 30 m; feeds on zooplankton, primarily copepods and crustacean larvae; does not stray far from its burrow; may be seen as solitary fish or in pairs.

HELFRICH'S DARTFISH

Nemateleotris helfrichi Randall & Allen, 1973

Dorsal rays VI + I,29–31; anal rays I,26–28; pectoral rays 20–21; pelvic rays I,5; longitudinal scale series about 140–160; body depth 4.9–5.6 in standard length; elongate anterior part of first dorsal fin variable in length, 2.3–3.5 in standard length; caudal fin slightly emarginate with rounded lobes, 4.5–5.5 in standard length; lavender, gradually shading posteriorly nearly to white and anteriorly on head to bright yellow; top of head from interorbital to origin of first dorsal fin with a narrowing band of bright magenta, merging with violet on dorsoanterior quadrant of iris; elevated anterior part of first dorsal fin orange and black with a broad, pale blue leading edge; rays of second dorsal and anal fins tipped with yellow or orange; caudal fin pale yellow. Largest specimen, 6.3 cm. Ryukyu Islands and Ogasawara Islands, islands of Micronesia and Polynesia except the Hawaiian Islands and Pitcairn Islands; type locality, Tahiti. Reported from depths of 29–69 m; rare in less than 40 m; typically found on steep seaward-reef slopes over rubble and sand substrata.

Sulawesi

A popular aquarium fish, like others of the genus. Constantly flicks its long first dorsal fin a short distance fore and aft. Senou & Ota (2002) illustrated a hybrid of *Nemateleotris decora* and *N. magnifica* from the Ryukyu Islands.

CRESTED DARTFISH
Parioglossus formosus (Smith, 1931)
Dorsal rays V-VI (rarely V) + I,13–15; anal rays I,13–15; pectoral rays 15–17; pelvic fins separated, the rays I,4 (true of all species of *Parioglossus*); branched caudal rays 13; longitudinal scale series 66–78; gill rakers 3–4 + 12–14; body moderately elongate, the depth about 5.5 in standard length (also generic); nuchal crest prominent in males, a low fold in females; third and fourth dorsal spines prolonged in males, not in females; caudal fin truncate to slightly emarginate in females, pointed and bilobed in males, the lower lobe longer; brown, shading to white ventrally, with a broad dark stripe from eye along lower side of body to end of lower part of caudal fin; a second median dorsal stripe from head, ending in upper part of caudal fin. Largest specimen, 4.6 cm. Indo-Malayan region north to Ryukyu Islands, south to Western Australia and southern Queensland, east to Palau, Vanuatu, and Fiji; type locality, Gulf of Thailand; occurs on shallow sheltered reefs and mangrove habitats, often in small aggregations.

NAKED DARTFISH
Parioglossus nudus Rennis & Hoese, 1985
Dorsal rays VI + I,15–18; anal rays I,16–17; pectoral rays 16–18; branched caudal rays 11; no scales on head or body; no head pores; gill rakers 1–3 + 10–12; nuchal crest low in both sexes; first dorsal fin low, without prolonged spines; caudal fin slightly forked; life color unknown; in preservative pale with a dusky patch on midside of caudal peduncle and base of caudal fin; a diffuse dark band on edge of preopercle; a dusky area below eye

RAO'S DARTFISH
Parioglossus raoi (Herre, 1939)
Dorsal rays VI + I,14–16; anal rays I,16–17; pectoral rays 14–16; branched caudal rays usually 13; longitudinal scale series 70–85; gill rakers 3–4 + 12–14; nuchal crest present in both sexes, higher in males; third and fourth dorsal spines prolonged in males, not in females; caudal fin of females truncate to slightly emarginate, of males more emarginate, the lobes about equal or the lower a little longer; yellow to brown with a black stripe as narrow as or narrower than pupil from eye along lower part of body, curving up to end of lower lobe of caudal fin; another black stripe in upper part of caudal fin; a large, bright blue spot on first dorsal fin between fifth and sixth spines. Largest specimen, 3.4 cm. Andaman Islands (type locality), southern Ryukyu Islands, Philippines, Indonesia, New Guinea, Pohnpei, Fiji, and Tonga; occurs in shallow mangrove areas and along protected rocky shores. Randall (1995a) extended the range to the Gulf of Oman and Persian Gulf; this population lacks the blue spot in the dorsal fin and warrants further study.

and as a band from eye to upper lip. Largest specimen, 2.7 cm. Known from the Philippines, Palau (type locality), Papua New Guinea, Solomon Islands, and Fiji; collected from coral reefs in 5–37 m.

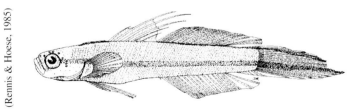

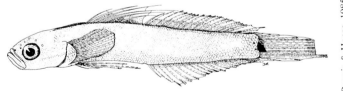

STRIPED DARTFISH
Parioglossus taeniatus Regan, 1912
Dorsal rays VI + I,14–16; anal rays I,15–16; pectoral rays 16–19 (rarely 19); branched caudal rays 13; longitudinal scale series 76–86; gill rakers 3–4 + 13–15; nuchal crest present in both sexes, higher in male; second to fourth dorsal spines prolonged and filamentous in males; third dorsal spine longest in females, but not prolonged; caudal fin round to slightly emarginate in females, the lobes elongate in males; life color not reported; a narrow dark stripe from eye to end of lower caudal lobe, the upper edge of stripe along midline of side of body; an oblique dark bar across upper part of caudal fin. Largest specimen, 3.4 cm. Recorded from Aldabra (type locality), Philippines, Palau, Vanuatu, and Fiji, in silty sand of estuaries and mangroves.

TRIANGLESPOT DARTFISH
Parioglossus triquetrus Rennis & Hoese, 1985
Dorsal rays VI + I,15–17; anal rays I,15–17; pectoral rays 17–19; branched caudal rays 13; longitudinal scale series 83–95; gill rakers 2–4 + 11–14; nuchal crest a low fold in both sexes; third to fifth dorsal spines prolonged and filamentous in males over 20 mm standard length, none prolonged in females; caudal fin truncate in females, also in males except for a prolongation of the thirteenth and fourteenth rays in individuals longer than 18 mm standard length; a black, triangular (occasionally rectangular) spot at base of sixth to eleventh caudal rays; a median dorsal brown line from snout along back to base of caudal fin. Largest specimen, 2.9 cm. Known only from mangroves of Fiji to 1.5 m.

Palau

Oman

(Rennis & Hoese, 1985)

(Rennis & Hoese, 1985)

(Rennis & Hoese, 1985)

Marshall Islands/juvenile

Maldive Islands

Line Islands/subadult

Negros, Philippines

Gunung Api, Indonesia

TWOTONE DARTFISH

Ptereleotris evides (Jordan & Hubbs, 1925)

Dorsal rays VI + I,23–26 (rarely 23); anal rays I,23–26 (rarely 26); pectoral rays 21–24; pelvic fins separated, the rays I,4 (true of all *Ptereleotris*); scales very small, cycloid (except for a few posteriorly that may have 1 or 2 weak cteni), mostly embedded, and nonoverlapping (also generic); body depth 5.2–6.9 in standard length; anterior part of second dorsal and anal fins elevated, the longest ray 1.2–1.4 in head length; first dorsal fin lower than second and without prolonged spines; caudal fin emarginate; pale bluish to greenish gray, gradually shading to black posteriorly; iridescent blue markings on operculum; lobes of caudal fin blackish to dark reddish, the broad centroposterior region whitish or pale yellowish; first dorsal fin yellow distally; second dorsal and anal fins blackish with black margins; juveniles with a large, oval black spot ventrally on posterior caudal peduncle and caudal-fin base. Largest examined, 13.8 cm. Red Sea and east coast of Africa to the Line, Society, Austral, and Pitcairn Islands; Japan (type locality, Wakanoura) to Great Barrier Reef, New South Wales, Lord Howe Island, and New Caledonia. Typical habitat exposed outer-reef areas in 2–15 m; adults usually seen in pairs, and juveniles in aggregations. More than others of the genus, this species tends to swim away from danger rather than rush to the vicinity of its burrow. *Ptereleotris tricolor* Smith from Mozambique is a synonym.

THREADFIN DARTFISH

Ptereleotris hanae (Jordan & Snyder, 1901)

Dorsal rays VI + I,24–26; anal rays I,22–25; pectoral rays 21–24; body depth 6.45–8.0 in standard length; a median, broad-based, retrorse barbel on chin, followed by a row of 3–5 very small barbels (may be only bumps); first dorsal fin about equal to highest part of second dorsal except for the prolonged second spine of some individuals; caudal fin slightly rounded, occasionally truncate centrally, adults with 2–6 trailing filaments (longest filament may be two-thirds or more of the standard length); pale blue to light bluish gray with a narrow, pale salmon pink stripe posteriorly on lower side of body (pink stripe may be contained with a broad, dark bluish stripe that extends full length of body); a light red to violet bar, usually edged in bright blue, at lower pectoral-fin base. Reaches 12 cm (not including caudal filaments). Southern Japan (type locality) to Western Australia, Great Barrier Reef, and New South Wales, east to islands of Micronesia, Line Islands, and Samoa Islands; adults often seen in pairs occupying the same burrow. Randall & Hoese (1985) discussed the possibility that 2 different species are being identified as *Ptereleotris hanae*.

SPOTTAIL DARTFISH

Ptereleotris heteroptera (Bleeker, 1855)

Dorsal rays VI + I,29–33; anal rays I,27–30; pectoral rays 21–24; body depth 6.2–7.8 in standard length; first dorsal fin nearly as high as second, the third and fourth spines longest, but not prolonged, 1.9–2.4 in head length; caudal fin emarginate with rounded corners; light blue to pale bluish gray; caudal fin whitish to yellow with a large, oval, dusky to black spot (faint or absent in juveniles); a faint, narrow, salmon pink bar, edged in blue, at pectoral-fin base. Largest specimen, 12 cm. Red Sea south to Natal, east to the Hawaiian Islands, Line Islands, Marquesas Islands, and Society Islands; Ryukyu Islands to Great Barrier Reef and New South Wales; type locality, Banjarmasin, Borneo. Collected from depths of 7–46 m; usually found on sand-rubble substrata near reefs; sometimes observed in aggregations, especially juveniles and subadults that often share the same burrow.

BLACKBARBEL DARTFISH
Ptereleotris melanopogon Randall & Hoese, 1985
Dorsal rays VI + I,26–28; anal rays I,23–25; pectoral rays 22–23; body depth 6.1–7.2 in standard length; a prominent median barbel on chin, followed by a median row of 3–4 small barbels (may be only small bumps on juveniles); first dorsal fin with second spine filamentous, varying from 2.7–5.4 in standard length; rest of fin equal in maximum height to second dorsal fin; caudal fin broadly rounded, 3.8–4.9 in standard length; pale bluish gray with a poorly defined, broad, dark brown stripe from behind eye along lower side of body to end of caudal fin (stripe black in caudal fin); stripe on body of juveniles and subadults narrower, darker, and more distinct; a broad blackish bar from eye across corner of mouth onto chin; barbel on chin black; a curved orange-red spot at lower pectoral-fin base. Largest specimen, 16.2 cm. Known only from the Marquesas Islands; collected from sand or sand and rubble bottoms in 21.5–41.5 m.

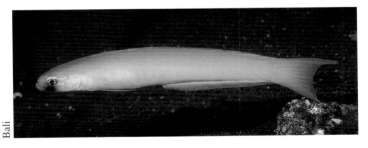

MONOFIN DARTFISH
Ptereleotris monoptera Randall & Hoese, 1985
Dorsal rays VI + I,35–39; anal rays I,33–37; pectoral rays 23–25; body depth 6.05–7.05 in standard length; no barbel on chin; dorsal fin low and continuous with only a slight indentation between spinous and soft portions, the soft portion a little higher than spinous; caudal fin emarginate, the corners narrowing to short filaments in adults; pale greenish yellow with a large, diffuse blue area on side of abdomen; a broad blackish bar below eye; iridescent blue-green markings on operculum; dorsal fin with an orange margin; anal fin with a blue margin and broad red submarginal band; upper and lower edges of caudal fin light orange-red. Reaches 15.5 cm. Seychelles and Oman to Line Islands and Society Islands; Sagami Bay, Japan, to Great Barrier Reef, Vanuatu, New Caledonia, Lord Howe Island, and New South Wales; no records from Micronesia; type locality, Taiwan. Known from depths of 6–15 m; often seen in colonies.

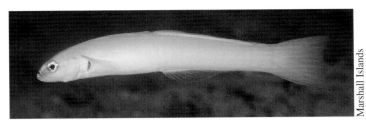

SMALLSCALE DARTFISH
Ptereleotris microlepis (Bleeker, 1856)
Dorsal rays VI + I,25–29; anal rays I,24–27; pectoral rays 21–24; body depth 5.5–7.0 in standard length; no barbel on chin, but a median fleshy ridge that narrows to a thin fold posteriorly; first dorsal fin low, the spines strongly curved posteriorly, the fifth spine longest, but not prolonged, 1.1–1.4 in head length; caudal fin emarginate, the corners angular; pale gray to bluish gray, usually with 2 faint orange lines posteriorly on side of body that converge slightly as they pass into caudal fin; a narrow black bar edged in pale blue on lower half to two-thirds of pectoral-fin base; pale blue lines and spots on postorbital head. Attains 12 cm. Red Sea and Zanzibar to Line Islands, Tuamotu Archipelago, and throughout Micronesia; Ryukyu Islands to Great Barrier Reef, New South Wales, and New Caledonia; type locality, Banda, Indonesia. Usually encountered in the protected waters of lagoons and bays over sand or sand and rubble substrata; collections from depths of 1–22 m; pairs may occupy the same burrow, but often many individuals share the same refuge.

ZEBRA DARTFISH
Ptereleotris zebra (Fowler, 1938)
Dorsal rays VI + I,27–29; anal rays I,25–28; pectoral rays 23–26; body depth 4.8–6.0 in standard length; a well-developed median barbel on chin, its length about half head length; first dorsal fin lower than second dorsal due to strong posterior curvature of spines; caudal fin slightly emarginate; pelvic fins usually equal to or slightly longer than head (pelvics in other species herein 1.1–1.5 in head); light yellowish to greenish gray, the body with about 20 narrow orange to pink bars, edged with blue or purple; a broad, blue-edged purple bar extending from eye to chin; 2 narrow, oblique, pale blue bands on opercle; an orange-red bar edged in bright blue at pectoral-fin base; dorsal fins with a deep blue to black margin. Largest specimen examined, 11.4 cm. Red Sea and Seychelles to Line Islands and Marquesas Islands; Ryukyu Islands to Great Barrier Reef, New South Wales, Lord Howe Island, and New Caledonia; type locality, Luzon. Occurs on exposed seaward reefs in 1.5–10 m, mostly from 2 to 4 m; usually encountered in aggregations over hard bottom; often many individuals shelter in the same hole. Adults, presumably males, display by lowering and expanding the pale pelvic fins and the chin barbel.

Orbicular Platax, *Platax orbicularis*, Sabah

SPADEFISHES
(EPHIPPIDAE)

This small family is represented by 2 species of the genus *Chaetodipterus,* 1 in the Atlantic and the other in the eastern Pacific, the monotypic *Parapsettus* from the eastern Pacific, and 5 Indo-Pacific genera; *Platax* is the largest with 5 species. The common name spadefish applies to the genus *Chaetodipterus.* Unfortunately the common name most often given to the species of *Platax* is batfish. This, however, is the official English common name for the fishes of the family Ogcocephalidae (Robins et al., 1991). I have proposed (Randall, 1995a) that platax be used as the common name for the species of *Platax,* as the French have done. Family characters are as follows: a deep compressed body; a small, terminal nonpro- tractile mouth; teeth small, in bands in jaws, none on palate; posterior nostril elongate; gill membranes broadly attached to isthmus; gill opening restricted to the side; scales small to moderate, cycloid to ctenoid; base of median fins densely scaled; dorsal fin with V-IX spines and 18–39 soft rays; anal fin with III spines and 15–29 soft rays; caudal fin slightly rounded, truncate, or slightly double emarginate; pelvic fins I,5, their origin below pectoral-fin base, with a scaly axillary process; vertebrae 24. This family and the Scatophagidae have been reclassified from the suborder Percoidei to the Acanthuroidei (Tyler et al., 1989; Winterbottom, 1993). Only two species of the family are known from islands of the South Pacific treated here, both in the genus *Platax.* Kishimoto et al. (1988) reviewed the genus *Platax,* with emphasis on Japanese species.

Bali

ORBICULAR PLATAX
Platax orbicularis (Forsskål, 1775)

Dorsal rays V,34–39; anal rays III,25–29; pectoral rays 16–18; lateral-line scales 44–52; scales finely ctenoid; top of head not scaled; body of juveniles very deep, the depth greater than standard length; depth progressively less with growth, that of large adults to 1.4 in standard length; teeth tricuspid, the middle cusp largest; chin with 5 sensory pores on each side (4 in *Platax pinnatus*); dorsal and anal fins of juveniles greatly elevated, gradually shortening with growth; caudal fin of juveniles slightly rounded, of adults slightly double emarginate; juveniles light reddish brown to brownish yellow with a dark bar on head through eye; adults silvery gray, usually with a few scattered black spots on body, a broad dark brown bar anteriorly on body, and a narrower one on head passing through eye. Reaches 40 cm. Occurs throughout the tropical Indo-Pacific region except the Hawaiian Islands; type locality, Red Sea. The young are found inshore in sheltered waters of bays and lagoons, often in mangrove habitats; observed to lie on their side and resemble drifting leaves (Randall & Randall, 1960); adults may be seen as solitary individuals or in small schools; diet omnivorous and varied.

Sulawesi/juvenile

569

Red Sea

Red Sea/juveniles

BLUNTHEAD PLATAX

Platax teira (Forsskål, 1775)

Dorsal rays V,29–34; anal rays III,21–26; pectoral rays 16–18; lateral-line scales 56–66; scales finely ctenoid; top of head not scaled; body of juveniles very deep, the depth greater than the standard length; depth progressively less with growth, that of large adults 1.4 in standard length; dorsal profile of head of adults from front of snout to well above eye nearly vertical (other species with a more sloping profile); teeth tricuspid, the lateral cusps nearly as large as middle one; chin with 5 sensory pores on each side; dorsal and anal fins of juveniles greatly elevated, gradually shortening with growth; caudal fin of juveniles slightly rounded, of adults slightly double emarginate; juveniles silvery gray with a very broad, dark brown bar posteriorly on body extending into dorsal and anal fins; a broad, dark brown bar anteriorly on body, and a narrower one on head through eye; adults with posterior half of body gray-brown, containing a dark bar in its anterior part; rest of body pale gray with a broad, dark brown bar from nape to abdomen, enclosing pectoral-fin base; head pale gray with a narrow, dark brown bar from angularity of dorsal profile through eye to chest; a black blotch generally larger than eye on side of abdomen; outer margin of median fins blackish, the caudal with a dark bar at base; pelvic fins yellowish brown. Attains about 70 cm. Red Sea (type locality), Persian Gulf, and east coast of Africa to the western Pacific from Hokkaido to Sydney and Norfolk Island, east to Fiji and islands of Micronesia except the Marshall Islands. The young have been found drifting with masses of algae or flotsam far at sea.

SCATS
(SCATOPHAGIDAE)

This Indo-Pacific family consists of 2 genera, the monotypic *Selenotoca* and *Scatophagus*, with at least 4 species. Family characters as follows: body deep and compressed; head with a steep dorsal profile and a concavity above eye; mouth small, terminal, and non-protractile; teeth small, in several rows in jaws; no teeth on roof of mouth; gill membranes united, forming a narrow fold across isthmus; scales very small, ctenoid, extending onto head and basally on soft portion of median fins; dorsal fin with X-XI strong spines (not including a procumbent spine) and 15–18 soft rays; anal fin with IV stout spines and 13–16 soft rays; caudal fin with 14 branched rays, slightly rounded to slightly double emarginate; pectoral fins short; pelvic fins I,5, their origin slightly posterior to pectoral-fin base, with a scaly axillary process; vertebrae 23; bones of head without spines or serrae, but the postlarva has a bony shield on the head with a suprascapular and a preopercular spine. Found in protected waters that vary from fully saline to fresh; at least 1 species can reproduce in fresh water. Often seen in small aggregations. The spines inflict painful wounds and are believed to be venomous. The name *Scatophagus* is from the Greek meaning feeding on dung; it refers to these fishes being observed to feed on excrement.

Aquarium photo

SPOTTED SCAT

Scatophagus argus (Linnaeus, 1766)

Dorsal rays XI (not including the hidden procumbent spine), 16–18; anal rays IV,14–15; pectoral rays 17; lateral-line scales about 95; body depth 1.5–1.7 in standard length; third or fifth dorsal spine longest; penultimate dorsal spine shorter than last spine; ground color variable, often silvery or silvery yellowish green, with numerous well-separated, dark brown to black spots (may be larger than eye on small fish); juveniles more colorful, orange-red dorsally on head and body, with dark bars that break into spots with growth. Attains 30 cm. Persian Gulf and India to western Pacific from Japan to New South Wales, east to New Caledonia and Fiji; type locality, India. Usually found in estuaries or mangrove sloughs; feeds on benthic algae, small invertebrates, and offal. T. R. Roberts (pers. comm.) believes that *S. atromaculatus* (Bennett), currently regarded as a synonym of *S. argus*, is a valid species distinct in having the spots on the body primarily in oblique rows. Specimens of this form have been collected in New Caledonia and Fiji.

MOORISH IDOL FAMILY (ZANCLIDAE)

See account of the single species of the family.

MOORISH IDOL

Zanclus cornutus (Linnaeus, 1758)
Dorsal rays VII,40–43; anal rays III,33–35; pectoral rays 19; body very deep, the depth 1.0–1.4 in standard length, and very compressed; third dorsal spine extremely elongate and filamentous, usually longer than standard length; snout narrow and prolonged; mouth small; teeth slender, slightly incurved, and in a single row in jaws; adults with a bony projection in front of each eye, larger in males; scales very small, each with a vertical row of erect cteni that curve posteriorly, giving the skin a texture like

Hawaiian Islands

fine sandpaper; broad middle zone of body yellow and white, bordered by 2 very broad black bars, the anterior covering head except snout, its posterior margin from dorsal-fin origin to pelvic fin base, the posterior across posterior one-fourth of body except yellow caudal peduncle, and extending into dorsal and anal fins; snout white with a black-edged yellow saddle, black lips and chin; caudal fin largely covered by a black bar edged in white anteriorly and pale blue posteriorly. Attains 22 cm. Wide-ranging in the Indo-Pacific and tropical eastern Pacific; not known from the Red Sea; type locality, Indian seas. During 3 visits to Easter Island, the author saw only a single large adult individual. Omnivorous, but feeds more on benthic invertebrates than algae, especially sponges; difficult to maintain in an aquarium. The unusually large postlarval stage (may reach 8 cm) has a stout, curved preorbital spine on each side of the head. It was described as a separate species by Linnaeus, *Z. canescens*. This spine is shed during transformation from the postlarval to the juvenile stage (Randall, 1955a). Strasburg (1962) illustrated and described the postlarval stage.

Tuamotu Archipelago (night)

572

Convict Surgeonfish, *Acanthurus triostegus*, Maldive Islands

SURGEONFISHES
(ACANTHURIDAE)

The surgeonfishes are aptly named for the sharp spine or spines on the side of the caudal peduncle. There are 80 species, of which 73 occur in the Indo-Pacific region. The family is divisible into 3 subfamilies, the Acanthurinae, which includes the genera *Acanthurus*, *Ctenochaetus*, *Paracanthurus*, and *Zebrasoma*, in which the caudal spine is single and folds into a horizontal groove; the Nasinae, represented by the genus *Naso*, in which caudal armament consists of 1 or 2 fixed, blade-like spines; and the Prionurinae, also with 1 genus, *Prionurus*, in which there are 3 to 10 fixed spines on each side. The species of *Naso* are called unicornfishes because of the horn-like rostral projection on the forehead of many of the species. The species of *Ctenochaetus* are called bristletooths because of their numerous comb-like teeth. Those of the genus *Zebrasoma* are called tangs (also a few species of *Acanthurus* have been given this common name), and the species of *Prionurus* are called saw-

tails. In addition to the caudal spines, the family characters include a deep compressed body; the eye high on the head; a single unnotched dorsal fin of IV-IX spines and 19–33 soft rays; an anal fin with II or III spines (only *Naso* with II) and 18–28 soft rays; pelvic fins with I spine and 3 or 5 soft rays (*Naso* and *Prionurus* with 3); very small ctenoid scales; a small terminal mouth with a single row of close-set incisiform teeth that may be spatulate with denticulate edges (*Acanthurus* and *Zebrasoma*), acute with or without serrate edges (*Naso*), or numerous and flexible with expanded denticulate incurved tips (*Ctenochaetus*). All of the surgeonfishes have a very long intestine; the species of *Ctenochaetus* and some of *Acanthurus* have a thick-walled gizzard-like stomach. Most of the surgeonfishes graze or browse on algae, but a few species of *Acanthurus* and many of *Naso* feed on zooplankton; the species of *Ctenochaetus* are detritus feeders. The acanthurid fishes that are primarily herbivorous may at times rise above the substratum to feed on zooplankton when it is abundant. A few, notably *Acanthurus mata*, *A. xanthopterus*, and

Marshall Islands

Line Islands

Guam

EYESTRIPE SURGEONFISH
Acanthurus dussumieri Valenciennes in C & V, 1835

Dorsal rays IX,25–27; anal rays III,24–26; pectoral rays 16–17 (usually 17); adults with up to 20 upper and 22 lower teeth; body depth 1.9–2.1 in standard length; large adults with a strongly convex forehead; caudal spine 3.0–5.0 in head length; caudal fin lunate, the caudal concavity 5.0 or less in standard length of specimens longer than 30 cm standard length; stomach gizzard-like; yellowish brown with irregular longitudinal blue lines on head and body; a broad yellow band across front of interorbital and continuing behind eye as a large irregular spot; opercular membrane black; sheath of caudal spine white, the socket edged in black; dorsal and anal fins of adults largely yellow with a blue line at base and a blue margin (fins of juveniles fully striped with blue); caudal fin deep blue with numerous small blackish spots, the basal part of the lobes orange-yellow. Reported to 54 cm. East coast of Africa to Hawaiian Islands and Line Islands; southern Japan to Great Barrier Reef, Lord Howe Island, Norfolk Island, and as juveniles to northern New Zealand; also reported from Western Australia; type locality, Mauritius. Generally found on seaward reefs, usually at depths greater than 10 m; submarine observations in Hawai'i to 131 m (Chave & Mundy, 1994). Feeds on the algal film on compact sand, but also grazes algae from the hard substratum of reefs.

WHITESPOTTED SURGEONFISH
Acanthurus guttatus Forster, 1801

Dorsal rays IX,27–30; anal rays III,23–26; pectoral rays 15–17; adults with 12 upper and 14 lower teeth; body very deep, the depth 1.5–1.6 in standard length; caudal spine small; caudal fin slightly emarginate, the caudal concavity contained 14–17 times in standard length; gray-brown with a white bar from nape across operculum, another on anterior body, and sometimes a third narrow one in middle of body; numerous white spots on posterior two-thirds of body and dorsal and anal fin, and adjacent part of dorsal fin; basal half of caudal fin pale yellow, the outer half black; pelvic fins bright yellow. Attains 28 cm. Islands of the western Indian Ocean to western Pacific from the Ryukyu Islands to the Great Barrier Reef of Australia and New Caledonia, east to Hawaiian Islands and Pitcairn Islands; type locality, Tahiti. Lives in the surge zone of exposed reefs or rocky shores, usually in small schools. The white spots on the body may help to conceal it, as it often swims in the swirling white bubbles produced by surf. Browses mainly on filamentous algae, but ingests some calcareous species such as *Jania*.

WHITEBAR SURGEONFISH
Acanthurus leucopareius (Jenkins, 1903)

Dorsal rays IX,25–27; anal rays III,23–25; pectoral rays 16; adults with up to 18 upper and 20 lower teeth; body depth 1.7–1.85 in standard length; caudal fin emarginate, the caudal concavity of adults 10–11 in standard length; gray-brown with a white band, broadly bordered by dark brown, from front of dorsal fin across posterior operculum, the anterior brown border passing through eye; very small blue spots anteriorly on body that coalesce into irregular lines posteriorly; a small black spot at rear base of dorsal fin; caudal fin brownish yellow with a white bar at base. Reaches 25 cm. Antiequatorial; in the Northern Hemisphere from the Hawaiian Islands to Minami-tori-shima (Marcus Island), Mariana Islands (common in the north but rare at Guam) to southern Japan, where it ranges from the Ogasawara Islands to Wakayama Prefecture; in the Southern Hemisphere from Easter Island, Pitcairn Islands, Austral Islands, and Rapa to New Caledonia; type locality, O'ahu. An inshore species of reefs or rocky substrata; occasionally seen in feeding aggregations that overcome the territorial damselfishes and surgeonfishes that are unable to protect their algal supply from so many intruders at once.

Easter Island

Ogasawara Islands

Great Barrier Reef/juvenile

Bali

LINED SURGEONFISH
Acanthurus lineatus (Linnaeus, 1758)

Dorsal rays IX,27–30; anal rays III,25–28 (rarely 25); pectoral rays 16; large adults with up to 14 upper and 16 lower teeth; body moderately elongate, the depth in adults about 2.2 in standard length; caudal spine very long, 1.9–2.0 in head length; caudal fin strongly lunate, the caudal concavity 3.3–4.5 in standard length; upper three-fourths of body bright yellow with narrow black-edged bright blue stripes that continue obliquely and narrowly onto head and posteriorly into dorsal fin; lower one-fourth of body lavender to bluish white; caudal fin yellow basally with 2 dark-edged, blue vertical lines, the rest of fin dark purplish gray (mainly yellow in juveniles) with a narrow blue margin and a curved blue line in middle of fin that continues as inner margin of caudal lobes. Reaches 38 cm. East Africa to French Polynesia and Pitcairn Islands; southern Japan to central New South Wales and Western Australia; type locality, "Indes." Known in Hawai'i from two individuals. Generally seen at depths of 1–3 m on exposed outer-reef areas; territorial and very aggressive; the caudal spine is venomous. Craig et al. (1997) reported that *lineatus* accounted for 39% of the total weight of artisanal catches of coral-reef fishes in 1994 in American Samoa. They determined that spawning occurs year-around but peaks in October–February; 79–80% of the total growth is attained in the first year, followed by slow growth; age to at least 18 years.

Solomon Islands

SPOTTEDFACE SURGEONFISH
Acanthurus maculiceps (Ahl, 1923)

Dorsal rays IX,24–25; anal rays III,23–24; pectoral rays 16; upper teeth of adults to 18 and lower teeth to 20; body depth 2.0–2.2 in standard length; snout of large adults convex; caudal spine 2.5–3.2 in head length; caudal fin of adults lunate, the caudal concavity to 3.3 in standard length; body brown to gray-brown with numerous very fine, pale yellow, lengthwise lines except on abdomen and chest; a horizontal black band, narrowly rimmed in yellow, at upper end of gill opening, extending posterior to gill opening little more than an eye diameter, the short anterior part either yellow or black; head and nape with numerous, small, pale yellow spots, mostly round to oblong, some interconnected; sheath of caudal spine white, the socket broadly edged in black; dorsal fin with narrow yellow bands and a black line at base; caudal fin with an irregular white bar at base and a narrow, white posterior margin; a large yellow area in upper outer part of pectoral fins. Reported to 40 cm. Maldive Islands to the Line Islands and Samoa Islands; Ryukyu Islands to Great Barrier Reef and Solomon Islands; type locality, New Britain. Generally found in outer-reef areas from 1 to at least 30 m, either as solitary individuals or in small groups.

ELONGATE SURGEONFISH
Acanthurus mata (Cuvier, 1829)

Dorsal rays IX,24–26; anal rays III,23–24; pectoral rays 16–17 (usually 17); mouth small; adults with up to 24 upper and 26 lower teeth; body depth of subadults about 2.1 in standard length, decreasing to 2.5 in large adults; snout short, 6.6–6.9 in standard length; caudal peduncle narrow, the least depth 7.7–9.5 in standard length; caudal spine small; caudal fin deeply emarginate, the caudal concavity 5.5–8.0 in standard length of adults; stomach not gizzard-like; gray to brown with lengthwise blue lines on head and body; a small blackish spot at upper end of gill opening, preceded by a yellow band that continues in front of eye as a double band. Reaches 50 cm. Red Sea and Gulf of Oman south to Natal, east to French Polynesia; southern Japan to Western Australia, New South Wales, and New Caledonia. Named *mata* (erroneously as *meta* by Cuvier, but corrected by Valenciennes in C & V, 1835) for the native name given by Russell (1803) for this species on the Coromandel coast of India. More inclined than other surgeonfishes to enter turbid waters. Feeds above the bottom on zooplankton, often in small schools. Capable of quickly changing its color to pale blue, as when visiting a cleaning station. Often misidentified as *Acanthurus bleekeri* Günther, a junior synonym.

Great Barrier Reef

GOLDRIM SURGEONFISH
Acanthurus nigricans (Linnaeus, 1758)

Dorsal rays IX,28–31; anal rays III,26–28; pectoral rays 16; mouth small and somewhat protruding, with at most 10 upper and 12 lower teeth; body depth 1.7–1.85 in standard length; caudal-spine length 2.5–3.0 in head length; caudal fin slightly emarginate, the caudal concavity 10–18 in standard length; black with a white spot broader than eye below and adjacent to eye; a narrow white band around mouth except dorsally; a yellow band at base of dorsal and anal fins that broadens posteriorly to nearly full height of fins; caudal fin whitish with a yellow bar in posterior one-third; capable of quickly becoming yellow on about posterior half of body. Largest specimen examined, 21.3 cm. Ryukyu Islands to Great Barrier Reef and New Caledonia, east to the Hawaiian Islands, islands of French Polynesia except Rapa, and the tropical eastern Pacific; only Western Australia, Christmas Island, and Cocos-Keeling Islands in the Indian Ocean; type locality unknown. An aggressive species typically found on exposed outer-reef areas just below the zone of heavy surge; feeds on filamentous algae. The acronurus larval stage is large, to 8 cm. Hybridizes with *Acanthurus achilles*, *A. japonicus*, and *A. leucosternon* (Randall & Frische, 2000). Debelius & Kuiter (2001) illustrated the hybrid of *leucosternon* and *nigri-*

Line Islands

cans as an undescribed species of *Acanthurus*. Often identified in the older literature as the synonyms *A. glaucopareius* Cuvier and *A. aliala* Lesson. The common name Whitecheek Surgeonfish is also used in the aquarium trade.

Great Barrier Reef

BLACKSTREAK SURGEONFISH
Acanthurus nigricauda Duncker & Mohr, 1929

Dorsal rays IX,25–28; anal rays III,23–26; pectoral rays 17; a specimen 22.6 cm in standard length has 19 upper and 22 lower teeth; body depth of adults 2.0–2.2 in standard length; caudal spine of adults 2.8–4.5 in head length; caudal fin increasingly lunate with growth, the caudal concavity to 3.6 in the standard length; stomach gizzard-like; brown without lines on body or spots on head; a slightly tilted black band extending backward from a little before upper end of gill opening, the ends usually rounded; caudal spine edged in black, the black continuing as a long pointed streak anterior to spine; dorsal and anal fins with a blue margin, the dorsal with a dark reddish line at base that broadens and becomes bluish to purplish anteriorly and extends medially onto nape; caudal fin blackish with a white bar at base and a narrow, white posterior margin; about outer third of pectoral fins yellow. Reported to 40 cm. East coast of Africa to the Society Islands and Tuamotu Archipelago; Ryukyu Islands to the Great Barrier Reef and New Caledonia; Scott Reef off the northwestern coast of Australia; type locality, Massau Island, Bismarck Archipelago. Usually seen over sand near coral reefs or rocky bottom, where it grazes on the surface algae and ingests some sand. Capable of rapidly changing its ground color to light grayish blue. Usually identified in the older literature as *Acanthurus nigricans* or *A. gahhm*, valid names for other species.

BROWN SURGEONFISH

Acanthurus nigrofuscus (Forsskål, 1775)

Dorsal rays IX,24–27 (rarely 27); anal rays III,22–24; pectoral rays 16–17; large adults with 14 upper and 16 lower teeth; body depth 2.0–2.3 in standard length; caudal-spine length about 3 in head length; caudal fin lunate, the caudal concavity of adults 4.5–6.0 in standard length; brown to pale lavender-brown, with or without fine, lengthwise, pale bluish lines or rows of dots; head, nape, and chest with small orange spots; lips blackish; a black spot larger than pupil at rear base of dorsal fin, and a smaller spot at rear base of anal fin; edge of caudal-spine socket narrowly blackish; caudal fin with a narrow, white posterior margin. Attains 21 cm. Red Sea (type locality) and east coast of Africa to the Pitcairn Islands and Hawaiian Islands; southern Japan to central New South Wales (as juveniles), Lord Howe Island, and Norfolk Island; south off Western Australia to Rottnest Island. Among the smallest of surgeonfishes, but aggressive. Generally abundant on shallow coral reefs or rocky bottom. Very large spawning aggregations in the Red Sea in the late after-

Hawaiian Islands

noon documented by Myrberg et al. (1988). Invalid names sometimes used for this common species include *Acanthurus elongatus* (Lacepède), *A. matoides* Valenciennes, *A. rubropunctatus* Rüppell, *A. bipunctatus* Steindachner, *A. flavoguttatus* Herre, and *Hepatus lucillae* Fowler.

Johnston Island

BLUELINED SURGEONFISH

Acanthurus nigroris Valenciennes in C & V, 1835

Dorsal rays IX,23–27; anal rays III,22–25; pectoral rays 15–16; adults with up to 12 upper and 14 lower teeth; body depth 1.8–2.0 in standard length; caudal-spine length about 4 in head length; caudal fin emarginate, the caudal concavity 6.7–10.5 in head length (5.8–7.5 in the Hawaiian Islands); brown with irregular, lengthwise blue lines on body, one-fourth or less the width of brown interspaces, those on snout passing from eye to mouth (fewer blue lines on smaller individuals; a specimen of 5.1 cm in standard length has only 11 on body); a small black spot at rear base of dorsal and anal fins; no black edge on caudal-spine socket; caudal fin with a very narrow, blue or white posterior margin, and often with a broad whitish bar at base. Reaches 25 cm. Occurs at the islands of Oceania from the Hawaiian Islands (type locality) and Pitcairn Islands to Micronesia and the Great Barrier Reef. A record from the Seychelles is a misidentification of *Acanthurus nigrofuscus*. The population in the Hawaiian Islands and Johnston Island differs in having higher fin-ray counts (dorsal soft rays 24–27, compared with 23–26 elsewhere; anal rays 23–25, compared with 22–24), higher gill-raker counts, and a more deeply emarginate caudal fin.

New Britain

DROPOFF SURGEONFISH

Acanthurus nubilus (Fowler & Bean, 1929)

Dorsal rays VI-VII (usually VII),25–27; anal rays III,23–24; pectoral rays 16–17; mouth small; adults with up to 24 upper and 28 lower teeth; body depth 1.8–2.2 in standard length; snout short, its length 6.8–7.2 in standard length; caudal-spine length 2.5–3.0 in head length; caudal fin deeply emarginate, the caudal concavity 4.5–9.5 in standard length; body with alternating lengthwise lines of pale blue and orangish brown or dull orange; head, nape, and chest pale blue with numerous small, close-set, orangish brown or orange spots; a broad, light yellowish zone around caudal spine; dorsal and anal fins with a linear pattern similar to that of body; anterior nostril in a small white spot. Largest specimen examined, 26 cm. Known from Indonesia (type locality, Sulawesi), Philippines, Guam, Solomon Islands, and New Caledonia across the South Pacific to the Pitcairn Islands; a specimen from the Mozambique Channel first identified as *nubilus* proved to be *Acanthurus mata*. Occurs on steep drop-offs well away from the substratum, feeding on zooplankon at depths of 25 to at least 62 m; can quickly change its color from brown to pale blue, and the caudal fin can shift from brown to white.

Tahiti/subadult

Marshall Islands

ORANGEBAND SURGEONFISH
Acanthurus olivaceus Forster, 1801

Dorsal rays IX,23–25; anal rays III,22–24; pectoral rays 16–17 (usually 17); adults with up to 20 upper and 22 lower teeth; body depth 2.0–2.4 in standard length; large males with a distinctly convex snout; caudal spine of adults large, up to 2.5 in head length; caudal fin of adults lunate, the caudal concavity 4.0–5.0 in standard length; stomach gizzard-like; grayish brown to olive brown with a broad, horizontal, bright orange band, widely rimmed in deep blue or purple, extending posteriorly from upper end of gill opening; an orange line at base of dorsal fin; caudal fin with small blackish spots and a large, crescentic white area posteriorly in central part of fin; can quickly assume a color pattern with the head and anterior half of body abruptly paler than the posterior half; young bright yellow; orange shoulder band develops before the change from yellow to brown. Reaches about 35 cm. Southern Japan to northern New South Wales, and Lord Howe Island, east in Oceania to the Hawaiian Islands, Society Islands (type locality, Tahiti), and Tuamotu Archipelago. In the eastern Indian Ocean at Christmas Island, Cocos-Keeling Islands, and south on the coast of Western Australia to Ningaloo Reef. Usually encountered grazing over sand near reefs, sometimes in small aggregations; submarine observations to 62 m (Chave & Mundy, 1994). Hybridizes with *Acanthurus nigricauda* and *A. tennentii* (Randall et al., 2001).

Line Islands/juvenile

Marshall Islands

MIMIC SURGEONFISH
Acanthurus pyroferus Kittlitz, 1834

Dorsal rays VIII,27–31; anal rays III,24–28; pectoral rays 15–16 (usually 16); adults usually with 16 upper and 18 lower teeth, but one with 21 lower teeth; body depth 1.8–2.0 in standard length; snout length 4.6–5.0 in standard length; mouth protruding, hence dorsal profile of snout concave; caudal spine 2.5–4.5 in head length; dorsal and anal fins high for the genus; caudal fin of adults lunate, the caudal concavity 3.5–5.0 in standard length; caudal fin of juveniles rounded; stomach round and gizzard-like; adults dark brown, sometimes changing to yellowish tan anteriorly, with an orange bar behind upper end of gill opening extending diffusely below base of pectoral fin; a broad black band from chin along edge of operculum, sometimes enclosing eye; lips black, nearly encircled by a narrow white band; caudal fin with a prominent, yellow posterior margin; outer half of pectoral rays yellow; nostrils in a white spot; juveniles entirely bright yellow or as mimics of the small angelfishes *Centropyge flavissima* and *C. vrolikii*. Largest specimen examined, 29 cm. Wakayama Prefecture, Japan, to New South Wales, east to Line Islands and islands of French Polynesia except Rapa; in the Indian Ocean at Christmas Island, Cocos-Keeling Islands, and Scott Reef off Western Australia; type locality, Ulea = Woleai Atoll, Caroline Islands. Mimicry of *Centropyge flavissima* first noted by Randall & Randall (1960) in Tahiti; its basis later determined as the extreme wariness of the angelfish model. *Acanthurus celebicus* Bleeker is a synonym.

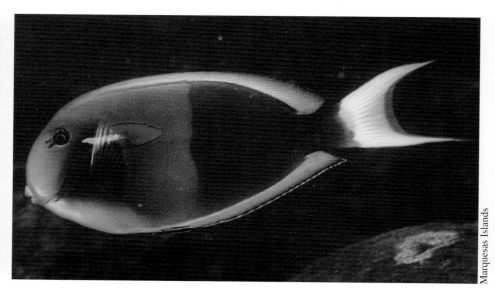

Marquesas Islands/subadult

Marquesas Islands

MARQUESAN SURGEONFISH

Acanthurus reversus Randall & Earle, 1999

Dorsal rays IX,24–25; anal rays III,23–24; pectoral rays 16–17; a specimen 21.6 cm in standard length with 19 upper and 20 lower teeth; body depth 2.1–2.2 in standard length; caudal spine 2.3–2.65 in head length; caudal fin of adults lunate, 3.35–4.7 in standard length; dark brown with an orange streak, edged in deep blue, extending posteriorly from upper end of gill opening, the blue broadening and continuing posterior to the orange a distance about equal to length of orange streak; dorsal fin with an orange line at base; caudal fin pale yellow with a black border that is broadest posteriorly in central part; juveniles bright yellow. Largest specimen, 34 cm. Endemic to the Marquesas Islands. One collected by the author at Takaroa Atoll in the northern Tuamotu Archipelago (where *Acanthurus olivaceus* is common) is regarded as a stray from the Marquesas Islands. Named *reversus* from the Latin in reference to the reversal of the color pattern of the caudal fin of *A. olivaceus*, its closest relative. Like *A. olivaceus*, the head and anterior half of body are often much paler than the posterior, the demarcation vertical and abrupt. A common inshore species at all of the islands of the Marquesas.

Sangiang, Indonesia/subadult

Maldive Islands

THOMPSON'S SURGEONFISH

Acanthurus thompsoni (Fowler, 1923)

Dorsal rays IX,23–26; anal rays III,23–26; pectoral rays 17; mouth small; adults with 20–21 upper and 24 lower teeth; body elongate for the genus, the depth 2.2–2.4 in standard length; dorsal profile of head distinctly convex; snout short, 7.9–8.2 in standard length; caudal-peduncle depth 2.2–2.5 in head length; caudal spine small; caudal fin deeply emarginate, the caudal concavity of adults 5.0–9.0 in standard length; usually uniform brown to dark brown with a darker brown spot in axil of pectoral fin and extending a short distance below (difficult to see on dark specimens), and a small black spot at rear base of dorsal fin; caudal fin white (colored like the body in the Hawaiian Islands); capable of rapidly changing color to pale grayish blue. Reported to 27 cm. East Africa to the Hawaiian Islands (type locality) and Pitcairn Islands; in the western Pacific from Kochi Prefecture, Japan, to the Great Barrier Reef and New Caledonia. Feeds on zooplankton well above the bottom, or in the case of drop-offs, well away from the wall. Although reported to occur as deep as 119 m (Chave & Mundy, 1994), it is generally seen in less than 30 m and may occur in as little as 4 m. *Acanthurus philippinus* Herre is a synonym.

CONVICT SURGEONFISH

Acanthurus triostegus (Linnaeus, 1758)

Dorsal rays IX,22–25; anal rays III,19–22; pectoral rays 14–16; maximum number of teeth in jaws, 16 upper and 18 lower; body depth 1.8–1.9 in standard length; caudal spine small; caudal fin truncate to slightly emarginate; light olivaceous gray dorsally, shading to white ventrally, with 5 narrow black bars on body and 1 on head through eye. Largest specimen, 27 cm, from Midway, but rarely exceeds 20 cm. Occurs throughout the Indo-Pacific region except for the seas around the Arabian Peninsula; also found in the tropical eastern Pacific; type locality, "Indies." The Hawaiian population regarded by some authors as a species, *Acanthurus sandvicensis* Streets, here considered a subspecies. Planes & Fauvelot (2002) studied the genetic structure of *A. triostegus* throughout the Pacific and found 5 populations, none of which were given nomenclatural recognition other than to note that the Hawaiian population had been regarded a subspecies. Randall (1961e) published on the biology in the Hawaiian Islands. Group spawning occurs at dusk; peak spawning from 12 days before to 2 days after full moon; spawning ceases during winter months. Duration of larval life determined as 2.5 months; juveniles abundant in tidepools, which they first enter as the

Tuamotu Archipelago

acronurus larval stage at night at an average standard length of 2.6 cm (total length 3.1 cm); transformation to the juvenile stage takes 4–5 days. Juveniles grow at a rate of 12 mm per month; at a standard length of 10–12 cm, growth decreases to 1.1 mm per month.

Bali

YELLOWFIN SURGEONFISH

Acanthurus xanthopterus Valenciennes in C & V, 1835

Dorsal rays IX,25–27; anal rays III,23–25; pectoral rays 16–17 (usually 17); a specimen 32 cm in standard length has 18 upper and 21 lower teeth; body depth 1.95–2.25 in standard length (body more elongate with growth); dorsal profile of head convex; caudal spine small, 4.4–5.7 in head length; caudal fin deeply emarginate to lunate, the caudal concavity 4.0–7.0 in standard length; stomach gizzard-like; color pattern can change quickly from uniform purplish gray to one with alternating, very irregular, lengthwise bands of dark yellowish gray and light blue-gray about 2 scales in width; a broad yellow band extending anteriorly to eye and an irregular one posterior to eye, extending narrowly to upper end of gill opening; a broad, pale blue area around caudal spine; dorsal and anal fins with a pale blue band at base and 4 or 5 lengthwise light blue bands alternating with

dull yellow; outer one-third of pectoral fins yellow. The largest species of the genus; recorded to 62.5 cm (24.5 inches). East coast of Africa to the Hawaiian Islands and French Polynesia; southern Japan to the Great Barrier Reef and New Caledonia; in the eastern Pacific from Clipperton Island and lower Gulf of California to Panama and the Galápagos Islands; type locality, Seychelles. Occurs in a variety of habitats, the juveniles mainly in protected inshore waters, often where turbid, the adults mainly in lagoons and bays but also in outer-reef areas; generally found in deeper water than most surgeonfishes (reported to a depth of 120 m), but may also be seen in only a few meters. Feeds predominately on the film of algae on compact sand but will also graze on hard surfaces. Synonyms include *Teuthis crestonis* Jordan & Starks from Mexico, *Hepatus aquilinus* Jordan & Seale from Western Samoa, and *Acanthurus reticulatus* Shen & Lim from Taiwan.

583

Marshall Islands/juvenile

Maldive Islands

TWOSPOT BRISTLETOOTH

Ctenochaetus binotatus Randall, 1955

Dorsal rays VIII,24–27; anal rays III,22–25; pectoral rays 15–17; pelvic rays I,5 (true of other species of the genus); 32–46 upper teeth and 36–48 lower teeth (in specimens 8–15 cm in standard length; a 3.5-cm juvenile has 22 upper and lower teeth); margins of lips smooth; body depth 1.9–2.3 in standard length; caudal fin of adults lunate, the caudal concavity 3.9–5.8 in standard length (in specimens larger than 8 cm standard length); dark orangish brown with slightly irregular, longitudinal blue (sometimes pale yellow) lines on body following scale rows, breaking into very small spots anteriorly; iris blue; a prominent black spot at rear

base of dorsal and anal fins and extending onto adjacent body; caudal fin of juveniles usually abruptly bright yellow; body of juveniles brown to orangish brown with straight, dark brown stripes that angle downward as they pass posteriorly (a 3.6-cm juvenile with 11 dark stripes). Largest specimen, 20 cm. East Africa to the Tuamotu Archipelago; southern Japan to the Great Barrier Reef and New Caledonia; not reported from the Red Sea, Gulf of Oman, Persian Gulf, Hawaiian Islands, Marquesas Islands, Rapa, Pitcairn Islands, and Easter Island; type locality, Luzon. A species of coral reefs and adjacent sand-rubble areas; known from the depth range of 2–53 m. *Ctenochaetus oculocoeruleus* Fourmanoir from Vietnam is a synonym.

Marshall Islands/juvenile

Marshall Islands

BLUELIP BRISTLETOOTH

Ctenochaetus cyanocheilus Randall & Clements, 2001

Dorsal rays VIII,25–28; anal rays III,22–26; pectoral rays 16–17 (rarely 17); 34–46 upper teeth and 38–52 lower teeth (in specimens 8.5–12 cm standard length); margins of lips smooth to finely papillate; body depth 1.8–1.95 in standard length; caudal fin emarginate, the caudal concavity 7.8–10.8 in standard length (in specimens larger than 8 cm). Orangish brown to dark brown with bluish longitudinal lines following scale rows; chest with a bluish cast; head, anterior body above pectoral-fin base, and chest with very small, pale yellowish spots; lips blue; eyes narrowly rimmed with dull yellow (often present only posteriorly); median fins dark brown, the dorsal with bluish lines extending in

from body; young bright yellow. Largest specimen, 17.7 cm. Ogasawara Islands south through the Philippines and Indonesia to the Great Barrier Reef and New Caledonia, east to Samoa Islands and Marshall Islands (type locality, Enewetak Atoll). Collected from depths of 1.5 to 30 m on coral reefs or adjacent habitats. In his revision of the genus, Randall (1955d) applied the name *C. strigosus* (Bennett) to 1 wide-ranging Indo-Pacific species, but noted population differences. Randall & Clements (2001) divided *strigosus* into a complex of 4 species, one of which was *C. cyanocheilus* and one *C. flavicauda*. The fourth is found in the Indian Ocean; all share certain features such as dentition, yellow ring around the eye, and a yellow juvenile stage.

WHITETAIL BRISTLETOOTH

Ctenochaetus flavicauda Fowler, 1938

Dorsal rays VIII,26–28 (modally 26, rarely 28); anal rays III,23–26; (usually 24); pectoral rays 16–17 (rarely 17); upper teeth 34–46, and lower teeth 40–48 (8–12 cm standard length); margin of lips smooth; body depth 1.8–2.0 in standard length; caudal fin of adults emarginate, the caudal concavity 5.05–8.8 in standard length. Head, nape, and anterior body orangish brown with very small yellow spots; rest of body orange with irregular, bluish gray, longitudinal lines, this linear pattern extending into dorsal and anal fins; lips purplish; rim of posterior half of eye bright yellow; posterior caudal peduncle and caudal fin abruptly pure white just behind caudal spine; juveniles all yellow or brown with a white caudal fin. Largest specimen examined, 16 cm. Known from the islands of French Polynesia, Pitcairn Islands, Cook Islands, Phoenix Islands, Line Islands, and Niue (M. P. Francis, pers. comm.); type locality, Takaroa Atoll, Tuamotu Archipelago. Inappropriately named *flavicauda* in the belief that the caudal fin was yellow in life. The size of fish that change from the yellow juvenile stage to the adult color pattern is variable. Harry (1953) was cut on the hand by the caudal spine of this species at Raroia Atoll in the Tuamotu Archipelago. He experienced immediate acute pain, and swelling within minutes; the pain persisted for a week.

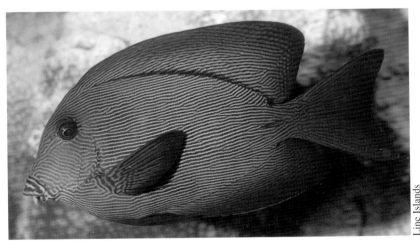

HAWAIIAN BRISTLETOOTH

Ctenochaetus hawaiiensis Randall, 1955

Dorsal rays VIII,27–29 (modally 28); anal rays III,25–26; pectoral rays 15–16 (rarely 15); lower teeth nearly twice as numerous as upper teeth; 20–31 upper teeth and 36–56 lower teeth (8.5–21 cm standard length); margin of lips crenulate; body depth 1.8–2.05 in standard length; caudal fin of specimens 8.5–22 cm in standard length, slightly emarginate, the caudal concavity 8.3–26 in standard length. Color of adults dark olive brown (appearing almost black underwater) with numerous fine, yellowish gray longitudinal lines on head, body, and dorsal and anal fins (those on head and anteriorly on dorsal and anal fins oblique); a small black spot at rear base of dorsal fin, and a very small one at rear base of anal fin (not readily visible on dark specimens); juveniles orange with narrow, dark gray-blue, chevron markings on body that extend basally into dorsal and anal fins, where they branch irregularly; head orange with a reticular pattern of dark gray-blue lines; outer posterior part of dorsal and anal fins deep bright blue; caudal fin orange to yellow with narrow, light blue bars or rows of spots. With growth, the chevrons lighten, become irregular, and additional irregular lines are added, resulting in a reticular pattern on body. Attains 28 cm. Occurs throughout most of Oceania from the Hawaiian Islands (type locality, island of Hawai'i), and Pitcairn Islands to the islands of Micronesia (including Palau), Wake, and Minami-tori-shima (Marcus Island). Juveniles are generally found in coral-rich areas at depths greater than 15 m; adults may range into shallow water, but also occur deeper; 1 was speared in 61 m by the author at Tetiaroa Atoll, Society Islands. Sometimes given the common name Black Bristletooth. The colorful juvenile stage, called the Chevron Tang, is popular in the aquarium trade.

Line Islands/juvenile

Line Islands

BLUESPOTTED BRISTLETOOTH

Ctenochaetus marginatus (Valenciennes in C & V, 1835)
Dorsal rays VIII,26–29 (modally 27); anal rays III,24–26 (usually 25); pectoral rays 16–17 (usually 17); upper teeth 36–59, and lower teeth 42–68 (7.6–22.5 cm standard length); margin of lower lip usually crenulate or papillate, especially posteriorly; body depth 1.85–2.15 in standard length; longest dorsal soft rays in anterior half of the fin (longest in posterior half on other species); caudal fin emarginate, the caudal concavity 6.5–8.0 in standard length (8 cm standard length or larger). Adults brown with very small blue spots on head and body, those posteriorly on body tending to form longitudinal rows; dorsal and anal fins with alternating dark brown and narrow pale blue or yellowish longitudinal bands (4 anteriorly and 8 posteriorly); base of anal fin with a pale blue band. Attains 29 cm. Occurs in the central Pacific in the Marshall Islands, Kiribati, Line Islands, eastern Caroline Islands (type locality, Lukunor Island), Phoenix Islands, Johnston Island, and the Marquesas Islands. Also known from the tropical eastern Pacific. Typically found in shallow water of outer-reef areas exposed to wave action, often in rapidly moving schools, but also ranges into deeper water. *Ctenochaetus cyanoguttatus* Randall is a synonym.

Taiwan/juvenile

Coral Sea

STRIPED BRISTLETOOTH

Ctenochaetus striatus (Quoy & Gaimard, 1825)
Dorsal rays VIII,27–31; anal rays III,24–28; pectoral rays 16–17 (usually 17); upper teeth 32–50, and lower teeth 36–62 (8.3–20.7 cm standard length); margin of lips smooth; body depth 1.9–2.3 in standard length; caudal fin of adults lunate, the caudal concavity 3.7–6.0 in standard length. Adults dark gray-brown to orangish brown with numerous longitudinal, pale bluish lines following scale rows and extending into basal part of dorsal and anal fins; nape and a broad zone around orbit with numerous very small, orange-yellow spots; outer part of dorsal fin with alternating, narrow, longitudinal, dark brown and pale bluish bands, most evident in soft portion; anal fin also with bands, but more obscure. This species can change from dark brown to light tan but still retains the linear pattern. Juveniles and subadults with a small black spot at rear base of dorsal fin. Small juveniles with 8 to 12 narrow red bands on body that angle downward as they pass posteriorly; tips of caudal lobes red. Largest specimen examined, 26 cm. Red Sea and east coast of Africa to the Pitcairn Islands and the islands of French Polynesia except the Marquesas; southern Japan to the Great Barrier Reef and New Caledonia; type locality, Guam. The most common surgeonfish at most localities where it occurs. Consumption of this species in French Polynesia has caused an illness similar to ciguatera, although the cases are not severe. Yasumoto et al. (1971) determined that this fish (and *Acanthurus lineatus*) may contain 2 toxins, one fat-soluble and the other water-soluble. The fat-soluble toxin was determined by column chromatography to be ciguatoxin. The water-soluble toxin, found in the liver, was later termed maitotoxin (derived from the Tahitian name Maito for this species). Harry (1953) reported pain from being injured by the caudal spine of this species, though not as severe as that from the caudal spine of *Ctenochaetus flavicauda*.

586

New Britain/juvenile

Luzon

ORANGETIPPED BRISTLETOOTH
Ctenochaetus tominiensis Randall, 1955
Dorsal rays VIII,24–27 (usually 25 or 26); anal rays III,22–25 (usually 23 or 24); pectoral rays 15–16 (usually 16); 26–32 upper teeth, and 28–33 lower teeth (in specimens 6.5–10.8 cm in standard length); edge of lips crenulate; body depth 1.85–2.1 in standard length; dorsal and anal fins distinctly angular posteriorly; caudal fin lunate, the caudal concavity 4.15–5.5 in standard length. Orangish brown with faint, narrow, bluish gray, longitudinal lines on body, more evident posteriorly; a black spot at rear base of dorsal and anal fins and on adjacent body, the dorsal spot largest (larger than pupil); nostrils white; lips dark brown; outer part of soft portions of dorsal and anal fins bright orange; caudal fin white; juveniles as small as 3 cm still have orange-tipped dorsal and anal fins and a white caudal fin. Largest specimen, 17.5 cm. East Indies, northern Great Barrier Reef, Solomon Islands, Palau, Vanuatu, and Fiji; type locality, Gulf of Tomini, Sulawesi. Typically found in coral-rich, outer-reef areas where not exposed to heavy surf.

Sulawesi/juvenile

Aquarium photo

PALETTE TANG
Paracanthurus hepatus (Linnaeus, 1766)
Dorsal rays IX,19–20; anal rays III,18–19; pectoral rays 16; pelvic-fin rays I,3; an adult 20.4 cm in standard length with 14 upper and 17 lower teeth; scales on head between eye and mouth and on cheek enlarged to tuberculate plates; body depth of adults 2.1–2.4 in standard length; a single folding spine on side of caudal peduncle, but not in a distinct socket like that of species of *Acanthurus*, its length 3.3–4.0 in head length; caudal fin of juveniles slightly rounded, of adults truncate with a short pointed tip at upper and lower corners; strikingly colored bright blue with a black band curving dorsoposteriorly from eye, broadening on body, continuing to full width of caudal peduncle, and containing a large, elliptical blue area centered above tip of pectoral fin; caudal fin yellow with broad black upper and lower margins, the yellow extending forward to enclose caudal spine and narrowing to a point a spine's length in front of spine; juveniles colored like adults. Attains about 26 cm. East coast of Africa to the islands of Micronesia, Line Islands, and Samoa Islands; in the western Pacific from Kochi Prefecture, Japan, to northern New South Wales; type locality, Ambon, Molucca Islands. Typically found in clear water on exposed outer-reef areas or in channels where there is moderate to strong current. Feeds on zooplankton, but also browses on benthic algae. Adults difficult to approach underwater; juveniles shelter among branches of live coral, hence making them relatively easy to collect. Usually called the Blue Tang in the aquarium trade, but this is the official common name of the western Atlantic *Acanthurus coeruleus*.

LONGNOSE TANG

Zebrasoma rostratum (Günther, 1875)

Dorsal rays IV-V (rarely IV),23–25; anal rays III,19–20; pectoral rays 15; pelvic rays I,5 (true of other *Zebrasoma*); a specimen 17 cm in standard length with 18 upper and 18 lower teeth; body depth of adults 1.9–2.1 in standard length; front of snout very prolonged, the dorsal profile to eye concave, the ventral profile nearly horizontal to curvature of chest; dorsal fin very elevated, the longest soft ray of adults 2.7–3.3 in standard length; males with a patch of bristle-like setae on side of body in front of caudal spine; caudal fin truncate to slightly rounded; appears totally black underwater, but closer inspection reveals the body as dark brown with a very fine, irregular, linear pattern below the lateral line; a pale blue line often present at base of dorsal fin; caudal spine hyaline, the sheath bright white. Largest specimen examined, 26.5 cm. Endemic to the following islands of central and southeastern Oceania: Rose Atoll, American Samoa (Wass, 1984), Society Islands (type locality), Rapa (Randall et al., 1990), Tuamotu Archipelago, Marquesas Islands, Line Islands, and the

Line Islands/Aquarium photo

Pitcairn Islands (Randall, 1999a); recently reported as a stray to the Hawaiian Islands. An uncommon coral-reef species known from the shallows to depths of at least 25 m. Hybridizes with *Zebrasoma scopas* (Randall et al., 2001).

Marshall Islands/juvenile

Marshall Islands

BRUSHTAIL TANG

Zebrasoma scopas (Cuvier, 1829)

Dorsal rays IV-V (rarely IV),23–25; anal rays III,19–21; pectoral rays 14–16; body very deep, the depth varying from 1.4 in standard length in small juveniles to 1.75 in large adults; mouth protruding, the dorsal profile of snout and ventral profile of head strongly concave; a dense patch of bristle-like setae posteriorly on side of body, the setae longer in males than in females the same size; dorsal fin very elevated, the longest dorsal ray 2.0 in standard length in small juveniles to 3.5 in large adults; caudal fin truncate, rounded in juveniles; dark brown, often shading to yellowish brown anteriorly, with pale blue dots on head and anterior body that form rows of fine dashes, and by midbody

solid irregular lines; sheath of caudal spine bright white; fins dark brown except pectorals with clear membranes; juveniles dark brown with 18 vertical, pale yellow lines on body, scattered dots anteriorly, and no horizontal lines. Largest specimen examined, 21.5 cm; males tend to be larger than females. East coast of Africa to the Pitcairn Islands; Suruga Bay, Japan, to Great Barrier Reef, Lord Howe Island, Norfolk Island, and New Caledonia; type locality, Banda, Indonesia; not reported from the Marquesas Islands, Hawaiian Islands, Red Sea, Oman, and Persian Gulf. A common coral-reef species at most localities where it occurs. Hybridizes with its close relative, *Zebrasoma flavescens* (Bennett) (Randall et al., 2001).

Marshall Islands

SAILFIN TANG
Zebrasoma veliferum (Bloch, 1795)

Dorsal rays IV,29–33 (rarely 29); anal rays III,23–26; pectoral rays 15–17; adults with up to 16 upper and 18 lower teeth; body depth of adults 1.8–2.0 in standard length; front of snout protruding, its dorsal profile concave; ventral profile of head more concave; dorsal fin extremely elevated, the longest ray 2.1–2.5 in standard length; caudal spine not broadly joined to the body posteriorly as in other species of the genus; no patch of bristle-like setae in front of caudal spine; caudal fin truncate; body and head posterior to eye dark gray-brown with vertical yellow lines and 6 narrow pale bars (white anteriorly and pale gray posteriorly), the yellow lines within pale bars much brighter than those in dark interspaces; head anterior to eye bar light gray with numerous close-set, small white spots; dorsal and anal fins dark brown, the soft portions with pale blue-green lines paralleling curved outer border of fins; caudal fin yellow with a white bar at base, a thin blue posterior margin, and a black submarginal line; juveniles with narrow gray and yellow bars, shading to black posteriorly; head with 2 black bars. Largest specimen recorded, 39.5 cm. Sagami Bay, Japan, to Sydney, New South Wales (as juveniles); east in Oceania to the Hawaiian Islands and Pitcairn

Fiji/juvenile

Islands; all of Micronesia and all of French Polynesia except the Marquesas Islands; type locality, seas of East Indies. The similar *Zebrasoma desjardinii* (Bennett) occurs in the Indian Ocean. Usually encountered as solitary individuals, but occasionally in pairs, on coral reefs or over rocky bottom; feeds on benthic algae. Pair spawning documented by Thresher (1984).

589

Banda Islands, Indonesia

Kenya/juvenile

Negros, Philippines/subadult

UNICORNFISHES (NASINAE)

WHITEMARGIN UNICORNFISH
Naso annulatus (Quoy & Gaimard, 1825)
Dorsal rays V,28–29; anal rays II,27–28; pectoral rays 17–19; pelvic rays I,3 (true of other *Naso*); body depth varying from about 2.2 in standard length of subadults to 3.0 in large adults; a long, tapering, bony process (or horn) anterior to eye of adults that can project nearly a head length in front of mouth; horn first appearing as a bump in individuals about 20 cm long; dorsal profile of snout to base of horn forming an angle of about 60° to horizontal axis of head and body; side of caudal peduncle with 2 bony plates that develop knife-like keels in adults; caudal fin truncate in subadults, scalloped in adults, the large males with a long trailing filament from each corner; light bluish gray or brown, paler ventrally, without any dark markings on head or body; edge of lips broadly white; juveniles and subadults with a white ring around caudal peduncle and a white posterior edge on the caudal fin, the subadults developing a black submarginal zone in fin; rays of caudal fin of adults distally blackish, the narrow membranes and filaments white. Attains at least 100 cm. Red Sea and East Africa to Hawaiian Islands, Marquesas Islands, and Tuamotu Archipelago; Suruga Bay, Japan, to Lord Howe Island and Norfolk Island (Francis, 1993); type locality, Timor. Also reported from Clipperton Island in the eastern Pacific (Robertson & Allen, 1996). Adults on steep drop-offs in more than 25 m, usually in small aggregations; feeds on zooplankton. *Naso herrei* Smith is a synonym.

Maldive Islands

Maldive Islands/male

HUMPBACK UNICORNFISH

Naso brachycentron (Valenciennes in C & V, 1835)

Dorsal rays IV-V,28–30; anal rays II,27–28; pectoral rays 17; body depth 2.3 (in subadults) to 2.7 in standard length; a hump developing at about 20 cm in length on back below origin of soft portion of dorsal fin, thus the dorsal profile from above the eye to the origin of the soft dorsal of adults is distinctly concave; dorsal profile of snout forming an angle of about 45° to horizontal axis of head and body; adult males with a long tapering horn anterior to eye that may extend before mouth; adult females with only a prominent bump before eye; 2 peduncular plates, those on

adults with a sharp keel ending in a forward-projecting point; head and upper half of body gray, the lower half whitish to pale yellowish, the demarcation irregular; often with a few small, pale blue spots behind eye; large males may have dark bars on lower side. Reported to 90 cm. East coast of Africa to French Polynesia; Ryukyu Islands to the Great Barrier Reef, Vanuatu, and New Caledonia; only Guam and Palau in Micronesia; type locality, Waigeo (Waigiou) off Irian Jaya. Not common; may be seen in shallow reef areas, but difficult to approach. Occasionally encountered in small aggregations. *Naso rigoletto* Smith from Mozambique is a synonym.

Marshall Islands/juvenile

Marshall Islands

LINED UNICORNFISH

Naso brevirostris (Cuvier, 1829)

Dorsal rays VI,27–29; anal rays II,27–29; pectoral rays 16–17; body depth from 2.0 in standard length of subadults to 2.7 in adults; a broad-based, tapering horn before eye of adults, extending as much as a head length in front of mouth (first appearing as a bump in individuals about 10 cm in length); dorsal profile of snout above mouth very short and nearly vertical; 2 peduncular plates on each side, the keels only moderately developed; caudal fin truncate to slightly rounded; ground color varying from light bluish gray to olivaceous brown; a series of dark gray vertical lines on body, ending as rows of spots ventrally; head with small

dark spots or a reticular pattern of lines; horn with oblique dark lines; opercular membrane white; edges of lips pale blue; caudal fin mainly whitish; one color phase with anterior one-fourth of body abruptly pale. Reported to 60 cm, but any over 50 cm would be exceptional. Occurs throughout the Indo-Pacific region except Oman and the Persian Gulf; in the eastern Pacific from the Galápagos Islands (McCosker & Humann, 1996); no type locality given. Feeds on benthic algae when young, but with the development of the horn, the food habits shift principally to zooplankton. Robertson (1982) reported feeding in part on the feces of fusiliers (Caesionidae) at Palau. Submarine observations of adults to 122 m (Chave & Mundy, 1994).

GRAY UNICORNFISH

Naso caesius Randall & Bell, 1992

Dorsal rays VI-VII,27–30; anal rays II,28–31; pectoral rays 16–18; 94 upper and 88 lower teeth in a specimen 53.7 cm in standard length; body depth of adults 2.5–3.0 in standard length; dorsal profile of head smoothly convex without any protuberance; side of caudal peduncle with 2 keeled bony plates, the blade-like keels not pointed; caudal fin emarginate in young, truncate in adults; bluish gray to dark gray-brown; caudal fin uniformly bluish; lower lip colored like body; upper surface of tongue not black; lower-limb gill rakers entirely pale; capable of quickly displaying a pattern of vertically elongate blotches on about upper two-thirds of body that may be either darker or paler than the ground color. Largest specimen, 62.5 cm. Reported from the Great Barrier Reef and Osprey Reef and the Chesterfield Islands in the Coral Sea (Kulbicki et al., 1994), New Caledonia, Fiji, Tuvalu, Society Islands, Pitcairn Islands, and Micronesia (type locality, Enewetak Atoll). Previous to its description, not distinguished from the closely related *Naso hexacanthus* with

Marshall Islands

which it sometimes schools. First detected by Lori Bell Colin at Enewetak when she observed 2 different male courtship patterns in the same aggregation. Named *caesius* from the Latin for bluish gray.

Marshall Islands

Bali/juvenile (night)

SLEEK UNICORNFISH

Naso hexacanthus (Bleeker, 1855)

Dorsal rays VI (rarely V or VII),26–29 (modally 27); anal rays II,27–30 (rarely 27 or 30); pectoral rays 17–18 (usually 17); body depth of adults 2.6–3.0 in standard length; dorsal profile of head sloping and smoothly convex; interorbital space strongly convex with a slight median ridge; 2 large peduncular plates, the keels with a forward-projecting point in adults; caudal fin emarginate in young, truncate in adults; brown to bluish gray, the ventral half of body yellowish gray to yellow, the demarcation along middle of side often abrupt and irregular; edge of opercle and preopercle usually with a dark brown band; margin of lower lip broadly white; upper surface of tongue of adults black; gill rakers blackish basally; caudal fin blue with a broad, brownish yellow, posterior border that narrows toward corners of fin; capable of rapidly changing to light grayish blue overall, as when at a cleaning station; males in courtship quickly display a broad, bluish white zone on nape and anterior upper part of body, followed by narrow bars of the same color that extend onto lower side. Reaches 75 cm. Occurs throughout most of the Indo-Pacific; type locality, Ambon; not reported from Oman, Persian Gulf, India, or Sri Lanka. Reported in the eastern Pacific from Clipperton Island and Cocos Island, Costa Rica. Adults usually seen in schools on outer-reef escarpments, where they feed on zooplankton; they come to the reef for parasite removal at *Labroides* cleaning stations and to sleep at night. Depth range, 6–229 m. *Naso vomer* Klunzinger and *N. thorpei* Smith are probable synonyms (Randall & Bell, 1992).

Red Sea/male courtship color

Hawaiian Islands/juvenile

Coral Sea

ORANGESPINE UNICORNFISH

Naso lituratus (Forster, 1801)

Dorsal rays VI,28–31 (modally 30); anal rays II,29–31 (modally 30); pectoral rays 17–18 (usually 17); teeth of adults incisiform with rounded smooth ends, 30–35 in jaws; body depth 2.2–2.7 in standard length (more elongate with growth); no horn or protuberance on forehead; dorsal profile of snout of adults nearly straight, forming an angle of about 45° to horizontal axis of head and body; 2 peduncular plates, each with a large, sharp, forward-projecting keel; caudal fin emarginate, adult males with a trailing filament from each corner; dark grayish brown, the peduncular plates and keels and area surrounding them brilliant orange; a narrow, curved yellow band from corner of mouth to below eye, the snout in front of yellow band black; lips orange; a yellow area above and behind eye; dorsal fin mainly black, the black continuing as a pointed projection onto nape, with a pale blue line at base and a broad outer white zone on soft portion, narrowing onto spinous part; anal fin mainly orange; dorsal and anal fins with a narrow blue margin and black submarginal line; caudal fin with a yellow submarginal band posteriorly. Reported to 46 cm. Suruga Bay, Japan, to Great Barrier Reef and New Caledonia, east to the islands of Oceania except Easter Island; type locality, Tahiti; reported in the eastern Pacific from Clipperton Island; in the eastern Indian Ocean south on the Western Australian coast to Ningaloo Reef (21°55′S). Illustrated in color from Christmas Island by Allen & Steene (1988: fig. 459); replaced by *N. elegans* (Rüppell) in the rest of the Indian Ocean. Browses on benthic algae on coral reefs or rocky bottom, especially leafy types such as *Sargassum, Pocockiella,* and *Dictyota*. Usually encountered in less than 30 m, but reported as deep as 90 m. Sometimes seen in large aggregations. Juveniles and subadults are popular in the aquarium trade.

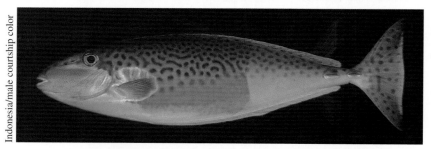

Cebu, Philippines

Indonesia/male courtship color

Bali (night)

SLENDER UNICORNFISH
Naso lopezi Herre, 1927

Dorsal rays V,28–31; anal rays II,27–30; pectoral rays 17; pelvic rays I,3; up to 70 upper and 65 lower teeth; body elongate in adults, the depth varying from 3.3 in standard length in a 25-cm specimen to 4.0 in large adults; dorsal and ventral profiles of head equally convex, with no protuberance on forehead; anterior interorbital space and adjacent space between nostrils nearly flat medially; snout long, 1.6–1.7 in head length; scales on cheek large for the genus; peduncular plates of moderate size, the keels without a forward-projecting point; caudal fin emarginate in young, truncate to very slightly double emarginate in adults (when fully spread); gray, paler ventrally, the upper half of body and caudal fin with numerous small, dark gray to black spots (larger and sometimes joined as short bands on some individuals; spots may be faint in subadults); a large pale area around pectoral fin, sometimes containing dark reddish bars; 2 broad black bands in anal fin (pigment mainly on membranes). Attains 50 cm. Andaman Sea and western Pacific from southern Honshu to Great Barrier Reef; east to Guam and New Caledonia; type locality, Ambil Island off Manila Bay, Luzon. Occurs off outer-reef escarpments as solitary fish or in small groups; feeds on zooplankton. Comes to the reef at night to sleep.

Hawaiian Islands/juvenile

Hawaiian Islands

SPOTTED UNICORNFISH
Naso maculatus Randall & Struhsaker, 1981

Dorsal rays VI-VII (rarely VII),26–28; anal rays II,26–28; pectoral rays 16–18; a 43.5-cm standard length specimen with 70 upper and 65 lower teeth; body depth 2.3 in standard length of subadults (about 30 cm standard length) to 3.3 in large adults; no protuberance on forehead, the dorsal and ventral profiles of head evenly convex; 2 peduncular plates with semicircular, blade-like keels; caudal fin emarginate; pale gray to gray-brown with numerous small, dark gray spots on head and body except ventrally; an irregular, dark gray line following lateral line; juveniles and subadults with fewer and relatively larger spots, some of which are joined to form short irregular lines; dorsal and anal fins with bluish white rays and dark gray membranes; caudal fin colored like body basally, becoming pale blue distally (as a narrow blue margin on subadults). Reported to 60 cm. Antitropical in the Pacific; known from the Hawaiian Islands (type locality, O'ahu), Wakayama Prefecture to Ogasawara Islands in Japan, Lord Howe Island, Chesterfield Islands, and New Caledonia. Reported in the main Hawaiian Islands from depths of 76–120 m (Chave & Mundy, 1994) and in southern Japan from depths of 43–220 m (Okamura, 1985); occurs in scuba-diving depths in the cooler sea of the Northwestern Hawaiian Islands; also in diving depths at Lord Howe Island and New Caledonia.

594

SINGLESPINE UNICORNFISH
Naso thynnoides (Valenciennes in C & V, 1835)
Dorsal rays IV-V (rarely V),28–30; anal rays II,28–30; pectoral rays 16–18; 80–90 upper teeth and 70–80 lower teeth in adults; body depth 2.8–3.2 in standard length; dorsal profile of head convex without a protuberance; a broad, median flat area in anterior interorbital space and adjacent space between nostrils; oblique groove on snout below nostrils reaching halfway from eye to mouth; a single peduncular plate, the keel small and approximately semicircular; caudal fin emarginate; gray, paler ventrally, with about 30 narrow, dark bluish gray bars on body and irregular spots on head; a broad, diffuse yellow stripe on side of body; peduncular plate and keel dusky; caudal fin bluish gray. Largest specimen examined, 28.5 cm. East coast of Africa to the Tuamotu Archipelago and islands of Micronesia except the Marshalls; in the western Pacific from the Ryukyu Islands to the Great Barrier Reef; type locality, Dorey Harbor, New Guinea. Semipelagic; usually seen in small, roving aggregations feeding on zooplankton. Occurs both in the protected waters of lagoons and in exposed outer-reef areas, from the shallows to least 40 m (but generally more than 10 m); comes to *Labroides* cleaning stations and sleeps on reefs at night, at which time it takes on a disruptive mottled color pattern.

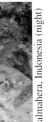

Tuamotu Archipelago

Halmahera, Indonesia (night)

Great Barrier Reef

BULBNOSE UNICORNFISH
Naso tonganus (Valenciennes in C & V, 1835)
Dorsal rays V,27–30; anal rays II,26–28; pectoral rays 16–18; teeth in jaws denticulate near tips, increasing in number with age, 22–46 in each jaw; body depth of adults varying from 2.25 in standard length of a 25-cm subadult to 3.0 in large adults; dorsal profile of body of adults with a pronounced convexity beneath spinous portion of dorsal fin; adults with a very large bulbous protuberance at front of head, which on large males extends anterior to mouth; 2 peduncular plates, the keel on each large with a forward-projecting point; caudal fin emarginate in young to truncate in adults (when fin is spread); gray to olivaceous, becoming paler ventrally, with numerous very small black spots on about upper half to three-fourths of body and on nape (large adults lose the dark spots except for a large V-shaped area of very small spots centered beneath hump on back); dorsal fin blackish basally (black mainly on membranes), with a very broad pale blue margin; caudal fin with a very narrow, bluish white posterior margin and a broad submarginal blackish zone; pectoral fins with a broad submarginal black band. Reaches at least 60 cm. East Africa to the Samoa Islands and throughout Micronesia; Ryukyu Islands to the Great Barrier Reef and New Caledonia; reported (as *Naso tuberosus*) from Western Australia south to Cape Cuvier by Allen & Swainston (1988); type locality, Tongatapu, Tonga. Johnson (2002) distinguished this species from the closely related *N. tuberosus* from the western Indian Ocean, which differs in having modally fewer dorsal and anal rays and a large semicircular black spot on the chest.

Gulf of Aqaba, Red Sea

BLUESPINE UNICORNFISH
Naso unicornis (Forsskål, 1775)

Dorsal rays VI,27–30; anal rays II,27–30; pectoral rays 17–18; depth of body varying from about 2.0 in standard length of subadults to 2.4–2.6 in adults; a tapering, bony, horn-like process in front of eye that does not extend anterior to mouth (horn first appearing as a bump anterior to eye in fish of about 12 cm); dorsal profile of snout to base of horn straight and forming an angle of about 45° to horizontal axis of head and body; 2 peduncular plates, each with a large sharp keel ending in a foward-projecting point; caudal fin emarginate in young, truncate with a filament from each corner in adults; males reported to have a longer horn, larger peduncular keels, and longer caudal filaments than females of the same size; yellowish to olivaceous gray dorsally, paler ventrally; a blue area sometimes present around pectoral fin; peduncular plates and keels blue; lips whitish or blue; dorsal and anal fins with a blue margin; caudal fin orangish basally, shading to gray, with a broad, pale greenish posterior border; caudal filaments edged in blue; one transient color phase with a blotchy

Hawaiian Islands/subadult

pale greenish zone beneath spinous portion of dorsal fin that narrows and ends beneath pectoral fin. Reported to reach 70 cm. Occurs throughout the Indo-Pacific region; type locality, Red Sea. Primarily an inshore fish of coral reefs and rocky shores; will enter surprisingly shallow water for so large a fish in its quest of leafy algae such as *Sargassum*. The keris larval stage, about 4 cm total length, has black spots on upper half of body.

Marshall Islands

BIGNOSE UNICORNFISH
Naso vlamingii (Valenciennes in C & V, 1835)

Dorsal rays VI,26–27; anal rays II,27–29; pectoral rays 17–19; body depth varying from about 2.2 in standard length of subadults to 2.5–2.6 in adults; a prominent convex protuberance on forehead of adults centered just below level of lower edge of eye; 2 peduncular plates, each with a large keel having a forward-projecting point in adults; dorsal fin elevated and nearly uniform in height, the first dorsal spine 1.5–1.7 in head length; caudal fin slightly emarginate in young, showing the start of a filament from each corner of fish as small as 15 cm; fin of adults truncate to slightly rounded with long filaments; ground color of adults may change rapidly from dark gray-brown to pale bluish gray; vertical, dark bluish lines on side of body with small, dark bluish spots above and below; head with small, dark bluish spots and

596

a broad blue band extending anteriorly from eye; lips blue; caudal fin bluish basally, gray in broad middle zone, with a broad yellowish border; caudal filaments and upper and lower edges of fin blue; dark bluish markings can be altered in an instant to brilliant blue, as during courtship or when visiting a cleaning station; one transient color phase displays a broad, pale bluish zone anteriorly on upper part of body; young with scattered, small blue spots. Attains about 55 cm. East coast of Africa to the Society Islands and Tuamotu Archipelago; Kii Peninsula, Japan, to Great Barrier Reef and New Caledonia. Not known from the Red Sea, Oman, Persian Gulf, India, or Hawaiian Islands; 1 record from the Galápagos Islands (McCosker & Humann, 1996); type locality, Molucca Islands. Usually seen in open water in outer-reef areas, especially near drop-offs, but may also occur in lagoons; depth range 4–50 m. Feeds mainly on zooplankton.

Palau/juvenile

Lord Howe Island

SAWTAILS (PRIONURINAE)

YELLOWSPOTTED SAWTAIL
Prionurus maculatus Ogilby, 1887
Dorsal rays IX,24–26; anal rays III,23–25; pectoral rays 17–18; pelvic rays I,5; body depth of adults 2.2–2.3 in standard length; head length 3.2–3.7 in standard length; mouth slightly protruding, the dorsal profile of snout straight to slightly concave, forming an angle of about 45° to horizontal axis of head and body; 3 lateral peduncular plates, each with a low lateral keel; caudal fin slightly emarginate to truncate; bluish gray with numerous small yellow spots on head and body, especially dorsally; peduncular plates black with blue keels, often with a white saddle-like mark above last plate; caudal fin gray with yellow spots on basal half; juveniles with yellow spots on back, the side of body with narrow yellow bars that break up into vertical rows of spots with growth. Largest collected by author, 43.5 cm. New South Wales to southern Queensland (only the Capricorn Group and Swains

Lord Howe Island

Reefs on the Great Barrier Reef), Lord Howe Island, Norfolk Island, New Caledonia (Laboute & Grandperrin, 2000), Kermadec Islands, and northern New Zealand (Francis, 1993); type locality, Port Jackson, Sydney, New South Wales. Generally found in protected waters, often in aggregations, but also occurs in outer-reef areas. Reported from the depth range of 2–30 m; feeds on benthic algae.

Spiny Rabbitfish, *Siganus spinus,* with *Scolopsis lineatus,* Tukungbesi Islands, Indonesia

RABBITFISHES
(SIGANIDAE)

The rabbitfish family is included with the acanthurids, *Zanclus,* ephippids, scatophagids, and *Luvarus* in the suborder Acanthuroidei. It consists of a single genus, *Siganus,* which was revised by Woodland (1990), who also provided many references on the biology of these fishes. He recognized 27 species, all of which occur in the Indo-Pacific region; he classified them in two subgenera, *Siganus* and *Lo,* the latter for the 5 species with protruding snouts. Two more species appear to be undescribed. Diagnostic characters for the Siganidae are as follows: body ellipsoid and compressed; a continuous dorsal fin with XIII spines (not including a procumbent spine) and 10 soft rays; anal fin with an unusual VII spines and 9 soft rays; dorsal and anal spines alternate left and right of the midline as they fold down; pelvic fins inserted slightly posterior to pectoral-fin base, with an initial and a terminal spine and 3 soft rays between, the inner spine connected by membrane to the abdomen; caudal fin truncate to forked; scales cycloid, very small, and partly embedded; a small, terminal to slightly inferior nonprotractile mouth with a broad upper lip; a single row of bicuspid incisiform teeth in jaws; no teeth on vomer or palatines; and 23 vertebrae. All of the spines, including even the procumbent one, are venomous, the venom glands lying in an anterolateral groove on each side. Wounds from the spines are extremely painful, as the author can confirm from more than one such contact; however, the wounds are not as serious or the pain as long-lasting as that inflicted by the spines of many of the scorpaenid fishes. All of the species are at least partly herbivorous, but several feed heavily on benthic invertebrates such as sponges and tunicates. Siganids are inshore fishes; 14 species are usually found in small schools in seagrass beds or over algal flats; the others are associated with coral reefs and are often encountered in pairs. When at rest on the bottom or asleep at night, they assume a different color pattern, usually a disruptive one of dark blotches. The eggs of most rabbitfishes are sticky and demersal; those of *Siganus argenteus* are pelagic (and those of *S. spinus* are presumed to be), which may explain the broad distribution of these 2 species. Because of rapid growth, herbivorous food habits, and tasty flesh, some of the rabbitfishes have been candidates for aquaculture. Their venomous spines make handling these fishes difficult.

FORKTAIL RABBITFISH
Siganus argenteus (Quoy & Gaimard, 1825)

Dorsal rays XIII,10; anal rays VII,9; pectoral rays 17–19; pelvic rays I,3,I (true of other *Siganus*); scale rows above lateral line 16–22; midventral region of chest naked; body elongate for the genus, the depth 2.4–3.0 in standard length; head moderately pointed; dorsal spines slender, the fourth to eighth longest, 2.5–3.5 times longer than last dorsal spine; second to fourth dorsal soft rays longest, but shorter than longest dorsal spines; caudal fin strongly forked; light blue to bluish gray or brown with numerous small yellow spots that may join to form narrow stripes, especially ventrally on body, or a reticular pattern; a short blackish bar at upper edge of gill opening. Largest specimen, 44 cm. The most wide-ranging of the Siganidae, from the Red Sea and coast of East Africa to the Line Islands, islands of French Polynesia, and the Pitcairn Islands; Ryukyu Islands to the Great Barrier Reef and New Caledonia; type locality, Guam. Usually seen in small aggregations; moves in open water more than other rabbitfishes. Named from the silvery late postlarval (or prejuvenile) stage, which is unusually large (may reach 7.5 cm). *Amphacanthus rostratus* Valenciennes is a synonym based on the adult. Popper & Gundermann (1975) published on the ecology and behavior.

Okinawa (artificial reef)

Bali

CORAL RABBITFISH
Siganus corallinus (Valenciennes in C & V, 1835)

Dorsal rays XIII,10; anal rays VII,9; pectoral rays 16–17; scale rows above lateral line 16–23; body moderately deep, the depth 1.7–2.3 in standard length; snout somewhat protruding, the dorsal and ventral profiles concave, 1.9–2.0 in head length; fifth to eighth dorsal spines longest, 1.1–1.4 times times longer than last dorsal spine; longest dorsal soft ray equal to or slightly longer than longest dorsal spine; caudal fin forked; yellow with numerous very small, dark-edged, pale blue spots; a triangular dark smudge extending dorsoposterior to eye and sometimes one onto snout; fins yellow. Reaches 30 cm. Seychelles (type locality) and Maldive Islands to Vanuatu and New Caledonia; Ryukyu Islands to Great Barrier Reef; replaced by *Siganus trispilos* Woodland & Allen in Western Australia. Juveniles occur in small aggregations in shallow seagrass beds and among shallow branching corals, often with other juvenile siganids and scarids; as adults they are seen in pairs on reefs down to about 10 m feeding mainly on benthic algae.

Great Barrier Reef/juvenile

Papua New Guinea, with *Labroides dimidiatus*

Palau/juvenile

Great Barrier Reef (night)

PENCILSTREAKED RABBITFISH
Siganus doliatus Cuvier, 1830

Dorsal rays XIII,10; anal rays VII,9; pectoral rays 16–17; scale rows above lateral line 19–26; body moderately deep, the depth 1.8–2.2 in standard length; snout short, 2.0–2.2 in head length, the dorsal and ventral profiles nearly straight; caudal fin emarginate in juveniles to moderately forked in adults; yellow dorsally and posteriorly, white ventrally, with vertical blue lines of width about equal to the yellow interspaces on most of body, becoming horizontal on chest and caudal peduncle; top of peduncle mainly yellow; head yellow with very irregular blue lines; 2 oblique orangish brown bands, one from nape through eye to chin (sometimes faint on nape), and the other from below base of fifth dorsal spine to upper base of pectoral fin; caudal and dorsal fins yellow. Attains 25 cm. Eastern Indonesia and Western Australia to Great Barrier Reef, Palau, Caroline Islands, New Caledonia, Fiji, and Tonga; described from the Molucca Islands and Vanikoro in the Santa Cruz Islands. Adults occur in pairs on shallow reefs; juveniles in small aggregations, often with other juvenile siganids and scarids, usually in *Acropora* thickets with dense algal growth at base. Very closely related to *Siganus virgatus* (Valenciennes) from the Philippines and Sulawesi to India; apparently the 2 hybridize in areas of overlap in Indonesia.

Flores, Indonesia (night)

Cebu, Philippines

DUSKY RABBITFISH
Siganus fuscescens (Houttuyn, 1782)

Dorsal rays XIII,10; anal rays VII,9; pectoral rays 15–17; scale rows above lateral line 18–26; cheeks sometimes naked, but usually at least a few scales scattered on lower half; midline of chest naked; body depth 2.3–2.9 in standard length; snout length 3.0–3.6 in standard length; the dorsal profile of head slightly convex; caudal fin emarginate in juveniles to moderately forked in adults; brown to olivaceous or brownish yellow dorsally, silvery gray or yellowish ventrally, with small, well-spaced, pale blue spots dorsally and white spots on side and ventrally, some white spots horizontally oblong; approximate horizontal rows of pale blue spots above lateral line varying from 3 in subadults to 6 in large adults (those in adults about 3 mm in diameter); a dark blotch a little smaller than eye often present behind upper end of gill opening and below lateral line. Attains 32 cm. Indo-Malayan region and Andaman Islands north to Japan (type locality) and Korea, south to New South Wales and Rottnest Island, Western Australia; east to Palau, Yap, Vanuatu, New Caledonia, and Lord Howe Island; often found in seagrass beds where it grazes algae from the seagrass blades.

GOLDLINED RABBITFISH

Siganus lineatus (Valenciennes in
  C & V, 1835)

Dorsal rays XIII,10; anal rays VII,9; pectoral rays 16–17; scale rows above lateral line 18–27; body moderately deep, the depth 1.9–2.2 in standard length; dorsal profile of snout nearly straight, the length 1.8–2.2 in head length; caudal fin slightly forked; pale blue with narrow, wavy, variously broken, orange-yellow stripes on body except ventrally (may be mainly as spots dorsally on body); a bright yellow spot as large as or larger than eye below rear base of dorsal fin; head and nape with irregular bands of yellow and pale blue, the blue narrower there. Recorded to 43 cm. Western Australia to Queensland, Great Barrier Reef, New Caledonia, and Vanuatu north to eastern Indonesia, New Guinea, Palau, and the Caroline Islands; described from Waigeo, Indonesia, and Vanikoro, Santa Cruz Islands. A separate population in India and Sri Lanka warrants further investigation. Juveniles occur in small schools in mangrove areas and seagrass beds; adults usually seen in small groups in protected waters where there is coral or hard substratum; feeds mainly on benthic algae, sometimes on sponges. Very closely related to *Siganus guttatus* (Bloch), which differs in being entirely spotted with orange-yellow; hybrids of the 2 might be expected in areas where both occur.

Great Barrier Reef

BLACK RABBITFISH

Siganus niger Woodland, 1990

Dorsal rays XIII,10; anal rays VII,9; pectoral rays 16–17; scale rows above lateral line 18; body depth 2.0–2.3 in standard length; snout strongly protruding, the dorsal and ventral profiles strongly concave, the snout length about 2 in head length; caudal fin very slightly forked; black, the outer part of pectoral fins broadly yellow; posterior edge of median fins very narrowly whitish. Largest specimen, 22.5 cm. Known only from Tonga (type locality, Vava'u); not common. Type specimens collected by the author. One of 5 species placed in the subgenus *Lo*.

Tonga

BLUELINED RABBITFISH

Siganus puellus (Schlegel, 1852)

Dorsal rays XIII,10; anal rays VII,9; pectoral rays 16–17 (rarely 15 or 17); scale rows above lateral line 18–25; body depth 2.3–2.6 in standard length; dorsal profile of head above upper lip nearly straight; snout length 1.95–2.0 in head length; caudal fin moderately forked; body yellow with wavy blue lines that are mostly vertical anteriorly and horizontal posteriorly; head yellow, grading to white on edge of gill cover, with an oblique blackish band from chin through eye to nape where spotted with black; fins yellow. Attains about 38 cm. Ryukyu Islands to Great Barrier Reef and New Caledonia, east to Marshall Islands, Caroline Islands, and Kiribati; in the eastern Indian Ocean from reefs off northwestern Australia and the Cocos-Keeling Islands; type locality, Ternate, Molucca Islands. Closely related to *Siganus puelloides* Woodland & Randall from the Andaman Sea and Maldive Islands; juveniles inshore of outer-reef flats and shallow coral heads; adults nearly always encountered in pairs, the pair bonding first showing at a length of about 10 cm. Juveniles feed on fine filamentous algae, the adults on coarser algae, along with sponge. *Siganus cyanotaenia* (Bleeker) is one of five synonyms.

Marshall Islands

601

Bali

GOLDSPOTTED RABBITFISH
Siganus punctatus (Forster, 1801)
Dorsal rays XIII,10; anal rays VII,9; pectoral rays 16–18 (rarely 18); scale rows above lateral line 23–27; body depth 1.9–2.3 in standard length; dorsal profile of head nearly straight; snout length 1.9–2.1 in head length; caudal fin deeply forked; bluish gray to light blue with numerous small, dark-edged orange spots on head, body, and caudal fin; a dark gray blotch larger than eye often present behind upper end of gill opening (orange spots visible within); a pale saddle-like mark sometimes present on caudal peduncle (also not obscuring orange spots). Reaches 40 cm. Ryukyu Islands to Great Barrier Reef, New South Wales, and New Caledonia, east to Tonga (type locality), Samoa Islands, and throughout Micronesia; also Western Australia and Cocos-Keeling Islands. Adults occur in pairs; found on coral reefs from a few to 50 m; feeds mainly on benthic algae.

SPINY RABBITFISH
Siganus spinus (Linnaeus, 1758)
Dorsal rays XIII,10; anal rays VII,9; pectoral rays 16–18 (rarely 16 or 18); scale rows above lateral line 14–18; body moderately elongate, the depth 2.3–2.8 in standard length; dorsal profile of snout convex; snout short, its length 2.5–2.7 in head length; caudal fin truncate (of juveniles slightly emarginate); whitish with a labyrinth of narrow brown bands over head and body; fins translucent, mottled with dark brown. Smallest of the siganid fishes; largest reported, 24 cm, but seldom exceeds 19 cm. Western Australia and Andaman Sea, including Sri Lanka, to Society Islands and throughout Micronesia; Ryukyu Islands to Great Barrier Reef and New Caledonia; type locality, Java. Adults in small groups up to about 20 individuals roam the outer reefs, grazing on benthic algae. The young recruit at times in huge numbers

Bali

to shallow reefs; in Guam this takes place in spring (Kami & Ikehara, 1976). Like *Siganus argenteus,* the late postlarval stage is large compared with that of other species of *Siganus,* to at least 4.5 cm.

Fiji/juvenile

Fiji/Aquarium photo

FIJI RABBITFISH
Siganus uspi Gawel & Woodland, 1974
Dorsal rays XIII,10; anal rays VII,9; pectoral rays 16–17; scale rows above lateral line 17–22; body depth 2.0–2.2 in standard length; snout strongly protruding, the dorsal and ventral profiles very concave; snout length about 2 in head length; caudal fin very slightly forked; body dark brown, the posterior one-fourth, caudal fin, and adjacent dorsal and anal fins abruptly bright yellow; head and chest black with an oblique white band from throat to nape, containing light brown dots and a fine reticular pattern. Largest specimen, 24 cm. Known only from Fiji except for 1 unconfirmed sight record from New Caledonia.

VERMICULATE RABBITFISH

Siganus vermiculatus (Valenciennes in C & V, 1835)
Dorsal rays XIII,10; anal rays VII,9; pectoral rays 16–17; scale rows above lateral line 17–26; body moderately deep, the depth 1.9–2.2 in standard length; dorsal profile of snout to eye straight; snout short, about 2.4–2.5 in head of adults (more than 3 in juveniles); caudal fin slightly forked; body whitish, covered with vermiculating, dark brown lines; median fins gray-brown, the caudal with many small, dark brown spots. Attains 45 cm. Indo-Malayan region west to Sri Lanka and India, east to Guam, Palau, Woliae in Caroline Islands, and Fiji; type locality, New Guinea. Gundermann et al. (1983) studied the biology in Fiji. Adults form breeding aggregations on the seventh or eighth days of the lunar month; the eggs are demersal and sticky; metamorphosis to the juvenile stage takes place 23–25 days after hatching. The fry occur in small schools around mangrove roots; adults move in and out of mangrove sloughs with the tide, grazing on algae off the mangrove roots. This species is a prime candidate for aquaculture because it is herbivorous, commands a high price in the market, is very tolerant of a wide range of temperature and salinity, grows rapidly, and reaches large size for the genus.

Sulawesi

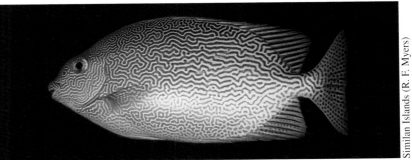

Similan Islands (R. F. Myers)

Redang, Malaysia

FOXFACE

Siganus vulpinus (Schlegel & Müller, 1845)
Dorsal rays XIII,10; anal rays VII,9; pectoral rays 16–17 (usually 16); scale rows above lateral line 16–20; body moderately deep, the depth 1.9–2.4 in standard length; dorsal profile of snout concave, that of ventral profile of head strongly concave; snout long, 1.7–1.95 in head length; caudal fin slightly forked to truncate; body and median fins yellow to an approximate vertical demarcation below the third to fourth dorsal spines, then gray; head and chest black with a broad, oblique white band from throat and edge of operculum to behind eye. Attains 25 cm. Indo-Malayan region south to Great Barrier Reef, east to Vanuatu, New Caledonia, and islands of Micronesia except the Mariana Islands; type locality, Ternate, Molucca Islands. Juveniles occur in small schools inshore; individuals begin to form pairs at about 12-cm length and are presumed to remain bonded through life; typically found in luxuriant coral areas of protected waters, each pair with a territory; limited data suggest that the diet is benthic algae. The similar *Siganus unimaculatus* ranges from the Philippines to Japan.

603

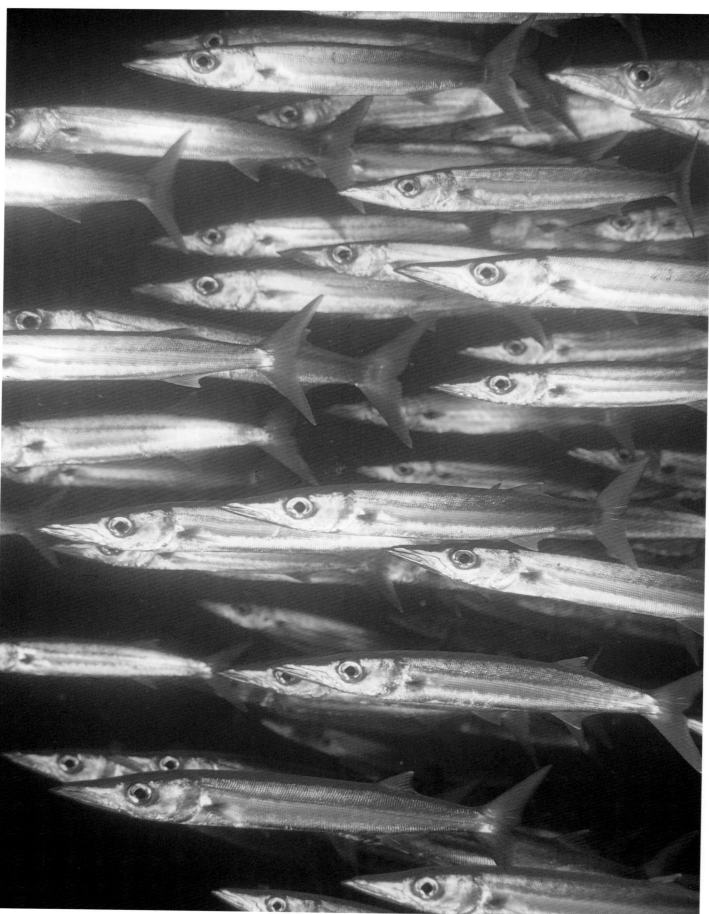

Bigeye Barracuda, *Sphyraena forsteri*, Solomon Islands

BARRACUDAS
(SPHYRAENIDAE)

The barracudas were formerly believed to be allied with the threadfins (Polynemidae) and mullets (Mugilidae), partly because of having 2 widely separated dorsal fins. They are currently classified in the perciform suborder Scombroidei, along with the cutlassfishes, snake mackerels, tunas, and billfishes (Johnson, 1986). The barracudas are very distinctive in having an elongate little-compressed body, strongly pointed head with projecting lower jaw, large mouth with compressed teeth of variable size in jaws and on palatines, some as long fangs. The first dorsal fin consists of V spines, set near the middle of the standard length, the second dorsal with I,9 rays about half the distance to the caudal fin, with the anal fin of II,8–9 rays below; the caudal fin is forked or double or triple emarginate; the pelvic fins have I,5 rays, their base distinctly posterior to that of the pectoral fins. The scales are small and cycloid, the lateral line conspicuous and nearly straight. Gill rakers are either absent or number only 1 or 2. As the dentition indicates, these fishes are predaceous, feeding mainly on fishes and squids. Some are diurnal and others are nocturnal, forming semistationary schools during the day. Although barracudas have attacked humans, this danger is greatly exaggerated. In clear water without anything that might attract a barracuda such as a wounded fish struggling on the end of a spear or a shiny object, there is no reason to fear a barracuda. The family consists of a single genus, *Sphyraena*, and about 20 species worldwide in tropical to temperate seas. Six species are treated here. One other, *S. putnamae* Jordan & Seale (type locality, Hong Kong) (*putnamiae* of some authors), may occur in the western part of the South Pacific, but it needs to be more convincingly diagnosed from *S. qenie*. Senou (1992) distinguished *putnamae* by having wavy bars that reach the dorsal and ventral contours of the body, whereas the bars of *qenie* are supposedly confined to the side of the body between horizontal lines at the start of the lateral line and the lower edge of the pectoral-fin base; his photographic illustrations do not confirm this (the extent of the dark bars in photographs depends on how the light strikes the silvery body). Senou in Carpenter & Niem (2001b) separated *putnamae* by having chevron markings in contrast to bars that are oblique in the upper half for *qenie*, but both species have chevron markings in his illustrations. He added that the last dorsal soft ray is longer than the penultimate ray in *putnamae* but not in *qenie*; however, his drawings do not show this difference. Senou included New Caledonia in his distribution map of *putnamae*, but this species is not listed from the island by Laboute & Grandperrin (2000).

School of Blackmargin Barracuda, *Sphyraena qenie,* with a surgeonfish (*Acanthurus xanthopterus*) feeding on their feces, Sabah

Sulawesi

GREAT BARRACUDA

Sphyraena barracuda (Walbaum, 1792)

Dorsal rays V + I,9; anal rays II,8; pectoral rays 13–15; lateral-line scales 69–90; no gill rakers (rough platelets present on gill arches but without spinules); body depth 6.0–8.2 in standard length; eye small for the genus; cartilaginous knob at front of lower jaw not well developed; teeth erect and contiguous; origin of first dorsal fin over rear base of pelvic fins; caudal fin emarginate with 2 rounded lobes in middle of posterior margin; tip of pectoral fins extending beyond base of pelvic fins; dark green to dark gray on back, silvery on side and ventrally, usually with a few scattered black spots, mainly on lower posterior two-thirds of body; 18–22 oblique dark bars on back, more evident in juveniles and subadults than in adults; caudal fin with 2 large black spots, one covering a major part of each lobe of fin. Reported to 1.7 m; world angling record, 38.5 kg, from the Philippines. Occurs throughout the Indo-Pacific region and the tropical and subtropical Atlantic (type locality, Bahamas). Future studies may

Hawaiian Islands/juvenile

determine that the Indo-Pacific form is a different species, in which case the name would be *Sphyraena commersonii* Cuvier. Juveniles generally found in calm inshore waters such as the mangrove habitat; adults usually solitary. Responsible for most attacks by barracudas on humans, nearly always a result of provocation (as by spearing) or taking place in murky water when a limb might be mistaken as prey. One of the worst offenders for causing ciguatera fish poisoning; large fish of this species should not be eaten where ciguatera is known. The biology was studied by De Sylva (1963).

Bali

Bahrain

YELLOWTAIL BARRACUDA

Sphyraena flavicauda Rüppell, 1838

Dorsal rays V + I,9; anal rays II,9 pectoral rays 14; lateral-line scales 72–90; gill rakers 2; body depth 6.8–8.3 in standard length; eye large; corner of preopercle with a prominent membranous flap; maxilla ending about a pupil width before eye; teeth erect, separated by a space greater than tooth width; origin of first dorsal fin behind a vertical at tip of pectoral fin; caudal fin forked; silvery green dorsally, shading to silvery on side, usually with a longitudinal series of short blackish bars on anterior part of lateral line, but extending above it posteriorly; a narrow brown stripe sometimes visible on side of head and lower side of body; lateral line yellowish brown; fins yellowish, especially the caudal, which may be dark-edged; a blackish blotch at base of pectoral fins. Attains about 40 cm. Red Sea (type locality) to Guam and Samoa Islands; Ryukyu Islands to Great Barrier Reef and New Caledonia. Usually seen by day in small aggregations; probably nocturnal.

Lombok, Indonesia

BIGEYE BARRACUDA
Sphyraena forsteri Cuvier in C & V, 1829

Dorsal rays V + I,9; anal rays II,9; pectoral rays 14–15; lateral-line scales 112–123; no gill rakers, but spinules on 10–20 tubercles of lower limb of first gill arch; body depth 6.9–7.7 in standard length; eye very large; corner of preopercle rounded, without a projecting flap; maxilla reaching to below anterior edge of eye; teeth closely spaced, those posteriorly in lower jaw angling backward; origin of first dorsal fin slightly posterior to base of pelvic fins; caudal fin forked with a small inner lobe on each major lobe; bluish gray dorsally, silvery gray on side and ventrally; a large blackish blotch in axil of pectoral fins and usually extending slightly above pectoral-fin base; median fins dusky, the tips of second dorsal and anal fins white. Attains 65 cm. Occurs throughout the Indo-Pacific region except the Hawaiian Islands; described from a drawing of a specimen from Tahiti; neotype from New Guinea. Nocturnal; usually seen in schools by day.

Marshall Islands

HELLER'S BARRACUDA
Sphyraena helleri Jenkins, 1901

Dorsal rays V + I,9; anal rays II,8; pectoral rays 13–14; lateral-line scales 120–135; a single gill raker at angle of first gill arch; body depth 7.0–8.0 in standard length; eye large; corner of preopercle rounded, without a projecting flap; maxilla reaching to within a half orbit diameter of edge of eye; teeth well spaced, the first 2 pairs in upper jaw angling inward; origin of dorsal fin over origin of pelvic fins; tip of pectoral fins well short of a vertical at origin of dorsal fin; caudal fin forked with a slight convexity on each side of midline; silvery with iridescence and 2 longitudinal brassy stripes on side of body in life. Attains 80 cm. Widepread at islands of Oceania, including the Hawaiian Islands (Oʻahu, type locality) and Easter Island; Senou in Carpenter & Niem (2001b) gave the range to the western Pacific and indicated that Indian Ocean records are uncertain. Nocturnal; forms nearly stationary schools by day.

Fiji

PICKHANDLE BARRACUDA
Sphyraena jello Cuvier in C & V, 1829

Dorsal rays V + I,9; anal rays II,9; pectoral rays 14–15; lateral-line scales 130–140; no gill rakers (platelets on lower limb of first gill arch rough but without spinules); body slender, the depth 7.9–8.9 in standard length; eye not large; corner of preopercle rounded, without a projecting flap; maxilla reaching to below anterior edge of eye; teeth erect; origin of first dorsal fin slightly posterior to base of pelvic fins; caudal fin deeply forked without inner lobes; dusky blue-green on back, silvery on sides and below with about 20 slightly oblique dark bars about equal in width to pale interspaces, those posterior to second dorsal fin faint; caudal fin yellow. Attains about 140 cm. Red Sea and east coast of Africa to western Pacific from Taiwan to Great Barrier Reef, New Caledonia, and Fiji; type locality, India. Diurnal; solitary or in small schools.

Palau

BLACKMARGIN BARRACUDA
Sphyraena qenie Klunzinger, 1870

Dorsal rays V + I,9; anal rays II,8; pectoral rays 15; lateral-line scales 120–130; no gill rakers, but gill arch with numerous spinules; body depth 6.0–7.9 in standard length; eye not large; corner of preopercle rounded, without a projecting flap; maxilla reaching to or slightly beyond a vertical at anterior edge of eye; teeth in jaws erect and close-set; origin of dorsal fin over rear base of pelvic fins; tip of pectoral fins reaching to or beyond rear base of pelvic fins; caudal fin forked with a distinct, small inner lobe to each side of middle of fin of adults; gray dorsally, silvery below, with about 18 slightly sinuous dark gray bars on body, broader than silvery interspaces dorsally and narrower ventrally; caudal fin yellowish gray with a black margin; axil of pectoral fin blackish. Reaches 140 cm. Occurs throughout the tropical Indo-Pacific region; type locality, Red Sea; two sight records for Hawai'i. Usually seen by day in large semistationary schools. See family account for discussion of the similar *Sphyraena putnamae*. The usual common name is Blacktail Barracuda, but this is misleading because only the margin of the caudal fin is black.

Indian Mackerel, *Rastrelliger kanagurta*, Sudan, Red Sea

TUNAS AND MACKERELS
(SCOMBRIDAE)

This well-known family of fishes includes species that are the basis for some of the world's most important commercial fisheries; many of these fishes are also highly prized as game fishes. A total of 15 genera and 49 species is recognized in the family (Collette & Nauen, 1983; Collette et al. in Moser et al., 1984). These fishes are divided into 2 subfamilies, the Gasterochismatinae (for 1 species, *Gasterochisma melampus* of southern temperate waters) and the Scombrinae. The latter consists of 4 tribes, the tunas (Thunnini), the bonitos and dogtooth tuna (Sardini), the Spanish mackerels (Scomberomorini), and the mackerels (Scombrini). The family is characterized by having a streamlined, fusiform to elongate body with a narrow caudal peduncle that is reinforced by 2 or 3 keels on each side. The mackerels of the genera *Scomber* and *Rastrelliger* have 2 keels on the caudal-fin base; the remaining species have a large midlateral keel on the peduncle and caudal-fin base, in addition to the 2 on the caudal-fin base. The caudal fin is forked to lunate, and stiff. There are 2 dorsal fins, each depressible into a groove, and 5 to 12 finlets behind the second dorsal and anal fins; the pelvic fins of 6 soft rays are inserted beneath the base of the pectoral fins. The scales are cycloid, small to moderate in size; the body may be fully covered with scales or naked except some species having an anterior corselet of thick scales on the body. The mouth is large, the teeth variable in size, but none as canines. The species of *Scomber* and *Rastrelliger* have transparent adipose tissue that covers the anterior and posterior part of the eye. The body color is usually green or blue dorsally, silvery on the sides, often with a distinctive pattern of dark bands or spots. The mackerels filter zooplankton from the sea with their long gill rakers; the tunas, bonitos, and Spanish mackerels feed mainly on small fishes, especially schooling species such as the clupeoids; squids may also be important in the diet. Scombrids, in general, are schooling species and epipelagic. Only those that commonly occur inshore are included in this volume.

DOUBLE-LINED MACKEREL

Grammatorcynus bilineatus (Rüppell, 1836)

Dorsal rays XI-XIII + 10–12 + 6–7 finlets; anal rays 11–13 + 6–7 finlets; pectoral fins short, with 22–26 rays; caudal peduncle and fin base with 3 keels, the middle one largest; body and most of head covered with moderately small scales; no prominent anterior corselet; 2 lateral lines, the second branching off the first beneath the third dorsal spine, passing ventrally along the body, and rejoining the first below the last dorsal finlet; gill rakers 19–24; eye large, 7–9% of fork length; maxilla reaching to below middle of eye; 20–30 slender conical teeth in jaws and a patch of small teeth on vomer and palatines; dorsal fins well separated; metallic blue-green, shading to silvery with iridescence below. Attains 65 cm and a weight of about 3.5 kg. Reported from the Red Sea (type locality), Andaman Sea, Indo-Malayan region, north to Ryukyu Islands, south to Western Australia and Queensland, and east to Fiji and throughout Micronesia; solitary or in schools; usually seen cruising along steep outer-reef slopes; feeds on small fishes and the larger crustacean larvae.

Gulf of Aqaba, Red Sea

Marshall Islands

DOGTOOTH TUNA

Gymnosarda unicolor (Rüppell, 1836)

Dorsal rays XIII-XV + 12 + 6–7 finlets; anal rays 12–13 + 6 finlets; pectoral rays 25–28; body naked posterior to corselet except for lateral line, dorsal-fin base, and median caudal keel; lateral line undulating; gill rakers 11–14; maxilla reaching slightly posterior to middle of eye; conical teeth in jaws, those in upper jaw large; 2 patches of villiform teeth on tongue; dorsal fins adjacent; a single large interpelvic process; gray-blue on back, silvery below; no dark markings except a broad blackish border anteriorly on first dorsal fin; tips of second dorsal and anal fins whitish. All-tackle angling record, 131 kg, 206 cm fork length (hence about 220 cm total length), from Kwan-Tall Island, Korea. Indo-Pacific except the Hawaiian Islands, but found mostly around oceanic islands or continental areas such as the Red Sea (type locality) with well-developed reefs and clear water. Patrols the drop-offs of coral reefs as solitary individuals or in small groups, preying mainly on schooling fishes. Randall (1980a) examined the stomachs of 17 adult specimens from the Marshall Islands; among the prey, *Caesio* sp., *Pterocaesio* sp., *Cirrhilabrus* sp., *Naso brevirostris*, and *N. vlamingii*; mackerel scads (*Decapterus*) are also reported from stomachs. Six of 13 fish tested for ciguatera at Enewetak Atoll were mildly toxic (Randall, 1980a). *Gymnosarda nuda* (Günther) is a synonym.

610

INDIAN MACKEREL

Rastrelliger kanagurta (Cuvier, 1816)

Dorsal rays IX-XI + 11–13 + 5 finlets; anal rays 11–12 (initial rudimentary spine not counted) + 5 finlets; pectoral rays 19–22; body entirely covered with scales, those anteriorly larger but not developed as a corselet; gill rakers very long (visible when mouth open), 30–46, the longest rakers with numerous spinules; body depth 3.4–4.0 in standard length; body moderately compressed; mouth large, the maxilla extending posterior to rear margin of eye; teeth in jaws very small, none on vomer or palatines; interpelvic process small; silvery blue-green dorsally with 2 rows of blackish spots above lateral line, silvery on sides and ventrally, sometimes with golden reflections; 2 or 3 narrow yellowish stripes often visible on side of body. Reported to 38 cm, but any over 30 cm would be exceptional. The most wide-ranging of the 3 species of the genus, Red Sea (and into the Mediterranean via the Suez Canal) south to Natal and east to Palau, Caroline Islands, and Samoa Islands; southern Japan to Queensland; type locality, Vishakhapatnam, India. Occurs in schools of vari-

Lombok, Indonesia

able size; feeds by swimming with mouth open through concentrations of zooplankton; the author once observed 3 adults swim through the spawn of the wrasse *Thalassoma amblycephalum* to strain the ova (also reported for *Thalassoma* sp. by Colin, 1976). An important commercial fish in Asian waters. Jones & Rosa (1967) provided a synopsis of biological data for the species.

Papua New Guinea

NARROWBARRED SPANISH MACKEREL

Scomberomorus commerson (Lacepède, 1800)

Dorsal rays XV-XVIII + 15–20 (usually 16–17) + 8–10 finlets; anal rays 16–21 (usually 18–19) + 7–12 finlets; pectoral rays 21–24; body fully scaled; lateral line bent downward below second dorsal fin, wavy posteriorly; gill rakers 0–1 + 2–6; vertebrae 42–45; body elongate, the depth 3.4–4.0 in fork length, and compressed; mouth large, the maxilla exposed on cheek and extending to below rear margin of eye; teeth in jaws large, compressed, and triangular; teeth present on vomer and palatines; second dorsal fin higher than anterior part of first dorsal; bluish gray dorsally, shading to silvery ventrally, with numerous narrow, irregular dark bars; median and pectoral fins gray to dark gray; second dorsal and anal fins tipped with white. Reported to 245 cm; the all-tackle angling record, 44.9 kg, from Natal. Red Sea (and Mediterranean via the Suez Canal) and east coast of Africa to Fiji; Japan to Tasmania; no type locality given. An inshore pelagic species capable of long migrations; feeds mainly on fishes, especially clupeoids. Observed by the author only as solitary individuals.

LEFTEYE FLOUNDERS
(BOTHIDAE)

The Bothidae is the largest family of flatfishes of the order Pleuronectiformes. The fishes of this family, with few exceptions, have the eyes on the left side (sinistral). There are no teeth on the vomer or palatines, and no spines in the fins; the dorsal fin originates above or before the upper eye; the dorsal and anal fins are not joined to the caudal fin; the pectoral and pelvic rays are unbranched, the pelvics with 6 or fewer rays; the pelvic fin of the blind side is short-based; the pelvic fin on the ocular side lies on the ventral edge of the body and has a long base, extending well anterior to the fin of the blind side; there is no supramaxilla; the preopercle has a free margin; there is a single lateral line on the ocular side, highly arched over the pectoral fin (the one on the blind side may be faint or absent); the caudal fin is often rhomboid; the anus is on the blind side. Males may have 1 or more spines on the head, and the eyes may be farther apart. Most species occur on open sand or mud substrata, but a few may be found in rocky or coral-reef areas. These fishes are masters of camouflage and can quickly change their color pattern as when moving to an environment of different color. Also they are able to bury quickly in the sediment. All are carnivorous, usually ambushing their prey of small fishes and crustaceans. The family is represented by 20 genera and at least 115 species. Norman's monograph of the flatfishes (1934) has long been the most useful reference for the Bothidae and related families. Many species have been described since 1934, others await description, and no doubt some remain to be discovered.

Panther Flounder, *Bothus pantherinus*, Hawaiian Islands

LURING FLOUNDER
Asterorhombus fijiensis (Norman, 1931)

Dorsal rays 71–82; anal rays 55–62; pectoral rays 11–12; pelvic rays 6; lateral-line scales 52–60; scales ctenoid on ocular side, cycloid on blind side; gill rakers palmate (short and broad, the margins with strong spinules), 0 + 8–9; body depth 1.85–2.0 in standard length; lower eye in advance of upper; orbit diameter 1.4–2.0 in snout length; interorbital broader in males than females; maxilla to below anterior edge of lower eye, its length on ocular side 2.25–2.5 in head length; no spines on head; teeth uniserial in both jaws; first ray of dorsal fin slightly prolonged, its distal part expanded and fringed; light brown, finely mottled with dark and light spots, with about 5 vertical rows of a few dark blotches, generally small and faint, with 1 blotch from 2 posterior rows in midline of body. Largest specimen, 11 cm. Known from Rowley Shoals, Western Australia; Okinawa; Fiji (type locality, Levuka Island); and the illustrated specimen from the Chesterfield Bank, Coral Sea; collections from as little as 3 m. Amaoka et al. (1994) concluded that the first dorsal ray is used as a lure in the same way as the illicium of antennariid fishes; they referred to the ray as the illicium and its expanded fringed tip as the esca. They noted that the illicium can be moved forward so that the esca is in front of the mouth. One might expect other species of *Asterorhombus* with a long first dorsal ray to do the same.

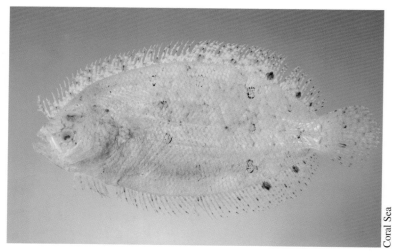

Coral Sea

LONGLURE FLOUNDER

Asterorhombus filifer Hensley & Randall, 2003

Dorsal rays 81–87; anal rays 63–68; ocular-side pectoral rays 11–12, of blind side 9–11; pelvic rays 5–6; lateral-line scales 56–67; gill rakers palmate, 0–2 + 6–11; body depth 2.0–2.3 in standard length; lower eye a little in advance of upper; each eye with a small tentacle; interorbital broader in males than in females; snout slightly longer than orbit diameter; maxilla reaching to or a little beyond a vertical at anterior edge of lower eye; no spines on head; teeth uniserial in both jaws; first ray of dorsal fin separate from remainder of fin and prolonged, varying from 0.8–1.7 in head length, its posterior membrane broad and smooth-edged; light brown, densely mottled with small, dark brown and white spots; a row of brown blotches a little larger than pupil along dorsal and ventral edges of body, and 4 vertical rows of larger brown blotches, the largest and darkest in last row on lateral line; elongate first dorsal ray with 4 dark spots, the

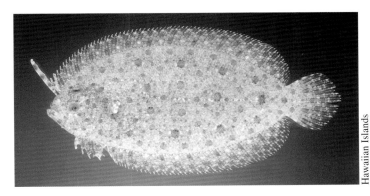

Hawaiian Islands

outer 2 across width of membrane. Largest specimen, 13 cm. Described from specimens from the Comoro Islands, Seychelles, Mauritius, Philippines, Great Barrier Reef, New Caledonia, Marshall Islands, Society Islands, and Hawaiian Islands (type locality, Midway); collections from depths of 4–57 m on sand.

INTERMEDIATE FLOUNDER

Asterorhombus intermedius (Bleeker, 1866)

Dorsal rays 77–83; anal rays 55–62; pectoral rays 11–12; pelvic rays 6; lateral-line scales 45–50; scales ctenoid on ocular side, cycloid on blind side; gill rakers palmate, 0 + 8–9; body depth 2.15–2.4 in standard length; lower eye a little in advance of upper; snout slightly longer than orbit diameter; maxilla reaching to or a little beyond anterior edge of lower eye, its length on ocular side about 2.5 in head length; no spines on head; teeth uniserial in both jaws; first ray of dorsal fin slightly prolonged; brown, finely mottled with lighter and darker brown, 5 vertical rows of dark brown and orange blotches, the first row including a spot on opercle, the largest blotch in last row on lateral line; rays of median fins irregularly banded, white to dark brown; a row of dark blotches (pigment mainly on rays) along base of dorsal and anal fins. Largest specimen, 16 cm. Reported from Seychelles, Mal-

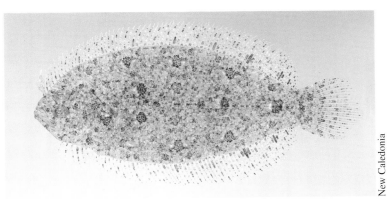

New Caledonia

dive Islands, Indonesia (type locality, Manado, Sulawesi), southern Japan, Monte Bello Islands, Western Australia, Queensland, New Caledonia, and Tonga. Shirai & Kitazawa (1998) described the use of the first ray in feeding.

FLOWERY FLOUNDER

Bothus mancus (Broussonet, 1782)

Dorsal rays 95–103; anal rays 75–81; pectoral rays of ocular side 10–11; lateral-line scales 85–97; scales weakly ctenoid or cycloid on ocular side, cycloid on blind side; gill rakers short, 9–11 on lower limb; body depth 1.7–2.05 in standard length; interorbital width of males 2.0–2.8 times eye diameter, of females 1.1–2.1 times eye diameter; anterior edge of upper eye above (in young) or behind posterior edge of lower eye; maxilla reaching to below or a little beyond anterior edge of lower eye; mature males with a strong spine on snout, another on lower orbital ridge, and 3 or 4 small spines on upper orbital ridge; short tentacles on eyes of males; pectoral fin of ocular side of mature males greatly pro-

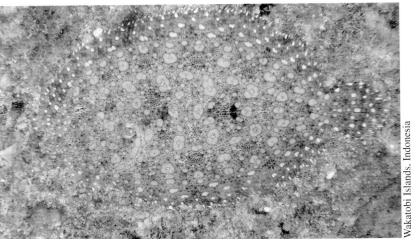

Wakatobi Islands, Indonesia

longed, the longest filamentous rays may reach to or beyond base of caudal fin; light brown with small pale spots, black dots (sometimes grouping to form blotches), and many dark-edged, roseate, pale blue spots, some approaching size of eyes, and often with pale yellow centers; 3 dark blotches along straight part of lateral line; median fins with black dots, white spots of variable size, and white-tipped rays; eyes spotted. Largest col-

lected, 48 cm. Occurs throughout the Indo-Pacific region and the tropical eastern Pacific; type locality, Tahiti; generally found adjacent to or within coral reefs, sometimes at rest on coral rock; reported from depths of 1–84 m. The author collected 24 adults for food-habit study, only 3 of which were empty; 88% of the food material was fishes (including acanthurids, mullids, mugilids, and labrids), and the rest crabs and shrimps.

Papua New Guinea/male

PANTHER FLOUNDER
Bothus pantherinus (Rüppell, 1830)
Dorsal rays 85–95; anal rays 66–72; pectoral rays of ocular side 9–11; lateral-line scales 80–92; scales weakly ctenoid or cycloid on ocular side, cycloid on blind side; gill rakers short, 6–9 on lower limb; body depth 1.7–2.0 in standard length; interorbital width of male about equal to eye diameter, less in female; anterior edge of upper eye above or a little behind middle of lower eye; maxilla reaching to below anterior half of lower eye; mature males with 1 or more bony tubercles or short spines on snout and on edge of eye; 1 or more short tentacles on eyes; pectoral fin of ocular side of males greater than about 15 cm, very long, with filamentous rays that may reach beyond base of caudal fin; light gray-brown, finely mottled with brown, with roseate, dark-edged pale spots (may be partly pale blue), dark brown or brownish yellow spots nearly as large as eye, and numerous small, yellow to brownish yellow spots (usually 1 in center of each pale roseate

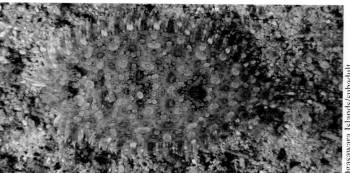

Ogasawara Islands/subadult

spot); a large dusky blotch on straight part of lateral line; eyes spotted. Reported to 30 cm. Indo-Pacific; type locality, Red Sea; occurs from the shallows to depths of at least 60 m; found more on silty sand in protected waters than on white sand near well-developed coral reefs.

TWOSPOT DWARF FLOUNDER
Engyprosopon grandisquamum (Temminck & Schlegel, 1846)
Dorsal rays 79–89; anal rays 59–68; pectoral rays of ocular side 10–12; lateral-line scales 36–46; scales ctenoid on ocular side, cycloid on blind side; gill rakers short, 5–7 on lower limb; body depth 1.6–2.1 in standard length; interorbital space of males 0.7–1.7 eye diameters in width, of females, 0.7–0.9; anterior edge of upper eye above middle of lower eye; maxilla reaching to below anterior edge of lower eye; teeth in upper jaw biserial, somewhat enlarged anteriorly, in lower jaw uniserial; a spine on front of snout and on upper edge of eyes of males, small or absent in females; light brown, finely mottled and spotted with dark brown, orange-yellow, and whitish; a prominent blackish spot centered on uppermost and lowermost branched rays of caudal fin. Reaches 15 cm. Japan (type locality) to New South Wales, west to the Nicobar Islands, Andaman Sea, Maldive Islands, Natal, and Gulf of Oman, east to New Caledonia; depth range 7–100 m.

New Caledonia

LARGESCALE DWARF FLOUNDER
Engyprosopon macrolepis (Regan, 1908)

Dorsal rays 76–85; anal rays 58–63; pectoral rays of ocular side 11–13; lateral-line scales 43–51; scales ctenoid on ocular side, cycloid on blind side; gill rakers short, 0 + 6–8; body depth 1.8–2.2 in standard length; eyes large, 2.8–3.8 in head length; interorbital space of males broad, to 3.3 in head length; anterior edge of upper eye of males above middle to anterior one-third of lower eye, of females over anterior one-fourth of lower eye; maxilla reaching to below anterior edge of lower eye; teeth in jaws uniserial; males with prominent rostral and anterior orbital spines; ocular side brown, densely mottled with spots of various shades of brown, black, and white; blind side of males blackish except for head. A small species; the largest, 7.5 cm total length. The holotype was collected at Cargados Carajos (St. Brandon's Shoals) in the Indian Ocean; other localities include Red Sea, Gulf of Aden, Maldive Islands (*Engyprosopon* sp. of Randall & Anderson, 1993), Philippines

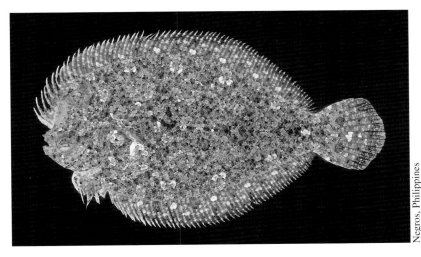

Negros, Philippines

(basis for redescription by Hensley & Randall, 1990), and New Caledonia (record from Amaoka et al., 1993, who reviewed the genus for the New Caledonia and Chesterfield Bank area); depth range, 3–91 m.

CRESTED FLOUNDERS
(SAMARIDAE)

This small Indo-Pacific family of 4 genera was classified as a subfamily in the Pleuronectidae. Chapleau & Keast (1988) and Chapleau (1993) elevated it to a family, but some authors continue to treat these flatfishes as a subfamily. Like the pleuronectids, the eyes of these fishes are on the right side (dextral). This is also true of the soles (Soleidae), but they are easily distinguished by having the edge of the preopercle scaled over. Most of the characters given for the Bothidae (and Pleuronectidae) apply to the Samaridae, such as no teeth on the palate, no fin spines, and the origin of the dorsal fin above or in front of the upper eye. One fundamental early difference of the Samaridae (and the Pleuronectidae) is the lack of an oil globule in the egg, which is present in the bothids. The characters separating samarids from pleuronectids are mostly osteological, such as the absence of postcleithra. The majority of the samarids occur in moderately deep water. All are small, none exceeding 22 cm, and most less than 12 cm. Two species are known inshore in the South Pacific area.

COCKATOO FLOUNDER
Samaris cristatus Gray, 1831

Dorsal rays 73–88, the first 10–15 greatly prolonged; anal rays 49–60; pectoral rays on ocular side 4, the fin missing or rudimentary on blind side; both pelvic fins with 5 rays, those on ocular side prolonged, the membranes of first 1–3 rays expanded at tips; lateral line of ocular side with 63–82 scales, of blind side absent or rudimentary; scales on ocular side ctenoid, those on blind side weakly ctenoid or cycloid; gill rakers 2–5 + 7–11; body depth 2.5–3.0 in standard length; head length 3.7–5.3 in standard length; eyes on right side and close together; teeth small, in

Sulawesi

a narrow band; ocular side brown with dark brown blotches, pale spots, and roseate markings; prolonged dorsal rays white except for a blackish band near base. Reported to 22 cm. Indian Ocean to western Pacific from Taiwan and South China Sea to northern Australia and New Caledonia; type locality, China. Occurs on sand to mud bottoms from depths of 15–70 m. *Samaris cacatuae* Ogilby, *S. ornatus* von Bonde, and *S. delagoensis* von Bonde are synonyms.

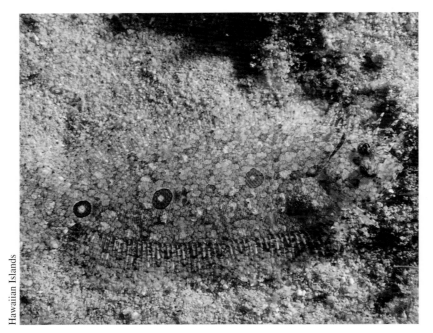

Hawaiian Islands

THREESPOT FLOUNDER

Samariscus triocellatus Woods in Schultz et al., 1966
Dorsal rays 62–70; anal rays 47–56; pectoral rays of ocular side 5, of blind side 1 (rudimentary); pelvic rays 5; lateral line nearly straight, the pored scales 71–76; body depth 2.4–3.1 in standard length; head length 3.6–4.3 in standard length; eyes close together, separated by a bony ridge; dorsal and anal fins elevated, the longest dorsal ray 5.2–5.9 in standard length; caudal fin rounded, longer than head, 3.4–3.8 in standard length; brown, mottled with light and dark blotches; 3 dark brown circles about the size of eyes along lateral line. Attains 7 cm. East coast of Africa to the Great Barrier Reef, Fiji, and the Hawaiian, Society, Marquesas, Pitcairn, Caroline, and Marshall Islands (type locality, Bikini Atoll); occurs in coral reefs, generally under ledges or in small caves, on sand or hard substratum; depth range, 5–30 m. May be seen at times moving its pectoral fin in an erect position, which is conspicuous because it is largely black.

SAND FLOUNDERS
(PARALICHTHYIDAE)

Body ovate; head length 3.0–4.4 in standard length; eyes on left side, separated by a bony ridge; 2 nostrils on each side, the anterior with a posterior flap; mouth moderately large, the teeth in jaws uniserial; scales cycloid or ctenoid; lateral line well developed on both sides, arched above pectoral fin, with a supratemporal branch on head reaching dorsal margin; gill rakers palmate; dorsal fin origin above or anterior to eyes; caudal fin rhomboid, separate from dorsal and anal fins; pectoral fins not elongate, the middle 6–9 rays on ocular side branched, none branched on blind side; pelvic fins short-based, nearly equal, the fin of ocular side at most slightly anterior to fin of blind side, the last 3 or 4 rays branched. Some authors such as Norman (1934) have classified this family as a subfamily of the Bothidae.

Persian Gulf

LARGETOOTH FLOUNDER

Pseudorhombus arsius (Hamilton, 1822)
Dorsal rays 71–84; anal rays 53–62; pectoral fin of ocular side with 11–13 rays; scales ctenoid on ocular side, cycloid on blind side; lateral-line scales 69–81; supratemporal branch of lateral line extending to between eighth and twelfth dorsal rays; gill rakers pointed, longer than broad, 1–7 + 8–15; body depth 1.8–2.3 in standard length; head length 3.3–3.6 in standard length; maxilla reaching to below posterior edge of lower eye; some pairs of moderately large canine teeth in both jaws, more widely spaced in lower jaw; brown, mottled and blotched with darker brown; a large, dark brown blotch at juncture of straight and curved parts of lateral line, often with 1 or 2 blotches more posteriorly on lateral line. Reported to 45 cm. Persian Gulf and east coast of Africa to Fiji and islands of Micronesia; southern Japan to New South Wales and New Caledonia; type locality, Ganges estuary; occurs on shallow, muddy sand or sandy substrata, including brackish areas. *Rhombus polyspilus* Bleeker is one of 9 synonyms.

616

SOLES
(SOLEIDAE)

Soles are flatfishes that have the eyes on the right side of the head (like the right-hand flounders of the family Pleuronectidae) but are most easily distinguished by lacking a free margin to the preopercle. The nostrils are widely separated, the anterior tubular; the mouth is usually ventral and curved; teeth in the jaws are on the blind side in a villiform band, absent or obsolete on the ocular side; the lateral line is straight on the body; the scales are either cycloid or ctenoid; blind side of the head with cutaneous cirri or small flaps; gill rakers absent or obsolete; eyes small; caudal fin rounded, not attached to dorsal or anal fins; pectoral fins sometimes absent; pelvic fins free from anal fin, with 4–5 rays. The family consists of about 20 genera and 90 species, worldwide in tropical to temperate seas except American waters, but mostly on continental shelves or the shores of large islands such as the East Indies. A second family of soles, the Achiridae, is restricted to the New World. Clark & George (1979) revised the soles of the genus *Pardachirus* and described the glands that produce a powerful toxin under stress that is repelling to predators. Randall & Meléndez (1987) found a comparable toxin in *Aseraggodes bahamondei* at Easter Island; it was also discovered recently by the author in one of the Hawaiian species of the genus. Some soles are buried in sediment during the day but emerge for foraging at night. *Aseraggodes melanostictus* (Peters), described from one specimen from Bougainville taken in 40 fathoms (73.5 m), has been recorded from the Marshall Islands, Guam, and the Society Islands, but doubt remains of the identifications at these islands. *Aseraggodes* is in need of revision.

PEACOCK SOLE
Pardachirus pavoninus (Lacepède, 1802)

Dorsal rays 62–73; anal rays 48–55; caudal rays 18; pectoral fins absent; pelvic rays 5; lateral-line scales 76–95; scales weakly ctenoid to cycloid, none on dorsal or anal fins; vertebrae 38–41; body depth 1.9–2.3 in standard length; head length about 5 in standard length; eye diameter 6–8 in head length; interorbital space narrow, slightly less than one eye diameter in width; a fringe of cirri on ventral edge of head; gray to gray-brown with many irregular, roundish, pale gray to nearly white spots containing 1 or more small black spots; spaces between large spots with small black spots and small white or yellow spots. Attains about 30 cm. Indo-Malayan region, west to Andaman Sea and Sri Lanka, north to southern Japan, south to New South Wales, east to Tonga and Samoa Islands; only Palau in Micronesia; no type locality. Known from depths of 1–40 m; usually found on sand or silty sand in which it buries readily with just the eyes and anterior nostril above the substratum.

BANDED SOLE
Soleichthys heterorhinos (Bleeker, 1856)

Dorsal rays 87–102; anal rays 77–87; caudal rays 18, branched; pectoral rays of ocular side 7–9, of blind side 6–8; pelvic rays 4; lateral-line scales of ocular side 110–122; scales ctenoid; vertebrae 50; body elongate, the depth 2.7–3.5 in standard length; head length 6.0–6.8 in standard length; eyes small and nearly contiguous; tubular anterior nostril longer than eye; fringe of cirri on ventral edge of head; whitish to pale brown with numerous wavy, dark brown lines or narrow bands across body and dorsal and anal fins, these fins with a white margin and a broad, pale blue submarginal zone except posteriorly where the blue is largely replaced with black; caudal fin with a broad black outer border, sometimes with a pale edge. Reaches 14 cm. Reported from the Red Sea, Andaman Islands, Indo-Malayan region, north to Japan, south to New South Wales and New Caledonia, east to

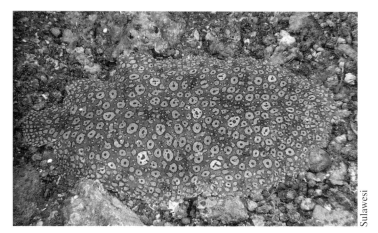

Sulawesi

Sulawesi

Fiji, Mariana Islands, Marshall Islands, and Samoa Islands; type locality, Ambon, Molucca Islands. Occurs inshore in protected reef areas or reef flats; buries readily in sand; juveniles have been mistaken for flatworms.

Titan Triggerfish, *Balistoides viridescens*, female guarding her nest, Bali

TRIGGERFISHES
(BALISTIDAE)

The Balistidae is one of the nine families of the order Tetraodontiformes (for a review of osteology and phylogeny, see Tyler, 1980). Triggerfishes are named for the mechanism by which the stout first dorsal spine can be locked in an erect position by the small second spine; if one pushes down on the second spine (the trigger), the first can be depressed. These fishes have a moderately deep and compressed body, the eye set high on the head, a long snout, and a small non-protractile mouth with close-set chisel-like teeth, 8 in the outer row and 6 in an inner row that serve to buttress the outer teeth; the gill opening is a short slit anterior to the upper base of the pectoral fin; the skin is tough and rough to the touch, comprised of non-overlapping scales, each with a broad area of small tubercles at the center; most species have a patch of enlarged modified scales behind the gill opening; some have rows of small, forward-curved spines posteriorly on the side of the body. There are two dorsal fins, the first of III spines (the third spine is usually very small), the second dorsal and anal fins only as soft rays, nearly all branched; the caudal fin consists of 12 principal rays, the median 10 branched; there are no pelvic fins (they are replaced by the tip of the long, depressible pelvic bone, which is encased in 4 segments of modified scales termed the pelvic rudiment). Triggerfishes are usually solitary; their usual mode of swimming is by undulating the second dorsal and anal fins; the caudal fin is used only for rapid movement. When threatened, they often seek a hole in the reef with an entrance through which they can barely pass; once inside they erect their first dorsal spine and depress the pelvic bone to lock themselves in position. At night they sleep in this or a similar hole. Although the mouth of balistid fishes is small, the jaws are powerful and the teeth strong and sharp; these fishes are able to reduce large prey to small pieces. Most feed on invertebrates with hard skeletal parts such as crabs, mollusks, and sea urchins. Therefore, they are not compatible in an aquarium with many of these invertebrates. Some balistids such as *Odonus niger* and the species of *Canthidermis*, *Melichthys*, and *Xanthichthys* feed heavily on zooplankton. In the case of *Melichthys*, benthic algae is also a major part of the diet; in addition, some have been observed to feed on the excrement of other fishes. Triggerfishes lay demersal eggs, which are aggressively defended by the female parent (Fricke,

1980). Many species make a nest by excavating a shallow crater in sand; the eggs are deposited in the center of the crater. Divers should not venture close to a guarding female of the larger species, especially *Balistoides viridescens* (note the threatening pose in the photograph to the left) and *Pseudobalistes fuscus*. The author had his leg bitten by a female of *B. viridescens*, and his camera attacked by another. These and other attacks were documented by Randall & Millington (1990). The larger species of triggerfishes have been reported as ciguatoxic. The Balistidae consists of 12 genera and 37 species. Randall & Klausewitz (1973) revised the genus *Melichthys*, Randall et al. (1978b) the genus *Xanthichthys*, and Matsuura (1980) reviewed the Japanese species of the family. Schneidewind (2002) published a well-illustrated book on the balistid fishes of the world. In the species accounts here, the rudimentary upper ray is included in the pectoral-ray count.

Flores, Indonesia/juvenile

Papua New Guinea

STELLATE TRIGGERFISH

Abalistes stellatus [Anonymous, 1798] (ex Commerson)
Dorsal rays III + 25–27; anal rays 24–25; pectoral rays 15–16 (rarely 16); enlarged osseous scales present behind gill opening; caudal peduncle very slender and tapering, the width greater than least depth (peduncle as deep or deeper than long in other balistid fishes); a long oblique groove before eye; first dorsal spine long, 1.6–1.9 in head length; third dorsal spine not short, about one-third length of first spine; front of second dorsal and anal fins not elevated; caudal fin double emarginate, the lobes longer with growth; whitish with numerous close-set spots that are dark brown dorsally and grade to dull yellow ventrally; 3 large, oblong

white spots on back, and a smaller spot dorsally on caudal peduncle; large adults dark brown dorsally, speckled with small white spots and flecks, the lower half of body with small, dull yellow spots, some of which anastomose to a reticular pattern. Reaches about 50 cm. Red Sea and east coast of Africa to western Pacific from Suruga Bay, Japan, to Great Barrier Reef and New South Wales, east to New Caledonia, Fiji, and Palau; description based on Commerson's manscript, so type locality may be Mauritius. *Balistes stellaris* Bloch & Schneider is a synonym. Occurs on open, silty sand or mud bottoms, generally with scattered small patches of rock or coral; reported from depths of 10–120 m; difficult to approach underwater.

Tahiti/juvenile

Marshall Islands/small female

Bali/male

ORANGELINED TRIGGERFISH

Balistapus undulatus (Park, 1797)

Dorsal rays III + 24–27 (rarely 24 or 27); anal rays 20–24; pectoral rays 13–15; no long groove before eye; 2 rows of strong antrorse spines on and slightly before caudal peduncle; front of second dorsal and anal fins not elevated; caudal fin slightly rounded; body and posterior head dark olive-green with oblique, curved orange lines; a very large, round black spot enclosing peduncular spines (lacking in Indian Ocean fish); a broad orange band adjacent to upper lip, with a narrow orange band above, and a similar band on chin with a black line below, the bands continuing obliquely across head, merging and reaching below pectoral-fin base; head above bands with oblique orange and bluish lines in females, lacking in males; caudal fin banded with olive green and orange. Attains 30 cm. Red Sea and east coast of Africa to Line Islands, Marquesas Islands, Society Islands, Tuamotu Archipelago, and all of Micronesia; Wakayama Prefecture to Great Barrier Reef and New Caledonia; type locality, Sumatra. Coral reefs from the shallows to at least 50 m. Diet variable: tips of branching corals, sea urchins, heart urchins, crabs, shrimps, mollusks, brittlestars, polychaete worms, tunicates, sponges, hydrozoans, and algae.

Hawaiian Islands

FINESCALED TRIGGERFISH

Balistes polylepis Steindachner, 1876

Dorsal rays III + 26–28; anal rays 25–26; pectoral rays 14–15; a deep oblique groove before eye; no horizontal grooves on cheek; no spines or longitudinal ridges posteriorly on side of body; third dorsal spine extending well above dorsal profile of body; front of second dorsal and anal fins strongly elevated; caudal fin double emarginate, the lobes prolonged in adults; light olive brown to bluish gray, the scale edges dark; no distinct markings. Reported to 76 cm. The most abundant triggerfish in the eastern Pacific, ranging from northern California (in warm years) to Peru and the offshore islands such as the Galápagos; type locality, Magdalena Bay, Baja California; once regarded as a waif to the Hawaiian Islands, but now represented by breeding individuals (Randall & Mundy, 1998). One individual reported from the Marquesas Islands (Randall & Earle, 2000).

620

Seram, Indonesia

CLOWN TRIGGERFISH

Balistoides conspicillum (Bloch & Schneider, 1801)

Dorsal rays III + 25–27; anal rays 21–23; pectoral rays 15; a deep groove before eye; region around lips fully scaled; 3 or 4 rows of small antrorse spines posteriorly on side of body; front of second dorsal and anal fins not elevated; caudal fin rounded, the corners acute; black with very large, round white spots on ventral half of body; a broad yellow zone on back from behind eye to below origin of second dorsal fin, densely spotted with black; a transverse white band across snout in front of eye; lips and adjacent zone around mouth orange-yellow, edged posteriorly by a black line and a yellow line; first dorsal fin black; an orange-yellow band at base of second dorsal and anal fins; caudal fin black with a broad yellow crossband; juveniles with smaller white spots over most of body and a larger orange-yellow area at front of head. Reaches 50 cm. East Africa to Samoa Islands, Line Islands, and throughout Micronesia; Sagami Bay, Japan, to Great Barrier Reef, New South Wales, Lord Howe Island, and New Caledonia; type locality, Indian seas. Usually found on seaward coral reefs from depths of 3–75 m, but not common at any locality. Sometimes identified as *Balistoides niger* (Bonnaterre), but this name invalid as a homonym. A popular aquarium fish in spite of its being destructive to invertebrates and aggressive to other fishes (meaning it is best in a tank by itself).

Mauritius/juvenile

621

Bali

TITAN TRIGGERFISH

Balistoides viridescens (Bloch & Schneider, 1801)

Dorsal rays III + 25–26; anal rays 22–24; pectoral rays 15; a deep groove before eye; a scaleless area around lips, continuing and narrowing posterior to corner of mouth; about 5 rows of antrorse spines posteriorly on side of body; second dorsal and anal fins slightly elevated anteriorly; caudal fin rounded to slightly double emarginate; scales of body with central tuberculate part dark brown (hence forming a diamond-shaped spot), the edges greenish white; broad zone around spines posteriorly on body greenish white, the spines brown and yellow; interorbital and adjacent nape and snout brown with yellow spots, continuing and narrowing below eye to upper end of gill opening; rest of head yellowish, becoming pale bluish below level of mouth; a broad, dark brown band across snout above upper lip, joined farther back by an equally broad band that continues narrowly well posterior to mouth; second dorsal, anal, and caudal fins yellowish with broad, dark brown basal and terminal bands; juveniles whitish with small black spots on body and large blackish blotches dorsally; an oblique, dusky-edged white line from above to behind mouth provides separation from the similar juvenile of *Pseudobalistes flavimarginatus*. The largest of the triggerfishes; reaches 75 cm. Tropical Indo-Pacific except the Persian Gulf, Oman, and the Hawaiian Islands; type locality, Mauritius. Feeds

Guam/juvenile

mainly on sea urchins, heart urchins, coral, crabs, mollusks, and tube worms. Wary of divers except when a female is guarding the nest. If an adult is encountered that does not retreat, but faces you with first dorsal spine erect (as in the photo in the family account), do not venture closer; the result could be an attack.

BLACK DURGON
Melichthys niger (Bloch, 1786)

Dorsal rays III + 30–34; anal rays 28–30; pectoral rays 15–17; a deep groove before eye; rows of scales on head between corner of mouth and upper end of gill opening 20–25; dorsal and ventral profiles of head convex; depth of body at origin of anal fin 2.4–2.8 in standard length; prominent longitudinal ridges following scale rows posteriorly on body; second dorsal and anal fins moderately elevated anteriorly; caudal fin varying from slightly rounded to double emarginate or truncate with prolonged lobes; dark greenish gray with black longitudinal lines following scale rows; a broad zone across interorbital and adjacent snout and nape often crossed by alternating blue and black lines (a color feature turned on and off); base of second dorsal and anal fins with a pale blue line (at a distance, fish seem entirely black except for these 2 pale lines). Largest examined, 32 cm; silvery late postlarval stage recorded to the extraordinary size of 17 cm. Circumtropical, but not listed from many areas where might be expected, such as the Red Sea, Great Barrier Reef, and Pitcairn Islands; type locality, China. Typically found on exposed seaward reefs from just below the surge zone to 75 m; maintains a position well above the substratum, but quickly retreats to a hole in the reef when threatened. Diet about 70% algae (both benthic and drifting, the benthic especially calcareous reds), the rest mainly zooplankton. *Balistes radula* (Solander) and *B. piceus* (Poey) are among the synonyms.

Hawaiian Islands

Banda Islands, Indonesia/subadult

New Britain

PINKTAILED DURGON
Melichthys vidua (Solander in Richardson, 1845)

Dorsal rays III + 31–35; anal rays 27–31; pectoral rays 14–16; a deep groove before eye; rows of scales on head between corner of mouth and upper end of gill opening 28–32; dorsal and ventral profiles of head convex; depth of body at origin of anal fin 2.3–2.6 in standard length; slight longitudinal ridges following scale rows posteriorly on body; second dorsal and anal fins very elevated anteriorly; caudal fin truncate to slightly emarginate; dark brown, often with a yellowish cast; scaled basal part of caudal fin white, the outer part pink, the upper and lower edges narrowly black; second dorsal and anal fins whitish with broad black borders; pectoral fins yellow. Largest specimen, 34 cm. South Africa and Réunion to Hawaiian Islands, Line Islands, Marquesas Islands, Tuamotu Archipelago, Society Islands, and throughout Micronesia; Iwate Prefecture, Japan, to Great Barrier Reef and New Caledonia; also to Galápagos Islands and Cocos Island, Costa Rica (Garrison, 2000); type locality, Tahiti. Usually seen on seaward reefs; depth range, 4–145 m (Chave & Mundy, 1994). Stomach contents of 6 adults examined by the author: 62% benthic algae of many species, the rest crabs, unidentified crustaceans, bivalve mollusks, octopus, sponge, and fish remains. The prejuvenile can reach the remarkable length of at least 16 cm. *Pachynathus nycteris* Jordan & Evermann and *Oncobalistes erythropterus* Fowler are synonyms based on this stage (Randall, 1971). Hybrids reported of this species and the Indian Ocean *Melichthys indicus* Randall & Klausewitz (Randall et al., 2002d).

Mauritius/juvenile

Marshall Islands

Maldive Islands

REDTOOTH TRIGGERFISH
Odonus niger (Rüppell, 1836)

Dorsal rays III + 33–36; anal rays 28–31; pectoral rays 15–16; a deep groove before eye; dorsal profile of head slightly convex, the ventral profile strongly convex; mouth upturned, the chin protruding; 2 upper teeth prolonged, visible when mouth closed; about 7 longitudinal rows of small spines on posterior half or more of body; second dorsal and anal fins strongly elevated anteriorly; caudal fin lunate, the lobes prolonged in large adults; blue to purplish blue; outer margins of second dorsal, anal, and cau- dal fins light blue, the caudal sometimes streaked with pink; teeth red; 2 narrow, dark blue bands extending anterior to eye, and often a broader blue stripe across head from corner of mouth; head yellowish gray in one transient color phase. Attains 40 cm (including long caudal-fin lobes). Red Sea (type locality) and East Africa to Line Islands, Marquesas Islands, and Society Islands; Sagami Bay, Japan, to Great Barrier Reef and New Cale- donia. Usually seen over outer-reef slopes, often in large aggrega- tions well above the substratum feeding on zooplankton; quickly retires to a hole in reef when approached.

Gulf of Aden

YELLOWMARGIN TRIGGERFISH
Pseudobalistes flavimarginatus (Rüppell, 1829)

Dorsal rays III + 24–27; anal rays 23–25; pectoral rays 15–16 (usually 16); a deep groove before eye; shallow near-horizontal grooves on cheek above level of mouth; 5 or 6 longitudinal rows of small spines posteriorly on side of body; second dorsal and anal fins slightly elevated anteriorly; caudal fin rounded in young, becoming emarginate in adults, the lobes prolonged in large adults; body light grayish yellow, the scale centers as dark yellowish gray, diamond-shaped spots, sometimes with a yellow dot in center on posterior scales; head gray dorsally, spotted with black on interorbital and nape, the lower half and chest pale orange-yellow; 2 or more horizontal, dark brown streaks behind and below eye; outer margins of second dorsal, anal, and caudal fins yellow; small juveniles pale with small black spots and black blotches around eye, under both dorsal fins (extending into front half of first dorsal), and caudal peduncle; larger juveniles whitish to pale orange-yellow with small black spots on body and postorbital head. Reported to 60 cm. Red Sea (type locality) and east coast of Africa to Society Islands, Tuamotu Archipelago, and the islands of Micronesia; Sagami Bay, Japan, to Great Barrier Reef and New South Wales. Lagoons and protected bays from depths of 2–50 m; nests in open areas of sand (sometimes several nests in the same vicinity). Very shy; although

Papua New Guinea/juvenile

females guarding nests have been reported as attacking divers, the author has observed the guarding fish leave the nest rather than stand ground. Food habits similar to those of *Balistoides viridescens*.

Maldive Islands

BLUESTRIPED TRIGGERFISH

Pseudobalistes fuscus (Bloch & Schneider, 1801)

Dorsal rays III + 25–27; anal rays 21–24; pectoral rays 15–16 (usually 15); a deep groove before eye; lower cheek with shallow near-horizontal grooves; broad region around mouth scaleless; no spines posteriorly on side of body; second dorsal and anal fins strongly elevated anteriorly; caudal fin rounded in young, becoming emarginate in adults, the lobes prolonged in large adults; adults dull yellow, the edges of scales unevenly blue, resulting in oblique blue lines on side of body and a blue reticulum elsewhere on body; head dull yellow with small blue spots and irregular lines, the shallow grooves dusky; a narrow, submarginal blue band in second dorsal, anal, and caudal fins; small juveniles white above, yellow below with small black spots and 4 large black blotches dorsally, the first across interorbital; larger juveniles with blue spots (first appearing in black blotches), and still larger juveniles yellow with blue spots coalescing to form stripes. Reaches 55 cm. Red Sea and East Africa to Society Islands, Pitcairn Islands, and throughout Micronesia; Wakayama Prefecture, Japan, to Great Barrier Reef and New Caledonia; no type locality given. Found on coral reefs, in both lagoon and seaward zones, to depths of at least 50 m. Feeds heavily on sea urchins and a variety of other benthic invertebrates. Fricke (1980) observed it turn over *Diadema* by ejecting a stream of water to expose the more vulnerable oral side. Females guarding nests are dangerous; Fricke wrote that 2 divers had to be hospitalized with serious bites, and several others, including himself, were also "badly bitten" in the Red Sea.

Indonesia/juvenile

Mauritius/subadult

Line Islands/juvenile

Tahiti

LAGOON TRIGGERFISH
Rhinecanthus aculeatus (Linnaeus, 1758)

Dorsal rays III + 23–26; anal rays 21–23; pectoral rays 13–14; no deep groove before eye; (true of other *Rhinecanthus*); dorsal and ventral profiles of head nearly straight (also generic); 3 horizontal rows of black antrorse spines posteriorly on side of body, the upper 2 rows longest; second dorsal and anal fins not elevated anteriorly (generic); caudal fin rounded, the corners angular; white with a large blackish area over much of upper side of body, with oblique black bands extending from it to base of anal fin, and a broad oblique band to origin of second dorsal fin; a black band containing 4 blue lines across interorbital, continuing below with 3 blue lines; a yellow area around mouth enclosing a blue line at base of upper lip, the yellow continuing as a narrowing band to below pectoral-fin base; anus black. Reaches 25 cm. Found throughout the tropical Indo-Pacific region; type locality, India. Typical habitat, lagoon reef flat where dominated by sand; analysis of stomach contents of 5 adults by the author revealed algae, detritus, mollusks, crabs, shrimps, other crustaceans, polychaetes and other worms, heart urchins, fishes, corals, tunicates, foraminifera, and unidentified eggs. Also known as the Picassofish.

Coral Sea/subadult (R. C. Steene)

Tahiti

HALFMOON TRIGGERFISH
Rhinecanthus lunula Randall & Steene, 1983

Dorsal rays III + 25–26 (usually 26); anal rays 22–24; pectoral rays 14; 3 horizontal rows of small antrorse spines posteriorly on side of body, the upper row short, not continuing onto caudal peduncle, the lower 2 extending to base of caudal fin; caudal fin of adults slightly double emarginate; gray dorsally, white ventrally; anus black with a large blackish area extending above it; a broad black bar, edged in pale blue, across caudal peduncle; a curved, pale blue band containing a black line extending from rear base of second dorsal fin; a blue band containing 3 narrow black bands across interorbital, continuing with 2 black bands below eye, narrowing to a black band at pectoral-fin base, where edged posteriorly in orange; a yellow band at base of upper lip, continuing from corner of mouth nearly to base of pectoral fin; first dorsal fin black except for first spine; caudal fin white with a black crescent preceded by a broad yellow area; juvenile as illustrated. Attains 28 cm. Subtropical South Pacific from Pitcairn Islands to Queensland; type locality, Tahiti. Not common; occurs in outer-reef areas, generally in more than 10 m.

626

Hawaiian Islands/juvenile

Hawaiian Islands

WEDGE TRIGGERFISH
Rhinecanthus rectangulus (Bloch & Schneider, 1801)
Dorsal rays III + 22–25; anal rays 20–22; pectoral rays 13–14; 4–5 (rarely 5) horizontal rows of small antrorse spines posteriorly on side of body; caudal fin rounded, the corners angular; light brown dorsally, white ventrally on head and abdomen, with a broad, oblique black band from anus and base of anal fin, enclosing pectoral fin, and narrowing as it extends nearly vertically to eye; a broad blue band across interorbital containing 3 black lines; caudal peduncle crossed by a black bar, the front end continuing in a wedge shape, edged in gold, anteriorly on body; 2 separate gold lines anterior and parallel to wedge, the lower line forming a border on large, oblique black band; a blue band across base of upper lip, and a red band at base of pectoral fins. Attains 25 cm. Occurs throughout the tropical Indo-Pacific region from the Red Sea and east coast of Africa to Hawai'i and the Pitcairn Islands; type locality, Indian Ocean. Common in the shallow outer-reef environment exposed to surge; like others of the genus, difficult to approach. Randall (1985b) analyzed the stomach contents of 12 adults, revealing a great variety of small benthic organisms: algae and detritus (18.5%), crabs (13.5%), polychaete worms (9.5%), brittlestars (9%), sea urchins and heart urchins (6.5%), sipunculid worms (5%), bivalve mollusks (4%), and the rest tunicates, shrimps and other crustaceans, foraminifera, eggs, and sponges. Also known as the Reef Triggerfish.

Hawaiian Islands/juvenile

Hawaiian Islands

SCIMITAR TRIGGERFISH
Sufflamen bursa (Bloch & Schneider, 1801)
Dorsal rays III + 27–30; anal rays 24–27; pectoral rays 13–15; longitudinal scale rows 43–50; head scale rows 27–30; a deep groove anterior to eye (true of other *Sufflamen*); dorsal and ventral profiles of head nearly straight (also generic); enlarged osseous scales behind gill opening (generic); a series of longitudinal ridges bearing small spinous tubercles on body following scale rows, the upper ridges extending to rear of pectoral fins; third dorsal spine showing above dorsal profile of body (generic); second dorsal and anal fins not elevated anteriorly (generic); caudal fin truncate to slightly rounded; gray to brown with faint, narrow dark stripes following scale rows; a scimitar-shaped band, that can be varied by the fish from dark brown to yellow, from in front of lower base of pectoral fin through posterior part of eye to nape, and an oblique band passing dorsally from behind gill opening; a white line from corner of mouth to origin of anal fin; edge of pelvic flap and pelvic rudiment blackish. Reaches 24 cm. Occurs throughout the tropical Indo-Pacific region except the seas of the Arabian Peninsula; type locality, Indian Ocean; a common coral-reef species reported from depths of 3–90 m. Stomach contents of 14 adults reported by Randall (1985b) to consist of algae and detritus (17%), crabs (15%), bivalve mollusks (12.4%), gastropods (9.5%), sea urchins and heart urchins (7.5%), polychaete worms (6%), sipunculids (5.5%), the rest damselfish and other eggs, tunicates, chitons, amphipods, isopods, shrimps, and other small crustaceans. Also known as the Lei Triggerfish and the Scythe Triggerfish.

Taiwan/juvenile

Coral Sea

FLAGTAIL TRIGGERFISH
Sufflamen chrysopterum (Bloch & Schneider, 1801)
Dorsal rays III + 26–28; anal rays 23–26; pectoral rays 13–15; longitudinal scale rows 41–47; head scale rows 23–28; a series of longitudinal ridges bearing small spinous tubercles on body following scale rows, the ridges extending forward to below middle of second dorsal fin; caudal fin truncate to slightly rounded with acute corners; yellowish gray to dark brown with a narrow, light yellow band from posterior edge of eye to below pectoral-fin base; lower head and abdomen often deep purplish blue; caudal fin yellowish brown with a broad, pure white border on margins. Attains 22 cm. East coast of Africa to Samoa Islands and islands of Micronesia; in the western Pacific from Izu Peninsula, Japan, to Great Barrier Reef, New South Wales, Lord Howe Island, and New Caledonia; type locality, India. Closely related to *Sufflamen albicaudatus* (Rüppell) from the Red Sea. Occurs on both lagoon and seaward reefs from depths of 1 to at least 30 m.

Sulawesi/juvenile

Hawaiian Islands

BRIDLED TRIGGERFISH
Sufflamen fraenatum (Latreille, 1804)
Dorsal rays III + 27–31; anal rays 24–28; pectoral rays 14–16; longitudinal scale rows 43–54; head scale rows 25–32; a series of longitudinal ridges bearing small spinous tubercles on body following scale rows, the ridges extending forward to below front of second dorsal fin; caudal fin slightly rounded in juveniles, truncate to slightly double emarginate in adults; yellowish to grayish brown with a narrow yellow band at base of upper lip; adult males with a narrow, yellow to pink, oblique band from corner of mouth across lower part of head, linked under chin with a transverse band of the same color; a black spot on first interspinous membrane of dorsal fin; a broad whitish bar often present across base of caudal fin and adjacent caudal peduncle. Reported to 38 cm. Occurs in the Indo-Pacific from the southern Red Sea and east coast of Africa to the Hawaiian Islands and Pitcairn Islands; no type locality given. A common species usually found over rubble and sand bottoms in the vicinity of reefs; depth range 12–183 m; the most wary of the genus. Stomach contents of 10 adults: sea urchins and heart urchins, including *Diadema*, *Eucidaris*, and *Echinometra* (20.4%), fishes (18.9%), bivalve mollusks (13.9%), tunicates (10%), brittlestars (7.4%), crabs (7.1%), mantis shrimps (3.5%), algae and detritus (3.1%), and the rest sipunculids, shrimps, gastropods, sponges, amphipods, bryozoans, foraminifera, and ostracods (Randall, 1985b). *Balistes capistratus* Shaw is a synonym.

GILDED TRIGGERFISH

Xanthichthys auromarginatus (Bennett, 1832)
Dorsal rays III + 27–30; anal rays 24–27; pectoral rays 13–15; longitudinal scale rows 42–47; head scale rows 17–20; a deep groove anterior to eye (true of other *Xanthichthys*); dorsal and ventral profiles of head moderately convex (also generic); enlarged osseous scales behind gill opening (generic); 5 horizontal grooves separating scale rows on cheek; a series of longitudinal ridges bearing small spines on body following scale rows, extending forward to pectoral fins; third dorsal spine short, not showing above dorsal profile of body (generic); second dorsal and anal fins elevated anteriorly (generic); caudal fin varying from slightly rounded to truncate, emarginate, and slightly double emarginate; gray-brown with a small, pale blue to white blotch in center of each scale, the spots larger ventrally than dorsally; base of lips narrowly blackish; edge of gill opening black; first dorsal fin black, and a dark brown band at base and outer margin of second dorsal and anal fins; caudal fin of females with a brown border all around, broadest centroposteriorly; border of caudal, second dorsal, and anal fins in males bright yellow; males with a large blue area on cheek, extending forward to enclose mouth. Largest specimen, 22 cm. Islands of the western Indian Ocean to the Hawaiian Islands, islands of Micronesia and the Society Islands (Randall et al., 2002a); in the western Pacific from Ryukyu Islands to the Great Barrier Reef and New Caledonia; there appear to be no records from continental areas except the Great Barrier Reef, and none from the East Indies; type locality, Mauritius. Occurs on seaward coral reefs from 15 to at least 70 m (not common in less than 30 m); feeds on zooplankton, especially calanoid copepods.

Hawaiian Islands/female

Hawaiian Islands/male

BLUELINE TRIGGERFISH

Xanthichthys caeruleolineatus Randall, Matsuura & Zama, 1978
Dorsal rays III + 26–27; anal rays 23–25; pectoral rays 13; longitudinal scale rows 40–43; head scale rows 22–23; 5 or 6 oblique grooves separating scale rows on cheek; median tubercles of scales slightly enlarged posteriorly on side of body, forming weak longitudinal ridges that do not extend anterior to second dorsal fin; caudal fin of adults deeply emarginate; light brown, the scale edges darker, with an irregular, pale blue line from pectoral-fin base to upper base of caudal fin; body above line darker brown, the scales with a vertically elongate white spot or short line; grooves on cheek blue; membrane of first dorsal fin partly black; caudal fin light red with bright red lobes; sexual dichromatism not documented. Largest specimen collected, 42 cm, from Baker Island in the central Pacific. Described from specimens from Agalega Islands in the Indian Ocean, Izu Islands, Ryukyu Islands, Minami-tori-shima (Marcus Island), Line Islands, Marquesas Islands, and Tuamotu Archi-

Hawaiian Islands

pelago (type locality, Manihi Atoll); range extended to Maldive Islands, Cocos-Keeling Islands, Sumatra, Coral Sea, American Samoa, Galápagos Islands, Isla del Coco, and Hawaiian Islands (Randall & Mundy, 1998); known from depths of 13–200 m, the main population is probably below 80 m.

CROSSHATCH TRIGGERFISH

Xanthichthys mento (Jordan & Gilbert, 1882)
Dorsal rays III + 29–31; anal rays 27–28; pectoral rays 12–14; longitudinal scale rows 43–48; head scale rows 19–21; 5 oblique grooves separating scale rows on cheek; a series of longitudinal ridges bearing small spines on body following scale rows, not extending anterior to second dorsal fin; caudal fin slightly emarginate; yellowish gray, the scale edges dark brown; shallow grooves on cheek blue; a dark brown band at base of second dorsal and anal fins; females with a broad orange border on second dorsal and anal fins and a broad, bright yellow border on caudal fin with a submarginal blue band to posterior margin; males with a yellow border on second dorsal and anal fins, the caudal fin reddish with a narrow, bright red margin all around and a blue submarginal line; males with a small bright blue spot on each scale of body. Reaches 30 cm. Antitropical in the Pacific; in the north from southern Japan, Minami-tori-shima (Marcus Island), Wake Island, Hawaiian Islands, Clipperton Island, Revillagigedo Islands (type locality), north to southern California; in the south from Easter Island, Pitcairn Islands, and Rapa; also in the eastern Pacific from the Galápagos Islands and Cocos Island, Costa Rica. Found in outer-reef areas and drop-offs; depth range 6–131 m; feeds on zooplankton.

Scrawled Filefish, *Aluterus scriptus*, Ogasawara Islands

FILEFISHES
(MONACANTHIDAE)

The filefishes are named for their tough abrasive skin; they are called leatherjackets in Australia. The family is very closely related to the Balistidae, and some authors have classified it as a subfamily of the Balistidae. The filefishes differ from the triggerfishes in having a longer and more slender first dorsal spine (which also can be locked in an erect position), a very small second dorsal spine (absent in a few species), and no third spine; the body is more compressed; there are 6 outer teeth in the jaws reinforced by an inner row of 4 teeth; there are nonoverlapping scales as in the Balistidae, but instead of nodules in the center of each scale, there is a cluster of spinules that obscures the scale outlines and gives the skin a sandpaper-like texture; the spinous knob at the end of the pelvic bone, called the pelvic rudiment, is encased in three or fewer pairs of modified scales; it is fixed or movable, but absent on some species. The body depth can be increased more than in balistids by depressing the pelvic bone and stretching the loose skin of the pelvic flap above it; because of the variation in maximum body depth, measurements of depth are taken from the origin of the anal fin. The soft rays of the dorsal and anal fins are unbranched; the uppermost pectoral ray is rudimentary but included in the counts given here; the caudal fin is usually rounded. Filefishes are more secretive than triggerfishes; many tend to match their surroundings in color, and some have small cutaneous flaps or cirri that enhance the camouflage. Most species are omnivorous and tend to feed on a wide variety of benthic plant and animal life; some species feed freely on very noxious sponges and coelenterates that are avoided by other fishes. Some filefishes are sexually dimorphic, especially with respect to spines or setae on the side of the caudal peduncle (typically larger in males). There are about 31 genera and 95 species of monacanthids in the world. Australia has 28 of the genera (Hutchins, 1977) and 54 of the species. The genus *Cantherhines* was revised by Randall (1964) and Hutchins & Randall (1982). The genus *Pervagor* was revised by Hutchins (1986), and the genus *Paramonacanthus* by Hutchins (1997).

SEAGRASS FILEFISH

Acreichthys tomentosus (Linnaeus, 1758)

Dorsal rays II + 26–30; anal rays 25–29; pectoral rays 10–13; vertebrae 20; body depth at origin of anal fin 1.85–2.1 in standard length (females deeper bodied than males); setae on scales posteriorly on body longer, in males still longer and forming a distinct patch; scattered small cirri on head and body, some fringed; dorsal profile of head concave; 4 inner teeth of upper jaw notched; first dorsal spine somewhat curved, originating above middle of eye; no groove in back behind first dorsal fin; pelvic rudiment movable; gray-brown, olivaceous, or grass green, finely mottled and spotted with white and dark brown, usually with an irregular, dark-edged white band extending posteriorly from gill opening; a similar smaller band behind eye. Reported to 11.5 cm. Sri Lanka to Indo-Malayan region, north

Papua New Guinea

to Ryukyu Islands, south to New Caledonia, east to Palau and Fiji; type locality, America (in error); typically found in seagrass beds or algal flats in protected waters. Also known as the Matted Filefish.

SCRAWLED FILEFISH

Aluterus scriptus (Osbeck, 1765)

Dorsal rays II + 43–49; anal rays 46–52; pectoral rays 14–16; body depth at anal-fin origin 2.7–3.1 in standard length; dorsal and ventral profiles of head concave; mouth slightly upturned, the lower jaw projecting; gill opening oblique; first dorsal spine long and slender, not followed by a groove; caudal fin round and very long, its length 1.6–3.0 in standard length; spinous pelvic rudiment embedded; light bluish gray to olive or brown with scattered, small black spots, and blue or blue-green spots and short irregular bands; capable of rapid color changes. Reaches 75 cm. Cosmopolitan in all warm seas; type locality, "China Sea." Diet highly varied, some fish feeding mainly on algae or seagrass, but most on hydrozoans (including the stinging coral *Millepora*), gorgonians, tunicates, toxic zoantharians such as *Palythoa*, gastropods, and sponges. A second species of the genus, *A. monoceros* (Linnaeus), should

Bali

be expected in the South Pacific area, but the author is not aware of any definite records. It is easily distinguished from *scriptus* by having a truncate to slightly emarginate caudal fin that is shorter than the head length and lacking any blue or black markings.

BROOM FILEFISH

Amanses scopas (Cuvier, 1829)

Dorsal rays II + 26–29; anal rays 22–25; pectoral rays 13; body deep, the depth at anal-fin origin 1.9–2.1 in standard length; dorsal profile of snout straight to slightly concave; caudal peduncle deep, the depth about equal to caudal-fin length; males with a group of 5 or 6 long quill-like retrorse spines on side of body below posterior half of second dorsal fin; females with a dense mass of long setae at the same location, resembling the bristles of a toothbrush; dorsal spine nearly straight, about as long as snout, originating over front part of eye, and folding partially into a groove on back; front of second dorsal and anal fins not elevated; caudal fin rounded, about 5 in standard length; pelvic rudiment immobile; brown with up to 12 narrow, dark brown bars on side of body anterior to the posterior spines or setae; caudal fin and base of pectoral fins dark brown; membranes of second dorsal, anal, and pectoral fins clear, the rays yellow; lips not covering teeth, which are conspicuously white. Largest specimen examined, 19 cm. Red Sea and east coast of Africa to the Society Islands, Tuamotu Archipelago, and throughout Micronesia; south-

Maldive Islands/male with *Labroides dimidiatus*

ern Japan to Great Barrier Reef; type locality, Mauritius. Often seen in pairs; very shy. Harmelin-Vivien (1979) examined the alimentary tract contents of 6 specimens from Madagascar; all contained fragments of madreporarian corals.

BARRED FILEFISH

Cantherhines dumerilii (Hollard, 1854)

Dorsal rays II + 34–39; anal rays 29–34; pectoral rays 14–15 (rarely 14); vertebrae 19 (true of other *Cantherhines*); body depth at origin of anal fin 2.2–2.4 in standard length; 2 pairs of prominent antrorse spines on side of caudal peduncle, larger in males; dorsal profile of snout straight; first dorsal spine originating over front half of eye and fitting partially into a groove in back (also generic), the spine straight and long, about equal to snout length; anterior part of dorsal and anal fins somewhat elevated, the longest dorsal ray 1.9–2.2 in snout length; pelvic rudiment immobile (generic); grayish brown with 8–14 darker brown bars on posterior half to two-thirds of side of body; edge of opercular membrane black; lips dull pink with a narrow brown edge; second dorsal and anal fins translucent with yellow rays; caudal spines and caudal fin of males orange, the rays brown basally; juveniles and subadults may have many small white spots. Largest collected, 37.5 cm. Indo-Pacific and tropical eastern Pacific; type locality, Mauritius. Stomach contents of 8 specimens examined by the author: mainly coral, especially *Acropora*, but also *Pocillopora*, *Montipora*, and *Leptoseris*; sometimes feeds on echinoids, bryozoans, mollusks, sponges, and algae; often seen in pairs.

Hawaiian Islands/female

Palau/male

Bali

Sulawesi (night)

SPECTACLED FILEFISH

Cantherhines fronticinctus (Günther in Playfair & Günther, 1867)

Dorsal rays II + 32–35; anal rays 30–32; pectoral rays 12–13; body depth at origin of anal fin 2.0–2.3 in standard length; no spines on side of caudal peduncle; dorsal profile of snout concave; first dorsal spine nearly equal to snout length; longest dorsal ray 2.4–2.8 in snout length; caudal fin moderately long, 3.1–3.9 in standard length; color variable but often light brown with dark brown blotches tending to merge to form 3 main stripes on body, with a lesser stripe above and below; 2 transverse, dark brown bands across interorbital, the anterior much broader than the posterior; caudal peduncle mainly pale; a mottled dark bar at base of caudal fin; edges of caudal fin usually dark brown. Attains about 24 cm. East coast of Africa (type locality, Zanzibar) to the Indo-Malayan region, north to Sagami Bay, Japan, south to Lord Howe Island and New Caledonia, east to Mariana Islands and Marshall Islands. Closely related to *Cantherhines verecundus* in the Hawaiian Islands, *C. longicaudus* in the Cook Islands and Society Islands, and *C. rapanui* in Easter Island.

633

LONGTAIL FILEFISH

Cantherhines longicaudus Hutchins & Randall, 1982

Dorsal rays II + 35–36; anal rays 31–33; pectoral rays 13; body depth at origin of anal fin about 2.0 in standard length; no spines or setae on side of caudal peduncle; dorsal profile of snout concave; first dorsal spine 1.3–1.4 in snout length; longest dorsal ray 1.35–1.8 in snout length; caudal fin long, 2.9–3.1 in standard length; usual color dull yellow with 5 rows of indistinct dusky blotches on body and a dusky bar from eye across gill opening to upper end of pectoral-fin base; second dorsal and anal fins with yellow rays and translucent membranes; caudal fin with yellow rays and brownish yellow membranes. Largest specimen, 17.5 cm. Known only from the Society Islands (type locality, Tahiti), Tuamotu Archipelago, and Rarotonga, Cook Islands.

HONEYCOMB FILEFISH

Cantherhines pardalis (Rüppell, 1837)

Dorsal rays II + 32–36; anal rays 29–32; pectoral rays 13–15; body depth at origin of anal fin 2.1–2.3 in standard length; adult males with a dense patch of brush-like setae on and slightly anterior to side of caudal peduncle; dorsal profile of snout concave; first dorsal spine varying from slightly shorter to slightly longer than snout length; front of second dorsal and anal fins not elevated, the longest dorsal ray 1.8–2.4 in snout length; caudal fin rounded and relatively short, 4.4–5.0 in standard length; color can be altered to 3 basic patterns: dark brown, light gray-brown with 5 poorly defined dark stripes that converge on the anterior caudal peduncle, and gray with numerous orange-brown spots so close-set as to give a honeycomb effect; all 3 phases have in common a bright white spot dorsally on caudal peduncle, and a smaller white spot ventrally; wide-ranging from the Red Sea (type locality) and coast of East Africa to the Marquesas Islands; Sagami Bay, Japan, to Great Barrier Reef, New South Wales, and Lord Howe Island; the species previously identified as *Cantherhines pardalis* from Rarotonga, Rapa, and the Pitcairn Islands proved to be *C. sandwichiensis*, otherwise known only from the Hawaiian Islands and Johnston Island. *Cantherhines pardalis* is closely related to *C. pullus* (Ranzani) from the Atlantic. Kawase & Nakazono (1994) studied the reproduction.

SQUARETAIL FILEFISH

Cantherhines sandwichiensis (Quoy & Gaimard, 1824)

Dorsal rays II + 33–36; anal rays 30–32; pectoral rays 13–15; body depth at origin of anal fin about 2.4 in standard length; patch of brush-like setae on side of caudal peduncle of male poorly developed; dorsal profile of snout nearly straight; first dorsal spine over anterior edge of eye, about equal to snout length; front of second dorsal and anal fins elevated, the longest dorsal ray (sixth or seventh) 1.5–1.8 in snout length; caudal fin short, 5.2–5.8 in standard length, and truncate (slightly rounded when broadly spread); brown to gray, sometimes with very small white spots of variable size on body, and irregular dark and pale lines around eye; dusky zone around mouth; membranes of caudal fin dark brown. Largest specimen, 19.4 cm. Antitropical: Hawaiian Islands (type locality) and Johnston Island in the north, and Rarotonga, Rapa, and Pitcairn Islands in the south. Feeds mainly on algae and detritus but also ingests tunicates, corals, sponges, bivalve mollusks, and foraminifera.

Fiji

LONGNOSE FILEFISH

Oxymonacanthus longirostris (Bloch & Schneider, 1801)
Dorsal rays II + 31–35; anal rays 29–32; pectoral rays 11–13; body elongate, the depth at origin of anal fin 3.1–3.3 in standard length; snout long, tapering, and tubular; mouth slightly upturned; setae on caudal peduncle of male long; first dorsal spine over posterior half of eye, shorter than snout, folding into a groove in back; second dorsal spine minute; second dorsal and anal fins not elevated anteriorly; caudal fin short and slightly rounded; pelvic rudiment small and immobile; bright green, shading to pale green or nearly white posteriorly, with 7 longitudinal rows of bright orange spots on body and posterior part of head, some of which may be joined to form elongate spots; first dorsal spine, front of head, and tubular part of snout orange; pelvic flap orange, the male with a large white-dotted black patch above

and a lesser one below the orange; female may have some black with the orange but the black not white-dotted and the orange not as bright; second dorsal and anal fins translucent; caudal fin pale green to whitish with a black spot larger than pupil. Attains 10 cm. East coast of Africa to the Samoa Islands and islands of Micronesia; Ryukyu Islands and Ogasawara Islands to Great Barrier Reef and Lord Howe Island; type locality, East Indies. An obligate coral-polyp feeder; usually seen feeding on corals of the genus *Acropora* on reefs without heavy surge at depths from less than 1 to at least 30 m. Large adults occur in male-female pairs; subadults often seen in small groups. Barlow (1987) described the spawning and early development. The eggs are green and adhesive, laid in blue-green algae; they hatch in 53.5 hours just after sunset. Replaced in the Red Sea by the closely related *Oxymonacanthus halli* Marshall.

MIMIC FILEFISH

Paraluteres prionurus (Bleeker, 1851)
Dorsal rays II + 25–28; anal rays 22–25; pectoral rays 11–12 (usually 12); body depth at origin of anal fin 2.0–2.4 in standard length; dorsal profile of snout straight or slightly concave; adult males with a broad, elliptical, dense patch of setae posteriorly on body, ending in 2 pairs of antrorse spines on caudal-fin base; origin of first dorsal spine over posterior half of eye, shorter than snout, the tip connected by membrane nearly to origin of second dorsal fin; spine usually held nearly hidden in groove in back; pelvic rudiment very small or absent; no ventral flap; white with black dots except on ventral fourth of body; a black band across posterior half of interorbital ending behind lower part of eye; a broad black bar below first dorsal fin tapering to end on abdomen; a similar black bar below fifth to fifteenth dorsal soft rays, ending above origin of anal fin; a short, triangular black bar below posterior one-third of second dorsal fin and dorsal part of caudal peduncle; caudal fin mainly yellow. Reaches 10 cm. Oman and coast of East Africa to Fiji, Tonga, Niue, and the islands of Micronesia; Suruga Bay, Japan, to Great Barrier Reef

Tonga

and New South Wales; type locality, Banda Islands, Indonesia. Replaced by *Paraluteres arqat* Clark & Gohar in the Red Sea. As noted by Clark & Gohar (1953), *P. prionurus* mimics the toby *Canthigaster valentini* (Bleeker), a poisonous species usually avoided by predators.

SHORTSNOUT FILEFISH
Paramonacanthus curtorhynchos (Bleeker, 1855)

Dorsal rays II + 33–36; anal rays 30–32; pectoral rays 11–13; body depth at origin of anal fin 1.9–3.2 in standard length (more elongate with growth, and males more elongate than females); dorsal profile of snout slightly concave to straight in females, convex in large males, the snout length 3.7–4.1 in standard length; no spines or long setae on side of caudal peduncle; fringed cutaneous cirri scattered on head and ventrally on body; origin of first dorsal fin over posterior edge of eye, 1.3–1.7 in head length; second dorsal and anal fins elevated anteriorly, the longest dorsal ray 1.7–3.2 in head length (ray longer in males); caudal fin rounded, the second ray prolonged as a filament in males; pelvic rudiment narrow and movable; whitish to pale yellowish with dark brown to dusky blotches that tend to form 2 longitudinal stripes or several irregular bars, or a combination of both; head with broad irregular dark bands radiating from eye, one of which crosses interorbital; first dorsal spine with 5 or 6 dark crossbands; caudal fin with 2 broad dark bars. Largest specimen, 11.3 cm. Formerly identified as *Paramonacanthus japonicus* (Tilesius), but this is now known to be a distinct Japanese species for which the valid name is *P. oblongus* (Temminck & Schlegel). *Paramonacanthus curtorhynchos* does not range to Japan (J. B. Hutchins, pers. comm.); it occurs in the

Sulawesi/female (night)

Sulawesi/male (night)

Indo-Malayan region (type locality, Ambon, Molucca Islands), south to Western Australia and Queensland, west to the Bay of Bengal, and east to Palau, New Caledonia, and Fiji; found in protected habitats, generally on open, silty sand bottoms.

YELLOWEYE FILEFISH
Pervagor alternans (Ogilby, 1899)

Dorsal rays II + 31–34; anal rays 27–31; pectoral rays 12–13 (usually 13); vertebrae 19 (true of other *Pervagor*); body depth at origin of anal fin 2.2–2.5 in standard length; setae on body increasing in length posteriorly, those of male with forward-curved tips (also generic); dorsal profile of snout concave (generic); first dorsal spine long, nearly straight, with 4 rows of prominent curved spines, its origin over middle to anterior half of eye (generic); length of first dorsal spine 1.2–1.6 in head length; front of second dorsal and anal fins not elevated (generic), the longest dorsal soft ray 2.7–3.1 in head length; caudal fin rounded (generic), 1.4–1.8 in head length; pelvic rudiment movable, with stout spines (generic); brown to dark brown with darker brown dots forming irregular longitudinal lines on body; sometimes shading to brownish orange on caudal peduncle; no dark blotch around gill opening; eye and a variable amount of orbital rim yellow; second dorsal and anal fins with light brown rays, the mem-

Lord Howe Island

branes pale orange basally with rows of pale blue dashes; caudal fin orange, streaked longitudinally with dark brown, with a broad dark brown outer band. Largest specimen, 18 cm. Apparently anti-equatorial: Marshall Islands in the north and southern Queensland, Great Barrier Reef, New South Wales (type locality, Maroubra Beach), Lord Howe Island, Norfolk Island, New Caledonia, Tonga, and Niue in the south.

Hawaiian Islands

ORANGETAIL FILEFISH
Pervagor aspricaudus (Hollard, 1854)

Dorsal rays II + 31–35; anal rays 28–32; pectoral rays 12–13 (usually 12); body depth at origin of anal fin 2.1–2.5 in standard length; length of first dorsal spine 1.0–1.2 in head length; longest dorsal soft ray 2.5–2.8 in head length; caudal fin 1.5–1.8 in head length; brown, shading posteriorly in about middle of body to orange, each scale with a dark brown dot, thus forming irregular longitudinal dotted lines; no large black blotch around gill opening; second dorsal and anal fins with longitudinal rows of yellow and pale blue lines; caudal fin bright orange-yellow with an outer blackish and yellow band. Largest specimen, 11.5 cm. Reported from Mauritius, Maldives, Christmas Island, Great Barrier Reef, New Caledonia, Ryukyu Islands, southern Taiwan, Marshall Islands, Minami-tori-shima (Marcus Island), Hawaiian Islands, and Johnston Island; type locality unknown. Maximum depth recorded, 23 m; like others of the genus, very secretive.

BLACKBAR FILEFISH
Pervagor janthinosoma (Bleeker, 1854)
Dorsal rays II + 29–34; anal rays 26–30; pectoral rays 11–13
(usually 12); body depth at origin of anal fin 2.2–2.5 in standard length; length of first dorsal spine 1.0–1.3 in head length;
longest dorsal soft ray 2.3–2.8 in head length; caudal fin
1.3–1.6 in head length; gray, shading posteriorly to yellowish
gray, with traces of faint, dotted, dark longitudinal lines; a
large black blotch enclosing gill opening and extending vertically upward to behind lower part of eye; second dorsal and
anal fins with narrow, irregular, blue and yellow bands; caudal
fin orange with a broad yellow posterior border containing
irregular dark blue to black lines paralleling margin. Largest
specimen, 13.5 cm. South Africa, Comoro Islands, Mauritius,
Western Australia, Indo-Malayan region (type locality,
Ambon), north to southern Japan, south to Great Barrier Reef,
New South Wales, and Norfolk Island, east to Mariana Islands,
Caroline Islands, Kiribati, Fiji, and Tonga; occurs on shallow
coral reefs to about 15 m.

Ambon, Indonesia

BLACKMARGIN FILEFISH
Pervagor marginalis Hutchins, 1986
Dorsal rays II + 30–32; anal rays 27–29; pectoral rays 12;
body depth at origin of anal fin 2.3–2.5 in standard length;
head length 2.9–3.1 in standard length; eye diameter 3.0–3.3
in head length; length of first dorsal spine 1.0–1.3 in head
length; longest dorsal soft ray 2.6–2.7 in head length; caudal
fin 1.4–1.5 in head; gray with a black dot on each scale of
head and body; a broad black bar across interorbital, enclosing eye and gill opening and ending at pectoral-fin base; first
dorsal fin black; second dorsal and anal fins with dark brown
rays and pale membranes; caudal fin with a broad black border all around, the center bright orange. Largest specimen,
8.2 cm. Known only from the Marquesas Islands (type locality, Nuku Hiva) and the Line Islands; depth range 2–23 m.
Closely related to the allopatric *Pervagor aspricaudus*, which
differs in having a longer head when comparing specimens of
the same size, a smaller eye diameter (3.2–4.0 in head length),
and in color.

Marquesas Islands

BLACKHEAD FILEFISH
Pervagor melanocephalus (Bleeker, 1853)
Dorsal rays II + 30–33; anal rays 27–30; pectoral rays 12–13
(usually 12); body depth at origin of anal fin 2.1–2.3 in standard length; length of first dorsal spine 1.0–1.2 in head
length; longest dorsal soft ray 2.4–2.7 in head length; caudal
fin 1.3–1.5 in head length; head and anterior body to below
midinterdorsal space dark gray to nearly black; rest of body
orange; gill opening enclosed in a black blotch that continues
dorsally to level of eye and ventrally to cover base of pectoral
fin; second dorsal and anal fins with yellow rays, the membranes narrowly banded with blue and yellow; caudal fin
orange with wavy, dark blue to black lines in about outer
one-fourth of fin. Largest specimen, 10.5 cm. Indo-Malayan
region (type locality, Solor), north to Ryukyu Islands and
Ogasawara Islands, south to Great Barrier Reef, and east to
Marshall Islands, Palau, Fiji, Tonga, and Samoa Islands
(Wass, 1984); recorded from depths of 8 to 40 m; usually
found deeper than 20 m.

Sulawesi

637

Alor, Indonesia/juveniles

Adonara, Indonesia (night)

RHINO FILEFISH

Pseudalutarius nasicornis (Temminck & Schlegel, 1850)
Dorsal rays II + 46–51; anal rays 44–48; pectoral rays 12–13; body elongate for a filefish, the depth at origin of anal fin about 6 in standard length in juveniles and about 3.5 in adult males; origin of first dorsal fin in advance of eye, the spine slender, longer than snout, and depressible into a groove on back; second dorsal spine minute; second dorsal and anal fins low; caudal fin small and rounded; no pelvic rudiment or pelvic flap; white to pale gray with a midlateral, dark brown stripe from front of snout through eye to end in a dark brown spot at caudal-fin base; a second dark brown stripe from dorsally on snout along back, narrowing and ending dorsally on caudal peduncle; a large, dark brown to black spot or broad bar covering most of caudal fin; males may have stripes variably joined and broken by pale bars; small yellow spots often present ventrally on body. Attains 18 cm. East coast of Africa to the Indo-Malayan region, north to Japan (type locality), south to Queensland and New South Wales, east to New Caledonia and Guam; occurs in protected waters, generally in seagrass or algal beds or soft corals; known from depths of a few to 68 m. Very secretive, generally hidden among plants or soft coral with head down.

BOXFISHES AND COWFISHES
(OSTRACIIDAE)

The boxfishes and cowfishes (also known as trunkfishes) are unique in possessing a bony carapace made of polygonal plates, with gaps for the mouth, gill opening, anus, caudal peduncle, and fins. The carapace may be triangular, quadrangular, pentagonal, hexagonal, or nearly round in cross-section. Some species have sharp spines that project from the carapace; those of the genus *Lactoria* have 2 hornlike spines from the front of the head, hence their common name, cowfishes. Other characteristics for the family include a small mouth that is low on the head; thick lips; teeth in a single row in the jaws, conical to incisiform with rounded tips; no teeth on the palate (true of all tetraodontiform fishes); gill opening restricted to a slit extending dorsally from in front of the pectoral-fin base; no spines in the fins; a single dorsal fin in posterior position; and no pelvic fins. As would be expected from their bony armor and boxy shape, the ostraciids are slow swimmers; their usual mode of progression is a sculling of the dorsal and anal fins; the caudal fin is brought into action when they need to move faster. The author has observed cowfishes swim directly backward when threatened,

thus keeping their sharp "horns" facing the intruder. Ostraciid fishes feed on a wide variety of benthic invertebrates, particularly sessile forms such as tunicates, sponges, and alcyonarians; many also ingest large amounts of algae. Some have been observed to jet a stream of water from the mouth to move sand away from fossorial prey such as polychaete worms. Although the bony carapace alone would seem to be enough to discourage a predator, especially those with protruding sharp spines, some boxfishes are known to secrete a skin toxin called ostracitoxin when under stress (Thomson, 1964; Boylan & Scheuer, 1967). If a boxfish is placed in a small volume of water with other fishes and harassed, the other fishes will die; if the level of the toxin is high enough, the boxfish will die as well. The family is divisible into 2 subfamilies, the Aracaninae (some authors prefer to make this a separate family) with the carapace rigid ventrally only at lateral edges, and the Ostraciinae with the carapace entirely rigid ventrally. There are no known representatives of the Aracaninae in inshore waters of islands of the South Pacific. A total of 14 genera and 34 species is recorded for the Ostraciidae (synoptic review by Trubschenck, 1981). Counts of the pectoral rays given here include the rudimentary upper ray.

Sulawesi/juvenile

Guam

LONGHORN COWFISH
Lactoria cornuta (Linnaeus, 1758)

Dorsal rays 8–9; anal rays 9; pectoral rays 10–11; a pair of sharp "horns" about twice eye diameter in adults extending anteriorly and slightly upward from front of carapace at level of upper edge of eye; a second pair of spines extending posteriorly, one from each side of rear of carapace; dorsal profile of snout nearly vertical; caudal fin very long, 1.5–2.0 in standard length, and truncate (though often ragged on the trailing edge); color variable but usually olive to yellowish gray with pale blue spots on the side; ventral part of carapace may be orange-yellow; caudal fin often with pale spots and sometimes indistinct dusky spots. Reported to 46 cm. Occurs from the Red Sea and east coast of Africa to the Marquesas Islands, Society Islands, and Tuamotu Archipelago; only the Mariana Islands in Micronesia; Korea and Shizuoka Prefecture to Great Barrier Reef, New South Wales, and Lord Howe Island; type locality, India. Usually found in lagoons or protected bays in seagrass beds or substrata with heavy algal cover, occasionally more in the open on sand or silty sand bottoms; reported to depths of 100 m.

Hawaiian Islands

Izu Islands, Japan

SPINY COWFISH
Lactoria diaphana (Bloch & Schneider, 1801)

Dorsal rays 9; anal rays 9; pectoral rays 10–11; carapace of 5 ridges, the median one with a small, thorn-like spine in middle of body and a smaller one to the side on the lateral ridge; a broad-based spine extending anteriorly from upper edge of each eye; lower lateral ridge ending on each side in a retrorse spine; ventral surface of carapace broadly convex; body depth 2.5–2.7 in standard length; caudal fin slightly rounded; light greenish gray with a few dark brown blotches and variously marked with small black spots; ventral part of carapace whitish. Reaches 25 cm. Wide-ranging but with few records from East Africa to the Hawaiian Islands, Cook Islands (M. P. Francis, pers. comm.), and Easter Island; in the western Pacific from southern Japan and the Mariana Islands to Lord Howe Island, New Caledonia, and Kermadec Islands; records in the eastern Pacific from southern California to Peru. Leis & Moyer (1985) illustrated the larval stages. They noted that this species reaches 10 cm or more as a larva and, surprisingly, can be mature and complete its life cycle while pelagic far from land.

THORNBACK COWFISH
Lactoria fornasini (Bianconi, 1846)

Dorsal rays 9; anal rays 9; pectoral rays 11–12 (rarely 12); carapace basically quadrangular in cross-section but with a median ridge on back bearing a large, thorn-like spine in the middle; bottom of carapace slightly convex; a pair of sharp horns extending anteriorly and slightly upward from carapace in front of upper edge of eyes, generally shorter than orbit diameter; a similar short pair of spines posteriorly, one from each rear corner of carapace; dorsal profile of head forming an angle of about 45° to horizontal axis of body; caudal fin rounded; light brown to brownish yellow with a few indistinct, large brown blotches, many irregular bright blue lines, and scattered, small, bright blue spots. Maximum length, 15 cm. Wide-ranging from the east coast of Africa to Rapa and the Hawaiian Islands; Miura Peninsula, Japan, to the Great Barrier Reef, New South Wales, and Lord Howe Island; apparently absent from many of the oceanic islands of the Indian and Pacific Oceans; type locality, Mozambique; observed more on rubble and sand bottoms than in coral reefs.

Bali/male

Mauritius/juvenile

Maldive Islands/subadult

Maldive Islands/female

YELLOW BOXFISH

Ostracion cubicus Linnaeus, 1758

Dorsal rays 9; anal rays 9; pectoral rays 11; carapace quadrangular in cross-section, the sides concave, broader at base than dorsally, and without a median ridge (true of other *Ostracion*); carapace depth of very small juveniles about 1.5 in standard length, of large adults about 3; a bony protuberance anteriorly above upper lip (small in juveniles); caudal fin rounded (generic); small juveniles yellow with round black spots nearly as large as pupil; black spots more numerous and relatively smaller with growth; with further growth, yellow changes to brown, and white spots appear, circled with small black spots or rimmed in black; mature males variable in color with small blue and black spots on body of carapace, yellow grooves separating some polygonal plates on cheek and lower side of body, and fin rays blue with small black spots. Reported to 45 cm. Occurs throughout the Indo-Pacific from the Red Sea and east coast of Africa to the Hawaiian Islands (where only a stray) and the islands of French Polynesia, including northern New Zealand; type locality, India. Stomach contents of 7 adults consisted mainly of didemnid tunicates and algae (including *Halimeda* and coralline reds), with lesser amounts of sponge, polychaete worms, bryozoans, small crustaceans, and small mollusks.

640

SPOTTED BOXFISH
Ostracion meleagris Shaw, 1796

Dorsal rays 9; anal rays 9; pectoral rays 11; no bony protuberance on snout; no low ridge ventrally at anterior edge of carapace; gill opening not short, greater than distance from its upper end to eye; females dark brown with small white spots; some spots on side of body of large females elongate; dorsal side of carapace of males brown with small white spots as in females; side of carapace blue to purple with many round to oblong, black-edged, bright orange spots, the spots of upper side at superior ridge larger, semicircular or oblong, and variously connected posteriorly to form an irregular yellow stripe that continues onto upper edge of caudal peduncle; a large, light brown area often present below eye. Reaches 15 cm. Occurs from the east coast of Africa (but not the Red Sea or Persian Gulf) to the Hawaiian Islands and Pitcairn Islands; in the western Pacific from Japan to New South Wales and Lord Howe Island; also found in the tropical eastern Pacific; type locality, Southern Ocean. Harmelin-Vivien (1979) examined the stomach contents of 4 specimens from Madagascar, finding mainly foraminifera, amphipods and other small crustaceans, algae, and tunicates; the author found only tunicate material in 1 adult. *Ostracion lentiginosus* Bloch & Schneider and *O. sebae* Bleeker are synonyms, and *Ostracion camurum* Jenkins from Hawai'i, with males of slightly different color, is currently regarded as a synonym.

SOLOR BOXFISH
Ostracion solorensis Bleeker, 1853

Dorsal rays 9; anal rays 8–9 (usually 9); pectoral rays 9–10 (usually 10); top of carapace nearly flat, the bottom slightly convex, the 4 ridges sharp; caudal fin rounded; top of carapace of female dark brown finely dotted with yellow or pale bluish gray; side of carapace and caudal peduncle with a broad reticular pattern of dark brown separated by lines of pale bluish gray or yellow; head below eye, chest, and pectoral region dull yellow with dark brown spots; fins pale yellow, the caudal with dark brown spots; males with top of carapace dark gray to black with irregular, fine, pale blue or blue-green lines and dots, the upper side of carapace with blue-edged black stripes, the rest light purple with pale blue spots broadly rimmed in black on posterior half (the spots sometimes nearly confluent) and a black-edged, pale blue band forming an L-shape (on its side) from eye to gill opening and extending forward onto side of head; fins pale purplish gray, the caudal with dark brown streaks on base. Reaches 11 cm. Philippines, Indonesia (type locality, Solor), and northern Great Barrier Reef, east to Palau and Fiji (where rare); also reported from Christmas Island, Indian Ocean (Allen & Steene, 1979). Difficult to approach underwater.

Bali/male

Kenya/female

Luzon/male

Papua New Guinea/female

Hawaiian Islands/juvenile

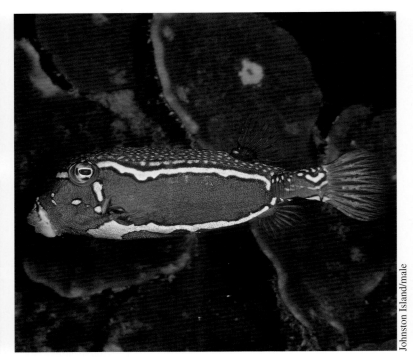
Johnston Island/male

Marquesas Islands/female

WHITLEY'S BOXFISH

Ostracion whitleyi Fowler, 1931

Dorsal rays 9; anal rays 9; pectoral rays 11; a low ridge ventrally at anterior end of carapace (around lower lip); gill opening short, equal to or less than distance from its upper end to eye; females brown dorsally on carapace and upper third of side with small white spots, white on ventral surface of carapace and lower edge of side with small dark brown spots, the 2 spotted areas on side separated by a broad white stripe (often bordered by dark brown or black); large females with more numerous and relatively smaller white spots; caudal fin with small, dark brown spots on rays; males deep blue with small white spots dorsally on carapace, the side next to the superior ridge with an irregular, black-edged white stripe, and a comparable stripe just above inferior ridge; ventral surface of carapace white with blue areas, the largest enclosing anal fin; a curved, black-edged white bar extending ventrally from lower posterior part of eye. Largest specimen, 15.5 cm. Known from the Society Islands, Tuamotu Archipelago, Marquesas Islands (type locality), Hawaiian Islands (where rare), and Johnston Island. First described as *Ostracion ornatus* by Guichenot in Hollard, but invalid as a homonym; Fowler provided the new name *whitleyi*.

HUMPBACK TURRETFISH

Tetrosomus gibbosus (Linnaeus, 1758)

Dorsal rays 9; anal rays 9; pectoral rays 11; carapace triangular in cross-section; a large, blade-like ridge middorsally on carapace, elevated above middle of ridge to a broad-based spine; inferior ridge of carapace with a series of 5 retrorse spines, the first below gill opening small; ridge over eye with a small spine; jaws with 10 upper and 8 lower teeth; caudal peduncle slender; caudal fin rounded; yellowish gray to olivaceous with large, poorly defined white spots; a dark brown blotch on side of large middorsal spine and 5 dark blotches along inferior ridge, the first ventrally on side of head, the second enclosing base of pectoral fin; caudal peduncle white with large, dark brown spots; some indiviudals (perhaps males) with small blue spots on head and anterior body. Reaches 30 cm. Red Sea south to Natal, east to the western Pacific from southern Japan to Queensland and New Caledonia; type locality, India. *Tetrosomus concatenatus* Bloch, from the western Pacific to east coast of Africa, has two small spines on the dorsal ridge of the carapace.

Adonara, Indonesia

Stellate Puffer, *Arothron stellatus*, Red Sea

PUFFERS
(TETRAODONTIDAE)

The puffers, also known as blowfishes, are named for their ability, when provoked, to inflate themselves by drawing water (or air if taken out of water) into a highly distensible ventral diverticulum of the stomach. They are characterized further by teeth fused to beak-like dental plates (with a median suture), a slit-like gill opening in front of the pectoral-fin base, tough skin without typical scales (small spinules are often present, especially ventrally, and their pattern may be important in classification); no spines in the fins; a single, short-based dorsal fin posterior in position, and a comparable anal fin below or behind the dorsal; caudal fin with 10 principal rays and no procurrent rays; no pelvic fins; and no ribs. Puffers are found in all tropical to warm temperate seas, usually in shallow water, but some occur at moderate depths; a few are pelagic. Most species are solitary, but some form small aggregations. These unusual fishes are well known for producing a powerful toxin, tetrodotoxin, in their tissues, especially in the liver and ovaries (Halstead, 1967). The toxin varies greatly in the different species, some being safe to eat, others potentially lethal. Also the toxin can vary with the geographical area and the reproductive state. The family is divisible into two subfamilies, the Tetraodontinae and the Canthigasterinae (reviewed by Allen & Randall, 1977). Species of the former, with 18 genera and 95 species, have rounded bodies, a conspicuous lateral line, the gill opening usually extending below the midbase of the pectoral fin, and 17–29 vertebrae. The Canthigasterinae, popularly known as tobies or sharpnose puffers, have laterally compressed bodies, an elongate pointed snout, an inconspicuous lateral line, a small gill opening (the lower end generally at or above the midbase of the pectoral fin), an erectile ridge of skin middorsally and midventrally, and 17 vertebrae. It consists of a single genus, *Canthigaster*, with 27 brightly colored species, 25 of which occur in the Indo-Pacific region; they are known to produce a repelling skin toxin and are rarely eaten by predators. Counts of fin rays given here include the rudimentary ray anteriorly in the dorsal and anal fins and dorsally in the pectoral fins.

Sarosa Island, Indonesia

BLUESPOTTED PUFFER

Arothron caeruleopunctatus Matsuura, 1994

Dorsal rays 11–12; anal rays 10–12; pectoral rays 18–19; small spinules on head and body except on posterior caudal peduncle, around eye, gill opening, and base of dorsal and anal fins; snout length 4.9–5.2 in standard length; interorbital space flat, the bony width 2.4–2.9 in head length; nasal organ consisting of 2 fleshy flaps from a common base (characteristic of the genus); origin of anal fin posterior to origin of dorsal fin (also generic); caudal fin rounded (generic) and relatively short, 4.0–5.0 in standard length; pale yellowish brown dorsally, white ventrally, with numerous small, dark-edged, pale blue spots, more close-set ventrally on body, where ground color may be black in patches; thin, pale blue and dark brown rings around eye; median fins with pale blue spots, those on dorsal and anal fins may be confined to base. Reported to 80 cm. Known from the Marshall Islands (type locality), Japan, Papua New Guinea, Indonesia, Maldive Islands, Réunion, and the Great Barrier Reef (where first photographed underwater by the author in 1981); specimens have been collected from depths of 2–45 m.

STRIPEBELLY PUFFER

Arothron hispidus (Linnaeus, 1758)

Dorsal rays 10–11; anal rays 10–11; pectoral rays 17–19; small spinules on head and body except snout and posterior caudal peduncle; snout short and obtuse, 2.0–2.3 in head, and about 7 in standard length; bony ridge over eye extending above level of interorbital space; bony interorbital width 2.6–3.1 in head length; caudal fin 3.4–4.3 in standard length; gray to olivaceous or brown with well-separated, small white spots, shading to white below, usually with dark stripes ventrally on head and abdomen, and sometimes with short dark bars on ventral part of head and body; region around gill opening black with a circle and arcs of white or yellow. Largest specimen, 48 cm. Occurs throughout the Indo-Pacific region, including Lord Howe Island, Hawaiian Islands, and all of French Polynesia, but not reported from the Pitcairn Islands; ranges to the tropical eastern Pacific; type locality, India. Seen more often in sand and rubble areas than in coral reefs; feeds on algae and detritus, mollusks,

Hawaiian Islands

tunicates, sponges, corals, zoanthids, crabs, tube worms, sea urchins, brittlestars, sea stars (including the crown-of-thorns), hermit crabs, and hydroids. Sometimes called the Whitespotted Puffer or Stars and Stripes Puffer.

STRIPED PUFFER
Arothron manilensis (Procé, 1822)

Dorsal rays 9–11 (usually 10); anal rays 9–10 (usually 10); pectoral rays 16–19; head and body largely covered with small spinules (may be embedded); snout short, 1.9–2.3 in head length; bony interorbital width 2.4–3.0 in head length; caudal fin long, its length 2.25–3.2 in standard length; brownish to greenish gray on back, whitish to pale yellowish ventrally, with 8–20 narrow dark stripes on body, the stripes reddish to black dorsally and brownish yellow to light reddish brown ventrally; upper stripes curving downward on head to be continuous or nearly so with lower stripes on body; caudal fin broadly edged with blackish. Largest specimen recorded, 31 cm. Western Australia and western Pacific from Ryukyu Islands to New South Wales, east to islands of Micronesia, Fiji, Tonga, and Samoa Islands; 1 record from the Hawaiian Islands, and 1 atypical specimen from Tahiti. Occurs in shallow protected waters, generally where the sea is somewhat turbid and the bottom silty sand or mud, with or without heavy ben-

Papua New Guinea

thic plant growth; it readily penetrates brackish habitats. Often misidentified as *A. immaculatus* (Bloch & Schneider), which differs in lacking stripes and having a shorter caudal fin (Randall, 1985c).

New Britain

MAP PUFFER
Arothron mappa (Lesson, 1831)

Dorsal rays 11–12; anal rays 10–11; pectoral rays 17–19; heavy bodied for the genus, the maximum depth (not inflated) as much as 1.7 in standard length; head and body with small spinules except for region around mouth, base of fins, and caudal peduncle; snout short, its length about 7 in standard length; interorbital space nearly flat; caudal fin short, its length 4.2–5.1 in standard length; upper two-thirds of body light yellowish gray with highly irregular black bands, many forming a reticulum; a large, irregular black blotch around gill opening; lower one-third of body white with a faint reticulum of yellow or gray and a large, irregular black blotch containing white spots below pectoral fin; irregular black lines radiating from eye; caudal fin with small white spots arranged in irregular vertical rows. Attains 60 cm. East coast of Africa to islands of Micronesia and Samoa Islands; Sea of Japan and Ryukyu Islands to Great Barrier Reef and New Caledonia; type locality, New Guinea. A coral-reef species; not common. Hiatt & Strasburg (1960) examined the digestive tract material of 2 adults from Arno Atoll, Marshall Islands: mainly sponges but also fragments of tunicates, gastropods, and algae (including *Halimeda*, *Valonia*, and corallines).

Hawaiian Islands

Line Islands/yellow phase

Coral Sea

Sulawesi

GUINEAFOWL PUFFER
Arothron meleagris (Lacepède, 1798)
Dorsal rays 10–13 (usually 11 or 12); anal rays 11–13; pectoral rays 17–21 (modally 19); small spinules on head and body except for most of snout and chin, caudal peduncle, and an area of variable size on back (spinules best developed on ventral half of body); gill rakers 5–19; snout short, 2.1–2.2 in head length, and about 7–8 in standard length; bony interorbital width 6.1–9.2 in standard length; caudal fin about 4.5–5.0 in standard length; dark brown to black dorsally, usually a little lighter ventrally, with numerous small white spots on head, body, and fins; fins of some individuals with pale outer margins; a second rare color phase is bright yellow with a few widely scattered small black spots; sometimes there are patches of the typical *meleagris* color pattern, especially on dorsal and anal fins. Reaches 32 cm. Oman and east coast of Africa to the Hawaiian Islands, all of French Polynesia, and the Pitcairn Islands; reported from Ryukyu Islands, Lord Howe Island, and New Caledonia, but there appear to be no records for the East Indies or the Great Barrier Reef; type locality given as Asia; wide-ranging in the tropical eastern Pacific. Gut contents of 6 adult specimens were examined by the author. Two from the Marshall Islands had eaten only *Acropora hyacinthus*; 4 from the Hawaiian Islands contained mainly coral fragments (*Porites compressa*, *Pocillopora meandrina*, and *Montipora verilli*, 80–90% by volume), along with sponges, gastropods, zoanthids, and algae.

BLACKSPOTTED PUFFER
Arothron nigropunctatus (Bloch & Schneider, 1801)
Dorsal rays 9–12 (modally 10, rarely 9 or 12); anal rays 10–12 (usually 11, rarely 12); pectoral rays 16–20 (modally 18); pattern of spinules similar to that of *A. meleagris*; gill rakers 11–40; snout short, 2.0–2.5 in head, and about 7–8 in standard length; bony interorbital width 8.1–12.0 in standard length; caudal fin 3.0–4.0 in standard length; color variable, gray to dark brown dorsally, whitish to bright yellow ventrally, but always with scattered black spots of different size, usually none larger than pupil; a transverse pale band generally present across dorsal part of snout separating dark area around eye and one around mouth; anus black. Largest specimen, 29.5 cm. Oman and east coast of Africa to islands of Micronesia and Samoa Islands; Ryukyu Islands and Ogasawara Islands to Great Barrier Reef and New South Wales; type locality, Tranquebar, India; replaced in the Red Sea by *Arothron diadematus* (Rüppell). Harmelin-Vivien (1979) examined the gut contents of 4 specimens from Madagascar; they had eaten mainly coral with a substantial amount of sponge. Seven examined by the author from the Marshall Islands also fed mainly on coral (*Acropora* and *Montipora*) with small amounts of sponge, tunicate, zoanthid, and algae.

Bali, with *Labroides bicolor*

STELLATE PUFFER

Arothron stellatus (Bloch & Schneider, 1801)

Dorsal rays 11–12; anal rays 11; pectoral rays 17–20; small spinules on head and body except top of snout, base of fins, and side of caudal peduncle, most evident ventrally; snout short, 1.7–2.7 in head length; bony interorbital width 2.2–2.4 in head length; caudal fin 4.0–5.0 in standard length; adults white with small black spots on head, body, and fins, those on pectoral-fin base and around gill opening largest (spots more numerous and relatively smaller with growth); juveniles often yellow to orange with small black spots and broad, irregular, oblique black bands on abdomen. Attains at least 90 cm. Red Sea, Oman, and east coast of Africa to Society Islands, Marquesas Islands, Tuamotu Archipelago, and islands of Micronesia; Japan and southern Korea to Great Barrier Reef, New South Wales, Lord Howe Island, and New Zealand; type locality, Mauritius. Gut contents

Papua New Guinea/juvenile

of 6 adults examined by the author: sea urchins (*Echinometra* and *Diadema*), sponges, coral, stinging coral (*Millepora*), starfish (*Linckia multifora*), crabs (including *Etisus splendidus*), hermit crabs, and algae (including *Halimeda*). *Arothron alboreticulatus* (Tanaka) is a probable synonym (Matsuura in Masuda et al., 1984).

ELONGATE PUFFER

Lagocephalus sceleratus (Gmelin, 1789)

Dorsal rays 11–13; anal rays 9–12; pectoral rays 16–18; 2 lateral lines, the lower in a ventrolateral ridge that extends from front of chin to lower base of caudal fin; small spinules dorsally on head and body nearly to caudal fin, and ventrally to anus; body very elongate, the depth 4.5–6.0 in standard length; front of head bluntly rounded; caudal peduncle long and tapering, broader than deep; dorsal and anal fins narrow-based, slightly falcate, and pointed; anal fin nearly directly below the dorsal; caudal fin deeply emarginate; greenish gray dorsally with small dark spots, silvery white ventrally, with a broad silver stripe on lower side. Reaches at least 85 cm; reported to over 100 cm. Red Sea and Persian Gulf to South Africa, east to New Caledonia, Fiji, and Samoa Islands (Wass, 1984, listed a specimen from 100 m); Sagami Bay to western and eastern coasts of Australia; type locality given as American and Pacific Ocean (the former in obvious error). Occurs over sand or mud bottoms, usually at greater than diving depths (night photo of subadult here taken in 18 m). Dangerously poisonous to eat.

Sulawesi/subadult (night)

Gulf of Aqaba, Red Sea

Hawaiian Islands

Tahiti

Sulawesi

AMBON TOBY

Canthigaster amboinensis (Bleeker, 1865)

Dorsal rays 11–12 (usually 12); anal rays 10–11 (usually 11); pectoral rays 16–17 (usually 17); a ridge of skin middorsally on body (characteristic of the genus); snout conical and attenuate (also generic); caudal fin slightly rounded (generic); brown dorsally on head and body, shading to whitish ventrally, with small, pale blue spots on body and basally on caudal fin; small brown spots on lower side mixed with the blue, and blue lines radiating from eye except ventrally; cheek with numerous close-set, pale blue spots or irregular lines. Attains 15 cm. East coast of Africa to the Hawaiian Islands, Marquesas Islands, Society Islands, and islands of Micronesia; Izu Islands, Japan, to Great Barrier Reef, and New South Wales; one specimen found in the Galápagos Islands; type locality, Ambon, Molucca Islands. Occurs in outer-reef areas just below the surge zone; fast swimming and difficult to approach; Allen & Randall (1977) reported the stomach and gut contents of 4 specimens as algae (43.6%), polychaetes (12.7%), echinoids (12%), ophiuroids (8.2%), tunicates, mostly didemnids (4.8%), gastropods (4.7%), coral (3.7%), bivalve mollusks (2.1%), and the rest amphipods, sponges, foraminifera, sipunculids, and unidentified animal material.

BENNETT'S TOBY

Canthigaster bennetti (Bleeker, 1854)

Dorsal rays 9–10; anal rays 8–10; pectoral rays 15–16 (usually 15); a broad, diffuse, dark gray to greenish brown stripe on upper side of body, the back pale yellowish to greenish gray with small pink spots anteriorly, oblique pink lines and small blue spots posteriorly, and a large, blue-edged black spot at base of dorsal fin; head with small pink spots and transverse pink and pale blue lines on chin; region around eye yellow to pink with blue lines extending anteriorly and posteriorly; fins translucent gray. Attains 10 cm. East coast of Africa to the Society Islands, Tuamotu Archipelago, and throughout Micronesia; southern Japan and Taiwan to Great Barrier Reef, New South Wales, and Lord Howe Island; type locality, Ambon, Molucca Islands; known in the eastern Pacific from a single specimen from the Galápagos Islands. Usually seen in shallow protected waters on sand-rubble bottoms or in seagrass or algal beds; 85% of the stomach contents of 3 from New Guinea consisted of algae, the rest various benthic invertebrates (Allen & Randall, 1977).

FINE-LINED TOBY

Canthigaster compressa (Procé, 1822)

Dorsal rays 8–10; anal rays 8–9 (usually 9); pectoral rays 15–18; brownish orange, the dorsal part of head and body with fine wavy blue lines, the rest of head and body densely covered with very small spots that are pale blue dorsally and white ventrally; base of dorsal fin and adjacent back with a black spot circled by a blue and black line; dorsal and anal fins transparent with dark-edged rays; caudal fin orange with very small blue spots forming vertical rows. Attains 11 cm. Indo-Malayan region (type locality, Manila Bay), north to Taiwan, Ogasawara Islands, and Ryukyu Islands, south to Vanuatu and New Caledonia, east to Palau and Guam. An inshore species of protected habitats, generally in silty dead-reef areas and harbors.

CROWN TOBY
Canthigaster coronata (Vaillant & Sauvage, 1875)

Dorsal rays 9–10 (usually 10); anal rays 9–10 (usually 9); pectoral rays 16–17 (usually 17); white with 4 short, broad, dark brown to black bars, the first across interorbital and enclosing rear part of eye, the second with its lower anterior corner at upper end of gill opening, the last 2 triangular and oblique; numerous small yellow spots usually present on head and body, many concentrated at edges of dark bars; short blue and yellow lines extending anteriorly and posteriorly from eye; upper and lower edges of caudal fin broadly bordered by dark brown, at least basally. Reaches 13.5 cm. Red Sea, Oman, and east coast of Africa to Hawaiian Islands (type locality), and islands of Micronesia; Sagami Bay, Japan, to Great Barrier Reef, New South Wales, New Caledonia, and Western Australia; usually found on sand or sand and rubble bottoms, often in the vicinity of reefs, generally at depths greater than 15 m, and reported to 120 m (Chave & Mundy, 1994). Allen & Randall (1977) analyzed the stomach and gut contents of 12 specimens: algae and detritus (13.3%), gastropods (11.9%), crabs (10.0%), bivalve mollusks (9.7%), polychaetes (8.9%), sponges (7.7%), sipunculids (7.0%),

Hawaiian Islands

echinoids (3.3%), foraminifera (2.4%), and the rest amphipods, shrimps, isopods, and unidentified. *Canthigaster cinctus* Jordan & Evermann is a synonym. Red Sea and Indian Ocean population with blue instead of yellow spots and shorter dark bars; further study may demonstrate that it is a distinct (and undescribed) species.

LANTERN TOBY
Canthigaster epilampra (Jenkins, 1903)

Dorsal rays 10; anal rays 9; pectoral rays 16–18 (usually 17); dorsal part of body to base of dorsal fin brown, soon shading ventrally and posteriorly to pale yellow, densely covered with small, dark-edged blue spots; abdomen and ventral part of head nearly white; region around eye brownish yellow with black-edged blue lines radiating from eye except ventrally where horizontal and curved; blue lines around mouth and on chin; a prominent yellow spot rimmed with blue above gill opening; a narrow blue band midventrally from chin to anus; caudal fin yellow with blue lines. Attains 11 cm. Christmas Island (Indian Ocean); western Pacific from Ryukyu Islands and Ogasawara Islands to Great Barrier Reef and New Caledonia; east to Hawaiian Islands (type locality, Maui) and Society Islands; occurs on coral reefs, often in or near caves in drop-offs, generally at depths greater than 25 m.

Ambon, Indonesia

GREENSPOTTED TOBY
Canthigaster janthinoptera (Bleeker, 1855)

Dorsal rays 9–10 (usually 9); anal rays 9–10 (usually 9); pectoral rays 16–18 (usually 17); dark orangish brown with numerous small, blue-green spots; a narrow orange area around eye crossed by dark-edged blue lines from eye; a few dark-edged blue lines sometimes present dorsally on caudal peduncle; dorsal and anal fins transparent with dark-edged rays; caudal fin uniform pale brownish gray. Reported to 9 cm. East coast of Africa to Line Islands, islands of French Polynesia except Rapa, and the Pitcairn Islands; Ryukyu Islands and Ogasawara Islands to Great Barrier Reef, New South Wales, Lord Howe Island, and New Caledonia; also to Western Australia; type locality, Ambon, Molucca Islands; one specimen reported from the Galápagos Islands (Robertson et al., 2004). A very cryptic coral-reef species; usually found in caves. From the color pattern, it seems related to the endemic Hawaiian *Canthigaster jactator* (Jenkins) and the eastern Pacific *C. punctatissimus* (Günther).

Tonga

MARQUESAN TOBY

Canthigaster marquesensis Allen & Randall, 1977

Dorsal rays 9–10 (usually 10); anal rays 9; pectoral rays 17–18 (rarely 18); dark brown dorsally, white on side and ventrally, with a slightly irregular midlateral stripe from behind pectoral fin nearly to caudal-fin base; stripe crossed posteriorly by oblique blue lines, these extending above and below stripe in some specimens; a dark brown spot at base of dorsal fin partly surrounded by a blue line; a yellow zone around eye with black-edged blue lines radiating from eye except ventrally; front of snout, chin, caudal fin, and adjacent caudal peduncle yellow with blue lines. Largest specimen, 11 cm. Known only from the Marquesas Islands (type locality, Nuku Hiva); collected from depths of 15–42 m. Closely related to *Canthigaster epilampra*, differing in color, slightly more slender body, and a longer caudal peduncle on the average.

SHY TOBY

Canthigaster ocellicincta Allen & Randall, 1977

Dorsal rays 9; anal rays 9; pectoral rays 16; brownish orange, shading to whitish on abdomen, with 2 broad, dark brown bars between eye and dorsal fin, the first bordered by white and enclosing gill opening and pectoral fin; bars crossed by faint blue lines; head anterior to dark bars with blue lines, those on snout vertical, those on cheek curving posteriorly; blue lines extending out from eye except ventrally where rimming eye; body posterior to bars with blue spots on side and blue lines dorsally and ventrally; a large, dark brown spot below dorsal fin, rimmed and crossed by blue lines; caudal fin brown with faint, longitudinal blue bands. Largest specimen, 6.5 cm. Known from Solomon Islands (type locality, Florida Island), Philippines, New Caledonia, Fiji, southern Great Barrier Reef, and recently discovered in Tahiti (Randall et al., 2002a); collected from depths of 20–53 m. Extremely secretive; generally seen at the back of caves.

RAPA TOBY

Canthigaster rapaensis Allen & Randall, 1977

Dorsal rays 10–11; anal rays 9–10 (usually 9); pectoral rays 16–18; gray-brown, shading to yellowish brown posteriorly, with numerous very small, dark-edged blue spots except dorsally between eye and dorsal fin; snout and chin with dark-edged blue lines; short, black-edged blue lines radiating from eye except ventrally; caudal fin bright yellow with broken, vertical, dark-edged blue lines. Largest specimen, 12.5 cm. Known only from the island of Rapa in French Polynesia; collections from depths of 12–31 m. Related to *Canthigaster epilampra*, differing in color pattern and a higher average dorsal-ray count.

SOLANDER'S TOBY

Canthigaster solandri (Richardson, 1845)

Dorsal rays 8–10; anal rays 8–10; pectoral rays 15–18 (usually 17); brown to brownish orange dorsally, shading to white or pale yellow ventrally, with numerous bright blue spots that are progressively smaller and more close-set ventrally; blue lines radiating from eye except ventrally, where horizontal; a large black spot, usually rimmed in bright blue, at base of dorsal fin; caudal fin brown with small blue spots basally, grading posteriorly to orange with vertical blue lines; a midventral blue band on body. Reaches 11.5 cm. Oman and east coast of Africa to Hawaiian

Marquesas Islands

Cebu, Philippines

Rapa

Tahiti

Islands (only 2 specimens known), Society Islands, Tuamotu Archipelago, Rapa, Samoa Islands, and throughout Micronesia; type locality given as Polynesia. Replaced by *Canthigaster papua* (Bleeker) in the Indo-Malayan region and eastern Australia, and by *C. margaritata* (Rüppell) in the Red Sea. A coral-reef species, more common in bays and lagoons than in exposed shores; reported to depths of 36 m, but usually in less than 15 m. The most common toby at many areas where it occurs; often seen in pairs. Allen & Randall (1977) reported the food of 8 specimens as algae and detritus (58.4%), tunicates (16.8%), coral (11.1%), foraminifera (3.6%), and the rest bryozoans, crabs, ophiuroids, gastropods, sponges, polychaetes, and unidentified. Harmelin-Vivien (1979) provided similar food-habit data for 75 specimens from Madagascar (as *C. margaritatus*). Also known as the Spotted Sharpnose Puffer.

Guam

Great Barrier Reef

MODEL TOBY

Canthigaster valentini (Bleeker, 1853)

Dorsal rays 9; anal rays 9; pectoral rays 16–17 (usually 16); white with small, brownish orange spots and 4 dark brown bars, the first from nape to posterior edge of eye (except next to eye where orange-yellow with blue lines extending posteriorly from eye), the second from middle of back, narrowing and curving around gill opening and pectoral-fin base to abdomen, the third from in front of dorsal fin, also narrowing onto abdomen, and the fourth short and triangular on caudal peduncle, extending dorsally onto caudal fin; top of snout with transverse rows of dusky yellow spots or lines; base of dorsal, anal, and pectoral fins orange; a midventral blue band on body; caudal fin yellow, often with orange spots at base, the lower edge with a blackish band on about proximal one-third of fin. Reaches 10 cm. East coast of Africa to the Society Islands, Tuamotu Archipelago, and all of Micronesia; southern Japan to Great Barrier Reef, New

South Wales, Lord Howe Island, and New Caledonia; type locality, Ambon, Indonesia. Its occurrence in the Galápagos Islands is curious because it remains unknown from Line Islands and the Phoenix Islands. A common coral-reef species from the shallows in protected areas to depths of at least 55 m. Feeds mainly on algae, foraminifera, and tunicates, to a lesser extent on gastropods, ophiuroids, bryozoans, echinoderms, polychaetes, and crustaceans (Harmelin-Vivien, 1979). Gladstone (1987a, 1987b) studied the reproduction in the Great Barrier Reef; males maintain a harem of up to 7 females; spawning occurs in mid-morning, the eggs laid on algae; hatching takes place around sunset 3–5 days later; duration of larval life 64–113 days. This toxic species serves as the model for the mimicking filefish *Paraluteres prionurus*. The demersal ova are not eaten by reef fishes, indicating the presence of a repelling substance (Gladstone, 1987c). *Tetrodon taeniatus* Peters from Mozambique is a synonym.

651

PORCUPINEFISHES AND BURRFISHES
(DIODONTIDAE)

Like the puffers, the diodontid fishes are able to inflate themselves by drawing water into the highly distensible ventral diverticulum of the stomach. They have the added protection of formidable sharp spines. These spines may be short with 3 or 4 roots, hence fixed, as found in the species of *Chilomycterus* and *Cyclichthys* (called burrfishes), or long and 2-rooted as in *Diodon*, hence angling outward when the fish is inflated. Also like the puffers, diodontids have the teeth fused to beak-like dental plates, a short vertical gill opening anterior to the pectoral-fin base, no spines in the fins, a single dorsal fin posterior in position, and no pelvic fins. In addition to the prominent spines, diodontid fishes differ from puffers by lacking a median suture to the dental plate, having larger eyes, and broader pectoral fins (often with the posterior margin emarginate). Most species are nocturnal, tending to hide in caves or beneath ledges during the day. Their power-ful jaws and strong dental plates enable them to crush the shells of mollusks and hermit crabs, tests of sea urchins, and exoskeletons of crabs and other crustaceans, their principal nocturnal prey. Care should be taken when handling these fishes, not only because of their sharp spines, but also because they are capable of inflicting a severe bite. There are reports of persons poisoned from eating diodontid fishes (Halstead, 1967), presumably from tetrodotoxin, but they also can cause ciguatera. Diodontids occur in all tropical to warm temperate seas; most species are found on coral reefs or rocky substrata, but a few range over sedimentary bottoms, and *Diodon eydouxii* Brisout de Barneville is pelagic. The larval stage of species of *Diodon* is very large, which partially explains their broad distributions. The family consists of 6 genera and 19 species. The genus *Diodon* was revised by Leis (1978).

Hawaiian Islands

SPOTTED BURRFISH
Chilomycterus reticulatus (Linnaeus, 1758)
Dorsal rays 12–14; anal rays 11–14; pectoral rays 19–22; scattered, short immobile spines on head and body; light gray to light brown dorsally, shading to white ventrally, with widely distributed small black spots on body, 2 indistinct dark bars on head, the first below eye, and 2 on body; fins with numerous small black spots. Largest specimen collected by the author, 69.7 cm, from Tonga. Young pelagic to about 20 cm. Circumglobal, mainly in subtropical to warm temperate seas; type locality, India. *Chilomycterus affinis* Günther, described from a 15-inch stuffed specimen of unknown locality, is a synonym.

LONGSPINED PORCUPINEFISH

Diodon holocanthus Linnaeus, 1758

Dorsal rays 13–15; anal rays 13–14; pectoral rays 21–25; spines 2-rooted and erectile (characteristic of the genus); 12–16 spines in an approximate row from front of snout to dorsal fin; spines very long, those medially on forehead usually longer than longest spines posterior to pectoral fins; no spines on caudal peduncle; a pair of short tentacles on chin, and a few elsewhere on head and body; head broad, the width 2.6–4.6 in standard length; posterior rays of anal fin nearly reaching base of caudal fin; light brown to olivaceous dorsally with a few to numerous small black spots, white ventrally; a dark brown bar from above to below eye; a broad, transverse, dark brown band on occipital region of head, and another on back before dorsal fin; a large, oval dark spot above pectoral fin, and one at base of dorsal fin; fins without dark spots or with only a few basally on caudal fin. Attains 38 cm. Circumglobal, but mainly in subtropical or warm temperate seas; appears to be antitropical in Oceania; type locality, India. Known from a few to at least 100 m; more inclined

Okinawa

than *Diodon hystrix* to venture away from the shelter of coral reefs. Stomach and gut contents of 3 adults consisted of gastropods, echinoids (including *Eucidaris* and *Echinometra*), crabs, and hermit crabs.

Marshall Islands

PORCUPINEFISH

Diodon hystrix Linnaeus, 1758

Dorsal rays 14–17; anal rays 14–16; pectoral rays 21–25; 16–20 spines in an approximate row from front of snout to dorsal fin; spines on forehead shorter than longest spines posterior to pectoral fins; 1 or more small spines dorsally on caudal peduncle; no small spine pointing downward below eye; no small tentacles on chin; head very broad, the width 2.4–3.3 in standard length; posterior rays of anal fin reaching to about midlength of caudal peduncle; light brown to olivaceous dorsally, with many small black spots, white ventrally; fins yellowish gray with small black spots. Largest specimen collected, 71 cm. Circumglobal in tropical to warm temperate seas; type locality, India. Nocturnal; alimentary tracts of 12 adults examined for food-habit study by Randall (1985b): 3 were empty, the others contained gastropods (42.3%), crabs (27.3%), hermit crabs (14.9%), sea urchins and sand dollars (13.7%), bivalve mollusks (1.7%), and a few foraminifera.

Lombok, Indonesia

Gulf of Aden

Ogasawara Islands

BLACKBLOTCHED PORCUPINEFISH
Diodon liturosus Shaw, 1804

Dorsal rays 14–16; anal rays 14–16; pectoral rays 21–25; 16–21 spines in an approximate row from front of snout to dorsal fin; spines on forehead much shorter than those behind pectoral fins; a short, downward-pointing spine below front of eye; no spines on caudal peduncle; a pair of short tentacles usually present on chin; a short tentacle may be present above eye; head broad, its width 3.3–4.2 in standard length; posterior rays of anal fin nearly reaching base of caudal fin; light yellowish brown dorsally, shading to white ventrally; small black spots associated with spines on side of body; a broad, dark brown bar, sometimes white-edged, extending ventrally from eye and a short distance above; a broad, transverse, white-edged, dark brown bar across occipital part of head, and one in line with it across operculum; a large, irregular, white-edged, oval, dark brown spot above pectoral fin, 1 on back before dorsal fin, and 1 at base of dorsal fin; a dark brown transverse band at front of chin. Attains 50 cm. Occurs from the Red Sea (Randall, 1994), Oman, and east coast of Africa to the Society Islands and islands of Micronesia; Wakayama Prefecture, Japan, to Great Barrier Reef, New South Wales, and New Caledonia; type locality, "Indian seas." *Diodon maculatus* Duméril and *D. bleekeri* Günther are synonyms.

GLOSSARY

Acronurus: the late postlarval stage of surgeonfishes of the genera *Acanthurus*, *Ctenochaetus*, and *Zebrasoma*. This is the form that comes inshore from the open ocean to transform to the juvenile stage. It was first proposed as a genus before its larval nature was realized.

Adipose: fatty; in fishes in reference to a small fin without rays dorsally on the body posterior to the dorsal fin (found in a few groups such as catfishes and lizardfishes); also used to describe the thick transparent tissue covering or partially covering the eye in some families such as the tunas and mackerels and the threadfins.

Allopatric: in reference to a species with different geographical distribution; the opposite of sympatric.

Anal fin: the fin along the ventral part of the body supported by rays in bony fishes; usually commences just behind the anus (vent).

Annelid: referring to an animal of the phylum Annelida, the segmented worms; includes the marine bristle worms known as polychaetes.

Antitropical: referring to the distribution of an organism north and south of, but not within, the tropical zone.

Antrorse: directed forward, as in reference to the direction of a spine; the opposite of retrorse.

Auxiliary scales: small scales found on other scales; more often seen on the head and nape than on the body of those fishes that have them.

Axil: the acute angular space between a fin and the body; usually used in reference to the underside of the base of the pectoral fin (equivalent to the armpit of humans).

Band: a linear marking, broader than a line, generally used in reference to an oblique or curved marking that is neither vertical (a bar) or horizontal (a stripe).

Bar: an elongate, vertical, straight-sided color marking.

Barbel: a slender fleshy process usually found anteriorly on the head of fishes, especially the chin.

Benthic: referring to the benthos, the fauna and flora of the sea bottom.

Biserial: in two rows; often used to describe teeth in jaws.

Branchial: referring to the gills.

Branchiostegal rays: the slender rib-like bones that support the gill membranes; they in turn are supported by bones of the hyoid complex.

Buccal: referring to the mouth.

Carnivore: a flesh-eating animal.

Cartilage: a translucent, somewhat flexible, structural tissue of embryos of all vertebrates; retained as the skeletal tissue of adult sharks and rays, but largely replaced by bone in higher vertebrates.

Caudal fin: tail fin; the term tail alone properly refers to that part of a fish posterior to the anus.

Caudal peduncle: the part of the body of a fish between the posterior base of the anal fin and the base of the caudal fin.

Cephalic: referring to the head.

Character: a characteristic; a distinguishing feature.

Chordate: an animal of the phylum Chordata, which possess a notochord; includes tunicates, cephalochordates (such as amphioxus), and vertebrates.

Ciguatera: an illness from eating a fresh fish (even when fully cooked) that has ciguatoxin in its tissues. The toxin is produced by a benthic dinoflagellate that is eaten incidentally by algal-feeding fishes and invertebrates and passed on to carnivorous fishes that accumulate the toxin to dangerous levels.

Ciliates: one-celled animals of the phylum Protozoa, class Ciliata, that are propelled with numerous hair-like structures termed cilia.

Circumtropical: in reference to the distribution of an organism that is found worldwide in the tropics.

Cirri: the plural of cirrus, a tendril or very short filament.

Clasper: the paired intromittent organ of elasmobranch fishes; develops in males along the medial edge of the pelvic fins.

Cleithrum: the largest and most anterior bone of the pectoral girdle.

Commensal: an organism that lives on or within another that is not harmful to its host organism, but the host derives no benefit.

Community: an assemblage of animals and plants living together in one habitat.

Compressed: laterally flattened; often used in reference to the shape of the body of a fish—in this case clearly narrower than deep; the opposite of depressed.

Copepod: a small to microscopic aquatic animal of the subclass Copepoda, class Crustacea; may be free-living (benthic or pelagic), commensal, or parasitic. A major component of the zooplankton.

Coronet: a prominent protuberance or group of spines on the top of the head of seahorses.

Cranial: in reference to the brain or skull.

Crenate: referring to a margin that is serially notched or scalloped.

Crustacean: an animal of the class Crustacea, phylum Arthropoda; includes crabs, lobsters, shrimps, and copepods.

Cryptic: in reference to an animal that tends to remain hidden.

Ctenoid scales: scales of bony fishes with tiny tooth-like projections along the posterior margin and exposed part of the scales. Collectively these little teeth (called cteni) impart a rough texture to the surface of the scales.

Cusp: a protuberance on the biting surface of a tooth; for a molar it would be a blunt projection, but in a shark it could be the large, pointed, main part of the tooth; a small secondary projection may be called a cusplet.

Cycloid scales: scales of bony fishes, the edges and exposed part of which are smooth.

Demersal: living on the sea bottom.

Dentary: a large paired bone forming the front of the lower jaw.

Depressed: dorsoventrally flattened; the opposite in body shape to compressed.

Depth: when used in reference to the structure of a fish, it means the maximum height of the body excluding the fins.

Dermal: pertaining to the skin, specifically to the connective tissue layer below the epidermis.

Detritus: in a geological sense, small particles of inorganic sediment, but in the biological connotation, mainly fine organic material, which may include living matter such as diatoms and bacteria.

Distal: outward from the point of attachment; the opposite of proximal.

Dorsal: toward the back or upper part of the body; the opposite of ventral.

Dorsal fin: the median fin along the back that is supported by rays.

Echinoderm: an aquatic marine animal of the phylum Echinodermata, radially symmetrical with a skeleton composed of calcareous places (may be reduced to spicules); many move with numerous tube feet; includes starfishes (seastars), brittlestars, sea urchins, and sea cucumbers.

Ectoparasite: a parasite living on the external part of an animal or within the gill chamber.

Elasmobranch: in reference to the subclass Elasmobranchii of the class Chondrichthyes; includes all true sharks, skates, and rays.

Emarginate: concave; used to describe the shape of the posterior border of a caudal fin that is inwardly curved.

Endemic: in reference to an animal or plant restricted to an area such as an island or group of islands.

Epidermis: the outer layer of the skin.

Euryhaline: showing a broad tolerance to a wide range of salinity; the opposite of stenohaline.

Eurythermal: showing a broad tolerance to a wide range of temperature; the opposite of stenothermal.

Exserted: projecting beyond the adjacent parts. In the case of fin rays, refers to those that project free of membrane beyond the others.

Falcate: curved like a sickle or scythe.

Family: a major entity in the classification of animals and plants consisting of a group of related genera. Family names end in "idae." If used as an adjective, the "ae" is dropped, thus Acanthuridae as an adjective becomes acanthurid. Related families group to form orders.

Fimbriate: fringed, as along a margin or around an orifice.

Finlet: a small fin made up of a single, much-branched soft ray that follows

the dorsal fin of scombroid fishes such as tunas and mackerels (Scombridae) and certain jacks (Carangidae), often in a series.

Foraminifera: an order of single-cell animals of the phylum Protozoa, mostly tiny, which are covered by a shell; they may be benthic, pelagic, or commensal.

Forked: inwardly angular, used in describing the shape of a caudal fin that is divided into two equal lobes, the posterior margin of which is relatively straight.

Fork length: the straight-line measurement of a fish with a forked caudal fin from the front of the snout to the end of the middle caudal-fin rays; used especially for fishes such as tunas and many jacks for which the measurement of the standard length is difficult because of the presence of keels or scutes to strengthen a narrow caudal peduncle.

Fossa: a pit or depression.

Fossorial: refers in fishes, such as spaghetti eels and many snake eels, to those living beneath the surface of sedimentary bottom.

Frenum: a fold of membrane that restrains motion; in many gobioid fishes a transverse membrane linking the pelvic spines, which may serve as the anterior part of a pelvic sucking disc.

Fusiform: spindle-shaped; used in reference to the body shape of a fish that is elongate and cylindrical or nearly so, tapering at both ends.

Gape: in fishes, the length of the mouth.

Genus: a group of related species. The first word of a scientific name (always capitalized).

Gill arch: the bony and cartilaginous support for the gill filaments (where the gaseous exchange of respiration takes place). Usually there are four pairs of gill arches in bony fishes.

Gill opening: the opening posteriorly (and often ventrally as well) on the head where the water of respiration is expelled. Bony fishes have a single gill opening whereas cartilaginous fishes (sharks and rays) have five to seven; the gill openings of sharks and rays are usually called gill slits.

Gill rakers: stout protuberances of the gill arch on the opposite side from the red gill filaments; they function in retaining food organisms; fishes feeding on very small animals tend to have numerous and long gill rakers.

Gonad: a reproductive organ (ovary of females, testes in males).

Gonochoristic: in reference to animals that maintain separate sexes throughout life.

Gular plate: a ventral bony plate that lies between the right and left bones of the lower jaw; found only in primitive teleost fishes such as those of the genera *Megalops* (tarpons) and *Elops* (ladyfishes).

Haemal: referring to blood.

Haremic: referring to male that maintains a harem; a mode of reproduction often found in fishes.

Head length: the straight-line measurement from the front of the upper lip to the membranous posterior end of the operculum.

Herbivore: a plant-feeding animal.

Hermaphrodite: an organism with reproductive organs of both sexes, or one that changes from one sex to another.

Holotype: the primary museum specimen on which the description of a new species is based.

Humeral: referring to the shoulder region (i.e., the region just above and immediately behind the upper end of the gill opening).

Hyoid complex: a series of bones that form the paired gill arches that support the gill filaments and gill rakers; they lead medially and anteriorly to the tongue.

Ichthyocide: a substance that is lethal to fishes; the most commonly used is rotenone.

Ichthyology: the study of fishes.

Illicium: the modified first dorsal spine of frogfishes, anglerfishes, and related families that is used as a lure to attract prey to the vicinity of the mouth; the fleshy tip of the lure is termed the esca.

Imbricate: overlapping; typical arrangement of most fish scales.

Incisiform: chisel-like; used to describe teeth that are flattened with sharp edges like the front teeth of some mammals, including humans.

Intermaxilla: the anterior upper-jaw bone of eels; a shorter name for the premaxilloethmovomer bone; bears the longest teeth in morays.

Interorbital space: the region on the top of the head between the eyes; the usual measurement taken of this space is the least width.

Invertebrate: an animal lacking a vertebral column; includes the vast majority of animals on earth such as corals, worms, starfishes, and insects.

Isthmus: the narrow anterior throat region of a fish.

Keel: a lateral strengthening ridge posteriorly on the caudal peduncle or base of the caudal fin; typically found on swift-swimming fishes with a narrow caudal peduncle.

Keris: the late postlarval stage of unicornfishes (genus *Naso*). This is the form that comes inshore from the open ocean to transform to the juvenile stage. It was first proposed as a genus before its larval nature was realized.

Labial: referring to the lips.

Lamina: a thin plate or layer; the plural is laminae.

Lateral: referring to the side or directed toward the side; the opposite of medial.

Lateral line: a sensory organ of fishes that consists of a canal along the side of the body communicating via pores through scales (when present) to the exterior; functions in perceiving vibrations from a distance.

Lateral-line scales: the pore-bearing scales of the lateral line. The count of these scales (generally from the upper end of the gill opening to the base of the caudal fin) is an important character in the identification of fishes.

Lectotype: a museum specimen from the original type series of a new species designated by a later author as the equivalent to the holotype. This is needed when the original author failed to indicate which of his specimens was the holotype.

Leptocephalus: the transparent, ribbon-like, late larval stage of eels and a few other families of primitive teleost fishes. The juvenile stage following transformation is shorter than the leptocephalus.

Lumen: the central cavity of a duct or organ.

Lunate: sickle-shaped; used to describe the shape of a caudal fin that is deeply emarginate with narrow lobes.

Mandible: the lower jaw of vertebrates.

Maxilla: a bone of the upper jaw that lies posterior to the premaxilla; in the higher fishes, the maxilla is excluded from the cleft of the mouth, and only the premaxilla bears the teeth.

Medial: toward the middle or median plane of the body; the opposite of lateral.

Median fins: those fins lying in the median (middle) plane of a fish, hence the dorsal, anal, and caudal fins.

Meristic: pertaining to animal parts that occur in a series, hence are countable, such as the fin rays or scales of fishes.

Molariform: in reference to teeth that are like the molars of mammals, hence very blunt without sharp cusps; these are teeth used for crushing.

Mollusk: an animal of the phylum Mollusca; unsegmented with a muscular "foot" and visceral mass; often protected with one or two shells; includes gastropods (snails and nudibranchs), pelecypods (bivalves such as clams and oysters), cephalopods (squids and octopuses), and amphineurans (chitons).

Monotypic: having a single type or representative, such as a genus with one species or a family with one genus.

Morphology: the branch of biology dealing with the form and structure of animals and plants. In reference to an organism it means the features that collectively comprise its structure.

Muciferous: referring to a tissue or organ that secretes mucus.

Nape: the dorsal region of the head posterior to the occiput.

Neotype: a specimen selected to replace a lost holotype, preferably from or near the type locality.

Neritic: refers to that part of the ocean over the continental (or insular) shelf (generally taken from the low-tide mark to a depth of 200 m).

Occiput: the dorsoposterior part of the cranium.

Ocellated: having ocelli.

Ocellus: an eye-like spot; in fishes generally a black spot rimmed in white or blue. The plural is ocelli.

Olfactory: pertaining to the sense of smell.

Omnivore: an animal that feeds on both plant and animal material.

Opercle: the most posterior and generally the largest of the external bones comprising the operculum (gill cover).

Operculum: gill cover; comprised of four external bones, the opercle, preopercle, subopercle, and interopercle.

Orbit: the external opening of the eye. The diameter is measured instead of the eyeball itself for an expression of eye size. The diameter measurement should be qualified as bony or fleshy, the latter being the larger.

Orbital: referring to the orbit or eye.

Order: a major unit in the classification of organisms; an assemblage of related families. The ordinal word ending in the Animal Kingdom is "iformes."

Organ: a combination of tissues performing a major function or functions.

Organism: a living entity, whether unicellular or multicellular, plant or animal.

Origin: the beginning; often used for the anterior end of the dorsal or anal fin at the base; also used in zoology to denote the more fixed attachment of a muscle (the other end being the insertion).

Osteological: in reference to a study of the bony skeletal parts of an animal.

Oviparous: producing eggs that hatch after leaving the body of the mother; this is the mode of reproduction in the great majority of bony fishes.

Ovoviparous: producing eggs that hatch within the body of the female; the mode of reproduction of most sharks and rays.

Ovum: an egg; the plural is ova.

Paired fins: a collective term for the pectoral and pelvic fins.

Palatine: one of a pair of bones forming part of the roof of the mouth, each behind and lateral to the vomer and often bearing teeth.

Papilla: a small fleshy protuberance.

Paratype: a specimen of a new species regarded by the author as the same as the holotype, the primary specimen on which the description is based.

Pectoral fin: the fin usually found on each side of the body just behind the gill opening; in primitive fishes, such as the tenpounders and sardines, the fin is low on the body.

Pelagic: pertaining to the open sea; oceanic (hence not living inshore or on the bottom).

Pelvic fin: one of a pair of juxtaposed fins ventrally on the body; varies in position from abdominal (not far from the anus) in more primitive fishes to thoracic or jugular in more advanced fishes. Sometimes called ventral fin.

Peritoneum: the membranous lining of the body cavity of an animal; its color in fishes may be of diagnostic importance.

Pharyngeal: in reference to the pharynx or throat region.

Phylogeny: the evolutionary history of an organism or a group of organisms; an extended family tree.

Phytoplankton: the plants of the plankton.

Plankton: collective term for the pelagic animals and plants that live above the bottom and drift passively with currents.

Postlarva: the late pelagic stage in the larval development of a fish.

Premaxilla: the more anterior bone forming the upper jaw; in the higher fishes it extends backward and bears all of the teeth of the jaw. It is this part of the upper jaw that can be protruded in many fishes.

Preopercle: a boomerang-shaped external bone of the head that forms the posterior and lower part of the cheek region; the most anterior bone of the opercular series comprising the gill cover.

Preoral: the distance from the front of the mouth to the tip of the snout (used for fishes like sharks with an overhanging snout).

Procurrent caudal rays: the small upper and lower caudal-fin rays that precede the principal caudal-fin rays (that extend to the rear margin of the fin). Often it is necessary to dissect or take an X-ray of the fin to determine the correct number of procurrent rays.

Produced: drawn out to a point; lengthened.

Protandrous: referring to an organism that commences maturity as a male and changes later to a female.

Protogynous: referring to an organism that begins mature life as a female and changes later to a male.

Protrusible: protractile; capable of being projected, as in the upper jaw of many fishes.

Proximal: toward the center of the body; opposite of distal.

Pterygion: a Greek word meaning wing or fin; often used in combined form with another word to describe a fin condition in fishes.

Pterygoids: a series of three bones that form part of the inner side and roof of the mouth of fishes.

Ray: the supporting element of the fins; includes spines and soft rays. Also an animal of a major group of cartilaginous fishes.

Recurve: to curve backward; often used in reference to the shape of a tooth.

Retrorse: curving backward; often used in reference to a spine; the opposite of antrorse.

Rhomboid: wedge-shaped; often used in reference to the shape of a caudal fin of which the middle rays are longest and the sides of the fin are more or less straight.

Rounded: refers to a caudal fin of which the terminal border is smoothly convex.

Scute: a modified scale that is thicker, usually enlarged, and often bears a sharp spine.

Segmented rays: the soft rays of the fins that bear cross striations, at least distally.

Serrate: notched along a free margin like the edge of a saw.

Sessile: permanently attached.

Seta: a bristle or bristle-like structure; the plural is setae.

Simple: not branched (in reference to soft rays of fins).

Siphonophore: a "jellyfish" of the order Siphonophora of the class Hydrozoa; the Portuguese man-of-war (*Physalia physalis*) is the best-known species.

Snout: the region of the head in front of the eye; the snout length is measured from the front of the upper lip to the front edge of the eye.

Soft ray: a segmented fin ray composed of two closely joined lateral parts; nearly always flexible and often branched.

Somatic: referring to the body.

Species: the fundamental unit in the classification of animals and plants consisting of a population of individuals that freely interbreed. The word species is both singular and plural.

Spine: unsegmented bony process consisting of a single element that is usually rigid and sharp-pointed; those spines that support fins are not branched.

Spiracle: a small opening between the eye and the first gill slit of a shark or ray that leads to the pharyngeal cavity; a vestige of an embryonic gill slit; absent in many sharks but functional as an intake of respiratory water in rays.

Standard length: the straight-line length of a fish from the front of the upper lip to the base of the caudal fin (posterior end of the vertebral column). This is the length most often used in documenting measurements of various anatomical parts of a fish by ratios.

Stenohaline: referring to an organism that is unable to withstand much change in salinity; the opposite of euryhaline.

Stripe: an elongate, horizontal, straight-sided color marking.

Subopercle: an elongate external bone that is one of four comprising the operculum; lies below the opercle and forms the ventroposterior margin of the gill cover.

Suborbital: referring to the region below the eye.

Superior: referring to a part of the body being above another; the opposite of inferior.

Supraorbital: referring to the region above the eye.

Swimbladder: the hydrostatic organ of bony fishes; consists of a tough-walled sac just beneath the vertebral column; also known as the gasbladder.

Sympatric: in reference to species that live in the same geographical area.

Symphysis: the articulation of two bones in the median plane, often in reference to the anterior joint between the bones of the two sides of the jaws; symphyseal is the adjective.

Synonym: an invalid scientific name of an organism usually due to its being proposed at a later date than the accepted name.

Tail: that part of the body of a fish posterior to the anus; the fin at the end of the tail is the caudal fin (not the tail).

Tapetum lucidum: a shiny layer of tissue in the eye behind the retina containing reflective guanine crystals that increases visual acuity in low light conditions; found in most sharks and many nocturnal or deep-dwelling bony fishes.

Taxon: a unit in the classification of organisms; the plural is taxa.

Tholichthys: a late larval stage of chaetodontid and scatophagid fishes characterized by strong bony plates that cover the head.

Thoracic: refers to the thorax or chest region.

Total length: the maximum straight-line measurement of a fish.

Transverse scales: vertical series of scales at the greatest depth of the body (often counted obliquely).

Tribe: a taxonomic category between the subfamily and genus. When used in a scientific name, it is placed in parentheses.

Truncate: square-ended; often used to describe the shape of a caudal fin that has a vertically straight posterior margin.

Trunk: that part of the body of a fish between the head and the anus, hence the part that contains the viscera. The part beyond the anus is the tail (the fin at the end of the tail is the caudal fin).

Tubercle: a small, firm, knob-like protuberance.

Type locality: the locality where the holotype (the specimen on which a new species description is based) was collected.

Uniserial: occurring in a single row.

Urohyal: an elongate, flat, unpaired bone lying inside the lower jaw.

Vascular: pertaining to blood vessels.

Ventral: toward the lower part of the body; the opposite of dorsal.

Vertebra: one of the segmental units of the axial skeleton of a vertebrate animal.

Vestigial: rudimentary; a small structure that was once more fully developed.

Villiform: resembling villi, the tiny finger-like projections found on membranes such as those on the inner surface of the intestine; often used to describe a dense band of very small, close-set, conical teeth.

Viviparous: producing living young that develop from nourishment directly from the mother.

Vomer: a median bone, usually bearing teeth, forming the anterior part of the roof of the mouth.

Zooplankton: the animals of the plankton.

REFERENCES

Allen, G. R. 1975a. The biology and taxonomy of the cardinalfish, *Sphaeramia orbicularis* (Pisces; Apogonidae). *J. R. Soc. West. Aust.* 58 (3): 86–92.

———. 1975b. *Damselfishes of the South Seas.* T.F.H. Publications, Neptune City, NJ. 240 pp.

———. 1985a. *Fishes of Western Australia.* Pacific Marine Fishes, Book 9:2205–2534. T.F.H. Publications, Neptune City, NJ.

———. 1985b. Snappers of the world. *FAO Fish. Synop.,* no. 125, vol. 6: vi + 208 pp.

———. 1991. *Damselfishes of the World.* Mergus Publishers, Melle, Germany. 271 pp.

———. 1995. *Lutjanus rufolineatus,* a valid species of snapper (Pisces, Lutjanidae) with notes on a closely allied species, *Lutjanus boutton. Rev. Fr. Aquariol.* 22 (1/2): 11–13.

Allen, G. R., and S. Bailey. 2002. *Chrysiptera albata,* a new species of damselfish (Pomacentridae) from the Phoenix Islands, central Pacific Ocean. *Aqua* 6 (1): 39–43.

Allen, G. R., and W. E. Burgess. 1990. A review of the glassfishes (Chandidae) of Australia and New Guinea. *Rec. West. Aust. Mus. Suppl.* no. 34:139–205.

Allen, G. R., and A. R. Emery. 1985. A review of the pomacentrid fishes of the genus *Stegastes* from the Indo-Pacific, with descriptions of two new species. *Indo-Pac. Fishes,* no. 3:1–31.

Allen, G. R., and R. H. Kuiter. 1976. A review of the plesiopid fish genus *Assessor,* with descriptions of two new species. *Rec. West. Aust. Mus.* 4 (3): 201–215.

———. 1978. *Heniochus diphreutes* Jordan, a valid species of butterflyfish (Chaetodontidae) from the Indo-West Pacific. *J. R. Soc. West. Aust.* 62 (1): 11–18.

Allen, G. R., and J. E. Randall. 1977. Review of the sharpnose puffers (subfamily Canthigasterinae) of the Indo-Pacific. *Rec. Aust. Mus.* 30 (17): 475–517.

———. 2002. A review of the *leuocogaster* species complex of the Indo-Pacific pomacentrid genus *Amblyglyphidodon,* with descriptions of two new species. *Aqua* 5 (4): 139–152.

Allen, G. R., J. E. Randall, and B. A. Carlson. 2003. *Cirrhilabrus marjorie,* a new wrasse (Pisces: Labridae) from Fiji. Aqua 7 (3): 113-118.

Allen, G. R., and D. R. Robertson. 1994. *Fishes of the Tropical Eastern Pacific.* University of Hawai'i Press, Honolulu. xix + 332 pp.

———. 2002. *Halichoeres salmofasciatus,* a new species of wrasse (Labridae) from Isla del Coco, tropical eastern Pacific. *Aqua* 5 (2): 65–72.

Allen, G. R., B. C. Russell, B. A. Carlson, and W. A. Starck II. 1975. Mimicry in marine fishes. *Trop. Fish Hobbyist* 25 (1): 47–56.

Allen, G. R., and W. F. Smith-Vaniz. 1994. Fishes of the Cocos (Keeling) Islands. *Atoll Res. Bull.,* no. 412:1–21.

Allen, G. R., and R. C. Steene. 1979. The fishes of Christmas Island, Indian Ocean. Special Publication Australian National Parks and Wildlife Service, Canberra. 81 pp.

———. 1987. *Reef Fishes of the Indian Ocean.* T.F.H. Publications, Neptune City, NJ. 240 pp.

———. 1988. *Fishes of Christmas Island, Indian Ocean.* Christmas Island Natural History Association, Australia. 197 pp.

Allen, G. R., R. Steene, and M. Allen. 1998. *A Guide to Angelfishes & Butterflyfishes.* Odyssey Publishing, Perth. 250 pp.

Allen, G. R., and R. Swainston. 1988. *The Marine Fishes of North-Western Australia.* Western Australian Museum, Perth. vi + 201 pp.

Allen, G. R., and F. H. Talbot. 1985. Review of the snappers of the genus *Lutjanus* (Pisces: Lutjanidae) from the Indo-Pacific, with the description of a new species. *Indo-Pac. Fishes,* no. 11:1–87.

Amaoka, K., E. Mihara, and J. Rivaton. 1993. Pisces, Pleuronectiformes: Flatfishes from the waters around New Caledonia—a revision of the genus *Engyprosopon. Résultas Campagnes Musorstom* 11:377–426.

Amaoka, K., H. Senou, and A. Ono. 1994. Record of the bothid flounder *Asterorhombus fijiensis* from the western Pacific, with observations on the use of the first dorsal-fin ray as a lure. *Jpn. J. Ichthyol.* 41 (1): 23–28.

Anderson, R. C., J. E. Randall, and R. H. Kuiter. 1998. New records of fishes from the Maldive Islands, with notes on other species. *Ichthyol. Bull. J. L. B. Smith Inst. Ichthyol.,* no. 67, part 2:20–32.

Araga, C., H. Masuda, and T. Yoshino. 1988. New records of the labrid fish genus *Suezichthys* from Japan. *Publ. Seto Mar. Biol. Lab.* 33 (4/6): 173–178.

Arnold, D. C. 1956. A systematic revision of the fishes of the teleost family Carapidae (Percomorphi, Blennioidea), with descriptions of two new species. *Bull. Br. Mus. (Nat. Hist). Zool.* 4 (6): 245–307.

Baissac, J. de B. 1976. Poissons de mer des eaux de l'Ile Maurice. *Proc. R. Soc. Arts Sci. Mauritius* 3 (2): 191–226.

Baldwin, C. C., and D. G. Johnson. 1999. *Paxton concilians:* A new genus and species of pseudamine apogonid (Teleostei: Percoidei) from northwestern Australia: The sister group of the enigmatic *Gymnapogon. Copeia* 1999 (4): 1050–1071.

Baldwin, C. C., D. G. Johnson, and P. L. Colin. 1991. Larvae of *Diploprion bifasciatum, Belonoperca chabanaudi* and *Grammistes sexlineatus* (Serranidae: Epinephelinae) with a comparison of known larvae of other Epinephelinae. *Bull. Mar. Sci.* 48 (1): 67–93.

Baldwin, C. C., and W. L. Smith. 1998. *Belonoperca pylei,* a new species of seabass (Teleostei: Serranidae: Epinephelinae: Diploprionini) from the Cook Islands with comments on relationships among diploprionins. *Ichthyol. Res.* 45 (4): 325–339.

Barlow, G. W. 1987. Spawning, eggs and larvae of the longnose filefish *Oxymonacanthus longirostris,* a monogamous coralivore. *Environ. Biol. Fishes* 20 (3): 183–194.

Bath, H. 1992. Revision der Gattung *Praealticus* Schultz & Chapman 1960 (Pisces: Blenniidae). *Senckenb. Biol.* 72 (4/6): 237–316.

———. 2001. Osteology and morphology of fishes of the subfamily Salariinae and its junior synonym Parablenniinae (Pisces: Blenniidae). *Stuttg. Beitr. Naturkd. Ser. A (Biol.),* no. 628:1–42.

Bauchot, M. L. 1963. Catalogue critique des types de poissons du Muséum National d'Histoire Naturelle. *Publ. Mus. Natl. Hist. Nat.,* no. 20:1–195.

Bell, L. J., and P. L. Colin. 1985. Mass spawning of *Caesio teres* (Pisces: Caesionidae) at Enewetak Atoll, Marshall Islands. *Environ. Biol. Fishes* 15 (1): 69–74.

Bellwood, D. R. 1994. A phylogenetic study of the parrotfish family Scaridae (Pisces: Labroidei), with a revision of genera. *Rec. Aust. Mus. Suppl.* 20:1–86.

Bellwood, D. R., and J. H. Choat. 1989. A description of the juvenile colour patterns of 24 parrotfish species (family Scaridae) from the Great Barrier Reef. *Rec. Aust. Mus.* 41:1–41.

———. 1990. A functional analysis of grazing in parrotfishes (family Scaridae): The ecological implications. *Environ. Biol. Fishes* 28:189–214.

Bergman, L. M. 2004. The cephalic lateralis system of cardinalfishes (Perciformes: Apogonidae) and its application to the taxonomy and systematics of the family. Ph.D. diss., University of Hawai'i, Honolulu. 373 pp.

Bleeker, P. 1865. *Atlas Ichthyologique des Indes Orientalis Néêrlandiaises.* Vol. 5. Fréderic Muller, Amsterdam. 152 pp.

Bloch, M. E., and J. G. Schneider. 1801. *Systema Ichthyologiae.* Sauderiano Commissum, Berlin (reprinted by J. von Cramer, Lehre, 1967). lx + 584 pp.

Böhlke, E. B. 1982. Vertebral formulae for type specimens of eels (Pisces: Angulliformes). *Proc. Acad. Nat. Sci. Phila.* 134:31–49.

——————. 1995. Notes on the muraenid genera *Strophidon, Lycodontis, Siderea, Thyrsoidea,* and *Pseudechidna,* with a redescription of *Muraena thyrsoidea* Richardson, 1845. *Proc. Acad. Nat. Sci. Phila.* 146:459–466.

——————. 1997. Notes on the identity of elongate unpatterned Indo-Pacific morays, with description of a new species (Muraenidae, subfamily Muraeninae). *Proc. Acad. Nat. Sci. Phila.* 147:89–109.

Böhlke, E. B., and J. E. McCosker. 1997. Review of the moray eel genus *Scuticaria* and included species (Pisces: Anguilliformes: Muraenidae: Uropterygiinae). *Proc. Acad. Nat. Sci. Phila.* 148:171–176.

——————. 2001. The moray eels of Australia and New Zealand, with the description of two new species. *Rec. Aust. Mus.* 53:71–102.

Böhlke, E. B., and J. E. Randall. 1999. A review of the moray eels (Anguilliformes: Muraenidae) of the Hawaiian Islands, with descriptions of two new species. *Proc. Acad. Nat. Sci. Phila.* 150:203–278.

Bowen, B. W., A. L. Bass, L. A. Rocha, W. S. Grant, and D. R. Robertson. 2001. Phylogeography of the trumpetfishes *(Aulostomus):* Ring species complex on a global scale. *Evolution* 55 (5): 1029–1039.

Boylan, D. B., and P. J. Scheuer. 1967. Pahutoxin: A fish poison. *Science* (Washington, D.C.) 155:52–56.

Briggs, J. C. 1955. A monograph of the clingfishes. *Stanford Ichthyol. Bull.* 6: iv + 224 pp.

Brock, R. E. 1972. A contribution to the biology of *Gymnothorax javanicus* (Bleeker). M.S. thesis, University of Hawai'i, Honolulu. 121 pp.

Bruce, R. W., and J. E. Randall. 1985. Revision of the Indo-Pacific parrotfish genera *Calotomus* and *Leptoscarus.* *Indo-Pac. Fishes,* no. 5:1–32.

Burchmore, J. J., D. A. Pollard, M. J. Middleton, J. D. Bell, and B. C. Pease. 1988. Biology of four species of whiting (Pisces: Sillaginidae) in Botany Bay, New South Wales. *Aust. J. Mar. Freshwater Res.* 39:709–727.

Burgess, W. E. 1974. Evidence for the elevation to family status of the angelfishes (Pomacanthidae), previously considered to be a subfamily of the butterflyfish family Chaetodontidae. *Pac. Sci.* 28 (1): 57–71.

Burridge, C. P. 2004. *Cheilodactylus (Goniistius) francisi,* a new species of morwong (Perciformes: Cirrhitoidea) from the Southwest Pacific. *Rec. Aust. Mus.* 56:231–234.

Burridge, C. P., and A. J. Smolenski. 2004. Molecular phylogeny of the Cheilodactylidae and Latridae (Perciformes: Cirrhitoidea) with notes on taxonomy and biogeography. *Mol. Phylogenet. Evol.* 30:118–127.

Burridge, C. P., and R. W. G. White. 2000. Molecular phylogeny of the antitropical subgenus *Goniistius* (Perciformes: Cheilodactylidae: *Cheilodactylus*): Evidence for multiple transequatorial divergences and non-monophyly. *Biol. J. Linn. Soc.* 70 (3): 435–458.

Cabanban, A. S. 1984. Some aspects of the biology of *Pterocaesio pisang* (Bleeker, 1853) (Pisces: Caesionidae) in the central Visayas. M.S. thesis, College of Science, University of the Philippines. 69 pp.

Cantwell, G. E. 1964. A revision of the genus *Parapercis* family Mugiloididae. *Pac. Sci.* 18 (3): 239–280.

Carlson, B. A. 1992. The life history and reproductive success of the Coral Blenny, *Exallias brevis* (Kner, 1868). Ph.D. diss., University of Hawai'i, Honolulu. 337 pp.

Carpenter, K. E. 1987. Revision of the Indo-Pacific fish family Caesionidae (Lutjanoidea), with descriptions of five new species. *Indo-Pac. Fishes,* no. 15:1–56.

——————. 1988. Fusilier fishes of the world. *FAO Fish. Synop.,* no. 125, vol. 8: vi + 75 pp.

Carpenter, K. E., and G. R. Allen. 1989. Emperor fishes of the world. *FAO Fish. Synop.,* no. 125, vol. 9: v + 118 pp.

Carpenter, K. E., and V. H. Niem (eds.). 1999a. *The Living Marine Resources of the Western Central Pacific.* Vol. 3. *Batoid Fishes, Chimaeras and Bony Fishes Part 1 (Elopidae to Linophrynidae).* Food and Agriculture Organization of the United Nations, Rome. vi + 1398–2068 pp.

——————. 1999b. *The Living Marine Resources of the Western Central Pacific.* Vol. 4. *Bony Fishes Part 2 (Mugilidae to Carangidae).* Food and Agriculture Organization of the United Nations, Rome. v + 2069–2790 pp.

——————. 2001a. *The Living Marine Resources of the Western Central Pacific.* Vol. 5. *Bony Fishes Part 3 (Menidae to Pomacentridae).* Food and Agriculture Organization of the United Nations, Rome. iv + 2791–3379 pp.

——————. 2001b. *The Living Marine Resources of the Western Central Pacific.* Vol. 6. *Bony Fishes Part 4 (Labridae to Latimeriidae),* . . . Food and Agriculture Organization of the United Nations, Rome. v + 3381–4218 pp.

Carpenter, K. E., and J. E. Randall. 2003. *Lethrinus ravus,* a new species of lethrinid fish (Perciformes) from the western Pacific and eastern Indian Ocean. *Zootaxa* 240:1–8.

Castle, P. H. J., and J. E. Randall. 1999. Revision of Indo-Pacific garden eels (Congridae: Heterocongrinae), with descriptions of five new species. *Indo-Pac. Fishes,* no. 30:1–52.

Chapleau, F. 1993. Pleuronectiform relationships: A cladistic reassessment. *Bull. Mar. Sci.* 52 (1): 516–540.

Chapleau, F., and A. Keast. 1988. A phylogenetic reassessment of the monophyletic status of the family Soleidae, with comments on the suborder Soleoidei (Pisces: Pleuronectiformes). *Can. J. Zool.* 66:2797–2810.

Chave, E. H. 1979. General ecology of Hawaiian cardinalfishes. *Pac. Sci.* (1978) 32 (3): 245–270.

Chave, E. H., and B. C. Mundy. 1994. Deep-sea benthic fish of the Hawaiian Archipelago, Cross Seamount, and Johnston Atoll. *Pac. Sci.* 48 (4): 367–409.

Chave, E. H., and H. A. Randall. 1971. Feeding behavior of the moray eel *Gymnothorax pictus. Copeia* 1971 (3): 570–574.

Choat, J. H., and J. E. Randall. 1986. A review of the parrotfishes (family Scaridae) of the Great Barrier Reef of Australia with description of a new species. *Rec. Aust. Mus.* 38:175–228.

Choat, J. H., and D. R. Robertson. 1975. Protogynous hermaphroditism in fishes of the family Scaridae, pp. 263–283 in R. Reinboth, *Intersexuality in the Animal Kingdom.* Springer-Verlag, Berlin.

Clark, E. 1980. Distribution, mobility, and behavior of the Red Sea garden eel. *Natl. Geogr. Soc. Res. Rep.* 12:91–102.

Clark, E., and A. George. 1979. Toxic soles, *Pardachirus marmoratus* from the Red Sea and *P. pavoninus* from Japan, with notes on other species. *Environ. Biol. Fishes* 4 (2): 103–123.

Clark, E., and H. A. F. Gohar. 1953. The fishes of the Red Sea: Order Plectognathi. *Publ. Mar. Biol. Stn. Al Ghardaqa,* no. 8:1–80 (plus text in Arabic).

Clark, E., and R. Petzold. 1998. Spawning behavior of the collared knifefish, *Cymolutes torquatus* (Labridae) in Papua New Guinea. *Environ. Biol. Fishes* 53:459–464.

Clark, E., and J. F. Pohle. 1992. Monogamy in tilefish. *Natl. Geogr. Res. Explor.* 1992:276–294.

Clark, E., J. F. Pohle, and B. Halstead. 1998. Ecology and behavior of tilefishes, *Hoplolatilus starcki, H. fronticinctus* and related species (Malacanthidae): Non-mound and mound builders. *Environ. Biol. Fishes* 52:395–417.

Clark, E., J. F. Pohle, and D. C. Shen. 1990. Ecology and population dynamics of garden eels at Râs Mohammed, Red Sea. *Natl. Geogr. Res.* 6 (3): 306–318.

Clark, E., and M. Pohle. 1996. *Trichonotus halstead,* a new sand-diving fish from Papua New Guinea. *Environ. Biol. Fishes* 45:1–11.

Clark, E., M. Pohle, and J. Rabin. 1991. Spotted sandperch dynamics. *Natl. Geogr. Res. Explor.* 7 (2): 138–155.

Clarke, T. A., and L. A. Privitera. 1995. Reproductive biology of two Hawaiian pelagic carangid fishes, the bigeye scad, *Selar crumenophthalmus,* and the round scad, *Decapterus macarellus. Bull. Mar. Sci.* 56 (1): 33–47.

Colborn, J., R. E. Crabtree, J. B. Shaklee, E. Pfeiler, and B. W. Bowen. 2001. The evolutionary enigma of bonefishes (*Albula* spp.): Cryptic species and ancient separations in a globally distributed shorefish. *Evolution* 55 (4): 807–820.

Cole, K. S., and D. R. Robertson. 1988. Protogyny in the Caribbean reef goby *Coryphopterus personatus:* Gonad ontogeny and social influences on sex-change. *Bull. Mar. Sci.* 42 (2): 317–333.

Cole, K. S., and D. Y. Shapiro. 1990. Gonad structure and hermaphroditism in the gobiid genus *Coryphopterus* (Teleostei: Gobiidae). *Copeia* 1990 (4): 996–1003.

Colin, P. L. 1976. Filter feeding and predation on the eggs of *Thalassoma* sp. by the scombrid fish *Rastrelliger kanagurta. Copeia* 1976 (3): 596–597.

Collette, B. B. 1974. Geographic variation in the central Pacific halfbeak, *Hyporhamphus acutus* (Günther). *Pac. Sci.* 28 (2): 111–122.

Collette, B. B., and H. M. Banford. 2001. Status of the eastern Pacific agujon needlefish *Tylosurus pacificus* (Steindachner, 1876) (Beloniformes: Belonidae). *Rev. Biol. Trop.* 49 Suppl. 1:51–57.

Collette, B. B., and C. E. Nauen. 1983. Scombrids of the world. *FAO Fish. Synop.,* no. 125, vol. 2: vii + 137 pp.

Collette, B. B., and N. V. Parin. 1978. Five new species of halfbeaks (Hemiramphidae) from the Indo-West Pacific. *Proc. Biol. Soc. Wash.* 91 (3): 731-747.

Compagno, L. J. V. 1984. Sharks of the world. *FAO Fish. Synop.,* no. 125, vol. 4, part 1: viii + 655 pp.

———. 2001. Sharks of the world: An annotated and illustrated catalogue of shark species known to date. Vol. 1. Bullhead, mackerel and carpet sharks (Heterodontiformes, Lamniformes and Orectolobiformes). *FAO Species Catalogue for Fishery Purposes,* no. 12, vol. 2: viii + 269 pp.

Corsini, M., G. Kondilatos, and P. S. Economidis. 2002. Lessepsian migrant *Fistularia commersonii* from the Rhodes marine area. *J. Fish Biol.* 61:1061–1062.

Craig, P. C., J. H. Choat, L. M. Axe, and S. Saucerman. 1997. Population biology and harvest of the coral reef surgeonfish *Acanthurus lineatus* in American Samoa. *Fish. Bull.* 95:680–693.

Cressey, R. F. 1981. Revision of Indo-West Pacific lizardfishes of the genus *Synodus* (Pisces: Synodontidae). *Smithson. Contrib. Zool.,* no. 342: iii + 53 pp.

Cressey, R. F., and E. A. Lachner. 1970. The parasitic copepod diet and life history of diskfishes (Echeneidae). *Copeia* 1970 (2): 310–318.

Cuvier, G., A. G. Desmarest, J. Geoffroy Saint-Hilaire, et al. 1827. *Planches de Seba. Locuplentissimi rerum naturalium Thesauri Accurata Descriptio. Accompaignées d'un text explicatif mis au courant de la Science et rédigé par M. le Baron Cuvier et une réunion de savants.* Ouvrage publié par les soins de M. E. Guérin; 5ème livraison. F. G. Levrault, Paris. 8 pp.

Cuvier, G., and A. Valenciennes. 1828–1850. *Histoire Naturelle des Poissons.* Vols. 1–22. Paris (reprinted by A. Asher & Co., Amsterdam, 1969).

Dawson, C. E. 1981. Review of the Indo-Pacific pipefish genus *Doryrhamphus* Kaup (Pisces: Syngnathidae), with descriptions of a new species and a new subspecies. *Ichthyol. Bull. J. L. B. Smith Inst. Ichthyol.,* no. 44:1–27.

———. 1985. *Indo-Pacific Pipefishes (Red Sea to the Americas).* Gulf Coast Research Laboratory, Ocean Springs, MS. 230 pp.

De Beaufort, L. F. 1940. *The Fishes of the Indo-Australian Archipelago.* Vol. 8. E. J. Brill, Leiden. xv + 508 pp.

Debelius, H., and R. H. Kuiter. 2001. *Doktorfische und ihre Verwandte Acanthuroidei.* Verlag Eugen Ulmer, Stuttgart. 208 pp.

De Sylva, D. P. 1963. Systematics and life history of the great barracuda *Sphyraena barracuda* (Walbaum). *Stud. Trop. Oceanogr.* (Miami) 1: vii + 179 pp.

DiSalvo, L. H., J. E. Randall, and A. Cea. 1988. Ecological reconnaissance of the Easter Island sublittoral marine environment. *Natl. Geogr. Res.* 4 (4): 451–473.

Doi, M., M. H. M. Nawi, N. R. N. Lah, and Z. Talib. 1991. Artificial propagation of the grouper, *Epinephelus suillus* at the marine finfish hatchery in Tanjong Demong, Terengganui, Malaysia. *Publ. Dep. Fish., Minis. Agric.,* no 167: vii + 41 pp.

Donaldson, T. 1986. Courtship and spawning of the hawkfish *Cirrhitichthys falco* at Miyake-jima, Japan. *Jpn. J. Ichthyol.* 33 (3): 329–333.

———. 1989a. Pair spawning of *Cephalopholis boenack* (Serranidae). *Jpn. J. Ichthyol.* 35 (4): 497–500.

———. 1989b. Facultative monogamy in obligate coral-dwelling hawkfishes (Cirrhitidae). *Environ. Biol. Fishes* 26:295–302.

———. 1995. Courtship and spawning of nine species of wrasses (Labridae) from the western Pacific. *Jpn. J. Ichthyol.* 42 (3/4): 311–319.

Dooley, J. K. 1978. Systematics and biology of the tilefishes (Perciformes: Branchiostegidae and Malacanthidae), with descriptions of two new species. *NOAA Tech. Rep. NMFS Circ.* 411: v + 78 pp.

Dor, M. 1984. *Checklist of the Fishes of the Red Sea.* The Israel Academy of Sciences and Humanities, Jerusalem. xxi + 427 pp.

Dunlap, P. V., and M. J. McFall-Ngai. 1984. *Leiognathus elongatus* (Perciformes: Leiognathidae): Two distinct species based on morphological and light organ characters. *Copeia* 1984 (4): 884–892.

Eschmeyer, W. N. 1997. A new species of Dactylopteridae (Pisces) from the Philippines and Australia, with a brief synopsis of the family. *Bull. Mar. Sci.* 60 (3): 727–738.

———. 1998. *Catalog of Fishes.* 3 vols. California Academy of Sciences, San Francisco. 2905 pp.

Eschmeyer, W. N., and K. V. Rama Rao. 1973. Two new stonefishes (Pisces, Scorpaenidae) from the Indo-West Pacific, with a synopsis of the subfamily Synanciinae. *Proc. Calif. Acad. Sci.* 39 (18): 337–382.

Eschmeyer, W. N., K. V. Rama-Rao, and L. E. Hallacher. 1979. Fishes of the scorpion-fish subfamily Choridactylinae from the western Pacific and the Indian Ocean. *Proc. Calif. Acad. Sci.* 41 (21): 475–500.

Eschmeyer, W. N., and J. E. Randall. 1975. The scorpaenid fishes of the Hawaiian Islands, including new species and new records (Pisces: Scorpaenidae). *Proc. Calif. Acad. Sci.* 40 (11): 265–334.

Evermann, B. S., and A. Seale. 1907. Fishes of the Philippine Islands. *Bull. Bur. Fish.* (1906) 26:51–110 + i–vi.

Fautin, D. G., and G. R. Allen. 1992. *Field Guide to Anemonefishes and Their Host Anemones.* Western Australian Museum, Perth. viii + 157 pp.

Fishelson, L. 1990. *Rhinomuraena* spp. (Pisces: Muraenidae): The first vertebrate genus with post-anally situated urogenital organs. *Mar. Biol. (Berl.)* 105:253–257.

———. 1992. Comparative gonad morphology and sexuality of the Muraenidae (Pisces, Teleostei). *Copeia* 1992 (1): 197–209.

Fourmanoir, P. 1961. Requins de la cote ouest de Madagascar. *Mém. l'Inst. Rech. Sci. Madag. Sér. F* 4:1–81.

———. 1970–1971. Notes ichthyologiques (no. 4). *Cah. O.R.S.T.O.M. Sér. Océanogr.* 8 (2): 19–33.

Fourmanoir, P., and P. Laboute. 1976. *Poissons de Nouvelle Calédonie et des Nouvelles Hébrides.* Les Editiones du Pacifique, Papeete. 376 pp.

Fowler, H. W. 1927. Fishes of the tropical central Pacific. *Bernice P. Bishop Mus. Bull.* 38:1–32.

———. 1959. *Fishes of Fiji.* Government of Fiji, Suva. 670 pp.

Fowler, H. W., and S. C. Ball. 1924. Descriptions of fishes obtained by the *Tanager* Expedition of 1923 in the Pacific islands west of Hawaii. *Proc. Acad. Nat. Sci. Phila.* 76:269–274.

———. 1925. Fishes of Hawaii, Johnston Island, and Wake. *Bernice P. Bishop Mus. Bull.* 26:1–31.

Francis, M. P. 1993. Checklist of the coastal fishes of Lord Howe, Norfolk, and Kermadec Islands, Southwest Pacific Ocean. *Pac. Sci.* 47 (2): 136–170.

Francis, M. P., R. V. Grace, & C. D. Paulin. 1987. Coastal fishes of the Kermadec Islands. *N. Z. J. Mar. Freshwater Res.* 21:1–13.

Fraser, T. H. 1972. Comparative osteology of the shallow water cardinal fishes

[Perciformes: Apogonidae] with reference to the systematics and evolution of the family. *Ichthyol. Bull. J. L. B. Smith Inst. Ichthyol.,* no. 34:1–105.

Fraser, T. H., and G. R. Allen. 2001. A new species of cardinalfish in *Neamia* (Apogonidae, Perciformes) from Mauritius, Indian Ocean, with a review of *Neamia octospina. Rec. West. Aust. Mus.* 20:159–165.

Fraser, T. H., and E. A. Lachner. 1985. A revision of the cardinalfish subgenera *Pristiapogon* and *Zoramia* (genus *Apogon*) of the Indo-Pacific region (Teleostei: Apogonidae). *Smithson. Contrib. Zool.,* no. 412: iii + 46 pp.

Fraser, T. H., and J. E. Randall. 2003. Two new species of deeper-dwelling *Apogon* (Perciformes: Apogonidae) from Micronesia and South Pacific Ocean. *Zootaxa* 117:1–11.

Fraser-Brunner, A. 1933. A revision of the chaetodont fishes of the subfamily Pomacanthinae. *Proc. Zool. Soc. Lond.* 103:543–599.

Fricke, H. W. 1980. Mating systems, maternal and biparental care in triggerfish (Balistidae). *Z. Tierpsychol.* 53:105–122.

Fricke, R. 1983. *Indo-Pacific Callionymidae.* J. Cramer, Braunschweig, Germany. x + 774 pp.

———. 1994. *Tripterygiid Fishes of Australia, New Zealand and the Southwest Pacific Ocean (Teleostei).* Koeltz Scientific Books, Königstein, Germany. ix + 585 pp.

———. 1997. *Tripterygiid Fishes of the Western and Central Pacific (Teleostei).* Koeltz Scientific Books, Koenigstein, Germany. ix + 607 pp.

Fritzsche, R. A. 1976. A review of the cornetfishes, genus *Fistularia* (Fistulariidae), with a discussion of intrageneric relationships and zoogeography. *Bull. Mar. Sci.* 26 (2): 196–204.

———. 1981. A new species of pipefish (Pisces: Syngnathidae: *Micrognathus*) from Tahiti. *Proc. Biol. Soc. Wash.* 94 (3): 771–773.

Garman, S. 1913. The Plagiostomia (sharks, skates, and rays). *Mem. Mus. Comp. Zoöl.* 36: xiii + 515 pp.

Garrick, J. A. F. 1982. Sharks of the genus *Carcharhinus. NOAA Tech. Rep. NMFS Circ.* 445: vii + 194 pp.

Garrison, G. 2000. Peces de la Isla del Coco. Instituto Nacional de Biodiversidad, Costa Rica. 393 pp.

Gilbert, C. R. 1967. A revision of the hammerhead sharks (Family Sphyrnidae). *Proc. U.S. Natl. Mus.* 119:1–83.

Gill, A. C. 2004. Revision of the Indo-Pacific dottyback fish subfamily Pseudochrominae (Perciformes: Pseudochromidae). *Smithiana Monogr.* 1:1–213.

Gill, A. C. and A. J. Edwards. 2003. *Pseudoplesiops wassi,* a new species of dottyback fish (Teleostei: Pseudochromidae: Pseudoplesiopidae) from the West Pacific *Zootaxa* 291:1–7.

Gill, A. C., and R. Fricke. 2001. Revision of the western Indian Ocean fish subfamily Anisochrominae (Perciformes, Pseudochromidae). *Bull. Nat. Hist. Mus. Lond. Zool. Ser.* 67 (2): 191–207.

Gladstone, W. 1987a. Role of female territoriality in the social and mating systems of *Canthigaster valentini* (Pisces, Tetraodontidae): Evidence from field experiments. *Mar. Biol. (Berl.)* 96:185–191.

———. 1987b. The courtship and spawning behaviors of *Canthigaster valentini* (Tetraodontidae). *Eviron. Biol. Fishes* 20:225–261.

———. 1987c. The eggs and larvae of the sharpnose pufferfish *Canthigaster valentini* (Pisces, Tetraodontidae) are unpalatable to other reef fishes. *Copeia* 1987 (1): 227–230.

Godkin, C. M., and R. Winterbottom. 1985. Phylogeny of the family Congrogadidae (Pisces; Perciformes) and its placement as a subfamily of the Pseudochromidae. *Bull. Mar. Sci.* 36 (3): 633–671.

Goeden, G. B. 1978. A monograph of the coral trout *Plectropomus leopardus* (Lacépède). *Res. Bull. Queensl. Fish. Serv.* 1:1–42.

Gon, O. 1987. *Apogon sphenurus* Klunzinger, 1884, a senior synonym of *Neamia octospina* Smith et Radcliffe, 1912, with redescription of the species. *Jpn. J. Ichthyol.* 34 (1): 91–95.

———. 1993. Revision of the cardinalfish genus *Cheilodipterus* (Perciformes: Apogonidae), with desciption of five new species. *Indo-Pac. Fishes,* no. 22:1–59.

Gon, O., and J. E. Randall. 2003. Revision of the Indo-Pacific cardinalfish genus *Archamia* (Perciformes: Apogonidae), with description of a new species. *Indo-Pac. Fishes,* no. 35:1–46.

Goren, M., and I. Karplus. 1980. *Fowleria abocellata,* a new cardinal fish from the Gulf of Elat—Red Sea (Pisces, Apogonidae). *Zool. Meded. (Leiden)* 55 (20): 231–234.

———. 1983. Preliminary observations on the scorpion fish *Scorpaenodes guamensis* and its possible mimic the cardinal fish *Fowleria abocellata. Dev. Ecol. Environ. Qual.* 2:327–336.

Gorlick, D. L. 1980. Ingestion of host fish surface mucus by the Hawaiian cleaning wrasse, *Labroides phthirophagus,* and its effect on host species preference. *Copeia* 1980 (4): 863–868.

Gosline, W. A. 1955. The osteology and relationships of certain gobioid fishes, with particular reference to the genera *Kraemeria* and *Microdesmus. Pac. Sci.* 9 (2): 158–170.

Greenfield, D. W. 2001. Revision of the *Apogon erythrinus* complex (Teleostei: Apogonidae). *Copeia* 2001 (2): 459–472.

Greenfield, D. W., and K. Matsuura. 2002. *Scorpaenodes quadrispinosus:* A new Indo-Pacific scorpionfish (Teleostei: Scorpaenidae) *Copeia* 2002 (4): 973–978.

Grove, J. S., and R. J. Lavenberg. 1997. *The Fishes of the Galápagos Islands.* Stanford University Press, Stanford. ix + 863 pp.

Gundermann, N., D. M. Popper, and T. Lichatowich. 1983. Biology and life cycle of *Siganus vermiculatus* (Siganidae, Pisces). *Pac. Sci.* 37 (2): 165–180.

Halstead, B. W. 1967. *Poisonous and Venomous Marine Animals of the World.* Vol. 2. U.S. Government Printing Office, Washington, D.C. xxxi + 1070 pp.

———. 1970. *Poisonous and Venomous Marine Animals of the World.* Vol. 3. U.S. Government Printing Office, Washington, D.C. xxv + 1006 pp.

Haneda, Y., and F. H. Johnson. 1958. The luciferin-luciferase reaction of a fish, *Parapriacanthus beryciformis,* of newly discovered luminescence. *Proc. Natl. Acad. Sci.* 44 (2): 127–129.

———. 1962. The photogenic organ of *Parapriacanthus beryciformis* Franz and other fish with the indirect type of luminescent system. *J. Morphol.* 110:187–198.

Haneda, Y., and F. I. Tsuji. 1976. The luminescent system of pony-fishes. *J. Morphol.* 150 (2): 539–552.

Hansen, P. E. H. 1986. Revision of the tripterygiid fish genus *Helcogramma,* including descriptions of four new species. *Bull. Mar. Sci.* 38 (2): 313–354.

Hardy, G. H. 1983. A revision of the fishes of the family Pentacerotidae (Perciformes). *N. Z. J. Zool.* 10:177–220.

Harmelin-Vivien, M. L. 1979. *Ichtyofaune des Recifs Coralliens de Tulear (Madagascar): Ecologie et Relations Trophiques.* Thèse, Université d'Aix-Marseille II. 165 pp. + annex of 154 tables.

Harmelin-Vivien, M. L., and C. Bouchon. 1976. Feeding behavior of some carnivorous fishes (Serranidae and Scorpaenidae) from Tuléar (Madagascar). *Mar. Biol. (Berl.)* 37:329–340.

Harry, R. R. 1953. Ichthyological field data of Raroia Atoll, Tuamotu Archipelago. *Atoll Res. Bull.,* no. 18:1–190.

Hashimoto, Y., K. Shiomi, and K. Aida. 1974. Occurrence of a skin toxin in coral-gobies *Gobiodon* spp. *Toxicon* 12:523–528.

Helfrich, P., and P. M. Allen. 1975. Observations on the spawning of mullet, *Crenimugil crenilabis* (Forskål), at Enewetak, Marshall Islands. *Micronesica* 11 (2): 219–225.

Helfrich, P., T. Piyakarnchana, and P. S. Miles. 1968. Ciguatera fish poisoning I. The ecology of ciguateric reef fishes in the Line Islands. *Occas. Pap. Bernice Pauahi Bishop Mus.* 23 (14): 305–382.

Hensley, D. A., and J. E. Randall. 1990. A redescription of *Engyprosopon macrolepis* (Teleostei: Bothidae). *Copeia* 1990 (3): 674–680.

Hiatt, R. W. 1947. Food-chains and the food cycle in Hawaiian fish ponds.—Part I. The food and feeding habits of mullet

(*Mugil cephalus*), milkfish (*Chanos chanos*), and the ten-pounder (*Elops machuata*). *Trans. Am. Fish. Soc.* 74:250–261.

Hiatt, R. W., and D. W. Strasburg. 1960. Ecological relationships of the fish fauna on coral reefs of the Marshall Islands. *Ecol. Monogr.* 30:65–127.

Hioki, S., and K. Suzuki. 1995. Spawning behavior, eggs, larvae, and hermaphroditism of the angelfish, *Apolemichthys trimaculatus,* in captivity. *Bull. Inst. Oceanic Res. Dev., Tokai Univ.* 16:13–22 (in Japanese).

Hioki, S., Y. Tanaka, and K. Suzuki. 1995. Reproductive behavior, eggs, larvae, and sexuality of two angelfishes, *Genicanthus watanabei* and *G. bellus,* in an aquarium. *J. Fac. Mar. Sci. Technol. Tokai Univ.* 40:151–171 (in Japanese).

Hobson, E. S. 1974. Feeding relationships of teleostean fishes on coral reefs in Kona, Hawaii. *Fish. Bull.* 72 (4): 915–1031.

Hoese, D. F. 1975. A revision of the gobiid fish genus *Kelloggella. Rec. Aust. Mus.* 29 (17): 473–484.

Hoese, D. F., and H. K. Larson. 1994. Revision of the Indo-Pacific gobiid fish genus *Valenciennea,* with descriptions of seven new species. *Indo-Pac. Fishes,* no. 23:1–71.

Holleman, W. 1987. Description of a new genus and species of tripterygiid fish (Perciformes: Blennioidei) from the Indo-Pacific, and the reallocation of *Vauclusella acanthops* Whitley, 1965. *Cybium* 11 (2): 173–181.

———. 1991. A revision of the tripterygiid fish genus *Norfolkia* Fowler, 1953 (Perciformes: Blennioidei). *Ann. Cape Prov. Mus. Nat. Hist.* 18 (2): 227–243.

———. 1993. *Ucla xenogrammus,* a new genus and species of Indo-Pacific fishes (Perciformes: Tripterygiidae). *Spec. Publ. J. L. B. Smith Inst. Ichthyol.,* no. 55:1–9.

Homma, K., and H. Ishihara. 1994. Food habits of six species of rays occurring at Pohnpei (Ponape) Island (E. Caroline Islands), FSM. *Chondros* 5 (1): 4–8.

Homma, K., Y. Takeda, and H. Ishihara. 1991. Survey of rays in Pohnpei Island, Federated States of Micronesia. *Rep. Jpn. Soc. Elasmo-branch Stud.,* no. 28:1–7 (in Japanese).

Hori, K., N. Fusetani, K. Hashimoto, K. Aida, and J. E. Randall. 1979. Occurrence of a grammistin-like toxin in the clingfish *Diademichthys lineatus. Toxicon* 17:418–424.

Howland, H. C., J. M. Christopher, and J. E. McCosker. 1992. Detection of eyeshine by flashlight fishes of the family Anomalopidae. *Vision Res.* 32 (4): 765–769.

Hubbs, C. L. 1944. Species of the circumtropical fish genus *Brotula. Copeia* 1944 (3): 162–178.

Humphreys, R. L., Jr. 1980. Feeding habits of the kahala, *Seriola dumerili,* in the Hawaiian Archipelago. Proceedings of the Symposium on Status of Resources

Investigations in the Northwestern Hawaiian Islands. *Sea Grant Misc. Rep.* 80–4:223–240.

Hutchins, J. B. 1977. Descriptions of three new genera and eight new species of monacanthid fishes from Australia. *Rec. West. Aust. Mus.* 5 (1): 3–58.

———. 1986. Review of the monacanthid fish genus *Pervagor,* with descriptions of two new species. *Indo-Pac. Fishes,* no. 12:1–35.

———. 1997. Review of the monacanthid fish genus *Paramonacanthus,* with descriptions of three new species. *Rec. West. Aust. Mus. Suppl.* no. 54:1–57.

Hutchins, J. B., and J. E. Randall. 1982. *Cantherhines longicaudus,* a new filefish from Oceania, with a review of the species of the *C. fronticinctus* complex. *Pac. Sci.* 36 (2): 175–185.

Imamura, H. 1996. Phylogeny of the family Platycephalidae and related taxa (Pisces: Scorpaeniformes). *Species Diversity* 1 (2): 123–233.

———. 2000. An alternative hypothesis on the phylogenetic position of the family Dactylopteridae (Pisces: Teleostei), with a proposed new classification. *Ichthyol. Res.* 47 (3): 203–222.

Ishihara, H., K. Homma, Y. Takeda, and J. E. Randall. 1993. Redescription, distribution and food habits of the Indo-Pacific dasyatidid stingray *Himanura granulata. Jpn. J. Ichthyol.* 40 (1): 23–28.

Ivantsoff, W., and L. E. L. M. Crowley. 1991. Review of the Australian silverside fishes of the genus *Atherinomorus* (Atherinidae). *Aust. J. Mar. Freshwater Res.* 42:479–505.

Iwatsuki, Y., S. Kimura, H. Kishimoto, and T. Yoshino. 1996. Validity of the gerreid fish, *Gerres macracanthus* Bleeker, 1854, with designation of a lectotype, and designation of a neotype for *G. filamentosus* Cuvier, 1829. *Ichthyol. Res.* 43 (4): 417–429.

Iwatsuki, Y., S. Kimura, and T. Yoshino. 2001. Redescription of *Gerres longirostris* (Lacepède, 1801) and *Gerres oblongus* Cuvier in Cuvier and Valenciennes, 1830, included in the *Gerres longirostris* complex (Perciformes: Gerreidae). *Copeia* 2001 (4): 954–965.

James, P. S. B. R. 1975. A systematic review of the fishes of the family Leiognathidae. *J. Mar. Biol. Assoc. India* 17 (1): 138–172.

Jewett, S. J., and E. A. Lachner. 1983. Seven new species of the Indo-Pacific genus *Eviota* (Pisces: Gobiidae). *Proc. Biol. Soc. Wash.* 96 (4): 780–806.

Johannes, R. E. 1981. *Words of the Lagoon.* University of California Press, Berkeley. xi + 245 pp.

John, C. M. 1950. Early stages in the development of the sucker fish *Echeneis naucrates* Linn. *Bull. Cent. Res. Inst. Univ. Kerala India Ser. C Nat. Sci.* 1:47–55.

Johnson, G. D. 1986. Scombroid phylogeny: An alternative hypothesis. *Bull. Mar. Sci.* 39 (1): 1–41.

Johnson, J. W. 2002. A new species of unicornfish, genus *Naso* (Perciformes: Acanthuridae), with a review of the *Naso tuberosus* complex. *Aust. J. Zool.* 50:293–311.

Johnson, J. W., J. E. Randall, and S. F. Chenoweth. 2001. *Diagramma melanacrum* new species of haemulid fish from Indonesia, Borneo and the Philippines with a generic review. *Mem. Queensl. Mus.* 46 (2): 657–676.

Johnson, R. H. 1978. *Sharks of Polynesia.* Editions du Pacifique, Papeete. 170 pp.

Johnson, R. H., and D. R. Nelson. 1973. Agonistic display in the gray reef shark, *Carcharhinus menisorrah,* and its relationship to attacks on man. *Copeia* 1973 (1): 76–84.

Jones, G. 1985. Revision of the Australian species of the fish family Leiognathidae. *Aust. J. Mar. Freshwater Res.* 36:559–613.

Jones, S., and H. Rosa Jr. 1967. Synopsis of biological data on the fishes of the genus *Rastrelliger* Jordan and Starks 1908, with an annotated bibliography. *Proc. Symp. Scombroid Fishes, Mar. Biol. Assoc. India* 1 (3): 1109–1236.

Jordan, D. S., and M. C. Dickerson. 1908. On a collection of fishes from Fiji, with notes on certain Hawaiian fishes. *Proc. U.S. Natl. Mus.* 34:603–617.

Jordan, D. S., and B. W. Evermann. 1903. Descriptions of new genera and species of fishes from the Hawaiian Islands. *Bull. U.S. Fish Comm.* 22:163–208.

Jordan, D. S., and R. E. Richardson. 1908. Fishes from islands of the Philippine Archipelago. *Bull. Bur. Fish.* 27 (1907): 233–287.

Jordan, D. S., and A. Seale. 1906. The fishes of Samoa. *Bull. Bur. Fish.* (1905) 25:273–488.

Jordan, D. S., and D. S. Snyder. 1902. A review of the trachinoid fishes and their supposed allies found in the waters of Japan. *Proc. U.S. Natl. Mus.* 24:461–497.

Kami, H. T., and I. I. Ikehara. 1976. Notes on the annual juvenile siganid harvest in Guam. *Micronesica* 12:323–325.

Kanazawa, R. H. 1958. A revision of the eels of the genus *Conger* with descriptions of four new species. *Proc. U.S. Natl. Mus.* 108:219–267.

Karnella, S. J., and E. A. Lachner. 1981. Three new species of the *Eviota epiphanes* group having vertical trunk bars (Pisces: Gobiidae). *Proc. Biol. Soc. Wash.* 94 (1): 264–275.

Karplus, I. 1987. The association between gobiid fishes and burrowing alpheid shrimps. *Annu. Rev. Oceanogr. Mar. Biol.* 25:507–562.

Kawase, H., and A. Nakazono. 1994. Reproductive behavior of the honeycomb leatherjacket, *Cantherhines pardalis* (Monacanthidae) at Kashiwajima, Japan. *Jpn. J. Ichthyol.* 4 (1): 80–83.

Kendall, W. C., and L. Radcliffe. 1912. Reports on the scientific results of the expedition to the eastern tropical Pacific, in charge of Alexander Agassiz, by the U. S. Fish Commission Steamer "Albatross," from October, 1904 to March, 1905, Lieut. Commander L. M. Garrett, U. S. N., commanding. XXV. The shore fishes. *Mem. Mus. Comp. Zoöl* 35 (3): 77–171.

Kimura, S., Y. Iwatsuki, and T. Yoshino. 2001a. Redescriptions of the Indo-West Pacific atherinid fishes, *Atherinomorus endrachtensis* (Quoy and Gaimard, 1825) and *A. duodecimalis* (Valenciennes *in* Cuvier and Valenciennes, 1835). *Ichthyol. Res.* 48:167–177.

———. 2001b. Validity of the atherinid fish, *Atherinomorus vaigiensis* (Quoy and Gaimard, 1825), with comments on its synonymy. *Ichthyol. Res.* 48:379–384.

Kishimoto, H., K. Amaoka, H. Kohno, and T. Hamaguchi. 1987. A revision of the black-and-white snappers, genus *Macolor* (Perciformes: Lutjanidae). *Jpn. J. Ichthyol.* 34 (2): 146–156.

Kishimoto, H., M. Hayashi, H. Kohno, and O. Moriyama. 1988. Revision of Japanese batfishes, genus *Platax. Sci. Rep. Yokosuka City Mus.*, no. 36:19–38 (in Japanese).

Klausewitz, W. 1960. Die Typen und Typoide des Naturmuseums Senckenberg, 23: Pisces, Chondrichthyes, Elasmobranchii. *Senckenb. Biol.* 41 (5/6): 289–296.

Kon, T., and T. Yoshino. 1999. Record of the frogfish (Lophiiformes: Antennariidae), *Antennarius analis,* from Japan, with comments on its authorship. *Jpn. J. Ichthyol.* 46 (2): 101–103 (in Japanese).

Kritzer, J. B. 2002. Stock structure, mortality and growth of the decorated goby, *Istigobius decoratus* (Gobiidae), at Lizard Island, Great Barrier Reef. *Environ. Biol. Fishes* 63 (2): 217–218.

Kuiter, R. H. 1993. *Coastal Fishes of South-Eastern Australia.* University of Hawai'i Press, Honolulu. xxxi + 437 pp.

Kuiter, R. H., and J. E. Randall. 1981. Three look-alike Indo-Pacific labrid fishes, *Halichoeres margaritaceus, H. nebulosus* and *H. miniatus. Rec. Fr. Aquariol.* 8 (1): 13–18.

Kuiter, R. H., and T. Tonozuka. 2001. *Photo Guide: Indonesian Reef Fishes.* Zoonetics, Seaford, Australia.

Kulbicki, M., J. E. Randall, and J. Rivaton. 1994. Checklist of the fishes of the Chesterfield Islands (Coral Sea). *Micronesica* 27 (1/2): 1–43.

Kulbicki, M., and J. Rivaton. 1997. Inventaire et biogéographie des poissons lagonaires et récifaux de Nouvelle-Calédonie. *Cybium* 21 (1) Suppl.: 81–98.

Kulbicki, M., and J. T. Williams. 1997. Checklist of the shorefishes of Ouvéa Atoll, New Caledonia. *Atoll Res. Bull.*, no. 444:1–26.

Kuthalingam, M. D. K., and K. K. P. Menon. 1965. A note on the occurrence of *Xiphasia setifer* (Swainson) off Mangalore, west coast of India. *J. Mar. Biol. Assoc. India* 7 (1): 214–217.

Kuwamura, T. 1981. Life history and population fluctuation in the labrid fish, *Labroides dimidiatus,* near the northern limit of its range. *Publ. Seto Mar. Biol. Lab.* 26 (1/2): 95–117.

———. 1984. Social structure of the protogynous fish *Labroides dimidiatus. Publ. Seto Mar. Biol. Lab.* 29 (1/3): 117–177.

Laboute, P., and R. Grandperrin. 2000. *Poissons de Nouvelle-Calédonie.* Editions Catherine Ledru, Nouméa. 520 pp.

Lachner, E. A., and S. J. Karnella. 1980. Fishes of the Indo-Pacific genus *Eviota* with descriptions of eight new species (Teleostei: Gobiidae). *Smithson. Contrib. Zool.*, no. 315: iii + 127 pp.

Larson, H. K. 1983. Notes on the biology of the goby *Kelloggella cardinalis* (Jordan & Seale). *Micronesica* 19 (1/2): 157–164.

———. 1985. A revision of the gobiid genus *Bryaninops* (Pisces), with a description of six new species. *Beagle* 2 (1): 57–93.

———. 1990. A revision of the commensal gobiid fish genera *Pleurosicya* and *Luposicya* (Gobiidae), with descriptions of eight new species of *Pleurosicya* and discussion of related genera. *Beagle* 7 (1): 1–53.

Larson, H. K., and D. F. Hoese. 1980. The species of the Indo-West Pacific genus *Calumia* (Pisces: Eleotridae). *Proc. Linn. Soc. N.S.W.* 104 (1): 17–22.

Last, P. R., and J. D. Stevens. 1994. *Sharks and Rays of Australia.* CSIRO, Australia. 513 pp.

Lavondès, H., and J. E. Randall. 1978. Les noms de poissons marquisiens. *J. Soc. Océanistes* 34:79–112.

Leis, J. M. 1978. Systematics and zoogeography of the porcupinefishes (*Diodon,* Diodontidae, Tetraodontiformes), with comments on egg and larval development. *Fish. Bull.* 76 (3): 535–567.

Leis, J. M., and B. M. Carson-Ewart. 2000. *The Larvae of Indo-Pacific Coastal Fishes.* Brill, Leiden. xix + 850 pp.

Leis, J. M., and J. T. Moyer. 1985. Development of eggs, larvae and pelagic juveniles of three Indo-Pacific ostraciid fishes (Tetraodontiformes): *Ostracion meleagris, Lactoria fornasini,* and *L. diaphana. Jpn. J. Ichthyol.* 32 (2): 189–202.

Lobel, P. S. 1981. *Bodianus prognathus* (Labridae, Pisces), a new longnose hogfish from the central Pacific. *Pac. Sci.* 35 (1): 45–50.

Losey, G. S. 1972. Predator protection in the poison-fang blenny, *Meiacanthus atrodorsalis,* and its mimics, *Ecsenius bicolor* and *Runula laudandus* (Blenniidae). *Pac. Sci.* 26 (2): 129–139.

Lourie, S. A., J. C. Pritchard, S. P. Casey, S. K. Truong, H. J. Hall, and A. C. J. Vincent. 1999. The taxonomy of Vietnam's exploited seahorses (family Syngnathidae). *Biol. J. Linn. Soc.* 66:231–256.

Lubbock, R. 1975. Fishes of the family Pseudochromidae (Perciformes) in the northwest Indian Ocean and Red Sea. *J. Zool. (Lond.)* 176:115–157.

Major, P. F. 1973. Scale feeding behavior of the leatherjacket, *Scomberoides lysan* and two species of the genus *Oligoplites* (Pisces: Carangidae). *Copeia* 1973 (1): 151–154.

Markle, D. F., and J. E. Olney. 1990. Systematics of the pearlfishes (Pisces: Carapidae). *Bull. Mar. Sci.* 47 (2): 269–410.

Masuda, H., K. Amaoka, C. Araga, T. Uyeno, and T. Yoshino (eds.). 1975. *Coastal Fishes of Japan.* Tokai University Press, Tokyo. 382 pp.

———. 1984. *The Fishes of the Japanese Archipelago.* Vol. 1 (text: xxii + 437 pp.) and vol. 2 (plates). Tokai University Press, Tokyo.

Masuda, H., and Y. Kobayashi. 1994. *Grand Atlas of Fish Life Modes (Color Variation in Japanese Fish).* Tokai University Press, Tokyo (in Japanese). 465 pp.

Matsuura, K. 1980. A revision of Japanese balistoid fishes. I. Family Balistidae. *Bull. Natl. Sci. Mus. Ser. A (Zool.)* 6 (1): 27–69.

Matthews, C. P., M. Samuel, and M. K. Baddar. 1986. Sexual maturation, length and age in some species of Kuwait fish related to their suitability for aquaculture. *Kuwait Bull. Mar. Sci.* 8:243–256.

McCosker, J. E. 1970. A review of the eel genera *Leptenchelys* and *Muraenichthys,* with the description of a new genus *Shismorhynchus* and a new species, *Muraenichthys chilensis. Pac. Sci.* 24 (4): 506–516.

———. 1977a. The osteology, classification, and relationships of the eel family Ophichthidae. *Proc. Calif. Acad. Sci.* 41 (1): 1–123.

———. 1977b. Fright posture of the plesiopid fish *Calloplesiops altivelis:* An example of Batesian mimicry. *Science (Washington, D.C.)* 197:400–401.

———. 1978. Synonymy and distribution of *Calloplesiops* (Pisces: Plesiopidae). *Copeia* 1978 (3): 707–710.

———. 1982. A new genus and two new species of remarkable Pacific worm eels (Ophichthidae, subfamily Myrophinae). *Proc. Calif. Acad. Sci.* 43 (5): 59–66.

———. 1998. A revision of the snake-eel genus *Callechelys* (Anguilliformes: Ophichthidae) with the description of two new Indo-Pacific species and a new callechelyin genus. *Proc. Calif. Acad. Sci.* 50 (7): 185–215.

———. 2002. Notes on Hawaiian snake eels (Pisces: Ophichthidae), with comments on *Ophichthus bonaparti. Pac. Sci.* 56 (1): 23–34.

McCosker, J. E., and P. H. Humann. 1996. New records of Galápagos fishes. *Not. Galápagos,* no. 56:18–22.

McCosker, J. E., and J. E. Randall. 2001. Revision of the snake-eel genus *Brachysomophis* (Anguilliformes:

Ophichthidae), with description of two new species and comments on the species of *Mystriophis. Indo-Pac. Fishes,* no. 33:1–32.

McCosker, J. E., and R. H. Rosenblatt. 1987. Notes on the biology, taxonomy, and distribution of flashlight fishes (Beryciformes: Anomalopidae). *Jpn. J. Ichthyol.* 34 (2): 157–164.

———. 1993. A revision of the snake eel genus *Myrichthys* (Anguilliformes: Ophichthidae) with the description of a new eastern Pacific species. *Proc. Calif. Acad. Sci.* 48 (8): 153–169.

McCulloch, A. R., and E. R. Waite. 1918. Descriptions of two new Australian gobies. *Rec. S. Aust. Mus. (Adelaide)* 1 (1): 79–82.

McKay, R. J. 1985. A revision of the fishes of the family Sillaginidae. *Mem. Queensl. Mus.* 22 (1): 1–73.

———. 1992. Sillaginid fishes of the world (family Sillaginidae). *FAO Fish. Synop.,* no. 125, vol. 14: vi + 87 pp.

Melton, R. J., J. E. Randall, N. Fusetani, R. S. Weiner, R. D. Couch, and J. K. Sims. 1984. Fatal sardine poisoning: A fatal case of fish poisoning in Hawaii associated with the Marquesan sardine. *Hawaii Med. J.* 43 (4): 114, 116, 118–120, 124.

Michael, S. W. 1998. *Reef Fishes.* Vol. 1. Microcosm, Shelburne, VT. 624 pp.

Mito, S. 1955. Breeding habits of a percoid fish, *Plesiops semeion. Sci. Bull. Fac. Agric. Kyushu Univ.* 15:95–99 (in Japanese).

Mohr, E. 1937. Revision der Centriscidae (Acanthopterygii Centrisciformes). *Dana-Rep. Carlsberg Found.* no. 18:1–69.

Mooi, R. D. 1990. Egg surface morphology of pseudochromoids (Perciformes: Percoidei), with comments on its phylogenetic implications. *Copeia* 1990 (2): 455–475.

———. 1995. Revision, phylogeny, and discussion of biology and biogeography of the fish genus *Plesiops* (Perciformes: Plesiopidae). *R. Ont. Mus. Life Sci. Contrib.,* no. 159: iv + 107 pp.

———. 1998. A new species of the genus *Pempheris* (Teleostei: Pempherididae) from Rapa Iti, French Polynesia. *Pac. Sci.* 52 (2): 154–160.

Morgans, J. F. C. 1982. Serranid fishes of Tanzania and Kenya. *Ichthyol. Bull. J. L. B. Smith Inst. Ichthyol.,* no. 46:1–44.

Moser, H. G., W. J. Richards, D. M. Cohen, M. P. Fahay, A. W. Kendall Jr., and S. L. Richardson (eds.). 1984. Ontogeny and systematics of fishes. *Spec. Publ. Am. Soc. Ichthyol. Herpetol.,* no. 1: ix + 760 pp.

Motomura, H. 2001. Redescription of *Polydactylus sexfilis* (Valenciennes *in* Cuvier and Valenciennes, 1831), a senior synonym of *P. kuru* (Bleeker, 1853) with designation of a lectotype (Perciformes: Polynemidae). *Ichthyol. Res.* 48:85–89.

———. in press. First record of a scorpion-fish (Scorpaenidae), *Scorpaenopsis ramaraoi,* from New Caledonia. *Cybium.*

Motomura, H., Y. Iwatsuki, and T. Yoshino. 2001a. A new species, *Polydactylus siamensis,* from Thailand and redescription of *P. plebeius* (Broussonet, 1782) with designation of a neotype (Perciformes: Polynemidae). *Ichthyol. Res.* 48:117–126.

Motomura, H., S. Kimura, and Y. Iwatsuki. 2001b. Distributional range extension of a clupeid fish, *Sardinella melanura* (Cuvier, 1829), in southern Japan (Teleostei: Clupeiformes). *Biogeography* 3:83–87.

Motomura, H., and H. Senou. 2002. Record of *Polydactylus sexfilis* (Perciformes: Polynemidae) from Hachijo-jima, Izu Islands, Japan with comments on morphological changes with growth and speciation of related species. *Bull. Kanagawa Prefect. Mus. Nat. Sci.,* no. 31:27–31.

Moyer, J. T., and M. J. Zaiser. 1981. Social organization and spawning behavior of the pteroine fish *Dendrochirus zebra* at Miyake-jima, Japan. *Jpn. J. Ichthyol.* 28 (1): 52–69.

Munday, P. L., A. S. Harold, and R. Winterbottom. 1999. Guide to coral-dwelling gobies, genus *Gobiodon* (Gobiidae) from Papua New Guinea and the Great Barrier Reef. *Rev. Fr. Aquariol.* 26 (1–2): 53–58.

Mundy, B. C. in press. Checklist of the fishes of the Hawaiian Archipelago. *Bishop Mus. Bull. Zool.*

Murdy, E. O. 1985a. Revision of the gobiid fish genus *Istigobius. Indo-Pac. Fishes,* no. 4:1–41.

———. 1985b. A review of the gobiid fish genera *Exyrias* and *Macrodontogobius,* with description of a new species of *Exyrias. Indo-Pac. Fishes,* no. 10:1–14.

———. 1989. A taxonomic revision and cladistic analysis of the oxudercine gobies (Gobiidae: Oxudercinae). *Rec. Aust. Mus. Suppl.* 11:1–93.

Myers, R. F. 1989. *Micronesian Reef Fishes.* 1st ed. Coral Graphics, Guam. vi + 298 pp., 144 pls.

———. 1999. *Micronesian Reef Fishes.* 3d ed. Coral Graphics, Guam. vi + 330 pp., 192 pls.

Myrberg, A. A., Jr., W. L. Montgomery, and L. Fishelson. 1988. The reproductive behavior of *Acanthurus nigrofuscus* (Forskal) and other surgeonfishes (Fam. Acanthuridae) off Eilat, Israel (Gulf of Aqaba, Red Sea). *Ethology* 79:31–61.

Nakabo, T. (ed.). 2002. *Fishes of Japan with Pictorial Keys to the Species.* English Ed. 2 vols., 1749 pp. Tokai University Press, Tokyo.

Nakazono, A., H. Nakatani, and H. Tsukahara. 1985. Reproductive ecology of the Japanese reef fish, *Parapercis snyderi. Proc. Fifth Int. Coral Reef Congr., Tahiti* 5:355–360.

Nelson, J. S. 1985. On the interrelationships of the genera of Creediidae (Perciformes: Trachinoidei). *Jpn. J. Ichthyol.* 32 (3): 283–293.

———. 1986. Some characters of Trichonotidae, with emphasis on those distinguishing it from Creediidae (Perciformes: Trachinoidei). *Jpn. J. Ichthyol.* 33 (1): 1–6.

———. 1994. *Fishes of the World.* 3d ed. John Wiley & Sons, New York. xvii + 600 pp.

Nelson, J. S., and J. E. Randall. 1985. *Crystallodytes pauciradiatus* (Perciformes), a new creediid fish species from Easter Island. *Proc. Biol. Soc. Wash.* 98 (2): 403–410.

Noguchi, T., and Y. Hashimoto. 1973. Isolation of tetrodotoxin from a goby *Gobius criniger. Toxicon* 11:305–307.

Noguchi, T., H. Kao, and Y. Hashimoto. 1971. Toxicity of the goby, *Gobius criniger. Bull. Jpn. Soc. Sci. Fish.* 37 (7): 642–647.

Norman, J. R. 1934. *A Systematic Monograph of the Flatfishes (Heterosomata).* British Museum (Natural History), London. vii + 459 pp.

Notarbartolo-di-Sciara, G. 1987. A revisionary study of the genus *Mobula* Rafinesque, 1810 (Chondrichthyes: Mobulidae) with the description of a new species. *Zool. J. Linn. Soc.* 91:1–91.

Okamura, O. (ed.). 1985. *Fishes of the Okinawa Trough and Adjacent Waters.* II. Japan Fisheries Resource Conservation Association, Tokyo (in Japanese). 417–781 pp.

Okamura, O., and K. Amaoka. 1997. *Sea Fishes of Japan.* Yama-kei Publisher, Tokyo (in Japanese). 783 pp.

Ormond, R. F. G. 1980. Aggressive mimicry and other interspecific feeding associations among Red Sea coral reef predators. *J. Zool. (Lond.)* 191:247–262.

Orr, J. W., and R. A. Fritzsche. 1993. Revision of the ghost pipefishes, family Solenostomidae (Teleostei: Syngnathoidei). *Copeia* 1993 (1): 168–182.

Orr, J. W., R. A. Fritzsche, and J. E. Randall. 2002. *Solenostomus halimeda,* a new species of ghost pipefish (Teleostei: Gasterosteiformes) from the Indo-Pacific, with a revised key to the family Solenostomidae. *Aqua* 5 (3): 99–108.

Paepke, H.-J. 1999. *Bloch's Fish Collection in the Museum für Naturkunde der Humboldt Universität zu Berlin: An Illustrated Catalog and Historical Account.* A. R. G. Gantner, Ruggell/Liechtenstein. 216 pp.

Palsson, W. A., and T. W. Pietsch. 1989. Revision of the acanthopterygian fish family Pegasidae (order Gasterosteiformes). *Indo-Pac. Fishes,* no. 18:1–38.

Parenti, P., and J. E. Randall. 2000. An annotated checklist of the species of the labroid fish families Labridae and Scaridae. *Ichthyol. Bull. J. L. B. Smith Inst. Ichthyol.,* no. 68:1–97.

Parin, N. V. 1967. Review of marine needlefishes of the West Pacific and Indian Oceans. *Tr. Okeanol. Inst.*

84:3–83 (in Russian; English translation, 1967, in *Natl. Mar. Fish. Serv. Syst. Lab. Transl.* no. 68).

Parin, N. V., B. B. Collette, and Y. N. Shcherbachev. 1980. Preliminary review of the marine halfbeaks (Hemiramphidae, Beloniformes) of the tropical Indo-West Pacific. *Trans. P. P. Shirshov Inst. Okeanol.* 97:7–173 (in Russian; English translation, 1982, by Al Ahram Center for Scientific Translations).

Pietsch, T. W., and D. B. Grobecker. 1978. The complete angler: Aggressive mimicry in an antennariid anglerfish. *Science* (Washington, D.C.) 201:369–370.

———. 1987. *Frogfishes of the World: Systematics, Zoogeography, and Behavioral Ecology.* Stanford University, Stanford, CA. xxii + 420 pp.

Planes, S., and C. Fauvelot. 2002. Isolation by distance and vicariance drive genetic structure of a coral reef fish in the Pacific Ocean. *Evolution* 56 (2): 378–399.

Popper, D., and N. Gundermann. 1975. Some ecological and behavioural aspects of siganid populations in the Red Sea and Mediterranean coasts of Israel in relation to their suitability for aquaculture. *Aquaculture* 6:127–141.

Poss, S. G., and W. N. Eschmeyer. 1978. Two new Australian velvetfishes, genus *Paraploactis* (Scorpaeniformes: Aploactinidae), with a revision of the genus and comments on the genera and species of the Aploactinidae. *Proc. Calif. Acad. Sci.* 41 (18): 401–426.

Privitera, L. A. 2001. Reproductive biology of the coral-reef goby, *Asterropteryx semipunctata*, in Kaneohe Bay, Hawai'i. *Environ. Biol. Fishes* 65:287–310.

———. 2002. Characteristics of egg and larval production in captive bluespotted gobies. *J. Fish Biol.* 58:1211–1220.

Pyle, R. L. 2003. A systematic treatment of the reef-fish family Pomacanthidae (Pisces: Perciformes). Ph.D. diss., University of Hawai'i, Honolulu. xv + 422 pp.

Pyle, R. L., and J. E. Randall. 1994. A review of hybridization in marine angelfishes (Perciformes: Pomacanthidae). *Environ. Biol. Fishes* 41:127–145.

Randall, H. A., and G. R. Allen. 1977. A revision of the damselfish genus *Dascyllus* (Pomacentridae), with the description of a new species. *Rec. Aust. Mus.* 31 (9): 349–385.

Randall, J. E. 1955a. Fishes of the Gilbert Islands. *Atoll Res. Bull.*, no. 47: xi + 243 pp.

———. 1955b. An analysis of the genera of surgeon fishes (family Acanthuridae). *Pac. Sci.* 9 (3): 359–367.

———. 1955c. A revision of the surgeon fish genera *Zebrasoma* and *Paracanthurus*. *Pac. Sci.* 9 (4): 396–412.

———. 1955d. A revision of the surgeon fish genus *Ctenochaetus*, family Acanthuridae, with descriptions of five new species. *Zoologica* 40 (4): 149–166.

———. 1956. A revision of the surgeon fish genus *Acanthurus*. *Pac. Sci.* 10 (2): 159–235.

———. 1958. A review of the labrid fish genus *Labroides*, with descriptions of two new species and notes on ecology. *Pac. Sci.* 12 (4): 327–347.

———. 1959. Report of a caudal-spine wound from the surgeonfish *Acanthurus lineatus* in the Society Islands. *Wassmann J. Biol.* 17 (2): 245–248.

———. 1960a. New fishes for Hawaii. *Sea Front.* 6 (1): 33–43.

———. 1960b. The living javelin. *Sea Front.* 6 (4): 228–233.

———. 1961a. A technique for fish photography. *Copeia* 1961 (2): 241–242.

———. 1961b. Let a sleeping shark lie. *Sea Front.* 7 (3): 153–159.

———. 1961c. A record of the kyphosid fish *Sectator ocyurus* (= *azureus*) from the Society Islands. *Copeia* 1961 (3): 357–358.

———. 1961d. Observations on the spawning of surgeonfishes (Acanthuridae) in the Society Islands. *Copeia* 1961 (2): 237–238.

———. 1961e. A contribution to the biology of the convict surgeonfish of the Hawaiian Islands, *Acanthurus triostegus sandvicensis*. *Pac. Sci.* 15 (2): 215–272.

———. 1963a. A fatal attack by the shark *Carcharhinus galapagensis* at St. Thomas, Virgin Islands. *Caribb. J. Sci.* 3 (4): 201–205.

———. 1963b. Review of the hawkfishes (family Cirrhitidae). *Proc. U.S. Natl. Mus.* 114:389–481.

———. 1963c. Notes on the systematics of parrotfishes (Scaridae), with emphasis on sexual dichromatism. *Copeia* 1963 (2): 225–237.

———. 1964. A revision of the filefish genera *Amanses* and *Cantherhines*. *Copeia* 1964 (2): 331–361.

———. 1971. The nominal triggerfishes (Balistidae) *Pachynathus nycteris* and *Oncobalistes erythropterus*, junior synonyms of *Melichthys vidua*. *Copeia* 1971 (3): 462–469.

———. 1973. Tahitian fish names and a preliminary checklist of the fishes of the Society Islands. *Occas. Pap. Bernice Pauahi Bishop Mus.* 24 (11): 167–214.

———. 1975. A revision of the Indo-Pacific angel-fish genus *Genicanthus*, with descriptions of three new species. *Bull. Mar. Sci.* 25 (3): 393–421.

———. 1977. Contribution to the biology of the whitetip reef shark (*Triaenodon obesus*). *Pac. Sci.* 31 (2): 143–164.

———. 1980a. A survey of ciguatera at Enewetak and Bikini, Marshall Islands, with notes on the systematics and food habits of ciguatoxic fishes. *Fish. Bull.* 78 (2): 201–249.

———. 1980b. Revision of the fish genus *Plectranthias* (Serranidae: Anthiinae) with descriptions of 13 new species. *Micronesica* 16 (1): 101–187.

———. 1981a. A review of the Indo-Pacific sand tilefish genus *Hoplolatilus*

(Perciformes: Malacanthidae). *Freshwater Mar. Aquarium* 4 (12): 39–46.

———. 1981b. Two new Indo-Pacific labrid fishes of the genus *Halichoeres*, with notes on other species of the genus. *Pac. Sci.* (1980) 34 (4): 415–432.

———. 1982. A review of the labrid genus *Hologymnosus*. *Rev. Fr. Aquariol.* 9 (1): 13–20.

———. 1983a. A review of the fishes of the subgenus *Goniistius*, genus *Cheilodactylus*, with description of a new species from Easter Island and Rapa. *Occas. Pap. Bernice Pauahi Bishop Mus.* 25 (7): 1–24.

———. 1983b. Revision of the Indo-Pacific labrid fish genus *Wetmorella*. *Copeia* 1983 (4): 875–883.

———. 1985a. Fishes, pp. 462–481 in B. Delesalle, R. Galzin, and B. Salvat (eds.), *Fifth International Coral Reef Congress, Tahiti.* Vol. 1. *French Polynesian Coral Reefs.*

———. 1985b. *Guide to Hawaiian Reef Fishes.* Harrowood Books, Newtown Square, PA. 70 pp.

———. 1985c. On the validity of the tetraodontid fish *Arothron manilensis* (Procé). *Jpn. J. Ichthyol.* 32 (3): 347–354.

———. 1987. Introductions to the marine fishes of the Hawaiian Islands. *Bull. Mar. Sci.* 41 (2): 490–502.

———. 1992. Review of the biology of the tiger shark (*Galeocerdo cuvier*). *Aust. J. Mar. Freshwater Res.* 43:21–31.

———. 1994. Twenty-two new records of fishes from the Red Sea. *Fauna Saudi Arabia* 14:259–275.

———. 1995a. *Coastal Fishes of Oman.* University of Hawai'i Press, Honolulu. xiii + 439 pp.

———. 1995b. *Fusigobius* Whitley, a junior synonym of the gobiid fish genus *Coryphopterus* Gill. *Bull. Mar. Sci.* 56:795–798.

———. 1997a. The parrotfish *Scarus atropectoralis* Schultz, a junior synonym of *S. xanthopleura* Bleeker. *Rev. Fr. Aquariol.* 24 (1–2): 49–52.

———. 1997b. Life color of 13 Indo-Pacific gobies of the genus *Eviota*. *I.O.P. Diving News* 8 (7): 4–7.

———. 1998a. Zoogeography of shore fishes of the Indo-Pacific region. *Zool. Stud.* 37 (4): 227–268.

———. 1998b. First record of the lizardfish *Synodus rubromarmoratus* Russell and Cressey from Hawaii and Japan. *I.O.P. Diving News* 9 (12): 6–7.

———. 1998c. Revision of the Indo-Pacific squirrelfishes (Beryciformes: Holocentridae: Holocentrinae) of the genus *Sargocentron*, with descriptions of four new species. *Indo-Pac. Fishes*, no. 27: 1–105.

———. 1999a. Report on fish collections from the Pitcairn Islands. *Atoll Res. Bull.*, no. 461: 1–36.

———. 1999b. Revision of the Indo-Pacific labrid fishes of the genus

668

Pseudocheilinus, with descriptions of three new species. *Indo-Pac. Fishes,* no. 28:1–34.

————. 1999c. Revision of the Indo-Pacific labrid fishes of the genus *Coris,* with descriptions of five new species. *Indo-Pac. Fishes,* no. 29:1–74.

————. 2001a. Notes on the scorpaenid genus *Rhinopias. I.O.P. Diving News* 12 (9): 5–7.

————. 2001b. Revision of the generic classification of the hawkfishes (Perciformes: Cirrhitidae), with descriptions of three new genera. *Zootaxa* 12:1–12.

————. 2001c. Four new damselfishes (Perciformes: Pomacentridae) from the Marquesas Islands. *Copeia* 2001 (1): 92–107.

————. 2001d. Five new Indo-Pacific gobiid fishes of the genus *Coryphopterus. Zool. Stud.* 40 (3): 206–225.

————. 2002a. *Surgeonfishes of the World.* Mutual Publishing and Bishop Museum Press, Honolulu. x + 123 pp.

————. 2002b. Two new damselfishes of the genus *Pomacentrus* from the South-West Pacific. *Aqua* 5 (4): 167–176.

————. 2003a. Review of the sandperches of the *Parapercis cylindrica* complex (Perciformes: Pinguipedidae), with descriptions of two new species. *Bishop Mus. Occas. Pap.,* no. 72:1–19.

————. 2003b. *Thalassoma nigrofasciatum,* a new species of labrid fish from the Southwest Pacific. *Aqua* 7 (1): 1–8.

————. 2004a. Five new shrimp gobies of the genus *Amblyeleotris* from islands of Oceania. *Aqua* 8 (2): 61–79.

————. 2004b. Revision of the goatfish genus *Parupeneus* (Perciformes: Mullidae), with descriptions of two new species. *Indo-Pac. Fishes,* no. 36:1–68.

Randall, J. E., K. Aida, T. Hibiya, N. Mitsuura, H. Kamiya, and Y. Hashimoto. 1971. Grammistin, the skin toxin of soapfishes, and its significance in the classification of the Grammistidae. *Publ. Seto Mar. Biol. Lab.* 19 (2/3): 157–190.

Randall, J. E., K. Aida, Y. Oshima, K. Hori, and Y. Hashimoto. 1981a. Occurrence of a crinotoxin and hemagglutinin in the skin mucus of the moray eel *Lycodontis nudivomer. Mar. Biol. (Berl.)* 62:179–184.

Randall, J. E., and G. R. Allen. 1973. A revision of the gobiid fish genus *Nemateleotris,* with descriptions of two new species. *Q. J. Taiwan Mus. (Taipei)* 26 (3 & 4): 347–367.

————. 2003. *Paracheilinus rubricaudalis,* a new species of flasherwrasse (Perciformes: Labridae) from Fiji. *Aqua* 7 (3): 103–112.

Randall, J. E., G. R. Allen, and D. R. Robertson. 2003a. *Myripristis earlei,* a new soldierfish (Beryciformes: Holocentridae) from the Marquesas and Phoenix Islands. *Zool. Stud.* 42 (3): 405–410.

Randall, J. E., G. R. Allen, and R. C. Steene. 1977. Five probable hybrid butterfly

fishes of the genus *Chaetodon* from the central and western Pacific. *Rec. W. Austr. Mus.* 6 (1): 3–26.

————. 1997a. *Fishes of the Great Barrier Reef and Coral Sea.* 2d ed. University of Hawai'i Press, Honolulu. xx + 557 pp.

Randall, J. E., and R. C. Anderson. 1993. Annotated checklist of the epipelagic and shore fishes of the Maldive Islands. *Ichthyol. Bull. J. L. B. Smith Inst. Ichthyol.,* no. 59:1–47.

Randall, J. E., P. Bacchet, R. Winterbottom, and L. Wrobel. 2002a. Fifty new records of shore fishes from the Society Islands and Tuamotu Archipelago. *Aqua* 5 (4): 153–166.

Randall, J. E., and C. C. Baldwin. 1997. Revision of the serranid fishes of the subtribe Pseudogrammina, with descriptions of five new species. *Indo-Pac. Fishes,* no. 26:1–56.

Randall, J. E., C. C. Baldwin, and J. T. Williams. 2002b. *Pseudogramma xanthum,* a new replacement name for a serranid fish from the subtropical South Pacific Ocean with description of the species. *Zootaxa* 40:1–8.

Randall, J. E., and M.-L. Bauchot. 1999. Clarification of the two Indo-Pacific species of bonefishes, *Albula glossodonta* and *A. forsteri. Cybium* 23 (1): 79–83.

Randall, J. E., M.-L. Bauchot, and M. Desoutter. 1987. *Heliases ternatensis* Bleeker, 1856 (currently *Chromis ternatensis;* Osteichthyes, Perciformes): Proposed conservation, and adoption of the name *Chromis viridis* (Cuvier, 1830) for the fish commonly called *C. caerulea* (Cuvier, 1830). Case 2516. *Bull. Zool. Nomencl.* 44 (4): 248–250.

Randall, J. E., and L. J. Bell. 1992. *Naso caesius,* a new acanthurid fish from the central Pacific. *Pac. Sci.* 46 (3): 344–352.

Randall, J. E., and A. Ben-Tuvia. 1983. A review of the groupers (Pisces: Serranidae: Epinephelinae) of the Red Sea, with description of a new species of *Cephalopholis. Bull. Mar. Sci.* 33 (2): 373–426.

Randall, J. E., and V. E. Brock. 1960. Observations on the ecology of epinepheline and lutjanid fishes of the Society Islands, with emphasis on food habits. *Trans. Am. Fish. Soc.* 89 (1): 9–16.

Randall, J. E., and R. W. Bruce. 1983. The parrotfishes of the subfamily Scarinae of the western Indian Ocean with descriptions of three new species. *Ichthyol. Bull. J. L. B. Smith Inst. Ichthyol.,* no. 47: 1–39.

Randall, J. E., and K. D. Clements. 2001. Second revision of the surgeonfish genus *Ctenochaetus* (Perciformes: Acanthuridae), with description of two new species. *Indo-Pac. Fishes,* no. 32: 1–33.

Randall, J. E., N. Downing, L. J. McCarthy, B. E. Stanaland, and A. B. Tarr. 1994. Fifty-one new records of fishes from the Arabian Gulf. *Fauna Saudi Arabia* 14:220–258.

Randall, J. E., and J. L. Earle. 1999. *Abudefduf conformis* and *Plectroglyphidodon*

sagmarius, two new damselfishes (Pomacentridae) from the Marquesas Islands. *Cybium* 23 (4): 333–343.

————. 2000. Annotated checklist of the shore fishes of the Marquesas Islands. *Occas. Pap. Bishop Mus.,* no. 66:1–39.

————. 2002. Review of Hawaiian razorfishes of the genus *Iniistius* (Perciformes: Labridae). *Pac. Sci.* 56 (4): 389–402.

————. 2004. *Novaculoides,* a new genus for the Indo-Pacific labrid fish *Novaculichthys macrolepidotus. Aqua* 8 (1): 37–43.

Randall, J. E., J. L. Earle, and D. R. Robertson. 2002c. *Iniistius auropunctatus,* a new razorfish (Perciformes: Labridae) from the Marquesas Islands. *Cybium* 26 (2): 93–98.

Randall, J. E., and A. R. Emery. 1971. On the resemblance of the young of the fishes *Platax pinnatus* and *Plectorhynchus chaetodonoides* to flatworms and nudibranchs. *Zoologica (N.Y.)* 56:115–119.

Randall, J. E., and W. N. Eschmeyer. 2001. Revision of the Indo-Pacific scorpionfish genus *Scorpaenopsis,* with descriptions of eight new species. *Indo-Pac. Fishes,* no. 34:1–79.

Randall, J. E., and J. Frische. 2000. Hybrid surgeonfishes of the *Acanthurus achilles* complex. *Aqua* 4 (2): 51–56.

Randall, J. E., and M. Goren. 1993. A review of the gobioid fishes of the Maldives. *Ichthyol. Bull. J. L. B. Smith Inst. Ichthyol.,* no. 58:1–37.

Randall, J. E., and D. W. Greenfield. 1996. Revision of the Indo-Pacific holocentrid fishes of the genus *Myripristis,* with descriptions of three new species. *Indo-Pac. Fishes,* no. 25:1–61.

————. 2001. A preliminary review of the Indo-Pacific gobiid fishes of the genus *Gnatholepis. Ichthyol. Bull. J. L. B. Smith Inst. Ichthyol.,* no. 69:1–17.

Randall, J. E., and P. Guézé. 1980. The goatfish *Mulloidichthys mimicus* n. sp. (Pisces, Mullidae) from Oceania, a mimic of the snapper *Lutjanus kasmira* (Pisces, Lutjanidae). *Bull. Mus. Natl. Hist. Nat.,* sér. 4, 2:603–609.

Randall, J. E., S. M. Head, and P. L. Sanders. 1978a. Food habits of the giant humphead wrasse. *Environ. Biol. Fishes* 3 (2): 235–238.

Randall, J. E., and P. C. Heemstra. 1985. A review of the squirrelfishes of the subfamily Holocentrinae from the western Indian Ocean and Red Sea. *Ichthyol. Bull. J. L. B. Smith Inst. Ichthyol.,* no. 49:1–27.

————. 1991. Revision of Indo-Pacific groupers (Perciformes: Serranidae: Epinephelinae), with descriptions of five new species. *Indo-Pac. Fishes,* no. 20:1–332.

Randall, J. E., and G. Helfman. 1972. *Diproctacanthus xanthurus,* a cleaner wrasse from the Palau Islands, with notes on other cleaning fishes. *Trop. Fish Hobbyist* 20 (11): 87–95.

———. 1973. Attacks on humans by the blacktip reef shark (*Carcharhinus melanopterus*). *Pac. Sci.* 27 (3): 226–238.

Randall, J. E., and D. F. Hoese. 1985. Revision of the Indo-Pacific dartfishes, genus *Ptereleotris* (Perciformes: Gobioidei). *Indo-Pac. Fishes*, no. 7:1–36.

Randall, J. E., H. Ida, K. Kato, R. L. Pyle, and J. L. Earle. 1997b. Annotated checklist of the inshore fishes of the Ogasawara Islands. *Monogr. Nat. Sci. Mus.*, no. 11:1–74.

Randall, J. E., H. Ida, and J. T. Moyer. 1981b. A review of the damselfishes of the genus *Chromis* from Japan and Taiwan, with description of a new species. *Jpn. J. Ichthyol.* 28 (3): 203–242.

Randall, J. E., and J. W. Johnson. 2000. *Perca lineata* and *P. vittata* established as valid species of *Plectorhinchus* (Perciformes: Haemulidae). *Mem. Queensl. Mus.* 45 (2): 477–482.

Randall, J. E., and R. K. Kanayama. 1972. Hawaiian fish immigrants. *Sea Front.* 18 (3): 144–153.

Randall, J. E., and M. Khalaf. 2003. Redescription of the labrid fish *Oxycheilinus orientalis* (Günther), a senior synonym of *O. rhodochrous* (Günther), and the first record from the Red Sea. *Zool. Stud.* 42 (1): 135–139.

Randall, J. E., and W. Klausewitz. 1973. A review of the triggerfish genus *Melichthys*, with description of a new species from the Indian Ocean. *Senckenb. Biol.* 54 (1/3): 57–69.

Randall, J. E., and R. H. Kuiter. 1989. The juvenile Indo-Pacific grouper *Anyperodon leucogrammicus*, a mimic of the wrasse *Halichoeres purpurascens* and allied species, with a review of the recent literature on mimicry in fishes. *Rev. Fr. Aquariol.* 16 (2): 51–56.

Randall, J. E., and M. Kulbicki. 1998. Two new cardinalfishes (Perciformes: Apogonidae) of the *Apogon cyanosoma* complex from the western Pacific, with notes on the status of *A. wassinki* Bleeker. *Rev. Fr. Aquariol.* 25 (1–2): 31–40.

Randall, J. E., and E. A. Lachner. 1986. The status of the Indo-West Pacific cardinalfishes *Apogon aroubiensis* and *A. nigrofasciatus*. *Proc. Biol. Soc. Wash.* 99 (1): 110–120.

Randall, J. E., E. A. Lachner, and T. H. Fraser. 1985a. A revision of the Indo-Pacific apogonid fish genus *Pseudamia*, with descriptions of three new species. *Indo-Pac. Fishes*, no. 6:1–23.

Randall, J. E., and P. S. Lobel. 2003. *Xyrichtys halsteadi*, a new labrid fish from the central and western Pacific. *Bull. Mar. Sci.* 72 (3): 971–977.

Randall, J. E., P. S. Lobel, and E. H. Chave. 1985b. Annotated checklist of the fishes of Johnston Island. *Pac. Sci.* 39 (1): 24–80.

Randall, J. E., and R. Lubbock. 1981. A revision of the serranid fishes of the subgenus *Mirolabrichthys* (Anthiinae: *Anthias*), with descriptions of five new species. *Contrib. Sci. Mus. Nat. Hist. Los Angeles Cty*, no. 333:1–27.

Randall, J. E., K. Matsuura, and A. Zama. 1978b. A revision of the triggerfish genus *Xanthichthys*, with description of a new species. *Bull. Mar. Sci.* 28 (4): 688–706.

Randall, J. E., and J. E. McCosker. 1992a. Revision of the fish genus *Luzonichthys* (Perciformes: Serranidae: Anthiinae), with descriptions of two new species. *Indo-Pac. Fishes*, no. 21:1–21.

———. 1992b. Two new damselfishes of the genus *Chromis* (Perciformes: Pomacentridae) from the South Pacific. *Proc. Calif. Acad. Sci.* 47 (12): 329–337.

———. 1993. Social mimicry in fishes. *Rev. Fr. Aquariol.* 20 (1): 5–8.

———. 2002. *Parapercis lata*, a new species of sandperch (Perciformes: Pinguipedidae) from the central Pacific. *Proc. Calif. Acad. Sci.* 72: 1–19.

Randall, J. E., and R. Meléndez. 1987. A new sole of the genus *Aseraggodes* from Easter Island and Lord Howe Island, with comments on the validity of *A. ramsaii*. *Occas. Pap. Bishop Mus.* 27:97–105.

Randall, J. E., and J. T. Millington. 1990. Triggerfish bite—a little-known marine hazard. *J. Wilderness Med.* 1:79–85.

Randall, J. E., and B. C. Mundy. 1998. *Balistes polylepis* and *Xanthichthys caeruleolineatus*, two large triggerfishes (Tetraodontiformes: Balistidae) from the Hawaiian Islands, with a key to Hawaiian species. *Pac. Sci.* 52 (4): 322–333.

Randall, J. E., R. F. Myers, and R. Winterbottom. 2002d. *Melichthys indicus* x *M. vidua*, a hybrid triggerfish (Tetraodontiformes: Balistidae) from Indonesia. *Aqua* 5 (2): 77–80.

Randall, J. E., and S. G. Poss. 2002. Redescription of the Indo-Pacific scorpionfish *Scorpaenopsis fowleri* (Pietschmann) and reallocation to the genus *Sebastapistes*. *Pac. Sci.* 56 (1): 57–64.

Randall, J. E., R. L. Pyle, and R. F. Myers. 2001. Three examples of hybrid surgeonfishes (Acanthuridae). *Aqua* 4 (3): 115–120.

Randall, J. E., and H. A. Randall. 1960. Examples of mimicry and protective resemblance in tropical marine fishes. *Bull. Mar. Sci. Gulf Caribb.* 10 (4): 444–480.

———. 1963. The spawning and early development of the Atlantic parrot fish, *Sparisoma rubripinne*, with notes on other scarid and labrid fishes. *Zoologica (N.Y.)* 48 (2): 49–60.

———. 2001. Review of the fishes of the genus *Kuhlia* (Perciformes: Kuhliidae) of the central Pacific. *Pac. Sci.* 55 (3): 227–256.

Randall, J. E., and H. Senou. 2001. Review of the Indo-Pacific gobiid fish genus *Lubricogobius*, with description of a new species and a new genus for *L. pumilus*. *Ichthyol. Res.* 48:3–12.

Randall, J. E., K.-T. Shao, and J.-P. Chen. 2003b. A review of the Indo-Pacific gobiid fish genus *Ctenogobiops*, with descriptions of two new species. *Zool. Stud.* 42 (4): 506–515.

Randall, J. E., and D. C. Shen. 2001. First records of the gobioid fishes *Gunnellichthys monostigma* and *Nemateleotris decora* from the Red Sea. *Fauna Saudi Arabia* 19:491–495.

Randall, J. E., and Y. Sinoto. 1978. Rapan fish names. *Occas. Pap. Bernice Pauahi Bishop Mus.* 24 (15): 291–306.

Randall, J. E., C. L. Smith, and M. N. Feinberg. 1990. Report on fish collections from Rapa, French Polynesia. *Am. Mus. Novit.*, no. 1966:1–42.

Randall, J. E., D. G. Smith, J. T. Williams, M. Kulbicki, G. Mou Tham, P. Labrosse, M. Kronen, E. Clua, and B. S. Mann. 2004. Checklist of the shore and epipelagic fishes of Tonga. *Atoll Res. Bull.*, no. 502:1–35.

Randall, J. E., M. M. Smith, and K. Aida. 1980. Notes on the classification and distribution of the Indo-Pacific soapfish, *Belonoperca chabanaudi* (Perciformes: Grammistidae). *Spec. Publ. J. L. B. Smith Inst. Ichthyol.*, no. 21:1–7.

Randall, J. E., and A. B. Tarr. 1994. *Trichonotus arabicus* (Perciformes: Trichonotidae), a new species of sand diver from the Arabian Gulf and Oman. *Fauna Saudi Arabia* 14:309–316.

Randall, J. E., and L. Taylor. 1988. Review of the Indo-Pacific fishes of the serranid genus *Liopropoma*, with descriptions of seven new species. *Indo-Pac. Fishes*, no. 16:1–47.

Randall, J. E., and J. van Egmond. 1994. Marine fishes from the Seychelles: 108 new records. *Zool. Verh. (Leiden)* no. 297: 43–83.

Randall, J. E., M. W. Westneat, and M. F. Gomon. 2003c. Two new labrid fishes of the genus *Oxycheilinus* from the South Pacific. *Proc. Calif. Acad. Sci.* 54 (20): 361–370.

Randall, J. E., and A. Wheeler. 1991. Reidentification of seven tropical Pacific fishes collected and observed by the Forsters during the voyage of HMS *Resolution*, 1772–75. *Copeia* 1991 (3): 760–767.

Ray, C., and C. W. Coates. 1958. A case of poisoning by the lion fish. *Copeia* 1958 (3): 235.

Reinboth, R. (ed.). 1975. *Intersexuality in the Animal Kingdom*. Springer Verlag, Berlin. 446 pp.

Rennis, D. S., and D. F. Hoese. 1985. A review of the genus *Parioglossus*, with descriptions of six new species (Pisces: Gobioidei). *Rec. Aust. Mus.* 36:169–201.

Rensch, K. H. 1999. *A Dictionary of Polynesian Fish Names*. Archipelago Press, Canberra. ix + 372 pp.

Robertson, D. R. 1982. Fish feces as fish food on a Pacific coral reef. *Mar. Ecol. Prog. Ser.* 7: 253–265.

———. 1983. On the spawning behavior and spawning cycles of eight surgeonfishes from the Indo-Pacific. *Mar. Biol. (Berl.)* 9:193–223.

Robertson, D. R., and G. R. Allen. 1996. Zoogeography of the shorefish fauna of Clipperton Atoll. *Coral Reefs* 15:121–131.

Robertson, D. R., J. S. Grove, and J. E. McCosker. 2004. Tropical transpacific shore fishes. *Pac. Sci.* 58:507–565.

Robertson, D. R., and G. Justines. 1982. Protogynous hermaphroditism in four Caribbean reef gobies. *Environ. Biol. Fishes* 7 (2): 137–142.

Robertson, D. R., N. V. C. Polunin, and K. Leighton. 1979. The behavioural ecology of three Indian Ocean surgeonfishes *(Acanthurus lineatus, A. leucosternon* and *Zebrasoma scopas)*: Their feeding strategies, and social and mating systems. *Environ. Biol. Fishes* 4 (2): 125–170.

Robertson, D. R., R. Reinboth, and B. W. Bruce. 1982. Gonochorism, protogynous sex-change and spawning in three Sparisomatinine parrotfishes from the western Indian Ocean. *Bull. Mar. Sci.* 32 (4): 868–879.

Robins, C. R., R. M. Bailey, C. E. Bond, J. R. Brooker, E. A. Lachner, R. N. Lea, and W. B. Scott. 1991. Common and scientific names of fishes from the United States and Canada. 5th ed. *Am. Fish. Soc. Spec. Publ.* 20:1–183.

Rofen, R. R. 1958. The marine fishes of Rennell Island, pp. 149–218 in *The Natural History of Rennell Island, British Solomon Islands.* Danish Science Press, Copenhagen.

Rosa, I. L. 1993. Systematic study of the family Creediidae (Perciformes: Trachinoidei). Ph.D. thesis, University of Alberta. 185 pp.

Rosa, I. L., and R. S. Rosa. 1987. *Pinguipes* Cuvier and Valenciennes and Pinguipedidae Günther, the valid names for the fish taxa usually known as *Mugiloides* and Mugiloididae. *Copeia* 1987 (4): 1048–1051.

Russell, B. C. 1985. Revision of the Indo-Pacific labrid fish genus *Suezichthys,* with descriptions of four new species. *Indo-Pac. Fishes,* no. 2:1–21.

———. 1990. Nemipterid fishes of the world. *FAO Fish. Synop.,* no. 125, vol. 12: v + 149 pp.

Russell, B. C., G. R. Allen, and H. R. Lubbock. 1976. New cases of mimicry in marine fishes. *J. Zool. (Lond.)* 180:407–423.

Russell, P. 1803. *Descriptions and Figures of Two Hundred Fishes; Collected at Vizagapatam on the Coast of Coromandel.* Vol. 1. W. Bulmer & Co., Shakespeare Press, Cleveland-Row. vii + 78 pp.

Sadovy, Y., and A. S. Cornish. 2000. *Reef Fishes of Hong Kong.* Hong Kong University Press. xi + 321 pp.

Sadovy, Y., and T. J. Donaldson. 1995. Sexual pattern of *Neocirrhites armatus* (Cirrhitidae) with notes on other hawkfish species. *Environ. Biol. Fishes* 43:143–150.

Sadovy, Y., J. E. Randall, and M. B. Rasotto. in press. Skin structure in six dragonet species (Gobiesociformes; Callionymidae): Inter-specific differences in glandular cell types and mucus secretion. *J. Fish Biol.*

Saeed, B., W. Ivantsoff, and L. E. L. M. Crowley. 1993. A new species of the surf-inhabiting atheriniform *Iso* (Pisces: Isonidae). *Rec. West. Aust. Mus.* 16 (3): 337–346.

Said, M. Z. M., M. A. Ambak, and A. K. M. Mohsin. 1983. Some aspects of the fishery and biology of *Nemipterus tolu* C.V. off the Trengganu coast, South China Sea. *Pertanika* 6:108–111.

Sakai, K., and T. Nakabo. 1995. Taxonomic review of the Indo-Pacific kyphosid fish, *Kyphosus vaigiensis* (Quoy and Gaimard). *Jpn. J. Ichthyol.* 42 (1): 61–70.

———. 2004. Two new species of *Kyphosus* (Kyphosidae) and a taxonomic review of *Kyphosus bigibbus* Lacepède from the Indo-Pacific. *Ichthyol. Res.* 51:20–32.

Sano, M. 1989. Feeding habits of Japanese butterflyfishes (Chaetodontidae). *Environ. Biol. Fishes* 25 (1–3): 195–203.

Sano, M., M. Shimizu, and Y. Nose. 1984. Food habits of teleostean reef fishes in Okinawa Island. *Bull. Univ. Mus., Univ. Tokyo,* no. 25:1–128.

Sazima, I. 1998. Field evidence for suspension feeding in *Pseudocaranx dentex,* with comments on ram filtering in other jacks (Carangidae). *Environ. Biol. Fishes* 53:225–229.

Schmid, H., and J. E. Randall. 1997. First record of the tripletail, *Lobotes surinamensis* (Pisces: Lobotidae) from the Red Sea. *Fauna Saudi Arabia* 16:353–355.

Schneidewind, F. 1999. *Kaiserfische.* Tetra-Verlag GmbH, Bissendorft-Wulften, Germany. 262 pp.

———. 2002. *Drückerfische.* Tetra-Verlag GmvH, Bissendorf, Germany. 256 pp.

Schultz, E. T. 1986. *Pterois volitans* and *Pterois miles:* Two valid species. *Copeia* 1986 (3): 686–690.

Schultz, L. P. 1940. Two new genera and three new species of cheilodipterid fishes, with notes on the other genera of the family. *Proc. U.S. Natl. Mus.* 88:403–423.

———. 1943. Fishes of the Phoenix and Samoan Islands collected in 1939 during the expedition of the U.S.S. "Bushnell." *Bull. U.S. Natl. Mus.* 180: x + 316 pp.

———. 1950. Three new species of fishes of the genus *Cirrhitus* (family Cirrhitidae) from the Indo-Pacific. *Proc. U.S. Natl. Mus.* 100:547–552.

Schultz, L. P., and collaborators. 1953. Fishes of the Marshall and Marianas Islands. *Bull. U.S. Natl. Mus.* 202, vol. 1: xxxii + 685 pp.

———. 1960. Fishes of the Marshall and Marianas Islands. *Bull. U.S. Natl. Mus.* 202, vol. 2: ix + 438 pp.

Schwartz, F. J. 2001. Freshwater and marine fish family hybrids: A worldwide changing scene revealed by the scientific literature. *J. Elisha Mitchell Sci. Soc.* 117 (1): 62–65.

Seale, A. 1906. Fishes of the South Pacific. *Occas. Pap. B. P. Bishop Mus.* 4 (1): 1–89.

———. 1935. The Templeton Crocker Expedition to western Polynesian and Melanesian islands, 1933. No. 27. Fishes. *Proc. Calif. Acad. Sci.* 21 (27): 337–378.

Seba, A. 1758. *Locupletissimi rerum naturalium thesauri . . .* Vol. 3. Amstelaedami. 212 pp.

Seigel, J. A. 1982. Median fin-spine locking in the ponyfishes (Perciformes: Leiognathidae). *Copeia* 1982 (1): 202–205.

Senou, H. 1992. Identification of four species of barracudas with vertical bars on the body from underwater photographs. *I.O.P. Diving News* 3 (12): 2–5 (in Japanese).

Senou, H., and T. Kawamoto. 2002. First record of a frogfish, *Antennarius randalli* from Japan. *I.O.P. Diving News* 13 (4): 2–6.

Senou, H., Y. Morita, and O. Morishita. 1997. Six new records of fishes from Japan. *I.O.P. Diving News* 8 (2): 2–7 (in Japanese).

Senou, H., and M. Ota. 2002. A hybrid between *Nemateleotris magnifica* Fowler, 1938 and *N. decora* Randall et Allen, 1973. *I.O.P. Diving News* 13 (5): 1 (in Japanese).

Senou, H., and S. Ueda. 2002. A hybrid between *Labroides bicolor* Fowler et Bean, 1928 & *Labroides pectoralis* Randall et Springer, 1975. *I.O.P. Diving News* 13 (8): 1 (in Japanese).

Severns, M., and P. Fiene-Severns. 1993. *Molokini Island.* Pacific Islands Publishing, Wailuku, HI. 144 pp.

Shaklee, J. E., and C. S. Tamaru. 1981. Biochemical and morphological evolution of Hawaiian bonefishes *(Albula).* *Syst. Zool.* 30 (2): 125–146.

Shallenberger, R. J., and W. D. Madden. 1973. Luring behaviour in the scorpionfish, *Iracundus signifer. Behaviour* 47 (1–2): 33–47.

Shapiro, D. Y. 1981. Sequence of coloration changes during sex reversal in the tropical marine fish *Anthias squamipinnis* (Peters). *Bull. Mar. Sci.* 31 (2): 383–398.

Shen, S.-C. 1998. A review of the congrid eels of the genus *Ariosoma* from Taiwan, with description of a new species. *Zool. Stud.* 37 (1): 7–12.

——— (ed.). 1993. *Fishes of Taiwan.* Department of Zoology, National Taiwan University, Taipei (in Chinese). xx + 960 pp.

671

Shen, S.-C., and K. Y. Wu. 1994. A revision of the tripterygiid fishes from coastal waters of Taiwan with descriptions of two new genera and five new species. *Acta Zool. Taiwan* 5 (2): 1–32.

Shimada, K., and T. Yoshino. 1984. A new trichonotid fish from the Yaeyama Islands, Okinawa Prefecture, Japan. *Jpn. J. Ichthyol.* 31 (1): 15–19.

Shimizu, T., and T. Yamakawa. 1979. Review of the squirrelfishes (subfamily Holocentrinae: order Beryciformes) of Japan, with a description of a new species. *Jpn. J. Ichthyol.* 26 (2): 1–23.

Shirai, Y., and H. Kitazawa. 1998. Peculiar feeding behavior of *Asterorhombus intermedius* in an aquarium. *Jpn. J. Ichthyol.* 45 (1): 47–50.

Shpigel, M., and L. Fishelson. 1989. Food habits and prey selection of three species of groupers from the genus *Cephalopholis* (Serranidae: Teleostei). *Environ. Biol. Fishes* 24 (1): 67–73.

Smith, D. G., and E. B. Böhlke. 1997. A review of the Indo-Pacific banded morays of the *Gymnothorax reticularis* group, with descriptions of three new species (Pisces, Anguilliformes, Muraenidae). *Proc. Acad. Nat. Sci. Phila.* 148:177–188.

Smith, J. L. B. 1951. A case of poisoning by the stonefish, *Synanceja verrucosa*. *Copeia* 1951 (3): 207–210.

———. 1957a. Two rapid fatalities from stonefish jabs. *Copeia* 1957 (3): 249.

———. 1957b. The fishes of the family Scorpaenidae in the western Indian Ocean. Part I. The sub-family Scorpaeninae. *Rhodes Univ. Dep. Ichthyol. Ichthyol. Bull.*, no. 4:48–72.

———. 1958. The gunnellichthid fishes with description of two new species from East Africa and of *Gunnellichthys (Clarkichthys) bilineatus* (Clark), 1936. *Rhodes Univ. Dep. Ichthyol. Ichthyol. Bull.*, no. 9:123–129.

———. 1959a. Gobioid fishes of the families Gobiidae, Periophthalmidae, Trypauchenidae, Taenioididae, and Kraemeriidae of the western Indian Ocean. *Rhodes Univ. Dep. Ichthyol. Ichthyol. Bull.*, no. 13:185–225.

———. 1959b. Fishes of the family Lethrinidae from the western Indian Ocean. *Rhodes Univ. Dep. Ichthyol. Ichthyol. Bull.*, no. 17:283–295.

———. 1962a. The moray eels of the western Indian Ocean and the Red Sea. *Rhodes Univ. Dep. Ichthyol. Ichthyol. Bull.*, no. 23:420–444.

———. 1962b. Fishes of the family Gaterinidae of the western Indian Ocean and the Red Sea with a resume of all known Indo-Pacific species. *Rhodes Univ. Dep. Ichthyol. Ichthyol. Bull.*, no. 25:467–502.

Smith-Vaniz, W. F. 1976. The saber-toothed blennies, Tribe Nemophini (Pisces: Blenniidae). *Monogr. Acad. Nat. Sci. Phila.*, no. 19:1–196.

———. 1987. The saber-toothed blennies, Tribe Nemophini (Pisces: Blenniidae): An update. *Proc. Acad. Nat. Sci. Phila.* 139:1–52.

———. 1989. Revision of the jawfish genus *Stalix* (Pisces: Opistognathidae), with descriptions of four new species. *Proc. Acad. Nat. Sci. Phila.* 141:375–407.

Smith-Vaniz, W. F., and J. E. Randall. 1973. *Blennechis filamentosus* Valenciennes, the prejuvenile of *Aspidontus taeniatus* Quoy and Gaimard (Pisces: Blenniidae). *Not. Nat. (Phila.)*, no. 448:1–11.

———. 1994. *Scomber dentex* Bloch & Schneider, 1801 and *Caranx lugubris* Poey, 1860 (Pisces, Carangidae) proposed conservation by suppression of *Scomber glaucus* Linnaeus, 1758 and *Scomber adscensionis* Osbeck, 1771, and *Caranx ascensionis* Cuvier, 1822, respectively. *Bull. Zool. Nomencl.* 51 (4): 1–7.

Smith-Vaniz, W. F., and V. G. Springer. 1971. Synopsis of the tribe Salariini, with description of five new genera and three new species (Pisces: Blenniidae). *Smithson. Contrib. Zool.*, no. 73:1–61.

Snyder, D. B., J. E. Randall, and S. W. Michael. 2001. Aggressive mimicry by the juvenile of the redmouth grouper, *Aethaloperca rogaa* (Serranidae). *Cybium* 25 (3): 227–232.

Springer, V. G. 1966. *Medusablennius chani*, a new genus and species of blennioid fish from the Tuamotu Archipelago: Its implication on blennioid classification. *Copeia* 1966 (1): 56–60.

———. 1967. Revision of the circumtropical shorefish genus *Entomacrodus* (Blenniidae: Salariinae). *Proc. U.S. Natl. Mus.* 122:1–150.

———. 1968. The Indo-Pacific blenniid fish genus *Stanulus*, with description of a new species from the Great Barrier Reef (Blenniidae; Blenniinae; Salariini). *Proc. Biol. Soc. Wash.* 81:111–121.

———. 1972a. Synopsis of the tribe Omobranchini with descriptions of three new genera and two new species (Pisces: Blenniidae). *Smithson. Contrib. Zool.*, no. 130:1–31.

———. 1972b. Additions to revision of the blenniid fish genera *Ecsenius* and *Entomacrodus*, with descriptions of three new species of *Ecsenius*. *Smithson. Contrib. Zool.*, no. 134: iii + 11 pp.

———. 1976. *Cirrisalarias bunares*, a new genus and species of blenniid fish from the Indian Ocean. *Proc. Biol. Soc. Wash.* 89 (13): 199–204.

———. 1981. Notes on blenniid fishes of the tribe Omobranchini, with descriptions of two new species. *Proc. Biol. Soc. Wash.* 94 (3): 699–707.

———. 1982. Pacific Plate biogeography, with special reference to shore fishes. *Smithson. Contrib. Zool.*, no. 367: iii + 182 pp.

———. 1983. *Tyson belos*, new genus and species of western Pacific fish (Gobiidae, Xenisthminae), with discussions of gob-

ioid osteology and classification. *Smithson. Contrib. Zool.*, no. 390:1–40.

———. 1988. The Indo-Pacific blenniid fish genus *Ecsenius*. *Smithson. Contrib. Zool.*, no. 465: iii + 134 pp.

———. 1993. Definition of the suborder Blennioidei and its included families (Pisces: Perciformes). *Bull. Mar. Sci.* 52 (1): 472–495.

———. 2002. *Ecsenius niue*, a new species of blenniid fish, and new distribution records for other species in the Opsifrontalis species group. *Zootaxa* 72:1–6.

Springer, V. G., and M. F. Gomon. 1975. Revision of the blenniid fish genus *Omobranchus* with descriptions of three new species and notes on other species of the tribe Omobranchini. *Smithson. Contrib. Zool.*, no. 177: iii + 135 pp.

Springer, V. G., and J. E. Randall. 1974. Two new species of the labrid fish genus *Cirrhilabrus* from the Red Sea. *Isr. J. Zool.* 23:45–54.

Springer, V. G., C. L. Smith, and T. H. Fraser. 1977. *Anisochromis straussi*, a new species of protogynous hermaphroditic fish, and synonymy of Anisochromidae, Pseudoplesiopidae, and Pseudochromidae. *Smithson. Contrib. Zool.*, no. 252:1–15.

Springer, V. G., and W. F. Smith-Vaniz. 1972. Mimetic relationships involving fishes of the family Blenniidae. *Smithson. Contrib. Zool.*, no. 112:1–36.

Springer, V. G., and A. E. Spreitzer. 1978. Five new species and a new genus of Indian Ocean blenniid fishes, tribe Salariini, with a key to the genera of the tribe. *Smithson. Contrib. Zool.*, no. 268: iii + 20 pp.

Springer, V. G., and J. T. Williams. 1994. The Indo-West Pacific blenniid fish genus *Istiblennius* reappraised: A revision of *Istiblennius, Blenniella*, and *Paralticus*, new genus. *Smithson. Contrib. Zool.*, no. 565: iii + 193 pp.

Starnes, W. C. 1988. Revision, phylogeny and biogeographic comments on the circumtropical marine percoid fish family Priacanthidae. *Bull. Mar. Sci.* 43 (2): 117–203.

Steinitz, H. 1959. Observations on *Pterois volitans* (L.) and its venom. *Copeia* 1959 (2): 158–160.

Stepien, C. A., J. E. Randall, and R. H. Rosenblatt. 1994. Genetic and morphological divergence of a circumtropical complex of goatfishes: *Mulloidichthys vanicolensis, M. dentatus*, and *M. martinicus*. *Pac. Sci.* 48 (1): 44–56.

Strasburg, D. W. 1959. Notes on the diet and correlating structures of some central Pacific echeneid fishes. *Copeia* 1959 (3): 244–248.

———. 1962. Pelagic larval stages of *Zanclus canescens* from Hawaii. *Copeia* 1962 (4): 844–845.

———. 1966. Observations on the ecology of four apogonid fishes. *Pac. Sci.* 20 (3): 338–341.

———. 1967. *Gunnellichthys monostigma* and *Ecsenius bicolor,* new fish records from the Marshall Islands. *Copeia* 1967 (4): 839–841.

Suzuki, H., E. Ishida, and M. Ohashi. 2001. Reproductive behavior, eggs and larvae of two blenniid fishes, *Ecsenius bicolor* (Day) and *E. midas* (Starck), in the aquarium. *Sci. Rep. Mus. Tokai Univ.* 3:29–42.

Suzuki, K. 2001. Early life stages in three Japanese anthiine fishes (Serranidae: Teleostei). *Sci. Rep. Mus. Tokai Univ.* 3:113–120.

Swerdloff, S. N. 1970. Behavioral observations on Eniwetok damselfishes (Pomacentridae: *Chromis*) with special reference to the spawning of *Chromis caeruleus*. *Copeia* 1970 (2): 371–374.

Takeuchi, N., H. Hashimoto, and K. Gushima. 2002. Short-term foraging patterns of individual cornetfish, *Fistularia commersonii,* based on stomach content analysis. *Ichthyol. Res.* 49:76–80.

Talbot, F. H. 1960. Notes on the biology of the Lutjanidae (Pisces) of the East African coast, with special reference to *L. bohar* (Forskal). *Ann. S. Afr. Mus.* 435:549–573.

Tanaka, Y., and T. Ohyama. 1991. Reproductive behavior, egg and larval development of the hawkfishes *Oxycirrhites typus* and *Cirrhitops hubbardi,* in an aquarium. *Bull. Inst. Oceanic Res. Dev. Tokai Univ.* 11/12: 41–57 (in Japanese).

Thacker, C. 2000. Phylogeny of the wormfishes (Teleostei: Gobioidei: Microdesmidae). *Copeia* 2000 (4): 940–957.

Thomson, D. A. 1964. Ostracitoxin: An ichthyotoxic stress secretion of the boxfish *Ostracion lentiginosus*. *Science* (Washington, D.C.) 146:242–246.

Thresher, R. E. 1982. Courtship and spawning of the emperor angelfish *Pomacanthus imperator,* with comments on the reproduction by other pomacanthid fishes. *Mar. Biol. (Berl.)* 70:149–156.

———. 1984. *Reproduction in Reef Fishes.* T.F.H. Publications, Neptune City, NJ. 399 pp.

Thresher, R. E., P. L. Colin, and L. J. Bell. 1989. Planktonic duration, distribution, and population structure of western and central Pacific damselfishes (Pomacentridae). *Copeia* 1989 (2): 420–435.

Trott, L. B. 1970. Contributions to the biology of carapid fishes (Paracanthopterygii: Gadiformes). *Univ. Calif. Publ. Zool.* 89:1–60.

Trubschenck, C. H., III. 1981. A synopsis of the taxonomy and distribution of the boxfish families Aracanidae and Ostraciidae. M.S. thesis, California State University, Sacramento. iv + 210 pp.

Tyler, J. C. 1980. Osteology, phylogeny, and higher classification of the fishes of the order Plectognathi (Tetraodontiformes). *NOAA Tech. Rep. NMFS Circ.* 434: xi + 422 pp.

Tyler, J. C., G. D. Johnson, I. Nakamura, and B. B. Collette. 1989. Morphology of *Luvarus imperialis* (Luvaridae), with a phylogenetic analysis of the Acanthuroidei (Pisces). *Smithson. Contrib. Zool.,* no. 485:1–178.

Tyler, J. C., and C. L. Smith. 1992. Systematic significance of the burrow form in seven species of garden eels (Congridae: Heterocongrinae). *Am. Mus. Novit.,* no. 3037:1–13.

Van der Elst, R. 1981. *A Guide to the Common Sea Fishes of Southern Africa.* C. Struik, Cape Town. 367 pp.

Vari, R. P. 1978. The *Terapon* perches (Percoidei, Teraponidae), a cladistic analysis and taxonomic revision. *Bull. Am. Mus. Nat. Hist.* 159 (5): 175–340.

Waite, E. R. 1904. Additions to the fish-fauna of Lord Howe Island, no. 4. *Rec. Aust. Mus.* 5 (3): 135–186.

Wallace, J. H. 1967. The batoid fishes of the east coast of southern Africa. Part II: Manta, eagle, duckbill, cownose, butterfly and sting rays. *Oceanogr. Res. Inst. (Durban),* no. 16:1–56.

Waples, R. S. 1982. A biochemical and morphological review of the lizardfish genus *Saurida* in Hawaii, with description of a new species. *Pac. Sci.* (1981) 35 (3): 217–235.

Waples, R. S., and J. E. Randall. 1989. A revision of the Hawaiian lizardfishes of the genus *Synodus,* with descriptions of four new species. *Pac. Sci.* (1988) 42 (3–4): 178–213.

Wass, R. C. 1973. Size, growth, and reproduction of the sandbar shark, *Carcharhinus milberti,* in Hawaii. *Pac. Sci.* 27 (4): 305–318.

———. 1984. An annotated checklist of the fishes of Samoa. *NOAA Tech. Rep. NMFS SSRF*-781: 1–43.

Weber, M., and L. F. de Beaufort. 1913. *The Fishes of the Indo-Australian Archipelago.* Vol. 2. E. J. Brill, Leiden. xx + 404 pp.

Wellington, G. M., and B. C. Victor. 1989. Planktonic larval duration of one hundred species of Pacific and Atlantic damselfishes (Pomacentridae). *Mar. Biol. (Berl.)* 101:557–567.

Westneat, M. W., and P. C. Wainwright. 1989. Feeding mechanism of *Epibulus insidiator* (Labridae; Teleostei): Evolution of a novel functional system. *J. Morphol.* 202: 129–150.

Wheeler, A. C. 1955. A preliminary revision of the fishes of the genus *Aulostomus*. *Ann. Mag. Nat. Hist.,* ser. 12, 8:613–623.

Wheeler, J. F. G., and F. D. Ommanney. 1953. *Report on the Mauritius-Seychelles Fisheries Survey 1948–1949.* Her Majesty's Stationery Office, London. 145 pp.

Whitehead, P. J. P. 1962. The species of *Elops* (Pisces: Elopidae). *Ann. Mag. Nat. Hist.,* ser. 13, 5:321–329.

———. 1985. Clupeoid fishes of the world (suborder Clupeoidei). *FAO Fish. Synop.,* no. 125, vol. 7, part 1: x + 303 pp.

Whitehead, P. J. P., and W. Ivantsoff. 1983. *Atherina lacunosa* and the fishes described by J. R. Forster. *Jpn. J. Ichthyol.* 29 (4): 355–364.

Whitehead, P. J. P., G. J. Nelson, and T. Wongratana. 1988. Clupeoid fishes of the world (suborder Clupeoidei). *FAO Fish. Synop.,* no. 125, vol. 7, part 2: vii + 305–579.

Whitfield, P. E., T. Gardner, S. P. Vives, M. R. Gilligan, W. R. Courtenay Jr., G. C. Ray, and J. A. Hare. 2002. Biological invasion of the Indo-Pacific lionfish *Pterois volitans* along the Atlantic coast of North America. *Mar. Ecol. Prog. Ser.* 235:289–297.

Williams, J. T. 1988. Revision and phylogenetic relationships of the blenniid fish genus *Cirripectes*. *Indo-Pac. Fishes,* no. 17:1–78.

———. 1989. Frogfishes of the World: Systematics, Zoogeography, and Behavioral Ecology (book review). *Natl. Geogr. Res.* 5 (3): 277–280.

Winterbottom, R. 1984. A review of the gobiid fish genus *Trimma* from the Chagos Archipelago, central Indian Ocean, with description of seven new species. *Can. J. Zool.* 62:695–715.

———. 1985a. Revision and vicariance biogeography of the subfamily Congrogadinae (Pisces: Perciformes: Pseudochromidae). *Indo-Pac. Fishes,* no. 9:1–34.

———. 1985b. Two new gobiid fish species (in *Priolepis* and *Trimma*) from the Chagos Archipelago, central Indian Ocean. *Can. J. Zool.* 63:748–754.

———. 1993. Myological evidence for the phylogeny of recent genera of surgeonfishes (Percomorpha, Acanthuridae) with comments on the Acanthuroidei. *Copeia* 1993 (1): 21–39.

———. 1995. Red Sea gobiid fishes of the genus *Trimma,* with the description of two new species. *Rev. Fr. Aquariol.* 22 (3–4): 93–98.

Winterbottom, R., and M. Burridge. 1989. A new species of *Priolepis* (Pisces; Gobiidae) from the Pacific Plate, with biogeographic comments. *Can. J. Zool.* 67:2398–2402.

———. 1992. A revision of the *Egglestonichthys* and *Priolepis* species possessing a transverse pattern of cheek papillae (Teleostei; Gobiidae), with a discussion of relationships. *Can. J. Zool.* 70:1934–1946.

———. 1993a. A revision of the species of *Priolepis* possessing a reduced transverse pattern of cheek papillae and no predorsal scales (Teleostei; Gobiidae). *Can. J. Zool.* 71:494–514.

———. 1993b. A revision of the Indo-Pacific *Priolepis* species possessing a reduced transverse pattern of cheek papillae, and predorsal scales (Teleostei; Gobiidae). *Can. J. Zool.* 71:2056–2076.

Winterbottom, R., and A. R. Emery. 1981. A new genus and two new species of gobiid fishes (Perciformes) from the Chagos

Archipelago, central Indian Ocean. *Environ. Biol. Fishes* 6 (2): 139–149.

———. 1986. Review of the gobioid fishes of the Chagos Archipelago, central Indian Ocean. *R. Ont. Mus. Life Sci. Contrib.,* no. 142: v + 82 pp.

Winterbottom, R., A. R. Emery, and E. Holm. 1989. An annotated checklist of the fishes of the Chagos Archipelago. *R. Ont. Mus. Life Sci. Contrib.,* no. 145: vi + 226 pp.

Winterbottom, R., and D. F. Hoese. 1988. A new genus and four new species of fishes from the Indo-West Pacific (Pisces; Perciformes; Gobiidae), with comments on relationships. *R. Ont. Mus. Life Sci. Occas. Pap.,* no. 37:1–17.

Woodland, D. J. 1990. Revision of the fish family Siganidae with descriptions of two new species and comments on distribution and biology. *Indo-Pac. Fishes,* no. 19:1–136.

Yabuta, S. 1997. Spawning migrations in the monogamous butterflyfish, *Chaetodon trifasciatus. Ichthyol. Res.* 44 (2): 177–182.

Yabuta, S., and M. Kawashima. 1997. Spawning behavior and haremic mating system in the corallivorous butterflyfish, *Chaetodon trifascialis,* at Kuroshima Island, Okinawa. *Ichthyol. Res.* 44 (2): 183–188.

Yasumoto, T., Y. Hashimoto, R. Bagnis, J. E. Randall, and A. H. Banner. 1971. Toxicity of surgeonfishes. *Bull. Jpn. Soc. Sci. Fish.* 37 (8): 724–734.

Yogo, Y., A. Nakazono, and H. Tsukahara. 1980. Ecological studies on the spawning of the parrotfish *Scarus sordidus* Forsskal. *Sci. Bull. Fac. Agric. Kyushu Univ.* 34 (3/4): 105–114 (in Japanese with English summary).

Yoshino, T., T. Kon, and S. Okabe. 1999. Review of the genus *Limnichthys* (Perciformes: Creediidae) from Japan, with description of a new species. *Ichthyol. Res.* 46 (1): 73–83.

Zehren, S. J. 1979. The comparative osteology and phylogeny of the Beryciformes (Pisces: Teleostei). *Evol. Monogr.* 1:1–389.